SOCIETIES, NETWORKS, AND TRANSITIONS

A GLOBAL HISTORY

SOCIETIES, NETWORKS, AND TRANSITIONS

A GLOBAL HISTORY

Volume II: Since 1450

Third Edition

Craig A. Lockard

University of Wisconsin—Green Bay

CENGAGE
Learning·

Australia · Brazil · Mexico · Singapore · United Kingdom · United States

**Societies, Networks, and Transitions:
A Global History, Third Edition,
Volume II: Since 1450**
Craig A. Lockard

Product Director: Suzanne Jeans

Product Manager: Brooke Barbier

Senior Content Developer: Tonya Lobato

Associate Content Developer: Cara Swan

Product Assistant: Andrew Newton

Media Developer: Kate MacLean

Marketing Development Manager:
Kyle Zimmerman

Senior Content Project Manager:
Carol Newman

Senior Art Director: Cate Barr

Manufacturing Planner: Sandee Milewski

Intellectual Property Analyst: Jessica Elias

Production Service/Compositor:
Cenveo® Publisher Services

Text Designer: Alisha Webber/
Cenveo Publisher Services

Cover Designer: Anne Bell Carter/
A Bell Design Co.

Cover Image: Haiti. Port-au-Prince. Haitian
market scene. Naive art. Fresco.

For product information and technology assistance, contact us at
Cengage Learning Customer & Sales Support, 1-800-354-9706
For permission to use material from this text or product,
submit all requests online at **www.cengage.com/permissions**.
Further permissions questions can be emailed to
permissionrequest@cengage.com.

Library of Congress Control Number: 2013952675

Student Edition:

ISBN-13: 978-1-285-73385-2

ISBN-10: 1-285-73385-1

Cengage Learning
200 First Stamford Place, 4th Floor
Stamford CT 06902
USA

Cengage Learning is a leading provider of customized learning solutions with office locations around the globe, including Singapore, the United Kingdom, Australia, Mexico, Brazil, and Japan. Locate your local office at **international.cengage.com/region**.

Cengage Learning products are represented in Canada by Nelson Education, Ltd.

For your course and learning solutions, visit **www.cengage.com**.

Purchase any of our products at your local college store or at our preferred online store **www.cengagebrain.com**.

Instructors: Please visit **login.cengage.com** and log in to access instructor-specific resources.

Printed in the United States of America
1 2 3 4 5 6 7 18 17 16 15 14

Brief Contents

v

Contents

Maps

Features

PROFILES

WITNESS TO THE PAST

HISTORICAL CONTROVERSIES

"Awareness of the need for a universal view of history—for a history which transcends national and regional boundaries and comprehends the entire globe—is one of the marks of the present. Our past [is] the past of the world, our history is the first to be world history."[1]

—Geoffrey Barraclough

British historian Geoffrey Barraclough wrote these words over three decades ago, yet historians are still grappling with what it means to write world history, and why it is crucial to do so, especially to better inform today's students about their changing world and how it came to be. The intended audience for this text is students taking introductory world history courses and the faculty who teach them. Many of these students will be taking world history in colleges, universities, and community colleges, often with the goal of satisfying general education requirements or building a foundation for majoring in history or a related field. Most others will take world history in secondary schools, often as Advanced Placement courses. Like the contemporary world, the marketplace for texts is also changing. Both students, many of whom have outside jobs, and instructors, often facing expanded workloads, have increasing demands on their time. New technologies are promoting new pedagogies and a multiplicity of classroom approaches. Hence, any textbook must provide a sound knowledge base while also enhancing teaching and learning whatever the pedagogy employed.

To make this third edition even more accessible and reader friendly than the first two editions, we have streamlined and shortened the narrative. Based on instructor feedback, we have also moved the popular *Societies, Networks, and Transitions* essay features from the end of each part to the beginning in order to give them more prominence. Like the core chapter narrative, these essays are also shorter, more streamlined, and are now organized by theme so that students can easily grasp the major parallels and changes that take place over the timeframe of the part. I believe that these changes and additions enhance the book's presentation and clarity and enable it to convey the richness and importance of world history for today's students and tomorrow's leaders while also making the teaching of the material easier for both high school and college instructors using this text.

Twenty-first-century students, more than any generation before them, live in multicultural countries and an interconnected world. The world's interdependence calls for teaching a wider vision, which is the goal of this text. My intention is to create a meaningful, coherent, and stimulating presentation that conveys to students the incredible diversity of societies from earliest times to the present, as well as the ways they have been increasingly connected to other societies and shaped by these relationships. History may happen "as one darn thing after another," but the job of historians is to make it something more than facts, names, and dates. A text should provide

a readable narrative, supplying a content base while also posing larger questions. The writing is as clear and thorough in its explanation of events and concepts as I can make it. No text can or should teach the course, but I hope that this text provides enough of a baseline of regional and global coverage to allow each instructor to bring her or his own talents, understandings, and particular interests to the process.

I became involved in teaching, debating, and writing world history as a result of my personal and academic experiences. My interest in other cultures was first awakened in the multicultural Southern California city where I grew up. Many of my classmates or their parents had come from Asia, Latin America, or the Middle East. There was also a substantial African American community. A curious person did not have to search far to hear music, sample foods, or encounter ideas from many different cultures. I remember being enchanted by the Chinese landscape paintings at a local museum devoted to Asian art, and vowing to one day see some of those misty mountains for myself. Today many young people may be as interested as I was in learning about the world, since, thanks to immigration, many cities and towns all over North America have taken on a cosmopolitan flavor similar to my hometown.

While experiences growing up sparked my interest in other cultures, it was my schooling that pointed the way to a career in teaching world history. When I entered college, many undergraduate students in the United States, often as part of the general education requirement, were required to take a year-long course in Western Civilization that introduced students to Egyptian pyramids, Greek philosophy, medieval pageantry, Renaissance art, and the French Revolution, enriching our lives. Fortunately, my university expanded student horizons further by adding course components (albeit brief) on China, Japan, India, and Islam while also developing a study abroad program. I participated in both the study abroad in Salzburg, Austria, and a year-long student exchange with a university in Hong Kong, which meant living with, rather than just sampling, different customs, outlooks, and histories.

More teachers and academic historians now realize that the emphasis in U.S. education on the histories of the United States and western Europe, to the near exclusion of the rest of the world, was not sufficient for understanding the realities of the twentieth century nor is it today. For decades young Americans have been sent thousands of miles away to fight wars in countries, such as Vietnam and Afghanistan, that few Americans had ever heard of. Newspapers and television reported developments in places such as Japan and Pakistan,

[1]Main Trends in History. New York: Holmes and Meier, 1979, p. 153.

Egypt and Congo, Cuba and Brazil, which had increasing relevance for Americans. Over the past half century graduate programs and scholarship directed toward Asian, African, Middle Eastern, Latin American, and eastern European and Russian history also grew out of the awareness of a widening world, broadening conceptions of history. I attended one of the new programs in Asian Studies for my MA degree, and then the first PhD program in world history. Thanks to that program, I encountered the stimulating work of pioneering world historians from North America such as Philip Curtin, Marshall Hodgson, William McNeill, and Leften S. Stavrianos. My own approach, developed as I taught undergraduate world history courses beginning in 1969, owes much to the global vision they offered.

To bring some coherence to the emerging world history field as well as to promote a global approach at all levels of education, several dozen of us teaching at the university, college, community college, and secondary school levels in the United States and Canada came together in the early 1980s to form the World History Association (WHA), for which I served as founding secretary and later as a member of the Executive Council. The organization grew rapidly, encouraging the teaching, studying, and writing of world history not only in the United States but all over the world. The approaches to world history found among active WHA members vary widely, and my engagement in the ongoing discussions at conferences and in essays, often about the merits of varied textbooks, provided an excellent background for writing this text.

The Aims and Approach of the Text

Societies, Networks, and Transitions: A Global History provides an accessible, thought-provoking guide to students in their exploration of the landscape of the past, helping them to think about it in all its social diversity and interconnectedness and to see their lives with fresh understanding. It does this by combining clear writing, special learning features, current scholarship, and a comprehensive, global approach that does not omit the role and richness of particular regions.

There is a method behind these aims. For forty-five years I have written about and taught Asian, African, and world history at universities in the United States and, as a visiting professor, Malaysia. A cumulative seven years of study, research, teaching, or travel in Southeast Asia, East Asia, East Africa, and Europe gave me insights into a wide variety of cultures and historical perspectives. Finally, the WHA, its publications and conferences, and the electronic listserv, H-WORLD, have provided active forums for vigorously discussing how best to think about and teach world history.

The most effective approach to presenting world history in a text for undergraduate and advanced high school students, I have concluded, is one that combines the themes of connections and cultures. World history is very much about connections that transcend countries, cultures, and regions, and a text should discuss, for example, major long-distance trade networks such as the Silk Road, the spread of religions, maritime exploration, world wars, and transregional empires such as the

Persian, Mongol, and British Empires. These connections are part of the broader global picture. Students need to understand that cultures, however unique, did not emerge and operate in a vacuum but faced similar challenges, shared many common experiences, and influenced each other.

The broader picture is drawn by means of several features in the text. To strengthen the presentation of the global overview, the text uses a short but innovative essay feature entitled "Societies, Networks, and Transitions." Appearing at the beginning of each of the six chronological parts, this feature analyzes and synthesizes the wider trends of the era, such as the role of long-distance trade, the spread of technologies and religions, and global climate change. The objective is to introduce and amplify the wider transregional messages developed in the part chapters and help students to think about the global context in which societies are enmeshed. The essays also make comparisons, for example, between the Han Chinese, Mauryan Indian, and Roman Empires, and between Chinese, Indian, and European emigration in the nineteenth century. These comparisons help to throw further light on diverse cultures and the differences and similarities between them during the era covered. Finally, each essay is meant to show how the transitions that characterize the era lead up to the era discussed in the following part. Furthermore, several chapters concentrate on global rather than regional developments.

However, while a broad global overview is a strongly developed feature of this text, most chapters, while acknowledging and explaining relevant linkages, focus on a particular region or several regions. Most students learn easiest by focusing on one region or culture at a time. Students also benefit from recognizing the cultural richness and intellectual creativity of specific societies. From this text students learn, for instance, about Chinese poetry, Indonesian music, Arab science, Greek philosophy, West African arts, Indian cinema, Latin American economies, and Anglo-American political thought. As a component of this cultural richness, this text also devotes considerable attention to the enduring religious traditions, such as Buddhism, Christianity, and Islam, and to issues of gender. The cultural richness of a region and its distinctive social patterns can get lost in an approach that minimizes regional coverage. Today most people are still mostly concerned with events in their own countries, even as their lives are reshaped by transnational economies and global cultural movements.

Also a strong part of the presentation of world history in this text is its attempt to be comprehensive and inclusive. To enhance comprehensiveness, the text balances social, economic, political, and cultural and religious history, and it also devotes some attention to geographical and environmental contexts as well as to the history of ideas and technologies. At the same time, the text highlights features within societies, such as economic production, technological innovations, and portable ideas that had widespread or enduring influence. To ensure inclusiveness, the text recognizes the contributions of many societies, including some often neglected, such as sub-Saharan Africa, pre-Columbian America, Southeast Asia, and Oceania. In particular, this text offers strong coverage of the diverse Asian societies. Throughout history, as today, the great majority of the world's population has lived in Asia.

Organizing the Text

All textbook authors struggle with how to organize the material. To keep the number of chapters corresponding to the twenty-eight or thirty weeks of most academic calendars in North America, and roughly equal in length, I have often had to combine several regions into a single chapter to be comprehensive, sometimes making decisions for conveniences sake. For example, unlike texts that may have only one chapter on sub-Saharan Africa covering the centuries from ancient times to 1500 C.E., this text discusses sub-Saharan Africa in each of the six chronological eras, devoting three chapters to the centuries prior to 1500 C.E. and three to the years since 1450 C.E. But this sometimes necessitated grouping Africa, depending on the era, with Europe, the Middle East, or the Americas. Unlike texts that may, for example, have material on Tang dynasty China scattered through several chapters, making it harder for students to gain a cohesive view of that society, I want to convey a comprehensive perspective of major societies such as Tang China. The material is divided into parts defined as distinct eras (such as the Classical and the Early Modern) so that students can understand how all regions were part of world history from earliest times. I believe that a chronological structure aids students in grasping the changes over time while helping to organize the material.

Distinguishing Features

Several features of *Societies, Networks, Transitions: A Global History* will help students better understand, assimilate, and appreciate the material they are about to encounter. Those unique to this text include the following.

Introducing World History World History may be the first and possibly the only history course many undergraduates will take in college. The text opens with a short essay that introduces students to the nature of history, the special challenges posed by studying world history, and why we need to study it.

Balancing Themes Three broad themes—uniqueness, interdependence, and change—have shaped the text. They are discussed throughout in terms of three related concepts—societies, networks, and transitions; they are also clearly identified in the text via the use of "S," "N," or "T" icons. These concepts, discussed in more detail in "Introducing World History," can be summarized as follows:

- **SOCIETIES** Influenced by environmental and geographical factors, people have formed and maintained societies defined by distinctive but often changing cultures, beliefs, social forms, institutions, and material traits.

- **NETWORKS** Over the centuries societies have generally been connected to other societies by growing networks forged by phenomena such as migration, long-distance trade, exploration, military expansion, colonization, the spread of ideas and technologies, and webs of communication. These growing networks modified individual

societies, created regional systems, and eventually led to a global system.

- **TRANSITIONS** Each major historical era has been marked by one or more great transitions sparked by events or innovations, such as settled agriculture, Mongol imperialism, industrial revolution, or world war, that have had profound and enduring influences on many societies, gradually reshaping the world. At the same time, societies and regions have experienced transitions of regional rather than global scope that have generated new ways of thinking or doing things, such as the expansion of Islam into India or the European colonization of East Africa and Mexico.

Through exposure to these three ideas integrated throughout the text, students learn of the rich cultural mosaic of the world. They are also introduced to its patterns of connections and unity as well as of continuity and change.

"Societies, Networks, and Transitions" Minichapters A short, thematically organized feature at the beginning of each part assists the student in backing up from the stories of societies and regions to see the larger historical patterns of change and the wider links among distant peoples. This comparative analysis allows students to identify experiences and transitions common to several regions or the entire world and to reflect further on the text themes. Additionally, the feature provides an important overview of key developments in the subsequent set of chapters.

Historical Controversies Since one of the common misconceptions about history is that it is about the "dead" past, included at the end of each part is a brief account of a debate among historians over how an issue in the past should be interpreted and what it means to us today. For example, why are the major societies dominated by males, and has this always been true? Why and when did Europe begin its "great divergence" from China and other Asian societies? How do historians evaluate contemporary globalization? Reappraisal is at the heart of history, and many historical questions are never completely answered. Yet most textbooks ignore this dimension of historical study; this text is innovative in including it. The Historical Controversy essays will help show students that historical facts are anything but dead; they live and change their meaning as new questions are asked by each new generation.

Profiles It is impossible to recount the human story without using broad generalizations, but it is also difficult to understand that story without seeing historical events reflected in the lives of men and women, prominent but also ordinary people. Each chapter contains a Profile that focuses on the experiences or accomplishments of a woman or man, to convey the flavor of life of the period, to embellish the chapter narrative with interesting personalities, and to integrate gender into the historical account. The Profiles try to show how gender affected the individual, shaping her or his opportunities and involvement in society. Several focus questions ask the student to reflect on the

Profile. For instance, students will examine a historian in early China, look at the spread of Christianity as seen through the life of a pagan female philosopher in Egypt, relive the experience of a female slave in colonial Brazil, and envision modern Indian life through a sketch of a film star. For this edition I have prepared three new Profiles.

Special Coverage This text also treats often-neglected areas and subjects. For example:

- It includes several regions with considerable historical importance but often marginalized or even omitted in many texts, including sub-Saharan Africa, Southeast Asia, Korea, Central Asia, pre-Columbian North America, ancient South America, the Caribbean, Polynesia, Australia, Canada, and the United States.

- It includes discussions of significant groups that transcend regional boundaries, such as the caravan travelers and traders of the Silk Road, Mongol empire builders, the Indian Ocean maritime traders, and contemporary humanitarian organizations such as Amnesty International and Doctors Without Borders.

- It features extensive coverage of the roots, rise, reshaping, and enduring influence of the great religious and philosophical traditions.

- It blends coverage of gender, particularly the experiences of women, and of social history generally, into the larger narrative.

- It devotes the first chapter of the text to the roots of human history. After a brief introduction to the shaping of our planet, human evolution, and the spread of people around the world, the chapter examines the birth of agriculture, cities, and states, which set the stage for everything to come.

- It includes strong coverage of the world since 1945, a focus of great interest to many students.

Witness to the Past Many texts incorporate excerpts from primary sources, but this text also keeps student needs in mind by using up-to-date translations and addressing a wide range of topics. Included are excerpts from important Buddhist, Hindu, Confucian, and Islamic works that helped shape great traditions. Readings such as a collection of Roman graffiti, a thirteenth-century tourist description of a Chinese city, a report on an Aztec market, and a manifesto for modern Egyptian women reveal something of people's lives and concerns. Also offered are materials that shed light on the politics of the time, such as an African king's plea to end the slave trade, Karl Marx's *Communist Manifesto*, and the recent *Arab Human Development Report*. Five new primary source readings are included in this edition. The wide selection of document excerpts is also designed to illustrate how historians work with original documents. Unlike most texts, chapters are also enlivened by brief but numerous excerpts of statements, writings, or

songs from people of the era that are effectively interspersed in the chapter narrative so that students can better see the vantage points and opinions of the people then living.

Chapter Learning Aids

The carefully designed learning aids are meant to help faculty teach world history and students actively learn and appreciate it. A number of aids have been created, including some that distinguish this text from others in use.

Chapter Opening Features A chapter outline shows the chapter contents at a glance. The outlines include *focus questions* for each section to prepare students for thinking about the main themes and topics of the chapter. Chapter text then opens with a quotation from a primary source pertinent to chapter topics. An interest-grabbing vignette or sketch then funnels students' attention toward the chapter themes they are about to explore.

Thematic Icons Every major section within each chapter is now identified by helpful thematic icons that let students know which of the main themes, societies, networks, or transitions, are being discussed.

Timelines To help students grasp the overall chronological picture of the chapter, timelines highlight key dates and events for each of the major regions discussed in each chapter.

Special Boxed Features Each chapter contains a *Witness to the Past* drawn from a primary source, and a *Profile* highlighting a man or woman from that era. Questions are also placed at the end of the primary source readings and profiles to help students comprehend the material.

Maps and Other Visuals Maps, photos, chronologies, and tables are amply interspersed throughout the chapters, illustrating and unifying coverage and themes.

Section Summaries At the end of each major section within a chapter, a bulleted summary helps students to review the key topics.

Chapter Summary At the end of each chapter, a concise summary invites students to sum up the chapter content and review its major points.

Key Terms and Pronunciation Guides Important terms likely to be new to the student are boldfaced in the text and immediately defined. These key terms are also listed at the end of the chapter and then listed with their definitions at the end of the text. The pronunciation of foreign and other difficult terms is shown parenthetically where the terms are introduced to help students with the terminology.

New to This Edition

In developing this new edition, I have also benefited from the responses to the first two editions, including correspondence and conversations with instructors and students who used the text. Incorporating many of their suggestions, this third edition is somewhat shorter than the first and second editions. Each part now opens with the comparative "Societies, Networks, and Transitions" essays that provide students an overview of important themes in the coming set of chapters. The chapter structure is now streamlined by combining some materials and hence eliminating superfluous heads.

In addition to all these changes, I have updated the narrative to incorporate new scholarly knowledge and historical developments over the last three years and since the second edition was published. Hence, many chapters include new information. Paleontology, archaeology, and ancient history are lively fields of study that constantly produce new knowledge, and the chapters in Part I include updates on subjects such as human evolution, the spread of modern humans, the rise of agriculture, the emergence of states, and early human settlement in the Americas. Later chapters incorporate new material on such subjects as the development of Hinduism, Austronesian migrations, Ottoman naval expansion, the effects of climate change, and Native American revolts against colonialism. As most readers know, many important developments have occurred in the last few years, and hence the chapters in Part VI have required the most revision. As a result, Chapter 26 on the Global System includes, among other topics, new material on the global recession, increasing global warming, the rise of the BRICS nations, and the roles of social media. Chapter 27 on East Asia examines economic challenges, human rights protests in China, violence in Tibet and Xinjiang, changing Chinese and Japanese leadership, and North Korean developments and regional tensions. The discussion of Europe and Russia in Chapter 28 ponders recent economic challenges, immigration issues, separatist and rightwing movements, Vladimir Putin's government, and changing attitudes toward the European Union and euro currency. In Chapter 29 on the Americas, I have added material on such topics as the Barack Obama presidency, politics in various Latin American nations, and the first Latin American pope. New material in Chapter 30 on the Middle East and Africa includes Turkish politics, the "Arab spring" conflicts in Egypt and Syria, and politics in varied African nations. Finally, Chapter 31 addresses India's challenges, political transition in Burma, and politics and violence in various Southeast Asian nations such as Thailand. These chapters should give students a good introduction to the world in which they live.

Ancillaries

A wide array of supplements accompany this text to assist students with different learning needs and to help instructors master today's various classroom challenges.

Instructor Resources

Aplia™ is an online interactive learning solution that improves comprehension and outcomes by increasing student effort and engagement. Founded by a professor to enhance his own courses, Aplia provides automatically graded assignments with detailed, immediate explanations on every question. The interactive assignments have been developed to address the major concepts covered in *Societies, Networks, and Transitions* and are designed to promote critical thinking and engage students more fully in learning. Question types include questions built around animated maps, primary sources such as newspaper extracts, or imagined scenarios, like engaging in a conversation with a historical figure or finding a diary and being asked to fill in some blanks; more in-depth primary source question sets address a major topic with a number of related primary sources and questions that promote deeper analysis of historical evidence. Many of the questions incorporate images, video clips, or audio clips. Students get immediate feedback on their work (not only what they got right or wrong, but why), and they can choose to see another set of related questions if they want more practice. A searchable eBook is available inside the course as well so that students can easily reference it as they work. Map reading and writing tutorials are also available to get students off to a good start. Aplia's simple-to-use course management interface allows instructors to post announcements, upload course materials, host student discussions, e-mail students, and manage the gradebook; a knowledgeable and friendly support team offers assistance and personalized support in customizing assignments to the instructor's course schedule. To learn more and view a demo for this book, visit www.aplia.com.

MindTap Reader for *Societies, Networks, and Transitions* is an eBook specifically designed to address the ways students assimilate content and media assets. MindTap Reader combines thoughtful navigation ergonomics, advanced student annotation, note-taking, and search tools, and embedded media assets such as video and MP3 chapter summaries, primary source documents with critical thinking questions, and interactive (zoomable) maps. Students can use the eBook as their primary text or as a multimedia companion to their printed book. The MindTap Reader eBook is available within the MindTap and Aplia online offerings found at www.cengagebrain.com.

History CourseMate Cengage Learning's History CourseMate brings course concepts to life with interactive learning, study tools, and exam preparation tools that support the printed textbook. Use Engagement Tracker to monitor student engagement in the course and watch student comprehension soar as your class works with the printed textbook and the textbook-specific website. An interactive eBook allows students to take notes, highlight, search, and interact with embedded media (such as quizzes, flashcards, primary sources, and videos). Learn more at **www.cengage.com/coursemate**.

Instructor Companion Website This website is an all-in-one resource for class preparation, presentation, and testing for instructors. Accessible through Cengage.com/login with your faculty account, you will find an Instructor's Manual, Powerpoint presentations (descriptions below), and testbank files (please see Cognero description).

> **Instructor's Manual** Prepared by Janet Jenkins of Arkansas Tech University, this manual contains for each chapter: instructional objectives, chapter outlines, lecture suggestions, discussion topics, primary source analysis, and suggested writing assignments.
>
> **PowerPoint® Lecture Tools** Prepared by Janet Jenkins of Arkansas Tech University. These presentations are ready-to-use, visual outlines of each chapter. They are easily customized for your lectures. There are presentations of only lecture or only images, as well as combined lecture and image presentations. Also available is a per chapter JPEG library of images and maps.
>
> **Cengage Learning Testing, powered by Cognero®** for Societies, Networks, and Transitions was prepared by David Burrow of University of South Dakota and is accessible through Cengage.com/login with your faculty account. This test bank contains multiple-choice and essay questions for each chapter. Cognero® is a flexible, online system that allows you to author, edit, and manage test bank content for Societies, Networks, and Transitions, third edition. Create multiple test versions instantly and deliver through your LMS from your classroom, or wherever you may be, with no special installs or downloads required.

The following format types are available for download from Instructor Companion Site: Blackboard, Angel, Moodle, Canvas, Desire2Learn. You can import these files directly into your LMS to edit, manage questions, and create tests. The test bank is also available in PDF format from the Instructor Companion Website.

Companion Website This website for instructors features an Instructor's Resource Manual (instructional objectives, chapter outlines, lecture suggestions, discussion topics, primary source analysis, and suggested writing assignments) and PowerPoint presentations (lecture outlines, images, and maps). In addition, access to *HistoryFinder*, a searchable online database with thousands of assets, allows instructors to easily create exciting presentations for their classroom by downloading art, photographs, maps, primary sources, and audio/video clips directly into a Microsoft® PowerPoint® slide.

CourseReader CourseReader is an online collection of primary and secondary sources that lets you create a customized electronic reader in minutes. With an easy-to-use interface and assessment tool, you can choose exactly what your students will be assigned—simply search or browse Cengage Learning's extensive document database to preview and select your customized collection of readings. In addition to print sources of all types (letters, diary entries, speeches, newspaper accounts, etc.), their collection includes a growing number of images and video and audio clips. Each primary source document includes a descriptive headnote that puts the reading into context and

is further supported by both critical thinking and multiple-choice questions designed to reinforce key points. For more information visit **www.cengage.com/coursereader**.

Cengagebrain.com Save your students' time and money. Direct them to **www.cengagebrain.com** for choice in formats and savings and a better chance to succeed in your class. Cengagebrain.com, Cengage Learning's online store, is a single destination for more than 10,000 new textbooks, eTextbooks, eChapters, study tools, and audio supplements. Students have the freedom to purchase a-la-carte exactly what they need when they need it. Students can save 50 percent on the electronic textbook, and can pay as little as $1.99 for an individual eChapter.

Reader Program Cengage Learning publishes a number of readers, some containing exclusively primary sources, others a combination of primary and secondary sources, and some designed to guide students through the process of historical inquiry. Visit Cengage.com/history for a complete list of readers.

Custom Options Nobody knows your students like you, so why not give them a text that is tailor-fit to their needs? Cengage Learning offers custom solutions for your course—whether it's making a small modification to *Societies, Networks, and Transitions* to match your syllabus or combining multiple sources to create something truly unique. You can pick and choose chapters, include your own material, and add additional map exercises along with the Rand McNally Atlas to create a text that fits the way you teach. Ensure that your students get the most out of their textbook dollar by giving them exactly what they need. Contact your Cengage Learning representative to explore custom solutions for your course.

Student Resources

Student Companion Site This website features an assortment of resources to help students master the subject matter. It includes chapter outlines, glossary, flashcards, and learning objectives.

CourseMate The more you study, the better the results. Make the most of your study time by accessing everything you need to succeed in one place. Read your textbook, take notes, review flashcards, watch videos, and take practice quizzes online with CourseMate.

MindTap Reader MindTap Reader is an eBook specifically designed to address the ways students assimilate content and media assets. MindTap Reader combines thoughtful navigation ergonomics, advanced student annotation, note-taking, and search tools, and embedded media assets such as video and MP3 chapter summaries, primary source documents with critical thinking questions, and interactive (zoomable) maps. Students can use the eBook as their primary text or as a multimedia companion to their printed book. The MindTap Reader eBook is available within the MindTap found at www.cengagebrain.com.

Reader Program Cengage Learning publishes a number of readers, some containing exclusively primary sources, others a combination of primary and secondary sources, and some designed to guide students through the process of historical inquiry. Visit Cengage.com/history for a complete list of readers.

Cengagebrain.com Save time and money! Go to www .cengagebrain.com for choice in formats and savings and a better chance to succeed in your class. Cengagebrain.com, Cengage Learning's online store, is a single destination for more than 10,000 new textbooks, eTextbooks, eChapters, study tools, and audio supplements. Students have the freedom to purchase a-la-carte exactly what they need when they need it. Students can save 50% on the electronic textbook, and can pay as little as $1.99 for an individual eChapter.

Writing for College History, 1e [ISBN: 9780618306039] Prepared by Robert M. Frakes, Clarion University. This brief handbook for survey courses in American history, Western Civilization/European history, and world civilization guides students through the various types of writing assignments they encounter in a history class. Providing examples of student writing and candid assessments of student work, this text focuses on the rules and conventions of writing for the college history course.

The History Handbook, 2e [ISBN: 9780495906766] Prepared by Carol Berkin of Baruch College, City University of New York and Betty Anderson of Boston University. This book teaches students both basic and history-specific study skills such as how to read primary sources, research historical topics, and correctly cite sources. Substantially less expensive than comparable skill-building texts, *The History Handbook* also offers tips for Internet research and evaluating online sources.

Doing History: Research and Writing in the Digital Age, 2e [ISBN: 9781133587880] Prepared by Michael J. Galgano, J. Chris Arndt, and Raymond M. Hyser of James Madison University. Whether you're starting down the path as a history major, or simply looking for a straightforward and systematic guide to writing a successful paper, you'll find this text to be an indispensable handbook to historical research. This text's "soup to nuts" approach to researching and writing about history addresses every step of the process, from locating your sources and gathering information, to writing clearly and making proper use of various citation styles to avoid plagiarism. You'll also learn how to make the most of every tool available to you—especially the technology that helps you conduct the process efficiently and effectively.

The Modern Researcher, 6e [ISBN: 9780495318705] Prepared by Jacques Barzun and Henry F. Graff of Columbia University. This classic introduction to the techniques of research and the art of expression is used widely in history courses, but is also appropriate for writing and research methods courses in other departments. Barzun and Graff thoroughly cover every aspect of research, from the selection of a topic through the gathering, analysis, writing, revision, and publication of findings, presenting the process not as a set of rules but through actual cases that put the subtleties of research in a useful context. Part One covers the principles and methods of research; Part Two covers writing, speaking, and getting one's work published.

Rand McNally Historical Atlas of the World, 2e [ISBN: 9780618841912] This valuable resource features over 70 maps that portray the rich panoply of the world's history from preliterate times to the present. They show how cultures and civilization were linked and how they interacted. The maps make it clear that history is not static. Rather, it is about change and movement across time. The maps show change by presenting the dynamics of expansion, cooperation, and conflict. This atlas includes maps that display the world from the beginning of civilization; the political development of all major areas of the world; expanded coverage of Africa, Latin America, and the Middle East; the current Islamic World; and the world population change in 1900 and 2000.

Formats

The text is available in a one-volume hardcover edition, a two-volume paperback edition, and as an interactive ebook. *Volume I: To 1500* includes Chapters 1–14; *Volume II: Since 1450* includes Chapters 15–31.

Acknowledgments

The author would like to thank the following community of instructors who, by sharing their teaching experiences and insightful feedback, helped shape the third edition and accompanying ancillary program:

Milan Andrejevich, Ivy Tech Community College
Maria Arbelaez, University of Nebraska at Omaha
Natalie Bayer, Drake University
William Burns, George Washington University
David Burrow, University of South Dakota
Brent Carney, Eastern Gateway Community College
William Collins, Salem State University
John Dennehy, Massachusetts Maritime Academy
Ross Doughty, Ursinus College
Ashley Duane, Wayne County Community College
Sherrie Dux-Ideus, Central Community College-Hastings
Randee Goodstadt, Asheville-Buncombe Technical
    Community College
Aimee Harris-Johnson, El Paso Community College
Gregory Havrilcsak, University of Michigan-Flint
Michael Hinckley, Northern Kentucky University
Donna Hoffa, Wayne County Community College
Janet Jenkins, Arkansas Tech University
Kenneth Koons, Virginia Military Institute
Raymond Krohn, Boise State University

Elizabeth Littell-Lamb, University of Tampa
Chrissy Lutz, Fort Valley State University
Mary Lyons-Carmona, University of Nebraska-Omaha
John McCannon, Southern New Hampshire University
David K. McQuilkin, Bridgewater College
Kyriakos Nalmpantis, Kent State University
Victor Padilla, Wright College
Dave Price, Santa Fe College
Marsha Robinson, Miami University
Shelley Rose, Cleveland State University
Julie Smith, Mount Aloysius College
Michael Swope, Wayne County Community College
Kelly Thompson, Wayne County Community College
Ann Tschetter, University of Nebraska-Lincoln
James Williams, University of Indianapolis
Bryan Wuthrich, Santa Fe College

The author would also like to acknowledge the following instructors who lent their insight and guidance to the previous editions: Siamak Adhami, Saddleback Community College; Sanjam Ahluwalia, Northern Arizona University; David G. Atwill, Pennsylvania State University; Susan Autry, Central Piedmont Community College; Ewa K. Bacon, Lewis University; Brett Berliner, Morgan State University; Edward Bond, Alabama A&M University; Bradford C. Brown, Bradley University; Gayle K. Brunelle, California State University, Fullerton; Clea Bunch, University of Arkansas at Little Rock; Rainer Buschmann, California State University, Channel Islands; Jorge Canizares-Esguerra, State University of New York–Buffalo; Bruce A. Castleman, San Diego State University; Harold B. Cline, Jr., Middle Georgia College; Simon Cordery, Monmouth College; Steve Corso, Elwood-John Glenn High School; Dale Crandall-Bear, Solano Community College; Gregory Crider, Winthrop University; Cole Dawson, Warner Pacific College; Hilde De Weerdt, University of Tennessee, Knoxville; Anna Dronzek, University of Minnesota, Morris; Jodi Eastberg, Alverno College; James R. Evans, Southeastern Community College; Robert Fish, Japan Society of New York; Eve Fisher, South Dakota State University; Robert J. Flynn, Portland Community College; Gladys Frantz-Murphy, Regis University; Timothy Furnish, Georgia Perimeter College; James E. Genova, The Ohio State University; Deborah Gerish, Emporia State University; Rick Gianni, Purdue University Calumet; Kurt A. Gingrich, Radford University; Candace Gregory-Abbott, California State University, Sacramento; Paul L. Hanson, California Lutheran University; A. Katie Harris, Georgia State University; Timothy Hawkins, Indiana State University; Linda Wilke Heil, Central Community College; Mark Hoffman, Wayne County Community College District; Don Holsinger, Seattle Pacific University; Mary N. Hovanec, Cuyahoga Community College; Bram Hubbell, Friends Seminary; Jonathan Judaken, University of Memphis; Thomas E. Kaiser, University of Arkansas at Little Rock; Frances Kelleher, Grand Valley State University; Carol Keller, San Antonio College; Patricia A. Kennedy, Leeward Community College–University of Hawaii; Kim Klein, Shippensburg University; Rachel Layman, Lawrence North High School; Jonathan Lee, San Antonio College;

Thomas Lide, San Diego State University; Derek S. Linton, Hobart and William Smith Colleges; David L. Longfellow, Baylor University; Christine Lovasz-Kaiser, University of Southern Indiana; John Lyons, Joliet Junior College; Mary Ann Mahony, Central Connecticut State University; Erik C. Maiershofer, Point Loma Nazarene University; Afshin Marashi, California State University, Sacramento; Laurence Marvin, Berry College; Robert B. McCormick, University of South Carolina Upstate; Patrick McDevitt, University at Buffalo SUNY; Doug T. McGetchin, Florida Atlantic University; Bill Mihalopoulos, Northern Michigan University; W. Jack Miller, Pennsylvania State University—Abington; Edwin Moise, Clemson University; Kerry Muhlestein, Brigham Young University–Hawaii; Aarti Nakra, Salt Lake Community College; Peter Ngwafu, Albany State University; Monique O'Connell, Wake Forest University; Melvin Page, East Tennessee State University; Annette Palmer, Morgan State University; Nicholas C. J. Pappas, Sam Houston State University; Craig Patton, Alabama A & M University; Patricia M. Pelley, Texas Tech University; William Pelz, Elgin Community College; John Pesda, Camden County College; Paul Philp, John Paul II HS/Eastfield Community College; Jason Ripper, Everett Community College; Pamela Roseman, Georgia Perimeter College; Paul Salstrom, St. Mary-of-the-Woods; Sharlene Sayegh, California State University, Long Beach; Michael Seth, James Madison University; Rose Mary Sheldon, Virginia Military Institute; David Simonelli, Youngstown State University; Peter Von Sivers, University of Utah; Anthony J. Steinhoff, University of Tennessee–Chattanooga; Nancy L. Stockdale, University of Central Florida; Bill Strickland, East Grand Rapids High School; Robert Shannon Sumner, University of West Georgia; Kate Transchel, California State University, Chico; Sally N. Vaughn, University of Houston; Thomas G. Velek, Mississippi University for Women; Kurt Waters, Centreville High School; and Kenneth Wilburn, East Carolina University.

The author has incurred many intellectual debts in developing his expertise in world history, as well as in preparing this text. To begin with, I cannot find words to express my gratitude to the editors and staff at Cengage Learning—Brooke Barbier, Tonya Lobato, Carol Newman, and Jean Woy—who had enough faith in this project to tolerate my missed deadlines and sometimes grumpy responses to editorial decisions or some other crisis. I also owe an incalculable debt to my development editor on the first edition, Phil Herbst, who prodded and pampered and helped me write for a student, rather than scholarly, audience. Tonya Lobato adroitly supervised the second and third editions. Abbey Stebing ably handled photos; Charlotte Miller, maps; Yashmita Hota, general project management; and Cara Swan, the wealth of ancillary materials. I also owe a great debt to Pam Gordon, whose interest and encouragement got this project started, and Nancy Blaine, who skillfully oversaw the writing and revising of the first two editions. Ken Wolf of Murray State University prepared the initial drafts of several of the early chapters in the first edition and in other ways gave me useful criticism and advice. I am grateful to historians such as James Hastings, Edwin Moise, Michelle Pinto,

Rick Gianni, and Ibrahim Shafie who pointed out factual errors in the first two editions. I would also like to acknowledge the inspiring mentors who helped me at various stages of my academic preparation: Bill Goldman, who introduced me to world history at Pasadena High School in California; Charles Hobart and David Poston, University of Redlands professors who sparked my interest in Asia; George Wong, Bart Stoodley, and especially Andrew and Margaret Roy, my mentors at Chung Chi College in Hong Kong; Walter Vella, Robert Van Niel, and Daniel Kwok, who taught me Asian studies at Hawaii; and John Smail and Philip Curtin, under whom I studied comparative world history in the immensely exciting PhD program at Wisconsin. My various sojourns in East Asia, Southeast Asia, and East Africa allowed me to meet and learn from many inspiring and knowledgeable scholars. I have also been greatly stimulated and influenced in my approach by the writings of many fine global historians, but I would single out Philip Curtin, Marshall Hodgson, L. S. Stavrianos, William McNeill, Fernand Braudel, Eric Hobsbawm, Immanuel Wallerstein, and Peter Stearns. Curtin, Hobsbawm, and McNeill also gave me personal encouragement concerning my writing in the field, for which I am very grateful.

Colleagues at the various universities where I taught have been supportive of my explorations in world and comparative history. Most especially I acknowledge the friendship, support, and intellectual collaboration over three and a half decades of my colleagues in the interdisciplinary Social Change and Development Department at the University of Wisconsin–Green Bay (UWGB), especially Harvey Kaye, Lynn Walter, Larry Smith, Andy Kersten, Kim Nielsen, Andrew Austin, and the late Tony Galt, as well as members of the History faculty. I have also benefited immeasurably as a world historian from the visiting lecture series sponsored by UWGB's Center for History and Social Change, directed by Harvey Kaye, which over the years has brought in dozens of outstanding scholars. My students at UWGB and elsewhere have also taught me much.

I also thank my colleagues in the World History Association (WHA), who have generously shared their knowledge, encouraged my work, and otherwise provided an exceptional opportunity for learning and an exchange of ideas. I am proud to have helped establish this organization, which incorporates world history teachers at all levels of education and in many nations. Among many others, I want to express a special thank-you to longtime friends and colleagues in the WHA from whom I have learned so much and with whom I have shared many wonderful meals and conversations.

Finally, I need to acknowledge the loving support and intellectual contributions of my wife Kathy, who patiently, although not always without complaint, for the many years of the project put up with my hectic work schedule and the ever-growing piles of research materials, books, and chapter drafts scattered around our cluttered den and sometimes colonizing other space around the house.

About the Author

Craig A. Lockard is Ben and Joyce Rosenberg Professor of History Emeritus in the Social Change and Development Department at the University of Wisconsin–Green Bay, where he taught courses on Asian, African, comparative, and world history from 1975 to 2010. He has also taught at SUNY-Buffalo, SUNY-Stony Brook, and the University of Bridgeport, and twice served as a Fulbright-Hays professor at the University of Malaya in Malaysia. After undergraduate studies at the University of Redlands, during which he was able to spend a semester in Austria and a year as an exchange student at a Chung Chi College in Hong Kong (now part of the Chinese University of Hong Kong), the author earned an MA in Asian Studies at the University of Hawaii and a PhD in Comparative World and Southeast Asian History at the University of Wisconsin–Madison. His published books, articles, essays, and reviews range over a wide spectrum of topics: world history; Southeast Asian history, politics, and society; Malaysian studies; Asian emigration and diasporas; the Vietnam War; and folk, popular, rock, and world music. Among his major books are *Southeast Asia in World History* (2009); *WORLD* (2009); *Chinese Society and Politics in Sarawak: Historical Essays* (2009); *Dance of Life: Popular Music and Politics in Modern Southeast Asia* (1998); and *From Kampung to City: A Social History of Kuching, Malaysia, 1820–1970* (1987). He was also part of the task force that prepared revisions to the U.S. National Standards in World History (1996). Professor Lockard has served on various editorial advisory boards, including the *Journal of World History*, *World History Connected*, and *The History Teacher*, and as book review editor for the *Journal of Asian Studies* and the *World History Bulletin*. He was one of the founders of the World History Association, served as the organization's first secretary and several terms as a member of the Executive Council. He has lived and traveled widely in Asia, Africa, and Europe.

Note on Spelling and Usage

Transforming foreign words and names, especially those from non-European languages, into spellings usable for English-speaking readers presents a challenge. Sometimes, as with Chinese, Thai, and Malay/Indonesian, several Romanized spelling systems have developed. Generally I have chosen user-friendly spellings that are widely used in other Western writings (such as *Aksum* for the classical Ethiopian state and *Ashoka* for the classical Indian king). For Chinese, I generally use the *pinyin* system developed in the People's Republic over the past few decades (such as *Qin* and *Qing* rather than the older *Chin* and *Ching* for these dynasties, and *Beijing* instead of *Peking*), but for a few terms and names (such as the twentieth-century political leaders *Sun Yat-sen* and *Chiang Kai-shek*) I have retained an older spelling more familiar to Western readers and easier to pronounce. The same strategy is used for some other terms or names from Afro-Asian societies, such as *Cairo* instead of *al-Cahira* (the Arabic name) for the Egyptian city, *Bombay* instead of *Mumbai* (the current Indian usage) for India's largest city, and *Burma* instead of *Myanmar*. In some cases I have favored a newer spelling widely used in a region and modern scholarship but not perhaps well known in the West. For example, in discussing Southeast Asia I follow contemporary scholarship and use *Melaka* instead of *Malacca* for the Malayan city and *Maluku* rather than *Moluccas* for the Indonesian islands. Similarly, like Africa specialists I have opted to use some newer spellings, such as *Gikuyu* rather than *Kikuyu* for the Kenyan ethnic group. To simplify things for the reader I have tried to avoid using diacritical marks within words. Sometimes their use is unavoidable, such as for the premodern Chinese city of *Chang'an;* the two syllables here are pronounced separately. I also follow the East Asian custom of rendering Chinese, Japanese, and Korean names with the surname (family name) first (e.g., *Mao Zedong, Tokugawa Ieyasu*). The reader is also referred to the opening essay, "Introducing World History," for explanations of the dating system used (such as the Common Era and the Intermediate Era) and geographical concepts (such as Eurasia for Europe and Asia, and Oceania for Australia, New Zealand, and the Pacific islands).

Introducing World History

"A journey of a thousand miles begins with the first step."

—Chinese Proverb

This introduction helps you take the important "first step" toward understanding the scope and challenge of studying world history, presenting the main concepts and themes of world history to serve as your guide, while providing a foretaste of the lively debates among historians as they try to make sense of the past, and how societies' contacts with one another created the interconnected world we know today.

What Do Historians Do?

History, the study of the past, looks at all of human life, thought, and behavior. The job of the historian is to both describe *and* interpret the past. Most professional historians want to make sense of historical events. Two general concepts help in these efforts: continuity and change. The legal system in the United States, for example, is unlike any other in the world, but has also been shaped in part by both English and ancient Roman legal practices.

Historians face their greatest challenges in interpreting the past. Although most strive to support their generalizations with evidence, they often disagree on how an event should be interpreted, sometimes because of political differences. In 1992 a widely publicized debate marked the 500-year anniversary of the first cross-Atlantic voyage of Christopher Columbus to the Western Hemisphere in 1492. Some historians pictured Columbus as a farsighted pioneer who made possible communication between the hemispheres, while others saw him as an immoral villain who began a pattern of exploiting Native American peoples by Europeans. Similar debates raged about whether it was necessary for the United States to drop atomic bombs on Japan in 1945, killing thousands of Japanese civilians but also ending World War II.

Our understanding of the past often changes as historians both acquire new information and use old information to answer new questions. Only within the past sixty years, for example, have historians studied the diaries and journals that reveal the important role of women during the American Civil War. Recently some historians used long neglected sources to conclude that, a millennium ago, China had the world's most dynamic economy and sophisticated technology. Similarly, historians have recently discovered thousands of old books written in African languages, forcing a rethinking of literacy and scholarship in West African societies hundreds of years ago.

What history "tells us" is constantly evolving. New evidence, changing interests, and the asking of new questions all add up to seeing things in a new light. No text contains the whole or final truth. **Historical revision**, or changing understanding of the past, and the difficulties of interpretation also make history controversial. In recent years heated debates about what schools should teach about history have erupted in many countries, including Japan, India, France, Egypt, and the United States.

Historians bridge the gap between the humanities and social sciences. As humanists, historians study the philosophies, religions, literatures, and arts that people generated over the ages. As social scientists, historians examine political, social, and economic patterns, though frequently asking questions different from those asked by anthropologists, economists, political scientists, and sociologists, who are generally more concerned with the present and theoretical questions. Historians also study people in their many roles and stations in life, the accomplishments of the rich and famous as well as the struggles and dreams of common women and men.

Why Study World History?

World or global history, the broadest field of history, studies the human record as a whole and the experiences of people in all the world's inhabited regions—Africa, the Americas, Asia, Europe, and the Pacific Basin—and also helps us better understand individual societies by making it easier to look at them comparatively. Studying history on a global scale also brings out patterns of life, cultural traditions, and connections between societies that go beyond a particular region, such as the spread of Buddhism, which followed the trade routes throughout southern and eastern Asia. World history helps us comprehend both the "forest" ("big picture") and the "trees" (individual societies), allowing us to situate ourselves in a broader context.

This helps us understand our increasingly connected world. Decisions made in Washington, D.C., Paris, or Tokyo influence citizens in Argentina, Senegal, and Malaysia, just as events elsewhere often affect the lives of people in Europe and North America. World historians use the widest angle of vision to comprehend how diverse local traditions and international trends intermingle. Western phenomena such as McDonald's, Hard Rock Cafes, French wines, Hollywood films, churches, the Internet, cell phones, and text messaging have spread around the world but so have non-Western products and ideas, among them Mexican soap operas, Chinese food, Japanese cars, Indonesian arts, African rhythms, and the Islamic religion. We must remember that, for all their idiosyncrasies, each society develops in a wider world.

A global perspective also highlights the past achievements of all peoples. The history of science, for example, shows that key inventions—printing, sternpost rudders, the compass, the wheelbarrow, gunpowder—originated in China, and the modern system of numbering came from India, reaching Europe from the Middle East as "Arabic" numerals. Indeed, various peoples—Mesopotamians, Egyptians, Greeks, Chinese, Indians, Arabs—built the early foundation for modern science and technology; their discoveries moved along the trade routes. Importers of technology and ideas often modified or improved on them. For example, Europeans made good use of Chinese, Indian, and Arab technologies, as well as their own inventions, in their quest to explore the world in the fifteenth and sixteenth centuries. The interdependence among and exchanges between peoples is a historical as well as a present reality.

The World History Challenge

When we study world history, we see other countries and peoples, past and present, with which we may be unfamiliar. World history helps us to recognize how some of the attitudes we absorb from the particular society and era we live in shape, and may distort, our understanding of the world and of history. Coming to terms with this mental baggage means examining such things as maps and geographical concepts and acquiring intellectual tools for comprehending other cultures.

Broadening the Scope of Our Histories

During much of the twentieth century, many high school and college students in North America were taught some version of a course, usually called Western Civilization, that emphasized the rise of western Europe and the European contributions to modern North American societies. This course recognized the undeniably influential role of Western nations, technologies, and ideas in the modern world, but also reflected more available data on Europe and North America compared with the rest of the world. This approach often exaggerated the role that Europe played in world history before modern times, pushing Asian, African, and Native American peoples and their accomplishments into the background while underplaying the contributions these peoples made to Europe. Students usually learned little about China, India, or Islamic societies, and even less about Africa, Southeast Asia, or Latin America.

In the 1960s history teaching began to change in North America. The political independence of most Asian, African, and Caribbean nations from Western nations fostered a more sophisticated understanding of African, Asian, Latin American, Native American, and Pacific island history in North America and Europe, making it easier to write a history of the entire globe. As a result, world history courses, rare before the 1960s, became increasingly common in U.S. universities, colleges, and high schools by the late twentieth century and have proliferated in several other countries, such as Australia, Canada, South Africa, China, and the Netherlands.

Revising Maps and Geography

Maps not only tell us where places are; they also create a mental image of the world, revealing how peoples perceive themselves and others. For example, Chinese maps once portrayed China as the "Middle Kingdom," the center of the world surrounded by "barbarians," reflecting and deepening the Chinese sense of superiority over neighboring peoples. Similarly, 2,500 years ago, Greek maps showed Greece at the center of the inhabited world known to them.

Even modern maps can be misleading. For example, the Mercator projection (or spatial presentation) still used in many school maps and atlases in North America and elsewhere, is based on a sixteenth-century European model that distorts the relative size of landmasses, greatly exaggerating Europe, North America, and Greenland while diminishing the lands nearer the equator and in the Southern Hemisphere. Hence, Africa, India, Southeast Asia, China, and South America look much smaller than they actually are. In the United States, maps using a Mercator projection have often tellingly placed the Americas in the middle of the map, cutting Asia in half, suggesting that the United States, appearing larger than it actually is, plays the central role in the world. Some alternative maps give a more accurate view of relative size. For example, the oval-shaped Eckert projection uses an ellipse that shows a better balance of size and shape while minimizing distortion of continental areas. A comparison between the Mercator and Eckert world maps is shown on this page and the next.

Concepts of geographical features and divisions, such as continents, the large landmasses on which most people live, also shape mental images. The classical Greeks used the terms *Europe*, *Africa*, and *Asia* in defining their world 2,500 years ago; later Europeans transformed these terms into the names for continents. For centuries Western peoples have considered Europe a continent although Europe is not a separate landmass, and the physical barriers between it and Asia are not that significant. If towering mountain ranges and other geographical barriers mark off a continent, India (blocked off by truly formidable mountains) or Southeast Asia make better candidates than Europe. Seeing Asia as a single continent is also a problem, given its spectacular size and geographical diversity. Today world geographers and historians often consider Europe and Asia to constitute one huge continent, Eurasia, containing several subcontinental regions such as Europe, South Asia, and East Asia.

Popular terms such as *Near East*, *Middle East*, or *Far East* are also misleading. They were originally formulated by Europeans to describe regions in relationship to Europe. Much depends on the viewer's position; Australians, for example, often label nearby Southeast and East Asia as the "Near North." Few Western scholars of China or Japan today refer to the "Far East," preferring the more neutral term *East Asia*. This text considers the term *Near East*, long used for western Asia, as outdated, but it refers to Southwest Asia and North Africa, closely linked historically (especially after the rise of Islam 1,400 years ago), as the Middle East, since that term is more convenient than the alternatives. The text also uses the term *Oceania* to refer to Australia, New Zealand, and the Pacific islands.

Rethinking the Dating System

A critical feature of historical study is the dating of events. World history challenges us by making us aware that all dating systems are based on the assumptions of a particular culture. Many Asian peoples saw history as moving in great cycles of birth, maturation, and decay (sometimes involving millions of years), whereas Westerners saw history as moving in a straight

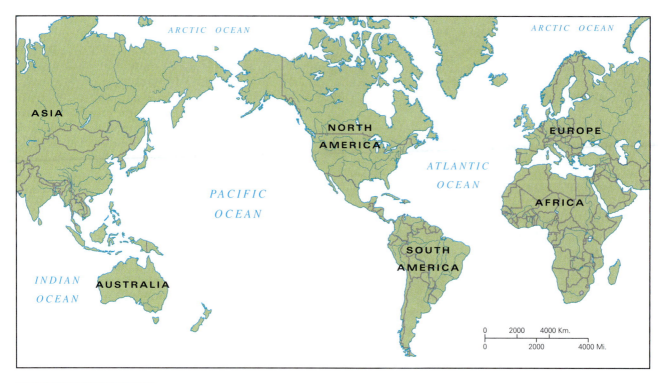

MERCATOR PROJECTION

line from past to future (as can be seen in the chronologies within each chapter). Calendars were often tied to myths about the world's creation or about a people's or country's origins. Hence, the classical Roman calendar was based on the founding of the city of Rome around 2,700 years ago.

The dating system used throughout the Western world today is based on the Gregorian Christian calendar, created by a sixteenth-century Roman Catholic pope, Gregory XIII. It uses the birth of Christianity's founder, Jesus of Nazareth, around 2,000 years ago as the turning point. Dates for events prior to the Christian era were identified as B.C. (before Christ); years in the Christian era were labeled A.D. (for the Latin *anno domini*, "in the year of the Lord"). Many history books published in Europe and North America still employ this system, which has spread around the world in recent centuries.

The notion of Christian and pre-Christian eras has no longer been satisfactory for studies of world history because it is rooted in the viewpoint of only one religious tradition, whereas there are many in the world, usually with different calendars. Muslims, for example, who consider the revelations of the prophet Muhammad to be history's central event, begin their dating system with Muhammad's journey, within Arabia, from the city of Mecca to Medina in 622 A.D. The Chinese chronological system divides history into cycles stretching over 24 million years. The Chinese are now in the fifth millennium of the current cycle, which corresponds more accurately than does the Gregorian calendar to the beginning of the world's oldest cities and states, between 5,000 and 6,000 years ago. Many other alternative dating systems exist. Selecting one over the others constitutes favoritism for a particular society or cultural tradition.

Therefore, most world historians and many specialists in Asian and African, and some in European, U.S., and Latin American history, have moved toward a more secular, or non-religious, concept, the Common Era. This system still accepts as familiar, at least to Western readers, the dates used in the Western calendar, but it calls the period after the transition a "common" era, since many influential, dynamic societies existed two millennia ago throughout the world, not only in the Judeo-Christian Holy Land. Two millennia ago, the beginning of the Common Era, the Roman Empire was at its height, Chinese and Indian empires ruled large chunks of Asia, and many peoples in the Eastern Hemisphere were linked by trade and religion to a greater extent than ever before. Several African and American urban societies also flourished. Hence this period makes a useful and familiar benchmark. In the new system, events are dated as B.C.E. (before the Common Era) and as C.E. (Common Era, which begins in year 1 of the Christian calendar). This change is an attempt at including all the world's people.

Rethinking the Division of History into Periods

To make world history more comprehensible, historians divide long periods of time into smaller segments, such as "the ancient world" or "modern history," each marked by certain key events or turning points, a system known as **periodization**. For example, scholars of European, Islamic, Chinese, Indonesian, or U.S. history generally agree among themselves on the major eras and turning points for the region or country they

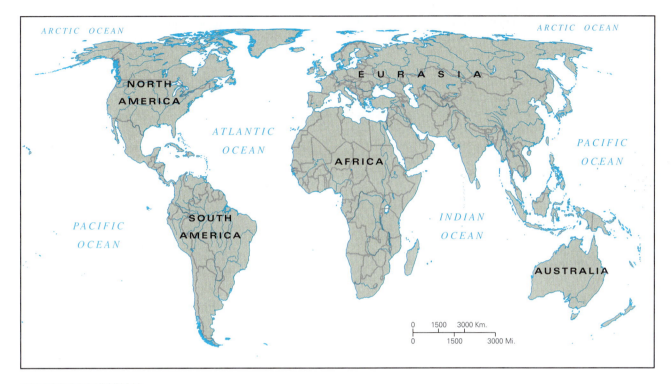

ECKERT PROJECTION

study, but world historians need a system that can encompass all parts of the world since most historic events did not affect all regions. For instance, developments that were key to eastern Eurasia, such as the spread of Buddhism, did not directly affect western Eurasia and Africa in these centuries; the Americas remained isolated from the Eastern Hemisphere until about 500 years ago.

Given the need for an inclusive chronological pattern, this book divides history into periods, each notable for significant changes around the world:

1. **Ancient (100,000–600 B.C.E.)** The Ancient Era, during which the foundations for world history were built, can be divided into two distinct periods. During the long centuries known as Prehistory (ca. 100,000–4000 B.C.E.), Stone Age peoples, living in small groups, survived by hunting and gathering food. Eventually some of them began simple farming and living in villages, launching the era of agrarian societies. Between 4000 and 600 B.C.E., agriculture became more productive, the first cities and states were established in both hemispheres, and some societies invented writing, allowing historians to better study their experiences and ideas.

2. **Classical (600 B.C.E.–600 C.E.)** The creation of more states and complex agrarian societies, the birth of major religions and philosophies, the formation of the first large empires, and the expansion of long-distance trade, which linked distant peoples, marked the Classical Era.

3. **Intermediate (600–1500 C.E.)** The Intermediate Era, comprising a long middle period or "middle ages" of expanding horizons that modified or displaced the classical societies, was characterized by increasing trade connections between distant peoples within the same hemisphere, the growth and spread of several older religions and of a new faith, Islam, and oceanic exploration by Asians and Europeans.

4. **Early Modern (1450–1750 C.E.)** During the Early Modern Era, the whole globe became intertwined as European exploration and conquests in the Americas, Africa, and southern Asia fostered the rise of a global economy, capitalism, and a trans-Atlantic slave trade while undermining American, African, and some other societies.

5. **Modern (1750–1945 C.E.)** Rapid technological and economic change in Europe and North America, Western colonization of many Asian and African societies, political revolutions and ideologies, world wars, and a widening gap between rich and poor societies distinguished the Modern Era.

6. **Contemporary (1945–present)** In the Contemporary Era we see a more closely interlinked world, including the global spread of commercial markets, cultures, and communications, the collapse of Western colonial empires, international organizations, new technologies, struggles by poor nations to develop economically, environmental destruction, and conflict between powerful nations.

Understanding Cultural and Historical Differences

The study of world history challenges us to understand peoples and ideas very different from our own. The past is, as one writer has put it, "a foreign country; they do things differently there."[1] As human behavior changes with the times, sometimes dramatically, so do people's beliefs, including moral and ethical standards. For example, in Asia centuries ago, Assyrians and Mongols sometimes killed everyone in cities that resisted their conquest. Some European Christians seven hundred years ago burned suspected heretics and witches at the stake and enjoyed watching blind beggars fight. Across the Atlantic, American peoples such as the Aztecs and Incas engaged in human sacrifice. None of these behaviors would be morally acceptable today in most societies.

Differences in customs complicate efforts to understand people of earlier centuries. We need not approve of empire builders, plunderers, human sacrifice, and witch burning, but we should be careful about applying our current standards of behavior and thought to people who lived in different times and places. We should avoid **ethnocentrism**, viewing others narrowly through the lens of one's own society and its values. Many historians perceive value-loaded words such as *primitive*, *barbarian*, *civilized*, or *progress* that carry negative or positive meanings as often matters of judgment rather than fact. For instance, soldiers on the battlefield may consider themselves civilized and their opponents barbarians. And progress, such as industrialization, often brings negative developments, such as pollution, along with the positive.

Today anthropologists use the term **cultural relativism** to remind us that, while all people have much in common, societies are diverse and unique, embodying different standards of proper behavior and thought. Hence, cultures may have very different ideas about children's obligations to their parents, what happens to people's souls when they die, or what constitutes pleasing music. We can still conclude that Mongol empire builders in Eurasia some eight hundred years ago were brutal; or that the mid-twentieth-century Nazi German dictator, Adolph Hitler, was a murderous tyrant; or that laws in some societies today that blame and penalize women who are raped are wrong. But cultural relativism discourages us from criticizing other cultures or ancient peoples just because they are or were different from us.

The Major Themes

This text uses certain themes to take maximum advantage of world history's power to illuminate both change and continuity as we move from the past to the present. Specifically, the author asked himself: What do educated students today need to know about world history to understand the globalizing era in which they live?

Three broad themes shaped around three concepts—societies, networks, and transitions—help you comprehend how today's world emerged.

1. **SOCIETIES** are broad groups of people that have common traditions, institutions and organized patterns of relationships with each other. Societies, influenced by environmental factors, were defined by distinctive but often changing cultures, beliefs, social forms, governments, economies, and ways of life.
2. **NETWORKS** are collections of links between different societies, such as the routes over which traders, goods, diplomats, armies, ideas, and information travel. Over the centuries societies were increasingly connected to, and modified by other societies, through growing networks forged by phenomena such as population movement, long-distance trade, exploration, military expansion, colonization, and the diffusion of ideas and technologies. Growing networks eventually fostered a global system in which distant peoples came into frequent contact.
3. **TRANSITIONS** are passages, changes, events, or movements that reshape societies and regions. Each major historical era was marked by one or more great transitions that were sparked by events or innovations that had profound, enduring influences on many societies and that gradually reshaped the world.

The first theme recognizes the importance in world history of the distinctiveness of societies. Cultural traditions and social patterns differed greatly. For example, societies in Eurasia fostered several influential philosophical and religious traditions, from Confucianism in eastern Asia to Christianity, born in the Middle East and later nourished both there and in Europe. Historians often identify unique traditions in a society that go back hundreds or even thousands of years.

The second theme acknowledges the way societies have contacted and engaged with each other through networks to create the interdependent world we know today. The spread of technologies and ideas, exploration and colonization, and global trade across Eurasia and Africa and then into the Western Hemisphere spurred this interlinking process. Today networks such as the World Wide Web, airline routes, multinational corporations, and terrorist organizations operate on a global scale. The third theme helps to emphasize major developments that shaped world history. The most important transitions include, roughly in chronological order, the beginning of agriculture, the rise of cities and states, the birth and spread of philosophical and religious traditions, the forming of great empires, the linking of Eurasia by the Mongols, the European seafaring explorations and conquests, the Industrial Revolution, the forging and dismantling of Western colonial empires, world wars, and the invention of electronic technologies that allow for instantaneous communication around the world.

With these themes in mind, the text constructs the rich story of world history. The intellectual experience of studying world history is exciting and will give you a clearer understanding of how the world as you know it came to be.

---

[1]P. I. Harley, quoted in David Lowenthal, *The Past Is a Foreign Country* (Cambridge: Cambridge University Press, 1985), p. xvi.

SOCIETIES, NETWORKS, AND TRANSITIONS

A GLOBAL HISTORY

PART IV

Connecting the Early Modern World, 1450–1750

CHAPTER OUTLINE

In 1552 a Spanish historian called the landing in the Americas by a naval expedition led by Christopher Columbus "the greatest event since the creation of the world."[1] It was a claim that ignored many previous achievements, yet the permanent connecting of the hemispheres that followed Columbus in fact reshaped the world, helping to make the Early Modern Era vastly different from the Intermediate Era that preceded it. History was now painted on a larger canvas, and peoples' horizons around the world rapidly expanded. In this new global age, greatly increased communication and mobility resulted in encounters, some friendly, others hostile, between societies once remote from each other, as travel and exploration revealed the resources of the inhabited world. The exchange among societies of people, diseases, ideas, technologies, capital, resources, and products now occurred on a greater scale than ever

before. Europeans forged a new world economy, while disrupting, changing, and sometimes destroying many of the societies they encountered, especially in the Americas and parts of Africa and Southeast Asia. Because of the growing contacts spanning the two hemispheres, for the first time in history an interconnected world became a reality. The links forged during the Early Modern Era laid a foundation for the building, often by force, of an even more integrated global system in the Modern Era.

Transitions
New Empires and Military Power

Increasing wealth and power, as well as more deadly weapons, allowed some Early Modern societies to build large empires that helped them acquire vast resources without relying chiefly on trade. Historians characterize most of these empires as "gunpowder empires" because they depended on bigger and better gunpowder weapons, including cannon mounted on ships, field artillery, and guns used by individual soldiers. Gunpowder empires dominated Eurasia and the Americas. Only a few European countries, however, had the means, including sea power, to envision dominating very distant societies in Africa, the Americas, Asia, and the Pacific in their quest for "gold, god, and glory."

As they spread around Eurasia and North Africa, gunpowder weapons changed warfare. In Europe—full of competitive, often hostile states—no

ruler had a monopoly on weapons. Hence rulers had an incentive to constantly improve their armaments, and as they did, the wars in Europe became far more deadly. The European powers used some of their weapons against each other. For example, the Dutch and Portuguese were bitter rivals for influence and territory in southern Asia and Brazil. With better ships and weapons, Europeans controlled Atlantic shipping and also gained considerable power over Indian Ocean trade, which brought them great wealth. As the English adventurer Sir Walter Raleigh recognized in 1608, "Who so commands the sea commands the trade of the world; who so commands the trade of the world commands the riches of the world."[2]

The maritime expansion of Europe contrasted sharply with that of the Chinese. Just as western Europeans turned outward and developed a naval technology to match that of the Chinese, the Chinese pulled back from their grand maritime expeditions of the early 1400s and turned inward, although some Chinese merchants continued to venture out to trade. China enjoyed huge budget surpluses until the late 1700s and did not need colonies or foreign trade to prosper. Moreover, the Chinese government often viewed merchants as a threat, whereas western European merchants had the support of their

[1]Francisco Lopez de Gomara, quoted in Roger Schlesinger, *In the Wake of Columbus: The Impact of the New World on Europe, 1492–1650* (Wheeling, IL.: Harlan Davidson, 1996), 23.

[2]Quoted in Peter J. Hugill, *World Trade Since 1430: Geography, Technology, and Capitalism* (Baltimore: Johns Hopkins University Press, 1993), vii.

governments, especially in England, the Netherlands, Spain, and France. The resulting political competition between European states fostered exploration and colonization.

Unlike Europeans, Asians took the development of their gunpowder arsenals only so far. The land-oriented Mughals ruling much of India saw little gain in developing naval armaments. With gunpowder weapons, the Qing dynasty greatly expanded China's land frontier deep into Central Asia and Tibet, thereby stabilizing their border regions. After that, secure in their power, the Qing emperors had little need to increase their offensive capability or challenge the Europeans in the oceans. Chinese firearms were adequate for ejecting the Dutch from Taiwan and the Russians from the Amur Valley in the 1600s, but two centuries later, European military technology far surpassed that of Asian powers, dramatically changing the hemispheric balance of power.

Societies
A Polycentric World

Despite the growth of empires, the Early Modern world had varied centers of political and economic power, a situation known as polycentrism. No one country or region could dominate all other rivals. European power was on the rise but remained limited in much of Asia, the Middle East, and large parts of Africa and the Americas, and the Pacific remained untouched by European exploration. For much of the era, the Ottoman Empire, Mughal India, and China were more politically, economically, and culturally influential in Eurasia than European societies. For example, many Muslims admired Mughal India, which became a destination for merchants, writers, and religious scholars. Hence, a Persian poet proclaimed: "Great is India, the Mecca of all in need. A journey to India is of essence to any man made worthy by knowledge and skill."[3]

The era was dynamic for many peoples. Across Eurasia varied societies experienced economic innovation, free markets, industrialization, and rising living standards. For example, cities such as Amsterdam in Holland, Isfahan **(is-fah-HAHN)** in Persia, and Ayuthia **(uh-YUT-uh-yuh)** in Siam were bustling trade crossroads, attracting merchants from all over Eurasia. Foreign merchants, such as the Dutch, Chinese, and Persians at Ayuthia, had to adapt to local customs to succeed. Sometimes, as in Siam, Tokugawa Japan, and Morocco, Europeans who disregarded local customs or threatened local governments were expelled.

The encounters between peoples fostered compromises and information exchange. Many Asians and Africans adapted ideas from other cultures to meet their own needs. Similarly, Spanish rule in the Americas survived only because the conquerors ultimately made compromises with Indian societies, including intermarriage. In the Spanish empire, as well as in other empires of the era such as the Ottoman and Mughal, laws recognized local customs, and different groups often maintained their own legal codes.

Science and technology remained creative all over Eurasia. The Chinese and British, for example, published important scientific books and invented new technologies, especially for the textile industry. New astronomical observatories were built in China, India, and the Middle East, although Europeans had by now developed a much keener interest than Asians in clocks and mathematics. Japan's fostering of schools gave it the world's highest literacy rate and an audience for a publishing industry. In addition, leaders of the European Renaissance, Reformation, and Enlightenment, Sufi mystics in the Ottoman and Mughal Empires, the Hindu bhakti **(BUK-tee)** movement in India, and some Chinese thinkers challenged accepted wisdom. Various European and Chinese philosophers emphasized reason, as did some Latin Americans. Indeed, some participants in the European Enlightenment were inspired by their growing knowledge of China, which was ruled by emperors who dabbled in philosophy. A French ambassador in 1688 praised Qing China for promoting "virtue, wisdom, prudence, good faith, sincerity, charity, gentleness, honesty [and] civility."[4]

Networks
The Emerging World Economy

With the opening of the Atlantic and Pacific Oceans to regular sea travel, connections spanning not just hemispheres but also the entire world were forged during the Early Modern Era. But, as with politics, these connections produced a polycentric structure in which both Europeans and Asians played important roles. Thanks to maritime expansion, western Europeans gradually created a global network of economic and political relationships that increasingly shaped the destinies of people around the world. Rather than the luxuries of earlier times, such as silks and spices, long-distance trade increasingly moved bulk items: essential natural resources, such as sugar and silver from the Americas, and manufactured goods, such as textiles from Europe and Asia. As traders moved commodities and capital faster and more cheaply over greater distances than ever before, western Europeans became the main beneficiaries of the increased communication and travel that shaped a gradual globalization of trade. Yet, European merchants were actually only a small part of global commerce; some Asian and African merchant groups also flourished, and some Asian states, particularly China and Siam, benefited from the increasing trade.

The capitalist market economy that gradually developed was increasingly centered on northwestern Europe, especially England and the Netherlands, but a half dozen other European countries were also enriched by trade (see map). For example, the Portuguese as well as the Dutch established regular maritime trade routes between Europe and Asia around Africa that allowed Europeans to avoid the overland routes through

[3]Quoted in Roger Savory, *Iran Under the Safavids* (Cambridge: Cambridge University Press, 1980), 205.

[4]Quoted in Gregory Blue, "China and Western Social Thought in the Modern Period," in *China and Historical Capitalism*, ed. Timothy Brook and Gregory Blue (New York: Cambridge University Press, 1999), 64.

DUTCH DIPLOMATS In this print, a Dutch delegation, eager to make an alliance with the Kongolese against the Portuguese, prostrate themselves before the Kongolese king, sitting on his throne under an imported chandelier, in 1642.

the Middle East, in the process harming their Muslim rivals by diminishing Persian and Ottoman commerce. The huge quantities of silver provided by the Spanish conquest of the Americas financed expansion of the European economy and, since Asian governments, especially China, valued silver, gave Europeans access to Asian markets. The Spanish establishment of a base at Manila in 1571 provided an essential economic link between eastern Eurasia and the Americas, forging a major foundation for a truly world economy.

But the transition to a European-dominated trading system took place over several centuries in Asia. Before the 1800s, when the transition was completed, Asia still boasted the bulk of world economic activity. The industries of China and India remained the twin pillars of Asian commerce well into the 1700s, and as late as 1775 Asians produced some 80 percent of goods. Many Asian societies imported raw materials from India (including raw cotton), China (especially silk), and Japan (copper) for production into exportable consumer goods. For example, Javanese women used beeswax

and dyes to transform Indian cloth into beautiful batik clothing. The economies of India and China dwarfed those of any other country. The most economically developed regions within China, Japan, India, and northwestern Europe may have enjoyed roughly comparable standards of living, including health and income levels. (See Historical Controversy: The Great Divergence between Europe and Asia).

Asian merchants, enjoying lower overhead and shrewd business skills, could often outcompete those from Europe and also traded over long distances. In the 1600s, for example, Arab and Persian traders remained influential at the main Mughal port, Surat, while north Indian merchants were found all over the Persian Gulf. European merchants competed best in Asia when they were supported by military force. Moreover, European-Asian trade relations often favored Asians. Since Asians had little interest in European manufactured goods such as clothing, which they considered inferior in quality to their own goods, Europeans bought Asian goods and resources such as Chinese tea with American silver and gold. Vast amounts

of American silver ended up in China, where it served as the basis of the monetary system and promoted economic growth. Meanwhile, Asian goods such as Indian textiles found a ready market around the world. Chinese goods transported from the Philippines were so much cheaper than Spanish ones in Peru that the Spanish viceroy complained it was "impossible to choke off the trade since a man can clothe his wife in Chinese silks for 25 pesos, whereas he could not provide her with clothing of Spanish silks with 200 pesos."[5]

Networks
Expanding Trade Networks

The growth of long-distance trade corresponded to the expansion of trade networks operated by different commercial communities. The rise of European power allowed Dutch, English, and French merchants to establish themselves in India, Southeast Asia, West Africa, eastern Europe, Russia, and the Caribbean Basin. Sephardic Jews, originally from Iberia, spread their trading networks throughout western Europe as well as in parts of South America, the Caribbean, and the Indian Ocean.

This growing commercial activity stimulated production for the market in mining and manufacturing but especially in tropical agriculture. The highly profitable plantations that sprung up around the Caribbean Basin, along the Atlantic coast of North and South America, and in the Philippines reflected the expansion of production. A growing trans-Atlantic slave trade from Africa provided cheap labor to the American plantations, enabling them to produce inexpensive calories for Europe in the form of sugar and, after 1700, abundant cotton for English textile mills. Slaves from various places also labored for Muslim enterprises in the Middle East and for European operations in southern Africa and Southeast Asia.

Groups specializing in trade were prominent in many lands. Traders of

---

[5]Quoted in Robert B. Marks, *The Origins of the Modern World: A Global and Ecological Narrative* (Lanham, MD: Rowman and Littlefield, 2002), 81.

EARLY MODERN TRADE ROUTES Between 1500 and 1700 the world economy developed and new trade routes proliferated. Major maritime routes linked Asia and the Americas across the Pacific; Europe, Asia, and the Americas across the Atlantic; and eastern and southern Asia with Africa and Europe across the Indian Ocean. © 2015 Cengage Learning

French or mixed French and Native American descent traveled deep into the North American continent contacting local peoples. Omani Arabs had a leading role in East African trade, while Muslim Hausa and Dyula Mandinka merchants traded in West Africa. Chinese remained active all over Southeast Asia, establishing permanent settlements in many cities and towns. For example, the Spanish in the Philippines depended on the large Chinese merchant class to supply many consumer goods. The Indian maritime trade network stretched westward to the Middle East and Northeast Africa and east to Southeast Asia and China. Meanwhile, Indian overland trade networks extended across Central Asia, Afghanistan, Tibet, Persia, the Caucasus states, and much of Russia. Armenian merchants based in Persia flourished in the overland trade from India to Central Asia and the Middle East, and from Persia to Russia, England, and the Baltic.

Transitions
Environmental Changes

Between 1300 and 1850 much of the world experienced a fluctuating "Little Ice Age," probably caused by a dimming sun and increased volcanic activity, that had significant consequences for many societies. In North America and Eurasia, this period brought cool temperatures, shorter growing seasons, and famine. For example, in the 1600s China often received either too much rain, which caused widespread flooding, or too little rain and late springs, which produced drought and reduced the growing season to allow for only one crop of rice rather than two. The lands bordering the North Atlantic saw much colder and wetter conditions, which diminished agricultural production and resulted in widespread starvation in much of Europe. Indeed, harsh weather conditions, combined with occasional outbreaks of bubonic plague, may have been one of the factors that spurred Europeans to seek new lands abroad. Climate change also affected tropical regions. For instance, West Africa had

abundant rain until 1700, when rainfall began diminishing, allowing desert to claim much of the Sahel and pushing savannah farming southward by several hundred miles.

Nonetheless, despite the poor weather, the distribution of new food sources and other resources was widening. Seaborne trade, especially from the Americas, also provided valuable resources, especially to coastal maritime states such as the Netherlands and Britain. The increased diffusion of resources fostered population growth. Indeed, American crops such as the potato helped Europe stave off even worse climate-related famines. Around the world the expansion of farming to sustain more people came at the expense of shifting cultivators, pastoralists, and food collectors, some of whom were killed or died off.

Partly because of the spread of food crops, especially from the Americas to Afro-Eurasia, world population increased significantly, from around 500 million to 750 million; China and India accounted for about half the total. Growth put severe pressure on land and resources. Expanding settlements and farming in frontier regions displaced woodlands, grasslands, and wetlands and reduced the variety of plant and animal life. As they had for millennia, people tapped the earth for underground resources, such as coal and iron ore. For farming and light industries, Early Modern economies relied chiefly on traditional power sources, such as people, animals, water, and wind.

Networks
The Exchange of Diseases, Animals, and Crops

As people in this era, especially Europeans and Africans, moved voluntarily or involuntarily to distant lands, they deliberately or accidentally brought with them species of animals, insects, bacteria, and plants that reshaped local ecosystems. These biological invasions, what historians have termed the Columbian Exchange, particularly accompanied the encounter between

Afro-Eurasia and the Americas. The European settlers in the Americas brought with them horses and food animals—pigs, chickens, sheep, and cattle—while ships returning to Europe carried with them American turkeys, which enriched Eurasian diets.

The exchange of diseases between the Eastern and Western Hemispheres had a greater impact on the Americas than on Eurasia and Africa. Native Americans had never experienced and hence never developed immunities to many Afro-Eurasian diseases, which now devastated the Americas. Smallpox brought the greatest known demographic catastrophe in world history, killing off around 90 percent of the peoples of the Americas. The disaster emptied productive land and paved the way for Europeans to settle the Americas and to import captive Africans to labor in mining and agriculture. Only in the highlands, such as the Andes Mountains in South America, did substantial concentrations of Native Americans survive. In contrast, only a few American diseases, especially syphilis, brought suffering to people in Europe and Africa.

Crop exchanges also proved momentous. Eurasian and African crops transformed some American regions. Most Native Americans had grown crops such as corn (maize) and potatoes on small plots, but settlers found that Afro-Eurasian crops such as wheat, rice, coffee, barley, and sugar were most successfully grown on large farms. Sugar had the most impact on the Americas, and vast acreage was devoted to its growth, mostly on plantations worked by African slaves and their descendants. Much of the sugar was exported to Europe for use to sweeten foods such as jam and breads and beverages such as tea and coffee.

American crops were adopted widely in the Eastern Hemisphere. Tobacco gained popularity in China and Europe. and many imports, such as tomatoes, made the once-bland European meals more varied. Potatoes became a mainstay of the European diet and the major crop grown in several societies. Maize (corn) could be grown on marginal land and proved a boon in Africa, Southwest Asia, and

dorling kindersley/Getty images

SMALLPOX VICTIMS IN THE AMERICAS Eurasian diseases accompanied the Europeans to the Americas, causing a catastrophic loss of life for the Native Americans, who had no immunity. As shown in this print from the 1500s, millions of people sickened and died from smallpox.

China. American chilies, hotter than Asian black peppers, proved hugely popular in South and Southeast Asian cooking, adding a sharp bite to curries and other foods. Peanuts became a key crop in West Africa. The new foods offered not only a more varied diet but also a healthier one.

Societies
Population Movements and Mixing

During the Early Modern Era, the growing networks of trade, information, and technology fostered changes in societies all over the world. Improved maritime technology made it possible for people to cross vast oceans and to do so in larger numbers than ever before. Global migration brought people with very different customs and values together, not always happily.

The largest population movement involved Europeans settling in the Americas and bringing with them enslaved Africans but few European

women. Since women comprised perhaps only a fifth of the Spanish and Portuguese who went to the Americas, men frequently sought partners among Native American and African women. Intermarriage or sexual contact between people from different ethnic groups produced new peoples with mixed cultural backgrounds, so that by 1750 in Latin America and in French colonies such as Louisiana a large part of the population blended European with Native American or African backgrounds. In turn, these groups' cultures often mixed the varying social influences, as in northeast Brazil, where people blended African religions and Catholic traditions. Unlike English North America, where any African ancestry usually meant classification as black, in much of Latin America a complex hierarchy of social categories developed based on gradations of skin color.

Migration and intermarriage also occurred in the Eastern Hemisphere. Dutch and Portuguese adventurers and merchants, most of them men, settled in southern Africa and the port cities of West Africa and South and Southeast Asia, often taking wives from the local population. The Portuguese settlers

raised their mixed-descent children as Portuguese-speaking Catholics, and Portuguese became the first language with global reach, spoken by a few million people in Brazil, coastal Africa, and southern Asia as well as Portugal. In coastal Africa the mixing of Europeans and Africans led to hybrid social groups. For example, the offspring of relations between Dutch men and African or Asian women were so common in South Africa that they became a distinct racial group, known as the Coloreds. As had been true for centuries, Arab and Indian traders also relocated to distant lands in Africa and Eurasia, often settling permanently and sometimes taking local wives. Many Chinese also moved into nearby territories such as Taiwan or settled in Southeast Asia, where they often married local women.

Societies
Changing Gender Relations

As the result of these changes, gender patterns were modified around the world. One-third of enslaved Africans taken to the Americas were women, some of whom were brought into close contact with slave-owning men, mostly white, who exercised control over their lives. The result was forced sexual activity and mixed-descent children. Since slave couples were often separated by sale, women held together many slave households, a social pattern that continued among many African Americans after the abolition of slavery. At the same time, Christian missionaries working among North American Indians often pursued policies that marginalized women in once-egalitarian cultures such as the Algonquians of eastern Canada and the Iroquois of New York. And in the parts of Africa most affected by slave trading, the absence of men in their productive years encouraged the remaining men to take multiple wives, a practice that may or may not have made life easier for women. Some women became active as slave traders, and women also played powerful roles in some of the newer kingdoms fostered by the trans-Atlantic slave trade, where they controlled access to the kings.

In much of Eurasia women experienced increasing subordination by men. Hence, women generally became more restricted in Mughal India, China, and Japan as patriarchal attitudes strengthened, largely as a result of internal factors. For example, as China's leaders turned more socially conservative, they imposed harsher laws against behavior considered deviant, such as homosexuality, and stressed the purity of women, which meant less freedom for women to leave home. More Chinese widows than ever before, forever faithful to their late husbands, frequently refused to remarry. In addition, Western missionaries and officials often sought to impose their own patriarchal prejudices on Asians. Hence, in Southeast Asia, the Spanish criticized Filipinos for tolerating adultery and premarital sex and punished those who engaged in these activities.

But there were exceptions to the growing restrictions on women. The Mughal emperor Akbar ordered that no woman could be forced by family or community pressures to immolate herself on her husband's funeral pyre. Many Chinese women from elite families published essays and poetry that were widely read and admired. One Chinese poet recalled how her father nurtured her talent: "Understanding that I was quite intelligent, He taught his daughters as he taught his sons, [advising us to] Develop together, support, and do not impede each other."[6]

Societies
Missionaries and Religious Change

The encounters between widely differing cultures around the world also had a religious dimension, forcing people to confront different belief systems while widening or sparking divisions in established faiths. Tensions simmering for several centuries finally fragmented Western Christianity into Catholic and diverse Protestant churches in the 1500s, spurring religious wars, militancy, and hostility toward non-Christians. Those in the majority often punished dissenters as heretics. Meanwhile, mystical Sufi orders became more influential in Islamic societies from Indonesia to West Africa. But the Sufis' popularity distressed dogmatists who despised mystical practices, fostering debate on Sufism's role and value among Ottoman, Mughal, and Central Asian Muslims. Another Islamic change was the Persian shift from the Sunni to the Shi'a branch of Islam, which caused many Sunnis to emigrate. At the same time, Muslims and animists lived side by side without conflict in parts of Africa, and in some European societies Protestants and Catholics learned to live in peace.

Several religions engaged in missionary activity. Christians actively sought converts in the Americas, Africa, and Asia; however, because Christian missionaries were often intolerant of local traditions and also fought among themselves, they were expulsed from Japan and China. In the Americas, one prominent Spanish clergyman strongly supported conquest and evangelization as a way of "civilizing" Native Americans, whom he described as "these pitiful men, in whom you will scarcely find any vestiges of humanness. They were born for servitude … [and] were justly conquered."[7] Despite such attitudes, Catholicism eventually triumphed in Latin America, Kongo, and the Philippines, while Protestant missionaries mostly concentrated on Catholic Europe, Southeast Asia, and North America, where they particularly targeted Native Americans and African slaves. But Christian missionary efforts had little success among Muslims, Theravada Buddhists, and Hindus. In contrast, Islam, which was not identified with unpopular Western conquest, attracted many converts in sub-Saharan Africa and southern Asia. Islam also spread into the Balkan societies under Ottoman control, and many Balkan peoples adopted the faith, forging a permanent divide between Christians and Muslims in the region.

Tensions sometimes led to secular approaches and tolerance rather than to religious zeal. To comprehend a changing world with diverse and challenging ideas, Chinese thinkers, European Enlightenment philosophers, and several Mughal emperors questioned religious dogmas and sought to broaden intellectual horizons. Theravada Buddhists generally respected all religions. Hence, when the French king, Louis XIV, sent a mission to King Narai of Ayuthia requesting that he and his people adopt Roman Catholicism, the Siamese monarch sent a letter back, arguing that God rejoiced not in religious uniformity but in theological diversities, preferring to be honored by different worships and ceremonies. And growing European knowledge of Chinese society, including Confucianism, led some thinkers to view China as an admirable, secular alternative model to the religious divisions and orthodoxies of Europe. In this way Asian ideas influenced some Europeans just as European ideas spread to some non-European peoples, a testament to an increasingly connected world.

[6]Quoted in Susan Mann, *Precious Records: Women in China's Long Eighteenth Century* (Stanford: Stanford University Press, 1997), 108.
[7]Juan Gimes de Sepulvida, in *1492: Discovery, Invasion, Encounter: Sources and Interpretations*, ed. Marvin Lunenfeld (Lexington, MA: D.C. Heath, 1991), 219—220.

15 Global Connections and the Remaking of Europe, 1450–1750

Universal History Archive/Getty Images

AMSTERDAM STOCK EXCHANGE During the seventeenth century, the Dutch port city of Amsterdam was the center of European commerce and played a key role in the world economy. The Amsterdam stock market, shown here in a painting from around 1754, attracted merchants and financiers from all over Europe.

"O, wonder! How many goodly creatures are there here! How beauteous mankind is! O brave new world That hath such people in't!"

— Miranda, in *The Tempest* by William Shakespeare, 1611[1]

European and world economies changed rapidly in the sixteenth century. Few places exemplified change more than the Flemish port city of Antwerp **(AN-twuhrp)**, with its fabulous Bourse **(boors)**, a huge building serving as a combination marketplace and stock exchange. The posted motto above its entrance read: "For the service of merchants of all nations and all languages." An economic boom enriched Antwerp's merchants and bankers, as well as the businesspeople from many lands who came to the Bourse to buy and sell. As many as twenty-five hundred ships from different lands anchored at one time in the harbor, many laden with gold and silver from the Americas. Every day goods went on sale in the Bourse, where bustling crowds of merchants, foreign visitors, and affluent local consumers thronged the rooms to buy Southeast Asian and Indian spices, American sugar, tin from England, Venetian glass, Spanish lace, German copper, paintings by great Flemish artists, and even the service of assassins or professional soldiers. Thus one great city linked the economies of Europe and the wider world. The Antwerp Bourse represented a postmedieval Europe shaped by overseas exploration, conquest, and expanding commerce, contributing the changes in life and thought that the English playwright Shakespeare referred to as a "brave new world."

In 1500, western Europeans were still medieval in many respects: dominated by the Roman Church, having little national identity, skeptical of science, minor participants in hemispheric commerce, and barely aware of distant lands. By the mid-1700s, however, Europe had undergone a profound economic, intellectual, and political transition, having conquered and settled the Americas and established colonies or trading networks in Asia and Africa. Wealth flowed into Europe, fostering investment in science and technology, while new knowledge of, and influences from, non-European cultures reshaped European thinking. The Catholic Church also faced severe challenges as secular ideas, including science, influenced some European thinkers. Such changes often produced long and bloody wars. By 1750 many Europeans had left their medieval institutions and beliefs behind and soon introduced even more profound changes to the world.

---

[1]From "The Tempest," *The Riverside Shakespeare*, 2nd ed. (Boston: Houghton Mifflin, 1997), 1684.

(T) Overseas Expansion and Capitalism

How did exploration, colonization, and capitalism increase Western power and wealth?

Many European societies established the foundations for dramatic changes in the 1400s and early 1500s. Europe's encounter with America and its riches, the growth of a trans-Atlantic slave trade, and the opening of direct trade with Asia all increased European wealth, fostering capitalism, an economic system in which property, exchange, and the means of production, such as factories, are privately owned. Capitalism gradually expanded its operations to a global level, so that by the 1600s valuable Asian spices and precious American metals and plantation crops poured into Europe. The economic revolution also led to stronger European states and reshaped most Europeans' daily lives.

capitalism An economic system in which property, exchange, and the means of production are privately owned.

Roots of Change

Some changes continued trends already apparent. During the 1400s, merchants flourished, cities grew larger, feudal social systems and values broke down, and commerce became part of everyday life. By 1500 cities such as Paris and London had grown to over 200,000; though still small by Asian standards, they enjoyed unique political power and autonomy, existing in a politically fragmented region rather than a centralized empire like China. City leaders could bargain with kings for advantages and autonomy. As middle classes bought more luxury goods, especially fine clothes, industries like textile manufacturing grew.

However, most Europeans were peasants working the soil, their lives organized around male-dominated households in

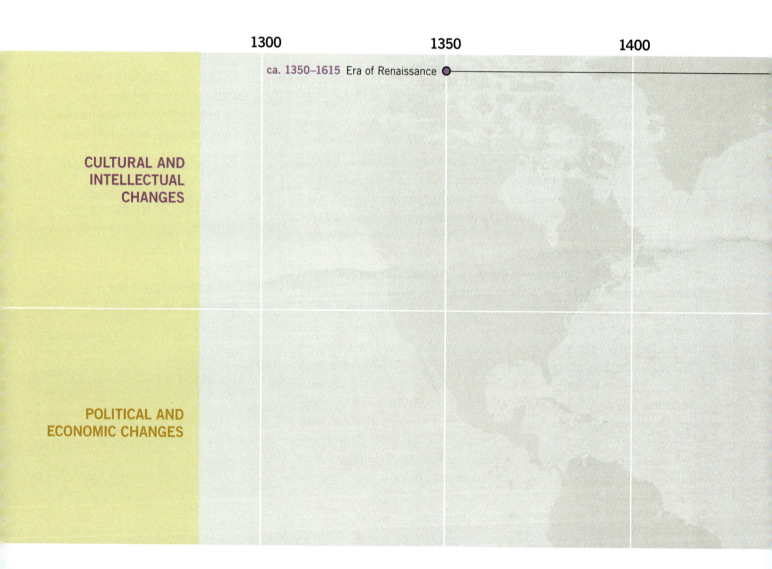

	1300	1350	1400

ca. 1350–1615 Era of Renaissance

CULTURAL AND INTELLECTUAL CHANGES

POLITICAL AND ECONOMIC CHANGES

which men tilled the fields while women had responsibility for the house, barn, and gardens. Although many peasants were now free or tenant farmers rather than serfs, they were still burdened by taxes and service obligations to lords and to the church. Yet, population growth and climate change also created economic change. Europe's population (excluding Russia) increased from 70 to 100 million between 1500 and 1600 and then to 125 million by 1750, fostering larger commercial markets. Global cooling began around 1300, reached its height in the late 1600s, and finally ended in the mid-1800s. This "Little Ice Age" brought winter freezing to canals and rivers, caused poor harvests, and helped motivate overseas explorers to seek better conditions and food sources elsewhere. Imported foods from the Americas, such as maize and potatoes, helped avert mass famine.

More favorable attitudes toward commerce gave merchants new status and power. They now enjoyed opportunity for making profit and to establish institutions, such as banks, that favored economic growth. Blessed with these advantages,

late medieval Europeans laid the foundation for an economic transition to capitalism that fundamentally altered Western life and later influenced the wider world. In the 1400s cities such as Venice and Genoa in Italy, and Bruges **(broozh)** and Antwerp in Belgium, became centers of capitalistic enterprise. Venetians and Genoese, fierce competitors, traded all over Europe, western Asia, and North Africa. However, the Catholic Church's condemnation of usury limited early capitalism; not until after 1500 did capitalism change dramatically, allowing the Antwerp merchants to build a Bourse as a marketplace for world products.

Western European politics also began to shift in the 1500s. Medieval Europe was politically fragmented, containing some five hundred states or ministates in 1500. Unlike in China, Ottoman Turkey, or Mughal India, no single bureaucratic imperial state dominated the economy and enforced conformity. During the 1500s, however, some small states, enriched by African, American, and Asian resources, gradually became integrated monarchies. Both merchants and monarchs

1500   **1600**   **1700**   **1800**

ca. 1517–1615 Protestant Reformation

1532 Formation of Church of England (Anglicans)

1534 Founding of Society of Jesus (Jesuits)

1536 Move of John Calvin to Geneva

1545–1563 Council of Trent

1558–1603 Elizabethan era in England

1572–1598 Wars of religion in France

1571 Defeat of Turks at Lepanto by "Holy League"

1588 English defeat of Spanish armada

1598 Edict of Nantes

1600–1750 Scientific Revolution

ca. 1600–1750 Baroque era

1675–1800 Enlightenment

1500–1770 Era of commercial capitalism

1533–1586 Reign of Ivan the Terrible in Muscovy

1588 Defeat of Spanish armada

1609 Dutch independence

1618–1648 Thirty Years War

1641–1645 English civil war

1648 Congress of Westphalia

1661–1715 Reign of Louis XIV in France

1682–1725 Reign of Peter the Great in Russia

1688–1689 Glorious Revolution and Declaration of Rights in England

1700–1709 Great Northern War

1701–1714 War of the Spanish Succession

1707 United Kingdom of England, Scotland, and Wales

resented the landed aristocracy's independence and cooperated to destroy their influence in bloody wars. For the first time since the Carolingians, large but competitive centralized European states developed, particularly in England and France, that fostered dynamic but unstable political systems.

New intellectual currents also led to broader horizons, especially improvements in mapmaking. In 1375 Abraham Cresques **(kres-kay)**, a Jewish cartographer on the Spanish island of Majorca **(muh-JOR-kuh)**, used Christian, Muslim, and Jewish traditions and travelers' accounts to produce a map that placed Jerusalem rather than Europe at the center of the world. Unlike Cresques, other mapmakers did not decenter Europe. Flemish mapmaker Gerardus Mercator's **(muhr-KAY-tuhr)** influential 1569 world map vastly exaggerated the size of Europe and North America while diminishing the size of Africa, India, China, and South America. In spite of these distortions, Mercator's approach, which pictures the earth as an uncurved rectangle intersected by straight lines for latitude and longitude, is still widely used.

Developments in technology and mathematics, often inspired by earlier Arab, Chinese, and Indian innovations, also brought change. Between 1450 and 1550 Europe surpassed the Arabs in technology and began catching up to China, with major improvements in shipbuilding, navigation, weaponry, and printing. European ships took advantage of Arab lateen sails, Chinese sternpost rudders, and, for navigation, the Chinese magnetic compass. Facing rougher, stormier waters than the placid Mediterranean, Atlantic coastal peoples built sturdier ships that gave them a naval advantage. Gunpowder weapons and printing processes, both invented in China, were improved, and the printing press disseminated knowledge to an increasingly literate audience. Europeans also blended the Indian numerical system and Arab algebra with their own insights to improve quantification.

"Gold, God, and Glory": Explorations and Conquests

The rise of Europe's world power resulted from overseas expansion and conquest (see Chapters 16–18). The phrase "gold, god, and glory" describes European motives. "Gold" was the material gain Europeans received by acquiring and selling Asian spices, African slaves, American metals, and other resources. A desire to directly connect with Asian trade spurred the first voyages of discovery in the 1400s. "God" refers to Christianity's crusading tradition, rivalry with Islam, disdain of non-Christian religions, and desire to convert the world to Christianity. Reflecting this view, a Catholic missionary in Spanish America argued that "it is a great thing that so many souls should have been saved and that so many evils, idolatries, and great offenses against God [by Native Americans] should have been halted."[2] "Glory" describes competing monarchies seeking to establish their claims to newly contacted territories, hence strengthening their position in European politics. Motivated by these three aims, various western European peoples expanded overseas and

gained control over widening segments of the globe. By the late nineteenth century Europeans dominated much of the world politically and economically.

During the 1400s seafaring Spaniards and Portuguese ventured out into the Atlantic and discovered the Azores, Madeira, and Canary island chains off Northwest Africa (see Map 15.1). These Iberians enjoyed a favorable location facing the Atlantic Ocean and North Africa, deep-sea fishing traditions, a history of aggressive crusading, and possession of Europe's best ships and navigation techniques. They also had economic motives. For centuries West African gold, passed through North Africa to southern Europe, had been used for coins, treasuries, and jewelry. Furthermore, the Portuguese sought to break the Venetian monopoly over the valuable trade from southern Asia through Persia and Egypt.

Maritime exploration required new technologies. The easily maneuverable Portuguese caravel could travel long distances, and Iberian-built galleons later provided much cargo space and room for larger crews. To chart sun and star positions, Iberian sailors used the Arab astrolabe **(AS-truh-labe)**. After learning how to mount weapons on ships, Europeans could overwhelm coastal defenses and defeat lightly armed ships. The Spanish in the Americas and the Portuguese in Africa and Asia, using artillery, naval cannon, and muskets, could control large territories whose inhabitants lacked guns. By the late 1500s, the English had built the most maneuverable ships and the best iron cannon, and by the 1700s European land and sea weapons had outclassed those of once militarily powerful China, India, Persia, and Ottoman Turkey. Europeans now threatened the great Asian states.

Intense competition between major European powers spurred increased exploration and a scramble for colonies, subject territories where Europeans could directly control primary production. In the 1400s the Portuguese began direct encounters with western Africa, and by 1497 they had reached East Africa and then sailed to India. Soon they seized key ports such as Hormuz on the Persian Gulf, Goa in India, and Melaka in Malaya. Meanwhile, the Spanish discovered a huge landmass to the west, soon named America, between Europe and Eastern Asia. Exploring the Americas and conquering many peoples, including the Inca and Aztec Empires, made Spain the most powerful European state in the 1500s. Portugal, England, France, and Holland also colonized in the Americas, sending emigrants to what they called "New World."

European states also established colonies or footholds in coastal Africa, carrying enslaved Africans to the Western Hemisphere to work on plantations growing cash crops, such as sugar, cotton, and coffee, for European consumption. Meanwhile, Portuguese, Dutch, and Spaniards colonized various Southeast Asian islands, including the Philippines, Java, and Indonesia's Spice Islands. American minerals, especially silver, supported European economic expansion and access to Asian trade. These developments enabled a massive transfer of resources, especially silver, gold, sugar, coffee, and spices, to Europe. The fortunes of trading ports such as Venice, Genoa,

---

[2]Franciscan friar Toribio de Montolinia, quoted in *1492: Discovery, Invasion, Encounter: Sources and Interpretations*, ed. Marvin Lunenfeld (Lexington, MA: D.C. Heath, 1991), 214.

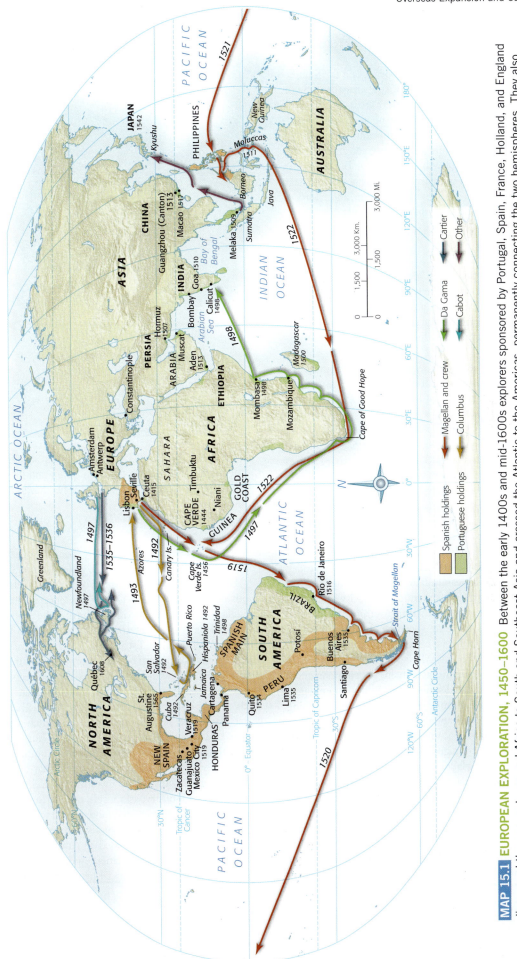

MAP 15.1 **EUROPEAN EXPLORATION, 1450–1600** Between the early 1400s and mid-1600s explorers sponsored by Portugal, Spain, France, Holland, and England discovered the sea route around Africa to South and Southeast Asia and crossed the Atlantic to the Americas, permanently connecting the two hemispheres. They also sailed across the Pacific Ocean from the Americas to Asia. © 2015 Cengage Learning

Lisbon, Seville, Antwerp, and Amsterdam rose or fell depending on overseas trade.

During the Early Modern Era, Europeans laid the foundations for their world dominance after 1750. Portugal and Spain prospered in the 1500s, while in the 1600s overseas trade helped Holland, England, and France become the most powerful European countries. By providing some Europeans with valuable human labor and natural resources, overseas trade and exploitation also contributed to the growth of capitalism. But European influence remained limited in many regions, as powerful Asian and African societies such as China, Siam, Japan, and Morocco successfully resisted or ignored European demands.

The Rise of Capitalism

Since its beginning in the Early Modern Era, capitalism has taken many forms and created new values around the world. Capitalism was revolutionary because, on a greater scale than before, money in the form of investment capital was used to make profits. Under capitalism, the drive for profit from privately owned, privately invested capital largely determined what goods were produced and how they were distributed. The various forms of capitalism had certain common features—the need for constant accumulation of additional capital, economic self-interest, the profit motive, a market economy of some sort, and competition—that shaped relations between people. Hence, carpenters that used to share their services on a barter basis and their profits with their guild now charged fees instead, competing for customers with other carpenters. Later capitalism included private ownership of the means of production, such as factories, businesses, and farms.

However, the profit motive, wealth accumulation, and competition contradicted some cultural values. Many cultures discouraged people from accumulating more wealth than their neighbors or working hard only to maximize income. Even today, some Asian, African, American Indian, and Latin American cultures value cooperation, religious piety, or generosity more than acquiring great wealth. Before capitalism governments siphoned off surplus wealth, with the elite spending their resources on luxuries such as the magnificent cathedrals, palaces, and pyramids that now impress tourists. Medieval merchant and craft guilds strictly regulated economic activity for the common good. By contrast, capitalists invested some profits in further exchange or production, fostering economic expansion and transforming small-scale trade into global capitalism.

While western Europe became increasingly capitalist, eastern European nobles discouraged capitalism. Allied with land-owning aristocracies facing labor shortages on their estates, kings in Poland, Lithuania, Prussia, and Russia mandated serfdom on the peasantries and forbade people to leave the land. Since they provided little support to merchants, capitalism did not expand and instead foreign merchants, including Dutch, Germans, Jews, and Armenians, gradually dominated eastern Europe's commerce. With chiefly agrarian economies, many once-vibrant cities declined into sleepy provincial towns, inhabited by many

THE PORT OF SEVILLE In the 1500s Seville became the main port for trade between Spain and its empire and a major cultural center. This view shows the busy river around 1590.

foreign-born merchants or their descendants. For example, many Polish and Lithuanian cities had large Jewish populations.

During the 1500s capitalism took hold in northwest Europe. The English, Flemish, and Dutch developed the most dynamic capitalism and soon eclipsed Italy, shifting the economic balance of power from the Mediterranean to the English Channel and North Sea. Enriched by distributing American silver and controlling Baltic grain, Antwerp became Europe's main financial capital. By the 1620s Amsterdam emerged as Europe's capitalist powerhouse, dominating much European and Asian trade and boasting amenities rare elsewhere, such as street lamps. In 1728 the English writer Daniel Defoe concluded that "the Dutch are the Middle Persons of Trade, the Factors and Brokers of Europe. They buy to sell again, and the greatest part of their vast commerce consists in being supply'd from all parts of the world that they may supply the world again."[3] Instead of investing in land, people invested in business and industry; as a result, the increased production of ships, arms, and textiles created more capital while the new materialism encouraged consuming goods from tea, coffee, and sugar to clocks, china, and glassware. Based on Arab models, coffee houses appeared in many European cities, especially in England, in the 1600s. They served multiple social networking and informational

Sanchez Coello, Alonso (1531-1589)/Museo de America, Madrid, Spain/Giraudon/The Bridgeman Art Library

---

[3]Quoted in Carlo M. Cipolla, *Before the Industrial Revolution: European Society and Economy, 1000–1700*, 2nd ed. (New York: W. W. Norton, 1980), 270.

functions as post offices, places to arrange business transactions, and venues for lively conversations and debates.

In this new capitalist era, the importation of American metals caused rising prices, which in turn meant that people needed more money. Increasing capital also encouraged the use of credit and banking. Attitudes toward charging interest for loans and seeking profit changed. Because the medieval church had denounced charging interest as usury, a mortal sin, good Christians could not become merchants or bankers. By the late 1500s, however, many rejected these church teachings, heeding the cynical saying that "he who takes usury goes to hell; he who doesn't goes to the poorhouse." Acceptance of interest reflected a gradual shift to an entirely different type of society.

Capitalism produced the **bourgeoisie (BUR-swah-zee)**, a new urban, mostly commercial, middle class ranging from small-scale merchants to financiers. Jacob Fugger **(FOOG-uhr)** (1459–1525) of Augsburg in southern Germany illustrated how an ambitious commoner could prosper from capitalism. A weaver's grandson and successful textile merchant's son, Fugger built a financial empire of banks, factories, silver mines, and farmlands, becoming Europe's richest man, loaning money to royal houses, and acquiring a castle and the title of count. He praised himself as "behind no one in attainment of extraordinary wealth, in generosity, purity of morals and greatness of soul."[4] His sons published the first newsletter for merchants and bankers, tracking European political and economic developments.

Capitalism continually changed in character and expanded in scope. Under **commercial capitalism**, dominant in western Europe between 1500 and 1770, most capital was invested in commercial enterprises such as trading companies, including the world's first joint-stock companies, run by directors chosen for their experience. These precursors of today's giant multinational corporations pooled their resources by selling shares, or stocks, to merchants and bankers, mobilizing great capital. Companies invested in diversified economic activities such as real estate, mining, and industry and employed many cashiers, bookkeepers, couriers, and middlemen skilled in languages. Few Asian or African merchants could compete with this collective power.

Commercial capitalism was also shaped by cooperation between governments and big business enterprises. England, Holland, France, and Spain pursued **mercantilism**, the practice of building a nation's wealth by expanding its reserves of precious metals such as gold and silver bullion. Under this system, trade was dominated by semimilitary, government-backed companies that were protected from competition. To attract other nations' bullion, these governments limited imports and increased exports. Some joint-stock companies obtained royal charters granting them monopolies and the right to colonize other lands in the state's name. In England such companies financed overseas exploration while supporting piracy against Spanish and French shipping. Spurred by mercantilism, commercial capitalism expanded into Africa, Asia, and the Americas.

> **bourgeoisie** The urban-based, mostly commercial, middle class that arose with capitalism in the Early Modern Era.
>
> **commercial capitalism** The economic system in which most capital was invested in commercial enterprises such as trading companies, including the world's first joint-stock companies.
>
> **mercantilism** An economic approach that emerged in Early Modern Europe based on a government policy of building a nation's wealth by expanding its reserves of precious metals.

MAKE SURE YOU UNDERSTAND THESE KEY POINTS BEFORE MOVING ON

- Europe's political decentralization fostered growing cities and the development of capitalism.

- Despite entrenched value systems that opposed an emphasis on accumulating wealth, capitalism took hold in western Europe, while eastern European leaders resisted it and instead mandated serfdom.

- Amsterdam established itself as capitalist Europe's center in the 1600s.

- Commercial capitalists, assisted by their country's mercantilist policies, increased their market power by pooling resources in such organizations as joint-stock companies.

aplia

The Renaissance and Reformation

How did the Renaissance and Reformation mark a crucial cultural and intellectual transition?

Two major movements, the Renaissance and Reformation, reshaped European thought and culture in the 1500s. During the Renaissance, a dramatic flowering in arts and learning beginning in Italy around 1350 (see Chapter 14), new philosophical, scientific, artistic, and literary currents developed that led to more creative, secular societies. In the 1500s gold and silver imported from the Americas provided more people with money to purchase art and books. Many historians believe that the Renaissance, sparked partly by trade with Asia and North Africa, provided a bridge between medieval and modern

---
[4]Quoted in Miriam Beard, *History of the Businessman* (New York: Macmillan, 1938), 239—240.

western Europe. At the same time, the **Reformation**, a movement to reform Christianity, spawned new Christian churches that provided alternatives to the Roman Catholic Church. Both movements helped undermine medieval society's pillars and changed cultural and religious life.

Renaissance Thought, Art, and Literature

During the Renaissance, thinkers and artists rediscovered Classical Greek and Roman ideas while consuming Chinese and Islamic products and ideas. The Renaissance promoted individualism, secularism, tolerance, beauty, creativity, and a philosophy, humanism, that emphasized humanity and its creations rather than God and a troubled Catholic Church that faced a confidence crisis, including leadership and clergy abuses. Some Renaissance thinkers favored church reform. The Dutch philosopher Erasmus **(uh-RAZ-muhs)** (1466–1536) advocated a more personal spirituality that tolerated diverse beliefs and the use of living languages rather than Latin, arguing that Jesus commanded people to love one another. The French humanist writer François Rabelais **(RAB-uh-lay)** (ca. 1494–1553) was even more critical, calling monks "a rabble of counterfeit saints, hypocrites, pretended zealots, who deceive the world."[5] By encouraging freedom of thought and offering critical insights, humanists also undermined the medieval attitudes that crippled scientific investigation. But popes rejected any doctrine or institutional changes.

Another humanist, the Florentine thinker Niccolò Machiavelli **(MAK-ee-uh-VEL-ee)** (1469–1527), provided guidance for European leaders in his influential political manual, *The Prince*, which studied power as separate from moral doctrine. Although claiming to draw on history's lessons, Machiavelli also used his experience as a diplomat for his ideas. *The Prince* argued that the ruler must always keep the end in mind, applying ruthless policies, such as deception and violence, in pursuing vital national interests. But, he argued, rulers ignore popular moral values at their peril; although a leader need not have piety, faith, integrity, and humanity, to avoid being hated he must seem to have them.

Interested in science, some thinkers employed direct experimental methods and observation. The Florentine Leonardo da Vinci **(lay-own-AHR-doh dah VIN-chee)** (1452–1519), painter, sculptor, architect, scientist, mathematician, and engineer, exemplified the versatile Renaissance personality and, in his knowledge about Muslim science and architecture, the Renaissance openness to varied influences. Polish astronomer Nicolaus Copernicus **(koh-PUR-nuh-kuhs)** (1473–1543) studied the skies and Islamic scholarship and suggested that the earth might not be the center of the universe. In 1507 Copernicus transformed astronomy and physics with his revolutionary "heliocentric," or sun-centered, theory of the solar

Reformation The movement to reform Christianity that was begun by Martin Luther in the sixteenth century.

system, refuting traditional ideas that the universe centered on the earth and the sun revolved around the planets. Fearing persecution by the church, he did not dare have his findings published until after his death.

The Renaissance spread Italian artistic influence, deepening the knowledge of humanity by more accurately representing real life in sculpture, painting, architecture, and literature. Some inspiration came from Islamic, Asian, and African artistic traditions; indeed, black Africans appeared in some paintings, including those with Christian themes. Italians such as the Venetian painter Giovanni Bellini (ca. 1430–1516) worked in or visited Muslim cities, spreading Italian influences but also returning with new perspectives. Rome replaced Florence as the hub of Italian art, attracting the eccentric Florentine Michelangelo Buonarroti **(mi-kuhl-AN-juh-loh bwawn-uh-RAW-tee)** (1475–1564), later famous for his realistic sculptures, paintings, and frescoes, especially the figures he painted on the ceiling of the Vatican's Sistine Chapel. Later Venice became Italy's main art center, where rich merchants and aristocrats offered artists generous financial support to produce landscapes and portraits rather than the once-common religious artworks. One Venetian, Titian **(TISH-uhn)** (ca. 1488–1576), contrary to Christian tradition, painted nudes and pre-Christian fables. Some women artists also gained a following. Artemisia Gentileschi (1593–ca. 1652), who survived rape by her art teacher and torture to test her allegations, painted heroic women from Greek mythology and the Bible. In the Low Countries, Pieter Bruegel **(BRU-guhl)** the Elder (ca. 1525–1569) painted realistic landscapes and sympathetic scenes of peasant and town life. El Greco **(ell GREK-oh)** (1541–1614), a native of Crete who studied in Italy before settling in Spain, blended Venetian, Byzantine, and Spanish traditions.

Growing secularism and humanism had literary consequences. During Queen Elizabeth I's brilliant reign in England (1558–1603), writers replaced concern for the hereafter with stories of human passions. The most famous, William Shakespeare (1564–1616), reflected the Elizabethans' celebration of the individual person and their nation. A prosperous businessman's son, Shakespeare acted in the theater and wrote histories, comedies, and tragedies that transcended time and place. Plays such as *Othello*, *Hamlet*, and *The Merchant of Venice* commented on the world beyond England, while other plays, such as *Henry V* and *Julius Caesar*, addressed English or ancient history. One of Shakespeare's best-known characters, Hamlet, voiced Renaissance exuberance: "What [a] piece of work is a man, how noble in reason, how infinite in faculties."[6] Another great writer, the Spaniard Miguel de Cervantes **(suhr-VAN-teez)** Saavedra (1547–1616), published the great novel *Don Quixote* **(kee-HO-tee)**, which portrayed Spain at the end of its golden age. A former steward and soldier who was once enslaved by pirates in Algiers, Cervantes became a purchasing agent and eventually was imprisoned for debt. The main character of his book, Don Quixote, sets out to battle dragons and evil men, right

---

[5]Quoted in H. O. Taylor, *Thought and Expression in the Sixteenth Century*, vol. 1 (New York: Macmillan, 1920), 175.
[6]From "Hamlet," *The Riverside Shakespeare*, 2nd ed. (Boston: Houghton Mifflin, 1997), 1204.

BRUEGEL'S *PEASANT WEDDING* Painted around 1567, Pieter Bruegel's *The Peasant Wedding* celebrates the rituals of peasant life, in this case a wedding dinner for a village. The Flemish artist may also have intended the painting of the feasting villagers as a satire on self-indulgence. The bride, composed and radiant, presides over the feast under a canopy.

injustice, and defend the oppressed, but mainly makes himself a grand nuisance. While Cervantes dignified the human spirit, like some Greek playwrights, he also satirized its plight.

Growing knowledge about other cultures inspired Europeans to rethink their assumptions about the world, stimulating debate about Native American society. In 1516, the English author Thomas More's (1478–1535) *Utopia* portrayed Native Americans as living in a paradise and European society as filled with poverty, injustice, hatred, and war. French writer Michel Eyquem de Montaigne **(mon-TANE)** (1533–1592) idealized Native American societies as "noble savages" uncorrupted by "civilization." Perhaps reflecting often hostile encounters between English settlers and Native Americans in Virginia, Shakespeare's play *The Tempest* mocked this idea by contrasting civilized Prospero and fierce, brutal Caliban **(KAL-uh-ban)** (an anagram for *cannibal*).

The Reformation and Religious Change

Questioning the old order also led to the Reformation (1517–1615), which transformed Europe's religious makeup and profoundly reshaped Western thought (see Map 15.2). Critics viewed the long-dominant Roman Church as corrupt, often led by incompetent popes who intervened rashly in political affairs and by church leaders and clergy who sometimes blatantly violated celibacy and poverty requirements. At the same time, the spreading literacy inspired some to examine Christian writings for themselves. Throughout the 1500s various groups sought church reform. Some, later called **Protestants**, broke completely with the Roman Catholic Church. By 1600 almost 40 percent of non-Orthodox Europeans, mostly in the north, had renounced Catholicism and adopted some form of Protestantism. Meanwhile, English and Dutch colonists carried Protestant faiths to North America. Eventually dozens of differing Protestant churches competed with each other and with Catholics for influence.

Martin Luther (1483–1546), a German, launched the movement that ended Western Christianity's unity. As conflicts between the Holy Roman Emperor, princes, and cities produced widespread discontent, many Germans began to resent the pope and bishops for leading luxurious lives. Luther, an Augustinian monk and later a University of Wittenberg **(WIT-n-burg)** professor, believed that nothing in scripture justified papal power and church rituals and concluded that only faith, not good works, could wipe away a person's sin and ensure salvation. In 1517 Luther distributed a paper attacking indulgences, clerical statements canceling punishment due for sins in exchange for lucrative cash contributions to the church. The paper prompted widespread discussion. After Pope Leo X excommunicated Luther in 1520 for refusing to retract his views, Luther translated the Bible into German and developed his doctrines,

Protestants Groups that broke completely with the Roman Catholic Church as the result of the Reformation.

MAP 15.2 REFORMATION EUROPE The Protestant Reformation reshaped Europe's religious landscape in the 1500s and early 1600s. By the mid-1550s some form of Protestantism had become dominant in much of northern Europe, England, and Scotland. Catholicism remained predominant in the southern half of western Europe and parts of eastern Europe. © 2015 Cengage Learning

Predominant religion in 1555
- Lutheran
- Calvinist (Reformed)
- Church of England
- Roman Catholic
- Orthodox
- Muslim
- Spread of Calvinism
- Huguenot center
- Ottoman Empire, 1566

ATLANTIC OCEAN

North Sea

Baltic Sea

Black Sea

Mediterranean Sea

Adriatic Sea

SWEDEN
- Helsinki
- Stockholm
- Riga

NORWAY 1536/1607
- Bergen

DENMARK
- Copenhagen

LITHUANIA

PRUSSIA

POLAND
- Warsaw

BRANDENBURG
- Hamburg
- Wittenberg, Birthplace of Martin Luther, 1483–1546
- Eisleben
- Erfurt
- Leipzig

SAXONY

HOLY ROMAN EMPIRE
- Prague, Jan Hus, 1369–1415
- Nuremberg
- Augsburg
- Munich
- Marburg
- Worms, Edict of Worms, 1521
- Speyer
- Stuttgart
- Zurich, Ulrich Zwingli, 1484–1531
- Strasbourg
- Basel

BOHEMIA

MORAVIA

AUSTRIA
- Vienna

HUNGARY
- Buda
- Pest
- Belgrade
- SERBIA

MOLDAVIA

WALLACHIA
- Danube R.

BESSARABIA

TRANSYLVANIA

BULGARIA

OTTOMAN EMPIRE

GREECE

NETHERLANDS
- Amsterdam, Penetration of Calvinism to England after 1558
- Münster
- Antwerp
- Brussels

FRANCE
- Birthplace of John Calvin, 1509–1564
- Noyon
- Paris
- Rennes
- Orléans
- Nantes, Edict of Nantes, 1598
- La Rochelle
- Bordeaux
- Toulouse
- Avignon
- Marseilles
- Geneva, John Calvin
- Council of Trent, 1545–1563
- Trent

ITALY
- Venice
- Milan
- Pavia
- Genoa
- Pisa
- Florence
- Rome, Roman Inquisition established, 1542
- Naples
- Bari

SCOTLAND 1560
- Edinburgh, John Knox, 1505–1572

ENGLAND 1536
- London
- Oxford, John Wyclif, 1320–1384
- Plymouth

IRELAND
- Dublin

SPAIN
- Madrid
- Toledo
- Granada
- Seville
- Barcelona
- Valencia
- Balearic Is.

PORTUGAL
- Lisbon

MOROCCO

ALGIERS

OTTOMAN EMPIRE

TUNIS

- Corsica
- Sardinia
- Sicily

Loyola, Birthplace of Ignatius Loyola, 1491–1556

400 Mi.
400 Km.
200
0

condemning Rome as "the greatest thief and robber that has ever appeared on earth or ever will. Poor Germans, we have been deceived."[7] In 1530 Lutherans formed a church rooted in the Augsburg Confession, a doctrinal statement arguing that the Bible was the only source of faith, that every believer had the freedom to interpret scripture, and that the cults of the Virgin Mary and the saints, priestly celibacy, and the monastic orders were misguided.

Lutheranism spread widely in northern Germany, Scandinavia, and the eastern Baltic coast. Many German city officials, princes, priests, professors, and common people supported the reform cause. But in 1524 a major conflict split the reform movement when peasants revolted against the landowning lords and church leaders. Unsuccessfully mediating between the sides, Luther then supported the nobles, who caused over 100,000 deaths in crushing the uprisings. In the end, the Lutheran Church became closely linked to many princely governments while the Holy Roman Emperor remained staunchly Catholic.

Inspired by Luther's example, non-Germans also founded Protestant movements. Calvinism was more radical in rejecting Catholic doctrine. Its founder, John Calvin (1509–1564), having been forced to leave France, settled in Geneva (juh-NEE-vuh), Switzerland. Unlike Luther, Calvin believed not in human free will but in predestination, the doctrine that God had already determined an individual's salvation or damnation at birth. Since good behavior and faith could not guarantee reaching Heaven, governments must enforce strict morality. Calvin attacked worldly pleasures such as dancing and playing cards, and his Geneva became a theocratic society, ruled by increasingly intolerant church leaders who burned some dissenters at the stake. Calvinism spread rapidly in Switzerland, England, and Holland, and in 1561 the Calvinist John Knox founded the Presbyterian Church in Scotland, where it became the dominant church.

In England, the initiative for religious change came from the king, Henry VIII (r. 1509–1547). Having no male heir with his wife Catherine of Aragon, a Spanish princess, Henry asked the pope to annul his marriage so he could marry Anne Boleyn (1501–1536), the much-courted daughter of English aristocrats. When Rome refused, in 1532 Henry rejected papal supremacy, announced his divorce, married Anne Boleyn, and appointed himself head of the English Catholic Church, which eventually became the Church of England. Later known as the Anglican Church, it retained much Catholic dogma and ritual. Suppressing both Calvinism and Rome-based power, Henry closed English monasteries and distributed their lands to his aristocratic and business allies. Growing disenchanted with Anne Boleyn, who bore him no sons, he beheaded her in 1536. Eventually married four more times, Henry generated religious strife. His son and successor, who died at sixteen, was succeeded by Henry's Catholic daughter by Catherine of Aragon, Queen Mary Tudor (TOO-duhr) (r. 1553–1558). Mary suppressed the Anglican Church, but it was restored when she died and was replaced by Elizabeth I (1533–1603), the daughter of Henry VIII and Anne Boleyn. When Elizabeth's successors persecuted English Calvinists (known as Puritans), some emigrated to Holland. From there one Puritan group, the Pilgrims, moved to North America in 1620 to seek more religious freedom, helping plant Puritan influence in the New England colonies.

Protestantism, Capitalism, and Catholic Reaction

Protestantism's emergence had many consequences. For example, historians debate how much Protestant doctrines supplied religious underpinnings for capitalist values. Calvinists believed that citizens demonstrated their fitness for salvation by being law-abiding, industrious, thrifty, and sober, all values supporting the capitalist order. Like Protestants, capitalists favored productive labor, frugality, wealth accumulation, and individualism. Although emerging in some Catholic societies, capitalism flourished especially in Protestant Holland, England, and northern Germany. The strongest capitalist societies featured intellectual diversity and produced some secularized free thinkers. The Reformation also opened doors to democracy. Although Luther and Calvin condemned other religious views, once people freely voiced their opinions on religion, they also wanted a voice in government. Similarly, women who became literate and could read the scriptures now gained some new options.

The Protestant challenge generated the **Counter Reformation**, a movement to confront Protestantism and crush Catholic Church dissidents using varied strategies, including the Holy Inquisition church court that had been formed in medieval times to combat heretical ideas (see Chapter 14). Several thousand suspected dissidents were burned at the stake in Spain, and the Congregation of the Index censored books, deciding which ones to forbid altogether. To outflank Protestantism, in 1534 the Spanish Basque former soldier, Ignatius Loyola (1491–1556), founded a highly disciplined missionary order, the Society of Jesus. One Jesuit, the Spanish Basque Saint Francis Xavier (ZAY-vee-uhr) (1506–1552), became a pioneering missionary in India, Southeast Asia, and Japan.

Despite harsh punitive measures, the Inquisition and Index did not suppress dissidence, prompting the pope to sponsor the Council of Trent (a city in northern Italy) to reconsider church doctrines. However, the council (1545–1563) reaffirmed most Catholic dogma, the value of both tradition and scripture, the church hierarchy and papal authority, and priestly celibacy, while imposing more papal supervision on priests and bishops and mandating that all clergy be trained in seminaries. The Trent reforms enabled Catholicism to recover some lost ground and to survive and flourish in a modified form.

But religious passions fostered intolerance. Religious minorities, such as Jews, French Protestants, and English Catholics, faced discrimination and sometimes violence. Several popes pursued anti-Jewish policies, while Luther advocated burning synagogues, arresting rabbis, and confiscating Jewish property. Facing expulsion from

Counter Reformation A movement to confront Protestantism and crush dissidents within the Catholic Church.

[7]Quoted in James Krokar et al., *Rhetoric and Civilization*, vol. 2 (Littleton, MA: Copley, 1988), 620.

their countries or segregation in city ghettoes, many Jews and minority Catholics and Protestants emigrated to other European countries or the Americas.

Religious Wars and Conflicts

Religious divisions also contributed to wars and conflicts from the late sixteenth through early eighteenth centuries. For example, religious tensions troubled Habsburg-ruled Spain, which controlled a vast empire in the Americas, Southeast Asia, Portugal, the Low Countries, and parts of Italy. King Philip II of Spain (r. 1556–1598), known as "the most Catholic of kings," put imperial resources toward defending the Catholic cause in Europe while spreading the faith abroad.

In the Low Countries, Philip's suppression of Calvinism antagonized businessmen and the nobility, who demanded autonomy and freedom of worship. Enraged Protestants attacked Catholic churches, and the execution of dissident leaders spurred a general revolt in 1566, with both Catholics and Protestants rallying behind the Calvinist leader, the Dutchman William of Nassau **(NAS-aw)**, Prince of Orange. Philip's occupation army executed over eleven hundred Protestants and sacked Antwerp. In 1579, Philip promised political liberty to the ten largely Catholic Flemish- and French-speaking southern provinces, forging the foundations of modern Belgium and Luxembourg. Then, when the English gave assistance to Low Country rebels and attacked Spanish shipping in the Americas, Philip II tried to invade England by sea in 1588, but he faced a determined foe in Queen Elizabeth I (see Witness to the Past: Queen Elizabeth I Rallies Her People). English ships outmaneuvered Spain's armada of 130 ships, triumphing when a storm in the English Channel devastated Spain's once-invincible fleet. The mostly Protestant, Dutch-speaking northern provinces broke away from Spain in 1588 and became fully independent in 1609, forming the Netherlands, popularly known as Holland.

Religious conflicts also raged across France, where the powerful Bourbon family led French Calvinists, or Huguenots **(HYOO-guh-nauts)**. In 1572, after the assassination of Calvinist leaders sparked Huguenot rioting in Paris, Catholic forces massacred thirty thousand Huguenots. In 1593 Henry of Bourbon (1553–1610), remarking that "Paris is well worth a mass," renounced Calvinism for Catholicism to become King Henry IV. In 1598 the Edict of Nantes **(nahnt)** recognized Catholicism as the state church but allowed Huguenots religious freedom.

WITNESS TO THE PAST

Queen Elizabeth I Rallies Her People

Few women ever enjoyed the power and respect of England's Renaissance queen, Elizabeth I, whose forty-five years of rule (1558–1603) marked a brilliant period for English culture, especially in literature and theater. On her death, the admiring playwright Ben Jonson wrote her epitaph: "For wit, features, and true passion, Earth, thou hast not such another." The queen may have been, as her detractors claimed, deceptive, devious, and autocratic, but her intelligence and formidable political skills helped her maneuver successfully through the snake pit of both English and European politics. One challenge was the deteriorating English-Spanish relations, which finally led to war. In 1588, as the powerful Spanish armada sailed toward the English coast, Elizabeth launched the English ships with a speech to her subjects that ironically played off her gender to reinforce her link with the English people. With the help of foul weather, the English defeated the Spanish, changing the fortunes of both countries.

My loving people. We have been persuaded by some that are careful for our safety, to take heed how we commit ourselves to armed multitudes, for fear of treachery, but I assure you, I do not desire to live to distrust my faithful and loving people. Let tyrants fear; I have always so behaved myself, that, under God, I have placed my chiefest strength and safeguard in the loyal hearts and good will of my subjects, and therefore I am come amongst you, as you see, at this time, not for my recreation and disport, but being resolved in the midst and heat of the battle, to live or die amongst you all, to lay down for my God, and for my kingdoms, and for my people, my honor and my blood, even in the dust.

I know I have the body of a weak and feeble woman; but I have the heart and stomach of a king, and of a king of England too; and I think foul scorn that...Spain, or any prince of Europe should dare to invade the borders of my realm; to which rather than any dishonor shall grow by me, I myself will take up arms, I myself will be your general, judge, and rewarder of every one of your virtues in the field.

I know already for your forwardness you have deserved rewards and crowns; and we do assure you in the word of a prince, they shall be duly paid you. In the meantime my lieutenant general shall be in my stead, than whom never prince commanded a more noble or worthy subject; no doubting but by your obedience to my general, by your concord in the camp, and your valor in the field, we shall shortly have a famous victory over those enemies of my God, of my kingdoms, and of my people.

THINKING ABOUT THE READING

1. How did Elizabeth justify the forthcoming battle with Spain?
2. What personal qualities did this Renaissance monarch suggest she could offer to her people in their time of peril?

Source: Charles W. Colby, ed., Selections from the Sources of English History (Harlow: Longmans, Green, 1899), 158—159. Quotation in introduction from A. L. Rowse, The Elizabethan Renaissance: The Life of the Society (New York: Charles Scribner's, 1971), 59.

Christian-Muslim conflicts also simmered, often resulting in political and military conflict. Muslim Ottoman Turks sought to expand their empire, which already included Greece, much of the Balkans, and Bulgaria (see Chapter 16). When some Balkan Christians embraced Islam, Holy Roman Emperor Charles V marshaled allies to defeat the Turks at Vienna in 1529. Later, in 1571, Spain, Rome, and Venice used advanced naval gunnery to destroy the Turkish fleet at the Battle of Lepanto (li-PAN-toh), off Greece, temporarily ending Turkish ambitions. In 1683, when the Turks besieged Vienna, Austria was saved by Polish intervention. Austrians pushed the Turks out of Hungary, ending Ottoman expansion in Europe and with it Christian fear of more losses to Islam.

MAKE SURE YOU UNDERSTAND THESE KEY POINTS BEFORE MOVING ON

- Renaissance humanists questioned the authority of the Catholic Church, while thinkers such as Machiavelli, Leonardo da Vinci, and Copernicus challenged accepted truths of morality, science, and astronomy.

- Renaissance artists such as Michelangelo aimed to represent humanity more realistically, and writers such as Shakespeare and Cervantes examined the concerns of individuals and the broad sweep of society.

- Martin Luther, who criticized the corruption of the Catholic Church, set the Reformation in motion; it was propelled by figures such as John Calvin, whose ideas were taken up by the Puritans, and King Henry VIII of England, who made England Protestant.

- In the Counter Reformation, the Catholic Church attempted to reassert its dominance, but ultimately it focused its energy on converting non-Europeans rather than combating Protestants.

aplia

Changing States and Politics

What types of governments emerged in Europe in this era?

Capitalism, Renaissance humanism, Protestant Reformation, and encounters with the wider world fostered new institutions, beliefs, and politics. The transition unleashed forces that consumed Europe in bloody wars: kingdoms torn asunder and reconfigured, old states declining, and new states gaining influence. These states were not nations in the modern sense but multiethnic entities ruled by royal families marrying across national lines. While in some states royal absolutism flourished, a few others developed representative governments with elements of democracy.

Regional Wars and National Conflicts

Various wars raged, some prompted by religious divisions, others by tensions between rival states and within large multinational empires such as Habsburg-ruled Spain and the Holy Roman Empire. Even after religious tensions subsided, warfare remained a constant reality. Continuing the religious wars and national rivalries of the 1500s, the Thirty Years War (1618–1648), a long series of bloody hostilities, claimed millions of lives and involved many countries. It began when Czech Protestants in the Holy Roman Empire revolted against Habsburg Catholic rulers who were trying to limit religious freedom. Eventually the fighting drew in German princes and mostly Lutheran Denmark and Sweden. Finally France, although mostly Catholic, went to war against its Habsburg rivals who ruled Austria and Spain. In 1648 the conflict ended after a four-year-long congress produced the Treaty of Westphalia (west-FALE-yuh), which reaffirmed religious freedom but failed to end Protestant-Catholic conflict. With Spain and the Holy Roman Empire militarily exhausted, France enjoyed unrivaled prestige after 1659. The Dutch also benefited because the long struggle had weakened their former ruler, Spain. After Westphalia, Europe fought wars with well-drilled professional soldiers, large warships, and more deadly cannon and rifles.

In the most widespread conflict, the War of the Spanish Succession (1701–1714), England, Holland, Austria, Denmark, Portugal, and some German states battled France and Spain over who would inherit the Spanish throne and how Spain's empire might be partitioned. War's human costs increased. Hence, one battle resulted in forty thousand French soldiers killed or wounded. The Treaty of Utrecht (YOO-trekt) ending the war transferred Spain's territory in Belgium and Italy to Austria. Once-prosperous Holland, by overextending itself, had damaged its economy. England received the most spoils, including the strategic Gibraltar peninsula at Spain's southern tip, which commanded the entrance to the Mediterranean Sea, as well as some French territory in eastern Canada. Utrecht fostered a new European system that maintained a power balance between rival states.

Absolutist and Despotic Monarchies

These conflicts and new mindsets created diverse political patterns by the seventeenth century, among them absolutism, a system of strong monarchial authority with all power placed under one supreme king or queen. Hoping to avoid chaos, Spain and Habsburg-ruled Austria, the Papal States of central Italy (governed by the Vatican), and the Turk-dominated Ottoman Empire all

> **absolutism** A system of strong monarchial authority in which all power is placed in a supreme authority, a king or queen.

TROOPS PLUNDERING A VILLAGE Common people suffered along with soldiers from European wars. This 1660 painting by Cornelis de Wael shows soldiers looting a village and seizing animals during the Thirty Years War.

exercised absolutist power. But French kings and Russian czars best represented this concentration of power.

For a time Europe was dazzled by the French absolute monarchy of King Louis XIV (r. 1661–1715), the envy of other rulers. French became the language of European diplomacy, and some European leaders, like Prussia's Frederick the Great, so admired aristocratic French culture that they spoke the language more than their native tongue. French art and architecture were imitated as far away as imperial Russia. By the mid-1600s France, with 18 million people, was western Europe's largest country, self-sufficient in agriculture, and with thriving industries. The king's mercantilism fostered royal-dominated industries and companies; he also revoked the Edict of Nantes, forbade Protestant pastors to preach, and closed Protestant schools and churches; as a result, 200,000 Huguenots emigrated to England, Holland, and North America.

Louis XIV believed he was the state and that his power derived from God, making him a monarch by divine right. Known as "the Sun King" for his court's brilliant extravagance and love of glory, he demanded obedience from all. Few French kings valued marital fidelity; Louis had many mistresses and children, legitimate and illegitimate. At Versailles **(vuhr-SIGH)**, a Paris suburb, some five thousand servants and courtiers lived at the Sun King's spectacular palace. Versailles became the center of French cultural life, regularly visited by French nobles and foreign leaders. Louis' brilliant finance minister, Jean Baptiste Colbert **(kohl-BEAR)**, complained that "every day is one long round of dances, comedies, music of all kinds, promenades, hunts and other entertainments."[8] The king gave annual allowances to a court composer and financed playwrights and ballet dancers.

To prevent Habsburg dominance, Louis XIV caused four major wars that proved financially ruinous and fell short of their objectives. The War of the Spanish Succession sapped the French treasury and military, enabling Austria, England, and Holland to counterbalance French power. Although France remained a major state, it lost some glory, and the French monarchy collapsed in revolution in the late 1700s.

In Russia, the czars developed a tyrannical government. After Russians freed themselves from Mongol domination, the brutal, paranoid Ivan **(ee-VON)** IV (r. 1533–1584), known as Ivan the Terrible, built a centralized state, fought wars with

[8]Quoted in *What Life Was Like During the Age of Reason* (Alexandria, VA: Time-Life Books, 1999), 18.

The Summer Palace, St. Petersburg (oil on canvas) (see also 88774), Russian School, (18th century)/State Russian Museum, St. Petersburg, Russia/Giraudon/The Bridgeman Art Library

SAINT PETERSBURG This painting shows the Summer Palace, built in 1744, of the imperial family in the Russian capital city of St. Petersburg, a major port that attracted many trading ships. The extravagant palace had 160 rooms.

neighboring Poland and Sweden, conquered the Tartar states founded by Mongols and Turks, and ordered the death or torture of Russians he considered enemies. Courting the landed nobility, Muscovite czars after Ivan tightly controlled the Russian Orthodox Church and a serfdom-based rural economy. Because serfs could be sold by their lords, they were little better than slaves. Czars also began extending their sovereignty toward the Black and Baltic Seas, sparking conflict with Poles and Lithuanians.

Enlightened but despotic, Peter I the Great (r. 1682–1725), nearly 7 feet tall, attempted to transform Russia into a modern state by copying Western technology and administrative techniques. He secretly toured Europe for eighteen months, visiting factories, museums, government offices, hospitals, and universities and even working as a carpenter in a Dutch shipyard to view advanced industrial and military technology. Upon returning to Russia, the czar hired foreign advisers and launched ambitious political, economic, military, and educational reforms. These Westernizing policies had mixed consequences. Some, such as banning beards, were superficial and unpopular. Peter also increased royal power, often harshly, at the expense of the church and nobility. He expanded Russia's frontiers, established industries, strengthened serfdom, formed a navy to protect his Baltic flank, and developed a more efficient government. Hating gloomy, medieval Moscow, he built a new capital on the Baltic, modeled on Amsterdam and Venice, and named it Saint Petersburg.

Wanting a stronger presence on the Sweden-dominated Baltic Sea, Peter forged a secret alliance with Denmark and Poland. During the Great Northern War (1700–1709), Russia and its allies finally forced the formidable Swedes to abandon the eastern Baltic to Russia. Russian forces then pushed south toward the Black Sea and the Straits of Bosporus, seeking permanent access to the Mediterranean Sea, which was open to shipping year-round (see Map 15.3). They also began acquiring territory in Siberia and Muslim Central Asia (see Chapter 16). Eventually Russia created a huge empire and exploited its resources. But although it developed a largely self-sufficient economy, it had limited trade with western Europe, with most czars after Peter fearing Western influence. Today Russia remains the last great land empire, ruling over various non-Russian peoples.

The Rise of Representative Governments

Some European countries moved toward greater political freedom. Iceland elected an assembly, Switzerland formed a multilingual, decentralized, and constitutional confederation of Catholic and Protestant districts, and Venice became a self-governing republic dominated by noble and merchant families. The Netherlands and England developed the most open and accountable governments. Enriched by sea trade, wealthy businessmen and many nobles played political roles and eventually demanded more influence.

MAP 15.3 **RUSSIAN EXPANSION, 1300–1750** Beginning in the 1300s the Russians expanded from a small remote northern state, based in Moscow, into an empire. By the mid-1700s the Russians had spread over a wide area and gained political domination over western Siberia, the northern Caucasus, and part of what is today the eastern Baltic region and the Ukraine. © 2015 Cengage Learning

	Principality of Moscow, ca. 1300
	Acquisitions by Ivan III's accession (1462)
	Acquisitions under Ivan III (1462–1505)
	Acquisitions by death of Ivan the Terrible (1584)
	Acquisitions by Peter the Great's accession (1689)
	Acquisitions under Peter the Great (1689–1725)
⭐	Major battle

The Netherlands enjoyed a prosperous golden age in the 1600s, building a colonial empire in the Americas, South Africa, Sri Lanka, and Southeast Asia while dominating the Atlantic, Baltic, and Indian Ocean trade. The Dutch East India Company, a large joint-stock company formed in 1602, made huge profits monopolizing the spice trade from southern Asia; importing Chinese silks and porcelain, Japanese art, Indian cotton textiles, and precious metals; and investing in Dutch industry. Holland's climate of freedom and tolerance also attracted people escaping persecution, such as Portuguese Jews, or seeking a more open intellectual atmosphere. At the same time, the wealth produced by Amsterdam, which served as a major world trade hub, fostered an innovative republican political system, as the predominantly Protestant Netherlands became a republic linked by assemblies of delegates. But tensions continued because the powerful Nassau family held the top post of Stadhouder General, which controlled the army and navy and sought more authority, while the merchant elite favored provincial autonomy.

Pursuing empire, England sent Protestant settlers to some districts in its mostly Catholic colony of Ireland and established colonies in North America and the Caribbean. Meanwhile, the English East India Company, founded in 1601, undertook commerce and conquest in Asia. Empire and growing profits from international trade fostered profound political changes. In addition, two upheavals in the 1600s secured first a republic and then a constitutional monarchy, defining royal and parliamentary rights. After Elizabeth I died without an heir, she was replaced by the Stuarts, Scotland's royal family. With absolutist ambitions, they made Anglicanism the only recognized faith, thereby antagonizing Puritans and Presbyterians. The English civil war began in 1641, when Parliament condemned Stuart despotism. Oliver Cromwell (1599–1658), a zealous Puritan convinced he was doing God's will, led parliamentary troops who defeated royalist forces in 1645. The Stuart king Charles I was beheaded.

Parliament then abolished the monarchy and proclaimed a republican Commonwealth (1649–1660) dominated by Cromwell. The royalist defeat proved a turning point as Puritans favoring capitalism and property rights ended lingering feudalism. But the Puritan Parliamentary majority, who were fanatics determined to root out "godlessness," established laws based on the biblical edicts of Moses and, impatient with constitutional government, expelled Presbyterians from Parliament. Eventually Cromwell became dictator, imposing Puritan morality, banning newspapers, executing dissidents, and crushing a Catholic rebellion in Ireland by burning crops and massacring thousands of Irish resistors. On Cromwell's death Parliament restored the Stuarts after they accepted individual religious freedom.

However, Protestant-Catholic conflicts resumed, eventually leading to a stronger Parliament, dominated by Anglicans, that offered the kingship to Dutch Stadhouder William of Orange, a zealous Protestant. Meanwhile, riots forced pro-Catholic James II (r. 1685–1688) to flee to France. In the Glorious Revolution (1688–1689), Parliament decreed William and his wife, Mary, sovereigns after they accepted a Bill of Rights recognizing the right of petition and requiring parliamentary approval of taxes to support the monarchy and army. The Toleration Act followed, establishing freedom of religion.

Although the Glorious Revolution modified royal power, the government represented only the landed nobility, wealthy merchants, and property owners. In 1707 England, Scotland, and Wales officially combined as the United Kingdom, often known as Great Britain. English supremacy exploited ethnic minorities, for example, by clearing feisty Scottish highlanders from their lands and banning their Celtic language, Gaelic (**GAY-lik**).

In colonized Ireland, Protestant English and Scottish settlers acquired land, while laws denied the majority Irish Catholics the right to education, property, and political office.

Rising New States, Declining Old States

Capitalism, religious change, warfare, and shifting political fortunes fostered several powerful new states while harming several longtime powers (see Map 15.4). Habsburg-ruled, German-speaking, Catholic Austria became a major empire after the Thirty Years War, governing Czechs, Croats, Slovenians, Hungarians, and some Italians, Romanians, and Serbs. Sweden became independent of once-mighty Denmark in 1520, forging a hereditary but not absolutist monarchy with a national assembly and Lutheranism as the state religion. Although the Swedes dominated Baltic trade, the Dutch eventually outcompeted them. Under King Gustavus Adolphus (r. 1611–1632), a brilliant military strategist, Sweden conquered parts of Poland, Prussia, and the eastern Baltic. By 1721, however, Russia and Prussia had displaced the Swedes from all their eastern Baltic possessions except Finland.

Prussia, a mostly German-speaking eastern Baltic state, became independent from Poland in 1660. Under King Frederick the Great (r. 1740–1786), an authoritarian but constitutional monarch, Prussia built a formidable standing army and rapidly expanded at the expense of Poland, Austria, and the Holy Roman Empire. A brilliant strategist, Frederick was ruthless but also a fine musician who enjoyed conversations with philosophers.

Several older states declined. Holy Roman Emperors, elected by leading princes, were figureheads who presided symbolically over some three hundred states representing assorted Germans, eastern Europeans, and Italians. The French writer Voltaire (**vawl-TARE**) mocked the incoherent entity as neither holy nor Roman nor an empire. In 1740 Austria and Prussia began a 130-year struggle for regional dominance. Meanwhile, the pope, the Habsburgs, and the Holy Roman Empire ruled the many small Italian states. In 1569 predominantly Catholic Poland and Lithuania formed a combined republican commonwealth under elected kings and noble-dominated national and local assemblies. The commonwealth enjoyed economic prosperity and religious tolerance, and its large Jewish communities enjoyed many legal rights. But by the mid-1600s it struggled amid rebellion and invasion by Russians, who slaughtered Jews. Catholics turned on Protestants, and after 1717 Russia dominated Poland and annexed Lithuania. Catholicism became crucial to Polish and Lithuanian identity.

MAKE SURE YOU UNDERSTAND THESE KEY POINTS BEFORE MOVING ON

- Louis XIV of France, the archetypal absolutist monarch, lived in astounding luxury and wielded great power.

- Russian czars from Ivan the Terrible on exercised tight control while expanding Russia's territory, traditions that Peter the Great continued while pushing to modernize and Westernize his country.

- The Dutch were successful colonial merchants and instituted a decentralized republican system of government that was strained by the military power held by the Nassau family.

- Through a series of struggles between Parliament and monarchs, English political power became more equally shared, though it was still held largely by wealthy aristocrats and merchants.

MAP 15.4 EUROPE IN 1740 By the mid-1700s France and Great Britain were the most powerful western European states. While once powerful Spain and Portugal had lost influence and the Germans and Italians remained divided, Prussia, Sweden, Russia, and Habsburg-ruled Austria were gaining strength. © 2015 Cengage Learning

French Bourbon lands
Spanish Bourbon lands
Austrian Habsburg lands
Prussian lands
Great Britain
Boundary of the Holy Roman Empire
Russian Empire
Russian gains, by 1725
Ottoman Empire, 1722

ATLANTIC OCEAN

GREAT BRITAIN
SCOTLAND
Edinburgh
ENGLAND
London
Thames R.
Dublin
IRELAND

North Sea

NORWAY
Oslo

KINGDOM OF DENMARK
DENMARK

S W E D E N

Baltic Sea

NORWAY

Moscow
RUSSIAN EMPIRE

St. Petersburg
INGRIA
ESTONIA
LIVONIA
Riga
LITHUANIA
Smolensk
Kiev
UKRAINE

Don R.
Dnieper R.
Dniester R.

CRIMEA

Black Sea

POLAND
Warsaw
Vistula R.

EAST PRUSSIA

BRANDENBURG-PRUSSIA
Berlin
Oder R.
Elbe R.
SAXONY
SILESIA
BOHEMIA

HANOVER
UNITED NETHERLANDS
Utrecht
Rhine R.
PALATINATE
LORRAINE
Strasbourg
SWITZERLAND

HOLY ROMAN EMPIRE
BAVARIA
Danube R.
AUSTRIA
Vienna

MOLDAVIA
TRANSYLVANIA
WALLACHIA
Danube R.
BULGARIA
Buda Pest
HUNGARY
CROATIA
SLAVONIA
BOSNIA
SERBIA
Belgrade
HERZEGOVINA
MONTENEGRO
ALBANIA

Constantinople
O T T O M A N E M P I R E

Aegean Sea
GREECE

N

Paris
Seine R.
Loire R.
FRANCE
Garonne R.
Toulouse
Rhône R.
Marseilles

SAVOY
Po R.
MILAN
GENOA
MODENA
TUSCANY
PAPAL STATES
Rome

REPUBLIC OF VENICE
Adriatic Sea

KINGDOM OF NAPLES
Naples

Corsica (Genoa)
Sardinia (Austria)
Sicily (Savoy)

Mediterranean Sea

Minorca (Gr. Br.)
Balearic Is.

CATALONIA
Ebro R.
SPAIN
Madrid
Tagus R.
Duero R.

PORTUGAL
Lisbon

GIBRALTAR (Gr. Br.)

10°E
50°N
40°E
30°E
60°N
10°W

300 Mi
300 Km.
0 150
0 150

© 2015 Cengage Learning

The Transformation of Cultures and Societies

How did major intellectual, scientific, and social changes help to reshape the West?

Voyages of discovery and colonization altered Europeans' world-view, broadened horizons, and fostered intellectual change. In England, Scotland, Switzerland, Poland-Lithuania, and especially the Netherlands, some religious tolerance and diversity undermined barriers to free thought. Science, philosophy, and technology proceeded with fewer obstacles than elsewhere, while the Islamic world, China, and India produced less creative thought than before. Nevertheless, European thinkers borrowed Islamic and Asian ideas. Meanwhile, capitalism spurred by overseas expansion reshaped social patterns, creating an increasingly urban society.

Arts and Philosophy

In the 1600s the Renaissance and Reformation led to an extravagant artistic movement. One new style, the **baroque** ("contorted" or "grotesque"), shocked people by limiting restraints on expression while questioning accepted ideas. In Italy Roman sculptor Gianlorenzo Bernini **(buhr-NEE-nee)** (1598–1680) emphasized freedom through expressive, sensuous marble statues and fountains. Commercial bounty also led to Dutch artistic breakthroughs, as wealthy Dutch merchants commissioned artworks celebrating personal success, Protestant values, and the material world to decorate their houses, town halls, and guild halls. Painters catered to this taste, offering realistic pictures of everyday life, group portraits, landscapes, and the interiors of well-appointed houses. Nearly every Dutch family of means owned at least one original piece of art. Unlike earlier Renaissance artists, Dutch artists viewed their work as a capitalist enterprise, often producing for the market rather than individual patrons.

Many Dutch painters concentrated on landscapes, still lives, and domestic scenes, rejecting medieval preoccupation with religious themes. The paintings of Rembrandt van Rijn (1606-1669) and Jan Vermeer (1632–1675) conveyed emotion, immediacy, personality, and individuals' thoughts and feelings. Influenced by baroque interest in emotions and light, Rembrandt portrayed the pain, power, and pride of humankind by manipulating the direction, distance, and intensity of light and shadow to reveal nuances of mood and character. Reflecting a growing world economy, some Dutch paintings also showed imported foreign products such as Chinese bowls, Turkish carpets, Southeast Asian spices, and American tobacco.

Not all creative people represented baroque attitudes. German Lutheran composers George Frederick Handel (1685–1750) and Johann Sebastian Bach (**BAHCH**) (1685–1759) produced popular works that appealed to a wide audience. Settled in London, Handel wrote his famous choral work, *The Messiah*, while Bach composed pieces for both Protestant and Catholic churches. His cantata about a young woman so madly in love with coffee that her father feared she would never find a husband memorialized the growing fad for such imported products.

In philosophy and science, the questioning of accepted ideas led to the greatest speculation in Europe since the Classical Greeks. For example, former English politician Francis Bacon (1561–1626) sought to eliminate intellectual restraints on science by applying reason and separating philosophy from theology. With a famous maxim: "Knowledge is power," Bacon developed the scientific method: developing an idea, testing it experimentally, and drawing conclusions. These ideas, unsettling at the time, greatly influenced later thinkers.

Modern philosophy's founding father, René Descartes **(DAY-cart)** (1596–1650), promoted a rationalist view of the world. Born in France, Descartes traveled widely and served in both Dutch and Bavarian armies. Viewing human rationality as founded on a distinction between mind and body, he wanted to sweep away traditional learning and establish a new system of knowledge. The only thing he could not doubt was his own existence, writing: "While I wanted to think everything false, it was absolutely necessary that I, who was thinking thus, must be something. I think, therefore I am."[9] Besides philosophy, Descartes studied mathematics, optics, physics, and physiology.

On a more somber note, the pessimistic English political thinker Thomas Hobbes (1588–1679) believed that society was not perfectible, even using reason or Christian teachings; with no government to control humanity's anarchic, power-seeking instincts, life was "solitary, poor, nasty, brutish, and short."[10] His disturbing book, *The Leviathan* (**la-VIA-thin**), provided a new view of the relationship between the state and the individual, arguing that people needed despotic power to control them. Truth, reason, and justice were artificial attributes created by social convention and language. Although many condemned Hobbes's royalist slant and apparent atheism, his idea of a social contract between citizens and rulers influenced later thinkers.

Science and Technology

The **Scientific Revolution** (ca. 1600–1750), an era of rapid advance in knowledge, particularly in mathematics and astronomy, built on the work of Bacon and Descartes to gain a new understanding of the natural and physical world. European scientists demolished the medieval view of earth's position in the cosmos and laid the groundwork for intellectual and industrial transitions. Although religious conflicts and despotic monarchs often made it dangerous to offer new ideas, advances occurred in many areas.

The Scientific Revolution derived partly from imported Asian and Islamic ideas and

baroque An extravagant and, to many, shocking European artistic movement of the 1600s that encouraged release from restraints of thought and expression.

Scientific Revolution An era of rapid European advance in knowledge, particularly in mathematics and astronomy, that occurred between 1600 and 1750.

---

[9]Quoted in Charles Blitzer, *Age of Kings* (New York: Time-Life Books, 1967), 119.
[10]From Hobbes, *The Leviathan*, Chapter 13 (oregonstate.edu/instruct/ph1302/texts/hobbes/leviathan-c.html).

technologies. European scientists were familiar with the writings of earlier Muslim thinkers and, thanks to reports from Jesuit missionaries, Chinese scientific traditions and inventions. French King Louis XIV sent a mission to China to acquire scientific and technical knowledge. As Europeans assimilated and improved imported models while creating new ones, leadership in scientific and technological leadership gradually shifted from China and the Middle East to Europe.

Astronomers made some of the most significant discoveries. While also improving telescopes, German mystic Johannes Kepler (1571–1630) used mathematics to confirm that all the planets revolved around the sun. The Italian Galileo Galilei **(gal-uh-LAY-oh gal-uh-LAY-ee)** (1564–1642) proved Copernicus's theories experimentally. By adapting spectacles, invented in Holland, in 1609 Galileo built the first telescope, with which he discovered that the moon had mountains, Jupiter had four large moons, and our solar system was but a small part of a Milky Way galaxy containing countless stars. These findings were dangerous, especially since Galileo insulted critics, mocked conventional wisdom, and criticized the biblical view of astronomy as ignorant. In 1615 the Catholic Church summoned the scientist to Rome to be tried for heresy and forced him to publicly recant his views to leave prison. When he continued writing, Inquisition officials placed him under house arrest for life.

Later, Sir Isaac Newton (1642–1727), a mathematics professor at Cambridge University, synthesized Bacon's methodologies, Descartes' mathematics, Galileo's discoveries, and other scientific findings to discover some fundamental laws of physics. A famous epitaph by the poet Alexander Pope proclaimed Newton's importance: "Nature and Nature's laws lay hidden in night; God said, 'Let Newton be!' and all was light."[11] In 1687 Newton's book *Mathematical Principles of Natural Philosophy*, describing all the motions of the planets, the comets, the moon, and the sea, revealed the connection, especially the law of universal gravitation, that tied together varied parts of the physical world into an ordered whole. Newton's ideas dominated Western scientific thinking for the next two hundred years.

Scientific discoveries led to new technology. Useful items like the watch, the lead pencil, the thermometer, concrete, the slide rule, and the first mechanical calculator to perform multiplication, division, and much more appeared. The Dutchman Christian Huygens **(HYE-guhnz)** introduced a more accurate clock. In the early 1700s, an English farmer, Jethro Tull, using a two-millennia-old Chinese model, developed a drill to sow seeds, the first step toward rural mechanization. Perhaps inspired by Chinese models, Englishman Thomas Newcomen invented the first crude steam engine to pump water from mines. Finally, by the 1730s England's textile industry efficiently produced cotton products with spinning machines that were similar to much older Chinese machines.

The Enlightenment

Another development of this era was the **Enlightenment** or Age of Reason, a philosophical movement based on science and reason that rejected many traditional ideas. The Enlightenment began in 1675 and continued until 1800. Scholars debate whether it was a single movement across Europe or rather separate intellectual experiences in different countries. The movement owed something to Bacon, Descartes, and Newton as well as to growing European knowledge of Native American societies and secular Chinese thought. In 1687 a French observer wrote that the Confucian "moral system is infinitely sublime, simple, sensible. Never has Reason appeared so well developed with so much power."[12] In fact, some historians call Confucius the Enlightenment's patron saint. The Enlightenment replaced unquestioning religious faith with observed fact, suggested that objective truth could be established through reason, and took human destiny away from God and placed it in human free will. Many Enlightenment thinkers admired Christianity's moral authority but opposed organized churches' dogmatic attitudes. Some adopted **deism**, believing in a benevolent God who designed the universe but does not intercede in its affairs.

In England, France, and Scotland, new notions of tolerance, individual rights, and the citizen-state relationship emerged. The Enlightenment spread humanistic secularism, promoted critical approaches to knowledge, and addressed gender issues such as women's education and marriage equality. For example, in France Louise d'Epinay (1726–1783) condemned gender discrimination and negative female stereotypes, arguing that both women and men "struggle against pain, difficulties, obstacles [and] have the same nature."[13] Some male thinkers also favored women's education and equality. Yet, gender issues were often marginalized, with many Enlightenment thinkers accepting the era's prejudices.

A major Enlightenment thinker was the Englishman John Locke (1632–1704), a physician who lived for a decade in France and Holland. Locke made experimental science studies that led him to proclaim the value of **empiricism**, which stressed experience and the testing of propositions rather than reason alone to acquire knowledge. Empirical approaches later became common in the social and natural sciences. Locke's influential political theories also provided a foundation for modern democratic states and notions of human freedom. He condemned absolute monarchy and advocated defending freedom through cooperation for common goals, allowing the state only limited powers over individuals. He also stated that people had the right to oppose a state that suppressed freedom and self-government. But although Locke favored individual rights, such as separation of church and state, he also favored restricting political participation to people with property. Many of his ideas became influential not only in England but also among the founders of the United States. In the Declaration of Independence in 1776, Thomas Jefferson enshrined Locke's view that people were entitled to life, liberty, and property.

Enlightenment A philosophical movement based on science and reason that began in Europe in the late seventeenth century and continued through the eighteenth century.

deism Belief in a benevolent God who designed the universe but does not intercede in its affairs.

empiricism An approach that stresses experience and the testing of propositions rather than reason alone in acquiring knowledge.

[11]Quoted in Norman Davies, *Europe: A History* (New York: Harper, 1996), 599.

[12]Quoted in John M. Hobson, *The Eastern Origins of Western Civilisation* (Cambridge: Cambridge University Press, 2004), 194.

[13]From Dena Goodman and Kathleen Wellman, eds., *The Enlightenment* (Boston: Houghton Mifflin, 2004), 167.

The French Enlightenment was expressed by intellectuals known as philosophes (fill-uh-SOHF) (philosophers). In Paris, educated women such as Madame Maria-Therese Geoffrin (JOFF-rin) (1699–1777) operated salons (sa-LAW): elegant rooms where thinkers and artists gathered for conversation. Baron de Montesquieu (maw-tuh-SKYOO) (1689–1755), attacking religious dogma and arbitrary, absolutist power, proposed a republican government with checks and balances, including separation of powers between the executive, legislature, and judiciary. Colonists in North America widely discussed his ideas. The best-known philosophe, Voltaire (1694–1778), a poet, dramatist, and historian, believed that science, empiricism, and rational behavior led to happier lives. Occasionally imprisoned in France, he spent many years in England, Switzerland, and Prussia. Voltaire viewed China as an admirable model, a despotic but secular, benevolent state contrasting with absolutist France. A deist, he supported tolerance toward other views but fiercely attacked established religion and disliked the Jews for their separation, often involuntary, from mainstream society. Challenging gender discrimination, Voltaire's friend and then lover, Emilie du Chatelet (EM-ih-lee de SHA-the-lay) (1706–1749), wrote works on mathematics, natural philosophy, and the ideas of scientists such as Newton (see Profile: Emilie du Chatelet, Enlightenment Scientist).

Capitalism and Rural Society

Capitalism gradually reshaped rural society and turned many peasants into a displaced labor force. In sixteenth-century England, King Henry VIII seized Catholic Church land and distributed some to wealthy businessmen who bought land as an investment, turning agriculture from subsistence living to commercial venture. In addition, hard-hearted landowners increased demands on peasants or shifted to more profitable sheep raising, ejecting peasants from the land. As a result, landless English peasants became tenant farmers and poor farm workers for big landlords. Some former peasants found jobs in towns, became rural craftsmen, or became rural vagabonds drifting around the countryside and resorting to any measures, including crime, to stay alive. Nursery rhymes reveal their plight and the country's negative, "blame the victim" attitudes: "Hark hark the dogs do bark, the beggars are coming to town. Some give them white bread, and some give them brown, and some give them a good horsewhip and send them out of town." While feudal people believed that individual well-being resulted from the inequitable manor system, under capitalism people were considered responsible for their own condition. Some communities imprisoned debtors and flogged the homeless.

While land loss ruined many peasant lives, it also created a labor pool for fledgling industries, giving England an advantage over the labor-short Dutch and over the French, who were reluctant to abandon feudal laws protecting peasants. Businessmen gave crafts production to displaced peasants, paying for each item they made, undermining guilds, and destroying medieval concepts of economic justice. Eventually these trends reached other western European societies. Nothing like the forced peasantry's impoverishment happened elsewhere. The Chinese and Ottoman imperial

power could curb landowner and merchant greed, preventing land seizures. Thus western European peasants, many heavily consuming alcohol as an escape, fared worse than peasants in Islamic societies.

The great rich-poor contrast, amplified by famine and devastating wars, sparked uprisings, such as the bloody 1524 peasant revolt in Germany. In England, the civil war fostered widespread discontent and radical movements such as the Levellers, led by lower-class soldiers who advocating equality, democracy, and complete religious freedom: in their 1648 manifesto, they pleaded, "May the pressing needs of our stomachs reach Parliament and the City [London]; may the tears of our starving babies be preserved; may the cries of their tender mothers begging for bread to feed them be graven in metal."[14] Life became increasingly dangerous and unhealthy. Bandits and mercenary soldiers attacked travelers, merchant convoys, and villages. Many fled to overcrowded cities, which were filled with beggars, drunks, trash-filled streets, polluted water, human waste stench, and disease. In the 1600s one-third of London's children died before the age of one. In France people said that nine-tenths of people die of hunger, one-tenth of indigestion.

Families and Gender Relations

For northern Europe's growing middle classes, the nuclear family of parents and their natural-born children, rare in medieval times, became more common, unlike southern and eastern Europe's large extended families. Societies increasingly recognized childhood as a distinct life phase, inventing toys and games while opening more schools, mostly for boys. However, at least half of children left their families by their early teens, many to become apprentices or servants with other families.

Women's economic roles and status shifted. With more consumer goods, women could now purchase rather than produce such items as cotton clothing. Men now made much higher wages than women, diminishing women's social status. Whereas many medieval women never married but worked in diverse occupations, now women were encouraged to look chiefly to marriage, motherhood, and the home. While northwest European women married in their twenties, early teenage brides were common elsewhere. Still, between 10 and 20 percent of people never married, and the Roman Catholic Church encouraged church vocations over marriage. At the Council of Trent church leaders rejected Protestantism's married clergy, denouncing the notion that "it is better and happier to be united in matrimony than to remain in virginity and celibacy."[15]

Women's experiences varied. Many Dutch women enjoyed liberated lives, some becoming merchants. Elsewhere, some women engaged in trade. German Jewish merchant Glukel of Hameln (HAH-muhln) (1646–1724), the mother of eight, traveled widely to trade fairs. But few women controlled financial resources. Some women wrote fiction, plays, poems, memoirs, and diaries, but most could not get their work published. A few educated French women, like Emilie du Chatelet, achieved intellectual and cultural influence.

philosophes The intellectuals who fostered the French Enlightenment.

[14] Quoted in Frederic Delouche et al., *Illustrated History of Europe: A Unique Portrait of Europe's Common History* (New York: Barnes and Noble, 2001), 247.

[15] Quoted in Diarmaid MacCulloch, *The Reformation: A History* (New York: Penguin, 2005), 609.

Emilie Du Chatelet, Enlightenment Scientist

Emilie du Chatelet overcame gender stereotypes and expectations to transform herself from wife, mother, and court figure into one of the French Enlightenment's more influential mathematicians and scientists. Born in Paris in 1706 to an aristocratic family that, defying the nobility's dislike of educating girls, encouraged her intellectual pursuits, she was freed by her wealth to pursue the life of the mind. Her father presided over weekly salons in their home, where she could listen to conversations between learned and talented men and also arranged for prominent thinkers to tutor her. She became fluent in four languages (German, Italian, Latin, and Greek) and also learned riding and fencing.

In 1725 the nineteen-year-old married thirty-four-year-old Marquis Florent-Claude du Chatelet-Lomont, a military officer who proved a pragmatic, tolerant spouse with whom she had three children. Now with the title of marquise, she indulged avidly in court social life at Versailles, enjoying dancing, acting, opera singing, and harpsichord playing. Yet, the high spirited, passionate, determined young woman refused to give up her intellectual pursuits, including translating Greek and Latin philosophy and plays and studying mathematics. Receiving little support from the scientific establishment because of her gender, she continuously fought prejudice. A freethinker who criticized conventional religion—the marquise considered Jesus "a pious fraud"—du Chatelet strongly advocated women's education, writing,

> I feel the full weight of the prejudice which so universally excludes us from the sciences;...there is no place where we are trained to think....Let the reader ponder why, at no time in the course of so many centuries, a good tragedy, a good poem, a respected tale, a fine painting, a good book on physics has ever been produced by women. Why these creatures whose understanding appears in every way similar to that of men, seem to be stopped by some irresistible force, this side of a barrier. Let the people give a reason, but until they do, women will have reason to protest against their education....

In 1733, while her husband pursued his career and acquired mistresses, the marquise began a long friendship and then romantic relationship with the French Enlightenment's leading but controversial figure, Voltaire, who had recently returned from exile in England. They moved to her country house in northeastern France, where they maintained an intense intellectual collaboration. Many prominent thinkers visited the home. The collaboration and idea exchange proved fruitful for both. She published an important work in physics, including a paper on fire that explored the nature of light and infrared radiation, and a pioneering textbook that, among other subjects, explored the scientific method. The two coauthored *The Elements of the Philosophy of Newton*, introducing Newton's theories to readers who lacked knowledge of higher mathematics. Her last and greatest project, published after her death, was the grueling translation, with an insightful commentary, of Newton's seminal *Principia Mathematica* from Latin into French. Her analysis of Newton's ideas foreshadowed modern concepts of kinetic energy.

Eventually the marquise's romance with Voltaire faded. In 1748 she fell in love with the much younger courtier and poet Marquis de Saint Lambert, but she died in 1749 at age forty-three shortly after a difficult pregnancy and birth of their daughter. Remaining her close confidant, Voltaire was crushed by her death. His earlier poem memorialized her: "Here's a portrait of my Émilie: / She's both a beauty and a friend to me. / Her keen imagination is always in bloom. / Her noble mind brightens every room. / She's possessed of charm and wit.../ She has, I assure you, a genius rare."

GABRIELLE-EMILIE-DE-BRETEUIL-MARQUISE-DV-CHASTELET-LORRAINE·

DEA/G DAGLI ORTI/Age Fotostock

PORTRAIT OF EMILIE DU CHATELET The multi-talented enlightenment thinker, a philosopher, mathematician, and scientist, was pictured here at her desk pondering her current writing or translation project.

THINKING ABOUT THE READING

1. How did Marquise du Chatelet become a scientist?
2. How did her relationship with Voltaire shape her career?
3. What were some of her major contributions to knowledge?

Note: Quotations from Karen Frenkel, "Why Aren't More Women Physicists?" *Scientific American*, January 14, 2007 (http://www.scientificamerican.com/article.cfm?id=why-arent-more-women-phys); and https://eee.uci.edu/clients/bjbecker/RevoltingIdeas/emilie.html#divine.

At the opposite extreme, many Russian women were, as a German visitor claimed, "most miserable; for men consider no woman virtuous unless they live at home, and be so closely guarded that she go out nowhere."[16] Few lower-class women found paid work except as servants in affluent households. Some women faced worse problems. Millions believed in magic, astrology, prophecy, ghosts, and witches, thought to destroy crops and cause personal misfortunes. The execution or banishment from the community of thousands of women suspected of witchcraft, often after horrific ordeals, provided a diversion from wars and religious conflicts. In a Polish trial, a suspected witch was stripped naked, bound hand and foot, and suspended from the ceiling before confessing.

More restrictive views of sexuality promoted punishing women and men who defied convention. Often prompted by churches, governments regulated sexual and moral behavior to encourage family life, prosecuting adultery and premarital sex.

Yet, premarital pregnancy rates ranged from 10 to 30 percent. Condemned by Catholic and Protestant churches, homosexuals faced severe sanctions, including execution. With erratic law enforcement, especially in tolerant England and Scandinavia, male homosexuals congregated in large cities. Antisodomy laws in Catholic countries often ignored the nobility and clergy, some of whom advocated same-sex relationships. Some influential men were possible or probable homosexuals, among them Leonardo da Vinci, Michelangelo, Francis Bacon, and several popes and kings such as Prussian Frederick the Great, and many European kings had same-sex bedmates. Fewer lesbians were public. Yet, the cosmopolitan, flamboyant Swedish queen Christina (1626–1689), an outspoken supporter of the French Enlightenment and science who spoke some ten languages, had a long affair with one of her ladies-in-waiting and, after abdicating her crown, maintained an active sexual life in Rome with both men and women.

MAKE SURE YOU UNDERSTAND THESE KEY POINTS BEFORE MOVING ON

- The extravagant baroque style that followed the Renaissance emphasized artistic freedom, while Dutch painters eschewed religious themes for natural ones.

- Bacon and Descartes emphasized the role of reason in science and philosophy, respectively, while Thomas Hobbes developed a pessimistic political philosophy.

- Advances in astronomy, particularly those made by Galileo, greatly antagonized Catholic officials,

while Isaac Newton discovered fundamental laws of physics.

- Locke, Montesquieu, and Voltaire were among the prominent thinkers of the Enlightenment, a movement that favored reason over unquestioning faith.

aplia

[16]Quoted in Robert Wallace, *Rise of Russia* (New York: Time-Life Books, 1967), 140.

CHAPTER SUMMARY

During the Early Modern Era many agrarian, feudalistic societies in Europe were reshaped. The Portuguese and Spanish pioneered maritime exploration and flourished from their American, African, and Asian conquests. The Dutch, English, and French also developed overseas empires that brought them considerable wealth. Meanwhile, the growth of trade, capitalism, and mercantilism created a new commercial orientation while shifting economic and political power to the countries of the Atlantic seaboard. The Renaissance, which spread humanist and secular values, and then the Reformation changed Europe's philosophical and religious terrain, challenging the Roman Church. By the mid-1500s Protestant churches dominated much of northern Europe. These challenges generated a Counter Reformation within the Catholic Church.

Wars raged during much of the era and contributed to political changes. France and Russia developed absolutist monarchies, whereas England and Holland enjoyed greater political freedom. Powerful new states such as Austria and Prussia emerged while older states such as the Holy Roman Empire declined. The discovery of new lands as well as the changing political, religious, and economic forces renewed interest in scientific discovery and a stress on individual rights, leading to the Enlightenment. The Scientific Revolution produced such revolutionary thinkers as Newton and allowed Europe to surpass China and the Middle East technologically. Capitalism made many rural peasants homeless, and family life, including the status of women, also changed.

KEY TERMS

capitalism (p. 346)
bourgeoisie (p. 351)
commercial capitalism (p. 351)
mercantilism (p. 351)
Reformation (p. 352)

Protestants (p. 353)
Counter Reformation (p. 355)
absolutism (p. 357)
baroque (p. 363)
Scientific Revolution (p. 363)

Enlightenment (p. 364)
deism (p. 364)
empiricism (p. 364)
philosophes (p. 365)

16 New Challenges for Africa and the Islamic World, 1450–1750

Janissaries and the parade musicians arriving, from 'Sur-Nama' (vellum), Turkish School, (16th century)/Private Collection / The Bridgeman Art Library

OTTOMAN JANISSARY SOLDIERS AND MUSICIANS ON PARADE The Ottoman rulers periodically sponsored parades in Istanbul featuring soldiers, musicians, and various occupational groups, including storytellers, glassblowers, taxidermists, potters, merchants, and even executioners. This painting of one parade is from the 1500s.

Warriors will fight scribes for the control of your institutions; wild bush will conquer your roads; your soil will crack from the drought; your sons will wander in the wilds. Yes, things will fall apart.

—Igbo ancestral curse[1]

Things fell apart for many Africans in the Early Modern Era, including Ayuba Suleiman Diallo **(ah-YOO-bah SOO-lay-mahn JAH-loh)**, both victim and beneficiary of the era's new challenges. In 1731 the thirty-year-old educated prince from Bondu, a West African kingdom, visited Senegambia, at Africa's western tip, on a trading mission. There he was captured by enemies, sold to the British as a slave, and eventually shipped to a tobacco plantation in Maryland. After he attempted to escape, Thomas Bluett, an English entrepreneur, recognized his ability to read and write Arabic and his connections to West African commercial life. Bluett emancipated Diallo, took him to London, and presented him at the royal court. The British hoped he might help their commercial activity in Senegambia. Agreeing to act as middleman in obtaining more slaves, Diallo returned to Bondu and resumed his life while profiting as a British trading partner.

Ayuba Suleiman Diallo's story represents the changing Atlantic world as Europe, Africa, and the Americas became increasingly linked in unprecedented ways. Diallo's West Africa now included English, Portuguese, Dutch, and French companies seeking gold, gum, hides, ivory, and especially slaves. Goree **(go-ray)** Island, near present-day Dakar **(duh-KAHR)**, became a major slave collection center. Diallo's story is unique because he gained freedom quickly and eventually returned home. But the ancient Igbo curse proved prophetic for the many Africans shipped off as slaves. Meanwhile, many other Africans remained untouched by slave trading and other disruptive European activities, pursuing traditional ways of life, expanding and flourishing or declining and decaying from local conditions unrelated to European activities along the coasts.

The growing European power was also felt in Central Asia and the Islamic Middle East (western Asia and North Africa). By the 1500s Islam, the monotheistic religion originating in Arabia a millennium earlier, dominated huge chunks of Afro-Eurasia, from Africa's westernmost fringe to central Indonesia and the southern Philippines, linking widespread peoples through its political ideas, trade networks, and literary traditions. While experiencing changes, these Islamic societies maintained long-standing traditions and largely controlled their own destinies. Meanwhile, non-Islamic societies had increasing trade connections and conflicts with the powerful Ottoman Empire, which ruled much of western Asia, North Africa, and southeastern Europe, and a new Persian state, the Safavid Empire.

[1]Quoted in Ali Mazrui, *The Africans: A Triple Heritage* (Boston: Little, Brown, 1986), 11.

S Sub-Saharan African Societies

How did the larger sub-Saharan African societies and states differ from each other in the sixteenth century?

Many African societies flourished in the 1500s, forming great states and engaging in extensive long-distance trade (see Chapter 12). While many were Muslim, others mixed monotheism, polytheism, and animism. The attraction of Europeans to African human and natural resources posed new challenges and changed Africa's relationship to the world. In the 1400s the Portuguese commenced exploratory voyages down the West African coast, foreshadowing dramatic changes to come.

The West African States

The last great Sudanic empire, Songhai **(song-GAH-ee)**, remained strong through much of the 1500s (see Map 16.1). Based at Gao on the Niger River, Songhai's empire stretched 1,500 miles from east to west. Songhai's people blended Islam with local customs. For example, Arab visitors were shocked by the fact that Sudanic women enjoyed high social status and considerable personal liberty, dominating village markets. In some cities women were free to have lovers as they desired.

Within the Songhai Empire, Timbuktu became a major terminus for the trans-Saharan trade, shipping gold, ivory, and slaves to North Africa for Arab and European markets. A major center of Islamic scholarship, Timbuktu boasted schools, libraries, well-stocked bookstores,

and universities teaching theology, law, and literature. An early-sixteenth-century Arab visitor, Leo Africanus, reported that Timbuktu had "numerous judges, doctors of letters, and learned Muslims. The king greatly honors scholarship. Here too, they sell many hand-written books. More profit is had from their sale than from any other merchandise."[2] The Islamic University of Sankore at Timbuktu, employing well-known Arab scholars on its faculty, drew its student body from throughout the Islamic realm. Scholars have found thousands of crumbling books, written in Arabic and several African languages, in forgotten Timbuktu storage rooms (see Chapter 12). Many were written in Ajami, a simplified Arabic-based alphabet invented by West Africans to write their own languages such as Hausa and Wolof.

Songhai's leadership deteriorated amidst succession struggles, and in 1591 a Moroccan invasion caused Songhai's collapse, ending the era of large western Sudanic empires. But several other West African societies exercised regional influence and profited from trade. For example, Sudanic kingdoms formed by the Mandinka, Bambara **(bahm-BAH-rah)**, and Mossi peoples in the upper Niger Basin had effective, cavalry-based armies. The Dyula **(JOO-lah)**, a Mandinka Muslim mercantile clan, operated throughout West Africa, moving goods such as gold and salt with caravans of porters,

---

[2]Quoted in Basil Davidson, ed., *African Civilization Revisited* (Trenton, NJ: African World Press, 1991), 118.

	1300	1350	1400	1450	1500	1550
SUB-SAHARAN AFRICA			1482 First Portuguese-Kongo encounter			
			1487 Portuguese discovery of Cape of Good Hope			
			1497 Portuguese encounters with East Africa			
			1505 Portuguese pillage of Kilwa			
			1507–1543 Rule of Alfonso I in Kongo			
			1514 First African slaves to Americas			
			1526–1870 Trans-Atlantic slave trade			
			1575 End of Portuguese technical assistance to Kongo			
MIDDLE EAST				1501–1736 Safavid Persia		
			1514–1517 Ottoman conquest of Syria, Egypt, and Arabia			
			1520–1566 Suleiman the Magnificent			
			1529 First Ottoman siege of Vienna			
			1554–1659 Sa'dian dynasty in Morocco			

Werner Forman/Universal Images Group/Getty Images

PORTUGUESE VISITORS TO BENIN This bronze plaque, one of many decorating the Benin royal palace, depicts two Portuguese men, possibly a father and son, likely traders or officials, who began visiting the kingdom in the late 1400s. The plaque was probably fashioned around 1575.

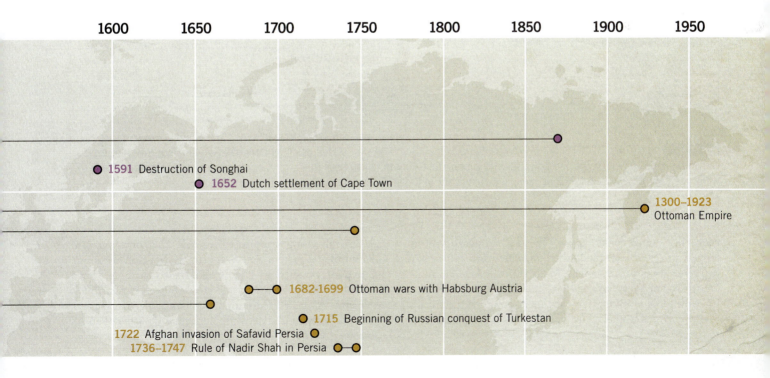

1600	1650	1700	1750	1800	1850	1900	1950

1591 Destruction of Songhai

1652 Dutch settlement of Cape Town

1300–1923 Ottoman Empire

1682-1699 Ottoman wars with Habsburg Austria

1715 Beginning of Russian conquest of Turkestan

1722 Afghan invasion of Safavid Persia

1736–1747 Rule of Nadir Shah in Persia

MAP 16.1 **AFRICAN STATES AND TRADE, 1500–1700** Some African states, such as Songhai, Kanem-Bornu, Benin, Lunda, Buganda, and Ethiopia, remained powerful in this era. West African coastal societies were increasingly drawn into world trade, while the East African coastal cities remained significant in Indian Ocean trade. © 2015 Cengage Learning

Legend:
- Buganda
- Kongo
- Monomotapa
- Kingdom of Songhai, ca. 1500 C.E.
- Kingdom of Kanem-Bornu, ca. 1500 C.E.
- Hausaland
- Kingdom of Ethiopia
- Main coastal trading areas

canoe fleets, and donkey trains. The first European visitors tapped into these well-established trade networks and weekly markets held in various towns. Many societies were matrilineal, with some West Africans having women chiefs or queens. Queen mothers of kings enjoyed great power, and Africans often venerated women elders for their wisdom and closeness to the ancestors.

Several strong trade-based Islamic kingdoms arose in the central and eastern Sudan. Kanem-Bornu (KAH-nuhm-BOR-noo), centered on Lake Chad, traded slaves to North African Arabs for horses. In the late 1500s and early 1600s, King Idrus Aloma (IH-dris ah-LOW-ma), a devout Muslim, extended his Islamic state while importing guns and Turkish musketeers from the Ottoman Empire. Kanem-Bornu declined

Bantu Trading Cities and Kingdoms

By the sixteenth century peoples speaking closely related Bantu languages dominated much of eastern, central, and southern Africa. City-states along the East African coast forged the closest ties to hemispheric networks, becoming thriving trade centers where Bantu settlers and Arab immigrants created a Swahili culture mixing African and Islamic traditions. Indonesians, Indians, Persians, and Arabs visited East Africa, bringing ideas, products, technologies, and immigrants. Some cities boasted large stone and mortar buildings with terraces, towers, trees, and gardens. Prosperous Kilwa and Malindi, with their royal courts, mosques, and luxury goods, were part of the great Indian Ocean trading network dominated by seafaring Arabs and Indian Muslims. Ships from Arabia, Persia, and India regularly visited Swahili ports, which collected goods from Africa's interior, such as iron, ivory, tortoise shell, leopard skins, gold, and slaves, to be exchanged for Chinese porcelain, glass beads, and Indian cotton. Portuguese visitors to Malindi reported that the "king wore a robe of damask trimmed with green satin, and a rich turban. He was seated on two cushioned chairs of bronze, beneath a round sunshade of crimson satin attached to a pole. Two trumpets of ivory made sweet harmony."[4]

Other major Bantu states emerged inland. On the southeastern plateau bordering the Zambezi (zam-BEE-zee) River, the Shona people exported gold and ivory to the Middle East and India. By 1500 the once-great Shona kingdom of Zimbabwe had collapsed, replaced by competing kingdoms. By the 1700s Buganda (boo-GON-da), in the fertile rolling hills west of Lake Victoria in southeastern Uganda, had a well-developed bureaucracy, powerful military, and extensive trade with coastal cities. As the kingdom grew in wealth and influence, it saw a flourishing of art, poetry, dance, and philosophy. By 1500 another state, the large Kongo kingdom along the Congo River and Atlantic coast in northern Angola and western Congo, ruled 2.5 million people from a royal capital containing some thirty thousand residents. To the east the Luba (LOO-buh) and Lunda kingdoms built substantial empires in the southern Congo. Located far inland and with access to trade networks running through Central Africa, they resisted European power into the nineteenth century.

Most Bantu societies in southern Africa combined farming with cattle herding and formed small states led by chiefs. The largest, the Xhosa (KHO-sa) and Zulu, lived along the Indian Ocean coast. Around fifty thousand Khoikhoi (KOI-KOI), non-Bantu pastoralists Europeans later called

THE SWAHILI PORT OF MOMBASA Mombasa was one of the major port cities along the East African coast that had flourished for several centuries before the arrival of Europeans. This engraving is from 1572.

only in the later 1700s. Other states included the fiercely competitive Hausa city-states of what is now northern Nigeria, eastern Niger, and southern Chad. These states manufactured cotton cloth and leatherwork, some sold as far away as Europe, and Hausa merchants traded around West Africa. Although Islam gradually became the dominant faith, Hausa women, like those in other savannah states such as Songhai, played vital political and social roles. For instance, Queen Amina of Zaria (ZAH-ree-uh) extended her city's power while building effective walled defenses against rival states and raiders.

Non-Muslim states occupied the Guinea Coast from today's Ghana to eastern Nigeria. For example, the small Akan (AH-kahn) states of the Volta (VAWL-tuh) River Basin prospered from mining and trading gold to the north. In western Nigeria's Yoruba states, each based on a large city ruled by a king or prince, women exercised influence and could elect a representative to the chiefs' council. Oyo, the most powerful Yoruba kingdom, with a cavalry force equipped with bows, javelins, and swords, flourished until the late 1700s under able kings. Another prosperous Guinea kingdom, Benin (buh-NEEN) in south-central Nigeria, shared many cultural and political traditions with the Yoruba. European visitors admired the capital city of wide streets and large wooden houses with verandas. A Dutch merchant marveled at the royal palace, which had galleries "as big as those on the Exchange at Amsterdam [supported by] wooden pillars encased with copper where their victories are depicted."[3]

[3]Quoted in Basil Davidson, *Africa in History* (New York: Touchstone, 1995), 176–177.
[4]Quoted in Derek Nourse and Thomas Spear, *The Swahili: Reconstructing the History and Language of an African Society, 800–1500* (Philadelphia: University of Pennsylvania Press, 1985), 82.

Hottentots (HOT-n-TOTS), also lived around the Cape of Good Hope at Africa's southern tip.

Africa in the Hemispheric System

Africans had long played key roles in the hemispheric economic system, but rising European power between 1450 and 1600 presented serious challenges, reshaping their role in the world. Often lacking the environmental advantages and interregional connections that benefited parts of Eurasia and North Africa, sub-Saharan Africans were especially vulnerable to European and Arab power. By 1500 Eurasian and North African societies had invented or borrowed cutting-edge technologies such as printing and gunpowder weapons while developing productive economies. But few Africans encountered the Chinese technology and Indian mathematics that spurred Middle Eastern and European progress. Furthermore, much of sub-Saharan Africa had marginally fertile soils, scarce exploitable minerals, and few good harbors.

West and East Africans had supplied gold, ivory, and other commodities to the Middle East and Europe for centuries. Although this trade increased European interest in Africa, few Europeans and Africans made direct contact with each other. By 1500 Islam had largely replaced Christianity in Nubia. Christianity flourished only in remote, mountainous Ethiopia, where the Amharic (ahm-HAHR-ik) people's state and church, related to Eastern Orthodoxy, had survived for fifteen hundred years, building splendid churches, often on steep mountainsides. Islamic expansion cut off the Ethiopians from Europe.

Direct contacts between Europe and sub-Saharan Africa began in the early 1400s, when Portuguese ships began exploring down West Africa's coast seeking gold, Christian allies against Islam (based on murky recollections of Ethiopian and Nubian Christians), and a sea route to China and Southeast Asia, the sources of valuable silk and spices. Europeans' ignorance of black Africa fostered the myth of **Darkest Africa** waiting to be "opened" to the "light of Western civilization." Europeans also perplexed Africans. In southern Nigeria, the first appearance of white men along the coast shocked a local fisherman, who reportedly "raced home [in a panic] and told his people what he had seen; whereupon he and the rest of the town set out to purify themselves, [to] rid themselves of the influence of the strange thing that had intruded into their world."[5]

After establishing control in the Americas, Europeans sought large numbers of enslaved Africans to do their work. As in other world regions, slavery had existed in many African societies, and Africans had also exported slaves for centuries. Muslim Arab and Berber merchants acquired slaves in the Sudan and transported them via caravan across the Sahara to North Africa for sale to Arab or, sometimes,

Darkest Africa Those areas of Africa least known to Europeans but, in European eyes, awaiting to be "opened" to the "light of Western civilization."

European owners. At the same time, an Arab-run trade from East Africa shipped slaves northward to Arabia, the Persian Gulf, Persia, and India. Over twelve centuries Muslim slave traders moved perhaps 10 to 15 million enslaved Africans north. Europeans also tolerated slavery. Slaves from eastern Europe, particularly Russians and Greeks, had for centuries been dispatched by the Byzantines and then by the Ottomans from the Black Sea region and Balkans to Spain, Portugal, Italy, France, Central Asia, and the Middle East. By the 1400s and 1500s black slaves became increasingly common in Europe, especially Iberia. Slavery had no particular "racial" identity yet. But developing plantation economies in the Americas focused more attention on Africa as a slave source. Europeans did not invent the African slave trade, but they soon transformed it.

The Portuguese and Early African Encounters

The Portuguese were the first Europeans to directly encounter sub-Saharan Africans. Equipped with the world's most advanced ships and gunpowder weapons, they began exploring West Africa's coastline in the early 1400s (see Chapters 12 and 14) and soon discovered and settled the uninhabited Azores and Madeira Islands. By 1471 they had reached the modern nation of Ghana, where they tapped into the gold trade from Akan states, calling the region the Gold Coast. Shifting from exploration to exploitation, they then colonized the Cape Verde Islands, the nearby coastal region of Guinea-Bissau, and the small islands of Sao Tome (tuh-MAY) and Principe near Nigeria, establishing trading forts to obtain gold, ivory, and slaves. In the 1480s the Portuguese sent Catholic missionaries and skilled craftsmen to Kongo in South-Central Africa, thus beginning a long relationship with that prosperous kingdom. The Portuguese and Kongolese enjoyed similar standards of living and held similar views of government, both favoring strong monarchy. The Kongolese king, much of the elite, and some of the people adopted Christianity, blending it with their own religious concepts. But many commoners, maintaining their traditional beliefs, rejected the new religion.

In 1487 Bartolomeu Dias (ca. 1450–1500) led an expedition that sailed round Africa's southern tip into the Indian Ocean. After months at sea, he reached the Cape of Good Hope, where he and his thirsty sailors helped themselves at a watering hole without asking permission. The resident Khoikhoi threw stones, and Dias killed a herdsman with a crossbow, an encounter that foreshadowed European-African conflicts to come. But Dias's adventure intensified Portuguese interest in both Africa and Asia. Believing Dias had discovered the best route to Asia and its fabulous goods, Portugal's king rebuffed Christopher Columbus when the Italian sailor sought sponsorship to sail west. Even when Columbus returned from his first voyage in 1492 and announced, incorrectly, that he had found a sea route to India, the skeptical Portuguese pursued the route

[5]Quoted in Michael Pearson, *The Indian Ocean* (New York: Routledge, 2003), 119.

around Africa. More Portuguese exploration followed, eventually reshaping the hemispheric trade system. In 1497 four ships commanded by Vasco da Gama (**VAS-ko dah GAH-ma**) (ca. 1469–1525), after surviving hurricanes and mutinies, sailed around the Cape and then up the East African coast, visiting the Swahili trading cities of Mozambique, Mombasa, and Malindi. There his hats and cloaks, being of poorer quality than Asian and Arab products, failed to entice the Swahili merchants, who had no interest in his meager trade goods. Refocusing his attention on India, da Gama engaged a skillful pilot and sailed from Malindi to southwestern India. The Indians also told him his merchandise was unworthy and could not compete with more valuable, better-made products from India, China, Indonesia, and Persia, but da Gama had located the sea route to the East. After acquiring a small cargo of spices and precious stones, he returned home in triumph. In the following years, often using force, the Portuguese set up trading bases around the Indian Ocean, where their warships attempted to limit maritime commerce by their Arab, Ottoman, Persian, and Indian rivals.

MAKE SURE YOU UNDERSTAND THESE KEY POINTS BEFORE MOVING ON

- Songhai, the last great Sudanic kingdom with its trading city Timbuktu, produced many scholars of Islam, but its society was much more open to contributions from women than was Arab society.

- West African states were extremely varied and included the strict Islamic kingdom of Kanem-Bornu, the Hausa traders, the Yoruba in western Nigeria, and the prosperous kingdom of Benin.

- In Bantu-speaking East Africa, coastal city-states such as Kilwa and Malindi grew wealthy from the sale of goods from across Africa to Arabia, Persia, and India; the Shona exported gold and ivory; and Buganda traded extensively with East African coastal cities.

- Enslavement of many people—for example, Africans by Africans, Africans by Arabs, eastern Europeans by western Europeans—was widespread when western Europeans began to obtain African slaves.

- The Portuguese were the first to contact sub-Saharan Africa, where they established relations with the Kongo kingdom, and to reach East Africa and India by sailing around the Cape of Good Hope.

Early European Imperialism and the Trans-Atlantic Slave Trade

What were the consequences of African-European encounters and the trans-Atlantic slave trade?

As they made ever-longer journeys along the West African coast, Portuguese ships fostered trade but also conflict and destruction. The Portuguese eventually colonized the Kongo and became active in East Africa, undermining coastal trading cities. Meanwhile, the Dutch gained a foothold in South Africa. These activities eventually made possible the trans-Atlantic slave trade, which affected millions of Africans who were captured, transported, and sold in the Americas. Those who profited were the African states where slaves were obtained, the American societies that imported slave labor, and European and North American merchants, shippers, and planters. These experiences fostered a new global system of trade and empire that harmed some African societies. By the 1700s the gulf in wealth, power, and development, once narrow, between Africa and Eurasia had grown very wide, greatly influencing the relationship between European and African peoples.

Kongo, Angola, and the Portuguese

The Portuguese greatly impacted Kongo and the surrounding region. The Kongolese were open to foreign influence and ruled by an enlightened king and dedicated Christian,

Alfonso I (r. 1507–1543). A Portuguese merchant noted that "the grandees of the court began to dress like Portuguese, wearing mantles, capes, cloaks of scarlet silk, hats, and velvet and leather sandals."[6] Alfonso, using Portuguese weapons to expand his empire, clearly wanted to modernize the kingdom along Western lines with Portuguese help. But the Portuguese became less concerned with political alliance and more interested in acquiring enslaved Kongolese, which they commenced to do in 1514. Although opposed in principle, Alfonso sold slaves in exchange for goods and services he regarded as essential to his kingdom's progress. In Kongolese tradition, owners must treat slaves well. However, demands for slaves multiplied as the Portuguese developed sugar plantations on Sao Tome'. In their new colony in Brazil, across the Atlantic from Kongo, they set up many more plantations, multiplying the need for enslaved labor. Since Alfonso and his successors permitted only a modest slave trade, the Portuguese resorted to armed raids to capture slaves. Alfonso repeatedly asked the Portuguese to halt these coercive activities, which were damaging and depopulating his country (see Witness to the Past: A Kongolese King Protests the Slave Trade), but his pleas were unsuccessful. Alfonso grew disillusioned with the

---

[6]From Roland Oliver and Caroline Oliver, eds., *Africa in the Days of Exploration* (Englewood Cliffs, NJ: Prentice-Hall, 1965), 111.

WITNESS TO THE PAST

A Kongolese King Protests the Slave Trade

In the early sixteenth century Kongolese king Alfonso I, who had embraced Catholicism and welcomed the Portuguese to his kingdom, wrote over twenty letters in Portuguese to Portugal's king, creating the earliest known African commentary on European activities in Africa. Some letters complained of aggressive Portuguese activities and asked that the king halt slavers from obtaining Kongolese citizens. They also requested Portuguese educational, medical, and religious assistance. The letters, usually polite in tone, revealed gradually diminished hopes as friendly early encounters turned into Portuguese plunder and exploitation. These are excerpts from several letters written in 1526.

Sir, Your Highness should know how our Kingdom is being lost in so many ways that it is convenient to provide the necessary remedy, since this is caused by the excessive freedom given by your factors and officials to the men and merchants who are allowed to come to the Kingdom to set up shop with goods and many things which have been prohibited by us....

And we cannot reckon how great the damage is, since the mentioned merchants are taking every day our natives, sons of the land and the sons of our noblemen and vassals and our relatives, because the thieves and men of bad conscience grab them wishing to have the things and wares of this Kingdom which they are ambitious of; they grab them and get them to be sold; and so great, Sir, is the corruption and licentiousness that our country is being completely depopulated, and Your Highness should not agree with this nor accept it as in your service. And to avoid it we need from...[your] Kingdoms no more than some priests and a few people to teach in schools....It is our will that in these Kingdoms there should not be any trade of slaves nor outlet for them....And as soon as they are taken by the white men they are immediately ironed and branded with fire....

It happens that we have continuously many and different diseases which put us very often in such a weakness that we reach almost the last extreme; and the same [thing] happens to our children, relatives and natives owing to the lack in this country of physicians and surgeons who might know how to cure properly such diseases. And as we have got neither dispensaries nor drugs which might help us in this forlornness, many of those who had already been confirmed and instructed in the holy faith of Our Lord Jesus Christ perish and die; and the rest of the people in their majority cure themselves with herbs and breads and other ancient methods, so that they put all their faith in the mentioned herbs and ceremonies if they live....And this is not much in the service of God....We beg of you to be agreeable and kind enough to send us two physicians and two apothecaries and one surgeon, so that they may come with their drug-stores and all the necessary things to stay in our kingdoms, because we are in extreme need of them all.

THINKING ABOUT THE READING

1. What do these examples of letters tell us about Portuguese slaving activities and growing power in the Kongo?
2. What did Alfonso believe his kingdom needed from the Portuguese?
3. Why were the Portuguese unlikely to grant Alfonso's requests?

Source: Basil Davidson, ed., *African Civilization Revisited: Chronicles from Antiquity to Modern Times* (Trenton, N.J.: Africa World Press, 1991), pp. 223–226. This excerpt has been reprinted with the permission of Africa World Press in Trenton, NJ.

---

rapacious Portuguese, who halted their cooperation with the Kongo government in 1575.

Eventually the Portuguese turned to conquest. Establishing a base at Luanda (**loo-AHN-duh**) in 1580, they began a war against a vassal state of Kongo, Ndongo (**uhn-DONG-go**), whose ruler, called the Ngola, gave the name Angola (**ahng-GO-luh**) to the region. Like the Kongolese, Ndongo warriors were skilled but armed only with arrows and lances against Portuguese guns, cannon, and steel swords. Queen Nzinga (**en-ZING-a**) of Ndongo (1624–1663), born a slave in the royal court, proved a formidable adversary. This brilliant diplomat, eloquent debater, and skilled warrior who dressed as a man and had a harem of men, led her troops into battle and also shrewdly negotiated to preserve her kingdom while demanding equal treatment with Europeans. Her charismatic personality rallied her people. After years of diplomacy alternating with war, the pragmatic Nzinga made peace, a victim of Portugal's superior arms and ruthless quest for gold and slaves.

After her death Ndongo became the foundation for Portugal's colony of Angola.

In the early seventeenth century both Portuguese and African mercenaries began raiding Kongo. The Christian monarchy sent moving appeals for help to the papacy, which ignored most appeals, though it pursued some with the Portuguese government. The ensuing civil wars in Kongo generated more captives for sale as slaves. Aiming to reform Kongolese political life while ending warfare and slavery, a charismatic Kongolese woman, Dona Beatriz Kimpa Vita, led a spiritual movement combining Catholic and traditional elements, but in 1706 Catholic missionaries had her burned at the stake.

Eventually most Kongolese were incorporated into Portuguese Angola, many abandoning Christianity. Angola and Kongo became deeply enmeshed in the trans-Atlantic slave trade, which, by the later 1600s, had grown much larger than the Arab and Black Sea slave trades. Angola and Kongo, the major suppliers of slaves to Brazil, became the Americas'

The meeting of Queen Nzinga of Ndongo and Joao Correia de Sousa the Portugese govenor of Luanda in 1622 (engraving). Dutch School, (17th century)/Private Collection/The Bridgeman Art Library

QUEEN NZINGA This drawing by an Italian priest, Father Cavazzi, shows the formidable Queen Nzinga of Ndongo, in Angola, sitting on her throne, wearing a crown topped by a Christian cross and bracelets befitting her royal dignity while giving an order to attendants.

largest source of enslaved men and women, accounting for some 35 to 40 percent of the total.

Eastern Africa and the Portuguese

Portuguese activity also extended into eastern Africa. In 1502 Vasco da Gama, leading twenty ships, occupied the cities of Mozambique and Sofala. To establish commercial control, Portuguese forces attacked, plundered, and occupied other Swahili trading cities, burning some to the ground. In Mombasa, wrote a Portuguese eyewitness, "everyone started to search the houses, forcing open the doors with axes and iron bars. A large quantity of cotton cloth, rich silk and gold embroidered clothes was seized."[7] Much of the population fled Kilwa, which the Portuguese pillaged in 1505, leaving only stone ruins. Using conquered cities as bases and ruthless methods, such as attacking and sinking Arab, Persian, and Indian ships, Portugal gradually gained partial control of the Indian Ocean maritime trading network while seizing key trading ports in the Persian Gulf, India, Malaya, Indonesia, and China and eastern Indonesia's Spice Islands, the main source for priceless clove and nutmeg supplies.

Portugal's East African ports never prospered, declining into poverty as many traders fled elsewhere. Fanatical Christians, the Portuguese suppressed the Islamic Swahili culture, burning books that contained epic poems, religious writings, and historical chronicles. While dominating coastal commerce for a century, their power over Indian Ocean maritime trade gradually diminished. As their influence waned all over the coast except in Mozambique, Arabs from Oman, on Arabia's northeast coast, filled the power vacuum, overrunning Portuguese settlements in the late 1600s and establishing a sultanate on Zanzibar, an island off Tanzania. Omani Arabs now supervised the lucrative slave and ivory trade to the Middle East and India, maintaining their political and commercial position into the late 1800s.

Eventually Portuguese adventurers, seeking gold on the plateau, moved up the Zambezi River to the largest Shona kingdom, Monomotapa **(MO-no-mo-TOP-a)**, while gradually taking control of the lower Zambezi Valley. Because many Portuguese died from tropical diseases such as malaria, the Shona held out until 1628, when a decaying Monomotapa became a virtual Portuguese puppet state.

While trying to control the gold trade, however, the Portuguese destroyed it. Neighboring African states overrunning Monomotapa forced the Portuguese out of the plateau, but the gold fields became less productive. The Portuguese then concentrated their efforts on coastal Mozambique, with the settlers, especially in the Zambezi Valley, often marrying

---

[7]From Basil Davidson, ed., *The African Past: Chronicles from Antiquity to Modern Times* (New York: Grosset and Dunlap, 1964), 136.

African women and adopting aspects of local culture and customs. Mozambique supplied slaves to the Indian Ocean islands and the Americas, but on a small scale relative to West and Central Africa. Only in the nineteenth century did Portugal gain firm control over the settlers, solidifying their Mozambique colony.

In the 1520s the Portuguese intervened briefly in Ethiopia, with its ancient Christian culture, when they sent a small force to help the Ethiopians successfully repulse an Ottoman-backed invasion by Muslim neighbors. Then in the early 1600s Portugal dispatched Jesuit missionaries to convert the king from the state church to Catholicism. He adopted the new faith and began reforming Ethiopian society and church. When both the church and population resisted, however, civil war erupted, the pro-Portuguese king abdicated, missionaries and other Portuguese were expelled, and Ethiopia went back to its old ways and faith. These Portuguese activities and interventions were the first of many later attempts by zealous Westerners to change African society, often harming local people.

South Africa and Dutch Colonization

European activity also affected Africa's southern tip. South Africans' social, political, and economic evolution differed greatly from that of most sub-Saharan Africans. In 1652 the Dutch established a settlement, Cape Town, at the Cape of Good Hope to provision Dutch ships sailing between Europe and Dutch operations in Indonesia (see Chapter 18). Dutch farmers arrived, trading with local Khoikhoi people, but, since they had guns, they soon seized what they wanted. In 1659 the Khoikhoi rose against the Dutch. After crushing this resistance, the Dutch claimed Khoikhoi land and eventually enslaved or killed all the Khoikhoi. Expanding their control, the Dutch also imposed white supremacy rule over resident Africans. Needing labor for their farms and households, they imported slaves from Madagascar, Mozambique, and Indonesia. Masters and slaves lived close together, spawning the mixed-race (known as "Colored") population of today. But whites maintained political, legal, and economic superiority.

Continued Dutch immigration fostered rapid population growth. Some Dutch, chafing at governmental rules, looked eastward for new land. Many adopted the Bantus' pastoralism, herding cattle and sheep. As some Dutch settlers, later called **Boers** ("farmers"), expanded east seeking farmland in the 1700s, their encounters with the Xhosa and later the Zulu peoples generated bitter conflicts over land that lasted for nearly half a century. Thousands of Africans and some Boers died in the fighting. Nonetheless, Boer migrations in cattle-drawn wagons, known as **trekking**, became a tradition, occurring whenever some Boers wanted to flee government restraints. But eventually the Dutch government extended its influence into the lands settled by Boer trekkers.

Boers Dutch farming settlers in South Africa in the eighteenth century.

trekking The migrations of Boer settlers in cattle-drawn wagons into the interior of South Africa whenever they wanted to flee government restraints.

Middle Passage The slave's journey by ship from Africa to the Americas.

The Trans-Atlantic Slave Trade

Modern relations between people of African and European ancestry have often originated in the nineteenth-century European expansion and trade in African slaves, which forged a global distribution of power and privilege determined by skin color. The trans-Atlantic slave trade—usually dated from 1526, when the first large shipments to the Americas began, to 1870, when it was completely abolished—fostered both commerce and cultural change in the lands bordering the Atlantic Ocean (see Map 16.2). The value of plantations and mines in Europe's new American colonies created a labor market not easily filled by free men and women, European slaves and criminals, or coerced Native Americans, especially since Native American populations declined massively during European conquest and colonization. African slaves provided the lowest available cost option, creating the racial basis of trans-Atlantic slavery. This ruthless exploitation of Africans was easily rationalized by their different cultures and appearance.

In the early 1600s Portuguese, Spanish, French, Dutch, Danish, and English colonists in North America began obtaining enslaved West Africans and shipping them across the Atlantic to meet the limitless demands of the American plantation economies. The West African coastal region's fragmentation into many small states precluded unified resistance, enabling European slavers to manipulate rivalries between states. Furthermore, the region's sedentary population was familiar with tropical agriculture and mining. Profits soared as the volume of transported Africans increased. European forts to obtain, store, and ship slaves soon dotted the West African coast from Senegal down to Angola, while holding centers, such as Calabar in Nigeria, Goree in Senegambia, and especially Luanda in Angola, processed slaves for sale. Europeans traded cotton goods, guns, iron, rum, and tobacco for slaves, often with local African chiefs' cooperation, but sometimes they acquired Africans directly by force, as in Kongo and Angola.

Perhaps some 25 to 30 million Africans were originally enslaved for the trade but many never reached the Americas. Between 9 and 12 million Africans, most between twelve and thirty years old, were landed in the Americas over four centuries, possibly a third women, to be sold at auction. Millions died in holding cells in West Africa or on the notorious **Middle Passage**, the slave's journey by ship from Africa to the Americas. Those surviving the Middle Passage faced a bleak future, to be sold without regard to personal ties, mostly to sugar, cotton, or coffee plantations. The trans-Atlantic slave trade reached its peak between 1700 and 1800, with perhaps 100,000 Africans a year shipped to the Americas, some 40 percent from Angola-Kongo and 35 percent from Nigeria.

The Middle Passage lasted one or two months on notoriously overcrowded, disease-ridden slave ships. Conditions were terrible, as this description by an American observer attested:

The [naked] men were shackled two by two, the right wrist and ankle of one to the left wrist and ankle of another. The women—usually regarded as fair prey for the sailors—spent the night between decks, in a space

MAP 16.2 **TRANS-ATLANTIC SLAVE TRADE, 1526–1870** While the Arab-run slave trade from West and East Africa to North Africa and western Asia continued, the trans-Atlantic slave trade was far larger in scope. Millions of Africans were transported across the Atlantic, the greatest number ending up in Brazil and the West Indies. The majority of slaves came from what is today Angola, Congo, and Nigeria. © 2015 Cengage Learning

partitioned off from that of the men. All the slaves were forced to sleep without covering on bare wooden floor. In a stormy passage the skin over their elbows might be worn away to the bare bones. Every man was allowed a space six feet long by sixteen inches wide (and usually about two feet seven inches high).[8]

Olaudah Equiano **(oh-LAU-duh ay-kwee-AHN-oh)**, an Igbo seized in Nigeria in the 1750s, described the intolerable stench of the hold and the floggings on the deck for misconduct, which sometimes resulted in death. The voyages' mortality rates averaged between 5 and 25 percent. Slavers debated whether cramming as many slaves as possible into the ships (known as "tight pack") or carrying slightly fewer slaves ("loose pack") would land the greater number of slaves for eventual sale. Many slaves committed suicide before reaching the Americas. Equiano remembered when two Igbos chained together jumped overboard in despair; many crews installed nets along the sides to catch jumpers. Mutinies were also frequent. In 1839 slaves seized control of a small Spanish ship, the *Amistad*, bound from Sierra Leone to Cuba. Led by a Mande chief's son, Joseph Cinque, the ringleaders picked the locks on their chains, then killed the captain and some crew members. After months at sea, and not knowing how to sail the ship home, they found their way to New York. Tried for mutiny in the United States, Cinque and his comrades were eventually freed by the courts.

The superiority Europeans felt toward Africans resulted in **racism**, a set of beliefs, practices, and institutions based on devaluing groups that are supposedly biologically different. To rationalize the trade, Europeans invented the cruel fiction that Africans were subhuman savages unworthy of civilized treatment. For instance, in 1589 the English adventurer Richard Hakluyt described Africans as "a people of beastly living, without a God, law, religion, or common wealth."[9] Western scholars argued that Africans were naturally inferior to Europeans in intelligence. Slave traders and owners felt little guilt, believing God ordained the inequality of peoples. Some even thought slavery helped Africans by exposing them to Western values and Christianity.

> **racism** A set of beliefs, practices, and institutions based on devaluing groups that are supposedly biologically different.

[8]Malcolm Cowley and Daniel Mannix, "The Middle Passage," in *The Atlantic Slave Trade*, ed. David Northrup (Lexington, MA: D.C. Heath, 1994), 99, 101.

[9]Quoted in R. A. Houston, "Colonies, Enterprise, and Wealth: The Economies of Europe and the Wider World in the Seventeenth Century," *Early Modern Europe: An Oxford History*, ed. Euan Cameron (New York: Oxford University Press, 1999), 165.

THE MIDDLE PASSAGE This painting from the era vividly shows the overcrowded conditions on the ships that carried African slaves, packed like sardines, on the "Middle Passage" across the Atlantic to the Americas. Such brutal conditions resulted in the deaths of many slaves and eventually prompted reformers to demand the end of the slave trade.

The Slave Trade and African Societies

The trans-Atlantic slave trade's impact on Africa varied from region to region. Some coastal West and Central Africans succumbed to chronic raiding, kidnapping, and warfare, in an "enslave your neighbor or be enslaved" syndrome. European guns traded for slaves resulted in plundered villages and broken families. Over three-quarters of the Africans in the Americas were Kongolese, Angolans, Yorubas, Igbos, and Akans, leaving their societies badly disrupted. In Angola, European settlers later seized land in depopulated districts. By linking Atlantic Africa closely to Europe and the Americas, the slave trade created an **Atlantic System**, a large network spanning western and Central Africa, North America's east and gulf coasts, the Caribbean Basin, and South America's Atlantic coast.

Although mainly seeking slaves, Europeans also coveted gold and cloth. Soon Western merchants monopolized coastal trade, but some Africans and people of mixed African and European ancestry also flourished as merchants and slave traders. Other Africans refused to cooperate in slave trading, dealing with Europeans on their own terms. Hence, Benin's kings prohibited selling

Atlantic System A large network that arose with the trans-Atlantic slave trade; the network spanned western and Central Africa, the east and gulf coasts of North America, the Caribbean Basin, and the Atlantic coast of South America.

male slaves and instead obtained firearms needed to protect the state by trading cotton textiles, mostly made by women, as well as pepper, ivory, and beads. Some states such as Dahomey **(duh-HO-mee)**, whose powerful army included women soldiers, prospered by cooperating with the slave traders at the expense of their neighbors. Along the Gold Coast, the Ashante **(a-SHAN-tee)** had formed a state in the seventeenth century under their great king Osei Tutu **(OH-say TOO-too)**, who introduced a constitution making other chiefs members of the king's advisory council. With access to gold fields, a powerful military force, and firearms acquired from Europeans, by the mid-1700s the Ashante dominated a large area while trading gold to North Africa and slaves to the Europeans.

The slave trade fostered economic, social, and political change in Africa. The most far-reaching changes occurred along the coast from Senegambia to Angola, sometimes reaching several hundred miles inland. Some states, such as Kongo, declined, while others, such as Ashante, rose in power. Most West and Central African societies far from the coast, such as Kanem-Bornu, had little direct contact with European slavers or coastal states. However, Arab slave trading badly disrupted some East African regions, even reaching the eastern Congo River Basin. Meanwhile, the Sudan region supplied slaves for North Africa, while the Portuguese and Dutch colonization in southern Africa foreshadowed the division of sub-Saharan Africa by several European nations in the 1800s. In general economic terms, the trans-Atlantic slave trade, by integrating Africa into the world economy as a supplier of human and later natural resources, created imbalances that hindered local industries. Yet, the European presence also fostered the diffusion of American food crops, such as maize and peanuts, to Africa. Some African artists incorporated Western ideas and Christian symbols into their work, while some African traditions influenced Western artists. The European intrusion involved imperialism, the control or domination, direct or indirect, of one state or people over another. Often imperialism led to colonialism, government by one society over another society. The Cape Verde Islands, Angola, and parts of Senegambia, Mozambique, and South Africa became Western colonies in this era. But the full-blown Western colonial scramble for Africa only began with Europe's

rapid industrialization, which accelerated the need for natural resources such as peanuts, palm oil, gold, timber, and cotton for processing into industrial or commercial products, as well as for new markets to consume these goods.

Racism made Africans and their descendants in the Americas a permanent underclass, treated with contempt. The first Europeans to encounter great African states like Benin, Kongo, and Kilwa in the late 1400s and early 1500s were awed by their prosperity and marveled at how even the poorest were treated with dignity. Yet by the 1700s Europeans and North Americans viewed Africa as in desperate need of Western tutelage, setting the stage for, and justifying, colonization. Meanwhile, the Islamic Middle East also encountered rising Western power, but, for most societies, with less dramatic consequences.

MAKE SURE YOU UNDERSTAND THESE KEY POINTS BEFORE MOVING ON

- After the Portuguese conquered both Angola and Kongo, these areas became the major source of slaves for the trans-Atlantic slave trade.

- Millions of West African slaves were shipped to North America because they were the cheapest form of labor available to work the farms and mines and because the Native American population had been decimated.

- The conditions of the Middle Passage, from West Africa to America, were horrific, and many slaves died, committed suicide, or mutinied en route.

- The slave trade led to racist views, as many Europeans justified it by claiming that Africans were inherently inferior or arguing that it benefited slaves by exposing them to Western culture and religion.

aplia

The Ottomans and Islamic Imperial Revival

What factors made the Ottoman Empire such a powerful force in the region?

The Islamic Middle East did not experience the jarring transitions felt by many Africans. While European nations established maritime supremacy, Islamic states remained major land powers. The greatest, the Turkish Ottoman Empire, eventually ruled much of southeastern Europe, Asia's western fringe, and much of North Africa while nearly conquering much of eastern and central Europe. By the 1700s, however, the Ottomans and other Middle Eastern states suffered from chronic warfare, poor leadership, growing rigidity, and a superiority complex toward the upstart Europeans. These Islamic societies soon became targets of European imperialism.

The Ottoman Empire, Government, and Economy

Ottoman Turks gained power over much of the once-great Byzantine Empire in the 1300s. Islamic power was conclusively demonstrated by the conquest of the Byzantine capital, Constantinople, in 1453, when the center of Orthodox Christianity was transformed into a Muslim city, later known

as Istanbul. By 1512 the Ottomans controlled Anatolia, Bulgaria, Greece, Albania, Serbia, and Romania. If their invasion of southern Italy had succeeded, Europe's history might have been very different. During the sixteenth century the Ottomans also defeated Persian forces, added Syria, Lebanon, Palestine, and Egypt to their domains, and controlled much of the Mediterranean.

The Ottoman golden age under Sultan Suleiman (**SOO-lay-man**) the Magnificent (r. 1520–1566), a just lawgiver but merciless conqueror, brought military expansion and a diminishing of Christian power. Suleiman's forces invaded the eastern Balkans and areas north of the Danube River, defeating the Hungarians and besieging Vienna; they also occupied Egypt and then the North African coast. After Suleiman defeated the Persians and incorporated Iraq, his empire stretched from Algeria to the Persian Gulf and from Hungary to Armenia (see Map 16.3). But the Ottomans

imperialism The control or domination, direct or indirect, of one state or people over another.

colonialism Government by one society over another society.

MAP 16.3 **THE OTTOMAN AND SAFAVID EMPIRES, 1500–1750** By the later 1500s the Ottoman Empire included large parts of western Asia, southeastern Europe, southern Russia, and North Africa. The Ottomans' major rivals, the Safavids, controlled Persia and parts of Iraq, the Caucasus, Afghanistan, and Central Asia. © 2015 Cengage Learning

never controlled much of the Arabian peninsula. During the 1500s Ottoman ships also challenged the Portuguese in the Indian Ocean with some success, operating as far east as the Straits of Melaka before eventually pulling back.

Suleiman's reign revived the Islamic glory that had faded with the Iraq-based Abbasid Empire's downfall in the 1200s. Ottoman sultans claimed to restore the caliphate, the blending of political and religious power claimed by early Islamic leaders to be ordained by God. In 1538 the Ottoman ruler boasted of his wide-ranging power: "I am God's slave and sultan of this world. I am head of Muhammad's community …who sends his fleets to the seas of Europe, the Maghrib [northwest Africa] and India."[10]

Suleiman's strategic position involved him in conflicts. Sometimes the Ottomans allied with France or with northern European Protestants against the Habsburgs, who ruled Austria and a large area of eastern Europe. Ottoman success owed much to advanced gunpowder weapons, especially cannon, that were

often built and operated by Hungarian Christians in Ottoman service, as well as to an effective navy with ships often designed and crewed by Christian mercenaries. Controlling overland trade routes between Europe and the Indian Ocean, Ottomans sold spices and other products from India, Southeast Asia, and China to Venetians and other Europeans.

For decades able sultans, governing through an imperial council headed by a prime minister and officials chosen on merit, allowed Arabs and other non-Turks to serve as officials and military officers. A Habsburg envoy wrote, "No distinction is attached to birth among the Turks. Honors, high posts, and judgeships are the rewards of great ability and good services."[11] The ruling elite resided in beautiful palaces with many servants and large harems of wives and concubines.

As they recruited administrators and soldiers from Christian peoples, the sultan's agents selected Christian youth for training, essentially making them slaves required to embrace Islam. The most talented attended the palace school, where

[10]Quoted in Halil Inalcik, *The Ottoman Empire: The Classical Age, 1300–1600* (London: Phoenix Press, 2000), 41.

[11]Quoted in Arthur Goldschmidt, Jr., *A Concise History of the Middle East*, 4th ed. revised and updated (Boulder, CO: Westview Press, 1991), 129.

they learned to read and write Arabic, Persian, and Turkish in preparation for administration. This group produced most Ottoman prime ministers. The other conscripts joined the well-armed, well-paid, highly disciplined elite military corps of infantrymen known as janissaries ("new troops"), who lived in barracks and were forbidden to marry.

The Ottoman Empire had a flourishing commercial economy. Istanbul and other major cities served as transregional trade centers where merchants from different lands bought or sold European woolens, Persian silk, Chinese porcelain, Indian spices and textiles, Arab sugar, and Anatolian iron. Artisan and merchant guilds controlled many economic activities. But international trade mostly involved luxuries, with the empire largely self-sufficient in necessities such as food.

Ottoman Society, Culture, and Thought

Ottoman society and culture were marked by diversity and prosperity. The empire's multiethnic population, about evenly divided between Christians and Muslims, contained some 50 million people at its peak, dwarfing the largest European country, France, which had perhaps 15 million. The sultans governed sizable Jewish, Greek Orthodox, and Armenian Christian communities through their own religious leaders, laws, and courts. Although facing some legal disabilities, religious minorities generally enjoyed a toleration rare in that era. Vibrant urban social life revolved around coffeehouses, public baths, and taverns. An Ottoman observer of one coffeehouse wrote: "Some read books and fine writings, some were busy with backgammon and chess, some brought new poems and talked of literature. Pious hypocrites said: 'People have become addicts of the coffee-house; nobody comes to the mosques.'"[12]

Many immigrants, including Jews and Muslims fleeing persecution in Spain, brought valuable expertise and international connections. European merchants and technicians, exempted from Ottoman taxes and laws, enjoyed commercial advantages over local-born competitors. Many Christian peasants from southern and eastern Europe immigrated or welcomed Ottoman conquest, which generally brought them a better life. Some Balkan peasants said that the Turk's turban was better than the pope's tiara.

Despite patriarchy, women had a higher status in Turkish than in Arab society. Royal women exercised political clout, influencing princes brought up in royal harems while financing buildings and social service activities. Upper-class women often owned land, managed businesses, and controlled wealth. Women also took their grievances to Islamic courts, which protected their rights to inheritance and property. Having sons provided even more security. Since men usually died younger, women often headed households. Yet, men could also abuse and more easily divorce women, and sometimes families punished or killed women suspected of illicit sexual activity.

Istanbul attracted artists and artisans from all over Europe and the Middle East. For example, Suleiman the Magnificent welcomed humanist thinkers from Italy, while Sultan Mehmed II (1432–1481) had the most famous Venetian artist, Giovanni Bellini, decorate his palace with paintings. Ottoman architects, such as the innovative Pasha Sinan, designed beautiful domed mosques and other public buildings, combining form with function (see Profile: Pasha Sinan, Ottoman Architect). In this creative environment, Ottoman and European architects and artists influenced each other. One sultan who admired Italian art tried to woo two of the greatest talents, Michelangelo and Leonardo da Vinci, to work in Istanbul. Meanwhile, Ottoman medicine remained vibrant, while Ottoman scholars published much on astronomy, mathematics, and geography and produced world maps more sophisticated than European maps. However, by the 1700s the Ottomans had fallen behind western Europe in science, and Ottoman intellectuals remained largely disinterested in and uninformed about scientific and technological developments elsewhere. The emphasis on law and theology rather than science in higher education inhibited technological innovation.

In religious life, various mystical Sufi sects, seeking to personally experience God, had large followings. Seyh Bedreddin (SAY beh-DREAD-en), who founded an order of practitioners known as dervishes, wrote: "Ecstasy came to me, and I remained in wonderment at God's presence. The mystic who has perceived God spreads to the whole universe; he is one with the mountains and streams. There is no here or hereafter; everything is a single moment."[13] To achieve a trancelike state, dervishes danced feverishly, whirling around faster and faster while their long skirts billowed out, creating a hypnotic effect. Some Sufi sects operated with official support; critics suspected others, including the dervishes, of political disloyalty and modifying too many Islamic principles.

Perhaps as the religious establishment became closer to the state, Islam became more rigid in the Ottoman realms and Middle East. Most religious leaders emphasized memorization rather than analyzing sacred texts, punished deviation from orthodoxy, and increasingly opposed technological innovation. Meanwhile, Christian minorities flocked to schools established by Christian missionaries from Europe and North America. Some of these schools, by teaching commercial and technical subjects, exposed them to knowledge from the wider world.

Ottoman Decline and the West

Eventually the Ottomans faced new challenges that undermined the state and reduced the empire. Ottoman armies effectively battled European and Persian rivals into the 1670s, when they annexed part of the Ukraine. However, in 1683 Austria and its allies repulsed the last Ottoman attack on Vienna. Soon the Ottomans were pushed south of the Danube River, lost the Ukraine and southern Greece, and

> **janissaries** ("new troops") Well-armed, highly disciplined, and generally effective elite military corps of infantrymen in the Ottoman Empire.

[12]Ibrahim Pecevi, quoted in Philip Mansel, *Constantinople: City of the World's Desire, 1453–1924* (New York: St. Martin's, 1995), 171.

[13]Quoted in Inalcik, *Ottoman Empire*, 189.

ceded Hungary to the rival Habsburgs. As its military practices and technology fell behind, reducing fear of Ottoman power, European diplomats began calling the empire "the sick man of Europe." Janissary military discipline weakened, and as officers spent winters in Istanbul, military campaigns were limited to warm weather months. Eventually sultans eliminated the training system for young men and led campaigns personally, exhausting their energy. In addition, the Ottoman navy had once enjoyed advanced technology, but by the 1600s European ships were better armed and more maneuverable. Ottoman weaponry, especially artillery, stagnated just as European military technology rapidly improved.

Compared to China or the emerging European states, the Ottoman state was not very centralized, making imperial control difficult to maintain. Government through religious communities or provincial leaders focused peoples' loyalty on their ethnic group or region rather than the Ottoman state. Kurds, a Sunni Muslim ethnic group occupying a large region in today's eastern Turkey, northern Iraq and Syria, and northwest Iran, increasingly resented Turkish control. In addition, many Arabs and Balkan Christians who once welcomed Ottoman rule began to think of their own peoples as repressed nations. Ottoman citizens disliked higher taxes, growing corruption, bureaucratic bloat, and increasing peasant poverty. Finally, the ruling elite exercised more power over weak or incompetent sultans, some of whom were mentally unstable or despots. "Ibrahim the Mad" proved particularly tyrannical, once ordering the drowning of 280 concubines who angered him; he was deposed and executed. With weaker male leaders, senior palace women gained more influence, supporting one or another of the factions that contended for favor.

Ottoman sultans also had difficulty controlling restless provinces in North Africa and western Asia, brutally crushing occasional rebellions during the 1600s. Although formally remaining vassals of Istanbul, leaders of Ottoman descent in Algeria and Tunisia became increasingly independent. In Mesopotamia and Egypt, Ottomans ruled through local Arab leaders, who sought more autonomy. By the mid-1700s Ottoman supremacy had deteriorated, while the Russians pressured Ottoman territory north of the Black Sea.

Rising western Europeans, Habsburgs, and Russia posed not only military but also economic challenges. Western Europe's growing wealth and role in Asian trade weakened Anatolia's historic middleman position as Portuguese and Dutch ships carrying Asian resources around Africa to Europe's Atlantic ports gradually reduced trade flowing through Ottoman ports. With little official support to merchants, who were mostly Greeks, Armenians, and Jews, the once self-sufficient empire became increasingly dependent on imports from Europe. Western merchants also gradually controlled large sectors of the Ottoman economy. Large Western trading firms, armed with great capital and better business methods and backed by their own governments, ultimately reduced the Ottomans to a secondary power in the emerging global trade system.

The rising European power sparked fierce debates within the empire. Reformers interested in European products and customs favored importing some European technology but struggled against conservatives, who preferred the status quo and maintained a Muslim superiority complex regarding once-upstart Europeans. Many reformers looked to the era of Suleiman the Magnificent for inspiration. In this fashion the creaking Ottoman state limped into the twentieth century.

MAKE SURE YOU UNDERSTAND THESE KEY POINTS BEFORE MOVING ON

- The Ottoman Empire was culturally and religiously diverse; religious minorities were allowed a measure of self-governance, and many immigrants were attracted by the empire's tolerance.

- The Ottoman Empire attracted and encouraged a range of artists and thinkers from across Eurasia, though state support for Islam may have caused it to become more rigid and close-minded.

- Though the Ottoman Empire remained strong through much of the seventeenth century, its military discipline, weaponry, and political stability soon began a gradual decline.

- As Europeans began to trade directly with Asia, the Ottomans lost their traditional role as middlemen and became increasingly dependent on European imports.

aplia

Ⓢ Persia, Morocco, and Central Asia

Ⓣ *How did the Persian and Central Asian experience differ from that of the Ottomans?*

Like the Ottomans, Islamic societies from Morocco to Central Asia underwent significant changes. Persian leaders, thinkers, and officials had long influenced the Islamic world, and Persian was widely spoken by Muslim elites from Istanbul to India. In the early sixteenth century a Shi'ite dynasty, the Safavids, revived Persian culture and became an internationally recognized power. In northwest Africa, Morocco developed formidable military prowess, while various Islamic societies in Central Asia struggled to maintain Silk Road trade networks while facing pressure from the expanding Russian Empire.

Pasha Sinan, Ottoman Architect

One of world history's most innovative architects, Pasha Sinan (1491–1588), served as royal architect to Ottoman sultans for fifty years, during which time he perfected the Ottoman style. Sinan's work reflected the mixing of Christian and Muslim cultures in Istanbul, the former Byzantine city of Constantinople. Thanks in part to Sinan, Istanbul's architecture symbolized the grandiose Ottoman spirit. Sinan designed over three hundred works, ranging from grand government buildings and mosques taking years to build to fountains, tombs, bridges, and baths.

Born into a Christian Greek family in central Anatolia and selected for the Ottoman military in 1512, Sinan was converted to Islam and trained as a janissary warrior, after which he fought in various military campaigns. During his military service he developed a reputation for his engineering skills. For example, he devised ways to float artillery across lakes and to quickly build a bridge across the Danube River. In 1538 the great sultan Suleiman the Magnificent appointed Sinan royal architect, based in Istanbul. In this highly visible post, Sinan developed, procured funding for, and supervised the construction of projects viewed by millions. To succeed, he needed the skills of a visionary, planner, administrator, and manager.

Istanbul was filled with inspiring architecture from Byzantine times, including the beautiful cathedral of Hagia Sophia, with its huge dome. Fascinated by these domed structures, Sinan concentrated on incorporating them into his own architecture. The Hagia Sophia church, with its ascending hierarchy of sanctity ending at the altar, had been built for the Byzantine emperor Justinian a thousand years earlier and so reflected the Byzantine world-view and Greek Orthodox Church values. Sinan sought to outdo the architects who built Hagia Sophia while adapting the dome structure to an Islamic house of worship, providing open spaces where all could face Mecca from an equal position. Sinan experimented constantly in pursuit of his vision.

Trying to incorporate Hagia Sophia's best features into an Islamic setting, Sinan designed several great mosques in Istanbul. The Suleimaniye (**SOO-lay-man-iya**) mosque, finished in 1557, sits atop a high hill, dominating the city and proclaiming Islam's triumph. A sixteenth-century English traveler, John Sanderson, believed the mosque passed "in greatness, workmanship, marble pillars, and riches all the churches of [Christian] emperors [and merited] to be matched with the 7 Wonders of the [ancient] World." The main dome is surrounded by over four hundred lesser domes. This huge complex included several of Istanbul's most elite schools.

Sinan's last great mosque, the Edirne (**eh-DURN-a**), completed in 1575, had a dome surpassing that of Hagia Sophia. Sinan considered it his masterpiece and boasted that "architects among Christians say that no Muslim architect would be able to build such a large dome. With the help of God I erected a dome higher and wider than Hagia Sophia." In designing this mosque, Sinan tried to assert what he considered the superiority of Islam over Christianity and brought Ottoman architecture to its highest point. The mosque expressed the imperial Ottoman achievement and the splendor of Islam.

Various rich Ottomans, to show their piety and provide themselves with a burial place, endowed mosques. Imperial family women and the wives of wealthy Ottoman officials also financed mosques, among other good works. Sinan designed some of these mosques and built great tombs to commemorate the powerful men and women of his day. He also designed parts of the sultan's great palace, the Topkapi Sarai (**sah-RYE**) (Abode of Felicity). This huge complex boasted beautiful interiors and contained a series of pavilions, gardens, courts, treasuries, reception halls, baths, kitchens, and other buildings. Begun by Sinan, it was constructed over several centuries with no particular master plan. The palace and the grand mosques remain as testimonies to Sinan's talents and Ottoman cultural vibrancy in the 1500s.

© Nickolay Vinokurov /Shutterstock.com

SULEIMANIYE MOSQUE Between 1548 and 1557 Sinan designed and supervised the building of one of Istanbul's most magnificent mosques, the Suleimaniye, honoring God and Sinan's patron, Sultan Suleiman the Magnificent, who was buried in the mosque. Overlooking the Straits of Bosporus, the mosque complex contains schools, shops, and a hospital.

THINKING ABOUT THE PROFILE

1. What does Sinan's career tell us about the Ottoman system?
2. How did Sinan's architecture reflect a mixing of Islamic and Christian traditions?

Notes: Quotations from Andrew Wheatcroft, *The Ottomans* (New York: Viking, 1993), 143; and Aptullah Kuran, *Sinan: The Grand Old Master of Ottoman Architecture* (Washington, DC: Institute of Turkish Studies, 1987), 168–169.

The Safavid Empire

The Safavid dynasty in Persia was founded in 1501 by a Turkish group from Azerbaijan (**AZ-uhr-bye-ZHAHN**) in the Caucasus Mountains who belonged to a militant Shi'ite Sufi order. Led by a charismatic thirteen-year-old boy, Isma'il (1487–1524), they invaded and began conquering Persia, then a center of Sunni practice. Isma'il claimed descent from Muhammad and Sassanian princes. A Venetian diplomat described the youth as "of noble presence and a truly royal bearing, as in his eyes and brows there was something so great and commanding, which plainly showed that he would someday become a great ruler."[14] Isma'il, believing himself an agent of God, mandated the conversion of Persians to Shi'ism. Tensions between the majority Sunni and minority Shi'a had simmered since the Islamic community divided centuries earlier, and the Safavids used force when necessary on reluctant Sunnis, confiscating property and executing religious leaders. The shift to Shi'ism took some years, with many Sunni families emigrating to India, Central Asia, or Ottoman territories. Many Persians, however, enjoyed the rich Shi'ite ceremonies and wanted to differentiate themselves from the hated Sunni Ottomans. Eventually Persians came to view Shi'ism as central to Persian identity, and today most Iranians are Shi'ites of Persian or Azeri Turkish background.

The Safavids, while establishing a strong political system, never acquired the gunpowder-based military power of the Ottomans. Safavid armies rode on horseback and viewed guns as both awkward and unmanly, an attitude that left them vulnerable to Ottoman and Portuguese gunpowder weapons. The Portuguese seized and held the strategic port of Hormuz (**hawr-MOOZ**), on Persia's southeast coast, for decades, and in 1514 the Ottomans occupied Safavid lands in Armenia and Anatolia. Battle losses to the hated Ottomans demoralized Safavid military leaders; Isma'il, unable to cope with defeat, became an alcoholic recluse in his palace. Although soon regaining their confidence, the Safavids did not attempt to expand their empire. They also adopted many governmental practices long common in the region. Like the Ottomans, they acquired slave boys, primarily from Christian peoples, especially Armenians and Georgians, for administrative or military training, and over time they adapted to local Persian customs.

Safavid rule reached its peak under Shah (king) Abbas (**ah-BAHS**) I (r. 1587–1629), who consolidated his power by manipulating or executing his enemies, including Sufi leaders. His capital, Isfahan (**is-fah-HAHN**), became a beautiful, tree-shaded city of some 1 million people, filled with mosques, public baths, parks, and a great bazaar that one visitor described as "the surprisingest piece of Greatness in Honor of Commerce that the world can boast of."[15] The shah kept men away a few days each year so that the normally secluded women could visit the bazaars and promenade in the evening on Isfahan's spectacular main boulevard, lined with gardens, pavilions, and a water channel. Shah Abbas enjoyed visiting the city's teahouses, listening to poets and storytellers and chatting with citizens.

Many peasants worked the king's land, receiving a share of the crop. Tolerant in religion, Abbas admitted Christian missionaries and maintained good relations with European powers, importing English advisers to train his military forces and manufacture modern cannon and muskets. Soon he waged successful wars against invading Ottomans and Uzbeks, and he also recaptured Hormuz from Portugal. Europeans sought Persia as an ally against their mutual Ottoman enemy.

By the eighteenth century Safavid sultans had become weaker, Shi'ite religious officials had become stronger, and the empire's economy had declined. Unable to control the clergy or trust their sons plotting for the throne, later Safavid rulers often turned to alcohol and concubines for comfort, while corruption grew rampant. In 1722 Afghans seized Isfahan and then repulsed invading Ottoman forces. Isfahan was nearly destroyed. In 1736 a new Persian leader, Nadir Shah (1688–1747), drove out the Afghans, established a vigorous new state, and marched his armies into Ottoman lands and north India, plundering the major city, Delhi. But Nadir Shah proved ruthless against suspected foes while economic collapse exposed millions to famine. After ill-advised efforts to reconvert Persians back to Sunni Islam, Nadir Shah was assassinated in 1747, and his empire soon collapsed. In the decades to follow, Persia divided into smaller states while Western pressure intensified.

Persian Economy, Society, Culture, and Thought

Safavid Persia flourished economically for several centuries from long-distance trade by land and sea. Persian merchants remained active in Indian Ocean trade, operating as far away as China, Southeast Asia, and East Africa. Meanwhile, foreign merchants flocked to Isfahan's great bazaar, where artisans produced fine carpets, textiles, metalwork, and ceramics. Armenian settlers based in Persia made and exported silk while operating lucrative gold and silver crafts industries, and they also competed fiercely with Dutch, English, Portuguese, and Indian merchants in parts of Eurasia. The Armenian network radiated outward from New Julfa (**JOOL-fa**), near Isfahan, and was run by a merchants' council. Sharing a common culture and Christian religion, Armenian merchants played key roles in the overland trade from India to Central Asia and the Middle East. The New Julfa Armenian network eventually stretched eastward to India, Burma, Java, and China; westward to Venice, Marseilles, Amsterdam, and London; and northward through Russia to northern Europe. English, Dutch, and French merchants visited Persian ports, whetting European appetites for more extensive trade. By cooperating with these traders, Persians counteracted Ottoman control of overland routes.

In patriarchal Persian society, women were largely restricted to the home and expected to veil themselves when leaving the household. Yet, they often had more influence than Arab women. Royal women in harems raised royal sons and

[14]From John J. Saunders, ed., *The Muslim World on the Eve of Europe's Expansion* (Englewood Cliffs, NJ: Prentice-Hall, 1966), 35.
[15]Quoted in Francis Robinson, *The Cultural Atlas of the Islamic World Since 1500* (London: Stonehenge, 1987), 49.

Ellen Mack/Flickr Open/Getty Images

THE SPLENDOR OF SAFAVID ISFAHAN Isfahan was one of the Early Modern world's most beautiful cities. This view shows the city's central Naqsh-e Jahn Square, flanked by the Imam Mosque in the distance and the Ali Qapu Palace on the right.

tried to shape government policies, and some women became wealthy, owning land and businesses. Even in seclusion, they used agents to help run their enterprises and manage property or money. Poor women had no such opportunities.

Like some Muslim rulers in India, Renaissance European princes, and Chinese emperors, Safavid shahs, often themselves artists and poets, patronized art and literature. The major cities, especially Isfahan, became centers for writers, craftsmen, and artists, and Persia's style of miniature paintings spread to the Ottoman and Mughal Empires. In 1525 the Safavid sultan commissioned an ambitious, decade-long project to produce an illustrated version of an old epic poem recounting Persian history. The completed version contained 258 paintings by many artists. Poetry also thrived, with well-known Persian poets recruited by Muslim Indian courts, some using Persian as an official language. Finally, carpet weaving became both an art form and a national industry, while government-run factories produced silks, brocades, velvets, and other fabrics.

Persian Shi'ism underwent some changes. The Safavids encouraged passion plays and annual religious processions commemorating the tragic death of the prophet Muhammad's grandson, Husayn, in the Battle of Karbala in 680, which split the Islamic community. During these events, hundreds of men fulfilled vows of faith by beating their bodies with chains while chanting religious dirges. With Sufi influence

gradually declining and religious teachers emphasizing their own authority over that of the Quran, Islamic leaders enjoyed greater power and more wealth than elsewhere in the Islamic world. Even the shahs claimed divine backing, giving the state a theocratic cast. But tensions over religious power between the shahs and Shi'ite leaders continued to simmer.

Moroccan Resurgence and Expansion

While Ottomans and Safavids dominated much of the Islamic world, Moroccans on Africa's far northwestern fringe forged a strong Islamic state and conquered an empire. Moroccan society comprised Berbers, Arabs, and an influential Jewish community, many of whom had migrated across the Strait of Gibraltar to Morocco as a result of the gradual Christian triumph in Iberia. Jews invigorated commercial life. Morocco traded with North Africa, West Africa, and Europe, and Venetian and Genoese ships regularly visited Moroccan ports, exchanging metals, textiles, spices, hardware, and wine for leather, carpets, wool, grain, sugar, and African slaves.

Encounters with the Portuguese brought the Sa'dians to power in Morocco. Portugal's cultivation of sugar on the Atlantic islands undermined Moroccan sugar production, and the establishment of Portuguese forts along the coast threatened the Moroccan government. In response, Sufi movements organized coalitions to resist the Portuguese. With Sufi and tribal support, in 1554 the Sa'dians, a Moroccan family claiming descent from the prophet Muhammad, conquered the country, ruling until 1659. The greatest Sa'dian leader, Sultan Ahmad al-Mansur (man-SOOR) (r. 1578–1603), recruited mercenary European and Turkish soldiers familiar with firearms and modern artillery. After buying ships, cannon, and gunpowder from the Netherlands and England, both Portugal's rivals, Moroccans captured the coastal Portuguese ports. Claiming to serve the Islamic world's interests, al-Mansur planned an invasion of West Africa: "The Sudan, being a very rich country and providing enormous revenues, we can now increase the size of the armies of Islam and strengthen the battalions of the faithful."[16] In 1591 Moroccan forces seized the trading city of Timbuktu in Songhai, undermining that Sudanic state, and gained control of the trans-Saharan trade. But facing disappointing profits, Moroccans withdrew in 1618.

After the Sa'dian system fragmented, a new Moroccan dynasty, the Alawis (uh-LAH-wees), also claiming descent from the prophet Muhammad, came to power in 1672. This dynasty still rules Morocco today. Sufi influence continued to expand, but powerful Sufi movements sometimes clashed with royal governments. Alawi-ruled Morocco traded even more heavily with Europe, North Africa, and the Sudan.

Central Asia and Russian Expansion

Russian imperial expansion into Central Asia and Ottoman territories fostered the most direct and long-lasting Muslim-European confrontations. Russians had long coveted Central Asia's dry lands, where long-distance trade flourished in Silk Road hubs such as Bukhara (boo-CAR-ruh) and Samarkand (SAM-ar-kand). Central Asia also contained large Muslim communities where Sufi masters often gained political power. As the remnants of the Mongol Empire broke up, Russia extended its power into Siberia and then into the Black Sea region and Central Asia. Seeking resources and land for possible Russian settlement, it acquired a great land-based

Cossacks Tough adventurers and soldiers from southern Russia who were descendants of Russians, Poles, and Lithuanians fleeing serfdom, slavery, or jail.

territorial empire. This eastward and southward Russian expansion over huge distances was a saga comparable to later westward expansion by the United States and Canada across North America. Key players were the Cossacks (KOS-aks), tough, hard-drinking adventurers and fierce soldiers from southern Russia who were descended from Russians, Poles, and Lithuanians fleeing serfdom, slavery, or jail.

The expansion east across sparsely populated Siberia to the Pacific coast began in the 1500s and accelerated into the eighteenth century. In 1689 conflict with China forced Russians to temporarily abandon the Amur (AH-moor) River Basin north of China (see Chapter 18); however, they added other Siberian territory, often overcoming fierce local resistance. Siberia yielded the Russians furs, metals, and forest products. Seeking direct access to maritime trade routes, Russian leaders also coveted the Black Sea and the Straits of Bosporus, through which Russian ships could reach the warm Mediterranean. The southward thrust meant confronting Tartars (TAHR-tuhrz), Muslim descendants of Mongols. In the 1400s and 1500s Tartars, Russians, Ottoman Turks, Poles, and Lithuanians fought for control of southern Russia. After seizing the Tartar state of Kazan (kuh-ZAN) and slaughtering many residents, the Russians dominated the northern Caspian Sea and direct trade between the Baltic lands and Persia through Russia.

Turning toward Muslim Central Asia, settled largely by Turkish peoples and often known as Turkestan, by the early 1700s the Russians had gained territory occupied by the Kazakhs (kah-ZAHKS), a pastoral people, and by 1864 they controlled all Kazakh lands to the eastern border with China. They then targeted the Silk Road cities but faced formidable opponents in the Uzbeks (OOZ-beks), a people of mixed Turkish, Persian, and Mongol ancestry. Since they promoted Sunni Islam, Uzbek sultans were enemies of the Shi'ite Safavids. When Safavid hostility closed Persia to Uzbek trade, the Silk Road cities declined, and the Uzbeks and their neighbors earned smaller revenues while sultans lost power to tribal chiefs. In the early 1700s Persians gained control of some Uzbek territory and much of Afghanistan. But by the later 1800s an expanding Russia had conquered all of southern Turkestan.

MAKE SURE YOU UNDERSTAND THESE KEY POINTS BEFORE MOVING ON

- Under the Safavids, Persia was a major exporter of silk and remained a major conduit of trade, and its beautiful capital, built by Shah Abbas I, attracted merchants from many countries.

- The Safavid Empire patronized art and literature, and Safavid artists became famous for their miniature painting and their carpet weaving.

- Safavid religious leaders, increasingly relying on their own authority rather than that of the Quran, eventually

became more influential as the power of Safavid rulers declined and then collapsed.

- Morocco, the far western outpost of Islam, absorbed many fleeing Iberian Muslims and grew into a powerful state that, under the Sa'dians, eventually defeated the Portuguese.

aplia

---

[16]Quoted in Ralph A. Austen, *Trans-Saharan Africa in World History* (New York: Oxford University Press, 2010), 58.

CHAPTER SUMMARY

The overseas expansion of Europe affected different regions in different ways but was only one of the forces at work in most societies. Various African societies, among them Songhai, Kanem-Bornu, the Hausa states, Benin, and Buganda, remained strong in the 1500s. Eventually, however, the Europeans' arrival set in motion forces that reshaped parts of Africa, especially societies along the western and eastern coasts, and many Africans became linked more closely to Europe and the Americas. The Portuguese undermined Kongo, Angola, and the East African city-states and established the first European colonies in sub-Saharan Africa, Angola, and Mozambique. With the trans-Atlantic slave trade, which arose in the sixteenth century, various Europeans procured slaves in West and Central Africa and shipped them across the Atlantic to meet the limitless demands of the American plantations.

This trade benefited a few African societies but devastated others, creating chronic conflict along the West African coast.

Several Islamic societies remained powerful, including the empires of the Ottomans, Safavids, and Morocco. The Ottomans, who were Sunni Turks, built an empire over much of western Asia, North Africa, and southeastern Europe, reuniting a large part of the Islamic world. At their zenith they had a powerful military, flourishing economy, and vibrant cultural life. The Safavids fostered a lively culture and economy in Persia and converted the Persians from Sunni to Shi'a Islam, increasing the rivalry with the Ottomans. Sa'dian Morocco repulsed the Portuguese and built a regional empire. But by the early 1700s these great Islamic states as well as Muslim societies in Central Asia experienced new challenges, some posed by Russian expansion into Muslim lands.

KEY TERMS

Darkest Africa (p. 374)
Boers (p. 378)
trekking (p. 378)
Middle Passage (p. 378)

racism (p. 379)
Atlantic System (p. 380)
imperialism (p. 381)
colonialism (p. 381)

janissaries (p. 383)
Cossacks (p. 388)

17 Americans, Europeans, Africans, and New Societies in the Americas, 1450–1750

De Eſpañol, y Meſtiſa; Caſtiſa.

Scala/Art Resource, NY

A MESTIZO FAMILY The intermarriage of Europeans and Indians was common in Latin America, especially in Mexico. This Mexican painting, by the eighteenth-century artist Las Castas, shows a Spanish man, his Indian wife, and their mixed-descent, or *mestizo*, daughter.

Truly do we live on earth? Not forever on earth; only a little while here. Although it be jade, it will be broken. Although it is gold, it is crushed.

—Aztec poem on the meaning of life, CA. 1500[1]

In the sixteenth century Spanish colonists in Mexico trained an Aztec historian, Chimalpahin Cuahtlehuanitzin **(chee-MAL-pin QUAT-al-WANT-zen)**, how to read and write in the Western alphabet. Using this alphabet with his native Nahuatl **(NAH-waht-l)** language, he recorded the Mexican world just before European invaders brought change. He wrote of Aztec victories over neighboring peoples and of Aztec kings improving their great capital, Tenochtitlan **(teh-noch-TIT-lan)**, with temple rebuilding and aqueducts to convey fresh water. But Cuahtlehuanitzin also reported ominous developments. In 1519 reports reached Tenochtitlan of pale-skinned men in huge boats arriving on the eastern coast from the sea, where gods might come from. Aztec legends claimed that, centuries earlier, a Toltec king driven into exile had become a god, Quetzalcoatl **(kate-zahl-CO-ah-tal)** ("the plumed serpent"), who promised to return some day and seek revenge. Dressed in metal, with unfamiliar but lethal metal weapons, and riding on large animals as tall as a house, these strange men seemed suspiciously godlike. The god's reappearance would threaten the Aztec social order. Cuahtlehuanitzin wrote that 1492 had been unusually bad, bringing an eclipse of the sun, volcanic eruptions, and widespread famine. But Aztecs were not prepared for the arriving Europeans or for a terrible and unknown disease that began killing off the people. Within two years, these men from afar, with horses, metal armor, and gunpowder weapons, had conquered the Aztec Empire, giving new meaning to the broken jade and crushed gold in the Aztec poem.

The first Europeans claimed to have discovered a "new world," but it was actually an old, long-populated one. By destroying or reshaping many long-existing societies, the exploratory voyages by Christopher Columbus and the conquests by European adventurers *created* a "new world." During the 1500s Spaniards and Portuguese conquered and colonized large areas of Latin America containing millions of people, and the English, French, and Dutch followed in North America and the Caribbean. Thanks to these incursions, few regions experienced more changes than the Americas, and the two hemispheres became closely linked. European exploration also led to encounters between Europeans and Pacific island societies. The resulting transitions affected both sides of the Atlantic, forging a complex exchange of crops and animals, peoples and cultures.

[1]Quoted in Michael C. Meyer and William L. Sherman, *The Course of Mexican History*, 2nd ed. (New York: Oxford University Press, 1983), 86.

(N)(S) Early American-European-Pacific Encounters

How did encounters between Europe and the Americas increase in the 1500s?

American peoples had developed diverse ways of life long before European voyages of exploration permanently connected the two hemispheres. But after Christopher Columbus began the historic change in 1492, various European nations first explored and then gradually conquered and settled the entire Western Hemisphere, drawing the Americas closer to Europe. This exploration also spilled over into the Pacific Ocean.

American Societies in 1500

Before 1500 American peoples, in adapting to different environments, had developed distinctive institutions, customs, and survival strategies. Hunting, gathering, and fishing societies mostly inhabited the North American Great Plains, the Pacific Northwest coast, Alaska, northern Canada, and Central and South American tropical forests. Small-scale farmers were concentrated in eastern North America, parts of the North American desert and Amazon Basin, and southeastern Brazil. The most complex societies flourished from intensive farming in Mesoamerica (Mexico and northern Central America) and the Andes region of western South America (see Chapter 12). By 1500 the Aztecs of central Mexico were Mesoamerica's most powerful society, and the Inca (**IN-kuhz**), centered in central Peru, controlled most of the Andes

region. Like their predecessors, the Aztecs and Inca lived in cities, farmed, and worked metals and fibers for tools, decoration, and weapons.

The Aztecs, through military conquest and well-organized government, completed their empire building in 1428. Aztec warfare relied on disciplined battle formations, shrewd tactics, and deadly weapons such as bows and arrows, stone-bladed broadswords, spears, and spear-throwers. But the Aztecs only loosely controlled their empire and faced military confrontations with rival societies, especially the Tlaxcalans (**tlax-CALL-uns**) on their eastern fringe. Cruel Aztec imperialism and extensive human sacrifice created enemies, some of whom later cooperated with the Spanish to overthrow Aztec power.

In 1440 the Inca completed their conquest of an empire larger than the Roman or Han Chinese Empire, stretching nearly 2,500 miles north to south, much of it above 8,000 feet in altitude. The Inca state was the Americas' most dynamic and integrated, geared for conquest and paternalistic regimentation. In the later 1500s the writer Garcilaso de la Vega (**GAHR-suh-LAH-so duh luh VAY-guh**), son of a Spanish captain and Inca princess, acknowledged the misery of people colonized by the Inca but praised their highly productive farming system and generosity, which "had attained perfection. No thoughtful man can fail to admire so noble a government."[2]

---

[2]From Lewis Hanke, ed., *History of Latin American Civilization: Sources and Interpretations*, vol. 1 (Boston: Little, Brown and Company, 1973), 64.

	1400	1430	1460	1490	1520	1550
EXPLORATION		1492 First Columbian voyage ●				
		1494 Treaty of Tordesillas ●				
		1497 John Cabot's landing in North America ●				
		1513 Balboa's sighting of Pacific Ocean ●				
		1519–1521 Magellan's circumnavigation of the globe ●				
LATIN AMERICA					1428–1521 Aztec Empire	
	1440–1532 Inca Empire ●					
		1500 Portuguese claim to Brazil ●				
		1521 Spanish conquest of Aztecs ●				
		1532 First permanent Portuguese settlement in Brazil ●				
		1532-1535 Spanish conquest of Inca ●				
NORTH AMERICA			1524 French claim of Canada ●			

Partly because of climate change, some societies had long passed their peak. The last Maya cities of southern Mexico and northern Central America had collapsed, but some 5 to 6 million Mayan-speaking people lived in villages, remnants of a once-vibrant 2,000-year-old society. In North America, Cahokia (**kuh-HOE-key-uh**), the main Mississippian city, was deserted by 1250, and by the 1400s the Anasazi (**ah-nah-SAH-zee**) and other southwestern desert societies had abandoned their major settlements. However, the Taino (**TIE-no**) in the Caribbean islands and the farming peoples along the Atlantic coasts of North America and Brazil had flourishing societies.

While the first European settlers wrongly considered the Americas largely empty land, by 1492 the Western Hemisphere's population probably numbered between 60 and 75 million people,

COLUMBUS LANDING IN THE AMERICAS This early nineteenth century painting by an Italian artist imagines Christopher Columbus landing in the Caribbean and presenting gifts to the first local peoples greeting him on the beach.

and perhaps even over 100 million, the majority in the Andes region and densely populated Mesoamerica. But European invasion changed that. Americans, isolated for many

millennia from the Eastern Hemisphere, had no immunity to the diseases brought by Europeans and later African slaves. Hence, the West brought a terrible mortality. Native

| 1580 | 1610 | 1640 | 1670 | 1700 | 1730 | 1760 | 1790 |

ca. 1605–1694 Palmares maroon state

1587 First English colony at Roanoke
1604 First French settlement in Acadia (Canada)
1607 First permanent English settlement in Virginia
1608 French settlement at Quebec City
1624 Dutch settlement at New York
1627 Colony of New France
1713 English control of Acadia
1739 Stono Rebellion in South Carolina
1755 Deportation of French Acadians to Louisiana
1759 English defeat of French in Quebec

Americans also had no metal swords or firearms to resist Europeans.

Bridging the Atlantic and the Columbian Voyages

The stormy Atlantic Ocean was the major barrier between the hemispheres, but a few Europeans steadily overcame the challenge. The first known contact between Americans and Europeans had no long-lasting impact. In the tenth century some Norse Vikings, sailing west from Iceland, established several small farming settlements in southern Greenland. By around 1000 a few of these hardy Norse sighted eastern Canada and explored the coast. They built a small village on the large island of Newfoundland, where they harvested fish and cut timber. After conflicts with Native Americans erupted, the Norse abandoned the Newfoundland settlement, but Greenland Norse apparently made occasional trading and lumbering expeditions to eastern Canada, as shown by Norse artifacts scattered across eastern Canada and the Arctic islands. The Greenland settlements collapsed by 1450 as the result of factional disputes, conflicts with native Inuit (**IN-yoo-it**) people, deforestation, and colder climates that made farming impossible. Portuguese ships occasionally visited Iceland, possibly learning of the Canada settlement and circulating this knowledge in Europe.

The Norse may not have been the only people to spot the North American coast. As cold weather brought poor harvests and reduced fish catches along Europe's Atlantic coast, some desperate Portuguese, Basque, Danish, English, Breton, and Moroccan fishermen ventured further out in North Atlantic waters seeking cod, whales, and sardines. Some probably reached the fish-rich Grand Banks off Newfoundland. A few scattered non-Norse European artifacts found in eastern North America suggest that some coastal people may have encountered Europeans, landings apparently unreported in Europe.

Later the quest for riches, national glory, and Christian converts encouraged other Europeans to explore the Atlantic (see Chapter 15). While Portuguese expeditions concentrated on the African route to the East (see Chapters 16 and 18), Christopher Columbus hoped to sail westward from Europe to Asia. Contrary to myth, many educated Europeans accepted that the earth was round and hence could be circumnavigated.

The first explorer to brave the Atlantic to reach Asia, Christopher Columbus (see Chapter 16), came under the Spanish flag. Columbus (1451–1506), born in Genoa, had lived for many years in Lisbon, which had a large Genoese merchant community. His connections helped him marry Donha Felipa Moniz, the aristocratic daughter of the governor of Portuguese-settled Madeira. Columbus worked in Madeira, visited the Canary and Azores Islands farther out in the Atlantic, likely sailed to Iceland and down the West African coast on Portuguese ships, and was probably familiar with the Norse discoveries and Portuguese fishermen's tales.

Inspired by the writings of thirteenth-century Italian adventurer Marco Polo, who traveled in Asia and sojourned in China, Columbus, a devout Christian, hoped to find the sea route to the silk- and spice-rich lands of China and Southeast Asia and to introduce Christianity to China. But his inaccurate maps vastly underestimated the earth's size and the distance to Asia. Rebuffed in Portugal, Columbus eventually convinced the Spanish monarchs, King Ferdinand and Queen Isabella, to finance his exploration in hopes of establishing direct ties to Asia. Commanding ships far smaller than the Chinese explorer Zheng He's great junks in the early 1400s, Columbus, believing he had discovered outlying regions of Asia, surveyed much of the Caribbean and some of the South American coast in four voyages over the next decade (see Map 17.1).

On his first voyage, Columbus reached the Bahamas, where he encountered the Taino, a friendly Arawak (**AR-uh-wahk**)-speaking people who lived on Caribbean islands but wore few clothes in the tropical heat, shocking the straight-laced Spanish. Some lived in towns built around Mesoamerican-style plazas. The Taino smoked cigars, slept in hammocks, possessed a little gold, combined fishing with corn (maize) and manioc cultivation, and carried on interisland trade in large canoes capable of holding up to 150 people. Taino women did the farming and often served as community leaders, confounding the patriarchal Spanish. Often resisting incursions by Caribs (**KAR-ibs**), a warlike group originating in South America, the Taino may have welcomed a potential ally. Columbus developed favorable views of the hospitable, patient, and peaceable Taino, seeing them as innocent children of nature: "They are uncovetous people [who] love their neighbors as themselves."[3] Later, when Columbus encountered Taino noncooperation or armed resistance to Spanish demands, he changed his views.

Columbus then sailed on to the island he called Hispaniola (**HIS-puhn-YO-luh**), today the home of Haiti and the Dominican Republic. Leaving a small colony of Spaniards there, Columbus landed on Cuba. Thinking Cuba might be China, he dispatched a small party to search for the Chinese ruler. They returned only with mysterious dried leaves called *tobacos*, which local people smoked. Later other Europeans took tobacco back to Europe, starting a smoking fad. Taking six Taino Indians to present at court, Columbus and his crew sailed back to Spain, where he was feted as a hero and promoted to admiral.

Although not finding China, Columbus launched a new era of exploration. Spanish authorities planned a second voyage and, to counteract a possible Portuguese challenge, persuaded the pope to issue the Treaty of Tordesillas (**tor-duh-SEE-yuhs**) in 1494 giving Spain the rights to most of the Americas; the Portuguese received Africa and Brazil. Both Iberian countries promised to evangelize and colonize the "heathen" peoples they encountered. During his four voyages, Columbus explored much of the Caribbean region. Bringing Spanish colonists with him in 1493, he established the first permanent European settlement in the Americas on Hispaniola, where he

---

[3]Quoted in Oliver Cox, "The Rise of Modern Race Relations," in *Racial Conflict, Discrimination, and Power*, ed. William Barclay et al. (New York: AMS Press, 1976), 91.

MAP 17.1 **THE AMERICAS AND EARLY EUROPEAN EXPLORATION** The several voyages across the Atlantic led by Columbus explored the Caribbean Basin and set the stage for Spanish conquest of many American societies, most notably of the Aztec and Inca Empires. © 2015 Cengage Learning

exploited the local Taino through forced labor and then slavery. As Columbus wrote, "The Indians of this island are its riches, for it is they who dig and produce the bread and other food for the [Spanish] Christians and get the gold from the mines, and perform all the services and labor of men and of draft animals."[4] Columbus also explored the Cuban and Jamaican coasts and sighted Puerto Rico. On his third voyage, in 1498, he found Trinidad and the Venezuelan coast. But his mismanagement as Hispaniola governor and his failure to discover vast riches brought disgrace, and he was ordered home under arrest.

However, Queen Isabella allowed Columbus one final voyage to find a strait leading to India. This expedition in 1502 explored the Central American coast and encountered a Maya trading raft Columbus thought might be Chinese. He now spoke of the Caribbean islands as the "West Indies," separate from the eagerly sought "East Indies" (India and Southeast Asia). After being shipwrecked for a year on Jamaica, he returned to Spain and died in 1506, a broken man.

Eventually Europeans referred to Native Americans as "Indians," confusing American peoples with those of India. The label remains controversial, and some activists prefer terms such as *Native American* or *First Nations* to *Indian*. The term *America* derives from an Italian merchant, Amerigo Vespucci (**ves-POO-chee**) (1454–1512), who claimed to have made several voyages to the Western

[4]Quoted in Herman J. Viola, "Seeds of Change," in *Seeds of Change: A Quincentennial Commemoration*, ed. Herman J. Viola and Carolyn Margolis (Washington, DC: Smithsonian Institution Press, 1991), 13.

Hemisphere. His letters to powerful European princes described a "new world" soon known as "Amerigo's land," which became *America*.

The Continuing Search for Wealth

Exploration soon became a multinational effort involving the English, French, Portuguese, and Spanish. By 1525 European expeditions had explored the Atlantic and Caribbean coasts from eastern Canada to South America's southern tip. Some explorers sought to enrich themselves and the European monarchs who sponsored them. Others hoped to gain God's favor through Christian missionary activity. An English expedition led by another Genoese, John Cabot, and possibly financed in part by a London-based Italian bank, claimed North America's Atlantic coast in 1497, setting off a fruitless search for a northwest sea passage connecting the Atlantic Ocean through North America to the Pacific. In 1500 Portugal claimed Brazil, which fell within the longitudes awarded to it in the Treaty of Tordesillas, and began settlements. By 1511 Spain controlled Cuba, Puerto Rico, and Jamaica. In 1513 a Spanish expedition led by Vasco Nunez de Balboa **(bal-BOH-uh)** crossed Panama and sighted the Pacific Ocean. The French claimed eastern Canada in 1524 with a voyage led by an Italian, Giovanni da Verrazano **(VER-uh-ZAH-no)**.

These brave explorers and their crews hoped to become rich but were just as likely to perish from violence, disease, or storms. A Spanish expedition led by a Portuguese captain, Ferdinand Magellan **(muh-JELL-un)** (1480–1521), finally discovered the only practical sea route to Asia via the Americas in 1520. With the Spanish monarch financing the search for a possible Pacific route to the Spice Islands via the Americas, Magellan's five ships sailed down the Atlantic, rounded South America's southern tip, and then survived a torturous trip through the stormy strait known today as the Strait of Magellan. They continued on across the Pacific, a long, difficult journey during which they spotted no inhabited islands before Guam **(gwahm)**, the crewmen living off rat meat and boiled leather for months. Eventually the expedition reached the Philippine Islands, where Magellan was killed in a clash with local people. Magellan's one surviving ship, with eighteen crew members and a valuable cargo of cloves from the Spice Islands, continued on westward around Africa to Spain. Having thus gained a better idea of world geography, Europeans turned to conquering and settling the Americas.

Some explorers, greedy for quick wealth, engaged in piracy and looting. The Spanish conqueror of Aztec Mexico, Hernán Cortés, admitted that Spaniards "suffer an affliction of the heart which can only be cured by gold."[5] As governor of Hispaniola, Columbus executed the Taino who refused to supply gold. Harsh exploitation generated Taino attacks on Spaniards,

prompting Columbus to enslave Taino rebels and their families and ship them to Spain in chains. Later Spaniards raided other islands for slaves. Within thirty years all the Taino on Hispaniola, and many elsewhere, had been enslaved or killed, had died of disease or overwork, or had committed suicide because of their suffering. A Spanish priest lamented that many Caribbean islands were ruined "by men who wished to depopulate them and to kill the Indians who lived there. They were laid to waste."[6]

New Horizons and Exploration in the Pacific

The continued search for a sea route to Asia led to exploration of the Pacific Basin, which was inhabited by Pacific islanders, scattered across many island chains, who had developed diverse cultural and political traditions. The larger mountainous islands provided varied food sources for farming and fishing and supported states led by kings or powerful chiefs. For example, the eight inhabited Hawaiian Islands, divided into four rival chiefdoms, contained perhaps 200,000 people. Some 100,000 to 150,000 Maori **(MOW-ree)**, organized into chiefdoms, lived on the two main New Zealand islands. By contrast, people living on small atolls only a few feet above sea level relied chiefly on resources from the sea.

Many island societies traded over vast distances. Warfare and destruction of their fragile environments were common problems. Hence, over the centuries Polynesian settlers deforested remote Easter Island in the eastern Pacific, sparking chronic civil war for control of scarce resources. Most Pacific islanders, like indigenous Americans, had no direct contact with Asia for millennia, making them vulnerable to Eurasian diseases later brought by Europeans.

In the 1500s and 1600s Spanish, Portuguese, English, and Dutch expeditions discovered many islands and Australia, but the islands had few easily exploitable resources compared to Asia and the Americas. Although Spanish ships annually sailed between the Philippines and Mexico beginning in 1565 (see Chapter 18), Europeans made little effort to colonize the vast Pacific region. They did not locate some island chains, including Hawaii, until the later 1700s, when English settlement in Australia also began. Magellan's ships, chancing on Guam, clashed with local Chamorro **(chuh-MOR-oh)** people, the first of many unhappy Pacific Islander–European encounters. Spain colonized Guam in 1663, founding a Catholic mission. But 90 percent of the Chamorros died over the next two decades, mostly from disease. In 1671 a demoralized Chamorro chief complained to a missionary that "the Spanish would have done better to remain in their own country. We have no need of their help to live happily. They treat us as gross barbarians."[7]

---

[5]Quoted in L. S. Stavrianos, *Lifelines from Our Past: A New World History*, rev. ed. (Armonk, NY: M.E. Sharpe, 1997), 96.

[6]Alonso de Zuazo, quoted in Kathleen Deagan and Jose Maria Cruxent, *Columbus's Outpost Among the Tainos: Spain and America at La Isabela, 1493–1498* (New Haven, CT: Yale University Press, 2002), 210.

[7]Magá Lahen Hurao, quoted in Geoffrey C. Gunn, *First Globalization: The Eurasian Exchange* (Lanham, MD: Rowman and Littlefield, 2003), 194.

MAKE SURE YOU UNDERSTAND THESE KEY POINTS BEFORE MOVING ON

- From 1000 on, Norse from Greenland intermittently settled in Newfoundland, and other Europeans may have crossed the Atlantic in search of fish long before Columbus discovered America.

- Beginning in 1492, Christopher Columbus explored the Caribbean and the South American coast under the impression that they were outlying areas of Asia, opening up exploration of the Americas.

- Columbus focused on the island of Hispaniola, where he enslaved the native Taino, and gradually gave up on the idea that he had discovered an Atlantic route to Asia, which was later discovered by Magellan.

- European nations divided up the Western Hemisphere according to the Treaty of Tordesillas, and as Europeans explored the Americas, some seeking riches and others converts, their diseases and their habit of enslaving or killing the local people decimated native populations.

The European Conquest of the Americas

How did Europeans conquer and begin settling the American societies?

European explorations and the search for riches led to colonization of the Americas. Native Americans, divided into often-hostile societies, lacked guns to resist the thousands of Spanish adventurers who roamed the Americas in the 1500s, many of whom, known as **conquistadors** (kon-KEY-stuh-dorz), engaged in armed conquest. While Spain conquered Mexico and the Andes and the Portuguese annexed Brazil, the English, French, and Dutch later obtained footholds in North America, the Caribbean, and South America's northeast coast. By 1750 various European powers firmly controlled many American societies.

The Fall of the Aztec and Inca Empires

Seeking to conquer the rich Aztec Empire, in 1519 Hernán Cortés **(kor-TEZ)** (1485–1547) and 550 soldiers from Spanish-controlled Cuba landed on Mexico's east coast, where they founded the settlement of Veracruz **(VER-uh-KROOZ)**. Native Americans were shocked by the Spanish guns: "A thing like a ball of stone comes out its entrails; it comes out shooting sparks and raining fire….If the cannon is aimed against a mountain, the mountain splits and cracks open."[8] Cortés defeated and then forged an alliance with the Tlaxcalans, long-time Aztec enemies. Impressed by Spanish power, the Tlaxcalan nobles adopted Christianity, and their soldiers joined Cortés. After defeating several peoples, Cortés and his growing force marched west through the mountains into the Valley of Mexico, heart of an Aztec Empire of 25 million. With its gleaming temples and canal network, the Aztec capital, Tenochtitlan, astonished the Spanish. Perhaps initially confusing Cortés with Quetzalcoatl and the Spaniards with gods, the Aztec leader, Moctezuma II **(mock-teh-ZOO-ma)**(r. 1502–1520), warmly greeted them. Taking advantage of this friendliness, Cortés arrested Moctezuma. With sixty Spanish soldiers supplied with horses and guns, and many Indian allies, Cortés temporarily controlled the capital.

Angered by the Spaniards' arrogant behavior and seizure of gold, Aztec mobs killed or captured some Spaniards. Either enraged Aztecs or his Spanish captors killed Moctezuma, no longer a credible leader. But the Aztecs' less deadly weapons and military goals—securing captives for sacrifice rather than killing opponents—put them at a disadvantage to the Spanish, and many died as the Spaniards fought their way out of the city. Some Spaniards, loaded down with stolen Aztec gold, fell into canals and drowned. Returning to the coast, Cortés recruited more Aztec enemies and Spanish soldiers from Cuba. Armed with deadly muskets, cannon, steel swords, crossbows, and horses, his enlarged army—around 1,000 Spaniards and 10,000 Indian allies—laid siege to Tenochtitlan. The Aztecs resisted fiercely while a smallpox epidemic, inadvertently spread by the Spaniards, ravaged their population. In 1521 the Spanish occupied the city, capturing Moctezuma II's successor as emperor while revengeful Tlaxcalans massacred thousands of city residents. Aztec poets, who once addressed their violent culture in melancholy verses, now bemoaned their destruction, one lamenting that "broken spears lie in the roads; we have torn our hair in our grief. The houses are roofless now, and their walls are red with blood."[9]

Spaniards now ruled the Aztec Empire, using efficient Aztec administration to collect tribute from former Aztec subjects. Seeing possibilities for wealth, Spanish conquerors pushed south from Mexico to seize Central America, Panama, and, a few years later, northern South America. Others moved north as far as New Mexico and northern California. By 1750 Spain's empire included a third of what later became the United States, stretching from San Francisco through Santa Fe and San Antonio all the way to Saint Augustine in Florida.

Ten years later another conquistador, Francisco Pizarro (ca. 1476–1541), explored South America's west coast. In 1531 his forces marched into the

conquistadors The leaders of Spanish soldiers engaged in armed conquest in the Americas.

---

[8]Quoted in Jon T. Davidann and Marc J. Gilbert, *Cross-Cultural Encounters in Modern World History* (New York: Pearson, 2013), 16.
[9]Quoted in Jane MacLaren Walsh and Yoko Sugiura, "The Demise of the Fifth Sun," in Viola and Margolis, *Seeds of Change*, 41.

Codex Duran: Pedro de Alvarado (c.1485-1541) companion-at-arms of Hernando Cortes (1485-1547) besieged by Aztec warriors (vellum), Duran, Diego (16th century)/Biblioteca Nacional, Madrid, Spain/The Bridgeman Art Library

CODEX OF AZTEC RESISTANCE Illustrations in a book published around 1580 revealed a local perspective on the Spanish conquest of the Aztec Empire. This illustration shows Aztec warriors besieging a Spanish force in Tenochtitlan and the difference in weapons technology.

Andes to conquer the Inca. As in Mexico, smallpox had already wiped out millions of Inca, including many leaders; in addition, the empire was divided by a civil war between two rivals for the throne. With only 160 Spaniards but artillery and horses, Pizarro captured Atahualpa (**AH-tuh-WAHL-puh**), one of two rival claimants, and killed thousands of Inca, many unarmed. Pizarro demanded and received gold and silver for ransom, then executed Atahualpa. Ignoring pleas from Catholic priests to treat the Inca with more leniency, Pizarro retorted that he had come to take Inca gold, not spread Christianity. The conquistadors converted the Inca capital, Cuzco (**KOOZ-ko**), into a Spanish settlement and founded the city of Lima along the Pacific coast. Soon Spain gained control over much of Peru, Ecuador, Bolivia, and Chile, brutally crushing Indian uprisings. Pizarro and his men placed themselves at the top of the efficient Inca administrative system. Supporters of a rival Spanish leader later murdered Pizarro.

Colonization of Brazil and the Caribbean

The Portuguese established small trading posts along coastal Brazil, which was blessed by regular rainfall, striking natural beauty, and a benign climate. While the Portuguese obtained and shipped brazilwood, an excellent dye for European textiles, they initially remained more focused on exploiting African and Asian wealth than on exploiting the Americas. In 1532 the Portuguese founded a permanent colony along Brazil's southern coast and awarded land grants to private entrepreneurs. Facing not large settled societies but seminomadic food collectors and small farmers, they considered the Indians potential slaves who could be forced

Paulistas Portuguese slavers from the southern Brazilian settlement at São Paulo.

to work. Portuguese from the settlement at São Paulo (**sow PAU-low**), known as Paulistas, raided for slaves deep into the interior. The colonial government combatted these activities, and expanded its control in the interior, only in 1680.

In the seventeenth century the Dutch gained control over much of northeastern Brazil, setting up plantations to grow huge quantities of sugar for the European market. But the Portuguese eventually expelled their rivals and took over the profitable northeast, building a city, Salvador da Bahia, at Bahia (**ba-HEE-a**).

While Spain colonized Cuba, Puerto Rico, and much of Central and South America's Caribbean coast, the Dutch, English, and French all founded Caribbean colonies. Expelled from Brazil, the Dutch moved to several small Caribbean islands and also established Dutch Guiana (**ghee-AHN-a**) (now Suriname) in northeastern South America. The French seized Haiti (**HAY-tee**), the western half of Hispaniola, where they developed plantations as a major wealth source. They also seized French Guiana and the islands of Guadeloupe (**GWAD-e-loop**) and Martinique (**mahr-ten-EEK**). Meanwhile, England made Jamaica, Barbados (**bahr-BAY-doz**), British Guiana (now Guyana), and later Trinidad their colonial linchpins.

In the Caribbean, European piracy became a major economic activity, often directed at Spanish settlements or the Spanish galleons hauling rich cargoes of silver, sugar, or imported Asian goods to Europe. In 1670 the English pirate Sir Henry Morgan led fourteen hundred men to brazenly sack Panama City, where warehouses stored wealth from Asia and Latin America. The Spanish burned the city rather than allow buccaneers to seize it. Some pirates, such as Morgan, John Hawkins, and Sir Francis Drake, became respected figures in England, celebrated for the wealth they captured from rival countries. In 1577 Drake (ca. 1540–1596) sailed from England on a secret mission for Queen Elizabeth I that eventually took him around the entire world while outflanking and plundering the Spanish Empire. Drake's fleet sailed through the Strait of Magellan and up the Pacific coast to Mexico and San Francisco Bay, and perhaps as far north as the Columbia River, looting unsuspecting Spanish settlements and treasure-laden ships along the way. Drake then sailed across the Pacific to the Spice Islands and around Africa to England. Like other explorers, he lost many crewmen to scurvy, the deadly Vitamin C deficiency caused by lack of fresh fruits and vegetables; the cause was only discovered two centuries later. Drake also helped defeat the Spanish armada sent against England in 1588, a battle that decisively shifted European political power. Drake's swashbuckling career illustrated how the world had changed after 1492.

The English, French, and Indians in North America

English and French colonizing efforts on North America's eastern seaboard undermined often matrilineal and sometimes matriarchal Native American farming societies, who generally enjoyed good health and nutritious diets. Indians soon disdained Europeans as unintelligent, physically weak, and smelly. While Indians valued personal cleanliness, the English and French seldom bathed. Nonetheless, Indians usually offered hospitality, traded with, and sought allies among the newcomers. But Europeans established settlements, wearing out their welcome.

Coveting land and wanting to outflank rival countries, England planted settlements up and down the Atlantic coast. The first, at Roanoke in Virginia in 1587, failed, but a colony established in 1607 at Jamestown in Virginia succeeded. As settlements struggled to survive in the unfamiliar land, farming families were sent from England. In many cases only generous Native Americans sharing knowledge or supplying food enabled colonists to survive. England also acquired the Dutch settlement at New York, which was founded in 1624 but was unable to recruit enough settlers from Holland to offset English immigration.

The French established their first settlement in Acadia (today the Canadian province of Nova Scotia) in 1604, which was followed by outposts along the Saint Lawrence River at Quebec (**ke-BEK**) City and Montreal, forming the basis for New France, a colony, established in 1627, that covered much of eastern Canada. French Jesuit missionaries (known as "Black Robes") traveled widely, as far west as today's Illinois, to convert Native Americans to Catholicism. Using canoes, French explorers and trappers, known as **voyageurs** (**voi-uh-ZHUR**), established trading outposts throughout the Great Lakes and Mississippi River Basin. To counter English and Spanish expansion, in 1699 the French founded New Orleans, which became the base for French activities and territorial claims in Louisiana and the Mississippi Valley (see Map 17.2).

English colonies north of Maryland developed largely as agricultural economies of free white settlers. Many English and French settlers exploited two valuable commodities, fish and fur. The seas off New England and eastern Canada teamed with cod, which became a major part of European diets. As cod stocks off Europe diminished, fishermen established

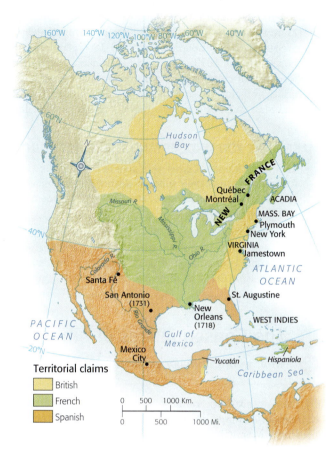

MAP 17.2 THE ENGLISH AND FRENCH IN NORTH AMERICA, CA. 1700 While the English colonized much of the Atlantic coast of North America, the French concentrated on what is today eastern Canada and the interior of North America, including the Great Lakes and the Mississippi and Ohio River Basins. © 2015 Cengage Learning

coastal North American bases. Later English and French settlers moved inland seeking beavers, whose fur became popular in Europe for women's and men's coats and hats. Fur remained Canadians' major export until the nineteenth century.

Both French and English settlement disrupted Indian tribes (now known as "First Nations" in Canada). The French generally maintained better relations with local peoples, allying with tribal leaders. Nonetheless, most Native Americans, dying from disease or armed conflict, were pushed north and west or eventually forced onto reservations. In the early 1700s English colonists forced various tribes, among them the Tuscarora (**tus-kuh-ROR-uh**) and Delaware, to move west of the Appalachian Mountains, foreshadowing worse treatment to come.

Yet, some proved formidable opponents. The Iroquois (**EAR-uh-coy**) Confederation, a complex political coalition formed in the 1500s, united five once-warring longhouse-dwelling tribes living between Lake Erie and the Hudson River in upstate New York. They shared a common enemy, the Huron of southern Ontario, who established a rival

voyageurs French explorers and trappers in North America.

confederation. Around 1500 on Lake Ontario's northern shore, the Huron built the region's largest town, surrounded by a massive stockade, that housed some 1500-1800 people in 100 longhouses. By the 1690s, the pantribal Iroquois government had a council of chiefs and an oral constitution that required unanimity for any decision. Some scholars credit Iroquois political ideas, such as a representative congress and freedom of speech, as influencing the later United States constitution. The effective Iroquois military alliance generally defeated rival tribes while holding off or outmaneuvering European arrivals for many years. Later it supported England in conflicts against France, which was allied with the Huron and Algonquins (**al-GAHN-kwinz**). Eventually the Iroquois, Huron, and Algonquins, like other Native Americans, were colonized.

MAKE SURE YOU UNDERSTAND THESE KEY POINTS BEFORE MOVING ON

- The Spanish under Cortés were able to conquer the Aztecs because of their superior weaponry, their alliances with other American peoples, and a smallpox epidemic that ravaged the Aztecs.

- From their base in Mexico, the Spanish pushed north and south, and Pizarro conquered the Inca, the Spanish proceeding to rule much of South America with great cruelty, using the Inca administrative system.

- The Spanish, Portuguese, Dutch, French, and English all struggled for colonial control of the Americas, with pirates from each country preying on other countries' ships.

- Many North American colonies thrived on fish and fur, while others practiced agriculture, and all eventually pushed native peoples off their lands.

aplia

The Consequences of American Colonization

What were the major consequences of European colonization of the Americas?

By the late sixteenth century Spaniards had explored and claimed an empire stretching from northern California and the Rocky Mountains to southern Chile and Argentina, forming local governments and founding cities. Meanwhile, England, France, and Holland held Caribbean Basin and North American territory. Despite many similarities, American colonies differed, but everywhere Native Americans suffered from the colonists' diseases, faced Christian missionary activity, and experienced violent repression of their resistance and culture.

The Columbian Exchange

The **Columbian Exchange** refers to the transfer of diseases, animals, and plants between hemispheres. The most catastrophic of these transfers was the transmission of virulent Eastern Hemisphere microbes to the Americas, which caused massive depopulation and suffering. Although often healthier than Eastern Hemisphere peoples, Native Americans had suffered from polio, hepatitis, tuberculosis, many intestinal parasites, and syphilis. Yet, only syphilis, a sexually transmitted disease, made any serious impact when carried to Europe, being more an unpleasant nuisance than a mass killer. In contrast, Native Americans had no immunity to Eastern Hemisphere

Columbian Exchange
The transportation of diseases, animals, and plants between the hemispheres that resulted from European exploration and conquest.

diseases like measles, typhus, influenza, and especially smallpox, which was widespread in Europe. As a result, these diseases reduced their population by around 90 percent. No group remained untouched. A Maya writer reported that "great was the stench of the dead. The dogs and vultures devoured the bodies. We were born to die!"[10] Men died at higher rates than women, leaving widows to support households and young girls to grow up without protection by fathers and male relatives.

American population numbers began recovering as the most resistant individuals survived and immigrants from Europe and Africa, with some immunity, married Native Americans, producing less susceptible children. Eventually Native American populations grew, and today descendants of Maya, Inca, and other peoples are numerous in Central and South America's highlands and forests. Recent research suggests that the massive mortality allowed American forests to expand, reducing carbon dioxide and perhaps sparking the Little Ice Age that especially impacted Europe.

The Columbian Exchange affected both hemispheres. European immigrants imported their political systems, social institutions, religious beliefs, and urban forms to the Americas as well as Eurasian plants such as wheat, orange trees, and grape vines and domesticated animals such as horses, pigs, chickens, goats, and sheep. Native Americans found some imports useful. For example, Spanish horses enabled some North American Great Plains tribes to hunt buffalo more effectively. Other arrivals were inadvertent. Barrels of dirt carried west on English ships as ballast were dumped on arrival to make space for tobacco headed for England. The dirt carried, among other bugs, earthworms, which had been killed off in parts of North America during the Ice Age, and their tunnels helped the soil. American products also moved eastward across the Atlantic, including drugs such as quinine and coca and crops such as tobacco, rubber, American cotton, potatoes, tomatoes,

[10]Quoted in Noble David Cook, *Born to Die: Disease and New World Conquest, 1492–1650* (Cambridge: Cambridge University Press, 1998), vi.

WITNESS TO THE PAST

WITNESS TO THE PAST

Spanish Men and Inca Women

In many parts of Latin America, Spaniards married or cohabitated with Native American women, fostering a mixed, or mestizo, population. In Peru some Spaniards deliberately sought to marry Inca princesses, perhaps to establish local connections in a factionalized colonial society. This account from the early seventeenth century by the Peruvian historian Garcilaso de la Vega, himself the product of such a match, describes an Inca princess unenthusiastic about her Spanish suitor, a captain from a modest background. Her ambivalent response has been viewed by some historians as representing a mixed attitude common in Latin America toward the imposition of European culture: contempt for many European customs and the brutal conquest but also admiration of some European values and Europeans' military power.

...a daughter of [Inca leader] Huaina Cápac and herself...the owner of the Indians [workers], was married to a very good soldier called Diego Hernández, a very worthy man, who was said in his youth to have been a tailor....[Before the marriage] the princess learned this and refused the match, saying that it was unjust to wed the daughter of Huaina Cápac with a...tailor. Although the Bishop of Cuzco as well as...other personages who went to attend the ceremony of betrothal, begged and pleaded with her, it was all to no purpose. They then sent to fetch her brother....When he came, he took his sister into a corner of the room and told her privately that it was impolitic for her to refuse the match, for by doing so she would render the whole of the [Inca] royal line odious in the eyes of the Spaniards, who would consider them

mortal enemies and never accept their friendship again. She agreed, though reluctantly, to her brother's demands, and so appeared before the bishop, who wished to honor the betrothed by officiating at the ceremony.

When the bride was asked through an Indian interpreter if she consented to become the bride and spouse of the aforesaid, the interpreter said "did she want to be the man's wife?" for the Indian language had no verb for consent or for spouse, and he could therefore not have asked anything else.

The bride replied in her own tongue:... "Maybe I will, maybe I won't." Whereupon the ceremony continued...They were still alive and living as man and wife when I left Cuzco.

Other marriages of this kind took place throughout the empire, and were arranged so as to give allocations of Indians to [Spanish] claimants and reward them with other people's properties. Many, however, were dissatisfied, some because their income was small and others because their wives were ugly; there is no perfect satisfaction in this world.

THINKING ABOUT THE READING

1. What does the reading tell us about social attitudes among Inca and Spaniards in colonial Peru?
2. What do we learn about the treatment of women?
3. How might the princess's attitude be seen as a form of resistance?

Source: Based on Garcilaso de la Vega, *Royal Commentaries of the Incas and General History of Peru,* Part Two. Translated by Harold V. Livermore (Austin: University of Texas Press, 1966), pp. 1229–1230. Copyright © 1966 by the University of Texas Press.

and maize (corn), increasing Europe's food supply. Widely grown, potatoes and corn helped end famine in Europe, while South American chilies became mainstays of South and Southeast Asian cooking, making spicy foods even hotter. Finally, American gold and silver financed Spain's empire and reshaped the Eurasian economy.

The Spanish Empire and New Latin American Societies

Conquered Americans paid the costs of conquest. In Spanish America and Portuguese Brazil, some Europeans made great fortunes by exploiting people, land, minerals, animals, and plants. Spanish and Portuguese seized all the riches, forced or persuaded Indians to adopt Christianity, destroyed their religious centers, murdered Indian leaders who refused to cooperate, and discouraged or suppressed local languages in favor of Spanish or Portuguese. While many peoples resisted, these efforts were usually futile. European settlers learned from native people how to survive and also intermarried or had sexual relations with local women, producing people of mixed descent.

While the Spanish appropriated American political structures, they also introduced their own institutions and ways. Some Spanish settlements became large cities, such as Havana, Buenos Aires, Lima, and Mexico City, the last built on the site of Tenochtitlan. Spain divided its vast empire into two smaller divisions (viceroyalties): New Spain (governed from Mexico City) and Peru (governed from Lima), each headed by a Spain-born viceroy who held great power. In 1739 Colombia, Ecuador, Venezuela, and Panama became part of the Bogota-based New Granada Viceroyalty. Smaller political units, called **audiencias**, were judicial tribunals with administrative functions. Spaniards held all key political offices, from governors down to local mayors.

Spain sometimes faced resistance. Maya Yucatán fell only in 1545 after a long, bitter military struggle, and sporadic Indian resistance continued in Peru for two centuries; the last major rebellion, in 1780–1781, involved over ten thousand Inca descendants led by Tupac Amaru II (**TOO-pack ah-MAR-oo**), named after an Inca emperor executed by the Spanish. In New Mexico resentment by some Pueblo peoples against Spain and the Catholic

audiencias Judicial tribunals with administrative functions that served as subdivisions of viceroyalties in Spanish America.

Church, which repressed Native American customs and executed or enslaved many people, led to several revolts. In 1680, a respected shaman, Popé (ca. 1630–1692), once imprisoned for suspected "witchcraft" and hoping to restore traditional culture, led a tribal coalition that pushed the Spanish out of the area. Although the Spanish returned and brutally crushed the Pueblo rebels, they adopted a more cooperative policy.

Distinctive societies gradually emerged in Spanish America and Brazil, now called Latin America. The **creoles** (**KREE-awl**), people of Iberian ancestry born in Latin America, were the key group. The mixing of peoples fostered **mestizos**, who blended white and Indian ancestry, and **mulattos**, a mix of African with white or Indian ancestry or both (see Witness to the Past: Spanish Men and Inca Women). While most creoles enjoyed high status, mixed groups held a social status between Europeans at the top and Indians and Africans at the bottom, and they eventually represented a sizable population in many colonies. Mexico and Peru developed large mestizo groups, while mulattos were especially prominent in Brazil and Cuba. Monopolizing wealth and power, people born in Europe (**peninsulares**) viewed creoles, mestizos, and mulattos with condescension or contempt as rustics. A Mexico-born scholar with Spanish parents complained that Europeans "think that not only the original Indian inhabitants but also those of us who were, by chance, born in [the Americas] either walk on two legs by divine dispensation or that they are hardly able to discover anything rational in us."[11]

Spanish America produced many talents, among them the creole Mexican nun Sor (Sister) Juana Inez de la Cruz (1651–1695), a renowned poet, playwright, philosopher, and scientist influenced by European Enlightenment thinkers. To pursue her intellectual interests, the well-born Sor Juana chose life in a convent over marriage, eventually collecting Mexico's largest private library. Sor Juana struggled against patriarchal customs, arguing that "like men, do women not have a rational soul? Shall they not enjoy the privilege of the enlightenment of letters? Why is she not as able to receive as much learning and science?"[12]

Despite creative, broad-minded figures like Sor Juana, Latin American culture owed more to Iberian Catholic traditions than to a western Europe reshaped by the Renaissance, Enlightenment, and Reformation. To suppress what they considered dangerous ideas, the church had to approve all printed matter entering the colonies. Universities, which trained creole men for careers as colonial officials and priests, taught largely in Latin and employed clerics as instructors. Attacking heresy, the ruthless Holy Inquisition tried suspected secret Jewish or Protestant sympathizers. *Conversos*, Jews forced to convert to Christianity in Spain, faced investigation, imprisonment, and sometimes gruesome executions. Most hid their identity, often even from their children. In recent years hundreds of Latin Americans, Mexican Americans, and Spaniards, rediscovering their converso ancestry, have embraced the Jewish identity and faith.

Latin American writers examined the conflicted Spain–Latin America relationship, describing a mix of good and evil, sun and shadow, as in the bullfight ring. While the elite looked toward Europe for inspiration, the majority favored preserving pre-Columbian languages, beliefs, and ways of life. Women faced the greatest dilemmas under patriarchal Spanish rule. They enjoyed new food sources, such as chickens and pigs, but they clung to their native dress and pride. Flexibility and adaptability aided survival. Since men had higher mortality rates, women often headed households. Some Indian and mestizo women engaged in commerce, worked in domestic service, tended animals, or made clothing, such as by carding, spinning, and weaving wool from sheep.

Christian Missions, the Black Legend, and Native Americans

Both Spain and Portugal pledged to spread Catholicism. Although enjoying mixed success, missionaries, frequently militant in their faith, gave Indians a superficial Christianity, changing local gods into Christian saints. Sometimes missionaries altered people's settlement and economic patterns. The Spanish Franciscan missionary Fray Junipero Serra (1713–1784), traveling by foot, established mission stations along coastal California from San Diego to San Francisco. He converted many while encouraging, sometimes requiring, seminomadic hunters and gatherers, like the Chumash (**CHOO-mash**), to live in towns and cultivate European crops.

Building forts near mission stations extended Spanish control, but missionaries often faced resistance. Many Inca women openly rejected Catholicism. A Spanish observer complained: "They do not confess, attend catechism classes, or go to mass. Returning to their ancient customs and idolatry, they do not want to serve God or the [Spanish] crown."[13] Native Americans could also put their stamp on Christianity. While some historians doubt the story, an Aztec peasant in 1531 supposedly saw a vision of the Virgin Mary at an Aztec mother-goddess shrine. Officials built a church there honoring "Our Lady of Guadalupe," and the image of the Virgin as Indian woman became a potent symbol of Mexican nationalism.

Missionary activity sometimes proved disastrous. In Yucatán, missionaries controlled many Maya and, intolerant of non-Christian beliefs, destroyed Maya books and religious symbols. In 1562 priests, suspecting that converts still secretly worshiped Maya gods, launched a terrible inquisition, torturing 4,500 Indians, 158 of whom died. One witness reported that "the friars ordered great stones attached to their feet, and so they were left to hang, and if they did not admit to [worshiping]

creoles People of Iberian ancestry who were born in Latin America.

mestizos Groups in Latin America that blended white and Indian ancestry.

mulattos Groups in Latin America that blended African ancestry with white or Indian ancestry or both.

peninsulares Europe-born residents in Latin America who monopolized wealth and power.

[11]From Hanke, *History of Latin American Civilization*, 388.

[12]Quoted in Jonathan C. Brown, *Latin America: A Social History of the Colonial Period* (Belmont, CA: Wadsworth, 2000), 146.

[13]Quoted in Marysa Navarro and Virginia Sanchez-Korrol, "Latin America and the Caribbean," in *Restoring Women to History* (Bloomington, IN: Organization of American Historians, 1988), 23.

© iStockphoto.com/hrstklnkr

INDIAN SLAVERY Spain's enemies publicized cases of Spanish brutality toward Native Americans. This sixteenth-century engraving, by the Dutch observer Theodore de Bry, portrays the misery of Native Americans subjected to slavery and forced labor.

But intolerant people reflecting Catholic-Protestant conflict in Europe (see Chapter 15) won the battle over how to treat Indians. Most Spaniards considered Indians justly conquered and born for servitude. A Spanish scholar expressed contempt for Indians as "naturally lazy and vicious, in general a lying, shiftless people [whose] chief desire is to eat, drink, worship heathen idols, and commit bestial obscenities."[15] These harsh attitudes also affected women. In 1625, an Indian writer in Peru charged that white men exploited both women's labor and their bodies: "In the mines, Indian women are made into concubines, daughters of Indian men are kidnapped. In the villages, [Spanish men convert] single women, married women, all women into prostitutes. Parish priests have concubines. There is no one who takes these women's side."[16] This contempt and economic need led to the drafting of Indians to work in mines or farms. Although eventually the church treated Indians indulgently and paternalistically, as children needing guidance, their quality of life—health, morale, leisure, and joy—mostly declined, generating alcoholism and despair. Today many Latin American Indians remain dominated politically, socially, and economically by creoles and mestizos.

idols, they were flogged as they hung there and had burning wax splashed on their bodies."[14] The church punished the priest in charge but later appointed him bishop. Homosexuals, who were tolerated by many Native American peoples, including Maya and Caribs, also were brought before the Inquisition or sometimes executed without trial, the Spanish claiming that the widespread homosexuality sanctioned treating Native Americans like animals.

Spanish actions fostered the **Black Legend** of brutality toward Native Americans, including the repression of native religions, the execution of rebels, and forced labor. Although the Black Legend exaggerated Spanish atrocities, Spain's enemies eagerly passed along such stories. In fact, disease killed far more Indians than murder and brutality. Furthermore, other Europeans were often as intolerant and forceful with local peoples. And while many Spaniards saw Native Americans as savages needing to be Christianized and ruled, some Catholic clerics advocated humane policies and sought to protect them. The Dominican friar Bartolomé de Las Casas **(lahs KAH-suhs)** (1474–1566), although an ardent missionary, proclaimed that Indians were humans like Spaniards, bemoaning their treatment. Spanish lawyer Francisco de Vitoria questioned Western colonization, suggesting that policies should always promote Indian welfare and interests and not only Spanish profits. In 1637 the Jesuits in Uruguay **(YOOR-uh-gwye)** even armed Indians to help protect them against slave raiders.

English and French Colonies in North America

The English and French expanded and competed in North America (see Map 17.2). By the mid-1700s the territory from New England to Georgia was divided into thirteen English colonies administered by appointed English governors. Immigration to these colonies increased, not only from England but also from Scotland, Ireland, Germany, and the Netherlands. Some from poor or criminal backgrounds arrived as indentured laborers, working on farms or in businesses, workshops, or households to repay their passage. By 1730 the thirteen colonies contained around 500,000 whites. Although African slaves or their descendants, some 20 percent of the population, were concentrated in the South, some also lived in northern colonies.

English colonies enjoyed intellectual and religious diversity. Influenced by English and French Enlightenment thinkers, educated colonists espoused democratic ideals and reason. Many English Protestant dissenters sought religious freedom, and Puritans influenced colonial culture, implanting Calvinist values extolling work and commerce. In 1695 Puritan preacher Cotton Mather

Black Legend The Spanish reputation for brutality toward Native Americans, including the repression of native religions, execution of rebels, and forced labor.

[14]Quoted in Felipe Fernandez-Armesto, *Millennium: A History of the Last Thousand Years* (New York: Scribner's, 1995), 300.

[15]Gonzalo Fernandez de Oviedo, quoted in L. S. Stavrianos, *Global Rift: The Third World Comes of Age* (New York: William Morrow, 1981), 83.

[16]Guzman Poma de Ayala, quoted in Brown, *Latin America*, 183.

Johnson Hall by Edward Lamson Henry (1841–1919), 1903. Oil on canvas 21 1/4 X 37 inches. Albany Institute of History and Art Purchase 1933.44

JOHNSON HALL This grand house, built in the mid-eighteenth century by American fur trader William Johnson in what is now upstate New York, became a meeting place for Native American tribes, such as the Iroquois, who were allied with the British against the French.

vigorously praised labor: "How can you ordinarily enjoy any rest at Night, if you have not been well at work in the Day? Let your Business ingross the most of your time."[17] Puritans also maintained patriarchal attitudes. John Winthrop, the Massachusetts colony's first governor, argued that women lost their reason if they concentrated on reading and writing instead of household affairs. Society viewed men as public and women as private beings. Yet, colonial life also fostered gender role changes. Although deeply engrained deference to men remained and although husbands had legal right to their wife's property, wages, and the couple's children, many women worked in the fields alongside men, and a few managed farms or plantations.

England and France clashed for decades over control of eastern Canada, part of a larger, globe-spanning English-French competition for access to fish and fur sources and for influence in Europe, the Caribbean, and southern Asia. Eventually England triumphed over France in North America, taking control of Acadia in 1713, and in 1755 England deported much of the Acadian French population to the French colony of Louisiana, forming the French-speaking Cajun **(KAY-juhn)** community. In 1759 English forces defeated the French near Quebec City and captured Montreal, acquiring New France. But French cultural influence remained strong in Quebec, and in 1774 England allowed the French in Quebec to hold public office, speak their language, and freely practice Catholicism.

Both French and the English Canadians settled down to farming. French immigration to Canada largely ended, but the French Canadian population, especially in Quebec, increased dramatically and today totals more than 7 million, one-fourth of Canadians. Until the mid-twentieth century the Catholic Church in Quebec encouraged early marriage and large families. French Canadians always felt threatened by the dominant English, a feeling that perhaps fostered cultural conservatism.

European-Indian relations reflected both conflict and alliance. Indians often fought settler occupation of their land, and the English and French had to deal carefully with the stronger tribes. But some Indians were drawn into the English-French struggle for global influence. The Huron allied with the French, the Iroquois allied with the English, and some tribes opposed both. European-Indian alliances largely reflected trading partnerships. As French fur traders ventured into the interior, setting up trading posts, they often intermarried with Indians, producing the **Metis (may-TEES)** people of mixed French and Indian descent. Today Metis communities are scattered around Canada. In contrast, English colonists tended to immigrate as families, reducing intermarriage with Indians.

Encounters with Europeans reshaped Indian life, making it much more difficult. An English observer, Robert Beverley, noted that "they have on several accounts to lament the arrival of the English [who] have taken away great part of their country, and consequently made everything less plenty among them."[18] Indians mistrusted Europeans, who often broke treaties. But although often repelled by European culture, they desired European goods, especially metalwork and guns. A few tribes, like the Cherokee in the Carolinas and Georgia, adopted

Metis People in Canada of mixed French and Indian descent.

[17]Quoted in Robert Heilbroner and Aaron Singer, *The Economic Transformation of America, 1600 to the Present*, 3rd ed. (Fort Worth, TX: Harcourt Brace, 1994), 68.
[18]Quoted in David Freeman Hawke, *Everyday Life in Early America* (New York: Harper and Row, 1988), 120.

European influences, such as new farming methods. This change often disadvantaged women, who once enjoyed high status because they did most of the farming. Christian missionaries also brought change, although they had less success in North America than in Latin America. For example, among matrilineal societies like the Huron and Cherokee, patriarchal Christian marriage practices undermined women's power and freedom by emphasizing wives' obedience to husbands. Spousal abuse often increased as men unable to support their families turned on their wives. But Some Indians responded creatively. The Cherokee still honor Sequoyah, who created a Cherokee writing system.

MAKE SURE YOU UNDERSTAND THESE KEY POINTS BEFORE MOVING ON

- As a result of American colonization, huge numbers of Native Americans died from smallpox, and many animal and plant species were exchanged between Europe and the Americas in the Columbian Exchange.

- The Spanish exploited the resources of their American colonies and ruled them harshly, inspiring several rebellions and fostering the "Black Legend."

- In the Spanish American colonies, a recognizable culture developed, more rigidly Catholic than in Europe and featuring American-born Spanish (creoles) and mixed-race peoples (mestizos and mulattos).

- In their attempts to convert Native Americans to Catholicism, the Spanish and Portuguese often trampled on Native American customs and beliefs, crushing perceived resistance harshly.

aplia

New Economies, Slavery, and the Atlantic System

How were the new American economies and the trans-Atlantic slave trade connected?

Latin America and northern English America developed different economic and social systems. In much of Latin America, the Caribbean, and the southern colonies of North America, European rule produced an inequitable economic relationship between the colonizing countries and their colonies, which supplied natural resources for the growing world economy. Plantations and mines depended chiefly on slave labor imported from Africa (see Chapter 16). In contrast, the northern English colonies in North America emphasized commerce and family farming, gradually moving toward economic independence. The trans-Atlantic slave trade and emerging American plantation zone linked West Africa, the Americas, and Europe into a larger Atlantic System, a triangular trade moving enslaved Africans to the Americas, largely for plantation labor growing sugar, cotton, and tobacco for shipment to Europe. European merchants used lucrative proceeds from slave labor to purchase guns, rum, textiles, and other commodities for shipment to Africa to obtain more enslaved labor. Profits from the slave trade and the enterprises it served also influenced European economic development.

Economic Change in Latin America

Latin American colonies chiefly exported natural resources (see Map 17.3). In the Andes and Mexico, the Spaniards developed rich gold and silver mines, coercing Indians to do the work. Indian silver miners in the main Andean mining center, Potosi (**po-tuh-SEE**), Bolivia, found life difficult, "working twelve hours a day, going down to where night is perpetual, the air thick and ill smelling. When they arrive at the top out of breath, [they] find a mineowner who scolds them because they did not bring enough load."[19] By the late 1600s Mexican mines produced over half of the hemisphere's mineral wealth, and Brazilian mines, mostly worked by African slaves, supplied over half of the world's gold. While benefiting few Native Americans, mining enriched merchants, filled royal treasuries, and linked colonies to the world economy. Much of the exported gold ultimately passed through Spain and Portugal to northern Europe as payment for manufactured goods, enriching Flanders, Holland, and England. American silver also bought Europeans access to Asian markets. And a large portion of American silver was shipped to China to purchase desirable Chinese products such as silk and tea.

Cattle and horses brought from Europe made ranching a major economic activity, especially in Argentina, Brazil, and Venezuela's grasslands, providing great incomes for monarchs, merchants, and investors. As Indians perished, Europeans obtained good land. Vast cattle ranches, known as **haciendas**, were often over 1 million acres in size. To ensure Indian labor, Spain imposed the **encomienda** ("entrustment"), the Crown's grant to a colonial Spaniard of Indians from whom he extracted tribute. Clergy instructed Indians in Christianity in exchange for providing labor. In theory protecting Indians, this system fostered many abuses. A Spanish Franciscan condemned cruel mine owners who pursued profit at the expense of encomienda workers: "The Indian slaves who up to the present have died in these [gold] mines cannot be counted. Gold, in this land, was adored as a god."[20] Because of abuses, Spanish monarchs sometimes abandoned the

> **haciendas** Vast ranches in Spanish America.
>
> **encomienda** ("entrustment") The Crown's grant to a colonial Spaniard in Latin America of a certain number of Indians from whom he extracted tribute.

[19]Quoted in Salvador de Madariaga, *The Rise of the Spanish American Empire* (New York: Macmillan, 1947), 90–91.

[20]From Fray Toribio Motolinia, "The Ten Plagues of New Spain," in *Indian Labor in the Spanish Indies*, ed. John Francis Bannon (Boston: D.C. Heath, 1966), 45.

MAP 17.3 THE ATLANTIC ECONOMY The Atlantic economy was based on a triangular trade in which African slaves were shipped to the Americas to produce raw materials that were chiefly exported to Europe, where they were turned into manufactured goods and exported to Africa and the Americas. © 2015 Cengage Learning

encomienda, relenting when Spanish colonists protested. The institution was reformed but still allowed temporary conscription of Indian labor until the later 1600s.

Despite early Spanish and Portuguese successes, eventually an increasingly stagnant Latin American economy fell behind vibrant North America. Initially, Latin America enjoyed many advantages over British North America: rich mines, abundant fertile land, and larger population. By the 1700s Latin Americans, unlike North Americans, had built a half dozen large cities and several fine universities and had produced great wealth, although it was inequitably distributed. But the rise of single-product, slave-based plantations, which, like mining or ranching, fostered specialized economic production for a world market, thwarted development in Latin America, the Caribbean, and southern English colonies by creating monocultures dependent on producing and exporting one chief commodity. Monocultures depended on the colonizing country buying their resource, such as sugar, silver, or beef, in return for supplying food and other necessities. Such plantation-, mining-, or ranching-based economies cannot generate overall development, defined as growth in diverse economic areas that benefits the majority of people. Enriching only a minority, they prosper or decline depending on world prices for their export commodity. Thus, with few alternative forms of employment or ways to generate wealth, plantation and mining societies in the Americas created significant poverty.

The Plantation Zone and African Slavery

Plantations became economically dominant in tropical and subtropical areas of the South American mainland, the Caribbean islands, and southeastern North America. By the later 1600s, the richest Andean and Mexican silver mines were exhausted, and plantations flourished by growing sugar, coffee, cotton, bananas, and sisal (a tough fiber used to make rope) for North America and Europe. This transition created the plantation zone, an area from Virginia and Kentucky southward through the West Indies and Central America to central Brazil and Peru in which economies relied on enslaved African labor. On Caribbean islands, sugar planting transformed whole economies. Initially European settlers founded self-sufficient farms that grew diverse crops in islands such as Jamaica, Barbados, Hispaniola, Cuba, and Puerto Rico. But in the mid-1600s sugar growing, being much more profitable, expanded. Since sugar needed plentiful land and cheap labor, slaves replaced white farmers. Whites became planters, migrated to North America, or became pirates.

American sugar growing fostered transitions in Europe. Europeans, especially Venetians, had earlier imported sugar from Arabs and Southeast Asia, and to satisfy increasing demand, the Portuguese grew sugar on small Atlantic islands such as Madeira. The search for more land for sugar production boosted the imperial appetite. American plantations and cheaper supplies transformed sugar from a rare luxury to a European dietary staple that sweetened bland foods and provided more calories for undernourished working classes. Sugar also helped foster an industrial economy in Britain because sweetened foods such as jam sandwiches and tea enabled people to take lunches to work and stay all day rather than go home for a large midday family meal.

Caribbean islands and some coastal districts in Brazil, the Guianas, Venezuela, Colombia, and Mexico became essentially sugar "factories," relying on mass production of raw sugar by enslaved workers. A seventeenth-century saying noted that "without sugar, no Brazil; without slaves, no sugar; without Angola, no slaves."[21] Southern English colonies of North America differed only in producing more varied crops, including cotton, rice, and tobacco as well as sugar. Enslaved people of African ancestry were numerically dominant in the plantation zone of southeastern North America, the Caribbean Basin, and coastal South America. A debilitating tropical disease spread by mosquitos, malaria had come to the Americas in the veins of African slaves, who had some degree of resistance. Hence, ndemic malaria infestation tended to correlate with the plantation zone, including in North America.

Africans occupied the bottom of the social ladder, where life was extremely harsh. On some sugar plantations, perhaps half the slaves died within two or three years of arrival. Such high mortality rates required constant importation of new slaves from Africa. Between 1500 and 1850 some 11 to 12 million Africans were brought into the Americas, especially to the plantation zone. Most went to Caribbean islands and Brazil, which today has the Americas' largest population of African descent. However, on a smaller scale African slaves were also used in northern English colonies such as New York, New Jersey, and Massachusetts and as far south as Peru and Argentina. Between 1500 and 1850 Brazil imported some 40 percent of all enslaved Africans, followed by the British Caribbean (21 percent), French Caribbean (15 percent), Spanish America (15 percent), and British North America (5 percent). About one-third of all people of African descent live in the Western Hemisphere today. Descendants of enslaved Africans constitute the large majority of people in Jamaica, Haiti, Barbados, the Bahamas, and most other Caribbean islands; half the population of Trinidad, Belize, Suriname, and Guyana; and substantial minorities in Brazil, Cuba, Puerto Rico, the Dominican Republic, Panama, Venezuela, Colombia, and the United States.

Slave Life and African American Cultures

Marketplace imperatives, not humane considerations, governed the lives of African slaves and their unfree descendants. Unlike many African societies, colonial Americans gave enslaved people few if any legal or customary rights, treating them as cost items in the production process, bought and sold at their owner's whim. Since markets for plantation crops constantly expanded,

monocultures An economy dependent on the production and export of one chief commodity.

development Growth in a variety of economic areas that benefits the majority of people; the opposite of monoculture.

plantation zone A group of societies with economies that relied on enslaved African labor; the plantation zone stretched from Virginia and Kentucky southward through the West Indies and the east coast of Central America to central Brazil and the Pacific coast of Colombia.

[21]Quoted in Stuart B. Schwartz, "Brazil," in *A Historical Guide to World Slavery*, ed. Seymour Drescher and Stanley L. Engerman (New York: Oxford University Press, 1998), 101.

slave owners sought maximum profit regardless of human consequences. Enslaved Africans died from mistreatment, disease, infant mortality, and disrupted family life, while slave women faced rape or sexual harassment by male owners and slaves. Encouraged by the Catholic Church to marry, many slaves formed families, even though they could be broken up by sale. In Brazil most slaves labored on sugar, coffee, and tobacco estates, and the average Brazilian sugar plantation owned between eighty and one hundred slaves. Some worked as mule drivers, sugar makers, household servants, or even low-level managers, but most were field hands expected to produce three-quarters of a ton of sugar a year each. Slave owners recovered the cost of purchasing and maintaining slaves after about three years but had little incentive to maintain the health of slaves unable to work hard.

CARIBBEAN SUGAR MILL On a West Indian plantation this windmill crushed sugar cane into juice, which was boiled down in the smoking building on the right to produce sugar granules. Such plantations were the dominant economic activity on the Caribbean islands and in parts of South America, Central America, and southeastern North America.

Africans and their descendants often resisted. Some, like the Brazilian woman Caetana, risked severe punishment by defending their interests (see Profile: Caetana, Slave Rebel Against Patriarchy). Some slaves, known as **maroons** in the English Caribbean, escaped from plantations and established African-type societies, often mixing varied ethnic traditions, in the interior of Brazil, Colombia, Jamaica, Haiti, Dutch Guiana, and some southern colonies in North America. Women led several of the ten major maroon societies in Brazil. With colonial governments sending military forces to recapture or control maroons, some communities enjoyed only temporary independence. The largest maroon state formed in northeast Brazil, where around 1605 rebellious slaves established Palmares **(paul-MARYS)**, with an African-style king and chiefs and a population of perhaps thirty thousand people. Palmares resisted nearly annual Portuguese assaults before being crushed in 1694. Slave revolts also erupted in Haiti, Mexico, the North American colonies, and elsewhere, all brutally repressed and their leaders executed. The 1739 Stono Rebellion in South Carolina, the deadliest North American uprising, largely involved recently imported Kongolese.

Some slaves were eventually freed, a process known as *manumission*. Manumission was rare in English colonies and more common in Latin America, especially Brazil, where women, mulattos, and local-born children were most likely to be freed. In both English and Latin America, a few slaves earned enough to buy their own freedom, and some slave owners gave favored slaves an inheritance. Free blacks filled niches in Latin American life, and enslaved and freed people of color constituted two-thirds of people in parts of Brazil and Cuba. While racism remained influential, Latin Americans tended to rank people by occupation and status as well as skin color, fostering a flexible social order. In contrast, English colonies rigidly divided people largely by skin color and whether they had any African ancestry.

Harsh slave life notwithstanding, unique African American cultures emerged. Africans and their descendants frequently mixed Western and African customs, some creating hybrid religions based on both African and Christian beliefs. The ceremonies of Haitian voodoo, Cuban *santaria* **(san-tuh-REE-uh)**, and Brazilian *candomblé* **(can-dum-BLAY)** involved West African practices such as animal sacrifice and worship of African spirits and gods. Yet, many followers of these faiths also revered the Christian God and saints. Combining African rhythms with local European and sometimes Native American musical traditions, African Americans laid foundations for popular twentieth-century musical forms, including North American jazz and blues; Caribbean salsa, reggae, and calypso; and Brazilian samba. A few even developed new languages, such as the Gullah **(GULL-uh)** dialect of the Georgia Sea Islands, which mixes English and African words.

In addition, African American cultures influenced other American ethnic groups. African words enriched locally spoken English, French, Spanish, and Portuguese. Brazilian Portuguese, for instance, contains many Kongolese and Yoruba words. Many non-Africans also enjoyed African folktales and traditions, such as the Brer Rabbit stories of the southern United States and the Angolan-based *capoiera* martial arts of Brazil, involving music and physical movements. In agriculture and manufacturing, Africans introduced several crops, including watermelons, black-eyed peas, okra, and rice, and contributed their knowledge

maroons Slaves who escaped from plantations and set up African-type societies in the interior of several American colonies.

Caetana, Slave Rebel Against Patriarchy

Thanks to a fascinating Brazilian court case in the 1830s, we learn about a remarkable female slave, Caetana, who challenged patriarchy. Caetana was born around 1818 on a large Rio Clara plantation owned by Captain Luis Mariano de Tolosa, in the Paraiba (par-uh-EE-buh) River Valley in southeastern Brazil. The plantation life Caetana experienced had not changed dramatically since the 1700s. At Rio Clara about half of the 134 slaves had been born in Africa while the other half, like Caetana, were Brazilian.

By 1835 coffee had become a major cash crop. Both men and women planted, maintained, and harvested the thirty thousand coffee bushes, often with children in tow. Some slaves raised other crops, tended cattle, or worked as artisans such as carpenters, blacksmiths, and stonemasons. The house

WOMEN SLAVES IN BRAZIL This 1861 painting shows a personal maid, much like Caetana, instructing slave girls in making lace on a Brazilian plantation. Such slave girls often wore colorful skirts and, like the instructor, earrings.

Source: Fundacao Biblioteca Nacional, Rio de Janeiro

slaves who worked in Tolosa's mansion did less strenuous indoor work such as cooking, cleaning, laundering and ironing clothes, carrying water, emptying kitchen slop and human waste, delivering messages, nursing infants, or taking care of the older Tolosa children. In exchange for better food and medical care than was given field hands, they were expected to be obedient and loyal.

Caetana lived in a close-knit relationship to kin, including her mother, Pulicena, and her sister, married to the freeborn mulatto, Joao Ribeira da Silva, probably a supervisor of field hands. Caetana was also close to her aunt, the freed slave Luisa Jacinta, whose husband, Alexandre, served as Caetana's godfather and male authority figure. Caetana grew up speaking Portuguese with no direct knowledge of African ways or the terrible Middle Passage across the Atlantic. From a young age she served in the Tolosa house as a personal maid to the Tolosa women, including two daughters, and was trusted and allowed into their private quarters.

In 1835 Tolosa, without consulting her, ordered Caetana, then around seventeen, to marry Custodio, a slave in his mid-twenties, in a wedding blessed by the Catholic Church. Custodio was a master tailor who may have cut and sewn rough cotton clothes worn by slaves and probably also made clothes for the Tolosa family. Like many slave owners, Tolosa may have believed that slave marriages fostered social stability and diminished the threat of rebellion. Perhaps he also feared that an unmarried house slave, representing unyoked female sexuality, might be a bad influence on his two daughters, twelve and two years old, and temptation for his three adolescent sons. Most adult slave women

at Rio Clara were married. Caetana, however, refused Tolosa's order, saying, according to court records, that she felt "a great repugnance for the state of matrimony" and found Custodio especially distasteful. In the end she obeyed, succumbing to her family's pleas and fearing Tolosa's threats to punish her by assigning her to field work or selling her to another plantation. But after priests performed the ceremony and the couple moved into her aunt and uncle's house, she refused to sleep with Custodio, humiliating and enraging him.

After her uncle and godfather, Alexandre, threatened to beat her if she did not submit to her husband, and with few options, Caetana fled to Tolosa's mansion and pleaded to end the marriage. Her rebellion was apparently not against plantation slavery as such but against male authority over her. Caetana's action against the entire system of male power—slave owner, uncle, husband, church—threw Rio Clara into turmoil. After his threats to sell Caetana or reassign her to onerous field work failed, Tolosa relented, giving her protection from her husband and asking a church court to issue an annulment. In court, Caetana complained that she was "reduced to the hard necessity of obeying solely from fear of grave punishment and lasting harm." The legal case took five years, including appeals, with the church ultimately refusing the annulment request.

We do not know why, against such long odds, she rebelled, why she despised marriage, or what ultimately happened to Caetana. Perhaps she envied unmarried free women, who were often respected, or the chaste nuns in the convents. The records do not indicate whether she continued to evade the marriage, but it seems unlikely she complied. She might have been sold to another plantation, before or after Tolosa died in 1853. What we do know is that Caetana bravely refused a demand to do something against her will.

THINKING ABOUT THE PROFILE

1. What does Caetana's experience tell us about life on a Brazilian plantation?
2. What does her rebellion tell us about the Brazilian system of patriarchy?

Note: Quotations from Sandra Lauderdale Graham, *Caetana Says No: Women's Stories from a Brazilian Slave Society* (New York: Cambridge University Press, 2002), 2, 57.

of blacksmithing and ironworking. African cultural forms and values probably survived most strongly in Brazil, Haiti, and Caribbean islands such as Cuba, Jamaica, and Trinidad. Especially in Brazil, the Portuguese eventually accepted the many African influences brought by thousands of African arrivals every year, creating a mixed African and European culture. In contrast, Spanish American and North American authorities often repressed African music and religion, with some success.

Economic Growth in English North America

Many English North American colonies developed different economic, and eventually political, systems than monoculture colonies. Some historians contrast English culture, which was energized by capitalism and religious diversity, with Spain and Portugal's semimedieval Catholic cultures, which inhibited Latin Americans because they discouraged resistance to authority, accepted poverty as God's will, and distrusted new ideas. Other historians emphasize colonial policies, pointing out that the northern English colonies enjoyed more autonomy than Spanish colonies. Others agree that both cultural and colonial patterns were influential but stress the colonial economies and social diversity they fostered. With northern English colonies lacking mines to fill galleons with gold and silver, a large Native American labor force to exploit, the soil or climate for profitable tropical crops, or open grasslands for ranching, slaves mostly worked for farms, businesses, or households. The immigrant European population, mostly farmers, artisans, and merchants, were never dependent on slave plantations and the severe social inequality they fostered.

Economic conditions fostered differing administrative policies. England allowed its colonies from New Jersey north through New England considerable freedom to build diversified economies for the local market. Being more concerned with its valuable plantation-dominated colonies such as South Carolina, Virginia, and Jamaica, the world's largest sugar producer in the 1700s, England imposed fewer restrictions on New York or Massachusetts. Merchants from Boston, Providence, and New York competed with the English in the Caribbean to obtain sugar and molasses, which was converted to rum and shipped to Africa for slaves. Some North Americans amassed huge slave trade profits to invest in their own broad-based economies. Thus while northern English colonies moved toward development, the southern English colonies, Latin America, and the Caribbean maintained largely undiversified, monoculture economies. The result was that those colonies with the most abundant natural and human resources to exploit had the greater short-term economic growth but less long-term development than the resource-poor northern English colonies. Some highly profitable colonies, such as Haiti, Jamaica, Peru, Bolivia, and Guatemala, are now among the world's poorest countries, and northeast Brazil is one of Brazil's poorest regions, while the less profitable northern English colonies eventually became among the world's most developed regions.

The Americas, the Atlantic System, and European Wealth

As discussed in Chapter 16, increasingly close economic ties and trans-Atlantic migration, voluntary and forced, created an Atlantic System spanning western and Central Africa, North America's east and gulf coasts, the Caribbean Basin, and coastal zones of South America. The system was defined by trans-Atlantic shipping, plantations, slavery, and the prominence of Africans and their descendants in the Americas. Ultimately, this system spurred European capitalism and wealth. Slave trading and plantation economies provided enormous capital to Europeans and North Americans while underpinning the prosperity of eighteenth-century cities such as Bristol and Liverpool in England and Nantes in France, as well as Boston, Providence, Charleston, Savannah, and New Orleans in North America. With the slavers, cooperating African chiefs and merchants, plantation owners, shipbuilders, and other groups linked directly or indirectly to the trade reluctant to abandon a lucrative activity, the trade endured for four hundred years, finally ending only in the 1870s.

The Atlantic System contributed to European industrialization and colonialism. Profits invested in enterprises and technology in England, the Netherlands, France, and North America financed economic development and later spurred rapid industrialization in England. Some individuals and companies linked to the slave trade and plantations invested in industrial technology. For example, Glasgow merchants known as the "tobacco lords," who were tied to North American tobacco plantations, established printing companies, tanneries, and ironworks while also investing in cotton textile plants and coal mines in Britain. However, the vast profits earned from overseas commerce did not always result in substantial development. Spain and Portugal largely squandered opportunities, becoming poor countries within Europe, while the Dutch and English pursued wiser investment policies.

Spain, the most powerful European country of the 1500s, reaped vast riches from American silver mines and galleons bringing Chinese goods and tropical products from the Philippines to Mexico. But Spain used this wealth poorly, failing to promote its own economic improvement. Thus, in the end, exploitation of the Americas hurt Spain. With American bullion causing severe inflation, Spain imported lower-priced products from other European countries. Moreover, Spaniards leaving for the Americas and Asia created a labor shortage at home. Because peasants and merchants in Spain were heavily taxed for large colonial investments, Spanish investment did not spur capitalism; most Spanish merchants bought land rather than investing in trade or industry. By 1600 Spain was bankrupt. A Spanish official charged that the country had wasted its wealth on frivolous spending rather than manufacturing: "the cause of [our] ruin is that riches ride on the wind, instead of [producing] goods that bear fruit. Spain is poor because she is rich [in gold and silver]."[22] Much of the silver ended up elsewhere in Europe or in China. China benefitted initilly but eventually the flood of silver caused inflation and unrest, contributing to the collapse of the Ming dynasty. Colonial wealth also tempted Spain's monarchy to pursue expensive and ultimately futile wars in Europe.

Portugal was second only to England in slave trading, and Brazil became the world's largest exporter of gold, diamonds, and sugar and a major producer of coffee and cotton. But the Portuguese also squandered their colonial wealth, building

---

[22]Gonzalez de Cellorigo, quoted in Jonathan Williams, *Money: A History* (New York: St. Martin's, 1997), 162.

magnificent churches and monasteries rather than financing local industry. As a small country with a small population, Portugal had a tiny domestic market and hence little incentive to build local industries. Investment in Brazil was more profitable.

Holland and England did much better investing their profits than the Spanish and Portuguese. Becoming a major banking center and boasting the world's largest commercial fleet, during the 1600s the Dutch earned vast profits from selling Indonesian coffee and spices to other Europeans and invested much of it in their domestic economy. Much Portuguese and Spanish wealth ended up in Holland. Replacing the Dutch as Europe's and the Atlantic system's dominant power by the end of the 1600s, England enjoyed the most long-term success, benefiting from profits earned in the Americas and India. Wealth flowed into Liverpool, Glasgow, and Bristol from the slave, tobacco, and sugar trades, enriching businessmen and bankers who could mobilize capital for investment in trade, technology, and manufacturing. These factors gave England unique advantages that it fully exploited in the 1700s and 1800s.

Transforming and linking the Americas to the rest of the globe reshaped world history. Conquering Native Americans, acquiring American resources, and trading slaves gave some Europeans decided economic advantages over China, India, and the Ottoman Empire. The profits from American metals, often mined by Native Americans, and American crops, chiefly grown by African slaves, shifted world economic power and added to European political and military strength. By the late 1700s Britain had surpassed China in wealth, living standards, and power.

MAKE SURE YOU UNDERSTAND THESE KEY POINTS BEFORE MOVING ON

- Using Indian labor imposed through the encomienda system, Spanish colonists became wealthy at first through ranching and mining gold and silver, but their economies eventually suffered from lack of diversification.

- Plantations run with African slave labor and focused on producing a single product—sugar in Latin America and the Caribbean, cotton in southeastern North America— also eventually created impoverished societies.

- African slaves in the Americas were treated as commodities, and resistance to slavery was rarely successful, though freed slaves had somewhat more success in Latin America than they did in North America.

- The slave trade and plantation economies helped spur European capitalism and were extremely profitable to Europeans and North American colonists.

aplia

CHAPTER SUMMARY

The Columbian voyages unleashed powerful forces around the Atlantic basin, generating a great historical transition. European explorers seeking a route to Asia and then conquerors seeking wealth brought the Americas and their peoples into a permanent relationship with the Eastern Hemisphere. The Spanish, Portuguese, English, and French built vast colonial empires in the Americas, using their superior military power to subjugate American peoples. The majority of Native American people perished from disease and other causes; American societies, including the great Aztec and Inca Empires, were destroyed and placed under European colonial control; survivors saw their lives changed enormously. The Native American and mixed-descent peoples had to adjust to colonial rule, Africans to the trauma of servitude, and the European colonizers and settlers to cultural resistance.

The economic evolution of the Americas, especially mining and plantation agriculture, created a tremendous market for labor. Mine owners conscripted Native American workers, and planters exploited enslaved Africans and their descendants. The slave trade linked the Americas closely to the larger world. The emerging Atlantic System closely connected Europe, West Africa, and the Americas, mostly to the benefit of Europe and European colonists. Some colonists in English North America built more diversified economies, in contrast to the monocultures of the Caribbean and Latin America. Spain and Portugal initially prospered from their conquests but later squandered the resources they obtained, while the English and Dutch capitalized on their activities to achieve greater wealth and power. American history was thus not only a dynamic saga of indigenous development but also the story of increasing integration into larger global processes.

KEY TERMS

conquistadors (p. 397)
Paulistas (p. 398)
voyageurs (p. 399)
Columbian Exchange (p. 400)
audiencias (p. 401)
creoles (p. 402)

mestizos (p. 402)
mulattos (p. 402)
peninsulares (p. 402)
Black Legend (p. 403)
Metis (p. 404)
haciendas (p. 405)

encomienda (p. 405)
monoculture (p. 407)
development (p. 407)
plantation zone (p. 407)
maroons (p. 408)

Japanese School (16th century)/The Art Gallery Collection/Alamy

"SOUTHERN BARBARIANS" This painting on a sixteenth-century Japanese screen, decorated with gold leaf, depicts the arrival of Portuguese ships and their crews in the port of Nagasaki. Various representatives have left the ship, with porters carrying gifts for Japanese officials and merchants.

> *The Portuguese saw that Melaka was magnificent, and its port exceedingly crowded. The people gathered around to see what the Portuguese looked like, and they were all surprised by their appearance. [But] these [Portuguese] know nothing of manners.*
>
> —Malay Chronicles[1]

Sultan Mahmud Shah (MA-mood shah) (r. 1488–1511), the

Malay ruler of Melaka, the great trading state on the Malay Peninsula's southwest coast, had a problem. In 1509 five well-armed Portuguese ships, flying banners bearing a cross and full of menacing pale-skinned men with unclear intentions, had anchored off his city on an exploratory visit prompted by Melaka's fame as a treasure-trove of Asian goods that fetched huge profits in Europe. They did not act like the peaceful Asian merchants that regularly arrived, nor did they bring the customary gifts for the sultan and his officials. Curious Melakans gathered around a Portuguese envoy, twisting his beard, taking off his hat, and grasping his hand. The Portuguese violated local customs, antagonized Melaka officials, and alarmed influential local Indian traders, who feared competition. The Portuguese considered Sultan Mahmud Shah arrogant and treacherous. Fighting between Portuguese sailors and Malays broke out. After Melakans arrested Portuguese sailors shopping in town, the remaining force, unprepared to assault the heavily defended city, sailed away, vowing revenge.

Two years later forty Portuguese ships, mounted with cannon and carrying hundreds of soldiers armed with deadly muskets, returned to capture the city. The sultan led the defense mounted on his elephant. Gaining the upper hand after a bloody month-long assault, the Portuguese commander, Admiral Affonso de Albuquerque (al-ba-KER-kee), told his soldiers to expel the "Moors" (Muslims); his men then slaughtered much of the population and looted the city. This episode previewed both the conflicts and connections forged between Europeans and Asians over the next four centuries. Many eastern and southern Asians had better success than the Melakans in deflecting the Europeans competing with each other and with Asians for markets and resources. The Portuguese in the 1500s, the Dutch in the 1600s, and the English in the 1700s established some control over the Indian Ocean maritime network and colonized a few areas, such as Melaka. But, despite their deadly gunpowder weapons, Europeans did not yet enjoy a clear military and economic advantage over the stronger Asian states; thus their regional influence remained modest. Furthermore, Asian countries could be reached only by long and dangerous voyages from Europe. Hence, most Asian societies escaped the transitions reshaping the Americas and parts of Africa in this era. Yet, by the mid-1700s most great Asian states were under stress or collapsing from internal problems and destabilizing Western activities.

[1] Quoted in Anthony Reid, "Early Southeast Asian Categorizations of Europeans," in *Implicit Understandings*, ed. Stuart B. Schwartz (Cambridge: Cambridge University Press, 1994), 275.

413

Mughal India, South Asia, and New Encounters

What were the major achievements and failures of the Mughal Empire?

Muslim conquerors and Hinduism shaped India's culture. The Mughals **(MOO-guhlz)**, Muslim Central Asians of mixed Mongol-Turkish descent, ruled much of India during this era, reaching their height in the later 1500s and early 1600s. They fostered artistic and religious innovations and a prosperous economy fueled by international trade. As pressures from European states mounted in the early 1700s, however, the Mughals rapidly declined.

The Rise and Decline of the Mughal Empire

In 1526 Babur **(BAH-bur)** (1483–1530), an ambitious, learned, and gifted poet in the Persian language who descended from Genghis Khan and Tamerlane, led twelve thousand troops from Afghanistan and conquered much of north India. The Mughal dynasty (see Map 18.1) that he formed restored India's imperial grandeur. Mughal India had few rivals in military strength, government efficiency, economic

Urdu A language developed in Mughal India that mixed Hindi, Arabic, and Persian and was written in the Persian script.

power, and arts patronage. A French visitor to the imperial court wondered whether any other monarch possessed more gold, silver, and jewels, and the English used the term *mogul* to mean someone of extreme wealth.

Like earlier Indian governments, the Mughals managed a highly diverse society. Buddhism, reduced to minor status in India, thrived in Tibet and on Sri Lanka (Ceylon). Most Indians practiced Hinduism, a religion of varied beliefs and practices, and perhaps a quarter embraced Islam. Muslim states had ruled parts of the subcontinent since the ninth century. Polytheistic Hinduism and monotheistic Islam offered starkly different visions of the cosmic and social order. But while Hindus and Muslims often disagreed, in many villages they lived side by side, sharing many customs. Indians were also divided by caste and hundreds of different regional languages, such as Bengali in the northeast and Tamil in the southeast. The adaptable Mughals used **Urdu**, a mix of Hindi, Arabic, and Persian written in the Persian script, as their language of administration.

Babur's grandson Akbar **(AK-bahr)** (r. 1556–1605) became the most outstanding Mughal ruler (see Profile: Akbar,

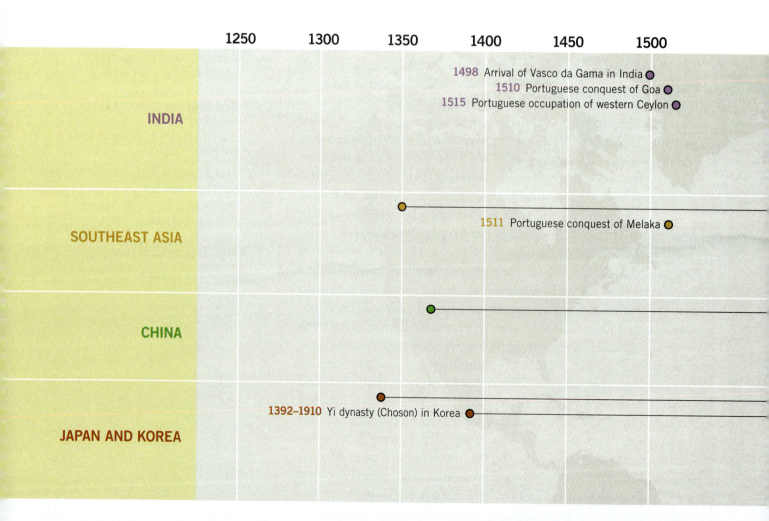

	1250	1300	1350	1400	1450	1500

INDIA

1498 Arrival of Vasco da Gama in India ◉
1510 Portuguese conquest of Goa ◉
1515 Portuguese occupation of western Ceylon ◉

SOUTHEAST ASIA

1511 Portuguese conquest of Melaka ◉

CHINA

JAPAN AND KOREA

1392–1910 Yi dynasty (Choson) in Korea ◉

Mughal Ruler). Akbar, whose name means "Very Great," expanded Babur's empire over all of north India and deep into south India. After winning the support of various Hindu groups, some from the Hindu warrior caste, the Rajputs **(RAHJ-putz)**, Akbar gave Hindus high government positions, removed extra taxes imposed by earlier Muslim rulers on non-Muslims, promoted religious toleration and compromise between communities, and strictly checked bribery and corruption while seeing that laws were justly administered. He tried to abolish what he considered pernicious social customs, such as *sati* (burning the wife on the husband's funeral pyre), child marriage, trial by ordeal, and enslaving prisoners of war. Akbar's India also enjoyed an enlightened criminal code; all citizens could appeal to the ruler if they believed themselves wrongly convicted or mistreated in courts.

Akbar presided over a golden age of peace and prosperity, but his successors had less tolerance and wisdom. With their many wives and concubines, Muslim rulers produced numerous ambitious male heirs to the throne and hence created unstable succession. Akbar was succeeded by Jahangir **(ja-HAN-gear)** ("World Seizer"), a rebellious son who poisoned Akbar and occupied the throne. Like some other royal Mughal women, his Persian wife, Nur Jahan **(nur ja-HAN)**, had considerable power at court and strongly influenced her husband; writing that he only needed wine and meat to be happy, Jahangir handed government business over to Nur Jahan. While Jahangir generally pursued Akbar's wise policies, his son, Shah Jahan (r. 1628–1658), promoted Islam, destroyed several Hindu temples, and assembled a harem of five thousand concubines. Sitting on his splendid jewel-encrusted Peacock Throne in Delhi, Shah Jahan doubled the tax bills, but his extensive building projects and unsuccessful military campaigns in Afghanistan and Central Asia virtually bankrupted the state. Eventually his even more intolerant son, Aurangzeb **(ow-rang-ZEB)** (r. 1658–1707), imprisoned Shah Jahan and greatly expanded the empire in the south while also undermining the state and its revenues.

Endless wars and extravagant royal spending finally drained the Mughals' state coffers and military strength. Once sufficient to keep Europeans and other enemies at bay, the armed forces now lacked naval power. Although the Mughal army had some 1 million soldiers equipped with gunpowder weapons such as muskets and field artillery that rivaled European arms, as well as thousands of battle elephants, by the early 1700s it lacked the money to match European military capabilities. Increasing taxes on both merchants and peasants also sparked increasing opposition, while Aurangzeb's ruthless, intolerant, and corrupt policies alienated both Muslims and non-Muslims. The dogmatic Aurangzeb placed higher taxes on non-Muslims and persecuted—sometimes executed—Hindu and Sikh leaders. One pious Muslim wrote that "bribery is

MAP 18.1 **THE MUGHAL EMPIRE, 1526–1761** By the mid-1600s the Mughals, a Muslim dynasty based in north India, controlled much of the Indian subcontinent. However, some ports fell under European rule. The Portuguese had a colony at Goa, and, by the early 1700s, the British had established outposts at Bombay, Calcutta, and Madras, while the French occupied Pondicherry. © 2015 Cengage Learning

merchants. When Safavid Iran conquered Mughal-controlled Afghanistan, factionalized Mughal leaders could not respond. In 1761 Hindu and Sikh insurgents finally defeated Mughal rulers, who continued to govern a small territory from Delhi until 1857.

Mughal decline and near demise opened India to penetration and eventual European conquest. Anti-Mughal forces could not unite, leaving India fragmented and vulnerable. Growing Hindu-Muslim divisions also facilitated the gradual establishment of European domination. After annexing parts of India in the 1700s, the English encouraged religious rivalry to fragment opposition, but they also had trouble subduing the Sikhs. The religious divide greatly shaped contemporary South Asia, which was divided into rival Hindu and Muslim nations.

Indian Economy, Society, Religion, and the Arts

India in this era was one of the world's major manufacturing societies. Demand continued for Indian textiles all over Eurasia and parts of Africa, while India's iron industry produced high-quality steel and cannon. By 1750 India still accounted for one-quarter of the world's industrial output and was the largest textile producer. Efficient farming, benefiting from investments in reservoirs and irrigation, produced large yields of wheat and rice, as well as cash crops such as cotton, indigo, pepper, sugar, and opium that supplied markets at home or abroad. India's population doubled between 1500 and 1750. While for centuries India had been a core of the Afro-Eurasian networks, trading fine fabrics such as cashmere and gingham to Europe and the Middle East for gold and silver, in the 1600s an influx of American silver, used by European merchants to obtain Indian products, tripled the money supply and benefited the Mughal treasury, allowing construction of ambitious but expensive buildings and imperial roads linking the empire.

Indian merchants and bankers expanded their commercial networks over vast distances, from Arabia, Persia, Northeast Africa, and the Red Sea to Malaya, Sumatra, Siam, and China. Hindu and Muslim merchants from Gujerat (**goo-juh-RAHT**) in northwest India were leading traders and financers around the Indian Ocean, including Melaka. Thousands of Indians also traded across Central Asia, Afghanistan, Tibet, the Caucasus states, and Russia, establishing, for example, commercial dominance at the Russian trading port of Astrakhan (**AS-truh-kan**) on the Caspian Sea.

Indian merchant networks enjoyed vast capital, sophisticated credit and financing arrangements, and reputations for shrewdness, often competing successfully against European and Asian rivals. Some merchants in Surat (**SOO-raht**), the main Gujerat port, were among the world's richest entrepreneurs. A Dutch diplomat wrote that merchants of Bengal were "exceptionally quick and experienced. They are always sober, modest, thrifty, and cunning in identifying the source for their profit."[3]

Caste and gender divisions divided Indian society. Most Hindu merchants belonged to various subcastes (*jati*) that moved

everywhere; mean people have become governors, May God damn the tyrant! In this world he is an infidel; in the next he is in hell."[2]

Revolt eventually led to the dismantling of the Mughal state as regions broke away. Aurangzeb's imperial expansion significantly increased his already huge army's size, creating logistical problems in supplying troops just as anti-Mughal forces were becoming bolder. Marathas (**muh-RAH-tuhz**), a Hindu group from western India, raided the faltering empire in the later 1600s, using guns given by disenchanted Hindu

Akbar, Mughal Ruler

During the early Mughal period, India was ruled by Akbar, one of history's most respected political leaders, who came to power at thirteen after his father died. A contemporary of Queen Elizabeth I of England and Shah Abbas of Persia, Akbar was also a possible epileptic (like Julius Caesar and Napoleon) and subject to bouts of depression. Rather than his ruthless military conquests, his greatness lay in his skills as an administrator and his ability to respect and blend India's diverse traditions. Always seeing himself as an Indian rather than a foreign ruler, he worked hard to accommodate all the strands of Indian culture and religion into a unified country. Although raised a Muslim, he married a Christian and two Hindu princesses, winning non-Muslim support and symbolizing acceptance of India's religious diversity.

Foreign visitors were charmed by Akbar. A Jesuit missionary who visited India in the early 1580s wrote that he was

> of a stature and type of countenance well suited to his royal dignity, so that one could easily recognize even at first glance that he is the king. He creates an opportunity almost every day for any of the common people or of the nobles to see him and converse with him. It is remarkable how great an effect this courtesy and affability has in attaching to him the minds of his subjects.

Visionary, energetic, and versatile, Akbar lived to the fullest, becoming a skilled metalworker, draftsman, polo player, and musician. Although himself illiterate, he had an insatiable love of learning and had books of all kinds read to him. His personal library included twenty-four thousand volumes. He also patronized poets, musicians, painters, and architects, even honoring his architects and artisans by having them build a new capital at Fatepuhr Sikri near Agra, where he then lived. Akbar greatly enjoyed the lovely gardens constructed around Mughal buildings in the capital and elsewhere, featuring shade trees, fountains, and pools. To show Hindus his respect, he encouraged Hindi literature and even appointed a Hindi court poet. In response to orthodox Muslims who criticized his support of Hindu court painters, some of whose subject matter violated Islamic prejudices against human images, he argued that God loved all beauty.

Although the Mughals were officially Muslims, Akbar espoused complete freedom of religion, not just for political expediency but also because he was an enlightened man with a restless, inquiring mind. Investigation of the mysteries of creation, he claimed, should be done according to the light of reason. He believed that all faiths had something truthful to offer and that all religions were untrue when they denied other religions' sincerity of purpose. Once a week, representatives of all religions held debates in the palace at his invitation; when Jesuit missionaries arrived from the West, they stayed with Akbar for several years and joined in the spirited debates. Indeed, Akbar had the Christian gospels translated into Persian and even attended the occasional mass out of curiosity.

AKBAR The great Mughal emperor, Akbar, enjoyed pomp and circumstance. This miniature painting shows him entertaining guests at a reception in his palace.

Akbar never completely bought into any religion totally, believing that no one faith had a monopoly on truth. He remained skeptical and found some beliefs in all of them that he thought contradicted reason. Later in life he adopted the Hindu custom of vegetarianism and gave up his favorite sport of hunting. Influenced by the inclusive spirit of Sufi mysticism, in the end he created his own religion, incorporating what he saw as the best features of all religions. But, since he would not impose his views on others, Akbar's religion found few takers and died with him.

THINKING ABOUT THE PROFILE

1. How did Akbar foster Indian cultural life?
2. How could Akbar afford to show so much tolerance of other religions?

Note: Quotation from Rhoads Murphey, *A History of Asia*, 4th ed. (New York: HarperCollins, 2003), 178.

up or down in the larger *vaisya* caste grouping, which ranked below the priests (*brahmans*) and warriors in a system that had evolved for over two thousand years. Women's influence depended on their caste and family situation. In north India both Muslim and Hindu women were often kept in seclusion, expected to be chaste and obedient to fathers and husbands in a patriarchal, patrilineal society. Yet, some Mughal court women exercised influence. Khanzada Begum (1478–1545), Babur's oldest sister, successfully interceded with rebellious brothers to end a family split and to keep Babur's son, Humayun, on the throne, avoiding bloodshed. Mughal women also had financial resources, which they often devoted to endowing mosques and supporting religious scholars.

The coming of Islam and the conversion of many Indians had dramatically changed India's religious and cultural environment. Muslims resisted assimilation into the tolerant Hindu fold, remaining disdainful of Hindus and the caste system, and the two groups never formed a single people. Yet, many upper-caste north Indian Hindus adopted some Muslim customs, such as the veiling and secluding of women. The early Mughals, especially Akbar, mostly left Hindus free to practice their own faith and customs. However, less tolerant later rulers deepened the religious divide. At the same time, as mysticism became increasingly popular among both Muslims and Hindus, Muslim rulers welcomed Indian, Arab, and Persian Sufi masters to their courts to compose songs, poems, and sermons that facilitated communion with God. Sufis preached a personal bond between each believer and God, with some Sufi movements, such as the Chishtiya **(CHIS-tee-ya)**, avoiding association with secular powers. The Indian Chishti saint Nizam al-Din Awliya **(KNEE-zam al-DIN aw-LEE-ya)** wrote that "my room has two doors. If the sultan comes through one door, I will leave through the other."[4] Akbar's and Jahangir's Sufi sympathies horrified Muslim dogmatists, who regarded mystics as heretics.

Hinduism continued to evolve. Many Hindus, particularly from lower castes, had gravitated toward the mystical bhakti **(BUK-tee)** devotional movement. Some bhakti groups opposed the caste system, ignoring high-caste brahmans and sympathizing with the poor. Often bhakti worship involved commitment to a particular Hindu god, such as Shiva or Vishnu, and many bhakti poets were women. Most famously, Mirabai **(MEERA-buy)** (ca. 1498–ca. 1546), a Rajput widowed at a young age, refused to commit sati and spent the rest of her life writing praises to Vishnu. Bhakti women like Mirabai could defy social conventions and even become saints, while Muslim women were more likely than men to honor and visit the graves of Sufi sheiks. Mysticism forged a gradual accommodation between some Muslims and Hindus venerating both Sufi and bhakti saints. Finally, between the fourteenth and seventeenth century Hindu thinkers increasingly treated

Sikhs Members of an Indian religion founded in the Early Modern Era that adopted elements from both Hinduism and Islam, including mysticism.

diverse schools of thought, such as Vedanta, yoga, bhakti, and Shiva worship, as belonging to a single system of belief and practice, separate rivers leading to the ocean of Brahman, the absolute reality. This melding laid the foundation for the modern concept of Hinduism as a coherent religion rather than loosely connected, often rival sects and beliefs.

Other Indians blended or transcended Hinduism and Islam by forming new religions. The largest new faith, the **Sikhs** ("Disciples"), adopted elements, including mysticism, from both Hinduism and Islam. Eventually Sikhs numbered several million people, mostly living in northwest India's Punjab region. The founder, Guru Nanak **(GOO-roo NAN-ak)** (1469–1539), born a Hindu and influenced by bhakti movements, argued that devotion was not enough; people were saved by their deeds alone: "God will not ask a man his tribe or sect, but what he has done. There is no Hindu and no Muslim. All are children of God." The nine spiritual leaders who followed Nanak refined the faith during Mughal times. Arjan (1563–1606) established the holy scripture, which announced: "I do not keep the Hindu fast, nor the Muslim Ramadan. I have broken with the Hindu and Muslim. I shall put my heart at the feet of one Supreme Being."[5] Akbar granted Sikhs land for a great temple in Amritsar **(uhm-RIT-suhr)** in the Punjab.

Like Muslims, Sikhs worshiped one universal and loving God, rejected the caste system and priests, promoted egalitarianism, forbade alcohol and tobacco, and stressed discipline, hard work, and charity for the needy. Sikhs also developed distinctive customs. Observant men sported beards, wore steel bracelets, and carried a dagger or sword at all times. Prohibited from cutting their hair, many men wore a turban. Sikh women enjoyed greater freedom than Hindus and Muslims. Persistent persecution by Mughal leaders after Akbar led Sikhs, once pacifists, to become militaristic and excellent soldiers, well represented in modern India's military and police forces. The Sikhs also became skilled and practical farmers.

Indian arts flourished in this period. For example, the distinctive Mughal school of miniature painting, based on Persian models, represented a synthesis between Islamic and Hindu cultures, while the Indian-Persian architectural style, known as Indo-Islamic, made lavish use of mosaics, domes, and gateways in building tombs, mosques, forts, and palaces. The Mughal elite lived in large houses with courtyards, trees, gardens, water basins, and handsome subterranean apartments furnished with large fans to escape the heat. In his spectacular Delhi palace audience hall, Shah Jahan had inscribed: "If on earth be an Eden of bliss, it is this, it is this, it is this!"[6] East of Delhi, at Agra **(AH-gruh)**, Shah Jahan left another legacy, the Taj Mahal **(tahzh muh-HAHL)**. Often considered the world's most beautiful building, the Taj is a marble mausoleum with pools, archways, domes, and minarets. It took 22,000 workers twenty-two years to complete this final resting place for Shah Jahan's favorite wife and close political adviser, Mumtaz Mahal **(MOOM-taz muh-HAHL)**.

[4]Quoted in Francis Robinson, *The Cultural Atlas of the Islamic World Since 1500* (London: Stonehenge, 1992), 39.
[5]The quotes are from Rhoads Murphey, *A History of Asia*, 4th ed. (New York: Longman, 2002), 185; and Michael Edwardes, *A History of India* (New York: Farrar, Straus and Cudahy, 1961), 191.
[6]Quoted in Edwardes, *History of India*, 190.

South Asia and European Challengers

When the Mughals, the last great precolonial Indian rulers, collapsed, the power vacuum was filled by Europeans. Spurred by interest in southern Asia as a source of spices and textiles, the Portuguese sought a sea route around Africa and the Spanish sponsored the Columbian voyages across the Atlantic in search of "the Indies." The Portuguese were the first Europeans to arrive in India directly by sea around Africa. They came from a country with superior naval technology, missionary zeal, and a compelling appetite for wealth but a standard of living little if any higher than that of many Indians, Southeast Asians, and Chinese.

Following the Indian Ocean maritime trade route from East Africa, a fleet captained by Vasco da Gama (ca. 1469–1525), using a pilot hired in East Africa, possibly a Muslim Gujerati, reached the southwestern Indian port of Calicut in 1498. Upon encountering merchants from as far away as Northwest Africa, da Gama quickly realized both Asia's economic potential and the small value of his European goods. With one military advantage over Indians—mounted cannon on his ships— he was able without force to obtain a cargo of spices, which he later sold in Europe at 3,000 percent profit. In 1500 a second Portuguese fleet returned to Calicut. After sailors fought Arabs and local people, the Portuguese bombarded Calicut to rubble and destroyed the less maneuverable Indian and Arab ships defending the city.

Like all the European powers following them to Asia, the Portuguese employed violence to enforce their power and acquire wealth. Seeking to control trade from Asia to the West, they established fortified settlements at strategic locations around the Indian Ocean, including Hormuz (hor-MOOZ) at the entrance to the Persian Gulf, Mombasa in East Africa, Diu (dee-YOU) in northwest India, Goa on India's southwestern coast, and Melaka in Malaya. In 1515 they occupied Colombo (kuh-LUM-bow), a Sri Lankan port that exported cinnamon. At the same time, Portuguese warships extorted payments from Ottoman, Arab, Indian, and Indonesian merchant ships in the Indian Ocean. In 1502 Vasco da Gama, using terrorism, attacked, plundered, and burned an Arab passenger ship carrying over three hundred people, including several of Calicut's richest merchants and many women and children, killing all aboard.

But the Portuguese, while aggressive, were also often ineffectual. Despite devoting some eight hundred ships and controlling several key ports, the ambitious Portuguese found competing with wily Asian merchants difficult and never completely dominated Indian Ocean commerce. While Asian merchants often outmaneuvered or evaded Portuguese ships, Asian states resisted Portuguese demands. Their zealous Catholicism also caused turmoil. Da Gama had told Calicut leaders that he sought "Christians and spices," a useful shorthand for understanding Portuguese motives, and the Portuguese hostility to Islam sometimes fostered persecution of Islamic institutions and believers in Portuguese-held territories. By introducing chilies from the Americas, however, the Portuguese made a lasting contribution to South and Southeast Asian cooking, making spicy food even hotter. In Goa Portuguese and local Indians created a fiery hot dish, *vindaloo*, combining European vinegar, American potatoes, chilies, and local ingredients, that became a fixture of South Asian cuisine.

By 1750 European influence and Indian-European trade remained modest. But the Portuguese activity foreshadowed an increasingly active European presence, as Holland, France, and England all attempted to shape parts of South Asia. The overextended Portuguese struggled to sustain their power against these European rivals with larger populations and better ships and gunpowder weapons. Portuguese men settled in Goa and Colombo, marrying local women and creating mixed-descent, Portuguese-speaking Catholic communities. But Portugal later lost all its other South and West Asian footholds, retaining only Goa as a colony until 1961, when India assumed control.

In the early 1600s the Dutch, destroying Portuguese power in South and Southeast Asia, gained partial control over the Indian Ocean commerce. With government

The horse market, miniature from Storia do Mogor (History of the Mughal Empire) in India by Niccolò Manucci (1638-1717), India 18th Century./De Agostini Picture Library/A. Dagli Orti/The Bridgeman Art Library

THE MUGHAL HORSE MARKET This eighteenth century miniature painting by shows Mughal men buying and selling horses, especially valuable for military purposes.

backing, Amsterdam merchants formed the well-financed, private Dutch East India Company in 1602, with its own armed fleet working in conjunction with Dutch operations. In the 1640s the Dutch seized some of Sri Lanka's coastal regions from the Portuguese. They remained there, often intermarrying with local people, until the British ousted them in the early 1800s and colonized Sri Lanka.

France also joined the competition, establishing a trading presence at Surat and Calcutta while building a military and commercial base at the southeast coast town of Pondicherry (pon-dir-CHEH-ree) in the later 1600s and early 1700s. Long-standing English-French political and commercial rivalries spilled over into conflict during the Seven Years War (1756–1763), during which the two nations fought in Europe, North America, the Caribbean, and Asia. The fierce battles for dominance in Southeast India destabilized the region's politics.

Eventually England, with a rapidly growing commercial economy, became the main threat to the Mughals, Dutch, and French. In 1600 British investors formed the British East India Company, and Company traders visited various ports. The English established a fort at Madras (muh-DRAS) (today known as Chennai) on India's southeast coast and a trading base at Surat in northwest India, where they forged a commercial alliance with the Parsis (PAHR-seez), Zoroastrian descendants of Persian refugees. In 1717 the English established bases at Bombay (today called Mumbai) and Calcutta (Kolkata), both sparsely populated backwaters, for collecting and exporting textiles, indigo, and saltpeter (an ingredient for gunpowder). Many Parsis left Surat for better prospects in Bombay, again working closely with the English for their mutual benefit.

Elsewhere English officials still had to negotiate with Mughals or local princes for trading privileges. When banditry grew rapidly as Mughal authority collapsed, the law and order in English-run ports attracted Indian settlers. Competition from Indian textile imports spurred English textile manufacturers to cut costs, helping stimulate English industrialization. By the mid-eighteenth century the English were strong enough to treat local rulers with less deference and expand their control into surrounding regions, often using military force against Indian resistance. From their Calcutta base in Bengal, they began their long military conquest, continually weakening what little remained of Mughal authority and eventually controlling nearly all of South Asia except a few small enclaves, such as Portuguese Goa and French Pondicherry. South Asians had often been conquered by outsiders of different cultural and religious backgrounds, such as the Mughals. But now India faced a major new challenge.

MAKE SURE YOU UNDERSTAND THESE KEY POINTS BEFORE MOVING ON

- The Muslim Mughal Empire attained great riches and, especially under Akbar, maintained an enlightened rule over religiously diverse India, but it began to decline after the fall of Akbar.

- The Indian economy, already strong, expanded greatly as extensive foreign trade brought an influx of silver and enriched entrepreneurs.

- Tensions existed between Indian Muslims and Hindus, though some were able to bridge the gap through mysticism and others joined sects such as the Sikhs that blended or transcended the dominant religions.

- The Dutch, French, and English all competed with each other and with the Portuguese for dominance of trade with India, with the English growing increasingly strong by the mid-eighteenth century.

aplia

Southeast Asia and Global Connections

How did Southeast Asia become more fully integrated into the world economy?

Diverse peoples, religions, ideas, and products had long met in cosmopolitan Southeast Asia, the region south of China and east of India. Southeast Asians participated in hemispheric trade, and most adopted Theravada Buddhism, Confucianism, or Islam. The Portuguese arrival at Melaka inaugurated a new era as European adventurers, traders, missionaries, and soldiers reshaped Malaya, the Philippine Islands, and parts of Indonesia. However, in most of Southeast Asia Western influence remained weak until the nineteenth century.

Southeast Asian Transitions and Societies

Southeast Asians experienced commercial growth, political change, increasingly productive agriculture, and expansion of Islam and Buddhism in this era, opening their cultures to the outside world. Increasing connections with European, Chinese, Arab, and Indian merchants spurred commerce between the 1400s and 1700s, with Southeast Asia remaining an essential hub in maritime trade linking East Asia with India and the Middle East. Merchants from the Middle East, Central Asia, Africa, and India stopped in the region's ports to exchange goods or wait for monsoon winds to shift.

This economic dynamism enhanced regional ports such as Melaka, Ayuthia (ah-YUT-uh-yuh) in Siam, Hoian (hoy-AHN) in Vietnam, Pegu (peh-GOO) in Burma's Irrawaddy Delta, and Banten (BAN-ten) in West Java. Thanks to increasing trade and the wealth this created, urban merchants gained political influence. Agriculture also remained a major activity, with new crops and rice varieties spurring population growth. Meanwhile, Theravada Buddhism dug deeper roots on the mainland, and Islam spread throughout the Malay Peninsula, Indonesian islands, and the southern Philippines.

Larger, more centralized states such as Burma, Siam, and Vietnam absorbed smaller neighboring states and remained vigorous (see Map 18.2). The kings of Ayuthia, a Theravada Buddhist state, governed much of Siam from 1350 to 1767, participating in maritime trade while expanding influence into Cambodia and small Lao **(laow)** states along the Mekong River. But Ayuthia's competition with Burma, Vietnam, and the largest Lao state, Lan Xang **(lan chang)**, for regional dominance occasionally sparked wars. In the 1560s a Burmese army ravaged Siam and sacked Ayuthia, carrying back to Burma thousands of Siamese prisoners reflecting diverse occupational skills: actor, actress, architect, artist, blacksmith, carpenter, coiffeur, cook, coppersmith, goldsmith, lacquer ware maker, painter, perfume maker, silversmith, stone carver, wood carver, and veterinarian.

Ayuthia eventually recovered and flourished. King Narai **(na-RY)** (r. 1656–1688) fostered a cultural renaissance, promoting literature and art, often with a Buddhist emphasis. Since Buddhist monks sponsored many village schools, Siam enjoyed one of the premodern world's highest literacy rates, providing writers an audience. For example, a long poem by Sri Mahosot **(shree ma-HO-sut)** describes courtship rituals of young people along the Ayuthia riverside during the evening: "O beautiful night! Excited voices on the riverbank. Couples closely embraced, they stare at each other. There is smiling, touching, singing in chorus, looking eye to eye. There is excitement, craving and longing forever."[7]

Reflecting hierarchy, the Siamese royal family and aristocracy remained aloof from commoners and a large slave class, while women operated village and town markets. But Siamese society was also tolerant. In 1636 a Dutch trader contrasted Siamese Buddhist tolerance with zealous Christian and Muslim proselytizing, observing that the Siamese did not condemn any "opinions, but believe that all, though of differing tenets, living virtuously, may be saved, all services which are performed with zeal being acceptable to the great God. And the Christians [and Muslims] are both permitted the free exercise of their religions."[8] Ayuthia's openness to merchants and creative people from abroad also made it a vibrant crossroads of goods and ideas. A French visitor in the 1680s wrote that "since all nations are well received in Siam…free [to] exercise…their religion…scarcely a single nation…is not found there."[9]

However, increasing activity by English, French, and Dutch traders proved challenging. King Narai sent three diplomatic missions to Louis XIV in France to obtain Western maps and scientific knowledge while employing foreigners as officials, including a Persian Muslim as prime minister and a Greek merchant, Constantine Phaulkon **(FALL-kin)**, as superintendent of foreign trade. After learning that the opportunistic Phaulkon and French officials planned to convert Narai to Christianity and station French troops, in 1688 Ayuthia executed Phaulkon and expelled French diplomats, missionaries, and merchants

from Siam. The Siamese, who once welcomed foreign traders, now mistrusted Europeans. Dutch traders remained but faced fierce competition, especially from Chinese.

Trade networks fostered Islamic expansion. Southeast Asian Muslims often made the long pilgrimage to Mecca, and some sent their sons to the Middle East for study, reinforcing links between the regions. Various societies adapted Islam to their own cultures. Hence many Javanese superimposed Islam, often Sufism, on the existing Hinduism and mystical animism (spirit worship), producing an eclectic, tolerant mix. Some other peoples, including most Malays, embraced a more orthodox Islam. Muslim merchants, who preferred ports with Muslim rulers, enriched these states. Mixing Islam and maritime trade encouraged connections to the wider world. For example, Hamzah Fansuri **(HOM-sah fan-SIR-ee)**, a Sufi poet from Sumatra famed for his mystical and romantic writings who once lived in Ayuthia and then Baghdad, was a follower of an earlier Spain-born mystic, Ibn al-Arabi (1165–1240), who taught, like Vedanta Hinduism, that all reality is one and everything that exists is part of the divine.

Rooted in patriarchal Arab traditions, Islam diminished women's rights and traditional independence in some Indonesian societies. Acheh **(AH-cheh)** in northern Sumatra, where four successive women ruled in the 1600s, now prohibited women from holding royal power. Yet, Muslim royal courts on Java and other islands were filled with hundreds, sometimes thousands, of women—wives, concubines, attendants, guards, or textile workers making *batik*, the beautiful cloth produced by a wax and dying process. Batik arts later spread throughout the world.

Southeast Asia's wealth and resources, especially spices such as cloves, nutmeg, and pepper, attracted European merchants and conquerors. The process began with the Portuguese, whose occupation of Melaka began a powerful and destabilizing European presence that transformed Southeast Asia between 1500 and 1914. As the victorious admiral Albuquerque boasted: "Melaka is the source of all the spices and drugs which the [Muslims] carry every year to [the Middle East]. Cairo and Mecca will be entirely ruined, and Venice will receive no spices unless her merchants go and buy them in Portugal."[10] A few years later the Portuguese brutally conquered the Spice Islands, known as Maluku **(muh-LOO-ku)** (Moluccas), in northeast Indonesia, gaining control of the valuable spice trade to Europe. The sultanate of Acheh in northern Sumatra forged an anti-Portuguese military alliance from 1530 to 1570 with the distant Ottoman Empire, but Ottoman naval power in the Indian Ocean remained weak and proved short-lived.

The Portuguese employed brutal force against rivals and challengers. Jesuit missionary Saint Francis Xavier, a Spaniard, described Portuguese behavior in the Spice Islands as little more than discovering new ways of conjugating the verb *to steal*. But, as in India, Portuguese power proved short-lived. Like the East African ports the Portuguese occupied

[7]Quoted in Klaus Wenk, *Thai Literature: An Introduction* (Bangkok: White Lotus, 1995), 14—16.

[8]Joost Schouten, quoted in Michael Smithies, *Descriptions of Old Siam* (Kuala Lumpur: Oxford University Press, 1995), 19.

[9]Father Tachard, quoted in Victor Purcell, *The Chinese in Southeast Asia*, 2nd ed. (London: Oxford University Press, 1965), 90.

[10]Quoted in Nicholas Tarling, "Mercantilism and Missionaries: Impact and Accommodation," in *Eastern Asia: An Introductory History*, ed. Colin Mackerras, 3rd ed. (Frenches Forest, NSW, Australia: Longmans, 2000), 115.

MAP 18.2 **SOUTHEAST ASIA IN THE EARLY MODERN ERA** Much of Southeast Asia remained independent, able to deflect European ambitions, but the Portuguese had captured the port of Melaka, Timor, and the Moluccas (Maluku), and the Spanish had colonized the Philippines. In the 1600s the Dutch displaced the Portuguese from Melaka and the Moluccas and ruled part of Java from Batavia. © 2015 Cengage Learning

earlier, Melaka languished because Muslim merchants faced higher taxes and intolerance of Islam, and in 1641 the Dutch replaced the Portuguese in Melaka. However, a small Catholic, Portuguese-speaking community still lives there. For several centuries Portuguese became a trading language in some Asian coastal regions, from Basra in Iraq to Vietnamese ports, and the Indonesian and Malay languages contain words of Portuguese origin.

Portuguese activities spurred the Spanish, Dutch, English, and French to compete for markets, resources, Christian converts, and power in Southeast Asia. The Spanish conquered the Philippines, the Dutch gained some control of Indian Ocean maritime trade and conquered Java and the

Spice Islands, and the English mainly sought trade relations. Beginning in 1615, the French sought trade with Vietnam and also dispatched Catholic missionaries, who recruited a small Vietnamese following. The French also changed the Vietnamese writing system, which was Chinese; to undercut Confucian influence, French missionaries created a romanized Vietnamese alphabet, and in the twentieth century this became the official writing system. Despite these influences, Southeast Asian states such as Siam, Vietnam, Burma, and Acheh were strong enough to resist over three hundred years of persistent effort by Westerners to gain complete political, social, and economic domination, which they achieved only by 1914.

The Philippines Under Spanish Colonization

The greatest Western impact before 1800 came in the Philippine Islands. The first Spanish ships to reach the islands in 1521, commanded by Ferdinand Magellan, were part of the first successful effort to circumnavigate the world. Magellan pressured the Filipinos he encountered to adopt Christianity, ordering a local chief to burn all his peoples' religious figures and replace them with a cross. These arrogant demands resulted in his death during a skirmish with hostile Filipinos. Today, on the Cebu Island beach where Magellan died, a memorial honors Lapulapu (**LAH-pu-LAH-pu**), the chief leading the attack, as the first Filipino to repel European aggression.

When, after visiting the Spice Islands, Magellan's ships returned to Spain, they had proved that Asia could be reached by sailing west from Europe. But Magellan had also chanced upon an archipelago inhabited by diverse peoples speaking over a hundred Malay languages and scattered across seven thousand islands, with the majority living on the two largest, Luzon (**loo-ZON**) and Mindanao (**min-duh-NOW**). The largest Filipino political units were villages led by chiefs. Muslims occupied the southernmost islands, but most Filipinos mixed belief in one supreme being with animism; Spaniards considered them immoral devil worshipers. While little cultural influence from India or China reached these remote islands, a few hundred Chinese traders lived in major towns, and some Filipino maritime traders traveled as far as Melaka and Burma. Many Filipinos used a simple writing system.

Four decades after Magellan, the Spaniards returned to conquer and evangelize the Philippines, which they renamed after their monarch, Philip II, known as "the most Catholic of kings." The militarily superior Spanish had little trouble conquering and co-opting local chiefs, but they never completely pacified the Muslims (**Moros**) in the south. Today some southern Muslims seek independence from the Christian-dominated Philippines. As a potential base for trade with China, the Spaniards set up their colonial government in Manila, located in Luzon along a fine natural harbor.

The Spanish ruled over the Philippines for nearly three centuries (1565–1898), imposing Catholicism and many aspects of Spanish culture on Filipinos with a policy known as **Hispanization**. The Catholic Church governed various regions and acquired great wealth as priests collected taxes and sold crops such as sugar. With missionary efforts financed by the Spanish crown, several Catholic religious orders competed to gain the most converts. To better control and evangelize, missionaries required people to move into towns, and the church controlled what little formal education existed, emphasizing religious doctrine. As in Latin America, Spaniards destroyed nearly all pre-Spanish writings as "pagan." Eventually around 85 percent of Filipinos adopted Roman Catholicism.

However, Filipinos disgusted the Spanish by incorporating their animist traditions into Catholicism, such as by transforming friendly spirits into Christian saints and magic into miracles attributed to Jesus or the Virgin Mary. Some Filipinos

MESTIZO FAMILY IN PHILIPPINES This painting shows three well-dressed Mestizos in Manila in the eighteenth century. Mestizos of Spanish and Chinese background played key roles in colonial life.

used religious festivals to subtly protest Spanish rule, rewriting Spanish passion plays on the life and death of Jesus into plays expressing anticolonial sentiments; for example, they presented Jesus as a social activist of humble background tormented by a corrupt ruling class. Given Spanish conquerors' contempt for the common people, few Filipinos could rise in the church hierarchy or in government.

The Philippine colonial economy, based on plantation agriculture and tenant farming, implanted a permanent gap between extraordinarily rich landowners and impoverished peasants. Emphasizing lucrative cash crops, such as sugar and hemp, for sale on the world market, Spanish officials, corporations, and Catholic orders owned most farmland, with the Filipino tenant farmers and plantation workers living almost like medieval European serfs. Peasant revolts became common. Priests and landowners told Filipinos their religious duty was to labor hard for others, receiving their just rewards later in heaven.

But although the Spanish created a country and expanded the economy, they did not construct a cohesive society; instead, regional and ethnic loyalties remained dominant. Spaniards occupied the top spots, mostly living in Manila

Moros The Spanish term for the Muslim peoples of the southern Philippines.

Hispanization The process by which, over nearly three centuries of Spanish colonial rule beginning in 1565, the Catholic religion and Spanish culture were imposed on the Philippine people.

and often in luxury, and few outside the church learned local languages. As in Latin America, many returned to Spain after acquiring wealth. Below them were Filipino families descending from chiefs and mixed-descent mestizos, the result of unions between Spanish men with Filipinas. Chinese immigrants worked as merchants and craftsmen, some becoming rich but most remaining middle class, and many Chinese became Catholic. Chinese men frequently married Filipinas, fostering a Chinese mestizo community. As a result, many Philippine leaders today have Chinese or Spanish mestizo ancestry. But while the Spanish needed Chinese as middlemen, they also despised, feared, persecuted, and sometimes expelled them. Spanish forces occasionally slaughtered residents of Manila's large Chinatown.

Most Filipinos, whom Spaniards called **Indios** (Indies people), occupied the lowest social status and faced many legal restrictions; hence, they were prohibited from dressing like Spaniards. While Filipinos retained close family ties, Filipinas lost their high position in pre-Spanish society because the Spanish culture and church devalued women. Female priestesses integral to Filipino animism were pushed to society's margins by Catholic priests, one of whom described the priestesses as "loathsome creatures, foul, obscene, truly damnable. My task [is] to reduce them to order."[11] But despite male prejudice and narrowing gender roles, Filipinas still controlled family finances and engaged in small-scale trade.

Indonesia and the Dutch

In the seventeenth century the Dutch arrived, replacing Portugal as the region's dominant European power. Holland was Europe's most prosperous society during the 1600s, thanks partly to its trade and conquests in Asia, especially Indonesia. In 1595 a Dutch fleet visited the Spice Islands and returned with spices. Over the following several decades the Dutch, after bloody battles, dislodged the Portuguese from most of their scattered outposts, including Maluku. In 1641 they finally captured Portuguese-controlled Melaka, but the city never recovered its earlier glory. The Dutch sought wealth but, unlike the Portuguese and Spanish, cared little about spreading their culture and religion.

Over three hundred years the Dutch gradually controlled the Indonesian islands, except for Portuguese-ruled Timor. They ruthlessly eliminated all competition, such as by massacring English residents on Ambon **(am-BOHN)** Island in 1623. In 1659, as Dutch forces attacked and occupied the prosperous trading city of Makassar **(muh-KAS-uhr)**, in southeast Sulawesi **(SOO-la-WAY-see)**, the city's sultan asked: "Do you believe that God has preserved for your trade alone islands which lie so distant from your homeland?"[12]

Indios The Filipinos at the bottom of the Spanish colonial social structure, who faced many legal restrictions.

Both sides sparked conflict, but the militarily superior Dutch often slaughtered their Indonesian opponents by the thousands. Well-organized, resourceful, and shrewd, they allied themselves with one state against a rival state, sometimes drawing them into civil wars or sparking stiff resistance. For example, Shaikh Yusuf (ca. 1624–1699), a Sulawesi-born, Arabia-educated spiritual adviser to the sultan of Banten in western Java, led two thousand followers into an unsuccessful holy war against the Dutch in 1683.

For several centuries the Dutch East India Company, which had great capital and large resources for pursuing profit, administered the Indonesian bases. With Holland ten months away by boat, the Company had little guidance and few restraints as it pursued a trade monopoly in Southeast Asia. If Spice Islanders grew restless, Dutch forces might exterminate them or carry them off as slaves to Java, Ceylon, or South Africa, as happened in 1621 to the Banda (BAN-duh) Islands' fifteen hundred people. To increase demand and reduce supply, the Dutch sometimes chopped down spice-growing trees and bushes, leaving the population with no income.

Eventually the Dutch concentrated on the rich island of Java, which enjoyed a flourishing mercantile economy, living standards comparable to those of many western Europeans, several competing sultanates, skillful traders, and large cities with multiethnic populations drawn from throughout Asia. Javanese artisans were noted for their fine craftsmanship, and the island's smiths made perhaps the world's finest steel swords. Javanese women were prominent in business alongside the men, as an English observer noted: "It is usual for a husband to entrust his pecuniary affairs entirely to his wife. The women alone attend the markets, and conduct all the buying and selling."[13]

Capitalizing on Java's political divisions, the Dutch slowly extended their power after establishing a base at a village they renamed Batavia, on the northwestern coast, in 1619. Batavia later grew into today's Jakarta. By 1800 the Dutch controlled most of Java, ruling some districts through local aristocrats. They also invited more Chinese traders to come to Java, where they had operated for centuries. Over time, Dutch and Chinese entrepreneurs slowly displaced Javanese merchants, once major players in the Asian economy.

Soon Holland concentrated on making Indonesia a source of wealth, forcing the rice-growing peasants in the west Java and Sumatra highlands to grow coffee through annual quotas. Coffee, domesticated in Ethiopia and grown in southern Arabia, had become a popular beverage in both the Middle East and Europe. The Dutch made huge profits from monopolizing the world coffee trade, enough to finance much of Holland's later industrialization. Thus Westerners called coffee "java."

Inequality characterized colonial society. Europeans occupied the top layer, followed by mixed-descent Eurasians and

[11]Pedro Chirino, quoted in Carolyn Brewer, "From Animist 'Priestess' to Catholic Priest: The Re/gendering of Religious Roles in the Philippines, 1521–1685," in *Other Pasts: Women, Gender and History in Early Modern Southeast Asia*, ed. Barbara Watson Andaya (Honolulu: Center for Southeast Asian Studies, University of Hawaii at Manoa, 2000), 69.
[12]Quoted in Felipe Fernandez-Armesto, *Millennium: A History of the Last Thousand Years* (New York: Scribner, 1995), 234.
[13]Thomas Stamford Raffles, quoted in Anthony Reid, *Southeast Asia in the Age of Commerce, 1450–1680*, vol. 1 (New Haven, CT: Yale University Press, 1993), 164.

BATAVIA The Dutch built a port they called Batavia on the northwest coast of Java, shown in this painting from ca. 1656 which features the fortress. Batavia grew rapidly as the political and commercial center of the Dutch empire in Southeast Asia.

the co-opted aristocracy, who encouraged peasants to treat aristocratic officials with great awe. The middle class was mostly Chinese. Like the Spaniards, the Dutch feared the growing Chinese community, sometimes massacring Chinese in Batavia. Denied real power, Javanese royal courts turned inward, creating more fluid, graceful, and stylized royal dances and intricate batik fabrics.

Many Dutch found Javanese culture seductive, taking local wives, owning slaves, dressing in Javanese clothes, and indulging in delicious spicy curries, now enriched by American chilies. Most Dutch lived in Batavia, which was built to resemble a city in Holland, with close-packed, stuffy houses and stagnant canals poorly suited to the tropical climate. The puritanical Dutch wore heavy woolen clothes but bathed only once a week. Like many Southeast Asian cities, Batavia had a multiethnic society.

Southeast Asians and the World Economy

With the Portuguese, Dutch, and Spanish exporting luxury items and natural resources from their colonies, Southeast Asia became an even more crucial part of the world economy, reshaping global commerce. After the founding of Manila in 1571, the first hub linking Asia and the Americas across the Pacific and soon a multicultural crossroads of the East Asian, Southeast Asian, and American markets, Asian products, including Chinese silk and porcelain, were exported directly to Mexico and from there to Europe. Spanish galleons then returned to Manila from Mexico with European goods, mail, personnel, and vast amounts of silver to pay for Asian goods, draining Spanish imperial coffers and enriching Asian treasuries. Over half the silver mined in the Americas ended up in China. American silver spurred Asian economies, encouraging increased production of Philippine sugar, Chinese tea, and Indian textiles.

In this highly speculative, "riches or ruin," Manila galleon trade, Spanish businessmen bet their fortunes that the galleons would arrive in Mexico safely. Pirates, storms, and other obstacles made voyages dangerous, and some never completed their trips. This unpredictability fostered a "get rich quick" mentality rather than a long-term strategy for Philippine prosperity.

In spite of the changes, Southeast Asians retained considerable continuity with the past. The West was not yet dominant in either political or economic spheres, except in a few widely scattered outposts such as Melaka, the Spice Islands, and the Philippines. Europeans still had to compete with Chinese, Arab, Indian, and Southeast Asian merchants. The Vietnamese, continuing their long expansion down the Vietnamese coast, annexed the Mekong Delta in the 1600s, while the Siamese forced the French to leave. Only by the eighteenth century did Southeast Asian societies, suffering from internal strife and increasingly expensive government structures, begin to collapse under the weight of accelerating Western military and economic activity.

MAKE SURE YOU UNDERSTAND THESE KEY POINTS BEFORE MOVING ON

- Increased trade in Southeast Asia led to greater political centralization and increased the influence of major world religions such as Islam and Buddhism.

- Europeans, beginning with the violent Portuguese and later including the Spanish, Dutch, English, and French, were attracted by Southeast Asia's riches and resources.

- The militaristic Dutch came to dominate Indonesia, particularly Java, which they turned into a highly profitable coffee exporter.

- As a result of European colonization, Southeast Asia entered the world economy, though European speculators often focused on making quick money rather than strengthening the region's economy for the long term.

aplia

Early Modern China and New Challenges

What factors enabled China to remain one of the world's strongest and most dynamic societies?

Two dynasties, the Ming followed by the Qing **(ching)**, ruled China between the overthrow of the Mongols in the 1300s and the advent of a republic in 1912, together making these centuries one of the great eras of orderly government and social stability (see Map 18.3). During this time China remained one of the most industrialized societies, boasting a vibrant culture and economy. Although encounters with Europeans indicated the challenges ahead just as China experienced political and technological decay, no other country could match the size, wealth, and power of Early Modern China.

The Later Ming Dynasty

China under the Ming (1368–1644) remained dynamic. The imperial political system, administered by mandarins, was supported by highly productive agriculture and the world's largest, most diversified commercial economy. Although heavily regulated, commerce provided numerous products and services. Along with silk and tea, cotton textiles were produced and exported to Japan and Southeast Asia for silver and spices. Rebuilding of the Grand Canal facilitated shipment and stimulated manufacturing. For centuries a world leader in science and technology, in the late Ming and early Qing periods China developed color woodblock printing, as well as better cotton gins, spinning wheels, and other technologies for textile and silk production.

Yet, Ming China turned somewhat inward, concentrating on home affairs and defending the northern borders. Always self-sufficient and self-centered, China became increasingly ethnocentric; the Ming court, viewing foreign states mainly as tribute providers, ended the great maritime voyages of the early 1400s. Although some foreign merchants still came and Chinese merchants illegally went to Southeast Asia, the later Ming encouraged isolation, in contrast to earlier Tang, Song, and Yuan cosmopolitanism. Chinese were not patrolling the seas when the first Portuguese ships arrived.

Eventually misrule and other mounting problems precipitated dynastic change. Crop failures and a terrible plague tied to climate change killed millions in north China and around Eurasia, and in the 1590s the treasury became depleted after Ming military forces defended their Korean vassal from Japanese invasion. Meanwhile, Japanese and Chinese pirates ravaged the southern coast and peasant revolts erupted. These problems opened the doors to the Manchus **(MAN-chooz)**, a seminomadic pastoral people from Manchuria just northeast of China whose forces swept into China on horseback, routing the Ming. It took several decades to occupy and pacify the country, with Ming loyalists holding out in the south and on the large offshore island of Taiwan for several decades.

Qing Empire, Society, Thought, and Culture

The new Manchu-installed Qing dynasty ruled from 1644 to 1912. The first Qing rulers, exceptionally able, governed, like much their Chinese predecessors, through the mandarin bureaucracy, patronizing Confucianism but also added their own innovations. Although forbidding intermarriage with

Chinese, the Manchus knew that to succeed they needed to adopt Chinese institutions and culture to win Chinese support. Thus, like most earlier foreign rulers, they assimilated Chinese ways and relied on scholarly degree holders educated in Confucian classics for administration. Yet, they governed with a smaller bureaucracy and lighter taxes than the Ming.

Some Qing emperors were outstanding managers, aware of their awesome responsibility. The reflective Kangzi (**kang-shee**) (r. 1661–1722), a writer and painter exemplifying the Confucian ideal of virtuous ruler, wrote that "giving life to the people and killing people—these are the powers that an emperor has. He knows that administrative errors in government bureaus can be rectified, but that a criminal who is executed cannot be brought back to life any more than a chopped string can be joined together again."[14] Kangzi toured the provinces inspecting public works and joining hunting expeditions. To bring Manchus and Chinese together, his imperial robes included elements of Manchu horse-riding attire and Chinese dragon motifs. His son and successor, Yongzheng (**young-cheng**) (r. 1723–1735), improved social conditions, ordering anyone held in hereditary servile status (slavery) anywhere in the empire to be freed.

The Manchus created the greatest Eurasian land empire since the Mongols. Qing armies reasserted Chinese control of the western and northern frontier, annexing Mongolia, Tibet (long a Chinese tributary state), and Xinjiang (**shin-chang**) ("New Dominions"), a desert region inhabited by Turkish-speaking Muslims. While Tibetans shared with Manchus and Mongols the mystical version of Buddhism called Lamaism (**LAH-muh-iz-uhm**), they differed culturally from the Chinese. The Qing also incorporated Taiwan, which was inhabited by Austronesian peoples, and the Chinese began immigrating there in the 1600s.

---

[14]Quoted in Jonathan S. Spence, *Emperor of China: Self-Portrait of Kang-Hsi* (New York: Vintage, 1975), 29.

MAP 18.3 **QING CHINA AND EAST ASIA IN THE EARLY MODERN ERA** Qing China remained the colossus of eastern Eurasia, controlling a huge empire that included Tibet, Xinjiang, and Mongolia. Korea and Vietnam remained tributary states of China, but the Russians expanded into eastern Siberia. The Japanese partly secluded themselves from the outside world. © 2015 Cengage Learning

Roger Viollet Collection/Getty Images

ENTRANCE OF EMPEROR KANGZI IN BEIJING The Qing emperor Kangzi had one of the longest reigns in Chinese history. In this print of Beijing from 1670, crowds gather as Kangzi prepares for public celebrations.

The Qing retained China's examination system. Ming and Qing China owed their political and social stability partly to the gentry, landlords and moneylenders who dominated rural life in this agrarian-based bureaucratic empire by combining political office with land ownership. Able to afford tutors, gentry men received a formal education and held scholarly degrees. The mid-Qing novel, *The Story of the Stone*, revealed the expectations for gentry sons: "A boy's proper business is to read books in order to gain an understanding of things, so that when he grows up he can play his part in governing the country."[15]

Together the gentry and Manchu rulers promoted the status quo. However, some gentry could not negotiate the dynastic change. An example is the celebrated late Ming essayist, poet, historian, and degree holder Zhang Dai (**chang die**) (1597–1680), who lived a comfortable life while supporting a wife, several consorts, and eight or ten children. Zhang spent his ample leisure time at a lakeside villa in Hangzhou (**hahng choh**), visiting tourist sites, collecting handcrafted lanterns, playing the lute, and participating in a crab-eating club. However, the Zhangs ran afoul of changing political winds during the dangerous Ming-Qing transition and were reduced to poverty.

Women had a complex status in patriarchal Qing society. The elite debated women's education, and some intellectuals encouraged it. Some women from gentry and merchant families, educated informally, read and even wrote literature. However,

elite women were hobbled by footbinding, a custom that was introduced half a millennium earlier but that only became widespread during the Ming. In the lower classes, peasant women, usually illiterate, played key economic roles, for example, by improving and promoting spinning and weaving tools. Men planted but women picked the cotton, processed it into yarn, and wove the finished product for sale. An eighteenth-century government report observed that "whole peasant families assemble, young and old; the mother-in-law leads her son's wives, the mother supervises her daughters; when the wicker lantern is lit and the starlight and moonlight come slanting down, still the click-clack of the spindle-wheels comes from the house."[16] But many peasant women were gradually marginalized as their menfolk or large commercial farmers, seeking greater profits, took over their livelihood. Some women in coastal villages even joined, and sometimes commanded, pirate fleets.

Chinese attitudes toward homosexuality fluctuated. Visiting Europeans were shocked by Chinese tolerance toward homosexuality, which was fiercely punished in Europe. However, some Chinese scholars, blaming the Ming downfall on lax morality, convinced the Qing to penalize homosexuality. Yet, Qing punishments were mild, and repression gradually ebbed. At least half of Qing emperors are thought to have had same-sex bedmates. Homosexual relationships also did not preclude marriage and family; one Qing emperor with a male lover fathered twenty-seven children with his wives and concubines.

Philosophy contributed to Ming and Qing stability. Most Chinese followed the eclectic mix of Confucianism, Buddhism, and Daoism that had evolved in the Classical Era. Nonetheless, during the Ming and early Qing Confucian thought enjoyed a renaissance with an interpretation of Confucianism known as neo-Confucianism, which incorporated elements of Buddhism and Daoism, stressed rational thinking, and reemphasized people's natural goodness.

Like European Renaissance and Enlightenment thinkers, Ming and Qing philosophers sought knowledge regardless of whether it conformed to religious doctrine. Like Sir Francis Bacon and Rene Descartes, the neo-Confucian Wang Yang-Ming (1472–1529) pondered the unity of knowledge and

---

[15]Quoted in Richard J. Smith, *China's Cultural Heritage: The Ch'ing Dynasty, 1644–1913* (Boulder, CO: Westview Press, 1983), 210.

[16]Quoted in Francesca Bray, "Towards a Critical History of Non-Western Technology," in *China and Historical Capitalism*, ed. Timothy Brook and Gregory Blue (New York: Cambridge University Press, 1999), 184.

conduct and wondered how people know the external world, concluding that "whatever we see, feel, hear, or in any wise conceive or understand is as real as ever."[17] Like Bacon and John Locke, scholars contended that the mind is reason. Others critically studied the past. Like Enlightenment thinkers, a few Chinese scholars studied knowledge from other societies. Philosopher and poet Tai Chen made comparative studies of Chinese and Western mathematics. However, neo-Confucianism became the new orthodoxy, limiting Chinese interest in alternative ideas. Some Qing scholars argued that no more writing was needed because the truth had been made clear by ancient thinkers: just practice their teachings. By the 1700s, few Chinese intellectuals showed interest in practical inquiry or technological development. Thus, although neo-Confucianism contributed to the unparalleled continuity of Chinese society, it fostered an intellectual conformity that was hostile to originality or ideas from outside.

China's art and literature, in contrast, remained creative. As they had for centuries, artists painted landscapes featuring misty distances, soaring mountains, and angular pine trees. However, many innovative painters also drew on Daoist mysticism, creating fanciful, untraditional scenes. The eccentric Zhu Da (ca. 1626–1705) painted bizarre nature: huge lotuses in ponds, birds with wise-looking eyes, surging landscapes. In literature, Qing authors wrote some of China's greatest fiction. Failing the civil service examinations, some scholars became writers. *The Scholars*, by Wu Jingzi (**woo ching-see**), satirized the examination system and revealed the foibles of the pompous and ignorant. The 1,300-page *The Story of the Stone*, by Cao Xueqin (**tsao swee-chin**), used a large, declining gentry family to discuss, and sometimes satirize, Qing life. Meanwhile, Qing scholars compiled the world's greatest encyclopedia, five thousand volumes long.

China and the World Economy

China had flourishing industrial production, extensive foreign trade, and the world's largest and best-integrated commercial economy (see Witness to the Past: A Chinese Official's Duties). Encouraged by government taxation policies, the fertile lower Yangzi (**yahng-zeh**) Basin gradually became China's industrial heartland, commercial hub, and most prosperous region. Cities like Nanjing and Suzhou enjoyed living standards comparable to those in England and Holland, both enriched by overseas colonization. A French visitor in the early 1700s, amazed that China's internal trade vastly exceeded the commerce of all Europe, wrote that the Chinese put "merit ceaselessly in competition with merit, diligence with diligence, and work with work. The whole country is like a perpetual fair."[18] Heavy Qing investment in infrastructure, such as canals and dams, also expanded the economy.

CHINESE CERAMICS China became famous for its porcelain products, much desired around the world. This tea service, painted with peonies, is from the eighteenth century.

A major force in the international economy, China exported porcelain, cotton textiles, silk, tea, quicksilver, and zinc, receiving silver from Europeans as payment. Its resources and market for imports influenced economic decisions made in Southeast Asia, the Middle East, Europe, and the Americas. At the same time, the population grew from the introduction of American crops such as corn (maize), sweet potatoes, and peanuts, as well as from Chinese development of a new fast-growing rice. China's population numbered some 100 million in 1500 and reached 250 or 300 million by 1750, a quarter of the world total. Several major cities had over a million residents, including Nanjing (**nahn-JING**), Beijing, and Guangzhou (**gwong-joe**) (known in the West as Canton).

However, despite this economic dynamism, full-scale capitalism and industrialization did not develop. The Tang, Song, and Ming commercial revolutions and technological advances failed to foster the revolutionary changes that transformed western European feudalism into capitalism. One reason was that, unlike England and Holland, China lacked an overseas empire to provide investment capital. Another basic difference from Europe was the continuity of Chinese traditions, with successive dynasties continuing the essential Han pattern until 1912. The bureaucracy-gentry, often contemptuous of merchant values, could absorb the effects of economic growth, keeping merchants politically weak, whereas in Europe economic growth undermined the old system. With population growth, China also had no labor shortage that might spur technological innovation. China's economy satisfied basic needs well.

Unlike early modern Europe, where business enterprises increasingly influenced politics, the imperial government restricted and taxed merchants. Although a wealthy Chinese merchant class existed and laws encouraged markets, the

[17]Quoted in John A. Harrison, *The Chinese Empire* (New York: Harcourt Brace Jovanovich, 1972), 335.
[18]Jean-Baptiste DuHalde, quoted in Carolyn Blunden and Mark Elvin, *The Cultural Atlas of China* (Alexandria, VA: Stonehenge, 1991), 144.

WITNESS TO THE PAST

A Chinese Official's Duties

Chen Hongmou (1696–1771) had a long career serving the Qing dynasty as a provincial governor in various provinces. In the following excerpts from some of his letters and other writings, he discusses the duties of an official from the perspective of Confucian ideals in a highly bureaucratic empire.

We in official service ought to look at all matters from the point of view of what is best for the people's livelihood. We must plan for the long term, rather than for the moment. We should concentrate on the substantial and practical, rather than disguising our inaction with empty words. To do otherwise would violate the court's basic principle that officials exist for the good of the people....

The way of shepherding the people involves no more than educating and nurturing them....By "nurturing" I mean construction and maintenance of irrigation works, encouragement of land reclamation, and patronage of community granaries....If the people can be made to produce a surplus, store it, and allow it to accumulate over the years, their well-being will be ensured. By "education" I mean promoting civilized behavior, diligently managing public schools, and widely distributing classical texts. Schools are the fountainheads of popular customs. If educational practice is correct, popular customs will be virtuous....

Therefore, officials must look to the long term, not the present, and in so doing put the interests of the people ahead of their own [career] concerns....In governing, good intentions and good policies alone are insufficient. There are those policies that sound admirable but that prove impossible to implement in practice....If the local official truly approaches each matter from the standpoint of the people's livelihood, in carrying out any new policy he will first thoroughly canvas local public opinion on the matter. He will then consider every aspect of its implementation, noting in which aspects it is advantageous to the people and in which aspects it will cause them hardship. If the advantages outweigh the hardships, implement it.

The court appoints officials for the benefit of the people. Officials must cherish the people and exercise their authority to the fullest in their behalf. It is no accident that the formal title of a district magistrate is "one who *knows* the district," nor that he is referred to as the "*local* official"...there should be no matter within their locality about which he does not know....Their relationship is exactly like that of a family....

I have drawn up the following list of items a local official should keep in mind in determining how to conduct himself.

1. *Maintain genuine commitment....*With genuine commitment, your energies will never flag; without it, whatever ability you possess will be wasted.
3. *Provide exemplars of civilized behavior.* Magistrates should make regular tours of the countryside, to investigate local customs, good and bad, and to meet with local community leaders to clarify for their benefit what is considered legal and proper.
6. *Keep a tight rein on your clerks.* Failure to control their predations will inevitably generate popular resentment....
8. *Prevent harassment of the people.* Evil government functionaries and local tyrants will inevitably come up with ways to harass the people...No matter how hardworking the magistrate, and how well intentioned the laws, such harassments can be prevented only through constant and diligent scrutiny....

THINKING ABOUT THE READING

1. What do the excerpts tell us about Confucian ideals of government?
2. How did officials promote political stability?
3. What challenges did an official confront?

Source: Sources of Chinese Tradition: From 1600 Through the Twentieth Century, compiled by Wm. Theodore de Bary and Richard Lufrano, 2nd ed., vol. 2 (New York: Columbia University Press, 2000), 162–167. © 2000 Columbia University Press.

government, fearing that powerful merchants might threaten the regime, circumscribed their activities. Industrialists and merchants organized themselves into government-certified guilds responsible for their members' behavior. Although many Song dynasty mandarins had come from merchant backgrounds and protected their families and business generally, by the Qing this was no longer true. The government also maintained monopolies over producing and distributing essential commodities, including arms, textiles, pottery, salt, iron, and wine.

Reflecting a centralized, agriculture-based empire, Ming emperors stopped Zheng He's overseas voyages, prohibited emigration, and ordered Chinese merchants to return home. However, wily Chinese merchants, especially from mountainous Fujian (**fu-JEN**) province on the southeast coast, continued going abroad, remaining prominent in Southeast Asian and Japanese trade. Since Fujian offered poor conditions for farming, Fujian men, as a Chinese official commented,

"made fields from the sea." But, unlike European rivals, they received no official support and often had to bribe local Chinese officials. Thus Chinese energies focused inward at a fateful turning point in world history, leaving the world's oceans open to Western enterprise.

China's Encounters with the West

Although turning inward in the later Ming, China did not cut itself off completely from the outside world. In the 1500s and 1600s European ships seeking silk, tea, porcelain, lacquer ware, and other products reached Chinese shores. The Portuguese landed on the China coast in 1514, beginning a troubled relationship with China while earning reputations as pirates and religious fanatics. With their naval forces spread thinly around Asia and Africa, the Portuguese could not match Chinese armed junks. But in 1557, to stop the piracy, the emperor allowed a Portuguese trading base at a small unpopulated peninsula, Macao (**muh-cow**), near Guangzhou on the southeast coast. With Qing decline, Portugal transformed Macao from trading base into the first Western colony on Chinese soil.

Christian missionaries, especially Jesuits, became active in late Ming China. In 1583 the most influential Jesuit, Italian Matteo Ricci (**ma-TAY-o REE-chee**) (1552–1610), a brilliant scholar and linguist trained in law, mathematics, and geography, arrived to study the Confucian classics and foster interest in Christianity among Confucian scholars. Impressing officials with his great learning, Ricci began training young scholars for the civil service exams. Eventually the emperor allowed Ricci and his Jesuit colleagues to settle in the capital, Beijing. Ricci became a scientific adviser to the imperial court, helping improve clocks, calendars, and astronomical observations. On Ricci's death the Chinese buried him with honors in Beijing. Yet, Ricci converted only a few to his faith.

Thanks to Jesuits, some Chinese leaders became interested in Western scientific knowledge. The emperor Kangzi wrote:

> *I often worked several hours a day with [the Jesuits]. I examined each stage of the forging of a cannon. I worked on clocks and mechanics. [Father] Pereira taught me to play a tune on the harpsichord....I also learned to calculate the weight and volume of spheres, cubes, and cones, and to measure distance and the angles of riverbanks.*[19]

A few Chinese even visited Europe. The Christian convert Michael Alphonsus Shen demonstrated chopstick techniques for French king Louis XIV and catalogued Chinese books in the Oxford University library. With more wealth and advanced technology than Europe, China much impressed the Italian Jesuits, whose letters describing Chinese ideas and inventions circulated widely in Europe. Jesuits lived like mandarins and wore Chinese clothing, and their admiration of Chinese traditions also led them to harmonize Christianity with Chinese philosophy, both to attract support from Chinese scholars and to avoid Christian doctrines incompatible with Confucianism.

However, despite Jesuit activity, by 1700 only some 100,000 Chinese had become Catholics, a tiny percentage of the vast population. Less tolerant missionaries who followed the early Jesuits made even less progress, and after the pope prohibited mixing Christianity and Confucianism, the faith became less appealing. Many Chinese also considered Christianity intellectually false

and resented the arrogant missionary enterprise. The emperor Yongzheng asked the missionaries: "What would you say if I sent a troop of Buddhist monks into your country to preach their doctrines? You want all Chinese to become Christians. Shall we become subjects of your king? You will listen to no other voices but yours."[20] In the early 1700s the Qing banned Christianity for undermining such Chinese traditions as ancestor worship, persecuted converts, and expelled missionaries.

Before 1800 China, being militarily and economically strong, could rebuff Western demands. But relations with the Dutch and Russians suggested trouble to come. The Dutch, who established a base on Taiwan in 1624, were expelled in 1662 by stronger Ming resistance forces that moved to the island. In 1683 the Qing took control of Taiwan, but the Dutch remained active in the China trade. Meanwhile, Russian expeditions crossed sparsely populated Siberia, seeking trade with China as well as sable fur, and over time they consolidated control of the region. Russian forces fought and lost several battles to China in their quest for a gateway to the Pacific through the Amur River Valley, an area in eastern Siberia north of the Manchu homeland and under loose Qing suzerainty. But the Qing granted the Russians commercial privileges in the Treaty of Nerchinsk of 1689, the first treaty between China and a European power, symbolizing things to come. Russia maintained its ambitions in eastern Siberia, occasionally testing Qing power.

Needing little from outside, China controlled its relations with European powers before the 1800s, restricting foreign trade to a few border outposts and southern ports, especially Guangzhou (Canton), and refusing diplomatic relations with Western nations. Willing to absorb useful technologies to improve mapmaking and astronomy, the Chinese were less interested in foreign ideas like Christianity. By the mid-Qing, China was also increasingly self-centered and complacent, underestimating the Western challenge.

China's internal problems mounted just as Western economic, industrial, and military power increased; foreign pressures intensified in the later 1700s, when the West eclipsed an overconfident China within a few decades. Having lived under foreign rulers such as the Manchus, the Chinese understood political subjugation but could not comprehend foreign forces prompting them to rethink their cultural traditions, which they believed superior and which they wanted to preserve at all costs. During the later 1800s the 2,000-year-old imperial system declined rapidly.

MAKE SURE YOU UNDERSTAND THESE KEY POINTS BEFORE MOVING ON

- During the Ming dynasty, China maintained its economic power, but it turned increasingly inward and antiforeign and was ultimately undermined by plague, famine, and pressures from Japan.

- The Qing dynasty was established by foreign Manchus, who assimilated to many Chinese ways, amassed the greatest Eurasian land empire since the Mongols, and added Taiwan to China's holdings.

- Chinese neo-Confucians incorporated elements of Buddhism and Daoism in their thinking and, like their

European contemporaries, emphasized reason, but over time neo-Confucianism hardened into a new orthodoxy and discouraged the growth of new ideas.

- China's economy remained extremely strong but never developed full-scale capitalism or industrialization, perhaps because it lacked an exploitable overseas empire, and perhaps because the government failed to encourage entrepreneurship.

aplia

[19]Quoted in Spence, *Emperor of China*, 72–73.

[20]Quoted in Joanna Waley-Cohen, *The Sextants of Beijing: Global Currents in Chinese History* (New York: W.W. Norton, 1999), 55.

(T)(S) Continuity and Change in Korea and Japan

How did Korea and Japan change during this era?

Although neighbors, the Koreans, Japanese, and Chinese developed very different societies. Korea faced little Western pressure, with local issues and conflicts with Japan being far more important. For a brief period Japan encountered a significant European presence, but when the experience proved destabilizing, the Japanese became aloof from the West.

Choson Korea, Ashikaga Japan, and European Encounters

Korea and Japan remained more isolated than China from the wider world. Koreans mixed Chinese influences with local traditions, adapting and modifying Chinese political models, Confucian social patterns, and Mahayana Buddhism. The Yi **(YEE)** dynasty (1392–1910), which called its state Choson, ruled over five centuries. Strongly Confucian, Choson borrowed Chinese models and maintained close relations with China. The early Yi era enjoyed progress in science, technology, writing, and literature. However, Choson was also damaged by factional disputes and a disastrous Japanese invasion.

The invasion occurred in 1592, when a Japanese army of 160,000 attempted to conquer the peninsula and captured the capital, Seoul (soul). Aided by China, the Koreans eventually prevailed by inventing the world's first ironclad naval vessels, which cut Japanese supply lines and forced Japanese withdrawal. But the invasion destroyed countless buildings, weakened the government, and generated severe economic problems.

Maintaining their power, the Yi abandoned or modified some customs borrowed from China while modifying the rigid social class system. As agriculture became more productive, the population reached 7 million by 1750. Commerce and the merchant class expanded. Yet, growing dissention fostered movements for change that grew during the 1700s.

Japan was East Asia's most unique society, exemplified by its samurai **(SAH-moo-rie)** warrior class, its distinctive mix of Buddhism, Confucianism, and Shinto, and its long history of adapting foreign influences. But by 1500 Japan under the Ashikaga **(ah-shee-KAH-gah)** Shogunate (1338–1573) was experiencing rapid economic change, population growth, and then civil war, which strained the political and social system. Ashikaga shoguns, military leaders who dominated the imperial family in Kyoto and the central government, never had much power beyond the capital.

As technological advances improved agriculture, tripling production per acre, Japan's population doubled from 16 million in 1500 to 30 million in 1750. Increased productivity stimulated trade and urban growth; by 1600 Kyoto contained some 800,000 people. Urban merchants and craftsmen organized themselves into guilds with monopoly rights to sell or make a product, earning higher status and more freedom than

most Japanese enjoyed. Active merchants spurred foreign and domestic trade, with Japan supplying silver, copper, swords, lacquer ware, rice wine, rice, and other goods to Asia. Only a few Japanese diplomats and Buddhist monks had ever ventured to Korea and China, but now Japanese traders and pirates visited Korea, China, and Southeast Asia. Japanese settled in Vietnam, Cambodia, Siam, and the Philippines; one even became a governor in Siam. If economic and military expansion had continued, the Japanese might have challenged Europeans for influence in Southeast Asia and perhaps even developed capitalism. But growing political turmoil and civil war turned Japan in a different direction.

Political power became increasingly decentralized, as several hundred daimyo, great territorial landowning magnates with supporting samurai forces, increasingly dominated rural Japan. The daimyo's rise precipitated a century-long civil war from the mid-1400s into the late 1500s, mostly involving hand-to-hand conflict between samurai wielding long, slightly curved, two-handed swords with great efficiency, supported by commoner spearmen. A famous poet offered a retrospective on the fleeting nature of the fighters' causes: "The summer grasses! All that is left of the warrior's dream!"[21]

Three successive shoguns, brutal warlords and devotees of the refined tea ceremony, gradually restored order. The first, Oda Nobunaga **(OH-da no-boo-NAG-ga)** (1534–1582), of daimyo background, proved a brilliant military strategist, once defeating an army of 25,000 with his own small force of 2,000 men. He usually performed a folk dance and then sang a delicate verse about life's transience before leading his samurai into bloody battles. Hideyoshi Toyotomi (1536–1598), of peasant origins and with ambitions abroad, dreamed of conquering China and demanded unsuccessfully that the Philippines' Spanish governor send him tribute. When Koreans refused his request to use Korea as a base for invading China, he instead attacked Korea in 1592; as already discussed, fierce Korean resistance repulsed his forces. The last of the three, Tokugawa Ieyasu **(ee-yeh-YAH-soo)** (1542–1616), one of Hideyoshi's chief generals, ended the civil war and became shogun in 1603.

During the civil war European traders and missionaries arrived in Japan, sparking cultural exchange and conflict. In 1542 the Portuguese reached Japan, causing a sensation, as we learn from a Japanese observer:

> *There came on a [merchant ship] a creature one couldn't put a name to, that [appeared to have] human form at first [glance], but might as well be a long-nosed goblin. Careful inquiry [revealed] that the creature was called a "Padre." The first thing one noticed was how long the nose was! It was like a wartless conch-shell.[22]*

---

[21]Matsuo Basho, quoted in Noel F. Busch, *The Horizon Concise History of Japan* (New York: American Heritage, 1972), 64.

[22]Quoted in Ronald P. Toby, "The 'Indianess' of Iberia and Changing Japanese Iconographies of Other," in Schwartz, *Implicit Understandings*, 326.

Europeans were equally astonished by Japan. An Italian Jesuit in the 1500s struggled with cultural differences:

Japan is a world the reverse of Europe. Hardly in anything do their ways conform to ours. They eat and dress differently. Their methods of doing business, their manner of sitting down, their buildings, their domestic arrangements are so unlike ours as to be beyond description or understanding.[23]

Despite mutual astonishment, Europeans had an economic, religious, and military impact. The Portuguese traded Chinese silk for Japanese gold, and soon Spanish and Dutch merchants arrived. Spanish Jesuit missionary Francis Xavier (1506–1552) began promoting Christianity in 1549. Thanks to Spanish and Portuguese missionaries, by 1600 perhaps 300,000 of the 18 million Japanese were Christians. Some daimyo on the southern island of Kyushu (**KYOO-shoo**) converted to gain closer relations with European traders and to acquire advanced gunpowder weapons. But many Japanese resented the missionaries' intolerance of Japanese faiths and customs and could not comprehend the fierce competition between Portuguese and Spanish priests and between rival Catholic orders. Meanwhile, Japanese leaders viewed the Christian communities, often armed by missionaries, as posing a threat.

Thanks to the warfare, the Japanese were now more open to borrowing from outside, but they adopted what was useful to them: Western technologies. For example, they acquired, then quickly improved, Portuguese and Spanish muskets. Such European guns sharpened warfare and, since even nonsamurai could obtain them, helped break down social class lines. In addition, the deadly violence resulting from guns often prompted peasants to seek solace in religion, some adopting Christianity. Japanese leaders became alarmed by this superior Western military and naval technology and the surprising effectiveness of Christian missionaries.

The Tokugawa Shogunate: Stability, Seclusion, and Society

Tokugawa Ieyasu, a great warrior, master strategist, and able administrator, but also cruel and treacherous, ended the civil war with a smashing victory in the Battle of Sekigahara, which involved at least eighty thousand soldiers on each side. After subduing his rivals, he established the Tokugawa Shogunate (1608–1868) at Tokyo, then known as Edo. Presiding over premodern Japan's most centralized state, the Tokugawa government mixed authoritarian centralization with a hierarchical social system led by samurai, somewhat resembling medieval European feudalism. A samurai scholar instrumental in developing the code of chivalry (*Bushido*; see Chapter 11) claimed that farmers, merchants, and artisans were too busy to master the warrior ways, while the samurai "is one who does not cultivate, manufacture, engage in trade. The business of the samurai consists in reflecting on his own station in life, in discharging loyal service to his master, in devoting himself to duty above all."[24] While the government and samurai ran the country, the imperial family in Kyoto remained powerless. To discourage rebellion, shoguns required some members of each daimyo family to live in Edo as hostages.

To stop the conflict between various Europeans and Catholic orders, the Tokugawa government eventually declared a seclusion policy, closing off Japan from Western pressure, ordering home Japanese traders in Southeast Asia, ejecting Western missionaries and merchants, and breaking the power of Christian communities. The shogun warned the Portuguese and Spanish that they should justly be killed, but he would spare their lives if they left Japan and never returned. When Japanese Christians rebelled in 1637, Tokugawa forces massacred thirty-seven thousand of them. But trade with China, Korea, and Southeast Asia continued, with Japan exporting its main mineral resource, silver. Meanwhile, several thousand Chinese merchants lived in Japanese ports, especially Nagasaki.

After 1639 a few Dutch traders, interested in commerce rather than Christian conversions, were allowed to keep a base on a small island, Deshima (**DEH-shi-ma**), in Nagasaki (**nah-gah-SAH-kee**) Bay. For the next two centuries Deshima served as Japan's only link to the Western world. The Dutch East Indies Company's Deshima station chief reported in 1650 that the many restrictions and humiliations they endured were worth the gains because Japan was the most profitable of the company's operations.

Tokugawa leaders believed that society could be frozen, but under the surface new social forces and tensions simmered. Even with restricted travel between cities or regions, merchants evaded the rules. Rapid population growth strained the country's resources, and peasant protests, riots, and uprisings became common. Led by Tokyo and Osaka, each with over a million inhabitants by 1800, cities became prosperous commercial centers, while merchants and their values became more influential.

Unlike some Asian women, Japanese women, never secluded, participated in community life. Some were literate, and a few became noted writers. European visitors in the 1500s were surprised that elite women had more independence than their European contemporaries. Nonetheless, the Tokugawa tried to restrict women. Women had few legal or property rights, faced arranged marriages, and were encouraged to be dependent on men. Severe laws against adultery punished only women. The Tokugawa advised peasants that "however good looking a wife may be, if she neglects her household duties by drinking tea or sight-seeing or rambling along the hillside, she must be divorced."[25]

Distinctive new cultural forms emerged. In major cities entertainment districts developed that were known as the "floating world," containing restaurants, theaters, geisha houses, and brothels. A playwright described a lively district in Osaka: "Through the thronged streets young rakes were strolling, singing folk-songs as they went, reciting fragments of puppet dramas, or imitating famous actors at their dialogues. From the

[23]Quoted in Edward Seidenstecker, *Japan* (New York: Time Inc., 1961), 58.
[24]Yamaga Soko, quoted in Conrad Totman, *A History of Japan* (Oxford: Blackwell, 2000), 221.
[25]Quoted in Mikiso Hane, *Modern Japan: A Historical Survey*, 2nd ed. (Boulder, CO: Westview Press, 1992), 36.

Werner Forman/Art Resource, NY

KABUKI THEATER The urban middle classes, especially the merchants and samurai, enjoyed kabuki drama. This eighteenth-century print by one of the most acclaimed artists, Moronobu, shows the audience enjoying a play about a vendetta involving two brothers.

upper rooms of many a teahouse floated the gay plucking of a *samisen* [lute]."[26] Master artist Moronobu **(more-oh-NOH-boo)** introduced colorful woodblock prints, known as **ukiyo-e (oo-kee-YO-ee)**, that celebrating the floating world and achieved wide distribution, making famous the actors, geishas, and courtesans portrayed. Later, landscapes, such as views of Mount Fuji, became popular woodcut themes. By the 1800s many European artists collected and were influenced by these prints.

New theater forms included the **bunraku** puppet theater and the racy **kabuki** drama, the favored entertainment of the urban merchant class. Kabuki featured gorgeous costumes, beautiful scenery, and scripts filled with violent passion. Men played all the roles. Professional female impersonators, highly honored, spent years mastering the voice, gestures, and other aspects of femininity. Seventeen-syllable **haiku** poems also became popular. Haiku portrayed the passage of time or briefly summarized some action or scene through a series of images. Hence, the samurai-turned-wanderer and greatest haiku poet, Matsuo Basho **(BAH-show)** (1644–1694), described a sudden event on a quiet pond: "An old pond. Frog jumps in. Sound of water." Another Basho poem commented on changing seasons and human emotions: "No blossoms and no moon, and he is drinking *sake* [rice wine], all alone."[27] The Japanese did not need to be lonely on a dark winter's night to appreciate Basho's delicate word art.

Tokugawa Japan largely enjoyed security, stability, and peace for 250 years, but at a price. Although commerce thrived, Japan, like China, experienced no political transformation or social rejuvenation and thus was vulnerable to

ukiyo-e Colorful Japanese woodblock prints that celebrated the life of the "floating world," the urban entertainment districts.

bunraku The puppet theater of Tokugawa Japan.

kabuki The all-male and racy drama that became the favored entertainment of the urban population in Tokugawa Japan.

haiku The seventeen-syllable poem that proved an excellent vehicle for discussing the passage of time and the change of seasons in Early Modern Japan.

[26]Chikamatsu Monzaemon, quoted in *What Life Was Like Among Samurai and Shoguns* (Alexandria, VA: Time-Life Books, 1999), 118.

[27]The haiku are from Conrad Schirokauer, *A Brief History of Chinese and Japanese Civilizations*, 2nd ed. (San Diego: Harcourt Brace Jovanovich, 1989), 373; and Harold G. Henderson, *An Introduction to Haiku: An Anthology of Poets from Basho to Shiki* (Garden City, NY: Doubleday Anchor, 1958), 40.

a later return of Western power. The Tokugawa had merely papered over the cracks. When the West intruded in the mid-nineteenth century, the latent tensions boiled over and the Tokugawa lost their grip on power. But Japan, unlike China, was able to respond creatively. Whereas Chinese feared cultural change more than political conquest, the Japanese were more afraid of conquest. Their history of borrowing from abroad made them uniquely prepared to assimilate Western techniques and customs to Japanese traditions, as they had done with Chinese, Korean, and Western imports in earlier eras. China and Japan eventually met the challenge from the West in very different ways.

MAKE SURE YOU UNDERSTAND THESE KEY POINTS BEFORE MOVING ON

- The Chinese helped Korea to rebuff a 1592 Japanese invasion, but as a result Korean culture began to liberalize and shed some customs borrowed from China.

- Ashikaga Japan saw tremendous economic and population growth, but it was undermined by a lengthy civil war, during which European merchants made incursions and introduced guns and Christianity, upsetting Japan's social order.

- The Tokugawa Shogunate ended Japan's civil war, restored strict order, and expelled European missionaries and traders, with the exception of a small group of Dutch traders who were uninterested in missionary work.

- Despite the Tokugawa leaders' attempt to halt change, the Japanese economy grew rapidly, tensions in Japanese society increased, and Japan's culture flourished in the urban "floating world" and in new theatrical and literary forms.

CHAPTER SUMMARY

European expansion had much less impact in most of southern and eastern Asia than it had in the Americas and Africa. Many Asian societies remained strong and militarily powerful, able to manipulate or deflect the Europeans who came in search of valuable trade resources and products. Mughal India, especially under the tolerant Akbar, developed creative art and architecture and a prosperous export economy. By the 1700s, however, the Mughals had weakened from overspending and religious intolerance as new challenges mounted. While various Southeast Asian states remained strong, the Portuguese and then the Dutch successively captured Melaka and the Spice Islands, and the Dutch gradually conquered Java. The Spanish carved out a colony in the Philippines and began exporting Asian goods from Manila to the Americas, helping build a world economy.

Increasing commerce more closely tied Southeast Asia to the growing world economy.

China during the late Ming and early Qing remained among the world's most powerful and prosperous countries, with outstanding leaders, extensive industry, and the world's largest commercial economy. However, while it remained creative in arts and philosophy, overpopulation and declining support for merchants eventually hindered China just as European pressures increased. Both Japan and Korea imposed policies of partial seclusion. After welcoming Western traders and missionaries, Japan restricted their access. The Tokugawa Shogunate maintained a rigid social and political system but also fostered a creative culture. Hence, European activity was only one of many factors influencing Asian societies.

KEY TERMS

Urdu (p. 414)
Sikhs (p. 418)
Moros (p. 423)

Hispanization (p. 423)
Indios (p. 424)
ukiyo-e (p. 434)

bunraku (p. 434)
kabuki (p. 434)
haiku (p. 434)

The Great Divergence Between Europe and Asia

In recent years historians have debated the roots of Europe's rise to world leadership, power, and wealth while other societies, especially in Asia, lost the political and economic leadership they once enjoyed—what some call "the great divergence." To many historians the surprising rise of Europe during the Early Modern Era needs explaining. It was not inevitable; history could have turned out very differently.

The Problem

How, why, and when Europe rather than a major Asian society like China came to dominate the world remain some of the principal questions of modern world history. If several Asian societies had an edge in power and wealth over other societies during most of the Intermediate Era, then why was the world so very different by 1800? Some western European societies, especially Britain, moved toward an unprecedented level of industrialization while once-influential Asian societies, including China, increasingly faced challenges from the West. And when did western Europe begin to diverge from other dynamic, commercialized economies, especially China's? The debate divides into several schools of thought.

The Debate

Many historians argue that the great divergence began in the Intermediate Era, when western Europe developed unique advantages that intensified after 1500. They contend that social, cultural, and political factors gave Europeans an advantage. David Landes believes Europe enjoyed a superior social heritage because its values and institutions promoted economic growth. In his view, European countries prospered because they were vital and open, valuing both hard work and knowledge, and these values led to increased economic productivity and positive attitudes toward change. Rodney Stark emphasizes what he considers a tradition unique to Christianity of stressing reason and progress. Offering another explanation, scholars such as E. L. Jones and Nathan Rosenberg stress the political pluralism represented by fiercely competing states. The chronic warfare between states stimulated a quest for increased revenues and more effective weapons. Furthermore, the flexibility of Western institutions, including the shift toward more representative government in England and Holland, made it easier to take advantage of overseas discoveries. Niall Ferguson contends that after 1400 western Europeans developed several "killer applications"— competition, consumerism, science, the work ethic, and modern medicine—that other societies lacked. In contrast to dynamic Europe, Landes and Jones argue, the rest of the world was static. China, in their view, had by 1700 reached an economic, political, and intellectual dead end, possessing wealth and power but introducing few inventions leading to any breakthroughs.

Other historians reject the notion of European social and cultural superiority. James Blaut and Andre Gunder Frank contend that the key to Europe's rise was not a unique culture but European countries' acquisition of wealth, especially in precious metals, from their conquests in the Americas. Between 1500 and 1800 the colonized Americas supplied 85 percent of the world's silver and 70 percent of the gold, a huge windfall to European merchants and governments, who sold much of it to China in exchange for tea, silk, porcelain, and other valuable Chinese exports. The rise of the slavery-based plantation economy in the Americas produced additional profits for the Western colonizers. The sale of profitable American minerals and cash crops such as sugar not only stimulated European capitalism but also gave Europeans new advantages as they tapped into the lucrative Asian market. Blaut also believes that Europe benefited from being much closer than was Asia to the Americas.

Many who dispute the claim that Western social and cultural traditions or the pluralistic state system provided a decisive advantage agree that Europeans capitalized on events, such as the American conquests and the acquisition of Asian and Middle Eastern technology, to foster economic growth. Scholars such as John Hobson, Alan Smith, L. S. Stavrianos, and Eric Wolf have shown that western European economies were rapidly commercializing from late medieval times and produced a full-blown commercial capitalism between 1450 and 1800 that helped generate a more widespread and powerful world economy. Nonetheless, while Europeans developed better weaponry and business organization, some historians conclude that Europe had no real advantage over China until the late eighteenth or early nineteenth centuries, when industrialization gave the British and later some other western Europeans a vastly superior technology.

Many historians disagree that China was at a dead end and in economic decline. They argue that China's commercial economy dwarfed all others, making China a major player in world trade. Chinese merchants and craftsmen were intensely competitive, hardly constrained by the Ming and Qing state. Indeed, China's commercial economy grew rapidly from the early Ming to the mid-1700s, producing abundant export products that were eagerly sought by merchants from all over Afro-Eurasia. In 1800 China still produced a third of all the world's manufactured goods and imported over half of all the silver mined in the Americas. Moreover, before 1800 Chinese in the commercialized core regions may have enjoyed as long life spans and as high, if not higher, standards of living and per capita incomes as northwest Europeans. Scholars also question whether other Asian societies, including India, were in decline, even though their states were clearly weakening. By 1800 India could not match China's economy but still produced around a quarter of the world's industry, about the same as Europe. Indian historian Prasannan Parthasarathi, viewing advanced regions of Europe and Asia as more alike than different, credits competition from Indian textiles and wood shortages from deforestation with prompting new spinning technologies and coal use in Britain. With their many exports and imports, China and India remained the engines for the Eastern Hemisphere trading system well into the 1700s. In the early Mughal era India enjoyed a far larger, more productive economy than England. Although the Mughal state was collapsing by the early 1700s, Indian manufactured goods still attracted a vigorous

The China Tea Trade, 1790-1800 (oil on canvas), Chinese School/© Peabody Essex Museum, Salem, Massachusetts, USA/The Bridgeman Art Library

THE CHINESE TEA TRADE This fanciful painting, from the 1790s, shows tea estates in the mountains, boat transport of tea to the coastal ports, and warehouses where it was stored in chests for shipment abroad.

international trade. R. Bin Wong, Kenneth Pomeranz, Jack Goldstone, Andre Gunder Frank, and Parthasarathi suggest that eighteenth-century China, India, western Europe, and perhaps Japan had comparable levels of economic development. Indian scholar Amiya Kumar Bagchi agrees, stressing that western Europeans enjoyed no decisive advantage over China and India in economic production, consumption, and growth before Britain's Industrial Revolution and that China only fell behind in the 1850s. Furthermore, he argues, most Europeans saw little improvement in their lives until the late nineteenth century.

In asking why sustained economic growth began first in northwestern Europe rather than in eastern Asia, Pomeranz argues that the densely populated Yangzi River Delta of China, Japan's Tokyo region, and possibly even India's Gujerat region were similar in many respects to the northwest European core regions, England and the Netherlands, in the seventeenth and eighteenth centuries, and that all these regions were facing similar ecological and demographic stress, such as overpopulation. The great divergence came in the 1800s, he suggests, when one country, England, developed fossil fuels, especially its coal industry, for power while increasingly reaping the benefits of cheap, often slavery-produced resources from the Americas. China had used coal many centuries before Europe, but its remaining coal reserves were remote from major population centers.

The availability of slave-produced American wealth and easily tapped coal reserves, Pomeranz suggests, put first England and then northwestern Europe on a completely new development path unavailable to China, Japan, and India, changing world history.

Evaluating the Debate

This debate will likely thrive for years, making thoughtful arguments on all sides. Some scholars see the rise of the West as inevitable, a result of certain advantageous trends building for centuries, while others argue that things could have turned out differently had Western nations not been able to exploit American resources and China had sustained its dynamism. The Industrial Revolution in Europe, beginning in the late 1700s, which gave Europeans the technology and wealth to achieve global dominance, may have been the product of long-standing and unique European attitudes, or it may have resulted from a late shift in global economic power, fueled by American resources, that favored Europe and undermined China and India. Whether or not Europe was exceptionally enterprising or simply lucky in finding useful resources, the new, expanded world economy that emerged between 1500 and 1800 benefited primarily western Europe and later North America, but it eventually touched everyone, bringing about changes in many aspects of life around the world.

(Continued)

437

1. What are some of the advantages many historians think Europeans possessed?
2. Why do some historians believe the great divergence between Asia and the West did not come until after 1750?
3. How did Western expansion into the Americas give some European countries an advantage over Asian countries in the global economy?

Exploring the Controversy

Historians emphasizing Europe's social, cultural, and political advantages include David S. Landes, *The Wealth and Power of Nations: Why Some Are So Rich and Some Are So Poor* (New York: Norton, 1998); Rodney Stark, *The Victory of Reason: How Christianity Led to Freedom, Capitalism, and Western Success* (New York: Random House, 2005); E. L. Jones, *The European Miracle: Environments, Economies and Geopolitics in the History of Europe and Asia*, 3rd ed. (Cambridge: Cambridge University Press, 2003); Niall Ferguson, *Civilization: The West and the Rest* (New York: Penguin, 2012); and Nathan Rosenberg and L. E. Birdzell, Jr., *How the West Grew Rich* (New York: Basic Books, 1986). On the rise of the European-dominated world economy, see Alan K. Smith, *Creating a World Economy: Merchant Capital, Colonialism, and World Trade*, 1400–1825 (Boulder, CO: Westview Press, 1991);

L. S. Stavrianos, *Global Rift: The Third World Comes of Age* (New York: William Morrow, 1981); and Eric Wolf, *Europe and the Peoples Without History* (Berkeley: University of California Press, 1983). Scholars dubious of innate European advantages include Andre Gunder Frank, *ReORIENT: Global Economy in the Asian Age* (Berkeley: University of California Press, 1998); James Blaut, *The Colonizer's Model of the World: Geographical Diffusionism and Eurocentric History* (New York: Guilford Press, 1993); Amiya Kumar Bagchi, *Perilous Passage: Mankind and the Global Ascendancy of Capital* (Lanham, MD: Rowman and Littlefield, 2005); and John M. Hobson, *The Eastern Origins of Western Civilization* (New York: Cambridge University Press, 2004). On China's continuing strength, see Kenneth Pomeranz, *The Great Divergence: China, Europe, and the Making of the Modern World Economy* (Princeton: Princeton University Press, 2000); and R. Bin Wong, *China Transformed: Historical Change and the Limits of European Experience* (Ithaca, NY: Cornell University Press, 1997). On India, see Prasannan Parthasarathi, *Why Europe Grew Rich and India Did Not* (New York: Cambridge University Press, 2011). For an excellent discussion of the great divergence debate and related issues, see David D. Buck, "Was It Pluck or Luck That Made the West Grow Rich?" *Journal of World History* 10, no. 2 (Fall 1999): 413–430; and Jack Goldstone; *Why Europe? The Rise of the West in World History, 1500–1850* (New York: McGraw-Hill, 2009).

PART V

Global Imbalances in the Modern World, 1750–1945

CHAPTER OUTLINE

The imbalances in wealth and power between the world's societies in the nineteenth century became even wider in the early twentieth century, shaped in part by revolutions and innovations in western Europe and North America. After lengthy travels in the South Pacific, Asia, Africa, and Europe, in 1900 American writer Mark Twain, author of beloved novels about Tom Sawyer and Huckleberry Finn, became a critic of the Western imperialism that increased these imbalances, including U.S. colonization of the Philippines. At the same time, Twain was being transported by the products of capitalism and industrialization, which created Western wealth and inspired new technologies such as the steamships and railroads that conveyed resources, products, and travelers like Twain over great distances.

Just as Spain and Portugal controlled Latin America until the early 1800s, by 1914, thanks in part to deadly new weapons, a half dozen Western nations ruled, or influenced the governments of, most Asian, African, and Caribbean peoples. Yet, other societies were not passive actors simply responding to the West. In whatever part of the world they lived, people were linked to a global system that, however imbalanced politically and economically, promoted the movement of products, ideas, institutions, technologies, and people, on a larger scale than ever before, across political boundaries. By the 1930s people around the world, often using borrowed Western ideas such as nationalism and Marxism, were challenging Western political and economic power.

Transitions
Global Empires

Powerful societies had formed empires since ancient times, but over the centuries successive empires grew larger and more complex. In the mid-1700s over two-thirds of the world's people lived in one of several large, multiethnic Eurasian or American empires based largely on military power, especially gunpowder weapons. While most empires depended on agriculture, the British and Dutch empires relied more on world trade. Many of the eighteenth-century empires had crumbled by the early twentieth century. The Spanish, Portuguese, and British lost most of their territories in the Americas, and the Habsburg and Ottoman Empires were dismantled after World War I. In their place, modern empires emerged. Between 1870 and 1914, Britain and France established overseas empires on a grander scale than ever before in history, ruling colonies in Africa, Asia, and the Pacific; Holland and Portugal still controlled large holdings in Southeast Asia and Africa, respectively; while Russia now controlled a vast expanse of Eurasia. On a smaller scale, Germany, Japan, and the United States also forged territorial empires. A huge portion of the globe, divided up into colonies or spheres of influence by the West, was incorporated into a Western-dominated world economic system. Influential British imperialist and author Rudyard Kipling summarized the rationale for exercising imperial power: "That they should take who have the power, And they should keep who can."[1]

Like empires throughout history, modern imperial states, whatever their democratic forms at home, punished dissent in their colonies. Sometimes protests, such as those led by Mohandas Gandhi in India, forced Western colonizers to modify their policies, and some Western critics, like Twain, criticized colonialism. A nineteenth-century English wit

---

[1] Quoted in L. S. Stavrianos, *Lifelines from Our Past: A New World History*, rev. ed. (Armonk, NY: M.E. Sharpe, 1997), 114.

charged that "the moment the very name of Ireland is mentioned, the English seem to bid adieu to common feelings, common prudence and common sense, and to act with the barbarity of tyrants and the fatuity of idiots."[2]

Societies
Nations, Nationalisms, and Revolutions

Whether parts of empires or not, all over the world societies struggled to become nations that enjoyed self-government and a common identity. But Western peoples formed the most powerful nations, many aided by strong government structures and democratic practices that fostered debate; they also enjoyed economic dynamism, possessed advanced weapons, and engaged in fierce rivalries with each other. By the later 1800s the United States matched European capabilities and had similar imperial ambitions. Americans believed in their nation's Manifest Destiny, articulated by an influential U.S. politician: "God has marked the American people as his chosen nation to finally lead in the regeneration of the world."[3] By contrast, few people in Asian or African colonies, with often arbitrary borders, shared any sense of common identity, let alone a national mission; colonial governments were unpopular and usually viewed by the colonized as illegitimate. The ethnic diversity of most colonies—Dutch Indonesia and the Belgian Congo each contained several hundred ethnic groups—inhibited nationalist feeling and thus the formation of nationalist movements. Still, despite the barriers, nationalism spread, often encouraged by travel, exile, or education. Venezuelan Simon Bolivar, Filipino Jose Rizal (rih-ZALL) (1861–1896), and Vietnamese Ho Chi Minh (1890–1969), all disenchanted with colonial restrictions, embraced a nationalist agenda while living in Europe. By 1900 Japan was a role model of nationalism and modernization for many Asians.

But nationalism was not always an imported sentiment. Many Asians had a sense of identity similar to nationalism long before the nineteenth century. People in Korea, Japan, and Vietnam, for example, had long enjoyed some national feeling based on shared religion, a common language, bureaucratic government, and the perception of one or more common enemies. Reflecting such national feeling, in 1898, Hawaii's last monarch, Queen Liliuokalani (luh-lee-uh-ohkuh-LAH-nee), pleaded with the United States not to colonize the islands, since her people's "form of government is as dear to them as yours is precious to you. Quite as warmly as you love your country, so they love theirs."[4] U.S. leaders ignored her pleas and annexed Hawaii. To resist colonial strategies, nationalists sought ways to regain the initiative and achieve sovereignty. Indian nationalist Jawaharlal Nehru expressed the search for a successful anticolonial strategy: "What could we do? How could we pull India out of this quagmire of poverty and defeatism, which sucked her in?"[5]

Some societies needed major rebellions and revolutions to transform old discredited orders and create new nations. The American and French Revolutions of the later 1700s began an Age of Revolution and inspired people elsewhere to take up arms against unjust or outdated governments. During the mid-nineteenth century the Taiping (TIE-ping) Rebellion against China's Qing dynasty and the Indian Rebellion against the British East India Company, although they ultimately failed, provided fierce challenges to established governments in the world's two most populous societies. Early in the twentieth century, other revolutions overturned old governments and built nations in Mexico, Turkey, and China; the Chinese Revolution ended two thousand years of imperial control and established the foundation, however unstable, for a modern republic. The Russian Revolution of 1917 installed the world's first communist government, inspiring communist movements and revolutionary nationalists around the world.

The aftermath of World War I also generated new revolutionary upheavals and ideologies. Old states collapsed in eastern Europe, fascism spread in Germany and Japan in the economic shambles caused by the Great Depression, and Spain erupted in civil war. In 1914 Marxism, the revolutionary socialist vision developed by Karl Marx (1818–1883), had relatively little influence outside of Germany and Russia, but by 1945 the ideology had mass support in many societies. Communist revolutionary movements percolated in China, Korea, Indonesia, and Vietnam.

Transitions
Change in the Global System

During the Modern Era the global system expanded and changed as networks of trade and communication linking distant societies grew in number and extent. Western influence increased. For example, textbooks in French colonial schools, where the students were Africans, Afro-Caribbean, Arabs, Asians, or Pacific islanders, celebrated the history of the French—"our ancestors the Gauls"—while children in the U.S.-ruled Philippines, a tropical and predominantly Catholic land, learned English from books showing American youngsters throwing snowballs, playing baseball, and attending Protestant church services. However, Western cultural influence was weak in some colonized societies, especially Muslim ones such as Egypt and northern Nigeria.

Countries gained or lost power in the global system depending on their wealth, type of government, and access to military power (see Historical Controversy: Modernization or World-System?). In 1750, Western overseas expansion, including military conquests, had already reshaped the Americas and some regions of Africa and southern Asia. Chinese, Indians, and western Europeans were the richest peoples at

[2]Rev. Sydney Smith, quoted in Frederic Delouche et al., *Illustrated History of Europe: A Unique Portrait of Europe's Common People* (New York: Barnes and Noble, 2001), 289.

[3]Senator Albert Beveridge of Indiana, quoted in Henry Allen, *What It Felt Like Living in the American Century* (New York: Pantheon, 2000), 7.

[4]Quoted in Scott B. Cook, *Colonial Encounters in the Age of High Imperialism* (New York: Longman, 1996), 100.

[5]From Clark D. Moore and David Eldridge, eds., *India Yesterday and Today* (New York: Bantam, 1970), 170.

QUEEN VICTORIA AS VIEWED BY A NIGERIAN ARTIST This wooden mask from nineteenth century southeastern Nigeria features a sculpture of the British monarch, to be fixed in a basketry cap and worn on the head during dance or funeral ceremonies.

this time, the Chinese accounting for a third and India and western Europe each accounting for a fourth of the world's total economic production. By 1914, however, after a century and a half of Western industrialization, imperial expansion, and colonization, the global system had become more divided than ever before into rich and poor societies. Falling well behind the Western powers, India and China were now among the poorer countries. Meanwhile, a few Western nation-states—especially Great Britain, the United States, Germany, and France—had grown rich and powerful, enjoying substantial influence around the world and over the global economy. Because of their unparalleled military power, all four of these nations ruled colonial empires, from which they extracted valuable resources; played a leading role in world trade; and tried to spread, with some success, their cultures and ideas. Some Western nations and Japan occupied an intermediate

category. Most Western colonies in Asia, Africa, and the Caribbean and Latin American nations had little economic or political power in the world.

By 1914 living conditions and governments in rich countries differed dramatically from those in poor societies. Many Western nations boasted diversified economies, industrialization, high literacy rates, urbanization, large middle classes, independent mass media, competing political parties, and efficient, well-financed, often democratic governments. By contrast, the poor societies, especially Western colonies in Asia and Africa, where many people worked lands owned by foreign landlords or planters, were not industrialized and people earned meager wages. Few had access to formal education or democracy, and middle classes remained small. Economic growth was often determined by foreign investment and markets for cash crops and minerals rather than by local needs. Western domination, however, did not preclude cultural and scientific achievements by colonized people. For example, although their country was a British colony, various Indian writers, mathematicians, biochemists, and astrophysicists won international renown and even Noble Prizes.

Between 1914 and 1945 the global system underwent further changes. Wars were now sometimes world wars, titanic struggles that reshaped world politics, fought on a greater scale than ever before and on battlefields thousands of miles apart. World Wars I and II were the deadliest conflicts in history. The United States became the world's richest, most powerful nation, while Germany temporarily lost wealth and power because of its defeat in World War I. Then during World War II, Germany, Italy, and Japan—all middle-ranking nations by the 1930s—challenged the rich nations—Britain,

France, and the United States. Several Latin American nations and Turkey enjoyed enough economic growth and stability of government to move into the middle-ranking category by the 1940s.

Networks
The World Economy, Inequality, and Industrialization

European influence on the world economy increased in the 1700s and 1800s when Western traders, supported by their governments, sought new natural resources and markets in the tropical world, thereby creating a truly global economy. By 1914 the entire world was enmeshed in a vast economic exchange that particularly benefited the more powerful nations. People often produced resources or manufactured goods—Middle Eastern oil, Indonesian coffee, British textiles—for markets thousands of miles away. Europe's Industrial Revolution, which provided manufactured goods to trade for resources, dramatically reshaped the Western economies in the 1800s but only slowly spread to other regions.

Imperialism and colonialism enabled the transfer of wealth to the imperial nations to finance their own development. Many colonies developed economies that produced and exported only one or two primary resources, such as rice and rubber from French Vietnam, rubber and tin from British Malaya, sugar from Spanish Cuba, copper from British Northern Rhodesia (Zambia), and cocoa from the British Gold Coast. Most of these resource exports were transformed into consumer goods, such as rubber tires and chocolate candies, and sold in stores in Western nations to the profit of their merchants. Societies specializing in producing one or two natural resources were especially vulnerable to a changing world economy and the whims of Western consumers.

The world economy widened the wealth gap between societies. In 1500 the differences in per capita income and living standards between people in the richer regions—China, Japan, Southeast Asia, India, Ottoman Turkey, and western Europe—had probably been minor. These peoples were roughly only two to three times better off materially than the farmers and city folk of the world's poorest farming societies. By 1900 the wealth gap between the richest and poorest societies had grown to about 10 to 1. This trend accelerated throughout the twentieth century, in part because the wealth produced in Western colonies seldom contributed to local development. Hence, by the 1950s the Belgian Congo still lacked all-weather roads linking the major cities and had only a few schools and health clinics for its millions of people.

Modern industrialization benefited Western nations. China and India had once been the world's leading manufacturing countries, and knowledge of Chinese mechanical devices probably stimulated several British inventions. Between 1750 and 1850, Britain took the lead in industrialization, and by the mid-1800s it was producing about half of the world's manufactured goods while China and India fell behind. Various other European nations, the United States, and Japan industrialized in the later 1800s. Industrialization gradually spread beyond Europe and North America, but at a highly uneven impact and pace. Western policies commonly discouraged other societies, especially colonies, from maintaining or opening industries that might compete with Western manufacturers. Hence, the British saw India not only as a market for their goods but also as a source of cash crops, such as jute and opium. In 1840 a British official boasted that his nation had "succeeded in converting India from a manufacturing country into a country exporting raw materials."[6] Although China, Persia, Egypt, the Ottoman Empire, and Mexico introduced textile industries in the nineteenth century, the British, nominally proponents of free trade, used stiff tariffs on imports to Britain to stifle many of these industries, thereby opening doors for the export of British fabrics and clothing to these countries.

Societies
Migrations

People have always been pushed to relocate by necessity or drawn to new lands by opportunity. But the rise of a modern world economy, and its constant quest for resources, markets, and labor, accelerated migration. Modern transportation networks, linked by larger and faster ships and later airplanes, facilitated the movement not only of commodities but also people. Rapid population growth also spurred migration. Between 1800 and 1900 the world population grew from 900 million to 1,500 million, with two-thirds of these people living in Asia. Some people escaped poverty and overcrowding by moving into nearby frontier regions, where they often mixed with local people, fostering hybrid cultures. Many others, more than 100 million between 1830 and 1914, left for distant lands. Some, such as enslaved Africans transported to the Americas, were taken from their homes unwillingly. In contrast, millions of Europeans and Asians sought, and often found, a better life in other countries.

The major movement of Africans resulted from the trans-Atlantic slave trade, which reached its height between 1760 and 1800. During these years over 70,000 people a year were herded onto crowded slave ships and shipped from Africa. Between 1800 and 1850 the annual export of Africans to the Americas ranged between 36,000 and 66,000. The great majority of Africans were landed in Brazil and the Caribbean islands, where people of African ancestry today account for a large part of the population. But the gradual abolition of slavery in the Americas eroded the trade. Abolition resulted in part from the efforts of some Western governments, often prompted by humanitarian organizations and Christian missionaries. Some abolitionists had themselves been slaves, such as Mary Prince, a slave from the British West Indies who was taken to London and freed; she argued eloquently in 1831: "All slaves want to be free. They work night and day, sick or well, till we are quite done up."[7] By the early 1900s slavery had declined significantly or been abolished in Africa, the Middle East, and Southeast Asia. The end of plantation slavery in the Americas opened the doors to recruitment of impoverished workers from Asia, who chiefly came voluntarily but under restrictive contracts that limited their rights by requiring them to work for years under harsh conditions.

Between 1500 and 1940 some 68 million people left Europe, creating new societies in the Americas, Australia, New Zealand, and southern Africa. The largest movement came in the nineteenth and early twentieth centuries. For example, between 1820 and 1930 some 32 million Europeans moved to the United States, the major destination. The tendency to look toward Europe for inspiration was especially strong in Argentina, Chile, Canada, Australia, and New Zealand, where many immigrants and their descendants tended to maintain their native languages, churches, and social customs and to identify with their homeland. As a result, the numerous Italians in Argentina's capital, Buenos Aires, often spoke Italian, while Anglo-Argentines sent their children to private English-medium schools. Similarly, Canadians, Australians, and New Zealanders commonly revered the British crown.

During this era, peoples from eastern and southern Asia—Chinese, Japanese, Koreans, Indians, Javanese, Filipinos—also emigrated in large numbers, usually by ship to distant shores. Many went in response to the demand among Western colonies and American nations for a labor force for the mines and plantations that supplied their wealth. As a result, Chinese mined tin in Southeast Asia and gold in California and Australia, while Indians worked on rubber plantations in British Malaya and sugar plantations in South Africa, Fiji in the South Pacific, Trinidad, and the Guianas in

[6]Quoted in Richard H. Robbins, *Global Problems and the Culture of Capitalism* (Boston: Allyn and Bacon, 1999), 90.
[7]Quoted in Pamela Scully, "Race and Ethnicity in Women's and Gender History in Global Perspective," in *Women's History in Global Perspective*, ed. Bonnie G. Smith, vol. 1 (Urbana: University of Illinois Press, 2004), 207.

ASIAN AND EUROPEAN MIGRATION, 1750–1940 During this era millions of Europeans emigrated to the Americas, South Africa, Australia, and New Zealand. Millions of Asians, especially Chinese and Indians, left their homes to work or settle in Southeast Asia, Africa, the Pacific islands, and the Americas. © 2015 Cengage Learning

Major migrations

Chinese
Japanese
Indian
European
Lebanese

South America. Immigrants often died from overwork or ill health and, as happened with Chinese in the western United States and Australia, sometimes suffered from violent attacks by local people who resented their presence. Yet, many Asians survived to raise families in their new homes. Today approximately 40 to 45 million Asians live outside, and often thousands of miles away from, their ancestral homelands. Chinese and Indians constituted the great majority of Asian migrants, settling in Southeast Asia while also establishing communities, often large, in the Americas, the Pacific and Indian Ocean islands, and parts of Africa. Their descendants became a vital presence in the world economy as merchants, miners, and plantation workers.

Today the majority of Chinese in Southeast Asia, the South Pacific and Indian Ocean islands, the Caribbean, and Latin America are engaged in commerce. A Chinese man who settled in New Zealand in the 1920s recalled the hard work that brought him success: "My generation really worked for a living. We had to open the shop at 7 A.M. and we closed [at] 1 A.M. Then we had to clean the shop. It was seldom before 2 A.M. before we got to bed."[8] The descendants of Chinese immigrants have constituted the most dynamic economic sector in Southeast Asia, with their money and initiative spurring the economic growth since 1970.

Networks
The Spread of Technologies

The modern global system owed much to innovations in technology. Improved methods of communication and transportation allowed people, ideas, and products to travel farther and faster than ever before, enhancing networks of power and exchange. For much of history, communication over long distances had been slow, depending largely on beasts of burden carrying riders or pulling wagons, and later on sailing ships. In 500 B.C.E. a message carried by successive riders on horses could travel the 1,800-mile length of

the Persian Empire in nine days. Two millennia later, in the 1600s, it took Dutch ships some nine months to sail from Amsterdam to Dutch-ruled Java to deliver news and orders. Thanks to the Industrial Revolution, communications changed dramatically. In 1844 the first telegraph messages were exchanged between Washington and Baltimore. By 1861 submarine telegraph cables linked Britain to North America, prompting a poet to write: "Two mighty lands have shaken hands, Across the deep blue sea; the world looks forward with new hope, Of better times to be."[9] The invention of the telephone in 1876 and radio in 1895 further increased the potential for communications. By the 1920s radio transmissions had become commonplace in industrial nations and British broadcasts could reach Canada, South Africa, India, and Australia.

Some technologies conveyed people and commodities as well as messages, transforming peoples' lives around the world. Railroads carried goods and passengers, with telegraph messages smoothing their journeys by passing on traffic and weather information. By 1869 railroads connected the Pacific and Atlantic coasts of North America, and by 1903 determined travelers could ride the 9,000 miles between Paris and Siberia's Pacific coast. Steamships also linked the world. The opening of the 105-mile Suez Canal in 1869 and the 51-mile Panama Canal in 1914, both of which cost the lives of thousands of workers during their construction, greatly reduced travel times for many sea journeys and also made it easier and cheaper to ship resources from Asia and

SINGAPORE'S CHINATOWN By the early 1900s Singapore, a major Southeast Asian port and commercial crossroads, was predominantly Chinese in population. The bustling streets were lined by shops, workers' quarters, theaters, brothels, and street hawkers.

Latin America to Europe and North America. Now it only took a few weeks to sail from Shanghai or Singapore to New York or London. In the early 1900s motor cars and buses continued the revolution in land transportation, allowing people to more easily commute to city jobs and downtown stores or to travel between cities. After World War I thousands of middle-class Europeans and North Americans owned their own cars, and in the 1930s the first commercial air flights began, making long-distance journeys even faster.

New technologies devoted to warfare made it easier to kill more people and at a greater distance. Most of these weapons remained largely a monopoly of Western nations and Japan during this era, facilitating imperialism and contributing to the imbalances in

[8]Quoted in Ng Bickleen Fong, *The Chinese in New Zealand* (Hong Kong: Hong Kong University Press, 1959), 96.
[9]Quoted in J. R. McNeill and William H. McNeill, *The Human Web: A Bird's-Eye View of World History* (New York: W. W. Norton, 2003), 217.

global power. For example, white adventurers and settlers used the rifle invented by the American Philo Remington (1816–1889), which was effective at 1,500 yards, to defeat, and seize the lands of, the Native Americans and the Australian Aborigines. In 1878 an Argentinean observed that the Remington rifle has left "the land strewn with the bodies of those [local Indians] who dared to oppose it."[10] Effective rifles also proved devastating in Africa against warriors armed only with spears and arrows. Military weaponry quickly improved, including more powerful repeating guns. During World War I, since Western armies had an array of repeating weapons and field artillery as well as armored tanks and battleships, the two rival alliances in that war inflicted terrible casualties on each other. With air power in World War II, the methods of warfare were now more indiscriminate in their targets and more lethal than ever before in history. In 1945 the United States used the most deadly weapon in history, the atomic bomb, to force Japanese surrender and end World War II.

Networks
The Spread of Mass Cultures

The revolution in communications and transportation technologies contributed to the creation and spread of mass cultures, popular entertainments appealing to a large audience that often crossed class divisions and national borders.

People were increasingly exposed to cultural products, such as films and music, and pastimes, such as sports, that were common in other regions of their countries or imported from abroad. The media disseminated mass culture, reporting on film stars and sports events or playing popular music. As literacy rates rose, the print media gained particular influence. Newspapers made available news and opinions in hundreds of languages. Popular books, from Arab detective novels to romances written in South Africa's Xhosa **(KHO-sa)** language, competed with classic works of philosophy and religion for the hearts and minds of readers.

By spreading cultural influences into other societies, mass communications and increased travel often fostered Westernization. Some organizations, such as the Red Cross, and social movements, such as feminism, crossed borders. American film stars such as Charlie Chaplin, born in Britain, became known throughout the world, and U.S.-born jazz musicians often made a living playing the nightclubs of Europe and Asia, where they inspired local musicians to take up jazz. Many societies adopted and excelled in Western sports. European football (soccer) became an international sport, played and watched all over the world. Influences from non-Western cultures also spread, contributing to a creative cultural mixing. For example, in the eighteenth and nineteenth centuries the growing Western interest in Chinese painting, Japanese prints, Indonesian gamelan music, and African woodcarvings influenced Western arts. Later, in

the 1930s, Indian films and popular music became popular in Southeast Asia and the Middle East. Cuban music, a mix of African and Western traditions, developed a large following in West and Central Africa, where it blended with local styles.

As people followed world events in newspapers and radio newscasts, global crises became more widely known. An avid news follower, the Trinidad calypso singer who humorously called himself Atilla the Hun, appraised the devastation in the world of the later 1930s:

> All we can hear is of unrest, riots, revolutions; There is war in Spain and China. Man using all his skill and ingenuity making weapons to destroy humanity. In the [Italian invasion of Ethiopia] it is said, over six hundred thousand maimed and dead. The grim reaper has taken a gigantic toll. Why all the bloodshed and devastation, Decimating the earth's population? Why can't this warfare cease? All that the tortured world needs is peace.[11]

Soon after Atilla's plea, World War II raised the level of violence even further, providing a fitting end to a turbulent, violent era during which the world's people had become more closely linked into a common global system.

[10]Quoted in L. S. Stavrianos, "The Global Redistribution of Man," in *World Migration in Modern Times*, ed. Franklin D. Scott (Englewood Cliffs, NJ: Prentice-Hall, 1968), 170.
[11]Quoted in Gordon Rohlehr, *Calypso and Society in Pre-Independence Trinidad* (Port of Spain: Gordon Rohlehr, 1990), 80–81.

19 Modern Transitions: Revolutions, Industries, Ideologies, Empires, 1750–1914

Hulton Archive/Getty Images

CRYSTAL PALACE EXPOSITION OF 1851 Attracting more than 6 million visitors, the Great Exhibition, held at the Crystal Palace in London in 1851, showcased industrial products and the companies that produced them from all over the world but especially from Europe. This painting shows the inauguration, opened by Queen Victoria.

From this foul drain the greatest stream of human industry flows out to fertilize the whole world. From this filthy sewer pure gold flows. Here humanity attains its most complete development and its most brutish.

—French writer Alexis de Tocqueville on Manchester, England, 1835[1]

On a spring day in 1851 Londoners celebrated their era's technological achievements. People of all social classes, from bankers and nobles to sailors, day laborers, and barmaids, headed for the spectacular new Crystal Palace in Hyde Park for the official opening, led by Queen Victoria, of the Great Exhibition celebrating "The Works of Industry of All Nations." The less affluent walked while the wealthy rode in horse-drawn carriages or steam-powered buses. Some came by railroad from other British cities or by steamships from France and Belgium to honor progress. The first "world's fair" featured displays by fourteen thousand firms showcasing British industrial leadership and the mineral basis such as coal and iron ore. The hall of machinery contained inventions that were revolutionizing British life: power textile looms, hydraulic presses, printing presses, marine engines, and locomotives that could attain an unimaginable 60 miles per hour. Another hall featured industrial products that British merchants sold all over the world, including fine wool, cotton, linen, and silk textiles. Manchester, condemned as a "foul drain" but praised for fostering development, made many products. Nearly half of the exhibitors represented other European and North American countries, illustrating industrialization's spread.

Since its beginning three-quarters of a century earlier, industrialization was already transforming Europe's social and physical landscapes. The British, enamored with progress, considered modern industry, economic growth, and creative science humanity's triumph over the natural world. Industrialization certainly enhanced European and North American economic and military power around the world. Political revolutions and new ideologies also redefined Europe and the Americas between 1750 and 1914. Great Britain, France, Germany, and Russia emerged as the main European powers, while the United States became the strongest American country. But the trends yielded mixed blessings. The British writer Charles Dickens, commenting on the French Revolution, summed up the era: "It was the best of times, it was the worst of times. It was the age of wisdom, it was the age of foolishness, it was the season of light, it was the season of darkness, it was the spring of hope, it was the winter of despair."[2] These trends had also sparked a renewal of imperialism, with various European nations acquiring or expanding empires in Asia and Africa.

[1] Quoted in Eric Hobsbawm, *The Age of Revolution, 1789–1848* (New York: New American Library, 1962), 44.
[2] From Charles Dickens, *A Tale of Two Cities* (New York: Bantam, 1989), 1.

The Age of Revolution

How did the Caribbean and Latin American revolutions compare with those in North America and Europe?

The **Age of Revolution** (1770s–1840s) refers to the period when violent upheavals rocked North America, Europe, the Caribbean, and Latin America as revolutionaries seized power through armed violence. While political revolutions changed governments' personnel and structure, social revolutions transformed both the political and social order. The American Revolution launched the era, ending British colonial rule and forming a new, more democratic government. The French Revolution, the major social revolution, overthrew discredited royalty and aristocratic privilege, inspiring other peoples to seek radical changes in states, ideologies, and class structures. As in British North America, dissatisfaction with colonialism festered in the Caribbean and Spanish America, sparking revolutions and wars of independence.

Age of Revolution The period from the 1770s through the 1840s when revolutions rocked North America, Europe, the Caribbean, and Latin America.

1700   **1750**   **1800**

EUROPE

1770s–1840s	Age of Revolution
1770s–1870s	First Industrial Revolution
1774	James Watt's first rotary steam engine
1776	Adam Smith's *The Wealth of Nations*
1789–1815	French Revolution
1791–1792	Constitutional state in Poland-Lithuania
1800	British Act of Union
1804	Crowning of Napoleon as emperor of France
1810–1811	Height of Napoleon's empire
1815	Defeat of Napoleon at Battle of Waterloo; Congress of Vienna
1821–1830	Greek war of independence

THE AMERICAS

1770s–1840s	Age of Revolution
1773	Boston Tea Party
1776	American Declaration of Independence
1776–1783	American Revolution
1783	Britain's recognition of U.S. independence
1787	U.S. constitutional convention; Northwest Ordinance for forming new states
1791–1804	Haitian Revolution
1808	Move of Portuguese royal family to Brazil
1810–1811	First Mexican revolution
1810–1826	Spanish-American wars of independence
1816	Argentine independence
1821	Founding of Gran Colombian republic by Bolívar
1822	Mexican independence; Dom Pedro emperor of Brazil

These revolutions, brutal but momentous events in modern world history, had much in common. Though often well educated and from middle-class or upper-class backgrounds, revolutionary leaders mobilized disenchanted peasants and urban workers. Many revolutions, including the French, moved from moderate to more extreme actions such as purging dissidents, rivals, or opponents. Although they replaced repressive and inequitable systems, few revolutionaries satisfied their people's demands.

British Colonialism and the American Revolution

In the late 1700s Europeans and Latin Americans watched fascinated as disaffected citizens in the thirteen British colonies in North America ended colonial rule and established the United States. American revolutionary leaders, proclaiming Enlightenment political theories such as democracy and personal freedom, formed a new representative government.

In the mid-1700s Britain's hold on these colonies seemed strong. Each colony from New Hampshire to Georgia had unique institutions and economies. The southern colonies depended largely on plantation slavery, while the northern colonies had a more balanced economy that combined commerce and manufacturing with farming. Only 2 million persons lived in the colonies; the largest town, Boston, had twenty thousand residents. A fifth of the colonial population was African American, mostly slaves concentrated in the southern plantation zone. White American colonists, generally prosperous,

1850   1900   1950   2000

1830–1831 Wave of revolutions across Europe

1831 Formation of Young Italy movement by Mazzini

1845–1846 Irish potato famine

1848 Wave of revolts across Europe; *The Communist Manifesto* by Marx and Engels

1851 Great Exhibition in London

1859–1870 Unification of Italy

1862–1871 Unification of Germany

1870s–1914 Second Industrial Revolution

1830 Independence of Colombia, Venezuela, and Ecuador

1839 Division of Central American states

enjoyed considerable self-government and religious toleration, voted for local assemblies and mayors if they were adult males with sufficient property, faced much lighter taxes than people in Britain, and eagerly consumed British culture.

But tensions increased. Many colonists, claiming the label of Americans, felt divorced from Britain and increasingly resented British policies, such as taxation without representation in the British Parliament. Britain also placed more restrictions than before on local American manufacturing. Clumsy British attempts to raise taxes, enforce long-ignored laws, and reserve coveted land west of the Appalachians for Indians angered many colonists, prompting boycotts of British goods. In 1773, protesters of a higher tea tax, dressed as Indians, raided three British ships in Boston harbor and dumped their cargo of tea overboard, an event known as the Boston Tea Party.

Clashes increased between colonists favoring independence, or Patriots, and those opposed, called Loyalists. Most Patriot and Loyalist leaders were wealthy lawyers, physicians, journalists, merchants, and landowners. Patriot leaders, admiring European Enlightenment thinkers such as John Locke in England and Baron de Montesquieu in France, favored democracy and a republic. The writings of antiroyalist Englishman Tom Paine (1737–1809), a sailor and teacher turned journalist, promoted independence, church-state separation, social equality, women's rights, abolition of slavery, and other ideas then considered radical. Paine's passionate pamphlet *Common Sense*, urging Americans to oppose tyranny and forcibly free themselves to "begin the world over again," helped galvanize public opinion against colonialism.

The colonies' many competing churches and schools of thought fostered intellectual diversity. Some Patriots were devout Protestants or Catholics, others free thinkers. Some, including Paine, Thomas Jefferson, James Madison, Benjamin Franklin, and George Washington, were deists, believing in an impersonal creator who left humanity alone, and were often suspicious of organized churches. Patriot leaders reflected their times: some owned slaves, smuggled, took mistresses, had illegitimate children, and, like many male colonists, drank heavily.

After preliminary American-British skirmishes, delegates met, and on July 4, 1776, approved the Declaration of Independence from the British crown, written largely by Thomas Jefferson (1743–1826), a Virginia planter. The Declaration stated, "We hold these truths to be self-evident, that all men are created equal, that they are endowed by their Creator with certain inalienable Rights, that among these are Life, Liberty and the pursuit of Happiness."[3] Perhaps a third of colonists remained Loyalists, and many others, especially less affluent whites, were neutral or apathetic. A revolutionary army organized and commanded by George Washington (1732–1799), a wealthy Virginia farmer and decorated veteran of earlier wars against France and its Indian allies, then fought the British and their allies for six bitter years, described by Tom Paine as "the times that try men's souls."

During the war, Patriot women raised funds, served as cooks and nurses in army camps, and engaged in sabotage and spying. A few, disguising themselves as men, joined the combat. Britain's rivals, France and Spain, aided the Patriot cause. Many Indians, resenting colonists for aggressively occupying Indian lands, and some black slaves, promised their freedom by a British general, supported Britain. Some Loyalists and British officials also accused Patriots of hypocrisy, wanting their freedom while maintaining slavery and exploitation for nonwhites. But the American defeat of British forces at Yorktown, Virginia, in 1781 proved decisive, and Britain recognized American independence in 1783. Despite their democratic values, after the war Patriots treated Loyalists harshly, confiscating their land and jailing them. Ultimately 100,000 Loyalists were expelled or fled to Canada or England.

The thirteen former colonies formed an independent federation, the United States of America, and the founders then debated the relative powers of states and a national government that could unite them. The first weak confederation proved unworkable. Seeking a stronger central government, in 1787 delegates approved a constitution, mostly written by James Madison (1751–1836), a well-educated Virginian, that established an elected president and a congress presiding over a federal system that granted the states many powers. Delegates then elected war hero Washington (g. 1789–1797), admired for his integrity and managerial skills, as the republic's first president. The first elected congress approved ten constitutional amendments, known as the Bill of Rights, enshrining Enlightenment values such as freedom of speech, assembly, press, and religion.

However, the new republic made no effort to transform the social order by challenging slavery, recognizing Native American claims to land, or expanding voting rights even to all white men, much less non-white men and all women. Although some Patriots, including Washington, freed their slaves and most northern states gradually abolished slavery, blacks fighting for Britain were often executed or reenslaved; some left for Canada. Indians watched bitterly as free Americans claimed and settled most Indian land east of the Mississippi River after the U.S. Congress approved the Northwest Ordinance, allowing frontier settlements to join the United States. Women did not gain equal rights with men, despite sacrificing to win independence and managing their absent husbands' shops, businesses, and farms during the war. However, new laws made it somewhat easier for women, like men, to obtain a divorce.

Americans, believing they had formed a society unique to history, an idea known as American "exceptionalism," considered themselves the world's most democratic, individualistic, enterprising, prosperous, technological, and self-determining society, unhindered by history's burdens. Yet, Americans also contended that their ideas and institutions were relevant for everyone, agreeing with Puritan Massachusetts governor John Winthrop's claim in 1630 that his new society constituted a "City upon a Hill, [with] the eyes of all people upon us."[4]

---

[3]From David A. Hollinger and Charles Capper, eds., *The American Intellectual Tradition: A Sourcebook*, vol. 1, 2nd ed. (New York: Oxford University Press, 1993), 131.

[4]Quoted in William Appleman Williams, *America Confronts a Revolutionary World, 1775–1976* (New York: William Morrow, 1976), 15, 25.

Jefferson declared America a standing monument and example for the world. These attitudes remained powerful in American thought.

The French Revolution

The French Revolution electrified Europe by replacing the monarchy with a republic and spreading values of liberty and social equality, but it also generated terrible violence, despotic leaders, and long years of war, reshaping Europe. The Revolution preached "liberty, equality, and fraternity" and a fairer wealth distribution, and the middle classes took over government in the name of the common people. But the Revolution also plunged Europe into a prolonged crisis and wars between France and its European rivals, who feared the spread of radical ideas and sought to restore French royal government.

The Revolution had many causes. Aiding the anti-British cause in the American War of Independence worsened long-standing financial problems rooted in an unjust economic system that badly needed reform. Exempting Roman Catholic clergy and privileged nobility from most direct taxes put the entire burden on artisans and peasants. Several bad harvests, food shortages, high prices, and high unemployment spurred resentment. People believed, erroneously, that the difficulty the poor had in buying bread led Marie-Antoinette, the king's wife, to contemptuously remark: "Let them eat cake."

To calm rising passions, King Louis XVI (1754–1793) called the Estates General, a long-dormant consultative body including representatives of the clergy, the nobility, and finally a Third Estate comprising elected representatives from the middle classes and peasants. The Third Estate's leaders, representing most of the population, demanded influence reflecting their numbers. Stalemated in the Estates General, Third Estate delegates, some inspired by Enlightenment thinkers and the American Revolution, formed a rival national assembly and began writing a new French constitution. In response, the king called in the army to restore order, provoking anger and violence.

The Revolution erupted in Paris in 1789 after armed crowds stormed the Bastille, the royal prison and hated symbol of tyranny, releasing prisoners and seizing gunpowder and cannon. The date of the bloody but inspirational Bastille attack (July 14) later became France's national holiday. As both men and women took up arms, the terrified nobility fled. Third Estate members, after forming a new Constituent Assembly, adopted the Declaration of the Rights of Man and of the Citizen, which was strongly influenced by the English Bill of Rights of 1689 and the new United States constitution. The Declaration announced that all people everywhere had a natural right to liberty, property, equality, security, religious toleration, and freedom of expression, press, and association. A new constitution made the king bound by laws and subject to an elected assembly, outlawed slavery, and reorganized and weakened the church, confiscating the higher clergy's vast wealth. French political reform inspired other Europeans. In 1791 reformers in Poland-Lithuania reshaped the state, expanding voting rights. But Russia, supported by Polish nobility, crushed the reformist government.

With several European states demanding restoration of royal power, French leaders declared war in 1792. The army recruited volunteers, identifying the defense of France with revolutionary ideals and proclaiming that "young men shall go forth in battle, married men shall forge weapons, women shall make tents and clothing, and shall serve in hospitals."[5] A national convention, elected by universal male suffrage, made France a republic, ending the monarchy. In the name of the

Storming of the Bastille on 14th July 1789 (oil on panel), French School, (18th century)/Musee de la Ville de Paris, Musee Carnavalet, Paris, France/The Bridgeman Art Library

STORMING THE BASTILLE This painting celebrates the taking of the Bastille, a castle prison in Paris that symbolized hated royal rule, by armed citizens and soldiers. The governor and his officials are led out and will soon be executed.

---

[5]Quoted in Peter N. Stearns, *Life and Society in the West: The Modern Centuries* (San Diego: Harcourt Brace Jovanovich, 1988), 164.

world's people, France crusaded to end absolute monarchies and social inequality in Europe. With patriotic enthusiasm the French public rallied behind the revolutionary government, singing a song, the *Marseillaise* (mar-sye-EZ), that was written as a call to oppose tyranny and that is now France's national anthem. In 1793 revolutionaries executed King Louis XVI for treason.

Military conflict intensified internal dissent and economic problems in France. Some leaders emphasized preserving the Revolution's libertarian principles. However, a more radical faction, the Jacobins (JAK-uh-binz), believing these rights had to be postponed, seized the state and imposed a dictatorship to promote internal security. The Jacobins' Committee of Public Safety used terror against real or imagined opponents, often cutting off their victims' heads in public. They executed perhaps forty thousand French citizens, mostly rebellious peasants and provincial leaders, and arrested tens of thousands more, often on flimsy evidence. The Jacobins' leader, Maximilien Robespierre (1758–1794), a lawyer and once an idealistic humanist, became the most zealous promoter of terror against alleged counterrevolutionaries, some his former allies. As the violence and radicalism intensified, sowing dissention, some Jacobin leaders, including Robespierre, were executed. The terror abated when Jacobins lost power in 1795, but several constructive Jacobin policies endured, including guaranteeing all children the right to public education.

Although not all its accomplishments proved long-lasting, the Revolution created a new order that inspired generations of revolutionaries to come. Much of the vocabulary of modern politics emerged, including terms such as *conservative* and *right-wing*, referring to those who favored retaining the status quo or restoring the past, and *liberal* and *left-wing*, meaning progressives wanting faster change. Revolutionary France also transformed warfare by introducing conscription and promotion through the ranks. France turned the countries it occupied or conquered, such as Belgium, into "sister republics" where revolutionary governments promoted human rights.

But the Jacobins' terrible violence undermined personal liberty, dampening the Revolution's appeal. The French trauma of anarchy and despotism turned North Americans against revolutions. Observers also debated whether the "Rights of Man" included women. Olympe de Gouges (1748–1793), a French butcher's daughter, published a manifesto complaining that women were excluded from decision making and tried to organize a female militia to fight for France, but she was executed by the Jacobins. A British campaigner for women's rights, Mary Wollstonecraft (1759–1797), wrote the *Vindication of the Rights of Women* in 1792, calling for equal opportunities in education and society. But despite the efforts of reformers, women remained excluded from active citizenship in France and nearly everywhere else.

Jacobins A radical faction in the French Revolution that believed civil rights had to be set aside in a crisis and that executed thousands of French citizens.

The Napoleonic Era and a New European Politics

The terror and shifting war fortunes fostered a promonarchy resurgence. Antiroyalists turned to ambitious General Napoleon Bonaparte (BOW-nuh-pahrt) (1769–1821), a lawyer's son and brilliant military strategist from the French-ruled island of Corsica. A lowly artillery officer once imprisoned for alleged Jacobin ties, he rapidly rose through the ranks through political connections and charisma to command major military victories in France, Italy, Austria, and Egypt. In 1799 Bonaparte became First Consul, the most powerful political office. With many believing that only a dictator could provide stability, in 1804 Bonaparte crowned himself emperor in a regal coronation attended by the pope, an event that harkened back a millennium to Charlemagne's crowning. Quickly promoting reconciliation and economic prosperity, Bonaparte made the Revolution's core values permanent by standardizing revolutionary laws, including citizens' equality before the law. However, his dictatorial tendencies betrayed French liberty. Developing a taste for the trappings of royal power, he divorced his childless wife, the popular Empress Josephine, and married an eighteen-year-old Austrian princess, Marie-Louise, hoping for an heir.

Wars soon resumed. In 1805 Britain, the dominant sea power, allied with Austria, Prussia, and Russia against France. France won most land battles and occupied much of western Europe. Bonaparte's family now ruled Spain, Naples, and some German states. But armed resistance in Spain and German states, a costly invasion of Russia resulting in a humiliating retreat, and an invasion of France by rival powers sapped Bonaparte's military strength. Bonaparte abdicated and was imprisoned on an Italian island. He escaped and regrouped his forces, but he finally lost to British and Prussian armies at Waterloo, a Belgian village, in 1815. The Bourbon family reclaimed the French throne, and Bonaparte spent his remaining years in exile.

With revolutionary France and Napoleon's empire defeated, the victorious allies met in 1815 at the Congress of Vienna to remold the European state system and partly restore the status quo (see Map 19.1). Europeans preferring monarchy and church-state alliance rejoiced at the French defeat. The men overthrowing French control in Naples sang, "Naples won't stay a republic. Here's an end to equality. Here's an end to liberty. Long live God and his Majesty."[6] Dominated by Austria, Britain, Russia, and the revived royalist France, the Congress reaffirmed pre-Napoleonic borders and restored most rulers displaced by revolutionaries and reformers. However, thirty-nine German states moved toward national unity, forming the German Confederation. Russia invaded Poland-Lithuania, destroying the constitutional government and partitioning the nation between Russia and Prussia.

Once the revolutionary genie was out of the bottle, however, all the established order's best efforts could not put it back again. Revolutionary ideas combined with popular discontent

---

[6]Quoted in Eric Hobsbawm, *Workers: World of Labor* (New York: Pantheon), 34.

MAP 19.1 EUROPE IN 1815 With the Napoleonic wars ended, the Congress of Vienna redrew the map of Europe. France, Austria, Spain, Britain, and a growing Prussia were the dominant states, but the Ottoman Turks still ruled a large area of southeastern Europe. © 2015 Cengage Learning

with despotism, and frequent wars unsettled Europe as various revolutions broke out in 1830–1831. The French overthrew despotic Bourbon king Charles X and installed his more progressive cousin, Louis-Philippe (1773–1850), as a constitutional monarch, recognizing some liberties. Uprisings in several German and Italian states and Poland sought voting rights, while peasant rebellions caused by poverty and unemployment rocked Britain.

Poor harvests, rising unemployment, massive poverty, and a desire for representative government sparked even more turbulent revolts in 1848. These upheavals began in France, forcing increasingly unpopular Louis-Philippe to

abdicate, and soon spread to Austria, Hungary, and many German and Italian states. German students met in city marketplaces, demanding elected parliaments and civil liberties such as free speech and press. Some places workers demanded better conditions. But conservative regimes soon violently crushed these uncoordinated movements. A French observer said that "nothing was lacking" in the repression in Paris, "not grapeshot, nor bullets, nor demolished houses, nor martial law, nor the ferocity of the soldiery, nor the insults to the dead."[7] Still, the uprisings spread democratic ideas, and parliamentary power increased in countries such as Denmark and the Netherlands. To prevent revolutionary outbursts,

[7]Quoted in Michael Elliott-Bateman et al., *Revolt to Revolution: Studies in the 19th and 20th Century European Experience* (Manchester, England: Manchester University Press, 1974), 87.

many European governments also began considering social and economic reforms, such as higher wages, to improve people's lives.

Caribbean Societies and the Haitian Revolution

Most small Caribbean islands and the Guianas in northeast South America were British, French, or Dutch plantation colonies inhabited chiefly by slaves of African ancestry. In these colonies, Afro-Caribbean peoples mixed European cultural forms and languages with African traditions. Hence, in British-colonized Jamaica, Barbados, and Antigua, most adopted Christianity and Anglo-Saxon names. The first successful Caribbean movement to overthrow colonialism occurred in Haiti, where slaves fought their way to power.

Slave revolts were common throughout the colonial era, but only the Haitian Revolution overthrew a regime. In 1791 some 100,000 Afro-Haitians, inspired by the French Revolution's slogans of liberty and equality, rose up against the oppressive society and French planters. They were led by Toussaint L'Ouverture **(too-SAN loo-ver-CHORE)** (1746–1803), a freed slave who envisioned a republic of free people. Raised a Catholic, Toussaint had learned French and Latin from an older slave.

For a decade Afro-Haitians fought the French military and anti-French British and Spanish forces hoping to capitalize on the turmoil. By 1801 Toussaint's forces controlled Haiti and had freed the slaves. But Napoleon Bonaparte sent in larger forces and captured Toussaint, who died in a French prison. In 1804 Afro-Haitians defeated Napoleon's army and established the Western Hemisphere's second independent nation after the United States. Around the Americas the Haitian Revolution cheered slaves and abolitionists but alarmed planters more determined to preserve slavery. The United States, still a slave-owning nation, withheld diplomatic recognition of the black republic. As French planters were either killed or fled, ex-slaves took over sugar production. But the promise of a better life for Haitians proved short-lived; Toussaint's successor, the Africa-born Jean Jacques Dessalines **(de-sah-LEEN)** (1758–1806), ruled despotically, beginning two centuries of tyranny.

Latin America's Independence Wars

Spain and Portugal ruled much larger and more populous American empires than Britain. By 1810 some 18 million people lived under Spanish rule from California to South America's southern tip, including 4 million Europeans, 8 million Indians, 1 million blacks, and 5 million people of mixed descent. Corruption ran deep, with planters, ranchers, mine owners, bureaucrats, and church officials benefiting from the Spanish government's opposition to any major changes. All preferred a system that sent raw materials, such as silver

and beef, to Spain rather than develop domestic institutions or markets.

Unlike British North America, Spain allowed little self-government, maintained economic monocultures, and imposed one dominant religion: Roman Catholicism. In addition, Latin American social conditions fostered disunity and inequality. American-born whites, called creoles, resented influential newcomers from Spain but also feared that resistance against Spain might get out of control and threaten their position. Meanwhile, the huge underclass of Indians, enslaved Africans, and mixed-descent people faced growing unemployment and perhaps the world's most inequitable wealth distribution. Even thought was repressed, as a rigid Catholic Church wary of dissent discouraged intellectual diversity. The Inquisition, considering any literature espousing equality and liberty seditious, punished "heretics." Local critics accused church and state of "[keeping] thought in chains."[8]

Given these political and social inequalities, revolts punctuated Spanish colonial rule. In Mexico a Maya revolt against high taxes and church repression in 1761 spurred Spanish reprisals, and in the 1780s, a mass uprising led by the wealthy, well-educated mestizo Tupac Amaru II (1740–1781), who claimed descent from an Inca king and dressed in royal Inca clothing, spread over large areas of Peru and into neighboring Andean regions. Tupac and Michaela Bastidas, his feisty wife and brilliant strategist, organized a broad-based coalition that seized much of the colony. They sought an independent state, with Tupac as king, where Indians, mestizos, and creoles would live in harmony. Many peasant followers revived Inca religion and attacked Catholic churches and clergy. However, the better-armed Spanish defeated the rebel bands, executing Tupac and his family.

Eventually, dissatisfaction exploded into wars of national independence (1810–1826). Creole merchants and ranchers, criticizing Spain's commercial monopoly, increasing taxes, and colonial favoritism toward those born in Spain, also wanted a government role. Creoles often felt more loyalty to their American region than distant Spain. Some were also inspired by the Enlightenment and the American and French Revolutions. Britain, pressuring Spain and Portugal to open Latin American markets to British goods, secretly aided anticolonial groups. Meanwhile, Spain experienced domestic political problems, including French occupation during the Napoleonic wars.

With Spain refusing serious political concessions, two separate independence movements began in Venezuela and Argentina, led respectively by Simon Bolivar **(bow-LEE-vahr)** and Jose de San Martin. From a wealthy Caracas family that owned slaves, land, and mines, Bolivar (1783–1830), a charismatic Spain-educated lawyer and free thinker who admired rationalist Enlightenment thought, offered an inclusive view of his Latin American people: "We are a microcosm of the human race, a world apart, neither Indian nor Europeans, but a part of each."[9] Bolivar spent time in Haiti and Jamaica, where he gained sympathy for blacks, and in 1816 he

---

[8]Jose de San Martin, quoted in Edwin Early, *The History Atlas of South America* (New York: Macmillan, 1998), 76.
[9]Quoted in Carlos Fuentes, *The Buried Mirror: Reflections on Spain and the New World* (New York: Houghton Mifflin, 1992), 252.

akg-images

SIMON BOLIVAR The main leader of the anti-Spanish war of independence in northern South America, Bolivar came to be known as "the Liberator," a symbol of Latin American nationalism and the struggle for political freedom.

Chile in 1818. In 1824 San Martin and Bolivar cooperated to liberate Peru, where royalist sympathies were strongest.

As in North America, some women enthusiastically served as soldiers and nurses in the fight for liberation. For example, Policarpa Salavarrieta helped Bolivar as a spy until she was captured by the Spanish. Before her execution in Bogota's main plaza, she exclaimed: "Although I am a woman and young, I have more than enough courage to suffer this death and a thousand more."[10] Generally, however, women still lived in patriarchal societies that offered few new legal or political rights.

Although these wars for liberation were eventually successful, their aftermath was complicated. Economies were damaged while people fled the fighting. Moreover, the new creole-dominated governments often forgot promises made to the Indians, mestizos, mulattos, and blacks who had constituted most of the revolutionary armies. While some slaves gained freedom, slavery was not abolished. Unlike in the United States, Latin America's new leaders also largely failed to form democratic governments. Bolivar could not hold his own country together; in 1830 Gran Colombia broke into Colombia, Ecuador, and Venezuela. Meanwhile, Uruguay and Paraguay split from Argentina, and Bolivia from Peru. Disillusioned, Bolivar concluded that Latin America was ungovernable.

Mexico and Brazil also experienced political change, though less violently (see Map 19.2). In 1810 two progressive Mexican Catholic priests, creole Manuel Hidalgo and mestizo Jose Maria Morelos **(moh-RAY-los)**, mobilized peasants and miners to launch a revolt promoting independence, abolition of slavery, and social reform. Creole conservatives and royalists suppressed that revolt, but a compromise between factions brought Mexico independence in 1822 under a creole general, Agustin de Iturbide **(ah-goos-TEEN deh ee-tur-BEE-deh)** (1783–1824), who proclaimed himself emperor. However, the anti-Spanish alliance of creoles, mestizos, and Indians unraveled, and a republican revolt ousted Iturbide. Central American peoples split off from Mexico, by 1839 splintering into five states.

By the late 1700s Brazil was the wealthiest part of the Portuguese empire, but only white plantation and gold mine owners benefited from this wealth. Since Brazil accounted for a quarter to a third of all Africans arriving in the Americas, blacks vastly outnumbered Native Americans. Disgruntled Afro-Brazilians demanding a better life faced many setbacks,

formed an army in 1816 to liberate northern South America, offering freedom to slaves who aided his cause. After many setbacks, Bolivar's forces triumphed. In 1821 the resulting republic of Gran Colombia united Colombia, Ecuador, and Venezuela. San Martin (1778–1850), a former Spanish army colonel, helped Argentina gain independence in 1816 and

[10]Quoted in E. Bradford Burns and Julie A. Charlip, *Latin America: A Concise Interpretive History*, 7th ed. (Upper Saddle River, NJ: Prentice-Hall, 2002), 75.

MAP 19.2 **LATIN AMERICAN INDEPENDENCE, 1840** By 1840 all of Latin America except for Cuba and Puerto Rico, still Spanish colonies, had become independent, with Brazil and Mexico the largest countries. Later the Central American provinces and Gran Colombia would fragment into smaller nations, and Argentina would annex Patagonia. © 2015 Cengage Learning

including defeat of a 1799 revolt in the northeastern state of Bahia **(buh-HEE-uh)**. Yet, Brazil enjoyed a nearly bloodless transition to independence. In 1808 the Portuguese royal family and government sought refuge in Brazil to escape the Napoleonic wars, and in the coming years Brazilians increasingly viewed themselves as separate from Portugal. A royal family member, Dom Pedro (1798–1834), severed ties with Portugal completely in 1822, becoming emperor of Brazil as Pedro I. But despite a new elected parliament, most Brazilians had no vote, Pedro I governed autocratically, and Brazilian politics was dominated by merchants, landowners, and the royal family.

MAKE SURE YOU UNDERSTAND THESE KEY POINTS BEFORE MOVING ON

- After a first failed attempt at confederation, the thirteen American colonies agreed upon a system that balanced federal and state powers, but the American Revolution did little to change the social order and did not extend equal rights to blacks, women, and Indians.

- The French Revolution, which aimed to wrest control from the nobility and the clergy, achieved some of its progressive goals and was an inspiration to some societies, but it led to a period of war and widespread terror.

- After over a decade of revolutionary struggle, the Afro-Haitian slaves won their freedom from the French, but they soon fell under the control of an African-born despot.

- Rising dissatisfaction among South Americans, particularly creoles, led to successful independence movements throughout the continent, though the newly free nations had trouble forming representative and democratic governments.

- After Mexico obtained its independence, the coalition that had opposed the Spanish fell apart, while members of the Portuguese royal family who fled to Brazil helped it to obtain its independence peacefully.

aplia

The Industrial Revolution and Economic Growth

How did industrialization reshape economic and social life?

The **Industrial Revolution**, a dramatic transformation in the production and transportation of goods, reshaped economic, political, and social patterns of Europe and later North America and Japan. In perhaps the greatest transformation since settled farming, urbanization, and the first states arose millennia ago, for the first time in history the shackles were taken off societies' productive power and people became capable of a rapid, constant, and seemingly limitless increase in goods and services. In the late 1700s Britain made breakthroughs in productivity that then crossed the English Channel to western Europe and the Atlantic to North America, eventually transforming Europe's limited power of 1750 into Western domination over much of the world by 1914.

The Age of Machines

The Industrial Revolution had deep roots. The Renaissance, Reformation, Scientific Revolution, and Enlightenment generated new ways of thought and understandings of the natural and physical world, while newly discovered lands, animals, plants, peoples, and cultures stimulated curiosity about the world. At the same time, commercial capitalism and conquest overseas formed political and economic links between the Americas, the African coast, some Asian societies, and western Europe, allowing Europeans to acquire natural resources and great wealth overseas for investment in new technologies and production of more commodities for the world market.

Great Britain became the world's leading trading nation. By the early 1700s British inventors had experimented with steam power and spinning machines, and accelerating world demand then spurred Britain to replace India as the main cotton textiles supplier. Britain had many advantages: a diverse intellectual atmosphere, a reasonably democratic political system, favorable terrain for building transportation networks, abundant raw materials like coal and iron, and many water sources to run machines. Between the 1780s and 1830s Britain dominated industrialization, thanks partly to its profits from British-controlled Caribbean islands, North American colonies, and trading posts in India. Some British companies, enriched by the trans-Atlantic slave trade and by sugar, cotton, and tobacco plantations in the Americas, often invested their excess capital in new British industries. The English Midlands east of Liverpool, a slave trade port, and northern Wales, near rich coal and iron ore fields, became the center of British industry (see Map 19.3).

Machines now produced goods and performed more human tasks, reshaping peoples' lives. Instead of things being made by hand by people or animals, aided by simple tools, they were made by increasingly complicated chemical processes and machines moved by energy derived from steam and other inanimate sources. By tapping the earth's resources and turning them into commodities,

Industrial Revolution A dramatic transformation in the production and transportation of goods.

MAP 19.3 INDUSTRIAL TRANSFORMATION IN ENGLAND British industrialization mostly occurred near coalfields and iron ore deposits, spurring the rise of cities such as Birmingham, Leeds, Liverpool, and Manchester. © 2015 Cengage Learning

the Industrial Revolution created both material richness and misery. Between the 1770s and 1914 sprawling and polluted industrial cities such as Manchester displaced peasant holdings, country estates, and domestic workshops, widening the gap between the few rich and the many poor. After the late 1700s Europe's material culture changed more than it had in the previous 750 years. Today industrialized societies use transportation, wear fabrics, and employ building materials inconceivable in 1750. As one measure of change, consider some English words that first appeared between 1780 and 1850: *industry, factory, middle class, working class, engineer, crisis, statistics, strike,* and *pauper.*

The Industrial Revolution triggered continual technological innovations and led to increasing economic activity, as inventions in one industry stimulated inventions in others. New cotton machines created demand for more plentiful and reliable power than that provided by water wheels and horses. The steam pump invented in 1712 was inefficient, but in 1774 Scottish inventor James Watt (1736–1819), financed by a wealthy merchant, produced the first successful rotary steam engine. Useful in many industrial activities, steam engines provided power for textile mills, iron furnaces, flour mills, and mines. In powering railroads and steamships, steam power also conquered time and space, bringing the

Mansell/Time & Life Pictures/Getty Images

INDUSTRIAL SHEFFIELD This mid-nineteenth century illustration of one of the key English industrial cities, Sheffield, shows the smokestacks and factories, many specializing in producing steel and metal goods, that dominated the landscape.

world much closer together. Watt's backer, Matthew Boulton, claimed he had to sell steam engines to all the world to make money.

The need for more iron, steel, and coal for the new machines and engines led to improvements in mining, metalworking, and then transportation to move coal and ore. Eventually people accepted technological and economic growth as normal. British novelist William Thackeray celebrated the changes in 1860: "It is only yesterday, but what a gulf between now and then! *Then* was the old world. Stagecoaches, riding horses, pack-horses, knights in armor, Norman invaders, Roman legions. But your railroad starts a new era."[11] Mechanization also provoked fear. Between 1815 and 1830 Luddites, British anti-industrialization activists, most of them skilled textile workers, invaded factories and destroyed machines in a mass protest against mechanization. After British troops stopped the destruction, wrecking machines became a crime punishable by death. Industrialization also affected environments. Recent studies suggest that carbon emissions from factory smokestacks and black smog were already warming the climate by melting Alpine glaciers, which helped end the Little Ice Age by 1850.

For decades Britain, the world's richest, most competitive nation, enjoyed a reputation as the world's workshop. Factories mass-produced goods of better quality and lower price than traditional handicrafts, giving British merchants marketable goods and incentives to sell them to the world to recoup heavy investments in machinery and materials. By the mid-1800s Britain produced two-thirds of the world's coal, half the iron, four seventh of its steel, and half the cotton cloth and other manufactured goods. A British poet boasted that "England's a perfect World, hath Indies, too, Correct your Maps, Newcastle [a center of the coal industry] is [silver rich] Peru."[12] No other state could threaten Britain's economic and political position.

However, between the 1830s and 1870s the British also helped spread the Industrial Revolution by investing some profits in western Europe. Capitalizing on its mineral reserves, prosperous trading cities, and a strategic location, Belgium industrialized in the early 1800s and built a railroad system to transport coal, iron, and manufactured goods. By the 1830s the French government

Luddites Anti-industrialization activists in Britain who destroyed machines in a mass protest against the effects of mechanization.

---

[11]Quoted in John R. Gillis, *A World of Their Own Making: Myth, Ritual, and the Quest for Family Values* (New York: Basic Books, 1996), 65.

[12]Quoted in Fernand Braudel, *The Perspective of the World: Civilization and Capitalism, 15th–18th Century* (New York: Harper and Row, 1984), 553.

also helped fund industrial activity. In the German states, political fragmentation before 1870 discouraged industrialization except in several coal-rich regions, and some countries, including Portugal, Spain, and Austria-Hungary, remained largely agricultural. By 1914, however, industrialization was widespread around Europe and in North America and Japan, and large numbers of people lived in cities and worked in factories.

Industrial Capitalism and Society

Industrialization and the vast increase in manufactured goods transformed commercial capitalism, dominated by large trading companies, into industrial capitalism centered on manufacturing. European industrial firms exported manufactured goods and imported raw materials, such as iron ore, to make more goods. Since economic success depended on large, steady turnover of goods, advertising developed to create demand. Banking and financial institutions also expanded operations, while government policies supported the industrialists, bankers, and financiers, maximizing private wealth.

Economic philosophers praised and justified British-style capitalism. Scottish professor and Enlightenment supporter Adam Smith (1723–1790) helped formulate modern economics theory, known as neoclassical economics. In his book *The Wealth of Nations* (1776), Smith advocated the policy of laissez faire, which opposed government interference in the marketplace through laws regulating business and profits. Instead, Smith believed in self-interest, arguing that the marketplace's "invisible hand" would turn the entrepreneur's individual greed into a rising standard of living for all. He also introduced the idea of a permanently growing economy, reinforcing long-standing Western views of progress, of history leading to a better future.

Smith's free trade philosophy refuted medieval attitudes condemning mercantile activity and helped end Early Modern mercantilism. Free traders believed that Britain should serve as the world's industrial center, with raw materials flowing in and manufactured goods flowing out. But Smith saw capitalism's potential for both good and evil: free enterprise did not necessarily generate prosperity for all, since the prosperity of the manufacturer and society might differ. Smith encouraged businesses to pay their employees high wages, writing that "no society can surely be flourishing and happy of which the far greater part of its members are poor and miserable. [They should be] well fed, clothed and lodged."[13]

Around 1870, the Second Industrial Revolution commenced, characterized by technological change, mass production, and specialization and led by the United States and Germany. Application of science to industry improved electrical, chemical, optical, and automotive industries, bringing new inventions such as electricity grids, radio, internal combustion engines, gasoline, and flush toilets. By 1900 Germany was Europe's main producer

laissez faire Restriction of government interference in the marketplace, such as laws regulating business and profits.

of electrical goods and chemicals. Assembly lines of separate specialized tasks became common; for example, an automobile worker might only install wheels. The Second Industrial Revolution promoted a shift from many competitive enterprises to giant monopolies led by fabulously wealthy tycoons.

Concentrating capital in "big business" gave a few businessmen and bankers, such as the Krupp family in Germany and the Rockefellers in the United States, vast economic power and control over many industries. Hence, Alfred Krupp (1812–1887), Europe's leading manufacturer of arms, also owned steel mills and mines. Factories, some now producing such useful innovations as aluminum and electrical power, required heavy capital investment to start, eliminating many small businesses and fostering monopolies. In the late 1800s a long depression also undermined competition, encouraging businesses to merge or cooperate and fix prices to moderate slumps. These economic changes generated a drive to colonize more of the world to ensure access to resources and markets.

The Industrial Revolution affected both men and women and all social and economic classes (see Chapter 20). Mainly agricultural a century earlier, by 1900 Europe had a greater division of labor, growing social problems, most people living in cities, and machines replacing many human workers. The factory system compelled millions to migrate from the countryside into overcrowded, unhealthy cities with high rates of alcoholism, prostitution, and crime. City people crowded into festering slums, worked long hours for low wages, and learned new lifestyles. French writer Alexis de Tocqueville (**TOKE-vill**) described the atmosphere of Manchester in 1835:

> The footsteps of a busy crowd, the crunching wheels of machinery, the shriek of steam from boilers, the regular beat of the looms, the heavy rumble of carts, these are the noises from which you can never escape in the somber half-light of these streets. Crowds are ever hurrying this way and that, but their footsteps are brisk, their looks preoccupied, and their appearance somber and harsh.[14]

Factories, mines, and cities reshaped European life. Many factory workers labored fourteen- or even eighteen-hour days under rigid discipline, with no insurance for accidents, ill health, or old age, and many children worked seven days a week in mines or factories. In mid-nineteenth-century English cotton mills, adult men were about one-quarter of workers, women and girls over half, with the rest boys under eighteen. Workers such as the English coal miner Tommy Armstrong sometimes used songs to express their solidarity with each other and resentment of those they worked for (see Profile: Tommy Armstrong, Bard of the English Coal Mines).

Gradually many people considered themselves members of a social and economic class with interests in opposition to other classes. Working classes, such as coal miners and factory workers, were the largest group, while middle classes

---

[13]Quoted in Peter Gay, *Age of Enlightenment* (New York: Time, Inc., 1966), 105–106.

[14]Quoted in Peter Hall, *Cities in Civilization* (New York: Fromm International, 1998), 310.

Tommy Armstrong, Bard of the English Coal Mines

Tommy Armstrong (1849–1919) was one of the most famous song-makers from Britain's industrial working class. From a poor family and with little formal schooling, Armstrong began working in the mine pits around Durham in north England's Northumbrian region at age nine. Since the youngster was born with crooked legs, his older brother William carried him to work on his back. Working first as a trapper-boy, opening ventilation doors for coal and miners to pass through, he later went on to more demanding jobs in the pits.

In the later 1800s many miners in Durham and elsewhere composed rhymes and songs. Armstrong began writing song lyrics at age twelve. Eventually he married, but miners' wages barely covered expenses for his overworked wife and fourteen children, prompting Armstrong to seek additional money by writing songs and having them printed. He then sold single sheets with lyrics, known as broadsides, in pubs to raise money for his family and buy beer for himself. The Tyneside balladeer, as he was known, referring to the nearby Tyne River, developed a legendary thirst. His son claimed, "Me dad's Muse was a mug of beer." Armstrong engaged in song duels with rival songwriters and even made up verses about people in the houses he passed on his way home from work or pub. His songs usually reflected social class and social criticism. One of them encouraged educating the young, in part to avoid trouble with the law: "Send your bairns [children] to school, Learn them all you can. Make scholarship your faithful friend, and you'll never see the school-board man [truant officer]." He set his songs to folk and music-hall tunes as well as to Irish melodies brought by the thousands of Irish immigrants to the mines.

Armstrong became renowned for writing songs reflecting the miner's increasingly radical views, and his ballads memorialized mining disasters, usually to raise money for union funds or relief of orphans and widows. For example, in 1882, after an explosion killed seventy-four miners, Armstrong produced a song commemorating the lost men: "Oh, let's not think of tomorrow lest we disappointed be. Our joys may turn to sorrow as we all may daily see. God protect the lonely widow

Source: Northern Recording Company, UK

TOMMY ARMSTRONG Known as the "Pitman's (coalminer's) Poet," Armstrong worked in the coalfields around Durham, in England, and wrote many songs celebrating the miners' struggles for a better life.

and raise each dropping head; Be a father to the orphans, never let them cry for bread." Conscious of his responsibility, he claimed that "when you're the Pitman's [coalminer's] Poet and looked up for it, if a disaster or a strike goes by without a song from you, they say: What's with Tommy Armstrong? Has someone let out all the inspiration?"

Armstrong was especially productive in the last two decades of the 1800s when strikes were common and the Miners' Union grew rapidly from 36,000 to over 200,000 members. As struggles between miners and mine owners became more bitter, the union grew more assertive and organized. Armstrong wrote strike songs to give information and courage to miners, but also to collect money for hungry families of strikers. Some of the worst conflicts erupted in 1892, when the Durham miners were asked to take a large pay cut. When the union refused, workers were locked out of their workplaces, prompting one of Armstrong's most famous songs: "In our Durham County I am sorry for to say, That hunger and starvation is increasing every day. For want of food and coals, we know not what to do, But with your kind assistance, we will stand the battle through. Our work is taken from us now, they care not if we die, For they [the mine owners] can eat the best of food, and drink the best when dry." After months of labor strife, the union pragmatically agreed to a lower pay reduction. The songs of Tommy Armstrong and other industrial balladeers provide a chronicle of the Industrial Revolution and the ways it shaped the lives of millions of people.

THINKING ABOUT THE PROFILE

1. How did Armstrong's life reflect the working conditions and often hardships imposed on workers by the Industrial Revolution?
2. What did the songs of industrial balladeers like Armstrong tell us about how working-class people confronted the realities of industrial society?

Note: Quotations from A. L. Lloyd, *Folk Song in England.* Copyright © 1967 by International Publishers. Reprinted with permission of International Publishers Co./New York.

included businesspeople, professionals, and prosperous farmers. A salaried labor force, today known as "white-collar" workers, emerged to handle sales and paperwork. Hence, some ninety thousand British women worked as secretaries by 1901. Middle classes, proud of their keen work ethic, attributed poverty to poor work habits and lack of initiative. Meanwhile, in many countries beleaguered aristocrats struggled to maintain dominance over governments and churches. In this developing situation, the obvious gap between haves and the have-nots encouraged crime.

MAKE SURE YOU UNDERSTAND THESE KEY POINTS BEFORE MOVING ON

- The Industrial Revolution began in England and gradually spread throughout western Europe and North America.

- Some people marveled at the technological changes brought by the Industrial Revolution, while others, such as the Luddites, resisted them.

- The Second Industrial Revolution ushered in an age of specialization and mass production and favored monopolistic corporations that could afford enormous investments in new technology.

- As a result of the revolution, new classes arose—the working class; the middle classes, including a new secretarial force; and the aristocrats—and the gap between the haves and the have-nots widened.

aplia

Nationalism, Liberalism, and Socialism

How did nationalism, liberalism, and socialism differ from each other?

Modern Europe produced three new ideologies—nationalism, liberalism, and socialism—that still shape our world. An **ideology** is a coherent, widely shared system of ideas about the social, political, and economic realm. Nationalism fostered unified countries, liberalism encouraged democratic governments, and socialism sparked movements to counteract industrial capitalism's power and the social dislocations generated by industrialization.

Nations and Nationalism

Nationalism, a primary loyalty to, and identity with, a nation bound by common culture, government, and shared territory, greatly influenced Europe and the Americas. Nationalists insisted that support for country transcended loyalty to family, village, church, region, social class, monarch, or ethnic group. Many peoples increasingly felt citizenship in a nation, such as France or Italy, that shared a common identity separate from, and they felt often better than, other nations. For example, a Swiss newspaper proclaimed in 1848 that the "nation [Switzerland] stands before us as an undeniable reality. The Swiss of different cantons [small self-governing states] will henceforth be perceived and act as members of a single nation."[15]

ideology A coherent, widely shared system of ideas about the nature of the social, political, and economic realm.

Nationalism A primary loyalty to, and identity with, a nation bound by a common culture, government, and shared territory.

Some historians perceive the nation as an "imagined community" in the minds of people living in the same society.

While nationalism provided a cement bonding all citizens to the state, it also fostered wars with rival nations. Because it united people who shared many traditions and a sense of common destiny, nationalism appealed particularly to rising middle classes and intellectuals struggling for more political power; they claimed the nation included all the people, regardless of social status. The India-born English poet Rudyard Kipling captured this perception of collective identity and the nation's special nature: "If England was what England seems, An' not the England of our dreams, But only putty, brass an' paint, 'Ow quick we'd drop 'er! But she ain't!"[16]

Most historians credit modern nationalism's birth to late-eighteenth- and early-nineteenth-century France and Great Britain. French revolutionaries claimed that all sovereignty emanated from the nation, rather than individuals or groups, and the British increasingly viewed themselves as one nation composed of several peoples. Although England and Wales united in 1536 under English monarchs and were joined by Scotland in 1707, no Britain yet existed; the peoples sharing the island identified as English, Scottish, or Welsh. But the spread of English power nearly suffocated Scottish and Welsh cultures and languages. Although some Welsh and Scots remained wary of England, eventually most accepted membership in Great Britain, a linking formalized in the British Act of Union in 1800.

---

[15]Quoted in Oliver Zimmer, *A Contested Nation: History, Memory and Nationalism in Switzerland, 1761–1891* (Cambridge: Cambridge University Press, 2003), 119.

[16]Quoted in W. Raymond Duncan et al., *World Politics in the 21st Century*, 2nd ed. (New York: Longman, 2004), 311.

LIEBIG COMPANY'S FLEISCH-EXTRACT UND-PEPTON.

Bismarck-
Kaiser-Proclamation zu Versailles, 18. Jan. 1871.

Gesetzl. geschützt.   Siehe Rückseite.

Culture Club/Getty Images

BISMARCK AND GERMAN UNIFICATION This advertisement for Liebig's Meat Extract, published in 1899, celebrates Germany's Chancellor Otto von Bismarck's proclamation of German unification in 1871, a source of German pride.

Nationalism also transformed Europe's political landscape. Multinational states with ethnically diverse populations dominated much of Europe in 1750. One royal family, the Vienna-based Habsburgs, ruled Austria, Hungary, the Czech lands, Belgium, and parts of Italy. In contrast, nationalism fostered **nation-states**, politically centralized countries with defined territorial boundaries, such as Italy, Belgium, and Norway. By 1914 only the Russian and Habsburg-ruled Austro-Hungarian empires remained major multinational European states.

Greeks, Italians, and Germans eventually created unified nations, partly through violence. Greeks, long part of the Turkish-dominated Ottoman Empire, served in the Ottoman government and dominated commerce in Ottoman-ruled western Asia. But some Greeks sent their sons to western Europe to study. Returning home with nationalist ideas, they organized an uprising for independence in 1821, killing many Turks. The Ottomans responded by massacring Greek villages, pillaging churches, and hanging the Greek Orthodox Church leader in Istanbul, inflaming western European opinion. When British, French, and Russian intervention helped Greece became independent in 1830, other restless Ottoman subjects were inspired. In 1862 Romania also became independent.

Unlike the Greeks, Italians, divided into many small states ruled by Habsburgs, the Holy Roman Empire, or the pope, long dreamed of unity. In 1831 the fiery Giuseppe Mazzini **(jew-SEP-pay mots-EE-nee)** (1805–1872), an exiled Genoese political philosopher, founded the Young Italy movement advocating one Italian nation. He also promoted republican government and women's rights, radical ideas in Italy. Nationalists and democrats elsewhere, inspired by Mazzini, formed organizations such as Young Poland. In 1859 nationalists began an armed struggle for Italian unity. Forces under Giuseppe Garibaldi **(gar-uh-BOWL-dee)** (1807–1882), who had nurtured his passions during years of exile in South America, created the kingdom of Italy in 1861. In 1870 Italian troops entered the last Papal State, Rome, reuniting Italy for the first time since the Roman Empire. The job of creating Italians who shared a common national vision took longer.

German unification also came in stages. In 1862 Prussian prime minister Otto von Bismarck (1815–1898) brought together many northern German states under Prussian domination. From the landed nobility, Bismarck spent his youth gambling and womanizing before beginning a rapid political ascent. Hostile to business and democratic political rights, he united the Germans through warfare, a policy of "blood and iron." Successful wars with Denmark, Austria (1866), and France added all the German-speaking territories west of Austria.

nation-states Politically centralized countries with defined territorial boundaries.

In 1871 King William I of Prussia was declared *kaiser* (emperor) of a united Germany, now one of Europe's major powers.

Some peoples could not satisfy their nationalist aspirations. Poles frequently but unsuccessfully rebelled against their Russian and German rulers, and Jewish minorities, scattered around Europe, often had little in common. Many East European and Russian Jews, largely restricted to all-Jewish villages and urban neighborhoods known as ghettoes, often maintained conservative cultural and religious traditions. Especially in Germany, France, and Britain, many also moved toward assimilation with the dominant culture. Reacting against widespread anti-Semitism, other Jews gravitated to revolutionary groups or to **Zionism**, a movement founded by Hungarian-born journalist Theodor Herzl **(HERT-suhl)** (1860–1904) that sought a Jewish homeland. In 1948 Zionists formed the state of Israel in Palestine.

Another oppressed people were the Irish, whose simmering opposition to harsh, centuries-long English rule sometimes erupted in violence. England attempted to destroy the Irish language, religion, poetry, literature, dress, and music. As an Irish folk song from 1798 protested, "She's the most distressful country that ever yet was seen. [The English] are hanging men and women for the wearing of the green [Ireland's unofficial national color]."[17] Much of Ireland's farming land belonged to rich English landlords. After 1800 England mounted even more restrictive laws, deporting thousands who resisted to Australia. In addition, the British army recruited many poor, jobless Irish men to fight in colonial wars abroad. Irish ballads memorialized men going out to fight, mothers or wives greeting their wounded men when they returned, and families grieving for those who would never return. Then during the 1840s, when the potato crop failed for several successive years because of a fungus blight, one and a half million Irish died from starvation while British policies discouraged food exports to Ireland and English landlords ejected Irish peasants, replacing subsistence food growing with more profitable sheep raising. Millions of Irish sought escape from poverty and repression by emigrating to the Americas and Australia.

But the Irish continued to rebel against British rule. The Fenians **(FEE-nians)**, a secret society dedicated to Irish independence, were transformed by 1905 into Sinn Fein **(shin FANE)** (Gaelic for "Ourselves Alone"). Sinn Fein extremists formed the violent Irish Republican Army (IRA), which organized a rebellion on Easter Monday, 1916, during which some fifteen hundred volunteers seized key buildings in Dublin and proclaimed a republic. English troops quickly crushed the rising, executing the ringleaders and jailing two thousand participants, but Sinn Fein, the IRA, and terrorism still bedeviled the English colonizers.

Zionism A movement that sought a Jewish homeland.

liberalism An ideology that favored emancipating the individual from all restraints, whether governmental, economic, or religious.

parliamentary democracy Government by representatives elected by the people.

Liberalism and Parliamentary Democracy

Another ideology offered a vision of democracy and individual freedom. Influenced by Enlightenment thinkers such as John Locke and Baron de Montesquieu, **liberalism** preached the emancipation of individuals from all governmental, economic, or religious restraints. Liberals, mainly of middle-class background, favored representative government, the right to vote, and basic civil liberties such as freedom of speech, religion, assembly, and the press. Scottish philosopher John Stuart Mill (1806–1873) eloquently defended free expression, writing that no one should restrict what arguments a legislature or executive should hear. Liberal politicians fought against slavery, advocated religious toleration, and worked for more popular participation in government.

Democratic decision making was an old idea. Village democracies allowing many residents to voice their opinions and shape decisions had long existed in various tribal and stateless societies of Asia, Africa, and the Americas. Classical Greeks and Romans also introduced democratic institutions, but they restricted political rights to a small minority of male citizens. Representative institutions later appeared in England, Holland, Switzerland, Iceland, and Poland. By the nineteenth century liberal democracy implied choice and competition, usually between contending political parties and policies, within a constitutional framework that allowed voters free choice. Eventually some nations, including Britain, adopted **parliamentary democracy**, government by representatives elected by the people. Liberalism proved particularly popular in Britain and the United States, underpinning the U.S. Constitution and Bill of Rights. To protect against tyranny, the nation's founders mandated a separation of executive, legislative, and judicial powers.

British democracy gradually grew as royal power declined over several centuries. After coming to power at eighteen, Queen Victoria (r. 1837–1901) reigned over Britain for sixty-four years, providing, with her German-born husband Prince Albert, models of morality and stability. But even the respected Queen Victoria no longer had much power and exercised influence mostly behind the scenes. Prime ministers, elected by the majority of Parliament members, now made national and foreign policy. Democracy gradually widened as the elected House of Commons exercised more power than the appointed and hereditary House of Lords. Both houses featured lively debate between political parties.

But democratic access remained somewhat limited in Britain, and reformers wanted average people to have more voice in the electoral system. The Reform Act of 1832 increased the number of voters to all upper- and middle-class males. The major working-class protest movement, Chartism, called for universal adult male suffrage, secret ballots, and salaries for Parliament members so that people without wealth could run for office. Some Chartists, led by Elizabeth Neesom, advocated women's right to participate in government. Chartists used demonstrations, strikes, boycotts, and riots to support their demands; however, because the wealthy

[17]Quoted in Patrick Galvin, *Irish Songs of Resistance* (New York: Folklore Press, n.d.), 84.

feared radical ideas such as wealth redistribution, these actions had little success.

Socialism, Marxism, and Social Reform

While liberals favored preserving wealth and property rights while fearing radical popular movements, a third ideology encouraged protest. In contrast to liberalism's individual liberty, socialism offered a vision of social equality and the common, or public, ownership of economic institutions such as factories. Socialism grew out of the painful social disruption accompanying the Industrial Revolution. Utopian socialists in Britain, France, and North America, many influenced by Christian ideals, offered visions of cooperative societies that promoted the common good. A few even founded communal villages that were based on community service and that renounced personal wealth. For example, British industrialist Robert Owen (1771–1858) founded a model factory town around his cotton mill and later established a model socialist community, New Harmony, in Indiana. Some proponents of women's rights, such as Emma Martin (1812–1851) in Britain and Flora Tristan (1801–1844) in France, stirred controversy by promoting socialism as the solution to female oppression. Clergymen opposed to feminism and socialism urged their congregations to disrupt Martin's speeches, and outraged mobs chased and stoned her.

The ideas of Karl Marx (1818–1883), known as Marxism, had the most long-lasting influence on socialist thought and became a major intellectual and political influence around the world. Marx, a German Jew with a passion for social justice, studied philosophy at the University of Berlin and then worked as a journalist before settling in London. His German friend, Friedrich Engels (1820–1895), who managed his father's cotton factory in England and introduced Marx to English industrial workers' degraded conditions, collaborated in writing and editing some of Marx's books. In *The Communist Manifesto* (1848), Marx claimed that the downtrodden could redress the wrongs inflicted upon them through violent socialist revolution, seizing power from capitalists and creating a new society (see Witness to the Past: The Communist View of Past, Present, and Future). Marx argued that revolutionary peoples can change inequitable political, social, and economic patterns inherited from the past. He opposed nationalism, writing that working people, having common interests, needed to cooperate across borders. In 1864 Marx helped form the International Workingmen's Association to work toward those goals.

Marx was a product of his scientific age and considered his ideas as laws of history, writing in his influential, three-volume *Capital* that historical change resulted from struggle between antagonistic social classes. All social and economic systems contain contradictions dooming them to conflict, which generates a higher stage of development. Hence, confrontation between nobles, merchants, and serfs undermined feudalism, leading to capitalism. Eventually, Marx predicted, this process would replace capitalism with socialism, where all would share in owning the means of production and the state would serve common people rather than privileged classes; and then communism, where the state would wither away and all would share the wealth, free to realize their human potential without exploitation by capitalists or governments. Such a vision of redistributing wealth and power proved attractive to many disgruntled Europeans and later around the world.

Economists and historians have debated Marxian ideas ever since. He believed that the nature of the economic system (such as feudalism with medieval manors or capitalism with factories) and technology determined all aspects of society, including religious values, social relations (such as family patterns), government, and laws. Hence, capitalism constantly destroyed older industries, transforming the instruments and means of production, and thus the whole relations of society. This caused instability. Marx also argued that religion, the "opiate of the people," discouraged protest but encouraged fatalistic acceptance of life's inequalities in hopes of a better afterlife. He criticized capitalism for fostering extremes of wealth and poverty, furnishing wealth to farm, mine, factory, and business owners as well as to the urban-based, mostly commercial, middle class Marx called the bourgeoisie. Marx observed that the industrial working class, the proletariat, grew more miserable as wealth became concentrated in giant monopolies in the later 1800s.

Marxist ideas attracted a wide following, first in Europe and later in various American, Asian, and African countries, sometimes stimulating unrest. In 1871, following a disastrous war with Germany and election of a conservative government, Marxists, republicans, and other groups briefly gained control of Paris. The Paris Commune, as this government was called, experimented with socialist programs such as better wages and working conditions. The French government attacked Paris with ruthless force; in response Commune supporters (Communards) burned public buildings and killed the Catholic archbishop. French soldiers' brutality horrified a British reporter: "Paris the beautiful is Paris the ghastly, the battered, the burning, the blood-splattered."[18] When the dust cleared, 38,000 Communards had been arrested, 20,000 executed, and 7,500 deported to the South Pacific. Later rebels across Europe hoisted Marxist banners for radical redistribion of power and privilege.

By promising a more equitable society, Marxism became a major world force, with socialist parties forming all over Europe in the late 1800s and early 1900s. More radical socialists soon split off and established parties calling themselves communist. While many poor people or industrial workers envied the rich and thought life unfair, family, religion, and social connections also inhibited them from joining radical movements or risking their lives in a rebellion that might fail. An English pub toast reflected the

socialism An ideology offering a vision of social equality and the common, or public, ownership of economic institutions such as factories.

proletariat The industrial working class.

---

[18]Quoted in S. C. Burchell, *The Age of Progress* (New York: Time, Inc., 1966), 120.

WITNESS TO THE PAST

The Communist View of Past, Present, and Future

In 1848 Karl Marx and Friedrich Engels published The Communist Manifesto *as a statement of beliefs and goals for the Communist League, an organization they had founded. In this excerpt Marx and Engels outlined their view of history as founded on class struggle, stressed the formation of the new world economy, and offered communism as the alternative to an oppressive capitalist system. They ended their summary of contemporary society's problems by imploring the working class to take its future into its own hands through unity and revolution.*

A specter is haunting Europe—the specter of communism. All the powers of old Europe have entered into a holy alliance to excise this specter.... Where is the party in opposition that has not been decried as communistic by its opponents in power?...The history of all hitherto existing society is the history of class struggles.... Oppressor and oppressed stood in constant opposition to one another, carried on in an uninterrupted, now hidden, now open fight, a fight that each time ended, either in a revolutionary reconstitution of society at large, or in the common ruin of the contending classes.

In the earlier epochs of history, we find almost everywhere a complicated arrangement of society into various orders, a manifold gradation of social rank. In ancient Rome we have patricians, knights, plebeians, slaves; in the Middle Ages, feudal lords, vassals, guild-masters, journeymen, apprentices, serfs; in almost all these classes, again, subordinate gradations. The modern bourgeois [middle class] society that has sprouted from the ruins of feudal society has not done away with class antagonisms. It has but established new classes, new conditions of oppression, new forms of struggle in place of the old ones.

Our epoch, the epoch of the bourgeoisie, possesses, however, this distinctive feature: it has simplified the class antagonisms. Society as a whole is more and more splitting up into two great hostile camps, into two great classes directly facing each other: bourgeoisie and proletariat (working class).... The discovery of America, the rounding of the Cape [of Good Hope], opened up fresh ground for the rising bourgeoisie. The East Indian and Chinese markets, the colonization of America, trade with the colonies, the increase in

the means of exchange and in commodities generally, gave to commerce, to navigation, to industry, an impulse never before known, and, thereby, a rapid development to the revolutionary element in the tottering feudal society.... Meantime the markets kept ever growing, the demand ever rising. Even manufacture no longer sufficed. Thereupon, steam and machinery revolutionized industrial production. The place of manufacture was taken by the giant, modern industry, the place of the industrial middle class, by industrial millionaires....

Modern industry has established the world market, for which the discovery of America paved the way.... The bourgeoisie, by the rapid improvement of all instruments of production, by the immensely facilitated means of communication, draws all, even the most barbarian, nations into civilization. The cheap prices of its commodities are the heavy artillery with which it batters down all Chinese walls.... It compels all nations, on pain of extinction, to adopt the bourgeois mode of production.... It creates a world after its own image....

[The Communists] have no interests separate from those of the proletariat as a whole.... The immediate aim of the Communists is...the formation of the proletariat into a class; the overthrow of the bourgeois supremacy; and the conquest of political power by the proletariat.... The Communists disdain to conceal their views and aims. They openly declare that their ends can be attained only by the forcible overthrow of all existing social conditions. Let the ruling classes tremble at a Communistic revolution. The proletarians have nothing to lose but their chains. They have a world to win. WORKING MEN OF ALL COUNTRIES, UNITE!

THINKING ABOUT THE READING

1. What did Marx and Engels identify as the opposing classes in European history?
2. What developments aided the rise of the bourgeoisie to power?
3. What is the goal of the communists?

Source: From *The Communist Manifesto*, trans. 1880. *http://www.anv.edu.au/polisci/marx/classics/manifesto.html.*

desires for more immediate pleasures: "If life was a thing that money could buy, the rich would live and the poor might die. Here's to oceans of wine, rivers of beer, a nice little wife and ten thousand a year."[19] North Americans had a weaker sense of social class, and Marxism never became as influential in the United States as in parts of Europe. Furthermore, Marx mistakenly believed that socialist revolution would first erupt in leading capitalist nations such as Britain and Germany. Instead the first successful socialist revolution came, over three decades after Marx had died, in Russia.

In contrast to revolution, some Marxists favored a more gradual, evolutionary approach of working within constitutional governments to establish social democracy, a system mixing capitalism and socialism within parliamentary frameworks. The first Social Democratic Party, formed in Germany in 1875, criticized Marxist revolutionaries. Its leader, Eduard Bernstein (1850–1932), argued that socialists should work less for the better future and more for the better present. Shared socialist views and class backgrounds in various countries fostered the founding of the Second International Workingmen's

---

[19]Quoted in Reginald Nettel, *Sing a Song of England: A Social History of Traditional Song* (London: Phoenix House, 1969), 183.

Association by nonrevolutionary socialist parties in 1889, with the goal of world peace, justice, and social reform.

Social Democrats and Marxists actively supported labor unions and strikes to promote worker demands. Despite strong employer opposition, unions gradually gained legal recognition as worker representatives in many nations. In Britain, France, Germany, Holland, and Sweden, trade unions and labor parties acquired enough political influence to legislate for better working conditions. In the later 1800s governments implemented social reforms that laid foundations for state-run welfare systems. Many European nations legislated the length of the workday, working conditions, and safety rules. To tackle poverty, Germany and Britain introduced health and unemployment insurance and created old-age pensions. Thus, contrary to Marx's expectations, life for many European workers improved considerably by the early 1900s. But many people still worked in dangerous and unhealthy conditions or faced a ten-hour working day, and child labor continued.

MAKE SURE YOU UNDERSTAND THESE KEY POINTS BEFORE MOVING ON

- With the rise of nationalism, the inhabitants of a given country came to identify with each other as distinct from, and often better than, the inhabitants of other countries.

- Liberalism, which favored maximizing individual liberty, was particularly influential in Britain and the United States.

- Socialism aimed to achieve economic equality through common ownership of industry, and its major proponent, Karl Marx, argued that history is driven by class struggle and that capitalism would inevitably give way to a communist society.

- Social Democrats, who rejected Marx's revolutionary ideas and instead favored working to better the lot of workers within a capitalist democracy, managed to greatly improve working conditions by the early 1900s.

aplia

The Resurgence of Western Imperialism

What factors spurred the Western imperialism of the later 1800s?

The Industrial Revolution provided economic incentives, and nationalism provided political incentives, for European merchants and states to exploit other lands, enriching their own nations and thwarting rival nations' ambitions. Initially Britain dominated the growing world economy. But economic, political, and ideological factors eventually fostered resurgent imperialism, leading European nations to colonize and dominate much of Asia and Africa, reshaping the global system. With the entire world connected by economic and political networks, history now transcended regions and became truly global.

British Trade, Industrialization, and Empire

The quest for colonies diminished in the early Industrial Revolution, even for Great Britain, which feared no competitor in world trade and had none. British free traders, wanting neither economic nor political restrictions, viewed acquiring more colonies as too expensive. Britain already controlled or had access to valuable American, African, Asian, and Pacific territories. Although it lost its thirteen North American colonies, Britain gained French Canada and Australia. Furthermore, Britain's Spanish and Portuguese rivals suffered graver losses; independence for their Latin American colonies opened doors for British commercial activity.

British merchants benefited from new technologies that enabled them to compete all over the world. No longer dependent on trade winds, British ships reached distant shores faster. The first steam-powered ships, in 1813, took 113 days to travel from England around Africa to India; in contrast, sailing ships took eight or nine months. Completion of the Suez Canal linked the Mediterranean Sea and the Red Sea in 1869, dramatically cutting travel time; Britain, the canal's major shareholder, extended its influence to East Africa and Southeast Asia. By 1900 the England-India trip took less than twenty-five days, more efficiently transporting resources, goods, and people.

Although it pragmatically preferred peaceful commerce, Britain obtained some colonies between 1750 and 1870 by seizing territories or fighting wars when governments refused to trade or could not protect British commerce. For example, as states in India grew weaker and banditry increased, the British began expanding their influence and gradually gained direct control or indirect power over most of India. They also established footholds in Malaya, Burma, China, and South Africa. But the British preferred undercutting their rivals' economic power, as they did in Argentina, Brazil, and Chile. They flooded India with cheap manufactured goods, greatly diminishing India's crafts and industries for their own benefit. British industrialists and merchants opposed any attempts to foster rival enterprises, such as textile mills, in Asian and African states.

However, the British advantage in world markets gradually diminished as economic leadership changed during the later 1800s. Britain often invested profits earned from India and its Caribbean colonies in other nations, especially the United States, Canada, and Australia, all settled largely by

LIPTON TEA European imperial expansion brought many new products to European consumers. Tea, grown in British-ruled India, Sri Lanka (Ceylon), and Malaya, became a popular drink, advertised here in a London weekly magazine.

British immigrants. This investment helped the United States become a serious competitor. Increasingly the United States and Germany gained on Britain. Because British investors earned more profits investing abroad than at home, Britain's industrial plants became increasingly obsolete. In 1860 Britain was the leading economic power, with France a distant second followed by the United States and Germany. By 1900, however, the United States was at the top, followed by Germany and then a fading Britain and France.

As industrializing Germany, France, and the United States became more competitive with Britain, their growing competition renewed the quest for colonies abroad. Domestic economies dominated by large monopolies stimulated empire building by piling up huge profits, and hence excess capital, that needed investment outlets abroad to keep growing. Furthermore, by the 1880s some wealth began filtering down to European working classes, stimulating new consumer interests in tropical products such as chocolate, tea, soap, and rubber for bicycle tires. Businessmen in Britain, Germany, Italy, France, Belgium, and the United States, seeking new opportunities to exploit Africa, Asia, and the Pacific, pressured their governments to pursue colonization.

National rivalries also motivated imperialism. Nations often seized colonies to prevent competing nations from gaining opportunities. While expanding British control in southern Africa, British imperialist Cecil Rhodes (1853–1902) remembered his Oxford University professor, the philosopher and art critic John Ruskin's, advice: "This is what England must either do, or perish: found colonies as fast and as far as [it] is able, seizing every piece of waste ground [it] can get [its] foot on."[20] National rivalries and intense competition for colonies also planted the roots of European conflict. By the early 1900s Germany and Austria-Hungary had forged an alliance, prompting Britain, France, and Russia to do likewise, setting the stage for future wars.

The Scramble for Empire and Imperial Ideologies

Conflicts between European powers fostered renewed Western imperialism between 1870 and 1914, resulting in colonialism or, less commonly, neocolonialism. New colonies brought profits for business interests while strengthening a nation's power in competition with rival nations. The result was the greatest land grab in world history: a handful of European powers dividing up the globe among themselves. Imperial Western nations conquered or impacted millions of Africans, Asians, and Pacific

---

[20]Quoted in Robert A. Huttenback, *The British Imperial Experience* (New York: Harper and Row, 1966), 101.

islanders, bringing them into the Western-dominated world economic system.

Many peoples fiercely resisted conquest. Vietnamese, Burmese, and various Indonesian and African societies held off militarily superior European armies for decades. Even after conquest, guerrilla forces often attacked European colonizers. For fifteen years after France annexed Vietnam, anticolonial fighters refused to surrender, preferring to fight to the death. Countless revolts punctuated colonial rule, from West Africa to the Philippines. Western ambitions also sometimes faced frustration. Ethiopians defeated an Italian invasion force, while Afghan slaughter of British occupiers discouraged direct colonization. The Japanese prevented Western political domination by modernizing their own government and economy, and the Siamese (Thai) deflected Western power by using skillful diplomacy and selective modernization.

Despite these efforts, by 1914 Western colonial powers controlled 90 percent of Africa, 99 percent of Polynesia, and 57 percent of Asia (see Map 19.4). The British Empire, the world's largest, included fifty-five colonies containing 400 million people, ten times Britain's population, inspiring the boast that "the sun never sets on the British Empire." France acquired the next largest empire of twenty-nine colonies. Germany, Spain, Belgium, and Italy joined in the grab for African colonies, and between 1898 and 1902 the United States took over Hawaii, Samoa, Puerto Rico, and the Philippines. Russia also continued its Eurasian expansion begun in the Early Modern Era (see Chapter 23).

New technologies facilitated and stimulated imperial expansion. Industrialization gave Europeans better weapons to enforce their will against Asians and Africans, including repeating rifles and machine guns, such as the lightweight, quick-firing Maxim Gun. A British writer boasted: "Whatever happens we have got the Maxim Gun, and they have not."[21] The discovery of quinine to treat malaria helped European colonists and officials survive in tropical Africa and Southeast Asia. Later, better communication and transportation networks, such as steamship lines, colonial railroads, and undersea telegraph cables, helped consolidate Western control and more closely connected the world. In 1866 a speaker, praising the new trans-Atlantic cable linking Europe and North America, noted that on the statue of Christopher Columbus in Genoa, Italy, was the inscription: "There was one world; let there be two." Now, with the cable, "There were two worlds and [now] they [are] one."[22]

Western imperialism forged globe-spanning networks of interlinked social, economic, and political relationships. Hence, decisions made by a government or business in London or Paris affected people in faraway Malaya or Madagascar, while silk spun in China was turned into dresses worn by fashionable women in Chicago and Munich. Westerners also enjoyed advantageous trade relations with, or strong influence over, countries such as China, Siam, Persia, and Argentina, known as neocolonialism. Western imperialism changed world power arrangements. In 1750 China and the Ottoman Empire remained among the strongest countries, but by 1914 they could not match Western military and economic power. In 1500 the wealth gap between more economically and less developed Eurasian and African societies was small, and China and India dominated world trade and manufacturing. By 1914 the gap in total wealth and personal income between industrialized societies, whether in Europe or North America, and most other societies, including China and India, had grown very wide.

Supporters of imperialism embraced a new ideology, Social Darwinism, that was based on ideas about the natural world developed by British scientist Charles Darwin, who described a struggle for existence among species (see Chapter 20). Social Darwinists, interpreting this struggle as survival of the fittest, applied this notion to the human world of social classes and nations. Industrialized peoples considered themselves most fit and the poor or exploited less fit. A German naval officer wrote in 1898 that "the struggle for life exists among individuals, provinces, parties and states. The latter wage it either by the use of arms or in the economic field. Those who don't want to, will perish."[23] Social Darwinists stereotyped Asian and African societies as "backward," upholding their own nations as "superior" peoples with the right to rule. As most Westerners took innate inequality for granted, Western racism and arrogance increased. Hence, whereas many Western observers once admired the Chinese and Enlightenment thinkers viewed China as a secular, efficient government model, by the 1800s Europeans and North Americans scorned "John Chinaman" and the "heathen Chinee." Intellectual and political leaders popularized these stereotypes. Cecil Rhodes boasted, "I contend that we British are the finest race in the world, and that the more of the world we inhabit the better it is for the human race."[24]

This self-proclaimed superiority legitimized "improving" other people by bringing them Western culture and religion. The French proclaimed their "civilizing mission" in Africa and Indochina, the British in India claimed they were "taking up the white man's burden," and Americans colonized the Philippines claiming condescendingly to "uplift" their "little brown brothers." Western defenders argued that colonialism gave "stagnating" non-Western societies better government and drew them out of isolation into the world market. A British newspaper in 1896 claimed that "the advance of the Union Jack means protection for weaker races, justice for the oppressed, liberty for the down-trodden."[25] However, most people in Asia, Africa, and the Pacific opposed colonialism, seeing the terrible toll on their lives. Indian nationalist leader Mohandas Gandhi, educated in Britain, reflected the resentment. When asked what he thought about "Western civilization," he reportedly replied that civilizing the West would be a good idea.

[21]Hillaire Beloc, quoted in Eric Hobsbawm, *The Age of Empire, 1875–1914* (New York: Vintage, 1987), 20.

[22]Quoted in John Steele Gordon, *A Thread Across the Ocean: The Heroic Story of the Transatlantic Cable* (New York: Perennial, 2003), 215.

[23]Quoted in Winnifred Baumgart, *Imperialism: The Idea and Reality of British and French Colonial Expansion, 1880–1914* (New York: Oxford University Press, 1986), 88.

[24]Quoted in L. S. Stavrianos, *Global Reach: The Third World Comes of Age* (New York: William Morrow, 1981), 263.

[25]Quoted in Baumgart, *Imperialism*, 52.

MAP 19.4 **THE GREAT POWERS AND THEIR COLONIAL POSSESSIONS IN 1913** By 1913 the British and French controlled huge empires, with colonies in Africa, southern Asia, the Caribbean zone, and the Pacific Basin. Russia ruled much of northern Eurasia, while the United States, Japan, and a half dozen European nations controlled smaller empires. © 2015 Cengage Learning

The colonial powers and their possessions

- Germany
- France
- Great Britain
- Belgium
- Netherlands
- Portugal
- Italy
- Spain
- Russia
- United States
- Japan
- Major shipping route

MAKE SURE YOU UNDERSTAND THESE KEY POINTS BEFORE MOVING ON

- Even after losing thirteen of its North American colonies, Britain continued to dominate the world economy through its other holdings and its technological advantages, but it gradually lost ground, especially to the United States.

- As Germany, France, and the United States became more competitive with Britain, the powers competed for colonies that could provide natural resources for their industries and power over their rivals.

- In the renewed scramble for colonial domination, many African, Asian, and Pacific peoples resisted Western imperialism, but the technological advantage of Western nations often proved insurmountable.

- Westerners rationalized imperialism and colonization as good for the colonized, who were offered the fruits of Western culture in exchange for their independence.

CHAPTER SUMMARY

The years between 1750 and 1914 were an age when revolutions reshaped economies, governments, and social systems in Europe and the Americas. Colonists in North America overthrew British rule and established a republic that included democratic institutions. The French Revolution ended the French monarchy and brought the middle classes to power. Although the Revolution was consumed in violence and then modified by Napoleon Bonaparte's dictatorship, the shock waves reverberated around Europe, carrying with them new ideas about liberty and equality. The American and French Revolutions also inspired peoples in the Caribbean and Latin America. Haitians ended slavery and forced out the French colonial regime and planters, and in South America creoles waged successful wars of independence against Spanish rule.

The Industrial Revolution, which began in Britain in the late 1700s, transformed societies profoundly, reorienting life to cities and factories and producing goods in unparalleled abundance. Until the 1850s Britain enjoyed unchallenged economic power. With the spread of industrialization, positions of world economic leadership began to change. New ideologies contributed to the creation of new states and government structures. Nationalism introduced new ideas of the nation and provided a glue to bind people within the same nation. Liberalism promoted increasing freedom and democracy. Socialism addressed the dislocations industrialization created and sought to improve life for the new working classes by forging a system of collective ownership of economic property. Capitalism, industrialization, and interstate rivalries in the West also generated a worldwide scramble for colonies and neocolonies in the later 1800s, allowing Western businesses to seek resources and markets abroad. This imperialism brought many more societies into a global system largely dominated by the West.

KEY TERMS

Age of Revolution (p. 448)
Jacobins (p. 452)
Industrial Revolution (p. 457)
Luddites (p. 459)
laissez faire (p. 460)

ideology (p. 462)
nationalism (p. 462)
nation-states (p. 463)
Zionism (p. 464)
liberalism (p. 464)

parliamentary democracy (p. 464)
socialism (p. 465)
proletariat (p. 465)

The Art Archive at Art Resource, NY

AUSTRALIAN GOLD RUSH The discovery of gold in southeastern Australia set off a gold rush in the 1850s. Hoping to strike it rich, miners, often from other countries such as China, flocked to the gold fields, and immigration to Australia boomed.

Of course, some day we [Americans] shall step in. We are bound to. We shall be giving the word for everything: industry, trade, law, journalism, art, politics, and religion. We shall run the world's business whether the world likes it or not. The world can't help it, and neither can we, I guess.

—American millionaire in Joseph Conrad's novel *Nostromo* (1904)[1]

In 1871 a thirty-three-year-old Japanese samurai and Confucian scholar, Kume Kunitake (1839–1931), began a three-week voyage on an American steamship to San Francisco as part of an official information-gathering Japanese delegation to the United States and then Europe. Visiting factories, museums, schools, churches, public parks, and scenic mountains around the country, Kume recorded his perceptive impressions of Western life but also filtered them through Japanese cultural concepts, concluding that "customs and characteristics of East and West are invariably different." Although admiring U.S. democracy, he also perceived potential disorder, since Americans were "careless about official authority, each person insisting on his own rights." Kume recorded Americans' friendliness but also brashness, ambition, and sense of destiny, attitudes satirized four decades later by Polish-born British novelist Joseph Conrad in *Nostromo*. Traveling around Europe, Kume noted how Europeans treasured and even imitated Japanese art. He loved the cafes, theaters, and art museums of Paris. But this ardent Confucian rationalist considered Christianity irrational and the Christian Bible full of "absurd tales." Kume contrasted splendid churches with people's poverty. But he preferred Europe's constitutional monarchies to the untidy U.S. republic, viewing rapidly industrializing Germany as Japan's natural model. Returning home by ship, Kume's delegation passed through Western colonies such as Ceylon, Singapore, and Hong Kong, Kume writing that "Europeans treated the natives with arrogance and cruelty."[2]

Kume's observations reflect the revolutions, industrialization, nation building, and overseas imperialism that reshaped European social, cultural, and intellectual patterns in this era. By 1914 the United States, Canada, and Mexico occupied all of North America; Latin America was divided into many countries large and small; and while some Caribbean societies were independent, many remained colonies. Europeans also settled the Pacific region known today as Oceania, Australia, and New Zealand and colonized the smaller Pacific islands. Although vast distances and unique characteristics separated Europe, the Americas, and Oceania, similar patterns of capitalism, migration, and nation building shaped their societies.

---

[1]Quoted in Joseph Conrad, *Nostromo* (Garden City, NY: Doubleday, Page, and Company, 1924), 77.
[2]The Kume quotes are from Donald Keene, *Modern Japanese Diaries: The Japanese at Home and Abroad as Revealed Through Their Diaries* (New York: Columbia University Press, 1998), 90–115.

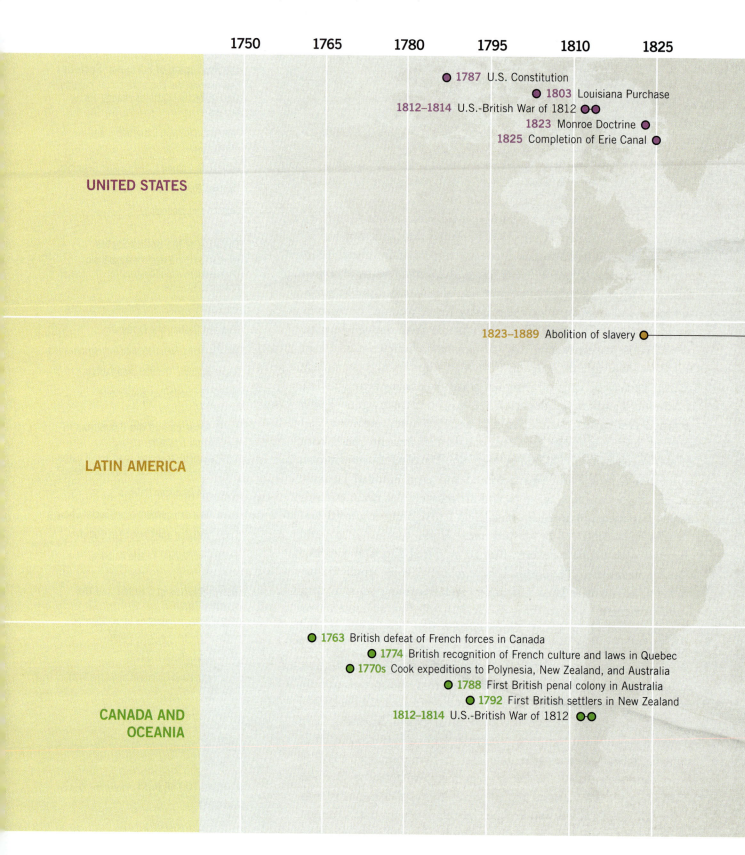

	1750	1765	1780	1795	1810	1825

UNITED STATES

● **1787** U.S. Constitution
● **1803** Louisiana Purchase
1812–1814 U.S.-British War of 1812 ●●
1823 Monroe Doctrine ●
1825 Completion of Erie Canal ●

LATIN AMERICA

1823–1889 Abolition of slavery ●——————

CANADA AND OCEANIA

● **1763** British defeat of French forces in Canada
● **1774** British recognition of French culture and laws in Quebec
● **1770s** Cook expeditions to Polynesia, New Zealand, and Australia
● **1788** First British penal colony in Australia
● **1792** First British settlers in New Zealand
1812–1814 U.S.-British War of 1812 ●●

1840   1855   1870   1885   1900   1915   1930   1945

1846–1848 U.S.-Mexican War
1848 U.S. acquisition of Texas, California, and New Mexico
1849 California gold rush
1861–1865 Civil War
1862 Lincoln's Emancipation Proclamation
1867 U.S. purchase of Alaska from Russia
1869 Completion of transcontinental railroad
1898 U.S. incorporation of Hawaii
1898–1902 Spanish-American War
1902 U.S. colonization of Philippines
1903 First powered flight by Wright Brothers

1842 End of trans-Atlantic slave trade by most nations
1861–1872 Benito Juarez president of Mexico
1862–1867 French occupation of Mexico
1876–1911 Diaz dictatorship in Mexico
1879–1884 War between Chile and Peru-Bolivia
1886 Abolition of slavery in Cuba
1889 Brazilian republic
1889 Abolition of slavery in Brazil
1895–1898 Cuban revolt against Spain
1898–1902 Spanish-American War
1901 Platt Amendment to Cuban constitution
1910–1920 Mexican Revolution
1912 U.S. intervention in Nicaragua
1914 Completion of Panama Canal
1901 Platt Amendment to Cuban constitution
1910–1920 Mexican Revolution
1912 U.S. intervention in Nicaragua
1914 Completion of Panama Canal

1840s–1900s Western colonization of Pacific islands
1850 Treaty of Waitangi
1851 Discovery of gold in Australia
1867 Canadian Confederation
1885 Canadian transcontinental railroad
1901 Australian Commonwealth
1907 New Zealand self-government

The Reshaping of European Societies

How and why did European social, cultural, and intellectual patterns change during this era?

Thanks to destabilizing revolutions in political and economic life (see Chapter 19), modern Europeans lived in a world of cities, new occupations, and rising populations, prompting millions of people to emigrate to the Americas, southern Africa, and Oceania seeking work and a better life. Industrialization transformed social structures and family systems. Thought, art, and science reflected and also shaped the new Europe, resulting in innovations that influenced peoples around the world.

Population Growth, Emigration, and Urbanization

In the Modern Era, expanding economies, better public health, and new crops such as American potatoes lowered mortality rates and fostered population growth, as people married earlier and in larger numbers than in Early Modern times. Europe's population (including Russia) grew from 100 million in 1650 to 190 million in 1800 and to 420 million in 1900. This growth created problems. English clergyman and economist Thomas Malthus argued in 1798 that without the checks of poverty, disease, war, and famine, the population would outgrow its means of subsistence. In some regions overpopulation indeed brought bleak poverty and underemployment, a trend that accelerated when small family farms were replaced by large farms that needed fewer workers. But urban and industrial growth also provided new employment opportunities.

Population growth and poverty spurred migration within Europe and emigration overseas. Many Poles, for example, moved to northern France and western Germany, while Irish immigrants built railroads, canals, and roads in England. Emigration cut Ireland's population by half between 1841 and 1911. In eastern Europe and Russia, Jews migrated because they became public scapegoats for unresolved problems and were sometimes subjected to violent, usually coordinated mob attacks known as pogroms (from the Russian word meaning "roundup"). As a result, many sought better lives in western Europe and the Americas. In all, some 45 million Europeans emigrated to the Americas, Australia, New Zealand, Algeria, and South Africa to escape their difficulties (see Map 20.1).

Internal migration also occurred as rural people moved to industrial cities. By 1900, 90 percent of Britons lived in towns and cities, the world's highest rate. Manchester, the center of the British cotton industry, grew tenfold between 1800 and 1900, while London increased from 900,000 to 4.7 million, Paris from 600,000 to 3.6 million, and Berlin from 170,000 to 2.7 million. Urbanization fostered social problems. Rapidly expanding cities lacked social services such as sanitation, street cleaning, and water distribution. Huge numbers lived in poverty, crammed into overcrowded housing in crime-ridden slums with high disease rates, overflowing privies, and littered streets. As the English poet William Blake wrote: "Every night and every morn, some to misery are born." Most Europeans' standard of living did not rise much until the 1880s, when incomes began improving and several countries, including Britain and Germany, began building a social safety net for their citizens. By 1900 British and French workers earned nearly twice their wages in 1850.

Western European rural life also changed. New agricultural technology and practices fostered better yields, more mechanization, and improved animal breeding, while market agriculture largely displaced subsistence production. But peasants often earned low wages, and many small farmers lost their land to highly capitalized, mechanized operations. Occasional famines also occurred, notably in Ireland and Russia. Some feudal traditions remained influential in eastern Europe, especially Russia and Poland, where landed gentry retained authority over peasant lives.

Social Life, Families, and Gender Relations

In the Modern Era Europeans enjoyed wider social horizons than their ancestors. After 1870 mass-distribution newspapers, organized football (soccer) leagues, widespread vacation travel, and other activities connected peoples within and between nations. The world's first cinema opened in Paris in 1896, launching a film industry that became popular entertainment in Europe and then the world. People also enjoyed more options in life choices: where to live, work, or worship and whom to marry. Choice brought more personal freedom but also more social instability. Some viewed these changes as liberation; others concluded they fostered anxious uncertainty.

Industrialization reshaped sexual attitudes, particularly in Britain. The middle class, considering unbridled passion a sign of bad character, increasingly discouraged sexual activity before marriage while limiting it within marriage. In contrast, working classes experienced higher illegitimacy rates and more frequent sexual relations. Marital infidelity flourished in urban slums, fostering negative middle-class stereotypes of the poor. A British factory girl in 1909 complained, "I wanted no one to know that I was a factory girl because I was ashamed at my position. I was always hearing people say that factory girls were loose-living and corrupt."[3]

Home life and families changed. During the Early Modern Era many in Britain and Holland began living in

---

[3] Quoted in Frederic Delouche et al., *Illustrated History of Europe* (New York: Barnes and Noble, 2001), 312.

MAP 20.1 **EUROPEAN EMIGRATION, 1820–1910** Pushed by rapid population growth and poverty, millions of Europeans left their homes to settle in the Americas (especially the United States), North and South Africa, Siberia, Australia, and New Zealand. The British and Irish accounted for the largest numbers of emigrants, nearly 17 million combined.

© 2015 Cengage Learning

nuclear families, usually including just parents and their children. During the 1800s nuclear families became common in northern Europe, especially among middle classes, while large extended families remained the norm in southern and eastern Europe. Unlike in earlier centuries, families now included few nonrelated members. In the 1700s western Europeans began choosing their partner and marrying for love rather than to meet family demands or economic need. Married men and women often spent more time with their same-sex friends than their spouses, with the line between friendships and homosexual relationships sometimes becoming murky.

Family life was also redefined. By the later 1800s some men and women, criticizing marriage as stifling and old-fashioned, lived out of wedlock with lovers. Prominent artistic and political people, such as popular French actress Sarah Bernhardt, openly had affairs or, like fiery German socialist Rosa Luxemburg, lived openly with same-sex partners.

Homosexuals occupied all levels of society but often faced discrimination and persecution. The Irish poet, novelist, and playwright Oscar Wilde (1854–1900), married father of two, was tried and imprisoned in 1895 for engaging in homosexual relationships, known as sodomy. Increasing attention to homosexuality and the first scientific studies of it sparked heated and ongoing debates as to whether the behavior was rooted in nature or a perversion.

The industrial economy was hard on families, particularly women and children. Seldom viewed as breadwinners, women typically earned only 25 percent of men's wages. Single mothers found it especially difficult to earn a living, with some forced into prostitution for survival. Many women and children did hard manual labor in cotton mills and mines. In 1838 a liberal British Parliament member reported: "I saw a cotton mill, a sight that froze my blood, full of women, young, all of them, some large with child, and obliged to stand twelve hours each day. The heat was excessive in some of the rooms, the stink pestiferous. I nearly fainted."[4] By the early 1900s, when machines did more factory work, fewer women and far fewer children worked full-time in the industrial sector.

The Industrial Revolution, by moving the workplace from home to factory, put men and women into separate work worlds, thereby increasing women's dependence on men and men's power over their wives. No longer needed in economic production, middle-class women lost their roles as direct producers and became instead home managers ("housewives"). Middle-class men, believing that women belonged at home as submissive helpmates, encouraged them to cultivate their beauty and social graces to please men. While men dominated political, social, economic, and religious spheres, women's roles were increasingly restricted to marriage, motherhood, and child rearing. Often women, without legal standing, could not divorce their husbands. Meanwhile, upper- and middle-class women limited their number of children by practicing artificial birth control. By 1900, however, women enjoyed longer life expectancies and devoted fewer years to childbearing and child rearing.

In the later 1800s European women gained more legal rights and economic opportunities. Some women became secretaries, telephone operators, department store sales clerks, and occasionally professionals. The Netherlands had Europe's first woman physician in 1870, France the first woman lawyer in 1903. Leading professionals such as Italian educator Maria Montessori **(mon-ti-SAWR-ee)** (1870–1952), whose innovative schools allowed children to develop at their own pace; Polish-born French scientist Marie Curie (1867–1934), who won a Nobel Prize in physics in 1903; influential German composer and pianist Clara Schumann (1819–1896); and British nurse Florence Nightingale (1820–1910), who revolutionized nursing practices, provided role models. In 1867 the University of Zurich in Switzerland admitted women, soon followed by universities in France, Sweden, and Finland.

"CONVICTS AND LUNATICS" The movement for women's right to vote, or suffrage, was particularly strong in Britain. This poster, designed by the artist Emily Harding Andrews for the Artist's Suffrage League around 1908, shows a woman graduate, deprived of basic political rights, treated similarly to a convict and a mentally disturbed woman.

Library of Congress Prints and Photographs Division/LC-USZC4-6888

feminism A philosophy promoting political, social, and economic equality for women with men.

suffragettes Women who press for the same voting rights as men.

Seeking more rights, some women espoused **feminism**, a philosophy promoting political, social, and economic equality for women with men. The first feminist movements emerged in Britain and Scandinavia, where activists, later known as **suffragettes**, pressed for equal voting rights with men. In 1896 Finland introduced female suffrage. British suffragettes led by Emily Pankhurst (1858–1928) campaigned for voting rights, giving speeches, canvassing door-to-door, and demonstrating. In southern and eastern Europe, however, feminists had only a small following.

---

[4]Quoted in Louise A. Tilly and Joan W. Scott, *Women, Work, and Family* (New York: Holt, Rinehart and Winston, 1978), 64.

Thought, Religion, and Culture

Europe's industrial, political, and social changes fostered new intellectual and cultural directions. Philosophers such as the Germans Immanuel Kant (1724–1804) and Friedrich Nietzsche (NEE-chuh) (1844–1890) debated Enlightenment values. Kant believed that experience alone was inadequate because the mind ultimately shapes perceptions, imposing structure on the sensations we see. Kant doubted that a perfect society was possible, arguing that "man wishes concord, but nature, knowing better what is good for his species, wishes discord."[5] Nietzsche rejected Enlightenment notions of progress, perceiving a growing cultural decadence caused by Christian values and democratic ideas. Unlike Enlightenment thinkers, Nietzsche perceived no fundamental moral and scientific truth, but rather misconceptions developed by each culture trying to understand the world. With no absolute truth, absolute good and evil cannot exist. Later extreme nationalists and racists distorted Nietzsche's ideas to persecute ethnic minorities, while many European and North American intellectuals, seeing truth as relative, argued that all knowledge was culturally constructed.

Religion also changed with the times. Gradually Protestants and Catholics learned to tolerate each other. In the later 1700s and early 1800s a religious revival inspired many European Protestants to move to the United States. Evangelicals stressed personal relations with God, favored missionary activity, and condemned behavior they considered sinful, such as social dancing and drinking. Soon new churches appeared. The charismatic British Anglican preacher John Wesley (1703–1791) founded the Methodist movement, later a church. The Society of Friends, or Quakers, emphasizing nonviolence, human dignity, and individual conscience, fought against slavery and for social and political freedom and humanitarian causes.

Many middle-class Protestants sought a liberalized faith stressing social tolerance rather than the hellfire and damnation preached by some evangelicals. As religion's relevance declined, by 1851 only half of England's population attended church. The divide between liberal and devout Europeans fostered public debates about religion's role in society. British evangelicals sought to ban alcohol and gambling and to require businesses to close on Sunday, but many Protestants and Catholics opposed these moves.

Roman Catholic and Greek Orthodox Churches also faced challenges. As a result of the French Revolution, Catholic clergy in France and Belgium lost their privileged status. France opened a public school system in the 1890s and mandated state neutrality toward religion in 1905. However, the Catholic Church strengthened dogma and organization, with popes reasserting their theological infallibility and announcing new doctrines such as the Virgin Mary's Immaculate Conception. The church remained a major spiritual force and landowner in Austria, southern Germany, Poland, Spain, Portugal, and Italy. Meanwhile, the Greek Orthodox world fragmented into national churches in Greece, Serbia, Romania, and Bulgaria.

During this era, a growing literate public with a desire for cultural products liberated writers, composers, and artists from dependence on wealthy patrons. Classical music enjoyed a golden age, producing compositions that are still enjoyed by audiences around the world. Austrian Wolfgang Amadeus Mozart (MOTE-sahrt) (1756–1791) wrote thirty-five symphonies, eight operas, and many concertos. Inspired by the Age of Revolution, some thinkers and artists also adopted romanticism, a philosophical, literary, artistic, and musical movement that questioned rationalist Enlightenment values, instead glorifying emotions, imagination, and heroism. Some romantics celebrated great figures such as Napoleon Bonaparte. German writer Friedrich Schiller (1759–1805) offered nationalist images, such as a poem turning the story of William Tell, a legendary Swiss resistance hero, into a manifesto for German political freedom. Romanticism inspired German composer Ludvig von Beethoven (1770–1827), whose much-admired *Ninth Symphony* set Schiller's poem, "Ode to Joy," to music.

Some writers and artists embraced another movement, realism, that portrayed a grimy industrial world filled with uncertainty and conflict. Liberal Spanish painter Francisco de Goya's (1746–1828) moving series on Napoleon's invasion of Spain portrayed not warfare's heroism but its horrors: orphans, pain, rape, blood, despair. British realist novelist and former factory worker Charles Dickens (1812–1870) revealed industrial life's hardships, capitalism's injustices, and the miseries of the poor.

Several significant movements reflecting Asian, African, and Pacific artistic influences shaped visual arts in the later 1800s. Modernism embraced progress, welcoming the future. Realistic landscape paintings, photography, and Japanese prints also contributed to the rise in France of impressionism, an artistic movement expressing immediate impressions aroused in momentary scenes that were bathed in changing light and color. Painters such as Claude Monet (moe-NAY) (1840–1926) and Pierre Renoir (ren-WAH) (1841–1919) achieved worldwide fame. Some French artists also rebelled against impressionism and returned to familiar shapes and compositions, including Paul Cezanne (say-ZAN) (1839–1906), famous for landscapes, still lifes, and portraits; Dutch-born Vincent Van Gogh (van GO) (1853–1890), who introduced intense primary colors and thick brushstrokes; and Paul Gauguin (go-GAN) (1848–1903), a former stockbroker whose richly

romanticism A philosophical, literary, artistic, and musical movement that questioned the Enlightenment's rationalist values and instead glorified emotions, individual imagination, and heroism.

modernism A cultural trend that embraced progress and welcomed the future.

impressionism An artistic movement that sought to express the immediate impression aroused by momentary scenes that were bathed in light and color.

---

[5]Quoted in T. W. C. Blanning, "The Commercialization and Sacralization of European Culture in the Nineteenth Century," in *The Oxford Illustrated History of Modern Europe*, ed. T. W. C. Blanning (Oxford: Oxford University Press, 1996), 147.

colored paintings often featured idyllic scenes of Polynesian life based on his long residence there, stimulating European interest in the wider world. Pablo Picasso (1881–1973), a young Spaniard in Paris, revolutionized Western art by integrating ideas from African sculpture and masks. The new art bore little resemblance to medieval art.

Science and Technology

The Modern Era saw spectacular achievements in science and technology. British naturalist Charles Darwin (1809–1882), after traveling for years around the world studying plants, animals, and fossils, formulated the theory of evolution emphasizing the natural selection of species. His book, *On the Origin of Species,* argued that all existing plant and animal species, including humans, evolved into their present forms over millions of years, during which time species either adapted to their environment or died out. Eventually evolution became the foundation for modern biological sciences. Although it was confirmed by many studies and accepted by most scientists, it also provoked controversy, as many churches saw evolutionary theory as degrading humans and negating religious faith.

Later in the Modern Era, the German-born Jewish physicist Albert Einstein (1879–1955) made discoveries that rank him with Galileo, Newton, and Darwin as a pathbreaking scientist. His papers on the theory of relativity, published in the early 1900s, provided the basis for modern physics, our understanding of the universe, and the atomic age. Einstein clarified space and time, showing that distances and durations are not, as Newton thought, absolute but affected by one's motion. His proving that matter can be converted into energy and that everything is composed of atoms made possible atomic energy. Einstein taught in Swiss, Czech, and German universities before immigrating to the United States in 1934.

Many other thinkers made technological discoveries that improved people's lives. Physicians introduced the first effective vaccines against deadly diseases such as smallpox that had long ravaged the world. In 1895 German physicist Wilhelm Rontgen **(RUNT-guhn)** (1845–1923) discovered x-rays, spurring progress in diagnosis and surgery. Together medical advances and improved sanitation fostered better public health. For example, thanks to cleaner water, Europe's industrial cities eradicated cholera. Meanwhile, electric batteries, motors, and generators provided new power sources. Italian Guglielmo Marconi (1874–1937) introduced wireless telegraphy and used his invention in 1901 to communicate between England and Canada, further connecting the world. Two Germans, Gottlieb Daimler and Karl Benz, became the "fathers of the automobile," producing the first petroleum-powered vehicle in the 1880s.

Meanwhile, some scientists worried about industrial pollution's effects on the environment. Observing that carbon dioxide emissions from coal-burning factories heated the atmosphere, Swedish scientist Svante Arrhenius identified a "greenhouse effect" that potentially threatened modern societies. Later scientific studies confirmed his fears. The world still struggles with the promise but also the perils of the technologies and industrial processes developed in this era.

MAKE SURE YOU UNDERSTAND THESE KEY POINTS BEFORE MOVING ON

- In Europe, better crops and health care produced larger populations, which led to increasing urbanization, impoverishment, and emigration.

- Industrialization made men more powerful and relegated women to the home, but in the late nineteenth century women began to gain legal rights and economic opportunities.

- While some Protestants attempted to stamp out behavior they considered sinful, Europeans as a whole became more secular and the Catholic Church's influence declined.

- Artists, writers, and composers became dependent on the public marketplace rather than wealthy patrons, and artistic trends such as romanticism, realism, modernism, and impressionism became dominant.

- Advances in science and technology led to the theory of evolution, greater understanding of the physical world, improved medical care, new sources of energy, and new concerns about pollution and its effects.

aplia

S The Rise of the United States

T *What impact did westward expansion, immigration, and industrialization have on American society?*

After the Revolution, Americans began building their new nation, establishing new government forms, reshaping economic patterns, fostering a new culture, and moving westward. They also conquered Native Americans, acquired Mexican territory, and became involved in the wider world. Between 1860 and 1914 the United States changed dramatically. The Civil War maintained the nation's territorial unity, ended slavery, and spurred federal government centralization, which, combined with economic protectionism, allowed the United States to duplicate the economic and political growth that mercantilism had fostered in Early Modern western Europe. Industrialization created more wealth, supported U.S. power, and reshaped American society. By 1900 the United States had a larger population than all but one European nation, boasted the world's most productive economy, owned half a continent, enjoyed a powerful, stable, democratic government, and exercised power abroad, all sustained by abundant natural resources.

The Early Republic and American Society

The new American republic—weak, disunited, and surrounded by hostile neighbors in British Canada and the Spanish American Empire—found nation building challenging. Seeking to unite the diverse states, Americans ultimately forged a distinctive representative democracy while constructing an economic framework to preserve independence and encourage free enterprise. The Constitution and Bill of Rights established a relatively powerful central government, elected by voters in each state, within a federal system that recognized each member state's lawmaking powers. By the mid-1800s all white adult males could vote, but the nation maintained slavery and excluded Native Americans and women from political activity.

Professing a love of freedom, Americans have had to constantly redefine the balance between the rights of the state and the individual and between the majority and the minority. The U.S. political system mixed liberalism, which underpinned the Bill of Rights, and fear of disorder. The founders made tyranny difficult by separating government powers into executive and legislative branches and an independent judiciary. But, wary of radicalism and shocked by the French Revolution's excesses, American leaders also discouraged attacks on the upper classes by limiting voting rights, such as through property and literacy qualifications, and by electing the president indirectly through the Electoral College, in which each state chose electors to cast their votes, producing results that have not always reflected the national popular vote.

American leaders wanted a sound economic foundation. While southern plantation interests favored free trade to market their crops abroad without obstacles, many founders, insisting that economic independence was necessary to safeguard political independence, preferred self-reliance and **protectionism**, using trade barriers to shield local industries from foreign competition. The first treasury secretary, West Indian–born Alexander Hamilton (1757–1804), established a national bank, favored tariffs to exclude competitive foreign goods, and provided government support for manufacturing. Continued conflicts with Britain sparked a temporary embargo of all foreign trade in 1807, stimulating domestic manufacturing to offset the lost imports.

Trade and border conflicts between Britain and the United States sparked the War of 1812 (1812–1814), during which the British captured the capital, Washington, burned down the White House, and repulsed a U.S. invasion of Canada. After some U.S. victories, the two sides negotiated peace. Industrialization proceeded in the Northeast, where the first large textile mills manufacturing finished cloth opened in New England. Northern industrialists favoring protectionist policies soon prevailed over southern planters wanting free trade. To move resources and products, Americans built over 3,300 miles of canals, including the Erie Canal across New York State, linking midwestern markets and resources to New York City.

Gradually American society diverged from Britain's. French writer Alexis de Tocqueville (1805–1859), visiting the United States in the early 1830s, noted Americans' commitment to democracy, individualism, and "unbounded desire for riches."[6] But he condemned slavery and feared that too much individualism and greed undermined community. De Tocqueville admired single American women's independence, marriage as voluntarily uniting loving equals, and married women's influence in the family. Nonetheless, men who believed women's place was in the home still controlled many women's lives.

Enslaved African Americans, mostly plantation workers, were concentrated in southern states, constantly replenished by new arrivals from Africa. They created spirituals, based partly on African rhythms and song styles, that used Christian images to indirectly express a longing for emancipation. In "Go Down Moses," the refrain emphasized "let my people go," just as Moses led the Hebrews in Egypt to freedom. The abolitionists Sojourner Truth (ca. 1797–1883) and Frederick Douglass (1818–1895), both former slaves, also eloquently advocated gender equality and women's suffrage. Many white Americans also wanted to eliminate slavery and other social ills. Sarah Grimke (1792–1873), a Quaker from a South Carolina slaveholding family, became an active abolitionist and feminist, rejecting the notion of different male and female natures (see Witness to the Past: Protesting Sexism and Slavery). Upon discovering that their deceased brother had fathered two sons with one of his slaves, Sarah and her sister Angelina flouted custom and laws by raising and educating their nephews.

Distinctively American religious and cultural beliefs often ignored rigid doctrines and dogmatic church leaders. Many secular Americans, indifferent to organized religion, tolerated diverse ideas. Others actively sought personal, intense religious experiences. Religious dissenters, such as Quakers and Methodists, had long flocked to North America. Protestant denominations multiplied, reinforced periodically by religious revivals. Yet, Puritan and Calvinist values remained influential, promoting hard work and criticizing music, dancing, and reading for pleasure.

Manifest Destiny and Expansion

The nation gradually expanded westward, acquiring abundant fertile land and rich mineral deposits, thus providing a counterpart to European imperialism in Asia and Africa (see Chapter 19). As pioneers crossed the Appalachian Mountains seeking new opportunities, Americans embraced **Manifest Destiny**, the conviction that their country's unmatched institutions and culture gave them a God-given right to expand over the continent. This idea was the religious sanction

> **protectionism** Use of trade barriers to shield local industries from foreign competition.
>
> **Manifest Destiny** Americans' conviction that their country's unmatched institutions and culture gave them a God-given right to take over the land.

---

[6]Alexis De Tocqueville, *Democracy in America and Two Essays on America* (New York: Penguin, 2003), xxxiii.

WITNESS TO THE PAST

Protesting Sexism and Slavery

Sarah Grimke and her younger sister, Angelina, daughters of a wealthy slaveholding family in Charleston, South Carolina, adopted the Quaker faith, which emphasized human dignity. Rejecting their elite status, they dedicated their lives to advocating women's rights and abolition of slavery. In 1837 they moved north, where they gave lectures before large audiences, often drawing criticism from churches for violating gender expectations and speaking out so publicly. In 1838 Sarah Grimke responded by writing letters to her critics using Christian arguments to defend women's right and obligation to voice their views. The letters, published together in one volume, became the first American feminist treatise on women's rights. The following excerpts convey some of Grimke's arguments.

Here then I plant myself. God created us equal; he created us free agents; he is our Lawgiver, our King and our Judge, and to him alone is woman bound to be in subjection, and to him alone is she accountable for the use of those talents with which her Heavenly Father has entrusted her.... As I am unable to learn from sacred writ when woman was deprived by God of her equality with man, I shall touch upon a few points in the Scriptures, which demonstrate that no supremacy was granted to man.... [In the Bible] we find the commands of God invariably the same to man and woman; and not the slightest intimation is given in a single passage, that God designed woman to point to man as her instructor....

I hope that the principles I have asserted will claim the attention of some of my sex, who may be able to bring into view, more thoroughly than I have done, the situation and degradation of women.... During the early part of my life, my lot was cast among the butterflies of the *fashionable* world; and of this class of women, I am constrained to say, both from experience and observation, that their education is miserably deficient; that they are taught to regard marriage as the one thing needful, the only notice of distinction; hence to attract the notice and win the attentions of men, by their external

charms, is the chief business of fashionable girls. They seldom think that men will be allured by intellectual acquirements, because they find, that where any mental superiority exists, a woman is generally shunned and regarded as stepping out of her "appropriate sphere," which, in their view, is to dress, to dance, to set out to the best possible advantage her person....To be married is too often held up to the view of girls as [necessary for] human happiness and human existence. For this purpose...the majority of girls are trained.... [In education] the improvement of their intellectual capacities is only a secondary consideration....Our education consists almost exclusively of culinary and other manual operations....

There is another class of women in this country, to whom I cannot refer, without feelings of the deepest shame and sorrow. I allude to our female slaves....The virtue of female slaves is wholly at the mercy of irresponsible tyrants, and women are bought and sold in our slave markets, to gratify the brutal lust of those who bear the name of Christians....If she dares resist her seducer, her life by the laws of some of the slave States may be...sacrificed to the fury of disappointed passion....The female slaves suffer every species of degradation and cruelty, which the most wanton barbarity can inflict; they are indecently divested of their clothing, sometimes tied up and severely whipped....Can any American woman look at these scenes of shocking...cruelty, and fold her hands in apathy, and say, "I have nothing to do with slavery"? *She cannot and be guiltless.*

THINKING ABOUT THE READING

1. What do the letters tell us about the social expectations and education for white women from affluent families?
2. In what way do Grimke's letters address the issue of slavery?

Source: Sarah M. Grimke, *Letters on the Equality of the Sexes, and the Condition of Woman* (Boston: Issac Knapp, 1838).

---

for U.S. nationalism and the thrust outward. In 1823 Secretary of State John Quincy Adams favored transforming the United States into "a nation, coextensive with the North American continent, destined by God and nature to be the most populous and powerful people ever combined under one social compact."[7]

After acquiring the Ohio territory in 1787, the new nation extended from the Atlantic to the Mississippi River. In 1803 President Thomas Jefferson (g. 1800–1809) astutely bought from France, in the Louisiana Purchase, much of the Midwest and South, doubling the country's size. Acquiring Florida and the Pacific Northwest added more. Some

Americans crossed vast prairies, deserts, and mountains to Oregon by wagon train. In 1848, after the U.S.-Mexican War, the United States obtained Texas, California, and New Mexico from Mexico. Then in 1849 gold discoveries near Sacramento prompted over 100,000 Americans, known as "49ers," to board sailing ships or covered wagons and head west for California, hoping to strike it rich. In California these "49ers" sometimes clashed with the long-settled Mexicans and immigrant Chinese. Finally, the 1867 purchase of Alaska from Russia eliminated all European rivals from North America (see Map 20.2). By 1913 the United States had grown to forty-eight states.

---

[7]Quoted in James Chase and Caleb Carr, *America Invulnerable: The Quest for Absolute Security from 1812 to Star Wars* (New York: Summit, 1988), 46.

AMERICAN PROGRESS This 1893 painting by the American artist John Gast extols progress and shows Americans, guided by divine providence, expanding across, and bringing civilization to, the forests and prairies of the Midwest and West. The painting reflects views held by many Americans of their destiny and special role in the world.

On the vast North American frontier, settlers developed new ways of life and ideas. Cattle ranching on the Great Plains fostered a new occupation: cowboys on horseback who guided large herds on long, lonely drives to railroad towns for shipment east. Cowboys—whites, Mexicans, African Americans, and men of mixed descent—often learned survival skills from Native Americans. Individualists sought adventure, social equality, and a better life in the West. But frontier life was often hard, especially on women. An Illinois farm wife, Sara Price, lamented her hardship in poetry: "life is a toil and love is a trouble. Beauty will fade and riches will flee. Pleasures will dwindle and prices they double, And nothing is as I would wish it to be."[8]

Westward expansion came at the expense of Mexicans, Spaniards, and Native Americans already there. Indians, viewing whites as invaders, often resisted violently. To whites, Indians represented an alien culture best restricted to

reservations. The U.S. Supreme Court ruled in 1831 that Indians' "relation to the United States resembles that of a ward to his guardian."[9] Eventually many Indians, even tribes living peacefully, were forcibly removed from their native lands. The Cherokee, farmers of Georgia and the Carolinas who had an alphabet, constitution, published newspaper, and good relations with their white neighbors, were forced into concentration camps and finally, in 1838, sent on a 1,200-mile forced march, the "Trail of Tears," to Oklahoma. Four thousand died from starvation or exposure. Some tribes resisted removal. The Seminole (**SEM-uh-nole**) in Florida, led by Chief Osceola (**os-ee-OH-luh**) (ca. 1804–1838), fought two wars with the U.S. army, attacking with guerrilla tactics and then retreating into the Everglades swamps. After Osceola was finally captured, Seminole resistance faded, and many were exiled to Oklahoma.

---

[8]From Peter Blood-Patterson, *Rise Up Singing* (Bethlehem, PA: Sing Out Publications, 1988), 246.
[9]Quoted in Walter L. Williams, "American Imperialism and the Indians," in *Indians in American History: An Introduction*, ed. Frederick E. Hoxie (Arlington Heights, IL: Harlan Davidson, 1988), 233.

The quest for resources and markets spurred territorial expansion into Latin America and the formation of empire. In 1823 Congress approved the Monroe Doctrine, a unilateral statement warning European nations against interfering in the Western Hemisphere and affirming U.S. commitment to shape Latin America's post-Spain political future. The doctrine claimed Latin America as an American **sphere of interest**, a region where one great power assumes responsibility for maintaining peace and monopolizes resources. The Monroe Doctrine forged complex links between the United States and Latin America, often provoking hostility, and set the stage for the United States as a world power.

sphere of interest An area in which one great power assumes responsibility for maintaining peace and monopolizes the area's resources.

After the U.S.-Mexican War of 1846–1848, the United States greatly expanded its national territory. Some 35,000 Americans and their slaves in the Mexican province of Texas, chafing at Mexican rule and its antislavery policies, rebelled in 1836 and pushed Mexican forces out, declaring themselves an independent republic. Soon Texans sought annexation to the United States, with proslavery southern states favoring and antislavery northern states opposed. The U.S. president and Congress moved to admit Texas to statehood in 1844, provoking Mexicans, who had never recognized Texan independence. The war that followed stirred divisive and passionate debate. Many Americans opposed the conflict. After President James Polk (1795–1849) ordered military action, a Massachusetts legislative resolution proclaimed "that such a war of conquest, so hateful, unjust and unconstitutional in its

MAP 20.2 U.S. EXPANSION THROUGH 1867 The United States expanded in stages after independence, gaining land from Spain, France, Britain, and Mexico until by 1867 the nation stretched from the Atlantic to the Gulf and Pacific coasts. During the same period Canadians expanded westward from Quebec to British Columbia. © 2015 Cengage Learning

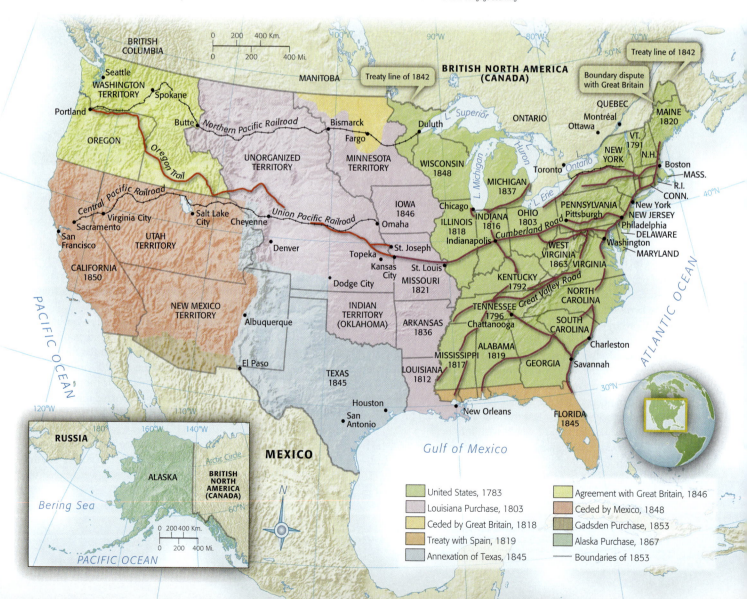

origin and character, must be regarded as a war against freedom, against humanity, against justice, against the Union."[10] The war ended when 14,000 U.S. troops invaded Mexico, capturing Mexico City. The United States then permanently annexed Mexican territories from Texas to California. However, the conflict had killed 13,000 Americans and 50,000 Mexicans, while fostering an enduring Mexican distrust of the United States.

Many Americans supported extending Manifest Destiny to Latin America and Asia. Polk wanted to seize California to increase profitable commerce with China. In 1853 Senator William Seward placed expansion in global perspective, advising Americans: "You are already the great continental power. But does that content you? I trust that it does not. You want the commerce of the world. The nation that draws the most from the earth and fabricates most, and sells the most to foreign nations, must be and will be the great power of the earth."[11] American traders participated in the lucrative China trade, including opium smuggling, while the United States Navy opened up reclusive Japan. Merchants from New England ports such as Salem (Massachusetts) established, and grew rich from, operations in Asian ports such as Macao and Madras, while U.S. traders, missionaries, adventurers, diplomats, and soldiers flocked to Asia (see Chapters 22–23).

Unlike Britain and Spain's territorial empires, during the nineteenth century the United States built an "informal" empire based on extending U.S. power through financial controls, trade, and military operations. American naval forces intervened in Southeast Asia almost annually from the 1830s through the 1860s. For example, in 1832 a U.S. naval expedition bombarded a port on the Indonesian island of Sumatra, whose officials had seized a private U.S. ship for illegal activities; U.S. officials boasted that the port demolition had "struck terror," forcing release of the ship. Some leaders advocated military action to gain trade agreements, an aggressive attitude that increasingly influenced U.S. policies during the century. Presidents also sought to obtain nearby Cuba from Spain, even financing Cuban revolts.

The Civil War, Abolition, and Industrialization

The Civil War (1861–1865) reshaped U.S. society by ending slavery. Many Americans believed that slavery mocked liberal democracy. By the early 1800s it had largely disappeared from northern states, and in 1810 the United States outlawed the slave trade. But slavery survived in the South. By 1860, the North boasted industries, banks, and great ports such as New York, Boston, and Philadelphia. By contrast, the South, inhabited by 350,000 white families and 3 million black slaves, had a monocultural economy that depended on exports to survive.

With the Civil War, the slavery-based southern plantation society tried to break free from the urbanization,

industrialization, and social change percolating in northern states. In 1860–1861 eleven southern states seceded from the union and formed the proslavery Confederate States of America. President Abraham Lincoln (1809–1865), an Illinois lawyer, wanting to end slavery and preserve the union, mobilized the military forces of the remaining states to resist secession. In 1862 his Emancipation Proclamation freed all slaves. The North's dynamic economy better mobilized resources for war, while northerners enjoyed a population advantage of nearly 4 to 1. After four years the North defeated the South.

Northern victory ultimately upended the plantation system, crushed southern self-determination, destroyed the South's economic link to Britain, confirmed protectionism as economic policy, and strengthened the federal government. Some 360,000 Union and 258,000 Confederate troops died, more than in all other wars fought by Americans combined. The South began to enjoy balanced economic development in the mid-twentieth century, with industries largely paid for by northern investors.

But emancipation did not eliminate the disadvantages faced by African Americans and other ethnic minorities. Many former slaves taught themselves to read, and some opened schools, expanding opportunities. Many also left plantations, but they found job prospects chiefly limited to sharecropping or physical labor. Moreover, long after slavery ended, African Americans faced laws restricting their rights and barriers to voting. Southern states, and some northern states, prohibited intermarriage and, unlike Latin America, offered no separate recognition for people of mixed ancestry, who were lumped with African Americans and treated as such. Any trace of African ancestry meant automatic relegation to inferior status. Skin color determined social class, and racial segregation was imposed in schools, housing, and public facilities. Those violating these laws and customs faced jail, beatings, or executions by white vigilantes. The journalist Ida B. Wells (1862–1931), born into slavery, sparked a long movement to end mob violence, including hangings (known as "lynchings"). Nevertheless, segregation remained the norm until the 1960s.

As expansion into central and western North America resumed, more Native Americans lost control of their destinies. Whites subdued the Great Plains with new technology, including six-shooters, steel ploughs, and barbed-wire fences. Settlers, railroad builders, and fur traders massacred 15 million bison, Great Plains tribes' chief subsistence source, while farmers and ranchers reshaped prairie and northern woodland environments. Indians resisted but eventually faced defeat. In 1890, the U.S. Army's massacre of three hundred Lakota Sioux followers of the Ghost Dance, an Indian spiritual revival movement, at Wounded Knee in South Dakota confirmed colonization of the West. Defeated and impoverished, Indians were put on government-controlled reservations, their children prohibited from speaking their native languages or practicing tribal traditions in boarding and public schools.

[10]Quoted in Simon Serfaty, *The Elusive Enemy: American Foreign Policy Since World War II* (Boston: Little, Brown, 1972), 13.
[11]Quoted in William Appleman Williams, *The Contours of American History* (Chicago: Quadrangle, 1966), 284.

Meanwhile, northern victory and protectionism improved material life and spurred great industrial growth in the later 1800s, as new food processing, textile, iron, and steel industries flourished and coal, mineral, and oil production expanded. In 1860 the United States ranked fourth among industrial nations, but by 1894 it ranked first and trailed only Britain as a world trader. Technological innovations changed economic life. Electric power and improved production methods turned out goods faster, more cheaply, and in greater quantities than ever before, increasing U.S. competitiveness. New American inventions such as typewriters, cash registers, adding machines, telegraphs, and telephones increased business productivity. Other American and European inventions—water-tube boilers, steam-powered forging hammers, portable steam engines, and internal combustion engines—revolutionized industry. Thomas Edison (1847–1931) perfected the light bulb, benefiting both the public and industry.

Improved transportation and communication networks reshaped life and population patterns. The transcontinental railroad, completed in 1869, opened western lands for settlement. Many workers who drove spikes and blasted passages

through rocks and mountains for the railroad tracks were African Americans, Chinese, or Irish. In 1903 Henry Ford's (1863–1947) motor company, manufacturing the first affordable cars, refined the mass-production assembly line. Orville and Wilber Wright achieved the first powered flight in 1903, launching the aviation age.

But industrialization also facilitated monopolistic concentration of industrial and financial resources similar to Europe's, worsening inequitable wealth distribution. A few fabulously wealthy tycoons such as John D. Rockefeller and J. P. Morgan, known to their critics as Robber Barons, influenced politicians, controlled much economic power, and paid workers subsistence wages. The Social Darwinist Rockefeller claimed that "the growth of large business is merely survival of the fittest and a law of God."[12] Many less affluent Americans also valued and hoped to acquire wealth, considering the United States a land of opportunity where anyone could succeed with hard work regardless of social background.

Industrial workers often experienced hard lives. In southern Appalachian and Ohio River Valley coal mines, work was

WOMEN TEXTILE WORKERS In both Europe and North America women became the largest part of the work force in the textile industry. These women, working in a New England spinning mill around 1850, endured harsh work conditions and the boring, often dangerous, job of tending machines.

Lewis Wickes Hine/Historical/Corbis

---

[12]Quoted in Robert Heilbroner and Aaron Singer, *The Economic Transformation of America, 1600 to the Present*, 3rd ed. (Fort Worth, TX: Harcourt Brace, 1994), 163.

dangerous, hours long, and wages low. Children worked alongside their parents, and miners often died young from breathing coal dust. Before the Civil War the New England textile industry also badly exploited women and children. Companies recruited teenage girls from poor rural families to work fourteen hours a day, six days a week in dark, hot mill rooms filled with cotton dust. The girls were housed in company dormitories, six to eight girls per room. By the 1880s the textile industry moved south to Virginia and the Carolinas, where wages were lower and people even more desperate for jobs.

Social Change, Thought, and Culture

Some 25 million Europeans immigrated to the United States between 1870 and 1916, initially largely northwestern Europeans—English, Irish, Germans, and Scandinavians—and later many southern and eastern Europeans—Italians, Greeks, Serbs, and Poles. Some businesses posted signs saying, "No Irish need apply." With many Jews fleeing persecution, by 1927 the American Jewish population totaled 4 million. In addition, thousands of Chinese, Japanese, and Filipino immigrants landed on the Pacific coast, where most of them faced discrimination. Asian immigrants, mostly living in western states, faced harsher restrictions and sometimes violence.

Once a mostly rural nation along the Atlantic coast, the United States became a transcontinental powerhouse. The federal government encouraged migration westward, giving free land to settlers in the Midwest. The country also became urbanized, with half the people living in cities, including metropolises such as New York and Chicago.

These decades also saw movements for economic and social change. Since factories produced more goods than Americans could consume, by the 1890s economic depression, panics, and bloody labor conflicts had led to working-class radicalism. Farmers and workers resented Robber Baron wealth and powerful large corporations and railroads. Many farmers went bankrupt, losing their land to banks. As a result, popular movements, some led by women, fought those with power and privilege. Labor unions first appeared in the 1820s; by midcentury textile mill girls were campaigning for better conditions and shorter workdays. Railroad union leader Eugene Debs (1855–1926) explained in 1893 that "the capitalists refer to you as mill hands, farm hands, factory hands. The trouble is he owns your head and your hands."[13] By the early 1900s the radical, Marxist-influenced Industrial Workers of the World (better known as Wobblies) had gained support among industrial workers, miners, and longshoremen. Union militants such as Irish immigrant Mary Harris ("Mother") Jones (1830–1930) organized coal miners and railroad workers, fighting big business power. Employers and their political allies, disparaging union members as communists, fought their demands.

Women, often working in factories, shops, and offices while also managing their homes, also struggled for their civil rights. Religious leaders urged women to be more pious, self-sacrificing, and obedient to men. Symbolizing this submission to male expectations, women wore stiff, uncomfortable whalebone corsets that constrained movement and accentuated their figure. Many wanted more options; banners carried by striking factory workers in 1912 read, "We want bread and roses too." Women gained basic privileges only after a long, nonviolent suffrage movement for the vote that declared that "all men and women are created equal." Suffragettes opposed a system that permitted women no rights to property or even to their own children after divorce. After seven decades of marching, publicizing their cause, and lobbying male politicians, they convinced Congress to approve women's voting rights in 1920.

During these years Americans created their own distinctive literary and intellectual traditions. Journalist Walt Whitman (1819–1892) celebrated democracy, the working class, and a broadminded view of sexual affection while addressing the impact of industrialization. Whitman described his dynamic, ethnically diverse nation as "a newer garden of creation, dense, joyous, modern, populous millions, cities and farms. By all the world contributed."[14] Inspired by European realism, Mark Twain (1835–1910), a former printer and riverboat pilot turned journalist, emphasized the underside of American life and character, was skeptical about technology's value, and opposed the increasing U.S. imperial thrust in the world.

American philosophy and religion went in new directions. Leading philosophers such as William James and John Dewey, breaking with European tradition, claimed that ideas had little value unless they enlarged people's concrete knowledge of reality, an approach known as pragmatism. While many Americans embraced secular and humanist views, others sought inspiration in religion. As the Protestant missionary impulse fostered religious and moral fervor, Americans became active as Christian missionaries around the world. Religious diversity also grew. In 1776 most Americans were Protestant, often Calvinist, but by 1914 the United States contained followers of many faiths, including some Buddhist and Muslim immigrants.

Mixing black and white traditions, Americans produced unique forms of music, especially blues and jazz. Derived from black plantation life, blues songs detailed personal woes in a harsh and racist world: lost love, police brutality, jail, joblessness, and oppression. Some songs celebrated black heroes such as the legendary hand driller John Henry, who allegedly died competing against a steam drill to build a railroad tunnel in the later 1800s. The blending of black blues with white folk music and popular music fostered several popular twentieth-century genres, including rock, rhythm and blues, and soul, that spread around the world.

American Capitalism and Empire

As in Europe, industrial capitalism led to imperialism and warfare. Repeated economic depressions from the 1870s through the 1890s, as well as difficult domestic problems, spurred demand for foreign markets and led many American businessmen, farmers, and workers to favor overseas conquests or interventions to improve national economic prospects. Others hoped to spread

[13]Quoted in Juliet Haines Mofford, ed., *Talkin' Union: The American Labor Movement* (Carlisle, MA: Discovery Enterprises, 1997), 24.
[14]From Mark Van Doren, ed., *The Portable Walt Whitman* (New York: Penguin, 1973), 210.

freedom and capitalism. The United States sent military forces to at least twenty-seven countries and territories between 1833 and 1898 to protect American economic interests or suppress piracy threatening U.S. shipping. Troops were dispatched to many Latin American nations, China, Indonesia, Korea, and North Africa, and for decades U.S. gunships patrolled several of China's rivers, protecting American businessmen and missionaries from Chinese who resented Western imperialism.

U.S. forces also brought the Hawaiian Islands, a Polynesian kingdom, into the U.S. empire. The growing American population in Hawaii of traders, whalers, planters, and missionaries resented the Hawaiian monarchy, while Queen Liliuokalani **(luh-lee-uh-oh-kuh-LAH-nee)** (1838–1917), a Hawaiian nationalist, wanted to restrict settler political influence. Although strong, resolute, and beloved by her people as a songwriter, she faced economic disaster when the U.S. Congress abandoned preferential treatment for Hawaiian sugar imports. In 1893 American settlers, aided by 150 U.S. troops, overthrew the monarchy, formed a provisional government, and sought affiliation with the United States. A heated American debate on direct colonization delayed annexation until 1898. The monarchy's end transformed the islands socially, as Japanese, Chinese, Korean, and Filipino immigrants become the main labor force, mostly working on plantations owned by American settlers and companies. By the 1930s, Asians constituted the large majority of Hawaii's population.

The major American conflict of this era, the Spanish-American War (1898–1902), pitted American against Spanish forces in several Spanish colonies and helped make the United States a major world power and empire. With President William McKinley (1843–1901) seeking foreign markets for America's surplus production, the United States coveted Spain's restless colonies: Cuba, Puerto Rico, Guam, and the Philippines. The war unleashed American nationalist fervor, one observer describing patriotism as oozing out of every boy old enough to feed the pigs. While the United States quickly triumphed against the hopelessly outmatched Spanish, 5,500 Americans died in Cuba, mostly of disease that caused, according to one surgeon, pale faces, sunken eyes, staggering gaits, and emaciated forms.

The war also changed Americans' outlook on the world. A future president, Woodrow Wilson, boasted about America's emergence as a major power: "No war ever transformed us quite as the war with Spain. No previous years ever ran with so swift a change as the years since 1898. We have witnessed a new revolution, the transformation of America completed."[15] However, to colonize the Philippines, the United States had to brutally suppress a fierce nationalist resistance by Filipinos opposing U.S. occupation, a struggle that resulted in thousands of Filipino and American deaths. Exercising power in the world proved costly, and many Americans protested the bloody U.S. invasion of distant islands (see Chapter 22). Colonization of the Philippines, Puerto Rico, and Guam, and economic and political domination over nominally independent Cuba, transformed the United States from an informal into a territorial empire much like the Netherlands and Portugal.

MAKE SURE YOU UNDERSTAND THESE KEY POINTS BEFORE MOVING ON

- Americans gradually pushed toward the West Coast, taking advantage of abundant natural resources and inflicting great suffering on Native Americans.

- The Monroe Doctrine announced that the United States saw Latin America as its own sphere of interest, off-limits to European powers.

- The bloody and divisive U.S.-Mexican War brought a large chunk of Mexican territory under American control.

- Millions of immigrants poured into the United States, seeking opportunity and often finding discrimination, while social movements arose seeking better treatment for workers and greater rights for women.

- To promote and protect American business interests, the U.S. military intervened in the affairs of many foreign countries and territories, most notably in the Spanish-American War, which brought the United States its first formal colonies.

Latin America and the Caribbean in the Global System

What political, economic, and social patterns shaped Latin America after independence?

Brazil and most of Spain's Latin American colonies won their independence in the early 1800s, although the Caribbean islands mostly remained colonies (see Chapter 19). But the new states, failing to forge enduring democracies or significant economic change, mostly experienced political instability and regional conflicts. By the 1870s expanding European markets increased demand for Latin American exports, though free trade policies also deepened economic monocultures. Black slaves gained their freedom, European immigrants changed the social landscape, and the United States increasingly exercised regional power.

New Latin American Nations

Latin Americans faced challenges in creating stable republics and political unity. While countries like Argentina, Brazil, and Mexico were large and unwieldy, others, like El Salvador and the Dominican Republic, were small and had limited resources. Some governments failed to win the allegiance of all the people, and civil wars often pitted those favoring federalism and regionalism against partisans of strong centralized government. Tensions between central governments and remote regions simmered. Meanwhile, frontier disputes led to occasional wars. After Chile fought Peru and Bolivia in 1837 and again in 1879–1884, it acquired territory from those two countries. Political instability also fostered military dictatorships. Although most countries adopted elections and U.S.-style constitutions, authoritarian governments often ignored their provisions.

Most leaders did not favor dramatic social and economic change. The upper class, mostly creoles, owned large businesses, plantations, and haciendas, while mestizos and mulattos constituted the small middle class of shopkeepers, teachers, and skilled artisans. Over half the population, including most Indians and blacks, were poor. Plantation agriculture and mining-based economies, with similar, highly unequal social structures, offered limited educational opportunities. Planters, ranchers, mine owners, merchants, and military officers dominated politics, often restricting political participation by poor nonwhites. In many countries military strongmen, known as caudillos, acquired and maintained power through force. Under the dictator Juan Manuel de Rosas (huan man-WELL deh ROH-sas) (1793–1877) in Argentina, police and thugs beat up, tortured, or murdered opponents, often poor peasants. For their armies, caudillos and regional leaders sometimes recruited local cowboys, skilled horsemen and fighters known as gauchos in Argentina and Uruguay that worked on large ranches.

Despite these problems, most nations established some stability by the 1850s. Many countries sought both "progress and order," usually under caudillos, but a few created multiparty systems. Liberals generally favored federalism, free trade, and separation of church and state, opposing the Catholic Church's institutional power for diminishing individual liberty. Conservatives sought centralization, trade protectionism, and maintenance of church power. Conflicts between these groups were sometimes violent.

Brazil was the only nation governed by a monarchy, which largely ignored popular aspirations toward abolishing slavery and forming a republic. As tensions simmered, the army seized power in 1889, exiled Emperor Dom Pedro II, and established a republic with a federal system that highly restricted suffrage. Most Brazilians gained neither property nor civil rights, many remaining desperately poor. Brazil maintained an authoritarian tradition that was repeatedly challenged by rebellions and regionalism.

Social and economic inequalities often spurred reforms and sometimes revolutions. The Mexican republic, founded in 1824, did not bring stability to this vast country that stretched from northern deserts to southern rain forests. Between 1833 and 1855 General Antonio Lopez de Santa Anna (1797–1876) led a series of dictatorships punctuated by civil war. Santa Anna also lost half of Mexico's territory, including Texas and California, in the disastrous U.S.-Mexican War (1846–1848), a humiliation still felt by Mexicans today. Growing social problems and Santa Anna's misadventures sparked upheaval. In 1861 Mexican liberals led by Benito Juarez (WAHR-ez) (1806–1872), a pragmatic but determined lawyer and Zapotec Indian, defeated conservatives and suspended foreign debt repayment, provoking a short-lived French occupation that installed a Habsburg, Maximilian of Austria (1832–1867), as Mexico's head. When France withdrew its troops, Maximilian's regime collapsed in 1867. Juarez again served as president until 1872, seeking social justice, fighting corruption, subordinating the church to the secular state, and assigning church and communal lands to individual peasant families. His reformist policies and Indian ancestry made Juarez Mexico's most honored leader and national symbol (see Profile: Benito Juarez, Mexican Reformer and President).

In 1876 Porfirio Diaz (DEE-ahs) (1830–1915), a mestizo, became Mexico's dictator. Diaz brought stability and economic progress while allowing foreign business interests and investors to control much of Mexico's economy, doing little to help the poor majority. Under his free enterprise policies many Indians sold their land to large haciendas and land companies to pay off debts, intensifying rather than ending the colonial legacy of landed estates owned by a small elite. The Diaz regime ended in civil war and the Mexican Revolution (1910–1920). Liberal creole Francisco Madero (1873–1913), a landowner's son educated in France and the United States, led one revolutionary faction. Another rebel leader, Pancho Villa (VEE-uh) (1877–1923), a former cowboy, attracted support chiefly from northern Mexico ranchers. In the south, charismatic mestizo and former peasant Emiliano Zapata (zeh-PAH-teh) (1879–1919) organized a peasant army, seizing haciendas and fighting the federal army.

After the defeat of Diaz, largely by Zapata's forces, the idealistic new president, Madero, was murdered by a rival, generating a free-for-all between diverse rivals. Sporadic violence engulfed Mexico, with all factions using ruthless tactics while alliances formed and collapsed. A novel recorded the confusion: "thinkers prepare the Revolution; bandits carry it out. At the moment no one can say with any assurance: 'So-and-so is a revolutionary and What's-his-name is a bandit.' Tomorrow, perhaps, it will be clearer."[16] Though Zapata was assassinated by a rival in 1919, his reputation lived on, making him the most celebrated revolutionary hero.

The fighting raised expectations for social change. Women played a critical revolutionary role, cooking and commanding troops, serving as spies and couriers, and shooting carbines and pistols. A constitution introduced in 1917 addressed women's rights, setting forth progressive goals such as an eight-hour workday

caudillos Latin American military strongmen who acquired and maintained power through force.

gauchos Cowboys in Argentina and Uruguay who worked on large ranches and were skilled horsemen and fighters.

---

[16]From Mariano Azuela's novel *The Flies*, quoted in Lesley Byrd Simpson, *Many Mexicos*, 4th ed. rev. (Berkeley: University of California Press, 1967), 298.

Benito Juarez, Mexican Reformer and President

Benito Juarez (1806-67) was one of Latin America's most extraordinary figures, rising to great achievements and high office despite extremely humble origins. President for five terms in a turbulent era of military conflicts and political divisions (1858 to 1872), Juarez was the only full-blooded Native American to ever serve as Mexico's president. Sometimes called modern Mexico's founding father, he struggled to preserve Mexico as a sovereign state while breaking with the Hispanic past, but he could not heal all the nation's ills and deep divisions.

A Zapotec Indian born into grinding poverty in a mountain village, San Pablo Guelatao, Oaxaca, in 1806, Juarez did not even speak Spanish until his teens. Orphaned at three and raised by an uncle, he worked in cornfields and as a shepherd until age twelve. Then, seeking a better life, he walked 41 miles to the state capital, Oaxaca city, where his sister worked as a cook for an immigrant Genoese merchant, Antonio Maza. Impressed with the boy's intelligence, industriousness, tenacity, and thirst for learning, a lay Franciscan brother paid his tuition to enter a seminary. Finding himself poorly suited for clerical training, Juarez entered the Institute of Science and Art and graduated with a law degree in 1834.

After joining the Oaxaca state congress, Juarez also practiced law, often defending poor Indian villagers who challenged wealthy hacienda owners and greedy clergy. Believing that Mexico's political and social system needed structural change, he joined the Liberal movement battling conservatives to shape the country's future. In 1843 Juarez, then thirty-seven, married seventeen-year-old Margarita Mazo (1826–1871), his first employer's illegitimate daughter. Together they had ten children. After holding various local and state offices and judgeships and serving in the national congress, Juarez was elected Oaxaca governor in 1847 and served until 1852, during which time he balanced the state budget, built rural schools, and promoted girls' education. Believing in popular sovereignty, he wanted "to protect mankind in the free development of his moral and physical faculties....no one individual, no sectional interest, and no class shall oppress the rest of society."

Between 1853 and 1855 Juarez and other liberal leaders, having been exiled by the returned caudillo, General Santa Anna, mostly lived in New Orleans, where he worked in a cigarette factory. When a liberal general overthrew Santa Anna, Juarez and his colleagues hurried home. While believing in God, Juarez opposed clerical power and corruption, and after being appointed secretary for justice, he sponsored legislation (known as the Juarez Law) subordinating military officers' and the clergy's traditional privileges to civil law. The law required the forced sale of church-owned lands not used for religious purposes. New laws also barred Indian villages from owning communal lands. Liberals hoped that selling and privatizing church and village lands would create a class of small private property holders, hence expanding the middle class and allowing increased tax collection.

A new constitution in 1857 proclaimed liberal ideals, guaranteeing church-state separation, secular education, abolition of slavery, equality before the law, and free speech, press, and assembly. Before this document, Catholicism was the state church and people could be jailed, even executed, for antigovernment writings. The changes provoked fierce church and conservative opposition, sparking Mexico's bloodiest civil war (1858–1861), the War of Reform, which pitted liberals against conservatives. Liberals eventually prevailed, but the fighting left Mexico exhausted, indebted, and broke. After being elected president in 1862, Juarez was forced to flee north during the French intervention (1862–1867). Led by Juarez, however, liberals eventually ousted the French puppet regime and regained control, but they now faced huge problems, including revolts, famine, and an empty treasury. From 1867 until his 1872 death at sixty-six from a heart attack, Juarez governed in an increasingly authoritarian manner, seeking improved relations with the United States while implementing educational, economic, and military reforms and conciliating enemies with an amnesty.

Today Mexicans view the tough-minded but practical Juarez as the greatest symbol of resistance to foreign intervention. He was controversial in his time and remains so today, fostering mythologies on both left and right. Supporters have celebrated a wise, visionary, strong, courageous model of patriotic integrity promoting democracy, legal equality, and rights and justice for indigenous Mexicans. Detractors have condemned him as a stubborn, anti-Christian dictator who undermined valuable traditions. Always convinced he was right, Juarez offered firm leadership when his nation badly needed it. Today a city (Ciudad Juárez) and many streets, schools, and businesses are named after him. A national holiday celebrating Juarez is held every March 21.

Library of Congress Prints and Photographs Division [LC-US262-7875]

MEXICAN PRESIDENT BENITO JUAREZ Juarez promoted social, cultural, and economic liberalization and fought French invasion.

THINKING ABOUT THE READING

1. What factors enabled Juarez's political rise?
2. How might his background have influenced his liberal views?
3. How have his policies and actions provoked disagreement about his legacy?

Note: Quotation from Brian Hamnett, *Juarez* (London: Longman, 1994), 77.

Armed Women "Soldaderas" (b/w photograph). Mexican Photographer, (20th century)/Private Collection/Peter Newark American Pictures/The Bridgeman Art Library

WOMEN REVOLUTIONARIES IN MEXICO Women joined men in fighting, and sometimes dying, for one or another faction during the Mexican Revolution. Many women hoped that the revolution would bring social change and a greater emphasis on improving women's political and economic rights.

and paid maternity leave. In 1920 the conflict wound down after claiming 1 million lives. While most Mexicans remained impoverished, former revolutionaries formed a government that brought political stability while opening opportunities for women to enter the business world and state governments.

Spanish-ruled Cuba also experienced revolt. By the later 1800s journalist and acclaimed poet Jose Marti (1853–1895), who had traveled and lived in Europe, the United States, and around Latin America, led an independence movement. Marti's writings promoting freedom, equality, and social justice helped inspire a Cuban revolt in 1895. Marti welcomed Afro-Cubans and women, who became the struggle's backbone. However, Marti was killed in the fighting, and U.S. intervention during the Spanish-American War sidetracked the revolution. Americans soon dominated the economy and strongly influenced Cuban governments.

Latin American Economic and Social Change

Like North Americans, Latin Americans debated free trade and involvement in the world economy as opposed to

protectionism and self-sufficiency. As exports and investments declined, Latin American leaders maintained plantation, mining, and ranching monocultures, concentrating on exporting raw materials—Ecuadorian cocoa, Brazilian coffee, Argentine beef, Cuban sugar, and Bolivian and Chilean ores— mainly to the United States and Europe. Since earnings from minerals and cash crops ebbed and flowed with world commodity prices, Latin Americans remained vulnerable, and by the twentieth century economic conditions were linked to fluctuating, "boom or bust" world prices for exports. Hence, politically unstable Central American countries whose economies depended on tropical agriculture were derisively called "banana republics."

Policies fostering growth but not development widened the gap between rich and poor. The poverty of most Indians and blacks gave them little purchasing power to support local industries. In addition, industrialization efforts in Brazil, Colombia, and Mexico in the 1830s and 1840s failed because of competition from European imports. North American, French, and especially British merchants and financiers used their economic power to dominate banking and the import trade for industrial goods while investing in mines and plantations, so that by the mid-1800s British businessmen and bankers controlled Brazilian and Argentine imports and exports. An Argentine nationalist complained that "English capital has done what English armies could not do. Today our country is tributary to England."[17] After 1890 the United States also became a powerful economic influence in Latin America.

Foreign corporations increasingly owned plantations and mines. For example, the U.S.-based United Fruit Company dominated Central American banana growing. Latin America became a major contributor to world commodity markets, producing some 62 percent of the world's coffee, 38 percent of the sugar, and 25 percent of the rubber by World War I. With powerful families or foreign corporations owning most usable land, inequalities grew, producing political unrest in the twentieth century. In parts of rural Brazil, landed families maintained peasants in semibondage through private armies and gunmen.

Yet, the abolition of slavery facilitated social change. Some leaders freed slaves who fought in the wars of independence. Between 1823 and 1854 slavery was legally abolished in most of Latin America and the Caribbean, and most European and American countries outlawed the trans-Atlantic slave trade. Spain finally granted Cuban slaves their freedom in 1886, while Brazilian abolitionists became more outspoken. Slave resistance, growing opposition by educated Brazilians, and plans to promote European immigration finally led to abolition in 1889. However, as in the United States, emancipation did not dramatically improve economic conditions. Many Latin American and Caribbean blacks shifted from slaves to low-status sharecroppers, tenant farmers, and laborers. A popular Brazilian verse lamented: "Everything in this world changes; Only the life of the Negro [black] remains the same. He works to die of hunger."[18]

Latin America's population doubled between 1850 and 1900 to over 60 million, as millions of European immigrants

[17]Quoted in Stanley J. Stein and Barbara H. Stein, *The Colonial Heritage of Latin America: Essays on Economic Dependence in Perspective* (New York: Oxford University Press, 1970), 151.
[18]Quoted in E. Bradford Burns, *Latin America: A Concise Interpretive History*, 5th ed. (Englewood Cliffs, NJ: Prentice-Hall, 1990), 213.

reshaped many societies. Italians, Spaniards, Germans, Russians, and Irish sought better economic prospects, especially in Argentina, Brazil, Chile, and Uruguay. As a result, today many people in Buenos Aires, Argentina, trace their roots to Italy. Continued immigration generated markets for European products and fashions.

Immigrants also came from overcrowded Asian and Middle Eastern lands. After abolition in Trinidad, British Guiana, and Dutch Guiana prompted labor-short planters to import workers from India, Indians eventually accounted for around half of the colony's populations. Japanese settled in Brazil, Peru, and Paraguay as farmers and traders, Arab Lebanese and Syrians developed trade diasporas throughout Latin America, Indonesians became plantation workers in Dutch Guiana, and Chinese flocked to Peru, Cuba, Jamaica, Trinidad, and the Guianas. Much cultural mixing occurred. For example, an Afro-Trinidadian might have a Spanish surname, belong to the Presbyterian Church, possess a Hindu love charm, enjoy English literature, and favor Chinese food. Moreover, people of Asian or Middle Eastern ancestry have sometimes headed Latin American or Caribbean governments.

Despite the newcomers, Latin American society remained more conservative than North American society. Creole elites dominated most countries, while European and Asian immigrants and mixed-descent people constituted the middle class. Many mulattos and most blacks and Indians remained lower class. Indians often withdrew into their village communities, limiting contact with national society. In 1865 a Mexican described the wide gap between whites and Indians: "The white is the proprietor; the Indian the worker. The white is rich; the Indian poor and miserable."[19] In Brazil, European, African, and mixed-descent people fostered a unique, multiracial society. Unlike in the United States, economic class and skin color did not always coincide, and intermarriage and cultural mixing were common. Millions of Brazilians of all backgrounds blended African religions with Catholicism, creating new sects. Yet blacks were also more likely to experience prejudice and poverty, as reflected in Rio de Janeiro's largely black hillside shantytowns.

Latin American and Caribbean Cultures

Latin Americans struggled to reconcile indigenous with imported European and African cultural traditions. Novelists focused on social themes. For example, Euclides da Cunha (KOO-nyuh) (1866–1909), acting as the spokesman for rising Brazilian nationalism and urban intellectuals, helped create a realistic Brazilian literature that described the life of the poor. Da Cunha's book *Rebellion in the Backlands* (1902), about a long uprising in the remote, impoverished northeast, challenged the nation's conscience

samba A Brazilian popular music and dance.

calypso A song style in Trinidad that featured lyrics addressing daily life and topical subjects.

and stimulated other authors to question accepted political wisdom. Radical Chilean essayist Francisco Bilbao praised freedom and rationalism while denouncing slavery, Catholicism, and U.S. expansionism. In contrast, a cosmopolitan new French-influenced literary and artistic movement, *modernismo* ("modernism"), flourished from 1880 to World War I as Latin America's most important literary innovation. Well-traveled Nicaraguan poet Ruben Dario (1867–1916), seeking ways to express Latin American experience, gave modernism its name and definition, his free verse expressing individualism and freedom. Dario offered escapist and fantastic images while stressing beauty as an end in itself. Living at various times in Chile, Argentina, Guatemala, Spain, and France, among other countries, he expressed a vision that transcended his nation to embrace the entire Latin American and Hispanic world.

Musicians and dancers produced creative cultural innovations. Mixing African and European traditions, the sensuous tango dance emerged in working-class bars and clubs of Buenos Aires, becoming Argentina and Uruguay's most popular music. Tango rhythms derived from African drumming, and the music featured the accordion-like *bandoneon*, carried by Italian immigrants. Becoming a symbol of lower-class identity, by the early 1900s tango achieved popularity in Europe's ballrooms and nightclubs. Brazil's unique music also blended European melody and African rhythms. **Samba**, a popular music and dance developed by Afro-Brazilian women from Bahia who settled in Rio de Janeiro's hillside shantytowns, became integral to Carnival, the three-day celebration before the long Christian period of fasting and penitence known as Lent.

Caribbean peoples also mixed African and European influences. On Trinidad, British officials, fearing the black majority, prohibited African-based musics, but two traditions reflecting Afro-Trinidadian identity defied British rule. **Calypso**, a song style featuring lyrics that addressed daily life and topical subjects, eventually became hugely popular in English-speaking eastern Caribbean islands. The second tradition, the pre-Lent Carnival, was a major festival that featured calypso songs, some of which questioned colonial policies. A song in the 1880s protested restrictions on music during Carnival: "Can't beat my drum, In my own native land. Can't have Carnival, In my native land."[20] By the 1920s informal calypso presentations in makeshift theaters had evolved into elaborate, heavily rehearsed shows.

The United States in Latin America

Latin Americans envied and feared the increasingly powerful United States, whose military forces occasionally intervened in Central America and the Caribbean. In 1856 William Walker, an American adventurer financed by influential U.S. businessmen, invaded Nicaragua with well-armed American mercenaries and proclaimed himself president, after which the United States granted his government diplomatic recognition. Walker introduced slavery before being forced out in 1857, becoming

---

[19]Quoted in Michael C. Meyer and William L. Sherman, *The Course of Mexican History*, 2nd ed. (New York: Oxford University Press, 1983), 416.

[20]Quoted in Lloyd Braithwaite, "The Problem of Cultural Integration in Trinidad," in *Consequences of Class and Color: West Indian Perspectives*, ed. David Lowenthal and Lambors Comitas (Garden City, NY: Anchor, 1973), 248.

a hated symbol of what Latin Americans often called "Yankee imperialism." Ruben Dario expressed this hatred when, outraged by the U.S. victory in Cuba, he addressed his critique of U.S. policies to President Teddy Roosevelt:

> *You are the United States, future invader of our naive America with its Indian blood, an America that still prays to Christ and still speaks Spanish....*
>
> *The United States is grand and powerful. Whenever it trembles, a profound shudder runs down the enormous backbone of the Andes. If it shouts, the sound is like the roar of a lion.*[21]

The Spanish-American War turned Cuba into a U.S.-dominated neocolony. The Platt Amendment to the Cuban constitution, imposed by the United States in 1901 and only repealed in 1934, integrated Cuban and U.S. economies and required U.S. congressional approval of any treaties negotiated by Cuba. The American military governor summarized the situation: "There is little or no real independence left to Cuba. She is absolutely in our hands, a practical dependency of the United States."[22] U.S. businessmen owned much of Cuba's economy, including railroads, banks, and mills, and Americans also acquired a naval base at Guantanamo Bay. Later Cuban nationalists blamed Cuba's squalid condition not on despotic Cuban governments but on the United States.

The United States became deeply involved in other Central American and Caribbean states as well. To build a canal across Central America linking the Pacific and Atlantic Oceans, Americans helped Panama secede from Colombia in 1903. Panama then leased a 10-mile-wide zone across the isthmus in perpetuity to the United States for the canal. Several thousand workers from Panama and Caribbean islands died in ten arduous years of construction. In 1914 the Panama Canal, 51 miles long, was completed, one of history's greatest engineering feats. Ships could now sail between the oceans safely and conveniently. In another intervention in 1912, Americans overthrew Nicaragua's president, who was suspected of inviting the British to build a rival canal. But unrest followed, prompting the United States to send in a military force that remained until 1933. U.S. soldiers also occupied Haiti (1915–1933) and the Dominican Republic (1916–1924) to quell unrest or maintain friendly governments. These interventions set the stage for more active U.S. imperial policies in the region.

MAKE SURE YOU UNDERSTAND THESE KEY POINTS BEFORE MOVING ON

- After gaining independence from Spain, Latin American nations were plagued by instability, undemocratic governments, and socioeconomic inequality along racial lines.

- Latin American economies tended to focus on the export of one or two natural resources, which created instability and made them susceptible to foreign domination.

- The abolition of slavery in Latin America did not greatly improve the economic conditions of former slaves, and millions of immigrants from Europe, India, Japan, and elsewhere flowed into Latin American countries.

- The tango developed in lower-class Buenos Aires, and samba was a result of cultural mixing in Rio de Janeiro, while Caribbean calypso was a legacy of resistance to British efforts to stamp out African-based music on Trinidad.

aplia

New Societies in Canada and the Pacific Basin

Why did the foundations for nationhood differ in Canada and Oceania?

The United States became the most powerful and prosperous of the American and Oceanic societies settled by Europeans, but the others also fostered democracies and growing economies. Canada expanded across North America to the Pacific. Western nations also colonized the island societies scattered around the Pacific Basin. In Australia and New Zealand, Britain established settler colonies.

Making a Canadian Nation

By 1763 Britain defeated the French and gained control of eastern Canada, including the main French colony, Quebec, but it had to forge stable relations with French Canadians, who maintained their language, culture, and identity. By 1774 Britain pragmatically recognized Catholic Church influence and French civil law in Quebec, while British colonists settled chiefly along the Atlantic coast and west of Quebec in Ontario. But relations between British and French Canadians remained uneasy; a British official in the 1830s concluded that Canada was "two nations warring in the bosom of a single state."[23] French power in North America ended in 1803, when the United States acquired the vast Louisiana territory, including the Mississippi River Basin long coveted by Americans.

American leaders hoped that Canada might eventually join the United States, but in the U.S.-British treaty of 1783 following the American Revolution, the United States recognized

[21]From *Selected Poems of Ruben Darío* by Ruben Dario, translated by Lysander Kemp, Copyright © 1965, renewed 1993. Reprinted by permission of the University of Texas Press.

[22]General Leonard Wood, quoted in Saul Landau, *The Dangerous Doctrine: National Security and U.S. Foreign Policy* (Boulder, CO: Westview Press, 1988), 80–81.

[23]Quoted in Louis Hartz, *The Founding of New Societies* (New York: Harcourt, Brace and World, 1964), 248.

British control north of the Great Lakes and the Saint Lawrence River. Many pro-British Loyalists moved to Canada, increasing the English-speaking population and promoting democratic reforms and representative assemblies. But relations between the United States and Canada remained tense for years. Americans feared that Canadians were aiding Native Americans who were resisting U.S. expansion in the Ohio region, where the powerful and charismatic Shawnee chief Tecumseh (1768–1813) gathered a large tribal alliance to drive the white settlers out of Ohio and reinvigorate Indian ways. Then during the War of 1812 Americans repeatedly invaded Canada but were repulsed. The war ended U.S. attempts to expand north while fostering a separate Canadian identity. In 1846 another treaty fixed the U.S.-Canada boundary in the west.

Canadians resumed building a democratic nation in peace while modifying British control. Between 1815 and 1850 Canada welcomed 800,000 British immigrants. Gradually reforms fostered a unified Canada, an elected national parliament, and waning British political influence. But fearing U.S. power, Canadians rejected complete independence in favor of self-rule within the British Empire. In 1867 leaders from Ontario, Quebec, New Brunswick, and Nova Scotia negotiated a Canadian Confederation that guaranteed provincial rights and preserved the French language wherever it was spoken. Canada became a **dominion**, a country having autonomy but owing allegiance to the British crown.

dominion A country having autonomy but owing allegiance to the British crown.

However, expansion of white settlement and political power westward fired resentment among Indians and mixed-descent, French-speaking Metis **(may-TEES)**. Combative Metis leader Louis Riel **(ree-EL)** (1844–1885) led two rebellions before being executed for treason. Eventually Manitoba and British Columbia joined the Confederation. Hoping to transform the 4 million Canadians into a unified nation, Canada's first prime minister, Scottish-born John MacDonald (g. 1867–1873, 1878–1891), promised to build a transcontinental railroad. Completed in 1885, the railroad crossed over 2,000 miles of forests, prairies, and high mountains. Putting many Native Americans on reservations allowed white settler migration to the western provinces. By 1905 Canada included all the present territory except Newfoundland.

Canada's economy and ethnic structure changed between the 1860s and 1914. Wheat grown in the Great Plains replaced beaver fur and fish as the major export. Gold strikes in the northwest and free land in western Canada attracted several million immigrants, many from eastern and southern Europe as well as China and Japan, enriching the ethnic mosaic. By 1911 Canadians controlled their own foreign affairs and diplomacy. Over the next several decades Canada encouraged industrialization and established warmer relations with the United States while maintaining the British monarch as symbolic head of state.

Exploration and Colonization of the Pacific Islands

The peoples on the small mountainous islands and flat atolls scattered across the vast Pacific Ocean Basin eventually experienced European expansion. Spain colonized Guam,

Hulton Archive/Getty Images

RIDING THE CANADIAN PACIFIC RAILWAY During the late nineteenth century Canadians and immigrants from many lands followed the railroad to settle the midwestern plains and western mountains. This illustration shows passengers aboard a sleeping car in 1888.

in the Marianas, in 1663, but otherwise European contact with Pacific islanders was minimal until the mid-1700s, when Britain and France raced to explore what they considered the last frontier. They eventually colonized, along with Spain, Germany, Russia, and the United States, all the inhabited islands. English captain James Cook (1728–1779), an agricultural laborer's son, led extensive explorations. Cook reached Tahiti, in eastern Polynesia, in 1769, recruiting a Polynesian high priest, Tupaia (ca. 1725–1771), whose navigational skills and command of several Polynesian languages greatly aided Cook's expedition. Tupaia drew up the charts that helped Cook map Polynesia, including New Zealand, and the Australian coast. Cook made two more expeditions and located the Hawaiian Islands in 1778. His early reports created an image of the South Sea islands as a "Garden of Eden" with amiable people, an image still surviving in popular culture, but Cook himself was killed in Hawaii after antagonizing local leaders.

European explorations spurred economic exploitation and Christian missionary activity. Russians established footholds in Alaska and the Aleutian Islands, where they hunted seals and sea otters to near extinction for their fur. Thousands of Aleuts died from the diseases brought by these Europeans. Deep-sea whaling lasted longer, attracting Western sailors. Western traders also sought Pacific island resources such as sandalwood, greatly valued in Asia for building furniture. Soon all of Fiji's sandalwood was gone. Meanwhile, Protestant and Catholic missionaries found mixed results. Samoans welcomed them, often adopting Christianity. Fijians initially rejected missionaries but later often pragmatically blended Christianity with their own traditions. One chief, Ratu Tui Levuka, reportedly said that his right hand was Methodist, his left hand Catholic, and his body heathen. Some islanders were hostile to outside influences. For instance, New Hebrides people killed the first missionaries who reached the islands.

With traders and missionaries opening the way, Western powers colonized all of the Pacific societies between the 1840s and 1900. France acquired many island chains, such as the Society Islands (including Tahiti), while Britain colonized various others, among them Fiji. Germans and Americans divided up Samoa. Germans seized most of Micronesia, and Britain and France controlled much of Melanesia. By 1875 smallpox, measles, and venereal diseases introduced by Western visitors and settlers to Hawaii had reduced the population from 150,000 to 50,000. Hawaii remained a Polynesian kingdom until 1893, when American settlers seized control.

The Rise of Australia and New Zealand

Britain colonized Australia and New Zealand (see Map 20.3 and Chapter 9). In 1788 the British began transporting convicts, often Irish, from overcrowded British jails to penal colonies they founded on Australia's southeast coast. Soon former convicts and discharged soldiers formed settlements and farms around Sydney. Agriculture, ranching, and mining underpinned the modern economy. Britain divided the continent into six colonies, with New South Wales and Victoria in the southeast having the largest populations.

British colonization disrupted the Aborigines, who were completely different from Pacific islanders in language, culture, and ways of life and whose nomadic ancestors had lived on the continent for thousands of years. Divided into hundreds of scattered tribes, Aborigines lived chiefly by fishing, hunting, and gathering. European settlers considered them an inferior, primitive people. Many Aborigines, resisting encroachments on their land, raided British settlements. While early British settlers killed as many as 20,000 Aborigines, European diseases such as smallpox and influenza killed the majority of Aborigines. By 1875 only 150,000 Aborigines remained, and whites forcibly settled their land. Eventually many Aborigines had little choice but to move to cities or work on white-owned cattle and sheep ranches. However, large numbers remained on tribal reservations, maintaining many of their traditions and beliefs.

Creating a common Australian identity and nationhood took over a century. Throughout the 1800s whites clung to coastal regions suitable for farming and ranching, avoiding the inhospitable desert interior. Gold discoveries in southeastern Australia in 1851 attracted settlers from Europe and Chinese and other Asians to seek their fortunes in Australia, creating resentments among whites. Violence between Europeans and Asians, especially in mining camps, prompted laws restricting Asian immigration. Meanwhile, white women struggled for influence in the male-dominated society. By the 1880s women's movements pressed for moral reform and suffrage; white women gained the right to vote in 1902. However, Aborigines gained voting rights only in 1962.

By 1890 Britain had turned all six of its Australian colonies into self-governing states, which formed the Commonwealth of Australia in 1901 (see Map 20.3). Like Canada, Australia became a self-governing, democratic dominion maintaining close political links with Britain, but it gradually formed its own identity. A transcontinental railroad system, completed in 1917, connected the vast country. Yet most white Australians lived in or near five coastal cities. Distance from European supplies fostered some local manufacturing, including steel production.

Colonizing New Zealand's two large mountainous islands, 1,200 miles east of Australia, came at the Polynesian Maori people's expense. They had lived on the islands, which they called Aotearoa, for hundreds of years, gradually dividing into sometimes warring tribes headed by chiefs. In 1792, when the first British settlers arrived, Maori numbered around 100,000. Some Maori used British newcomers for their own purposes. One chief, Hongi Hika (ca. 1772–1828), befriended a Protestant missionary, who took him to England. Returning with guns, Hongi and his warriors raided rival tribes. Maori intertribal warfare became more deadly, limiting cooperation to oppose the British.

As more British settlers came, territorial disputes with the Maori increased. The Treaty of Waitangi in 1850 between Britain and five hundred Maori chiefs seemingly confirmed Maori rights to their land and the authority of their chiefs while acknowledging British sovereignty. But English-language and Maori-language versions differed, the British claiming that the treaty gave them political and legal power. Disagreement over treaty provisions and British occupation of more Maori land provoked deadly wars that ended only in the 1870s. During these wars Britain skillfully exploited Maori tribal rivalries

MAP 20.3 **AUSTRALIA AND NEW ZEALAND** The British colonized and gradually settled Australia and New Zealand between the late 1700s and 1914. In 1901 the six Australian colonies became a federation, with a capital eventually built in Canberra.
© 2015 Cengage Learning

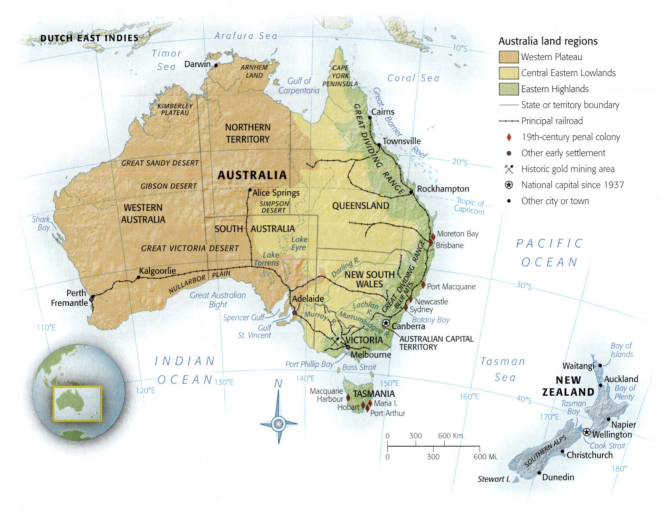

while employing heavy artillery and armored steamships. Eventually Maori resistance subsided, leading to an 1881 peace agreement that accorded Maori control over some districts.

Gradually British identity in New Zealand grew stronger. Gold discoveries in 1861 stimulated British immigration, so that by 1881 Maori comprised only 10 percent of the half-million population. High living standards, farming and sheep raising, and a growing government welfare system attracted immigrants. New Zealand prospered after 1882, when steamships, having acquired refrigerated holds, carried lamb and dairy products to Europe. A parliamentary government including Maori representatives was formed in 1852, and by 1893 all men and women enjoyed universal suffrage. New Zealand gained self-government as a British dominion in 1907, its alliance with Britain guaranteeing security. It remained an outpost of the British Empire well into the twentieth century.

MAKE SURE YOU UNDERSTAND THESE KEY POINTS BEFORE MOVING ON

- Canada had to contend with the challenge of forming a unified country that included French and English speakers, as well as with the threat of the neighboring United States.

- Western nations, starting with Britain and France but later including Russia, the United States, and Germany, colonized the Pacific islands and exploited their natural resources.

- Starting as penal colonies, British settlements in Australia expanded and pushed the native Aborigines off their land and then clashed with Asians who came to mine gold.

- British colonizers of New Zealand clashed repeatedly with the native Maori, ultimately deceiving them into signing away the rights to their land in the Treaty of Waitangi, which led to a series of wars that ended only in the late nineteenth century.

CHAPTER SUMMARY

During the Modern Era European populations grew and millions of people emigrated to the Americas and Oceania. More people lived in cities, where social problems and poverty increased. The industrial system influenced relations between men and women, as family life changed and European women lost status, fostering feminist movements. Reacting to political and social turbulence, some European thinkers abandoned Enlightenment ideas. The pace of scientific and technological innovation also increased.

Across the Atlantic, the new democratic republic in the United States gradually became a regional and then world power with a diversified economy and distinctive culture. The United States expanded westward, eventually incorporating large sections of North America, some of it acquired after war with Mexico. As Americans settled the frontier, they subdued Native Americans and fostered new social patterns. The Civil War temporarily divided the nation and ended slavery. In the aftermath, economic growth and industrialization spurred massive immigration from Europe and social movements to improve the lives of workers and women. Industrial capitalism also motivated Americans to increase their influence in the wider world, eventually leading to the Spanish-American War. The U.S. victory in that conflict made the United States a world power.

Other new nations arose in the Americas and Oceania during the Modern Era. After Latin Americans gained independence from Spain and Portugal, the new governments remained authoritarian and fostered little economic or social change. Latin American and Caribbean economies remained monocultures geared to exporting raw materials and under foreign domination. While millions of European immigrants arrived, most blacks and Indians remained poor. Social inequalities produced tensions and, in Mexico, a revolution. Latin American and Caribbean societies created unique cultures that reflected the mix of peoples from around the world. The United States also played an increasing role in the region, creating resentments that have lingered into the present.

Despite a division between French and English speakers, Canada expanded to the Pacific and became a nation with a self-governing democracy. Meanwhile, European powers colonized the Pacific islands. Europeans settled in Australia and New Zealand and, like Canadians, elected to remain tied to Britain even while developing their own democratic nations.

KEY TERMS

feminism (p. 478)
suffragettes (p. 478)
romanticism (p. 479)
modernism (p. 479)
impressionism (p. 479)

protectionism (p. 481)
Manifest Destiny (p. 481)
sphere of interest (p. 484)
caudillos (p. 489)
gauchos (p. 489)

samba (p. 492)
calypso (p. 492)
dominion (p. 494)

21 Africa, the Middle East, and Imperialism, 1750–1914

TOMB OF MUHAMMAD AHMAD IN KHARTOUM Muhammad Ahmad Ibn 'Abd Allah, known to history as the Mahdi ("Divinely Guided One"), used Islamic appeals to recruit a large army and lead opposition to the joint British and Egyptian rule in Sudan. He died soon after routing the British forces in 1885, but his tomb remains a popular place of pilgrimage and a symbol of Muslim resistance to Western power.

Isam Al-Haj/AFP/Getty Images

The power of these Europeans has advanced to a shocking degree and has manifested itself in an unparalleled manner. Indeed, we are on the brink of a time of [complete] corruption. As for knowing what tomorrow holds, I am blind.

—Moroccan historian Ahmad Ibn Khalid al-Nasri, 1860[1]

Fresh from victories in Italy and Austria, in 1798 French general Napoleon Bonaparte vowed to join illustrious European conquerors who had achieved glory in the Middle East. Alexander the Great had conquered Egypt and Persia, Roman and Byzantine emperors had controlled the eastern Mediterranean, and medieval Christian crusaders had established temporary western Asia footholds. In his mind, Europe hardly deserved his talents when the rich Muslim world beckoned. He planned to invade Egypt and then reduce the Ottoman Turks and Persians to French vassals. With four hundred ships carrying fifty thousand soldiers, Bonaparte quickly controlled northern Egypt. He also brought some five hundred French scholars to study Egyptian history, society, language, and environment. In the Nile River Delta they discovered the multilanguage Rosetta stone, a tablet from 196 B.C.E. that facilitated, for the first time, translating ancient Egyptian hieroglyphics. Seeking popular support, the French general confidently announced: "People of Egypt, I come to restore your rights; I respect God, His Prophet and the Quran. We are friends of all true Muslims. Happiness to the People!"[2] He also claimed to have liberated Egyptians from repressive Mamluk rulers. But Bonaparte's policies soon alienated Egyptians, who came to see the French as even worse. The ill-equipped French army withered in the desert heat. An attempt to conquer Syria having failed, Bonaparte left for Paris in 1799, another example of Westerners unsuccessfully attempting to control and change Muslim societies.

As Moroccan historian Ahmad Ibn Khalid al-Nasri had feared, the invasion, while unsuccessful, provided a harbinger of more conflicts resulting from European imperial thrusts in sub-Saharan Africa and the Middle East. Industrializing Europe's accelerating need for natural resources and new markets, combined with European political rivalries and powerful military technologies, sparked ruthless colonization. European colonialism generally lasted only a century or less, and sub-Saharan and North Africans often resisted Western power. Yet Western governments, technologies, and ideas reshaped African societies and their economies, cultures, and political systems while linking them closely to a European-dominated world economy. Although western Asian societies experienced less disruption, Ottomans lost their North African and European territories and, like Persians, struggled to meet challenges posed by European power.

[1]Quoted in Edmund Burke III, *Prelude to Protectorate in Morocco: Precolonial Protest and Resistance, 1860–1912* (Chicago: University of Chicago Press, 1976), xi.
[2]Quoted in Alan Palmer, *The Decline and Fall of the Ottoman Empire* (New York: Barnes and Noble, 1992), 58.

The Colonization of Sub-Saharan Africa

How did various Western nations obtain colonies in sub-Saharan Africa?

Between 1750 and the later 1800s the trans-Atlantic slave trade's diminishing importance gradually changed African-European relationships. The Western impact was uneven during the slave trade, which had drawn Africa into the world economy chiefly to supply slaves while impeding most trade involving other products. As demand for slaves waned and industrialization spread, Europeans increasingly sought African agricultural and mineral resources and more territories, precipitating the full-blown quest for colonies, what a British newspaper called the "scramble for Africa." European powers divided up Africa among themselves, often against fierce resistance, accelerating economic penetration. By 1914 colonization was complete.

The End of the Slave Trade and African Societies

For over three centuries the trans-Atlantic slave trade (1520–1870) dominated relations between Africa, Europe, and the Americas, but humanitarian opposition and economic concerns

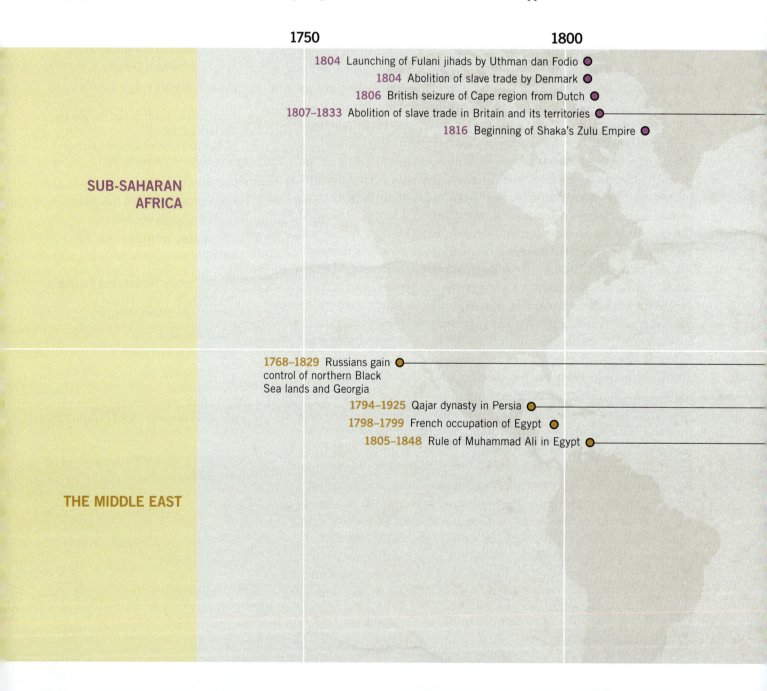

1750   1800

SUB-SAHARAN AFRICA

1804   Launching of Fulani jihads by Uthman dan Fodio
1804   Abolition of slave trade by Denmark
1806   British seizure of Cape region from Dutch
1807–1833   Abolition of slave trade in Britain and its territories
1816   Beginning of Shaka's Zulu Empire

THE MIDDLE EAST

1768–1829   Russians gain control of northern Black Sea lands and Georgia
1794–1925   Qajar dynasty in Persia
1798–1799   French occupation of Egypt
1805–1848   Rule of Muhammad Ali in Egypt

spurred abolitionist movements. British abolitionists hoped to open Africa to both Christian missionaries and trade in diverse commodities. Abolitionists also included Christians prompted largely by moral outrage at slavery and others influenced by visions of human equality. One sympathizer wrote that people "are not objects. Everyone has his rights, property, dignity. Africa will have its day."[3]

Africans and African Americans also struggled against slavery. Olaudah Equiano (1745–1797), an Igbo taken from Nigeria to Barbados and then Virginia, eventually purchased his freedom and campaigned in Europe for abolition. Equiano published a best-selling book chronicling his own horrific experiences and exposing self-proclaimed devout Christians mistreating their slaves. Slave revolts in the Americas, including Haiti's successful revolution (see Chapter 19), confirmed that many slaves were risking their lives for freedom. Meanwhile, the widely read poetry and Christian writings of Phyllis Wheatley (ca. 1753–1785), a Senegal-born slave in Boston who learned Latin and Greek and eventually won her freedom, undermined widespread notions that Africans were incapable of sophisticated thought.

There were also economic reasons. The Industrial Revolution made slavery uneconomical as overseas markets for factory-made goods became more desirable than cheap labor

[3]Quoted in John Iliffe, "Tanzania Under German and British Rule," in *Zamani: A Survey of East African History*, ed. B. A. Ogot, new ed. (Nairobi: Longman Kenya, 1974), 301.

1850   1900   1950

1838 Great Trek by South African Boers
1842 Ending of trans-Atlantic slave trade by most European nations
1847 First American freed slave settlement in Liberia
1870 Ending of trans-Atlantic slave trade
1874–1901 British-Ashante wars
1878 Belgian colonization in Congo
1884–1885 Berlin Conference on colonialism
1884–1885 Discovery of gold in South Africa
1898 French defeat of Samory Toure
1899–1902 Boer (South African) War
1905 Maji Maji Rebellion in Tanganyika
1912 Founding of African National Congress in South Africa

1830 Greek independence from Ottoman Empire
1830 French colonization of Algeria
1859–1869 Building of Suez Canal
1882 British colonization of Egypt
1890s–1915 Turkish genocide against Armenians
1897 First Zionist conference
1899 British protectorate over Kuwait
1905–1911 Constitutional revolution in Persia
1907–1921 Russian and British spheres of influence in Persia
1908 Young Turk government in Ottoman Turkey
1908 Discovery of oil in Persia
1911–1912 Colonization of Libya and Morocco

for plantations. Moreover, plantations became less profitable because so many colonies producing sugar flooded the market. African states also charged more to provide slaves. Investing in manufacturing proved more profitable.

Given these moral and economic factors, the slave trade and slavery ended in the Atlantic world in the nineteenth century. Denmark outlawed the trade in 1804, Britain in 1807, and then all British-controlled territories, including their plantation-rich Caribbean colonies, in 1833. Britain declared war on slave traders, intercepting slave ships in the Atlantic and returning the slaves to Africa. By 1842 most European and American countries made transporting slaves across the Atlantic illegal. The Civil War ended slavery in the United States in 1865. In the later 1880s Brazil and Cuba finally outlawed slavery.

The East African trade sending slaves to the Middle East and Indian Ocean islands, run chiefly by Omani Arabs, continued longer. In 1835 the Omani leader, Sayyid Sa'id **(SIGH-id SIGH-eed)** (r. 1806–1856), moved his capital to Zanzibar, an island just off the Tanzanian coast, where he built a commercial empire shipping ivory to India, China, and Europe and slaves to India, the Persian Gulf, and South Arabia. Omanis also profited from growing Indonesian cloves on slave plantations on Zanzibar. To obtain slaves and ivory, Omani and Swahili merchants expanded overland trade routes through Tanzania into the eastern Congo River Basin. In 1873 Britain convinced the sultan to close Zanzibar's slave market, but slavers still raided African villages for men to carry huge ivory tusks to the coast. Although Britain gained control of Zanzibar in 1890, some slave trading continued in parts of East and Central Africa until the early 1900s.

Even before abolition, freed slaves who chose, or were pressured, to return to Africa from the Americas established several West African states and port cities. The states' black founders and white financiers wanted the freed slaves to run their own lives while also setting up new centers of Western trade. The two largest settlements emerged in Sierra Leone and Liberia. In 1787 Britain settled four hundred former slaves around the fort at Freetown, the core of its Sierra Leone colony. More former slaves arrived in Freetown from Britain's West Indian colonies and British-ruled Canada, many of them former Loyalists during the American Revolution. Freed slaves from the United States first reached Liberia in 1847 and were joined by others after the Civil War. One of the first African nationalists, West Indian–born Edward Blyden (1832–1912), emigrated to Liberia after being denied admission to U.S. universities because he was black. Blyden believed that, given the racism in the Americas and Europe, people of African ancestry could realize their potential only in Africa.

However, some problems remained. Although descendants of former slaves governed an independent Liberia, U.S.-owned rubber plantations dominated its economy. Moreover, in both Sierra Leone and Liberia, local Africans often resented the freed slave settlers, who were mostly English-speaking Christians and who occupied valuable land, dominated commerce, and held political power. In recent decades conflicts between the two groups have torn apart both countries.

The decline of slave trading made Africa more accessible to Western explorers hoping to discover whether great rivers were navigable for commercial purposes. Scottish explorer Mungo Park (1771–1806), an English trading company doctor in West Africa, traveled along the Niger to open new sources of wealth for British industry. Obsessed with finding the source of Africa's greatest river, the Nile, adventurers finally located Lake Victoria in 1860. David Livingstone (1813–1873), a Scottish cotton mill worker turned medical missionary, spent over two decades traveling in eastern Africa, collecting information and opening the region to Christian missionary activity and Western trade. Although European adventurers claimed to have "discovered" inland African societies and geographical features, they usually followed long-established trading routes using local guides and actually discovered little that Africans and Arabs did not already know. Western views were shaped mostly by myths: ethnocentric stereotypes of intrepid white explorers struggling in hardship through virgin territories. Explorers also spread the notion of "Darkest Africa" awaiting salvation by Christian missionaries and Western traders.

In the 1800s European traders began obtaining various raw materials needed by the West, such as peanuts, palm oil, gold, timber, and cotton. They competed with dynamic West African merchants who set up cash crop plantations, many producing palm oil, the main lubricant for industrial machinery in Europe before the development of petroleum. To avoid African middlemen on the coast, British traders traveled up Nigeria's rivers to buy palm oil directly from Igbo **(EE-boh)** producers. With superior financial resources and their governments' support, European companies eventually undermined African merchants and states that were reluctant to grant trade concessions; by 1890, in the trading port of Lagos, only one African merchant could still compete with British merchants.

Some major developments derived largely from forces within African societies rather than relations with the West. For example, some militancy and political expansion were caused by tensions within the Sudan's Islamic societies. Conflicts between those wanting to purge pre-Islamic customs from Islamic practice and those mixing Muslim and African traditions broke out sporadically in West Africa. By the 1790s these conflicts spread to the Fulani, a pastoral and trading people scattered across the Sudan from Senegal to Chad. Some Fulani were devout Muslims, some nominal Muslims, and some animists.

Uthman dan Fodio **(AHTH-mun dahn FOH-dee-oh)** (1754–1817), a respected Fulani Muslim scholar, author of over a hundred books, and a Sufi mystic who lived in the Hausa states of northern Nigeria, criticized the Hausa rulers' religious tolerance and called for the conversion of non-Muslim Fulani, making Islam central to Sudanic life. His magnetic personality and Islamic zeal attracted a Fulani and Hausa following. But Uthman's attacks on high taxes and social injustice, as well as his promise to build an Islamic government, alarmed Hausa rulers. After an attempt was made on his life, Uthman launched a jihad (holy war) in 1804, during which he conquered the Hausa states and created a caliphate based in Sokoto **(SOH-kuh-toh)** city. Uthman divided his empire into small, Fulani-led states led by governors, known as *emirs*.

Interfoto/Alamy

AFRICAN MUSLIM WARRIOR While Western pressure on coastal societies increased, several Muslim peoples expanded their influence in the West African interior. Some military forces, having acquired Western arms in exchange for slaves and gold, conquered regional empires that flourished for a century or more.

Uthman's jihad and his vision of purified Islam sparked others to form several other jihadist states, often led by Fulani religious scholars, in the Sudan. The Islamic revival, continuing into the 1880s, spread a more orthodox Islam just as Western influence increased in Africa. But by the later 1800s, the Fulani states had declined and Sokoto's power had waned. The Fulani resisted French and British expansion but eventually could not stop it; however, Islam remained a vital force in the Sudanic zone.

European Conquest and Partition

Britain, France, Germany, Spain, Belgium, and Italy all acquired African colonies in the late 1800s, often through warfare or the threat of force (see Map 21.1). Several factors made this possible. Western companies sought their government's help to pressure states to admit Western merchants. In addition, advances in tropical medicine, especially the treatment of malaria with quinine, freed Europeans from high tropical mortality rates. Inventing more powerful weapons also gave Europeans huge military advantages over African

forces armed only with rifles or spears. When possible, Europeans achieved conquest peacefully through deceptive treaties, bribes, division of states, and attempts to convince leaders that resistance was futile. When Africans resisted, Europeans used ruthless force.

In 1878 Belgium's King Leopold took the lead in colonization, hiring Henry Stanley (1841–1904), a Welsh-born American and former Confederate soldier and journalist who had earlier searched successfully in East Africa to find David Livingstone. Stanley then explored the Congo River Basin, which King Leopold now commissioned him to acquire for Belgium. Soon other European powers joined the scramble to obtain colonies. In 1884–1885 these nations held a conference in Berlin to set colonization ground rules. To have a claim recognized, the colonizer had to announce its intent and then militarily occupy the territory. Agents of European governments such as Stanley asked African chiefs, who knew no Western languages, to sign treaties of friendship or protection, which actually signed over their land, or face war. But in most African traditions tribal members, not chiefs, owned the land. Fearing a slaughter or war with their neighbors, many chiefs signed. The Buganda king reflected African distress when he concluded that Europeans were coming to eat his country.

The colonial scramble came at a time of famine; rains failed, and smallpox and cholera epidemics killed millions. One French missionary reflected the despair: "wars, drought, famine, pestilence, locusts, cattle-plague! Why so many calamities in succession? Why?"[4] The military disparity in weapons and tactics played a major role. The British had the hand-cranked Gatling gun, which could fire hundreds of rounds per minute, and then the Maxim gun, a totally automatic machine gun invented in 1884. Europeans willingly slaughtered thousands. In Southwest Africa (today's Namibia), Germans killed all but 15,000 of the 80,000 Herero **(hair-AIR-oh)** after a 1904 rebellion. In Kenya, British military expeditions attacked villages for chasing away tax collectors or ambushing Western military patrols that intimidated potential resisters. A British officer boasted of giving orders that every living thing in a Gikuyu village, except children, should be killed without mercy because an Englishman had been killed nearby. Soldiers then burned all the huts and destroyed banana farms. They called establishing law and order, often by force, the "Pax Britannica," or British peace.

After centuries of rivalries and slave wars, Africans could not unite for common defense. Europeans took advantage, pitting state against state and ethnic group against ethnic group. Various independent kingdoms and village-based stateless societies existed in the region that became Nigeria. Thanks to the slave trade, some were already unstable; Yorubas engaged in bitter civil war for much of the 1800s. Between 1887 and 1903 Britain conquered or annexed these diverse societies, creating the colony Nigeria because it occupied both sides of the lower Niger River.

By 1914 European powers, by drawing boundaries and staking claims, had divided up the entire continent except for Ethiopia and Liberia. The French empire, concentrated in

---

[4]Francois Coillard, quoted in John Iliffe, *Africans: The History of a Continent* (New York: Cambridge University Press, 1995), 208.

MAP 21.1 AFRICA IN 1914 Before 1878 the European powers held only a few coastal territories in Africa, but in that year they turned to expanding their power through colonization. By 1914 the British, French, Belgians, Germans, Italians, Portuguese, and Spanish controlled all of the continent except for Ethiopia and Liberia. © 2015 Cengage Learning

North, West, and Central Africa, extended across the Sahara from Senegal to Lake Chad. The British had four colonies in West Africa, including Nigeria, but built most of their empire in eastern and southern Africa. The four German colonies were scattered, while Italy concentrated on Northeast Africa, including Somalia and Eritrea, and on Libya in North Africa.

Fierce competition for territories sometimes led to the brink of war over rival claims. Britain wanted to control

eastern Africa from Cairo in the north to the Cape of Good Hope, while Germans dreamed of a Central African empire. German colonization of Tanganyika spurred Britain to move into Kenya, Uganda, and Zanzibar. In South Africa, the brash British imperialist Cecil Rhodes (1853–1902), a clergyman's son who made millions in the South African diamond mining industry, led efforts to outflank Germany and Portugal by extending British influence into territories he arrogantly named Northern and Southern Rhodesia.

SAMORY TOURE Samory Toure, the ruler of a Mandinka state, led a military force that resisted French incursion into their West African region in the late nineteenth century, but he was eventually captured by the French. This photo shows him (front, left) in custody.

British settlers migrated to Southern Rhodesia (today's Zimbabwe) and Kenya, solidifying Britain's domination.

Although outgunned, many Africans offered spirited resistance to conquest. Mandinka leader Samory Toure (1830–1900), in the western Sudan, resisted French invasion for a decade. An inspirational military commander, he recruited a large, well-trained army from among Muslims and animists, building a revived Mandinka state modeled on Sundiata's earlier Mali empire. Finally, France defeated Samory's brave but exhausted force in 1898 and exiled him. In 1903 many in Fulani-ruled Sokoto died in battle against the British rather than surrender. In Muslim West Africa, mystical Sufi brotherhoods sometimes rallied opposition to France or Britain. When the French tried to rule Senegal's Wolof people through their kings and chiefs, resisters turned to Muslim clerics, especially Amadu Bamba Mbacke (AH-mah-doo BOM-ba um-BACK-ee) (ca. 1853–1927), founder of a peaceful Sufi order, the *Murids* ("learners seeking God"). France exiled him for many years but eventually realized it could only rule Senegal with Murid cooperation. While Amadu Bamba acknowledged French administration, he was allowed to expand the Murids. The only decisive African military triumph came in Ethiopia, fortified in high mountains. In 1896, reforming Emperor Menelik (MEN-uh-lik) II's (1844–1914) French-trained army of 80,000 men defeated an invasion force of 10,000 Italian troops.

In the Gold Coast (today's Ghana), the Ashante kingdom held off British forces for decades. Seeking to protect its coastal forts, Britain repeatedly clashed with the prosperous, powerful, expanding Ashante. In 1874 a large British force secured the coast and looted the capital, Kumasi, but effective Ashante resistance by forty thousand troops equipped with obsolete but serviceable muskets prevented them from pushing further into the interior. British forces withdrew from Kumasi but forced the Ashante to pay a large indemnity. The British then fomented civil war in Ashante territories, but the Ashante king refused British ultimatums to surrender. In 1896 three thousand well-armed British troops finally occupied Kumasi and exiled the king. However, resistance continued, often spurred by royal women such as queen-mother Yaa Asantewa (ca. 1840–1921). Outraged by British demands for the golden stool that symbolized Ashante kingship, she offered to lead Ashante forces if the men would not: "Is it true that the bravery of the Ashante is no more? I cannot believe it....We the women...will fight the white man...till the last of us falls in the battlefields."[5] Not until 1901 did the British manage to quell her rebellion, stamp out resistance, and fully incorporate the Ashante into their Gold Coast colony.

[5]Quoted in "Yaa Asantewaa" (http://ghanaweb.com/GhanaHomePage/people/pop-up.php?ID+175).

MAKE SURE YOU UNDERSTAND THESE KEY POINTS BEFORE MOVING ON

- Opposed by many Europeans on humanitarian and religious grounds, African slavery became less profitable than manufacturing as the Industrial Revolution gained momentum, and it was phased out by the end of the nineteenth century.

- With the end of the slave trade, Europeans began to explore Africa's interior and to take advantage of its vast store of natural resources.

- European nations rapidly colonized Africa by engaging in deceptive negotiations, by threatening and often carrying

out acts of violence, and by exploiting existing rivalries among groups of Africans.

- By 1914, all but a small portion of Africa had been divided up among the European powers, which sometimes feuded over control of various territories and sometimes met fierce resistance from Africans such as the Ashante.

aplia

The Colonial Reshaping of Sub-Saharan Africa

What were some of the major consequences of colonialism in Africa?

Western colonial domination from the 1880s to the 1960s reshaped sub-Saharan Africans' politics, society, culture, and economy. Whereas the trans-Atlantic and East African slave trades had devastated parts of Africa for four centuries, colonial conquests undermined all African societies' autonomy. Colonialism created artificial states while transforming Africans into subject peoples who enjoyed few political rights. Europeans also took some land as settlers. The largest settler colony, South Africa, experienced an unusual history: over three centuries of white supremacy introduced by Dutch colonizers and perpetuated by Britain. European immigrants also settled in British East Africa, the Rhodesias, and Portuguese colonies. Asian migrants joined them, often as traders. Colonialism allowed Western business interests to penetrate the continent, integrating Africa into the global system as a supplier of valuable raw materials.

Colonial States and African Societies

Colonial policies devised in London, Paris, Berlin, Lisbon, and Brussels introduced new kinds of governments, with each colonizing power seeking to achieve maximum control at minimum expense. France grouped its colonies into large federations, such as French West Africa, headed by one governor; Britain preferred to govern each colony, such as the Gold Coast and Nigeria, separately. Despite little understanding of, or interest in, African cultures, Europeans always held ultimate political authority, usually supervising administration; Africans had to obey decisions made by European bureaucrats.

direct rule A method of ruling colonies whereby a largely European colonial administration supervised all activity, even down to the local level, and native chiefs or kings were reduced to symbolic roles.

indirect rule A method of ruling colonies whereby districts were administered by traditional (native) leaders, who had considerable local power but were subject to European officials.

Under **direct rule**, administration was largely European down to the local level, with chiefs or kings reduced to symbolic roles. Under **indirect rule**, traditional kings or chiefs enjoyed considerable local power but were subject to colonial officials. Leaving much of African society intact, indirect rule caused less disruption, but African leaders had to consult with local European advisers on many matters. Indirect rule was inspired by pragmatism, there being too few European officials to administer large colonies. Colonizers sometimes strengthened chiefs or appointed chiefs where none previously existed, undermining village democracy.

Huge and unwieldy Nigeria, with some 250 distinct African ethnic groups, reflected both kinds of administration. Struggling to keep the largely Muslim north pacified, Britain needed cooperation from Hausa and Fulani emirs. Lord Lugard, the British governor, proclaimed that every emir "will rule over the people as of old time but will obey the laws of the [British] Governor,"[6] hence leaving the traditional Hausa-Fulani courts and social structure largely undisturbed. By contrast, in southern Nigeria, which was chiefly governed through direct rule, greater change occurred, including the introduction of Christian missions and cash crop farming. Some southerners adapted to these changes. The Igbo, particularly receptive to Christianity, became prominent in Nigeria's educated middle class. The Yoruba blended their rich artistic tradition and polytheism with imported English literary forms and Christianity, maintaining tolerance for divergent views. Rejecting fate and helplessness, Yoruba described their culture as a river that never rests, with swift-moving currents that can either run deep and quietly or be turbulent and overpowering.

However, many policies politically handicapped Africans. Supporters of Western colonialism claimed it provided "a school for democracy," but by 1945 only a few Africans enjoyed political rights or access to democratic institutions. A few thousand urban merchants and professionals in British Nigeria and Gold Coast voted for and served on city councils, while males

---

[6]Quoted in Iliffe, *Africans*, 200–201.

in French Senegal elected members of the colonial council and a representative to the French parliament. Meanwhile, African chiefs and kings, to keep their positions, implemented colonial policies, such as supervising cash crop agriculture and recruiting people for labor and war. Africans often viewed these privileged, wealthy leaders as little better than paid colonial agents.

Misunderstanding African ethnic complexities, to simplify administration colonizers identified people of similar culture and language as "tribes," even though these peoples were actually collections of subgroups without much historical unity. In reality, African peoples such as the Yoruba, Gikuyu, Igbo, Xhosa, and Mandinka were ethnic groups, not unlike the politically divided Italians, Irish, and Poles of early-nineteenth-century Europe. Thus colonial boundaries, often ignoring traditional ethnic relationships, created artificial countries such as Nigeria, Ghana (the former Gold Coast), Congo, and Mozambique, not nations built on shared culture and identity. Colonizers ignored local interests, sometimes dividing ethnic groups between two or more colonial systems. The Kongolese, once masters of a great kingdom, were split between Portuguese Angola and the Belgian and French Congos. Rival societies were sometimes joined, creating a basis for later political instability. In Nigeria the tensions between Igbo, Yoruba, Hausa-Fulani, and other groups have fostered chronic conflict since British rule ended. Other countries also experienced ethnic conflicts that sometimes provoked violence.

Several colonies heavily restricted African civil and economic rights, particularly South Africa, Portuguese-ruled Angola, and British-ruled Kenya and Southern Rhodesia. They reserved for immigrant white farmers the best land, such as Kenya's fertile highlands once dominated by the Gikuyu, and the most lucrative crops, such as coffee. At the same time, African farmers faced barriers in obtaining bank loans. European settlers participated in government and erected rigid color bars limiting contact between whites and Africans except as employers and hired workers, perpetuating white supremacy.

Europeans viewed African culture as irrational and static, with no history of achievement. An ethnocentric British scholar argued in 1920 that "the chief distinction between the backward and forward peoples is that the former are of colored skin."[7] This prejudice translated into demeaning ideas that Africans were unfit to rule themselves and badly needed Western leadership. Racist ideology spawned the French and Belgian idea of the "civilizing mission": Africans were children who could attain adulthood only by adopting the French language, religion, and culture. Europeans also imposed a color bar, excluding Africans from clubs, schools, and jobs reserved for Europeans.

Some colonies attracted Asian immigrants. Beginning in the 1890s Indians arrived to build railroads, work on sugar plantations, or become middle-level retail traders. They became East Africa's commercial middle class and played key economic roles in South Africa, the Rhodesias, Mozambique, and Madagascar. Cities such as Nairobi in Kenya, Kampala in Uganda, and Durban in South Africa had substantial Indian populations, their downtowns dominated by Indian stores and Hindu temples. In West and Central Africa, Lebanese became urban shopkeepers. Black Africans resented this growing Asian influence and wealth, and after independence many governments restricted Asian economic power. However, seeking to divide and rule, Europeans hoped that Africans would focus their resentment on Asian traders rather than European officials.

Europeans and Africans in South Africa

Conflicts between European settlers and Bantu-speaking Africans shaped South Africa. From their first settlement at Cape Town, established in 1652, the Dutch settlers, known as Boers (Dutch for "farmers"), expanded while establishing white rule over nonwhites that enforced physical separation of the groups in all areas of life. White supremacy became even more rigid in the late 1700s and early 1800s. Many Boers migrated by wagon trains east along the coast and into the interior, a journey they called trekking, seeking good farm land and escaping government restrictions on their freedom of action.

Trekking sparked conflicts for nearly half a century between Boers and Xhosa (KHO-sa) farmers and pastoralists in the eastern Cape region, during which time many Xhosa died. When fearing attack, trekkers pulled their wagons into a circle, known as a laager, that came to symbolize Boer resistance to new ideas and desire for separation from other peoples. The Boers' white supremacy, sanctioned by their strict, puritanical Calvinist Christian beliefs, ensured them a cheap labor supply for their farms and ranches. This economy, dependent on thousands of slaves of African and Asian origin, was threatened when the British annexed Cape Colony in 1806 and then in 1807 ended South African slavery and later granted voting rights to Africans and mixed-descent people, known as coloreds. These developments prompted more Boers to migrate into the interior.

Eventually migrating Boers faced the largest Bantu people, the Zulus. In the early 1800s some Zulus began expanding under an ambitious military genius, Shaka (ca. 1787–1828), who overcame the disadvantage of birth out of wedlock to gain fame as a courageous warrior and become a powerful chief. Shaka united various Zulu clans in Natal (nuh-TALL), along South Africa's Indian Ocean coast, into a powerful nation. Soil exhaustion, severe drought, population growth, and fears of potential Boer migration may all have provoked Zulu expansion. Shaka organized a disciplined army of some forty thousand warriors and invented effective new military tactics, such as dividing his troops into regiments armed with short, stabbing spears. In 1816 he began invading other groups' territories, wreaking widespread disruption and causing the deaths of thousands of Zulus and non-Zulus. After conquering much of the interior plateau, Shaka grew more despotic and was assassinated by his brother, and eventually the Zulu empire fell to the Boers. Ironically, by depopulating much of the

laager A defensive arrangement of wagons in a circle. Used by the Boers in South Africa in the eighteenth and nineteenth centuries to guard against attacks by native Africans.

---

[7]H. H. Johnston, quoted in M. E. Chamberlain, *The Scramble for Africa* (Harlow, UK: Longman, 1974), 96.

WAGGON ASCENDING THE UNCOMMOSS HILL, NATAL.

THE GREAT TREK Many Boers migrated into the South African interior in wagon trains. These migrants, known as trekkers, endured hardships but also eventually subjugated the local African peoples, taking their land for farming, pasturing, and mining.

mineral-rich interior plateau, Shaka's wars made it easier for Boers to later move in.

Some Bantus avoided Zulu or Boer conquest. For example, amidst the regional turmoil Moshoeshoe **(UM-shway-shway)** I created a kingdom for his branch of the Sotho **(SOO-too)** people, skillfully evading colonization for half a century (see Profile: Moshoeshoe I, Sotho Chief and State Builder). Eventually gaining British support allowed his Sotho kingdom to remain independent until 1871, when British-ruled Cape Colony absorbed it.

British-Boer conflict intensified. In 1838 many Boers began the Great Trek, heading in well-armed wagon caravans of several hundred families with their sheep and cattle into the interior. After many hardships and fighting with Zulus, they moved into the high plateau and formed two independent Boer republics, Transvaal **(TRANS-vahl)** and Orange Free State. Seizing cattle, the Boers forced conquered Africans to work on Boer farms. They consolidated control over Africans and dedicated themselves to preserving their culture and upholding unequal relations between white "master" and African

Moshoeshoe I, Sotho Chief and State Builder

Moshoeshoe I (ca.1786–1870), a paramount Sotho chief, built the most successful black-ruled state in nineteenth-century southern Africa thanks to his mental toughness, pragmatism, remarkable political and military skills, diplomacy, generosity, and fairness to subjects. As a youth his cattle-raiding successes earned him the nickname "the razor" for cutting away an opponent's herds as neatly as a shave. The son of a minor chief, by thirty-four he rose to clan chief and eventually settled with his followers on a defensible flat-top mountain, surrounded by a fertile valley, from where he warded off attacks.

The Sotho peoples, farmers and herders, were divided into several often feuding chiefdoms, but when Zulu and Boer military expansion caused regional chaos, many Sotho and non-Sotho refugees sought protection with Moshoeshoe, who wisely welcomed them into his community regardless of ethnic backgrounds. In building his own state, he generally avoided warfare and coercion, preferring peaceful negotiations when possible. "Peace is like the rain which makes the grass grow," he concluded, "while war is like the wind which dries it up."

Using diverse survival strategies, Moshoeshoe sent tribute, especially cattle, to potential aggressors, among them Zulus, to avoid war and built his Basuto state around cattle exchange and an inclusive administration; some Sotho rivals, ignoring diplomacy, were defeated. He understood cattle's key economic role and rewarded supporters with captured cattle for marriage gifts. Tapping polygamous traditions, he made many marriage alliances and probably had over a hundred wives himself. But his many sons and grandsons, who all needed administrative posts, later proved a strain when they schemed against each other for power in his waning years.

Moshoeshoe encouraged people to debate civic questions in public meetings, including in a crucial decision-making state-level assembly. Chiefdoms that joined his state were bound to Moshoeshoe through political marriages and councils and kept some local autonomy, making his state more a confederation than a centralized kingdom. Refugees could maintain their chiefs and traditions and rule themselves. His community grew from about 25,000 in 1833 to 80,000 by 1848.

Moshoeshoe also looked for help elsewhere. He invited Christian missionaries to his state and used them to acquire guns and horses. French Protestants from the Paris Evangelical Society greatly aided him, advising him on, and negotiating with, his British, Boer, and colored (mixed-race) adversaries. Missionaries created a Sotho written language, built churches and schools, and educated many Sotho youth. Moshoeshoe sent his own sons to the schools but, unwilling to abandon polygamy, never became a Christian. If one of his wives converted, he granted her a divorce. He also welcomed

a few British army deserters to teach firearm skills and technologies. French missionary Eugène Casalis, the state's unofficial foreign minister, described Moshoeshoe as having "an agreeable and interesting countenance, his deportment is noble and dignified, and a benevolent smile plays upon his lips." Furthermore, Casalis wrote:

"Being of a very observant disposition, he knew how to resist and how to yield at the right moment; procured himself allies, even among the invaders of his territory; set his enemies at variance with each other, and by various acts of kindness secured the respect of those even who had sworn his ruin."

For decades Moshoeshoe's state faced continuous military challenges from Zulus, Ndebeles, Sotho rivals, and Boers, but, while the attacks devastated the countryside, his forces successfully defended his bastion. Eventually Britain proved the most formidable opponent, respecting his regional power but disputing his territorial claims. In 1848 his forces beat back a British general who tried to annex his state. British forces withdrew after Moshoeshoe sent General George Cathcart a face-saving message: "I entreat peace from you—you have shown your power,—you have chastised,—let it be enough I pray you; and let me no longer be considered an enemy of the Queen." Soon recognizing his diminishing options and needing a counterweight to the encroaching Boers, Moshoeshoe humbly cultivated friendship and alliance with Britain as "fleas in the blanket of Queen Victoria." British support allowed his Sotho state to remain formally independent until 1871, when it was absorbed into Britain's Cape Colony. In 1884 it became Basutoland, a British protectorate separate from, and with more autonomy than, South Africa.

When Moshoeshoe died in 1870, his state's independence was compromised, his people were still not united, and much Sotho land was lost to Afrikaners. Yet, more skillfully than other southern African leaders facing similar challenges, he created a kingdom out of chaos and steered it to the best destiny open to it. In 1966, Basutoland gained its independence as Lesotho, and his family continued his legacy. One great-grandson became South Africa's first black Roman Catholic bishop; another, Moshoeshoe II, became Lesotho's king after independence.

KING MOSHOESHOE The pragmatic Sotho king built a kingdom that withstood Western pressure for decades.

Fotosearch/Getty Images

THINKING ABOUT THE PROFILE

1. What strategies led to Moshoeshoe's state-building success?
2. Why is he considered one of Africa's great leaders?

Note: Quotations from Leonard Thompson, *A History of South Africa* (New Haven: Yale University Press, 1990), 86 and 95; "Moshoeshoe of Lesotho, 'Africa's Greatest Leader,'" *afrol News* (http://www.afrol.com/features/35246); Donald Denoon, *Southern Africa Since 1800* (New York: Praeger, 1973), 57.

"servant." The Boers despised the British and considered black Africans an "inferior race" hostile to European values.

However, the discovery of gold and diamonds in the Boer republics spurred Britain to seek control there, leading to the South African War (1899–1902), often called the Boer War. The ensuing British victory intensified Boer resentment. The British burned farms, destroyed towns, and interned thousands, including women and children, in concentration camps, where twenty-six thousand Boers died of disease and starvation. Britain relied on African troops, thousands of whom died hoping the British would be less oppressive.

But African hopes were soon dashed. British and Boer leaders worked out a compromise, making the South African government a collaboration between the two groups. The regime extended discriminatory laws, restricted African civil and political rights, and put many Africans on reserves, rural lands with few resources from which workers could be recruited. The white-owned economy chiefly valued Africans as cheap unskilled labor; laws limited their movement and reserved desirable neighborhoods and jobs only for whites. Facing continued African resistance, the government built a police state to enforce its racial policies. Furthermore, British-Boer tensions simmered as thousands of British settlers eventually became a third of the white population. Boers began calling themselves Afrikaners (people of Africa) and their Dutch-derived language Afrikaans.

Christian Missions and African Culture

Supported by colonial governments, Christian missionaries, seeking to reshape African culture and religious life, established most of Africa's modern hospitals and schools. Mission doctors practiced Western medicine while denouncing African folk medicine. By teaching new agricultural methods, mathematics, reading, writing, and Western languages, mission schools gave a few Africans valuable skills for the colonial economy and administration. But critics complained that, while teaching Western values and European history, they ignored African history and derided African beliefs as superstition. Some African nationalists, themselves mission school graduates, claimed that these schools, as an Igbo writer put it, "miseducated" and "de-Africanized" them, perpetuating their status as "hewers of wood and haulers of water."[8] In addition, Africans who attended mission schools and adopted individualistic Western ways often became divorced from their village traditions, loosening their communities' social ties. Yet, before 1945 only 5 percent of children attended any government or mission school. Sierra Leone established the first modern African college in 1827, but before 1940 the few Africans who could attend a university mostly did so in Europe or the United States.

Millions of Africans adopted Christianity, some becoming devout Catholics or Protestants and others only accepting beliefs they liked while rejecting others. Africans often emphasized Bible passages calling for justice and equality.

Some African churches incorporated traditional practices and beliefs, such as men having more than one wife. Yorubas often added Christian and Muslim gods to their polytheistic pantheon. Christianity also marginalized once-influential female deities and shamans, reducing women's religious roles. Moreover, Christian leaders who required men to give up multiple wives left these women without support for their children. Yet, women often welcomed monogamy and favored Christian social values such as promoting girls' education.

Africans in the World Economy

Africa's economic transformation was as significant as its political reorganization. Extracting wealth required linking its economy closely to that of the colonizers. European businessmen now controlled the key economic institutions, including banks, import-export companies, mines, and plantations.

RUBBER COILS IN BELGIAN CONGO The Belgians colonized the Congo hoping to exploit its resources. This critical cartoon, published in the British satirical magazine *Punch* in 1906, shows a Congolese ensnared in the rubber coils of the Belgian king Leopold in the guise of a serpent. Rubber was the major cash crop, introduced by the Belgians to generate profits.

[8]Nnamdi Azikiwe, quoted in Minton F. Goldman, "Political Change in a Multi-National Setting," in *Dynamics of the Third World: Political and Social Change*, ed. David Schmitt (Cambridge: Winthrop, 1974), 172.

Since subsistence food growing was unable to produce enough revenues for governments or investors, colonial policies made Africans into producers for the world market and required that taxes be paid in cash. These policies promoted the growing of cash crops such as cotton, cocoa, rubber, and palm oil and the mining of copper, gold, oil, chrome, cobalt, and diamonds. If taxation did not spur changes, authorities resorted to forced labor, most notoriously in the Belgian Congo, which required much of the population to grow rubber for Belgian planters. An American missionary reported in 1895 that the Belgian policies "reduced the people to a state of utter despair. Each town is forced to bring a certain quality [of rubber]. The soldiers drive the people into the bush. If they will not go they are shot down, and their left hands cut off. The soldiers often shoot poor helpless women and harmless children."[9] Over half the Congolese died from overwork or brutality over a twenty-year period.

Linking Africans to the world economy often left them vulnerable, subjecting their livelihoods to fluctuations in world prices for the commodities they produced, which were determined by the whims of Western consumers and corporations. Colonies became markets for Western industrial products, displacing village handicrafts, while Africans became exporters of cash crops they did not consume, such as cocoa and rubber, and importers of goods they did not produce. Many cash crops dominating African lives, such as peanuts and rubber from South America or cocoa from Mexico, had been introduced from outside. A growing automobile culture in the West also fostered an oil-drilling industry along the West African coast, making these societies dependent on oil exports. As a result, colonies often became economic monocultures. Hence Northern Rhodesia (now Zambia) mostly exported copper, Senegal peanuts, and the Gold Coast cocoa. A local popular song from the 1960s well described Ghanaians' dependence on growing and selling cocoa: "If you want to send your children to school, build your house, marry, buy cloth [or] a truck, it is cocoa. Whatever you want to do in this world, it is with cocoa money that you do it."[10]

The colonial economy's opportunities and demands profoundly affected both men and women. Recruiting or forcing many men to migrate to other districts or colonies for mining or industrial labor established a permanent pattern of labor migration. South Africa's white-owned farms and mines recruited thousands of workers from Mozambique and British Central Africa on renewable one-year contracts, while men from the Sahel migrated to Ivory Coast and Gold Coast cocoa estates. These migrations disrupted family and village life. Male migrants lived in crowded dormitories or huts offering little privacy, enjoyed few amenities other than drinking beer in makeshift bars, and could visit their families back home for only a few days a year.

Many thousands of South Africans also moved to cities, especially the Transvaal mining center of Johannesburg, becoming temporarily or permanently removed from their farming villages. They experienced dreadful work conditions on white-owned factories and farms, and even worse in the mines, where safety regulations were few; hundreds of miners died each year. The Zulu poet B. W. Vilakezi described the miner's life in the early 1900s: "Roar, without rest, machines of the mines, Roar from dawn till darkness falls. To black men groaning as they labor, Tortured by their aching muscles, Gasping in the fetid air, Reeking from the dirt and sweat. The earth will swallow us who burrow. And, if I die there, underground, What does it matter? All round me, every day, I see men stumble, fall and die."[11]

In many African societies women had long played key roles as traders and farmers. As men migrated for work or took up cash crop farming, women's workload increased as they became responsible for less lucrative food production. Women's agricultural workweek in the German-ruled Cameroons increased from forty-five to seventy hours. Baule women of the Ivory Coast, who once profited from growing cotton and spinning it into thread, lost their position to Baule men when cotton became a cash crop and textiles an export item. In addition, women traders who had dominated town markets now faced competition from Indians or Lebanese. Some women responded with self-help organizations. Ashante market women in Kumasi organized themselves under elected leaders later known as market queens, promoting cooperation and settling disputes among themselves. Thanks to education, self-help, and ambition, some African women also supported themselves as teachers, nurses, and traders. But trying to preserve their families while fulfilling their new responsibilities overwhelmed many poor women.

African Responses and the Colonial Legacy

Africans responded to colonialism in various ways. In South Africa the small educated middle class of professionals and traders found ways to oppose white supremacy. Johannesburg lawyer Pixley ka Isaka Seme **(PIX-ley ka I-sa-ka SE-me)**, a graduate of Columbia University in New York, helped found the African National Congress in 1912 to promote African rights and cultural regeneration. In Nigeria many educated Igbos became cash crop farmers, merchants, professionals, or clerks. Other Africans dealt with change by enriching traditional ways. In the woodcarvings and elaborately carved doors he sculpted for Yoruba kings, the imaginative Yoruba artist Olowe of Ise **(oh-LO-way of ee-SAY)** (ca. 1875–1938) emphasized Yoruba themes and ideals and creatively added richly textured surfaces and the illusion of movement. Some Africans mixed Western and African ideas. The Black Zion movement in South Africa had Christian overtones, claiming that Jesus was African, but also promoted African traditions such as faith healing.

Sometimes traditional cultural forms expressed African sentiments. Combining dance and theater, Igbo women influenced their individualistic but patriarchal society by dancing and singing their grievances in a strategy known as "sitting on a man." Some dance performances encouraged noncooperation

[9]Rev. J. B. Murphy, quoted in Kevin Shillington, *History of Africa*, rev. ed. (New York: St. Martin's Press, 1995), 333–334.

[10]Quoted in Dennis Austin, *Politics in Ghana* (London: Oxford University Press, 1964), 275.

[11]Quoted in Tom Hopkinson, *South Africa* (New York: Time Inc., 1964), 93.

with colonial demands, such as increased taxes, or with excessive male Igbo chauvinism. When local leaders ignored dance messages, Igbo women took stronger action, including rioting. In South Africa Zulu workers reworked dance tunes to protest white domination. Sotho people transformed poetry praising influential people and ancestors into songs expressing male migrants' experiences in the mines and the women left behind in villages. And South African composers mixed Christian hymns with traditional Xhosa or Zulu choral music. The African National Congress adopted one such hymn, "God Bless Africa," as their official anthem. Later the song, with its uplifting message of hope, became the anthem of black empowerment:

> *Bless the youth, that they may carry the land with patience. Bless the wives and young girls. Bless agriculture and stock raising. Banish all famine and diseases. Fill the land with good health. Bless our effort, of union and self uplift, of education and mutual understanding.*[12]

Resistance strategies varied. Tax evasion and passive protest were rampant, especially in rural areas. Some Africans formed labor unions, which were usually illegal since colonial regimes protected Western-owned businesses. Strikes were common, especially among mine workers, but governments arrested strike leaders, jailing them along with political activists. Rebellions sparked by unpopular policies, such as new taxes or forced labor, punctuated colonial rule. The Maji Maji Rebellion in German-ruled Tanganyika in 1905 began as a peasant protest against a new cotton-growing scheme that forced people to work for only 35 cents a month. Africans' preference to grow their own food rather than be commercial farmers sparked a new religious cult, Maji Maji ("water medicine"), which used "magic water" in hopes of better crops. Sprinkling their bodies with magic water and believing it would make them immune from bullets, rebels occupied towns. Germans regained the towns with machine guns and in 1907 defeated the Maji Maji, killing twenty-six thousand Africans. However, the resistance caused the Germans to end forced labor.

Some historians contend that colonialism increased the land's productive capacity, built cities and transportation networks, brought advances in technology, and stimulated Africans to produce more wealth than ever before. Other historians disagree, arguing that colonial rulers stole land, exploited labor, gained profitable access to raw materials, shifted wealth back to Europe, limited Africa's economic growth, and created artificial, unstable countries. While colonial profits supported European industrialization and enriched businesses, Africans enjoyed little balanced economic growth that benefited the majority. One observer in the early 1900s noted that in Portuguese-ruled Mozambique a man "works…all his life under horrible conditions to buy scanty clothing for his wife and daughters. The men and boys can rarely afford proper clothing."[13] Moreover, many former colonies became economically vulnerable monocultures. Seventy-five years of Belgian colonialism in the Congo failed to build any paved road system linking the major cities or establish more than a handful of schools and medical clinics for the millions of Congolese. As a result, sub-Saharan Africa was the most impoverished region of the world at the end of the colonial era, a legacy difficult to overcome.

MAKE SURE YOU UNDERSTAND THESE KEY POINTS BEFORE MOVING ON

- Colonizers divided Africa into countries with artificial boundaries, sometimes splitting an ethnic group into more than one country and sometimes throwing rival groups into a single country, thus creating lasting tensions.

- Dutch settlers of South Africa, called Boers, pursued a policy of white supremacy in spite of more liberal British policies.

- Christian missionary schools provided a small minority of Africans with skills they could use in the colonial world but largely ignored and often damaged the native African culture.

- As African economies came to depend on a single commodity desired by Europeans, colonized Africans lost their subsistence skills and were often forced to work far from home.

- Blacks suffered greatly in white-dominated South Africa, but many resisted through poetry, music, dance, and political organizations such as the African National Congress.

aplia

Imperialism, Reform, and the Middle Eastern Societies

S *What political and economic impact did Europe have on the Middle East?*

Between 1750 and 1914 most Muslim societies suffered repeated challenges from western Europe and Russia. The Ottoman Empire remained the only significant power and, despite its remarkable ability to rejuvenate itself, fell behind the industrializing West. As Ottomans and Persians lost territories to expanding European empires, European economic penetration and cultural influences forced diverse responses.

---

[12]The lyrics are in David B. Coplan, *In Township Tonite: South Africa's Black City Music and Theater* (London: Longman, 1985), 44–45.

[13]Quoted in Leroy Vail, "The Political Economy of East-Central Africa," in *History of Central Africa*, ed. David Birmingham and Phyllis M. Martin, vol. 2 (New York: Longman, 1983), 233.

MAP 21.2 **THE OTTOMAN EMPIRE AND PERSIA, 1914** The Ottoman Empire once included much of southeastern Europe, western Asia, and North Africa. By 1914, after losing most of its European, Caucasian, and North African territories, it was restricted largely to parts of western Asia. © 2015 Cengage Learning

Challenges to the Ottoman Empire

During the Early Modern Era the Ottoman Turks forged a huge empire in southeastern Europe, western Asia, and North Africa. Many Muslims viewed the Ottoman sultan as the caliph, successor to the Prophet and the Islamic community's leader. But by 1750 Ottoman power had diminished from both Western pressure and internal problems. In the nineteenth century rising pressure from Europe and Russia undermined the empire and its more than 60 million people (see Map 21.2). The Russians had been expanding south toward the Black Sea since the 1500s. In 1768, defeating Ottoman forces, they gained partial control of the northern Black Sea coast. They later acquired the Crimean peninsula and in 1829 took over Georgia, a largely Christian Caucasus state. In 1853 Czar Nicholas I characterized the weakening Ottoman Empire as "the sick man of Europe," a reputation that would stick.

European powers schemed to outflank each other in dismantling the weakening empire. With European support, Greeks, Serbs, Romanians, and Bulgarians threw off Ottoman

rule in the 1800s (see Chapter 19). An Anglo-French fleet and the Russian army intervened to aid the Greeks, shifting the military balance. The 1830 treaty ending the war recognized Greek independence and gave autonomy to Serbia and Moldavia.

Weakened by military losses, the Ottoman government had difficulty satisfying the empire's multiethnic population. Because Turks had long benefited from tapping the varied peoples to enrich their state, non-Muslim minorities played major roles in commerce, the professions, and government. Generally tolerating minorities such as Kurds (mostly Sunni Muslims), Jews, and Arab Christians, Ottomans allowed each group to basically rule itself through its own religious establishment, such as the Greek Orthodox Church. Christians and Jews felt particularly secure in major Ottoman cities, with Jews generally enjoying more rights and prosperity than in Europe. Multiethnic Istanbul was described in 1873 as "a city not of one nation but of many. Eight or nine languages are constantly spoken in the streets and five or six appear on the shop fronts."[14] Various religious sects also settled in Lebanon's mountains, maintaining their traditions.

---

[14]Quoted in Andrew Wheatcroft, *The Ottomans* (New York: Viking, 1993), 146.

But some ethnic minorities became restless, especially in eastern Turkey and the Caucasus, where Turkish relations with Christian Armenians deteriorated. Armenians had long remained loyal Ottoman subjects, some holding high government positions, but nationalist and socialist ideas percolating in Europe inspired some to desire nationhood. With European and North American financial and moral support, Armenians founded their own schools, colleges, libraries, hospitals, presses, and charitable organizations. In the 1890s and early 1900s Ottomans responded to increasing Armenian assertiveness, including terrorist attacks, by seizing Armenian property, killing over 100,000 Armenians, and exiling thousands more. Many moved to North America. Then in 1915, during World War I, charging Armenians with supporting Russia, the government began removing Armenians from eastern Anatolia; in response Armenian nationalists declared a republic, after which the Ottoman army, aided by local Turks and Kurds, killed around a million Armenians. Many historians consider the violent assault a genocide, the singling out of one group for mass killing, but Turkish nationalists consider it an incidental side effect of war. The killings still complicate Armenian-Turkish relations. Surviving Armenians formed a small republic in the Caucasus, Armenia, that was absorbed by Russia in 1920.

To survive and match Western power, Ottoman sultans tried to reform and modernize, building a more secular and centralized government. However, Islamic religious leaders, the privileged Janissary military force, and the virtually independent governors of distant Arab provinces benefited from weak central authority. Gradually Ottoman leaders and thinkers recognized the need to obtain Western knowledge and aid. Reformist sultan Mahmud II (**MACH-mood**) (r. 1808–1839) tried to eliminate the Janissaries, who were once an effective fighting force but now a costly burden that resisted change. Mahmud recruited a new military force, crushed the Janissaries, and then slowly built a modern army trained by Prussian officers. His successors founded new schools that taught European learning and languages; the University of Istanbul became the Muslim world's first modern higher education institution. Replacing many older Islamic laws with laws based on French revolutionary codes, Ottoman rulers increasingly marginalized Islam and treated Islamic knowledge as irrelevant, demoralizing conservatives.

The centralized government and a modern, secular Ottoman nationality grew through the 1800s. To foster a national identity, Ottoman sultans declared all citizens equal before the law, announcing that "the differences of religion and sect among the subjects is something not affecting their rights of citizenship. It is wrong to make discriminations among us."[15] But attempts to involve the people in government largely failed; the reforms proved inadequate. In the 1880s a modernizing group, the **Young Turks**, emerged in the military and universities. Seeking to make Turkey a modern nation with a liberal constitution, in 1908 the Young Turks, espousing Turkish nationalism, led a military coup that deposed the old sultan. Under the facade of parliamentary government, they ruled as autocrats and military modernizers. During World War I, as an ally of Germany and Austria-Hungary, the Young Turks embraced a Turkish ethnic identity, secularization, and closer ties to the Western world. After defeat in World War I, the Ottoman Empire was dissolved, and Arab peoples once ruled by the Ottomans fell under British or French rule. By 1920 the Turks were struggling to hold on to their Anatolian heartland.

Egypt: Modernization and Occupation

The most extensive effort to deflect Western pressure through modernization came in Egypt, but only after minimizing Ottoman influence. Ottomans had governed the province through the Mamluks, a Muslim caste of Turkish origin whose corruption and repression gave French general Napoleon Bonaparte an excuse to invade the country. When Bonaparte abandoned his Egyptian adventure, Muhammad Ali (r. 1805–1848), a Turkish-speaking Albanian who led Ottoman forces that helped eject the French, became ruler. After being appointed viceroy by the Ottoman sultan, Muhammad Ali made Egypt effectively independent but was forced by European powers to remain loosely bound to the weakening Ottoman state. The charming sultan impressed Europeans with his talents: "If ever a man had an eye that denoted genius, [he] was the person. Never dead nor quiescent, it was fascinating like that of a gazelle; or, in the hour of storm, fierce as an eagle's."[16]

Muhammad Ali introduced ambitious reforms to transform Egypt into a European-style industrial nation. Using government revenues from increased agricultural exports, he established foundries, shipyards, factories (textile, sugar, and glass), a conscript army trained by Western instructors, a navy, and an arms industry. He also replaced Islamic with French legal codes, sent Egyptians to study technical subjects in Europe, fostered the first Arab newspapers, and established a state educational system that trained people for the military and bureaucracy. However, his programs ultimately failed to protect Egyptian independence and foster development. Unlike European nations, Egypt lacked iron and coal, and the work force was not used to industrial regimentation. Moreover, as Muhammad Ali and his successors welcomed Western investment, they also became more shackled to European finance. Finally, importing cheap British commodities stifled Egypt's textile and

Young Turks A modernizing group in Ottoman Turkey that promoted a national identity and that gained power in the early twentieth century.

[15]Quoted in Halil Inalcik, "Turkey," in *Political Modernization in Japan and Turkey*, ed. Robert E. Ward and Dankwart A. Rostow (Princeton: Princeton University Press, 1964), 57–58.
[16]Quoted in Afaf Lufti al-Sayyid Marsot, *Egypt in the Reign of Muhammad Ali* (New York: Cambridge University Press, 1994), 28.

MUHAMMAD ALI MEETS EUROPEAN REPRESENTATIVES Muhammad Ali, the Egyptian sultan who tried to modernize his state, cultivated ties with Western nations. This painting shows the sultan in 1839 meeting with representatives from several European governments.

handicraft manufacturing. Rather than buy finished textiles, Europeans wanted Egyptian raw cotton for processing in their own mills.

Like leaders of European nations, Muhammad Ali soon sought resources and markets through conquest. Egyptian armies moved south, conquering the Sudanic lands along the Nile River, and also into Ottoman-ruled Arabia, Palestine, Syria, and Greece. But this aggression alarmed European powers, who intervened to push the Egyptians back. Britain in particular sought to undermine Egypt to expand its regional influence and gain control of the Suez Canal, which was built as a French-Egyptian collaboration between 1859 and 1869. The 100-mile-long canal, a magnificent technological achievement whose construction cost thousands of Egyptian lives, linked the Mediterranean and Red Seas, greatly decreasing the shipping time between Europe and Asia. British merchant and naval ships became the canal's major users. In 1875 Muhammad Ali's grandson was forced by skyrocketing national debt to sell Egypt's share of canal ownership to the British government.

Egypt's bankruptcy and debt to European financiers and governments eventually led to a British takeover. While the country's political and commercial elite, including many Coptic Christians, were committed to modernization, most Egyptians, influenced by conservative Islamic ideas and leaders, opposed Western influence. To preempt other European powers' ambitions, in 1882 Britain, using local unrest and threats to European residents as an excuse, invaded the country, making Egypt part of Britain's growing worldwide empire.

Britain soon faced a challenge from the Sudanic region to Egypt's south (today the nation of Sudan). In 1881 the militant Arab Muslim Muhammad Ahmad (1846–1885) declared himself the Mahdi **(MAH-dee)** ("the Guided One") sent to restore Islam's purity and destroy the corrupt Egyptian-imposed government. He recruited an army, defeated Egyptian forces and their British officers, and then formed an Islamic state. However, the Mahdist government wasted money in wars. In 1898 British and Egyptian forces triumphed, forming a new state known as the Anglo-Egyptian Sudan, effectively a British colony.

Persia: Challenges and Reforms

More a diverse collection of tribes, ethnic groups, and religious sects than a nation, Persia, increasingly known as Iran, faced many problems. While Christian Armenians, Jews, Zoroastrians, and Sunni Kurds all sought increased autonomy, the majority of Persia's people, including Turkish-speaking Azeris in the northwest, were Shi'ites. Shi'ite clerics controlled education, law, and welfare, enjoying vast wealth from landholdings and tithes. After the Safavid collapse in 1736 and the following decades of turmoil, in 1794 one Persian tribe, the Qajars **(KAH-jars)**, established control from their base in Tehran, from where they ruled uneasily until 1925. Early Qajar rulers, unable to resolve most problems, became noted for greed, corruption, and lavish living. One extravagant shah married 158 wives, fathered nearly 100 children, and was survived by some 600 grandchildren. Top Shi'ite clerics engaged in power struggles with Qajar shahs. Shi'ites also persecuted as heretical the Bahai **(buh-HI)** religion. Founded in 1867 by the Persian Bahaullah **(bah-hah-oo-LAH)** (1817–1892) as an offshoot of Shi'ism, Bahai called for universal peace, the unity of all religions, and service to others. Shi'ites killed many Bahais and forced their leaders into exile.

Persia also faced continuous pressure from Russia and Britain. By the 1870s Russia had gained territory on both sides of the Caspian Sea, including the Caucasus, and between 1907 and 1921 it asserted a sphere of influence in northern Persia. At the same time, British power steadily grew in the Persian Gulf and along Arabia's Indian Ocean coast. Wanting to keep Russians away from the Persian Gulf and India, Britain asserted a sphere of influence in southeastern Persia, at the entrance to the Persian Gulf. British entrepreneurs soon monopolized Persian railroad construction and banking; the Anglo-Persian Oil Company (later British Petroleum), which struck oil in 1908, became Persia's dominant economic enterprise, with profits going chiefly to Britain. Persians considered the powerful British economic role a humiliation. Weak government combined with foreign pressure prompted reforms, and to restore central government power, some Qajar shahs rebuilt an army, established a Western-style college, introduced a telegraph system, and allowed Christian missionaries to establish schools and hospitals. But while some celebrated the reforms, they threatened the conservative Shi'ite clergy, who hoped to thwart modernization.

From 1905 to 1911 Persia enjoyed a constitutional revolution and democracy unique in the Middle East. Liberal Shi'ite clergy, allied with Tehran merchants, Armenians, and Western-educated radicals, imposed a democratic constitution that curbed royal power and provided for an elected parliament and freedom of the press. When a conservative, pro-Russian shah took power and attempted to weaken the parliament, liberal newspapers, writers, and musicians lampooned him and his allies, while troubadours performed songs about love of country, democracy, freedom, justice, and equality. However, Britain and Russia pressured Persia to grant them more influence, straining the progressive leadership. The constitutionalist forces split into pro-Western nationalists who sought separation of religious and civil power, land reform, and universal education, and Shi'ite clerics, who, alarmed at secularism, favored slower change. As violence increased in 1911, the royal government closed down the parliament, ending the democratic experiment. Aref Qazvini, a popular prorevolution songwriter, lamented the setback: "O let not Iran thus be lost, if ye be men of truth."[17] By then, Britain and Russia, stationing troops in Persia, had reduced Persia's political and economic independence.

Western Asia, Northwest Africa, and Europe

Declining Ottoman power and growing Western activity eventually reshaped the empire's eastern Arab provinces, especially Syria and Lebanon, an ethnically and religiously diverse region whose Arab and Armenian Christians, Sunni and Shi'ite Arabs, and Sunni Kurds had mostly lived in peace. By recognizing each community's autonomy, the Ottomans promoted religious tolerance. A British writer admired Lebanon's generally stable conditions: "every man lives in a perfect security of life and property. The peasant is not richer than in other countries, but he is free."[18] However, in the 1850s poverty and a stagnant economy led to conflicts, and the densely populated region around Mount Lebanon came under Western influence. The French developed a special relationship with Maronites **(MAR-uh-nite)**, Arab Christians seeking a closer connection with the Roman Catholic Church, while American Protestant missionaries established a college in Beirut, spreading modern ideas. Economic problems also encouraged emigration, especially of Lebanese Christians to the United States, and by 1914 perhaps 350,000 Syrians and Lebanese had emigrated to the Americas. In the United States many have governed states or served in Congress. Other Lebanese and Syrian Christians and Muslims moved to West Africa, Latin America, or the Caribbean. In the past half century people of Lebanese, Syrian, or other Arab ancestry have served as presidents of several Latin American and Caribbean nations, including Argentina, Ecuador, and Jamaica.

Under Ottoman rule, Iraq, the heart of ancient Mesopotamia, lacked political unity and prosperity. Ottoman Iraq included three provinces: a largely Sunni Arab and Kurdish north, a chiefly Sunni Arab center, and a Shi'ite Arab south. Iraqis suffered from major floods and repeated plague and cholera epidemics. A British official described Iraq as "a country of extremes, either dying of thirst or of being drowned."[19] Iraq also lacked order, foreign capital, widespread literacy, railroads, and steamships. Pirates attacked Persian Gulf shipping,

Bahai An offshoot of Persian Shi'ism that was founded in 1867; Bahai preached universal peace, the unity of all religions, and service to others.

---

[17]Quoted in Yahya Armajani and Thomas M. Ricks, *Middle East: Past and Present*, 2nd ed. (Englewood Cliffs, NJ: Prentice-Hall, 1986), 221.

[18]Quoted in Charles Issawi, *The Middle East Economy: Decline and Recovery* (Princeton: Markus Wiener, 1995), 126.

[19]Gertrude Bell, quoted in Emory C. Bogle, *The Modern Middle East: From Imperialism to Freedom, 1800–1958* (Upper Saddle River, NJ: Prentice-Hall, 1996), 103.

while Bedouin tribes raided land caravans. Yet, Western interest in Iraq's economic potential and strategic location grew. In 1899 Britain established a protectorate over the neighboring Persian Gulf kingdom of Kuwait **(koo-WAIT)**, which allowing it to station troops and agents. But both the British and Germans suspected that Iraq might have considerable oil, spurring Ottomans and foreign investors to pour money into Iraq.

The Ottomans never firmly controlled Arabic-speaking societies along Africa's Mediterranean coast from Libya to Algeria, and their proximity to Europe made them natural targets. In 1830 France embarked on full-scale colonization of Algeria. Abd al-Qadir **(AB dul-KA-deer)**, using Islamic appeals, united Arab and Berber opposition to the French. His resourceful followers quickly learned how to make guns. Facing years of determined resistance, France demoralized the Algerians, driving peasants off the best land and selling it to European settlers while relocating and breaking up tribes. Yet anti-French revolts erupted until the 1880s. Ruthless French conquest cost tens of thousands of French and hundreds of thousands of Algerian lives.

France intended to impose French culture, settlers, and economic priorities on Algeria. General Bugeaud, who conquered Algeria, conceded in 1849 that "the Arabs with great insight understand very well the cruel revolution we have brought them; it is as radical for them as socialism would be for us."[20] Between the 1840s and 1914 over a million immigrants from France, Italy, and Spain poured into Algeria, erecting a racist society similar to South Africa. Algeria was incorporated into the French state with European settlers given voting rights. Vineyard cultivation and wine production displaced food crops and pasture, mocking Islamic values prohibiting alcoholic beverages.

Gradually European power in Northwest Africa increased. In Morocco, Sultan Mawlay Hassan (r. 1873–1895), to preserve the country's independence, skillfully played rival European powers against each other. However, France and Spain, attracted by Morocco's economic potential and strategic position, had divided the country between them by 1912. Tunisia long enjoyed considerable autonomy under Ottoman rule, with the port city of Tunis prospering as a trade and piracy center. In 1881 France colonized Tunisia. The Italians conquered Libya, a sparsely populated, mostly desert land between Tunisia and Egypt, in 1911 and 1912. Islamic orders led repeated resistance efforts, and the resulting conflicts killed one-third of Libya's people. European colonialism now dominated all of North Africa.

MAKE SURE YOU UNDERSTAND THESE KEY POINTS BEFORE MOVING ON

- The Ottomans modernized their army, adopted French-style laws, and became increasingly secular, but their power began to wane under pressure from Russia and western Europe and also from the Armenians.

- After Napoleon left Egypt, an Ottoman-appointed governor, Muhammad Ali, attempted an ambitious and somewhat successful program of modernization; ultimately, however, Britain gained control of the Suez Canal and made Egypt a colony.

- Persia, fragmented under the rule of the Qajars, came to be dominated economically by Britain, and interference by both Britain and Russia helped to end a brief period of progressive rule.

- Westerners became increasingly influential in Syria and Lebanon, as well as in Iraq, which was undeveloped but attracted Western attention because of its economic potential.

- Europeans colonized Northwest Africa: first Algeria, where settlers established a racist society; then Morocco, which was shared by France and Spain; and finally Tunisia and Libya.

aplia

Middle Eastern Thought and Culture

How did Middle Eastern thought and culture respond to the Western challenge?

West Asians and North Africans responded to Western challenges in three ways. Some formed vibrant revivalist movements promoting a purer version of Islamic practice rooted in early Muslim tradition. Others mounted reform movements combining Islam with modernization and secularization. Early stirrings of Arab nationalism constituted a third response. While governments stagnated or struggled, revivalist, reform, and nationalist movements pumped fresh vitality into cultures and religious life. But no movement offered an effective resistance to Western economic and military power.

Islamic Revivalism

Islamic revivalism sought to purify religious practices by returning to a purer vision of

Islamic revivalism Arab movements that sought to purify Islamic practices by reviving what they considered to be a purer vision of Islamic society.

---
[20]Quoted in Eric R. Wolf, *Peasant Wars of the Twentieth Century* (New York: Harper and Row, 1969), 209.

Islamic society rooted in the faith's early years, embracing what followers regarded as God's word in the Quran and the Prophet Muhammad's sayings. Revivalists idealized the theocratic state of the early Mecca caliphs, which blended religion and government, and criticized as corrupt the scholarly and mystical additions that over the centuries had accured from Persian, Hindu, Indonesian, African, and European cultures. In many African and Southeast Asian societies, Muslims still consulted shamans skilled in magic and healing, revered Sufi saints, and permitted women to engage in trade and reject veiling. Muslim revivalists despised Sufism and its mystical practices, such as music and dance. Several Sufi brotherhoods eventually abandoned mystical beliefs and emphasized the Prophet Muhammad's original teachings.

While political leaders lost prestige and authority, revivalists allied to merchant and tribal groups seized the initiative. For example, Othman dan Fodio in West Africa and the Mahdist Army in Sudan interpreted the early Muslim idea of jihad, or struggle for the faith, as a call to wage holy war against Muslims who disagreed with them. Carried by scholars, merchants, and missionaries, revivalist Islam spread all over the Islamic world. Many sub-Saharan African, Indian, and Southeast Asian Muslims visited, studied, or sojourned in the Middle East, often embracing revivalist ideas. These movements stiffened resistance against French colonization in Algeria and West Africa and against Dutch colonization in Indonesia.

Revivalism had its greatest impact in Arabia, where it produced a militant movement in the 1700s called **Wahhabism** (wah-HAH-bi-zuhm). The founder, Muhammad Abd al-Wahhab (al-wah-HAHB) (1703–1792), led a long campaign to purify Arabian Islam. After studying Islamic theology in Medina and Iraq, al-Wahhab adopted a strict interpretation of Islamic law and promoted intolerance toward all alternative views, such as Sufism and Shi'ism, and those lax in their faith. In 1744 a key ally, Muhammad Ibn Saud (sah-OOD), a tribal chief, put together a fighting force to expand their influence, and during the later 1700s Wahhabis used military force to take over parts of Arabia. Advancing into Syria and Iraq, they occupied the city of Karbala and destroyed the major Shi'ite holy site. By 1805 Wahhabis controlled Mecca and Medina, Islam's two holiest cities, where they horrified non-Wahhabis by massacring the residents and trying to destroy sacred tombs to prevent saint worship. Egypt's governor, Muhammad Ali, used his European-style army and modern weapons to push Wahhabis back from the holy cities. However, Wahhabi ideas, puritanism, and zeal spread widely during the 1800s as Western power undermined Middle Eastern governments. Yet many Muslims condemned Wahhabi intolerance, extremism, and such practices as forced veiling of women.

Wahhabism A militant Islamic revivalist movement founded in Arabia in the eighteenth century.

In 1902 al-Wahhab and Ibn Saud's descendants launched a second expansion. The head of the Saud family, Abdul Aziz Ibn Saud (1880–1953), sent Wahhabi clergy to convince Bedouins to abandon nomadic ways and join self-sufficient farming communities that adopted extreme asceticism and literal interpretation of the Islamic legal code, the Shari'a. Wahhabi clergy beat men for arriving late for prayers. In 1925 the Saud family established Saudi Arabia, a state based on the Shari'a. Oil discoveries in 1938 gave the Saud family and their Wahhabi allies the wealth to maintain their control.

Modernist Islamic Thought

Some reformist Muslim thinkers, rejecting a rigid, backward-looking vision such as Wahhabism, promoted modernization to transform Islamic society and meet the Western challenges. Intellectuals argued that Muslims should reject blind faith and welcome fresh ideas, social change, and religious moderation. Modernists detested many conservative traditions. Qasim Amin **(KA-sim AH-mean)**, a French-educated Egyptian lawyer, argued that liberating women was essential to liberating Egypt, that acquiring their "share of intellectual and moral development, happiness, and authority would prove…the most significant development in Egyptian history." Women reformers such as Bahithat al-Badiya **(buh-TEE-that al-buh-DEE-ya)** echoed these sentiments (see Witness to the Past: Egyptian Women and Their Rights). The radical male Iraqi poet Jamil Sidqi az-Zahawi **(ja-MILL SID-key az-za-HA-wi)** identified the veil as symbolizing female exclusion, imploring women to "unveil yourself for life needs transformation. Tear it away, burn it, do not hesitate. It has only given you false protection!"[21]

Modernists believed that introducing change would be a straightforward process, that buying weapons and machines could strengthen their armies and industries to deflect Western pressure, enrich their countries, and avoid domestic unrest. But their dreams proved impractical; visionaries were ahead of largely conservative populations. Challenges increased as Western technical and economic capabilities grew. Like European Enlightenment thinkers, some modernists struggled with reconciling faith and reason. They worried that modernization required adopting Western philosophical and scientific theories, often contrary to Islamic beliefs about society, God, and nature. Belief in equality also contradicted Muslim women's low status, while notions of popular sovereignty and the nation troubled those who believed that only God could make laws or establish standards, which the state must then administer. Some reformers doubted whether Islam, which idealized a universalistic, multiethnic, God-guided community, was compatible with nationalism, which emphasized unity defined by a common state. Moroccan historian Ahmad Ibn Khalid al-Nasri worried that military

---

[21]The quotes are from Akram Fouad Khater, ed., *Sources in the History of the Modern Middle East* (Boston: Houghton Mifflin, 2004), 75; Wiebke Walther, *Women in Islam* (Princeton: Markus Wiener, 1993), 221.

WITNESS TO THE PAST

Egyptian Women and Their Rights

One of the leading women writers and thinkers in early-twentieth-century Egypt, Bahithat al-Badiya (1886–1918), advocated greater economic and educational rights for women in a rapidly changing society. She wrote at a time when Egyptian nationalists demanded independence from Britain and a modern state while intellectuals debated the merits of modernity as opposed to tradition. In 1909, in a lecture to an Egyptian women's club associated with a nationalist organization, Bahithat offered a program for improving women's lives. Struggling against male and Islamic opposition to women's rights, she sought a middle ground between Islamic conservatism and European secular liberalization.

Ladies, I greet you as a sister who feels what you feel, suffers what you suffer, and rejoices in what you rejoice....Complaints about both men and women are rife....This mutual blame which has deepened the antagonism between the sexes is something to be regretted and feared. God did not create man and women to hate each other but to love each other and to live together so the world would be populated....Men say when we become educated we shall push them out of work and abandon the role for which God has created us. But isn't it rather men who have pushed women out of work? Before, women used to spin and to weave cloth for clothes,...but men invented machines for spinning and weaving....In the past, women sewed clothes...but men invented the sewing machine....Women...[made bread] with their own hands. Then men invented bakeries employing men....I do not mean to denigrate these useful inventions which do a lot of our work....Since male inventors and workers have taken away our work should we waste our time in idleness or seek other work to occupy us? Of course, we should do the latter....

Men say to us categorically, "You women have been created for the house and we have been created to be breadwinners." Is this a God-given dictate?...No holy book has

spelled it out....Women in villages...help their men till the land and plant crops. Some women do the fertilizing, haul crops, lead animals, draw water for irrigation, and other chores....Specialized work for each sex is a matter of convention,...not mandatory....Women may not have to their credit great inventions but women have excelled in learning and the arts and politics....Nothing irritates me more than when men claim they do not wish us to work because they wish to spare us the burden. We do not want condescension, we want respect....

If we had been raised from childhood to go unveiled and if our men were ready for it I would approve of unveiling those who want it. But the nation is not ready for it now....The imprisonment in the home of the Egyptian woman of the past is detrimental while the current freedom of the European is excessive. I cannot find a better model [than] today's Turkish woman. She falls between the two extremes and does not violate what Islam prescribes. She is a good example of decorum and modesty....We should get a sound education, not merely acquire the trappings of a foreign language and rudiments of music. Our education should also include home management, health care, and childcare....We shall advance when we give up idleness.

THINKING ABOUT THE READING

1. How does Bahithat evaluate women's roles and gender relations in Egypt?
2. What does her moderate advice to Egyptian women suggest about Egyptian society and the power of patriarchy?

Source: Bahithat al-Badiya, "A Lecture in the Club of the Umma Party, 1909," trans. by Ali Badran and Margot Badran, in *Opening the Gate: A Century of Arab Feminist Writing,* ed. by Margot Badran and Miriam Cooke (Bloomington: Indiana University Press, 1990), pp. 228–238. Copyright © 1990 by Indiana University Press. Reprinted with permission of Indiana University Press.

cadets being trained in Western weapons and tactics "want to learn to fight to protect the faith, but they lose the faith in the process of learning how."[22] What role, modernizers wondered, could clerics and the Shari'a have in a world of machines and nations?

Egypt-based thinkers argued about Islam's compatibility with modernization. Persia-born teacher Jamal al-Din al-Afghani (1838–1895), believing that reason and science were not contrary to Islam, argued that rigid religious interpretations, intolerance of new ideas, and the weight of local traditions contributed to Arab backwardness. He lamented that "the Arab world still remains buried in profound darkness,"[23]

while rational interpretations of Islam would free Muslims for positive change. Strongly criticizing British imperialism and Arab leaders he viewed as puppets, he moved to Paris, where he published a weekly newspaper promoting his views. Another well-traveled thinker, Muhammad Abduh (**AHB-doo**) (1849–1905), wanted to reform his native Egypt and rejuvenate Islam. Although opposing wholesale Westernization, Abduh admired major European thinkers, contending that no knowledge, whatever its origin, was incompatible with Islam. A top Islamic jurist, he promoted modernist Islam at Al-Azhar University, the Middle East's most influential higher education institution.

---

[22]Quoted in Burke, *Prelude to Protectorate,* 38.
[23]From Khater, *Sources,* 34.

17 CAIRO. — Opera Square. — LL.

Hulton Archive/Getty Images

CAIRO OPERA HOUSE Hoping to demonstrate modernization, Egyptian leaders built an opera house in Cairo in the 1860s. One of the first pieces staged was an opera by Italian composer Giuseppe Verdi to celebrate the opening of the Suez Canal in 1869.

The Roots of Arab Nationalism and the Zionist Quest

During the 1800s an Arab national consciousness developed in response to Ottoman, British, and French domination. Some proposed a pan-Arab movement uniting Arabs from Morocco to Iraq in a common struggle for political and cultural independence. But diverse religious and group affiliations divided Arabs. Most were Sunni Muslims, but many Shi'ites lived in western Asia, and some Christians lived in Egypt, Lebanon, and Syria. Feuding patriarchal tribes sometimes disliked rival tribes as much as their Ottoman or European overlords. Many Arabs also remained loyal to Ottoman rule. In 1876, hoping to defuse ethnic nationalism, the Ottomans gave Arabs seats in the national legislature.

Yet, some thoughtful Arabs envisioned self-governing Arab nations. Arab nationalism emerged from a Syrian literary and cultural movement in the later 1800s that included Lebanese Christians; one published a poem calling on Arabs to "arise and awake." Abd-al-Rahman al-Kawabiki **(AB-dul-RAH-man al-KA-wa-BIK-ee)** (1849–1903), a witty Syrian who had studied in Egypt and Mecca and hated intolerance and injustice, criticized Ottoman despotism as contrary to Islam while promoting Arab politics. Arab nationalist groups formed all over the Ottoman Empire, but before World War I they were small and had little public influence.

While Islamic societies struggled against Western power, the Zionist movement (see Chapter 19) introduced

kibbutz A Jewish collective farm in Palestine that stressed the sharing of wealth.

another challenge. In Jewish ghettoes of eastern Europe, especially Poland and Russia, some thinkers sought a state for their long-persecuted, widely scattered people. Prayers in Jewish synagogues for worshiping "next year in Jerusalem," the ancient Hebrew capital in Palestine, endured for centuries. Few European Jews spoke Hebrew, and many rejected Zionism, identifying with the country where they lived. For others, Zionism functioned like nationalism. The first Zionist conference, held in Basel, Switzerland, in 1897, identified Ottoman-ruled Palestine as the potential Jewish homeland. Jews had long visited or settled in Palestine, and perhaps twenty thousand lived there in 1870. When the Ottomans prohibited Zionists from organizing a massive Jewish settlement, the Zionist leader, Hungarian-born journalist Theodor Herzl (1860–1904), proposed accepting a British offer for a temporary home in East Africa.

Soon militant Zionists promoted Jewish migration to Palestine without Ottoman permission or European governments' support. By 1914 some 85,000 Jews, many newcomers from Russia and Poland, lived in Palestine alongside some 700,000 Arabs. Committed to creating a socialist society, many immigrants established Jewish collective farms, each known as a **kibbutz**, whose members shared their wealth and promoted Hebrew rather than the German-based Yiddish widely spoken by central and east European Jews. International Zionist organizations funded Palestine settlement, buying land from absentee Arab and Turkish landowners. Zionists had a flag, an anthem, and an active Jewish press but no legal recognition in Palestine, setting the stage for future conflict with Palestinian Arabs, who resented the newcomers and their plans to acquire more land for a Jewish state.

MAKE SURE YOU UNDERSTAND THESE KEY POINTS BEFORE MOVING ON

- One response to European pressure was Islamic revivalism, which advocated a pure form of Islam, favored a theocratic state, and sometimes used violence.

- Revivalism was most influential in Arabia, where militant followers of al-Wahhab and Ibn Saud took over a number of cities and eventually formed Saudi Arabia.

- Some intellectuals tried to modernize their religion, but modern European ideas such as equality continued to clash with Islamic practices such as the subjugation of women, and Western nationalism was at odds with the idea of a universal brotherhood under God.

- Some tried to inspire Arab nationalism, but religious divisions and rivalries made this a difficult task.

- Muslims were also challenged by European Zionists, who moved to Palestine in spite of Ottoman objections and also in spite of the Palestinian Arabs, setting the stage for future conflict.

aplia

CHAPTER SUMMARY

Sub-Saharan Africa underwent extensive changes between 1750 and 1914. Ending the trans-Atlantic slave trade opened Africa to exploration and trade by Europeans. Industrial Europe's need for resources and markets fostered a "scramble for Africa" as various Western nations colonized African societies, sometimes by military force against protracted resistance. The French colonized a vast area of West and Central Africa; Britain forged a large empire in West, Central, and East Africa; and the Germans, Belgians, and Italians also acquired African colonies. European settlers flocked to colonies in southern and eastern Africa, most notably South Africa, establishing white supremacist societies. Colonialism created artificial, multiethnic countries. It replaced subsistence agriculture with cash crop farming, plantations, and mineral exploitation while enmeshing Africa in the world economy as a supplier of natural resources. Africans mounted strikes and rebellions against colonialism, but all such efforts were eventually defeated.

The Middle East also experienced European imperialism. The Ottoman Empire attempted to stall its decline with Western-style reforms, but it still lost territory and influence. Egypt attempted an ambitious modernization program, but it proved inadequate to prevent British colonization. In Persia, Western economic and political influence sparked reforms that were later rejected by Persian conservatives. France and Italy colonized North Africa, and French settlers displaced Algerians from valuable land. In response, some Muslims, most notably Wahhabis, pursued a revivalist strategy to purify the religion and reject Western influence, while modernist reformers sought to energize Muslim societies by adapting secular Western ideas to Islam. Arab nationalist movements also arose but remained weak before World War I. Finally, Jewish Zionists posed a threat to Palestinian Arabs by beginning to settle in Palestine, where they hoped to build a Jewish state.

KEY TERMS

direct rule (p. 506)
indirect rule (p. 506)
laager (p. 507)

Young Turks (p. 514)
Bahai (p. 516)
Islamic revivalism (p. 517)

Wahhabism (p. 518)
kibbutz (p. 520)

22 South Asia, Southeast Asia, and Colonization, 1750–1914

Leiden University Library, Codex Orientalis 7398: 2

DIPENEGARA This painting shows Prince Dipenegara, a Javanese aristocrat who led a revolt against the Dutch colonizers in the 1820s, reading, with several attendants at hand.

Rice fields are littered with our battle-killed; blood flows or lies in pools, stains hills and streams. [French] Troops … grab our land, our towns, roaring and stirring dust to dim the skies. A scholar with no talent and no power, could I redress a world turned upside down?

—Protest by Vietnamese poet Nguyen Dinh Chieu against French conquest, late nineteenth century[1]

In 1858, seeking to expand its empire and frustrated by the Vietnamese emperor's refusal to liberalize trade relations and protect Christian missionaries, France attacked Vietnam with military force, and over the next three decades it conquered the country against determined resistance. One of the strongest resisters was a blind poet, Nguyen Dinh Chieu **(NEW-yin dinh chew)** (1822–1888), who gave an oration honoring Vietnamese soldiers killed during a heroic battle: "You preferred to die fighting the enemy, and return to our ancestors in glory rather than survive in submission to the [Westerners] and share your miserable life with barbarians." The French retaliated, seizing Chieu's land and property. The poet, unbowed, refused to use Western products and forbade his children to learn the romanized Vietnamese alphabet developed by French Catholic missionaries. In painstakingly copied manuscripts spread throughout the land, Chieu promoted the struggle and heaped scorn on Vietnamese who collaborated with French occupiers: "I had rather face unending darkness, Than see the country tortured. Everyone will rejoice in seeing the West wind [colonialism], Vanish from [Vietnam's] mountains and rivers."[2] Chieu to become a physician, scholar, and teacher famous for epic poems sung in the streets that extolled love of country, friendship, marital fidelity, family loyalty, scholarship, and military arts. He rejected the French offer of a financial subsidy and the return of his family land if he supported their cause. Vietnamese continue to revere his stirring poems.

Using their enhanced military, economic, and technological power (see Chapters 19–20), and motivated by cultural arrogance, Britain, France, the Netherlands, and the United States colonized all of South and Southeast Asia except Thailand. Western domination proved a transforming experience, destroying traditional political systems, reorienting economies, and posing challenges for societies and their world-views. As Asian workers produced resources that spurred Western economic growth, these regions were introduced to Western ideas and technologies and became linked more closely to a European-dominated world economy. Resentment against colonialism simmered for decades; eventually some Asians asserted their peoples' rights to self-determination.

---

[1]From Huynh Sanh Thong, *An Anthology of Vietnamese Poems from the Eleventh Through the Twentieth Centuries* (New Haven, CT: Yale University Press, 1996), 88.
[2]The poem excerpts are in Helen B. Lamb, *Vietnam's Will to Live: Resistance to Foreign Aggression from Early Times Through the Nineteenth Century* (New York: Monthly Review Press, 1972), 134, 152.

(T) Forming British India

How and why did Britain extend its control throughout India?

By the early 1700s the Muslim Mughals who ruled much of India (see Chapter 18) were in steep decline, challenged by both Indians and Europeans. Mughal court splendors and India's valuable exports had earlier attracted Portuguese, Dutch, and British. But it was the British who took advantage as Mughal power declined. In the mid-1700s they began their conquest, and by the mid-1800s they controlled both India and the island of Sri Lanka. Unlike earlier conquerors from western and Central Asia, who often assimilated into Indian society, the British maintained their separate traditions.

Mughal Decline and the British

Europeans had long coveted South Asia for its spices and textiles. Even today, small, single-masted sailing barges ply the coastline between western India, the Persian Gulf, and East

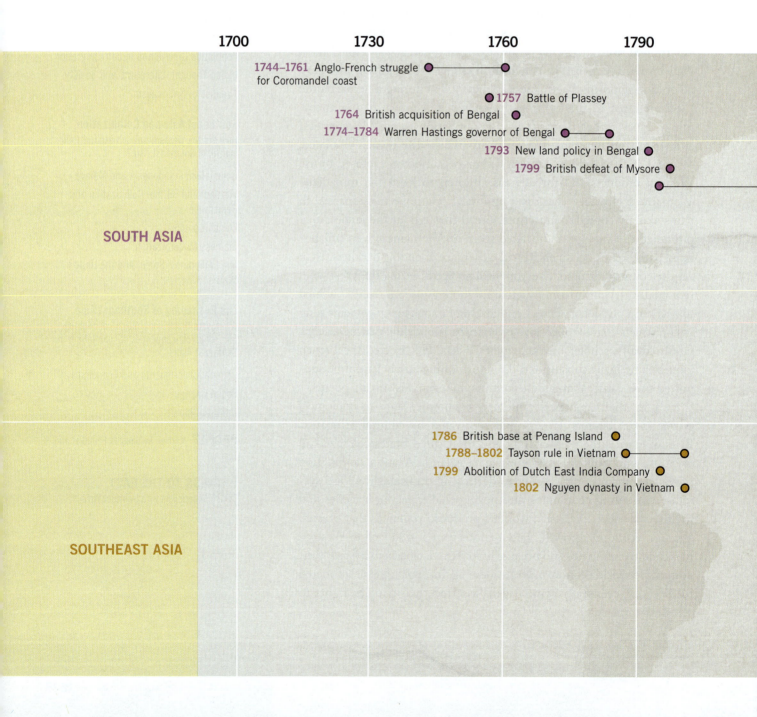

1700   **1730**   **1760**   **1790**

SOUTH ASIA

1744–1761 Anglo-French struggle for Coromandel coast

1757 Battle of Plassey

1764 British acquisition of Bengal

1774–1784 Warren Hastings governor of Bengal

1793 New land policy in Bengal

1799 British defeat of Mysore

SOUTHEAST ASIA

1786 British base at Penang Island

1788–1802 Tayson rule in Vietnam

1799 Abolition of Dutch East India Company

1802 Nguyen dynasty in Vietnam

Africa, ferrying merchandise with the coming and going of monsoon winds. Between 1500 and 1750 European powers controlled some of the Indian Ocean maritime trade but conquered only a few scattered outposts in South Asia. The Dutch, after destroying Portuguese power, concentrated on Sri Lanka and Indonesia. By 1696 the British possessed three fortified trading stations in India: Calcutta (now Kolkata) in Bengal, Madras (today known as Chennai) on the southeastern coast, and Bombay (today called Mumbai) on the west coast.

By 1750 many Indians had already broken away from weak and corrupt Mughal control, and the emperors sitting on the spectacular Peacock Throne in Delhi's Red Fort enjoyed little actual power beyond Delhi. As they consoled themselves with the royal harem or opium and as Mughal factions quarreled among themselves, the countryside became increasingly disorderly. Powerful new states arose, including those built by the **Marathas (muh-RAH-tuhs)**, a loosely knit, Hindu-led confederacy from west-central India, and the Sikh religious minority in northwest India. By 1800 Marathas ruled much of western India, while Sikhs under the dynamic Ranjit Singh **(RUN-ji SING)** (1780–1839) conquered

Marathas A loosely knit confederacy led by Hindu warriors from west-central India; one of several groups that challenged British domination after the decline of the Mughals.

1820   1850   1880   1910   1940

1796–1815 British colonization of Sri Lanka
1816 British protectorate over Nepal
1819 British occupation of all Maratha lands
1820s Beginning of British Westernization policy
1839–1842 First Anglo-Afghan War
1849 British defeat of Sikhs in Punjab
1850 Completion of British India
1857–1858 Indian Rebellion
1858 Introduction of colonial system in India
1877 Founding of Muslim college at Aligarh
1878–1880 Second Anglo-Afghan War
1885 Formation of Indian National Congress
1903 British invasion of Tibet
1906 Formation of All-India Muslim League

1819 British colony in Singapore
1824–1886 Anglo-Burman Wars
1830–1870 Cultivation system in Java
1858–1884 French conquest of Vietnam
1868–1910 Kingship of Chulalongkorn in Siam
1869 Opening of Suez Canal
1885–1886 Completion of British conquest of Burma
1887 Formation of Federation of Indochina
1898–1902 U.S. conquest of Philippines
1908 Dutch defeat of last Balinese kingdom

the Punjab and Kashmir. Mounted on sturdy ponies, the feared Marathas made plundering raids deep into central India against helpless Mughal armies. Without a powerful state to unite it, this diverse Indian society could not effectively resist European encroachments. Both Britain and France attempted to fill the power vacuum in southern India, supporting their respective Indian allies in the struggle for regional advantage. Ultimately, no Indian state gained enough power or acquired enough weapons to repulse the West.

Britain posed the gravest challenge, and one of the key events took place in Bengal, India's richest and most populous region that was ruled by governors who mostly ignored the Mughal government. Aliverdi Khan (r. 1740–1756) had left British trade unmolested. But his successor, Siraja Dowlah **(see-RAH-ja DOW-luh)** (ca. 1732–1757), considering the British bothersome leeches on his land's riches, alienated Western merchants and in 1757 rashly attacked trading stations. After capturing Calcutta, Dowlah's forces placed 146 captured British men, women, and children in a crowded jail known as the **Black Hole of Calcutta**. The next day only 23 staggered out, the rest having perished from suffocation and dehydration. The enraged British dispatched a force under Robert Clive

Black Hole of Calcutta A crowded jail in India where over a hundred British prisoners of a hostile Bengali ruler died from suffocation and dehydration in 1757. This event precipitated the beginning of British use of force in India.

(1725–1774) to regain holdings. A former clerk turned into daring war strategist, the ambitious Clive and his 3,200 soldiers defeated 50,000 Bengali troops at the Battle of Plassey in 1757, recapturing Calcutta. Allied with Hindu bankers and Muslim nobles unhappy with Siraja Dowlah, who was executed, by 1764 Clive controlled Bengal.

The mercantilist British government allowed the British East India Company (known as "the Company") to govern Indian districts as they were acquired, sharing the profits. The British, much like the former Mughal rulers, expected Indians to serve them, showing a lust for riches equal to Spanish conquistadors in the 1500s. As Bengal governor (1758–1760, 1764–1767), Clive sanctioned organized plunder; British merchants and officials drained Bengal's wealth while Company officials, including Clive, lived like kings. Praised by British leaders and celebrated in the press and schoolboy stories, Clive became the idol of every young Englishman dreaming of glory and wealth via India's battlefields and bazaars. The cry of "Go East," inspired by Clive's rags-to-riches story, fueled British imperialist ambitions. But Clive was eventually accused and later cleared of corruption and fraud charges, and at the age of forty-nine, depressed, he committed suicide.

To undo Clive's economic chaos and consolidate Britain's position, the Company appointed Warren Hastings as Bengal's governor-general (1774–1784). Hastings redesigned the revenue system, made treaty alliances, and annexed nearby districts to safeguard the British bases. A scholarly man influenced by

CLIVE MEETS INDIAN LEADERS In this painting, Robert Clive meets the new Bengali official, Mir Jafir, after the British victory in the 1757 Battle of Plassey. Clive supported Mir Jafir's seizure of power from the anti-British leader, Siraja Dowlah.

Enlightenment thought, Hastings respected Indians, unlike other British officials, and opposed colonizing all India. Like Britons, he argued, many Indians had intellect and integrity and should enjoy equal rights with the colonizers. His successors often disregarded his advice. Hastings himself, accused of corruption and forced out of office, lived the rest of his life in disgrace.

Expanding British India

Bengal success fueled further British expansion. The Company had authority to administer all British-controlled Indian territories while also seeking profit, but not for further annexation. Despite the ban, governor-generals authorized occupying more areas, often against opposition, to prevent trade disruption or to counteract European rivals. Some imperialists promoted Britain's "sacred trust" to reshape the world, viewing British authority, culture, religion, and free trade policies a great blessing for Asians. Reality often differed. In expanding, Britain mixed military force, extortion, bribery, and manipulation of India's diversity. British agents and merchants pitted region against region and Hindu against Muslim, aided by Indian collaborators, especially businessmen eager for access to the world market. Superior weapons and disciplined military forces overcame spirited resistance. British officers commanded mercenary Indian soldiers, known as **sepoys**; by 1857 Company forces comprised nearly 200,000 sepoy troops and 10,000 British officers and soldiers.

With France hoping to block British expansion, European wars involving the two nations were extended into a contest for India's southeastern Coromandel coast. Victory over the French in 1761 sparked British actions against other Indian states. In Mysore, a mostly Hindu state in south-central India, Haidar Ali Khan (r. 1761–1782), a devout Muslim and brilliant military strategist who modeled his army on Western lines, warned the British, "I will march your troops until their legs swell to the size of their bodies. You shall not have a blade of grass, nor a drop of water."[3] Only in 1799, after twenty years of bloody wars, was Mysore defeated.

Gradually Britain controlled western, central, and northern India. With the Maratha confederacy divided by rivalries, in 1805 the British occupied the Marathas' northern territories and entered Delhi, deposing the aged Mughal emperor. After taking the remaining Maratha lands in 1819, they turned to northwest India, which was dominated by Sikhs and Rajputs, a declining Hindu warrior caste. Admitting their weakness, the Rajputs now signed treaties giving Britain claims on their lands. The death of Sikh leader Ranjit Singh in 1839 shattered Sikh unity and undermined their powerful military state. In 1849, after a series of bloody British-Sikh wars, Britain finally triumphed and then stationed troops in the many small independent principalities scattered around India. By 1850, the British ruled all Indians directly or through princes who collaborated with them (see Map 22.1).

British expansion in India eventually fostered interventions in neighboring societies, including Sri Lanka **(Ceylon)**, the large, fertile island just south of India. Fearing that France might establish a base, in 1796 the British acquired Dutch-held territory there; by 1815, after conquering the last remaining Sri Lankan kingdom, Kandy, they controlled the entire island. They seized rice-growing land from peasants, established coffee, tea, and rubber plantations, and recruited Tamil-speaking workers from southeast India as laborers. By 1911 the poorly paid Tamil laborers and their families, constituting 11 percent of Sri Lanka's population, maintained their own customs, language, and Hindu religion and had little contact with the Buddhist Sinhalese majority. Since many Sinhalese considered both British and Tamils unwanted aliens, Sinhalese-Tamil tensions simmered and, after independence, sparked a long civil war.

Fearing that the Russians, who had already conquered Muslim Central Asia, coveted South Asia, the British attempted to secure India's land borders. First they invaded Nepal, a Himalayan kingdom, defeated Nepal's Hindu ruling caste and its fierce fighters, the Gurkhas **(GORE-kuhz)**, in 1814–1816, and made Nepal a British protectorate. Britain later recruited Nepalese soldiers, also known as gurkhas, to support British objectives around the world. Mountainous Afghanistan, an ethnically diverse Muslim region with little political unity, seemed particularly vulnerable to Russian expansion. However, Pashtun tribes in the south possessed fighting skills to oppose conquest. The British twice invaded Afghanistan and occupied the major eastern city, Kabul, but they faltered against fierce Pashtun resistance. In the first Afghan War (1839–1842), Pashtuns massacred most of the twelve thousand retreating British and sepoy troops and the civilians, including women and children, who accompanied them. Undeterred, Britain fought the second Afghan War (1878–1880). Concluding that Afghanistan could not be annexed by military force, Britain replaced a pro-Russian Pashtun leader with a pro-British leader who gave Britain control of Afghanistan's foreign affairs. These British thrusts helped mould Afghan's hatred of foreign invaders and rule.

India Under the East India Company

The British East India Company gradually tightened its control of India, shifting from sharing government with local rulers to administering through British officials. Sir Thomas Munro, Madras governor (1820–1827), arrogantly explained the imperial mission by claiming that British rule must continue until Indians, sometime in the distant future, abandoned their "superstitions" and became "enlightened" enough to govern themselves. In the 1820s, the Company began **Westernization**, a policy to spread Western culture and

> **sepoys** Mercenary soldiers recruited among the warrior and peasant castes by the British in India.
>
> **Westernization** A deliberate attempt to spread Western culture and ideas.

---

[3]Quoted in Sinharaja Tammita-Delgoda, *A Traveller's History of India*, 2nd ed. (New York: Interlink, 1999), 154.

MAP 22.1 **THE GROWTH OF BRITISH INDIA, 1750–1860** Gradually expanding control from their bases at Calcutta, Madras, and Bombay, the British completed their military conquest of the final holdout states by the 1850s. © 2015 Cengage Learning

ideas. Protestant evangelism, then strong in Britain, influenced reform ideas. Disregarding Indian traditions, British officials encouraged Christian missions and tried to ban customs they disliked. Many Indians agreed with prohibiting *sati*, the practice of widows throwing themselves on their husband's funeral pyre, but disliked tinkering with Muslim and Hindu law codes.

Orientalism A scholarly interest among British officials in India and its history that prompted some to rediscover the Hindu Classical age.

As part of Westernization, Britain established English-medium schools. Lord Macaulay (1800–1859), a reformer and cultural chauvinist, considered it pointless to teach Indian languages, declaring in 1832 that "a single shelf of a good European library is worth the whole native literature of India and Arabia." Reflecting racist views, Macaulay proposed creating "a class of persons Indian in blood and color but English in taste, opinions, morals and intellect."[4] Many Indians considered English schools a threat to both Hindu and Muslim customs; others believed they opened students to a wider world. Indians formed the first English-medium higher education institution, the Hindu College in Calcutta, in 1818.

Some scholarly Britons studied India and its history, reflecting an approach later called **Orientalism**. Warren Hastings, who promoted Indian culture, languages, and literature,

[4]The quotes are in Burton Stein, *A History of India* (Malden, MA: Blackwell, 1998), 265–266.

The British Raj Great Indian Peninsular Terminus (w/c on paper), Haig, Axel (1835–1921)/British Library, London, UK/The Bridgeman Art Library

BRITISH RULE IN INDIA This painting from the later 1800s presents the Great Indian Peninsular Terminus in Bombay, a massive train station but also the center of railroad administration for the Raj.

preferred reading the European and Asian languages he had mastered—Greek, Latin, Persian, and Urdu—to his regular duties. One official, William Jones (1746–1794), who mastered Arabic, Persian, and Sanskrit, became the most influential Orientalist scholar, but he often attempted to fit India into Western concepts of history and religion. Just as Christians and Jews considered the Bible historical truth, Jones treated ancient Vedic texts as accurate historical records rather than religious teachings and claimed that the Classical Greeks derived some ideas from the same ancient source as Classical Indian sages. Jones's views shaped scholarly understanding of Indian history and religion. Several religious movements based on Hindu concepts, such as reincarnation, also gained a small Western following. Scholars today debate whether "Hinduism" as a unified religion was "invented" during the early nineteenth century by British Orientalists, Christian missionaries, and Indian thinkers who applied Christian concepts such as sacred texts and

authority figures to this ancient, diverse faith with many earthy traditions, or whether instead Hindus accommodated or reshaped new ideas. By the later 1800s British nationalism and intolerance had largely replaced Orientalist respect for India.

The India-West encounter also fostered a Hindu social reform movement and philosophical renaissance led by the brilliant Bengali scholar Ram Mohan Roy (1772–1833). Seeing his sister die on a funeral pyre, and believing that customs such as *sati* and caste divisions were harmful, Roy hoped that the adoption of certain Western ways could reform and strengthen Hinduism. He cautioned against Hindu dogmatism, writing that Indian "youths [will] not be fitted to be better members of society by the Vedantic doctrines which teach them to believe that [since reality is illusion] all visible things have no real existence."[5] Roy may have been the first Hindu to describe India's eclectic religious tradition as "Hinduism." To better understand the world by studying non-Hindu religions,

[5]Quoted in Sugata Bose and Ayesha Jalal, *Modern South Asia: History, Culture, Political Economy* (New York: Routledge, 1998), 83–84.

Roy mastered their source languages—Hebrew, Greek, Arabic, and Persian—and thus became the first modern scholar of comparative religion. Roy and his followers tried to synthesize the best in Hinduism and Christianity; he also founded secondary schools, newspapers, and a Hindu reform organization. Admiring their knowledge and liberty, Roy wanted the British to promote modernization while also seeking Indian advice.

To make India more profitable, the Company built roads, railroads, and irrigation systems; most significantly for rural Indians, it revised land revenue collection. Britons simplistically viewed Indian rural society as stagnant, unable to provide tax revenues to support British administration. In precolonial times, most Indians, living in self-sufficient villages governed by families and castes, enjoyed considerable social stability and the hereditary right to use the land. One British observer wrote that "the village communities [have] everything they want within themselves. They seem to last when nothing else lasts. Dynasty after dynasty tumbles down; but the village communities remain the same."[6]

Company officials, seeking higher revenues, began collecting farmers' taxes in money rather than in a portion of the crop, as was done before. In 1793 British officials in Bengal converted Mughal revenue collectors, or **zamindars**, into landlords, thus giving them the additional rights to buy and sell land. Peasant farmers now became tenants to landlords and lost their hereditary rights to land. Many landlords sold their land rights to businessmen, absentee landlords who became enriched from the peasants' crops. In Madras, Governor Munro, mistakenly believing that peasants were or could become profit-seeking individualists like English farmers, made them deal directly with the government, paying taxes in cash but being subject to eviction for nonpayment. Both systems transformed a barter economy, with villagers exchanging their services or products with each other, into a money economy. Since some villagers earned more money, cash-based systems undermined peasant stability and security while benefiting a moneylender caste that eventually controlled much of the land. The Company also encouraged cash crops such as opium, coffee, rubber, tea, and cotton, often grown on plantations, rather than food crops.

zamindars Mughal revenue collectors that the British turned into landlords who were given the rights to buy and sell land.

Resistance: The 1857 Revolt

Despite Indian reform movements, most Indians resented the Company's Westernization and economic policies. Many once-prosperous families lost land or become indebted, while courts enforced laws based on British traditions, fueling hostility. Thanks to such grievances, local revolts were common. Furthermore, sepoys resented aggressive British attempts to convert them to Christianity. Sepoys in Bengal particularly disliked new army rifle cartridges, which had to be bitten off before being rammed down the gun barrel. A rumor spread that the cartridges were greased with beef and pork fat, violating dietary prohibitions of both cow-revering Hindus and pork-avoiding Muslims.

In 1857 one revolt, which the British called the Indian Mutiny and Indian nationalists later termed the first War of Independence, spread rapidly in north and northeast India, seriously challenging British authority. The revolt began among sepoys and soon fostered peasant and Muslim uprisings. A few members of princely families joined the rebel cause, and the widow of the Maratha ruler of Jhansi led her troops into battle dressed as a man. No rebel leaders envisioned a unified Indian nation, but many Indians perceived their customs and religions threatened by British policies. Some leaders attempted to unite Hindus and Muslims against their common British enemy. A few wanted to restore the Mughal order.

The rebels captured Delhi and besieged several cities. Both sides used ruthless tactics and committed massacres. Rebels murdered a thousand British residents when they occupied the city of Kanpur, and British troops recapturing Delhi engaged in widespread raping, pillaging, and killing. Muslim poet Ghalib mourned: "Here is a vast ocean of blood before me. Thousands of my friends are dead. Perhaps none is left even to shed tears upon my death."[7] The rebels could not overcome inadequate arms, weak communications, and lack of a unified command structure or strategy. Nor did they receive support from people in other parts of India. Linguistic, religious, cultural, and regional fragmentation made a united Indian opposition impossible. When the British captured the last rebel fort, held by the rani (queen) of Jhansi, in 1858, she was killed and the rebellion collapsed, although a few small rebel groups fought skirmishes until 1860.

MAKE SURE YOU UNDERSTAND THESE KEY POINTS BEFORE MOVING ON

- Fragmented after the decline of the Mughals, India was unable to resist encroachment by the Portuguese, Dutch, British, and French.

- Though initially opposed by the French, the British East India Company gradually expanded its control over India by employing local collaborators and playing groups off against each other, and by 1850 Britain controlled all of India.

- The British expanded into Sri Lanka, where they imported Tamils to work on the tea plantations; into

Nepal, where they recruited effective soldiers; and into Afghanistan, where they met fierce resistance but ultimately installed a friendly ruler.

- Though some Indians supported Westernization, periodic revolts occurred, and in 1857 the sepoys began a large rebellion that led to much bloodshed and eventually Indian defeat.

aplia

---

[6]Charles Metcalfe, quoted in David Ludden, *An Agrarian History of South Asia* (New York: Cambridge University Press, 1999), 161.
[7]Quoted in Tammita-Delgoda, *Traveller's History*, 167.

The Reshaping of Indian Society

How did colonialism transform the Indian economy and foster new ideas in India?

The 1857 revolt prompted Britain to replace the Company government with direct colonial rule. While the British felt betrayed, some officials viewed the troubles as symptoms of deeper discontents that called for change. The 1858 Government of India Act transferred sovereignty to the British monarch. In 1876 Queen Victoria was proclaimed Empress of India and head of the British *Raj*, named for the ancient title of Hindu kings. India became the brightest "jewel in the imperial crown," a source of fabulous wealth. The policies now pursued reshaped economic, intellectual, and social patterns, eventually inspiring movements reflecting a new sense of the Indian nation.

Colonial Government and Education

The British Raj bore many similarities to the Mughal system. Top British officials, the viceroys, lived in splendor in Delhi and then in a new capital at New Delhi, enjoying pomp and circumstance, including Mughal-style ceremonies. Despite health problems from tropical heat and diseases such as malaria, the British built palatial mansions, museums, schools, universities, and city halls and connected India with a network of roads, bridges, and railways; by 1900 India had over 25,000 miles of track, the world's fourth largest rail system.

Although British officials mistrusted Indians after 1857, they allowed traditional princes to keep their privileges and palaces in exchange for promoting acceptance of British policies. Deliberately pitting the Hindu majority against the Muslim minority, Britons favored one or the other group in law, language, and custom. For example, Hindus protested use of the main Muslim language, Urdu, in many north Indian courts, which exacerbated hatreds that remain today.

Local revenue supported a huge army of 200,000 men, mostly Indian volunteers, who were needed to keep the peace in India and fight British battles abroad. As part of the "Great Game" of strategic rivalry with Russia, Britain invaded Tibet in 1903; Lord Curzon (viceroy from 1899 to 1905) conceded, "It would be madness for us to cross the Himalayas and to occupy it [Tibet]. But it is important that no one else should seize it."[8] Tibetan leaders agreed not to concede territory to Russia or any foreign power.

Europeans typically believed that Western colonialism improved Asian and African societies. Rudyard Kipling (1865–1936), a Bombay-born, Britain-educated English poet and novelist, articulated this view: "Take up the White Man's burden—Send forth the best ye breed—Go, bind your sons in exile. To serve your captives' need."[9] Some policies reflected racism and Westernization. Much like colonized Africans, Indians were excluded from European-only clubs and parks as well as from high bureaucratic positions, enjoying no real power or influence. An expanded English-medium education system promoted British and often Christian values. But although English became the common language for educated Indians, only a privileged minority, mostly higher-caste Hindus, could afford to send their children, mostly boys, to English schools. By 1911 only 11 percent of men and 1 percent of women were literate in any language, and less than 2 percent of Indians were Christians. However, an emerging English-educated middle class, with a taste for European products and ideas, sent their sons and a few daughters to British universities. Acquiring notions like "freedom" and "self-determination of peoples" that contrasted with the nondemocratic Raj, this growing professional class organized social, professional, and political bodies concerned with improving Indian life and acquiring more political influence.

Economic Transformation

Britain transformed India's economy. Long an economic powerhouse and major cotton textile exporter, India still produced a quarter of all world manufactured goods in 1750. Two centuries later, conditions had changed. Many Indians were harmed by British policies, which were designed to drain Indian wealth to benefit Britain. Land policies commercialized agriculture, while tax and tariff policies diminished manufacturing. The land tax system exploited the peasantry, fostering one of contemporary India's greatest dilemmas, inequitable land ownership. Many fell hopelessly into debt. With peasants growing cash crops such as cotton, jute, pepper, or opium rather than food, famine killed millions as food supplies and distribution became more uncertain. Between 1870 and 1900 millions of south Indians perished from hunger when the Raj refused to divert excess food from north India.

Other changes affected rural life. Steamships freed shipping from the vagaries of monsoon winds, and the Suez Canal, opened in 1869, made shipping raw materials from India to Europe easier and much faster. The return ships brought cheap machine goods, undermining village craftsmen such as weavers and tinkers who could compete only by lowering prices, earning too little to support families. In addition, felling forests and plowing grassland to grow more cash crops placed massive pressure on the physical environment.

Many historians argue that British rule also led to a decline in manufacturing. Seeking new markets abroad for its industrial products, Britain denied India tariff protection for its more expensive handmade products, excluded Indian manufactured goods from Britain, and prohibited importing industrial machinery for Indians. Meanwhile, British products flooded India, destroying many skilled craftsmen's livelihood. Textile imports increased sixfold between 1854 and 1913, ruining millions of weavers, who, like metalworkers and glass

[8]Quoted in Judith M. Brown, *Modern India: The Origins of an Asian Democracy*, 2nd ed. (New York: Oxford University Press, 1994), 134.
[9]Quoted in Tammita-Delgoda, *Traveller's History*, 173.

blowers, often became farm laborers. Yet, industrial activity did not disappear completely; some Indians found ways to prosper. A few competed with British imports by manufacturing cotton textiles and initiating a modern iron and steel sector. Gujarati industrialist Jamsetji N. Tata (**JAM-set-gee TA-ta**) (1839–1904) built cotton mills, while his son, Sir Dorabji Tata (**DOR-ab-ji TA-ta**) (1859–1932), founded the Indian steel industry in 1907. Unable to get British funding, they raised money among Indian investors, later using their wealth to promote scientific education and found technical colleges.

By the late 1800s the limits on India's industries were generating heated controversy. Indian critics alleged that tariffs protecting British industries strangled Indian competition. The British-Indian wealth gap grew. By 1895 Britain's per capita income was fifteen times higher than India's, much more unequal than two hundred years earlier. Defenders contended that British rule brought investment, imported goods, railroads, and law and order. But critics questioned whether these innovations, enriching British merchants, industrialists, and collaborating Indian businessmen and landlords, benefited most Indians. Indian scholars attacked "The Drain" of wealth, arguing that British policies gave India "peace but not prosperity; the manufacturers lost their industries; the cultivators were ground down by a heavy and variable taxation; and the revenues were to a large extent diverted to England.[10] By 1948, after two centuries of British influence, most Indians remained poor.

Population Growth and Indian Emigration

Population growth worsened the peasants' plight. With peace and improved sanitation and health, India's population rose from perhaps 100 million in 1700 to 300 million by 1920. While encouraging agricultural productivity, the Raj provided economic incentives to have more children to help in the fields. But whereas Europe's population increase could be absorbed by industrialization or emigration to the Americas and Australia, India enjoyed neither industrial revolution nor increased food growing. Profiting from the cash crop system, Indian landlords discouraged innovation. In addition, growing population numbers far outstripped available food and land, creating dire poverty and widespread hunger.

This impoverishment created millions of desperately poor Indians who were recruited to emigrate to other lands. After abolition, former slaves often left American plantations, creating a market for Indian labor in Trinidad, British Guiana (today's Guyana), and Dutch Guiana (now Suriname). Plantations in Sri Lanka, Malaya, Fiji, the Indian Ocean island of Mauritius, and South Africa also wanted Indian labor. But travel was hazardous. For example, in 1884 a family of low-caste landless laborers—Somerea, a fifty-year-old widow, her two sons, a daughter-in-law, and four grandchildren—facing starvation in Bihar state, boarded a sailing ship at Calcutta bound for the distant Fiji Islands in the South Pacific. After three months the ship reached the

islands, but 56 of the 497 passengers had died from cholera, dysentery, typhoid, and a shipwreck. Somerea's family apparently survived the journey.

Many merchants, moneylenders, and laborers flocked to British Burma, Singapore, Malaya, and East Africa. Between 1880 and 1930 a quarter million people a year left India. Few returned. Most Indian emigrants, including Somerea's family, were indentured, having signed contracts obligating them to work for a period of years (usually three to five) to repay their passage. Somerea's family probably worked on a sugar plantation. Indenture contracts stipulated the number of days per week (six) and hours per day (usually nine to ten) to be worked. With high mortality rates and unfavorable indenture terms, critics considered the system another form of slavery. Earning only a few pennies a day, many Indians could never pay off their contracts.

Indians now played key economic roles in many countries. Cities such as Nairobi in Kenya, Rangoon in Burma, and Port of Spain in Trinidad had large Indian neighborhoods, and Indian trade networks reached around the Indian Ocean and Pacific Rim. The future leader of the Indian nationalist movement, Mohandas Gandhi (**GAHN-dee**), experimented with nonviolent resistance to illegitimate power while working among Indians in South Africa. Today people of Indian ancestry comprise half or more of the Mauritius, Trinidad, Guyana, Suriname, and Fiji populations and substantial minorities in Sri Lanka, Malaysia, Singapore, Burma, Kenya, and South Africa. Although many Indian emigrants succeeded in business or the professions, the majority still labor on plantations growing cocoa, rubber, tea, or sugar.

Indian Thought, Literature, and Society

Indian intellectuals responded to British rule and ideas in several ways. A few, like Ram Mohan Roy, wanted to combine the best of East and West while reforming customs, such as banning widow remarriage, that they considered corruptions of Hinduism. Their influence waned after 1900. Another group, hostile to Western ways, sought to revive Hindu culture and emphasized the past's glories, arguing that India needed nothing from the West. Influential teacher Swami Vivekananda (**SWAH-me VIH-vee-keh-NAHN-da**) (1863–1902) wanted to end British cultural and political domination: "O India, this is your terrible danger. The spell of imitating the West is getting such a strong hold upon you. Be proud that thou art an Indian, and proudly proclaim: 'I am an Indian, every Indian is my brother.'"[11]

Also a reformer, Swami Vivekananda condemned untouchable oppression and the conditions of the poor. His writings and lectures fostered Indians' pride in their culture and helped spread Hindu thought to the West. Visiting New York in 1893, he formed the Vedanta Society, which promoted a philosophical Hinduism based on the ancient *Upanishads*. Vedanta portrayed the Hindu holy books, the Vedas, which were compiled over 2,500 years ago, as the supreme source of

---

[10]Dadabhai Naoroji and R.C. Dutt, quoted in Ainslee T. Embree, *India's Search for National Identity* (New York: Alfred A. Knopf, 1972), 48–49.

[11]Quoted in Clark D. Moore and David Eldridge, eds., *India Yesterday and Today* (New York: Bantam, 1970), 154–155.

RABINDRANATH TAGORE Tagore was a leading thinker and writer in British India who achieved international fame. This photo was taken around 1917.

religious knowledge, although not necessarily authored by either God or humans. Vedanta ideas contributed to another movement, Theosophy, that attracted some Western followers by blending Hindu notions with Western spiritualist and scientific ideas. Theosophy promoted the idea that India was more spiritual than other societies.

Like Hindus, Muslims had to rethink their values and prospects. Although Britain left many Muslim institutions untouched, Muslims resented Christian missionary activity that was supported by British officials critical of Islam. With European and Hindu values increasingly dominating India, some Muslims pursued Islamic knowledge in the Middle East, coming home with Islamic revivalist ideas; some opened schools. In the northwest frontier and Bengal, dogmatic Wahhabis (see Chapter 21) opposed to modernization clashed with other Muslims, Christians, Sikhs, and Hindus.

In contrast, Muslim modernists, led by cosmopolitan Sayyid Ahmad Khan (1817–1898), wanted Muslims to gain strength: "the more worldly progress we make, the more glory Islam gains." Believing that Islam was compatible with modern science, in 1877 he founded a college at Aligarh (**AL-ee-GAHR**) that offered Western learning within a Muslim context. Trained for government jobs, Aligarh students studied many subjects in English and learned how to play the British game of cricket. Many later studied at top British

universities. A satirist observed Aligarh's secular atmosphere, where leaders "neither believe in God, nor yet in prayer. They say they do, but it is plain to see, What they believe in is the powers that be."[12] Aligarh graduates dominated Muslim political activity in India until independence.

Indian literature took on a more nationalist flavor. The Tagore family, wealthy Hindus from Calcutta, worked to awaken national pride and expand literary expression. Hugely influential, Rabindranath Tagore (**RAH-bin-drah-NATH ta-GORE**) (1861–1941) was a poet, educator, patriot, and internationalist whose writings won him the Nobel Prize for literature in 1913 (see Witness to the Past: Challenging British Imperialism with Spiritual Virtues). Tagore sought a new and freer India, "where the mind is without fear and the head is held high; Where knowledge is free; where the clear stream of reason has not lost its way into the dreary desert sand of dead habit; Into that heaven of freedom, let my country awake."[13]

British policies also affected society, including the caste system. Historians debate whether the elaborate modern caste system existed for centuries as a continually changing part of Indian life or was shaped by colonial-era officials seeking to classify Indians for administrative and census purposes. Before colonialism, Hindus in Bengal, Punjab, and south India generally placed less emphasis on formal differences among varied castes. But British policies, sharpening caste identities, classified people largely through caste affiliations, making the system more rigid and favoring higher castes to win their support. As different Indians increasingly came into contact with one another, some sought firmer social boundaries by further dividing castes. Much of India became more caste conscious than ever before; upper castes stressed their uniqueness, and lower castes emulated the upper castes to improve their social status. Envying the highest caste, other castes adopted brahman rituals and ideas, such as vegetarianism. Hence, some untouchable leather workers joined an anticaste movement but, like brahmans, avoided eating meat. Higher castes, trying to preserve their privileged positions, demanded that lower castes be excluded from government jobs. Meanwhile, Hindu thinkers disagreed about the caste system. Some reformers called for abolishing caste, while defenders praised the system's ideals of conduct and morality.

Gender relations changed in British India. Traditionally women and men performed separate but interdependent roles within patriarchal households: men ploughed; women tended house and garden; and both did transplanting and weeding. But both men and women lost work as absentee landlords emphasized cash crops rather than food. Lower-caste men emulated upper castes, often forcing women into seclusion. But new opportunities also arose for women. More girls attended school, becoming teachers, nurses, midwives, and even doctors. By the 1870s women published biographies of their experiences and struggles. For centuries girls had been married early with little choice of husband. Now a small minority of urban "new women" led more

Theosophy A nineteenth-century North American and European movement that blended Hindu thought with Western spiritualist and scientific ideas.

[12]The quotes are in Francis Robinson, *The Cultural Atlas of the Islamic World Since 1500* (Oxford: Stonehenge, 1992), 148–149.

[13]From Rabindranath Tagore, *Gitanjali: A Collection of Indian Songs* (New York: Macmillan, 1973), 49–50.

WITNESS TO THE PAST

Challenging British Imperialism with Spiritual Virtues

On the last day of the nineteenth century Rabindranath Tagore wrote a poem in Bengali protesting the brutal imperialism of Britain's war against the Boers in South Africa, driven, Tagore believed, by British nationalism. The poem suggested that patient cultivation of India's "spiritual virtues" would become a force in the world after reckless Western imperialism, sparked by nationalism, had lost its control over humankind. He echoed the views of many Hindu nationalists and reformers that Hinduism and India had a special devotion to peace and spiritual insights that could benefit the Western world. For this poem and other influential writings, Tagore won the Noble Prize for literature in 1913.

The last sun of the century sets amidst the blood-red clouds of the West and the whirlwind of hatred.

The naked passion of self-love of Nations, in its drunken delirium of greed, is dancing to the clash of steel and the howling verses of vengeance.

The hungry self of the Nation shall burst in a violence of fury from its own shameless feeding, for it has made the world its food.

And licking it, crunching it, and swallowing it in big morsels, It swells and swells,

Till in the midst of its unholy feast descends the sudden shaft of heaven piercing its heart of grossness.

The crimson glow of light on the horizon is not the light of thy dawn of peace, my Motherland.

It is the glimmer of the funeral pyre burning to ashes the vast flesh—the self-love of the Nation—dead under its own excess.

The morning waits behind the patient dark of the East, Meek and silent.

Keep watch, India.

Bring your offerings of worship for that sacred sunrise.

Let the first hymn of its welcome sound in your voice and sing

"Come, Peace, thou daughter of God's own great suffering.

Come with thy treasure of contentment, the sword of fortitude, And meekness crowning thy forehead."

Be not ashamed, my brothers, to stand before the proud and the powerful, With your white robe of simpleness.

Let your crown be of humility, your freedom the freedom of the soul.

Build God's throne daily upon the ample barrenness of your poverty.

And know that what is huge is not great and pride is not everlasting.

THINKING ABOUT THE READING

1. How does Tagore perceive nationalism?
2. How does he believe India should respond to Western power?

Source: From *Sources of Indian Tradition*, Vol. 2, William Theodore de Bary, ed. Copyright © 1958 Columbia University Press. Reprinted with permission of the publisher.

---

independent lives, marrying later, in their twenties or thirties, or sometimes not at all.

Indian and British reformers sought to improve women's lives and foster greater gender equality. A controversial marriage law in 1872 provided for both civil and cross-caste marriage. Britain also tried incremental reforms, such as allowing widow remarriage and raising the age of female consent from ten to twelve. But although reformers often supported marriages based on love, they also encouraged wives to show husbands and children self-sacrificing devotion. Some women considered progress inadequate. For example, the reformer father of Pandita Ramabai (1858–1922) defied tradition by educating her and declining to marry her off as a child. She then promoted education, urging women to take control of their lives. Ramabai's knowledge of Sanskrit won her comparison to *Saraswati*, the Hindu goddess of wisdom, and Calcutta University proclaimed her a Pandita ("learned"). She married a lawyer of low-caste background, a shocking move for a brahman woman. When a court sentenced a child bride to prison for refusing to have conjugal relations with a much older husband, Ramabai protested what she considered slavery: "Our only wonder is that a defenseless woman…dared to raise her voice in the face of the powerful Hindu law, the mighty British government, the 129,000,000 [Indian] men, the 330,000,000 gods of the Hindus; all these have conspired to crush her into nothingness."[14] She then traveled to England, becoming a Christian. Upon returning, Ramabai opened a school for girls, especially child widows, and a refuge for female famine victims. The mission she founded remains active today, providing housing, education, vocational training, and medical services for widows, orphans, and the blind.

The Rise of Nationalism

British leaders viewed India as their empire's centerpiece, to be ruled into the far future, but their rule inevitably produced nationalist reactions. The Western idea of the "nation," an inclusive feeling among people living within the same state

---

[14]Quoted in Geraldine Forbes, *Women in Modern India* (New York: Cambridge University Press, 1996), 49.

(see Chapter 19), was new for Indians, who perceived themselves joined by a common Hindu or Muslim culture rather than a centralized state. By establishing political unity, educating Indians in European ideas, but then largely excluding Indians from administration, Britain fostered national feelings but also anticolonial bitterness. Furthermore, by 1900 six hundred Indian newspapers were reporting on world events such as Irish independence struggles, the Japanese defeat of Russia, and the U.S. conquest of the Philippines, all of which inspired Indians to oppose British rule. In 1885 nationalists formed the Indian National Congress, which worked for peaceful progress toward self-government. But the Congress, scorned by Britons, mostly attracted well-educated professionals and merchants, especially Bengalis. Constitutional reforms in 1909 brought limited representative government but no true legislative and financial power.

By 1907 radical nationalists led by former journalist Bal Gangadhar Tilak **(BAL GAGN-ga-DAR TEA-lak)** (1856–1920) had transformed the Congress from a gentleman's pressure group into an active independence movement. Tilak fiercely defended Hindu orthodoxy and custom; however, many Indians disliked Tilak and remained wary of the Congress. For their part, Muslims perceived the Hindu-dominated Congress, particularly Tilak, as anti-Muslim. As Hindu-Muslim tensions increased, the All-India Muslim League, founded in 1906, sought unity for Muslims scattered around the country. Hindus constituted 80 percent of Indians; Muslims were a majority only in eastern Bengal, Sind, north Punjab, and west of the Indus Valley. Influential Muslim reformer and educator Sayyid Ahmad Khan opposed potential Hindu majority rule, arguing that "it would be like a game of dice, in which one man has four dice and the other only one."[15] The Muslim League's first great victory came in 1909, when British reforms guaranteed some seats in representative councils to Muslims. Enraged, the Congress charged divide and rule. Hindu-Muslim rivalries complicated the nationalist movement throughout the twentieth century, eventually leading to separate Hindu- and Muslim-majority nations, India and Pakistan, in 1949.

MAKE SURE YOU UNDERSTAND THESE KEY POINTS BEFORE MOVING ON

- After 1857, the British monarchy ruled India through the British Raj, which built palatial buildings, a large railroad system, and an expanded English-language school system, thereby educating Indians about Western ideals such as nationalism and sowing the seeds for an Indian revolution against Britain.

- Britain stifled Indian industry by using India as a market for British industrial products, and it turned Indian peasants into tenants who had to grow cash crops for Britain rather than their own food, thus destroying the centuries-old village economy and exacerbating famine and poverty.

- The caste system became more rigid under British rule, with lower castes imitating upper castes, upper castes trying to strengthen their privileges, and women facing greater restrictions in some cases and expanded opportunity in others.

- As Indian nationalists began to unite in their opposition to the British, members of the Hindu majority formed the Indian National Congress in 1885, but it was opposed by many Muslims, who formed the All-India Muslim League in 1906.

Southeast Asia and Colonization

How did the Western nations expand their control of Southeast Asia?

Like Indians, Southeast Asians experienced colonization imposed by Western military force. During the 1800s Western challenges became more threatening, and by 1914 all the major Southeast Asian societies except Siam were under Western colonial control. Indonesia, Vietnam, and Burma, where the Dutch, French, and British, respectively, increased their power, and the Philippines, controlled by the United States in 1902, faced the most changes. Thus Southeast Asian societies became tied even more to the larger world but lost their political and economic independence.

Colonialism in Indonesia and Malaya

Holland expanded its power in the Indonesian archipelago. The Dutch East India Company already controlled the Spice Islands (Maluku) and Java, territories that provided great wealth. In 1799 the Dutch abolished the Company because of debts and corruption and replaced it with a formal colonial government largely focused on Java and Sumatra. In 1830 the **cultivation system**, an agricultural policy that forced farmers on Java to grow sugar on their rice land and allowed the government to pay peasants a low fixed price for sugar, even when world prices were high, enriched the Dutch but ultimately impoverished many peasants. A Dutch critic described the results: "If anyone should ask whether the man who grows the products receives a reward proportionate to the yields, the answer must be in the negative. The

cultivation system An agricultural policy imposed by the Dutch in Java that forced Javanese farmers to grow sugar on rice land.

[15]Quoted in John McLane, ed., *The Political Awakening of India* (Englewood Cliffs, NJ: Prentice-Hall, 1970), 46.

MAP 22.2 THE COLONIZATION OF SOUTHEAST ASIA Between 1800 and 1914 the European powers gradually conquered or gained control over the Southeast Asian societies that had not been colonized in the Early Modern Era. Only Siam remained independent. © 2015 Cengage Learning

Government compels him to grow on *his* land what pleases *it;* it punishes him when he sells the crop to anyone else but *it.*"[16] Dutch-owned plantations growing sugar and other cash crops replaced the cultivation system in the 1870s.

In the later 1800s the Dutch turned to gaining control, and exploiting the resources, of other Indonesian islands such as Borneo and Sulawesi, sometimes using violence to impose their rule and suppress resistance (see Map 22.2). For example, between 1906 and 1908 they crushed the small kingdoms on Bali, an island just east of Java. After valiant Balinese resistance failed, the royal family of the largest kingdom committed collective suicide by walking into Dutch guns rather than surrender, shaming the Dutch and depriving them of any sense of victory. Holland also united the thousands of scattered societies and

dozens of states of the archipelago into the Dutch East Indies. But the diverse colony, governed from Batavia (now Jakarta) on Java, promoted little common national feeling, making it difficult later to build an Indonesian nation with a shared identity.

Meanwhile the British became more active in Malaya, eventually subjugating the varied Malay states. Seeking a naval base, the British East India Company purchased Penang **(puh-NANG)** Island, off Malaya's northwest coast, from a cash-strapped sultan in 1786. In 1819 a visionary British East India Company agent, Jamaica-born Thomas Stamford Raffles (1781–1826), capitalized on local political unrest to acquire sparsely populated Singapore Island at the tip of the Malay Peninsula. A fine harbor and strategic location on the Straits of Melaka made Singapore a valuable base and a great

---

[16]Douwes Dekker, from Harry J. Benda and John A. Larkin, eds., *The World of Southeast Asia: Selected Historical Readings* (New York: Harper and Row, 1967), 127.

source of profit for British businessmen and government treasuries. Welcoming Chinese immigrants, it became the major Southeast Asian hub for both British and Chinese economic activity and networks, and by the 1860s it was mostly Chinese in population and the key crossroads of Southeast Asian commerce. After obtaining Melaka from the Dutch in 1824, Britain governed the three Malayan ports as one colony, the Straits Settlements.

Pressured by merchants, Britain soon extended its influence into the Malay states. Chinese immigrants in western Malaya contracted with Malay rulers to mine tin and gold, and Europe's growing demand for metals spurred British merchants to seek control of the mining. By the 1870s Britain, demanding order and security, threatened or forced Malay sultans to accept British advisers and then domination. Soon it achieved formal or informal control over nine sultanates, which, with the Straits Settlements, became British Malaya. The British also colonized the northern third of Borneo, creating the states of Sabah (British North Borneo) and Sarawak and imposing a protectorate over the Brunei sultanate. The historical Malay world of sultanates was now artificially divided between the British, Dutch, and Siamese.

British rule changed Malaya, encouraging pepper, tobacco, oil palm, and rubber planting on the west coast while attracting many Chinese and Indian immigrants. Malayan tin was used by Europeans and North Americans to make household utensils, tin cans, and barrels for food and oil storage. Malay villagers, pressured to plant rubber, lost their self-sufficiency. Britain maintained Malay sultans and aristocrats as symbolic and privileged local leaders, fostering a **plural society**, a medley of peoples—Malays, Chinese, and Indians—that mixed but did not blend. The different groups generally maintained their own cultures, religions, languages, and customs, confirming a Malay proverb: "raven with raven, sparrow with sparrow."

Vietnam and Burma: Colonization and Resistance

Vietnam fell to French colonialism after a bitter struggle. In 1771 three brothers from southern Vietnam launched the Tayson Rebellion. Social revolutionaries seeking a unified Vietnam and opposed to corruption and misrule, the Taysons fought against Vietnamese emperors and their French allies, using the slogan "seize the property of the rich and redistribute it to the poor."[17] In 1788 they defeated their foes and reestablished national unity, after which they sponsored economic expansion and rallied the people against Chinese invasion.

However, Tayson policies alienated some Vietnamese. In 1802, forces led by Nguyen Anh (**NEW-yin ahn**) (1761–1820) defeated the Taysons with French assistance and established a new imperial dynasty. But the Nguyen dynasty, unable to address social inequalities, proved unpopular. *The Tale of Kieu*, a 3,300-line poem still cherished by the Vietnamese, sympathetically portrays an intelligent, beautiful young woman, Kieu, who is forced by poverty to become a concubine and then a prostitute but maintains her sense of honor. Kieu symbolized the people mistreated by the upper-class Vietnamese and their French allies. Another critic was the outspoken, witty, sarcastic, and sometimes raunchy woman poet Ho Xuan Huong (**ho swan wan**), formerly a concubine to several high officials. Criticizing the imperial court and patriarchal Confucianism, she wrote freely about sex, championed women's rights, and attacked polygamy: "One wife gets quilts, the other wife must freeze. To share a husband … what a fate! I labor as a wageless maid."[18]

French Conquest

In 1858 the militarily powerful French, hoping to control the Mekong and Red River trade routes to China, began their arrogant "civilizing mission" to spread French culture and Christianity, launching bloody campaigns against determined but badly outgunned Vietnamese resistance. After first conquering the south, they moved north, facing opposition the whole way. Although victorious by 1884, the French faced prolonged, heroic resistance for another fifteen years from thousands of poorly armed rebels known as the **can vuong** (**kan voo-AHN**) ("aid-the-king"), who waged guerrilla warfare, just as their ancestors had against Chinese and Mongol invaders, often against hopeless odds. One of the rebel leaders rejected any compromise: "Please do not mention the word *surrender* any more. You cannot give any good counsel to a man who is determined to die." As a French witness admitted, the Vietnamese resisted fiercely: "We have had enormous difficulties in imposing our authority. Rebel bands disturb the country everywhere, appear from nowhere, arrive in large numbers, destroy everything, and then disappear into nowhere."[19] Rebels received food and shelter from local populations. In suppressing resistance, the French massacred thousands and executed surrendered or captured rebels. The can vuong rebels became powerful symbols of resistance for later generations of Vietnamese fighting colonialism and foreign invasion.

In 1887 France created the artificial Federation of Indochina, linking Vietnam, now divided into three separate colonies, with newly acquired Cambodia and Laos, all states with very different social, cultural, and political histories. While France maintained its rule by force, French commercial interests and settlers exploited natural resources and markets. The colonial regime destroyed the Vietnamese village's traditional autonomy, appointing leaders and raising taxes to finance administrative costs. Many peasants lost their land, or access to communal lands, to private landowners, investors,

plural society A medley of peoples who mix but do not blend, maintaining their own cultures, religions, languages, and customs.

can vuong ("aid-the-king") Rebel groups who waged guerrilla warfare for fifteen years against the French occupation of Vietnam.

---

[17]Quoted in Truong Buu Lam, *Resistance, Rebellion, Revolution: Popular Movements in Vietnamese History* (Singapore: Institute of Southeast Asian Studies, 1984), 11.

[18]From Huynh, *Anthology of Vietnamese Poems*, 214.

[19]The quotes are in Lamb, *Vietnam's Will to Live*, 229; Truong Buu Lam, *Patterns of Vietnamese Response to Foreign Intervention, 1858–1900*, Monograph Series No. 11, Southeast Asia Studies (New Haven, CT: Yale University Press, 1967), 8.

View of European shipping on the Saigon river, by T. Child, F. Beato and Charles E. Watkins, 1870s (albumen print)/Private Collection/Photo © Bonhams, London, UK/The Bridgeman Art Library

MARITIME TRADE IN FRENCH INDOCHINA Under French colonialism, Vietnam became more closely tied to the world economy. This photo from the 1870s shows European ships and warehouses on the Saigon River.

and rubber planters, mostly French. And although powerful French enterprises prospered, Indochina proved a financial burden for French taxpayers. Meanwhile, ruling through the traditional monarchies and aristocracies, France did little to promote economic development or improve living conditions in Cambodia and Laos.

As with French Indochina, Britain devoted decades to colonizing Burma and overcoming resistance. Aiming to expand its power in India, Britain coveted Burma's rich lands and contested Burmese claims to border regions. In three wars—1824–1826, 1851–1852, and 1885–1886—the British conquered Burma (today Myanmar), both sides suffering huge casualties. Vastly differing cultures and clashing strategic interests produced violent conflict, while the gradual loss of independence demoralized Burmans, the country's majority ethnic group. In losing territory, they felt an impending doom that they expressed in frenzied cultural activity, including drama, love poetry, and music. The court, fearing that the Burmese heritage might disappear if Britain triumphed, compiled *The Glass Palace Chronicle*, a history of Burma from earliest times.

Between 1853 and 1878 a new Burmese king, the idealistic Mindon, tried to salvage his country's prospects by pursuing modernization and seeking good relations with Britain. Mindon introduced steamships, promoted foreign trade, and tried to break down barriers between the court and the people. Worried he might succeed, the British tried to humiliate Mindon, and in 1886, their conquest complete, they exiled the royal family and abolished the aristocratic system. When some resisted colonial rule, the British, calling it "pacification," destroyed whole villages and executed rebel leaders. Burma became a province of British India, a humiliating fate. For the next fifty years Britain undermined Burmese Buddhism and cultural values, established Christian mission schools, and recruited non-Burman hill peoples into the government and army.

Siamese Modernization

Burma's traditional enemies, the Siamese (Thai), were the only Southeast Asians who maintained their independence. The vigorous new Bangkok-based Chakri dynasty ruled a strong Siam in the early 1800s. Seeing Burma's dilemma, able Chakri kings mounted a successful strategy to resist Western pressures. With Britain and France both coveting Siam but preoccupied with controlling Malaya, Burma, and Indochina, Siamese leaders had time to strengthen government institutions, improve economic infrastructure, cultivate a long-standing alliance with China, and broaden popular support. Farsighted Siamese kings, understanding changing Southeast Asian politics and rising Western power, promoted modernization, yielding to the West when necessary and consolidating what remained. They gave up claims to Laos and several Malay states. Siamese leaders also accepted commercial agreements opening the country to Western businesses. Recognizing Siamese determination and pressed by unrest in Burma and Indochina, Britain and France decided that conquering Siam would be too costly and left Siam as a buffer between Burma and Indochina.

Two kings and their advisers presided over Siam's policies. Scholarly, peace-loving Mongkut (**MAHN-kut**) (r. 1851–1868) had been a Buddhist monk and teacher who studied science and learned to read Latin. To discourage invasion, he signed treaties, often unfavorable for Siam, with Western powers, invited Western aid to modernize his kingdom, and hired Christian missionaries' wives to teach his wives and sons English. Mongkut's widely traveled son and successor, Chulalongkorn (**CHOO-lah-LONG-corn**) (r. 1868–1910), emphasized diplomacy and modernization, abolishing slavery, centralizing government services, strengthening the bureaucracy, establishing a Western-style government education system, and stimulating economic growth by encouraging Chinese immigration. Opening new land for rice production made Siam one of the world's leading rice exporters. Hence, Siam generally kept pace with its colonized neighbors in economic development, but under Siamese, not colonial, direction. When Chulalongkorn died in 1910, Siam (today Thailand) remained independent, avoiding political, cultural, and economic disaster under colonialism, and Western appetites for new colonies had waned.

The Philippines, Spain, and the United States

As in Latin America (see Chapter 19), hostility toward corrupt, repressive, economically stagnant Spanish rule simmered for decades in the Philippines. Many educated Filipinos of Spanish, indigenous, and mixed (mestizo) background resented colonial power, privileged immigrants from Spain, and Catholic Church domination. These anti-Spanish feelings were encouraged by the Chinese mestizo poet and novelist Jose Rizal (**ri-ZAHL**) (1861–1896), who lived for a time in Spain and Germany. Rizal's novels satirizing the government and church earned him official condemnation as a subversive heretic, and he was publicly executed for alleged treason in 1896. Rizal had earlier prophesied that "the day the Spanish inflict martyrdom [on me] farewell Spanish government."[20] Indeed, Rizal's death united varied opposition groups, turning nationalists toward revolution. One nationalist leader, Emilio Aguinaldo (**AH-gee-NAHL-doe**) (1870–1964), called on Filipinos to rebel: "Filipinos! Open your eyes! Lovers of their native land, rise up in arms, to proclaim their liberty and independence."[21] Women played active roles in the movement as soldiers, couriers, spies, and nurses. Gregoria de Jesus boasted that she "learned to ride,…shoot a rifle,…manipulate other weapons…sleep on the ground without tasting food…drink dirty water from mudholes."[22] Despite such heroic efforts, Spain contained the revolution by 1897, but it failed to crush scattered resistance.

The situation changed dramatically in 1898 when a U.S. fleet sailed into Manila Bay and destroyed the Spanish navy. Having engaged in occasional naval skirmishes in Southeast Asia throughout the 1800s, Americans now sought control of its resources and markets. The United States intervened in the Philippines as part of the Spanish-American War (see Chapter 20), the first of four ground wars it would fight in East and Southeast Asia over the next eight decades. The U.S. attack on Manila rejuvenated the revolutionaries led by Aguinaldo, who, receiving American support, soon controlled much of the country, declared independence, and established a semidemocratic republican government. But the factionalized leaders disagreed in their objectives, and Americans had other plans for the islands.

The U.S. decision to remain in the Philippines as a colonizer led Americans to suppress the nationalist revolution. U.S. president William McKinley, answering Rudyard Kipling's call to assume "the white man's burden", articulated Manifest Destiny, the notion that God supported U.S. expansion. Ignoring centuries of Filipino history and deep desire for independence, McKinley proclaimed: "It is our duty to uplift and civilize and Christianize and by God's Will do our very best by [the Filipinos]."[23]

But McKinley, admitting he could not locate the Philippines on a map, underestimated Filipino opposition to U.S. occupation. Some 125,000 American troops fought during the four-year Philippine-American War, during which over 5,000 Americans and 16,000 Filipinos died in battle. Another 200,000 Filipinos perished from famine and disease or in guarded compounds set up to keep villagers from helping the revolutionaries. Since Filipino soldiers often enjoyed active support from local people, Americans had to fight for every town. The elusive revolutionaries' guerrilla warfare demoralized American soldiers, who expected quick victory. While

[20]Quoted in David Joel Steinberg, *The Philippines: A Singular and Plural Place*, 3rd ed. (Boulder, CO: Westview, 1994), 64.

[21]Quoted in Teodoro A. Agoncillo, *A Short History of the Philippines* (New York: Mentor, 1969), 93.

[22]Quoted in Barbara Watson Andaya, "Gender, Warfare, and Patriotism in Southeast Asia and in the Philippine Revolution," in *The Philippine Revolution of 1896: Ordinary Lives in Extraordinary Times*, ed. Florintina Rodao and Felice Noelle Rodriguez (Quezon City: Ateneo de Manila Press, 2001), 11.

[23]Quoted in David Joel Steinberg et al., *In Search of Southeast Asia: A Modern History*, rev. ed. (Honolulu: University of Hawaii Press, 1987), 274.

Americans controlled towns, revolutionaries controlled the countryside. Both sides committed atrocities, including torture. Americans destroyed whole villages and looted Catholic churches, while Filipinos killed captured Americans. U.S. general Jacob Smith ordered his men to turn Samar Island into a "howling wilderness," to "kill and burn. The more you kill and burn the better you will please me."[24]

The war divided Americans. Supporters coveted Philippine resources and markets, and U.S. newspapers urged the slaughter of all Filipinos who resisted. But an organized protest movement opposed the war. In his rewriting of "The Battle Hymn of the Republic," the writer Mark Twain satirized American economic motives: "Mine eyes have seen the orgy of the launching of the Sword; He is searching out the hoardings where the strangers' wealth is stored; He hath loosed his fateful lightnings, and with woe and death has scored; His

lust is marching on." American critics also rejected imperialism: "We've taken up the white man's burden, of ebony and brown; Now will you tell us, Rudyard [Kipling], how we may put it down."[25]

By 1902, with revolutionaries defeated and many wealthy Filipinos supporting U.S. rule, the Philippines became an American colony. Americans reshaped the society of those they paternalistically called "our little brown brothers," establishing an elected legislature filled mostly by Filipinos. Unlike in most European colonies, the government fostered modern health care and education, producing many Filipinos fluent in English. But American rule ignored peasant needs while perpetuating Filipino landowners, who controlled millions of impoverished peasant tenants, and reinforcing the cash crop economy now linked to American economic needs.

MAKE SURE YOU UNDERSTAND THESE KEY POINTS BEFORE MOVING ON

- As the Dutch expanded their control over the Indonesian archipelago, they joined together vastly disparate cultures and disrupted the traditional economy.

- The British expanded control over the Malay Peninsula, which they used to supply raw materials such as tin and rubber, and Singapore, which became a key crossroads of Southeast Asian and India-China trade.

- After conquering Vietnam, the French faced fierce resistance from can vuong rebels, but they ultimately conquered the rebels and opened the country to exploitation by French commercial interests.

- As the British gradually conquered Burma, native Burmans attempted to preserve their culture, but after the British victory in 1886 the Burmese traditions were largely undermined.

- Siam (now Thailand) avoided colonization because of its fortunate geographical location and its farseeing leaders, who gave in to some Western demands and consolidated popular support.

The Reshaping of Southeast Asia

What were the major political, economic, and social consequences of colonialism in Southeast Asia?

Colonialism in Southeast Asia resembled that in India and Africa. Although some benefited, many others experienced worsening living conditions. A chant popular among Vietnamese peasants lamented the French seizure of resources: "Ill fortune, indeed, for power has been seized by the French invaders. It's criminal to set out the food tray and find that one has nothing but roots and greens to eat."[26] From a global perspective, colonialism linked Southeast Asia more firmly to a Western-dominated world economy. But colonial policies also affected political, social, intellectual, and cultural life. Like Indians, Southeast Asians responded to the challenges in creative ways.

Colonial Governments and Economies

Colonialism proved a shattering experience. The only colony with much self-government, the U.S.-ruled Philippines, had an elected legislature, but U.S. officials had to approve its decisions. Britain allowed some influential Malayans participation in local government and, in 1935, formed a Burmese legislature that included elected and appointed members. But France and Holland allowed little democracy. Colonialism often meant government by stodgy, autocratic European bureaucrats.

Colonial governments varied widely. As in sub-Saharan Africa (see Chapter 21), direct rule, which removed traditional

[24]Quoted in Daniel B. Schirmer, *Republic or Empire: American Resistance to the Philippine War* (Cambridge: Schenkman, 1972), 237.

[25]The quotes are in David Howard Bain, *Sitting in Darkness: Americans in the Philippines* (Baltimore: Penguin, 1986), 2; and Gary R. Hess, *Vietnam and United States: Origins and Legacy of War* (Boston: Twayne, 1990), 25.

[26]Quoted in Ngo Vinh Long, *Before the Revolution: The Vietnamese Peasants Under the French* (New York: Columbia University Press, 1991), v.

© Chronicle/Alamy

JAVA COFFEE PLANTATION This painting from the nineteenth century shows a European manager supervising barefoot laborers who are raking and drying coffee beans, a major Javanese cash crop.

leaders, such as Burmese kings, or made them symbolic only, as with the Vietnamese emperors, was used in Burma, the Philippines, and parts of Vietnam and Indonesia. Under indirect rule, mostly applied in Malaya, Cambodia, Laos, and some parts of Indonesia, colonialists governed districts through traditional leaders, such as Malay sultans or Javanese aristocrats, who frequently supported colonial rule. Colonial authorities played one ethnic group or one region off against another, creating problems that made national unity difficult after independence. As in Africa, colonial boundaries sometimes ignored traditional ethnic relationships and rivalries, fostering political instability. Countries such as Burma, Indonesia, and Laos were artificial creations rather than organic unities with culturally similar populations.

Colonialism transformed economic life. Since subsistence food farming could not produce enough revenues for colonial governments or investors, it was replaced by cash crop farming, plantations, and mines, which, along with banks and import-export companies, were mostly controlled by Western businessmen. Thus the colony's economy was tied more closely to

the colonizer. Under these conditions, Southeast Asia became one of the world's most valuable economic areas, with colonial taxation policies encouraging the cultivation of rubber, pepper, sugar, coffee, tea, opium, and palm oil; the cutting of timber; the mining of gold and tin; and the drilling for oil. Some key cash crops, such as rubber from Brazil and coffee from the Middle East, originated elsewhere. Many colonies became specialized monocultures emphasizing one or two major commodities—Malaya's rubber and tin, Vietnam's rubber and rice—but world prices fluctuated with unstable demand. These economic activities often harmed the natural environment, with forests cleared for plantations or logged for timber.

Rubber was a key crop. As the invention of bicycles and then automobiles opened markets for rubber tires, many now depended on rubber growing for their livelihood. Britain introduced rubber to Malaya, and it soon spread to Sumatra, Borneo, southern Thailand, Vietnam, and Cambodia, grown mostly on European-owned plantations. Malaya supplied over half the world's natural rubber by 1920. Plantation workers endured long hours, strict discipline, monotonous routine, and poor food, generally arising before dawn to tend rubber trees and trying to finish before the blazing tropical sun made hard physical work unhealthy. A Vietnamese writer described rubber estate workers: "every day one was worn down a bit more, cheeks sunken, eyes hollow. Everyone appeared almost dead."[27]

This economic growth benefited only a minority. Colonizers and the local officials and merchants cooperating with them gained wealth, and peasants on Java growing sugar and coffee initially earned new income. But costs rose faster than compensation, forcing peasants to grow more and work longer hours to earn the same profit as before. Peasants now depended on sugar or coffee profits for survival, but rising costs often impoverished them. They also faced disaster when world sugar and coffee prices declined and then, in the 1930s, collapsed altogether.

Social Change

As in India, colonial policies sparked rapid population growth, from perhaps 30 to 35 million people in 1800 to around 140 or 150 million by the late 1930s. Java experienced the greatest increases, from some 10 million in 1800 to 30 million by 1900 and 48 million by 1940, creating a burden for contemporary Indonesia. Dutch policies fostered better health care, people lived longer, and economic incentives encouraged larger families to provide more labor. However, women faced more hours working in the fields as well as increased expectations for bearing more children. Fast-growing populations, especially in Java, Vietnam, and the Philippines, resulted in smaller farm plots and more landless people.

Between 1800 and 1941 millions of Chinese and Indians immigrated to Southeast Asia to work as laborers, miners, planters, and merchants. The Chinese chiefly came from poor, overcrowded coastal provinces. Although some established businesses or joined relatives, many immigrated under indenture, a system that obligated them to work for years in mines, plantations, or enterprises. Chinese immigrants, mostly males, hoped to return to their native village wealthy and respected, but some remained poor, spending their lives as laborers, miners, or plantation workers. Many Chinese prospered as merchants, planters, and mine owners, often deciding to remain in Southeast Asia. Dominating retail trade, the Chinese became the commercial middle class, operating general stores, specialty shops, and restaurants in every town. Some cities, such as Kuala Lumpur (KWAW-luh loom-POOR) in Malaya, had largely Chinese populations. Since few unmarried women emigrated from China before World War I, many Chinese married local women or brought families from China, their descendants often adopting aspects of local culture and language. By adjusting to local conditions, the Chinese became a permanent presence in Southeast Asian life.

Indian immigrants had long come to Malaya as traders, craftsmen, and workers. Beginning in the 1880s, the British imported Tamils from southeast India to work on rubber plantations. Together Chinese and Indians eventually outnumbered Malays. Britain governed the various communities through their own leaders: Malay chiefs, Chinese merchants, and urban Indian traders. But this strategy separated and discouraged cooperation between the groups.

The changes particularly affected women, traditionally farmers, traders, and weavers. As men took up cash crop farming, women often had the increased workload of growing the family's food. With Chinese, Indian, and sometimes Arab men increasingly monopolizing small-scale trade, many women lost their role in the local marketplace and thus their status as family income earners. Women also lost their domination of weaving, spinning, and dyeing. Although this was hard work, even drudgery, women could weave at home with friends and relatives while caring for children. But after 1850, inexpensive factory-made textiles from Europe displaced local handwoven cloth, slowly forcing women out of the textile business. A Javanese noblewoman wrote in 1909 that "little by little [women] feel that their life is no longer of such value, considered by men only as ornaments as they are no longer contributing to the household coffers."[28] Women had to find other income sources that often took them away from home and children.

Influenced by European feminism, in the late nineteenth and early twentieth centuries some women joined movements asserting their rights. Hence, Siamese feminists opposed polygamy and supported girls' education. Today many Indonesians honor an inspirational Javanese woman, Raden Adjeng Kartini, whose writings and life influenced Indonesian feminism and nationalism (see Profile: Kartini, Indonesian Feminist and Teacher). Although she died young, the girls' schools she founded in 1900 multiplied. Like Kartini, other women struggled to cope with the changing world.

Southeast Asia already had large cities, but Western rule encouraged more rapid urbanization. Cities such as Manila, Jakarta, Rangoon (today Yangon), Singapore, Kuala Lumpur, and Saigon (today Ho Chi Minh City) grew as colonial capitals. Attracting migrants from nearby districts and immigrants, towns and cities offered diverse food stalls and restaurants and schools catering to different ethnic groups, as well as Muslim mosques, Christian churches, and Buddhist, Hindu, and Chinese temples. While most people maintained their own culture, some descendants of Chinese, Indian, and Arab immigrants assimilated into the surrounding society; friendships and even marriages crossed ethnic lines. For example, much of Thailand's political and economic elite has mixed Chinese-Siamese ancestry.

Cultural Change

Colonial governments differed in educating people and fostering indigenous cultures. Most colonies left education to Christian missions. Some Vietnamese, Indonesians, and

[27]Tran Tu Binh, *The Red Earth: A Vietnamese Memoir of Life on a Colonial Rubber Plantation*, translated by John Spragens, Jr. (Athens, OH: Center for International Studies, Ohio University, 1985), 26.
[28]Raden Ajoe Mangkoedimedjo, quoted in Norman Owen et al., *The Emergence of Modern Southeast Asia: A New History* (Honolulu: University of Hawaii Press, 2005), 197.

Kartini, Indonesian Feminist and Teacher

Inspirational social activist and teacher Raden Adjeng Kartini **(RAH-den AH-jeng KAR-teen-ee)** (1879–1905), usually known simply as Kartini, represented a feminist consciousness new to Indonesia while sharing the problems and facing the prejudices that Indonesian women encountered in the colonial system and their own societies. A Javanese aristocrat's daughter, she chafed against the confined lives of her social class, which expected young women to obey men, especially their fathers, without question, stay home, and train for marriage. However, Kartini's unusually liberal parents subscribed to Dutch-language newspapers, hired Dutch tutors for their sons and daughters, and then sent Kartini and her siblings to a Dutch-language primary school. Her brothers later moved on to a Dutch-language high school, and one even attended a university in Holland. A good student, Kartini keenly wanted to complete high school and study in Holland, but these experiences would have required her to leave home. Since Javanese customs discouraged aristocratic women from traveling without their families, her father would not permit it. Conforming to aristocratic custom, at puberty Kartini was restricted to the family's house and ordered to prepare for an arranged marriage by learning domestic skills.

But Kartini had larger ambitions. From her experience in Dutch school and friendships with Dutch women, she drew a model of personal freedom contrary to her Javanese society, including a commitment to educate women and give them more options in life. Eventually Kartini bowed to her parents' demands and entered an arranged marriage with a man she scarcely knew who already had two other wives; he agreed to support her plan to open a girls' school. Kartini sent a memorandum to the colonial government entitled "Educate the Javanese," and then, at twenty, she opened Indonesia's first girls' school, combining Javanese and Western values.

Kartini wrote fascinating letters to Dutch friends in Java and Holland that revealed much about her thinking. Her correspondents, often nonconformist career women with socialist leanings, known in Holland as "modern girls," encouraged Kartini's educational plans and thirst for knowledge. In 1899 she told a pen-friend, the radical feminist Stella Zeehandelaar: "I have been longing to make the acquaintance of a 'modern girl,' that proud independent girl who has all my sympathy." Mixing her Dutch friends' ideas with her own, Kartini's letters asserted women's right to education and freedom from polygamy and child marriage.

RADEN ADJENG KARTINI This painting, completed decades after Kartini's death, honors the young Javanese woman who founded girls' schools.

Courtesy, Photo Gallery, Indonesian Embassy, London

Like European feminists, in her letters Kartini criticized the constraints of marriage, family, and society, revealing serious doubts about the advantages of marriage in her own society: "But we must marry, must, must. Not to marry is the greatest sin which the Muslim women can commit. And marriage among us? Miserable is too feeble an expression for it. How can it be otherwise, when the laws have made everything for the man and nothing for the woman. When law and convention both are for the man; when everything is allowed to him." She thought women repressed: "The ideal Javanese girl is silent and expressionless as a wooden doll, speaking only when it is necessary." She also condemned religious prejudice, whether by Muslims or Christians: "We feel that the kernel of all religion is right living, and that all religion is good and beautiful. But, o ye peoples, what have you made of it?" But she had hope for change: "I glow with enthusiasm toward the new time which has come. My thoughts and sympathies are with my sisters who are struggling forward in the distant West."

Kartini died in childbirth at age twenty-five. Her Dutch friends later published Kartini's letters, ensuring her fame. Thanks partly to royalties from her published letters, the schools Kartini founded multiplied after her death, educating thousands of Indonesian girls in the twentieth century. But Kartini left a controversial legacy for Indonesians. Her schools filled a great need, for which many Indonesians are grateful. Although Kartini criticized Javanese culture and admired Western ideals, in 1964 the Indonesian president named her a national heroine and honored her as the nation's *ibu* ("mother"). But conservatives accused her of abandoning Islam and Javanese culture. Because of her close ties to Dutch friends, her detractors labeled Kartini an apologist for colonialism; some contrasted her unfavorably to Rahma El-Yunusiah, a devout Muslim woman from Sumatra who taught Arabic and the Quran and refused any contact with the Dutch. Nonetheless, today Kartini is honored as a proponent of Indonesian women's rights and a precursor of Indonesian nationalist sentiment.

THINKING ABOUT THE PROFILE

1. What does Kartini's life tell us about the challenges that faced Javanese women of her day?
2. How do Kartini's thoughts reflect the meeting of East and West?

Note: Quotations from Raden Adjeng Kartini, *Letters of a Javanese Princess*, edited with an introduction by Hildred Geertz (New York: W. W. Norton, 1964), 31, 34, 42, 45, 73.

Chinese and many hill peoples became Christian, but few Theravada Buddhists or Muslims abandoned their faiths. A few colonies established public schools, especially in the U.S.-ruled Philippines, which enrolled 75 percent of children in elementary schools. Independent Siam made public education widely available for both boys and girls. In contrast, French Indochina spent little public money on schools. However, some communities developed alternatives to Western education. Buddhist and Muslim groups expanded schools that taught from a non-Western perspective, while other schools mixed Eastern and Western ideas. Schools run by a mystical Javanese religious organization provided an alternative to both Islamic and Christian instruction, emphasizing Indonesian arts such as music and dance but also Western self-expression and social equality.

New cultural forms developed. Indonesian musicians mixed European string instruments with largely percussion Javanese gamelan orchestra rhythms, creating a romantic new popular music, *kronchong*. In the 1800s these sentimental songs were adopted by Indonesian sailors and soldiers, as well as by disreputable young men, known as kronchong crocodiles, who dressed flamboyantly, gambled, and drank heavily. By the early 1900s, however, kronchong had become respectable and it was eventually embraced by Indonesian nationalists as an anticolonial artistic weapon featuring topical and nationalist songs.

Cultural exchange was not one way. A few Western composers, observing performances by Javanese and Balinese gamelan orchestras, incorporated gamelan influences into their music. In most colonies, modern literature reflected alienation from colonialism and an awareness of rapid change. But since colonial regimes suppressed criticism, authors made their points indirectly to avoid censorship or arrest. Vietnamese writers used historical themes or critiques of Vietnamese society to discuss contemporary conditions, while Indonesian writers explored characters experiencing despair and disorientation because of the colonial system.

MAKE SURE YOU UNDERSTAND THESE KEY POINTS BEFORE MOVING ON

- Colonized Southeast Asian peoples were allowed very little autonomy and were frequently combined into countries with little ethnic or cultural unity.

- Economic life in colonies was reshaped to serve Western nations' needs for raw materials, especially rubber, and for markets for their goods, and in many cases this change led to destruction of the natural environment and the impoverishment of local people.

- Millions of Chinese immigrated to Southeast Asia, where many prospered as merchants and retailers, while Indians came to work in Malayan rubber plantations.

- Economic changes due to colonization forced women to grow food for their families and eliminated the market for their handmade textiles, thus taking away their traditional ability to earn an income.

- Education in colonies included both Western-style and more traditional schools, and cultural and artistic interchange between Westerners and colonized peoples produced new cultural forms, such as kronchong music.

aplia

CHAPTER SUMMARY

Change was more obvious than continuity in South and Southeast Asia. Gradually Britain extended its control over the Indian subcontinent, using military force but also outmaneuvering rivals, forging alliances, and intimidating small states into accepting British domination. By 1850 the British East India Company controlled all of India directly or indirectly. The Company introduced policies to reshape India's economy and culture, including a Westernizing education system. The rebellion of 1857, suppressed with great difficulty, shocked Britain into replacing the Company with colonial government rule. The new British Raj allowed little Indian participation in government. British policies transformed the Indian economy by favoring landlords at the expense of peasants and by suffocating traditional industries to benefit British manufactures. Population growth and poverty fostered emigration. The encounter with the West also prompted Indian thinkers to reassess their cultural traditions. Some Indians adopted Western influences, some rejected them, and others tried to mix East and West. Finally, unpopular British policies generated a nationalist movement that challenged British rule.

The European powers finished colonizing Southeast Asia. Using military force or threats, the Dutch became dominant throughout the Indonesian archipelago, reaping its wealth in part by compelling Javanese to grow cash crops. Britain gained control of Burma through warfare but needed less force in Malaya, which proved profitable as a source of minerals and cash crops. Against strong resistance the French occupied Vietnam, exploiting and reshaping rural Vietnamese society. The Americans displaced the Spanish as the colonial power in the Philippines after suppressing a nationalist revolution. While they maintained the cash crop economic system, they also fostered some political participation. Only Siam, led by perceptive kings, avoided colonization. Colonialism reshaped social patterns, undermining the economic activities of women, fostering urbanization, and promoting immigration of Chinese, who later became the commercial class. Southeast Asians responded by forming creative schools and unique cultural activities.

KEY TERMS

Marathas (p. 525)
Black Hole of Calcutta (p. 526)
sepoys (p. 527)
Westernization (p. 527)

Orientalism (p. 528)
zamindars (p. 530)
Theosophy (p. 533)
cultivation system (p. 535)

plural society (p. 537)
can vuong (p. 537)

23 East Asia and the Russian Empire Face New Challenges, 1750–1914

DEA/G. DAGLI ORTI/DeAgostini/Getty Images

TREATY BETWEEN JAPAN AND CHINA After an industrializing Japan defeated a declining China in a war over Japanese encroachments in Korea (1894–1895), diplomats from both nations met to negotiate a peace treaty. This painting shows the Chinese and Japanese representatives, easily identified by their different clothing styles, discussing the terms.

The sacred traditions of our ancestors have fallen into oblivion. Those who watch attentively the march of events feel a dark and wonderful presentiment. We are on the eve of an immense revolution. But will the impulse come from within or without?

—A Chinese official, 1846[1]

In 1820 Li Ruzhen (LEE ju-chen) (1763–1830) published a satiric novel boldly attacking Chinese social conditions. Set in the Tang dynasty, *Flowers in the Mirror* explored a sensitive topic only superficially discussed by male Chinese writers: relationships between the sexes. Li described a trip by three men to a country in which all the gender roles followed in China for centuries have been reversed, where men suffered ear piercing and footbinding pain, and endured hours every day putting on makeup, to please the women running the country. One of the men, Merchant Lin, is conscripted as a court "lady" by the female "king":

> *His [bound] feet lost much of their original shape. Blood and flesh were squeezed into a pulp, shrunk to a dainty size. With blood-red lipstick, and powder adorning his face, and jade and pearl adorning his coiffure and ears, Merchant Lin assumed a not unappealing appearance.*[2]

Li seemed an unlikely man to address so sympathetically women's daily challenges. A conventionally educated Confucian scholar who failed the civil service examinations, Li became a writer on language, political philosophy, mathematics, and astrology. But growing Western pressure to open China's borders to foreign trade, unchecked population growth, domestic unrest, political corruption, and growing opium addiction spurred Chinese scholars such as Li to reassess Chinese traditions, such as the social inequities that prevented women from participating in China's regeneration. Growing dissatisfaction, combined with Western intervention set the stage for the immense revolution that eventually transformed this ancient society.

Still powerful in the late 1700s, China in the 1800s experienced three military defeats, devastating rebellions, and increasing poverty. Eventually, revolutionary movements overthrew the imperial system. When Western ships forced Japan open in the 1850s, the old system fell, and Japan's new leaders launched an all-out modernization program to prevent Western domination. Meanwhile, Russia, perched on the borders of Europe, East Asia, and the Islamic Middle East and Central Asia, became Eurasia's largest territorial power.

[1]Quoted in Frederic Wakeman, Jr., *Strangers at the Gate: Social Disorder in South China, 1839–1861* (Berkeley: University of California Press, 1966), 126.
[2]Quoted in Jonathan D. Spence, *The Search for Modern China*, 2nd ed. (New York: W.W. Norton, 1999), 148.

The Zenith and Decline of Qing China

What were the causes and consequences of the Opium War?

Established by Manchus, the Qing **(ching)** (1644–1912) was the last dynasty in China's two-thousand-year-old imperial history. After reaching its zenith in the eighteenth century, Qing China experienced decay in the nineteenth as several catastrophic wars resulted in unequal treaties that increased Western penetration and fostered major rebellions. As China's economy changed, increasing poverty prompted millions to seek their fortunes abroad. Qing decline had as much to do with Europe's rise as with China's failures.

Qing China in an Imperial World

Eighteenth-century China, self-sufficient and self-centered, was one of the world's most powerful, prosperous, and technologically sophisticated societies. But the Manchus were more despotic than earlier Chinese rulers and forbade intermarriage with the Chinese. While the Chinese accepted Manchu rule, as they had tolerated alien rule in the past, they resented the ethnic discrimination. The Qing built a great empire, occupying predominantly Muslim Xinjiang **(shin-jee-yahng)**, a desert region west of China proper; conquering the Mongols; annexing Tibet; and adding the fertile island of Taiwan (Formosa), to which many Chinese migrated. This expansion stretched Qing military power and proved economically costly.

Yet the Qing generally maintained prosperity for nearly two centuries. New crops from the Americas, such as corn, sweet potatoes, and peanuts, increased food sources, while expanded cash cropping of cotton, tea, and American tobacco fostered growing concentration of land ownership. In 1830 China, with growing domestic trade, new textile factories, and increased copper mining, remained the world's largest commercial economy and produced a third of the world's manufacturing. Some historians see parallels with western Europe's economic development. Between 1700 and 1850 China's population nearly tripled, growing from 150 million to 432 million. Peasants responded to population pressure by farming marginal land and expanding their use of irrigation and fertilizer.

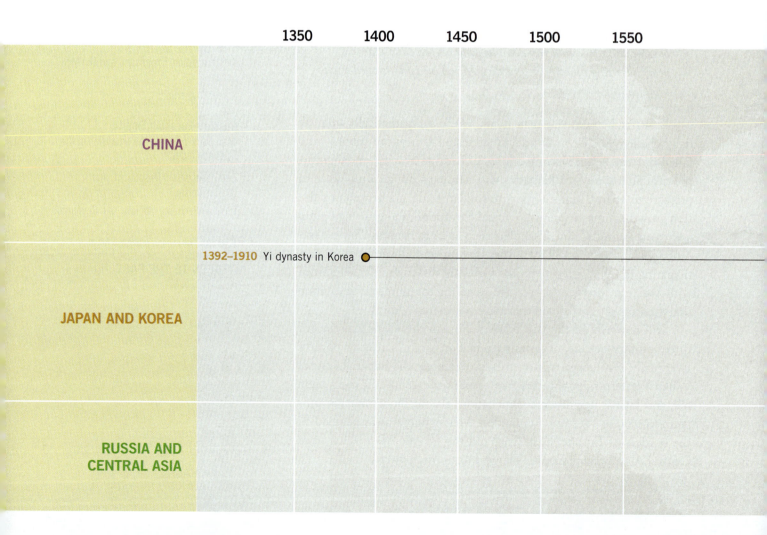

But population growth outstripped the growth of the food supply, straining resources and fostering corruption and Chinese resentment of the Qing government. Although in the 1700s living standards in more developed regions of China and western Europe were probably comparable, China's living standards deteriorated in the 1800s. As Chinese culture and society became more conservative, the Qing prohibited books and plays considered treasonable or subversive to traditional Chinese values. Some scholars, arguing that moral laxness caused dynastic collapses, applauded the crackdown. The Qing imposed harsher laws against homosexuality, which Chinese had generally tolerated, and increased social pressures on women to conform to gender expectations, such as by prohibiting widow remarriage. Imperial edicts emphasized Confucian moral virtues, heaping honor on filial sons, loyal officials, and faithful wives. Government-sponsored instructional books encouraged female obligations such as not laughing aloud, talking loudly, or swaying their skirts. Yet, women also read popular literature, such as the satirical novel *Flowers in a Mirror*. In a few central China villages, peasant women wrote their communications in a secret script, *nuxu* (**noo-shoe**), perhaps developed by and for women centuries earlier.

China's problems were caused by both internal decay and foreign pressure. Greedy officials took bribes to allow the smuggling and sale of narcotic drugs. Local rebellions against the Qing were suppressed at great cost. Meanwhile, European nations demanded more privileges, including freedom to travel inside China. Portugal gradually turned its base at Macao on the southern coast into a colony, and in the 1700s Dutch and English traders received permission to trade at the southern port of Guangzhou (**gwahng-jo**) (known to the British as Canton).

Eying profits, Chinese merchants in coastal cities often supported trade with Europeans. Some merchants specialized in **Chinoiserie** (**chin-WAH-zur-ee**), a Western vogue for Chinese ceramics, painting, lacquer ware, and decorative furniture whose quality Europeans could not duplicate. Western merchants and diplomats also commissioned Chinese artists to paint Chinese people, costumes, and city scenes using Western artistic techniques. In the early 1800s a merchant's guild, the **Co-hong**, had a monopoly on Guangzhou's trade with the West; its head, Howqua (**how-kwah**) (1769–1843), became one of the world's richest men, famous for his spectacular pleasure garden and lavish mansion, which employed five hundred servants.

Chinoiserie An eighteenth- and nineteenth-century Western vogue for Chinese painting, ceramics, lacquer ware, and decorative furniture.

Co-hong A nineteenth-century Chinese merchant's guild that had a monopoly on Guangzhou's trade with the West.

View of Canton, c.1800 (watercolour and gouache on paper), Chinese School, (19th century)/© Peabody Essex Museum, Salem, Massachusetts, USA/The Bridgeman Art Library

GUANGZHOU During the eighteenth century, the Western traders in China were restricted to one riverside district in Guangzhou (Canton), where they built their warehouses, businesses, and homes in European style.

Nevertheless, largely self-sufficient in food and resources and not needing foreign trade, Qing emperors refused to permit a more open trade system, restricting trade to a few ports such as Guangzhou and refusing diplomatic relations on an equal basis with the West. Knowing little of the Western world, the Chinese were confused by the diverse European nationalities. Moreover, viewing European merchants as barbarians bearing tribute, the Qing required visiting diplomats to perform the humiliating custom of prostrating themselves before the emperor. But the British, righteously believing that free trade would benefit China, sent a trade mission in 1793 requesting more access. The letter Emperor Qianlong **(chee-YEN-loong)** (r. 1736–1795) sent in response to King George III exemplified China's attitude toward foreign trade and the outside world. The emperor denied Britain permission to establish an embassy but commended the king for his respectful spirit of submission and humility in sending tribute: "Our dynasty's majestic virtue has penetrated into every country under heaven. Our celestial empire possesses all things in prolific abundance. It behooves you, O king, to display ever greater devotion and loyalty in the future, so that by perpetual submission to our throne, you may secure peace and prosperity for your country hereafter."[3]

Opium Trade and War

Half a century after Emperor Qianlong blithely dismissed the British request, two wars in the mid-1800s, in which Qing China suffered humiliating defeats, forcibly jarred the Chinese from their complacency, making clear that the world was

changing. Britain badly wanted more Chinese silk and tea, which were valued revenue sources for British merchants. But China, desiring little from the West, accepted only precious gold and silver bullion as payment. Between the 1760s and 1780s silver imports to China increased over 500 percent, presenting balance-of-payment problems for Western economies. Seeking a marketable product to alter this unfavorable trade disparity, the British turned to opium, an addictive drug grown in India and the Middle East.

The Chinese had used opium as a painkiller since the 1600s. By the later 1700s they smoked opium for pleasure by mixing it in a pipe with tobacco, and opium dens appeared where people could buy and use opium. The dreamy, relaxed experience produced by the drug temporarily relieved boredom, stress, physical pain, and depression, appealing to officials, wealthy women cooped up at home, busy clerks, anxious merchants, nervous soldiers, and overworked peasants. Highly addictive, it also produced severe withdrawal symptoms such as cramps and nausea.

The British grew opium as a cash crop in Bengal and soon found foreign markets around Asia. In fact, opium sales became an important revenue source for all European colonial governments in Southeast Asia. British and American traders, smuggling opium into China for huge profits, ignored the terrible moral and social consequences. Opium trading brought wealth and prominence to various British and American companies and families, helping support universities, schools, churches, and hospitals in cities such as Bristol (England) and Salem (Massachusetts). Between 1800 and 1838 opium imports increased sixfold, with 5 to 10 million Chinese becoming

---

[3]Quoted in Derk Bodde, *China's Cultural Tradition: What and Whither?* (New York: Holt, Rinehart and Winston, 1957), 62–63.

addicts. As the opium trade undermined Chinese society and impoverished families, one Chinese official concluded: "opium is nothing else but a flowing poison [which] utterly ruins the minds and morals of the people, a dreadful calamity."[4] Another argued that opium smokers should be strangled and the pushers and producers beheaded.

The emperor prohibited opium marketing, smuggling, and consumption, forcing British, American, and other Western traders to trade through the Co-hong merchant's guild in Guangzhou. But finding that officials could be bribed to overlook smuggling, the British doubled opium imports during the 1830s while also pressing for trading system reform. In response, the emperor appointed the mandarin Lin Zexu **(lin tsay-shoe)** (1785–1850) to go to Guangzhou and end the opium trade. Lin, an incorruptible Confucian moralist, wrote to Britain's Queen Victoria: "Suppose there were people from another country who carried opium for sale to England and seduced your people into buying and smoking it. Certainly you would be bitterly aroused."[5] But Chinese and British officials had very different mindsets about international relations and economic exchange. Lin's officials raided the Western settlement, seizing and destroying twenty thousand chests of opium worth millions of dollars.

In support of outraged Western traders, the British commenced what they called the Opium War (1839–1842). The British fleet raided up and down the Chinese coast, blockading and bombarding ports, including Guangzhou. The Chinese fought back, often resisting against hopeless odds, but they lacked the weapons to triumph. Europeans had now greatly surpassed once powerful China in naval and military technology. A few alarmed officials recognized Chinese military inadequacy. Lin Zexu wrote to a friend that China badly needed ships and guns like the British, but most officials rejected such ideas, remaining scornful of all things Western. Average Chinese reacted with rage. One placard in Canton in 1841 was addressed to "rebellious barbarian dogs. If we do not completely exterminate you we will not be manly Chinese able to support the sky over our heads. We are definitely going to kill you, cut your heads off, and burn your bodies in the trash."[6]

British preparations to assault a major Yangzi city, Nanjing, forced the Qing to negotiate for peace (see Map 23.1). In 1842 the Treaty of Nanjing, the first of a series of humiliatingly unequal treaties nibbling away at Chinese sovereignty, gave Britain permanent possession of Hong Kong, a sparsely populated coastal island downriver from Guangzhou; opened five ports to British trade; abolished the Co-hong and its trade monopoly; set fixed tariffs so China no longer controlled its economic policy; and gave the British **extraterritoriality**, or freedom from local laws. In addition, China was required to pay Britain's war costs. Soon other Western countries signed treaties with China giving them the same rights as Britain. Each successive treaty expanded foreign privileges. The Opium War became to the Chinese a permanent symbol of Western imperialism.

The Treaty System and Rebellion

The Opium War debacle soon sparked other wars, a treaty system opening China to the West, and rebellions. Britain remained dissatisfied with trade volume while China evaded its obligations, ensuring another conflict. When China imprisoned Chinese sailors for suspected piracy aboard a ship, *The Arrow*, registered in Hong Kong, Britain used the incident as a pretext to attack China, generating the Arrow War (1856–1860). France soon joined. Defeated again, China signed a new unequal treaty that opened more coastal and interior ports to Western traders, established foreign embassies in Beijing, and permitted Christian missionaries to enter interior China. Again forced to pay war costs, China fell deeper into debt. China had to abandon its claim to Vietnam, a longtime vassal state being colonized by France, and acquiesce in Russian takeover of eastern Siberia.

By restricting China's power to control its economy and make rules for Western residents, the treaty system deprived China of considerable autonomy. **International settlements**, zones in major Chinese port cities such as Guangzhou and Shanghai that were set aside for foreigners, restricted Chinese residence. Hence, a small riverfront island adjacent to downtown Guangzhou, accessible only by a footbridge, housed Western merchants, officials, and missionaries. Its mansions, warehouses, clubs, and churches served the largely British, American, and French population, with Chinese unwelcome except as servants and businessmen. However, some historians question the popular notion that signs in Shanghai's international settlement warning "no dogs or Chinese allowed" really existed.

The Opium and Arrow Wars and the treaty system forced the Chinese to debate responses. Some officials understood the need to learn from the West, examine Western books, build modern ships and guns, and study science, mathematics, and foreign languages. Provincial official and reformer Zeng Guofan **(zung gwoh-FAN)** (1811–1872) recommended making modern weapons and steamships. But, failing to see the magnitude of the challenges, few mandarins showed interest, one conservative rejecting Western knowledge as based largely on earlier Chinese discoveries.

While scholars debated, China's problems multiplied, especially in coastal provinces. To pay for wars, the Qing raised taxes, causing many peasants to lose their land; some turned to begging or banditry. Between 1800 and 1850 the Yellow River flooded twenty times and then changed course, wiping out hundreds of towns and villages. Meanwhile, Western cultural influence increased. American and British Christian missionaries opened most of China's

extraterritoriality Freedom from local laws for foreign subjects.

international settlements Special zones in major Chinese cities set aside for foreigners, where most Chinese were not allowed; arose as a result of China's defeat in the Opium and Arrow Wars.

[4]Chu Tsun, quoted in Hsin-Pao Chang, *Commissioner Lin and the Opium War* (New York: W.W. Norton, 1970), 89.
[5]Quoted in Mark Borthwick, *Pacific Century: The Emergence of Modern East Asia* (Boulder, CO: Westview Press, 1992), 97.
[6]Ssu-Yu Teng and John K. Fairbank, eds., *China's Response to the West: A Documentary Survey, 1839–1923* (New York: Atheneum, 1963), 26.

Western-type schools and hospitals, providing educational and health benefits to those with access to them. However, Christian missionaries—twenty-five hundred of them Americans by the 1920s—often lived well and were protected by Western military power, challenging Chinese religions and provoking negative opinions. Many Western residents, ethnocentric and proud of their "superior" Western civilization, mocked Chinese culture. For their part, the Chinese often distrusted the several hundred thousand Chinese Christians.

Deteriorating conditions eventually generated the Taiping Rebellion (1850–1864), the most critical of several midcentury upheavals against the Qing. Guangdong (**GWAHNG-dong**) province, on the southeast coast, experienced particularly severe social and economic dislocations, increasing popular unrest. Many peasant families, having no food surplus, were reduced to eating the chaff of the wheat. Economic insecurity,

famine, loss of faith in government, and a desire for social change fueled rebellion. The leader, Hong Xiuquan (**hoong shee-OH-chew-an**) (1813–1864), who failed the civil service examinations four times, had received confused visions in a trance. Later reading Christian tracts, he believed himself the younger brother of Jesus, appointed by God as the new Son of Heaven to exterminate evil. Impressed by Western military power but also proudly Chinese, Hong crafted a doctrine that blended Christianity and Chinese thought, a mixing of local and Western ideas typical in Asia and Africa as a response to Western disruption.

Hong promoted a new form of government, equal distribution of goods, communal property, and gender equality. The puritanical Hong prohibited opium use, polygamy, footbinding, prostitution, concubinage, and arranged marriages. He established the Taiping (Heavenly Kingdom of Great Peace)

MAP 23.1 **CONFLICTS IN QING CHINA, 1839–1870** During the mid-1800s Qing China experienced repeated unrest, including several major rebellions. The largest and most destructive, the Taiping Rebellion, engulfed a large part of southern and central China between 1850 and 1864. © 2015 Cengage Learning sect, rejecting Confucian traditions and promising a God-oriented utopia where all people were equal. Many Taiping men and women were, like Hong himself, Hakkas, a south China group with a distinctive dialect whose assertive women never bound their feet. Hong organized an army and in 1850 launched a rebellion, invoking Chinese nationalism: "We raise the army of righteousness to liberate the masses for the sake of China."[7] Soon he had attracted millions of poor and disaffected supporters.

Taiping armies conquered large parts of central and southern China, but they suffered from leadership conflicts, and their hostility to traditional Chinese culture cost them popular support. Conservative Confucians disliked their espousal of women's rights, which threatened the patriarchal family system, and intellectuals accused them of opening China to Westernization. Most of the educated elite rallied to the Qing and organized provincial armies. Westerners, while often sympathizing with the progressive Taiping social message, knew that a weak Manchu government made Western exploitation of China easier. Hence, various Western nations aided the Qing with money, arms, mercenary soldiers, and military advisers. The Taiping were defeated, and the conflict, which cost 20 million lives, left China devastated. An American missionary described

the destruction: "Ruined cities, desolated towns and heaps of rubble still mark their path. The hum of busy populations had ceased and weeds and jungle cover the land."[8] The Qing, now deeper in debt, were compelled to adopt even more conciliatory attitudes.

Economic Change and Emigration

China's encounters with the West generated economic changes. The extension of Western businesses into the interior stimulated the Chinese merchant class and small-scale Chinese-owned industries, such as match factories and flour mills, but merchants disliked Western economic domination and the weak government. Gradually a new working class formed in mines, factories, railways, and docks. The gulf between peasants and coastal merchants and workers was vast. Unequal treaties enabled Western economic penetration, with China's economy increasingly geared to Western needs. Westerners often operated government agencies, banks, railroads, factories, and mines, guarding them with Western police, and by 1920 foreign companies controlled most of China's iron ore, coal, railroads, and steamships. Western businessmen believed in a vast China market; one U.S. firm launched an advertising campaign to put a cigarette in the

Manufacture of Porcelain: Hand Modelling & Moulding (w/c and gouache on paper), Chinese School, (19th century)/© Peabody Essex Museum, Salem, Massachusetts, USA/The Bridgeman Art Library

MANUFACTURING PORCELAIN This nineteenth century painting shows Chinese artists and craftsmen making pottery and other objects, often for shipment abroad.

---

[7] Quoted in Jean Chesneaux et al., *China: From the Opium Wars to the 1911 Revolution* (New York: Pantheon, 1976), 123.

[8] S. Wells Williams, quoted in John A. Harrison, *China Since 1800* (New York: Harcourt, Brace and World, 1967), 42.

mouth of every Chinese man, woman, and child. Imported British textiles frequently displaced Chinese women from textile production. Although continuing to weave, women earned lower incomes than before.

Some scholars contend that Western economic imperialism spurred the growth of China's domestic economy, but others believe that Western competition ruined Chinese industries such as cotton spinning and iron and steel production, hurting China's ability to compete with the West. Western businesses enjoyed greater capital and support of Western governments and military power. At the same time, competition from other Asian countries diminished China's traditional exports. By 1900 India and Sri Lanka were the world's largest producers of tea and Japan of silk. The Qing had little money left for building economic institutions.

From the 1840s through 1920s, deteriorating economic, social, political, and environmental conditions in hard-hit southern coastal provinces prompted millions of Chinese to emigrate, usually to places where Western colonialism and capitalism were opening new economic opportunities. Several hundred thousand people a year left, usually for Southeast Asia but, in many cases, for Pacific islands such as Hawaii and Tahiti or for Australia, Peru, Cuba, North America, and South Africa (see Chapters 20 and 22). Chinese emigrants who joined or opened businesses in these new countries formed the basis for mostly urban middle-class Chinese communities. But many left China as part of the notorious "coolie trade"; Westerners called emigrant workers, whether Chinese or Indians, "coolies," a derogatory term. Under this labor system, desperate Chinese, recruited or coerced, became indentured workers in faraway places, signing contracts that required them to labor for years in harsh conditions on plantations, in mines, or in building railroads. Unmarried Chinese women began to emigrate in significant numbers only in the 1920s.

Thanks to this emigration, the societies where Chinese settled, especially in Southeast Asia, became more closely connected to China through economic and social networks. Chinese businesses overseas often had branches in China, and families in China maintained ties to relatives abroad. While some Chinese emigrants returned to their native villages with the wealth they earned, others never earned enough to return home, and many settled permanently abroad. Many emigrants and their descendants sustained Chinese culture and language, while others mixed Chinese and local customs. Today some 30 to 40 million people of Chinese ancestry live outside China, the large majority in Southeast Asia. Some finance businesses, industries, and educational institutions in China.

MAKE SURE YOU UNDERSTAND THESE KEY POINTS BEFORE MOVING ON

- In the eighteenth century, Qing China was still thriving on the strength of its agriculture, trade, and manufacturing, but its rapidly growing population began to intensify internal problems such as poverty and corruption.

- In the nineteenth century, China faced increasing problems as well as pressure from Westerners for greater trade opportunities, but the Qing refused to allow an open trading system, thus creating a severe trade imbalance between the West and the East.

- To solve this imbalance, the British began smuggling opium into China, and when China resisted the British defeated China in the Opium War and forced the Chinese to agree to highly unfavorable terms that allowed the British to trade in China.

- After another war, China was forced to set aside special areas exclusively for Westerners, called international settlements, and to also allow Christian missionaries into the country.

- Economic insecurity, famine, and Western interference eventually led to the Taiping Rebellion, a widespread and devastating revolt that was ultimately put down by the Qing with help from Western powers.

aplia

From Imperial to Republican China

Why did Chinese efforts at modernization fail?

Rebellions, government stagnation, poverty, and growing Western demands generated a crisis for the Qing. Some Chinese still concluded that China should reaffirm traditional ways, rejecting the West. But a growing number of reformers wanted to adapt useful Western technologies to Chinese ways. As setbacks mounted, some gave up on reform and organized revolutionary movements. Eventually revolutionaries overthrew the imperial system, but they could not solve China's problems.

Chinese Debates and New Challenges

China's elite divided over whether China should modernize. Conservatives dominating the bureaucracy advised holding fast to Confucian traditions, opposing railroads, underground mines, and other innovations that disrupted harmony between humanity and nature and put boatmen and cart drivers out of work. One conservative wrote it was "better to see the nation die than its way of life change."[9] Conservatives believed that the new technologies undermined social, economic, and even political values. Liberals, believing China had to adopt certain Western ideas to survive, streamlined central and regional governments, set up a foreign ministry, formed a college to train diplomats, and sent some students to schools in the West, especially the United States. Some argued that Confucius favored democracy and gender equality. Few liberals, however, wanted radical transformation, preferring to graft on some technological innovations. To most reformers, Western ideas such as political democracy and nationalism were not easily adapted to China's family-centered society. As one noted, "China should acquire the West's superiority in arms and machinery, but retain China's superiority in Confucian virtue."[10]

Reformers in the provinces, calling themselves "self-strengtheners," aimed to strengthen China by building arsenals and shipyards. By 1894 China had a better-trained army and sixty-five warships, but it was still insufficient against a fully industrialized enemy. Reforms failed to save the Qing because technological innovations generated new problems. New warships required coal to make steam power, which required improved coal-mining technology. Moving coal necessitated building railroads, which needed telegraphs to communicate train movements. Training workers for these new enterprises required technical schools. Furthermore, the new working class did not fit into the Confucian social categories of scholars, peasants, artisans, and merchants. Although Western advisers helped set up and run new industries and government departments, the new enterprises were often poorly run. Costly innovations further complicated the problems of a Chinese government financing a growing debt to Western nations and banks.

China's problems grew less manageable. China was too large, overpopulated, and saddled with a poorly led, bureaucratic, and overly conservative government. From 1861 to 1908 Empress Dowager Ci Xi (**zoo shee**) (1835–1908), the old emperor's concubine who became the regent of the new child emperor, dominated the imperial government. Forceful, and intelligent but also covetous, irresponsible, strong-willed and, like many at court, an opium smoker, she diverted money for building a modern navy to construct the magnificent Summer Palace, just outside Beijing, for her personal retreat. China's inability to deflect growing challenges fostered escapism among many thoughtful Chinese, expressed by a poet official: "I'll drink myself merry, Thrash out a wild song from my lute, And let the storms rage at will."[11]

Foreign economic and political pressures also placed constraints on what China could accomplish, fostering a siege mentality. By the late 1800s Western gunboats patrolled China's rivers, international settlements existed in major cities, Christian missionaries challenged Chinese values, and Westerners influenced the imperial government and economy. Some foreign powers dominated particular regions as spheres of influence, such as Britain in Guangdong and Germany in Shandong, acquiring resources, establishing enterprises, and manipulating local governments.

The United States, Britain, France, and Germany exercised power through **gunboat diplomacy**, the use of superior firepower to impose a foreign country's will on local populations and governments. Western gunboats patrolled some rivers and seacoasts in the late 1800s and early 1900s, protecting Western businessmen, missionaries, and diplomats whose activities generated Chinese hostility. Ignoring sovereign Chinese rights and outrage at foreign intrusion, a notorious U.S. naval force, the Yangzi Patrol, comprising shallow-draft gunboats, destroyers, and cruisers, patrolled hundreds of miles of the Yangzi River "to make every American feel perfectly safe in coming to live or to transact business, until such time as the Chinese themselves are able to afford these guarantees."[12] Americans also promoted free trade, generously funded Christian missionaries, and donated to humanitarian causes such as flood relief and orphanages. Yet China never became a full Western colony such as India or Vietnam, perhaps because too many foreign powers were involved. The United States promoted an "Open Door" policy that allowed equal access by all the foreign powers to China's vast markets and resources, enabling industrialized nations to avoid conflict and acquire wealth without the high political and military costs of conquering and governing China.

Wars, Reforms, and Nationalism

Growing foreign challenges soon included rapidly industrializing Japan. Seeking resources and markets, in the 1890s Japan intervened in Korea. A long-time vassal state, Koreans pleaded for help from China. The resulting Sino-Japanese War (1894–1895) ended in humiliating defeat with China forced to pay Japan an indemnity and recognize Korean independence; in 1910 Korea became a Japanese colony. The Qing, having been forced to cede to Japan the large island of Taiwan, populated largely by Chinese, had already lost influence over other tributary states, such as Vietnam (to France), Burma (to Britain), and the Ryukyu (**ree-OO-kyoo**) islands (to Japan). The defeat by Japan damaged Chinese pride and the Qing rulers' credibility.

A group of progressive reformers began advising the young Manchu emperor, Guangxu, and in 1898 he called for dramatic changes, later known as the 100 Days of Reform, that included economic modernization. But the Empress Dowager Xi Ci and her conservative allies blocked the proposals, arrested the reformers, placed the emperor under house arrest, promoted an antiforeign atmosphere, and encouraged Chinese to organize antiforeign militias. The ensuing tensions sparked the

gunboat diplomacy The Western countries' use of superior firepower to impose their will on local populations and governments in the nineteenth century.

[9]Hsu Tung, quoted in Joseph R. Levenson, *Confucian China and Its Modern Fate: A Trilogy* (Berkeley: University of California Press, 1968), 105.
[10]Quoted in Earl Swisher, "Chinese Intellectuals and the Western Impact, 1838–1900," *Comparative Studies in Society and History* 1 (October 1958): 35.
[11]Wang Pengyun, from Cyril Birch, ed., *Anthology of Chinese Literature* (New York: Grove Press, 1972), 294.
[12]Quoted in Lloyd Gardner, *Safe for Democracy: The Anglo-American Response to Revolution, 1913–1923* (New York: Oxford University Press, 1984), 318.

Library of Congress Prints and Photographs Division [LC-US262-5972]

SUN YAT SEN The main founder of the Chinese nationalist movement, Sun challenged the Qing government and formulated the ideology of the Chinese republic.

Boxer Rebellion, a Qing-backed popular movement in 1900 to drive foreigners out of China. While the Boxers ("Righteous Harmony Fists"), a predominantly peasant, anti-Western, anti-Christian secret society, attacked foreigners in north China, occupied Beijing, and besieged the foreign embassies, the Qing declared war on the foreign powers. But the British, Americans, and French organized an international force that routed the Boxers, occupied Beijing, and forced the Qing to pay another huge indemnity and permit foreign military forces in China. Europeans talked openly of dismantling China; Russians used the rebellion to occupy Manchuria.

The defeats generated frantic efforts at reform and modernization. Fearing China might soon be divided into colonies, the chastened Qing looked to Japan for models, abolished the two-thousand-year-old Confucian examination system, allocated more money to the military, strengthened provincial governments and former provincial and national assemblies (which met in 1909–1910), sent ten thousand students to Japan, and established modern Western-style schools. But the fifty-seven thousand state schools enrolled only a fraction of China's school-age children, and Manchus still monopolized decision making.

Reformist ideas also sparked movements among women. Some women studying in Japan formed the Encompassing Love

Society, which sought to make Chinese women full participants in society. Other women worked to raise female literacy and expand economic opportunities. Later executed as a revolutionary, feminist Qin Jin **(chin jin)** (1877–1907) left her arranged marriage for study in Japan and then started a women's magazine and pursued political activity. She wrote in a poem, "Our women's world is sunk so deep, who can help us? Unbinding my feet I clear out a thousand years of poison."[13] She hoped China would one day see free women "blooming like fields of flowers."

Gradually liberals who criticized Qing reforms as too slow became more influential. Many reformers familiar with European literature and scholarship were deeply impressed by Japan's modernization. The leading liberal, scholar and journalist Liang Qichao **(Li-ANG chi-CHAO)** (1871–1929), promoted modernization that blended Confucian values and Western learning. He supported industrialization, constitutional government, and a focus on the nation instead of culture. Liang's colleague, Kang Youwei **(KANG yoo-WAY)** (1858–1928), envisioned a world government, a welfare state, and the end of nationalist strife and gender discrimination. He also campaigned against footbinding, the longtime practice that severely hampered women, as expressed by a song passed among illiterate women: "Your body is so heavy a burden for your feet that you fear you may stumble in the wind."[14]

For some Chinese nationalists, most importantly Sun Zhong Shan (1866–1925), better known as Sun Yat-sen **(soon yot-SEN)**, the Boxer Rebellion fiasco showed the futility of reform from above, prompting them to organize revolution from below. Unlike liberal reformers Liang and Kang, Sun did not come from an upper-class mandarin background. Having no commitment to the traditional system, he identified with the poor and downtrodden, calling himself a coolie's son. Born near Guangzhou to a peasant family that supported the Taipings, at age thirteen Sun joined an elder brother in Hawaii, where he studied in an Anglican high school and became a semi-Christian. After later receiving a medical degree in British-ruled Hong Kong, he dressed in Western clothes and visited England, where he learned that Westerners often criticized their governments.

Convinced the Qing system was hopeless, Sun devoted his life to politics and became the Chinese Revolution's chief architect. In 1895 he founded a secret society dedicated to replacing the imperial system with a Western-style republic, and branches of the society were formed in China, Japan, and Hawaii (see Witness to the Past: Planning a Revolutionary New China). Facing arrest in China for treason, Sun traveled extensively, recruiting support among Chinese merchants in Southeast Asia, North America, and the treaty ports; among Chinese students in Japan; and among sympathetic military officers. Sun and his followers considered themselves nationalists, more interested in China as a nation than as a culture.

Sun began developing his program, the "Three Principles of the People." The first principle, nationalism, involved overthrowing the Qing, restoring ethnic Chinese to power, and reclaiming China's historical greatness. His second principle, republicanism, proposed constitutional democracy with

[13]Quoted in Jonathan D. Spence, *The Gate of Heavenly Peace: The Chinese and Their Revolution, 1895–1980* (New York: Viking, 1981), 52.

[14]Quoted in Ono Kazuko, *Chinese Women in a Century of Revolution* (Stanford, CA: Stanford University Press, 1989), 30.

WITNESS TO THE PAST

Planning a Revolutionary New China

In 1905 various radical Chinese groups, meeting in Japan, merged into one revolutionary organization, the Tongmen Hui *(Chinese Alliance Association), that was led by Sun Yat-sen and based in Tokyo. Most members were drawn from the ten thousand Chinese students enrolled in Japanese universities. Unhappy with the Qing and impressed by modernizing Japan, they sought to change China through revolution. In their founding proclamation, influenced by Western thought, they set out their agenda, visionary but vague, for a three-stage passage from military to constitutional government and a more equitable society.*

Since the beginning of China as a nation, we Chinese have governed our own country despite occasional interruptions. When China was occasionally occupied by a foreign race, our ancestors could always...drive these foreigners out...and preserve China for future generations....There is a difference, however, between our revolution and the revolutions of our ancestors. The purpose of past revolutions...was to restore China to the Chinese, and nothing else. We, on the other hand, strive not only to expel the ruling aliens [Manchus]...but also to change basically the political and economic structure....The revolutions of yesterday were revolutions by and for the heroes; our revolution, on the other hand, is a revolution by and for the people....everyone who believes in the principles of liberty, equality, and fraternity has an obligation to participate in it....

At this juncture we wish to express candidly and fully how to make our revolution today and how to govern the country tomorrow.

1. Expulsion of the Manchus from China....We shall quickly overthrow the Manchu government so as to restore the sovereignty of China to the Chinese.
2. Restoration of China to the Chinese. China belongs to the Chinese who have the right to govern themselves....
3. Establishment of a Republic. Since one of the principles of our revolution is equality, we intend to establish

a republic....all citizens will have the right to participate in the government, the president of the republic will be elected by the people, and the parliament will have deputies elected by and responsible to their respective constituencies....

4. Equalization of land ownership. The social and economic structure of China must be so reconstructed that the fruits of labor will be shared by all Chinese on an equal basis....

To attain the four goals..., we propose a procedure of three stages. The first...is that of military rule...[in which] the Military Government, in cooperation with the people, will eradicate all the abuses of the past; with the arrival of the second stage the Military Government will hand over local administration to the people while reserving for itself the right of jurisdiction over all matters that concern the nation as a whole; during the...final stage the Military Government will cease to exist and all governmental power will be invested in organs as prescribed in a national constitution. This orderly procedure is necessary because our people need time to acquaint themselves with the idea of liberty and equality..., the basis on which the republic of China rests....On...restoring China to her own people, we urge everyone to step forward and to do the best he can....Whatever our station in society is, rich or poor, we are all equal in our determination to safeguard the security of China as a nation and to preserve the Chinese people.

THINKING ABOUT THE READING

1. How does the proclamation use Western revolutionary and nationalist ideas?
2. How will revolution build a new China?

Source: Pei-Kai Cheng and Michael Lestz with Jonathan D. Spence, eds., The Search for Modern China: A Documentary Collection *(New York: W.W. Norton, 1999), 202–206.*

---

elected representative government, rather than the constitutional monarchy liberal reformers sought. The third principle, people's livelihood, envisioned an equitable economic status for all. Vague on details, Sun favored partial state control of the economy and the reshaping of China into a modern, wealthy, powerful nation. He did not support imitating Europe and the United States, but eventually, he hoped, the Chinese could look over their shoulders and find the West lagging far behind.

Chinese Revolution and Republic

Sun was raising money in the United States when, on October 10, 1911, some followers began the uprising. Soldiers in a Yangzi River city, Wuhan (**WOO-HAHN**), mutinied and

were soon joined by sympathizers in other cities. Within two months revolutionary soldiers controlled provinces in central and southern China. As Qing authority crumbled outside the north, Sun returned to China for the first time in sixteen years. With wide popular support, his nationalist message spread rapidly, especially among students, military officers, and Chinese in the treaty ports. Reorganizing his anti-Manchu secret society into a political party, the Guomindang (**gwo-min-dong**) (Chinese Nationalist Party), Sun gathered varied nationalists and liberal reformers. However, the revolutionaries agreed only on opposing the Qing, and Sun was not a forceful leader. When the Qing asked an ambitious general, Yuan Shikai (**yoo-AHN shee-KAI**) (1859–1916), to crush the revolutionaries, Yuan, in control of a large army, decided to replace the dynasty with his own rule by playing the Manchus off against the revolutionaries.

Two centers of power now existed. General Yuan held power in the north and influence over Qing leaders in Beijing, while the revolutionaries, controlling the Yangzi Valley and parts of south China, made plans for a provisional government. Seeking compromise to save China from civil war, Sun made Yuan president for arranging the five-year-old Qing emperor's abdication. In February 1912 the Qing dynasty and the two-thousand-year-old imperial system ended, and a republic was established in Nanjing. Symbolizing a change of direction, the new government adopted the Western calendar. But Sun underestimated Yuan's ambitions. Hoping to restore and lead an autocratic system, Yuan moved the capital back to Beijing.

During the first year, the republic's leaders established liberal institutions, including a constitution written by Sun providing for a two-chamber parliament and a president. In 1913, in China's first general election, a restricted electorate chose a national assembly and provincial assemblies, while a new women's suffrage movement, influenced by European feminists, pressed for equal rights for women. But although Sun's Guomindang won a majority of seats, it lacked consensus about the directions of change. The republican system failed to bring stability and liberty, dashing Sun's hopes. Convinced that China needed a strong leader, Yuan had Guomindang leaders assassinated, bought off, or, like Sun, forced into exile. Supported by much of the army, the imperial bureaucracy,

and foreign powers, who preferred a strongman to democratic uncertainties, Yuan outlawed the Guomindang, suspended parliament, and banned the women's suffrage movement. Sun and his closest followers moved to Japan, embittered and demoralized. Increasingly autocratic, Yuan announced plans to found a new dynasty.

Financial problems, constant pressure from foreign powers, and secession of regions occupied largely by non-Chinese delayed Yuan's plans. Moreover, growing nationalism made concessions to foreign powers unpopular. With China bankrupt, Yuan was forced to borrow heavily from foreign governments to keep the country afloat. In 1911 much of Mongolia declared independence and later became allied with Russia, while Tibet expelled the Chinese administration. Although China remained neutral during World War I, Japan, allied with Britain, occupied Germany's sphere of influence in the Shandong peninsula. In 1915 Japan presented Yuan with 21 Demands, including control of Shandong, more rights in Manchuria, and Japanese advisers to China's government. The 21 Demands sparked huge Chinese protests and boycotts against Japan and against Yuan for his inability to protect China's interests. His imperial restoration plans aborted, a humiliated Yuan died in 1916. Yuan's years in power had wrecked republican institutions, and his submission to Japan's 21 Demands suggested that China was even weaker than before. After Yuan's death, China fell into the abyss of prolonged civil war.

MAKE SURE YOU UNDERSTAND THESE KEY POINTS BEFORE MOVING ON

- In the debate over what China should do next, conservatives thought China should stick to its traditions, while liberals tried to modernize China, but their reforms failed to bring it to the technological and military level of the West.

- Sun Yat-sen, born to Chinese peasants but educated in Western schools, formed a secret society devoted to replacing imperial rule with a Western-style republic and set out three principles: nationalism, republicanism, and economic equality.

- A revolution inspired by Sun Yat-sen succeeded in toppling the Qing dynasty with the assistance of General Yuan Shikai.

- Yuan seized power after Sun Yat-sen's party won the republic's first election, but he was weakened by Japanese encroachment and the loss of influence over areas such as Mongolia and Tibet, and after his death China entered a period of civil war.

aplia

The Remaking of Japan and Korea

How did the Meiji government transform Japan and Korea?

In the later nineteenth century Japan met Western challenges more successfully than China and rapidly transformed itself into a powerful industrialized nation.. When the first Western ships demanded to open Japan, the Japanese were as far behind the West in military and industrial technology as other Asian societies. Yet, despite serious internal problems, Japan possessed significant strengths, and its response was radically different from China's; it avoided colonialism and became the only non-Western nation to successfully industrialize before World War II. Tokugawa shoguns, or military dictators, had

governed Japan since 1600, tightly controlling the country. A revolution ended Tokugawa rule and created a new government whose dramatic reforms helped Japan resist the West. Across the straits, Korea also faced severe challenges, eventually becoming a Japanese colony.

Late Tokugawa Japan

While China gradually lost some of its autonomy, Japan successfully met the challenge of Western intrusion, thanks partly to differences between these two ancient neighbors. Living in a geographically compact and linguistically homogeneous country, the Japanese shared a strong loyalty to the emperor as a national symbol, whereas China's vastness meant that loyalties were restricted largely to the family. The Chinese slowly assimilated or modified foreign ideas, such as Buddhism, whereas the Japanese readily borrowed from outside. Hence, Japanese leaders could more easily decide to import and adopt new ideas, technologies, and institutions.

The two neighbors also had different economic, political, and military systems. Japan's assertive merchant class rapidly expanded its scope and power, whereas China's government restricted commercial energies. Unlike in China's centralized empire, Tokugawa shoguns, based in Edo (today's Tokyo), had to balance the interests of regional landowning families while keeping the Kyoto-based emperor powerless. Although the samurai had lost their fighting edge, they still held a respected and influential position. Never successfully invaded, the Japanese felt vulnerable when encountering well-armed Westerners. Unlike the Chinese, Japanese leaders prized political independence far more than cultural purity, and hence, informed by Dutch traders of Western capabilities, were far more sensitive to the threat than China's elite.

Japan also benefited from openness to new ideas. Its many schools fostered high literacy rates, and it acquired Western knowledge from Dutch traders that included sciences such as medicine, physics, and chemistry. One reformer argued that "Dutch [Western] learning is not perfect, but if we choose the good points, what harm could come? What is more ridiculous than to refuse to discuss its merits?"[15] Although women generally suffered a low status, some gained an education. Poet and painter Ema Saiko (1787–1861) compared her reading with her father's: "My father deciphers Dutch books; His daughter reads Chinese poetry. Divided by a single lamp, We each follow our own course."[16]

Japanese also valued hard work, thrift, saving, and cooperation—attributes that facilitated modernization. Cities such as Edo and Osaka, already among the world's largest, offered flourishing commerce and diverse entertainments. A carnival in Edo in 1865 included many amusements, services, and vendors: kabuki theater, archery booths, fortune tellers, wandering balladeers, massage healers, barbershops, and peddlers of chilled water, sushi (raw fish), confectionery, stuffed fritters, dumplings, fried eel livers, toys, and lanterns.

Vigorous Tokugawa arts produced ceramics, jewelry, and furniture that achieved worldwide renown, enriching Dutch traders at Nagasaki. The Japanese also produced outstanding paintings and woodblock prints, the two greatest artists blending Japanese and imported art styles. Katsushika Hokusai (HO-koo-sie) (1760–1849) created thousands of paintings but was most famous for landscape prints such as the *Thirty-six Views of Mount Fuji*. He strove to improve his craft, predicting that "by ninety I will surely have penetrated

the mystery of life. At one hundred, I will have attained a magnificent level and at one hundred and ten, each dot of my work will vibrate with life."[17] Ando Hiroshige (AN-do hir-o-SHEE-gee) (1797–1858) concentrated on Tokyo scenes and landscapes emphasizing nature (see Profile: Hiroshige, Japanese Artist). The Japanese treatment of atmosphere and light in color prints influenced French impressionist painters of the later 1800s (see Chapter 20), especially influential Dutch artist Vincent van Gogh. Both Japanese prints and French impressionism asked viewers to look at an everyday scene in a new way.

Growing Problems and the Opening of Japan

By the early 1800s many Japanese blamed the Tokugawa for growing problems: inflation, increasing taxes, social disorder, and gradual samurai impoverishment. As daimyo families, burdened with heavy expenses, cut salaries, their samurai borrowed money from merchants to support their own families. In the 1830s Japan also experienced widespread famine, while growing social tensions fostered urban riots, peasant revolts, and plots to depose the shogun. Finally, the growing Western presence in the region worried officials. They knew that Russians were active in Siberia and the North Pacific and that British ships were sailing along Japan's coast. The shogun ordered samurai to fire on foreign ships approaching the coast. After China's defeat in the Opium War, Japan's shocked leaders encouraged samurai to develop more effective weapons. The Japanese considered Westerners money-grasping barbarians who did not understand proper social behavior. The samurai, vowing to resist to the death, pressured the shogun to deal firmly with the threat.

Tokugawa reforms, such as establishing a bureau to translate Western books and reducing the number of government officials to save money, failed to energize the system. Some provincial governments in the southwest attempted more daring changes, recruiting talented men to their administrations, emphasizing "Dutch studies," and even sponsoring industrial experiments, including an electric steam engine. Some samurai learned how to cast better guns and iron suitable for making modern cannon.

External threats arising in the 1850s made the need for change urgent. Americans provided the most dramatic attempt to break down Japanese seclusion. American ships occasionally visited the Dutch base at Nagasaki to trade. U.S. leaders also wanted Japan to protect shipwrecked sailors and provide fresh water and coal to ships sailing between California and China. In 1853 eleven U.S. warships commanded by Commodore Matthew Perry sailed into Tokyo Bay to deliver a letter from the U.S. president, Millard Fillmore, demanding that the shogun sign a treaty opening the country or face war when Perry returned the following year.

[15]Otsuki Gentaku, quoted in Mikiso Hane, *Modern Japan: A Historical Survey*, 2nd ed. (Boulder, CO: Westview Press, 1992), 59.

[16]Quoted in Patricia Fister, "Female *Bunjin*: The Life of Poet-Painter Ema Saiko," in *Recreating Japanese Women, 1600–1945*, ed. Gail Lee Bernstein (Berkeley: University of California Press, 1991), 109.

[17]Quoted in Matthi Ferrer, *Hokusai* (New York: Barnes and Noble, 2002), 9.

Hiroshige, Japanese Artist

Nineteenth-century Japanese artist Ando Hiroshige (1797–1858) gained a worldwide reputation for reflecting a distinctly Japanese vision of landscape and urban life. His work, like that of his four-decades-older contemporary, Katsushika Hokusai, portrayed old Japan on the eve of dramatic change, a Japan of rice fields, small shops, traveling peddlers, sedan chairs, samurai warriors, and dirt roads rather than the later Japan of factories, conglomerates, railroads, and steamships. By portraying scenery and diverse urban scenes, Hiroshige and Hokusai carried printmaking far beyond the early Tokugawa tradition, which emphasized life in the restaurants, teahouses, theaters, and bordellos of the "Floating World" entertainment districts.

Hiroshige was born into a samurai family in Edo (Tokyo) in 1797. Since his father was a member of the fire brigade, the family lived at the fire station. As a child, Hiroshige learned to read, write, and master martial arts, and he also developed a talent for poetry. Like other young samurai, he probably visited the Floating World to enjoy kabuki theater and patronize courtesans. In 1809 the twelve-year-old youngster succeeded to his father's position as a fireman. Underpaid and enjoying art more than firefighting, he began studying with several famous artists. From this time on he used the name Utagawa Hiroshige, a tribute to the Utagawa school of art in which he had been trained. Dutch traders at Nagasaki had introduced Western art to Japan, and Hiroshige probably assimilated ideas from imported Dutch etchings. The young artist was inspired by mountains, rivers, rocks, and trees and gained a working knowledge of different modes and techniques to use in depicting them. Influenced by Hokusai's pioneering work, Hiroshige favored rural landscapes and Edo scenes. At twenty-seven he passed on his fire brigade post to his son and pursued art full time.

Although having much in common, Hokusai and Hiroshige had different outlooks. Hokusai's landscapes divided attention between the setting and the people in it, usually workers such as weavers, carpenters, and spinners. By contrast, Hiroshige subordinated everything to the setting, especially to the mood established by weather, season, time of day, and angle of view. Influenced by Chinese art, Hiroshige portrayed the insignificance of humans against the vastness of nature. His rain and snow scenes are marvels of mood, showing mastery of light and subtle harmony, mixing fact with imagination.

Hiroshige's art often reflected his personal experiences. In 1832, while accompanying an embassy of the Tokugawa shogun to the imperial court in Kyoto, Hiroshige gathered material for his famous work, *The 53 Stations of the Tokaido*, which depicts scenes of villages, inns, and lakes along the Tokaido (Eastern Sea Route) highway connecting Tokyo and Kyoto.

The Road to Mount Fuji (woodblock print), Hiroshige, Ando or Utagawa (1797–1858)/Cragside, Northumberland, UK/National Trust Photographic Library/Derrick E. Witty/The Bridgeman Art Library

THE ROAD TO MOUNT FUJI This 1856 woodblock print from Hiroshige shows Edo's Surugacho Quarter, wth a street, lined by shops, running straight to the majestic mountain.

Hiroshige immortalized the highway, which skirted the Pacific coast of Honshu Island, where mountains sweep down to the sea, and then traversed inland through majestic snowcapped mountains and past beautiful Lake Biwa. A continued stream of people—daimyo and their processions, couriers, monks, pilgrims, merchants, adventurers, entertainers—traveled the well-maintained Tokaido to and from the shogun's court. Stations with inns, restaurants, brothels, and bathhouses flourished as rest stops for the bustling traffic.

Since many Japanese had money to indulge in art, Hiroshige's later collections of prints sold thousands of copies, and he remained a very popular artist. Townspeople loved this art reflecting daily life or the worldly dreams of the merchant class. Hiroshige produced some 5,500 different prints, sold individually or in collections such as the *53 Stations of the Tokaido* and *One Hundred Views of Famous Places in Edo*. However, his personal life was often troubled. Hiroshige, never prospering financially, was often pressed to finance his beloved nightly cup of rice wine. He married several times and sired several children. His eldest daughter's husband, known as Hiroshige II (1826–1869), continued Hiroshige's artistic tradition. At sixty Hiroshige became a Buddhist monk, not an unusual step for aging Japanese men. In 1858 he died at sixty-two of cholera during a great epidemic. On his deathbed, he discouraged his family from holding a lavish funeral by reciting an old verse: "When I die, Cremate me not nor bury me. Just lay me in the fields, to fill the belly of some starving dog."

Hiroshige was the last of the major Japanese print masters. Shortly after he died, Westerners opened up Japan, ending the secluded world that had nourished the woodblock prints and the artists who produced them. But Hiroshige prints continued to be traded around the world, giving foreigners their most vivid impressions of Japan. When Europeans imported the pictures in the late 1800s, they proved a revelation to artists looking for new ways to portray landscapes. Hence woodblock prints, born of isolation, became one of the first major cultural links between Japan and the outside world.

THINKING ABOUT THE PROFILE

1. How did Hokusai and Hiroshige's prints differ from earlier Japanese prints?
2. What do Hiroshige's life and art tell us about late Tokugawa Japan?

Note: Quotation from Julian Bicknell, *Hiroshige in Tokyo: The Floating World of Edo* (San Francisco: Pomegranate Artbooks, 1994), 50.

threat. On December 7, 1941, what President Franklin D. Roosevelt called "a date which will live in infamy," Japanese planes attacked the U.S. naval base at Pearl Harbor, Hawaii, destroying much of the U.S. Pacific fleet, killing twenty-four hundred Americans, and ending U.S. neutrality. Japanese military forces then invaded Southeast Asia, and within several months they controlled most of the region, had forced Americans out of the Philippines, and had jailed British and Dutch residents of their colonies. Bogged down and unable to expand their occupation of China, the Japanese badly needed Southeast Asian resources, especially oil and rubber from the Dutch East Indies (Indonesia). Meanwhile, the Western powers, preoccupied with the European war and with only modest military forces left in Asia, could not resist the Japanese advance.

Japanese leaders disagreed about challenging U.S. power. Some top military officers argued against the Pearl Harbor attack, knowing that the superior U.S. military and economic power could defeat Japan if Americans mobilized to do so. But

MAP 24.3 **WORLD WAR II IN EUROPE AND NORTH AFRICA** The Axis Powers, led by Germany and Italy, initially occupied much of Europe, and in 1941 they invaded the Soviet Union, but they were unable to hold their gains against the counteroffensive of the United States, Britain, the Soviet Union, and the Free French forces. © 2015 Cengage Learning

MAP 24.4 WORLD WAR II IN ASIA AND THE PACIFIC After invading China in 1937, Japan disabled the U.S. fleet at Pearl Harbor in 1941 and in 1941–1942 occupied most of Southeast Asia and the western Pacific. The United States and its allies pushed back the Japanese forces from their bases in the Pacific and bombed Japan from those bases, but Japan did not surrender until 1945, when the United States dropped atomic bombs on Hiroshima and Nagasaki. © 2015 Cengage Learning

other leaders, impressed by Hitler's quick victories, thought they could duplicate that success by immobilizing the U.S. fleet and gaining time to consolidate control of Asia and the Pacific. If Germany kept the United States focused on Europe, they thought Roosevelt might avoid a costly Asian war. They also assumed that Americans, addicted to creature comforts, lacked the will to mobilize. But the surprise Pearl Harbor attack proved a strategic blunder, uniting Americans in support of total, unrelenting war. Admiral Isoruku Yamamoto (**EE-so-ROO-koo YAH-muh-MO-toe**), the former university student in the United States who, understanding American strength, long opposed but eventually planned the attack, somberly told colleagues: "I fear all we have done is to awaken a sleeping giant and

fill him with a terrible resolve."[22] The admiral, who had predicted and feared a long war of attrition, died in 1943 when Americans shot down his plane in reprisal for Pearl Harbor.

Roosevelt had hoped to turn U.S. public opinion toward war and end his nation's isolationism, and Pearl Harbor served that purpose well. Historians remain divided about how much U.S. officials, including Roosevelt, knew about the forthcoming attack and whether they let it happen to shock the U.S. public. U.S. officials anticipated military conflict with Japan but apparently expected an assault on the Philippines, an American colony, rather than on Hawaii, where Japanese Americans constituted over half of the population. U.S. military intelligence had broken some Japanese codes but not those ordering the

[22]Quoted in George Donelson Moss, *America in the Twentieth Century*, 4th ed. (Upper Saddle River, NJ: Prentice-Hall, 2000), 257.

attack. The United States quickly mobilized, regearing the economy for war. A patriotic wave swept the country as America entered the war on both fronts.

The war affected American society. Six million women joined the work force, replacing the men going off to fight. Although many men objected, by 1943 the government encouraged women as their "patriotic duty" to take up jobs once considered unladylike, such as on factory assembly lines. A popular song celebrated "Rosie the Riveter" who was "making history working for victory." The song could have described Sybil Lewis, an African American from Oklahoma who moved to Los Angeles to work as a waitress, became a riveter making airplane gas tanks, and then worked as a shipyard welder. Anxious for workers, companies often hired African Americans, challenging prevailing racial attitudes; millions of southern blacks escaping segregation found jobs in northern and western cities. When the war ended, over 19 million American women had full-time paid jobs, and the black population of many American cities had doubled. After defeating fascism, more white Americans were also sympathetic to black demands for democracy.

But racism aimed at 110,000 Japanese Americans in western states, many U.S.-born or naturalized citizens, fueled a great invasion of civil liberties. Many Japanese Americans joined U.S. military units to fight in Europe, suffering heavy casualties. Nevertheless, suspecting but offering little proof that some Japanese Americans might be spies or support Japan's war effort, the U.S. government seized their property and sent them to sparse, remote internment camps, such as Manzanar in the harsh California desert, for the conflict's duration. Their property was never returned. With some exceptions, German and Italian Americans did not face similar treatment.

The End of the War

The U.S. entry reshaped the conflict. Through 1942 Germany dominated much of Europe and North Africa, while Japan controlled most of Asia east of India and large areas of the western Pacific. But in 1943 the tide began to turn. The Germans were defeated in North Africa, and Allied landings knocked Italy out of the war. In June 1944, British and American forces landed on five beaches at Normandy, on France's Atlantic coast. Although German defenses caused huge casualties, the Allies, including Free French forces under General Charles DeGaulle (1890–1970), finally began pushing the Germans back in France.

Germany was finally defeated by massive Allied ground offensives and aerial bombardments that demoralized the civilian population. The British firebombed several German cities; in Hamburg, a firestorm killed thirty thousand civilians. While the Soviet Red Army pushed Germans back in the east, U.S. and British forces retook Italy, France, and other Nazi-occupied countries. By December 1944, Allied forces reached Germany and the Allies gained command of the skies. Germany's war economy collapsed. As losses mounted, Hitler lost touch with reality, giving

orders to nonexistent army divisions. In spring 1945, British and U.S. armies moved into Germany from the west and the Red Army from the east; Hitler and his mistress, Eva Braun, committed suicide in their underground bunker in Berlin. Germany surrendered. Soon the liberation of concentration camps revealed the full extent of Nazi atrocities to a shocked world.

A major reason for Nazi defeat was Hitler's racist and imperialistic policies. Believing Germans racially superior to all other peoples, including conquered Slavs, Hitler brutally exploited occupied areas to supply Germany. Had the Germans patronized east Europeans and Russians, they might have won some support. Some Ukrainians, Russians, Lithuanians, and Latvians did in fact collaborate with Nazis because they hated communists more; they were pursued and punished for this collaboration after the war.

Japan's defeat was more dramatic. In 1942, Americans stopped Japan's advance at the battle of Midway Island, west of Hawaii, and began isolating Japanese bases in the Pacific. By mid-1944, pushing Japanese out of most of the western Pacific islands, they began launching bombing raids on Japan. By early 1945, U.S., Australian, and British forces started retaking Southeast Asia and China. Increasingly desperate, the Japanese navy organized suicide pilots, known as *kamakazi*, to crash their small fighter planes into U.S. warships. The invasion of Okinawa, in the Ryukyus Islands just south of Japan's main islands, killed 12,500 American troops, 110,000 Japanese soldiers, and 80,000 civilians, warning what invading Japan's main islands might entail. The Japanese, resisting demands for total surrender, could not agree with U.S. leaders on peace negotiations.

In August 1945, the United States forever changed warfare by dropping an atomic bomb on the Japanese city of Hiroshima, demolishing the city and killing eighty thousand people; thousands more were maimed or died later from injuries or radiation. Japan's cabinet, divided on surrender, debated whether Americans had more than one bomb. Three days later, a second bomb hit Nagasaki, killing sixty thousand civilians. Japanese emperor Hirohito (1901–1989) opted for surrender, asking his people to "suffer the insufferable, endure the unendurable," and cooperate with U.S. occupation. Historians debate Hirohito's role in Japan's militarization and wars, but Japan's leaders felt it imperative that the symbol of the nation not be punished or removed; eventually U.S. diplomats agreed. For the first time in its long history, Japan was defeated and successfully invaded. Disgraced, over five hundred military officers committed suicide. But a long-imprisoned Japanese leftist celebrated defeat: "Ah, such happiness, At somehow living long enough, To see this rare day, When the fighting has ceased."[23] World War II had ended.

Historians debate whether dropping atomic bombs, which caused so many civilian deaths, was necessary. Many contend that the Japanese would have fiercely resisted an invasion and hence the bombs saved many American and Japanese lives. Others argue that Japan was near surrender but that U.S. leaders misread its intentions and underestimated the growing propeace faction in government. Still others conclude that the

---

[23]Quoted in James L. McClain, *Japan: A Modern History* (New York: W.W. Norton, 2002), 515.

U.S. Air Force/AP Images

BOMBING OF NAGASAKI This photo shows the awesome power of the atomic bomb dropped by the United States on the Japanese city of Nagasaki in August 1945, three days after the atomic bombing of Hiroshima. Some sixty thousand Japanese died in the Nagasaki bombing.

United States rushed to defeat Japan because the Soviet Union was going to join the struggle to demand territory or a role in the occupation. Soviet forces had already moved into Manchuria as Japanese resistance collapsed. Furthermore, the Russians also seized the Kurile Islands and southern Sakhalin Island north of Japan; they remain in Russian hands today, complicating Russo-Japanese relations. Others point to the Soviet declaration of war, announced just after Hiroshima; Japanese leaders greatly feared communism and Soviet participation in occupation. Hoping to dissuade Soviet expansionism, the bomb proclaimed U.S. capabilities. Some historians argue that the Soviet entry into the war was at least as important as the atomic bombings in prompting Japan to surrender.

Japan lost the war primarily because of overstretched forces, failure to convert Southeast Asian resources into military and industrial products fast enough to defeat the larger, wealthier United States, and the use of authoritarian, brutal policies on subject peoples. Hence, Japanese troops, upon capturing China's capital in 1937, killed thousands of Chinese in an orgy of destruction known as the "Rape of Nanjing." Decades later the world learned that the Japanese had performed horrific medical experiments and used germ warfare on Chinese, killing perhaps half a million people, the only documented mass use of biological weapons in modern times. They also conscripted Korean and Filipina women for forced prostitution

and thousands of Indonesians for forced labor. In most cases Japan's military alienated Chinese and Southeast Asians; eventually most Southeast Asians looked on Japan as perhaps even worse than Western colonizers.

The Costs and Consequences of Global War

World War II took a terrible toll: approximately 15 million military and 35 million civilian deaths. Losing over 20 million people, or 10 percent of its population, Soviet Russia had one more bitter memory of invasions by countries to the west. Over 10 percent of Poles and Yugoslavs died. Britain lost 375,000 people and France 600,000. Strategic bombing blasted every major German city to rubble. Over 2 million Japanese military personnel and probably a million Japanese civilians died; 7 million Chinese were killed or wounded. Fighting on both fronts, some 300,000 American military personnel perished.

The economic devastation cleared the way for new global economic arrangements. In 1944, at a conference held in Bretton Woods, New Hampshire, representatives of forty-four countries established the postwar world economic order, including international monetary cooperation to prevent the financial crises that caused the Great Depression. The Bretton Woods Conference established the U.S.-dominated World Bank and International Monetary Fund to provide credit to states requiring financial investment. Bretton Woods also fixed currency exchange rates and encouraged trade liberalization, benefiting the United States.

World War II transformed world politics, removing the twin threats of German Nazism and Japanese militarism. Unlike after World War I, the victors treated the vanquished more generously. Germany, Italy, and Japan lost their colonies and were required to adopt democratic governments. U.S. forces occupied Japan for several years, while Germany was temporarily divided into sectors controlled by Russia, Britain, France, and the United States. But the Allies gave the defeated nations massive aid and guidance, speeding recovery. Meanwhile, Chinese, Korean, and Vietnamese communists capitalized on Japanese occupation to gain support. Japanese occupation undermined Western colonial rule throughout Southeast Asia. In India, nationalists jailed for opposing the wartime use of Indian troops became even more embittered against British rule (see Chapter 25). Soon devastating anticolonial or civil wars erupted in China, Korea, Indonesia, Vietnam, and Malaya.

In February 1945, Roosevelt, Churchill, and Stalin met at a conference at Yalta (**YAWL-tuh**), in Russia's Crimean peninsula, to determine the postwar political order. They proposed goals, an institutional structure, and a voting system for a new world organization, the United Nations. The Yalta Conference also divided Europe into anticommunist and communist spheres of interest. Western leaders, drained by war and seeking postwar stability, reluctantly agreed that the Soviet Union could dominate eastern Europe, stationing troops there and influencing its governments.

Rivalry between the two emerging superpowers, the United States and the USSR, complicated the new global political order. The United States, having never fought on its own soil, emerged much less devastated than other major combatants as well as politically and economically stronger. Now the dominant world power, Americans took the lead in protecting the global system. But with the USSR a military power with imperialist ambitions, U.S. leaders realized that thwarting Soviet ambitions required reconstructing Europe and Japan to restore political stability.

World political history between 1945 and 1989 revolved around conflicts between these two competing superpowers with very different governments and economies. The USSR replaced Germany in its domination of eastern Europe, where it installed communist governments, including in eastern Germany. World War II also increased communism's appeal worldwide, fostering communist regimes in Yugoslavia and North Korea and later in China and North Vietnam. Both Soviet and U.S. leaders viewed the world through the lens of their World War II experience. Soviets were paranoid about any threat from the West, while Americans perceived a repeat of Hitler's aggression anywhere they identified a political threat, such as in nationalist or communist-inspired revolutions. U.S.-Soviet rivalry created a world very different from that existing before World War II.

MAKE SURE YOU UNDERSTAND THESE KEY POINTS BEFORE MOVING ON

- Nazi Germany deliberately killed 6 million Jews and a half million Gypsies in death camps, along with millions of others; historians are divided on how much the German people knew about the death camps and how responsible they were for them.

- After Japan attacked Pearl Harbor, the United States entered the war in both Asia and Europe, and many women and blacks found work in professions that had until then been closed to them, while Japanese Americans were put in internment camps.

- After the United States entered the war, the Allies slowly began to win the war in Europe, and in the spring of 1945, with U.S. forces advancing from the west and the Soviets from the east, Hitler committed suicide and Germany surrendered.

- After Japan refused to agree to a total surrender despite serious setbacks, the United States dropped atomic bombs on Hiroshima and Nagasaki, killing, injuring, and sickening scores of thousands.

- World War II killed 50 million military personnel and civilians, but in its aftermath, Germany, Italy, and Japan were aided rather than punished, and the United States and the Soviet Union emerged as the world's dominant powers.

aplia

CHAPTER SUMMARY

War and its aftermath dominated the years between 1914 and 1929 in the industrialized Western nations. Growing tensions between European powers sparked World War I, with new weapons killing millions of civilians and soldiers alike. The terrible losses fostered widespread disillusionment and brought major political changes to Europe and the wider world. New nations were carved out of the German, Russian, Austro-Hungarian, and Russian Empires, while the United States emerged as a major world power. The communist Bolsheviks seized power in Russia and created the Soviet Union. Lenin forged a one-party state, and his successor, Stalin, imposed a brutal dictatorship that collectivized the economy, used Five-Year Plans to encourage industrialization, and modernized Russian society.

During the 1920s much of Europe, the United States, and Japan experienced liberal democracy and middle-class prosperity. However, in the 1930s, the Great Depression generated economic collapse, a sharp decline in world trade, and millions of unemployed workers. A few wealthy nations, especially the United States, pursued recovery through liberal reform and government spending, sustaining democracy despite economic hardship. But for Germany, Italy, and Japan, economic disaster fostered fascism, an ideology that favored an authoritarian state, extreme nationalism, and repression of minorities. The increasing aggression of fascist nations, seeking lands to exploit for their resources and markets, generated World War II. During the war, Nazi brutality perpetrated genocide against Jews and other minorities. Germany initially occupied eastern Europe and much of western Europe, while Japan invaded China and Southeast Asia. With the entry of the United States into the war, the Allies eventually won. The war cost 50 million lives and devastated Europe and much of Asia. The United States emerged as the world's major superpower, with the Soviet Union as its major rival.

KEY TERMS

Bolsheviks (p. 578)
soviets (p. 579)
Leninism (p. 581)
Marxism-Leninism (p. 581)
New Economic Policy (p. 581)

Stalinism (p. 581)
gulags (p. 582)
socialist realism (p. 582)
Great Depression (p. 583)
Dust Bowl (p. 586)

New Deal (p. 586)
cubism (p. 588)
fascism (p. 588)
Holocaust (p. 592)

MAO ZEDONG ORGANIZING COMMUNISTS IN CHINA This later artist's rendition shows the young Mao Zedong, the future Chinese communist leader, organizing a communist group in his native province, Hunan, around 1921. A portrait of Karl Marx decorates the wall.

What unhappiness strikes the poor, Who wear a single worn-out, torn cloth. Oh heaven, why are you not just? Some have abundance while others are in want.

—Peasant folk song protesting colonialism in Vietnam[1]

In 1911 Nguyen Tat Thanh (**NEW-win tat-tan**), from an impoverished village in French-ruled Vietnam, became a merchant seaman on a French ship, only returning to his homeland thirty years later. Hating colonialism, Nguyen dreamed of an independent Vietnam: "The people of Vietnam often wondered who would help them to remove the yoke of French control….I saw that I must go abroad and see for myself."[2] Nguyen visited North African and American ports, developing a distaste for America's white racism and admiration for its freedom. Nguyen moved to Paris, where he worked chiefly as a photo retoucher while developing an anticolonial movement among Vietnamese exiles. Adopting a new alias, Nguyen Ai Quoc (**NEW-win eye-kwok**) ("Nguyen the Patriot"), he joined Asian nationalists and French socialists to oppose colonialism.

Nguyen Ai Quoc became famous among Vietnamese exiles for trying to address the Paris Peace Conference delegates about self-determination for colonized people and changing France's treatment of its Southeast Asian colonies, with basic freedoms and representation in government The Western powers refused to permit his entry. Disillusioned with Western democracy, Nguyen helped found the French Communist Party, which promised to abolish the colonial system. He moved to the Soviet Union and later, under a new name, Ho Chi Minh (**ho chee-min**) ("He Who Enlightens"), led Vietnamese communist forces in their long struggle against French colonialism and then the Americans. Ho became a worldwide symbol of opposition to Western imperialism and of sympathy for peasants suffering under colonial policies.

Between 1914 and 1945 nationalistic Asians and Africans challenged the European imperialism, now weakened by World War I, that had reshaped their politics and economies. From Indonesia to Egypt to Senegal, rapid, often destabilizing change sparked nationalism aimed at overthrowing Western domination. Similar trends influenced independent countries such as Siam (now Thailand), Persia (now Iran), and China. During the unsettling Great Depression and World War II nationalist movements grew stronger, making a return to the world of the 1930s impossible.

[1]Quoted in James C. Scott, *The Moral Economy of the Peasant: Rebellion and Subsistence in Southeast Asia* (New Haven: Yale University Press, 1976), 236.
[2]Quoted in William J. Duiker, *Ho Chi Minh: A Life* (New York: Hyperion, 2000), 45.

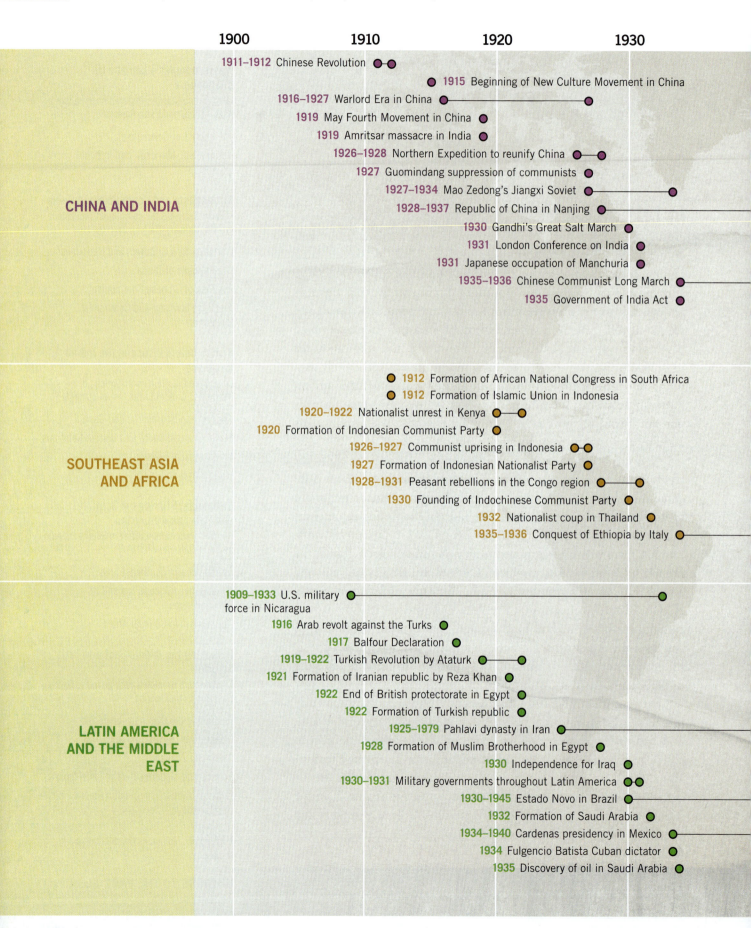

	1900	1910	1920	1930

CHINA AND INDIA

1911–1912 Chinese Revolution
1915 Beginning of New Culture Movement in China
1916–1927 Warlord Era in China
1919 May Fourth Movement in China
1919 Amritsar massacre in India
1926–1928 Northern Expedition to reunify China
1927 Guomindang suppression of communists
1927–1934 Mao Zedong's Jiangxi Soviet
1928–1937 Republic of China in Nanjing
1930 Gandhi's Great Salt March
1931 London Conference on India
1931 Japanese occupation of Manchuria
1935–1936 Chinese Communist Long March
1935 Government of India Act

SOUTHEAST ASIA AND AFRICA

1912 Formation of African National Congress in South Africa
1912 Formation of Islamic Union in Indonesia
1920–1922 Nationalist unrest in Kenya
1920 Formation of Indonesian Communist Party
1926–1927 Communist uprising in Indonesia
1927 Formation of Indonesian Nationalist Party
1928–1931 Peasant rebellions in the Congo region
1930 Founding of Indochinese Communist Party
1932 Nationalist coup in Thailand
1935–1936 Conquest of Ethiopia by Italy

LATIN AMERICA AND THE MIDDLE EAST

1909–1933 U.S. military force in Nicaragua
1916 Arab revolt against the Turks
1917 Balfour Declaration
1919–1922 Turkish Revolution by Ataturk
1921 Formation of Iranian republic by Reza Khan
1922 End of British protectorate in Egypt
1922 Formation of Turkish republic
1925–1979 Pahlavi dynasty in Iran
1928 Formation of Muslim Brotherhood in Egypt
1930 Independence for Iraq
1930–1931 Military governments throughout Latin America
1930–1945 Estado Novo in Brazil
1932 Formation of Saudi Arabia
1934–1940 Cardenas presidency in Mexico
1934 Fulgencio Batista Cuban dictator
1935 Discovery of oil in Saudi Arabia

1940   1950   1960   1970   1980

1937 Provincial elections in India

1937–1945 Japanese invasion of China

1942 Gandhi's Quit India campaign

1941–1945 Japanese occupation of Southeast Asia

1941 Formation of Viet Minh in Vietnam by Ho Chi Minh

1936 Britain-Egypt alliance

1936–1939 Civil war in Palestine

Ⓢ Western Imperialism and Its Challengers

Ⓝ *What circumstances fostered nationalism in Asia, Africa, and Latin America?*

The events that rocked industrialized nations—two world wars, the Russian Revolution, and the Great Depression—also affected Asians, Africans, and Latin Americans. These societies, enjoying little power in the global system, also suffered from destabilizing social and economic changes resulting from colonialism. Many disenchanted Asians and Africans adopted nationalism and Marxism to struggle for power.

The Impact of Colonialism

Western colonialism had a major impact on Asians, Africans, and Caribbean peoples. The slaughter during World War I undermined Western credibility and whatever moral authority Western peoples claimed to possess, while the deaths of thousands of Asians and Africans conscripted or recruited as soldiers and workers to support the war effort spurred resentment. Both France and Germany drafted men, often through harsh forced labor, from their African colonies; Britain sent Africans and Indians. Some 46,000 Kenyans died fighting for Britain, and at least 25,000 West Africans perished helping France on the front lines. Although British and French officials promised democratic reforms and special treatment for

NOTRE-DAME CATHEDRAL IN SAIGON Colonialism spurred cultural as well as economic and political change. Many Vietnamese became Roman Catholics.

war veterans, both broke these promises. Few families of dead African soldiers ever received any compensation.

Colonialism also reshaped societies, forming artificial states that often ignored regional social, economic, and historical realities (see Chapters 21–22). Colonies such as Dutch-ruled Indonesia, British Nigeria, and the Belgian Congo incorporated diverse, often rival ethnic groups with little feeling of national unity. To cover costs, colonial governments used varied, often unpopular methods, including higher taxes and forced labor. In Portuguese-ruled Mozambique, men and women unable to pay required taxes were assigned to plantations or mines in a system not unlike slavery. After months of labor they often received little more than a receipt saying they met their annual tax obligation. In Southeast Asia, opium and alcohol monopolies provided revenues for colonial governments. France required all Vietnamese villages to purchase designated amounts of these products, making some people opium addicts; by 1918 opium sales accounted for one-third of all colonial revenues. Villages that bought too little alcohol or made their own illicit beverages were fined.

Rising birthrates and declining death rates, the result of colonial economic policies and sometimes improved health and sanitation, led to rapid population growth in colonies such as India, Indonesia, the Philippines, and Vietnam, outstripping resources, exacerbating poverty, and stimulating emigration. Producing and exporting one or two primary commodities, such as rice and rubber from Vietnam, sugar from Barbados and Fiji, copper from Northern Rhodesia, and oil from Trinidad and Iraq, retarded later economic diversification. In addition, colonized peoples disliked Western colonizers' arrogance. Assuming their societies' superiority, Europeans and North Americans enshrined their racist attitude in the League of Nations Covenant, which considered colonized peoples unable to govern themselves. Western officials, businessmen, and planters in the colonies lived in luxury—with mansions, servants, and private clubs—while many local people endured dire poverty, often underfed and underemployed.

Yet, colonial governments built modern communications and economic infrastructures, often spurring economic growth. British India, Dutch Indonesia, and British East Africa built railroads that facilitated the movement of goods and people. Colonialism also increased urban growth. Hence, in 1890, to service its new East African Railroad, Britain opened a settlement with a hotel and bar at Nairobi, a Gikuyu village in the Kenyan highlands. Nairobi, with its cool climate, later became the colonial capital. Port cities founded by Western colonizers, such as Hong Kong, Jakarta in Indonesia, Singapore, Bombay (today's Mumbai), and Cape Town, became key world trade hubs. But critics questioned whether these developments benefited Asians and Africans.

Western capitalism also spurred resentment. Some non-European merchants, such as Chinese in Southeast Asia and Lebanese in West Africa, profited from the growing economic opportunities. But colonial policies, while promoting capitalist markets and expanded communications, eroded traditional political authority and also destabilized rural villages, fostering revolutionary responses in countries like Vietnam. Agricultural commercialization transformed traditional, often communal, landowning arrangements into competitive money-based private property systems, converting land into a commodity. In many colonies, among them British India, French Vietnam, and Portuguese Angola, powerful landlord classes now flourished at the expense of once-self-sufficient peasant farmers. The remaining peasant farmers had no control over fluctuating prices for their crops. Lacking money or connections to influential people, many peasants fell into dire poverty. A Vietnamese peasant later recalled the bitter colonial hardship: "My father was very poor. He and my mother, and all of my brothers and sisters, had to pull the plow. In the old days, people did the work of water buffalo."[3]

The Great Depression brought economic catastrophe to many nonindustrialized societies as demand for their resources plummeted. Prices for rubber, sugar, and coffee fell in Southeast Asia and Africa, Argentina's livestock and wheat prices collapsed, and Brazilians threw nearly worthless sacks of coffee beans into the sea. To protect Western investors, international agreements restricted rubber growing to large plantations, harming small farmers, rubber workers, and shopkeepers in Malaya, Sri Lanka, and the Belgian Congo. As these exports declined, colonial revenues fell. Because rubber and tin provided most tax revenues in British Malaya, huge budget cuts undermined such activities as education and road building.

Unequal landowning, growing mass poverty, declining economic opportunities, and foreign economic control generated political unrest. Hence, on Trinidad, the depression sparked strikes and labor unrest. Calypso singer Growling Tiger implored British officials not to ignore human suffering: "The authorities should deal much more leniently with the many unemployed in the colony; work is nowhere to be found but there is rent to pay while the money circulation decreases by the day."[4] Most colonial regimes harassed and jailed protest leaders.

Nationalism, Marxism, and Imperial Expansion

As a result of these hardships, ideologies of resistance, including nationalism and Marxism, became influential, fostering movements for independence. Since colonial governments jailed or exiled dissenters, nationalists organized underground. Nationalism appealed especially to educated middle-class lawyers, teachers, merchants, and military officers facing white racism. The few colonial universities offered a venue for nationalist-government conflicts and campus protests. In British Burma (today's Myanmar) during the 1920s and 1930s, male and female students at the University of Rangoon repeatedly went on strike to protest British policies; student leaders were often expelled.

Nationalism promoted a sense of belonging to a nation, such as Indonesia or Nigeria, that transcended parochial differences such as social class and religion. Whereas colonialism uprooted people from villages, families, customs, and traditions, nationalists sought to help the poor, often linking capitalism with foreign control. But the "nation" sometimes existed only in people's imagination: in multiethnic African, Southeast Asian, and Caribbean colonies, ethnic rivalries hindered a feeling of nationhood.

Some Asians, Africans, and Latin Americans seeking radical change, such as Ho Chi Minh, mixed nationalism with Marxism, providing an alternative to colonialism, capitalism, and discredited local traditions and leaders. Some young Asians, Africans, and West Indians studying in Europe and North America adopted Marxism after facing racism in the West and bleak employment prospects and political repression at home. Some gravitated to the communism imposed on and practiced in the Soviet Union (see Chapter 24), which addressed social inequality and political powerlessness. Many found Soviet communist leader Vladimir Lenin's theories persuasive; blaming colonial and neocolonial societies' poverty on industrialized nations imposing a capitalist system, Lenin divided the world into imperial countries (the exploiters) and dominated countries (the exploited). Thus many nationalists who once admired Western democracies now found inspiration in Soviet Russia. Although the USSR proved capable of following blatantly imperialistic policies, many accepted Lenin's theory of capitalism-based imperialism.

In contrast, many Muslims were less amenable to Marxism, communism, and secular nationalism. Some believed that revitalizing Islam required purging it of pre-Islamic features such as mysticism. Some adopted dogmatic and puritanical approaches, rejecting modernity and seeking to recreate the early Muslim society of the Prophet Muhammad's time. Other Muslims emphasized Sufism and its syncretic, tolerant approaches. Better transportation, especially steamship lines, enabled more to study in the Middle East or make pilgrimages to Mecca, meeting Muslims from around the world.

While anti-imperialist feelings increased, powerful nations expanded their imperial reach, intervening in less powerful countries. Britain and France took control of former Ottoman colonies in western Asia and German colonies in Africa, some of which had valuable resources, while Australia and Japan occupied German-ruled Pacific islands. Supported by colonial governments, Europeans continued to settle in Algeria, Angola, Kenya, South Africa, and Southern Rhodesia, dispossessing local people from their land. Moreover, Western military conquests in Africa had not ended. In 1935–1936 Italy invaded and brutally conquered the last independent African state, Ethiopia, killing some 200,000 Ethiopians. Despite spirited defense, Ethiopians succumbed to superior Italian aerial bombing and firepower.

Meanwhile, the United States exercised influence in the Americas. Americans owned a large share of Mexico's economy,

---

[3] Quoted in James W. Trullinger, *Village at War: An Account of Conflict in Vietnam* (Stanford, CA: Stanford University Press, 1994), 18.

[4] Dick Spottswood, liner notes to the album *Calypsos from Trinidad: Politics, Intrigue and Violence in the 1930s* (Arhoolie 7004, 1991).

including most of the oil industry. To support these interests, President Woodrow Wilson sent thousands of U.S. troops into Mexico to restore order during the Mexican Revolution. In Nicaragua U.S. Marines overthrew a hostile government and remained there from 1909 to 1933; Augusto César Sandino **(san-DEE-no)** (1895–1934) led a peasant resistance, becoming a hero to nationalist Central Americans. To protect U.S. investments in Central America, Americans often supported governments led by landowners and generals, such as the notoriously corrupt Nicaraguan dictator, Anastasio Somoza (1896–1956). President Franklin D. Roosevelt defended this policy, maintaining that "they may be SOBs, but they're our SOBs."[5] Repeated U.S. interventions fostered resentment against what Central Americans called "Yankee imperialism."

MAKE SURE YOU UNDERSTAND THESE KEY POINTS BEFORE MOVING ON

- World War I affected colonies in Asia, Africa, and the Caribbean as thousands of colonial subjects were forced to fight and die for France, Germany, and Britain.

- Colonial governments imposed heavy taxes and hard labor on the colonial peoples, who often lived in poverty while their Western counterparts lived in luxury, a state of affairs that was defended by the Western idea that the colonial peoples could not yet govern themselves.

- Western capitalism disrupted traditional rural life in many colonies, placing formerly self-sufficient farmers at the mercy of landowners and the world economy, which led to misery, political unrest, and activism during the Great Depression.

- Nationalism appealed to many frustrated colonial subjects, though many multiethnic colonies struggled to develop a sense of nationhood.

- Despite local opposition, Western nations expanded their colonial reach between 1900 and 1945: Italy brutally conquered Ethiopia, France and Britain took over former Ottoman colonies, and the United States continued to meddle in Central America.

aplia

Nationalism and Communism in China

How and why did the communist movement grow in China?

The Chinese Revolution of 1911–1912, ending the two-thousand-year-old imperial system (see Chapter 23), produced a republic Chinese hoped would foster renewed strength in the world. These hopes were soon dashed as China lapsed into warlordism and civil war, remaining nominally independent but subject to Western and Japanese forces. Alarm at China's domestic failures and continuing Western imperialism sparked resurgent nationalism, the formation of a communist party, and China's eventual reunification.

Warlords, New Cultures, and Nationalism

During the demoralizing Warlord Era (1916–1927), China was divided into territories controlled by rival **warlords**, local political leaders with their own armies that taxed and terrorized the population. Some warlords, calling themselves reformers, promoted education and industry. Others took bribes to favor merchants or foreign governments. Perhaps the most brutal, corrupt, and hated warlord, Zhang Zongchang, was known as the "Dogmeat General" because of his food preference. A children's ditty mocked his penchant for destruction and excess: "Zhang Zongchang, wicked and wasteful; Wrecks shoes, wrecks stockings, wrecks army equipment."[6] High taxes, inflation, famine, accelerating social tensions, and banditry made life difficult for most Chinese, increasing frustration.

Cities became enclaves of new intellectual, social, cultural, and economic thought. New schools and universities opened, and 4.5 million girls attended schools by 1919, although boys enjoyed more access to formal education. By the 1920s many women worked as nurses, teachers, and civil servants; however, few rural women became literate or enjoyed these new opportunities. Exposure to Western ideas in universities, many operated by Christian groups, led some students to question their own cultural traditions. Women activists and sympathetic men campaigned against footbinding, which largely disappeared except in remote areas by 1930. Chambers of commerce and labor unions also appeared.

A new movement originating at Beijing University in 1915, the **New Culture Movement**, rejected the discredited past and sprouted a literary revival. The university hired radical professors and encouraged the mixing of Chinese and Western thought, and university professors published the literary magazine *New Youth*, which attacked China's traditions, including Confucianism, for promoting conformity and discouraging critical thinking. The magazine's editor, Chen Duxiu **(chen too-shoe)** (1879–1942), emphasized republican government and science. Contributors,

warlords Local political leaders with their own armies.

New Culture Movement A movement of Chinese intellectuals started in 1915 that sought to wash away the discredited past and sprout a literary revival.

[5] Quoted in Lester Langley, *Central America: The Real Stakes: Understanding Central America Before It's Too Late* (New York: Dorsey, 1985), 23.

[6] Quoted in James Sheridan, *China in Disintegration: The Republican Era in Chinese History, 1912–1949* (New York: Free Press, 1975), 67.

while detesting Western imperialism, admired Western nations' liberal, open intellectual atmosphere, viewed modern science as liberation from superstition, derided the traditional Chinese family system for crushing individual rights, and advised women to seek equality with men.

Chinese rage against Western and Japanese imperialism increased in World War I's aftermath. China remained neutral until 1917 but sent 200,000 Chinese laborers to assist the Allies in France. Japan, which had occupied Germany's sphere of influence in the Shandong peninsula, in 1915 presented China with 21 Demands, including control of Shandong, increased rights in Manchuria, and appointment of Japanese advisers to China's government. The Western allies' decision to allow Japan to take over Shandong provoked a radical nationalist resurgence in 1919, the **May Fourth Movement**, that opposed imperialism and the ineffective, warlord-controlled Chinese government. Decrying social injustice and government inaction, students and workers, including many women, mounted mass demonstrations, strikes, and boycotts of Japanese goods. Merchants closed their businesses in sympathy. Capitulating to the protests, the government refused to sign the Versailles treaty. The new Soviet Union sided with China and renounced the special privileges obtained by the czars, winning Chinese admiration.

In 1921 Beijing University professors and students organized the Chinese Communist Party (CCP). Some party founders, such as *New Youth* editor Chen Duxiu, were Europe- or Japan-educated reformers who admired Western science and culture. Others were nationalists who, despising Western models, believed people could liberate China if mobilized for revolution. Soviet advisers, while encouraging the party to organize the urban working class, considered the Communists unlikely to become influential. But the Communists formed peasant associations, labor unions, women's groups, and youth clubs, enrolling some sixty thousand members by 1927. A Communist women's congress declared that "women…are still imprisoned in the yoke of the feudal ethical code and lead lives similar to prostitutes."[7]

Capitalizing on the resurgent nationalism, Sun Zhongshan, better known as Sun Yat-sen (1866–1925), whose revolutionary ideas helped overthrow the Qing dynasty (see Chapter 23), began to rebuild his Guomindang, or Nationalist Party. Receiving no help from Western nations, who benefited from China's disarray, Sun accepted Soviet advisers and military aid. In the mid-1920s Sun's Guomindang and the Chinese Communists worked together, in an alliance known as the United Front, to defeat warlordism. However, Sun's ideology grew more authoritarian; he concluded that China's 400 million people—in his view just "loose sand"—were not ready for democracy. Sun died of cancer in 1925, and was replaced by his brother-in-law, Jiang Jieshi, better known in the West as Chiang Kai-shek (**CHANG kai-shek**) (1887–1975). From a wealthy landowning family, Chiang was a conservative, probusiness soldier and patriot but indifferent to social change. Developing a close relationship with the United States, Chiang began building a modern military force.

The Republic of China

Between 1926 and 1928 Guomindang forces and their communist allies reunified China with a military drive, the Northern Expedition, that defeated or co-opted warlords. Foreign powers recognized Chiang's new Republic of China. However, tensions grew between leftwing and rightwing factions. Whereas the communists and leftist Guomindang leaders sought social change and mobilization of workers, the Chiang-led right wing allied with the antiprogressive Shanghai business community. In 1927, expelling communists from the United Front, Chiang began a reign of terror, killing thousands of leftists; survivors went into hiding or fled into the interior or abroad.

From 1928 to 1937 Chiang's Republic, based at Nanjing (**nahn-JING**) along the Yangzi River, launched a modernization program. The leaders, many Western-educated Christians, built railroads, factories, a banking system, and a modern army, streamlined government, fostered public health and education, and adopted new legal codes. But while promoting monogamy and equal inheritance for women, Chiang's government lacked power to implement them. Chiang negotiated the elimination of most unequal international treaties imposed by Western nations and Japan in the 1800s. The U.S. government, closely allied with Chiang, and private Americans, feeling paternalistic responsibility, provided generous political and financial support for modernization, funding schools, hospitals, orphanages, and Christian missions. In 1940 a prominent, ethnocentric U.S. senator, believing Americans could enrich and Westernize China, proclaimed: "We will lift Shanghai up, ever up, until it is just like Kansas City."[8]

The Republic faced daunting challenges. While the elite in big coastal cities prospered, Chiang was unable or unwilling to address the peasantry's growing poverty. Agricultural commercialization shifted more land to landlords, leaving half of China's peasants unable to support their families. One 1930s academic study of rural China described the desperate peasant as "a man standing up to his neck in water, whom the slightest ripple will drown."[9] Meanwhile, Chiang tolerated government corruption, rewarding his merchant and banker financial backers. As antigovernment sentiment grew, Chiang, influenced by European fascism, built an authoritarian police state, brutally repressing dissent. Another threat to Chiang's government came from Japan. Blaming the Chinese for a railway bombing secretly perpetrated by Japanese soldiers, in 1931 Japanese forces seized Manchuria, rich in mineral resources and fertile farmland, and established a puppet government under the last Manchu emperor, Henry Pu Yi (1906–1967) (see Map 25.1). As Japan gradually extended its military and political influence southward, Chiang, with inferior military power, followed an appeasement policy. His

May Fourth Movement A radical nationalist resurgence in China in 1919 that opposed imperialism and the ineffective, warlord-controlled Chinese government.

[7]Quoted in Christina Kelley Gilmartin, *Engendering the Chinese Revolution: Radical Women, Communist Politics, and Mass Movements in the 1920s* (Berkeley: University of California Press, 1995), 68–69.

[8]Kenneth Wherry of Nebraska, quoted in John Brooks, *The Great Leap: The Past Twenty-five Years in America* (New York: Harper and Row, 1966), 327.

[9]R. H. Tawney, quoted in Diane Lary, *China's Republic* (New York: Cambridge University Press, 2007), 107.

MAP 25.1 CHINESE COMMUNIST MOVEMENT AND CHINESE-JAPANESE WAR Japan occupied much of northern and eastern China by 1939. In 1935–1936 the Chinese communists made the famous 6,000-mile Long March from their base in Jiangxi in southern China to Yan'an in northwest China. © 2015 Cengage Learning

attempts to strengthen the military diverted scarce resources from economic development, while critics considered Chiang's reluctance to fight Japan unpatriotic.

Cultural life reflected China's challenges. Disillusioned by China's weakness and continued despotism, many intellectuals lost faith in both Chiang's regime and Chinese traditions.

The writer Lu Xun (LOO shun) (1881–1936), who studied in Japan and became proficient in several foreign languages, published satires on Chinese failures to meet challenges. Lu later formed a leftist writers' group and supported the communists. In criticizing both imperialism and greedy Chinese leaders, he argued, "Our vaunted Chinese civilization is only a feast of human flesh prepared for the rich and mighty, and China is only a kitchen where these feasts are prepared."[10] Ding Ling (1904–1985), one of China's first feminist writers, had fled her native village to avoid an arranged marriage, participated in the May Fourth Movement, and lived a liberated city life. Her early novels and short stories featured independent women unable to find emotional or sexual satisfaction. After the Guomindang killed her politically activist husband, she dedicated her writing to the revolutionary cause but later faced communist persecution for her feminism and reluctance to follow the party line.

The Rise of Chinese Communism

As communists surviving Chiang's terror rebuilt their movement, a younger party leader, Mao Zedong **(maow dzuh-dong)** (1893–1976), pursued his own strategy to mount revolution. From a peasant family dominated by an abusive father, Mao ran away from home to attend high school and later worked in the Beijing University Library. Embracing communism, he edited a radical magazine, became an elementary school principal, and organized workers and peasants. In 1927, as Chiang eliminated communists, Mao fled to rugged mountains in Jiangxi **(kee-ON-see)** province in south-central China, established a revolutionary base, the Jiangxi Soviet, and organized a guerrilla army out of peasants, bandits, and former Guomindang soldiers. Rejecting Soviet advice to depend on the urban working class, Mao instead relied on China's huge peasantry (see Witness to the Past: Peasants as a Revolutionary Base).

Mao believed that violence was necessary to oppose Chiang. Between 1928 and 1934 Mao expanded the Jiangxi Soviet, redistributing land from the rich to the poor. As Chiang's repression intensified, top Communist leaders joined Mao in Jiangxi.

Increasingly alarmed, Chiang's army blockaded the Soviet to keep out essential supplies, forcing Mao to reluctantly abandon his base. In 1935, seeking a safer base, 100,000 soldiers and followers broke through the blockade and began the Long March, an epic journey, full of hardship; Mao's Red Army fought their way 6,000 miles on foot and horseback through eleven provinces, crossed eighteen mountain ranges, forded twenty-four rivers, and slogged through swamps, losing 90 percent of their people to death or desertion. Finally in late 1936 the ragtag survivors arrived in a poor northwestern province and moved into cavelike homes in hills around dusty Yan'an **(YEH-nan)** city. The Long March saved the communists from elimination, making Mao the unchallenged party leader. Mao celebrated the achievement: "The Long March is the first of its kind in the annals of history [and has] proclaimed that the Red Army is an army of heroes."[11] But still vulnerable to Chiang's larger, better-equipped forces, they would be saved only by Japan's invasion of China in 1937, which forced Chiang to shift his military priorities to fighting

THE LONG MARCH In June, 1935 the Chinese Red Army crossed the Jiajinshan Mountain, the first of many snow-covered mountains encountered on their long, harrowing trek to northwest China.

the Japanese, allowing the communists to regroup and spread their message in wartime China.

Japanese Invasion and Communist Revolution

The Japanese invasion and disastrous war that followed altered China's politics as Chiang diverted modernization funds to the military. Mao captured the country's patriotic mood, proposing a united front against Japan; Chiang had to agree. The Japanese soon occupied the major north China and coastal cities. When Japanese forces captured the Republican capital, Nanjing, brutality, murders, and rapes that followed shocked the world; some 300,000, mostly civilians, died in the orgy of violence later called "the Rape of Nanjing." By the end of 1938 the Japanese controlled most of eastern China, including the best farmland and major industrial cities,

Jiangxi Soviet A revolutionary base, established in 1927 in south-central China, where Mao Zedong organized a guerrilla force to fight the Guomindang.

Long March An epic journey, full of hardship, in which Mao Zedong's Red Army fought their way 6,000 miles on foot and horseback through eleven Chinese provinces to establish a safe base.

[10]Quoted in *A Pictorial Biography of Luxun* (Beijing: Peoples Fine Arts Publishing House, n.d.), 157.

[11]Quoted in Stephen Uhalley, Jr., *Mao Tse-Tung: A Critical Biography* (New York: New Viewpoints, 1975), 55.

WITNESS TO THE PAST

Peasants as a Revolutionary Base

In 1926 Mao Zedong, one of the few communist leaders from a peasant background and with experience organizing peasants, became head of the Communist Party's "Peasant Department." Returning to his native Hunan province to attend a conference of local peasants, already noted for radical activism, Mao remained for some time investigating the peasantry's revolutionary potential. The report on his findings, published in April 1927, became a key document in twentieth-century Chinese history. Although he originally thought poor peasants lacked organization, he discovered that many were already involved in peasant associations that challenged the social and economic inequities of rural life, including patriarchal power over women. Mao wanted the party to support their efforts as part of their broader struggle against the Guomindang and cultural conservatism. This excerpt includes some of Mao's best-known thoughts on revolution and the oppression of women.

I called together for fact-finding conferences experienced peasants and comrades working for the peasant movement.... And many strange things there were that I had never seen or heard before. I think these conditions exist in many other places. All kinds of arguments against the peasant movement must be speedily set right....For the rise of the present peasant movement is a colossal event. In a very short time...several hundred million peasants will rise like a tornado or tempest, a force so extraordinarily swift and violent that no power, however great, will be able to suppress it....They will send all imperialists, warlords, corrupt officials, local bullies, and bad gentry to their graves....To march at their head and lead them? Or to follow at their rear, gesticulating at them and criticizing them? Every Chinese is free to choose...but circumstances demand that a quick choice be made.

All Power to the Peasant Association! The peasants attack as their main targets the local bullies and bad gentry and the lawless landlords, hitting in passing against patriarchal ideologies and institutions, corrupt officials in the cities, and evil customs in the rural areas....The revolt of the peasants disturbed the sweet dreams of the gentry....the fact is...that the broad peasant masses have risen to fulfill their historic mission, that the democratic forces in the rural areas have risen to overthrow the rural feudal power. The patriarchal-feudal class...has formed the basis of an autocratic government for thousands of years, the cornerstone of imperialism, warlordism and corrupt officialdom. To overthrow this feudal power is the real objective of the national revolution. What

Dr. Sun Yat-sen wanted to do in forty years he devoted to the national revolution but failed to accomplish, the peasants have accomplished in a few months. This is a marvelous feat which has never been achieved in the last forty or even thousand years. It is very good indeed....

For ages these people, with power in their hands, tyrannized over the peasants and trampled them underfoot; that is why the peasants have now risen in such a great revolt....a revolution is not the same as inviting people to dinner, or writing an essay, or painting a picture, or doing fancy needlework; it cannot be anything so refined, so calm and gentle, or so mild, kind, courteous, restrained, and magnanimous. A revolution is an uprising, an act of violence whereby one class overthrows another. A rural revolution is a revolution by which the peasantry overthrows the authority of the feudal landlord class....In the rural areas, there must be a great fervent revolutionary upsurge, which alone can arouse hundreds and thousands of the people to form a great force....

A man in China is usually subjected to the domination of three systems of authority: 1) the system of the state (political authority), ranging from the national, provincial, and country government to the township government; 2) the system of the clan (clan authority), ranging from the central and branch ancestral temples to the head of the household; and 3) the system of gods and spirits (theocratic authority)....As to women, apart from being dominated by the three systems mentioned above, they are further dominated by men (the authority of the husband). These four kinds of authority...represent the whole ideology and institutions of feudalism and patriarchy, and are the four great cords that have bound the Chinese people and particularly the peasants....In a word, then, the whole feudal-patriarchal system and ideology is tottering with the growth of the peasant's power....The abolition of the clan system, of superstitions, and of inequality between men and women will follow as a natural consequence of victory in political and economic struggles.

THINKING ABOUT THE READING

1. Why does Mao believe that the peasants were angry and demonstrated revolutionary potential?
2. How does he describe the status of women and how it can be improved?

Source: "Report on an Investigation of the Peasant Movement in Hunan," in *Selected Works of Mao Tse-Tung*, vol. 1 (Peking: Foreign Languages Press, 1965), 23–28, 44–46.

but, their forces overextended, they became bogged down, unable to expand control. Over 95 million Chinese ultimately became war refugees, sapping the rural economy as civilians fled. War and occupation undermined Chiang's government, enabling the communists to recruit support and setting the stage for major political changes in the later 1940s.

Chiang's government, along with a mass migration of Chinese, relocated inland to Chongqing (**CHUNG-king**), a Yangzi River city protected by high mountains. Unlike cosmopolitan coastal cities, Chongqing, with a depressing climate of fog and humidity, offered no bright lights or French restaurants. Fatigue, cynicism, and inflation discouraged the Guomindang's followers. Virtually broke but needing to support an army of 4 to 5 million men, Chiang's government taxed the peasants in areas it still controlled. Militarily ineffective, politically repressive, and economically corrupt, it offered limited resistance to the Japanese, killed and imprisoned opponents, and put its leaders' personal gain above the people's economic well-being. Although supporting Chiang, the United States could supply Guomindang-held areas only by difficult, mountainous routes from Burma and India. Moreover, Chiang often ignored U.S. military and political advice. As the war wore on, Chiang lost much popular support.

Meanwhile, the communists at Yan'an improved their prospects. Used to poverty, they had a more disciplined army with higher morale. While Chiang's much larger forces had the main responsibility to fight Japan, the communists mobilized, forging a close relationship with north China peasants and mounting guerrilla bands to harass the Japanese. Their unconventional struggle, called "**people's war**," combined military action and political recruitment. In Mao's military strategy, "the enemy advances, we retreat; the enemy halts, we harass; the enemy retreats, we pursue."[12] Politically communist activists also formed village governments and peasant associations and encouraged women's rights, punishing abusive husbands. Attracted by their message of social revolution and nationalism, thousands of Chinese, students, intellectuals, and writers such as Ding Ling flocked to Yan'an, joining the communist cause. By 1945 the party had 1.2 million members.

Communist experiences at Yan'an fostered **Maoism**, an ideology promoted by Mao that mixed Chinese ideas with Soviet Marxist-Leninism. Mao emphasized the subordination of the individual to group needs (a traditional Chinese notion), the superiority of political values over technical and artistic ones, and the belief in human will as a social force. To combat elitism, Mao introduced mass campaigns; everyone engaged in physical labor, such as building dams and roads. Sent into villages to teach literacy, intellectuals also learned from peasants. Mao expressed faith that politically educated people possessed the collective power to triumph over nature, poverty, and exploitation and build a new society.

The communists now dominated much of rural north China, where Mao's ideas on social change and economic justice gained support. When the war ended in 1945, they had improved their prospects while Chiang's Guomindang, although still a superior military force, was beset with problems and losing popular support. In 1949 the communists won a bitter civil war and established a government.

> **people's war** An unconventional struggle combining military action and political recruitment, formulated by Mao Zedong in China.

> **Maoism** An ideology promoted by Mao Zedong that mixed ideas from Chinese tradition with Marxist-Leninist ideas from the Soviet Union.

MAKE SURE YOU UNDERSTAND THESE KEY POINTS BEFORE MOVING ON

- After the end of the imperial system, rival warlords controlled China during a period of civil war, and intellectuals formed the New Culture Movement, which called for a modernized China that fostered individualism and equality rather than traditions such as Confucianism.

- Japan's aggressive demands after World War I enraged the Chinese, and some were attracted to communism, but Sun Yat-sen's successor, the pro-business Chiang Kai-shek, allied the nationalist movement with the United States.

- Chiang Kai-shek's Republic of China launched a modernization program, but it was hampered by a split with the communists, persistent rural poverty, and the Japanese seizure of Manchuria.

- The Chinese people lost faith in Chiang's government as it squeezed them for taxes to support a failing war against Japan, while Mao's communists instilled hope through guerrilla attacks on the Japanese and a promise of equality and progress through shared sacrifice.

aplia

British Colonialism and the Indian Response   S T

What were the main contributions of Mohandas Gandhi to the Indian struggle?

Indian resentment of British colonialism and social inequalities fueled a powerful nationalist movement. Those hoping that World War I would bring self-determination saw that British rhetoric about democracy did not apply to India. Growing opposition to British rule, spurred by the Indian National Congress, led to unrest, forcing Britain to modify some policies. Nationalism also set the stage for separate Hindu and Muslim nations after World War II.

---

[12]Quoted in John Meskill, "History of China," in *An Introduction to Chinese Civilization*, ed. John Meskill (Lexington, MA: D.C. Heath, 1973), 302.

The Nationalist Upsurge and Gandhi

During World War I the British Raj raised taxes and customs duties to finance the war, sparking several armed uprisings. Over 1 million Indians fought for Britain in France and the Middle East; 60,000 were killed and 70,000 wounded. Because of their sacrifices in a war they did not start, many Indians expected liberalization, perhaps self-government similar to Australia and Canada, both former colonies. Dashing these hopes, Britain declared it would maintain India as an integral part of its empire. However, World War I losses showed that British power was no longer unchallengeable.

With a severe economic slump heightening discontent, Britain clamped down on dissent, maintaining harsh wartime laws. In 1919, in the Punjab city of Amritsar, British officers, fearing a mass uprising, ordered their Indian soldiers to open fire on unarmed protesters at an unauthorized rally in a walled field, killing 400 protesters and wounding 1,000, including women and children. Indians greeted the Amritsar massacre with outrage, which intensified when the British hailed the commanding officer, General Dyer, as a national hero. Prominent Indians, many once pro-British, were appalled at the cruelty. The Nobel Prize–winning writer Rabindranath Tagore **(tuh-GAWR)** (1861–1941) wrote, "The enormity of the measures taken up for quelling some local disturbances had, with a rude shock, revealed to our minds the helplessness of our position as British subjects in India."[13]

The unrest brought forth new nationalist leaders, most notably Mohandas K. Gandhi **(GAHN-dee)** (1869–1948) (see Profile: Mohandas Gandhi, Indian Nationalist). After earning his law degree in Britain, Gandhi lived for twenty-two years in South Africa, where British rulers practiced racial segregation and white supremacy (see Chapter 21). To assert Indian immigrants' rights, Gandhi developed tactics of **nonviolent resistance**, noncooperation with unjust laws and peaceful confrontation with illegitimate authority. Influenced by his pacifist wife, Kasturbai, Gandhi adopted ideas against taking life that had been introduced twenty-five hundred years earlier by Jains and Buddhists and that were also promoted by Quakers, a pacifist Christian movement Gandhi encountered in England. Nonviolence—Gandhi often called it passive resistance—was, he wrote, "a method of securing rights by personal suffering; it is the reverse of resistance by arms."[14] Gandhi believed that violence was never justified. Meet the enemy with reason; if he responded with violence, this had to be endured in good spirit.

nonviolent resistance
Noncooperation with unjust laws and peaceful confrontation with illegitimate authority, pursued by Mohandas Gandhi in India.

After returning to India, in 1920 Gandhi became president of the Indian National Congress, mounting nonviolent mass campaigns against British political and economic institutions. Inspired by his example, huge numbers of ordinary people—factory workers, peasants, estate laborers—joined his movement, shaking colonial rule's foundations. Gandhi made mass civil disobedience—marches, sit-ins, hunger strikes, peaceful violation of law, refusal to pay taxes, boycotts of government and businesses—an effective nonviolent strategy. His Congress colleague, Jawaharlal Nehru **(JAH-wa-HAR-lahl NAY-roo)**, placed Gandhi's role in perspective: "Gandhi was like a powerful current of fresh air that made us stretch ourselves and take deep breaths, like a Whirlwind that upset many things but most of all the working of people's minds."[15]

Yet, some of Gandhi's ideas were outside mainstream nationalist thought, confounding allies. Gandhi opposed the global economic system, characterized by competitive capitalism and trade between societies with unequal power and wealth. He believed India should reject Western models and return to the self-sufficient, village-based precolonial economy, where people could spin their own cloth. He called industrialization "a machinery which has impoverished India. India's salvation consists in unlearning what she has learned during the past fifty years. The railways, telegraphs, hospitals, [and] lawyers have all to go."[16] Critics considered Gandhi's ideal of simple living a utopian fantasy, impractical, out of touch with the modern world, and unable to improve people's lives. Gandhi also insisted that society's lowest social group, untouchables, be included in political actions, distressing high-caste Hindus. Gandhi coined the term *harijans* (children of God) as a more dignified label to replace *pariahs*, the centuries-old term for untouchables. While not entirely rejecting the caste system, Gandhi wanted all people to enjoy the same dignity. In his conception, harijan toilet cleaners would have the same status as members of the priestly caste but continue cleaning toilets. Even untouchable leaders often considered Gandhi's views unrealistic and patronizing.

Thanks to Gandhi's efforts, during the 1920s the Congress developed a mass base, supported by people from all cultures, religions, regions, and social backgrounds. His tactics bewildered the British; while they claimed to uphold law, order, and Christian values, they clubbed hunger strikers, trampled nonviolent protesters with horses, and arrested Gandhi and other leaders. One Indian observer told British officials in 1930 that the Congress "has undoubtedly acquired a great hold on the popular imagination. On roadside stations where until a few months ago I could hardly have suspected that people had any politics, I have seen demonstrations and heard Congress slogans."[17] Each campaign led to British concessions and the growing realization that Britain could not hold India forever.

---

[13]Quoted in Sinharaja Tammita-Delgoda, *A Traveller's History of India*, 2nd ed. (New York: Interlink, 1999), 189.

[14]From Clark D. Moore and David Eldridge, eds., *India Yesterday and Today* (New York: Bantam, 1970), 174.

[15]Quoted in Martin Deming Lewis, ed., *Gandhi: Maker of Modern India?* (Lexington, MA: D.C. Heath, 1965), xii.

[16]Quoted in Hermann Kulke and Dietmar Rothermund, *History of India*, 3rd ed. (New York: Routledge, 1998), 135–136.

[17]Sir T. P. Sapru, quoted in Judith M. Brown, *Modern India: The Origins of an Asian Democracy*, 2nd ed. (New York: Oxford University Press, 1994), 280.

Mohandas Gandhi, Indian Nationalist

Few individuals have had as much impact on history as Mohandas Gandhi (1869–1948), who became Indian nationalism's leading figure in the 1920s by formulating ideas of nonviolent opposition to repressive colonial rule, influencing millions both inside and outside India. Gandhi was born into an affluent vaisya family in the western state of Gujarat; although vaisyas commonly engaged in commerce, his father was a government official. Like many traditionalist, devout Hindus, His parents arranged for him to marry at thirteen to Kasturbai Kapada (**KAST-er-by ka-PO-da**) (1869–1948), a rich merchant's daughter. Kasturbai proved a courageous helpmate in his later political activities.

Gandhi wanted to study law in London, but his family feared he would be corrupted there. He vowed to live a celibate life in England and never touch meat or wine. In England he read Indian works such as the *Bhagavad Gita* and Western books including the Christian Bible. He also learned about Western nationalism and democracy.

In 1893 Gandhi joined a large Indian law firm in South Africa, where the racist government and white minority mistreated the thousands of Indians recruited as laborers and plantation workers. With his wife's encouragement, he began helping local Indians assert their rights, for which he was jailed, beaten by mobs, and almost killed by angry opponents. South Africa's British rulers raised taxes on Indians, shut down Indian gatherings, and refused official recognition of Hindu marriages. Influenced by Kasturbai's advocacy of justice and nonviolence, Gandhi developed his nonviolent resistance strategy against oppressive rule, ideas that later inspired admirers throughout the world. Gandhi spread ideas of nonviolence by leading hunger strikes, public demonstrations, and mass marches; thousands of Indians, resisting oppression, willingly risked beating or arrest for their cause. In 1914, the colonial regime lifted the worst legal injustices. Gandhi was forty-five years old when the triumph earned him fame and the respected title of *Mahatma* (Great Soul) among Indians in South Africa and at home.

When World War I broke out, Gandhi, Kasturbai, and their four children returned to India. In 1915 Gandhi established a spiritual center in Gujarat training followers in nonviolence. Though deeply religious, he also believed everyone had to reach truth in his or her own way, writing that "there are innumerable definitions of God, because His manifestations are innumerable. But I worship God as Truth only. I have not yet found Him, but I am seeking after Him." Moved by the Indian masses' poverty and suffering, he took up their cause. The high-caste Gandhi adopted simple peasant dress and always traveled third class.

Bettmann/Corbis

GANDHI ADDRESSING CALCUTTA MEETING Mohandas Gandhi addressed some of his followers—many women as well as men—on a lawn following a meeting with British officials in Calcutta in 1931.

The massacre of Indian protesters at Amritsar in 1919 shook Gandhi's faith in British justice. In 1920 he became the leader of the Indian National Congress. Over the next three decades he was at times a religious figure, at other times the consummate politician, crafty and practical. He launched three great campaigns of civil disobedience, in 1920, 1930, and 1942. Each time Britain jailed him for long periods. His practice of fasting to protest oppression reflected his self-discipline, adding to his saintly image.

Gandhi's personal life was also troubled. His wife, Kasturbai, aided in his campaigns, but Gandhi was gone for long periods, neglecting her and their four children. When Gandhi took a lifelong vow of chastity in 1906, Kasturbai did also. Although both came from affluent families, the Gandhis agreed to live simply. Critics accused Gandhi of sometimes humiliating his wife by, for example, asking her to do menial tasks such as cleaning toilets. Arrested during Gandhi's "Quit India" campaign, Kasturbai, in failing health, died in her husband's lap in prison in 1944. Before passing away, she noted they had shared many joys and sorrows and asked that she be cremated in a sari (dress) made from yarn he had spun.

Gandhi helped lead India to independence from Britain. Shortly thereafter, trying to end accelerating Hindu-Muslim violence in 1948, a Hindu fanatic who opposed Gandhi's tolerant approach assassinated him (see Chapter 31). India's first prime minister, Jawaharlal Nehru, called Gandhi's death the loss of India's soul: "The light has gone out of our lives and there is darkness everywhere."

THINKING ABOUT THE PROFILE

1. How did Gandhi's South African experiences shape his political strategies?
2. How did Gandhi's ideas and activities have a great influence in the world?

Note: Quotations from Judith M. Brown, *Modern India: The Origins of an Asian Democracy,* 2nd ed. (New York: Oxford University Press, 1994), 211; and Rhoads Murphey, *A History of Asia,* 4th ed. (New York: Longman, 2003), 437.

The Great Depression collapsed prices for cash crops and rural credit, caused distress and suffering, and sparked a new Gandhi-led campaign in 1930, the Great Salt March. Gandhi and several dozen followers marched to the west coast, where they produced salt from seawater, breaking British laws since salt production was a lucrative government monopoly. Gandhi's action and arrest caught the popular imagination, sparking demonstrations, strikes, and boycotts. In quelling the unrest, the British killed 103, injured 420, and imprisoned 60,000 resisters. Released a few months later, Gandhi agreed to halt civil disobedience campaigns if Britain promoted Indian-made goods and held a conference to discuss India's political future.

Social Change: Caste and Gender Relations

Nationalist politics, economic dislocations, and rapid population growth affected India's social structure. India's population grew from 255 million in 1871 to 390 million in 1940. Trends reshaping the caste system continued, including more awareness of caste identities and lower castes adopting high-caste practices such as vegetarianism. Although Gandhi urged fair treatment, stronger caste identities fostered more discrimination against untouchables, perhaps a fifth of India's population. Untouchables responded, mounting movements promoting their rights. Dr. Bhimrao Ramji Ambedkar (**BIM-rao RAM-jee am-BED-car**) (1893–1956), who rose from one of the lowest groups, sweepers who cleaned village streets, to earn a Ph.D. and law degree from major U.S. and British universities, started schools, newspapers, and political parties. Rejecting Gandhi's policies as inadequate, he successfully lobbied to offer untouchables government jobs and scholarships for higher education. Later in life, believing untouchables could never flourish within Hinduism, Ambedkar led thousands of followers to adopt Buddhism, which by then had only a small following in India.

Attitudes toward women were also changing. Hindus increasingly favored widow remarriage, once forbidden, to help offset the higher Muslim birthrate. But greater emphasis on what traditionalists considered proper female conduct largely favored male authority. While the feminist movement remained weak, many women joined the Congress, and some demanded a vote equal to men for representative institutions. In 1915 poet Sarojini Naidu (1879–1949) became the first female Congress president. With British assent, all provincial legislatures granted women the franchise between 1923 and 1930. Educated women published magazines. Rokeya Hossain (1880–1932), a Bengali Muslim raised in seclusion who opened girls' schools and campaigned for equal rights, published a utopian short story, "Sultana's Dream," portraying men confined to seclusion because of uncontrolled sexual desires while women governed. Gandhi advocated gender equality, encouraged women's participation in public life, and urged women to abandon seclusion. But Gandhi usually offered women followers more menial tasks such as picketing and cooking, promoted women's traditional roles as wives and mothers, and believed women were especially suited to passive resistance. Some militant women joined men in terrorist organizations. Pritilata Waddedar (1911–1932), a brilliant Bengali university graduate, led and died in an armed raid on a British club that reportedly boasted a sign: "Dogs and Indians not allowed."

Hindu-Muslim Division

A growing Hindu-Muslim division posed a problem for nationalists. Although some Muslims supported the largely Hindu Congress, other Muslims pondered their role in India. While Gandhi respected all religions and welcomed Muslim support, Muslim leaders, fearing independence would mean Hindu domination, mounted their own nationalist organizations to work for a potential Muslim country. In 1930 student activists in Britain called their proposed Muslim nation Pakistan ("Land of the Pure") in Urdu. Some 20 percent of British India's population and largely concentrated in the northwest and Bengal, Muslims were divided by social status, ancestry, language, and sect. The great majority were Sunnis.

While Muslim leaders envisioned a state enshrining their religious values, Congress leaders were chiefly Western-oriented Hindu intellectuals. Jawaharlal Nehru (1889–1964), who succeeded Gandhi as Congress leader in 1929, wanted a secular state that was neutral toward religion and, unlike Gandhi, a modernized India. From a wealthy brahman family, charismatic with rare public speaking skills, Nehru was a Marxist-influenced product of an elite Western education who emphasized the common people's welfare. While Gandhi wanted to reshape society, Nehru and other Congress leaders focused on political independence. Few Indian nationalists shared the Chinese communist goal of radical social transformation.

By the 1930s the Muslim League, led by Western-educated Bombay lawyer Muhammed Ali Jinnah (**jee-NAH**) (1876–1948), a dapper figure in tailored suits who always spoke English and never learned Urdu, became a mass political movement competing with the Congress. Jinnah promoted a two-nations solution, arguing that it was a naive dream that Hindus and Muslims, with different values, could ever forge a common nationality. Jinnah's claim to speak for all Muslims outraged the Congress, which, with over a hundred thousand Muslim members, viewed itself as a national party representing all religions and castes. But Jinnah cultivated good relations with Britain and convinced regional Muslim leaders to support the Muslim League. The Congress, trying to marginalize the Muslim League, refused to form a coalition, a mistake in the long run.

The competing Congress and Muslim League visions complicated British efforts to introduce representative government. The rival organizations clashed in 1931, when Indian leaders and British officials met in London to discuss expanded elections. Various minorities, including

Muslims, Sikhs, and untouchables, demanded separate electorates to ensure they gained representation. Believing this would perpetuate British divide and rule, the Congress objected, but the minorities won provincial electoral rights. The electoral agreement failed to end anticolonial unrest and British counterviolence. However, in the Government of India Act of 1935, Britain introduced a new constitution that allowed 35 million property-owning Indians to vote for newly formed provincial legislatures. In the 1937 elections, the Congress won 70 percent of the popular vote and the majority of seats, defeating the Muslim League even in reserved Muslim seats. Jinnah redoubled his efforts to unite Muslims against the Congress. More Indians achieved leadership positions in the army, police, and civil service. However, British officials argued that communal divisions necessitated British rule to maintain order.

World War II and India

World War II, increasing the Hindu-Muslim divide, reshaped the nationalist dialogue. Britain committed Indian troops without consulting Congress leaders. In 1942 Gandhi, fearing Britain would not end its colonial rule, mounted a campaign demanding the British "Quit India." The British arrested the entire Congress leadership and 60,000 party activists, jailing many for the war's duration. Meanwhile, the rural poor and urban workers suffered as prices for essential goods soared; famine in Bengal killed 3 to 4 million people. In response, Nehru's main rival for Congress leadership, militant Bengali Marxist Subhas Chandra Bose (1895–1945), allied with imperial Japan and organized an Indian National Army, recruited from the British Indian army and Indian emigrants in Southeast Asia, that invaded India from Japanese-held Burma. The invasion failed, but many Indians saw Bose as a national hero.

Meanwhile, jailing Congress leaders allowed Jinnah to strengthen his Muslim League. The British cultivated Jinnah, who joined the government and demanded a separate Muslim state based on the Muslim-majority provinces. Rejecting Muslim separatism, the jailed Gandhi unsuccessfully urged Muslims to resist what he termed the suicide of partition. After World War II, the struggle between Indian nationalists and Britain, and between Hindus and Muslims, resumed, leading to the end of British rule and creating two separate independent nations, predominantly Hindu India and chiefly Muslim Pakistan.

MAKE SURE YOU UNDERSTAND THESE KEY POINTS BEFORE MOVING ON

- Mohandas Gandhi, the foremost Indian nationalist leader, promoted nonviolent resistance to British rule, including strikes, boycotts, and refusal to pay taxes, and won a massive popular following for the Indian National Congress.

- While even his Indian supporters considered some of Gandhi's ideas naive and utopian, campaigns such as the Great Salt March were highly effective in winning concessions from the British.

- Leaders of the untouchables, the lowest Hindu caste, pushed for and obtained greater opportunities, and women were allowed somewhat more freedom, though many Indian men, including Gandhi, did not see them as entirely equal to men.

- The British jailed tens of thousands of Indian National Congress activists after Gandhi objected to Indian troops being forced to fight in World War II.

- Muhammed Ali Jinnah created the Muslim League and fought for a separate country for Muslims, and eventually two countries gained independence: India and Pakistan.

Nationalist Stirrings in Southeast Asia and Sub-Saharan Africa

How did nationalism differ in Southeast Asia and sub-Saharan Africa?

As in India, nationalist movements and protests in Southeast Asia and sub-Saharan Africa, none as influential as the Indian National Congress, also challenged Western colonialism. In 1930 the Indonesian Nationalist Party, struggling against Dutch colonialism, urged Indonesians to zealously pursue national freedom. The plea symbolized nationalist assertions in Southeast Asia, especially French-ruled Vietnam. In sub-Saharan Africa nationalist movements, often based on ethnicity, were weaker.

Nationalism in Southeast Asia

The first stirrings of Southeast Asian nationalism, in the Philippines in the late 1800s, was thwarted by the American occupation. The United States reduced radical sentiments by promising eventual independence and co-opting nationalist leaders into the colonial administration. By 1941 nationalists had a large following in Vietnam, British Burma, and Indonesia, all experiencing oppressive colonial rule. In French-ruled

Cambodia and Laos and in British Malaya and Borneo, all colonies enduring less social, economic, and political disruption, nationalism was weaker.

In Burma (today's Myanmar), despite limited self-government by the 1930s, the majority ethnic group, the Burmans, hated British rule, British favoritism toward Christian ethnic minorities, and the large, economically dominant Indian community. The colony's schools encouraged students to adopt Western ways, including clothing styles, devaluing Buddhist traditions. Nationalist leaders, using Theravada Buddhism as a rallying cry, pressed for reform; some favored women's rights. A militant student movement emerged whose members called themselves thakins ("lords"), a symbol of youthful defiance. Their leaders, such as Aung San and U Nu, would lead the struggle for independence. When the Japanese invaded Burma in 1941, many Burmans welcomed them as liberators.

Although Siam (today's Thailand) was not a colony, nationalism emerged among the rising middle class of civil servants, military officers, and professionals, who resented the royal family and aristocracy's political domination. The Great Depression forced salary and budget cuts, further fueling middle-class discontent. In 1932 military officers, calling themselves nationalists, took power in a coup against the royal government, pressuring Siam's king, whose family had ruled since the late 1700s, to become a constitutional, mostly symbolic monarch. Military leaders ran the government through the 1930s, pursuing nationalist policies, renaming the country Thailand ("Land of Free People"), and promoting modern lifestyles, including dressing in Western fashion, with hats and shoes. Allying with imperial Japan, Thailand introduced fascist policies, militarizing schools and suppressing dissent.

The most powerful nationalist movement emerged in Vietnam, destabilized by French rule. The passionately revolutionary Phan Boi Chau (**FAN boy chow**) (1867–1940), from a mandarin family, inspired patriotism and resistance. Before dying in a French prison, he wrote, "It has been but a yearning to purchase my freedom even at the cost of spilling my blood, to exchange my fate of slavery for the right of self-determination."[18] But older Confucian scholars like Phan gradually lost influence to younger, urban, French-educated intellectuals of the Vietnamese Nationalist Party, which, with few other options, assassinated colonial officials and bombed French buildings. A premature uprising in 1930 proved a turning point, sparking greater French repression that destroyed or weakened major nationalist groups except for the better-organized

Viet Minh The Vietnamese Independence League, a coalition of anti-French groups established by Ho Chi Minh in 1941 that waged war against both the French and the Japanese.

lingua franca A language widely used as a common tongue among diverse groups with different languages.

communists, some of whose leadership was underground or, like Ho, living abroad.

Vietnamese communism owed much to Ho Chi Minh, a mandarin's son turned political activist who spent many years organizing the movement among Vietnamese exiles in Thailand and China. Believing revolution was the answer to economic exploitation and political repression, Ho favored equality for women and improving the lives of peasants and plantation workers. In 1930 he established the Indochinese Communist Party, uniting anticolonial radicals from Vietnam, Cambodia, and Laos. Vietnamese Marxists, imbued with nationalism, linked themselves to the patriotic Vietnamese rebels who for two thousand years had resisted Chinese, Mongol, and French conquerors. As one Marxist wrote: "Behind us we have the immense history of our people. There [are] still spiritual cords attaching us."[19] In 1941 Ho established the **Viet Minh** (Vietnamese Independence League), a coalition of anti-French groups that fought both French colonizers and the Japanese, who occupied Vietnam during World War II.

Nationalist activity also emerged in the Dutch East Indies. Diverse organizations sought freedom from Dutch rule while seeking to unite the colony's hundreds of ethnic groups. Some emphasized a unifying language. Malay, the mother tongue for many peoples in western Indonesia and a trading language elsewhere, was the archipelago's **lingua franca**, a widely used common tongue among diverse groups with their own languages. Nationalist intellectuals began using Malay, calling it Indonesian, which gradually became the language of magazines, newspapers, books, and education. Indonesians also reshaped religious traditions. Some Muslims, impressed with but also resenting Western power, sought to reform and purify their faith by eliminating older pre-Islamic influences, such as mysticism. *Muhammadiyah* ("Way of Muhammad") and its allied women's organization, *Aisyah*, criticized local customs, promoted the goal of an Islamic state, stressed Islam's five pillars, and favored segregating men and women in public, a custom most Indonesians ignored.

In 1912 Javanese batik merchants, mixing reformist religious ideas with nationalism, established the first true political movement, the Islamic Union; by 1919 it had 2 million members. As Marxism became influential, the colonial government arrested Marxists. Radical Marxists established the Indonesian Communist Party in 1920, attracting support from nondevout Muslim peasants and labor union members in Java. Overestimating their strength, the communists sparked a poorly planned uprising in 1926. The Dutch crushed the uprising, executing communist leaders.

Javanese aristocrats who rejected Islamic reform ideas established the Indonesian Nationalist Party in 1927, promoting a new national identity. The key founder, Sukarno (**soo-KAHR-no**) (1902–1970), from a wealthy aristocratic

[18]"Phan Boi Chau's Prison Reflections, 1914," in *Major Problems in the History of the Vietnam War: Documents and Essays*, ed. Robert J. McMahon (Lexington, MA: D.C. Heath, 1990), 32.

[19]Hoai Thanh, quoted in David Marr, "Vietnamese Historical Reassessment, 1900–1944," in *Perceptions of the Past in Southeast Asia*, ed. Anthony Reid and David Marr (Singapore: Heinemann, 1979), 337–338.

Javanese family, studied engineering and then dedicated his life to politics and a free Indonesia. Sukarno loved the shadow puppet stories popular on Java for centuries. Like these stories' characters, Sukarno (who had no first name) brought together contradictory ideas, such as Islamic faith and atheistic Marxism. In 1941 Sukarno wrote: "What is Sukarno? A nationalist? An Islamist? A Marxist?…Sukarno is a mixture of all these isms…a meeting place of all trends and Ideologies."[20] A spellbinding orator and nationalism's mass popularizer, he created a slogan: "one nation—Indonesia, one people—Indonesian, one language—Indonesian," designed a flag, and wrote a national anthem. Dutch authorities arrested Sukarno in 1929 and exiled him to a remote island prison for the next decade, making him a nationalist symbol. In his defense speech he stressed Indonesia's "grandiose past. Oh, what Indonesian does not feel his heart shrink with sorrow when he hears the stories about the beautiful past, does not regret the disappearance of that departed glory!"[21] With Sukarno imprisoned, the Nationalist Party and vision grew slowly throughout the 1930s.

The Japanese Occupation and Its Consequences

Japanese occupation from 1941 to 1945 boosted nationalism and weakened colonialism. Before 1941 colonial authority remained strong; only Vietnamese nationalism posed a serious threat. Then everything changed. Japan had already bullied Thailand and the Vichy-controlled French colonial regime in Vietnam to allow stationing of Japanese troops. Then a rapid Japanese invasion of Southeast Asia quickly followed the Pearl Harbor bombing in 1941. Easily overwhelming colonial forces, within four months Japan controlled major cities and heavily populated regions, shattering the mystique of Western invincibility. As an Indonesian writer remembered, the occupation "destroyed a whole set of illusions and left man as naked as when he was created."[22] European and American officials, businessmen, planters, and missionaries were either in retreat or prison camps. Japanese talked of "Asia for the Asians," and some anticolonial officers sympathized with Southeast Asian nationalists. But this rhetoric also masked Japanese desire for resources, especially rubber, oil, and timber from Indonesia, British Borneo, and Malaya.

Japanese domination was brief, less than four years, yet it fostered significant changes. Conflicts between ethnic groups often increased. In Malaya, Japanese policy allowed Malay officials to keep their jobs while Chinese often faced property seizures and arrest, creating antagonisms that persisted long after the war. Destroying the link to the world economy also caused hardship. Western companies closed, while Japanese seized natural resources and food. By 1944 living standards, crippled by food and clothing shortages, declined steeply. Japanese police harassed Southeast Asians, brutally punishing even minor violations of regulations. Japan also conscripted thousands of Southeast Asians: Javanese men became slave laborers, and Filipinas, termed "comfort women," served Japanese soldiers' sexual needs. As their war effort faltered, desperate Japanese became even more repressive.

Japanese rule directly or indirectly aided some Southeast Asian nationalists. Needing experienced local help, Japanese promoted Southeast Asians into government positions once reserved for Westerners. Purging Western cultural influences, they closed Christian mission schools, encouraged Islamic or Buddhist leaders, and fostered indigenous culture and local literature. Under colonialism most nationalists were in jail or exile, hence powerless; Japan freed nationalist leaders such as Sukarno, giving them official positions, if little actual power. Nationalists used radio and newspapers to spread their beliefs. Young people, recruited into armed paramilitary forces, became the basis for later nationalist armies in Indonesia and Burma, resisting the colonizers' return.

Some Southeast Asians actively opposed Japanese rule. Vietnamese communism might never have achieved power so quickly had the occupation not discredited the French administration and imposed great hardship on millions. Ho Chi Minh led the Viet Minh, now armed and trained by American advisers sent to help anti-Japanese forces. In 1944, the Viet Minh expanded their influence in northern Vietnam, attracting peasant support while attacking Japanese occupiers with guerrilla tactics. Japan exported scarce food to Japan while famine killed 2 million Vietnamese, spurring support for the Viet Minh, who organized local peasant-led village administrations.

As the United States gained military victories, bombing Japanese installations in Southeast Asia, Japanese encouraged Southeast Asians to resist reestablishing Western colonialism. Japanese officials helped Indonesian nationalists prepare for Indonesian independence and Burmese nationalists establish a government. Sukarno told his people: "Every city, every village, every house—yes, every heart must become a fortress [against the Dutch]."[23] Seeing Japan's prospects waning, some nationalists began secretly working with the Western Allies. Changing sides, the Burmese nationalist army helped push out Japanese forces. Tired of economic deprivation and repression, few Southeast Asians regretted Japan's defeat; some, especially in Malaya, British Borneo, and the Philippines, welcomed the renewed Western presence. Americans granted the Philippines independence under pro-U.S. leaders in 1946. But often the returning Westerners faced volatility, which produced dramatic political change in Vietnam, Indonesia, and Burma as nationalist forces successfully struggled for independence in the late 1940s and early 1950s.

---

[20]Quoted in J. D. Legge, *Sukarno: A Political Biography* (New York: Praeger, 1972), 341.

[21]From Harry J. Benda and John A. Larkin, eds., *The World of Southeast Asia: Selected Historical Readings* (New York: Harper and Row, 1967), 192.

[22]Sitor Situmorang, quoted in Harry Aveling, ed., *From Surabaya to Armageddon: Indonesian Short Stories* (Singapore: Heinemann, 1976), vii.

[23]Quoted in Berhard Dahm, *Sukarno and the Struggle for Indonesian Independence* (New York: Cornell University Press, 1969), 274.

Nationalism in Colonial Africa

The roots of the African struggle were planted in the interwar years, although African nationalists, lacking the Vietnamese or Indian mass base, had limited success overcoming major barriers to widespread popular support. Few regimes prepared their colonies for political and economic independence by permitting African participation in government or producing a large educated class. In addition, artificial colonial boundaries hindered nationalist organizing. Colonial regimes, using divide-and-rule strategies to govern diverse ethnic groups, made creating viable national identities and uniting all people difficult. For example, British Nigeria contained many often-rival ethnic groups. While some nationalists sought Pan-Nigerian unity, most found support only among particular regions or ethnic groups. In the 1940s a prominent Yoruba leader expressed the common fear that no Nigerian nation was really possible:

> *Nigeria is not a nation [but] a mere geographical expression. There are no "Nigerians" in the same sense as there are "English" or "French." The word "Nigerian" merely distinguish[es] those who live within the boundaries of Nigeria from those who do not.*[24]

World War I and unfulfilled expectations in its aftermath spurred nationalism. Britain, France, and Germany all drafted or recruited Africans to fight on European battlefields, where many thousands died. When survivors returned home, promises made about land or jobs proved empty while taxes increased. Returning Kenyan soldiers found that British settlers had seized their land. Harry Thuku **(THOO-koo)** (ca. 1895–1970), a Gikuyu, forged a diverse alliance to confront the British. When Britain arrested Thuku, rioting broke out, led by Gikuyu women; British forces killed many rioters. Anticolonial protests were also common in the Belgian Congo, sparking rebellions by peasant farmers upset at demands for unpaid labor. Women often led resistance. In Senegal Aline Sitoe Diatta (1920–1944) was exiled and later executed for leading an uprising when France conscripted her village's rice supplies. In Nigeria in 1929, tens of thousands of Igbo women, particularly palm oil traders, rioted to protest taxes. After the British killed thirty-two women, protests escalated; restoring order took months.

In the 1920s new urban-based nationalist organizations, pressing for African participation in local government, were led by Western-educated Africans including J. E. Casely Hayford (1866–1930), a British Gold Coast lawyer and journalist influenced by Gandhi. Some like Hayford favored a Pan-African approach, seeking support across colonial borders that they rejected as the basis

highlife An urban-based West African musical style mixing Christian hymns, West Indian calypso songs, and African dance rhythms.

pidgin English The form of broken English that developed in Africa during the colonial era.

for nations. But neither nationalists nor Pan-Africanists could overcome ethnic divisions and, unlike Indian and Vietnamese nationalists, the city-village gap. Furthermore, some African merchants, chiefs, and kings, profiting from links to the colonizers, discouraged protests.

Even with outrage at the brutal Italian invasion and occupation of Ethiopia in 1935–1936, nationalists had modest influence before World War II. West African nationalist currents were strongest in multiethnic capital cities, where they bred the grounds of new ideas. Urban-based trade union movements sponsored occasional strikes protesting colonial policies or economic exploitation. Hence, market women in Lagos, Nigeria, protested taxation and demanded voting rights. During World War II they refused to cooperate with price controls, forcing Britain to back down. Rural people also asserted their rights. During the 1930s cocoa growers in the British Gold Coast held back their crops to protest low prices.

New cultural trends enabled Africans to express their views, often critical, about colonial life. During the 1930s a musical style, created in the Gold Coast, spread into other British West African colonies, carried by guitar-playing Africans and West Indian sailors. **Highlife** mixed Christian hymns, West Indian calypso songs, and African dance rhythms. Later, West African musicians added Cuban, Brazilian, and American influences, especially jazz, continuing cultural links between West Africa and the Americas. Although closely tied to dance bands and parties, some highlife musicians addressed social and political issues and everyday problems. The very term *highlife* signified both envy and disapproval of Western colonizers and rich Africans living in mansions staffed by servants. Many highlife songs were sung in **pidgin English**, a broken English form mixing African and English words and grammar developed during the colonial era. Pidgin English then spread throughout British West Africa as a marketplace lingua franca among diverse urban populations.

Racial inequality and white supremacy sparked nationalism and resistance to oppression in South Africa. Early nationalists, such as the African National Congress (ANC) founders in 1912, came from the urban middle class. The ANC encouraged education and preached independence from white rule, but it did not directly confront the government until the 1950s. More militant resistance flourished in the mining industry, where strikes were endemic despite severe government repression. Resistance was often subtle, involving noncooperation or affirmation of African cultural forms. Music often expressed protest, usually veiled to avoid arrest. Knowing that few whites understood African languages, African workers filled mining camps with political music, offering messages such as "we demand freedom" and "workers unite." Road gangs worked to songs such as "We Say: Oh, the White Man's Bad." Zulu and Swazi workers, blending their traditions with Western influences, created new dances. Virile, stamping dancers laced their performances with provocative songs: "Who has taken our land from us? Come out! Let us fight! The land was ours. Now it is taken. Fight! Fight!"[25]

[24]Obafemi Awolowo, quoted in Chester L. Hunt and Lewis Walker, *Ethnic Dynamics: Patterns of Intergroup Relations in Various Societies*, 2nd ed. (Holmes Beach, FL: Learning Publications, 1979), 277.

[25]Quoted in Veit Erlmann, *African Stars: Studies in Black South African Performance* (Chicago: University of Chicago Press, 1991), 95–96.

Great Strike on the Rand (b/w photo), South African Photographer, (20th Century)/Private Collection/© Look and Learn/Elgar Collection/The Bridgeman Art Library

GREAT STRIKE IN THE SOUTH AFRICAN MINING DISTRICTS In 1913 18,000 white miners went on strike to demand recognition of their union and protest difficult working conditions and competition from African miners but police used violence to quell the protests, killing 20.

In South African cities jazz, adapted from African Americans, became a form of resistance and potent vehicle for protest, reflecting African rejection of racist Afrikaner culture. African American musicians such as trumpeter Louis Armstrong (1901–1971) and pianist Duke Ellington (1898–1974), popular in the 1930s, influenced South African jazz bands and new jazz-based musical styles. Educated urban Africans, envisioning a modern African culture, sometimes rejected African traditions, as one Johannesburg resident proclaimed:

Tribal music! Chiefs! We don't care about chiefs! Give us jazz and film stars, man! We want Ellington, Satchmo [Louis Armstrong], and hot dames! Yes, brother, anything American. You can cut out this junk about [rural homesteads] and folk-tales—forget it! You're just trying to keep us backward![26]

The preferred music of the small black professional and business class, jazz ultimately symbolized black nationalism in South Africa.

MAKE SURE YOU UNDERSTAND THESE KEY POINTS BEFORE MOVING ON

- Southeast Asian nationalism was strong in places such as Burma, which experienced harsh colonial rule, and even emerged as a rallying cry in Siam, which was never colonized but where a military coup overthrew the royal government.

- Vietnamese resistance to French rule was continued by the terrorist Vietnamese Nationalist Party, which the French harshly repressed, and the Viet Minh, a coalition led by the communist Ho Chi Minh.

- A variety of groups representing Muslims, women, and communists worked toward independence for the Dutch East Indies.

- Although African nationalist movements were hampered by the existence of rival ethnic groups within artificial colonies, anger over the poor treatment of Africans who had fought in World War I inspired many, especially in cities, to work for independence.

- In South Africa, nationalists opposed the repressive white supremacist government through education, strikes, and, most pervasively, music.

aplia

---

[26]Quoted in Charles Hamm, "'The Constant Companion of Man': Separate Development, Radio Bantu and Music," *Popular Music* 10, no. 2 (May 1991): 161.

Ⓣ Remaking the Middle East and Latin America

What factors promoted change in the Middle East and Latin America?

Nationalism also influenced Middle Eastern and Latin American peoples. While North Africans experienced Western colonial rule, Turkey remained independent and Arabs in western Asian territories controlled by Ottoman Turks stagnated economically. The transfer of Ottoman-ruled Arab territories to Britain and France sparked nationalist resentment and reshaped Arab politics. In Latin America, two world wars and the Great Depression caused turmoil, fostered dictatorships, and spurred nationalism.

Reshaping the Ottoman Territories

After World War I the Turkish-dominated Ottoman Empire, Germany's ally, was dismantled. Still independent, the Turks, sharing German hatred of expansionist Russia, also dreamed of liberating Russian-controlled lands in the Caucasus and Central Asia, where many spoke languages related to Turkish. However, Caucasus peoples, especially Christian Armenians, desired independence. Suspecting them of aiding Russia, the Turks turned on Armenians in eastern Anatolia (see Chapter 21), deporting more than a million, chiefly to Syria and Iraq; perhaps another million died of thirst, starvation, or systematic slaughter by the Ottoman army. These sufferings created permanent Turkish-Armenian hostility.

World War I hardships also spurred Arab nationalism against Ottoman rule; hunger and disease affected millions of Arabs, with 200,000 dying in Syria alone. Syrian unrest precipitated fierce repression, during which dissidents were sent into exile or hanged for treason. The most serious challenge came in Arabia, where Sharif Hussein ibn Ali (1856–1931), the Arab ruler of the Hejaz, the western Arabia region including Mecca and Medina, shifted his loyalties from the Ottomans to Britain, who promised to support Arab independence. In 1916, at British urging, Sharif Hussein launched an Arab revolt. British officers, including the flamboyant Lt. T. E. Lawrence (famous as "Lawrence of Arabia"), advised Sharif Hussein's tribal forces as they attacked Ottoman bases and communications. Britain also invaded and occupied southern Iraq, an Ottoman province with a strategic position and potential oil wealth.

However, postwar developments crushed dreams, fostering turmoil. Arab nationalists such as Sharif Hussein were unaware that Britain, France, and Russia had made secret agreements that ignored Arab interests. The czarist Russians planned to incorporate Istanbul and nearby territories into their empire, while Britain and France agreed to partition Ottoman provinces in western Asia between them. Russian plans had to be modified after communists took power and signed a peace treaty with Germany allowing the Russian-controlled Caucasus territories to be returned to the Ottomans. But with Ottoman defeat, British troops occupied much of Iraq and Palestine, French troops controlled the Syrian coast, and Russians regained control of the Caucasus, including Armenia.

The Versailles treaty dismembered the Ottoman Empire (see Map 25.2). Turkey's neighbors—Greeks, Italians, and Armenians—made claims on Anatolia and adjacent islands, while European Zionists asked for a Jewish national home in Palestine (see Chapter 21). The Allies promised eventual independence to the Kurds, a Sunni Muslim people who were distinct from both Arabs and Turks and who inhabited a large, mountainous region of western Asia, including southeast Turkey. Both Syria and Iraq declared their independence. However, the League of Nations, dominated by Western countries, awarded France control over Syria and Lebanon and gave Britain control over Iraq, Palestine, and Transjordan (today Jordan), under what the League called mandates, in theory less permanent than colonies. Considering mandates as a new colonialism, Arab nationalists in Syria proposed a democratic government; some favored granting women the vote, which few Western nations had done. Ignoring Syrian views, French forces, after facing armed resistance, exiled nationalist leaders. Despite promises, the Allies also ignored Kurdish desires for their own nation, dividing them between Turkey, Persia (Iran), Iraq, and Syria; Kurds remained the world's largest ethnic group without their own state.

The Ottoman Empire's center, Turkey, saw the most revolutionary changes. Disastrous defeat and the humiliating agreements that followed left Turks helpless, bitter, and facing a Greek invasion and Arab secession. But the daring war hero and ardent nationalist later known as Kemal Ataturk (**kuh-MAHL AT-uh-turk**) (1881–1938) led a spectacular Turkish resurgence. In 1919 Ataturk began mobilizing military forces in eastern Anatolia into a revolutionary organization to oppose the Ottoman sultan, discredited by defeats, restore Turkish dignity, and preserve Turkish-majority areas and Kurdish districts in eastern Anatolia. After establishing a rival Turkish government in Ankara, a central Anatolia city, Ataturk's forces fought both the sultan's government and Greek forces moving deep into Anatolia. Ataturk finally pushed the Greeks back; Turkey and Greece eventually agreed to transfer many Greeks living in Turkey to Greece and most Turks dwelling in Greece to Turkey. In 1922 Ataturk deposed the Ottoman sultan and founded a republic with himself as president.

Ataturk was and remains controversial among Turks. A religious agnostic, he violated Muslim customs with sexual promiscuity and heavy public drinking. A nationalist glorifying the pre-Islamic Turkish past, Ataturk dismissed Islamic culture as outdated and favored modernization, announcing that "our eyes are turned westward. We shall transplant Western institutions to Asiatic soil. We wish to be a modern nation with our mind open, and yet to remain ourselves."[27] Ataturk claimed that secularization and women's emancipation were Turkish traditions. In the 1920s he introduced reforms challenging

---

[27]Quoted in Hans Kohn, *A History of Nationalism in the East* (New York: Harcourt, 1929), 257.

MAP 25.2 PARTITION OF THE OTTOMAN EMPIRE Before 1914 the Ottoman Turks controlled much of western Asia, including western Arabia. After World War II the League of Nations awarded Iraq, Transjordan, and Palestine to Britain. Syria and Lebanon were given to France, and western Arabia was ruled by Arabs. Eventually the Saudi family, rulers of the Najd, expanded their rule into western Arabia and created Saudi Arabia. © 2015 Cengage Learning

Legend:
- Ottoman Empire in 1914
- British protectorate in 1914
- Area controlled under mandates from the League of Nations, 1920
- British Mandate
- French Mandate
- International boundaries, 1923

Muslim traditions, revamping the legal system along Western lines, replacing Arabic-based script with a Western alphabet, prohibiting polygamy, abolishing Islamic schools and courts, removing reference to Islam as the state religion from the constitution, and granting women equal rights in divorce, child custody, and inheritance. While his government resembled a parliamentary democracy, he exercised near-dictatorial power, suppressing Kurdish language and culture. Ataturk left a deeply changed nation. While many reforms never reached villages, where Islam remained a strong influence, his secular approach remained popular with Turkish nationalists, including military officers.

Hulton Archive/Stringer/Getty Images

ATATURK WEDDING DANCE The Turkish leader Kemal Ataturk promoted and adopted Western fashions while defying Muslim customs. In this photo from around 1925, Ataturk dances with his daughter at her Western-style wedding.

Modern Iran, Egypt, and Iraq

Major changes also occurred in other Middle Eastern countries. The war's end left Britain with power to impose a protectorate over Persia, forcing the government to accept British loans, financial controls, advisers, and military forces. Growing Persian opposition in 1921 prompted Britain to support General Reza Khan **(REE-za kahn)** (1877–1944), a soldier seeking to end the corrupt, ineffective royal dynasty, establish a secular republic, and address economic underdevelopment. Secular Shi'ites, long struggling for more democracy to reduce the powerful Shi'ite clergy's domination, supported Reza Khan. But in 1925, at the urging of Shi'ite clerics, Reza Khan, abandoning republican government, formed the Pahlavi **(PAH-lah-vee)** dynasty, with himself as king (known in Persia as a shah).

Reza Khan promoted modernization and in 1935 renamed his nation Iran, symbolically breaking with the past. The shah created a large national army through conscription, built railroads, established government factories

producing textiles, sugar, cement, and steel, and took over the oil industry. Social changes outraged Muslim conservatives, such as introducing a Western law code, encouraging men to wear Western hats and clothes, and outlawing women's veiling in public. Women who wanted to wear the veil had to stay home. But while the modernists, merchants, and middle class supported Reza Khan's policies, poor Iranians saw little improvement; the landlord class expanded at peasant expense. When Reza Khan supported Germany during World War II, Anglo-Russian forces occupied Iran. Humiliated, Reza Khan abdicated in favor of his son, Muhammad Reza Pahlavi **(REH-zah PAH-lah-vee)** (1919–1980), who ruled until 1979.

British control of Egypt and Iraq also generated nationalism. In Egypt during World War I Britain imposed martial law, drafting peasants to build roads and dig trenches in war zones. A popular song castigated British officials for carrying off the peasants' corn, camels, and cattle. After the war the leading nationalist party, the secular *Wafd*, led by Saad Zaghlul **(sod ZOG-lool)** (ca. 1857–1927), who studied under Islamic modernists and then earned a French law degree, sought independence, representative government, civil liberties, and curtailed powers for the pro-British monarchy.

In 1919 the British arrested Wafd leaders. Enraged Egyptians—rich and poor, Muslims and Coptic Christians, men and women—responded with strikes, student demonstrations, sabotaging of railroads, and murder of British soldiers, forcing the release of Zaghlul, who then went to the Paris Peace Conference to plead for national self-determination but, like Vietnam's Ho Chi Minh, was ignored. Zaghlul was arrested again, but the resulting unrest forced Britain to grant Egypt limited independence in 1922. Nationalists saw this agreement as a sham, since Britain still controlled Egypt's defense and foreign affairs. In 1936 Britain, officially ending its occupation, still kept thousands of troops along the Suez Canal and shared with Egypt administration of Sudan to the south. Resentment of the continuing British presence increased during World War II.

Britain also struggled to control Iraq, an artificial creation uniting three Ottoman provinces dominated respectively by Sunni Kurds, Sunni Arabs, and Shi'ite Arabs. Describing their occupation as "liberation," the British promised an efficient administration, honest finance, impartial justice, and security. A plebiscite giving the appearance of popular support was manipulated to suggest pro-British sympathies. Hating occupation, in 1920 Shi'ite clerics seeking an Islamic state proclaimed holy war against the British, and various Shi'a and Sunni tribes rose in rebellion. The British, relying heavily on aerial bombing, suppressed the rebellion, killing some 10,000 Iraqis and flattening whole villages.

Shaken by the fierce resistance, Britain introduced limited self-government through an appointed Council of State. Skilled diplomacy by pro-Arab British archaeologist, writer, and diplomat Lady Gertrude Bell (1868–1926) defused tensions. Seeking a king for Iraq who would "reign but not govern," Britain installed a member of the Hashemite **(HASH-uh-mite)** royal family of Mecca, Sharif Hussein's son Faisal (1885–1935). In 1930 Faisal convinced Britain to grant Iraq independence, accepting continued British military bases and government advisers. By then oil discoveries made Britain unwilling to cut ties. Many Arabs considered Faisal and his successors British puppets, but Sunni Arab military autocrats influenced government more than the kings.

Islam and Zionism

European power and cultural influence concerned most Middle Eastern societies, but nationalist success came slowly. Thinkers debated how or whether to emulate Western nations. While envying industrialization and consumer goods, they disagreed about adopting Western patterns, such as freethinking, parliamentary democracy, and women's rights. Some favored Westernization, some preservation of Islamic traditions, and still others mixing of the two. Egypt, Iraq, Lebanon, Transjordan, and Syria adopted Western-style constitutions providing civil liberties and elected parliaments that proved limited and unrepresentative. Real power remained with European officials or kings with little respect for civil liberties.

Inspired by Western modernity, Arabs made progress in education, public health, industrialization, and communications, but change came slowly. Egypt's literacy rate rose from 9 percent in 1917 to only 15 percent in 1937. Some women asserted their rights. Huda Shaarawi **(HOO-da sha-RAH-we)** (1879–1947), from a wealthy Cairo family, was married off at thirteen to a much older cousin. Finding the marriage confining, she organized nonviolent anti-British demonstrations by women after World War I, then publicly removed her veil, shocking Egyptians. The Egyptian feminist movement she founded succeeded in raising the minimum marriage age for girls to sixteen and increasing women's educational opportunities.

Debates over Westernization fostered new intellectual currents. A blind Egyptian writer, Taha Husayn (1889–1973), educated in Islamic schools but also at the Sorbonne in Paris, challenged orthodox Islam and, in 1938, proclaimed that Westernizing Arab culture fit with Egypt's traditions: "I want our new life to harmonize with our ancient glory." In contrast, the **Muslim Brotherhood**, founded in 1928 by schoolteacher Hasan al-Banna (1906–1949), reflected popular reaction against Westernization. Al-Banna despised Western values, arguing that it "would be inexcusable for us to turn aside from the path of truth—Islam—and so follow the path of fleshly desires and vanities—the path of Europe."[28] The Brotherhood, strictly interpreting the Quran, also accepted modern technology and favored a more active public role for women. Expressing widespread resentment against Western films, bars, and figure-revealing fashions, the Brotherhood developed a following in Sudan and western Asia.

The most extreme anti-Western reaction, and the one that eventually dominated Arabia, was the puritanical Wahhabi movement, which opposed shaving beards, smoking tobacco, and drinking alcohol, seeking a return to early Islam uncorrupted by centuries of change. The Wahhabis' influence grew when their ally, tribal chief Abdul Aziz Ibn Saud **(sah-OOD)** (1902–1969), expanded Saudi family power in central and eastern Arabia (see Chapter 21). By 1932 his forces had taken western Arabia and the holy cities from the Hashemites and formed Saudi Arabia. As king, Abdul Aziz strictly enforced Islamic law, establishing Committees for the Commendation of Virtue and the Condemnation of Vice to monitor personal behavior. Policemen used long canes to enforce attendance at daily prayers, punish alcohol use and listening to music, and harass unveiled women. Yet, Saudis also welcomed Western material innovations such as automobiles, medicine, and telephones. Wealth from the world's richest oil reserves, discovered in 1935, chiefly benefited the royal family and Wahhabi clergy.

Developments in Palestine, part of Ottoman-ruled Syria with a largely Arab population, created long-term problems. Britain took over after World War I. Meanwhile, the Zionist movement, seeking a Jewish homeland, emerged in Europe's Jewish ghettoes (see Chapters 19 and 21). The Zionist slogan—"a land without a people for a people without a land"—offered a compelling vision: take long-persecuted Jewish minorities and return them to Palestine, their ancient ancestral home. To reach this goal, Zionist leaders cultivated the British government. In 1917 the **Balfour Declaration** gave British support for establishing Palestine as a national home for the Jewish people. But Arabs had lived there for many centuries, building cities, cultivating orchards, and herding livestock. In Arab eyes, Jewish immigrants were European colonizers planning to dispossess them.

Thousands of European Jews migrated to Palestine with British support, some fleeing Nazi Germany, so that by 1939 Palestine's population of 1.5 million was one-third Jewish. Although Jewish settlers established businesses, industries, and productive farms, Arabs feared becoming a vulnerable minority in their own land. Zionist organizations bought the best land from absentee Arab landlords who disregarded the customary rights of villagers to use it, uprooting thousands of Arab peasants. As tensions increased, violence spread, bewildering the British. Sometimes armed clashes killed hundreds of Arabs and Jews; in 1936 a three-year civil war erupted, during which Arabs demanded an end to Jewish immigration and land sales to Jews, as well as plans for an independent Palestine. Britain proposed a partition into two states, removing thousands of Arabs from the Jewish side, but both groups rejected the proposal. In 1939 Britain limited Jewish immigration and banned land transfers; however,

Muslim Brotherhood An Egyptian religious movement founded in 1928 that expressed popular Arab reaction to Westernization.

Balfour Declaration A letter from the British foreign minister to Zionist leaders in 1917 giving British support for the establishment of Palestine as a national home for the Jewish people.

---

[28] The quotes are from Akram Fouad Khater, ed., *Sources in the History of the Modern Middle East* (Boston: Houghton Mifflin, 2004), 167, 176.

MAP 25.3 SOUTH AND CENTRAL AMERICA IN 1930 By 1930 Latin America had achieved its present political configuration, except that Britain, France, and Holland still had colonies in the Guianas region of South America, and Britain controlled British Honduras (today's Belize) in Central America. © 2015 Cengage Learning

the Holocaust during World War II spurred a more militant desire for a homeland where Jews could govern themselves.

Politics and Modernization in Latin America

Latin Americans, reliant on natural resource exports such as beef, copper, coffee, and sugar, were vulnerable to global political and economic crises and sometimes foreign interventions, as when U.S. military forces occupied Nicaragua from 1909 to 1933 and Haiti from 1915 to 1934. During the Great Depression, foreign investment fell and foreign markets closed, cutting some countries' foreign trade by 90 percent; by 1932 Latin America exported 65 percent less than in 1929. Economic downturns fostered political instability and military dictators, known as caudillos, all over the region (see Map 25.3).

In 1930–1931 armed forces overthrew governments in a dozen Latin American nations. European fascism influenced some new governments, particularly in Argentina and Brazil. Dictators amassed huge fortunes, repressed dissent, and often increased their governments' economic roles, beginning industries to provide products normally imported. In El Salvador President Maximiliano Hernandez Martinez massacred thirty thousand protesting Indian peasants; praising poverty, he claimed people who went barefoot could better receive the earth's "beneficial vibrations" than those with shoes. Some dictatorships continued for years. Collapsing sugar prices, which generated a massive Cuban strike, forced repressive rightwinger Gerardo Machado (r. 1925–1933) out of office, temporarily bringing leftwing nationalists and socialists to power. But the United States, disliking the new government for reforms that hurt influential American business interests, encouraged a coup by Sgt. Fulgencio Batista **(fool-HEN-see-o bah-TEES-ta)** (1901–1973) in 1934; Batista dominated Cuba for the next twenty-five years as a rightwing dictator.

The challenges also affected Chile, one of the most open Latin American nations. Although the military occasionally seized power for short periods, Chileans generally elected democratic governments and supported several political parties. The Great Depression helped reformist parties and social movements gain support; the squabbling leftist and centrist parties, united in a Popular Front, won the 1939 elections. Their reformist government, supported by labor unions, sponsored industrialization, while a growing women's movement allied with Chile's political left brought once-forbidden ideas into the patriarchal, strongly Catholic country. Demanding respect for Chilean women and ending "compulsory motherhood," feminists lobbied for prenatal health care, child-care subsidies, birth control, and the right to abortion, which was illegal but widely practiced. But while winning some basic legal rights, women still struggled for voting rights and could not get most of their social agenda approved.

Brazil experienced political change tinged with nationalism. In the 1920s middle-class reformers, challenging a corrupt ruling class that failed to listen to common people or assert Brazil's national interests in the world, sought official recognition of labor unions, a minimum wage, restraints on child labor, land reform, universal suffrage, and expansion of education to poor children. Worker unrest fostered labor unions. But the Great Depression prompted a civilian-military coup by Getulio Vargas **(jay-TOO-lee-oh VAR-gus)** (1883–1954) in 1930. A pragmatic former soldier, lawyer, and government minister, Vargas launched the **Estado Novo** ("New State"), a fascist-influenced, modernizing dictatorship, ruling until 1945. An anti-Vargas businessman described him as "intelligent, extremely perceptive, but also a demagogue who knew how to manipulate the masses."[29] While using torture and censorship to repress opponents, he nationalized banks, financed industrialization, and introduced social security, an eight-hour workday, a minimum wage, the right to strike, and the vote for literate eighteen-year-olds and working women, reforms popular with the lower classes. Gradually the dictator became more populist and nationalist. After the army deposed him in 1945, tensions between rightwing and leftwing Brazilians remained.

Progressive and nationalist ideas emerged in Mexico. After the decade-long Mexican Revolution (see Chapter 20), which ended in 1920, Mexico badly needed reconstruction funds but faced sharply reduced export earnings and a deepening economic slump. A popular song noted the hardship on common Mexicans: "The scramble to be president is one of our oldest haunts. But to eat a peaceful tortilla is all the poor man wants."[30] President Plutarcho Elias Calles **(KAH-yays)** (r. 1924–1928) stabilized the political system, creating a new party that brought together various factions. Yet many saw little improvement, and women remained largely excluded from public life. In 1934 Lazaro Cardenas **(car-DAYN-es)** (r. 1934–1940), an army officer with socialist leanings, was elected president. Cynical peasants doubted political leaders' promises to supply them with land; Cardenas fulfilled this dream, assigning land ownership to *ejidos* **(eh-HEE-dos)**, traditional agricultural cooperatives, who now apportioned land to their members. Cardenas hoped that the ejidos would build schools and hospitals and supply credit to farmers, uplifting Mexico's poorest social class. But agricultural production fell, and the promised government aid never materialized.

Other Cardenas reforms and nationalist economic policies made him popular. He encouraged a large labor confederation, allowing the working class to enjoy higher living standards and more dignity, and supported women's rights. After U.S.-owned oil companies ignored a Mexican Supreme Court order to improve worker pay, Cardenas nationalized the industry, spurring celebrations in Mexico but outraging U.S. leaders. Cardenas reorganized the ruling Party of Revolutionary Institutions around four functional groups: peasants, organized labor, military, and middle class. Thus Cardenas revitalized the Mexican Revolution, causing deep resentment among wealthy Mexican landowners and merchants and U.S. political and business leaders.

However, more moderate leaders after Cardenas reversed support for the ejidos, favoring instead individual farmers, ignored women's rights—women could not vote until 1953—and cooperated with the United States on immigration issues. While poor Mexicans had long moved to the United States, during World War II a binational agreement sent more Mexican workers north to fill industry, agriculture, and the service sector jobs left vacant by drafted American men. The flow northward of poor Mexicans became a floodtide after the war.

Estado Novo ("New State") A fascist-influenced and modernizing dictatorship in Brazil led by Getulio Vargas between 1930 and 1945.

---

[29]Severino Fama, quoted in Robert M. Levine, *The History of Brazil* (New York: Palgrave, 1999), 107.

[30]From Frederick B. Pike, ed., *Latin American History: Select Problems, Identity, Integration, and Nationhood* (New York: Harcourt, Brace and World, 1969), 319.

Cultural Nationalism in Latin America and the Caribbean

Cultural nationalism greatly affected Latin American and Caribbean societies. A literary approach, modernism, explored Brazil's rich cultural heritage. Rather than emulating European trends, modernist writers reflected Brazil's uniqueness. Poet, novelist, and critic Mario de Andrade (1893–1945) mixed words from regional dialects and Native American, African, and Portuguese folklore into his work. The more internationalist Oswald de Andrade (1890–1954), considering Brazil a creative cultural consumer, argued that Brazilians should mix ideas from all over the world. Nationalism also shaped Brazilian music. Afro-Brazilian and Indian religious rites and urban popular music inspired unconventional composer Heitor Villa-Lobos (1890–1959). Associated with Rio de Janeiro annual pre-Lenten carnival, *samba* music and dance became a symbol of Brazilian society while allowing the Afro-Brazilian lower classes to express themselves. Annual carnival processions grew increasingly extravagant, featuring elaborate floats, flamboyant costumes, and intricate group choreography. Professional samba groups competed for prizes, making samba a major social activity of Rio's shantytowns.

The progressive spirit spurred literary and artistic movements. Marxist-influenced writers such as Chilean poet Pablo Neruda **(ne-ROO-duh)** (1904–1973) bristled with anger over economic inequalities. Sometimes governments retaliated against dissident artists; Neruda wrote some of his greatest poetry in hiding or exile. Mexican artists, glorifying the country's mixed-descent, or mestizo, heritage, addressed the remaining Native American communities' poverty and powerlessness. In this tradition, several great artists painted, usually on public building walls, magnificent murals showing Mexican life, most notably Diego Rivera (1885–1957), a Marxist whose huge, realistic murals depicted peasants and workers struggling for dignity or emphasized conflicts between Indians and the Spanish colonizers. His wife, Frida Kahlo (1907–1954), a German Jewish immigrant's daughter, specialized in vivid paintings expressing women's physical and psychological pain, reflecting her own health problems and stormy personal relationships.

Caribbean intellectuals' search for an authentic West Indian identity required overcoming the reluctance to acknowledge African influences. Adopting British and French stereotypes, West Indians often associated Africa with the uncivilized. Some Afro-Caribbean intellectuals such as the Trinidadian Marxist C. L. R. James (1901–1989), rebuilding Afro-Caribbean pride by celebrating African roots, used literature, art, and music to challenge Western colonialism. James was a well-traveled historian, prolific writer, political theorist, critic, skillful cricket player, and activist in Trinidad politics, equally at home in the Caribbean, Europe, Africa, and North America, who inspired intellectuals around the world.

Charles Perry Weimer/Three Lions/Getty Images

BRAZILIAN FARM WORKERS These workers, some of them probably immigrants from Europe, planted sugar cane with cattle in 1930 near Recife in northeastern Brazil.

MAKE SURE YOU UNDERSTAND THESE KEY POINTS BEFORE MOVING ON

- In the post–World War I breakup of the Ottoman Empire, lands such as Iraq, Syria, and Lebanon that sought freedom were instead colonized by Britain and France, but Turkey revived under the leadership of Ataturk, who modernized the country and minimized the role of Islam.

- Reza Khan, the British-supported shah of Persia, attempted to modernize his country as Ataturk had Turkey, though with less success, while Britain, in reaction to violent opposition, granted Egypt and Iraq increasing measures of autonomy and independence.

- Vulnerable Latin American economies were greatly damaged during the Great Depression, which led to

instability and the rise of military dictators in many countries, while in Chile, instability led to a progressive, prolabor government.

- Impoverished and frustrated after a long revolution, many Mexicans were pleased by the rule of Lazaro Cardenas, who gave land to agricultural cooperatives, nationalized industries, and supported women's rights, but who was followed by less progressive leaders.

aplia

CHAPTER SUMMARY

During this era, nationalism became a strong force in the Western colonies and other dominated Asian, African, and Latin American societies. Two world wars and the Great Depression destabilized local economies, capitalism reshaped rural life for millions of peasants, and many Asians and Africans resented the Western powers. Nationalism, often blended with Marxism, gained support as a strategy to oppose Western domination. Nationalists reunified China after two decades of warlord violence but could not improve rural life or halt Japanese expansion, providing an opening for Chinese communists under Mao Zedong to gain support by offering a program to transform society. In India, nationalism opposing repressive British colonialism gained a mass following. Mohandas Gandhi mounted massive, nonviolent campaigns of civil disobedience, which undermined British rule. But Gandhi and other nationalist leaders, mostly Hindus, could not prevent the minority Muslims from seeking a separate nation.

Nationalism had an uneven history in Southeast Asia, sub-Saharan Africa, and the Middle East. In Vietnam, Ho Chi Minh organized effective communist resistance to the French, while in Indonesia, Sukarno led opposition to Dutch rule. During World War II nationalists in Vietnam, Indonesia, and Burma organized to oppose a resumption of Western colonialism when the war ended. While political nationalist organizations developed in Africa and black South Africans resisted white domination, nationalism was often more influential as a cultural force, especially in music. World War I left the Middle East in turmoil, as Britain and France extended their power into Arab societies once ruled by the Ottoman Empire. But the Turks, led by Kemal Ataturk, and Iran developed modern states open to Western influences. Muslim intellectuals debated whether to adopt Western ideas or maintain Islamic traditions. Arab conservatives, including the Wahhabis, used Islam to oppose any social or cultural changes. The rise of Zionist immigration to Palestine posed another challenge to the Arabs. In many Latin American nations, while progressive social and literary movements proliferated, economic problems intensified and dictators gained power. Nationalism permeated literary, musical, and artistic expression in both Latin America and the Caribbean.

KEY TERMS

warlords (p. 604)
New Culture Movement (p. 604)
May Fourth Movement (p. 605)
Jiangxi Soviet (p. 607)
Long March (p. 607)

people's war (p. 609)
Maoism (p. 609)
nonviolent resistance (p. 610)
Viet Minh (p. 614)
lingua franca (p. 614)

highlife (p. 616)
pidgin English (p. 616)
Muslim Brotherhood (p. 621)
Balfour Declaration (p. 621)
Estado Novo (p. 623)

Modernization or World-System?

Historians and social scientists in the West have vigorously debated which theories best explain the modern world, especially how it became interconnected. One influential approach uses the concept of modernization and focuses on individual societies. The other approach, world-system analysis, emphasizes the links between societies. This second approach has often interested world historians.

The Problem

The attempt by historians and historically oriented social scientists to understand societies and their changes over time has led to new intellectual approaches in the past several decades. Scholars have asked why some societies in the modern world, such as the United States, Britain, and Japan, became rich and powerful while others, such as Mozambique, Haiti, and Laos, remained poor and weak. Have societies developed as they did because of their own traditions or because of their connections to the larger world? Should we study societies as separate units, as the modernization approach advocates? Or should societies be examined as part of a larger system of exchange and power, or a world-system? Or are both of these approaches inadequate?

The Debate

During the 1950s and 1960s modernization theory was developed in the United States by scholars such as C. E. Black, W. W. Rostow, and Gabriel Almond. In their classification, most societies were traditional, retaining centuries-old political and economic institutions and social and cultural values. These societies had despotic governments, extended family systems, and fatalistic attitudes. In contrast, a few dynamic societies became modern by adopting liberal democracy, secularism, flexible social systems, high-consumption lifestyles, and free market capitalism. This modernization began in Europe between 1400 or 1500 and 1750, reaching its fullest development in the United States by the mid-twentieth century. All societies, these theorists asserted, were moving, rapidly or slowly, in the same direction toward U.S.-style modernization—some enthusiastically, others reluctantly—and this modernization was desirable.

Modernization theory was influential in the United States for several decades, but by the 1970s it began losing support among many historians. While the notion of modernity seemed helpful, critics found many flaws in the theory of modernization. They argued that it centered history on the West as the dynamic nursery of modernization and neglected other politically and economically successful societies, such as Qing China, Tokugawa Japan, and Ottoman Turkey. Although these societies had all either collapsed or struggled against Western imperialism during the nineteenth century, they had once flourished and fostered economic growth despite having few of the characteristics associated with modernity. Furthermore, critics contended, by emphasizing the individual trees (societies) at the expense of the larger forest (the global context), the theory failed to explain the interconnections of societies through various international networks and processes that created global imbalances, such as the transfer of wealth and resources—Indonesian coffee, Iraqi oil, West African cocoa, Latin American silver, Caribbean sugar—from colonies to colonizers.

Early modernization theory generally reflected the views of scholars who believe that U.S.-style individualism, democratic government, and free enterprise capitalism are the best strategies to promote personal freedom and economic growth, and who want to export these ideas to the world. Indeed, as historians like Nils Gilman and Michael Latham have shown, it strongly influenced U.S. foreign policies during the Cold War. Modernization theorists such as Rostow, an adviser to Presidents Kennedy and Johnson, considered challenges to U.S. influence and to capitalism, from Marxists and radical nationalists, to be diversions leading to despotic governments and an economic dead end. While agreeing that political and economic freedom were valuable ideas that generally benefited Western peoples, critics doubt that these are the foundation of modernity or applicable everywhere. By characterizing traditional societies as "backward" and blaming them for being this way, modernization theory, detractors believe, reflects Western prejudices about the world, such as the French "civilizing mission" and the U.S. notion of "Manifest Destiny," and supports the expansion of Western political power and economic investment into Asia and Africa on the grounds that it fosters "progress." Furthermore, critics argue, most societies are a mix of "traditional" and "modern" traits. For example, the "modern" United States has been a religious society from its beginning, arguably less secular than "traditional" China. Nor have Asians and Africans always found Western social and cultural models, such as nuclear families and Christianity, to be more appealing or useful than their own traditions; some, often inspired by Western ideas, have hoped to reform Muslim, Hindu, Confucian, or Buddhist traditions, but most have continued to find meaning in the beliefs and customs of their ancestors.

Challenging modernization theory's neglect of connections, scholars led by American sociologist Immanuel Wallerstein developed the concept of the "world-system," a network of interlinked economic, political, and social relationships spanning the globe. To Wallerstein the world-system, originating in Europe in the 1400s and based on a capitalist world economy, rival European states, and imperialism, explains growing Western global dominance after 1500. By 1914 Western military expansion, colonialism, and industrialization had enriched Europe and brought other societies into the modern world-system. An Africa specialist, Wallerstein views the modern world-system as more widely spread than the more limited networks, such as those of the Mongols and Arabs, that linked Afro-Eurasian societies prior to the 1400s.

In this view, modernization involves not only changes within societies but also their changing relationship to the dominant political powers and the world economy. For example, the Ashante kingdom became a West African power in the 1700s by trading slaves to the West, but, in the late 1800s, it was conquered and absorbed into the British colony of the

A JAPANESE VIEW OF WESTERNERS This Japanese woodcut print records the impression of a Western family living in Japan in 1860. The mother uses a sewing machine while her husband plays with the children.

Gold Coast (modern Ghana). Under British rule, the Ashante chiefly grew cocoa for export and thus were dependent on the fluctuations of the world price for cocoa. To understand modern Ghana, then, requires knowledge of the Ashante relations to both British colonialism and the world economy.

To describe the world political and economic structure, Wallerstein divided the world-system into three broad zones, or categories of countries: the *core*, *semiperiphery*, and *periphery*. In 1914 the core included the rich and powerful nations such as Britain, France, and the United States, which all benefited from industrialization, growing middle classes, democracy, a strong sense of nationhood, and political stability. They sometimes used their armies and financial clout to assert power over other societies, even independent ones such as China, where Western powers established spheres of interest patrolled by their gunboats. By 1914 Wallerstein's middle category, the semiperiphery, included countries such as Japan, Russia, and Italy, which were partially industrialized, politically independent nation-states but less prosperous and powerful than the core nations. Finally, the largest group in 1914, the periphery, comprised the colonized societies, such as French Vietnam, British Nigeria, and the U.S.-ruled Philippines, and the neocolonies such as Brazil, Thailand (Siam), and Iran (Persia). These societies were burdened with export economies based on natural resources, little or no industrialization, massive poverty, little democracy, and domination by more powerful core nations. Colonialism transferred wealth from the periphery to the core, which used the wealth for its own economic development. As Wallerstein acknowledges, the world-system is not rigid, and a few societies shifted categories over the centuries. For example, the United States was semiperipheral in 1800, but by 1900 industrialization and territorial expansion had propelled it into the core. By contrast, once-powerful China fell into peripheral status after 1800. But even with some movement up or down, Wallerstein argues, the core-semiperiphery-periphery structure still characterizes the world-system today.

If modernization theory predicts an increasing standardization around the world toward a Western-influenced pattern, world-system analysis suggests that the core and periphery, serving different functions in the world economy, have moved in opposite directions, toward wealth on the one hand and poverty on the other. Since the economic exchange between them was unequal, the periphery became dependent on the core for goods, services, investment, and resource markets, giving core societies, which exploited the resources of the periphery, great influence. For example, the Gold Coast's cocoa growers needed British markets, and British companies provided consumer goods to the shopkeepers, often Lebanese immigrants, who served these communities. The wealth and power of a country, then, reflect its political and economic position in the world-system.

Like modernization theory, world-system analysis has provoked controversy. Some scholars embrace a world-system approach but disagree with Wallerstein's version or consider both world-system and modernization theories too rigid. Whereas Wallerstein believes a world-system began only around 1500, Christopher Chase-Dunn and Thomas Hall emphasize a longer history with diverse intersocietal networks that can be called world-systems beginning in ancient times. Andre Gunder Frank and Barry Gills identify one single world-system existing for five thousand years, since, they argue, some form of capitalism began with the earliest states, such as Sumeria, in Afro-Eurasia. Some critics accuse Wallerstein, like the modernization theorists, of overemphasizing the West and underestimating the key roles played by Asians in the Afro-Eurasian economy in the past five hundred years.

(Continued)

Other critics are harsher. Some charge that Wallerstein's stress on exchange between countries downplays inequitable economies and class structures within countries—such as rapacious landowners, privileged aristocrats, tyrannical chiefs, and greedy merchants—hence shifting the blame for poverty to the world economy. Others, such as Daniel Chirot, question whether exploitation of the periphery explains the economic growth of the core. Critics also wonder whether terms such as *core* and *periphery* constitute a more sophisticated version of "modernity" and "tradition," marginalizing and perhaps demeaning poor societies. Finally, some think Wallerstein's focus on economic factors neglects politics and cultures, including religion, and places so much stress on the forest that it misses the trees. Yet, like many world historians, even some critics find that the general concept of an interlinked global system helps explain transnational economic relations, the impact of colonialism, the background to military interventions by more powerful countries, and the political turbulence of the poorer nations today.

Evaluating the Debate

The modernization and world-system theorists launched an ongoing debate about how world history can be understood, but some wonder if either approach fully explains modern history. Many world historians consider the once-dominant modernization theory inadequate for understanding the world as a whole. Some of these are attracted to one or another version of world-system analysis but often believe that many details of Wallerstein's approach are open to challenge. While, as modernization scholars recognize, each society has unique characteristics that shape its history, perceiving some sort of global system or systems that rise and fall over time helps us understand large-scale, long-term change and explains how thousands of small hunting and gathering bands twelve thousand years ago became the contemporary global community of nation-states.

THINKING ABOUT THE CONTROVERSY

1. How do modernization and world-system approaches explain the modern world and its diverse societies differently?
2. What are the major advantages and problems of each of the two approaches?

Exploring the Controversy

Among the major works of modernization theory are C. E. Black, *The Dynamics of Modernization: A Study in Comparative History* (New York: Harper and Row, 1966); and W. W. Rostow, *The Stages of Economic Growth: A Non-Communist Manifesto* (Cambridge: Cambridge University Press, 1960). On a history of the approach and its political influence, see Nils Gilman, *Mandarins of the Future: Modernization Theory in Cold War America* (Baltimore: Johns Hopkins University Press, 2007); and Michael E. Latham, *Modernization and Ideology: American Social Science and "Nation-Building" in the Kennedy Era* (Chapel Hill: University of North Carolina Press, 2000). Immanuel Wallerstein has summarized his ideas in *The Capitalist World-Economy* (New York: Cambridge University Press, 1979) and *World-Systems Analysis: An Introduction* (Durham, NC: Duke University Press, 2004). Alternative versions of the world-system concept include Christopher Chase-Dunn and Thomas D. Hall, *Rise and Demise: Comparing World-Systems* (Boulder, CO: Westview Press, 1997); and Andre Gunder Frank and Barry K. Gills, eds., *The World System: Five Hundred Years or Five Thousand?* (New York: Routledge, 1996). Daniel Chirot takes issue with much of world-system analysis in *Social Change in the Modern Era* (New York: Harcourt Brace Jovanovich, 1986). Excellent summaries and critiques of world-system analysis and competing ideas can be found in Thomas R. Shannon, *An Introduction to the World-System Perspective* (Boulder, CO: Westview Press, 1989); Alvin Y. So, *Social Change and Development: Modernization, Dependency, and World-System Theories* (Newbury Park, CA: Sage, 1990); Stephen K. Sanderson, ed., *Civilizations and World Systems: Studying World-Historical Change* (Walnut Creek, CA: Altamira Press, 1995); Pamela Kyle Crossley, *What Is Global History?* (Malden, MA: Polity Press, 2008); and Thomas D. Hall, ed., *A World-Systems Reader: New Perspectives on Gender, Urbanism, Cultures, Indigenous Peoples, and Ecology* (Lanham, MD: Rowman and Littlefield, 2000). For a provocative critique of these debates and the rise of the world economy by an Indian scholar, see Amiya Kumar Bagchi, *Perilous Passage: Mankind and the Global Ascendancy of Capital* (Lanham, MD: Rowman and Littlefield, 2005).

PART VI

Global System: Interdependence and Conflict in the Contemporary World, Since 1945

CHAPTER OUTLINE

The world has changed dramatically since 1945. Some observers describe these years as the most revolutionary age in history, reshaping whole ways of life and world-views. All regions of the world, opening to ideas and products from everywhere, have become part of a global village or global system. Indonesian thinker Soedjatmoko (**so-jat-MOH-ko**) perceived a world of collapsing "national boundaries and horrifying destructive power, expanding technological capacity and instant communication [in which] we live in imperfect intimacy with all our fellow human beings."[1] This interconnected and rapidly changing global society, and the people who shape it, have produced both great good and indescribable horrors.

[1]Kathleen Newland and Kamala Chandrakirana Soedjatmoko, eds., *Transforming Humanity: The Visionary Writings of Soedjatmoko* (West Hartford, CT: Kumarian Press, 1994), 186–187.

The contemporary world has become a global unity within a larger diversity. Linking distant societies, globalization fostered or intensified networks of exchange and communication: international trade pacts and electronic fund transfers, jet-speed travel and fax machines. Yet, even while becoming more closely linked, nations have difficulty working together to meet the challenges facing humanity. No clear international consensus has emerged on maintaining strong local cultures in the face of global influences, correcting the widening gap between rich and poor nations, and achieving a better balance between environmental preservation and economic development.

Transitions
Globalization and Its Impact

Over recent centuries the world's people have built a human web, or networked society, characterized by transnational connections and the institutions that foster them, such as the World Bank, the Internet, and religious missionaries. Around the world people speak, with fear or enthusiasm, of globalization. Some observers see the trend as dangerous folly, others as a boon, and still others have mixed feelings.

Globalization's roots go deep into the past. A thousand years ago an Eastern Hemisphere–wide economy based in Asia and anchored by Chinese and Indian manufacturing and Islamic trade networks represented an early form of globalization. The links between the hemispheres forged after 1492, during which Europeans competed with each other and with Asians for a share of the growing trade in raw materials, created a global economy. In the nineteenth century the Industrial Revolution, which produced desirable trade goods, and European imperialism, which spurred Western colonization of much of the world, extended the connections even further, aided by technological innovations such as steamships and transoceanic cables.

The integration of commerce and financial services today is more developed than ever before. Societies became more dependent on each other for everything from consumer goods and entertainments to fuels and technological innovations. For example, all over the world people consume Chinese textiles, U.S. films, Persian Gulf oil, Indian yoga, and Japanese electronics. Video-conferencing allows business partners in Los Angeles, Berlin, and Hong Kong to confer instantaneously with one another. Yet, while globalization affects every country to some degree, the great bulk of world trade and financial flow and activity is concentrated in, and has the largest impact on, the peoples of three huge interlinked blocs: North America, Europe, and a group of Asian nations stretching from Japan to India. This impersonal globalization, operating independent of governments, has had major impacts on societies, politics, economies, cultures, and environments. Whether they are seen as positive or negative consequences depends on the observer (see Historical Controversy).

Per capita income

- Over $20,000
- $10,000–$19,999
- $2,000–$9,999
- Under $2,000

One square represents $20 billion in GDP

The top fifty countries are named; the GDP of the top twelve is listed.

GLOBAL DISTRIBUTION OF WEALTH The countries of North America, northern Europe, and Japan have the most wealth and the world's highest per capita incomes, averaging over $20,000 per year. At the other extreme, many people in South America and most people in the poor countries of sub-Saharan Africa, South Asia, and the Middle East earn under $2,000 per year.

© 2015 Cengage Learning

To adapt and flourish in an interconnected world, people have had to become aware of international conditions. In North America, activists seeking to fight inequality or preserve the environment have urged people to think globally but act locally. Thinking globally, for example, would include understanding how rapid deforestation in the tropics—especially in the Amazon and Congo Basins, where rain forests recycle vast amounts of water into the air—diminishes rainfall around the world. Acting locally, Brazilian environmental and citizens' groups work to save their rain forests, while environmentally conscious North Americans and Europeans support organizations, businesses, and political leaders committed to improving the global environment.

Networks
The Globalization of Cultures

Global forces, symbolized by advertising for foreign-made goods and satellites miles up in the sky relaying information around the world, interact with local cultures, raising questions about national and local identity. As a result, local traditions and products sometimes get replaced, and imported and local cultures blend. People around the world consume global products, from fast food to fashionable footwear to action films, but still enjoy local cultural traditions (like Thai boxing or Japanese sumo wrestling) popular with earlier generations.

The inequitable relationship between the dominant West and the developing nations fostered the concept of cultural imperialism, in which the economic and political power of Western nations, especially the United States, enables their cultural products to spread widely. Some African writers called this pattern a "cultural bomb" because, they believe, Western products and entertainments destroy local cultures. For instance, big budget Hollywood films attract large audiences while local films, made on small budgets, cannot compete; local film industries often die as a result. To survive, local filmmakers adopt the formulas used by successful Hollywood filmmakers: sex and violence.

Popular culture produced in the United States, entertaining but also challenging to traditional values, emerged as the closest thing available to a global entertainment. The Monroe Doctrine—the early-nineteenth-century declaration by Congress that the United States would interfere in Latin American political developments—has now become, in the view of certain wags, the "Marilyn Monroe Doctrine," after the famous American actress who, for many non-Americans, symbolized U.S. culture in the 1950s. Some American icons, from basketball stars Michael Jordan and LeBron James to McDonald's and Kentucky Fried Chicken, became symbols of a new global modernity and capitalism. In 1989 two young East Germans crossed the Berlin Wall and discovered their first McDonald's restaurant. One of them remembered, "It was all so modern, the windows were so amazing. I felt like a lost convict who'd just spent twenty-five years in prison. I was in a state of shock."[2] Not even the Chinese, with one of the world's most admired cuisines, were immune to the appeal of modern U.S. marketing techniques and convenience for harried urbanites. In 1993 a famous roast duck restaurant in China's capital, Beijing, sent its management staff to study the McDonald's operation in British-ruled Hong Kong and then introduced its customers to "roast duck fast food." Today McDonald's franchises are found all over China. Yet, Chinese restaurants also flourish around the world.

Still, popular American and other Western entertainments often face opposition. Governments, from Islamic clerics running Iran to India's more democratic leaders, have attempted to halt or control the influx of what they consider destabilizing, immoral pop culture. In 1995 an Islamic political party in Pakistan even demanded, unsuccessfully, that the United States turn over to them American pop stars Madonna and Michael Jackson so that they could be placed on trial as "cultural terrorists" destroying humanity. Yet the rising world culture is not uniform. No total homogenization of expression and meaning has occurred.

Anglo-American cultural forms are not the only ones to reach a global audience. Mexican and Brazilian soap operas, Indian (Bollywood) films, Nigerian novels, African and Caribbean pop music, and Japanese comics and electronic games have been popular all over the globe. The cultural traffic flow is not one-way. In North America, western Europe, and Australia, people take up Indian yoga, Chinese *tai qi*, and other Asian spiritual disciplines; patronize Thai, Indian, Chinese, and Japanese restaurants; enjoy Brazilian and African pop music; learn Latin American dances; and master Asian martial arts, such as karate and judo. The meeting of global and local cultures fosters hybridization, the blending of two cultures, a process that can be either enriching or impoverishing. Record stores in Western cities set aside some of their display space to sell a hybrid form called "world music," popular music originating largely outside of the West that mixes Western influences with local and other traditions. Just like Western pop stars, some world musicians such as Brazilian singer-songwriter Caetano Veloso, Indian film diva Asha Bhosle (the most recorded artist in history), and Senegalese Youssou N'Dour, the descendant of griots, who mixes guitars with West African talking drums, perform around the world.

S ocieties
The North-South Gap

Globalization transcending national boundaries benefits some people but not all equally. The gap between rich and poor nations, and rich and poor people within nations, has grown and remains one of the world's major problems. In 1960 the richest fifth of the world's population had a total income thirty times the poorest fifth; by 2000 the ratio had more than doubled. Since World War II, nations on every continent improved their living standards and per capita incomes, lowered poverty rates, and increased their stake in the global economy, which has more than quintupled in size since 1950. But the world economy's rising tide has not lifted all ships, leaving some nations, especially in the southern lands near or below the equator, poor relative to the northern

countries. Over 1 billion people live in extreme poverty. Using a popular term for an underdeveloped nation, Jamaican reggae star Pato Banton reflected on the harshness of poverty in a 1989 song, "Third World Country":

> In a Third World country, the plants are green, it's a beautiful scene. Seems like a nice place for human beings. But there's people on the streets, no shoes on their feet. They gotta hustle to get a little food to eat. Things shouldn't be this way.[3]

The gap between the richest and poorest countries, often known as the North-South gap, has widened steadily. The difference in average per capita incomes between industrialized and nonindustrialized nations grew from 2:1 in 1850 to 10:1 in 1950 to 30:1 by 2000. Today the industrialized North contains under a quarter of the world's population but accounts for over three-quarters of its production of goods and services. Literacy rates, life expectancy, and food consumption also differ dramatically. On average, North Americans consume twice as many calories each day as Haitians and Bangladeshis. While overeating contributes to widespread obesity in industrialized nations, an eighth of the world's people are chronically malnourished, often suffering permanent brain damage because of it, and lack access to clean water. Fifteen million children die each year from hunger-related ailments. The 10 percent of people who live in the most industrialized nations consume two-thirds of the world's energy. Over 60 percent of the world's poorest people are women, who often struggle to compete with men for resources or are often prevented by local custom from working outside the home.

T ransitions
Building a New World Order

The challenge of development is only a part of a larger contemporary question: how societies, working together, can forge a new, more equitable world order.

---

[2]Daphne Berdahl, quoted in James L. Watson, ed., *Golden Arches East: McDonald's in East Asia* (Stanford, CA: Stanford University Press, 1997), xvii.
[3]From Banton's album, *Visions of the World* (IRSD-82003, 1989).

The old world order, built in the nineteenth century when powerful Western nations conquered much of Asia and Africa, was one in which a few rich nations politically and economically dominated most of the others. Even after World War II, decolonization, and the rise of revolutionary states such as China, a few nations, mostly in the West and East Asia, still held disproportionate power and influence. The United States has played the key role and borne the major costs in managing the global system through military alliances (such as NATO), trade pacts (such as GATT), and international organizations (such as the World Bank). The United Nations has been one major attempt at global cooperation but has had a mixed record.

The prospect of fostering a more equitable sharing of world resources raises questions about the availability of resources. Experts worry that the world's resources and environment could not support a Western standard of living for all the world. If every Chinese, Indian, Egyptian, and Peruvian, they argue, consumed the same products and calories as Americans, Swedes, or Japanese, world resources would quickly diminish. For all 7 billion people in today's world to live at a western European standard of living would require a 140-fold increase in the consumption of resources and energy. People in nations once poor but becoming developed, such as China, India, and Brazil, do not believe that the industrialized Western peoples have any more right to consume the world's resources than they do, and they want their fair share.

China's recent economic success shows the challenges ahead. By the early twenty-first century a China rushing toward development had become a huge consumer of the world's industrial, agricultural, and natural resources, energizing global trade but causing shortages elsewhere. For example, world oil prices have soared since 2000 in part because of China's increasing energy appetite as Chinese switch from bicycles to cars. If the Chinese consumed as much oil per capita as Americans, their demand would exceed the present world production. By 2006 Chinese consumed nearly twice as much meat and more than twice as much steel as Americans. China's living standards remain far below those of Japan and South Korea. Should they rise to that level, however, in the next decade or two, China will import vastly more resources than it does today, further stressing supplies. As occurred in the industrializing West earlier, rapid Chinese development, including the growing use of polluting fossil fuels, has also led to environmental degradation, including dangerous air and water pollution.

Networks
Building Sustainable Environments

The decades since the mid-twentieth century were unusual for the intensity of environmental deterioration and the centrality of human effort in causing it. By 2000 the challenge of a changing environment became obvious. On every continent, but especially in Eurasia and North America, gas-guzzling vehicles, smoky factories, coal-fired power plants, and large farming operations produce large amounts of carbon dioxide, methane, chlorofluorocarbons, and other pollutants that accumulate in the atmosphere, contributing to rising average temperatures that scientists call global warming. This climate change, if it continues, may have a greater impact—possibly catastrophic—on human life than any conventional war or other destructive human activities. Problems such as global warming raise the question of whether in the long term the natural environment can maintain itself and support plant, animal, and human life—a pattern known as sustainability.

Experts have wondered whether the world's resources—minerals, wild plants, food crops, fresh water—could sustain present living standards on a long-term basis. For the past several decades scientists have been alarmed at the human

Greenpeace, Osman Ugur/AP Images

PROTESTING GLOBAL WARMING People in societies around the world became alarmed at the increasing environmental damage brought by modern economic activity and exploitation of resources. This demonstration by environmental activists concerned with global warming, a potentially dangerous trend caused by burning fossil fuels such as coal that produces more carbon dioxide, took place in Turkey.

consumption of natural resources faster than nature can replenish them. Human activity has altered environments since prehistory, sometimes with catastrophic results. Environmental collapse triggered by agricultural practices or deforestation helped undermine the Mesopotamians, Romans, and Maya, among others. But modern industrial societies and rapidly growing populations encroach on their natural settings even more heavily than did earlier societies. In the twentieth century people used more energy than had been used in all previous history. Contemporary industrial and agricultural practices contributed to, among other pressing problems, air and water pollution, disposal of hazardous waste, declining genetic diversity in crops, deforestation, and a mass extinction of plant and animal species. With their heavy economic production and consumption, people today are borrowing from tomorrow.

The atmosphere faces particular dangers, including a measurable warming. Earth's climate changed little, with only minor fluctuations, between the last Ice Age, which ended 10,000 years ago, and the end of the eighteenth century, when the Industrial Revolution began in Europe, but it has been changing fast over the past two centuries. Since 1985, the world has experienced the highest average annual temperatures on record and unprecedented droughts. Blaming a Greenhouse Effect, human-made pollutants overheating the earth, scientists now largely agree that global warming has been increasing, although they debate its causes and dangers. In the pessimistic scenarios, the consequences of rising temperatures for many of the world's peoples are devastating. Earth gets baked, rich farmland turns to desert, food supplies diminish, forests wilt, Arctic and Antarctic ice and glaciers melt, and ocean levels rise, inundating low-lying islands, deltas, cities, and farm lands. Fresh water, already scarce, becomes even harder to find as lakes and streams dry up. Rising ocean temperatures damage fisheries and kill most protective coral reefs. The tropical countries, most still poor, contribute least to the problem but may experience the worst losses.

[4] Rene Dubos, *So Human an Animal* (New York: Scribner's, 1968), 270.

The environmental challenges, such as diminishing resources, global warming, and deforestation, reinforce the scientific concept, first popularized in the 1970s, of global ecology—the world, including human societies, as a complex web in which all living things interact with each other and their surroundings. Cultural, economic, political, and social activity affects livelihoods and environmental sustainability in what some term the "humanosphere." While organizations promoting environmental sustainability proliferate, the world's leaders often disagree on ways to better balance economic growth, which all nations desire, with environmental protection. Efforts to expand renewable energy sources, such as wind and solar, remain spotty.

Transitions
Understanding the Global Past

The study of history helps us understand today's news and views as they are reported in daily newspapers, broadcast on radio and television, and disseminated on the World Wide Web. Historians often describe their work as involving a dialogue between past, present, and future. A few years ago French scientist René Dubos argued: "The past is not dead history. It is living material out of which makes the present and builds the future."[4] Current global problems have their roots in the patterns of world history: the rise of cities, states, and organized religions; the expansion of trade and capitalism to global dimensions; the unprecedented mastery and altering of nature represented by the scientific, industrial, and technological revolutions; the proliferation of competitive, unequal nations; and the myriad of social, economic, political, and cultural connections between peoples encompassed in the expanding global system. While seeking to understand how the past shaped the present, historians also speculate on how current trends may shape the future.

World historians offer several ways of understanding the world of yesterday, today, and tomorrow. One view is that contacts and collisions between

different societies produce change. Whether through peaceful exchange or warfare or perhaps both, when societies encounter other societies they are exposed to different customs and ideas. Historians also emphasize continuity, the persistence of social, cultural, political, and religious ideas and patterns, as well as change, the transformations in ways of life, work, and thought. Continuities are common. For example, many Christians, Muslims, Jews, Buddhists, and Hindus still look at the world through the prism of traditional religious values forged millennia ago and still meaningful today. Hundreds of thousands of Christian and Muslim missionaries spread their message around the world, often making converts. Yet changes, too, are everywhere. Hence, most people engage in activities, face challenges, and use forms of transportation and communication nonexistent a few generations ago. As a result, missionaries and clerics often use radio, television, social media, and the Internet to spread their message. Another insight offered by global historians is that great transitions, such as the agricultural and industrial revolutions or, more recently, the rise of high technology, can turn history in new directions. Hence, thousands of years ago farming largely displaced hunting and gathering, two centuries ago industry transformed the world economy, and today instant communication and information bring distant peoples closer together.

The experiences of most societies over the past half century reveal a mix of change and continuity. For example, Western ideas have gained even greater influence in the world since 1945 than they had before. People in different lands have adopted Western ideas of government, such as constitutions and elections, although not necessarily the substance of democracy, along with Western-rooted ideologies and faiths: capitalism, socialism, nationalism, and Christianity. Western pop culture, from rock music to soft drinks and blue jeans, has spread widely, leading to what critics consider the "Coca-Colazation" of the world stemming from Western economic power, including advertising. Yet influences from the West are usually strongest in large cities and penetrate less deeply into the villages in Africa, Asia, Latin America, and the Middle East, where traditional ways reflect continuity with the past. As a result, city youth in Malaysia or Tanzania may follow the latest recordings from Western pop stars, but these recordings may be unknown to their rural counterparts. Yet the urban youth may also share with rural youth traditional views about family and faith, and rural youth may, like their city counterparts, own motorcycles, boom boxes, and cell phones that make their lives different from those of their parents.

As a result of the transition to globalizing technology, culture, and commerce, the contacts between societies and their interdependence have vastly increased since 1945. In different ways nuclear weapons, multinational corporations, earth-circling satellites, World Cup soccer, and cable news networks draw people together, willingly or not. Imperialists once claimed proudly that "the sun never set on the British Empire." By the 1990s observers noted that "the sun never sets on McDonald's." Today it never sets on smart phones or tablets and Twitter. Closer contact, of course, does not necessarily mean friendly relations and a less dangerous world; it can also bring collisions. Guided missiles and planes carrying bombs can reach 10,000 miles from their base. Over the past several decades over 60,000 Americans have died fighting in Vietnam, Afghanistan, and Iraq in support of U.S. foreign policies.

The contacts, changes, and transitions since 1945 created a global village, a single community of exchange and interaction. Even remote societies have become part of this global village. By the 1960s, for example, people living in the once-isolated interior of the island of Borneo, divided between Indonesia and Malaysia, could access the outside world through battery-powered transistor radios and cassette players, and also by means of visiting traders, Christian missionaries, and government officials. Borneo's interior people also often left their villages to find work at logging camps, oil wells, or plantations as their rain forest

environment and small farms rapidly disappeared, destroyed by international timber and mining operations that cut forests and stripped land to procure resources to ship to distant countries. As once-remote peoples are brought into the global system, and ethnic minorities are incorporated into nations, they find it harder to maintain their cultures and languages. Half of all languages are in danger of dying out over the next several decades, and less than 1 percent of languages are used on the Internet.

Transitions Toward the Future

Women and men created the present world from the materials of the past and are now laying the foundation for the future. As a Belgian scholar wrote a few years ago, "We cannot predict the future, but we can prepare it."[5] But this raises the question of what kind of future. The world's long history of war, inequality, and exploitation, even when seemingly offset by progress, does not foster optimism. Indeed, some respected experts predict human extinction if people do not adopt more sustainable ways, and scientific studies are more frequently pessimistic than optimistic about the future. Worried that we face environment collapse, one study concluded: "Our generation is the first to be faced with decisions that will determine whether the earth our children inherit will be habitable."[6] Yet, since 1945 humanity has produced many green shoots of hope, such as institutions (like the European Union) that

have created transnational unity or (like various United Nations agencies) international cooperation on global problems, economic development in many once impoverished nations, nongovernmental organizations working for human rights and a healthier environment, and women elected presidents or prime ministers in over two dozen nations.

A history not only of cruelty and exploitation but also of compassion and sacrifice provides hope in navigating troubled times. Remembering when people behaved magnificently may foster inspiration to answer the challenges. Historians sometimes view the past as a stream with banks. The stream is filled

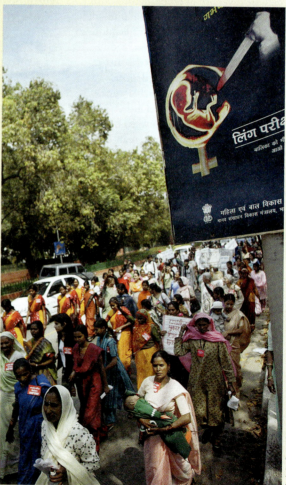

INTERNATIONAL WOMEN'S DAY 2005 Women around the world became more willing to assert their rights. Activists from diverse Indian nongovernmental organizations interested in women's rights marched in New Delhi, India's capital, in 2005 to mark International Women's Day.

Gurinder Osan/AP Images

[5] Ilya Prigogine, quoted in Federico Mayor and Jerome Bindé, *The World Ahead: Our Future in the Making* (New York: Zed Books, 2001), 1.
[6] Lester Brown et al., "A World at Risk," in *State of the World 1989* (New York: W.W. Norton, 1989), 20.

with people killing, bullying, enslaving, and doing other things historians usually record, while on the banks, unnoticed, women and men build homes, raise children, tend farms, settle disputes, sing songs, whittle statues, trade with their neighbors, and chat with travelers from other lands. Historians often ignore the banks for the stream, but what happens on the banks may be more reassuring.

Some observers, believing that cultural differences will increasingly drive international politics, forecast a clash of civilizations, such as between the Christian West and Islam, which are seen as irreconcilably opposed in worldviews. But simplistic formulas miss the complexity of the global order. None of the great religions and the cultures that they shaped are monolithic, the divisions among Christians or Muslims, Westerners or Middle Easterners, being as great as their differences with other traditions. No cultures or religions have a monopoly on values such as peace, justice, charity, tolerance, public discussion, and goodwill. In any case, nations generally shape their foreign policies according to their national interests rather than ideology. Furthermore, thanks to the many available information sources, people can become informed about why past societies, such as the Mesopotamians and Maya, destroyed their environments and collapsed, and how countries blundered into wars or failed to develop cooperative relations with their neighbors that maintained peace. These insights, if acquired, may help people today to avoid repeating the mistakes of the past and construct a better future.

Four centuries ago, the English playwright William Shakespeare wrote that the past is prologue to the present. The study of world history allows us to ask questions about the global future because we understand the changing patterns of the global past, including the building of societies, their interactions through networks, and the great transitions that reshaped humanity. These have led to an increasingly connected world in the past 1,500 years. The contemporary age has been marked by a complex mix of dividing and unifying forces, unique societies differing greatly in standards of living but linked into a global system of exchange. People today cannot yet know with certainty where the path will lead, but they can help build it. How nations, working together, deal with the world's many challenges will determine the shape of the future.

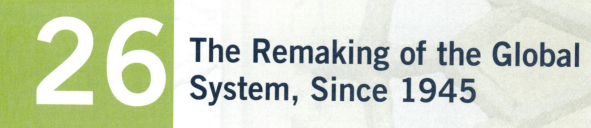

26 The Remaking of the Global System, Since 1945

"OUR WORLD IS NOT FOR SALE" In 2004 tens of thousands of activists from all over the world, under the banner of "Our World Is Not for Sale," marched on the streets of Mumbai (formerly Bombay), India's largest city, to protest economic globalization, racial and caste oppression, and the U.S.-led war in Iraq. The march reflected the globalization of social movements and political protests in the contemporary world.

636

One heart, one destiny. Peace and love for all mankind. And Africa for Africans.

—Bob Marley, reggae superstar[1]

In 1980, Jamaican reggae music star Bob Marley, a symbol of black empowerment, performed at Zimbabwe's celebration of independence from British rule. Marley's experience there reflected many late-twentieth-century political and cultural trends. His songs often dealt with issues such as poverty, racial prejudice, and asserting one's rights, realities for Zimbabweans, who had lived under an uncaring British colonial and then white supremacist government. But Marley's concert was disrupted by the local police, mostly whites, who used tear gas to disperse thousands of black Zimbabweans, often poor, outside the overcrowded stadium. The next night Marley, ignoring threats of violence against him, gave a free concert for 40,000 Zimbabweans. The violence and threats showed Marley that the social ills, economic inequalities, and ethnic hatreds he knew in Jamaica occurred elsewhere in the world. In Zimbabwe a black majority government would not solve them and made several of them worse.

Marley's career reflected a world interconnected as never before. An eloquent advocate of political and cultural freedom whose music was enjoyed around the world, Marley came from the slums of a small island of barely 2 million people; yet his music, an intoxicating mix of African, Caribbean, and North American traditions, touched hearts and minds across racial, political, religious, class, and cultural barriers. To the world, Marley personified reggae's progressive politics and spiritual quest.

Ancient thinkers such as the Buddha in India, Daoists in China, and the Greek philosopher Heraclitus claimed that nothing was permanent except change. Never was this more true than in the decades since 1945, when the pace of change quickened, the global economy grew dramatically, economic and cultural networks linked societies ever more closely, and ideas, technologies, and products flowed across porous borders, affecting people everywhere. Turbulent world politics reflected the conflict between the United States and the Soviet Union (USSR) as well as African, Asian, and Latin American struggles for decolonization and development. Since 1989, when the Soviet bloc collapsed, the world has groped toward a new political configuration while dealing with mounting economic, political, and environmental problems.

[1]Quoted in Adrian Boot and Chris Salewicz with Rita Marley as Senior Editor, *Bob Marley: Songs of Freedom* (London: Bloomsbury, 1995), 278.

T N Decolonization, New States, and the Global System

How did decolonization change the global system?

The contemporary world derived both from Western imperialism and the resistance waged against it. Asia, Africa, and Latin America became major battlegrounds between the United States and the Soviet Union, superpowers with much more military, political, and economic might than other countries. Asian, African, and Latin American struggles to end Western domination and develop economically also shaped the postwar era. Nationalist movements proliferated, sometimes sparking interventions by Western powers or the USSR, which were anxious to preserve their political and economic influence. Finally, the former colonies joined a global system marked by continued imbalances in wealth and power.

Nationalism and Decolonization

Nationalism became a powerful force in Western colonies (see Chapter 25). Three types of nationalist movements developed. In most colonized societies, the goal was ending colonial rule, but not necessarily major social and economic change. Colonial powers granted independence less reluctantly if nationalist leaders, in countries such as Nigeria and the Philippines, accepted continued Western control of mines, plantations, and other resources. In the second type, nationalist movements mounted by social revolutionaries inspired by Marxism sought both political independence and a new social order free of Western economic domination. Hence, in China the communists led by Mao Zedong reorganized Chinese society while limiting contact with the world economy and the United States. The third trend was represented by nationalist movements by long-repressed nonwhite majorities in white settler colonies such as Algeria and Zimbabwe, which struggled against domination by minority whites, who owned most land and resources.

The Great Depression and World War II intensified anticolonial feelings. Colonialism gradually crumbled, often after nationalist resistance led by charismatic figures such as

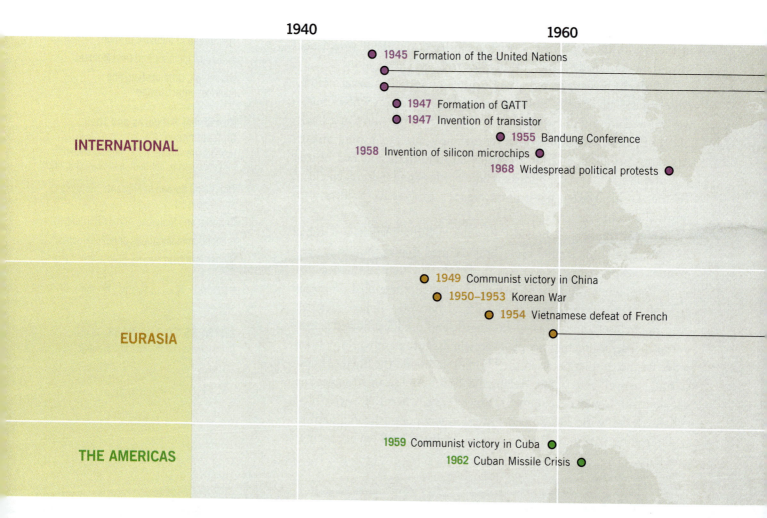

1940

1960

INTERNATIONAL

● **1945** Formation of the United Nations

● **1947** Formation of GATT
● **1947** Invention of transistor
● **1955** Bandung Conference
1958 Invention of silicon microchips ●
1968 Widespread political protests ●

EURASIA

● **1949** Communist victory in China
● **1950–1953** Korean War
● **1954** Vietnamese defeat of French

THE AMERICAS

1959 Communist victory in Cuba ●
1962 Cuban Missile Crisis ●

Mohandas Gandhi in India and Sukarno in Indonesia. Most Western colonizers realized that maintaining their control with military force was too expensive. In 1946 the United States began the decolonization trend, granting independence to the Philippines. Weary of suppressing nationalist resistance, Britain gave up its rule in India and Burma. Between 1946 and 1975 most Western colonies in Asia, Africa, and the Caribbean achieved independence (see Map 26.1).

Some colonizers agreed to decolonization only after failing to quell nationalist uprisings. Holland planned to regain Indonesia, a source of immense wealth, but battling a nationalist army proved bloody and demoralizing. Similarly, France had no plans to abandon profitable Vietnam and Algeria, but revolutionary uprisings forced it to leave. In Vietnam, heavy U.S. aid could not prevent humiliating French defeat by Ho Chi Minh's communist forces in 1954. The electrifying, ultimately successful anticolonial struggles by Indonesian, Vietnamese, and Algerian nationalists gave hope to colonized peoples elsewhere, warning Western powers of the heavy cost of opposing decolonization.

Both superpowers sought to capitalize on the nationalist surge. The Soviet Union generally supported nationalist movements, sometimes supplied arms to revolutionaries, and offered economic aid and diplomatic support to countries with strategic value or valuable resources, such as India, Egypt, and Indonesia. The United States followed a mixed policy on decolonization. Wanting trade and outlets for investment in Asia and Africa, Americans encouraged the Dutch to leave Indonesia and urged independence for some British colonies in Africa, but they also opposed communism and Soviet influence. Fearing leftwing nationalism, as in French-ruled Vietnam and Portuguese-ruled Mozambique, the United States supported continued colonial power, no matter how unpopular, helping finance French and Portuguese military efforts to suppress revolutionaries. Portugal stubbornly resisted decolonization until festering African rebellions, growing demoralization at home, and the toppling of its fascist dictator forced it to abandon its African empire in 1975.

Colonialism did not completely disappear. By the 1980s the major remaining territorial empire, the USSR, strained to repress the nationalist demands of the Baltic, Caucasus, and Central Asian peoples it ruled. The Soviet Empire was largely dismantled between 1989 and 1991, when the communist system collapsed. Britain and France retained direct control of a few islands, mostly in the South Pacific, South Atlantic, and Caribbean, and some outposts such as French Guiana in South America. The United States maintains a few territories that are mostly self-governing, including Puerto Rico and the

MAP 26.1 **DECOLONIZATION** Between 1946 and 1975 most of the Western colonies in Asia, Africa, and the Caribbean won their independence, with the greatest number achieving independence in the 1960s. The decolonization reshaped the political map, particularly of Africa, South Asia, and Southeast Asia. © 2015 Cengage Learning

1960 Year independence achieved

Former ruler

- Great Britain
- France
- Netherlands
- Italy
- Belgium
- Portugal
- United States
- Other

ATLANTIC OCEAN

PACIFIC OCEAN

INDIAN OCEAN

Arabian Sea

Bay of Bengal

Caspian Sea

Black Sea

Mediterranean Sea

Tropic of Cancer

Equator 0°

Tropic of Capricorn

GREAT BRITAIN

FRANCE

SPAIN

PORTUGAL

NETHERLANDS

BELGIUM

ITALY

JAPAN

NORTH KOREA 1948

SOUTH KOREA 1948 (From Japan)

PHILIPPINES 1946

BRUNEI 1984 (From Gr. Br.)

MALAYSIA 1963

SINGAPORE 1965 (From Malaysia)

INDONESIA 1949

TIMOR-LESTE 1999 (From Indonesia)

PAPUA NEW GUINEA 1975 (From Australia)

NORTH VIETNAM 1954 (Unified 1975)

SOUTH VIETNAM 1954

CAMBODIA 1953

LAOS 1949

MYANMAR (BURMA) 1947

PAKISTAN 1947, BANGLADESH 1973

INDIA 1947

PAKISTAN 1947

SRI LANKA (CEYLON) 1948

MALDIVES 1975 (From Gr. Br.)

SEYCHELLES 1976 (From Gr. Br.)

COMOROS 1975 (From France)

MAURITIUS 1968 (From Gr. Br.)

MADAGASCAR 1960

OMAN 1971

P.D.R. OF YEMEN 1967 (Unified 1990) YEMEN

KUWAIT 1961

BAHRAIN 1971 QATAR 1971

UNITED ARAB EMIRATES 1971

IRAQ 1932

JORDAN 1946

SYRIA 1944

LEBANON 1944 ISRAEL 1948

CYPRUS 1960

MALTA 1964 (From Gr. Br.)

EGYPT 1922

LIBYA 1951

TUNISIA 1957

MOROCCO 1956

WESTERN SAHARA 1975 (Morocco) (From Spain)

MAURITANIA 1960

CAPE VERDE 1975 (From Port.)

SENEGAL 1960

GAMBIA 1965

GUINEA-BISSAU 1974

GUINEA 1958

SIERRA LEONE 1961

LIBERIA 1820s

CÔTE D'IVOIRE 1960

GHANA 1957

BURKINA FASO 1960

MALI 1960

ALGERIA 1962

NIGER 1960

BENIN 1960

TOGO 1960

NIGERIA 1960

EQUATORIAL GUINEA 1968 (From Spain)

SÃO TOMÉ AND PRÍNCIPE 1975 (From Port.)

GABON 1960

CAMEROON 1960

CENTRAL AFRICAN REPUBLIC 1960

CHAD 1960

SUDAN 1956

ERITREA 1993 (From Ethiopia)

ETHIOPIA

DJIBOUTI 1977

SOMALIA 1960

REPUBLIC OF CONGO 1960

DEM. REP. OF CONGO 1960

UGANDA 1962

RWANDA 1962

BURUNDI 1962

KENYA 1963

TANZANIA 1964

ANGOLA 1975

ZAMBIA 1964

MALAWI 1964

MOZAMBIQUE 1974

ZIMBABWE 1980

BOTSWANA 1966

NAMIBIA 1990 (From South Africa)

SOUTH AFRICA (Republic 1961)

SWAZILAND 1968

LESOTHO 1966

0   1,000   2,000 Km.
0   1,000   2,000 Mi.

N

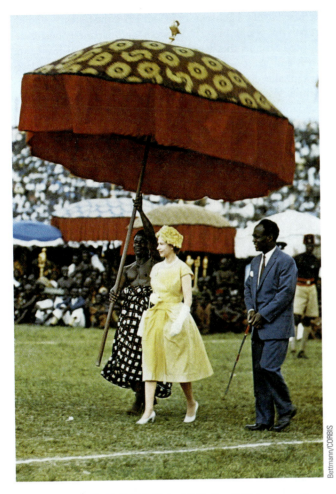

Bettmann/CORBIS

AFRICAN INDEPENDENCE In 1961 the British monarch, Queen Elizabeth II, made an official visit to newly independent Ghana, the former British colony of the Gold Coast. Here she walks under a ceremonial umbrella with the Ghanian president, Kwame Nkrumah.

Virgin Islands in the Caribbean and a few Pacific islands such as American Samoa and Guam.

Decolonization often produced neocolonialism, or continuing Western political and economic influence. In the Philippines, Americans maintained a major economic role, governments loyally supported U.S. foreign policies, and Filipinos avidly consumed American products and popular culture such as music, films, and fashions. Similarly, the French controlled much of the economy and advised the government in Cote d'Ivoire **(COAT dee-VWAHR)** (Ivory Coast), and many Ivoirians favored French cuisine, literature, and language. A West Indian–born writer offered a radical nationalist but oversimplified view of neocolonialism: "The colonial power says, 'Since you want independence, take it and starve' [after economic aid ends]. Other countries refuse to undergo this ordeal and agree to [accept] the conditions

of the former guardian power."[2] Some Asian and African intellectuals advocated "decolonizing the mind," to escape what Bob Marley called the "mental slavery" that kept formerly colonized people in awe of Western power, wealth, and culture. This sometimes meant building a nationalist culture reflecting local traditions or abandoning Western languages in literature. For example, Kenyan novelist Ngugi wa Thiongo **(en-GOO-gey wah they-ON-go)** switched from English to his native Gikuyu.

Social Revolutionary States

During the twentieth century, revolutionary activity in Asia, Africa, and Latin America, intensified by the drive to end Western domination, often engaged peasants impoverished by loss of land or declining crop prices. Amilcar Cabral **(AM-ill-car ka-BRAWL)** (1924–1973), the revolutionary leader in Portugal's colony of Guinea Bissau **(GIN-ee bi-SOW)**, advised other Marxist intellectuals to "always bear in mind that the people are not fighting for ideas, for the things in anyone's head. They are fighting to live better, and in peace, to guarantee the future of their children."[3] Between 1949 and 1980 social revolutionaries fought their way to power in China, Vietnam, Algeria, Cuba, Nicaragua, Angola, and Mozambique. Opposed by the United States, they looked to the USSR for political, economic, and military support. Revolutionary movements were also active, although ultimately frustrated, in various other Latin American and Southeast Asian countries.

Thinkers and activists around the world, such as the West Indian–born psychiatrist and writer Frantz Fanon (1925–1961), who joined the anti-French movement while working in colonial Algeria, often romanticized the revolutionaries' promise to create more just societies. While social revolutionary governments often raised the status and living standards of the poor, they also became bureaucratic, despotic, and intolerant of dissent, frequently compiling poor human rights records. Influenced by Stalinism, they had uneven relations with capitalist nations. These states usually limited their involvement with the world economy, instead creating planned economies in which governments rather than free markets drove policies. Nevertheless, many people welcomed the end of the uncaring, often repressive governments the revolutions replaced.

Social revolutionary approaches brought mixed results. Civil wars or rebellions sidetracked some revolutions. South Africa and the United States supported rebels in Angola who fought the Marxist government for over two decades, a struggle that cost over 200,000 lives, ruined the country, and diverted resources to the military. In contrast, between 1949 and 1978 communist China increased its economic potential and addressed social problems, even while it severely limited personal freedom. After 1978 China sparked even more rapid growth, modifying socialism with foreign investment

[2]Frantz Fanon, *The Wretched of the Earth* (New York: Grove, 1968), 97–98.

[3]Quoted in Goran Hyden, *Beyond Ujamaa in Tanzania: Underdevelopment and an Uncaptured Peasantry* (Berkeley: University of California Press, 1980), 202.

and free enterprise. China's shift, followed by that of Vietnam, toward market economies and participation in the world economy suggested that revolutions gained control of resources but could not raise living standards to the levels of richer nations. China and Vietnam discovered that free markets created more wealth than socialism but did not necessarily foster an equitable wealth distribution, breeding explosive social tensions.

A New Global System

A new global system emerged after 1945. A few great Western powers, led by Britain and France, dominated the prewar world, ruling over vast empires in Asia, Africa, and the Caribbean. Decolonization and the rise of the United States and Soviet Union to superpower status modified this pattern, dividing the world, some argued, into three categories characterized by different levels of economic development and power. The **First World** comprised the industrialized democracies of western Europe, North America, Australia–New Zealand, and Japan. The **Second World** referred to communist nations, led by the USSR and China. Most societies in Asia, Africa, Latin America, and the Caribbean, grouped as the **Third World**, were linked by mass poverty and Western colonization or neocolonialism. Some experts added a fourth category, the **Fourth World**, that comprised the poorest societies, with small economies and few exploitable resources, such as Laos, Afghanistan, Haiti, and Mali. However, critics contended that lumping the world's societies—with very different histories, cultures, and global connections—into a few categories was misleading. Furthermore, after the 1970s the global system changed, diminishing the descriptive value of the simplistic "three worlds" concept. Countries such as Malaysia, South Korea, Dubai (**doo-BYE**), Brazil, and Chile, once grouped with the Third World, achieved rapid economic growth, and the communist systems often collapsed. Today some specialists group the world geographically: a highly developed North (North America, Europe, northern Asia) and the developing South.

Most Western nations and Japan enjoyed new heights of prosperity from the 1960s through the 1980s. After World War II the United States offered generous aid and investment to its allies, restarting further economic growth in industrialized, diversified countries that already had literate, skilled, and mostly urban populations. Hence, western Europe and Japan recovered and prospered. Japan's economy increased fivefold between 1953 and 1973, the fastest economic growth in world history. Western and Japanese businesses invested around the world, spurring international trade, and Japan and West Germany became the second and third largest capitalist economies. By the 1970s several Western nations, such as West Germany, Sweden, Canada, and Australia, had standards of living similar to those in the United States but far more income equality.

Although economic growth rates often slowed after 1990, Western prosperity relative to the rest of the world continued. Every year the United Nations issues a Human Development Report that rates the quality of life of nations in the world by examining per capita income, health, and literacy. Generally Norway, Sweden, Australia, Canada, and the Netherlands have been rated the most livable nations. A hundred years earlier Norway and Sweden were among the poorest European countries. Sweden achieved the world's lowest poverty rate, largely because the state provides each citizen free education, subsidized health care, and other welfare benefits, and the economy grew steadily. The 2013 report ranks Norway, Australia, the United States, Netherlands, and Germany as the top five; three once-poor Asian societies made the top 20: South Korea (12), Hong Kong (13), and Singapore (19). The 2013 report ranks 45 nations, mostly in sub-Saharan Africa, as having the lowest quality of life—massive poverty, inadequate health care, and low literacy. The late Tanzanian president Julius Nyerere (**nye-RE-re**) put the gap between rich and poor nations in perspective: "While the United States is trying to reach the moon, Tanzania is trying to reach its villages."[4] Yet, some of the poorest African nations have also enjoyed modest economic growth.

In the later twentieth and early twenty-first centuries some nations had more political stability and resources to help their citizens thrive. Richer nations, usually benefiting from democracy, were nation-states with cohesive societies. However, some contained restless ethnic or religious minorities. For example, Basques in northern Spain, whose language and identity differ completely from those of the Spanish majority, sought autonomy or independence. But democratic governments mostly diminished social tensions, while generous social services prevented mass poverty. Many western European states, Canada, and New Zealand adopted ambitious welfare systems with comprehensive national health insurance, promoting social justice and equality. Poorer nations, having small budgets, limited resources, and often highly diverse populations, faced greater challenges in building stable nation-states. Abandoning communism and its safety net sometimes sparked violence, such as the repeated ethnic conflicts in Yugoslavia that produced brutal atrocities and forced expulsion of minorities. Only a few non-European nations, such as Sri Lanka and oil-rich Brunei and Saudi Arabia, tried to mount welfare states with free education and health care, but they struggled to pay for them.

First World The industrialized democracies of western Europe, North America, Australia–New Zealand, and Japan.

Second World The communist nations, led by the USSR and China.

Third World Societies in Asia, Africa, Latin America, and the Caribbean, which were shaped by mass poverty and a legacy of colonization or neocolonialism.

Fourth World The poorest societies, with very small economies and few exploitable resources.

---

[4]Quoted in Jennifer Seymour Whitaker, *How Can Africa Survive?* (New York: Harper and Row, 1988), 13.

MAKE SURE YOU UNDERSTAND THESE KEY POINTS BEFORE MOVING ON

- Between 1946 and 1975, most Western colonies achieved independence, in many cases as a result of violent opposition movements, though the United States continued to oppose leftist movements and the Soviet Union's vast colonial empire endured until 1989.

- Western nations maintained a great deal of influence over the economy and culture of many of their former colonies, which led some intellectuals to call for "decolonizing the mind."

- Revolutionary regimes, often inspired by Marxism, came to power in a number of Asian, African, and Latin American nations, though they met with mixed economic success and in some cases were embroiled in long-term civil war.

- The division of the world's nations into First, Second, and Third Worlds grew blurry as some Third World nations developed First-World-level economies and the Soviet Union collapsed, though democratic countries tended to be more stable and offer more support to their citizens.

aplia

Cold War, Hot Wars, and World Politics

What roles did the Cold War and superpower rivalry play in world politics?

A new global political configuration emerged after World War II. From 1946 to 1989 the two major superpowers, the United States and the USSR, engaged in the **Cold War**, competing for allies and engaging in occasional warfare against their rival's allies rather than each other directly. Americans enjoyed much greater influence and boasted more allies. While the Cold War did not lead to direct U.S.-Soviet military conflict, it produced chronic tensions and generated covert and military interventions by each superpower seeking to block gains by the other.

The Cold War: A Divided World

The world took on a bipolar political character. Nations practicing capitalism and often democracy, led by the United States, opposed those promoting socialist authoritarianism, led by the USSR and known as the Soviet bloc. For over four decades U.S.-USSR relations were a major factor in international affairs. Americans sought to contain communism, while the USSR worked to spread communism and undercut U.S. influence. For several decades leaders of nations such as Egypt, India, and Indonesia promoted nonalignment with either superpower. In 1955 leaders from twenty-nine nonaligned Asian and African countries met in Bandung, Indonesia, to promote a Third World bloc, but they had trouble sustaining unity.

The United States, the world's most powerful nation, enjoyed far greater wealth, military force, and cultural influence than any other nation. In 1945, Americans already had the atomic bomb, produced half the world's industrial output, and held two-thirds of the gold. Now they assumed a heavy financial and military burden to maintain their leading role in world affairs and promote economic growth, obtaining resources and preserving profitable markets.

By 1948 the Soviets controlled all of eastern Europe and were allied with communist Mongolia and North Korea. Perceiving the USSR as rivals for world influence, Americans tried to prevent communists from controlling China and then fought the Korean War (1950–1953) to stop North Koreans from forcibly reunifying the peninsula. Despite U.S. efforts, communist regimes came to power in China in 1949, North Vietnam in 1954, and Cuba in 1959. Furthermore, waging the Cold War and widely using military force, including a long war in Vietnam, cost the United States $4–5 trillion and some 113,000 American lives, mostly soldiers, between 1946 and 1989.

Historians debate whether the USSR ever posed a serious military threat and how much each side misinterpreted its rival's motives and actions. Remembering centuries of invasions from the west, and fearing the United States and its western European allies' combined military power, the USSR occupied eastern Europe as a buffer zone. Mistrusting Soviet leaders and despising communism, Americans viewed themselves as protecting freedom; the Soviets claimed they were helping the world's exploited masses and fighting imperialism.

Some historians believe the Cold War brought stability; others point to some eighty wars between 1945 and 1989, generating 20 million deaths and perhaps 20 million refugees. Cold War rivalries dragged in emerging nations, sparking upheavals that bankrupted economies and devastated societies. Varied small conflicts involved surrogates, governments, or movements allied to one superpower and fighting the troops from the other superpower. In Korea and Vietnam U.S. troops battled not Soviet armies but Soviet-supported local communist forces; the USSR sent military supplies and advisers to help Vietnamese communists fight first the French and then the United States, which supported a pro-Western government in South Vietnam after the French were defeated. Communists controlled Vietnam by 1975. Americans also used surrogates, such as the Islamic insurgents fighting the Soviets in Afghanistan in the 1980s. Insurgencies often used **guerrilla warfare**, an unconventional military strategy of avoiding full-scale direct

Cold War A conflict lasting from 1946 to 1989 in which the United States and the USSR competed for allies and engaged in occasional warfare against their rival's allies rather than against each other directly.

guerrilla warfare An unconventional military strategy of avoiding full-scale direct confrontations in favor of small-scale skirmishes.

confrontations in favor of small-scale skirmishes, including hit-and-run attacks, sniping, land mines, and roadside bombs.

Both superpowers intervened, both covertly and militarily, to protect their interests. The USSR sent military forces into Poland, Hungary, and Czechoslovakia to crush anti-Soviet movements and into Afghanistan to support a pro-Soviet government. Some invasions proved disastrous; the heavy losses and humiliating withdrawal from Afghanistan in 1989 contributed to the Soviet system's collapse. Communist parties became a strong presence in nations like Indonesia, India, and Chile, participating openly in politics, but they also launched unsuccessful insurgencies in countries such as Peru, Malaysia, and the Philippines. Meanwhile, the United States actively sought to shape the political and economic direction of Asian, African, and Latin American societies; Americans generously donated food, disaster and medical assistance, offered technical advice, supported democratic organizations, and sometimes promoted human rights. But other efforts destabilized or helped overthrow governments deemed unfriendly to U.S. business and political interests, including left-leaning but democratically elected regimes in Brazil, Chile, and Guatemala.

One of the earliest U.S. interventions came in 1953 in oil-rich Iran. A nationalist but noncommunist regime angered the Americans and British by nationalizing British- and U.S.-owned oil companies that sent most of their huge profits abroad and paid Iranian workers under fifty cents a day. In response, Britain and the United States imposed an economic boycott to prevent Iran from selling its oil abroad. American agents recruited disaffected military officers and paid Iranians to spark riots that paralyzed the capital, forcing the nationalists from power and installing a pro-U.S. but despotic government. For the first time ever the United States had overthrown a foreign government outside the Western Hemisphere. Ever since, many Iranians have hated the United States.

To critics, the U.S. interventions constituted imperialism. They often proved costly as well. The U.S.-Vietnam war cost vast sums of money, killed some fifty-eight thousand Americans and several million Vietnamese on all sides, and forced Americans to negotiate for peace and withdraw, harming U.S. prestige in the world. The war also created economic problems and political divisions in the United States, reducing American willingness to exercise military power. Meanwhile, the USSR and China spent scarce resources supplying their communist allies.

The Nuclear Arms Race and Global Militarization

The Cold War generated a superpower arms race and increased global militarization. Both superpowers developed first atomic and then **nuclear weapons**, explosive devices that

nuclear weapons Explosive devices that owe their destructive power to the energy released by either splitting or fusing atoms.

owe their destructive power to energy released by either splitting or fusing atoms, the most deadly result of the technological surge extending back

through Einstein to Newton and the Scientific Revolution. A nuclear explosion produces a powerful blast, intense heat, and deadly radiation. The United States dropped the first atomic bombs on Japan to end World War II. Both superpowers eventually developed even more deadly nuclear warheads, placing them on missiles. The growth of nuclear arsenals represented the most dangerous part of a larger trend toward expanding war-making ability by many nations.

Since 1945 the world has lived in the shadow of nuclear weapons; a small number could reduce whole countries to radioactive rubble. Einstein, fretting that unleashed atomic power changed everything except ways of thinking, worried that leaders would create a global catastrophe by rashly using these technologies. Fortunately these weapons were never used after 1945, although the world was close to nuclear confrontations on several occasions. For example, in 1962 President John F. Kennedy (1917–1963) demanded that the USSR remove nuclear missiles secretly planted in Cuba, 90 miles from Florida, but vetoed a U.S. invasion or nuclear attack that might have sparked all-out nuclear war. His firm stance created a tense crisis, ultimately forcing the Soviets to withdraw them. Years later we learned that a Soviet submarine commander armed but did not fire a nuclear missile at Florida, averting catastrophe.

The Cold War fostered a balance of terror, with both superpowers unwilling to use their weapons out of fear that the other would retaliate. Historians debate whether the nuclear arms race preserved peace by discouraging all-out U.S.-USSR military confrontations or unsettled international politics, wasting trillions of dollars. Britain, France, China, India, and Pakistan also constructed or acquired nuclear bombs, while Israel, Iran, and North Korea began nuclear programs. In 1987 the two superpowers negotiated their first treaty reducing nuclear arms, and today a nuclear conflict involving the United States, Britain, Russia, and China seems remote. But India-Pakistan relations remained tense and concerns grew about nuclear proliferation, especially if North Korea or Pakistan sold bombs to other countries or terrorist groups. Some outside the West argued that a few powerful nations' monopoly on such weapons was unfair.

The proportion of total world production and spending devoted to militaries grew dramatically during the Cold War. By 1985, the world spent more on military forces and weapons than the combined income of the poorest half of the world's countries. The two superpowers together, with 11 percent of the world population, accounted for 60 percent of military spending, 25 percent of the armed forces, and 97 percent of nuclear weapons. They also sold conventional weapons to other countries.

The wars since 1945 have caused enormous casualties, three-fourths of them civilians. Two million people died during China's civil war (1945–1949), 800,000 during India's violent partition (1948), 2 million during the American-Vietnamese War, 1 million during the Nigerian civil war (1967), and more than 2 million in Cambodian violence (1970–1978). Millions perished from genocide. Hence, in the 1990s members of the Hutu majority slaughtered minority Tutsis in Rwanda (**roo-AHN-duh**), and extremist Serbs killed Bosnian and Albanian

Muslims in Yugoslavia, in what they called "ethnic cleansing." The United States and western European nations sent in troops to restore order in Yugoslavia, punishing the worst human rights violators. Some think the ethnic or religion-based massacres in Sudan, Syria, and the eastern Congo constituted genocide.

Global Organizations and Activism

More than ever before in history, public and private organizations with a global reach and mission have promoted political cooperation and addressed various social, political, economic, and environmental issues. The largest effort to cooperate for the common good, the United Nations, founded in 1945 with fifty-one members, became a key debate forum and agency for improving global conditions. The United Nations Charter enumerated the founding principles: "To develop friendly relations among nations based on respect for … equal rights and self-determination of peoples and … strengthen universal peace." The founding members aimed to "save succeeding generations from the scourge of war, reaffirm faith in fundamental rights, and respect international law."[5] As colonies gaining independence joined, the organization grew to nearly two hundred member states. The United Nations has also sponsored humanitarian agencies such as the World Health Organization, which monitors diseases, funds medical research, and promotes public health, and the United Nations Children Fund (UNICEF), which promotes children's welfare and education. Such programs have dramatically reduced deaths from malnutrition and infectious diseases, helping increase average life expectancy from forty-five in 1900 to seventy in 2013, and have greatly reduced the risk of mothers dying in childbirth. However, critics believe that political differences have often obstructed the United Nations' work.

The five major powers of 1945 (the United States, China, Britain, France, and the USSR) have enjoyed permanent seats with veto power in the policymaking United Nations Security Council, and both superpowers have vetoed decisions challenging their national interests. Hence, the United States vetoed resolutions aimed at penalizing Israel and also blocked the communist government from occupying China's United Nations seat. The Security Council sometimes sent peacekeeping troops into troubled countries and discouraged, but could not prevent, states from resorting to force. To gain support for military action, nations often made their case before the Security Council and sometimes received support; a United States–led United Nations military force repulsed a North Korean invasion of South Korea. However, nations often ignored other nations' disapproval, as the United States did when it invaded Iraq in 2003. In recent years support has built to give several emerging nations, such as Brazil and India, and perhaps acknowledged powers like Japan, permanent Security Council seats.

Nations have also forged international agreements and treaties. In 1972 they banned biological weapons. In 1997, 132 nations prohibited the production, use, and export of land mines, which kill and injure civilians years after conflicts end. In 1997 most nations also signed the Kyoto Protocol, pledging to reduce the harmful gases contributing to global warming, but follow-up conferences failed to impose strict regulations on the world. In 2002 a treaty established an International Criminal Court to prosecute perpetrators of genocide, war crimes, and crimes against humanity. But the United States and several other industrial nations refused to ratify these modest efforts to reduce weapons, promote environmental stability, and establish accountability for international crimes.

Private organizations and activists have also addressed issues of peace, social justice, health, refugees, famine, conflict resolution, and environmental protection. For example, Doctors Without Borders offers medical personnel, and Amnesty International works to free political prisoners. Some religious leaders have promoted world peace, justice, and humanitarian issues. The Dalai Lama (b. 1935), the highest Tibetan Buddhist spiritual leader, won the Nobel Peace Prize in 1989 for promoting human rights, nonviolent conflict resolution, and understanding among different religions. In 1997 he pleaded, "We all have a special responsibility to create a better world. No one loses, and everyone gains by a shared universal sense of responsibility to this planet and all living things on it."[6] The Aga Khan IV (b. 1936), spiritual leader of a largely Indian Shi'ite Muslim sect, has funded schools and clinics all over the world. The World Council of Churches, supported by diverse Protestant and Eastern Orthodox churches, has encouraged interfaith cooperation and understanding. Several Catholic popes have favored interfaith dialogue and denounced war and capital punishment.

World Politics Since 1989

Between 1989 and 1991 the Soviet bloc disintegrated and communist regimes in eastern Europe and the USSR collapsed, ending the Cold War and the bipolar world it defined. Many historians conclude that no country or person "won" the Cold War, which was fueled by misconceptions and nearly bankrupted both sides. Other nations, especially Japan and West Germany, both protected by U.S. military bases, gained the most by investing heavily in economic growth. As U.S. and Soviet leaders deescalated tensions in the later 1980s, the United States became the sole superpower. By 2008 it spent as much on defense as all other countries combined and was the world's major supplier of arms. Some observers perceived a multipolar system in which the United States, despite its power, had to share political and economic leadership with western Europe and several Asian nations, especially China, Japan, and India. Since 2009 five influential nations—Brazil, Russia, India, China, and South Africa—known as the BRICS,

---

[5]The quotes are in Choi Chatterjee et al., *The 20th Century: A Retrospective* (Boulder, CO: Westview Press, 2002), 153, 306.

[6]Dalai Lama, *My Land and My People* (New York: Warner Books, 1997), x.

Sayyid Azim/AP Images

UNITED NATIONS PEACEKEEPERS IN CONGO The United Nations has regularly sent peacekeepers into troubled countries such as the Congo. This photo, from 2003, shows United Nations troops from Uruguay guarding a United Nations office while a Congolese woman and her four children, displaced from her village by factional fighting, seek United Nations help.

have increasingly cooperated in many areas, providing an alternative to the Western alliance.

The first major post–Cold War challenge for the United States came from Iraq's brutal dictator, Saddam Hussein (1937–2006), whose army invaded and occupied Iraq's small, oil-rich neighbor, Kuwait, in 1990. Opposing Iran's Islamic government, the United States had supported Saddam's military with weapons in the 1980s, when Iraq fought Iran. Now the United States organized an international coalition and, in 1991, quickly pushed the Iraqis out of Kuwait. U.S. president George H. W. Bush proclaimed a "new world order" led by the United States and based on American values, envisioning the United States as a world policeman.

A new world disorder characterized the 1990s. Ethnic and nationalist conflicts exploded in violence in Yugoslavia, eastern Europe, Sri Lanka, West Africa, and Rwanda. States with weak or dysfunctional governments, among them Haiti, Liberia, Sierra Leone, Congo, Sudan, and Somalia, experienced chronic fighting and civil war. Rising tides of religious militancy or conflict between rival faiths complicated politics in countries such as India, Indonesia, Pakistan, Algeria, Egypt, and Nigeria.

In particular, militant Islam demonstrated its potency in Iran, Sudan, and Afghanistan; extremists formed terrorist groups to fight moderate Islamic regimes, Israel, and Western nations. By the early 2000s Islamic radicals posed a greater challenge in southern Asia and the Middle East than declining communist movements. Aggressive dictators, such as Iraq's Saddam Hussein, and North Korea, which limited contact with the outside world, fostered regional tensions. In 2008–2009 a severe global recession added to the problems; businesses closed, world trade declined, and national economies floundered. Finally, the "Arab spring" (2011–2013) displaced or challenged various authoritarian regimes but also left in its wake violence and instability, from riots and terrorism to rival militias and civil wars, in countries like Egypt, Syria, Libya, and Yemen. The new world order promise of a peaceful world moving toward democracy foundered as proliferating regional, nationalist, religious, and ethnic conflicts, combined with economic collapse, produced a context for violence. Yet, wars between nations, and battle deaths, became less common than in the middle twentieth century, thanks to international sanctions, trade, and widening prosperity.

MAKE SURE YOU UNDERSTAND THESE KEY POINTS BEFORE MOVING ON

- During the Cold War, the United States and the USSR struggled for world control, with the United States generally favoring democracy and capitalism but also seeking access to resources and foreign markets, and the USSR supporting emerging communist regimes and movements.

- Though the United States and the USSR never fought directly, they were involved in wars in other countries, such as Vietnam, Korea, and Afghanistan, in which millions died, and they intervened in countries such as Guatemala, Iran, Poland, Hungary, and Czechoslovakia.

- The United States and the USSR participated in a massive arms race, spending trillions of dollars on

nuclear weapons, which led to widespread fear of mass destruction, though some argue that this fear helped prevent all-out war.

- The United Nations was formed with the goal of promoting world peace and human rights, and various agreements have been signed to ban biological weapons and land mines, to prevent global warming, and to facilitate an international justice system, though they have encountered opposition by the United States and some other industrial nations.

aplia

Globalizing Economies, Underdevelopment, and Environmental Change

T N

What were some of the main consequences of a globalizing world economy?

The world was increasingly characterized by **globalization**, a pattern in which economic, political, and cultural processes reach beyond national boundaries. This trend reduced barriers between countries, allowing for more collaboration, and more closely connected societies through worldwide commercial markets, finance, telecommunications, and exchange of ideas. However, globalization also widened inequalities between the richest and poorest nations, while industrialization and economic growth produced negative environmental consequences, including increased pollution and a warming climate. As a result of population growth, people expanded agriculture into semidesert areas and cut down rain forests, causing environmental deterioration.

The Transnational Economy

A world economy linking distant societies has been developing for the past twenty-five hundred years, but after 1945 globalization rapidly spread market capitalism and fostered flows of capital, goods, services, and people. The world's production of goods and services was 120 times higher in 2000 than in 1500; average personal income grew fourfold between 1900 and 2000. In the interconnected world, events occurring or decisions taken in one part of the world affect societies far away. Rising or falling prices on the Tokyo or New York stock exchanges quickly reverberate around the world, influencing stock markets elsewhere. Similarly, Western governments' sales of stockpiled rubber depress world prices, affecting rubber growers, and the businesses that supply them, in Malaysia, Sri Lanka, Brazil, and the Congo. Some transnational economic activity is illegal, especially the flow of narcotics. Heroin and cocaine smuggled into and sold in North America and Europe by transnational criminal syndicates originate largely in Asia and Latin America.

Americans are major globalization proponents and believe that open markets, investment, and trade lead to prosperity. By 2000 the United States produced nearly a third of the world's goods and services; Japan, the next largest economy, accounted for around a sixth. International observers described U.S. leadership metaphorically: when Americans sneeze, the rest of the world catches cold. However, economic growth and trade do not necessarily improve living conditions for everybody; well-functioning governments, legal and political rights, and health and education services are also required. Critics charge that globalization promises riches it cannot always deliver, distributing the benefits unequally. By the 1990s the United States and China gained the most from removing trade barriers and fostering competitive markets worldwide, sucking in investment capital, aggressively acquiring natural resources, and supplying diverse products to foreign markets. Surpassing Germany and then Japan, China became the world's second largest economy, producing clothing, housewares, and other consumer goods. Chinese invested in Africa, Latin America, and the Middle East and bought U.S.-based companies. But not all Chinese benefited. Some less efficient state-owned enterprises closed down, and peasants protested as their farmland was bulldozed to build foreign-owned factories, private housing developments, and golf courses for affluent Chinese.

A few other nations, such as India, Ireland, Singapore, and South Korea, capitalized on globalization, creating economic growth and becoming high-technology centers. However, Japan and some European nations struggled to compete in the globalizing economy, and some Asian, African, and Caribbean nations fell deeper into poverty. In addition, many people in developing nations—Mexican corn farmers, West African wheat growers, Pakistani textile workers—faced

globalization A pattern in which economic, political, and cultural processes reach beyond nation-state boundaries.

Ou Neakiry/AP Images

THE GLOBAL ECONOMY Cambodian Buddhist monks, following ancient traditions, collect their food from the devout in the capital city, Phnom Penh, while advertising for American cigarettes entices Cambodians into the global economy, despite government concerns about the health danger posed by tobacco products.

trade barriers and well-funded, technologically superior Western competitors. United Nations secretary general Kofi Annan **(KO-fee AN-uhn)**, a Ghanaian, contended in 2002: "Our challenge today is to make globalization an engine that lifts people out of hardship and misery, not a force that holds them down."[7]

Until recently Western industrial nations and Japan generally maintained a favorable position in the global economy, controlling most of the capital, markets, and international financial institutions such as banks; moreover, their corporations own assets in other nations. Hence, Americans control businesses, mines, and plantations in Latin America, Japanese operate factories in Southeast Asia, and the French maintain a large economic stake in West Africa. Capitalist systems in industrialized nations range from limited government interference, common in the United States, to mixed free markets and welfare states in western Europe, to close government-business relationships in Japan and South Korea. These contrast with many former colonies where power holders, often closely tied to foreign or domestic business interests, preside over largely poor populations. Hence, in the Congo, corrupt leaders have protected the Belgian-owned and local corporations who fund them. Rebel movements and brutal local warlords have added to Congolese misery.

As some once-poor countries have used the transnational economy to their advantage, some have achieved spectacular growth, leading many experts to proclaim the rise of the South (see Witness to the Past: Human Development and the Rise of the South). A few oil-rich nations, like Kuwait and the United Arab Emirates, use revenues to improve their citizens' lives.

Various Asian countries, much like Japan in the late 1800s, have combined market economies, cheap labor, and powerful governments to promote industrialization. By repressing opposition, they have ensured political stability and attracted foreign investment. Their emphasis on export-oriented growth—the production of consumer goods such as clothing, toys, electronics, and housewares for sale abroad, especially in Europe and North America—has fostered high growth rates and imported industrial jobs from Western countries or Japan. Beginning in the 1980s, China, South Korea, Taiwan, Malaysia, Thailand, Singapore, and eventually Vietnam created the world's fastest-growing economies, their major cities boasting well-stocked malls, freeways, diverse restaurants, and luxury condominiums. Elsewhere nations like Brazil, South Africa, Ghana, Turkey, and Chile enjoyed robust growth. But by 2014 some experienced slowing growth as foreign investment diminished.

Often the growing middle class and labor leaders have demanded political liberalization and a larger voice in government. By the 1990s Indonesians, South Koreans, Taiwanese, Thais, Ghanaians, Brazilians, and Chileans replaced dictatorships with democratic governments. Some Asian systems became development models by mixing capitalism, which creates wealth, with socialism, which can distribute wealth equitably. Their economic resurgence has restored the leading role some Asian societies enjoyed in the world economy for many centuries before 1800. But in the late 1990s many Asian economies crashed, then slowly rebounded until they were damaged again in 2008–2009 as the U.S. economic crisis affected Asia and the rest of the world.

WITNESS TO THE PAST

Human Development and the Rise of the South

The Human Development Report, *issued by the United Nations in 2013, focused on this century's shifting global dynamics with the rise of what they term the South, especially the more than forty developing countries with a fast-improving quality of life as measured by life expectancy, adult literacy, and standard of living. Although criticized for neglecting other criteria such as environmental health and political freedom, these annual reports provide a useful benchmark for quantitatively evaluating human development in each nation and territory.*

When developed economies stopped growing during the 2008–2009 financial crisis but developing economies kept on growing, the world took notice. The rise of the South, seen within the developing world as an overdue global rebalancing, has been much commented on since. This discussion has typically focused narrowly on GDP and trade growth in a few large countries. Yet there are broader dynamics at play, involving many more countries and deeper trends, with potentially far-reaching implications for people's lives, for social equity, and for democratic governance at the local and global levels…the rise of the South is both the result of continual human development investments and achievements and an opportunity for still more human progress for the world as a whole….

The rise of the South is unprecedented in its speed and scale. It must be understood in broad human development terms as the story of a dramatic expansion of individual capabilities and sustained human development progress in the countries that are home to the vast majority of the world's people….Although most developing countries have done well, a large number…have done particularly well…. Some of the largest countries have made rapid advances, notably Brazil, China, India, Indonesia, Mexico, South Africa, and Turkey. But there has also been substantial progress in smaller economies, such as Bangladesh, Chile, Ghana, Mauritius, Rwanda, and Tunisia….

For the first time in 150 years, the combined output of the developing world's three leading economies—Brazil, China, and India—is about equal to the combined GDP of the longstanding industrial powers of the North—Canada, France, Germany, Italy, the United Kingdom and the United

States. This represents a dramatic rebalancing of global economic power…. The South is now emerging alongside the North as a breeding ground of technical innovation and creative entrepreneurship…. All developing countries are not yet participating fully in the rise of the South. The pace of change is slower, for instance, in most of the 49 least developed countries, especially those that are landlocked or distant from world markets….

How have so many countries in the South transformed their human development prospects? … There have been three notable drivers of development: a proactive developmental state, tapping of global markets, and determined social policy and innovation…. Many countries in the South have demonstrated much success. But even in higher achieving countries, future success is not guaranteed. How can countries … continue their pace of progress? … The Report suggests four important areas to facilitate this: enhancing equity, enabling voice and participation, confronting environmental pressures and managing demographic change…. While environmental threats such as climate change, deforestation, air and water pollution, and natural disasters affect everyone, they hurt poor countries and poor communities most….

Investments in human development are justified not only on moral grounds, but also because improvements in health, education and social welfare are key to success in a more competitive and dynamic world economy … these investments should target the poor—connecting them to markets and increasing their livelihood opportunities. Poverty is an injustice that can and should be remedied by determined action…. The rise of the South is leading to a greater diversity of voices on the world stage.

THINKING ABOUT THE READING

1. What does the report identify as progress for many developing countries?
2. What factors have contributed to their growth and development?

Source: *Human Development Report 2013. The Rise of the South: Human Progress in a Divided World* (New York: United Nations Development Programme, 2013), 1–13.

Factories closed and revenues declined, causing massive unemployment and hardship. By 2013 many Asian nations, including China, had reestablished strong to modest growth. Historians debate whether China or India might eventually surpass the United States as the world's colossus.

Various institutions shaped the transnational economy, especially international lending agencies formed by the Allies in 1944 to aid postwar reconstruction. The World Bank funded development projects such as dams and agricultural schemes; the International Monetary Fund (IMF) regulated currency dealings and addressed financial problems. Many Asian, African,

Caribbean, and Latin American nations, not earning enough income to buy food and medicine, import luxuries, build dams, and improve ports, took out IMF or World Bank loans. Some fell deeply in debt. Moreover, the IMF, able to dictate economic policies to borrowing countries, favored Western investment and free markets rather than social services like schools and clinics. In 2013 the BRICS proposed to establish a new development bank to challenge the World Bank and IMF.

Trade agreements and trading blocs reflected unprecedented economic connectedness. Formed in 1947, the General Agreement on Trade and Tariffs (GATT) set rules for world trade, including tariffs and regulations. The World Trade Organization (WTO), founded by 124 nations in 1995, had stronger dispute-resolution capabilities than GATT. Regional trading blocs also formed. The European Common Market (now the European Union) eventually included most European nations. Major industrial nations cooperated to manage the global economy. By the 1990s economic officials from the seven richest industrial countries met regularly as the G7 (Group of 7), later joined by Russia to form the G8. Thanks to the 2008–2009 economic crisis and the need for concerted global action, G8 leaders permanently expanded to include 12 other countries with large economies, such as China, India, Brazil, Indonesia, South Korea, and Argentina. This new G20 grouping confirmed the changing world economic leadership, especially China's key role.

Giant business enterprises, known as **multinational corporations** because they operate all over the world, have gained a leading role in the global marketplace. Some 300 to 400 companies, two-thirds U.S.-owned, dominate world production and trade and are now the world's third largest economic force, greatly influencing governments. Multinationals set the world price for various commodities, such as coffee, copper, or oil; play one country off against another to get the best deal; and move manufacturing jobs. Multinationals have also created millions of jobs in poor countries. Increasingly women are the majority in the global assembly lines of factories producing for export. Supporters argue that outsourcing—moving jobs from high-wage to low-wage countries—creates middle-class jobs and employs people with few other job prospects. Critics contend that most jobs pay low wages, require long hours, and offer little future. For example, although the U.S.-based Nike Corporation creates needed jobs in Vietnam, Vietnamese employees, mainly women, work in unhealthy conditions, face sexual harassment, and are fired if they complain.

The Spread of Industrialization

Industrialization spread, especially to Asia and Latin America. Entrepreneurs or state agencies in, among others, China, India, South Korea, Brazil, and Mexico built textile mills, steel mills, and automobile plants; Chinese textiles, Indian steel, and South Korean cars found markets around the world. Meanwhile, the U.S. share of world industrial production fell from 50 percent in 1950 to 30 percent in the 1980s; Americans built over 75 percent of all cars in 1950 but less than 20 percent by the 1990s. Malaysians now drive Swedish Volvos, South Korean Hyundais, Japanese Toyotas, and Proton Sagas manufactured locally.

multinational corporations Giant business enterprises that operate all over the world, gaining a leading role in the global marketplace.

Third Industrial Revolution The creation of unprecedented scientific knowledge and new technologies.

Green Revolution Increased agricultural output through the use of new high-yield seeds and mechanized farming.

Technological innovations spurred economic growth. The so-called **Third Industrial Revolution** created unprecedented scientific knowledge and new technologies, making the First and Second Industrial Revolutions seem obsolete. Nuclear power, computers, automation, and robots displaced traditional smokestack industries like steel mills. Rocketry, genetic engineering, silicon chips, and lasers became commonplace. Space technology produced the first manned trips to the moon and unmanned crafts exploring the solar system. In 2005 a probe landed on Saturn's large, mysterious moon, Titan, sending back photographs of the surface. More powerful telescopes increased knowledge of the solar system and the universe, even discovering planets circling other stars. British poet Archibald MacLeish observed that astronauts on space capsules circling the planet did not perceive national boundaries or international rivalries, but only oceans and lands containing people with a common planetary home: "To see the Earth as we now see it, small and blue and beautiful in that eternal silence [of space] where it floats, is to see ourselves as rulers on the Earth together."[8]

The Third Industrial Revolution has potentially dramatic consequences. One component, the **Green Revolution**, has increased agricultural output from the use of new high-yield seeds and mechanized farming. Farmers able to afford these innovations can raise more crops a year. But in countries such as India, the Philippines, and Mexico, the Green Revolution, requiring more capital for seeds and machines but fewer people to work the land, often harmed poor peasants unable to afford the investment. In many industries, including automobile manufacturing, automation has taken over production, allowing companies to fire workers.

Industry became globalized. By the 1990s foreign-owned factories paying low taxes and wages relocated to industrial parks around the world. Hence, factories in northern Mexico, usually U.S.-owned and making goods largely for the U.S. market, employed a half million workers, mainly women. Service and information exchange industries also grew. More people worked in service enterprises, such as fast-food restaurants. Transnational computer networks, such as AOL and Google, helped people use the Internet for communication and knowledge acquisition. Responding to these trends, India, which graduates each year thousands of people fluent in English and skilled in computer technology, became a world center for offshore information and technical services. Increasingly consumers calling North American companies for computer technical support, product information, or billing questions reach people working in cubicles in India, Sri Lanka, or the Philippines.

Globalization comes with risks. Hoping to better compete, businesses have moved factories to countries with low wages and costs. Some Western and Japanese businesses shifted operations to South Korea or Taiwan, where average workers earn in a month what American or German workers earn in a week or ten days, yet produce as much. Others established operations in Asian, African, Latin American, or eastern European nations where workers earn even less. For example, in 1990 the

[8]Quoted in J. Donald Hughes, *An Environmental History of the World: Mankind's Changing Role in the Community of Life* (New York: Routledge, 2002), 206.

U.S. clothing maker Levi Strauss closed fifty-eight U.S. plants with over ten thousand workers while shifting half of its production to foreign countries.

Underdevelopment and Development

Uneven economic growth has contributed to a growing gap between the richest nations and poorest undeveloped nations. The gap was already wide in 1945, thanks to colonialism; a Guyanese historian argued that "the vast majority of Africans went into colonialism with a hoe and came out with a hoe."[9] Many Asian, African, and Latin American economies grew rapidly in the 1950s and 1960s, when the world economy boomed, but most declined in the 1970s and 1980s, as the world economy soured and world prices for many exports collapsed. The world economy revived for a few years, only to experience a dramatic downturn in the later 1990s and early 2000s. In 2008–2009 the world economy went into the worst crisis since the Great Depression. Many nations were severely affected, but some Asian countries and the United States began to recover by 2010.

Moreover, economic growth has not always fostered development, defined as growth that benefits the majority of the population. Some Asian nations have prospered from welcoming foreign investment, building schools, hospitals, and highways. Yet, foreign investment often does not create locally owned businesses. In Nigeria, for example, British enterprises still dominate banking, importing, and exporting; Western investment has gone mainly into cash crops and oil production, controlled largely by Western companies. Outraged that they gain little from the polluting oil wells around them, people in Nigeria's main oil-producing region have sabotaged operations, kidnapped foreign oil workers, and resorted to armed insurgency. Furthermore, foreign investment and aid have often lined the pockets of corrupt leaders, bureaucrats, and military officers.

Scholars debate how poor countries can better profit from their connections to the world economy and spur local efforts at development. The influential Indian economist Amartya Sen (b. 1933) helped run evening schools for illiterate rural children as a youth, prompting his studies of global poverty, famine, and social and gender inequality; he won the Nobel Prize in economics in 1998. Influenced by his first wife, a writer and political activist, Sen argues that women's literacy and employment are the best predictors of both child survival and fertility rate reduction, prerequisites for development in poor villages. His views on poverty and gender inequality influenced the United Nations when, in 2000, it developed an agenda for a new millennium to address the world's pressing problems by 2020. However, few poor countries have sufficient resources to seriously combat widespread poverty or promote women's empowerment.

Most of the poorest nations have suffered from some combination of rapid population growth, high unemployment, illiteracy, hunger, disease, corrupt or ineffective governments, and reliance on only a few exports. By the 1990s the richest fifth of the world's people received 80 percent of the total income while the poorest fifth earned less than 2 percent. Hence, in Guatemala, 90 percent lived below the official poverty line; nearly half had no health care, indoor plumbing, piped water, or formal education. By 2000 the world's three richest persons owned more assets than the forty-eight poorest nations together; 358 billionaires had a combined net worth equal to that of the bottom 45 percent of the world's population combined. A fifth of the world's people earned less than $1 per day, and one billion suffered from hunger in 2009, a problem made worse by global recession. Furthermore, despite preaching free trade, rich nations often blocked or restricted food and fiber imports from poor nations while heavily subsidizing their own farmers. Hence, wheat farmers in Mali, however industrious, cannot compete with French or U.S. wheat farmers, who enjoy financial support from their governments. The United Nations secretary general, Kofi Annan, laid out the organization's challenges in a world changed dramatically since the organization's formation over five decades earlier: "How can we say that the half of the human race which has yet to make or receive a phone call, let alone use a computer, is taking part in globalization? We cannot, without insulting their poverty.... We are plundering our children's heritage to pay for our present unsustainable practices. We must stop. Above all we need to remember the old African wisdom which I learned as a child—that the earth is not ours. It is a treasure we hold in trust for our descendants."[10]

Yet, non-Western nations can boast of many achievements. Between 1960 and 2000 they reduced infant mortality by half and doubled adult literacy rates. Among others, China, Sri Lanka, Malaysia, and Tanzania provided many social services, such as schools and clinics, to rural areas. Various countries implemented locally based development strategies. In sub-Saharan Africa, for instance, Burkina Faso (**buhr-KEE-nuh FAH-so**) and Niger (**nee-jer**) moved away from expensive prestige projects—such as building large dams to supply hydroelectric power—to small-scale labor-intensive projects aiding the environment, such as tree-planting campaigns; local cooperative banks provided credit to farmers. However, severe drought can still cause widespread starvation.

Women and their children face the harshest problems. Economic change has undermined the handicrafts that provide incomes for women while also fragmenting families: many men have to find work in other districts or countries, leaving their wives to support and raise the children. In Africa, men migrate each year from Burkina Faso to the Ivory Coast's cocoa plantations and logging camps and from Mozambique to South African mines. Meanwhile, women leave India, Sri Lanka, and the Philippines to work as domestic servants in the Persian Gulf states and Saudi Arabia, some facing sexual harassment or cruel employers. Asian and Latin American women work in homes and sweatshops in North America and Europe.

---

[9]Walter Rodney, *How Europe Underdeveloped Africa* (London: Bogle-L'Ouverture, 1972), 162.

[10]United Nations, *The Millennium Report* (*http://www.un.org/millennium/sg/report/state.htm*).

RICH AND POOR IN BRAZIL The stark contrast between the wealthy and the poor in many nations can be seen in the Brazilian city of Rio de Janeiro. Seeking jobs in expanding industries, millions of migrants flock to the city, building shantytown slums and squatter settlements on hillsides in view of luxury high-rise apartment and office buildings.

Development often leaves women behind because of their inferior social status and relative invisibility in national economic statistics. Many face social customs that accord them little influence and, in case of divorce, award their children to the father. An Indian folk song expressed the bitterness of village women who, after marriage, have no claim on their birth family's property: "To my brother belong your green fields, O father, while I am banished afar."[11] While women do 60 percent of the world's work and produce 50 to 75 percent of the food, they own only 1 percent of the property and earn 10 percent of the income. Most of poor women's labor—food preparation, cleaning, child rearing—is unpaid and demanding. In Senegal a typical rural woman, married at a young age, gets up at 5 A.M. to pound millet, the staple food, for an hour. She then walks a few hundred yards or perhaps several miles to get water from a well, makes breakfast for the family, goes to the village shop, makes the family lunch, takes food to family members working in the fields, does laundry, makes supper, and then pounds millet again before bed.

Some nations help women and children through bottom-up, grassroots policies. The Grameen **(GRAH-mean)** Bank in Bangladesh, which promotes self-help, provides an outstanding model. After meeting a woman matmaker who earned four cents a day, the economist Muhammad Yunus (b. 1940) concluded that conventional economics ignored rural poverty. Since few banks made loans to the poor, in 1983 Yunus opened the Grameen Bank, which makes loans under $100 on cheap terms to peasants, especially women, for buying tools they need to earn a living, like a cell phone for business or personal calls or bamboo to make chairs. Less than 2 percent of borrowers have defaulted. The women earning an income now enjoy higher social status, and many began using contraceptives, helping to lower the Bangladesh birthrate from 3 to 2 percent a year. Muhammad Yunus won the Nobel Peace Prize in 2006. Some other nations have borrowed the Grameen model, with mixed results.

Population, Urbanization, and Environmental Change

Rapid population growth and overcrowded cities exemplify global imbalance. Since 1945 the world's population grew faster than ever before in history (see Map 26.2). Two thousand years ago the earth had between 125 and 250 million people; roughly ten thousand generations later, in 1830, the world

---

[11]Quoted in Michael H. Hunt, *The World Transformed; 1945 to the Present* (Boston: Bedford/St. Martin's, 204), 428.

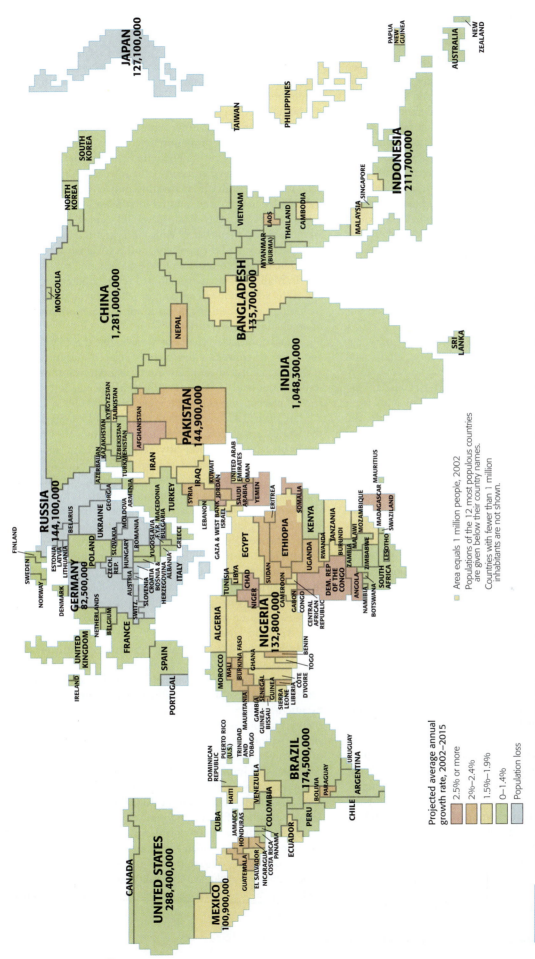

MAP 26.2 WORLD POPULATION GROWTH This map shows dramatically which nations have the largest populations: China, India, the United States, Indonesia, and Brazil. It also shows which regions experience the most rapid population growth: Africa, South Asia, and Central America. © 2015 Cengage Learning

Projected average annual growth rate, 2002–2015

- 2.5% or more
- 2%–2.4%
- 1.5%–1.9%
- 0–1.4%
- Population loss

Area equals 1 million people, 2002

Populations of the 12 most populous countries are given below their country names.

Countries with fewer than 1 million inhabitants are not shown.

CANADA

UNITED STATES
288,400,000

MEXICO
100,900,000

GUATEMALA
EL SALVADOR
NICARAGUA
COSTA RICA
PANAMA
HONDURAS
JAMAICA
CUBA
HAITI
DOMINICAN REPUBLIC
PUERTO RICO (U.S.)
TRINIDAD AND TOBAGO
VENEZUELA
COLOMBIA
ECUADOR
PERU
BOLIVIA
BRAZIL
174,500,000
PARAGUAY
CHILE
ARGENTINA
URUGUAY

IRELAND
UNITED KINGDOM
PORTUGAL
SPAIN
FRANCE
NETHERLANDS
BELGIUM
SWITZ.
NORWAY
SWEDEN
FINLAND
DENMARK
GERMANY
82,500,000
AUSTRIA
SLOVENIA
CZECH REP.
POLAND
HUNGARY
SLOVAKIA
CROATIA
BOSNIA & HERZEGOVINA
ALBANIA
ITALY
GREECE
YUGOSLAVIA
F.Y.R. MACEDONIA
BULGARIA
ROMANIA
MOLDOVA
UKRAINE
BELARUS
ESTONIA
LATVIA
LITHUANIA
RUSSIA
144,100,000
GEORGIA
ARMENIA
AZERBAIJAN
KAZAKHSTAN
KYRGYZSTAN
TAJIKISTAN
UZBEKISTAN
TURKMENISTAN
AFGHANISTAN
TURKEY
IRAN
PAKISTAN
144,900,000
NEPAL
INDIA
1,048,300,000
BANGLADESH
135,700,000
MYANMAR (BURMA)
SRI LANKA
CHINA
1,281,000,000
MONGOLIA
NORTH KOREA
SOUTH KOREA
JAPAN
127,100,000
TAIWAN
PHILIPPINES
VIETNAM
LAOS
THAILAND
CAMBODIA
MALAYSIA
SINGAPORE
INDONESIA
211,700,000

MOROCCO
ALGERIA
TUNISIA
LIBYA
EGYPT
MAURITANIA
MALI
NIGER
CHAD
SUDAN
SENEGAL
GAMBIA
GUINEA-BISSAU
GUINEA
SIERRA LEONE
LIBERIA
CÔTE D'IVOIRE
BURKINA FASO
GHANA
TOGO
BENIN
NIGERIA
132,800,000
CAMEROON
GABON
CONGO
CENTRAL AFRICAN REPUBLIC
DEM. REP. OF THE CONGO
ETHIOPIA
ERITREA
SOMALIA
UGANDA
RWANDA
BURUNDI
KENYA
TANZANIA
ZAMBIA
MALAWI
MOZAMBIQUE
ANGOLA
ZIMBABWE
NAMIBIA
BOTSWANA
SOUTH AFRICA
LESOTHO
SWAZILAND
MADAGASCAR
MAURITIUS

LEBANON
GAZA & WEST BANK
ISRAEL
SYRIA
IRAQ
JORDAN
KUWAIT
SAUDI ARABIA
YEMEN
UNITED ARAB EMIRATES
OMAN

AUSTRALIA
PAPUA NEW GUINEA
NEW ZEALAND

population reached 1 billion. By 1945 the population had risen to 2.5 billion; by 2011 it had more than doubled to 7 billion. Some experts worried about a "population bomb" overwhelming the world's water, food sources, forests, and minerals, which the earth's resources could not support. But fertility rates began dropping, especially in industrialized nations, thanks to widespread artificial birth control, such as contraceptive pills, better health care, and more women entering the paid work force. However, largely because of rapid African population growth, demographers now envision a world population of some 9 billion by 2050 and perhaps 11 billion by 2100, which will still impose a heavy burden on food supplies and services while intensifying social, economic, and environmental problems. Overpopulation and competition for limited resources have sparked violence in crowded countries such as Ethiopia, Rwanda, and El Salvador. Some studies have predicted a worldwide 50 percent rise in demand for food, 30 percent for water, and 50 percent for energy by 2030.

Most population growth in the past half century has occurred in Asia, Africa, and Latin America. China and India have the largest populations, over a billion people each. While Asia continues, as it has for millennia, to house at least 60 percent of humanity, Europe's share of population fell from a quarter in 1900 to an eighth. Because of falling birthrates, various European nations, Russia, China, and Japan have declining and aging populations, burdening working-age people to support elderly populations. Italy and Spain, which once had high birthrates, now claim the world's lowest fertility rates. North American birthrates have also dropped, but immigration offsets the decline. Between 1960 and 2009 the fertility rate in Mexico and Brazil tumbled by two-thirds. If African growth slows, as Asian and Latin American growth has, some experts forecast world population eventually falling.

Western nations, Japan, and recently China, enjoying high rates of resource consumption, including fossil fuels, harm the environment more than countries with large populations but low consumption rates. Owing to heavy energy use and metals-dependent innovations—air conditioners, central heating systems, gasoline-powered vehicles, refrigerators—the average American or Canadian consumes some twenty times, and the average Australian, German, or Japanese ten to fifteen times, more resources than the average Pakistani or Peruvian.

Rapid population growth has undermined economic development in overcrowded nations struggling with scarce food, health care, housing, and education. In countries like the Philippines, Pakistan, and Uganda, the school-age population has expanded faster than the resources to build new schools and hire teachers. Many countries cannot afford compulsory education. The increased food production caused by the Green Revolution averted mass famine, but by the 1990s harvests reached a plateau, producing only small food increases or sometimes even decreases. Fish catches have declined steeply, partly because of overfishing by high-technology Western and Japanese fleets. Providing new cropland requires massive forest clearing.

Recent advances in health and welfare could be reversed unless nations slow population growth and reduce poverty. Predominantly Islamic and Roman Catholic nations often discourage birth control and outlaw abortion as contrary to religious beliefs. Some other nations have pursued vigorous population control programs, increasing their economic potential. Thailand cut its birthrate by a fifth between 1980 and 2000. Using harsher means, overcrowded China dramatically reduced fertility by mandating only one child per family; couples flouting the laws faced stiff fines or, sometimes, forced abortions. The most successful campaigns targeted women, giving them better education, health care, and dignity independent of their roles as mothers. Many parents have traditionally viewed more children as insurance for their old age; in Mali the average woman had seven children, four surviving to adulthood. Economic development and affluence, including better health care to lower infant mortality, have often changed these attitudes.

Rural folk have often had to abandon their livelihoods and move to crowded cities such as Jakarta, Calcutta, Cairo, and Mexico City, where many live in shantytowns or on sidewalks. Cities held 10 percent of the world population in 1900 and 50 percent in 2000. Cairo grew from 900,000 in 1897 to 2.8 million in 1947 and 20 million in 2013. In 1950 most of the world's ten largest metropolitan areas were Western cities, headed by New York; fifty years later Asian and Latin American cities dominated the list. Tokyo, with 37 million people, was followed by Jakarta, Seoul, Delhi, and Shanghai. Colossal traffic jams make driving in Bangkok, Tokyo, Mexico City, and Lagos a nightmare. Struggling to provide needed services, cities dump raw sewage into bays and rivers. Today cities consume 75 percent of the world's resources and produce 75 percent of its trash. City life reshapes traditional ways. In a Peruvian pop song, a boy who migrated to Lima complains that his girlfriend has abandoned rural values: "You came as a country girl. Now you are in Lima you comb your hair in a city way. You even say, 'I'm going to dance the twist" [a popular dance from the United States]."[12]

Industrialization, population growth, and urbanization have posed unprecedented environmental challenges, increased competition for limited resources such as oil, timber, and tin, and contributed to a warmer, drier global climate. Over the twentieth century industrial output increased twentyfold and energy use fourteenfold. Industrialized nations and industrializing nations, such as China, South Korea, and Malaysia, paid the cost in noxious air, toxic waste, stripped forests, water pollution, and hotter climates. Some environmental disasters affected large populations. In 1957 an explosion in a Russian nuclear waste dump killed some 10,000 people, contaminated 150 square miles of land, and forced the evacuation of 270,000 people. A Japanese nuclear plant destroyed by an earthquake and tsunami in 2011 ruined a large area with radiation. A massive die-off among frogs and some ocean species, perhaps due to pollution and ecological instability, suggested that polluted environments are increasingly dangerous to life. Sea turtle

---

[12]Quoted in Eric Hobsbawm, *The Age of Extremes: A History of the World, 1914–1991* (New York: Pantheon, 1994), 365.

Wangari Maathai, Kenyan Environmental Activist

Wangari Maathai (**wahn-GAHR-ee muh-THIGH**), who won the 2004 Nobel Peace Prize for her environmental activism, was born in 1940 and grew up in Nyeri, a small village in Kenya, East Africa. As a young girl, fetching water from a small stream, she grew fascinated by creatures living in the stream and loved the lush trees and shrubs around her village. But over the years the stream dried up, silt choked nearby rivers, and once green land grew barren. She lamented the assault on nature. Girls in rural Kenya in the 1940s and 1950s commonly spent their youth preparing for marriage and children. But a brother convinced Wangari's parents to send the inquisitive girl to the primary school he attended.

After graduating from a Roman Catholic high school, Wangari won a scholarship to study in the United States, earning a B.A. in biology from a small Kansas college in 1964 and then completing an M.A. at the University of Pittsburgh in 1966. She credited her U.S. experience, including observations of anti–Vietnam War protests, with encouraging her interest in democracy and free speech. Returning home, she earned a Ph.D. at Nairobi University in 1971, the first East African woman to achieve that degree, and then joined the faculty to teach biological sciences. She became a dean and joined a local organization coordinating United Nations environmental programs.

Throughout her life Wangari faced and overcame gender barriers, including in her marriage to Mwangi Maathai; they had three children, but, their relationship souring, they divorced after he was elected to parliament in 1974. She attributed the breakup to gender prejudice: "I think my activism may have contributed to my being perceived as an [un]conventional [woman]. And that puts pressure on the man you live with, because he is then perceived as if he is not controlling you properly."

To stop the spread of desert in Kenya by planting trees, the dogged Wangari founded the Greenbelt Movement on Earth Day, 1977. Talking to women when she served on the National Council of Women, she learned they needed clean drinking water, nutritious food, and energy. Trees could provide for all these needs: stop soil erosion, help water conservation, bear fruit, provide fuel and building materials, offer shade, and also enhance the beauty of the landscape. Over ten thousand Kenyans, largely women, became involved, planting and nurturing more than 30 million trees and earning

WANGARI MAATHAI Wangari Maathai, winner of the 2004 Nobel Prize for peace, plants a tree outside the United Nations headquarters in New York in 2005. Earlier that day she challenged world leaders to dirty their hands by planting trees and working to stop the destruction of forests worldwide.

AP Images/Evan Schneider/The United Nations

a small income for each tree planted. The movement showed Kenyans that the health of their forests and rivers mattered for both their immediate and future well-being.

Realizing that logging contracts enriched leaders of corrupt governments, including Kenya's repressive regime, Wangari perceived the link between environmental health and good governance. As a result, the Greenbelt Movement launched civic education programs, linking human rights, ecology, and individual activism and helping thousands of women gain more control of their lives. Women took on local leadership roles, running tree nurseries and planning community-based projects. Thanks to the movement, she said, "women have become aware that planting trees or fighting to save forests from being chopped down is part of a larger mission to create a society that respects democracy, the rule of law, human rights, and the rights of women."

Wangari and her campaign to empower and educate rural women had many critics in Kenya, including the country's dictatorial president. She was threatened by violence, harassed, sometimes severely beaten, arrested over a dozen times, and had her public appearances broken up by police. When she led protests against the building of a 62-story tower that would destroy much of Nairobi's main public park in the mid-1970s, the police killed seven of her associates. Still, she continued to protest illegal forest clearing and the Kenya government's holding of political prisoners. Wangari's efforts inspired similar Greenbelt movements in the United States, Haiti, and over thirty other African countries; she became an international environmental spokesperson. In 2002, during the first fair elections in years, Wangari ran for the Kenyan parliament as a Green Party member, gaining election by a huge majority. From 2003-2005 she served as an Assistant Minister for Environment, Natural Resources, and Wildlife. In awarding her the Noble Peace Prize, the Nobel committee praised Wangari for taking a comprehensive "approach to sustainable development that embraces democracy, human relations, and women's rights," saying that she "thinks globally and acts locally." She celebrated winning the Noble Prize by planting a tree on the slopes of Mount Kenya, near her childhood home, and recommitting herself to the struggle for a better world. Wangari died of ovarian cancer in 2011.

THINKING ABOUT THE PROFILE

1. How did Wangari's activities help Kenyan women?
2. How did Wangari's efforts to protect the environment also foster change in the political and social realms?

Note: Quotations from Friends of the Greenbelt Movement North America website (http://gbmna.org/a .php?id).

populations decreased drastically in regions as far apart as Southeast Asia, the Persian Gulf, and Central America.

Deforestation reflects environmental destruction. In the twentieth century half of the world's rain forests were cut down; commercial loggers obtained wood for housing, farmers converted forests into farms, and poor people collected firewood. This destruction continues at a furious pace today. Between 1975 and 2000 a quarter of the Central American rain forest was turned into grasslands, often to raise beef cattle for North American fast-food restaurants. Three nations hold most of the world's remaining tropical rain forests: Brazil, Congo, and Indonesia. Clearing tropical land exposes thin topsoils to leaching of the nutrients by rains; after a few years the cleared land becomes unusable desert. Deforestation has enormous long-term consequences, from decreasing rainfall to losing valuable pharmaceuticals. Millions of species of plants and animals have disappeared in recent decades; more than eleven thousand species of plants and animals remain threatened with extinction. A quarter to half of all current species could disappear by 2100. Destroying forests, which absorb carbon dioxide, also contributed, along with carbon dioxide–producing fossil fuels and industrial pollution, to acceleration of global warming. Global temperatures today are the highest in four thousand years. Scientists worry that as glaciers and polar ice melt, ocean levels will rise substantially, flooding lowlands, river deltas, coastal cities, and small islands. Rising temperatures will also ruin good farmland as drought increases and make tropical regions unlivable.

Desertification, the transformation of once-productive land into useless desert, increased with government, market, and population pressure to expand agriculture onto marginal land. During the past half century, some 20,000 square miles of African land became desert every year. To combat the resulting farming failures, Africans used more pesticides, fertilizers, and irrigation, often with negative consequences. Drier climates diminish water supplies. One of Africa's largest lakes, Lake Chad, has lost 90 percent of its water since 1975. Deforestation and desertification also cause soil erosion; with less vegetation, rains wash away fertile topsoil and cause severe flooding. A regular reality in Africa, drought has forced millions to become refugees in other lands. With less rain, the Niger River in West Africa, where great trading cities once flourished, supports less farming than five centuries ago. In Nepal, farmers have stripped once-lush Himalayan mountainsides for wood. The rain then washes unimpeded down the slopes into rivers, causing, along with melting Himalayan glaciers, more destructive floods downstream in India and Bangladesh.

Movements to counter environmental decay have emerged. Some, such as the Sierra Club in the United States and the Malaysian Nature Society, appeal chiefly to middle-class people. Others, such as the Chipko tree protection movement in India and the Greenbelt movement in Kenya, bring middle-class urbanites and rural peasants together. In 2004 the Greenbelt leader and global environmental activist, Wangari Maathai, won the Noble Peace Prize (see Profile: Wangari Maathai, Kenyan Environmental Activist). The United Nations environmental program issues regular reports warning that environmental destruction, combined with poverty and population growth, threatens the long-term health of the planet and its people. Their most recent study by an international panel of scientists, released in 2013, concludes, "It is extremely likely that human influence on climate caused more than half of the observed increase in global average surface temperature from 1951 to 2010…. this has warmed the ocean, melted snow and ice, raised global mean sea level and changed some climate extremes."[13]

Desertification The transformation by which productive land is transformed into mostly useless desert.

MAKE SURE YOU UNDERSTAND THESE KEY POINTS BEFORE MOVING ON

- Globalization has boosted world economies and has reaped great rewards for countries such as the United States and China, but it has not always benefited the lives of poor people and has also led to continued foreign domination of some groups and nations by others.

- Industrialization has spread throughout Asia and Latin America, the Third Industrial Revolution has created powerful new technologies, the Green Revolution has allowed for increased agricultural production, while the service and information industries have grown rapidly.

- Women have faced great problems in the modern economy as they have been drastically underpaid for

their contributions, but grassroots programs such as the Grameen Bank have offered some increased economic opportunity.

- Over the past fifty years, the world population has exploded, especially in Asia, Africa, and Latin America, prompting fears that it will eventually outstrip available resources; while in more developed countries, fertility rates have dropped and populations have grown older.

[13]Quoted in Justin Gillis, "Climate Panel Cites Near Certainty on Warming," *New York Times*, August 20, 2013, p. A1.

New Global Networks and Their Consequences

How did growing networks linking societies influence social, political, and economic life?

Some scholars perceive a "spaceship earth" or global village, an interconnected world community in which all people, regardless of nationality, share a common fate. "Global village" boundaries are fluid, the inhabitants highly mobile. Globalization has reshaped politics and cultures, fostering movement of people, diseases, cultures, and religions. Increasingly both unity and diversity characterize the world, with common influences mixing with local traditions.

The Global Spread of Migrants, Refugees, and Disease

Today, many people live in nations filled with immigrants and their descendants from around the globe. Forty percent of Australians are immigrants or the children of immigrants. Thirty million people moved to labor-short western Europe between 1945 and 1975, chiefly from North Africa, West Africa, Turkey, South Asia, and the Caribbean. Similarly, 4 million Mexicans legally entered the United States, many filling low-wage jobs. Immigrants rapidly transformed cities such as Vancouver, Los Angeles, Sydney, and Paris into internationalized hubs of world culture and commerce. The many educated people moving to Western nations constitute a "brain drain" from poor countries. Hence, Indian doctors and Philippine nurses play key roles in North American health care. Cosmopolitanism—the blending of peoples and cultures—flavors cities closely linked to the world economy, such as Hong Kong, Singapore, São Paulo **(POU-lo)**, London, Dubai, and New York. While globalization of trade and jobs dissolves economic boundaries, governments increasingly impose tighter border controls to discourage illegal immigration, not always successfully.

The great majority of the over 100 million voluntary migrants to foreign countries have moved for economic rather than political reasons. Many migrants—some from impoverished regions such as Central America and South Asia, others from more prosperous nations such as South Korea and Taiwan—have sought better economic opportunities in the industrialized West. Small Indian- and Pakistani-run sundry goods and grocery stores, known as corner shops, have become fixtures in British cities. Millions of Asians and Africans work in the Middle East. Especially mobile, Filipinos migrated for short periods to other Southeast Asian nations and the Middle East, and more permanently to North America. Some 8 million Filipinos now live abroad. A Moroccan woman whose husband worked in Europe and rarely returned home expressed her distress: "Germany, Belgium, France and Netherlands, Where are you situated? I have never seen your countries, I do not speak your language. I am afraid my love forgets me in your paradise. I ask you, give him back to me."[14]

Political turbulence, wars, genocides, government repression, and famine created over 30 million refugees by 2012.

Desperate people fled nations engulfed in political violence, such as Sudan, Guatemala, Afghanistan, Somalia, Syria, Iraq, and Cambodia, and drought-plagued states like Ethiopia and Mali. Cubans, Chinese, Laotians **(lao-OH-shuhnz)**, and Vietnamese escaped communist-run states that restricted their freedoms. Others, among them Haitians, Chileans, Iranians, and Congolese, escaped brutal rightwing dictatorships or corrupt despotisms. Millions of refugees remained for decades, even generations, in squalid refugee camps, often fed and housed by international aid organizations. Many Palestinians have lived in refugee camps in Egypt, Jordan, and Lebanon for over six decades. Citizens in refuge countries often resented the refugees. By the 1990s many nations, especially in Europe, became more cautious in granting political asylum.

Diseases traveling trade and migration routes have produced major pandemics, or massive disease outbreaks, throughout history. Although modern medicine has eliminated diseases long plaguing humanity like smallpox, leprosy, and polio, other diseases, such as cholera and malaria, still bedevil people. Cholera, a bacterial disease, still kills several thousand people a year in poor countries; malaria, spread by mosquitoes, debilitates millions of people in tropical regions. Experts worry about several viral diseases, potentially killing millions, that pass from birds, poultry, and pigs to humans. Both United Nations agencies and private organizations have worked to reduce health threats and treat victims. But the travel of migrants, tourists, business people, armies, truck drivers, sailors, and others spreads diseases.

The most deadly contemporary scourge affecting nations rich and poor, autoimmune deficiency syndrome (AIDS), caused by a virus known as HIV, is partly spread through the increased trade and travel associated with globalization. The disease spreads through sexual contact, needle sharing by drug addicts, and selling or receiving blood. By 2011 some 34 million people around the world, two-thirds in Africa, were infected with either HIV or AIDS; 1.7 million died annually, leaving millions of orphans. As much as 30 percent of the adult population of some African nations was HIV positive. The disease is less catastrophic but still troublesome in richer countries. AIDS victims are often rejected by their families and communities, dying alone and neglected by society.

Cultures and Religions Across Borders

Cultural products and religions have spread across national borders and creatively mixed with local traditions. Popular culture, produced for commercial purposes and spread by mass media such as radio, television, and

> **global village** An interconnected world community in which all people, regardless of their nationality, share a common fate.

[14]From Hazel Johnson and Henry Bernstein, eds., *Third World Lives of Struggle* (London: Heinemann Educational, 1982), 173.

films, has become part of everyday life for billions of people. Western influences have been pervasive, although often superficial. Western videos, pop music recordings, jeans, and shopping malls attract many Asian, African, and Latin American youth, but their influence on rural areas is often more limited. No common world culture has emerged. India has developed the world's largest film industry, producing some one thousand films a year by 2002, three times more than the next largest producers, the United States and Japan. Cheap, often pirated, audio cassettes in the 1970s, videocassettes in the 1980s, and DVDs in the 1990s enabled even many more people to enjoy music and films while helping political or religious groups to spread their messages. Modern media have reshaped people's lives, especially in cities. One observer in the 1990s noted the global popularity of television:

> *Take a walk down any street, in any city or village, as the twilight fades and the darkness comes. Whether you are in London or Tokyo, Cairo or New York, Buenos Aires or Singapore, a small blue light will flicker at you from the unshuttered windows. These lights are the tiny knots in the seamless web of modern media.*[15]

Today file sharing and social media make these products even easier to obtain.

Popular musics reflect cultural mixing and the spread of mass media. Some popular styles, such as American jazz and Brazilian samba, emerged well before World War II, but most appeared after 1945. Rock, jazz, and rap, all African American forms, found audiences all over the world. Vaclav Havel (**VAH-slav HAH-vel**), leader of the movement that overthrew Czech communism, credited U.S. rock musician Frank Zappa's songs with inspiring his activism. Havel even wrote songs for a Czech rock group. Rebellious youth in Manila, Cape Town, Paris, Casablanca, and São Paulo use rap to express their feelings. The sudden death in 2009 of American pop musician Michael Jackson, known equally for his spectacular musical talents and bizarre lifestyle, illustrated U.S. popular culture's global influence. His passing and legacy dominated mass media in many nations for weeks, a star-studded memorial tribute was televised around the world, and millions of fans bought his recordings and memorabilia. Through their global reputations, pop stars also mount concerts to address issues like racism, political prisoners, famine, and African poverty. Bono, Irish rock band U2's lead singer, campaigns among world leaders for causes such as debt relief for poor nations.

Many musicians have mixed indigenous and imported influences, often from outside the West. Hence, Congolese popular music, which borrowed Latin American dance rhythms, gained audiences throughout Africa and Europe. Indian film music and Arab folk music influenced Southeast Asian and East African pop music. Even pop music that does not cross many borders can reflect creative blending. *Dangdut*, an Indonesian popular music, originated as a fusion of Western rock, Indian film music, and local folk music. The major dangdut star,

Rhoma Irama (**ROW-muh ih-RAH-muh**), sometimes faced arrest for political protests in songs addressing poverty, human rights abuses, struggles of the underdog, Islamic moral teachings, and betrayal of nationalist promises.

Although secular thought became more popular than ever before in history, over three-quarters of the world's people identify with one or another universal religion with roots deep in the past, including over 2.2 billion Christians, 1.6 billion Muslims, 1 billion Hindus, 500 million Buddhists, and 14 million Jews. Well over 1.5 billion practice a local faith, such as animism or Daoism, or profess no religion (see Map 26.3). Religion sometimes underlies national identity, as in Roman Catholic Poland and Ireland or Muslim Bangladesh and Pakistan. Religious leaders have debated how much, if at all, their faiths need to change to better engage the contemporary world. Pope John XXIII (pope 1958–1963) liberalized Catholic church practices, such as by having the mass in vernacular languages rather than Latin, and encouraged interfaith dialogue. Meanwhile, a controversial movement among Latin American Catholic clergy and laypeople, liberation theology, cooperated with socialist and communist groups to address poverty. Muslim liberals and militants have confronted each other over issues like the role of women, relations with non-Muslims, and basing their legal systems on Islamic law. In sub-Saharan Africa and Southeast Asia, some Muslims have become more devout, and more men have studied in the Middle East, often returning with more militant views.

The easy spread of ideas in the globalized world has worked to the advantage of portable creeds not dependent on one culture or setting. In Africa, polytheism and animism have faded while Christianity and Islam, promoted by missionary activity, have gained wider followings. Protestants have evangelized and gained ground in predominantly Catholic Latin America. Pentacostalism, an American-born Christian tradition promoting charismatic worship and faith healing, has developed large international followings. Protestants and Catholics compete with each other, and often with Muslims, in Africa, Southeast Asia, and East Asia. Christianity increasingly has become a non-Western faith, with far more believers in Africa, Asia, and Latin America than in Europe and North America. Christian and Muslim missionaries appeal to the downtrodden, promising both spiritual health and material wealth, often recasting their messages to recognize local cultural traditions.

Yet, organized religion has declined in East Asia and much of the West. Communist regimes discouraged religious observance; many Japanese found neither their traditional faiths nor imported religions relevant to their lives; and church attendance and membership in Europe, Canada, and Australia fell dramatically. Religious dogmas competed with changing social attitudes. Predominantly Catholic European nations legalized abortion and moved toward equal rights for homosexuals, challenging church policies. By 2013 nine European and six other nations approved same-sex marriage, among them Spain, Portugal, Belgium, Canada, South Africa, Brazil, and Uruguay.

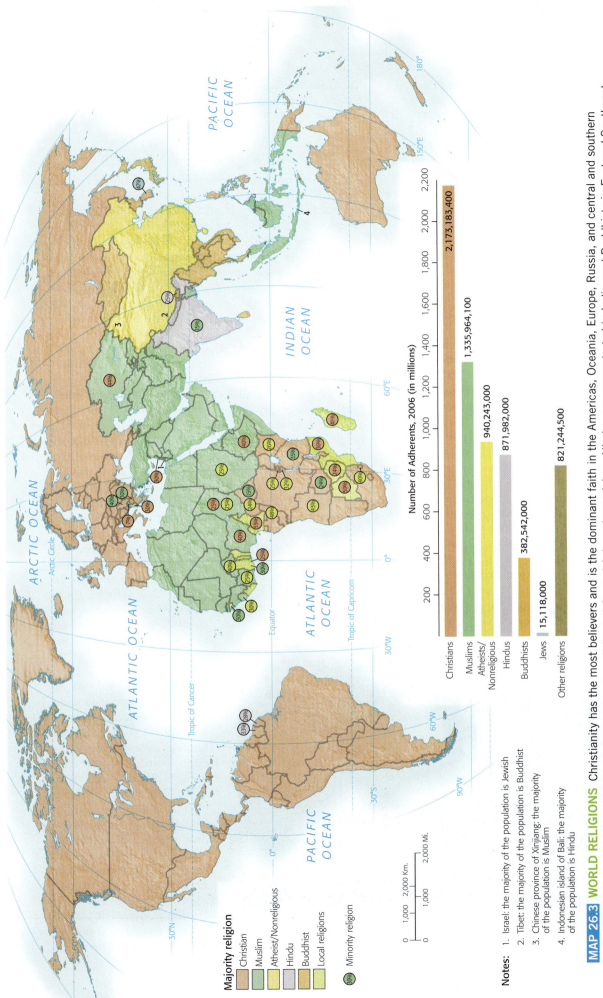

Majority religion

- Christian
- Muslim
- Atheist/Nonreligious
- Hindu
- Buddhist
- Local religions

(50%) Minority religion

Number of Adherents, 2006 (in millions)

Christians	2,173,183,400
Muslims	1,335,964,100
Atheists/Nonreligious	940,243,000
Hindus	871,982,000
Buddhists	382,542,000
Jews	15,118,000
Other religions	821,244,500

0   1,000   2,000 Mi.
0   1,000   2,000 Km.

Notes:
1. Israel: the majority of the population is Jewish
2. Tibet: the majority of the population is Buddhist
3. Chinese province of Xinjiang: the majority of the population is Muslim
4. Indonesian island of Bali: the majority of the population is Hindu

MAP 26.3 WORLD RELIGIONS Christianity has the most believers and is the dominant faith in the Americas, Oceania, Europe, Russia, and central and southern Africa. Most people in the northern half of Africa, western Asia, and Central Asia embrace Islam. Hindus are concentrated in India, and Buddhists in East and Southeast Asia. ©2015 Cengage Learning

Yet, homosexuality remains a crime in many countries and a capital offense in six African and Middle Eastern nations.

Tensions remain between different faiths. Sparked by political differences, some Christians and Muslims have attacked each other in Indonesia, the Philippines, Egypt, Lebanon, Yugoslavia, and Nigeria. Conflicts between Muslims and Hindus in India, Catholics and Protestants in Northern Ireland, and Sunni and Shi'ite Muslims in Pakistan and western Asia have generated sporadic violence. Some Sunni regimes have discriminated against or persecuted Shi'ites. Indeed, several countries, including China, Burma, Saudi Arabia, and North Korea, repress various religious groups. Religious militancy has also grown. Some Muslim militants have turned the notion of *jihad*, or struggle within believers to strengthen their faith, into holy war against unbelievers, secular Muslims, and countries or groups they consider anti-Muslim; they hope to turn secular states into Islamic ones. Often known as Islamists or jihadis, militants appeal especially to the embittered young and poor. Jihadis unsettle politics in and terrorize Muslim countries like Pakistan, Afghanistan, Nigeria, and Mali. Many Muslims oppose market capitalism and despise the West's revealing clothing styles, open romantic behavior, independent women, rebellious youth, and raunchy television programs and movies. At the same time, some Christians, especially in the United States, Latin America, and Africa, have turned to literal, fundamentalist interpretations of the Bible and promote proselytizing. Some Nigerian Protestant churches send missionaries to the United States and Europe, while South Korean Protestants evangelize in China. Conservative churches have often opposed secular culture, rejected scientific findings incompatible with biblical accounts, and condemned political and social movements promoting socialism, feminism, legalized abortion, and homosexual rights. Christian and Islamic militancy has sparked similar movements in Buddhism, Hinduism, and Judaism, pitting zealous believers against those with moderate, tolerant views.

Global Communications and Movements

A worldwide communications network has facilitated globalization. Radio in the early 1900s was followed by tape recording, television, and then transistors, fostering miniaturization of electronics. In 1953 portable transistor radios became available and soon reached even remote villages without electricity, opening them to world news and culture. By the 1960s in central Borneo, a densely forested island divided between Indonesia and Malaysia, isolated villagers listened to radio broadcasts from the United States, Britain, and Australia, some learning the songs of Western pop musicians like the British rock group The Beatles.

Technological breakthroughs have generated more rapid and widespread communications, creating a networked world. The first general-purpose computers were built in 1948; in 1958 the first silicon microchips made possible the first personal computers. By 2008 the world had nearly 800 million personal computers. By 2013 some 2.7 billion Internet users (40 percent of humanity), and countless web pages and blogs, were all part of a vast information superhighway. Every minute millions of e-mails, texts, and tweets are dispatched instantly via computer, smartphone, or tablets, often to foreign countries. An interested reader in Hong Kong, Ghana, or Finland can access online versions of newspapers, such as the *New York Times*, *Al Ahram* in Cairo, or the *Deccan Herald* in India. The rise of 24-hour cable news networks reaching worldwide audiences, such as U.S.-based CNN (Cable News Network) and the Arab-language Al Jazeera, based in the Persian Gulf state of Qatar, widened access to diverse views. Technologically literate people send music, video, and photos around the world via electronic media.

The rapid evolution of media and information technology has many consequences. Through fax communications, orbiting communications satellites, portable phones, electronic mail, and the World Wide Web, information can be transmitted outside governments' reach, diminishing their power to shape thinking. Hence, repressive states seeking to limit information flow, such as Iran, Cuba, Burma, and China, have banned satellite dish receivers and jammed access to controversial and dissident websites. These efforts

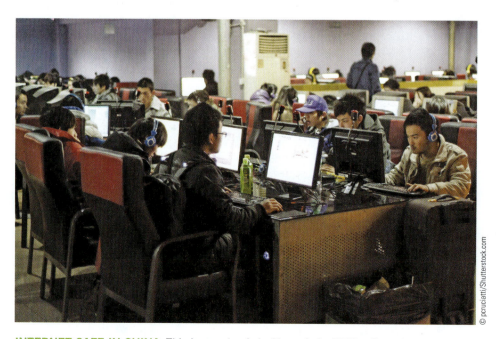

© pcruciatti/Shutterstock.com

INTERNET CAFE IN CHINA This jammed cafe in Chengdu in 2010 reflected the huge increase in users, who then numbered over 450 million in China.

have been only partly successful. Protesters in nations like China, Egypt, and Iran use cellphones, Twitter, and YouTube to coordinate their activities, spread their message, and circumvent government control of mass media. The U.S.-based social media site Facebook claims 1.15 billion members, 70 percent of them outside the United States. Some technologies, especially the World Wide Web, have enhanced the value of education and of English, now a world language like Latin two thousand years ago and Arabic one thousand years ago. Perhaps a quarter of the world's people know some English. Asian countries with many educated people fluent in English, such as India and Singapore, have an advantage in attracting high-technology industries. But in the poorest nations, only a lucky few have access to satellite dishes, fax machines, and networked computers. Furthermore, many nations resent the strong U.S. influence over the Internet.

Social and political movements originating in different countries transcend borders, linking to similar movements elsewhere. Diverse transnational organizations promote issues such as political prisoners, women's rights, and antiracism. Amnesty International, based in Britain, publicizes the plight of people imprisoned solely for their political views and activities, organizing letter-writing and pressure campaigns to seek their release. The World Social Forum, formed in 2001 and meeting annually in Brazil, brings together nongovernment organizations and activists who believe that globalization undermines workers' rights and environmental protection.

Movements or upheavals in one nation or region sometimes spread widely. During the 1960s, students, workers, and political radicals in many nations organized protests against the U.S. war in Vietnam, racism, unresponsive governments, capitalism, and other concerns. In 1968 demonstrations, marches, and strikes affected over a dozen countries, from the United States and Mexico to France, Czechoslovakia, and Japan. The same writers, music, and ideas often influenced young protesters. Some protesters revered leftist icons like Ho Chi Minh and Cuban revolutionary Che Guevara; others looked to noncommunists or even anticommunists, such as the dissidents who opposed Poland's communist regime. After the 1968 activism, environmental, peace, workers' rights, homosexual rights, and feminist movements grew, especially in industrialized nations.

Women have actively sought to expand their rights, placing women's issues on the international agenda. The United Nations periodically sponsors global conferences on women's issues such as gender equality. However, women activists, divided by culture and nationality, sometimes disagree on goals and strategies. In the United Nations' fourth World Conference on Women, held in China in 1995, the forty thousand delegates differed sharply on priorities. While delegates from rich nations favored expanding women's employment options, social freedom, and control over their bodies, Asian, African, and Latin American delegates emphasized their families' health and economic security.

One Indian delegate described U.S. delegates' goals as irrelevant to Indian women: "They ask for abortion rights. We ask for safe drinking water and basic health care."[16] Abortion has become legal in most Western and many Asian nations but remains controversial.

Despite disagreements, women have worked across borders on many issues. For example, women activists and their male supporters have fought the tradition, common in some Muslim societies, of jailing or killing women for adultery while exonerating the man responsible. In 2005 Mukhtaran Bibi (**MOOK-tahr-an BIH-bee**), an illiterate woman from an impoverished Pakistani village without electricity, gained worldwide sympathy for her resistance to male brutality. The tribal council ruled she be gang-raped to punish her family for a village dispute. Instead of following custom by ending the "disgrace" through suicide, she bravely pursued the rapists in court. They were convicted, and she used the money awarded her to start two village schools, one for boys and one for girls. When a higher court overturned the men's convictions, her courageous refusal to accept the verdict caused an international outcry. Men and women around the world, alerted by news accounts and Internet appeals, donated money and made her a symbol of the need for women's rights. Mukhtaran Bibi inspired millions everywhere with her courage and faith in education and justice.

Global Terrorism

Terrorism, which involves small-scale but violent attacks, often on civilian targets, that are aimed at undermining governments or demoralizing populations, has expanded to global dimensions, reshaping world politics. After 1945 Palestinians under Israeli control, Basque nationalists in Spain, and Irish nationalists in Britain, among others, engaged in terrorism for their causes. Some states sponsored terrorism against unfriendly governments or political movements. South Africa's white minority government financed insurgencies against Marxist governments in Angola and Mozambique during which thousands of civilians died. The United States sponsored terrorism against leftist-ruled Nicaragua in the 1980s, helping form a military force, the *Contras*, that often attacked civilian targets such as rural schools, day-care centers, and clinics. Some terrorist networks operate on a global level, with branches in many countries. The most active, formed by militant Islamists, has capitalized on widespread Muslim anger at Israel, their own governments, and U.S. foreign policies, attacking politicians, police, Western residents and tourists, and Israeli and U.S. targets.

Terrorism has increasingly threatened Middle Eastern countries. For example, the *Hezbollah* movement in Lebanon, formed by Shi'ite Arabs opposed to the U.S.-backed Lebanese government and support for Israel, used suicide bombers driving

Terrorism Small-scale but violent attacks aimed at undermining a government or demoralizing a population.

[16]Quoted in David Reynolds, *One World Divisible: A Global History Since 1945* (New York: W. W. Norton, 2000), 491.

explosive-filled trucks to destroy the U.S. Embassy and a Marine Corps base in Beirut in 1983, killing several hundred Americans. Later, to oppose Israeli occupation of Arab lands and demoralize Israelis, Palestinian militants detonated explosives in Israeli buses and businesses. Outraged, Israelis responded by killing or arresting Palestinians and expelling families of suspected militants from their homes. Divided by politics, Israelis and Palestinians shared the bitter experience of grieving for those lost in the chronic violence, among them innocent women and children.

When the Soviets intervened militarily in 1979 to support a pro-Soviet government in Afghanistan, Middle Eastern and Pakistani militants helped the Muslim Afghan resistance. In 1988 the most extreme foreign fighters came together in a jihadi organization, *Al Qaeda* ("The Base"), formed by the Saudi Osama bin Laden (1957–2011). From an extremely wealthy family and trained as an engineer, bin Laden used his wealth to support Afghan rebels, who were also funded and armed by the United States as part of its Cold War rivalry with the USSR. After the Soviets abandoned Afghanistan in 1989, bin Laden established Al Qaeda cells elsewhere, including Saudi Arabia, Egypt, and Iraq, whose government he viewed as corrupt or as suppressing Islamic militants. To recruit, support, and communicate with members, Al Qaeda took advantage of the information superhighway, using websites, e-mail, satellite phones, and videotapes of bin Laden's messages. Bin Laden, ruthlessly willing to kill innocent people, plotted terrorism against his former Afghan resistance ally, the United States, for maintaining military bases in Saudi Arabia, supporting repressive Arab governments, and being a close ally with Israel. Attacks on U.S. targets, including embassies, caused hundreds of casualties.

On September 11, 2001, Al Qaeda members hijacked U.S. commercial airliners and crashed them into New York's World Trade Center and the Pentagon near Washington, D.C., killing over three thousand people, mostly civilians. The attacks, shocking Americans and the world, prompted U.S. president George W. Bush to declare a war on terrorism. U.S. forces attacked Al Qaeda bases in Afghanistan and occupied the country, whose Islamist government shielded bin Laden; but Americans still faced resistance from Islamic militants. Americans finally killed bin Laden in his Pakistan hiding place in 2011.

In 2003 the United States, claiming that Saddam Hussein's Iraq was closely linked to Al Qaeda and possessed weapons of mass destruction, invaded Iraq, removed Saddam's brutal government, and imposed a U.S. military occupation supported chiefly by Britain. However, U.S. troops found no evidence of Al Qaeda ties or weapons of mass destruction. The occupation sparked an insurgency, unleashing sectarian divisions that hindered U.S. efforts to stabilize and rebuild Iraq. Islamists flocked to Iraq to attack Americans and destabilize the country. The U.S. invasion and occupation, and the resistance to it, killed over 100,000 Iraqis, resulted in 4,300 U.S. deaths and tens of thousands of wounded, and kept a large U.S. military force tied down in Iraq.

Eventually violence diminished and the last U.S. troops withdrew in 2011. But the war alienated many U.S. allies and, like the earlier U.S. conflict in Vietnam, was unpopular around the world. Meanwhile, Al Qaeda spawned loosely affiliated terrorist groups that launched terrorist attacks on several continents, from Spain and Britain to Indonesia, Kenya, Yemen, and Morocco. In 1993 a German historian had perceptively predicted the challenges ahead in the post–Cold War world: "We are at the beginning of a new era, characterized by great insecurity, permanent crisis and the absence of any kind of *status quo*. We must realize that we find ourselves in one of those crises of world history."[17]

---

[17]Michael Sturmer, quoted in Hobsbawm, *Age of Extremes*, 558.

MAKE SURE YOU UNDERSTAND THESE KEY POINTS BEFORE MOVING ON

- In the new global village, millions of people have immigrated to foreign countries seeking greater economic opportunity or an escape from insufferable conditions at home, including political repression, famine, and civil war.

- Modern medicine has eliminated many diseases, but cholera and malaria are still serious problems, and AIDS has seriously affected India, Southeast Asia, and especially Africa.

- Western consumer culture has spread around the world, while musical forms from different cultures have mingled and musicians and performers have expressed political and often controversial views.

- Worldwide communication has been facilitated by technologies such as radio, television, and the Internet, making a vast array of information available, even in countries such as China, Iran, and Cuba, whose governments have attempted to limit its availability.

- Terrorism, which was used throughout the twentieth century by groups such as the Palestinians, the Basques, and the Irish, has become more deadly, culminating in the radical Muslim group Al Qaeda's 2001 attack on the United States.

aplia

CHAPTER SUMMARY

The later twentieth century proved turbulent. Nationalism spread in Asia and Africa, leading to decolonization. During the 1950s and 1960s most of the Western colonies gained their independence through negotiations, the threat of violence, or armed struggle, and social revolutionaries gained power in some nations. However, the West maintained a strong economic presence in many former colonies. The rivalry between the United States and the USSR also shaped the global system, generating a Cold War in which the two superpowers faced each other indirectly or through surrogates. The powerful United States had a large group of allies and sometimes intervened in Asian and Latin American nations, while the USSR occupied eastern Europe. The collapse of the Communist bloc and then the USSR allowed the United States to become the world's lone superpower.

The world was also shaped by globalization, with its unprecedented flow of money, products, information, and ideas across national borders. The global economy grew rapidly but did not spread its benefits equally. As industrialization spread, most Western and some Asian and Latin American nations prospered, but many poor nations struggled to escape underdevelopment and raise living standards. A billion people remained mired in deep poverty. Meanwhile millions of people migrated, social and political movements addressed local and global problems, universal religions gained new converts, and the information superhighway and other technological innovations linked millions of people in new ways. New international terrorist networks also challenged governments and reshaped world politics.

KEY TERMS

First World (p. 642)
Second World (p. 642)
Third World (p. 642)
Fourth World (p. 642)
Cold War (p. 643)

guerrilla warfare (p. 643)
nuclear weapons (p. 644)
globalization (p. 647)
multinational corporations (p. 650)
Third Industrial Revolution (p. 650)

Green Revolution (p. 650)
desertification (p. 656)
global village (p. 657)
terrorism (p. 661)

East Asian Resurgence, Since 1945

THE CHINA STOCK EXCHANGE The East Asian nations enjoyed an economic resurgence in this era. Since the 1980s, China has boasted the world's fastest-growing economy and a booming stock exchange.

Wally McNamee/Corbis

Once China's destiny is in the hands of the people, China, like the sun rising in the east, will illuminate every corner with a brilliant flame, and build a new, powerful and prosperous [society].

—Mao Zedong, Chinese communist leader[1]

On October 1, 1949, Mao Zedong (1893–1976), the Chinese communist leader, was driven into Beijing accompanied by soldiers from the communist People's Liberation Army. Mao, a fifty-five-year-old peasant's son, had never been out of China and had spent the previous twenty-two years living in remote rural areas directing brutal warfare against Japanese invaders and the Chinese government. Ahead of Mao's car rolled a Sherman tank, originally donated by the United States to the Republic of China, headed by Jiang Jieshi **(Chiang Kai-shek)** (1887–1975), to help crush Mao's communist forces. But Chiang's army had lost, and the president had fled to the large offshore island of Taiwan. Mao climbed to the top of the Gate of Heavenly Peace, the entrance to the Qing emperors' Forbidden City overlooking spacious Tiananmen Square. Chinese jammed the square to hear their new ruler announce a new communist state, the People's Republic of China (PRC). Referring to a century of corrupt governments, humiliation, and domination by Western nations and Japan, Mao proclaimed: "The Chinese people have stood up. Nobody will insult us again."[2]

The People's Republic marked a watershed in Chinese and world history, ending China's severe political instability and an inability to defend against foreign imperialism. Given China's size and a population, any major transition there had global significance. By the early twenty-first century Mao was long gone and many of his policies discarded, but, with a booming economy, China had reclaimed some of the political and economic status it had lost two centuries earlier.

Other East Asians also enjoyed a resurgence. By the 1980s observers referred to the Pacific Rim, the economically dynamic Asian countries bordering the Pacific Ocean: China, Japan, South Korea, Taiwan, and several Southeast Asian nations. The center of gravity of world economic life began moving back toward a resurgent Asia. China, Japan, and their neighbors have remained major players in the global system.

Pacific Rim The economically dynamic Asian countries on the edge of the Pacific Basin: China, Japan, South Korea, Taiwan, and several Southeast Asian nations.

[1]Quoted in Jerome Chen, *Mao and the Chinese Revolution* (New York: Oxford University Press, 1967), 6.
[2]Quoted in Ross Terrill, *Mao: A Biography* (New York: Harper, 1980), 198.

Mao's Revolutionary China

T
S *How did Maoism transform Chinese society?*

The Chinese Revolution that brought the communists to power was one of modern history's three greatest upheavals. The French Revolution (1789), extolling the common peoples' rights, destroyed lingering feudalism throughout western Europe; the Russian Revolution (1917) charted a noncapitalist path to industrialization. Both events swept away old social classes and ruling elites. China's revolution remade a major world society while restoring its international status. Communist government made China the world's most experimental nation, introducing innovative policies to renovate Chinese life and overcome underdevelopment. China's new model of economic development differed from both Western-dominated capitalism and highly centralized Soviet communism. But conflict and

repression littered its path. Furthermore, like all societies, China remained partly ancient empire, partly modern nation, its leaders often behaving much like the old emperors in autocratically exercising power.

The Communist Triumph and the New China

Japan's defeat in 1945 sparked a fierce civil war between Mao's communists and Chiang Kai-shek's nationalist government to control China. Both Mao and Chiang were patriotic, autocratic, and power hungry. Chiang's 3.7-million-man army vastly outnumbered the 900,000 communist troops. The United States lavished military aid on Chiang, providing planes and trucks

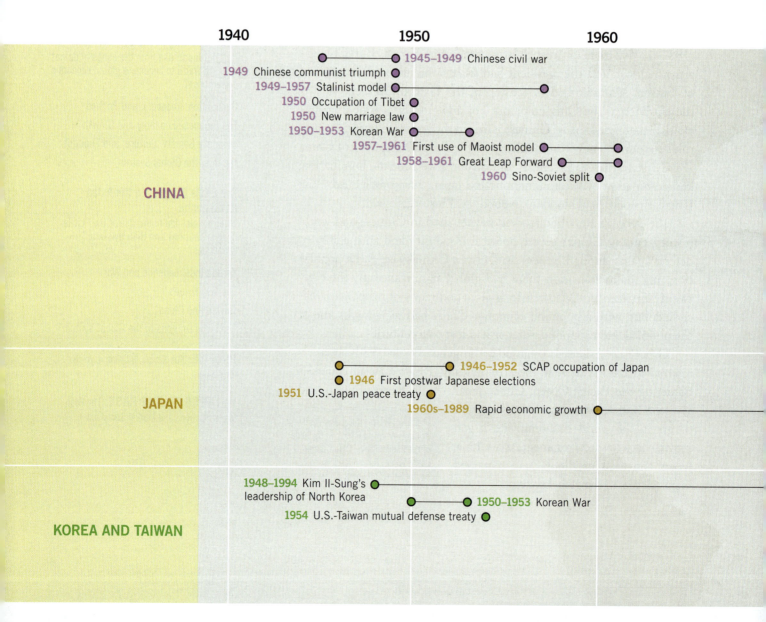

1940   **1950**   **1960**

CHINA

1945–1949 Chinese civil war
1949 Chinese communist triumph
1949–1957 Stalinist model
1950 Occupation of Tibet
1950 New marriage law
1950–1953 Korean War
1957–1961 First use of Maoist model
1958–1961 Great Leap Forward
1960 Sino-Soviet split

JAPAN

1946–1952 SCAP occupation of Japan
1946 First postwar Japanese elections
1951 U.S.-Japan peace treaty
1960s–1989 Rapid economic growth

KOREA AND TAIWAN

1948–1994 Kim Il-Sung's leadership of North Korea
1950–1953 Korean War
1954 U.S.-Taiwan mutual defense treaty

to help his soldiers occupy as much territory as possible. The communists, aided by the Soviet Union (USSR), concentrated on north China and Manchuria. Besides overstretching supply lines trying to block Mao's forces, Chiang's Republic experienced corruption and a rapid decline in the value of Chinese currency, demoralizing the population. Seeking change, many Chinese viewed the communists as a more honest alternative to Chiang's Nationalist Party.

Meanwhile, in the villages that they controlled, the communists promoted a social revolution, known as the "turning over," encouraging villagers to denounce local landlords, transferring land from richer to poorer peasants, replacing government-appointed leaders with elected village councils, and protecting battered wives. Encouraged to air their grievances, "speaking pains to recall pains" in village meetings, women warned abusive men to mend their ways or face punishment or arrest. Releasing pent-up rage against violent husbands or greedy landlords spurred excesses, such as angry crowds beating them to death.

The military and political tide turned against the Republic, and in 1948 Chiang's troops in Manchuria surrendered. The United States unsuccessfully pressured Chiang to broaden his political base with democratic reforms. Some American leaders recommended sending troops to help Chiang; others concluded that his regime had lost too much popular support to win the conflict. With the communists taking major cities, Chiang fled to the island of Taiwan in 1949, along with thousands of troops and 2 million supporters. On Taiwan, with massive U.S. aid and military protection, the relocated Republic of China developed a successful capitalist strategy for economic growth. Meanwhile, mainland China's history now moved in a very different direction.

The key question confronting PRC leaders was how to achieve rapid economic development in an overpopulated, battered country. Two decades of war had ruined the economy, leaving little capital for industrialization. China had no overseas empire to exploit, and the communists rejected loans and

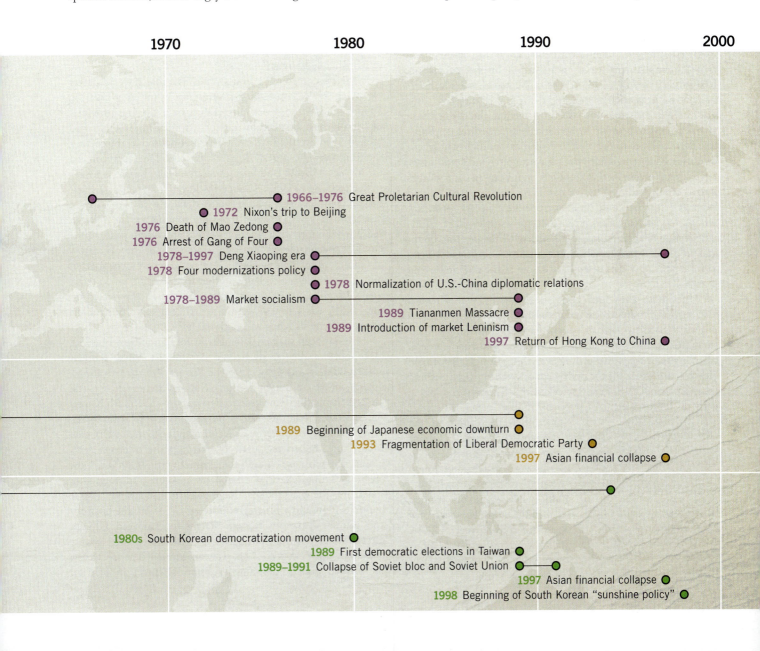

foreign investment that might reduce their independence. Furthermore, alarmed at Mao's policies and prompted by Cold War concerns, the United States launched an economic boycott to limit China's international trade, refused diplomatic recognition, and built military bases nearby. Isolated, China created its own economic and political development models.

Between 1949 and 1976 China followed two different economic development models. The first, Stalinism, based on Soviet-style central planning, heavy industry, a powerful bureaucracy, and a managerial system, dominated the early years (1949–1957). China received some Soviet aid but otherwise financed development through self-reliance, limiting contact with the global system. As in Meiji Japan and the USSR, the state took the lead, emphasizing austerity, making people work hard for low wages, abolishing private ownership of business and industry, and transferring land to poor peasants. Soon it collectivized the rural economy into cooperatives in which peasants helped each other and shared tools. As in the USSR, a privileged elite emerged in the government and ruling Communist Party, which cracked down on dissent.

In the late 1950s Mao, disenchanted with Stalinism, reintroduced Maoism, a unique synthesis of Marxism and Chinese thought emphasizing mass mobilization of the population. Maoism (1957–1961, 1966–1976) mobilized people for development projects, such as building dams and eliminating pests. For example, everyone was issued fly swatters and asked to kill as many flies as possible in hopes of reducing disease; people also planted trees to reverse the ecological instability of recent centuries. Mao reorganized the rural economy into **communes**, large agricultural units that combined many families and villages into a common administrative system for pooling resources and labor. A commune could build and operate a factory, secondary school, and hospital, tasks impractical for a single village. Communes raised agricultural productivity, eliminated landlords, and promoted social and economic equality. Locating industries in rural areas also kept peasants at home rather than migrating to cities.

The most ambitious policy, the **Great Leap Forward** (1958–1961), attempted to industrialize China rapidly and end poverty through collective efforts. Farmers and workers built small iron furnaces in their backyards, courtyards, and gardens, spending their free time turning everything from cutlery to old bicycles into steel. But the poorly conceived campaign, pushing the people too hard, nearly wrecked the economy and, along with disastrous weather, caused 30 million people to starve.

One of Mao's critics in the leadership charged: "Grains scattered on the ground, potato leaves withered; Strong young people have left to smelt iron, only children and old women reaped the crops; How can they pass the coming year?"[3] These failures diminished Mao's influence, bringing moderate policies in the early 1960s.

communes Large agricultural units introduced by Mao Zedong that combined many families and villages into a common system for pooling resources and labor.

Great Leap Forward Mao Zedong's ambitious attempt to industrialize China rapidly and end poverty through collective efforts.

Chinese Politics and the World

The Communist Party, led by Mao as chairman, dominated the political system, with party members occupying all key positions in the government and military. Using the slogan "Politics Takes Command," the communists emphasized ideology, making political values pervasive and requiring all Chinese to join political discussion groups monitored by party activists, who reported dissenters; political education was integrated into schools, work units, and even leisure activities. Placing group over individual interests, the party sought to eradicate inequalities and alter thought patterns and attitudes. To eliminate class distinctions, officials and intellectuals had to sporadically perform physical labor, such as laying bricks or spreading manure on farm fields, to understand workers' and peasants' experiences. The system required massive social control and a vast police apparatus that harassed, jailed, exiled, or killed millions of suspected dissenters. Even some communists, such as the outspoken feminist writer Ding Ling (1902–1986), were purged after losing official favor. In exchange for accepting its policies, the state promised everyone the "five guarantees" of food, clothes, fuel, education, and a decent burial. But over the years many thousands of people fled to British-ruled Hong Kong.

The PRC restored China's status as a major world power (see Map 27.1). Reasserting sovereignty in outlying areas, in 1950 Chinese troops occupied Tibet, once a Qing province. Culturally and historically distinct from China, Tibet had broken away in 1912. Most Tibetans opposed Chinese rule, sparking periodic unrest. Suppression of a Tibetan revolt led the highest Tibetan Buddhist leader, the Dalai Lama (b. 1935), to flee to India in 1959. Revered by devout Tibetans as a spiritual and political leader, he became a defiant symbol of Tibetan resistance, traveling the world to rally support for the Tibetan cause while promoting Buddhist ethics and world peace. China's leaders considered him a terrorist seeking the overthrow of Chinese rule and punished Tibetans who openly supported him. China failed to reclaim another former Qing-ruled territory, Mongolia, a communist state allied to, and protected by, the USSR; the Chinese were also irritated that Mongolians honored Genghis Khan as a national hero.

China faced major challenges in foreign affairs. In 1950, in support of the USSR-backed communist North Korean government, it was drawn into the Korean War (1950–1953), during which it fought United Nations forces led by the United States that were sent to defend pro-U.S. South Korea. After United Nations forces pushed North Korean forces toward China's border, the U.S. commander, General Douglas MacArthur, talked recklessly of carrying the offensive into China. The Chinese entered the conflict with 300,000 troops, pushing United Nations troops back south and forcing a stalemate. The war produced huge casualties, including several hundred thousand Chinese, reinforcing U.S.-Chinese hostility and mutual fear. The Korean stalemate improved China's international position, but relations with the United States remained tense. After a U.S.-Taiwan mutual defense treaty, the United States maintained substantial forces in Taiwan,

---

[3]Peng Dehuai, quoted in Craig Dietrich, *People's China: A Brief History*, 3rd ed. (New York: Oxford University Press, 1998), 130.

Peter Guttman/Encyclopedia/Corbis

HONORING CHAIRMAN MAO Since the beginning of communist rule in China in 1949, this giant portrait of Mao Zedong, the chairman of the Chinese Communist Party, has hung on the Gate of Heavenly Peace, the entrance to the Forbidden City of the Qing dynasty emperors, in the heart of Beijing.

United Nations membership and, in 1978, normalized diplomatic relations with China. Meanwhile, China developed better relations with noncommunist nations in Southeast Asia and Africa.

Cultural Revolution and Maoist Society

Mao was a complex figure, promoting women's rights but also sexually promiscuous, marrying several times and with many lovers. He seldom bathed or brushed his teeth. A poor public speaker, he nevertheless inspired millions to follow him. A poet and philosopher but also power hungry and ruthless, he made many enemies, even within the leadership. Although many of his initiatives ultimately failed or caused misery for millions, he played a powerful historical role, leading

South Korea, Japan, Okinawa, and the Philippines, while the U.S. Navy patrolled the waters off China. Using paranoia about this formidable U.S. military presence, Mao mobilized Chinese around his programs. Many U.S. allies recognized the Republic of China on Taiwan as China's official government, and the United States continued to veto communist efforts to gain China's United Nations seat.

In the late 1950s China-USSR tensions grew. The Soviet "peaceful coexistence" policy with the West enraged Mao, who labeled the United States "a paper tiger." Mao also opposed Soviet leader Nikita Khrushchev's **(KROOSH-chef)** 1956 exposure of Stalin's brutal excesses, which questioned communist dictators' abuse of power. By 1960 the Sino-Soviet split was official; the USSR withdrew advisers, technicians, and even the spare parts for the industries it helped build. The Chinese built up their military strength, tested their first atomic bomb, and occasionally clashed with Soviet forces on their border. To counterbalance the United States and the USSR, China sought allies and influence in Asia and Africa. Yet, despite fierce anti-U.S. and anti-Soviet rhetoric, Chinese leaders generally followed a cautious foreign policy.

During the 1970s Chinese foreign policy changed dramatically, symbolized by U.S. president Richard Nixon's trip to Beijing in 1972. Both nations shared a hostility toward the USSR, and the bitter U.S. experience in Vietnam had fostered rethinking in both countries. Chinese leaders perceived Americans as stepping back from Asian commitments, and hence a diminishing threat. The United States quit blocking Chinese

the communists to victory, reunifying China, focusing public attention on rural people, and placing his stamp on the world's most populous nation.

Dissatisfied with China's development and his eclipse, in the mid-1960s Mao regained his dominant status and resurrected Maoism and a Mao cult. In Mao's vision of a society comprising unselfish, politically conscious citizens, individuals inspired by the slogan "Serve the People" subordinated their own needs to the broader social order. Newspapers reported that, illuminated by Mao's revolutionary ideas, factory workers discovered better techniques for galvanizing, a food store manager doubled watermelon sales, and farmers learned to judge the right amount of manure to fertilize their plots. In 1966 the People's Liberation Army newspaper asserted, "The most powerful ideological weapon…is the great Mao [Zedong's] thought…the highest instruction for our actions…our telescope and microscope for observing and analyzing all things.…Chairman Mao is the radiant sun lighting our minds…[and his] thought is our lifeline."[4] Between 1966 and 1976 a radical Maoist movement convulsed and reshaped China like a whirl-

wind. The **Great Proletarian Cultural Revolution** represented Mao's attempt to implant his vision, destroy his enemies, crush the stifling bureaucracy, and renew revolutionary vigor (see Witness to the Past: Guidelines for the Cultural Revolution).

Great Proletarian Cultural Revolution A radical movement in China between 1966 and 1976 that represented Mao Zedong's attempt to implant his vision, destroy his enemies, crush the stifling bureaucracy, and renew the revolution's vigor.

[4]*The Great Socialist Cultural Revolution in China* (Peking: Foreign Languages Press, 1966), 3: 1, 17.

MAP 27.1 **CHINA AND TAIWAN** China is a huge country, divided into many provinces, and occupies a large part of eastern Eurasia. In 1949 the government of the Republic of China, defeated by the Chinese communists, moved to the island of Taiwan, off China's Pacific coast. © 2015 Cengage Learning

Nationalist retreat 1948–1949

--- Boundary uncertain

RUSSIA

KAZAKHSTAN

KYRGYZSTAN

TAJIKISTAN

AFGHANISTAN

PAKISTAN

UZBEKISTAN

TURKMENISTAN

MONGOLIA

INNER MONGOLIA

HEILONGJIANG

• Harbin

JILIN

LIAONING

• Dalian

NORTH KOREA

SOUTH KOREA

JAPAN

Sea of Japan (East Sea)

PACIFIC OCEAN

Yellow Sea

BEIJING Beijing ✪

Tianjin TIANJIN

HEBEI

SHANDONG

SHANXI

• Dazhai

Yanan •

SHAANXI

Xian •

NINGXIA

GANSU

XINJIANG

QINGHAI

TIBET

Lhasa •

NEPAL

BHUTAN

(INDIA)

BANGLADESH

INDIA

Indian claim

Chinese line of control

Yangzi R.

SICHUAN

Chengdu •

CHONGQING

YUNNAN

GUIZHOU

HUNAN

Changsha •

GUANGXI

GUANGDONG

Guangzhou

Shenzhen

HONG KONG

Macao

MACAO

HAINAN

VIETNAM

LAOS

THAILAND

BURMA (MYANMAR)

Bay of Bengal

South China Sea

Tropic of Cancer

20°N

PHILIPPINES

TAIWAN

Taipei •

East China Sea

FUJIAN

Xiamen •

JIANGXI

ZHEJIANG

Hangzhou •

SHANGHAI

JIANGSU

Nanjing •

ANHUI

HUBEI

Wuhan •

HENAN

Huang He R. (Yellow R.)

Xi R.

300 Mi.

300 Km.

60°E

80°E

100°E

120°E

140°E

N

WITNESS TO THE PAST

Guidelines for the Cultural Revolution

This document from 1966 sets out the goals that Chairman Mao Zedong had for the Great Proletarian Cultural Revolution as formulated by the Central Committee of the Chinese Communist Party. Mao had lost some of his power and influence in the aftermath of policy failures, especially the disastrous Great Leap Forward, that compromised his position. He hoped to restore his centrality to Chinese politics, promote revolutionary values hostile to capitalism, and destroy political enemies in the government and Communist Party, especially the President of China, Liu Shaoqi, and the Party Secretary-General, Deng Xiaoping, who had a more pragmatic vision for a socialist China. Mao called on young people and workers to join his cause and seize power from the established local leaders who opposed Mao or ignored his policies. With the outbreak of the Cultural Revolution many young, often idealistic Chinese formed or joined Red Guard units to change society, inspired by Mao Zedong's ideas and encouragement. Sometimes this meant harassing, removing, arresting, or even physically attacking those they believed opposed Mao or represented the status quo. Some Red Guards undertook to duplicate the Red Army's Long March in the 1930s, walking hundreds or even thousands of miles to demonstrate their commitment to the Maoist cause. The document applauds these efforts and proposes to make the groups promoting them a permanent part of Chinese society.

1. A New Stage in the Socialist Revolution

The Great Proletarian Cultural Revolution now unfolding is a great revolution that touches people to their very soul and constitutes a new stage in the development of the socialist revolution in our country, a deeper and more extensive stage....Although the bourgeoisie has been overthrown, it is still trying to use the old ideas, culture and customs, and habits of the exploiting classes to corrupt the masses, capture their minds, and endeavor to stage a comeback. The proletariat must do just the opposite: it must meet headon every challenge of the bourgeoisie in the ideological field and use the new ideas, culture, customs, and habits of the proletariat to change the mental outlook of the whole of society. At present our objective is to struggle against and crush those persons in authority who are taking the capitalist road, to criticize and repudiate the reactionary bourgeois academic "authorities" and the ideology of the bourgeoisie and all other exploiting classes, and transform education, literature, and art and all other parts of the superstructure that do not correspond to the socialist economic base, so as to facilitate the consolidation and development of the socialist system.

2. The Main Current and the Zigzags

The masses of the workers, peasants, soldiers, revolutionary intellectuals, and revolutionary cadres form the main force in this Great Cultural Revolution. Large numbers of revolutionary young people, previously unknown, have become courageous and daring pathbreakers. They are vigorous in action and intelligent. Through the media of big character posters and great debates, they argue things out, expose and criticize thoroughly, and launch resolute attacks on the open and hidden representatives of the bourgeoisie....Since the Cultural Revolution is a revolution, it inevitably meets with resistance. This resistance comes chiefly from those in authority who have wormed their way into the party and are taking the capitalist road. It also comes from the old force of habit in society. At present, this resistance is still fairly strong and stubborn. However, the Great Proletarian Cultural Revolution is, after all, an irresistible general trend. There is abundant evidence that such resistance will crumble fast once the masses become fully aroused....

9. Cultural Revolutionary Groups, Committees, and Congresses

Many new things have begun to emerge in the Great Proletarian Cultural Revolution. The cultural revolutionary groups, committees, and other organizational forms created by the masses in many schools and units are something new and of great historic importance. These cultural revolutionary groups, committees, and congresses are excellent new forms of organization whereby under the leadership of the Communist Party the masses are educating themselves. They are an excellent bridge to keep our party in close contact with the masses. They are organs of power of the Proletarian Cultural Revolution.

The cultural revolutionary groups, committees, and congresses should not be temporary organizations but permanent, standing mass organizations. They are suitable not only for colleges, schools, government, and other organizations but generally also for factories, mines, and other enterprises, urban districts, and villages....It is necessary to institute a system of general elections, like that of the Paris Commune, for electing members to the cultural revolutionary groups and committees and delegates to the cultural revolutionary congress.

THINKING ABOUT THE READING

1. Who does the document identify as the major social group threatening the revolution and its goals?
2. How can the threats be overcome?
3. What people and groups are allies in promoting Mao's revolutionary program and confronting his enemies?

Source: *Sources of Chinese Tradition: From 1600 Through the Twentieth Century*, compiled by Wm. Theodore de Bary and Richard Lufrano, 2nd ed., vol. 2 (New York: Columbia University Press, 2000), 474–475.

Workers and students known as **Red Guards** roamed around cities and countryside in groups, attacking and arresting anti-Mao leaders while smashing temples, churches, and party and government headquarters. Revolutionary committees led by students, workers, and soldiers ran cities, factories, and schools. Red Guards carried a little red book containing short quotations from Mao's writings, such as his claim that understanding Marxism requires contact with workers and peasants. One observer noted that "giant portraits of [Mao] now hung in the streets, busts were in every chamber, his books and photographs were everywhere on display."[5]

During this turmoil, industrial and agricultural production was disrupted, most schools were closed for two years, and thousands of people were killed, jailed, or removed from official positions. Millions were sent to remote rural areas to experience peasant life. Anti-Mao officials, intellectuals, and people with upper-class backgrounds faced public criticism and often punishment. A Chinese journalist whose grandparents were capitalists remembered attacks on her family: "Red Guards swarming all over the house and a great fire in our courtyard onto which were thrown my father's books, my grandparent's precious traditional furniture and my toys."[6] Soon even Mao was dampening the radical fervor.

The communists reshaped Chinese society. Mao promoted social equality, known as the **Iron Rice Bowl**, in which people, especially in villages, shared resources—food, draft animals, farm equipment—and peasants enjoyed dignity. Hence, Maoism often improved life for many poorer Chinese, especially in villages. Emphasizing preventive medicine, villagers trained as paramedics, known as barefoot doctors, addressed everyday health care, such as by distributing medication and setting broken bones. Where once famine and disease were common, most Chinese now enjoyed decent health care and adequate food. Mass education raised literacy rates to the levels of industrialized nations.

Trying to overturn Confucian-influenced patriarchy by raising women's status, Mao praised women for "holding up half the sky." A new marriage law abolished arranged marriages, forbade men from taking concubines, and made divorce easier; land reform empowered women, expanding their property rights. Women now enjoyed legal equality with men and greater access to education, worked for wages, and played a stronger public role, often leading local organizations. Women debated the proper balance between housekeeping and paid work and between furthering the revolution and caring for their husbands and children. Women activists sought democratic families, emphasizing love matches rather than arranged marriages, fostering closer emotional ties between husbands, wives, and children, and lessening male

Red Guards Young workers and students who were the major supporters of the Cultural Revolution in Mao's China.

Iron Rice Bowl A model of social equality in Mao's China in which the people, especially in the villages, shared resources and the peasants enjoyed status and dignity.

Liberation of Beijing in 1949 and declaration of the Republic of China, China, 20th century/De Agostini Picture Library/The Bridgeman Art Library

CHINESE POLITICAL ART The Communists used political art to rally popular support for their cause. This example celebrates the declaration establishing the Peoples Republic in Beijing in 1949.

domination. But rural areas remained more conservative. Moreover, few women held high national positions. Mao's last wife, Jiang Qing **(chang ching)** (1914–1991), a former film actress, wielded great power during the Cultural Revolution, but her radical policies made her unpopular. In 1976, after Mao's death, Jiang and her top party allies, the "Gang of Four," lost a power struggle and were imprisoned.

The communists often undermined traditional beliefs and culture. Calling religion a bond enslaving people, Mao controlled religious behavior and marginalized Christian churches, Buddhist monasteries, and Islamic mosques; by the 1970s a small minority openly practiced religion. Only religious leaders who cooperated with the state maintained their positions. Mao used the arts as a weapon in the class struggle, fostering a "people's art" created by and for common people. He wrote, "In the world today all culture, all literature and art belongs to definite political lines. Art for art's sake, art that stands above the class and party do not exist in reality."[7] During the Great Leap Forward, party activists collected literature written by common people and encouraged peasants and workers to compose poetry and songs. Peasants painted

[5]Quoted in Maurice Meisner, *Mao's China and After: A History of the People's Republic*, 3rd ed. (New York: Free Press, 1999), 281.

[6]Xue Xinran, *The Good Women of China: Hidden Voices* (New York: Anchor, 2002), 175.

[7]From Timothy Cheek, *Mao Zedong and China's Revolutions: A Brief History with Documents* (Boston: Bedford/St. Martin's, 2002), 116.

scenes of people at work, often in bright, cheerful colors conveying an optimistic tone. Part-time writers got time off from the factory to work on literary projects. A 1958 poem proclaimed: "Labor is joy, how joyful it is, Bathed in sweat and two hands full of mud. Like sweet rain, my sweat waters the land."[8] Critics considered art serving revolutionary goals political propaganda.

Politicization of the arts peaked during the Cultural Revolution, when elitism faced fierce attack. Red Guards sang new songs praising change and Chairman Mao, such as "The East is red, the sun has risen. China has produced a Mao Zedong; He is the great savior of the people."[9] Militant operas contained revolutionary themes, such as peasant dignity or Communist Party history. Dancers composed revolutionary ballets integrating Chinese martial arts, folk dances, and Russian ballet. For example, *The Red Detachment of Women* portrayed a company of women soldiers' experiences during the civil war.

After Mao died in 1976, the Chinese evaluated his legacy. The communists had restored China to great power status, renewing confidence after a century of imperialistic exploitation and invasion. No longer a doormat, China even had nuclear weapons. Once again, the Middle Kingdom exercised influence in the world. Whereas a generation earlier begging and prostitution were common, now most Chinese, though enjoying little material surplus, could satisfy their basic food, housing, and clothing needs in a healthier, more broadly based economy.

Mao's policies, however, also generated failures and political repression. Although controlling its economic destiny, China remained poor by world standards. Mao discouraged free enterprise and individual initiative; few private cars interfered with the bicycles most Chinese used to get to work or shopping. Chinese wanted better housing and more consumer goods now rather than in the distant future. With few luxuries or diversions, life was dull. Moreover, fierce punishment of dissenters and the Great Leap Forward and Cultural Revolution had ruined numerous lives. Disillusioned by government coercion, unfulfilled promises, and chaotic turmoil, many blamed Mao and his radicalism. Party reformers charged that Mao had lost touch with common people's lives. Often erratic policies made people cynical, only passively cooperating and avoiding commitment to a particular line. Many Chinese were ready for change. Since 1976 Chinese have continued to debate Mao's policies and role, with various political factions using him to legitimize their own agenda or power.

MAKE SURE YOU UNDERSTAND THESE KEY POINTS BEFORE MOVING ON

- After Japan was defeated in World War II, Chinese communists and nationalists fought a civil war in which Mao Zedong's communists triumphed by appealing to people's frustration with the corruption of Chiang Kai-shek's nationalists.

- Maoism emphasized mass mobilization of the people to industrialize and maximize output, but millions starved to death and many suffered under political repression.

- Mao reshaped Chinese society, improving literacy rates and health care, especially for rural people, expanding the rights of women, opposing traditional religious institutions and elitism, and encouraging the people to produce their own literature and art, but at the cost of many human rights abuses.

- While Mao restored China as a world power and brought many out of poverty, after his death in 1976 many Chinese wanted to join the modern world and gain increased access to material benefits.

aplia

ⓣ Chinese Modernization

What factors explain the dramatic rise of Chinese economic power in the world since 1978?

Deng Xiaoping **(dung shee-yao-ping)** (1904–1997), a long-time Communist Party leader who often clashed with Mao, came to power in 1978 and changed China's direction. Deng and his allies rejected Mao's self-sufficient, ideologically pure China outside the world economy, concluding that collectivized agriculture failed to raise productivity enough to finance the high technology and industry needed to make China a major power. In 1978 Deng, portraying China as at a turning point, announced the policy of four modernizations: the development of agriculture, industry, the military, and science and technology to turn China into a powerful nation by 2000. Deng's successors generally followed his pragmatic policies, transforming China into an economic powerhouse and modifying Maoist society.

Market Socialism and Repression

From 1978 to 1989 Chinese leaders pursued **market socialism**, mixing free enterprise, economic liberalization, and state controls to generate economic dynamism. This pragmatic approach, unlike Mao's,

> **market socialism** A Chinese economic program used between 1978 and 1989 that mixed free enterprise, economic liberalization, and state controls and that produced economic dynamism in China.

[8]Quoted in Hu Kai-Yu, *The Chinese Literary Scene: A Writer's Visit to the People's Republic* (New York: Vintage, 1975), 227.
[9]Quoted in Orville Schell, *Discos and Democracy: China in the Throes of Reform* (New York: Anchor, 1989), 101.

emphasized economic results rather than socialist values. Twice purged for opposing Mao, Deng loved a Chinese proverb: "It doesn't matter whether a cat is black or white, only if it catches mice." Using the market to stimulate productivity, China reentered the world economy to obtain capital investment to spur manufacturing. Like Meiji Japan, China now imported technology, foreign expertise, and capitalist ideas. Deng believed China had reached a plateau; moving to the next levels required wider international participation. Hence, he improved ties with the United States, Japan, western Europe, and noncommunist Southeast Asia. Dazzled by China's huge potential market of, as Western experts put it, 1 billion toothbrushes (for toothpaste) and 2 billion armpits (for deodorant), Western companies promoted increased trade.

Introducing capitalist ideas, such as offering workers better pay rather than ideological slogans, Deng's reforms sparked dramatic changes, permitting small private enterprises, then larger ones; ultimately both private and state-owned enterprises competed with each other. In agriculture, Deng replaced Mao's communes with the contract system, under which peasants could lease (but not buy) land to work privately. In many districts this free market generated soaring productivity; rural per capita incomes rose fourfold in the first decade. Tapping a skilled, industrious, but cheap labor force, many Western and Asian companies established manufacturing operations to produce goods such as shirts, underwear, and toys for export. China became a consumer society; even in small cities, shops stocked Japanese televisions and Western soft drinks. Over the next twenty-five years the economy quadrupled in size, and foreign trade increased ten times over.

Deng also loosened political and cultural controls. Intellectuals and artists enjoyed greater freedom, the press was enlivened, public debate widened, and organized religion was increasingly tolerated. Western popular culture, especially films, rock music, and discos, won a huge audience; foreign books and magazines became available; and foreign travelers backpacked in remote areas. The sentimental recordings of Taiwan's top female singer, Deng Lijun (**deyn lee-choong**), better known in Hong Kong, Japan, and Southeast Asia as Teresa Teng, were so widely heard in homes and restaurants that people said that "the day belongs to Deng Xiaoping but the night belongs to Deng Lijun."[10] Novels and short stories addressed the suffering during the Cultural Revolution. Popular writers developed huge audiences for stories with daring sexual themes. Chinese-made films won international acclaim, but creative directors, portraying China as anything but a communist paradise, skirmished with wary government censors. Rock musicians, especially ethnic Korean Cui Jian (**sway jen**), a former Beijing Symphony trumpeter, spoke for alienated urban youth. Dressed in battered army fatigues and a Mao coat style, Cui sang: "This guitar in my hands is like a knife. I want to cut at your hypocrisy till I see some truth." Cui's songs were indirect, focusing more on bureaucratic corruption, social problems, and young people's frustrations than politics; Chinese youth easily read between the lines for hidden meanings. One fan commented that "Cui Jian says things we all feel, but cannot say."[11]

Although many Chinese applauded ideological loosening and growing economic options, market socialism hid a dark underside. Many districts enjoyed few benefits from reorganizing rural life. Chinese authorities imposed one national policy rather than allowing districts and villages to find their own policy. Furthermore, Chinese social norms stress the concept of connections or relationships (known as *guanxi*) with other people, especially influential patrons, to increase one's power and wealth, but this emphasis can lead to corruption. Villagers with better land, political connections, or entrepreneurial skills benefited more, opening a rich-poor gap. Prices rose rapidly, and corruption increased as bureaucrats and party officials lined their pockets. Moreover, intraparty tensions increased; Stalinists and Maoists feared that economic liberalization undermined one-party rule and communism. The fall of communism in eastern Europe and the USSR in 1989 alarmed hardliners. But dissidents and some reformers, believing that strong controls inhibited initiative, pushed democracy as "the fifth modernization." At a Beijing site known unofficially as the "Democracy Wall," people put up posters expressing their criticisms. In response, party hardliners called for cracking down, arresting dissidents.

In 1989 tensions reached a boiling point, generating massive protests and government repression. Thousands of protesters, led by university students and workers, took over Tiananmen Square in downtown Beijing, demanding the most unpopular leaders' resignations, an end to government corruption, and the creation of a fully open system. Smaller demonstrations erupted in several other cities. In a festive spirit, street vendors gave free food and drink to demonstrators; rock musicians entertained the throngs. Party hardliners, with Deng's support, purged moderate party leaders and ordered the army to clear out the demonstrators, sparking the Tiananmen Massacre; the army killed hundreds and arrested thousands, while millions around the world watched on television. The courageous Beijing protesters had overestimated their popular support. Since many rural Chinese valued stability more than vague promises of a better world, the protesters miscalculated democracy's prospects in a country with an authoritarian political tradition.

Economic Change and Politics Since 1989

After the Tiananmen Massacre the communists modified market socialism into **market Leninism**, with the Chinese state, obsessed with stability, asserting more power over society while also fostering an even stronger market economy. The party reestablished control in political, social, and cultural life,

market Leninism A policy followed after the Tiananmen Massacre in 1989 whereby the Chinese communist state asserted more power over society while also fostering an even stronger market orientation in the economy than had existed under market socialism.

[10]Quoted in June Teufel Dreyer, *China's Political System: Modernization and Tradition* (New York: Paragon House, 1993), 345.

[11]The quotes are in Andrew F. Jones, *Like a Knife: Ideology and Genre in Contemporary Chinese Popular Music* (Ithaca, NY: East Asia Program, Cornell University, 1992), 97, 148.

tolerating less dissent than in the 1980s. China now did not fit the communist or capitalist model but was essentially a form of state capitalism. In many enterprises state agencies and private entrepreneurs shared ownership; the government owned shares in many companies or entered joint ventures with foreign businessmen, often favoring state-owned or -controlled businesses in contracts. Remembering the Cultural Revolution and the 1989 unrest, the Chinese often valued political stability over individual rights, such as unfettered free speech and participation in government, especially when there was overheated economic growth. This approach was typically Chinese; for two thousand years Chinese governments had promoted social and political harmony to discourage conflict.

However, the one-party state's control was not absolute. In some local elections officials permitted competition, and some dissenters still spoke out. Dissenters opposed but could not halt the environmentally damaging Three Gorges Dam project to control the Yangzi (**yahng-zeh**) River and provide electrical power, which forced several million people to move. However, the Chinese state, often arbitrary, has used the military and police to intimidate dissidents. Assertive dissidents face arrest, dampening public debate. China has executed thousands every year, mostly criminals but also some accused of economic misbehavior or political opposition. The state has also repressed the sometimes restless ethnic minorities, who constitute 8.5 percent of China's 1.35 billion population. Anxious to preserve national unity, China suppressed dissent in Tibet and among Muslim Turkish groups in Xinjiang (**shinjee-yahng**), in far western China, where people have sought autonomy, greater religious freedom, and limits on large-scale Chinese immigration; seething resentment periodically sparks self-immolations, riots, and interethnic violence, leaving hundreds of people dead or injured.

After 1980 China, abetted by a "get-rich-quick" mentality, generally enjoyed the world's fastest economic growth, often 10 percent a year. Deng claimed that to get rich was glorious. China's exports increased fifteenfold between 1980 and 2000. The party sought popular support by offering consumer goods and wealth rather than political reform, providing shops with ample consumer goods and households with spending money. In the early reform days, people wanted the "three bigs": bicycle, wristwatch, and sewing machine. Now they coveted televisions, washing machines, video recorders, and smartphones. Clearly benefiting from the mobility of capital and products with globalization, China moved ahead of Germany in 2009 and then Japan in 2011 to become the world's second largest economy; the U.S. economy remains three times larger. If high annual growth rates continue, China may eventually have the world's largest economy.

Although economic reforms improved living standards for many Chinese, they produced numerous downsides. Economic dynamism is concentrated in a few coastal provinces and special economic zones, where living standards approach those of Taiwan and South Korea. Half of Chinese now live in cities, many boasting towering skyscrapers and huge shopping malls with upscale shops. Charming old neighborhoods are often bulldozed, replaced by apartment blocks. Shanghai has more skyscrapers than any other world city and two of the three tallest buildings. Elsewhere, conditions have often deteriorated. Although laws discourage migration to another district without government permission, millions of peasants seeking jobs or a less rustic life have moved to cities, where they struggle and, considered nonresidents, have limited rights. Most single migrant factory workers live in crowded, company-owned dormitories, laboring twelve to fourteen hours a day, six to seven days a week. Their precarious position became clear in 2008, when the global economic crisis affected China as overseas markets collapsed. Thousands of factories closed, leaving millions of disillusioned workers without incomes and forced to return to their home villages. Yet, unlike many Western nations and Japan, China's economy still grew, albeit at a slower rate. Thanks to a huge government stimulus package and autocratic decision making, China's economy recovered and many workers found jobs. Labor shortages and worker resistance may eventually improve working conditions.

The Chinese have become great users of world resources, such as oil and coal, and major polluters of the atmosphere. China is now the number one producer of greenhouse gases causing global warming, just ahead of the United States. Mindful of the unhealthy air pollution choking China's cities and the fouled rivers and lakes fostered by industrialization, by 2009 China had placed more emphasis on developing cleaner, greener, and renewable energy sources such as wind and solar, yet it still relies heavily on coal-based power sources, leading the world in carbon emissions. Water supplies are badly overstretched and often polluted. With private cars clogging streets where bicycles once dominated and factories and coal-burning power plants polluting the air, smog blankets much of the country. By 2013 some local pollution emergencies, so severe and dangerous they were called "airpocalypses", paralyzed cities and closed schools and airports. Many feared consuming food produced from damaged, pesticide-saturated soils. Land and energy grow more expensive. China has devoted vast sums to a modern transportation network, including high-speed trains, city subway systems, and superhighways, but some are poorly built, causing accidents and collapses. Poorly regulated companies sell tainted food and milk.

Political and economic changes have influenced other areas of Chinese life. Newly rich entrepreneurs enjoy luxury cars, golf courses, and vacations abroad. China has several hundred thousand millionaires and some billionaires. A Chinese observer noted, "Walk around Beijing and what do you see? Buy a new Audi, look at this Rolex, you need some clothes from Gucci. Such things are simply unaffordable [for most]."[12] Party leaders' sons and daughters, known as "princelings," use their connections to advance in business or politics. Even the middle class, numbering 100 to 250 million and chiefly working in local or foreign businesses, enjoy a comfortable life. Some village leaders abuse their power and connections to amass wealth. The wealthy flaunt their affluence; the poor resent it.

---

[12]Law professor Zhou Guanquan, quoted in Dan Levin, "China's New Wealth Gives Old Status Symbol a Boost," *New York Times*, August 10, 2011, p. A6.

Street songs often mock the powerful: "I'm a big official, so I eat and drink, and I've got the potbelly to prove it. Beer, spirits, rice wine, love potions—I drink it all."[13] Since 2005 peasant protests against seizure of village land to build polluting factories, luxury housing, and golf courses have become frequent, numbering 180,000 annually by 2012, but most protest leaders are arrested. Meanwhile, the shift to market forces leaves millions unable to afford medical care and their children's schooling. Thanks to declining health care, especially in rural areas, between half a million and 1.5 million Chinese have HIV or AIDS. Some poorer Chinese long fondly for Mao and the Iron Rice Bowl. Yet, despite reduced job security and social services, people are now freer than before to travel, change jobs, enjoy leisure, and even complain.

The party, now with 70 million members, faces problems Mao could never have anticipated. Lacking a unifying figure like Mao or Deng, the leadership today is mostly a faceless group of longtime party members who rose through the ranks not by ideology but by tapping connections and forging alliances. Once claiming to uplift the working class and poor peasants, it now welcomes wealthy businessmen and professionals. Many with little faith in the communist vision still consider party membership helpful to their career prospects. Most young Chinese, preoccupied with seeking wealth, know little about the Tiananmen Massacre. Yet, powerful provincial leaders, promoting local economic growth, increasingly ignore Beijing. Chinese leaders must resolve inequalities, spreading wealth more equitably, to check growing social tensions. Some pessimists forecast more conflicts between rich and poor Chinese, or civil war between rich and poor regions. In 2012 new tensions emerged as China's elite installed a new leadership team, headed by Xi Jinping, and debated further reforms under the concept, influenced by both Confucian and Maoist slogans, of the "Chinese Dream" that emphasized China's strength and prosperity. The arrest and conviction of a powerful but controversial regional leader for corruption revealed deep party divisions between rival leaders and between factions favoring market reforms or addressing economic inequality. While promising more influence for the market, Xi also favored state owned companies and a stronger role for the Communist Party.

Chinese Society and Culture Since 1989

The government struggles to maintain social stability. Mao's China was one of the world's safest countries, but economic growth and the quest for wealth have generated a rapid increase in crime. The close connection between government and business corruption, underworld activity, and financial success has led to Chinese talking about the "Five Colors," or surest roads to riches: Communist Party connections, prostitution, smuggling, illegal drug dealing, and criminal gangs. Rampant drug dealing serves the growing numbers using narcotics for escape. Maintaining Confucian and Maoist attitudes, many Chinese view wealth as corrupting and mistrust rich business interests.

Although women's economic status has often improved, many still face restricted gender expectations. Feminist journalist Xue Xinran (**shoe shin-rahn**) argued that "Chinese women had always thought that their lives should be full of misery. Many had no idea what happiness was, other than having a son for the family"[14] Many scholars consider the long-suffering, submissive Chinese woman stereotype misleading; modern women are often strong-willed and resourceful. But women now receive little support because government policies are aimed at economic growth, not gender equality. Millions of rural women migrate to cities for industrial and service jobs, providing much of the labor force that has helped turn China into an economic giant. Wherever they live, women commonly work long hours. Few women occupy high positions in the government, Communist Party, or top business enterprises (see Profile: Xue Xinran, a Chinese Voice for Women).

Since China already had 1 billion people in the 1980s, a fifth of humankind, Deng Xiaoping introduced a one-child-per-family policy to stabilize the population. Critics complained that children without siblings, called "little emperors," were pampered and self-centered. The policy encouraged and sometimes mandated abortion; since traditional attitudes favoring sons remained, killing of female babies was widespread. Raising more boys than girls has fostered serious social consequences, as many men cannot find wives. By 2013 officials relaxed the rigid one-child policy for some families and abolished hated prison labor camps, but enforcement of the reform depended on local officials who often acquired income and influence from the old system.

Global entertainment and consumer culture also affect China, with Western popular culture becoming a powerful force among youth. Cui Jian and other rock musicians, some of whom participated in the Beijing student protest movement, now compete with heavy metal, punk, and rap musicians, and Chinese imitators of Anglo-American boy bands and girl groups enjoy a vast teen audience. The U.S. television program *American Idol* inspired hugely popular Chinese imitators such as *Super Girl*; wary, in 2011 the party limited "vulgar" entertainment on television. But in other areas the West continues to influence society. A Disney Resort in Shanghai will open in 2015. Numerous McDonald's outlets (one near Mao's mausoleum), Pizza Huts, Hard Rock Cafes, Walmarts, and some eighty-five thousand Avon agents selling American beauty products serve consumers. Homosexuals, who faced condemnation and discrimination under Mao, have slowly been coming out, even having hundreds of their own websites. Gay bars are common in large cities. South Korean popular culture and consumer products—music, clothing, television dramas, movies, cosmetics—have also become very fashionable among young Chinese. Much of the conversion of millions of Chinese

---

[13]Quoted in R. Keith Schoppa, *Revolution and Its Past: Identities and Change in Modern Chinese History* (Upper Saddle River, NJ: Prentice-Hall, 2002), 433.

[14]Xue Xinran, author interview in *Random House Reading Group for the Good Women of China* (http://www.randomhouse.co.uk/offthepage/guide.htm?command=Search&db+catalog/mai).

Xue Xinran, a Chinese Voice for Women

In the 1980s Xue Xinran (**shoe shin-rahn**), known professionally as Xinran, began working for a radio network and later became one of China's most successful and innovative journalists. A radio call-in show she launched in 1989 featured hundreds of poignant and haunting stories by women. Her huge audience and sensitive handling of callers made Xinran a role model and heroine for Chinese women. Her own life and career also revealed women's experiences.

Born in Beijing in 1958, Xinran had a difficult childhood complicated by the Cultural Revolution's turmoil. Her mother came from a capitalist, property-owning family. But Xinran's grandfather, although cooperating with the communists, lost his property and was imprisoned during the Cultural Revolution. Her mother joined the Communist Party and army at sixteen and was occasionally jailed or demoted in purges of those from capitalist backgrounds. Xinran's father, a national expert in mechanics and computing, was also from a once-wealthy family and had been imprisoned. When she was one month old, Xinran was sent to live with a grandmother, and she seldom saw her parents during childhood. Reflecting on her family, she wrote that, like many Chinese, her parents endured an unhappy marriage: "Did [my parents] love each other? I have never dared to ask." While working as an army administrator, Xinran married, had a son, PanPan, and later divorced.

Eventually Xinran became a radio journalist. But she had to persuade the station to let her begin a nightly call-in program, *Words on the Night Breeze*. Since 1949 the media functioned as a Communist Party mouthpiece, ensuring that it spoke with one identical voice. However, Xinran said, "I was trying to open a little window, a tiny hole, so that people would allow their spirits to cry out and breathe after the gunpowder-laden atmosphere of the previous forty years." The question that obsessed her was: What is a woman's life really worth in a China where footbinding was a recent memory but women now lived and worked alongside men? Xinran's compassion and ability encouraged callers to talk freely about feelings. For eight groundbreaking years, women called in and discussed their lives. Broadcast all over China, the program offered an unflinching portrait of what it meant to be a woman in modern China, including expectations of obedience to fathers, husbands, and sons. Women from every social status—daughters of wealthy families, wives of party

XUE XINRAN The Chinese journalist, Xue Xinran, explored the lives of Chinese women on her radio program and in her writings.

officials, children of Cultural Revolution survivors, homeless street scavengers, isolated mountain villagers—called in stories, often heartbreaking tales of sexual abuse, gang rape, forced marriages, and enforced separation of families.

The stories did not fit the image promoted by the Communist Party of a happy, harmonious society. She told, for instance, of Jingyi and her boyfriend, Gu Da, university classmates who fell passionately in love but were sent to work in different regions. They had planned to eventually marry but lost touch during the Cultural Revolution. For forty-five years Jingyi had first longed for and then searched for Gu Da. When they finally had a reunion in 1994, Jingyi was devastated to discover that Gu Da, despairing of ever seeing Jingyi again, had married another woman. Their saga provided a window on the disrupted personal and family ties common after 1949.

In Xinran's view, "When China started to open up [to the outside world], it was like a starving child devouring everything without much discrimination." In 1997 the conflict between what Xinran knew and what she was permitted to say caused her to give up her career and leave for Britain, where she hoped to find a freer life and reach a global audience. She first taught at the University of London and then became a columnist for a national newspaper, *The Guardian*. She published several nonfiction books based on the stories she learned in China. In *The Good Women of China: Hidden Voices* (2002), she revealed strong, resourceful characters who offered insights into China's past and present. Another book, *The Sky Burial* (2004), told the extraordinary story of an intrepid Chinese woman who spent thirty years searching rugged Tibet for her beloved husband, an army doctor who was reported killed. In *China Witness* (2008), Xinran traced China's traumatic modern history through candid interviews with aging Chinese. In 2002 Xinran married an Englishman, the literary agent Toby Eady. Every year she returns to China for reporting, and also sponsors a charity, The Mother's Bridge of Love, that helps disadvantaged children.

THINKING ABOUT THE PROFILE

1. Why did Xinran achieve such fame in China?
2. What does her journalism tell us about the experiences of Chinese women?

Note: Quotations from Xue Xinran, *The Good Women of China: Hidden Voices* (New York: Anchor, 2002), 3, 126, 227.

to evangelical Christianity is due to thousands of South Korean Protestant missionaries.

More than 485 million Chinese have gained some access to the wider world by becoming Internet users. E-commerce is also becoming much more popular; China's biggest online auction site had some 145 million registered members in 2009. To restrict the free flow of information and crack down on cyberspace, officials created "the Great Firewall," sometimes closing down Internet cafes and preventing Internet providers—local and Western—from allowing access to banned websites. Many thousands of computer-savvy security agents monitor the Internet for any sites or discussions deemed "dangerous" to public security. But websites and blogs proliferate rapidly, making complete monitoring difficult. By 2009 the government sought even stricter controls over the Internet and electronic tools such as Twitter, Facebook, and YouTube. The government also sometimes shuts down newspapers and magazines for daring reporting, but some brave journalists and officials have risked punishment by openly criticizing media micromanagement; some journalists and other writers refer to the limits imposed on them as "dancing with shackles." When liberal party members and intellectuals sign petitions and write articles protesting human rights abuses, they often lose their jobs or experience police surveillance. Yet, by 2012 some 2 million Chinese, including children of high officials, were studying abroad.

Policies toward religion have been inconsistent. After 1978 the government tolerated millions of Chinese returning to their ancestral faith, but it has cracked down on movements deemed a threat or that refuse to accept official restrictions. Officials arrest and sometimes execute leaders and members of the assertive, missionary *Falun Gong* meditation sect, a Daoist-Buddhist-Christian mix, and harass or close down rapidly proliferating independent Christian churches that do not seek government approval.

China in the Global System

China's relations with the wider world have been colored by humiliation from lost wars, foreign gunboats, civil wars, and Japanese invasions. Eventually the Chinese saw their nation again stand tall, strong, and increasingly rich. In 1997 they celebrated Hong Kong's peaceful return from British colonial control, rectifying the loss during the Opium War. Prosperous Hong Kong, whose towering skyscrapers, dazzling neon-lit waterfront, bustling shopping malls, and dynamic film industry symbolized East Asian capitalism, was incorporated under a "one nation, two systems" policy. Yet, a vocal and popular prodemocracy movement charges that China's occasional interference in Hong Kong politics threatens political freedoms. In 1999 Portugal returned its small coastal colony of Macao to Chinese control. Macao's economy is based on gambling casinos, a lucrative enterprise that the once-puritanical communists seem happy to tolerate.

Since 1976 China has pursued a pragmatic foreign policy to win friends and trading partners but to avoid entangling alliances. China gradually improved relations with the

United States and USSR and became increasingly active in the world, joining international institutions such as the World Trade Organization. Yet, China's military has been rapidly modernizing, augmenting the world's largest army (some 1.25 million troops) with enhanced naval and air power. In 2010 China began pressing claims to much of the South China Sea, which may have vast oil reserves; countries like Taiwan, Vietnam, Indonesia, and the Philippines also have claims in the area. Tensions simmer. China enjoys tremendous influence in the world economy, importing vast amounts of capital and natural resources, such as Zambian copper and Venezuelan oil, while exporting industrial products of every kind. Thousands of foreign investors from the West, Japan, Southeast Asia, South Korea, and even Taiwan have opened factories and negotiated joint ventures with Chinese firms. Meanwhile, China has supported the U.S. economy, becoming the major buyer of treasury bonds. Hundreds of Chinese enterprises buy companies in other nations or operate in Africa and Latin America, and many thousands of Chinese have followed them as workers or to open small businesses. China provides investment and loans to governments but expects cooperation in return. Thus China has become the world's most successful newly industrializing economy, buttressed by a vast resource base, a huge domestic market, and a resourceful labor force.

Yet China has met roadblocks in enhancing its global power. The communists threaten forced unification if Taiwan, enjoying a defense agreement with the United States, tries to declare a permanent break from China. Although economic and social links between China and Taiwan have increased, few in the island nation, which enjoys democracy and much higher living standards, want to merge with the mainland. Chinese relations with Japan also ebb and flow. The two nations have close economic ties but are natural rivals. The Chinese still resent Japanese brutality during World War II and fear contemporary Japanese nationalism. However, China has improved political and economic relations with once-bitter enemies such as South Korea and anticommunist countries like Malaysia, the Philippines, and Australia, which view China as the future regional power. In many Asian and some African and Latin American countries, many people are learning Chinese, and some ninety thousand foreign students study in China. Nonetheless, historical resentment of Japan and the West stokes Chinese nationalism, sometimes resulting in anti-Japan or anti-U.S. protest demonstrations. In 2013 China ranked second in military spending, a quarter of the U.S. total.

China has much lower overall living standards and far more poverty than North America, western Europe, Japan, and several industrializing Asian nations. Nevertheless, its tremendous size, population, natural resources, military strength, national confidence, and sense of history make it a major global power. China, rather than the United States, led global recovery from the 2008–2009 recession, suggesting that the world's economic center of gravity may be shifting to East Asia. Perhaps China has returned to its historical leadership as the Asian dragon and a major engine of the global economy. Experts debate whether either China or India might replace the United States as the major world power by 2050 or 2100. India has advantages, such as democracy, a free press, and a sounder financial system. Yet, China, with a far better infrastructure, might have better prospects, especially if the growing middle class fosters a more open political system. As during the long period of Chinese power and prosperity between 600 and 1800, China is once again a major force in world affairs. Still, many experts doubt that any country will match overall American power within the next several decades.

MAKE SURE YOU UNDERSTAND THESE KEY POINTS BEFORE MOVING ON

- Under Deng Xiaoping, China opened up to Western economic ideas and investment, gradually introducing private ownership and competition, as well as to political, religious, and cultural currents that had been suppressed under Mao.

- Although many supported Deng's reforms, they led to increasing corruption and a growing gap between rich and poor.

- Under market Leninism, the Chinese state increased political and social control while continuing to privatize the economy, which grew briskly, though there was stagnation in many rural areas and environmental damage in others.

- China has enjoyed a great recovery and return to world prominence in recent decades, though it still has uncertain relations with Taiwan and Japan, and its living standard remains much lower than that of many of its rivals.

aplia

The Remaking of Japan

T **S**

How did Japan rise from the ashes of defeat in World War II to become a global economic powerhouse?

In August 1945, Japan lay in ruins, its major cities largely destroyed by U.S. bombing, its economy devastated, and its people in psychological shock. Yet, within a decade Japanese had recovered from the World War II disaster. After several decades of world history's highest economic growth rates, what some called an "economic miracle," by the 1980s Japan was challenging the United States for world economic leadership. Stressing cooperation rather than individualism fostered economic and social stability in an overcrowded land (127 million in 2012). But beginning in the 1990s Japan has experienced political and economic uncertainty.

Occupation, Recovery, and Politics

The U.S. post–World War II occupation aided Japan's recovery. Emperor Hirohito **(here-o-HEE-to)** (1901–1989), still a revered figure, asked the Japanese to cooperate with the Allied forces, and by and large they did. The U.S.-dominated military administration, the Supreme Command of Allied Powers (SCAP), sought to rebuild rather than punish Japan. Japan lost Korea, Taiwan, and Manchuria, while the United States took control of the Ryukyu Islands, which were returned to Japan in the 1970s, and Micronesia. Hoping to democratize Japan by using the United States as a model while aiding economic recovery, SCAP dismantled the military, removed some civilian politicians, and tried and hanged seven wartime leaders as war criminals. Fearing that punishing the emperor, a member of an imperial family over fifteen hundred years old, would destabilize Japan, U.S. officials forced Hirohito to renounce his godlike aura and become a more public figure.

SCAP fostered political and social changes. Sustaining democracy required a more egalitarian society, with once-disadvantaged people sharing in the progress. A new constitution guaranteed civil liberties and forever renounced war as the nation's sovereign right. Democratic elections held in 1946 involved various competing political parties, and all adult citizens, including women, could vote. Women gained legal equality in society and marriage but were only partly freed from patriarchal expectations. New universities opened, providing greater access to higher education. The economy gradually recovered, using the same free markets mix introduced in the Meiji era, free from government intervention. Land reform subsidized the peasantry, making them strong government supporters and bringing prosperity to rural areas. Although SCAP attempted to break up entrenched economic power, large industrial-commercial-banking conglomerates still dominated manufacturing and foreign trade, making Japan more competitive in the world economy. But workers gained the right to unionize.

With the Chinese communist victory and the Korean War, Americans shifted their emphasis from restructuring Japanese society to integrating Japan into the anticommunist Western alliance, symbolized by the formal U.S.-Japan peace treaty and mutual defense pact in 1951. U.S. military bases have remained in Japan ever since. The SCAP occupation officially ended in 1952; its policies were most successful where U.S. and Japanese desires coincided or when they fit with Japanese traditions.

MAP 27.2 **JAPAN AND THE LITTLE DRAGONS** Japan fostered the strongest Asian economy through the second half of the twentieth century, but in recent decades the Little Dragons—South Korea, Taiwan, Hong Kong, and Singapore—have also had rapid economic growth. © 2015 Cengage Learning

Democratic government fit both criteria. It was not without precedent; the Japanese had enjoyed several decades of democracy before the Great Depression. Borrowing from abroad also reflected tradition; the Japanese were again receptive to importing Western culture. With conditions stabilized, Japanese leaders began capitalizing on peace to strengthen the nation.

Despite stresses, Japan's democratic political system has endured. Diverse political parties—socialists, communists, liberals, Buddhists, rightwing nationalists—have competed for parliamentary seats. But the center-right Liberal Democratic Party (LDP) has dominated politics, applying generally conservative, probusiness, pro-U.S. policies. The SCAP-imposed electoral system gave greater weight to rural voters, the backbone of LDP support. But although prime ministers negotiate with opposition parties and varied LDP factions, critics believe that a political system dominated by one party and wealthy kingmakers, who face little criticism from media largely owned by huge corporations, is at best a partial democracy.

The need to finance political careers by raising money from powerful corporations and criminal gangs has led to corruption. Bribery scandals sometimes force political leaders to resign, and a few have gone to prison. In 1993 the LDP fragmented in factional disputes but soon returned to power under a reform leader. In 2009, with Japan mired in severe recession and facing a huge national debt, the LDP experienced a huge defeat in national elections, losing power to the center-left Democratic Party, which promised reforms. But the Democrats proved unable to resolve the problems, and in 2013 voters gave the LDP a smashing victory under their leader, Shinzo Abe (b. 1954), a rightwing, promilitary, anti-China nationalist but economic populist who many hoped could energize the economy.

With a U.S. military alliance and bases for protection, Japan's military spending has long remained meager, providing more resources to the civilian economy and spurring rapid economic growth. While the Cold War superpowers invested in weapons and armies, Japan devoted its economic surplus largely to industrial development. However, leftist parties, labor unions, and militant student groups have long opposed the U.S. military presence as neocolonialism and fear that U.S. military interventions elsewhere will make Japan a potential target. Remembering World War II's horrors, especially the atomic bombings, which killed some 200,000 Japanese, many Japanese have favored pacifism. Yet, with U.S. support, Japan began increasing military spending in the 1980s, and it now has the world's fifth largest military budget, about one tenth that of the U.S.. Sending soldiers to support, in noncombat activities, the U.S. war in Iraq was widely unpopular and, to critics, violated the constitutional ban against engaging in war. Seeing China as a threat, Prime Minister Shinzo Abe, seeking a more assertive foreign policy, pledged to amend the constitution to increase Japanese military power.

JAPANESE PROTEST Political demonstrations are common in Japanese cities. During this protest in 2001, liberals and leftists criticized new middle-school textbooks, approved by the Education Ministry, that, the critics claimed, distorted history by emphasizing nationalist viewpoints and downplaying Japanese atrocities in World War II.

KAZUHIRO NOGI/AFP/Getty Images

The Japanese Economy and Growth

Adapting capitalism to its own traditions, Japan achieved phenomenal economic growth, its goods in demand on every continent only a century after it opened to the outside world. Wartime destruction required rebuilding basic industries using the latest innovations. Investing in high-tech fields, Japanese became world leaders in manufacturing products such as pianos, oil tankers, and automobiles, as well as electronics such as watches, televisions, and cameras. From the 1960s through the 1980s Japan enjoyed annual growth rates three times higher than those of all other industrialized nations. An industrial giant, in 2000 Japan produced some 16 percent of the world's goods and services, half the U.S. percentage, a particularly impressive figure considering that Japan has few mineral resources, limited productive farmland, and no major rivers for hydroelectric power. Consequently, the Japanese must import the minerals needed for industry, such as iron ore, tin, and copper. Oil obtained from Alaska, Southeast Asia, and the Middle East powers Japan's transportation.

Japan became known for innovative technologies and high-quality products. A magnificent mass transit system included state-of-the-art bullet trains that carry passengers at 125 to 150 miles per hour and always on time. Electronics manufacturers such as Sony, Atari, and Nintendo invented entertainment-oriented products, among them video and handheld game systems that are now part of life everywhere, especially for youth. Millions of people, from Boston to Bogotá, Barcelona to Bombay, drive Toyotas, Hondas, and other Japanese-made cars. Enjoying living standards equal to those of most western Europeans, Japanese became Western-style consumers, with most urbanites owning cars, televisions, washing machines, and air conditioners. One Japanese remembered his family's elation in the 1960s: "The first evening we turned on the television set we were so excited that we could not sleep. When the refrigerator arrived we kept opening and closing the door until Mother called us, and we sat transfixed watching the electric rice cooker after it was switched on. How 'high class' it was to live like this, we thought, eating bread browned in a toaster and spread with butter."[15]

The Japanese have also achieved the world's highest average life expectancy: seventy-nine for men, eighty-six for women. A more varied diet, including more meat and dairy products, has produced taller, healthier children. Western foods and beverages have become popular, and fast-food outlets such as McDonald's prove successful serving hamburgers and fries but also dishes adapted to local taste, such as teriyaki burgers and Chinese fried rice. Unlike in the 1920s, rural areas share in the prosperity; however, most rural youth have left their villages for the cities. Many workers make do with part-time jobs offering few benefits; a small but growing underclass have no permanent jobs or homes.

Japan's capitalist economy differs in fundamental ways from that of Western industrial nations. The national government and big business work together in a cooperative relationship known as **Japan, Inc.** (Japan Incorporated). The government regulates business, setting overall guidelines, sponsoring research and development, and leasing the resulting products or technologies to private enterprise. Most Japanese businesses accept the guidelines, taking a longer-term view of profitability than Western business leaders. But government-business cooperation occurs chiefly in international trade, the country's lifeblood, made easier by the dominating Japanese conglomerates that own diverse enterprises such as factories, banks, and department stores. Protectionist barriers and bureaucratic hurdles impede foreign businesses but aid Japanese businesses.

Economic growth has generated new problems. As in the West, industrialization has fostered wealth but harmed the environment. Pollution of rivers and bays has wiped out coastal fishing, and smoggy air sometimes prompts city residents to cover their noses and mouths with masks to avert respiratory difficulties. Toxic waste dumped by factories has killed or sickened thousands. In 2011 a horrific earthquake and tsunami devastated a northern coastal region, leaving twenty thousand dead or missing and ruining a major nuclear power plant, which continues to poison the nearby land and sea with radioactivity, forcing reconsideration of the role and safety of Japan's many nuclear power plants.

Japan's business and factory life has contributed to success. The system capitalizes on Japanese cultural values such as conformity, hard work, cooperation, thrift, and foresight, while adding innovations. While temporary workers and many employees in smaller businesses lack generous benefits and are vulnerable to layoffs, the 30 percent of workers in larger Japanese companies often enjoy lifetime job security and access to generous employer-provided welfare benefits such as health insurance, recreation, housing, and car loans. Many employees enjoy company-sponsored group tours abroad or vacation retreats. When corporations face financial trouble, top managers often accept responsibility, cutting their own pay rather than firing workers. Before the 1980s most workers remained with the same employer for life, but changing jobs became more common. To encourage identity with the corporate "family," employees gather together to sing the company anthem each morning before heading for their workstations. Japanese companies emphasize working in teams and "bottom-up" decision making through quality control circles and work groups; for example, a factory team that installs car engines will decide how best to undertake their tasks. Business offices are often organized around large tables, and white-collar employees work collaboratively rather than in small cubicles. Businesses and factories expect their employees to put company over personal interests, including regularly working overtime.

Japanese Society, Culture, and Thought

Urbanization and affluence have contributed to social change. Sixty percent of Japanese live in cities of over 100,000. With 36 million people, Tokyo is the world's largest metropolitan area, and its legendary traffic jams may take police several days to untangle. With city subways convenient but overcrowded, rush hour has evolved into "crush hour"; city employees equipped with padded poles push commuters into overflowing cars to allow the train doors to close. Yet, despite notorious Mafia-like organized crime syndicates, Japan's cities are the world's safest; experts attribute the low rates of violent crime in part to strict gun control.

The economy has changed men's lives. Most university-educated men want white-collar office jobs in major corporations where they can become **salarymen**, urban middle-class male business employees who commit their energies and souls to the company, accepting assignments without complaint and taking few vacations. The cover of a local book pictures a harried middle-aged salaryman eyeing the sundry items that define his work life: a computer, newspaper, lunch box, demanding boss, and subway strap. Many white-collar men are also known as "7-11 husbands," leaving for work at 7 A.M. and not returning until 11 P.M. After work they and their office mates socialize in restaurants, bars, and nightclubs while their wives take care

Japan, Inc. The cooperative relationship between government and big business that has existed in Japan after 1945.

salarymen Japanese urban middle-class male business employees who commit their energies and soul to the company, accept assignments without complaint, and take few vacations.

---

[15]Ito Masanori, quoted in Peter Duus, *Modern Japan*, 2nd ed. (Boston: Houghton Mifflin, 1998), 301.

of the home. In the 1980s one wife complained, "I don't know why Japanese men marry if they are never going to be home."[16]

While earning more money, gaining legal protections, and enjoying greater freedom, women struggle for full equality in a hierarchical society obsessed with patriarchy and seniority. They are expected to marry, work, and then retire to raise children, even though many remain in paid work. According to one young woman, when she graduated from a top university, "our bright appearance [for the graduation ceremonies] in vividly colored kimonos [traditional robes] was deceiving. Deep in our hearts we knew that our opportunities to use our professional education would be few."[17] As single women discovered they could support themselves, the average marriage age for women rose from twenty-two in the 1950s to twenty-seven in the 1990s. In recent years, many women have avoided marriage altogether, preferring to concentrate on their careers or leisure interests. The resulting decline in marriage rates and fertility alarms politicians.

Despite popular images of timid Japanese females, assertive feminist organizations and leaders have publicized women's issues, while working women have lobbied companies for equal treatment and pay. Some women have moved into middle management or prestige occupations like law, journalism, college teaching, and diplomacy. Yet, women earn 60 percent less than males and largely lack political and economic power; only a few attain political or corporate leadership positions. In 2014, only five percent of senior managers were women, compared to 15-20 percent in Europe and North America. Gender equality activists admire former schoolteacher and journalist Ichikawa Fusae (ee-CHEE-kah-wah foo-SIGH) (1893–1981), who organized the women's suffrage movement in the 1920s and served in parliament for twenty-five years after World War II, campaigning for women's equality and human rights. Although traditional arranged marriages remain common, many men and women select their own spouse. More Japanese marry late or end unhappy marriages in divorce. Declining marriage rates make it easier for homosexuals to find social acceptance. Japanese society has always tolerated homosexual behavior, but now more are open about their sexual orientation.

Urban housing remains cramped; the elderly complain of neglect by children with no room in their small homes. Birth control and abortion were widely practiced in overcrowded Japan for centuries, and after World War II these practices, along with lower marriage rates, stabilized the population for several decades. Yet, by 2000 a birthrate well below replacement standards and a rapidly aging population (23 percent over sixty-five) had heavily burdened a shrinking work force to pay for retirees' benefits and a generous health care system. Despite this problem, Japan has discouraged immigration to provide new workers. Thousands of Brazil-born Japanese who returned to their ancestral homeland, mostly to work in factories, often face resentment; those unemployed are encouraged to return to Brazil. Foreigners, mostly Chinese and Koreans, number less than 2 percent of the population, in contrast to Britain (5 percent), Germany (10 percent), United States (12 percent), and Australia (22 percent). Despite laws banning discrimination, prejudice persists against Koreans and the 1 to 3 million *Burakumin*, a despised underclass for centuries who traditionally did jobs considered unclean.

Youth face their own pressures, including difficult exams to get into the better kindergartens, grade schools, and secondary schools; entrance exams for top universities so rigorous they are known as "exam hell"; and expectations to conform to mainstream society's values. These have encouraged youth rebellion. Some join motorcycle gangs, roaring along highways by day and neighborhood streets by night, annoying middle-class families. University students often support leftwing political organizations protesting issues such as U.S. military bases or the destruction of farmland to build new airports or business developments; some others join rightwing nationalist groups. Many younger people resent the long hours and sacrifices expected of employees, especially since a high

Junko Kimura/Getty Images

JAPANESE WOMEN COMMUTERS A female passenger boards a train compartment reserved for women in a subway station in Tokyo. Tokyo's subways are usually jammed with passengers, and special cars allow women to travel without fear of possible sexual harassment.

[16]Quoted in James L. McClain, *Japan: A Modern History* (New York: W.W. Norton, 2002), 585.
[17]Misuzu Hanikara, from Richard H. Minear, ed., *Through Japanese Eyes*, vol. 2 (New York: Praeger, 1974), 88.

standard of living has already been achieved. But student activism has waned in recent years. Eventually, most young protesters return to the mainstream, taking jobs in the corporate or industrial world. Some who cannot conform emigrate to North America, Europe, or Latin America, seeking a more free-spirited life.

The Japanese debate the blending of traditional and modern cultures and beliefs, East and West, and its effect on cultural identity. Artists and writers ponder whether synthesizing foreign and local ideas has been the nation's salvation or bane. Some worry that Japan's adoption of foreign culture has imperiled its own distinctive legacy. Others contend that the Japanese need to become more global-minded, even encouraging immigration to create a multicultural nation.

Films, some achieving worldwide recognition, have frequently analyzed questions about Japanese identity and problems facing society. While Japan's film industry, the world's third largest, produces escapist films portraying samurai warriors and gigantic city-wrecking monsters, it also makes thought-provoking masterpieces, especially grand historical epics and introspective psychological or sociological studies. One of the most skillful directors, Kurosawa Akira (**kur-o-SAH-wa a-KEER-a**) (1910–1998), mixed a distinctive Japanese style and setting with universal themes. *Rashomon* (1950), for example, examines the relativity of truth through varied perspectives on one event, the killing and violation of a feudal lord's wife by a bandit. Another Kurosawa film, *Ikuru* ("To Live") (1952), explores life's meaning; a Japanese bureaucrat dying of cancer overcomes endless red tape to facilitate the building of a small neighborhood park.

The Japanese have the world's highest literacy rate (99.9 percent) and the largest numbers of newspaper readers, magazine subscribers, and bookstores per capita, fostering both popular and serious literature. Kawabata Yasunari (**ka-wa-BAH-ta yah-suh-NAHR-ee**) (1899–1972) became the first Japanese novelist, in 1968, to receive the Nobel Prize for literature. Directly addressing Japanese identity, the writings of Mishima Yukio (**me-SHE-mah YOO-kee-oh**) (1925–1970) portray an effete, decadent "nation of shopkeepers" who need to renew the Tokugawa period's martial values. His best novel concerns a disturbed young man torn, like Mishima himself, between old samurai and modern Westernized values. For Mishima, a conflicted homosexual and avid body builder, life became art; in 1970 he publicly committed suicide in samurai style, sacrificing himself for the "old beautiful tradition of Japan, which is disappearing day by day."[18] His action shocked the Japanese, but his message died with him; Japan continued developing a consumer society.

Continuity has long characterized Japanese popular culture. Every sport, art form, and religion appearing in the past fifteen hundred years still attracts practitioners or followers. The Japanese remain passionate about sumo wrestling, an old sport in which two large, paunchy men attempt to push each other out of a small ring. Yet, today many top wrestlers are foreigners, among them Mongolians, east Europeans, Turks,

and Polynesians. But while kabuki or bunraku, theatrical forms appearing in the 1600s, still attract devoted audiences, and young Japanese women preparing for marriage often master the even older tea ceremony, many more Japanese follow professional baseball teams; consume Japanese comics, or *manga* (**mahn-gah**), and animated films, or *anime*, which are popular worldwide; and flock to Japanese or Western films, discos, pinball palaces, and video-game arcades. Japanese creations like Transformers, Power Rangers, Hello Kitty, The Iron Chef, karaoke, ramen noodles, and sushi have achieved global popularity. Modern Japanese, avidly adopting foreign cultural forms, frequent nightclubs featuring, among other musical styles, local and imported versions of rock, jazz, reggae, country western, rap, and salsa.

Organized religion continues to decline, although some remain deeply religious. Militant Buddhist groups claim several million followers, and various new religions based on Buddhist or Shinto traditions, or mixing of the two, address material prosperity and family problems. Nonetheless, contemporary Japanese are a largely secular people. In censuses, less than 15 percent report any formal religious affiliation. Despite a tiny Christian population (2 percent), millions of non-Christians ardently celebrate Christmas as an opportunity to give and receive gifts; department stores feature elaborate Christmas displays, complete with Santa Claus and brightly decorated Christmas trees. However, weak religious influence has not fostered social breakdown. The Japanese remain among the world's most law-abiding, peaceful citizens; morality mostly derives from fear of shaming the family or group rather than fear of retribution by gods or ancestors. Reluctance to disgrace the family suggests that Confucianism remains important. Yet conforming to the group and its rules has downsides. Criticizing an old saying—"the nail that sticks up gets hammered down"—Japanese liberals have sought a less conformist society that nourishes rather than inhibits individual genius.

Japan in the Global System

The Japanese have had to readjust their global views and economic expectations over the past several decades. Like their North American and European counterparts, Japanese companies, seeking cheaper labor, have established factories in Southeast Asia, South Korea, and China, a practice that has cost Japan jobs. In 1989 Japan's economy went into a severe downturn, thanks to overvalued stocks precipitating a crisis on the Tokyo Stock Exchange, global recession, and competition from newly industrializing Southeast Asia. This crisis began what observers called a "Lost Decade" of economic stagnation during the 1990s, and lingering into the 2000s, that discredited the Japan Inc. model. Eventually policies fostering higher growth rates renewed business confidence, but the recovery remained incomplete. The global economic crisis of 2008–2009 undermined export-oriented Japan, causing recession, bank failures, bankruptcies, and huge drops in

---

[18]Mishima, quoted in Mikiso Hane, *Modern Japan: A Historical Survey*, 2nd ed. (Boulder, CO: Westview Press, 1992), 371.

consumer spending abroad, even affecting leading manufacturers like Toyota and Sony. Like U.S. corporations, Japanese corporations reacted to recent foreign competition and crises by slashing salaries, cutting benefits, and even firing employees, modifying the business system that brought prosperity for a half century. Some newly unemployed men, especially office workers, ashamed to admit their humiliation to friends and families, spend each workday on park benches or in coffee houses. The economic problems have caused disenchanted voters to turn out several governments.

While comfortable as an economic powerhouse, Japan remains reluctant to assert its political and military power in the world, remembering how the attempt to dominate eastern Asia brought it disaster during World War II. Japan's main concerns are the world economy's health and access to overseas resources and markets. Hence, the Japanese prefer peaceful rather than military solutions to world problems. Despite their strategic alliance, Japan and its main trading partner, the United States, remain keen economic rivals and sometimes engage in trade disputes. Japanese leaders have promoted peaceful exchange with China and South Korea, two countries with long memories of Japanese imperialism. However, relations with South Korea and China have often been strained; the Chinese have demanded that Japan accept responsibility for wartime atrocities. In 2012 tensions flared over ownership of tiny, uninhabited islands midway between the countries. Resurgent Japanese and Chinese nationalisms clash, fanned by opportunistic political leaders seeking to solidify popular support. As China and several other Asian nations rise economically, Japan faces more competition and the challenge of maintaining its position in the world economy.

MAKE SURE YOU UNDERSTAND THESE KEY POINTS BEFORE MOVING ON

- After World War II, a U.S.-led occupation of Japan (SCAP) worked to rebuild Japan's economy while demilitarizing the country and encouraging the return of democracy.

- The Liberal Democratic Party dominated Japanese politics for decades, with a brief break in the 1990s, and the presence of U.S. military bases within Japan was seen by some as neocolonialism but freed up resources to help fuel the economy.

- Relying on innovation and collaboration between government and big business, Japan's economy has grown at a phenomenal rate.

- Japan's cities have become increasingly congested, men are expected to devote all their energy to work, women struggle for equality and increasingly choose work over marriage, and students face the pressure of an arduous education system.

- Japanese have managed to blend their traditions with modern and foreign influences and have maintained a high degree of social order in spite of low participation in organized religion.

aplia

The Little Dragons in the Asian Resurgence

T
S

What policies led to the rise of the "Little Dragon" nations and their dynamic economies?

While China and Japan were rising to regional and global power, several of their East Asian neighbors achieved economic development. Known as the **Little Dragons** because of the strong Chinese cultural influence on these nations, South Korea, Taiwan, Singapore, and Hong Kong built rapidly growing, industrializing economies. Except for Hong Kong, a British colony until 1997 and a free enterprise bastion, these societies largely followed the Meiji Japan model of state-directed capitalism and were inspired by Japan's resurgence after World War II, which depended on participation in the world economy. Sharing the Confucian cultural heritage emphasizing hard work, discipline, cooperation, and tolerance for authoritarian governments, the Little Dragons all achieved export-oriented industrialization, raising incomes, reducing poverty, and improving health and education. For South Korea, this development followed after a brutal war, leaving a hostile, rigidly communist North Korea on the border. In China's shadow, Taiwan found its own path, while Singapore (see Chapter 31) and Hong Kong (now part of China) are city-states with largely Chinese populations.

Korean Independence and War

The Korean War (1950–1953) was rooted in Korean nationalism, which simmered, despite fierce repression, during a half century of harsh Japanese colonial rule (see Chapters 23 and 24). While introducing some economic modernization, Japan arrested or executed Korean nationalists, conscripted Korean women to serve Japanese soldiers, relocated thousands of Korean workers to Japan, and manipulated divisions within Korean society. Christians constituted one influential group that grew in numbers; by the 1940s a fifth of Koreans were Catholics or Protestants. Another group gravitated toward communism, some escaping to the USSR to

Little Dragons South Korea, Taiwan, Singapore, and Hong Kong, which were strongly influenced by Chinese culture and built rapidly growing, industrializing economies.

form a revolutionary movement. Most Koreans followed Buddhism and Confucianism. Although Christians, communists, and traditionalists all hated Japanese rule and worked underground to oppose it, they could not cooperate with each other, and no unified nationalist movement emerged.

Japan's crushing defeat in 1945 meant Korea's political liberation and a chance to reclaim independence, free of foreign interference. But the United States quickly occupied the peninsula's southern half and the Soviet Union the north, bisecting Korea and making it a Cold War hostage. As the USSR and United States imposed rival governments, unification quickly became impossible. With Soviet help, communists led by the ruthless Kim Il-Sung **(KIM ill-soon)** (1912–1994) established North Korea. A clever strategist, Kim built a brutal communist system, eliminated his opponents, and reorganized rural society. But the impatient Kim disastrously overestimated the south's revolutionary potential and misjudged Americans' determination to stop spreading Soviet influence. The United States helped create and then supported a South Korean state headed by Rhee Syngman **(REE SING-man)** (1865–1965). An autocratic, politically conservative Christian from a powerful landlord family, Rhee had lived in exile in the United States for over two decades. Unpopular with the non-Christian majority, Rhee imprisoned or eliminated his opponents, sparking a leftist rebellion supported by many factory workers and peasants that American troops helped crush. Although less repressive than North Korea, Rhee's South Korea held some thirty thousand political prisoners.

The Korean War was created from the mixing of revolution and nationalism into a Cold War–driven stew (see Map 27.3). Historians still debate the origins of this conflict, which helped shape East Asian politics for over half a century. Both states, threatening to reunify Korea with military force, initiated border skirmishes. In this highly charged context, North Korea, with Soviet and Chinese approval, invaded the South in 1950. The Western-dominated United Nations authorized a U.S.-led military intervention to support South Korea, turning the Korean crisis into a Cold War confrontation in which Americans committed the most troops, war materials, and funding. U.S. president Harry Truman secretly planned to strike North Korea with atomic weapons if the USSR entered the war. But while the Soviets gave military supplies and advice, they sent no combat troops.

United Nations troops, aided by U.S. air power, quickly pushed the North Koreans back across the north-south border. But the United Nations move into North Korea and push toward China's border sparked a massive Chinese intervention that drove back United Nations troops and turned a likely victory into bitter stalemate. U.S. leaders had underestimated the Chinese people's willingness to fight and their military capabilities. When the war ended in 1953 with peace talks, the north-south boundary, remaining roughly where it was before the war, was now a heavily fortified zone. The war killed 400,000 Korean troops and 1 to 2 million civilians, some 400,000 Chinese, and 43,000 United Nations forces, 90 percent of them American, while generating millions of refugees who wandered the countryside, seeking food and shelter. Both Koreas were left in economic shambles.

MAP 27.3 **THE KOREAN WAR** In 1950, North Korean forces crossed the 38th parallel and invaded South Korea, but they were then pushed back north by United Nations forces led by the United States. The intervention of China in support of North Korea pushed the United Nations forces south and produced a military stalemate, preserving the border between North and South Korea at the 38th parallel. © 2015 Cengage Learning

The Two Koreas

South Korea's postwar rise was nearly as dramatic as Japan's. Closely allied to the United States, South Korean governments ranged from highly repressive military dictatorships from the 1950s through the mid-1980s, to moderate semidemocracies

SOUTH KOREAN ECONOMIC GROWTH One of South Korea's major, most diverse enterprises, the Hyundai Corporation, formed in 1976, engages in shipping, manufacturing, and trade, producing, among other products, chemicals, machinery, and information and telecommunications equipment. The ships in this company dry dock are being readied to carry Hyundai-made cars to distant markets around the world.

in the later 1980s, and then to liberal democracies with free elections since the early 1990s. All regimes aimed at economic development. The dictator Park Chung Hee (1917–1979) argued in 1970, "My chief concern was economic revolution. One must eat and breathe before concerning himself with politics, social affairs, and culture."[19] Prohibited from forming unions, many South Koreans experienced brutal working conditions, especially miners and teenage girls recruited into factory work. Americans protected South Korean regimes, permanently stationing troops and supplying generous economic and military aid. Six decades after the war, some forty thousand U.S. troops remained in South Korea.

South Korea enjoyed enormous economic growth, investing in the Middle East, Southeast Asia, and Russia while exporting automobiles and electronic products. By the 1990s South Korea had become the first non-Western nation since Japan to join the ranks of advanced industrial nations, and it later became a member of the G-20 grouping of industrial powers and a high-technology model. Having acquired living standards they could only dream of two decades earlier, with nearly universal literacy, South Koreans now enjoy the world's highest rate of high-speed Internet access: some 75 percent of households are wired, far more than in North

America and Europe. Both boys and girls receive free education through age twelve; the adult literacy rate is 98 percent. South Korean women have benefited from new job options in the professions and business. With more women in the work force and self-supporting, marriage rates declined and average births per woman fell dramatically, from 6 in 1990 to 1.6 in 2005, worrying leaders. In response in 2010, some national and local governments began sponsoring dating parties to promote courtship.

Economic growth also fostered political change. Democracy movements, begun in the 1960s, often faced government repression. One dissident wrote that "bullets, nightsticks, and fists are not the only forms of violence. A nation with no expression of dissent is a nation in ruins."[20] In 1980 the dictatorship brutally crushed an uprising in a southern province. When some five hundred demonstrators demanded an end to martial law, paratroopers slaughtered the protesters and local people. Hundreds of thousands of enraged citizens drove the troops out of the city, only to face a much larger force that killed over two thousand people. Eventually, political tensions diminished. Governments fostered more liberalization, tolerated a freer press, and made overtures toward former Soviet and Chinese enemies. By the early 1990s, as the middle class

[19]Quoted in Frank Gibney, *The Pacific Century: America and Asia in a Changing World* (New York: Charles Scribner's, 1992), 231.
[20]Cho Se-hui, quoted in Bruce Cumings, *Korea's Place in the Sun: A Modern History* (New York: W.W. Norton, 1997), 337.

and organized labor grew, democracy flowered, though sometimes it was sullied by political corruption. South Koreans are proud of their freedom, their bustling cities, and their popular culture's influence in both China and Japan.

But while the country and its 50 million people (one-quarter of them Christians) have clearly outshined repressive North Korea, problems have arisen. Many rural people and unskilled workers did not share in the prosperity, while factories expected long hours from poorly paid workers. Frustrated at their prospects, thousands, many of them middle class, emigrated, especially to the United States. The economic slowdown beginning in 1997, and then the 2008–2009 global economic crisis, which cost many jobs, also spurred discontent. By 2011 business had largely rebounded, although it was a largely jobless recovery. Another problem is that while many South Koreans have welcomed U.S. bases, others consider them an affront to nationalism. Koreans yearn for reunification and an end to the peninsular cold war. After years of hostility, and owing partly to South Korean efforts to improve relations, North and South Korea finally achieved a wary peaceful coexistence. A dialogue known as the "sunshine policy," begun in 1998, fostered limited cross-border trade and some South Korean visits to family members in North Korea not seen since the early 1950s. Televised images of South Koreans tearfully embracing aging parents or siblings mesmerized the nation. Then in 2000 South Korean president Kim Dae-jung (**kim day-chung**) (1925–2009), a liberal reformer and former dissident, visited North Korea, an event unthinkable a decade earlier. Yet national reconciliation still remains a dream; South Koreans worry about North Korea's military capabilities and its quest to build nuclear weapons. Tensions increased after 2009, with a more conservative South Korean president skeptical of negotiations over these issues.

North Korea's leaders chose a completely different path from South Korea. The Korean War devastated the country, though North Korea quickly recovered with Soviet and Chinese aid. From 1948 until his death in 1994, Kim Il-Sung created a personality cult around himself as the "Great Leader." North Koreans were taught that they owed everything—jobs, goods, schooling, food, military security—to Kim. To ensure loyalty and deflect blame for failures, Kim purged many communist officials and jailed or executed thousands of dissidents. Kim mixed Stalinist economic planning and central direction, emphasizing heavy industry and weapons, with Maoist self-reliance. Hence, North Koreans did not enjoy the rising living standards of South Koreans, who live about ten years longer. Although North Korea contained most of Korea's factories and mines, built during Japanese colonial times, the huge military establishment drained resources to deter enemies and intimidate South Korea.

Like nineteenth-century Korea's Confucian kings, North Korea stressed group loyalty, ultranationalism, and independence from foreign influence. A small political and military elite, isolated from peasants' and workers' bleak lives, enjoyed comfortable apartments and sufficient food, controlling people through regimentation and restriction of information. To monitor activities and thoughts, the government required everyone to register at a public security office and urged people to spy on their families and neighbors. To prevent contrary views, radios received only the government station. Political prisoners and people caught fleeing to China or South Korea faced long terms in harsh concentration camps or execution. The economy declined rapidly, thanks to poor management, commodity shortages, and rigid policies. Satellite photos of the Korean peninsula at night revealed the stark differences in electrical power between brilliantly lit South Korea and completely dark North Korea. Even the capital city's lights were mostly turned off by 9 P.M. U.S. diplomatic and economic pressure isolated the regime, making North Korea totally reliant economically on the Soviet bloc; when it collapsed in 1989, Russia and China then demanded that North Korea pay cash for oil and other imports.

North Korea's problems increased after Kim Jong-Il (**chong-ill**) (b. 1942), known as the "Dear Leader," succeeded his deceased father in 1995. When the nation faced mass starvation, South Korea, Japan, and the United States, anxious to discourage desperate military action, sent food aid. Many people still died or were malnourished, and thousands fled to China seeking food and work. Yet the regime avoided collapse, even after inexperienced Kim Jong-Un, a virtual unknown thought to be around twenty-five years old, became leader after his father's death in 2011, continuing the family dynasty. Thanks to isolation and tight information control, few North Koreans traveled abroad, studied foreign languages, met foreigners, or encountered foreign publications, films, and music. Meanwhile, a small dissident movement, risking harsh reprisals, smuggled in food from China and videotapes, books, and music from South Korea. Estimates of political prisoners, held in brutal conditions, range from 80,000 to 200,000.

North Korea worried both regional and world leaders, with its military force twice as large as South Korea's and capable of building nuclear weapons. But with both Koreas possessing lethal military forces, South Korea boasting twice the population, and U.S. nuclear weapons in South Korea, all-out war became less likely, encouraging the search for common ground. Economic disasters, especially food shortages, sometimes softened North Korea's position; after 1998 South Korea actively sought better relations to reduce the threat from its dangerous northern neighbor and its unpredictable leaders. Indeed, isolated by its bellicose policies, North Korea relies mostly on trade with China and South Korea. North Korea's neighbors and the United States sought diplomatic ways to eliminate the possibility of a conventional war or a nuclear confrontation, but by 2008 tensions returned; often disapproving the regime's unpredictable behavior and bellicose rhetoric but fearing North Korean collapse, China remains the only major ally. North Korea has continued testing nuclear weapons and missiles, unsettling the region.

Taiwan and China

With the communist triumph on the mainland in 1949, Chiang Kai-shek and his nationalist government relocated to mountainous, subtropical Taiwan island, where they reestablished the Republic of China. Taiwan had only become a part of Chinese territory in the seventeenth and eighteenth centuries; in 1910 it became a Japanese colony. Japan ruled Taiwan less harshly than it did Korea, financing industrialization that produced higher living standards than in mainland China. After World War II China reclaimed the island, but in 1947 local resentment of Chiang's heavy-handed regime sparked an island-wide uprising. To quell the unrest, Chiang dispatched 100,000 troops that killed 30,000 to 40,000 Taiwanese, including many local leaders.

As the Republic collapsed in 1948–1949, Chiang and 2 million mainlanders took their government, Nationalist Party, remaining military forces, priceless national museum art collections, and China's national treasury to Taiwan. These mainlanders and their descendants eventually constituted 15 percent of the total island population, which numbered 23 million by 2012. Because the minority mainlanders dominated politics, the economy, and the military, the majority Taiwanese, although Chinese in culture and language, often considered the mainlanders colonizers. Hoping to retake the mainland, Chiang viewed Taiwan as a temporary refuge. After his death in 1975, many mainlanders (and their children), realizing that a return to the mainland was unlikely and that Taiwan might be their permanent home, cultivated better relations with the Taiwanese. However, two governments claiming to represent China created a long-term diplomatic problem for the world community. Both the People's Republic and the Republic on Taiwan regarded the island as an integral part of China rather than a separate nation, a "one China policy" endorsed by most of the world.

Learning from their China defeat and using generous U.S. aid, the Republic's leaders promoted rapid industrial and agricultural growth, more equitable wealth distribution, the land reform they neglected on the mainland, and access to credit facilities; as a result, the peasantry prospered. As in South Korea and Meiji Japan, Taiwan's economy mixed capitalism and foreign investment with government planning and investment. Light industry and manufacturing accounted for half the economic production and most exports. The world's third largest manufacturer of computer hardware, between the early 1970s and the late 1990s Taiwan enjoyed more years of double-digit growth than any other nation. Taiwanese companies established operations in Southeast Asia, China, Africa, and Latin America, and Taiwan's economic indicators far surpassed China's: a per capita annual income of $36,000, 99 percent of households owning a color television, 96 percent literacy, and a life expectancy of seventy-eight. Rapid development, however, brought environmental destruction, traffic congestion, political corruption, and a severe economic slowdown in 1997 and 2008–2009. Concrete high-rise buildings increasingly displace the lush greenery of the mountains around the capital, Taipei.

Modernization has challenged Chinese values and traditions. Small roadside cafés selling noodle soup and meat dumplings often close, unable to compete with U.S. fast-food restaurants and convenience stores selling Coca-Cola, hamburgers, and ice cream. Rampant materialism concerns those who believe that life should offer more than luxury goods and money. While Confucian values fostered material success, some worry that respect for parents and concern for community rather than the individual are threatened. Yet, traditional Chinese culture remains stronger in Taiwan than on the mainland. Most Taiwanese describe themselves as Buddhists, Daoists, Confucianists, or a mix of the three; some 5 percent are Christians, while several million others infrequently attend temples or churches.

Until the later 1980s Taiwan followed the authoritarian Little Dragon political model, with a police state holding numerous political prisoners. Chiang Kai-shek made it illegal to advocate permanent independence from China, and the PRC also opposed those favoring two separate Chinese nations. For four decades Chiang's Nationalist Party ruled, but in 1989, nudged by a growing middle class seeking liberalization, the party permitted opposition candidates to run in elections. Gradually the regime recognized civil liberties, including freedom of speech and press. The 2000 elections swept into office the Democratic Progressive Party (DPP), largely supported by native Taiwanese; many party leaders supported separate Taiwan nationhood, angering both nationalist leaders on Taiwan and mainland communist leaders. However, Taiwan's voters seemed less eager to confront China and in 2008 replaced the DPP government, beset by corruption, with the nationalists, who sought friendlier ties with China and remain in power today. However, in 2014 a proposed free trade pact with China enraged and energized the opposition, leading to massive protests by students and workers fearing more influence by the Peoples' Republic over the island.

China remains Taiwan's permanent challenge. Fearing an invasion to forcibly annex the island, Taiwan lavishly funded its military, kept a large standing army, bought the latest fighter jets and gunboats, and maintained a defense alliance with the United States. But in 1978 the United States recognized the PRC as China's only government, withdrawing diplomatic recognition from the Republic but maintaining a strong economic presence and commitment to defend Taiwan. In the later 1980s Taiwan and China began improving relations. Informal trade grew substantially; many Taiwanese visited the mainland for business or family reunions, while mainland tourists and students went to Taiwan. However, doubts about China's eventual liberalization and democratization, in addition to unease at occasional Chinese military exercises, precluded any serious negotiations on reunification. Any Chinese military action against Taiwan would alarm Japan and might draw in the United States. Taiwan's political future remains an open question, fiercely debated by Taiwanese and their several competing political parties.

The Little Dragons in the Global System

The rise of the Pacific Rim in the late twentieth century, including China, Japan, and the Little Dragons, reshaped the global system. The quarter of the world's population living along the western edge of the Pacific Basin outpaced the West and the rest of the world in economic growth while maintaining political stability. A global economy based three decades ago on the United States, western Europe, and Japan now has to accommodate China and the Little Dragons. Using the Meiji Japan model, the Little Dragons industrialized and then diversified into high technology to make computers and other electronics products, posing an economic challenge to Japan and the West. However, the Little Dragons have recently lost market share as China manufactures competing electronic products, fueling protests against trade pacts with China in Taiwan.

Some trends suggested that the Pacific Rim nations were becoming an Asian counterpart to the European Community, the free-trade zone formed by western European nations, perhaps fostering a **Pacific Century** dominated economically by Asian nations rather than European and North America in the twenty-first century. Many East and Southeast Asian nations worked on closer economic cooperation, with Japan and China forming the hubs. But in 1997 and again in 2008–2009, a severe economic meltdown hit South Korea, Taiwan, Japan, and industrializing Southeast Asia. As businesses closed, unemployment soared and economies went into deep recession. Yet, many economies rebounded by 2012. Thus both the Pacific Rim countries and the United States face uncertain futures but will likely play major roles in the future. In many respects, East Asia has returned to its historical role as a key engine of the world economy.

Pacific Century The possible shift of global economic power from Europe and North America to the Pacific Rim in the twenty-first century.

MAKE SURE YOU UNDERSTAND THESE KEY POINTS BEFORE MOVING ON

- South Korean governments have grown more tolerant of internal dissent and more open to relations with former enemies such as communist North Korea and China, though their primary emphasis has been on economic growth.

- After the Korean War, North Korea recovered with support from the USSR and China and was ruled as a repressive communist dictatorship with a centrally planned economy whose shortcomings led to widespread food shortages in the 1990s.

- With the communists ruling mainland China, the Nationalists took over Taiwan, which they ruled as a police state and turned into an economic powerhouse, but relations with mainland China have continued to be tense.

- China and the "Little Dragons" (Taiwan, South Korea, Singapore, and Hong Kong) grew rapidly in the late twentieth century, leading to predictions of a coming "Pacific Century," but several slowdowns dampened such expectations.

aplia

CHAPTER SUMMARY

After World War II, East Asia experienced revolutionary upheavals and dramatic economic development, generating a resurgence of the region's world influence. The communist triumph in China began a new era of change. After experimenting with a Soviet-style Stalinist development model, China's leader, Mao Zedong, imposed his own version of communism, emphasizing collective efforts, political values, mass mobilization, and rural communes. Then Mao sparked the Cultural Revolution, which created turmoil while attacking the bureaucracy and those who opposed his political and economic vision. After Mao's death, Deng Xiaoping led China in a new direction; his market socialism energized the economy but led to tensions and then repression. During the 1990s market Leninism continued the economic reforms, providing a basis for rapid growth. China became a world economic power, but the growing wealth inequalities and corruption have threatened to destabilize the nation.

The experiences of Japan and the Little Dragons differed from China's. After the World War II defeat and U.S. occupation, Japan rapidly rose to become an economic powerhouse, based on mixing political democracy with capitalism; government and business worked together. Japanese rebuilt their industries and fostered new forms of business and production. But social change came slowly, leaving Japan hierarchical. The Little Dragon nations of South Korea and Taiwan achieved industrial growth and prosperity by borrowing the Japanese model, mixing free markets with government intervention and eventually fostering democracy. North Korea chose Stalinism and isolation from the world. The dynamism of most East Asian nations suggests that they have recovered from the disasters they experienced from the mid-1800s to the mid-1900s resulting from Western imperialism, Japanese expansion, and war, but their overall prospects remain tied to the health of the world economy.

KEY TERMS

Pacific Rim (p. 665)
communes (p. 668)
Great Leap Forward (p. 668)
Great Proletarian Cultural Revolution
(p. 669)

Red Guards (p. 671)
Iron Rice Bowl (p. 671)
market socialism (p. 672)
market Leninism (p. 674)

Japan, Inc. (p. 682)
salaryman (p. 682)
Little Dragons (p. 685)
Pacific Century (p. 690)

28 Rebuilding Europe and Russia, Since 1945

FALL OF THE BERLIN WALL In 1989, as communist governments collapsed in eastern Europe, peaceful protesters climbed on top of the Berlin Wall, which had already been decorated with graffiti. The wall, which divided communist East and democratic West Berlin, was soon torn down.

This [united] Europe must be born. And she will, when Spaniards say "our Chartres," Englishmen "our Cracow," Italians "our Copenhagen," and Germans "our Bruges." Then Europe will live.

—Spanish writer Salvador de Madariaga, 1948[1]

French banker's son turned socialist politician Jacques Delors (deh-LOW-er) faced a challenge. Having lived through the Great Depression, World War II, and the Cold War, he now dedicated himself to building a united Europe and in 1985 became president of the European Commission, established to reconcile national loyalties with more political cooperation. In 1991, Delors convened the leaders of twelve closely linked European nations in Maastricht, Holland, a city full of historic buildings. Marshaling all his diplomatic skills, he prodded them to conclude a historic agreement for increased cooperation, affirming a dream of European unity that had long percolated among visionaries. Europeans, chastened by centuries of conflict, seemed ready to subordinate national interests to a common good. Delors asked leaders to transform the economic and political alliance begun in the late 1940s and expanded in the 1950s into a more comprehensive union.

In the same month the Soviet Union (USSR) dissolved. With their biggest communist rival no longer a threat, European leaders hoped that linking their countries would ensure a stable, peaceful future. In theory the European Union would stretch from the Atlantic to the western frontier of Russia, allowing goods and people to freely cross borders and to use a single currency, the *euro*. Voters in all member nations later ratified the Maastricht Treaty, though debates continued as new members joined. While facing road bumps, given the centuries of European strife, the European Union was a huge achievement.

From 1945 until 1990 three themes dominated European history: the Cold War shaped by the United States and the USSR, each with political and military power vastly exceeding that of all other nations; the rebirth of western European wealth and influence; and the movement toward European unity represented by Maastricht. After World War II, which left most countries in shambles, Europe became divided into mutually hostile political and military blocs. While eastern Europe came under Soviet domination, enduring authoritarian communist governments, much of western Europe recovered its prosperity under democratic governments that emphasized consensus rather than military might. After 1989, when the communist governments collapsed, this movement accelerated, opening the way for a new, interconnected Europe. But serious economic problems since 2007 have partly undermined progress, raising questions about Europe's future and identity.

[1]Quoted in Norman Davies, *Europe: A History* (New York: Harper, 1998), 1066.

Western Europe: Revival and Unity

What factors fostered the movement toward unity in western Europe?

After emerging from World War II economically bankrupt, western Europe rapidly recovered with American aid. Most western Europeans reestablished working multiparty democracies that guaranteed personal freedom. Beginning in 1947, however, Europe was split into two mutually hostile camps—western and eastern Europe—with rival military forces and different postwar reconstruction models. Gradually West Germany, France, and Britain led a rebuilt, increasingly unified western Europe and regained world influence, while economic prosperity blunted radicalism.

Marshall Plan A recovery program created for western Europe by the United States that aimed to prevent communist expansion and to spread liberal economic principles.

The Remaking of European Nations

World War II cost some 50 million lives, reduced major cities to rubble, and destroyed bridges, tunnels, and roads. Transportation, food, housing, and fuel were in short supply. Political boundaries redrawn after the war had displaced many people, including 10 million Germans who were forced to leave eastern Europe and move to Germany. Emotionally traumatized by wartime atrocities, Europeans saw their prestige in tatters. War crimes trials held in Nuremberg, Germany, in 1946 condemned Nazi leaders to death and declared crimes against humanity, especially genocide, indefensible.

But economic growth fostered a new Europe. In 1947 the U.S. secretary of state, World War II general George Marshall (1880–1959), proposed that Americans help restore Europe's economic health to achieve stability and guarantee peace. The **Marshall Plan** created a recovery program to prevent communist expansion and spread liberal economic principles, such as free markets. Between 1948 and 1952 the United States provided $13 billion, half going to Britain, France, and West Germany. In exchange, American business enjoyed greater

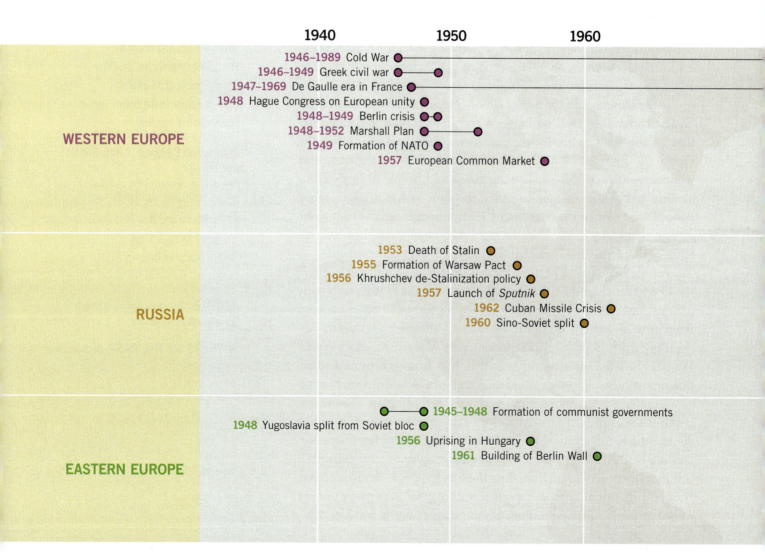

	1940	1950	1960

WESTERN EUROPE
- 1946–1989 Cold War
- 1946–1949 Greek civil war
- 1947–1969 De Gaulle era in France
- 1948 Hague Congress on European unity
- 1948–1949 Berlin crisis
- 1948–1952 Marshall Plan
- 1949 Formation of NATO
- 1957 European Common Market

RUSSIA
- 1953 Death of Stalin
- 1955 Formation of Warsaw Pact
- 1956 Khrushchev de-Stalinization policy
- 1957 Launch of *Sputnik*
- 1962 Cuban Missile Crisis
- 1960 Sino-Soviet split

EASTERN EUROPE
- 1945–1948 Formation of communist governments
- 1948 Yugoslavia split from Soviet bloc
- 1956 Uprising in Hungary
- 1961 Building of Berlin Wall

access to European markets. The Marshall Plan restored agriculture, industry, and international trade. The rapid economic resurgence from 1948 to 1965, unmatched in world history except for Japan's postwar recovery (see Chapter 27), also resulted from liberal democracy, modern production and managerial techniques, and advances in science, technology, transportation, and agriculture.

At the same time, British leader Winston Churchill (1874–1965) warned that Soviet expansionism had built "an iron curtain" across Europe, dividing western Europe from eastern Europe and pro-Western, capitalist West Germany from communist East Germany. This Cold War division stimulated western European cooperation. When delegates met in 1948 at the Hague in Holland and called for a democratic economic union, Churchill urged them to "design a United Europe, where men and women of every country will think of being European as of belonging to their native land, and wherever they go in this wide domain they will truly feel 'Here I am at home.'"[2]

The Hague Congress created a European assembly and human rights court, generating the "European Movement."

Western Europeans also committed to parliamentary democracy, including for the surviving constitutional monarchies—Belgium, Britain, the Netherlands, and the Scandinavian nations—where kings and queens symbolized their people but enjoyed little power. In the 1970s democrats overthrew longtime dictators in Spain, Portugal, and Greece. Britain, France, Italy, and West Germany became the most influential European nations.

New political alignments emerged. Political stability depended on improving relations between France and Germany and helping Germany recover from war. Although Charles De Gaulle (1890–1970), the crusty general and proudly nationalist French leader (1947–1969), imagined France "like the princess in the fairy stories, as dedicated to an exalted and exceptional destiny,"[3] he made French-German reconciliation the cornerstone of French policy. Similarly, West German leaders

---

[2]Quoted in ibid.
[3]Quoted in Felix Gilbert with David Clay Large, *The End of the European Era, 1890 to the Present*, 4th ed. (New York: W.W. Norton, 1991), 429.

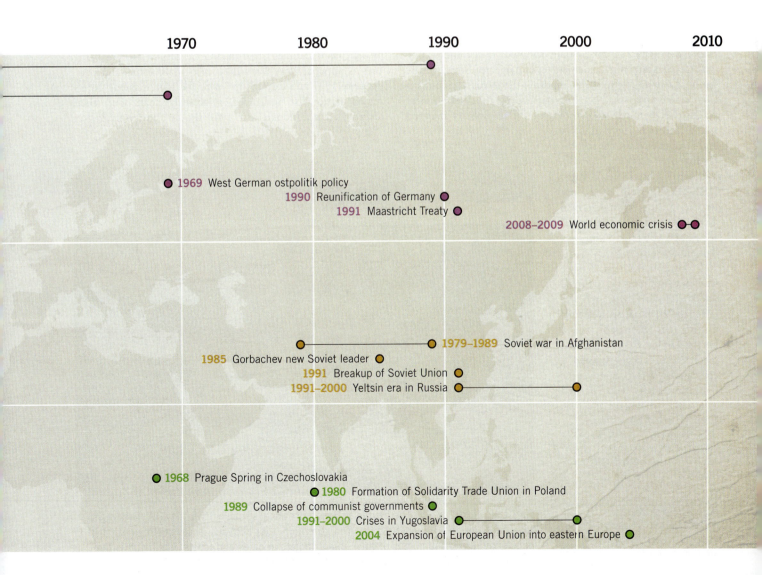

1970   1980   1990   2000   2010

1969 West German ostpolitik policy
1990 Reunification of Germany
1991 Maastricht Treaty
2008–2009 World economic crisis

1979–1989 Soviet war in Afghanistan
1985 Gorbachev new Soviet leader
1991 Breakup of Soviet Union
1991–2000 Yeltsin era in Russia

1968 Prague Spring in Czechoslovakia
1980 Formation of Solidarity Trade Union in Poland
1989 Collapse of communist governments
1991–2000 Crises in Yugoslavia
2004 Expansion of European Union into eastern Europe

sought a cooperative relationship. In the 1960s West German chancellor Willy Brandt (1913–1992), a fervent anti-Nazi who had fled Hitler, furthered Germany's reconciliation with its neighbors and accepted German responsibilities for the war and the new imposed borders, which awarded much German territory to Poland. Economic growth improved French-German relations. West Germany's economy was central to western European recovery; by 1960 West Germany, firmly allied with France, accounted for a fifth of the world's manufactured goods, surpassing Britain.

New political parties and movements took shape. Christian Democrats, conservatives backed by the Catholic Church who emphasized Christian values and traditional families, either formed governments or led oppositions in a half dozen countries, including West Germany and Italy. But, thanks partly to corruption scandals, by the 1990s they lost considerable support. On the left social democratic parties, favoring generous welfare programs to provide all citizens a safety net, came to power in several countries, including Britain and France, and moved toward state ownership of large industries such as steel and railroads. Eventually most social democrats, such as the British Labor Party, abandoned state ownership and economic planning for free markets.

Meanwhile, the western European communist parties declined rapidly, except in France, Italy, Portugal, and Spain. Seeking popular support, some adopted **Eurocommunism**, which embraced political democracy and rejected Soviet domination. Losing most of their support in the 1990s, communists fragmented into small feuding parties. By the 1980s a new political movement had an impact. The **Greens** rejected militarism and heavy industry and favored environmental protection over economic growth. Women such as Petra Kelly (1947–1992) were prominent leaders in the West German Green Party, helping it appeal to women voters and win parliamentary seats.

However, western Europe was not immune to political unrest. In the Greek civil war (1946-1949), conservatives supporting the monarchy, aided by the United States, defeated revolutionaries who wanted a communist state. Some ethnic minorities who desired independence or autonomy spurred violence and sometimes terrorism. For example, the Basque people, who live mostly in northern Spain and speak a language completely different from Spanish, have long sought their own nation. An underground Basque independence movement, ETA (for "Basque Homeland and Freedom"), has carried out assassinations and bombings. Many Catalans in northeast Spain also dream of their own country but are nonviolent. For decades the Catholic minority in Northern Ireland (Ulster), which was part of Great Britain, sought a merger with the largely Catholic Irish Republic, while the majority Protestants wanted to remain a British province. Extremist Catholic and Protestant paramilitary groups attacked each other and the British army, causing thousands of civilian deaths, but violence ebbed as relations between Britain and Ireland improved. In recent years other separatist movements—Scottish nationalists in the United Kingdom, Venetians, South Tyroleans, and the Lombardy region in Italy, Flemish in Belgium—have gained strength, motivated by economic crises.

Decolonization and the Cold War

Most European colonizers, gradually abandoning efforts to quell Asian and African nationalist movements, eventually gave up their colonial territories. Britain, whose empire occupied an area 125 times larger than Great Britain itself, realizing that its imperial glory was fading, recognized India's independence in 1947 and Burma's in 1948. The Dutch, facing determined nationalist resistance, reluctantly abandoned their lucrative colony, Indonesia, in 1950. By the mid-1960s Britain

Eurocommunism A form of communism in western Europe that embraced political democracy and free elections and that rejected Soviet domination.

Greens A political movement in western Europe that rejected militarism and heavy industry and favored environmental protection over economic growth.

JAVIER SORIANO/AFP/Getty Images

BASQUE TERRORISM The extremist Basque nationalist movement, the ETA, has waged a terrorist campaign against the Spanish government for decades, assassinating dozens of people and exploding bombs at government targets in cities and towns. The result is the sort of destruction shown here after an attack on the Madrid airport in 2006.

had turned over most of its African, Asian, and Caribbean colonies to local leaders, retaining only a few tiny outposts, such as Gibraltar, a strategically valuable peninsula on Spain's southern coast, and some tiny Caribbean and South Atlantic islands. British control of Gibraltar sometimes complicates relations with Spain. While postimperial Britain balanced a special relationship to the United States with closer European links, it continued to maintain economic ties to many former colonies. The British **Commonwealth of Nations**, established in 1931 and comprising fifty-four states by 2013, provided an ongoing formal connection and forum for cooperating and discussing issues of mutual interest.

By contrast, France and Portugal only grudgingly recognized the inevitable. In the 1940s many thousands died as France attempted to suppress nationalist rebellions in Algeria and Vietnam. Criticizing torture against Algerian rebels, anticolonial French philosopher Jean-Paul Sartre wrote: "We are sick, very sick. Feverish and prostrate, obsessed by old dreams of glory and the foreboding of its shame, France is struggling in the grip of a nightmare it is unable either to flee or to decipher."[4] In 1954, unable to defeat communist-led revolutionaries, France withdrew from Vietnam, and in 1962 it left Algeria, causing 800,000 embittered European settlers to flee to France. France retained a few small Caribbean, Pacific, and Indian Ocean islands and French Guiana. It eventually established close relations with many former colonies, including an enduring economic connection that critics considered neocolonialism because French business interests and advisers remained prominent. Meanwhile, Portugal wasted lives and wealth violently resisting African nationalist movements but, after democrats overthrew the long-standing fascist dictatorship, granted its African colonies independence in 1975.

Beginning in 1946, the Cold War shaped European roles in the world. The USSR helped install communist governments in eastern Europe and East Germany, while the United States assumed the military burden for protecting western Europe. In 1949 strong European and U.S. fears of possible Soviet attack spurred formation of the North Atlantic Treaty Organization, or **NATO**, a military alliance linking nine western European countries with the United States and Canada that would allow coordination of defense policies against the USSR and its communist allies, the **Soviet bloc**, to repulse any potential military attack across the "iron curtain" frontier. The United States established permanent military bases in NATO countries, especially West Germany. The Soviets responded in 1955 by forming the **Warsaw Pact**, a defense alliance linking communist-ruled eastern European countries with the USSR (see Map 28.1). Europeans worried that nuclear weapons could obliterate their cities in minutes and that a U.S.-USSR nuclear conflict might inevitably destroy Europe as well. By the 1980s senior NATO and Warsaw Pact officers had spent their careers preparing for a war that never came.

The Cold War and NATO were partly generated by Germany's postwar division. The United States, Britain, France, and the USSR each had an occupation zone and also divided up the German capital, Berlin. In 1948 the three Western powers united their occupation zones. Angered, the USSR blockaded Berlin to prevent supplies from reaching the city by land through Soviet-controlled East Germany, forcing a year-long airlift of food and fuel. In 1949 the USSR allowed the creation of the Federal Republic of Germany, or West Germany, while forming the communist German Democratic Republic, or East Germany. West Germany later joined NATO.

Cold War fears gradually slackened as the danger of actual war faded; western Europeans reappraised their policies toward both superpowers. Some, especially in Britain, promoted the U.S. alliance, but many Europeans resented what they considered irresponsible U.S. foreign policies. Most opposed the American war in Vietnam and U.S. interventions to overthrow left-leaning governments in Latin America, such as Guatemala (1954) and Chile (1973). In 1969 West Germany's Social Democratic, anticommunist chancellor Willy Brandt's **ostpolitik** ("eastern politics") policy, which sought reconciliation between West and East Germany and expanded dialogue with the USSR, fostered a thaw between West Germany and the Soviet bloc, giving hope to eastern Europeans who wanted more freedom. Gradually western Europeans rebuilt their own military forces, becoming less reliant on U.S. power. Despite the differences, the Western alliance and NATO remained strong because of mutual interests during the Cold War.

From Cooperation to European Community

Western Europe's role in the global system changed. Between the two world wars Europeans owned enterprises all over the globe, including Indian tea plantations, Malayan rubber estates, African mines, and South American railroads. But during the 1940s Europeans lost influence to the United States. Concluding they had no choice but to cooperate, in 1949 ten nations formed the Council of Europe, based on shared cultural heritage and democratic principles, which produced the European Convention on Human Rights, the root of a Europe-wide justice system and court. But some leaders wanted more. Jean Monnet **(MOAN-ay)** (1888–1979), a French economist, financier, and former League of Nations official often called the "Father of United Europe," and French prime minister Robert Schuman (1886–1963), who promoted French-German reconciliation, wanted to make war not only unthinkable but also impossible. To encourage better economic coordination, their European Coal and Steel Community (ECSC) formed in 1951 with six members, a first step for unity and peace. But some nations, including Britain, feared losing economic independence and declined to join.

Commonwealth of Nations A forum, established by Britain in 1931, for discussing issues of mutual interest with its former colonies.

NATO A military alliance, formed in 1949, that linked nine western European countries with the United States and Canada.

Soviet bloc The Soviet Union and the communist states allied with it.

Warsaw Pact A defense alliance formed in 1955 that linked the communist-ruled eastern European countries with the USSR.

ostpolitik A West German policy, promoted by Chancellor Willy Brandt, that sought a reconciliation between West and East Germany and an expanded dialogue with the USSR.

---

[4]Quoted in Harold James, *Europe Reborn: A History, 1914–2000* (New York: Longman, 2001), 248.

MAP 28.1 MILITARY ALLIANCES AND MULTINATIONAL ECONOMIC GROUPINGS, 1949–1989 Post–World War II Europe was divided by Cold War politics into communist and noncommunist blocs. Most western European nations joined the NATO defense alliance. Western Europeans also cooperated in economic matters. By 1989 the Common Market had expanded from six to eleven members. The Soviet bloc counterpart, COMECON, had eight members. © 2015 Cengage Learning

Participants in the Marshall Plan

Member of NATO,* formed in 1949

Member of COMECON,** formed in 1949, and the Warsaw Pact, organized in 1955

Member of the European Common Market, formed in 1958

Iron Curtain

* North Atlantic Treaty Organization
** Council for Mutual Economic Assistance

400 Mi.
400 Km.
200
200

UNION OF SOVIET SOCIALIST REPUBLICS

Exploded first atomic bomb, 1949

Moscow

FINLAND
Helsinki

SWEDEN
Stockholm

NORWAY
Oslo

Copenhagen

DENMARK

Berlin blockade, 1948–1949

Warsaw

POLAND

East Berlin

West Berlin

EAST GERMANY

Communist coup, 1948
U.S.S.R. invasion, 1968

Prague

CZECHOSLOVAKIA

Budapest

HUNGARY

Vienna

AUSTRIA

Joined NATO, 1955

Zones of occupation ended, 1955

Revolution, 1956

ROMANIA
Bucharest

BULGARIA
Sofia

YUGOSLAVIA
Belgrade

Tito-Stalin schism, 1948

Tiranë

ALBANIA

Left COMECON, 1961
Withdrew from WP, 1968

GREECE
Athens

Truman Doctrine, 1947
Joined NATO, 1952

TURKEY
Ankara

CYPRUS
Nicosia

Truman Doctrine, 1947
Joined NATO, 1952
Joined Common Market, 1981

Black Sea

Caspian Sea

Volga R.
Don R.
Dnieper R.
Danube R.

U.S. loan of $3.5 billion, 1946
Exploded first atomic bomb, 1952
Joined Common Market, 1973

UNITED KINGDOM
London
Dublin

IRELAND

Joined Common Market, 1973

North Sea

WEST GERMANY
Bonn

Amsterdam
NETHERLANDS
Brussels
BELGIUM
Paris **LUX.**

SWITZ.
Bern

FRANCE

Exploded first atomic bomb, 1960
Withdrew from NATO, 1966

ITALY
Rome

Corsica
Sardinia

Sicily

Balearic Is.

Joined Common Market, 1986

SPAIN
Madrid

Joined NATO, 1982
Joined Common Market, 1986

PORTUGAL
Lisbon

Joined Common Market, 1986

Mediterranean Sea

ATLANTIC OCEAN

Arctic Circle

ICELAND
Reykjavik

Joined Common Market, 1973

GDP per capita

- Over $40,000
- $30,000–40,000
- $25,000–29,999
- $20,000–24,999
- $15,000–19,999
- $10,000–14,999
- Under $10,000

MAP 28.2 **EUROPE'S GROSS DOMESTIC PRODUCT** The gross domestic product, or the official measure of the output of goods and services in a national economy, provides a good summary of a nation's economic production. In the early twenty-first century, Norway, Ireland, and Switzerland were the most productive European countries on a per capita basis, while former Soviet bloc nations had the weakest performance. © 2015 Cengage Learning

The Common Market, later known as the European Community (EC) and then the European Union (EU), was formed in 1957 with six members: France, Italy, West Germany, the Netherlands, Belgium, and Luxembourg. Removing tariff barriers facilitated free movement of capital and labor across borders. Inviting others to join, the EC added Britain, Ireland, and Denmark in 1973, creating unprecedented economic unity in the world's largest free trade zone. Monnet and Schuman dreamed of a Europe united politically: societies that depend on one another, they reasoned, won't go to war. But nationalism and disagreements occasionally flared up; member nations squabbled to get the best deal for their own farmers or businesses; and the British, an island people proud of their distinctive

traditions, periodically threatened to withdraw. Today many Britons still favor quitting the union. Some doubters, the "Euro-skeptics," believed cooperation went too far. Yet the EC greatly reduced old national tensions. Eventually an elected European Parliament, based in Brussels, Belgium, discussed shared issues and made policies encouraging cooperation and standardization. But critics believed the arrangements marginalized both the European and national parliaments.

The EC spurred growth, creating a consumer society in western Europe (see Map 28.2). With higher wages, greater purchasing power, and more available consumer products, families bought automobiles, washing machines, refrigerators, and televisions. More people worked in the service sector and fewer in agriculture; middle classes grew rapidly, while blue-collar workers shared middle-class aspirations. Consumer markets reached from Europe's sprawling cities into remote villages. A journalist's description of an old French village in 1973 revealed the change: "The last horse trod its streets in 1968. The water mill closed down in 1952. The washing machine replaced the wash house—and broke up the community of women—in the 1960s."[5] High-speed railroads and turnpikes linked peoples together; subways and commuter trains made city life more convenient. Yet prosperity did not eliminate all poverty or regional disparities. Industrialized northern Italy remained much wealthier than largely agricultural southern Italy.

Western Europe still faced economic problems. In 1971, with the U.S. economy undermined by the war in Vietnam, President Richard Nixon devalued the U.S. dollar, the Western nations' staple currency, a move that ended its parity with gold, destabilized world trade, and triggered soaring prices and trade deficits. Then in 1973 a quadrupling of oil prices brought European economies to a standstill; this was followed by a short oil export embargo by major oil-producing nations, who were angered by Western support of Israel. Frustrated motorists

waiting in long lines at gas stations showed how vulnerable prosperity could be in the global system. In addition, noxious air, toxic waste, and lakes and forests dying from acid rain—the price of industrialization—were environmental problems common to all industrial societies.

Costlier energy and growing competition from industrializing Asian nations and Japan also hurt European industries and workers. Factories built a century earlier, often decaying and inefficient, reduced operations or closed, causing high unemployment in industrial cities like Birmingham and Manchester in England. Jobless young people, living in bleak row houses or apartments and surviving on welfare payments, hung out on street corners, some turning to drugs or crime. By 1983 unemployment rates had risen to 10 percent, posing special problems to women, immigrants, and those just out of school. Some blamed their problems on immigrant workers, especially Arabs, Turks, and South Asians, whom they saw as competing with local people for jobs, boosting rightwing, anti-immigrant parties. Free market conservatives often regained political power, penalizing striking workers and weakening labor unions.

MAKE SURE YOU UNDERSTAND THESE KEY POINTS BEFORE MOVING ON

- World War II devastated western Europe's population, infrastructure, and economy, but it enjoyed a remarkable period of growth, aided by extensive U.S. funding under the Marshall Plan.

- A wave of decolonization followed World War II, and Germany and France overcame centuries of mutual hatred.

- The Cold War shaped European politics, with eastern Europe allied with the USSR and western Europe allied

with the United States, but over time some European leaders distanced themselves from U.S. policies and advocated dialogue with the USSR.

- Having been surpassed economically by the United States, European countries joined together in the European Community, which became the world's largest free trade zone and led to increased prosperity.

aplia

Western European Societies and Cultures

How did the rise of welfare states transform western European societies?

In the ashes of World War II the wartime British prime minister, Winston Churchill, wrote, "What is Europe? A rubble heap, a charnel house, a breeding ground for pestilence and hate."[6] Seeing the need for change, western European nations began reshaping their societies and improving the quality of life for all their citizens, often blending capitalism and socialism. The postwar economic boom allowed most states, influenced by socialism, to construct welfare programs that created political stability, ensured public health, and eliminated poverty for most citizens. As gender relations, family life, and sexual attitudes changed, musicians, philosophers, and churches addressed the new European cultures.

welfare states Government systems that offer their citizens a range of state-subsidized health, education, and social service benefits; adopted by western European nations after World War II.

Social Democracy and Welfare States

The rise of **welfare states**, government systems offering their citizens state-subsidized health, education, and social service benefits, and the high quality of life they fostered, owed much to an influential political philosophy. Social democracy derived from early-twentieth-century socialists who favored evolutionary rather than revolutionary change, eventually promoting a mix of liberal democracy, market economies, and a safety net for workers. Since 1945 social democratic parties have governed or been the dominant opposition in many Western countries. They have usually controlled governments in the Scandinavian nations of Denmark, Finland, Norway, and Sweden; have often governed in several other nations, including Britain, France, Netherlands, West Germany, Portugal,

---

[5]Quoted in Robert O. Paxton, *Europe in the Twentieth Century* (New York: Harcourt Brace Jovanovich, 1973), 576.
[6]Quoted in Davies, *Europe*, 1065.

and Spain; and have been influential in Australia, Canada, and New Zealand.

Social democracy fostered welfare programs, a mix of free markets and government regulation, parliamentary democracy and civil liberties, and labor unions, moderating the extremes of wealth and poverty. Hence, northern and central European workers gained more rights and protections than workers enjoy anywhere else. In West Germany they received generous pensions and seats on the boards of directors of the enterprises employing them. Valuing leisure, many Europeans believed they worked to live while Americans, who earn more, lived to work. By the 1990s both white-collar and blue-collar Europeans worked many fewer hours each year than Americans and Japanese and also enjoyed four to six weeks of paid vacations per year. During the most popular vacation month, August, beach and mountain resorts were jammed; with many employees gone, stores often offered limited services. The 35-hour workweek became the norm in France and West Germany; by 2000 the average German spent around 400 fewer hours a year on the job than the average American.

Many Europeans receive generous taxpayer-funded benefits from the state. Free education through the university level (but with stiff university entrance exams) helps people from working-class and farming backgrounds move into the middle and upper classes. Generous unemployment insurance removes the pain of job loss. Inexpensive, widely available day care (often even for infants) allows mothers to work outside the home for wages; custodial parents receive child support payments. France makes free preschool available beginning at age three. Universal health coverage, furnished inexpensively by the state or private sector, removes fear of serious illness, providing inexpensive prescription drugs and guaranteeing medical care to all citizens, greatly improving public health. Most western European nations spend much less than Americans do on health care yet often see better outcomes. Enjoying one of the world's best health care systems, the French live three years longer than Americans. Where Europeans once looked to the extended family for support, now they expect the welfare state to care for the elderly and incapacitated. In addition, with the most equitable distributions of income in the world, northern European nations have nearly eliminated slums and deep poverty. The Scandinavian nations, poor a century ago, developed the strongest social democratic traditions and became the world's most prosperous societies. Norway achieved the world's highest living standards, thanks to North Sea oil and a generous social safety net, even thriving during the 2008–2009 global economic crisis. In Sweden, Europe's most creative country in experimenting with social change, women, youth, and even animals have more rights and protections than elsewhere. In recent decades, Sweden, with the world's most level playing field and lowest poverty rate, has often enjoyed Europe's most dynamic economy.

All welfare states have faced problems, however. Funding them requires high taxes, often half of a citizen's annual income. Worker protections make it hard to fire workers, prompting companies to hire fewer people. Workers enjoy so much security that they may not need to strive harder, which has economic costs. Losing a job is less disastrous than for Americans because the welfare state insulates people from many effects of economic slumps, promoting social stability. Yet, many people with modest incomes, especially immigrants, live in drab apartment blocks or houses, often far from potential jobs and the best schools. Economic problems, joblessness, and racial discrimination occasionally spark rioting and vandalism by minority youth in countries like France, Britain, and even Sweden.

Beginning in the 1980s, the welfare states experienced more problems related to sporadic downturns in the world economy. For decades governments paid for social services by borrowing against future exports, practicing deficit spending. But falling export profits, and hence revenues, stressed the welfare systems, forcing cutbacks in benefits; nations also cut

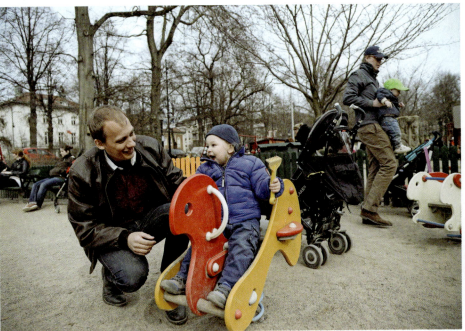

Jonathan Nackstrand/Getty Images

SWEDISH FATHER AND CHILD Swedes have been the most innovative Europeans in social policy, including adopting in 1975 a law requiring employers to grant parental leave. While women mainly take advantage of the law, some men, including this man with his child, take off the full allotted time.

defense spending. Companies downsized, putting pressure on unemployment programs. In some countries conservative parties gained power and began modifying the welfare systems. For example, in Britain, Prime Minister Margaret Thatcher (governed 1979–1990), a free market enthusiast and Europe's first woman prime minister, deeply divided Britons by cutting taxes, battling unions, and reducing health services while privatizing many industries, mass transit, and public housing; people now had to wait longer to receive medical attention. But the conservative regimes did not dismantle many welfare state institutions such as national health insurance, which remained hugely popular.

Unlike in the 1930s, these economic problems did not bring serious violence or political instability. While occasionally anti-immigrant or anti–European Union political parties gained followers, extremist rightwing and ultranationalist forces remained weak in most countries until recently. For example, the French National Front, demanding expulsion of Arab and African immigrants and secession from the EU, won 10 percent of the national vote in 1986, but its appeal faded; then the 2008–2009 economic crisis gave it new life while boosting similar parties in, among others, Britain and Greece. In general, however, the welfare state, which allows even the unemployed to receive basic necessities such as health care, provides stability. Hence, even most free market conservatives have accepted the welfare state's broad framework, although wanting to make it more efficient and cost-effective.

Social Activism, Reform, and Gender Relations

Occasional student and worker protests against capitalism, materialism, and mainstream society have erupted. In 1968, France faced widespread youth protests aimed at the aging, autocratic president Charles De Gaulle, an antiquated university education system, and the unpopular U.S. war in Vietnam, France's former colony. University students went on strike, protesters blocked traffic, and activists fought pitched battles with police, who responded with teargas and beatings. As public sentiment shifted toward the protesters, industrial workers called a general strike, bringing some 10 million workers into the streets. The protests soon spread to Italy and West Germany, where students resented conservative governments, staid bureaucracies, rigid university systems, and powerful business interests. Lacking strong public support, the protests soon fizzled, and governments did not fall. However, De Gaulle resigned a year later after the public rejected, in a referendum, his proposals to reorganize the French government.

Europeans have also dealt with social problems common to all industrialized nations, such as drug and alcohol abuse and high divorce rates. But European and American attitudes have often differed. For example, while the United States harshly punished drug use and trafficking, by the 1980s many western Europeans considered drug use and minor drug sales as social and medical rather than criminal issues. Some European countries even decriminalized marijuana use. Most nations abolished capital punishment and enacted strict gun control laws, often reducing violent crime by banning handguns.

Attitudes toward marriage and gender relations shifted. After World War II, governments tried to revitalize traditional marriage and family patterns, perceiving women as chiefly homemakers who should have many children. But in the 1960s and 1970s general access to birth control helped lead to the sexual revolution and changed attitudes toward sexual activity. The contraceptive pill, illegal in some Catholic countries until much later, gave women control over their reproduction and sexuality. The sexual revolution upset traditionalists, such as the rural Spanish woman who regretted the ease of pursuing sex outside of marriage: "If a boy wants to be alone with a girl there's no problem; they go off alone and whatever fires they have can burn."[7]

Changing social attitudes have eliminated or moderated the social shame of divorce, extramarital sex, and unmarried cohabitation, which were challenging to cultural taboos. Although sex scandals involving politicians are not unknown, especially in Britain, public criticisms of politicians who have openly extramarital relationships or children out of wedlock, a common practice in France and Italy, are rare. But even many Italians were outraged at the sex life and corrupt practices of conservative Prime Minister Silvio Berlusconi (governed 1994–1995, 2001–2006, 2008–2011), a media tycoon who boasted of his wild "bunga bunga" parties with young prostitutes and models. With pornography and obscenity laws relaxed, long-banned works, such as British author D. H. Lawrence's racy 1920s novel *Lady Chatterly's Lover*, were published. British poet Philip Larkin satirized the changes: "Sexual intercourse began, in nineteen sixty-three (Which was rather late for me)—Between the end of the *Chatterly* ban, And the Beatles' first LP."[8]

Inspired by feminist thinkers such as philosopher Simone de Beauvoir (**bo-VWAHR**) (see Profile: Simone de Beauvoir, French Feminist and Philosopher), growing women's movements pressed their agendas more effectively by the 1970s. An English women's group believed that "a world freed from the economic, social and psychological bonds of patriarchy would be a world turned upside down, creating a human potential we can hardly dream of now,"[9] benefiting both men and women. Feminists sought legal divorce, easier access to birth control, abortion rights, and reform of family laws to give wives more influence. Many Protestant countries adopted their ideas. In 1973 Denmark legalized abortion on request. Although Pope John Paul II (pope 1978–2005) reiterated long-standing church bans on contraception, abortion, and divorce, many Catholics ignored these conservative teachings. During the 1970s and 1980s most Catholic nations, including Italy and

---

[7]Quoted in Bonnie G. Smith, *Changing Lives: Women in European History Since 1700* (Lexington, MA: D.C. Heath, 1989), 509.

[8]Quoted in Richard Vinen, *A History in Fragments: Europe in the Twentieth Century* (New York: Da Capo, 2000), 370.

[9]Quoted in Bonnie S. Anderson and Judith P. Zinsser, *A History of Their Own: Women in Europe from Prehistory to the Present*, vol. 2 (New York: Harper Perennial, 1988), 334.

Simone de Beauvoir, French Feminist and Philosopher

Few thinkers had more influence on the study of women and contemporary women's movements than Simone de Beauvoir (1908–1986), the first systematic feminist philosopher and prolific writer of novels, essays, and autobiographical works. She was born in Paris to a middle-class family. Her father, a lawyer, and a devout, very traditional mother sent her to fashionable Roman Catholic girls' schools that taught her, she remembered, "the habit of obedience." She believed God expected her "to be dutiful." Her classmates aimed at marriage rather than careers. But World War I impoverished de Beauvoir's family, pushing Simone toward a career. During her teens she battled her parents for more freedom to leave the house on her own and alarmed them by becoming an atheist.

Simone loved the liberating intellectual atmosphere at the Sorbonne in Paris, the most prestigious French university, but found that, to succeed in her studies there, she had to overcome gender stereotypes: "My upbringing had convinced me of my sex's intellectual inferiority. I flattered myself that I had a woman's heart and a man's brain." Graduating at the top of her class, she then supported herself, first as a high school teacher and then as a writer. De Beauvoir began a romantic and intellectual partnership with Jean Paul Sartre, later to become Europe's most acclaimed philosopher, whom she met at the Sorbonne, becoming a vital contributor to Sartre's ideas and books. The two maintained an intense free union, their lifelong connection providing a model of an adult male-female relationship without wedlock or exclusive commitment. Both had lovers on the side.

De Beauvoir's life reflected the transformation of a privileged woman into a feminist icon. By the late 1940s she was Europe's most famous female intellectual. Throughout her life she enjoyed the new opportunities gained by women as French society liberalized: legal equality, educational opportunities, the vote, and diverse economic roles; she also saw the limits to these freedoms. Sartre suggested she write about what difference being a woman made in her life. The result, the pioneering 1,200-page study *The Second Sex*

(1949), challenged conventional thinking, becoming perhaps the most influential book on women ever written. The study, ranging through biology, history, mythology, sociology, and Marxist and Freudian theory, concluded that society's attitudes oppressed all women. Critically analyzing Western culture as dominated by males, she argued that women are not born inferior but are made to view themselves as such. De Beauvoir showed how, with their choices restricted, such as in careers, girls perceived their future differently than boys. Men took themselves as the model: "There is an absolute human type, the masculine. He is the Absolute— she is the Other." In her view, marriage denied women's individuality, becoming a contract of subjugation rather than an equal partnership. Her writings greatly influenced North American and European feminist movements. Later she addressed aging, including the way society dictated roles for the elderly.

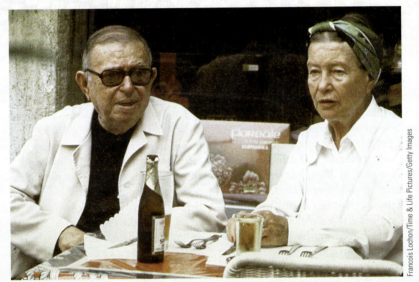

Francois Lochon/Time & Life Pictures/Getty Images

SIMONE DE BEAUVOIR AND JEAN PAUL SARTRE The French feminist thinker Simone de Beauvoir and her partner, the philosopher Jean Paul Sartre, were frequent visitors to the cafés of European cities and influential participants in the lively intellectual life of post–World War II Europe.

Disillusioned by slowly changing gender relations, in 1972 de Beauvoir became a feminist activist, acknowledging her solidarity with other women and contending they had to fight to improve their social condition. She became president of the French League of Women's Rights and editor of journals calling attention to problems of violence, sexual assault, and lack of easily available contraception in Europe and the world. In 1976 she addressed the International Tribunal of Crimes Against Women, noting, "You are gathered here to denounce the oppression to which women are subjected. Talk to the world, bring to light the shameful truths that half of humanity is trying to cover up." Admired by millions, de Beauvoir died in 1986 at age seventy-eight.

THINKING ABOUT THE PROFILE

1. How did de Beauvoir's personal life affect her ideas?
2. What were de Beauvoir's main arguments about how history and society shaped perceptions of gender?

Note: Quotations from Bonnie S. Anderson and Judith P. Zinsser, *A History of Their Own: Women in Europe from Prehistory to the Present*, vol. 2 (New York: Harper, 1988), 240, 169, 422; and Bonnie G. Smith, *Changing Lives: Women in European History Since 1700* (Lexington, MA: D.C. Heath, 1989), 519.

Spain, followed France, Britain, and Germany in legalizing both divorce and abortion.

Changes in work, politics, and family life affected both men and women, who now shared responsibility for financially supporting their families. By the 1980s women comprised half the work force in Sweden, a third in France and Italy, and a quarter in conservative Ireland. Women moved into the professions, business, and, having won the right to vote by 1945, even politics. As once-powerful male-dominated institutions such as the military and church declined in influence, more women supported socialist and liberal parties guaranteeing them and their children health care and education. Women occasionally headed governments in nations such as Britain, France, Germany, Iceland, Finland, Denmark, Portugal, and Norway. Even patriarchal Ireland in 1991 elected its first woman president, social democrat Mary Robinson (b. 1944), an outspoken law professor, feminist, single parent, and supporter of homosexual rights. Women political activists made their voices heard. In 1976 two Northern Ireland mothers, Mairead Corrigan (b. 1944) and Betty Williams (b. 1943), jointly shared the Nobel Peace Prize for their efforts to bridge the Catholic-Protestant divide and bring peace to their troubled land. Yet, some changes came slowly. So few women had achieved high business and industry positions that, in 2006, Norway's social democratic government, outraging corporate leaders, required that 40 percent of large private companies' board members must be women. The EU and several other nations have considered similar legislation. At the same time, less rigid gender roles have affected marriage patterns. In the 1970s the married heterosexual couple remained the norm; even rock stars known for their live-in girlfriends, such as Mick Jagger of the Rolling Stones, a popular British group, got married. Some celebrities, such as French rock star Johnny Halliday, changed spouses frequently. But by the 1980s more men and women remained single, often living on their own. In Scandinavia and Germany, singles accounted for between a quarter and a third of the adult population. Increasing personal independence and mobility fostered small nuclear families instead of the large extended families of old. As unhappy couples no longer needed to stay married, divorce rates more than doubled between 1960 and 1990.

Homosexuals began to enjoy equal rights. Homosexual subcultures in European cities had been active for decades but faced discriminatory laws and attitudes. In the 1950s many governments still prosecuted homosexuals, including respected figures in the arts, for consensual sexual activity. Between 1953 and 1965 West Germany convicted some 99,000 men of homosexual activity, jailing many of them. Although governments began eliminating antihomosexual laws by the 1960s, combating prejudice took longer. Hence, in 1974 a conservative Italian leader warned that "if divorce is allowed, it will be possible to have marriages between homosexuals, and perhaps your wife will run off with some pretty young girl."[10] Eventually most societies developed tolerant attitudes. Denmark recognized domestic partnerships in 1989.

Soon most of northern Europe had such laws providing legal protection, and discrimination ebbed. By 2013 ten nations, including Catholic Belgium, Portugal, and Spain, had legalized homosexual marriage; many others recognized domestic partnerships. Openly homosexual men and women served as high government officials or political leaders in nations as socially different as the liberal Netherlands and conservative Ireland. A black Muslim gay peer, Lord Alli, even sits in Britain's House of Lords. In 2009 Iceland, engulfed in economic collapse, chose the openly lesbian Johanna Sigurdarlottir, a leftwing former flight attendant and trade unionist, as prime minister.

Immigration: Questions of Identity

Responding to postwar labor shortages, several million immigrants settled in various European countries as "guest workers." Poorer southern Europeans, especially Italians, Greeks, and Portuguese, migrated to northern Europe seeking better jobs and pay, and they were soon joined by Turks, Algerians, Moroccans, West Africans, and West Indians fleeing even harsher poverty. Initially many were single men who were recruited for factory work and often housed in bleak shantytowns. Later entire families arrived. Many Indians, Pakistanis, and Bangladeshis also sought a better life in their former imperial power, Britain; others left Indonesia and Suriname, former Dutch colonies, for the Netherlands. By 2010 immigrants numbered 48 million and constituted nearly 10 percent of the European Union, including 12 percent in Germany, 11 percent in France, 11.5 percent in Britain, 12 percent in Spain, and 11 percent in the Netherlands. Major European cities such as Berlin, London, and Paris took on an international flavor; in 2013 nonwhites comprised half of London's population. Islamic culture flourished in cities like Hamburg (Germany) and Marseilles (France), where Arab- and Turkish-language radio stations had large audiences.

Immigrants contributed much to European societies. A large recording industry in Paris churned out music by Arab and African musicians, often for export to their homelands. Small Arab-run neighborhood grocery stores served vital functions in French urban life, and Indian and Pakistani sundry goods and grocery shops and restaurants became features of English and Irish city life. Observers remarked that Indian curry was the favorite British food; many Germans treasure currywurst, a mix of German fried pork sausage, American ketchup, and Indian curry powder. Nearly every Irish town boasted Chinese carry-out restaurants. In Britain many immigrants served as mayors, officials, doctors, professors, writers, and entertainers. People of Asian, Middle Eastern, and African descent were elected to parliaments in, among others, Britain, France, Germany, and the Netherlands. In 2007 two Muslim women, of Algerian and Senegalese background respectively, were named to the French cabinet. Asian and African cultural forms also influenced European culture. For example, in Britain the popular

---

[10]Amintore Fanfani, quoted in Vinen, *History in Fragments*, 493.

bhangra music blended Indian folk songs with Caribbean reggae and Anglo-American styles, such as rock, hip hop, and disco, becoming a lively dance music that was popular with both white and Indian youth. By the 1980s bhangra had spread to Indian immigrant communities in North America and the Caribbean and to India and Pakistan, sustaining Indian identity and encouraging Indian youth to have fun.

However, immigration posed problems of absorption into European society, fostering tensions between whites and nonwhites. Over the years, many Turks, Arabs, Africans, Jamaicans, and Pakistanis, often doing low-paying jobs nobody else wanted, then settled down, and they and their local-born children faced discrimination and sometimes violent attack by rightwing youth gangs. Neo-Nazis in Germany sometimes set fire to immigrant apartment buildings; young toughs in England boasted of "Paki-bashing," beating up South Asians; and Greek racists harassed or assaulted immigrants. In response, many immigrants retreated into their own cultures. While older immigrants often clung to the cultures and attitudes brought from their Asian or Middle Eastern villages, such as a husband's authority over his wife and arranged marriages, their children struggled to reconcile their conservative family and religious traditions with materialistic, individualistic, secular Europe.

Tensions mounted further after 1989. Vanishing jobs put both immigrants and local people on unemployment rolls or competing for scarce work. Illegal immigration also increased as people fled extreme poverty or harsh repression. Boarding rickety boats, desperate Albanians headed to Italy and Africans tried to reach Spain. Hence, anti-immigrant (especially anti-Muslim) movements emerged even in famously tolerant countries like Denmark and the Netherlands, especially after the terrorist attacks against the United States in 2001 and several since in Britain and Spain, shocking Europeans. To express their alienation, young people of Middle Eastern, South Asian, and African-Caribbean background often turned to musical forms from their ancestral countries, such as Algerian *rai* for Arabs and Jamaican dancehall and reggae for Afro-Caribbeans. Some immigrant youth adapted African American rap, writing lyrics in their own languages. For example, in France Senegal-born M. C. Solaar achieved popularity for songs chronicling the lives of young people of African ancestry. Facing particular hostility since 2001, some young Muslims, rejecting Western culture as immoral and criticizing the Islam their parents brought from North African, Turkish, or South Asian villages as corrupted by Sufi mysticism, became more devout and rigidly orthodox. The most alienated turned to militant Islamic groups for direction.

Reshaping Cultures, Thought, and Religion

Enriched by imports from around the world, western Europeans enjoyed a resilient cultural and intellectual life. American mass culture became widespread: cigarettes, Coca-Cola, and chewing gum symbolized postwar fashions; films and music reshaped cultural horizons. African American jazz musicians often settled in Europe, especially France and Scandinavia, to escape racism at home. In response, European governments tried to protect their languages and culture industries by mandating how much foreign music government radio stations could play. Young people also enjoyed non-Western popular entertainments, such as Caribbean reggae music, Latin American dances, and Japanese animated films. Yet Europeans often treasured entertainers that reflected local culture, such as the waiflike French singer Edith Piaf (1915–1963), known for her sad, nostalgic songs of lost love and lost youth, and the Greek composer-musician and liberal political activist Mikis Theodorakis (b. 1925).

After rock, an exciting, edgy music, emerged in the United States in the mid-1950s, it rapidly gained a huge European following, with American rock stars like Bill Haley, Buddy Holly, Elvis Presley, and Chuck Berry enjoying massive popularity. By the 1960s European musicians inspired by U.S. rock and blues, such as Francois Hardy in France and the Beatles and Rolling Stones in Britain, had reshaped local music scenes. The Beatles, young working-class men from gritty but cosmopolitan Liverpool, matured as musicians playing clubs in West Germany. "Beatlemania" reached around the world. Rock became known as "yeah yeah" music in nations as different as Brazil and Malaysia, after the Beatles lyric "she loves you yeah yeah yeah." The music and fashion of the Beatles and other rockers asserted youth identity. The Beatles' 1967 album, *Sgt. Pepper's Lonely Hearts Club Band*, became the prototype of the concept album, with a linking theme, cross-cultural musical explorations (including use of Indian instruments), and provocative lyrics, influencing popular musicians around the world.

By the mid-1970s a new style of rock, punk, expressed social protest. Although gaining a presence in North America and continental Europe, punk became especially influential in Britain, where working-class youth faced limited job options. The provocative songs of a leading punk group, the Sex Pistols, insulted the monarchy and offended British society's deeper values, delighting their fans. A leading punk magazine asserted: "[Punk] music is a perfect medium for shoving two fingers up at the establishment."[11] As punk's energy dissipated in the 1980s, many favored escapist dance music. But punk fostered creative new forms of rock in Europe and North America.

Cultural life was influenced not only by cultural imports but also by local developments, especially political liberalism and growing mass media such as television and cinema. Creative cinema from France, Italy, and Sweden found a global audience by depicting the humblest lives and psychological and social dilemmas common to people in a

bhangra A popular music that emerged in Britain from a blending of traditional folk songs brought by Indian immigrants with Caribbean reggae and Anglo-American styles, such as rock, hip hop, and disco.

---

[11] *Sniffin' Glue*, quoted in Peter Wicke, *Rock Music: Culture, Aesthetics and Sociology* (New York: Cambridge University Press, 1990), 148.

rapidly changing world. Literature reflected political change. Writers known as postcolonialists challenged the world-view shaped by Western dominance. For example, India-born British writer Salman Rushdie (b. 1947), a Cambridge University–educated former actor and advertising copywriter from a Muslim family, confronted Western ethnocentrism. Remembering the prejudice he faced in British schools, Rushdie criticized Western society but also challenged what he considered Islamic culture's antimodern sensibilities. His books *Shame* (1983), a satire on Pakistan's history, and especially *The Satanic Verses* (1988), a critical look at Islamic history, created an uproar among conservative Muslims, earning him death threats.

As Europeans struggled to understand World War II's horrors, which seemed to contradict the rational thought and tolerance building in Europe since the Enlightenment, some turned to secular philosophies. Reflecting disillusionment with Europe's violent history, **existentialism** speculated on the nature of reality, doubting whether objectivity is possible. Stressing class struggle, Marxism envisioned a noncapitalist future for societies. Organized religion declined, and churches struggled to remain relevant in an increasingly secular society.

French philosopher Jean Paul Sartre **(SAHRT)** (1905–1980) and Simone de Beauvoir (1908–1986), his longtime partner, transformed little-known existential thought into a philosophy with wide appeal. Sartre argued that women and men, defined by a reality they view as fate or imposed by others, should not let others determine their lives but find their own meaning, overcoming uncertainty about the world and their place in it. People must accept responsibility for their actions, sparking political engagement to create a better society. Sartre himself reached across political boundaries by becoming active in leftwing movements promoting world peace and banning nuclear weapons. He achieved fame unusual for a philosopher; when he died in 1980, thousands attended his funeral.

Other influential philosophies debated the nature of reality. Marxism emphasized social class and gender inequality, but as a political philosophy it lost many followers after the 1960s. Unlike Marxism's certitude about truth, an approach called deconstruction, pursued by Algeria-born Frenchman Jacques Derrida **(DER-i-dah)** (1930–2004), claimed that all rational thought could be taken apart and shown to be meaningless.

Derrida questioned the entire Western philosophical tradition and whether Western civilization was superior to other cultures. Inspired by Derrida, by the 1990s **postmodernism**, contending that truth is not absolute but constructed by people according to their society's beliefs, influenced literature and scholarship. Hence, notions of different male and female aptitudes or one literary work's superiority over another are not objective but merely subjective attitudes shaped by society. Even scholars, postmodernists argue, cannot completely escape their gender, social class, ethnic, and cultural prejudices. However, some thinkers rejected postmodernist notions that truth is relative and objectivity impossible.

Organized religious life and churchgoing declined, partly because World War II and postwar materialism destroyed many people's faith, often leaving churches semideserted. According to opinion polls, whereas some two-thirds of Americans had a moderate or strong religious faith and believed in God, less than half of western Europeans did; while 40 percent of Americans regularly attended church, only 10 percent of western Europeans did. Conflicts between rival churches diminished, Protestants and Catholics no longer lived in separate worlds, and ecumenical cooperation increased. Formed in 1948, the Switzerland-based World Council of Churches brought together the main Protestant and Eastern Orthodox churches. Appalled by the Holocaust, Christian thinkers, acknowledging their faiths' relationship to Judaism, began referring to Europe's *Judeo-Christian* heritage. Although Europe's Jewish population had decreased sharply from the Holocaust and postwar emigration to Israel and the Americas, Jews remained active in public life. By 2000 immigration and conversions made Islam the second largest religion after Catholicism in France, Belgium, and Spain.

Protestant churches struggled to maintain their influence, often paying a price for their close ties to the state. Governments often subsidized state churches, as in Scandinavia and Britain, and church-operated schools, which did not need to actively solicit support and hence could not generate religious passion. This view was expressed by a popular joke about a young British man joining the army, who wrote on his enlistment form "no religion" and was told, "We'll put you down as Church of England [Anglican] then."

The Roman Catholic Church also faced challenges. Reformist Pope John XXIII (pope 1958–1963) initiated convocations of church leaders, known as the Second Vatican Council (1962–1965), or Vatican II, which launched the most radical church changes since the 1500s. Reconciling the church with modernity, Vatican II gave the laity greater responsibility in worship, no longer required Latin in the liturgy, and removed blame from the Jews for the death of Jesus. Even after Vatican II, many Catholics ignored church teachings they disliked, such as banning artificial birth control. Some conservative Catholics turned to traditionalist movements opposing Vatican II, and some Catholic women, seeking more influence, advocated allowing women to become priests. As fewer European and North American men and women entered Catholic religious vocations, Asians, Africans, and Latin Americans comprised a growing share of the priesthood and religious orders. Hence, Catholic churches in Europe and North America increasingly imported parish priests from countries such as Nigeria or Mexico. Some observers predicted a Third World rather than a Western church of the future.

existentialism A philosophy, influential in post–World War II western Europe, whose speculation on the nature of reality reflects disillusionment with Europe's violent history and doubt that objectivity is possible.

postmodernism A European intellectual approach contending that truth is not absolute but constructed by people according to their society's beliefs.

MAKE SURE YOU UNDERSTAND THESE KEY POINTS BEFORE MOVING ON

- Large numbers of immigrants have come to western Europe to seek work and to take advantage of the welfare state, a mix of capitalism and socialism in which citizens benefit from an extensive social safety net but pay high taxes in return.

- The diversity of western Europe contributes to a rich cultural and intellectual environment, though tensions have often arisen between Europeans and immigrants, leading to problems with assimilation.

- In 1968, a wave of radical protest swept Europe that resulted in significant social changes and ushered in the sexual revolution.

- Rock music, originally imported from the United States, became extremely popular among European youth, as did punk, which expressed working-class frustrations, while other popular music showed Asian and African influences.

- Philosophies such as existentialism, which urged people to control their own lives, and postmodernism, which claimed that complete objectivity is impossible, became popular in postwar Europe, while organized religion became less influential.

aplia

Communism in the Soviet Union and Eastern Europe

What factors contributed to political crises in the Soviet Union and eastern Europe?

Like western Europe, the Soviet Union changed after World War II. Western Europeans struggled for centuries to understand Russia; Winston Churchill called Russia a riddle wrapped in a mystery inside an enigma. For several generations during the Cold War, the USSR was the major political, military, and ideological rival to North Americans and western Europeans. The Soviets feared U.S. ambitions and NATO military power, viewing themselves as more threatened than threatening. The USSR, the last great territorial empire, enjoyed substantial natural resources while maintaining a powerful state and a planned economy. But while communism modernized society, by the 1980s the Soviet system showed signs of decay.

Soviet Politics and Economy

The USSR emerged from World War II as the world's number two military and economic power, no mean achievement given the war's ravages: 20 million killed, millions left homeless, cities blasted into rubble, the countryside laid waste. The trauma helps explain hostility toward the West: Russians resented the sacrifices they had been forced to make because of Germany's conflict with Britain and France. These experiences reinforced traditional Russian paranoia about the West, prompting Russians to maintain a huge defense establishment and power in eastern Europe to keep the region as a buffer zone. But the stresses in the rigid Soviet political system led to some change over the decades.

Given Russia's key role in the victory over Nazism and the Russian occupation of eastern Europe, communist leader Josef Stalin (**STAH-lin**) (1879–1953) believed that the Soviets could deal as equals with the West. Soviet armies in eastern Europe helped establish communist governments there to create the Soviet bloc of nations, which was divided

from the West by heavily fortified borders. Stalin also kept control of Estonia, Latvia, and Lithuania, formerly independent Baltic nations occupied in World War II. In 1949 the USSR gained a key ally with the communist victory in China (see Chapter 27). By 1949 Soviet scientists, helped by information collected by spies in the United States, had built and tested an atomic bomb, keeping pace with the United States in the emerging arms race.

During Stalin's brutal rule, the paranoid dictator, imagining potential enemies everywhere, maintained an iron grip on power, exiling millions to Siberia; hundreds of others, including top Communist Party officials and military officers Stalin suspected of disloyalty, were convicted of treason in show trials and executed. The regime also maintained a tight rein on the arts, education, and science. Hence, party officials banned the poetry of Anna Akhmatova (**uhk-MAH-tuh-vuh**) (1888–1966), who courageously recorded the agonies of Stalin's purge victims, and detained her in a filthy hospital; they also imprisoned scientists whose research questioned theories favored by party-approved scientists in fields such as plant genetics; as a result, studies were flawed. Stalin also spread Russian language and culture in the empire's non-Russian regions, especially Muslim Central Asia.

Stalin's death in 1953 sparked rethinking and modest political change. Russian poet Evgeni Evtushenko remembered that "all Russia wept tears of grief—and perhaps tears of fear for the future."[12] Stalin's successor, Nikita Khrushchev (**KROOSH-chef**) (1894–1971), courageously began de-Stalinization in 1956 with a secret speech to a closed party congress session that was critical of Stalin's dictatorial ruling style, intolerance, abuse of power, and crimes. Khrushchev hoped that cleansing communism of the brutal Stalinist legacy would legitimize the system to his people and the world.

---

[12]Quoted in Ronald Grigor Suny, *The Soviet Experiment: Russia, the USSR, and the Successor States* (New York: Oxford University Press, 1998), 387.

The speech circulated underground throughout the Soviet bloc, stirring up dissent in eastern Europe. Suppression of a Polish strike killed or wounded hundreds, and twenty thousand Hungarians died in an abortive uprising against Soviet domination. De-Stalinization also divided the communist world—China broke its alliance with the USSR in 1960—perhaps planting the seed for the unraveling of the Soviet Empire and system three decades later.

Beginning a political thaw at home, Khrushchev promised that Soviet living standards would eventually equal those of Americans. It never happened, but Khrushchev produced some achievements. In 1957 the USSR shocked the world by launching *Sputnik*, the first artificial satellite to orbit earth; in 1961 cosmonaut Yuri Gagaran (**guh-GAHR-un**) (1934–1968) became the first man to fly aboard a rocket ship into earth orbit, returning a hero. In 1963, cosmonaut Valentina Tereshkova (**tare-esh-KO-va**) (b. 1937), daughter of a tractor driver and textile mill worker, became the first woman to fly in space. But Soviet repression, though less brutal than Stalin's, did not end: in 1957 Khrushchev prevented novelist Boris Pasternak (**PAS-ter-NAK**) (1890–1960) from publishing the novel *Dr. Zhivago*, a critical look at the Bolsheviks during the Russian Civil War that won a Nobel Prize after being smuggled to the West.

In 1964 Khrushchev was deposed. Leonid Brezhnev (1906–1982), a cautious bureaucrat, imposed a Stalinist system giving the state a hand in everything. Russians still found subtle ways to express their discontent, addressing their political powerlessness by passing jokes along to friends and relatives. In a popular joke, a man arrested for shouting "Brezhnev is an idiot" in Moscow's Red Square received fifteen days for hooliganism and fifteen years for revealing a state secret. Brezhnev led the country for two decades (1964–1982), and under him and his successors, the Soviet state, run mostly in secret by elderly, bureaucratic men, was intolerant of dissent. The secret police (KGB) monitored thought and behavior; most citizens endured Communist Party control as inevitable; and Russians learned how to avoid trouble. A few active dissidents, mostly intellectuals and artists, were often deprived of jobs and benefits; some were sent to remote Siberian prison camps, where poorly fed inmates spent their regimented days in hard labor. Many died there.

Some persecuted intellectuals had made notable achievements. In 1970 writer Alexander Solzhenitsyn (**SOL-zhuh-NEET-sin**) (1918–2008), a Red Army veteran imprisoned by Stalin, was forbidden to receive the Nobel Prize for literature because his novel, *One Day in the Life of Ivan Denisovich*, exposed the harsh labor camp life. He later fled to the United States. Another well-known dissident, Andrei Sakharov (**SAH-kuh-rawf**) (1921–1989), a physicist who helped develop the first Soviet atomic bomb but became disillusioned, was exiled to a remote city after championing human rights, democracy, and an end to the nuclear arms race. Sakharov won the Nobel Peace Prize in 1975 but was prevented from attending the ceremonies. Milovan Djilas (**JIL-ahs**) (1911–1995), a Yugoslav communist leader turned dissident, described the contrast between modern Europe's two great

political movements: "Fascism is a nightmare and madness; communism is force and taboo. Fascism is temporary, communism is an enduring way of life."[13]

While the Soviets achieved notable successes, they also experienced severe economic problems. Stalin's Five-Year Plans rapidly transformed the USSR from a backward to fairly modern society. To encourage more progress, Soviet leaders had three tools: the Communist Party, the bureaucracy, and the military. By the 1980s all three proved inadequate in directing a modern economy and society. The authoritarian party, tolerating little dissent, fostered rigidity. The cautious, overcentralized bureaucracy, anxious to preserve their perks and power, often bungled planning and management; officials planned the number of industrial products needed—from steel beams to dish pans—for five years ahead without adequate information. The military, large but inefficient and held together by brutal discipline, promoted incompetent officers and wasted resources.

Increasingly the economy struggled. The Soviets spent vast sums to achieve nuclear and military parity with the United States, building a massive defense establishment and arms industry that sucked money from other scientific and technological projects. Since Soviet factories could not supply consumer goods to meet growing demand, people often bought food and clothes through the black market from illegal vendors. Paying workers regardless of effort caused absenteeism and indifference; bored shop clerks seemed annoyed when shoppers interrupted their frequent tea breaks and gossip sessions. Failing to innovate high technology, Russians missed the personal computer revolution sweeping the West. By the 1990s few citizens or schools possessed computers. Although better off than most Asians, Africans, or Latin Americans, most Soviet citizens lived well below North American and western European standards.

Meanwhile, industrial pollution ravaged the environment, producing dying forests and lakes, toxic farmland, and poisoned air. Diverting rivers for farming and power caused the once large Aral Sea to practically dry up and diminished the world's largest inland body of water, the Caspian Sea. In 1986 the Chernobyl nuclear power station in the Ukraine exploded, causing numerous deaths and injuries, releasing radiation over Europe, and revealing the USSR's inadequate environmental protections.

When living standards rose under Krushchev in the 1950s, the Soviet people turned optimistic about communism. But Soviet leaders papered over problems, and by the 1970s fewer Soviet citizens believed in the communist future. People joked cynically: "Under capitalism man exploits man; under communism it's the other way around." In a supposedly classless society, the contrast between the party, government, and military elite's wealth and everyone else was striking. Communism fostered a favored elite that Djilas called a new class, enjoying special privileges denied to average citizens. Social decay was evident everywhere: drab working-class lives, rampant corruption and bribery, shortage of goods, widespread alcoholism, and demoralized youth seeking access to Western popular culture and consumer goods.

---

[13]Quoted in James, *Europe Reborn*, 279.

ARAL SEA As water from the rivers that supplied it was diverted for agriculture and industry, the Aral Sea in Soviet Central Asia lost over half its water between 1960 and 2000. This photo shows a stranded boat where rich lake fisheries once existed.

Eventually, military interventions proved costly. In 1979 Soviet armies invaded neighboring Afghanistan to prop up a pro-Soviet government. But the United States, along with Arab nations and Pakistan, actively aided the Afghan rebels, mostly militant Muslims, who were fighting the secular Afghan regime and Soviet occupation. Ultimately Afghanistan, where mountains and deserts made fighting difficult, proved a disaster, costing thirteen thousand Russian lives and billions of dollars; the Soviets withdrew their forces in 1989. Economic problems, restless subject peoples, and the cost of supporting a huge military and its widespread commitments contributed to major rethinking in the later 1980s.

The Soviet Union in the Cold War

Tensions between the United States and the USSR reached a height in the late 1940s through late 1950s. During the Korean War (1950–1953), the Soviets supplied communist North Koreans fighting the South Koreans and Americans. But from the late 1950s through late 1970s, Stalin's successors promoted a less aggressive "peaceful coexistence" toward the West and tensions eased somewhat, even though Soviet-backed forces took control of North Vietnam in 1954 and Cuba in 1959. In 1961 East Germany built a high, 27-mile-long wall around West Berlin, preventing disenchanted East Germans from fleeing to the West but also symbolizing fears of exposing them to Western culture and values. In 1962 a crisis caused by secretly placing Soviet nuclear missiles in Cuba, and the U.S. demand for the missiles' removal, brought the two superpowers to the brink of nuclear war. The Soviets withdrew the missiles, easing tensions. But the Soviets helped arm communist forces fighting U.S.-supported South Vietnam, Laos, and the Philippines in the 1950s and 1960s, conflicts that drew in U.S. advisers and troops.

The Soviets generally were more interested in the normal pursuit of allies, security, and political influence than in spreading communism. While supporting nationalist and revolutionary movements in Asia, Africa, and Latin America, often supplying weapons and advice, the Soviets mostly followed pragmatic policies, dispatching military forces only when their direct interests were threatened. After China broke with the USSR in 1960 and became a rival, Soviet and Chinese troops watched each other warily along their common border. Following the **Brezhnev Doctrine**, which asserted Moscow's right to interfere in the eastern European satellites to protect communist governments, the Soviets intervened militarily to suppress revolts in Poland and Hungary in the 1950s, liberalizing tendencies in Czechoslovakia in 1968, and Polish dissident movements in the 1970s and 1980s.

Soviet Society and Culture

Soviet society changed over the decades. Population surged from 180 million in 1950 to 275 million by the late 1980s. Soviet citizens, far healthier, better paid, and more educated than their predecessors in 1917, enjoyed social services unimaginable fifty years earlier: free medical care, old-age pensions, maternity leaves, guaranteed jobs, paid vacations, and day-care centers. In exchange for security, however, people had to accept state power and subordination of individual rights. Moreover, state-provided benefits, often termed "cradle to grave socialism," relieved individuals of responsibility for their own lives.

Education and social services shaped women's experiences. While few served in the Soviet hierarchy, most were in the paid work force and even constituted three-quarters of the number of doctors. Many young rural women migrated to the cities. While rural women often faced hard lives—no running water, indoor plumbing, central heating, or access to nearby shops—urban women also faced challenges. Besides working their jobs, lower-income women stood in long lines to buy food and necessities, took their kids to and from school, washed clothes and dishes in the bathroom sink, and sometimes prepared meals in communal kitchens. Because women increasingly divorced abusive husbands and abortion was legalized, families became smaller. Except in Central Asia, both birthrates and life expectancy fell dramatically. Schools perpetuated stereotypes of weak, passionate women and strong, rational men. Sometimes feminist activists were harassed, arrested, or deported.

Relations deteriorated between ethnic Russians, who constituted half the Soviet

> **Brezhnev Doctrine** An assertion by Soviet leaders of Moscow's right to interfere in Soviet satellites to protect communist governments and the Soviet bloc.

population by the 1980s, and diverse minorities chafing at Russian domination. In Central Asian republics such as Kazakhstan and Uzbekistan, newly built industrial cities attracted millions of ethnic Russians, who monopolized most managerial and professional positions. Thus communism brought relatively high living standards to Soviet Central Asia. But many Muslim peoples resented Russification of their cultures and weakening of Islamic practice. Most Baltic peoples hated Russian domination and the replacement of local languages with Russian; some Jews sought freedom to openly practice their religion or emigrate to Israel or North America.

The state marginalized organized religion, promoting atheism and denouncing Christianity as superstition. But the Russian Orthodox Church became an informal state agent; the clergy carefully avoided angering the Communist Party. Still, Russians often attended church and nurtured their faith; in the 1980s, when the state became more tolerant, millions returned to the church. Yet, many Russians remained skeptical of or indifferent to organized religion.

Soviet policies forced most cultural creativity underground. Intellectuals secretly exchanged copies of forbidden books and magazines, and writers published their work abroad illegally. Anti-Stalinist poets explored the breathing space between the official line and prison, while youth movements baffled Soviet and eastern European authorities. Considering Western rock degenerate, officials restricted innovative musicians, although few faced arrest. Vladimir Vysotski **(VLAD-eh-meer vih-SOT-skee)** (1938–1980), an irreverent singer-songwriter-actor-poet, expressed political disenchantment, avoiding arrest but not harassment. The urban intelligentsia admired Vysotski for songs exposing the Russian soul, extolling sex and liquor, and mocking Soviet corruption, hypocrisy, labor camps, and even politics: "But wait—let's have a smoke, better yet, let's drink to a time, when there will be no jails in Russia."[14] Cassette tapes of his unofficial concerts enjoyed wide underground distribution. After his death from cancer, hundreds of mourners left flowers at his Moscow grave every month for years.

Young people wanted cultural liberalization. By the 1960s some modeled themselves on the Anglo-American "hippie" counterculture, wearing jeans, bell-bottom pants, miniskirts, and peace medallions and listening to the Beatles or their Soviet clones. Rock music, spread by illicit cassettes, remained the chief escape from an oppressive society; some 160,000

SOVIET ROCK BAND For Soviet youth, rock music became a way of escaping the restrictions of Soviet life. This long-haired rocker from the 1980s wears a shirt with the communist symbol, the hammer and sickle, but the lyrics of rock bands often addressed the problems of Soviet life.

RIA-Novosti

underground rock and jazz bands existed by the 1980s. While few musicians challenged the system directly, like Vysotski they explored the fringes, mocking the bureaucracy or the absurdity of Soviet life. Rather than seeking to change the government, rock musicians and their audience sought to live beyond the police and bureaucracy.

Eastern Europe in the Soviet System

During the late 1940s the Soviets installed communist governments in each eastern European nation, sealing the region's fate for over forty years. Political parties were abolished, churches persecuted, and nationalistic leaders purged. In 1949 COMECON (Council for Mutual Economic Assistance) more closely integrated Soviet and eastern European economies. But while communism fostered industrialization in Romania and Bulgaria, people in more industrialized Czechoslovakia, Poland, and East Germany aspired to living standards closer

---

[14]Quoted in Timothy W. Ryback, *Rock Around the Bloc: A History of Rock Music in Eastern Europe and the Soviet Union* (New York: Oxford University Press, 1990), 35.

to those of western Europeans. To supply consumer goods and finance industrialization, governments built up huge debts. The increased industrial activity had serious environmental side effects. While the Soviets treated the satellite countries as neo-colonies, exploiting their resources, they also had to give them generous subsidies to maintain control.

Yugoslavia followed the most independent path, breaking with the USSR entirely in 1948. In 1945 the Yugoslav Communist Party, led by Marshal Josip Broz Tito **(TEE-toe)** (1892–1980), who had led the anti-Nazi resistance, won national elections. To avoid Soviet domination, Tito cooperated with the nonaligned nations while maintaining friendly relations with the West. Tito's unique form of communism, which experimented with worker rather than manager control of factories, created enough prosperity and popular support to neutralize Yugoslavia's powerful ethnic divisions.

Resentment of Soviet domination fostered unrest. After the Soviets crushed protest demonstrations in Poland in the early 1950s, a Polish poet daringly wrote: "They [the communists] ran to us shouting, 'Under socialism, a cut finger doesn't hurt.' But they [the people] felt pain [and] lost faith."[15] Poland, with its strong Catholic allegiances, was the most restless satellite, its workers demanding more public input into government. In 1956 Hungarian leaders tried to break with rigid communism, reinstating private property, inviting noncommunists into government, and declaring the country neutral. In response, a Soviet bloc force occupied Hungary and executed anti-Soviet leaders. But even under the new pro-Soviet leaders, Hungary remained open to the West and more tolerant of dissent than other satellites. While other eastern Europeans followed the Soviet pattern of highly centralized bureaucracies, Hungary's blend of state influence and free markets, known as market socialism, created the most prosperous Soviet bloc economy. Hungarians called it "goulash communism," after their favorite dish, a mix of pasta and meat.

Other disgruntled eastern Europeans later defied Soviet power. In Czechoslovakia in 1968 the reform-minded leader Alexander Dubček **(DOOB-check)** (1927–1993) fostered the "Prague Spring" and a shift to a more liberal "communism with a human face." Alarmed, the Soviets sent in Warsaw Pact troops and replaced Dubček and his supporters with repressive Soviet puppets. In Poland, the Soviets allowed Polish-born Pope John Paul II to make a triumphant visit in 1979, which sparked an outpouring of religious and nationalist fervor. In 1980 Polish shipyard workers led by Lech Walesa **(leck wa-LEN-za)** (b. 1943), an electrical engineer, went on strike. As food prices increased, thousands of women took to the streets, shouting, "We're hungry!" When dissidents formed the Solidarity trade union, aimed at economic liberalization, the government declared martial law, banning Solidarity. Even though illegal, Solidarity, with 9.5 million members by 1981, worked for both economic and political goals. As one leader put it: "What we had in mind was not only bread, butter and sausage but also justice, democracy, truth, legality, human dignity, freedom of convicts, and the repair of the republic."[16]

Soviet Decline and Reform

Soviet problems mounted, forcing a reappraisal of the political and economic system and the nation's place in the world. The USSR had steadily lost ground in world affairs to the United States and economic ground to Japan and West Germany, while China became a bitter rival. Conducting the Afghanistan war and subsidizing eastern European satellites drained Soviet wealth. By the mid-1980s the USSR had few close remaining allies outside the Soviet bloc, which was restless, and few Asian, African, or Latin American revolutionaries looked toward Moscow for inspiration. Soviet power was mostly military, whereas the United States and its Western allies also had cultural, economic, and technological influence. Around the world people studied English or French, not Russian; some observers found more power in rock music, videos, fast food, youth fashions, and global news networks than in the Soviet Red Army. Young people from Bangkok to Buenos Aires favored blue jeans and American adventure films; few knew or cared much about Soviet life. Some scholars concluded that the Beatles, McDonald's, and Cable News Network (CNN) were at least as crucial to winning the Cold War as U.S. military power.

Declining international influence, combined with spiraling social and economic problems and a stifling bureaucracy, ultimately produced younger, reform-minded Soviet leaders who introduced dramatic change. Having more contact with the outside world, these Soviet leaders realized their growing technological backwardness. The planned economy that had transformed Russia into a superpower now seemed a burden; a Communist Party permitting no political competition and a planned economy, run from the top, left little room for individual initiative or creativity. In 1985 Mikhail Gorbachev **(GORE-beh-CHOF)** (b. 1931) became Soviet leader. Realizing that the nation, facing escalating military costs, could not win an arms race or ever match the United States as a superpower, he hoped to preserve and energize communist rule by liberalizing the economy, decentralizing decision making, and relaxing ideological controls. Gorbachev introduced a dazzling series of reforms, developed closer relations with the West, and abandoned the ideological struggle with liberal democracies. In 1987 a U.S.–USSR treaty lessened the threat of nuclear war, and both countries destroyed their short- and long-range missiles. With his **glasnost** ("openness") policy, Gorbachev democratized the political system, arranged for free elections and a parliament including noncommunist parties, released most political prisoners, deemphasized the Communist Party's role, loosened state control of media and the arts, and invited scholars to talk truthfully about the Soviet past. Realizing the ruinous financial costs of maintaining unpopular eastern European governments, Gorbachev did not intervene to preserve them as they collapsed or were toppled in 1989.

glasnost The policy introduced in the Soviet Union by Mikhail Gorbachev to democratize the political system.

[15]Quoted in Davies, *Europe*, 1102.

[16]Quoted in James, *Europe Reborn*, 300.

WITNESS TO THE PAST

Restructuring Soviet Society

In 1987 Mikhail Gorbachev, Soviet Communist Party and government head, published a book, Perestroika, outlining his policy of economic restructuring to transform the inefficient, stagnant Soviet economy into one based on a decentralized market similar to Hungary and China's market socialism. The new policy gave greater autonomy to local government officials and factory managers and attempted to democratize the Communist Party itself. Causing a sensation, the book was ranked by some observers as the most important publication of the late twentieth century. By the early 1990s, with Gorbachev himself removed from office, the policy was eclipsed, but the book remained a testimony to the problems that led to the Soviet system's collapse. In this excerpt, Gorbachev defines perestroika.

Perestroika means overcoming the stagnation process, breaking down the braking mechanism, creating a dependable and effective mechanism for acceleration of social and economic progress and giving it dynamism.

Perestroika means initiative. It is the comprehensive development of democracy, socialist self-government, encouragement of initiative and creative endeavor, improved order and discipline, more glasnost (openness), criticism and self-criticism in all spheres of our society. It is utmost respect for the individual and consideration for personal dignity.

Perestroika is the all-round intensification of the Soviet economy, the revival and development of the principles of democratic centralism in running the national economy, the universal introduction of economic methods, the renunciation of management by injunction and by administration methods, and the overall encouragement of innovation and socialist enterprise.

Perestroika means a resolute shift to scientific methods, an ability to provide a solid scientific basis for every new initiative. It means the combination of the achievements of the scientific and technological revolution with a planned economy.

Perestroika means priority development of the social sphere aimed at ever better satisfaction of the Soviet people's requirements for good living and working conditions, for good rest and recreation, education and health care. It means unceasing concern for cultural and spiritual wealth, for the culture of every individual and society as a whole.

Perestroika means the elimination from society of the distortions of social ethics, the consistent implementation of the principles of social justice. It means the unity of words and deeds, rights and duties. It is the elevation of honest, highly-qualified labor, the overcoming of leveling tendencies in pay and consumerism.

This is how we see perestroika today. This is how we see our tasks, and the substance and content of our work for the forthcoming period. It is difficult now to say how long that period will take. Of course, it will be much more than two or three years. We are ready for serious, strenuous and tedious work to ensure that our country reaches new heights by the end of the twentieth century.

THINKING ABOUT THE READING

1. What did Gorbachev mean by perestroika?
2. What problems did the policy aim to solve?

Source: Adapted from Mikhail Gorbachev, *Perestroika* (New York: HarperCollins, 1987), pp. 34–35, 1987.

Admitting Soviet communism's faults, Gorbachev liberalized the economy using market mechanisms through **perestroika** ("restructuring") (see Witness to the Past: Restructuring Soviet Society). But the economic changes failed to take off. While many in the intelligentsia wanted democratization, the working classes mostly preferred consumer goods, which did not come. Meanwhile, top bureaucrats, including state enterprise managers, resisted changes that threatened their role. Conservatives in the Communist Party and secret police opposed reforms that might undermine their power. Soon the Soviet system collapsed.

perestroika ("restructuring") Mikhail Gorbachev's policy to liberalize the Soviet economy using market mechanisms.

MAKE SURE YOU UNDERSTAND THESE KEY POINTS BEFORE MOVING ON

- Although the Soviet economy grew under communism, it suffered from lack of innovation, inept planning, and an overemphasis on the military; and it created a privileged class of Communist Party and military insiders who lived much better than the common people.

- U.S.-USSR relations were strained by the Cuban Missile Crisis, the Berlin Wall, and Soviet support for communist Cuba and North Vietnam.

- Many non-Russians in Central Asia and the Baltics resented Russian domination and the devaluing of their own cultures.

- Much of eastern Europe was effectively colonized by the USSR, though Yugoslavia pursued an independent communist course, and citizens of Poland, Hungary, and Czechoslovakia mounted periodic challenges to Soviet rule.

- With the USSR losing ground economically and culturally, Soviet leader Mikhail Gorbachev introduced reforms designed to democratize the USSR, to liberalize its economy, and to allow eastern European countries greater self-determination.

aplia

Communist Collapse: A New Russia and Europe

How did the demise of the communist system contribute to a new Europe?

For over four decades the Cold War and the iron curtain provided the context for both western and eastern European politics. The breakup of the communist bloc of nations in 1989 and the USSR in 1991 reshaped the political and economic face of Russia, former Soviet territories, eastern Europe, and western Europe, creating hope but also uncertainties. Russia struggled to rebuild and revive its power. While wars tore apart Yugoslavia and Germany was reunited, western Europe pushed toward unification, including some of eastern Europe, but still faced conflicting forces of nationalism and cooperation. Most Europeans now chose governments through multiparty elections. Europe, though no longer having imperial power, is still important in the global system.

A New Russia and New Post-Soviet Nations

The sudden collapse of the Soviet empire and communism in Europe was a major development of twentieth-century history. In 1985 there were 5 million Soviet soldiers stationed from East Germany to eastern Siberia's Pacific coast, symbolizing imperial Soviet power's reach. Six years later the USSR and its satellite nations had unraveled, mostly without violence. Though the collapse was not a complete surprise, its pace was astonishing. While outside factors, including eastern European unrest and escalating U.S. defense spending, played a role, Soviet economic decline was probably the decisive cause. The collapse showed the failure of the Soviet system, founded on Leninism and strongly shaped by Stalinism. Democratic governments and decentralized capitalism had adjusted better to global changes than communist-planned economies, while nationalist yearnings among non-Russians had sapped the empire's foundations.

Gorbachev's greatest contribution was to face up to failure. By 1991 Gorbachev, unable to control the forces unleashed, had lost his credibility and resigned in disgrace, and he was replaced by Boris Yeltsin (1931–2007), a communist bureaucrat turned reformer with strong U.S. support. Yeltsin ended seven decades of communist rule by outlawing the Communist Party. Russians welcoming the party's demise toppled statues of Lenin and restored czarist names to cities renamed during Soviet times; Leningrad once again became Saint Petersburg.

Yeltsin acquiesced in breaking up the USSR while maintaining the unity of the largest Soviet republic, Russia, which stretched from the Baltic Sea through ten time zones to Siberia's eastern tip, only a few miles from Alaska (see Map 28.3). But glasnost had opened a Pandora's box. Ethnic hatreds, long suppressed by military force or tamed by the safety net, soon exploded. In 1991 all the fourteen Soviet republics outside of Russia, from Lithuania and the Ukraine in the west to Kyrgyzstan (**KER-giz-STAN**) in eastern Turkestan, declared independence, often under former communist officials whose autocratic, intolerant ruling style resembled the old Soviet system.

Most of the new nations struggled to achieve economic self-sufficiency and political stability. Some experienced conflict between rival ethnic or nationalist groups or fought each other over territorial claims, as did Christian Armenia and Muslim Azerbaijan. In three of the former Soviet republics—Georgia, Ukraine, and Kyrgyzstan—what observers called "colored revolutions" because their proponents symbolized their cause with a color, prodemocracy activists, with U.S. and western European encouragement, forced out dictatorial regimes. But the leaders soon lost support by becoming less democratic or antagonizing Russia. Conflict, sometimes violent, between those favoring close ties with the West and those preferring alliance with Russia have continued to destabilize Ukraine. In Central Asia militant Muslims launched insurgencies against secular post-Soviet governments and nominal Muslims, while Islam gained support among the disenchanted and marginalized, especially jobless young men. Islamic fervor forced or prompted many women to don the headscarf or veil and to dress and behave modestly. Meanwhile, millions of ethnic Russians in the former Soviet republics faced resentment for their relative affluence and ties to the former colonizer. In Latvia, for example, the indigenous Lett people make up only half the population, while Russians constitute a third. The Latvian government now requires everyone to learn the Latvian language, which was marginalized under Soviet rule.

In Russia Yeltsin faced many problems. Taking the advice of Russian free market enthusiasts and American advisers, he introduced "shock therapy": rapid conversion of the stagnant planned economy to market capitalism. This approach, while producing more consumer goods and a growing middle class, also created other dilemmas. Soviet officials converted the enterprises they managed into private companies, becoming Russia's new capitalists, while organized crime groups and a few well-placed former communists, known as oligarchs, now controlled many economic assets. Oil-rich Chechnya, a largely Muslim Caucasus region, declared independence from Russia in 1994. Fearing that Chechnya's independence would encourage other secession movements, Yeltsin tried to crush the separatists, producing a persistent quagmire with thousands of casualties. Secessionist sentiments still fester in several other predominantly Muslim Caucasus regions.

Russia's economic pain was widespread. Millions of workers, especially women, lost jobs as inefficient, obsolete Soviet industries closed. Conservatives encouraged women to stay home and tend to family obligations. With free higher education ended, families devoted their funds to their sons. Factory workers, miners, and state employees, such as teachers, were often not paid for years. As Yeltsin dismantled the welfare state, health care reductions, declining incomes, heavier drinking, and illegal drug use affected public health; men's

oligarchs Well-placed former communists who amassed enough wealth to gain control of major segments of the post–Soviet Russian economy.

MAP 28.3 THE DISSOLUTION OF THE SOVIET UNION In 1991 the leaders of Russia, who had abandoned communism, allowed the other fourteen republics to leave the Soviet Union, bringing an end to a vast federation that had endured for over seven decades. Even without the fourteen republics, Russia remained the world's largest nation in geographical size, stretching across ten time zones from the Pacific Ocean to the Baltic Sea. © 2015 Cengage Learning

life expectancy dropped from sixty-four in 1990 to fifty-nine in 2002. By 1992 inflation was 2,500 percent, devastating people on pensions and fixed incomes. According to a popular local joke, "All the good things the communists said about communism were false, but all the bad things they said about capitalism were true."

In 2000, with the Russian economy near collapse and free markets discredited, Yeltsin resigned in disgrace and was replaced by Vladimir Putin (b. 1952), who ended shock therapy and brought back stability after fifteen years of turbulence. A former secret police colonel who kept a portrait of Peter the Great in his office, Putin espoused capitalism and democratic reforms, including multiparty elections, but also pursued more authoritarian, socially conservative, and nationalist policies than Yeltsin. Political liberalism faded as Putin took control of much of the media, seizing or muffling opposition newspapers and television stations and prosecuting some oligarchs for alleged corruption. Some wealthy men were jailed; others fled into exile. The state took over many large private companies, turning the economy into a form of state capitalism not unlike Meiji Japan. Eventually improved tax collection

and higher prices for oil and natural gas exports fostered economic recovery, allowing Putin to assert Russian interests in the world. Putin outmaneuvered discredited pro-U.S. free market advocates, the rebuilt Communist Party, and extreme right-wing nationalists but also showed little patience with liberal, prodemocracy dissidents and protesters, arresting or harassing some of them.

The 2008–2009 global economic crisis brought a rapid drop in oil prices, while drastic revenue declines brought cutbacks and recession, hurting Putin's prestige and fomenting dissent. Political satire flourished, poking fun at leaders and policies even on broadcast media. Some 60 million of Russia's 140 million people now enjoy Internet access. As the economy rebounded, Putin's Russia became, with Brazil, China, India, and South Africa, part of the BRICS group of nations seeking an alternative to Western domination. However, by 2013 the economy, the world's eighth largest, had slowed to a standstill from a lag in foreign investment caused by resentment against endemic corruption and an expanding government economic role. Meanwhile, opposition to Putin grows but remains fragmented.

Putin's Russia has mixed autocratic government with openness to the outside world. The Russian Orthodox Church, for centuries closely connected to national identity and political power, regained influence, and even Putin claimed to be a believer. Within the church leadership, liberals promoted a tolerant and ecumenical view while conservatives denounced ecumenism, some even supporting anti-Semitic, anti-Muslim views and a return of the monarchy. With church encouragement, Putin greatly restricted homosexual rights, making public support of same-sex relations a crime in 2013. He also harassed feminists and some dissidents; in 2012 members of a controversial feminist punk rock group, Pussy Riot, were sentenced to prison for a public protest in a Moscow cathedral. These repressive actions generated protests from many nations, some groups calling unsuccessfully for an international boycott of the 2014 Winter Olympics in Sochi, Russia. Yet, in many places, Muslims—some 15 percent of the population—and Christians live in harmony. In 2009 Russian secondary schools began teaching Alexander Solzhenitsyn's long-banned book about Stalin-era Soviet labor camps, *The Gulag Archipelago*. Putin also sought good relations with Germany, France, the United States, and China, but he often opposed U.S. foreign policies, especially in the Middle East, and maintained alliances with authoritarian regimes such as Iran and Syria.

Problems remain. While the Russian middle class grew, the contrasts between rich and poor became stark as oil money flowed to the well connected. While elegantly dressed men and women in Moscow cavorted in fine restaurants and glitzy casinos, some remote towns went without heat and power. In addition, corruption, poverty, unaccountability, weak legal institutions, and the festering conflicts in the Caucasus stifled development. Russia ranks third in military spending, but its budget is only an eighth that of the United States. Some polls have showed that a majority of Russians preferred the communist years to the new Russia, many people expressing nostalgia for Stalin and Lenin.

The New Eastern Europe

The changes in the USSR resonated throughout eastern Europe. In the late 1980s Mikhail Gorbachev, who admired Hungarian market socialism, promoted reform because the USSR could no longer afford to subsidize these states. When it became clear that the USSR would not protect the largely unpopular eastern European governments, they fell like dominoes. Democratic movements once underground surfaced. Hungary adopted democracy, Solidarity came to power in Poland, and East Germans streamed across the border into West Germany. The world watched on television as Berliners gleefully knocked down the Berlin Wall, the symbol of Cold War division, carrying off its bricks as souvenirs. Soon the East German regime and the other communist governments

Peter Turnley/Turnley/Corbis

THE VELVET REVOLUTION Protesters took to the streets in Prague, Czechoslovakia, to protest communist government and demand democracy. These protests, known as the Velvet Revolution for their peaceful nature, were led by Václav Havel, pictured on the poster carried by a protester.

collapsed or were overthrown. After massive demonstrations forced communist leaders to resign in a largely peaceful "Velvet Revolution," Czechoslovaks elected as president playwright and former rock group lyricist Václav Havel (**vax-LAV hah-VEL**) (1936–2011), who had been frequently arrested for his prodemocracy activities. Havel announced, "Your government, my people, has been returned to you."[17]

The new democratic or semidemocratic governments replaced planned economies with market forces; eastern Europeans took up voting enthusiastically. Yet, reformers did not anticipate the results of their policies. Ending communism uncorked ethnic hatreds and rivalries going back centuries. Slovaks seceded from the Czechs, forming their own country; Romanians repressed the large Hungarian minority; several countries persecuted or avoided providing schools to the unpopular Romany (Gypsies); and prejudice against Jews intensified.

[17]Quoted in James Wilkenson and H. Stuart Hughes, *Contemporary Europe: A History*, 10th ed. (Upper Saddle River, NJ: Prentice-Hall, 2004), 559.

The rapid move to capitalism, while providing abundant consumer goods, also proved destabilizing, giving shock without therapy. While millions lost work as obsolete factories closed, western European or North American companies bought many of the remaining enterprises. Dazzled by Western consumer goods, eastern Europeans may have underestimated the risks accompanying Western-style capitalism. People missed communist-era free education, health care, and subsidized housing. Shops were full of attractive goods, but few people could afford to buy them. Only Poland and the Czech Republic enjoyed robust economic growth. While some economies gradually improved, pockets of high unemployment remained and the rich-poor gap widened. And severe pollution remained common in some countries, especially Bulgaria and Poland. The 2008–2009 world recession undermined many economies; most have not recovered.

Diverse political parties competed for power. Capitalizing on popular support for the social safety net, former Communist Party members, calling themselves reform communists, won some national elections, competing for power with free market advocates, pro-Western liberals, and rightwing nationalists. In a striking repudiation of the Soviet legacy, reform communists often supported joining the European Union and even NATO. Eventually most eastern European nations joined these groupings. Women have sometimes led many nations, among them Lithuania, Poland, Bulgaria, and Slovakia. Few anticommunists regretted the changes, however jarring they were. Adam Michnik, a leader of Polish Solidarity, concluded that "without the slightest hesitation it is much better to live in a country that is democratic, prosperous and thus boring."[18]

The greatest instability plagued Yugoslavia, an artificial federation of states that self-destructed in bloody civil wars (see Map 28.4). Created for political convenience after World War I, Yugoslavia contained antagonistic ethnic and religious groups. After Marshal Tito, the product of a mixed Croat-Serb marriage who kept the lid on ethnic hatreds, died in 1980, the nationalistic Orthodox Serbs tried to dominate the federation, while the Catholic Croats and Slovenians and the Bosnian and Albanian Muslims wanted independence for their regions. In 1991 the Serb-dominated Yugoslav army tried to stop Slovenia and Croatia from breaking away, but the United Nations sent in peacekeeping troops to secure their independence. In 1992 the Muslim majority in multiethnic Bosnia declared independence, opposed by minority Serbs and Croats. Bosnian Serb militias, aided covertly by the largest Yugoslav state, Serbia, massacred thousands of Muslims, using a new term for genocide, "ethnic cleansing." United Nations peacemakers and U.S. air strikes under NATO auspices forced a peace in 1995. The Bosnia conflict killed 200,000 people and generated 4 million refugees. In 1999 violence returned when the Albanian majority in Kosovo, Serbia's southern region, revolted; Serbs responded with ferocity, prompting another NATO-imposed settlement in 2000. Thousands of NATO troops remained in Bosnia and Kosovo, a symbol of unresolved challenges, but tensions still simmer.

Toward European Unity

Germany's reunification, the unity movement, and the 2008–2009 economic collapse dominated western Europe in the years after 1989. With the East German collapse, Germany was quickly reunified in 1990, but the results were mixed. For many East Germans, merging with prosperous West Germany offered access to a materially comfortable life. But reunification, which cost billions, threw the German economy into a tailspin. Before reunification West Germany enjoyed a long boom, but a decade later, the reunified nation's 80 million people were stuck in deep recession. Since Germany has western Europe's largest economy, the slump dragged down the rest of Europe. Many East German workers lost jobs as obsolete factories were closed or sold to West Germans, who often downsized the work force. The unemployment rate in the east was twice as high as in the west and wages much lower. As a result, some angry youth turned to rightwing, often neo-Nazi, groups that favored heavy metal rock music whose songs promoted hatred of foreigners and immigrants. Yet, Germany eventually recovered, becoming an export machine.

Worried by Germany's problems, western European leaders believed that hastening unification would stabilize postcommunist Europe. The Maastricht Treaty proposed economic and monetary union that required budgetary and wage restraint as a prelude. Most treaty signers adopted the euro as their currency. Unity was aided by other factors. Millions of Europeans were multilingual, moving easily between cultures, and many studied in other countries. This cosmopolitanism influenced the arts. The popular Greek singer Nana Mouskeri (**NA-na mouse-KUR-ee**) gained a large international audience by recording in English, French, German, Spanish, and Greek. The Eurotunnel, stretching 94 miles under the English Channel, made possible a three-hour train ride from London to Paris, symbolizing the decline of political and cultural borders.

The European Union (EU) doubled its membership from twelve nations in 1993 to twenty-eight by 2013, including ten former Soviet bloc states and republics. The Czech Republic, Poland, Hungary, and Estonia had joined in 2004. The Danish prime minister told prospective new EU members: "In 1989 brave and visionary people brought about the collapse of the Berlin Wall. They could no longer tolerate the forced division of Europe. Today we are giving life to their hopes."[19] The EU became a bloc of 500 million people (7.3 percent of the world) encompassing most of Europe and enjoying a combined economic power of 20 percent of global GDP in 2012, slightly larger than that of the United States. Before the 2008–2009 economic collapse, Ireland, whose poverty had long spurred emigration, became known as the "Celtic Tiger" because of its rapid growth. Many thousands of migrants from Europe and Asia moved to Ireland for jobs, fostering multiethnic neighborhoods in Dublin. Many Irish emigrants also returned home.

---

[18]Quoted in Vinen, *History in Fragments*, 520.
[19]Quoted in Wilkenson and Hughes, *Contemporary Europe*, 590.

Conducting a quarter of the world's commerce and economic production, the EU joined the United States and East Asia (especially China and Japan) in leading a tripolar world. However, critics called the EU a faceless bureaucracy with innumerable rules that compromised national independence; two of Europe's most prosperous nations, Norway and Switzerland, declined membership. The EU leaders were cautious in admitting former Soviet bloc states with weak economies and autocratic leaders. Largely Muslim Turkey long sought membership, fostering a debate about how to define Europe that spilled over into efforts to prepare an EU constitution. Amid much controversy, the proposed constitution rejected any mention of Europe's Christian heritage. After some shocking rejections, it was modified into a treaty forming a stronger executive and European parliament while promising

more democracy, transparency, and efficiency, winning most members' approval.

In the 1990s, stagnant economic conditions fostered austerity policies, unsettling politics and welfare states. Social democrats, who governed many nations in the early 1990s, now jockeyed with centrists, free market conservatives, Greens, anti-immigrant nationalists, and the fading communists for power. Attempts to roll back but not eliminate social benefits sometimes set off massive protests and long strikes. While many Europeans preferred to maintain what they termed the social market economy, even at the cost of slower economic growth, both the German and French governments replaced 35-hour workweeks with 40-hour workweeks to increase their competitiveness. Despite this change, some large companies continued to downsize or export jobs. Some critics compared

MAP 28.4 ETHNIC CONFLICTS IN EASTERN EUROPE Many of the nations in central and eastern Europe contain substantial ethnic minorities, and tensions between various groups have often led to conflict. In Yugoslavia, the conflicts between the major ethnic groups—Serbs, Croats, Bosnian Muslims, and Albanians—led to violence and civil war at the end of the twentieth century. © 2015 Cengage Learning

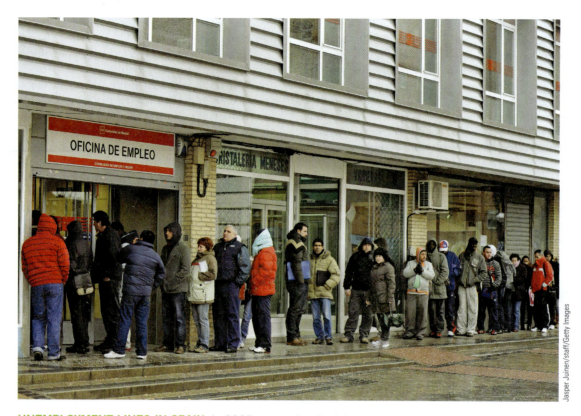

UNEMPLOYMENT LINES IN SPAIN In 2005 companies shed thousands of jobs when the Spanish property boom ended. Eventually over 3 million Spaniards were unemployed, 13 percent of the population.

Europe's sluggish social market economies unfavorably with the dynamic U.S. economy. Others contended that many European nations enjoyed a per capita income nearly as high as that in the United States, less inequality, universal health insurance, and a greater commitment to a high quality of life for all.

The 2008–2009 global economic crisis challenged both arguments. The crisis, the worst since the Great Depression, began in the United States with real estate, banking, and financial problems, discrediting the free-wheeling, antiregulatory U.S. economic model. But in 2009 the new Barack Obama U.S. administration stopped the free fall and fostered slow growth, enabling the United States to outperform most of Europe. European economies also went into steep decline, greatly stressing welfare states and demonstrating government inadequacies in resolving the problems. Germany, saddled with an indecisive coalition government, reacted slowly as deficits mounted. Iceland's economy collapsed from bank failures; as Ireland's economy rapidly plummeted, thousands of immigrants, losing jobs, returned home and many Irish emigrated. Indeed, the grim job market prompted many Arabs, Africans, and eastern Europeans to leave western European countries. Portugal, with a 14 percent unemployment rate, urged jobless citizens to emigrate to its former colonies like Brazil and Angola. Hundreds of

thousands of Europeans now live in campgrounds, vehicles, and cheap hotel rooms.

Since 2009 some economies, including Germany, the Netherlands, and the Scandinavians, have achieved healthy growth by lowering taxes and trimming social benefits while not abandoning the welfare state. However, most eastern European economies have remained deeply troubled. The recovery has also proved short-lived in most western European nations, sparking the severe austerity policies pushed by Germany, now the EU's leader under conservative Angela Merkel (b. 1954), an East German chemist who became chancellor in 2005. Germany's budget cuts and spending reductions generated widespread misery—cutting public sector salaries, eliminating public works projects, but still not generating growth or jobs. Austerity also stalled Britain's recovery; economic weakness and rising prices mixed with income stagnation fostered more poverty and hunger. Some poorer southern European economies, among them Italy, Spain, Portugal, and especially Greece, experiencing huge job losses and defunding of social services, needed EU loans and bailouts to pay their bills but had to adopt austerity and restructure to avert collapse. Some want Greece and perhaps other troubled countries, whose problems strain other Europeans' patience and finances, expelled from the euro zone. By 2013 most economies remained mired in problems, with high unemployment. While Germany weathered the stormy waters, France saw anemic growth, straining the French-German alliance and forcing the French to ponder whether they can afford their comfortable way of life or become more competitive in the world economy.

The economic damage strained the EU and its monetary system. The euro, a single currency shared by many EU nations, was adapted in prosperous times but lacked institutions to make it work in harsher conditions. The crises in poorer nations like Greece and Spain stressed the system, suggesting the need to reform the euro system. EU members debate whether to move toward further unity or step back and allow more national sovereignty and uniqueness. While some nations, like Iceland, consider applying for membership, many people in Britain want to withdraw. Thus, saddled with high joblessness and inflation, the EU's future may depend on economic recovery. A German journalist wrote in 2013 that Europe needs a new vision to cement emotional ties: "Perhaps the answer is to conceive of Europe in the flesh, with colors, smells, folklore, poetic force. And variety."[20]

Europeans also faced other challenges. A century earlier overcrowded and the world's greatest exporter of people, Europe now has a declining population, due mainly to the world's lowest birthrate: 1.2 children per woman. Population decline posed a long-term problem: with more people retiring from than entering the work force, younger workers had more responsibility for financing government services for the elderly. Yet, Europeans became increasingly hostile to Middle Eastern and African immigrants, many of them unemployed young men who resented discrimination and police harassment. Tensions simmered, sometimes sparking rioting and vandalism, thus raising the issue of what sort of integration of immigrants was possible. For example, neither Britain's permissive multiculturalism nor France's ardent secularism, prevented some conflict between Muslims and Christians. By the early twenty-first century, anti-immigrant parties became more influential, even in tolerant nations like Denmark and the Netherlands. Europeans still struggle to define their place in a changing world.

Europe and Russia in the Global System

With the end of the Cold War, Russia, western Europe, and the former Soviet bloc states searched for new roles in the world. Russia sought good relations with the EU, the United States, China, and the nearby Islamic nations, such as Iran, but also acted in its own self-interest, sometimes opposing U.S. or EU policies. NATO needed to redefine its mission as it added many former Warsaw Pact nations, discomforting Russia. After Russia warned NATO against admitting former Soviet republics such as Ukraine and Georgia, it reinforced its threat in 2008 by briefly invading Georgia, a small U.S. ally and former Soviet republic in the Caucasus, to protect pro-Russian enclaves. In 2014, after massive protests in Ukraine forced out a pro-Russian autocrat and installed pro-Western nationalists, many Russian

speakers in eastern Ukraine became restless. In response, Russia supported an uprising in the heavily Russian Yalta peninsula that allowed Russia to take control, provoking tensions with the U.S. and western Europe and more turmoil in eastern Ukraine. For their part, western Europeans seemed more reluctant than Americans to lavish money on the military or send armed forces into combat. The United States, not Europe, led the intervention to end the killing and restore order in Yugoslavia.

After 2000 Europe's relations with its military ally and main trading rival, the United States, became more complicated. As part of NATO and sharing the goal of combating international terrorism, some nations sent troops to Afghanistan after the 2001 terrorist attacks on the United States. But most Europeans mistrusted the U.S. decision to invade oil-rich Iraq in 2003, believing it had little to do with fighting terrorism and would destabilize the Middle East. European nations such as France and Germany criticized the U.S. invasion and occupation. Although their people strongly opposed the war, some close U.S. allies, such as Italy, Poland, and Spain, sent small token forces, but only Britain had a sizable military presence in Iraq. Along with the United States, NATO supplied aid and weapons to Libyan rebels in 2011 to successfully overthrow the autocratic Gaddafi regime, but most Europeans were reluctant to become involved in the complex Syrian civil war. In 2013 France sent troops to push back Islamist rebels in Mali.

Europeans disagreed on how best to respond to international terrorism and militant Islamic groups. Substantial Muslim immigrant populations complicated policies on the spread of militancy among some people of Arab or South Asian ancestry, especially unemployed youth. Some of the men who attacked the United States in 2011 had studied in Europe, where Islamic militants recruited them. Deadly terrorist attacks on commuter trains in Madrid in 2004 and the London subway in 2005, which killed several hundred people, showed the potential for terrorist violence but convinced many that Middle East interventions increased terrorist threats. In 2006, riots and demonstrations that occurred when a right-wing, anti-immigrant Danish newspaper published offensive cartoons insulting the Islamic prophet Muhammad showed shocked Europeans how tense Muslim-Western relations had become.

Europeans played key roles in resolving world problems. Before the 2008–2009 economic crisis, Europeans identified global warming as the major world problem, and some nations strongly encouraged alternative energy strategies. Hence Denmark now imports no Middle Eastern oil and aims to get 50 percent of all electricity from wind power by 2050. Europeans took the lead in developing international treaties on issues such as climate change, biological and chemical weapons, international criminal courts, and genocide. U.S. opposition to these treaties built resentment. Yet, since 2008 Europeans, mired in recession, have struggled to develop policies to combat global warming. European workers have also led movements against economic globalization, which they believe destroys jobs and livelihoods. Saying the

---

[20]Olivier Guez, "Are There Any Europeans Left?" *New York Times*, March 13, 2013, p. 4.

world is not for sale, French farmer José Bové drove a tractor into a McDonald's outlet, vandalizing it to protest against large global corporations often displacing local enterprises; Bové became a hero to Europeans opposed to globalization and the institutions promoting it.

With closer political and economic integration, Europe became much more than a geographical expression and a collection of separate countries sharing cultural traditions and a history. A few European leaders even envisioned a political federation, or united states of Europe, but many hurdles would have to be overcome first. However, the persisting economic problems of recent years have strained unity and raised questions about the future of the EU and the euro currency. Although Europeans have slowly rebuilt their shared institutions and values since 1945, nations still remain central to life. While Europe is no longer the powerhouse it had been in the nineteenth century, its peoples are carving out a new place in the world.

MAKE SURE YOU UNDERSTAND THESE KEY POINTS BEFORE MOVING ON

- The collapsing Soviet bloc and Soviet decay created problems for Mikhail Gorbachev, and he was replaced by Boris Yeltsin, who allowed independence for all the non-Russian Soviet republics, some of which ended up with authoritarian governments, and pursued a rapid shift to capitalism.

- With the fall of the USSR, formerly communist eastern Europe became more democratic, though many countries struggled economically and others suffered political upheaval, especially Yugoslavia, which experienced violent civil war and "ethnic cleansing."

- German reunification, celebrated at first, yielded mixed results, while the European Union grew to include many nations but faced questions over whether to admit non-Christian nations and over what form its constitution should take.

- European nations struggled to navigate the evolving world economy, to deal with Islamic terrorism, and to work out relations with each other and with the United States, whose 2003 invasion of Iraq was generally unpopular in most countries.

CHAPTER SUMMARY

Emerging shattered from World War II, western Europeans were determined to build a new Europe. Although the Cold War divided Europe, western Europeans rebuilt democracies and began a movement to foster unity. Sparked by French-German reconciliation, they established institutions for economic cooperation that eventually became the European Union, which established a single currency and a European parliament. Stability also resulted from the rise of welfare states, which guaranteed all citizens fair access to housing, health care, and education. Social democratic parties took the lead in creating the safety net, but supporting it became more costly because of growing economic problems and unemployment rates. Gradually family and gender relations changed, while millions of immigrants reshaped European societies.

After the war the Soviet Union maintained a communist-run government and economy, with a powerful state dominating life and work. The Soviets installed communist governments in eastern Europe and brutally repressed opposition, but they failed to foster much economic dynamism and lost ground in the Cold War to a more powerful U.S.–western Europe alliance. By the 1980s the Soviet system and Soviet bloc needed reform. Although communism generated modernization and improved living standards, ethnic minorities were restless, the bureaucracy was stifling, and the economy remained stagnant. Unsettling reforms resulted in the collapse of communism and the dismantling of the Soviet Empire in 1991. Since then the former communist nations have struggled to sustain capitalism and liberal democracy. Meanwhile, most European nations joined the European Union, the world's third largest economic power. Germany struggled to make reunification work, Russia debated a new role in the world, and the European Union sought the appropriate mix of cooperation and national sovereignty.

KEY TERMS

Marshall Plan (p. 694)
Eurocommunism (p. 696)
Greens (p. 696)
Commonwealth of Nations (p. 697)
NATO (p. 697)
Soviet bloc (p. 697)

Warsaw Pact (p. 697)
ostpolitik (p. 697)
welfare states (p. 700)
bhangra (p. 705)
existentialism (p. 706)
postmodernism (p. 706)

Brezhnev Doctrine (p. 709)
glasnost (p. 711)
perestroika (p. 712)
oligarchs (p. 713)

29 The Americas and the Pacific Basin: New Roles in the Contemporary World, Since 1945

AP Images/Kiichiro Sato

A NATURALIZATION CEREMONY Seeking political freedom or economic opportunities, immigrants flock to the United States, and many become citizens. At this ceremony, 800 residents, representing 88 countries, took the oath of citizenship in Columbus, Ohio, in April 2005.

It's curious. Our generals listen to the [U.S.] Pentagon. They learn the ideology of National Security and commit all these crimes [against the Argentine people]. Then the same [American] people who gave us this gift come and ask, "How did these terrible things happen?"

—President Raul Alfonsin of Argentina, 1984[1]

The women appeared one day in 1977 in the historic Plaza de Mayo, adjacent to the presidential palace in downtown Buenos Aires, Argentina. For several years the military government had waged a bloody campaign to eliminate dissidents, killing or abducting some thirty thousand people and arresting and torturing thousands more. Some may have belonged to outlawed leftist groups, but many simply held progressive ideas or were friends with regime critics. Initially only the feared secret police paid attention to the dozen or so frightened women who came once a week, standing in silent protest. A year later the peaceful protesters numbered more than a thousand. Wearing kerchiefs on their heads and sensible flat shoes, the mothers and grandmothers, pinning to their chests photographs of missing family members, victims of the state's terror, asked: Where were their missing children, husbands, pregnant daughters, and grandchildren? The "Mothers and Grandmothers of the Plaza de Mayo" challenged one of Latin America's most brutal tyrannies. Most were housewives fighting, as one put it, vicious armed forces, spineless politicians, complicit clergy, muzzled press, and co-opted labor unions. Their courageous protest inspired others in Argentina and around the world with hope and moral outrage at military repression. The gatherings continued weekly until 1983, when the regime fell and a civilian government could investigate the disappearances. Most never learned their loved ones' fates.

The Plaza de Mayo protest illustrates how some Latin Americans addressed the authoritarian governments they lived under, sometimes for decades. Latin American countries often shifted back and forth between dictatorship and democracy, neither system fostering widespread economic prosperity amid the stark rich-poor divide. Many Latin Americans also resented the United States, which often supported dictatorships that welcomed U.S. investment. The United States remained the hemisphere's dominant power while expanding its global influence. U.S. president Harry Truman (president 1945–1953) argued in 1947 that American political and business practices could thrive at home only if foreign countries embraced similar practices. Hence, the United States became the global workshop and banker, preacher and teacher, umpire and policeman. Between 1946 and 1989, it enjoyed unrivaled military might, economic power, and political-ideological leadership, contested only by the Soviet Union; it remains the major superpower today. Meanwhile, U.S. society increasingly differed from the societies of its North American neighbor, Canada, and the Pacific Basin countries of Australia and New Zealand.

[1]Quoted in James D. Cockcroft, *Latin America: History, Politics, and U.S. Policy,* 2nd ed. (Chicago: Nelson-Hall, 1996), 567.

N T The United States as a Superpower

How did the Cold War shape U.S. foreign policies?

Thanks to its size, power, and wealth, the United States has played a major world role, helping Europe and Japan recover from World War II, espousing and often promoting human rights and freedom, lavishing aid on allies, and providing leadership in a politically fragmented world. During the Cold War, competition with the Soviet bloc for allies and strategic advantage shaped U.S. policies, influencing the world's perceptions of Americans. Soviet domination of eastern Europe, communist victory in China, and the Korean War convinced Americans that communist expansion had to be thwarted. People around the world admired America's democratic ideals, prosperity, and technological ingenuity, but U.S. wars,

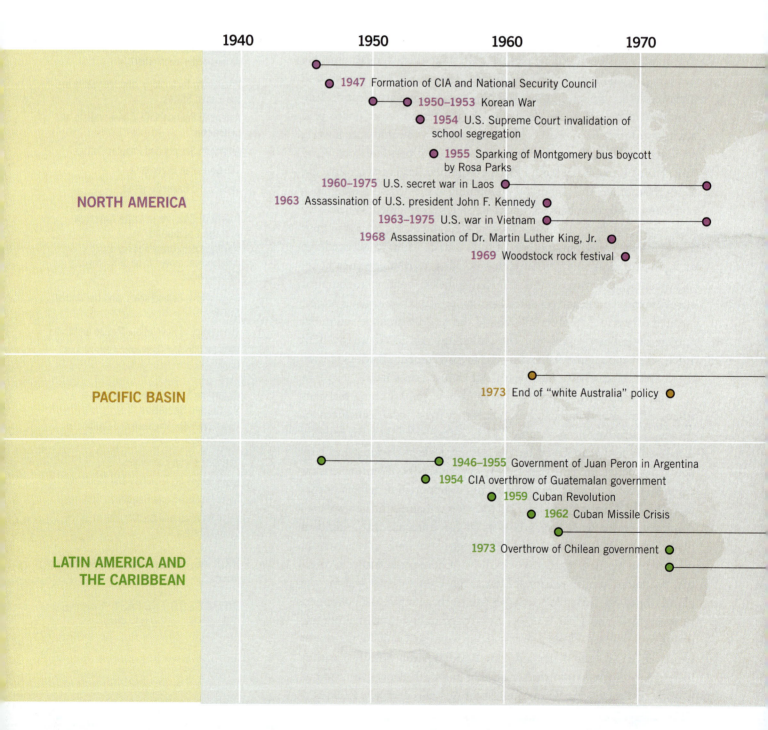

	1940	1950	1960	1970

NORTH AMERICA

1947 Formation of CIA and National Security Council
1950–1953 Korean War
1954 U.S. Supreme Court invalidation of school segregation
1955 Sparking of Montgomery bus boycott by Rosa Parks
1960–1975 U.S. secret war in Laos
1963 Assassination of U.S. president John F. Kennedy
1963–1975 U.S. war in Vietnam
1968 Assassination of Dr. Martin Luther King, Jr.
1969 Woodstock rock festival

PACIFIC BASIN

1973 End of "white Australia" policy

LATIN AMERICA AND THE CARIBBEAN

1946–1955 Government of Juan Peron in Argentina
1954 CIA overthrow of Guatemalan government
1959 Cuban Revolution
1962 Cuban Missile Crisis
1973 Overthrow of Chilean government

interventions, support for often authoritarian allies, frequent neglect of human rights, and globalization of capitalism fostered widespread hostility. After the Cold War, the United States and its allies faced new challenges.

The American Century and the Cold War

World War II was a watershed that forged Americans' vision of world politics. Increased political centralization and economic growth encouraged Americans to accept international involvements, promoting an activist foreign policy. As the global

powerbroker and policeman, the United States sought to block its main rival, the Soviet Union, from gaining influence in other countries. Victory over Nazism and Japanese militarism reinforced American confidence and sense of mission. In 1941, Henry Luce, publisher of the most influential U.S. news magazine, *Time*, declared that the twentieth century would be the American Century, imposing global duties and opportunities on Americans. Luce believed that America's idealistic Bill of Rights, magnificent industrial products, and technological skills would be shared with all peoples. His view, while arrogant, reflected a longtime belief in exporting Americans' values

1980   1990   2000   2010   2015

1946–1989 Cold War

1991 Gulf War
1994 Formation of NAFTA
2001 Al Qaeda terrorist attacks in United States
2002 Beginning of Afghanistan war
2003–2011 U.S. war in Iraq

1962–1990 Decolonization of Pacific islands

1988 Canadian Multiculturalism Act
1999 Formation of Nunavut in northern Canada

1964–1985 Military government in Brazil

1973–1989 Military government in Chile
1979–1989 Sandinista government in Nicaragua
1983 Restoration of Argentina's democracy
1990 U.S. invasion of Panama
1994 Formation of NAFTA
1998 Economic collapse in many nations
2000 Election of President Vicente Fox in Mexico
2002 Election of President Lula da Silva in Brazil

and institutions; their nation was the world's model. But U.S.-style capitalism and democracy proved difficult to implant where they had no roots.

After World War II the United States rebuilt defeated Germany and Japan, established global financial networks, lavished aid on western Europe to help stabilize democratic governments, used military forces to protect U.S. allies in Asia, and opposed radical nationalist and communist-led movements in Asia, Africa, and Latin America. For several decades, as the U.S. economy soared, the American Century idea seemed realistic. But U.S. economic superiority in the 1940s and 1950s derived from unusual conditions. Among the great powers, only the United States had not been bombed or financially drained and could maintain a modern industrial system. Americans alone could mass-produce the consumer goods needed by others. In 1950, the United States accounted for 27 percent of total world economic output. Supplying the world, Americans experienced an economic boom that lasted until the late 1960s and that helped to finance an activist foreign policy.

As the United States became the world economy's engine, it forged close trade links with Canada, western Europe, and Japan while sponsoring foreign aid programs and investment, especially in Asia and Latin America. Such aid and investment spurred an economic renaissance and political stability in western Europe and Japan. However, in developing nations the aid and investment often supported cash crop agriculture and mining, and reinforcing dependence on the export of natural resources promoted unbalanced growth. Later, U.S. investment developed light industry, especially textile factories, utilizing cheap labor in countries like Mexico and Thailand. Asian, African, and Latin American countries became key U.S. markets and acquired over a third of American exports by the 1990s, enriching U.S. corporations. However, American consumption of more foreign imports, from Japanese cars to Middle Eastern oil, contributed to chronic trade imbalances; Americans spent more for foreign products than they earned from exports, living beyond their means as globalization fostered outsourcing of manufacturing and jobs.

The Cold War generated long-term conflict between communism and capitalist democracy, with U.S. foreign relations shaped by the fear that the Soviet Union pursued global domination. Although the USSR, ruled by dictators, possessed formidable military might, Americans often overestimated the threat. The Central Intelligence Agency (CIA) and the National Security Council, both established in 1947, and other intelligence-gathering agencies operated in top secrecy, with little congressional oversight and ever larger budgets ($40 billion per year by the 1980s). The **domino theory**, which envisioned countries falling one by one to communism, shaped U.S. policy.

Anticommunism intensified after hard-drinking U.S. senator Joseph McCarthy (1909–1957) and his allies charged, without offering much proof, that communists had infiltrated the U.S. government and were shaping foreign policy. During McCarthyism, a campaign in the 1950s to identify suspected communists in the government, the military, education, and the entertainment industry, thousands of Americans who held leftwing political views were fired or blacklisted and condemned as "un-American." (Blacklisting prevented people from working.) For example, many university experts on Asia lost their positions for criticizing U.S. Asian policies, and some were forced to finish their careers overseas. McCarthy called hundreds before his Senate committee, from movie actors to State Department officials, and questioned them about their political activities or their friends' political views. In 1954 the U.S. Senate censured McCarthy for recklessly charging top military leaders with treason. To critics, McCarthy's investigation, a Cold War–driven hysteria, violated the Bill of Rights.

As a broad consensus emerged around opposing communism and Soviet power, most American leaders favored an activist foreign policy that relied on military power, but they disagreed on the approach. Some favored **multilateralism**, with the United States seeking a common front to coordinate foreign policies with allies in western Europe, Japan, and Canada, avoiding activities that might enflame world opinion. In contrast, most policymakers, and the presidents they served, favored **unilateralism**: acting alone in perceived American national interests even if key allies disapproved, as most did with the U.S. war in Vietnam. Unilateralists supported repressive allies such as the Philippines and the Congo; those who questioned the rationale, tactics, and cost of an activist policy were sidelined. Ultimately the costly interventions abroad, especially the frustrating war in Vietnam, generated debate about the goals, operation, and impact of U.S. foreign policy, undermining consensus and increasing dissent.

The main U.S. strategy, **containment**, which aimed at preventing communists from gaining power and the Soviets from gaining influence in other nations, generated wars in Korea and Vietnam and interventions in countries seeking to weaken or escape from Western economic and political domination. An influential, top secret 1950 government report, NSC-68, provided the rationale for activist policies, painting a bleak picture of the Soviet search for world supremacy: "The issues that face us are momentous, involving the fulfillment or destruction not only of this [U.S.] Republic but of civilization itself."[2] Sanctioning any tactics in the anticommunism struggle, NSC-68

domino theory A theory that envisioned countries falling one by one to communism and that became a mainstay of U.S. policy.

multilateralism A foreign policy in which the United States sought a common front and a coordination of foreign policies with allies in western Europe, Japan, and Canada, avoiding activities that might enflame world opinion against the United States.

unilateralism A foreign policy in which the United States acted alone in its own perceived national interest even if key allies disapproved.

containment The main U.S. strategy aimed at preventing communists from gaining power, and the USSR from getting political influence, in other nations during the Cold War.

---

[2] Quoted in Marilyn B. Young, *The Vietnam Wars, 1945–1990* (New York: HarperCollins, 1991), 25.

remained a foundation for U.S. military and intelligence policies abroad until the mid-1970s.

NSC-68 called for huge defense budgets and expansion of the nuclear weapons arsenal, paid for by tax increases and major reductions in social welfare spending; security took precedence at the expense of other priorities. The Soviets matched the U.S. military buildup, spurring costly escalation of military spending and more sophisticated weapons on both sides. Under the policy of **Mutually Assured Destruction** (MAD), the United States and USSR used fear of nuclear weapons as deterrence. Historians debate whether MAD prevented a direct military confrontation that might have sparked World War III. As Americans reacted to that fear in the 1950s, some built bomb shelters in their basements or backyards, while schools held mock air raid drills, with students learning to "duck and cover" under their desks to protect themselves from a nuclear attack.

Defense spending reshaped the U.S. economy. U.S. World War II commander and later president Dwight Eisenhower (g. 1953–1961) warned about the growing influence of what he termed the "military-industrial complex," an alliance of military leaders and weapons producers. Defense became an enormous business, employing a fifth of the industrial work force and a third of scientists and engineers by the 1960s and costing U.S. taxpayers hundreds of billions of dollars a year. The United States also sold weapons to allied nations, including dictatorships like Argentina, which sometimes used American weapons and police tactics against their own citizens to eliminate dissidents.

Between 1945 and 1975 U.S. power was unmatched in the world, with military bases in dozens of countries (see Map 29.1). Both the United States and the USSR intervened directly or indirectly in civil wars and revolutions to outflank the other. Americans employed military force, as in the long war in Vietnam and the invasion of the Dominican Republic in 1965, and covertly aided governments to suppress opposition or helped overthrow governments, sometimes democratically elected ones, that were considered unfriendly to U.S. economic or political interests. Some foreign observers applauded American efforts to suppress leftwing governments and movements; others criticized superpower imperialism. The U.S.-USSR rivalry persisted until many communist regimes collapsed in 1989.

U.S. power was diminished between the mid-1970s and early 1990s due to a resurgent western Europe and Japan, Soviet military strength, economic challenges from industrializing nations such as South Korea and China, damage done to the U.S. economy and prestige by the widely unpopular war in Vietnam, and the economic price for global power. With many costly military commitments, the nation's economic creativity sagged and industries became obsolete; defense spending diverted resources from the domestic economy. For over four decades Americans spent around $4 trillion on the Cold War rather than improving education and health care or meeting other needs. While the growing U.S. defense budgets helped undermine the USSR, which was unable to match the lavish spending, the ballooning federal deficits also made the United

States the world's largest debtor nation. President Bill Clinton (g. 1993–2001) eliminated the budget deficits, but the debts skyrocketed again under his successor, George W. Bush (g. 2001–2009).

The United States, Wars, and the Developing Nations

The 1949 communist victory in longtime ally China escalated U.S. concern about communist expansion, helping spark the Korean War (1950–1953) (see Chapter 27). Comparing North Korea's invasion to Nazi aggression and influenced by Americans' anticommunist mood, U.S. president Harry S. Truman signaled adoption of an interventionist foreign policy by deploying U.S. troops to Korea. By never consulting Congress, which had constitutional responsibility to declare war, Truman also made presidents supreme in decisions to go to war, enhancing executive branch power. Furthermore, Soviet support of North Korea and Chinese intervention deepened American fear of expanding communism. Despite 38,000 Americans killed and over 100,000 wounded, the war ended in stalemate, the first time Americans failed to decisively win a war since 1812. The intervention also reflected the idealistic American desire to spread democracy and free market capitalism around the world. However, South Korea did not become a democracy until the 1980s, over three decades after the war. U.S. military bases and nearly 30,000 troops remain in South Korea today.

The domino theory, predicting a communist sweep through Southeast Asia, as well as the desire to maintain military credibility and keep valuable Southeast Asian resources in friendly hands, also fostered support for the French effort to maintain colonial control (1946–1954) in Vietnam. When that effort failed, U.S. troops eventually fought Soviet- and Chinese-armed Vietnamese communist forces (see Chapter 31). Few U.S. leaders comprehended the historical and cultural factors that motivated the Vietnamese revolutionaries and their supporters. By the mid-1960s, U.S. president Lyndon B. Johnson (g. 1963–1969) had committed military forces and launched an intensive air war in North and South Vietnam and later in neighboring Cambodia and Laos. Using domino theory rhetoric, Johnson asserted that "if we don't stop the [communists] in South Vietnam, tomorrow they will be in Hawaii and next week they will be in San Francisco,"[3] very unlikely scenarios. Between 1963 and 1975, 2.5 million Americans served in Vietnam; 58,000 died and 300,000 were wounded.

As public support for the war ebbed in what seemed a quagmire, new president Richard Nixon (g. 1969–1973) negotiated a political settlement with North Vietnam and gradually withdrew U.S. forces. Thanks to a wartime policy of spending lavishly on both "guns and butter"—military and domestic needs—Americans struggled

> **Mutually Assured Destruction** A policy, known as MAD, in which the United States and the USSR used the fear of nuclear weapons to deter each other.

---

[3]Quoted in L. S. Stavrianos, *Global Rift: The Third World Comes of Age* (New York: William Morrow, 1981), 712.

MAP 29.1 U.S. MILITARY PRESENCE IN THE WORLD, 1945–PRESENT As the major superpower, the United States maintained several dozen military bases outside of North America while engaging in military operations in Latin America, Africa, Asia, the Middle East, and Europe. This map shows some of the major U.S. bases and military conflicts. © 2015 Cengage Learning

with huge deficits and other economic problems from the later 1960s into the 1990s. The war in Vietnam will ultimately have cost U.S. taxpayers $1 to 2 trillion. The unpopular, unsuccessful war also made Americans wary of supporting other military interventions that might become quagmires.

During the Cold War, decolonization, nationalism, the U.S.-Soviet struggle, and persistent poverty combined to make Asian, African, and Latin American societies prone to crises. The United States often favored decolonization that opened U.S. business opportunities, pressuring the Dutch to abandon Indonesia and Britain to grant most of its African colonies independence. But Americans opposed independence for colonies, such as French-ruled Vietnam and Portuguese-ruled Mozambique, where communists or leftists dominated nationalist movements. After decolonization, Americans

offered generous aid to friendly nations and victims of famine or natural catastrophes while funding the Green Revolution in agriculture, which improved food production. However, as already discussed, Cold War challenges involved Americans in long-term confrontations with communist-led China, North Vietnam, and Cuba, and interventions, sometimes with military force, to suppress leftist insurgencies and oppose left-leaning governments.

Some U.S.-supported governments lacked widespread popular support or lost their credibility, repressing and sometimes killing domestic opponents. Some interventions also removed democratic governments, as in Guatemala and Chile, or suppressed democratic movements. Hence, President Lyndon Johnson, fearing another Cuba, dispatched twenty thousand U.S. Marines into the Dominican Republic in 1965 to support a military government opposed by democratically elected leaders they had recently overthrown. Johnson consulted no other Latin American governments, and the antimilitary leaders were left-leaning but noncommunist reformers. Former Dominican president Juan Bosch (1909–2001) declared that "this was a democratic revolution smashed by the leading democracy in the world."[4] The United States also provided friendly governments or anti-leftist groups with weapons, military advisers, intelligence agents, and funding. Hence, during the 1970s and 1980s it aided pro-Western but often repressive governments combating leftist insurgents in El Salvador. In Laos (1960–1975), during the CIA's "secret war" hidden from Congress and the U.S. public, Americans recruited hill peoples to fight communist Laotian and North Vietnamese forces (see Chapter 31).

ON PATROL IN VIETNAM U.S. soldiers sought out National Liberation Front fighters and supporters in the villages, rice fields, and jungles of South Vietnam. They could not easily tell friend from foe and warily dealt with local people.

Some interventions involved covert destabilization. American agents worked underground to undermine or overthrow governments by spreading misinformation, subsidizing opposition political parties, providing weapons to the military, and facilitating assassinations of government leaders. U.S. clandestine activity undermined left-leaning democratic governments in Iran in the 1950s and Thailand and Chile in the 1970s, resulting in brutal dictatorships. Secretary of State Henry Kissinger, defending the U.S.-supported military coup against an elected Chilean government which respected civil liberties, explained, "I don't see why we [Americans] need to stand by and watch a country go communist due to the irresponsibility of its own people."[5] Only in the mid-1970s, with congressional hearings, did Americans learn of the U.S. role in Chile and other interventions, forcing debate on whether secret operations and foreign interventions unknown to the public are compatible with democracy and open, accountable government.

The United States in the Global System After 1989

The dissolution of the Soviet bloc in 1989 and the USSR in 1991 left the United States the dominant world power, although the European Union, Japan, and rising China and India also enjoyed great influence in the global system. But the absence of a rival superpower under the *Pax Americana*

("American Peace") did not mean there were no serious challenges in a world characterized by small, deadly conflicts. During the early 1990s, for example, the United States sent a few U.S. troops, under United Nations auspices, to stabilize Somalia, a famine-racked northeast African state engulfed in civil war, but a local warlord paraded the mutilated bodies of dead U.S. soldiers through the streets, forcing a U.S. withdrawal. In the aftermath, the United States declined to intervene to stop bloody ethnic conflicts and genocides in the African states of Rwanda, Liberia, and Sierra Leone. However, working with European allies, President Clinton sent U.S. forces to help end deadly civil wars in the former Yugoslavia. Clinton also established diplomatic ties and lifted the trade embargo imposed on Vietnam after 1975, improving relations.

Cold War policies sometimes came back to haunt Americans. For example, Iranians' resentment over the 1953 overthrow of their government still complicates U.S.-Iran relations. In another example, when the United States gave military and financial aid to Islamic rebels fighting Soviet troops and the pro-Soviet government in Afghanistan in the 1980s (see Chapter 30), some aid went to Arab volunteers fighting alongside the rebels, among them Saudi militant Osama bin Laden (1957–2011). After the defeated Soviets left Afghanistan in 1989, Muslim extremists called the Taliban ultimately took power, offering a base for bin Laden to form his global terrorist network, Al Qaeda ("the Base"). Al Qaeda plotted terrorist attacks against the United States, sometimes using leftover U.S. weapons (see Chapters 26 and 30). Iraq's ruthless dictator, Saddam Hussein, also used

---

[4]Quoted in Walter LaFeber, *America, Russia and the Cold War: 1945–1992*, 7th ed. (New York: McGraw-Hill, 1993), 248.

[5]Quoted in Cockcroft, *Latin America*, 531.

weapons acquired from the United States, his ally against Iran in the 1980s, to repress dissident groups and, in 1991, invaded oil-rich Kuwait. An American-led coalition pushed invading Iraqi forces out during the Gulf War. With an ever-expanding American appetite for oil, this war reflected a consistent U.S. policy to protect the oil flow from the Middle East to the West, sometimes by supporting dictatorial regimes.

The Al Qaeda terrorist attack on New York's World Trade Center and the Pentagon outside Washington, D.C., in September 2001, which killed nearly three thousand Americans, shocked the nation. The terrorists, young Muslim fanatics mostly from two close U.S. allies, Egypt and Saudi Arabia, attacked buildings symbolizing often-unpopular U.S. economic and military power. However, people in most countries, even if they disliked U.S. power, deplored the bombings and loss of innocent life.

The 2011 attack sparked new domestic and foreign policies. To prevent more domestic terrorism, the new U.S. president, George W. Bush (g. 2001–2009), introduced policies that critics believed infringed on civil liberties, such as preventive detention, interception of overseas phone calls, and monitoring of libraries. President Bush also declared war on international terrorism. But unlike the USSR during the Cold War, terrorist networks, having no clear command structure or military resources, could not be influenced by diplomacy. With international support, the United States invaded Afghanistan to destroy Al Qaeda terrorist bases, displacing the brutal Taliban government that tolerated their presence. Bush then announced a new doctrine of **preemptive war** sanctioning unilateral military action against potential threats: "We cannot let our enemies strike first .... The greater the threat, the greater the risk of inaction ... [we] will, if necessary, act preemptively."[6] Bush named Iraq, Iran, and North Korea as an "axis of evil" threatening their neighbors and world peace. Critics considered the Bush doctrine a rationale for acquiring an American empire through military action in violation of international law and the United Nations charter.

Acting on the doctrine of preemptive war, the Bush administration resumed unilateralist U.S. foreign policies. Rejecting opposition from the United Nations and key U.S. allies, among them Canada and Germany, in 2003 the Bush administration invaded and occupied oil-rich Iraq, ending Saddam Hussein's brutal regime. Using faulty or manipulated intelligence, Bush claimed that Iraq possessed weapons of mass destruction and aided Al Qaeda. But U.S. forces found no evidence for either claim. With poor U.S. planning for restoring stability, explosive ethnic and religious divisions threatened to explode into civil war, frustrating attempts to foster democracy. A mounting insurgency, suicide bombings, and foreign terrorists flocking to Iraq caused many thousands of U.S. casualties and complicated reconstruction, including of oil production and basic services, demoralizing Iraqis. Eventually, after 4,500 American and over 100,000 Iraqi deaths and some 32,000 Americans wounded, in 2008 conditions stabilized, violence diminished, and political conditions improved; the last U.S. troops left in 2011. Meanwhile, the U.S.-led NATO force in Afghanistan became bogged down amidst difficult terrain, contentious Afghan politics, cultural misunderstandings, and increased resistance from Islamist fighters led by a rejuvenated Taliban; 3,371 NATO troops had died by 2013, including 2,270 Americans. In both Afghanistan and Iraq, U.S. forces had to return to the counterinsurgency strategy used in Vietnam. The spiraling costs of the Iraq and Afghanistan wars and occupations (ultimately some $6 trillion), combined with large tax cuts and other expenses, ballooned U.S. budget deficits and the national debt. The Iraq war, unpopular in much of the world, and U.S. rejection of several international treaties, such as that on global warming, alienated many Western allies.

Because of its unparalleled economic and military might, the United States has assumed heavy burdens, maintaining military bases and operations around the world. By 2011 its arms sales accounted for three-quarters of all arm sales to other nations, earning some $66 billion per year. While western Europeans and East Asians generally concentrated on trade relations with other nations, Americans attempted to balance trade with confronting the nations they perceived as dangerous. By 2008 U.S. military spending accounted for half of all military spending worldwide, but the U.S. share dropped to about 40 percent in 2013. While anti-U.S. sentiments grew steadily in the early twenty-first century, no major coalition of nations emerged to oppose the U.S. role. By 2012, the United States was shifting attention to eastern Eurasia, where a rising China concerned many nations in the region.

The spiraling national debt (doubling between 2001 and 2008), expensive global commitments, a housing market crisis, and overly lax regulation of banks, corporations, and the stock market generated an economic meltdown in 2008–2009 that soon spread to the rest of the world. Millions of Americans lost their jobs and homes, consumer spending dropped dramatically, stock prices plummeted, pension funds dwindled, and state and local governments faced severe budget cuts. Bailing out major banks, the distressed automobile industry, and revenue-starved states added to federal budget deficits. While the severe recession was not as catastrophic as the Great Depression, it forced debate on the free-wheeling U.S. economic model and the heavy costs of the nation's global obligations. It remains unclear whether the United States will retain its dominance for decades or whether its growing burdens will reduce U.S. power as other nations, perhaps India or more likely China, surge ahead. As U.S. ideological supremacy and control of the global order diminish, some observers have proclaimed the end of the "American Century." Thanks to the world economic crisis, some experts have also perceived a transition under way toward a multipolar economy less dependent on U.S. leadership and consumption. Whatever the case, since the Romans two millennia ago, no other nation has been as dominant in military, economic, political, and social realms as the United States after 1990, forcing Americans to debate, as the Romans and Athenians did, whether democracy and imperial power are consistent.

preemptive war A U.S. doctrine, triggered by the 2001 terrorist attacks, that sanctioned unilateral military action against potential threats.

---

[6]*The National Security Strategy of the United States* (http://www.whitehouse.gov/nsc/print/nssall.html).

MAKE SURE YOU UNDERSTAND THESE KEY POINTS BEFORE MOVING ON

- For several decades after World War II, the United States enjoyed a period of economic growth and lavished economic aid on western Europe and Japan, helping them recover.

- During the Cold War, McCarthyism led to the persecution of many U.S. citizens for supposed communist sympathies, and defense spending became a key factor in the U.S. economy.

- On the basis of the domino theory, which argued that if communism wasn't stopped it would take over the world, the United States adopted an interventionist foreign policy and fought communists in Korea and Vietnam, but neither war achieved U.S. goals, and the Vietnam War severely crippled the U.S. economy.

- During the Cold War, the United States opposed not only communist movements but also noncommunist leftist movements in several countries, in many cases helping to replace them with brutal military dictatorships.

- After the Cold War ended, the United States continued to police the world and after 9/11 followed the doctrine of preemptive war, but the mixed results of its engagements and their high economic cost have raised the question of whether the United States can continue to combine democracy with interventionist foreign policies.

The Changing Societies of North America and the Pacific Basin Ⓢ

How and why are the societies of the United States, Canada, and Australia similar to and different from each other?

The United States, Canada, Australia, and New Zealand, all former British colonies with societies shaped by the many settlers from the British Isles, have shared a general prosperity, stable democracies, similar social patterns, and many cultural traditions. Millions of immigrants from around the world have helped to globalize their cultures, linking them more closely to other nations. But the largest and most powerful, the United States, has played a different role than the other countries, exercising more world power.

Prosperity, Technology, and Inequality in the United States

Living in the world's richest nation, many Americans have benefited from a growing economy and widespread affluence. During the 1960s, as many Americans worked in new automobile, aerospace, service, and information technology industries, production of goods and services doubled, while per capita income rose by half. By 2000 Americans produced a third of the world's goods and services and enjoyed a median annual family income over $40,000. Americans also owned the majority of the giant multinational corporations, such as Exxon-Mobil, General Motors, and Walmart, that played ever-larger roles in the globalizing world. However, this growth had downsides. With 4 percent of the world's population in 2011, Americans consumed around 30 percent of all the world's resources, such as oil and iron ore, and produced a large share of the chemicals, gases, and toxic wastes that pollute the atmosphere, alter the climate, and destroy the land. Yet, Americans lagged well behind most of western Europe, Japan, and several developing nations in meeting sustainable environmental goals. Americans

also worked longer hours than any industrialized people except the Japanese.

The rise of high technology and the decline of smokestack industries such as steel production reshaped the economy and workplace. Americans made innovations in medicine, space research, transportation, and electronics. Space satellites greatly improved weather forecasting, communications, and intelligence gathering; convenient and versatile, computers revolutionized life, being able to, as *Time* magazine concluded, "send letters at the speed of light, diagnose a sick poodle [and] test recipes for beer."[7] By 2008 many carried pocket-sized devices, once the stuff of science fiction novels, that could make telephone calls, send text messages, take photos, play music and films, and access news and weather. Today electronic devices, social media, and the Internet are much more advanced, with endless options.

Beginning in the 1970s, a growing economy improved life for some people, especially those trained in new technologies, but hurt millions of unskilled workers, younger workers, and children in single-parent households. Computers and robots increased efficiency but replaced workers. Industrialists won corporate bonuses for relocating factories and exporting jobs to Latin America or Asia, devastating factory-dependent communities while eliminating a quarter of manufacturing employment. By the early 2000s, although life for the majority of Americans remained comfortable compared to that in most other nations, male unemployment was the highest in five decades, and millions worked two jobs to support their families. Moreover, the United States generally ranked behind Scandinavia, Canada, and Australia for overall quality of life in the annual United Nations Human Development Reports. Some economists referred to a "winner-take-all economy" that

---

[7]Quoted in Walter LaFeber et al., *The American Century: A History of the United States Since 1941*, 5th ed. (Boston: McGraw-Hill, 1998), 519.

produced ever-more millionaires—nearly 6 million by 2012—but also a struggling middle class and more homeless people sleeping in city streets and parks. Except for the richest 1 percent, whose earnings skyrocketed, average incomes fell between 2001 and 2008. Northern European nations, Canada, and Australia fostered far more social mobility than the United States.

Unlike most industrialized nations, the United States also never developed a comprehensive welfare state or national health insurance. Thus a widening gap separated the richest and poorest thirds of Americans. Wealth inequality grew dramatically after 1980; by 2008, 13 percent of Americans lived below the poverty line, the industrialized world's highest rate; the gap between the richest and poorest 20 percent was three times wider than in Japan, the Netherlands, Sweden, or Germany. The economic crisis beginning in 2008 made things worse; by 2010 the top 1 percent of taxpayers enjoyed 93 percent of income growth, doubling their share of national income. Meanwhile, 15 percent lived in poverty. The gap was starkly revealed in 2005 when a devastating hurricane, Katrina, ruined New Orleans, rendered millions homeless, and killed several thousand people: most of the victims were black and poor, unable to afford transportation out of the area. The United States also leads the world in the percentage of its population and total number in prison.

Suburbanization deepened the inequalities. Following World War II many white families with young children sought affordable housing and a better life in suburbia, bedroom communities around major cities that built shopping malls, offered well-funded schools, and seemed immune from city violence. Supporting the trend, governments subsidized real estate developers. William Leavitt, who built vast suburban tracts around New York City, argued that no persons owning their own house and yard could be a communist because they were too busy working to pay the mortgage. The two-car, multitelevision family symbolized affluence. Affordable automobiles and government-funded highways made long commutes from central city jobs possible. Many jobs later moved to the suburbs, leaving the city cores to the local-born poor, often nonwhite, or immigrants. Increasing use of fossil fuels for gasoline, electricity, and heating caused pollution, while clearing land for housing and business development harmed the environment. Most suburbs lacked ethnic and cultural diversity, isolating residents from the stimulation and problems of big city life. Suburban living also intensified the trend toward two-parent, single-breadwinner nuclear families living apart from other relatives, encouraging mothers to stay at home. Until the mid-1960s the image of the fashionably dressed, stay-at-home suburban housewife, smiling proudly as she served breakfast to her husband and children, remained ingrained in the culture, even as more women needed to undertake paid work. Critics lambasted the conformity of life in standardized suburban tract houses, which, according to a 1950s song, resembled "little boxes. There's a green one, a pink one, a blue one and a yellow one. And they're all made out of ticky-tacky, And they all look just the same."[8]

American Political Life: Conservatism and Liberalism

Americans tended to alternate between political conservatism and liberalism. For most of the postwar years, political conservatives, allied with big business groups favoring low taxes and religious groups who disliked social and cultural liberalization, dominated the federal government and judiciary. Liberals, influential chiefly in the 1960s, 1990s, and after 2006, were generally supported by labor unions, environmentalists, and groups seeking social change and a stronger government safety net, such as women's and civil rights organizations.

The desire for stability after the Great Depression and a calamitous world war encouraged political and social conservatism throughout the 1950s; few questioned their government or prevailing social patterns. Americans who criticized U.S. foreign policy or favored social change faced harassment, expulsion from job or school, arrest, or grillings by congressional committees. More Americans than ever married, producing a "baby boom" of children born after the war. The mass media portrayed women as obsessed with bleaching their clothes a purer white and defined by kitchen, bedroom, babies, and home. Society expected homosexuals to remain deep in the closet; those who did not faced taunting, beatings, or arrest. The growing consumer economy emphasized pleasure and leisure activities like cocktail parties, backyard barbecues, and baseball games. Like their parents, teenagers became consumers, creating a market for youth-oriented clothes and music.

During the 1960s, many Americans became open to new ideas and lifestyles as liberalism became influential. The era saw the first people to walk on the moon; the Peace Corps sent idealistic young Americans to help developing nations as teachers, health workers, and agricultural specialists. Presidents John F. Kennedy (g. 1961–1963) and Lyndon B. Johnson (g. 1963–1969) launched programs to address poverty and racism. But the 1960s also fostered doubts, anger, and violence. Three national leaders were assassinated, including Kennedy in 1963. War in Vietnam, the African American civil rights movement, and issues of environmental protection and women's empowerment divided the nation; prowar "hawks" and antiwar "doves" competed for support; riots and demonstrations became common.

During these years many young people, chiefly middle class, rebelled against the values of their parents and established society. Popular folksinger Bob Dylan (b. 1941) sang: "Come, mothers and fathers, throughout the land, And don't criticize what you can't understand. Your sons and your daughters are beyond your command, Your old world is rapidly aging. Please get out of the new one if you can't lend your hand, For the times, they are a'changing."[9] High school and university students worked to change society and politics, registering voters, holding "teach-ins" to discuss national issues, and going door to door to spread their cause. Some youth forged a counterculture that often involved illegal drugs, such as marijuana,

---

[8]Folksinger Malvina Reynolds, quoted in Richard O. Davies, "The Ambivalent Heritage: The City in Modern America," in *Paths to the Present: Interpretive Essays on American Society Since 1930*, ed. James T. Patterson (Minneapolis: Burgess, 1975), 163.
[9]From Peter Blood-Patterson, ed., *Rise Up Singing* (Bethlehem, PA: Sing Out Publications, 1988), 219.

and casual sex, emblazoning "Make love, not war" on bumper stickers, posters, and buttons. During the "Summer of Love" in 1967 young people gathered in San Francisco to hear rock music and share comradery; the Woodstock rock music festival of 1969, which attracted over 300,000 to a New York farm to hear some of the most popular rock musicians, marked the zenith of both the youth counterculture and political activism.

In the 1970s, as the war wound down, the nation returned to more conservative values and politics. With the exception of the 1990s, when the moderate Bill Clinton held the presidency, conservatives maintained their dominance of American politics and the social agenda until 2009. President Ronald Reagan (g. 1981–1989), a popular former movie star and zealous anticommunist, symbolized conservative governance, weakening the labor movement and welfare system while taking a hard line toward the USSR. Religion remained a powerful force, with Americans more likely to attend churches and profess strong Christian beliefs than Canadians or most Europeans. By the 1980s conservative Catholics and evangelical Protestants had become influential in public life, helping elect conservatives to office. Experts debated whether Christian conservatism reflected a rejection of the Enlightenment emphasis on reason and tolerance or rather a search for personal spiritual experience and timeless rules. Many churches stressed membership in a supportive community or emphasized self-help. While Americans avidly consumed new technologies, such as cell phones and portable music players, substantial numbers mistrusted science, rejecting scientific explanations for the origins of the universe and human evolution in favor of biblical accounts. Yet, a fifth of Americans claimed no religious affiliation by 2012, and younger Americans increasingly identified themselves as belonging to no organized faith.

Observers found much to deplore and much to praise in post-1960s U.S. politics. Big corporations, billionaires, and other special interests increasingly financed political activity, fostering corruption and political apathy; generally around half of eligible voters voted in presidential elections, far lower numbers than in most other industrial democracies. However, a free media exposed government corruption, including presidential abuses of power. President Richard Nixon, facing impeachment, resigned in 1973 for sanctioning and then covering up illegal activities by his subordinates, and the Reagan and Clinton presidencies were marred by congressional hearings examining their misdeeds. The controversial, bitter 2000 and 2004 elections of Republican George W. Bush (g. 2001–2009) as president sharply divided Americans between the two major political parties and their divergent policies.

However, the apathy faded in 2008 during an exciting election campaign to replace Bush, who was widely disliked for the unpopular Iraq war, an inadequate response to Hurricane Katrina, spiraling national debt, controversial social and environmental policies, and the economic meltdown of 2008. Illinois senator Barack Obama (b. 1961), the Hawaii-born son of a black Kenyan father studying in the United States and a white mother from Kansas, won the Democratic nomination over New York senator Hillary Rodham Clinton (b. 1947), a

former First Lady. Obama had lived in Indonesia for a few years as a child. Mobilizing a coalition of racial minorities, women, youth, and labor unions, Obama won the presidency; his victory as the first nonwhite U.S. president electrified the world, suggesting that U.S. society was changing. Many Americans and non-Americans hoped for a less unilateral and aggressive U.S. foreign policy. Inheriting two wars and an economic crisis, and enjoying Democratic congressional majorities, Obama introduced New Deal–like policies to generate economic recovery, withdrew U.S. troops from Iraq, ordered the operation that killed Osama bin Laden, recognized homosexual rights, supported immigration reform, and guided a highly controversial health coverage plan ("Obamacare") through Congress. However, while a government stimulus package averted a complete crash and the economy began modest growth, reducing unemployment proved a challenge. Furthermore, the conservative Republican opposition, which controlled the House of Representatives and the majority of states after the 2010 midterm elections, blocked many of his initiatives and vowed to repeal "Obamacare," contributing to political gridlock. Obama also continued some controversial Bush era national security policies, including far-reaching electronic intelligence gathering at home and abroad and the use of military drones against alleged terrorists in southern and western Asia. Both policies alarmed civil libertarians and governments around the world. Whether Obama, reelected in 2012, had begun a new era of liberalism and economic resurgence remained to be seen.

American Society and Popular Culture

Social change affected ethnic minorities, families, women, and men. African Americans, over 10 percent of the population, faced various forms of discrimination and experienced much higher rates of poverty than whites. Until the 1960s southern states maintained strict racial segregation, forcing blacks to attend separate schools and even use different public drinking fountains than whites. In northern industrial cities racism and poverty often concentrated African Americans in run-down inner-city neighborhoods, known as ghettos.

The civil rights movement, organized in the 1950s, eventually forced courts, states, and the federal government to introduce reforms. In 1954 the Supreme Court outlawed segregated schools. A year later, in Montgomery, Alabama, seamstress and community activist Rosa Parks (1913–2005) bravely refused to follow the local custom to give up her front seat on a bus to a white man, sparking a mass movement for change. Reverend Martin Luther King, Jr. (1929–1968) led a bus boycott to protest her arrest and fine. Using nonviolent resistance pioneered by Mohandas Gandhi, King led a protest movement all over the South. While leading the 1963 March on Washington to demand equal rights, he presented his vision: "I have a dream. When we let freedom ring, all of God's children will be able to join hands and sing in the words of that old spiritual, 'Thank God almighty, we are free at last!'"[10] King's assassination by a white racist in 1968 shocked the nation, but the African American struggle inspired similar struggles elsewhere in the

---

[10]Quoted in George Donelson Moss, *America in the Twentieth Century*, 4th ed. (Upper Saddle River, NJ: Prentice-Hall, 2000), 409.

THE OBAMA PRESIDENTIAL CAMPAIGN President Barack Obama addressed a large campaign rally in Las Vegas, Nevada in November, 2012, on his way to re-election for a second term.

world, including black South Africans, Afro-Brazilians, and Australian Aborigines. African Americans gradually gained legal equality and voting rights, many moving into the middle and upper classes, although they were still more likely than whites to live in poverty, face unemployment, and be imprisoned. While they celebrated Obama's presidential victory as a sign of progress, they were also more likely to lose jobs and homes in the 2008–2009 recession. By 2013 some Republican governed states passed legislation that made voting harder particularly for minorities, students, and the poor (see Witness to the Past: Remembering Fifty Years of Civil Rights Progress).

Americans often boasted they live in a "melting pot" in which ethnic groups merged and lost their separate identities, which was often true for people of European ancestry. However, with many members of nonwhite ethnic groups maintaining their separate cultures, America increasingly became a multiracial, multicultural society. By 2013 the U.S. population of 317 million, the world's third largest, was more diverse than ever: 65 percent white, 15 percent Hispanic, 13 percent black, and 4.5 percent Asian; over 10 percent were foreign-born. American life took on a cosmopolitan flavor: Spanish became widely spoken; Latin American grocery stores, Asian restaurants, and African art galleries opened in communities throughout the country. Alaska and Hawaii, both with large nonwhite populations, became states in 1959, adding to the nation's diversity.

Ethnic groups grew through both legal and illegal immigration. Some immigrants labored for meager wages in crowded sweatshops in big cities, where bosses often allowed workers only one or two breaks during their shift and ignored city safety regulations. Chinese sewed clothing in New York City; Mexicans did the same in Los Angeles. Immigration marginalized Native Americans; many lived in cities, others on isolated reservations. Some joined movements seeking a return of lands seized by white settlers generations earlier. While a few tribes achieved prosperity by operating gambling casinos, most Native Americans remained poor.

Women's issues became more prominent. In the 1950s few women worked for high pay, colleges imposed strict quotas on female applicants, married women could not borrow money in their own names, there was no legal concept of sexual harassment, and men joked of keeping women "barefoot and pregnant." By the early twenty-first century conditions had changed dramatically, but it took a long struggle for gender equality. Beginning in the 1960s many women joined feminist movements demanding equal legal rights with men and improved economic status. In 1963 Betty Friedan's (1921–2006) passionate book, *The Feminine Mystique*, identified women's core problem as patriarchal society and unfulfilling housework stunting their growth. With slogans such as "Sisterhood Is Powerful," women came together in groups, such as the National Organization for Women (NOW), fighting for expanded opportunities. Women workers' median income climbed to 70 percent of men's, and the number of women with paid work more than doubled between 1960 and 2000. Women held governorships, federal cabinet posts, and United Nations ambassadorships, served in Congress, sat on the Supreme Court, and

WITNESS TO THE PAST

Remembering Fifty Years of Civil Rights Progress

In 2013 thousands of people of all backgrounds and ethnicities gathered in Washington to commemorate the fiftieth anniversary of the 1963 March on Washington led by Dr. Martin Luther King. John Lewis, then a young civil rights activist, spoke at the first march and then attended the commemoration as a Georgia congressman many years later, offering his memories of the turbulent era, the march, and how things have changed in fifty years.

When I look out over this diverse crowd and survey the guests on this platform ... [I] realize what Otis Redding sang about and what Martin Luther King, Jr. preached about. This moment in our history has been a long time coming, but a change has come. We are standing here in the shadow of Abraham Lincoln 150 years after he issued the Emancipation Proclamation and only 50 years after the historic March on Washington for Jobs and Freedom. We have come a great distance in this country in the 50 years, but we still have a great distance to go before we fulfill the dream of Martin Luther King, Jr. Sometimes I hear people saying nothing has changed, but for someone to grow up the way I grew up in the cotton fields of Alabama to now be serving in the United States Congress makes me want to tell them come and walk in my shoes. Come walk in the shoes of those who were attacked by police dogs, fire hoses and nightsticks, arrested and taken to jail.

I first came to Washington ... to participate in a Freedom Ride. In 1961, black and white people could not be seated together on a Greyhound bus, so we decided to take an integrated ride from here to New Orleans. But we never made it there. Over 400 of us were arrested and jailed in Mississippi during the Freedom Rides. A bus was set on fire in Anniston, Alabama. We were beaten and arrested and jailed, but we helped bring an end to segregation in public transportation. ... In 1963, we could not register to vote simply because of the color of our skin. We had to pay a poll tax, pass a so-called literacy test, count the number of bubbles in a bar of soap or the number of jelly beans in a jar. Hundreds and thousands of people were arrested and jailed throughout the South for trying to participate in the democratic process.... And that's why we told President Kennedy we intended to march on Washington, to demonstrate the need for equal justice and equal opportunity in America.

On August 28th, 1963, the nation's capital was in a state of emergency. Thousands of troops surrounded the city ... but the march was so orderly, so peaceful, it was filled with dignity and self-respect because ... Martin Luther King, Jr. taught us the way of peace ... love ... [and] nonviolence. He taught us to have the power to forgive, the capacity to be reconciled. He taught us to stand up, to speak up, to speak out, to find a way to get in the way. People were inspired by that vision of justice and equality, and they were willing to put their bodies on the line for a cause greater than themselves. ... The spirit of Dr. King's words captured the hearts of people not just around America but around the world. On that day, Martin Luther King, Jr. made a speech, but he also delivered a sermon. He transformed these marble steps of the Lincoln Memorial into a modern day pulpit. He changed us forever. ...

Fifty years later we can ride anywhere we want to ride, we can stay where we want to stay. Those signs that said "white" and "colored" are gone. And you won't see them anymore—except in a museum, in a book, on a video. But there are still invisible signs buried in the hearts in humankind that form a gulf between us. Too many of us still believe our differences define us instead of the divine spark that runs through all of human creation.... So I say to each of us today, we must never, ever give up.... We must keep the faith and keep our eyes on the prize.... And the dean of the civil rights movement once said, we may have come here on different ships, but we all are in the same boat now. So it doesn't matter whether they're black or white, Latino, Asian-American or Native American, whether we are or gay or straight—we are one people, we are one family, we are all living in the same house—not just the American house, but the world house. And when we finally accept these truths, then we will be able to fulfill Dr. King's dream to build a beloved community, a nation and a world at peace with itself.

THINKING ABOUT THE READING

1. How does Lewis describe conditions for African Americans in the early 1960s?
2. How much have things changed since the March on Washington?

Source: "Transcript: Rep. John Lewis' Speech on 50th Anniversary of the March on Washington," *Washington Post,* August 28, 2013 (http://www.washingtonpost.com/politics/transcript-rep-john-lewiss-speech-on-50th-anniversary-of-the-march-on-washington/2013/08/28/fc2d538a-100d-11e3-8cdd-bcdc09410972_story.html).

were serious candidates for president. Hillary Clinton became Obama's secretary of state, the third woman to hold that influential post. Today more women than men finish secondary school and attend universities, some joining highly paid, traditionally male occupations such as law, university teaching, engineering, and medicine. Women pursuing satisfying, well-paid careers, running for political office, and enjoying personal freedoms unimaginable to their great grandmothers owed their gains largely to the feminist movement and its male supporters. However, most employed women struggled to juggle work with family and housekeeping responsibilities. One young mother of two complained in the 1990s that "it's like twenty-four hours a day you're working. My day never ends."[11] Moreover, sexual harassment in the workplace, stalking, and rape remained serious problems. Scholars wrote of a "feminization of poverty" as many women headed single-parent families.

[11]Quoted in James T. Patterson, *America Since 1941: A History*, 2nd ed. (Fort Worth, TX: Harcourt, 2000), 254.

Some changes affected both women and men. Divorce became easier; over half of all marriages in the 1980s, and 40 percent in 2012, ended in divorce, fostering many single-parent households. As in Europe, many men and women never married, often living with partners and often having children out of wedlock. Americans remained deeply divided on abortion, long common but illegal before being declared legal by the Supreme Court in 1973. Americans also disagreed about homosexuality. By the 1960s gay men and lesbians actively fought harassment and legal discrimination, gaining greater acceptance; yet many, especially outside big cities, still faced hostility. Americans quarreled over allowing homosexuals to serve openly in the armed forces, marry, or establish legal partnerships, all patterns common in Europe and Canada but opposed by many Christian churches. By 2013 some states had legalized homosexual marriages, while many others passed laws forbidding it.

Once importers of culture from Europe, Americans became the world's greatest exporters of popular culture products. U.S.-made films, television programs, books, magazines, popular music, and sports reached a global audience. Various musical styles, including the Broadway musicals of songwriters such as Richard Rodgers and Oscar Hammerstein, the blues of singer Billie Holiday and guitarist B. B. King, the jazz of saxophonist John Coltrane and trumpeter Miles Davis, and the country music of singer-songwriters Hank Williams and Dolly Parton, spread far and wide.

But no music style had the power of rock, which in the 1950s and 1960s helped spark a cultural revolution, especially among youth, in the United States and abroad. The first exhilarating blasts of rock and roll from, among others, hip-swinging white singer Elvis Presley (1935–1977) (known as "Elvis the Pelvis") and inventive black guitarist Chuck Berry (b. 1926) defied the Eisenhower era's puritanical social and political conformity, often alarming adults. Rock music broke down social barriers, challenging sexual and racial taboos by appealing across social class boundaries. Inspired by black rhythm and blues, southern white country, and gospel music, early rock proclaimed that young Americans were less divided by race than their parents. Rock became the heart of the 1960s youth movement, when albums by key rock musicians, such as poetic American singer-songwriter Bob Dylan and the British group the Beatles, seemed infused with political meaning. Rock later lost its political edge but, evolving into forms such as punk, grunge, heavy metal, and Indie rock, remained at the heart of U.S. popular music.

African American music also addresses problems of American life. Soul music from artists like James Brown and Aretha Franklin promoted black self-respect and unity, paralleling black pride movements. In the 1980s rap music, emerging out of urban black ghettos, became the cutting edge of Western pop music. An eclectic mix of rock, soul, rhythm and blues, and Caribbean music, rap expresses urban black youth's tensions, concerns, and aspirations. The boastful, often angry tone highlights conflict between white and black, rich and poor, and male and female, outraging segments of both white society and the black middle class. Musicians in nations around the world adopted the rap style, often integrating it into their own traditions.

The Canadian Experience

Although sharing cultural traditions and a democratic spirit with Americans, Canadians remained proudly independent of their powerful southern neighbor, nurturing differences such as two official languages—English and French. Two main parties, one liberal and one conservative, dominated national elections, but, unlike in the United States, smaller leftwing, rightwing, and regional parties also played key roles, often governing Canadian provinces. The French Canadian nationalist Party Québecois (**KAY-be-KWAH**) often governed French-speaking Quebec, which contains a quarter of Canada's population, periodically holding votes on independence from Canada (see Map 29.2). In 1985 Quebec gained recognition as a distinct society with more provincial autonomy. Canadians still debate how much power to allocate to provinces and how much to the federal government.

Canadians, 35 million strong by 2013, cannot ignore their proximity to the United States, which is much larger and with vastly more global power. Former prime minister Pierre Trudeau (**troo-DOE**) (g. 1968–1984), a French Canadian, complained that sharing a border with the United States was "like sleeping with an elephant. No matter how friendly or even-tempered the beast, one is affected by every twitch and grunt."[12] Most Canadians live within a hundred miles of the U.S. border, with easy access to the U.S. mass media. Moreover, Americans own some 20 percent of Canada's economy. Some resent U.S. domination. In 1994 the North American Free Trade Agreement (NAFTA) further bound the Canadian, Mexican, and U.S. economies. Yet, despite usually friendly relations, Canadians often opposed U.S. foreign policies, including the wars in Vietnam and Iraq.

Canadians generally enjoyed prosperity, which fostered social stability. Agricultural, industrial, and natural resource exports helped finance rising living standards, while mining vast oil reserves in tar sands enriched western provinces but also caused serious environmental damage. Hence, Canada consistently ranked among the top five nations in the annual United Nations Human Development Index of life quality. Canadians recovered better than most from the 2008–2009 global economic collapse, with lower unemployment and higher household net worth than Americans. Unlike more individualistic Americans, Canadians, influenced by social democratic ideals, built a strong social safety net, including national health insurance. Generally more liberal on social and economic issues than Americans, they also approved same-sex marriage, banned the death penalty, and, in some provinces, decriminalized marijuana use. Organized religion's influence in public life has declined. In Quebec, where the Catholic Church once enjoyed great influence, even openly homosexual politicians enjoyed popular support and officials promoted secular policies. Quebec's birthrate, one of the world's highest in the 1940s, has fallen by over half, becoming one of the world's lowest.

Canadian society has become increasingly diverse, welcoming several million immigrants from all over the world, many from Asia and the Caribbean. In 2005 Haitian-born

---

[12]Quoted in Wayne C. Thompson, *Canada 1997* (Harpers Ferry, VA: Stryker-Post, 1997), 1.

MAP 29.2 CANADA The Canadian federation includes eleven provinces stretching from Newfoundland in the east to British Columbia and the Yukon in the west. In 1999 a large part of northern Canada, inhabited chiefly by the Inuit, became the self-governing region of Nunavut. © 2015 Cengage Learning

Michaelle Jean, a Quebec television journalist, became Canada's first female governor general, the official head of state representing the British monarch. Rather than following the American "melting pot" ideal, Canadian laws, especially the Multiculturalism Act of 1988, allow ethnic minorities to maintain their cultures and languages and also recognize the rights of Native Americans, known as the "First Nations," some of whom have pressed land claims. But some Canadians resent recognition of Portuguese Canadians or Chinese Canadians. To address the desire for autonomy of the Inuit, or Eskimo, peoples of the Arctic region, in 1999 the federal government transformed much of northern Canada into the self-governing territory of Nunavut **(NOO-nuh-voot)**. Canadians still debate how much to think of themselves as English, French, Japanese, or Inuit Canadians and how much to live comfortably with multiple identities.

The Pacific Basin Societies

The diverse societies scattered around the Pacific Basin experienced major changes as they adjusted to a new world. In the two largest, most populous countries, Australia and New Zealand, the majority population, descended from European, mainly British and Irish, settlers, identified with western European society. Australia became one of the world's most affluent nations, known to its people as the "lucky country" because of its abundant resources and high living standards. A comprehensive system of social welfare, health care, and education helped forge a quality of life that usually places Australia near the top in the annual United Nations Human Development Reports. However, Australians have also faced chronic high unemployment and areas of persisting poverty. Feminists complain that men dominate government, business, and churches, giving women less influence than in most Western nations. Many men hold traditional views on women. Conservative prime minister, Tony Abbott (g. 2013–), was once asked rhetorically, in a discussion about the rarity of women in powerful positions in Australia: "What if men are, by physiology or temperament, more adapted to exercise authority or to issue command?"[13] Nonetheless, women have won considerable gender equity; Australians elected the first woman prime minister, Julia Gillard (g. 2010–2013),

---

[13]Quoted in A. Odysseus Patrick, "Australia's Tony Abbott on Track to Win Prime Minister Post After Years in the Political Doldrums," *Washington Post*, September 3, 2013 (http://www.washingtonpost.com/world/asia_pacific/australias-tony-abbott-on-track-to-win-prime-minister-post-after-years-in-political-doldrums/2013/09/03/24aaae98-10c7-11e3-bdf6-e4fc677d94a1_st ory.html).

and boasted the richest Australian, mining magnate Gina Rinehart.

Australia's 23 million people are increasingly diverse; 20 percent speak a language other than English at home, and immigrants or their descendants are prominent in most fields, including sports. In 1973 the federal government, seeking better relations with Asian nations, abandoned restrictions on non-white immigration—known as the "white Australia" policy—in place since 1901, stimulating immigration from Asia and the Middle East; as a result, predominantly Asian neighborhoods developed in major cities. Newcomers from Europe continued to arrive. Hence, one of the major cities, Melbourne, boasted the world's largest Greek emigrant population. Eventually nearly a quarter of Australia's people were born abroad. Race relations improved as Aborigines, 2.5 percent of the population, often poor and facing discrimination, gained some self-determination and land rights for their tribal territories. One group blocked a dam project in the 1990s that threatened tribal land. Yet, those Aborigines living in run-down city neighborhoods have struggled in the largely white-owned urban economy. Occasional attacks on Arab and Indian immigrants by drunken white youth have also showed that racism has not been eliminated.

Changing global conditions have forced new economic thinking. Climate change threatens Australia more than most nations, sparking more catastrophic floods and fires. In addition, with an economy based primarily on exporting minerals, wheat, beef, and wool, Australia needs secure outside markets.

Formation of the European Union and NAFTA threatened traditional markets in Europe and North America, raising questions about the link to Britain. In a 1995 referendum, 55 percent of Australians supported remaining a constitutional monarchy under the British queen. Yet, Britain was far away, while Asia was, as Australians put it, the "near north." Torn between its European history and Asian geography, Australians established closer trade and investment links to Southeast Asia, East Asia, and the Pacific islands, fostering two decades of economic growth; by 2000, Asian nations, especially China, accounted for some 60 percent of Australia's export market. Thanks to a mining boom, Australia largely avoided recession during the global financial crisis, but growth slowed by 2013.

New Zealanders have long cultivated their British heritage and British patronage, but now they have also forged strategic and economic connections within the Asia-Pacific region. The economy traditionally relied heavily on tourism and export of agricultural products, mostly to Britain. But, suffering from a stumbling economy and jolted by Britain's membership in the European Community, New Zealand cultivated close relations with the United States and then with nearby Asian and Pacific countries, which by 2000 accounted for one-third of the nation's trade. While experiencing rising unemployment, New Zealanders were also helped by an elaborate social welfare system. Thanks in part to expanded educational opportunities, women gained new economic roles and served in politics. Former university professor Helen Clark (b. 1950) was the nation's first female prime minister (g. 1999–2008). In 2013

LION DANCE In recent decades, many Asians have settled in Australia. This Chinese dragon dance, in Melbourne's large Chinatown, celebrates the Chinese New Year.

Kylie McLaughlin/Lonely Planet Images/Getty Images

New Zealanders approved gay marriage. Closer ties to the Pacific region fostered increased immigration from Asia and the Pacific islands. The government also recognized the land rights of, and worked to end discrimination against, the native Maori minority, who sought to maintain their Polynesian culture while adding modern economic skills.

While Australians and New Zealanders long enjoyed independence, decolonization of many Pacific islands, spurred by the United Nations, came much later; between 1962 and 1980 nine independent Pacific nations were formed in Polynesia and Melanesia, and in 1990 the United States gave up control of some of its Micronesian territories. The new states ranged from republics such as Fiji to kingdoms like Tonga to groupings such as the Federated States of Micronesia. Not all Pacific islanders, however, became independent. Some French-ruled islands, such as Tahiti and New Caledonia, became semiautonomous French territories with representation in the French parliament, and many islanders resented what they considered disguised French colonialism. Most independent islands retained close ties to their former colonizer, as Micronesia did with the United States. Pacific islanders have remained dependent on fishing, tourism, and export of mineral and agricultural products to Japan, the United States, Australia, and New Zealand.

Islanders cooperated on common issues, forming regional organizations that promoted everything from duty-free trade to art festivals and fighting high-technology fishing fleets from industrialized nations. Opposing nuclear weapons testing, they joined with Australia and New Zealand to declare the Pacific a nuclear-free zone. The international Law of the Sea Treaty gave them more control of adjacent sea beds and their minerals. But some problems have defied solution. Thanks to rising sea levels, which threaten low-lying atolls and coastal plains, many islanders will have to relocate over the next century. The Tuvalo islands, with eleven thousand people and averaging only 3 feet above sea level, will be inundated by 2050.

Islanders have held on to some indigenous traditions while adapting to social and political change. While most became Christian, some pre-Christian customs remained important. For example, although Western Samoa, first ruled by Germany and then by New Zealand, has an elected parliament, clan chiefs still govern the villages. But poverty fostered migration to island cities, such as Suva in Fiji and Pago Pago in American Samoa, as well as emigration to Australia, New Zealand, Hawaii, and the mainland United States. More Samoans and Cook Islanders live abroad than at home; thousands of Tongans reside in California. The money migrants send back has become a valuable source of income. Some islands have experienced ethnic or regional conflict over political power and scarce land. Occasional military coups have rocked Fiji, resulting from tensions between descendants of Indian immigrants, nearly half the population, and native Fijians, who fear that Indians want to diminish traditional Fijian chiefs and challenge tribal rights to land.

MAKE SURE YOU UNDERSTAND THESE KEY POINTS BEFORE MOVING ON

- On average, U.S. residents are among the wealthiest in the world, yet in recent decades many industrial jobs have been moved overseas and the gap between rich and poor has grown wider, with the former often living in suburbs and the latter left behind in inner cities.

- After 1945 African Americans gained legal rights through the civil rights movement, immigrants made America more diverse, women increasingly entered the work force, and gays and lesbians became more visible but still struggled for equal rights.

- While Canada's culture and economy are strongly influenced by the United States, in many ways Canada resembles western Europe, with a strong social safety net and a more liberal attitude on social issues.

- Australia and New Zealand have maintained their traditional ties with Britain but have also traded increasingly with their Asian neighbors, while many Pacific islands have gained independence from former colonizers but still face challenges such as rising sea levels, poverty, and ethnic conflict.

aplia

Political Change in Latin America and the Caribbean

S
N

Why have democracy and economic development proved to be difficult goals in Latin America?

The Latin American and Caribbean peoples (see Map 29.3) had different experiences than North Americans and Pacific Basin societies. Social inequality, economic underdevelopment, and demands for change often generated revolutionary and progressive political movements in impoverished villages and shantytowns. Sometimes leftists gained power, launching reforms; only in Cuba did they remain in power for decades. A few Latin American countries and most small Caribbean islands enjoyed consistent democratic traditions; elsewhere military leaders or autocratic civilians often dominated governments. Most governments, whether democratic or dictatorial, proved unable to eliminate their nation's major problems.

MAP 29.3 MODERN LATIN AMERICA AND THE CARIBBEAN Latin America includes the nations of Central and South America and those Caribbean societies that are Spanish-speaking, including Cuba and the Dominican Republic. Brazil, Argentina, and Mexico are the largest Latin American nations. The peoples of the small Caribbean islands, mostly English- or French-speaking, also formed independent states. © 2015 Cengage Learning

Despotisms, Democracies, and the United States

Latin Americans struggled to raise living standards and expand political participation. Some paternalistic but authoritarian reformers mobilized workers and peasants for change, but they failed to empower the people or significantly improve their lives. The charismatic Juan Peron (**puh-RONE**) (1895–1974),

a former army officer, admirer of Benito Mussolini, and hypnotic public speaker, was elected Argentina's president in 1946 and proved to be an autocratic reformer who marginalized the legislature and crushed opposition. With help from his hugely popular wife, Evita Peron (1919–1952), a radio and stage actress from a poor family and a proponent of social justice, the nationalistic regime won working- and middle-class support, emphasized industrialization, and bought often foreign-owned banks, insurance companies, railroads, and shipping companies. Evita promoted women's issues. After Evita's death in 1952, corruption, growing unemployment, inflation, strikes, and human rights abuses sparked Peron's overthrow in 1955. The military mostly ruled Argentina from the 1950s through 1983, often killing opponents. Yet Peron's followers sustained a Peronist movement, chiefly working class, that often governed Argentina after democracy was restored.

Rightwing and leftwing forces jockeyed for power in Latin America. From the 1950s through the late 1980s, right-wing military governments and despots ruled most countries, suppressing labor unions, student protesters, and democracy activists to maintain stability. In some Central American countries such as El Salvador and Guatemala, organized death squads assassinated dissident peasants, liberal clergy, teachers, and journalists. Despite the repression, leftwing movements increased their strength. By 1979 the Sandinistas, a Marxist-led revolutionary movement, had defeated the long-standing dictatorship and gained control of Nicaragua. In 1970 the even more radical Shining Path emerged in Peru; its leaders, half of them women, mixed Maoist ideas with plans to emancipate impoverished Indians. Their rebellion terrorized Peruvians before being crushed in the early 1990s.

During the later 1980s, with rightwing rule largely discredited for not addressing mass poverty, many nations turned to democracy and free markets under centrist or moderate leftist leaders. In most cases they also could not resolve severe problems or diminish social inequalities. Some nations faced racial and ethnic tensions. Large Indian communities in Bolivia, Peru, Colombia, Mexico, and Guatemala, often allied with leftists, increasingly sought equal rights, a fairer share of wealth, and recognition of their cultures and aspirations. Hence, in 2005 Bolivia's resentful Indian majority elected as president Evo Morales (b. 1959), a former small-town soccer player who led coca farmers fighting a white-dominated government and U.S. opposition to coca growing. At an ancient temple's ruins, Morales participated in a spiritual ceremony steeped in his Aymara peoples' pre-Inca traditions. Walking barefoot up the pyramid steps, he donned a traditional tunic and cap, accepted a gold and silver baton from Aymara priests, and promised to "seek equality and justice" for the poor and eliminate vestiges of the colonial past. However, redistributing wealth and power from the white minority, reshaping the political system, and pursuing nationalistic economic policies generated conflict within Bolivia and U.S. opposition.

By the later 1990s, as disillusionment with capitalism increased, the left regained the political initiative, largely within a democratic context. After mobilizing poor workers and peasants, former general Hugo Chavez (1954–2013) was elected president of oil-rich Venezuela. Chavez introduced socialist policies to redistribute oil wealth to the poor, marginalized the congress, and controlled the courts, all actions that alienated the wealthy and middle class, who organized mass protests. Chavez called his policies the Bolivaran Revolution, linking them to the nineteenth-century, Venezuelan-born liberator. The United States moved to isolate the dictatorial,

pro-Cuba Chavez regime and support the opposition. Chavez lambasted U.S. leaders and foreign policies, provided aid and oil to other Latin Americans, and tightened his grip on politics and the media, but economic problems after 2009 eroded domestic support. His allies maintained power after Chavez died of cancer soon after his 2012 reelection; his death was mourned by the poor. Elsewhere, voters desperate for more equitable policies elected pragmatic leftist leaders in countries such as Argentina, Brazil, Chile, Ecuador, Uruguay, and El Salvador; some prosecuted or investigated human rights violations perpetrated under military rule. But experts debate whether imported economic ideas from the left or right will work for Latin Americans.

Latin Americans also had to deal with the United States and its powerful presence. Referring to longtime U.S. economic leverage, a leftist Nicaraguan leader lamented that his country's "function was to grow sugar, cocoa and coffee for the United States; we served the dessert at the imperialist dining table."[14] The United States acted not only as neighborhood bully at times but also as a leading trading partner, major source of investment capital, supplier of military and economic assistance, and inspiration to the region's democrats and free market enthusiasts. U.S. popular culture, particularly films and music, reached a huge audience, influencing local cultures. Moreover, millions of people seeking a better life have moved north to the United States legally or illegally. In 1999 the United States transferred control over the Panama Canal to Panama, yet U.S. military bases remained along the canal, symbolizing regional power.

Under the banner of anticommunism, Americans often intervened in Latin American and Caribbean countries, arousing much local resentment. For example, in 1954 a CIA-organized and armed force led by exiled Guatemalan military officers overthrew a democratically elected, reformist government led chiefly by liberals and socialists who were considered communists by American leaders for implementing land reform and encouraging leftist labor unions, angering U.S. business interests. The powerful United Fruit Company, closely connected to Eisenhower administration officials, controlled much of Guatemala's economy, especially the banana plantations. The democratic regime's removal cheered wealthy Guatemalans and U.S. corporations, but Guatemala's new leaders formed death squads that killed over 200,000 people, especially poor Indian peasants and workers, over the next three decades. By 1990, when the repression diminished, 90 percent of Guatemalans still lived in poverty, and one-third lacked adequate food.

U.S. leaders also used their power elsewhere, offering military assistance and advice to friendly governments against revolutionary movements in El Salvador, Honduras, and Colombia and employing covert operations to undermine or overthrow left-leaning governments in Brazil (1964), Chile (1973), and Nicaragua (1989). Most Americans were unaware of the covert activities until years later. Sometimes the United States dispatched military forces, as in the Dominican Republic (1965) and Grenada (1982). Although not inspired by anticommunism, in 1990 U.S. troops invaded Panama to remove and arrest

[14]Jaime Wheelock, quoted in Kyle Longley, *In the Eagle's Shadow: The United States and Latin America* (Wheeling, IL: Harlan Davidson, 2002), 291.

dictator Manuel Noriega (b. 1940), a longtime U.S. ally and well-paid CIA informant who was implicated in human rights abuses and drug smuggling. U.S. troops were also sent to Haiti in 1994 to support a reform government that replaced a brutal dictatorship, promoting stability as leftwing and rightwing forces intermittently battled for control, leaving Haitians more desperate.

The Legacy of Revolution: Mexico and Cuba

The early-twentieth-century Mexican Revolution inspired hopes of reducing social inequality, but the nation's leaders soon emphasized economic growth over uplifting the poor majority. Even today, in southern states where revolutionaries once promised liberty and justice, peasant men, wearing traditional white cotton pants and shirt, still use machetes to cultivate their tiny plots of corn. In Mexico's limited democracy, the Party of Revolutionary Institutions (PRI) controlled elections, often resorting to voter fraud. A broad coalition of factions led by businessmen and bureaucrats, the PRI fostered stability for decades while deflecting challenges to its power, usually by co-opting or arresting opponents. But in 1968 police fired on a large demonstration, killing hundreds of university students and other protesters.

By the 1980s the PRI began to falter as leftist and right-wing parties made some national gains. In the early 1990s a peasant revolt in a poor southern state, Chiapas, revealed starkly the PRI's failure to redress rural poverty. The 2000 election of a non-PRI president, Vicente Fox, ended the seven-decades-long PRI monopoly on federal power. Fox, a pro-U.S. rancher and free market conservative, could not foster much economic or social change, while the PRI still held power in many states and enjoyed a national power base. Gradually, however, a more open and pluralistic political system emerged, with stronger leftwing and rightwing parties contending with the PRI for support. In the 2008 elections another conservative edged out a leftist for the presidency, solidifying a multiparty system. But in 2012, with sixty thousand dead from rampant violence by drug cartels, crime syndicates, and a failed war on drugs, making life dangerous in many regions, the PRI returned to power under a new president, Enrique Peña Nieto.

Mexico's economic system also gradually opened, although corruption remained part of life. For decades the PRI mixed capitalism with a strong government role. However, with oil the major foreign revenue source, collapsing world oil prices in the 1980s damaged development prospects; open markets replaced protectionist policies. In 1994, after the North American Free Trade Agreement (NAFTA) helped integrate the U.S. and Mexican economies, many U.S.-owned factories opened on Mexico's side of the border. The majority of new workers, poorly paid young women housed in crowded dormitories or flimsy shacks, often complained of harassment or assault by male

Castroism Innovative socialist policies introduced by Fidel Castro to stimulate economic development in Cuba while tightly controlling its population.

workers or managers. Elsewhere many Mexicans lost jobs; peasant corn farmers could not compete with highly subsidized U.S. farmers. By 2000 half of the 100 million Mexicans lived on $4 a day or less, and the bottom 20 percent of Mexicans earned only 4 percent of the country's personal income. Even the urban middle class felt the economic pain as wages stagnated. Whereas in 1980 Mexico's economy was nearly four times larger than South Korea's, by 2005 a dynamic South Korea had pushed ahead. At the same time, Mexico's population quadrupled between 1940 and 2000. In recent years Mexico has become Latin America's largest exporter of manufactured products, income inequality has declined, and more people have joined the middle class. These trends attracted migrants from the United States, Asia, and Latin America; between 2000 and 2010 the foreign-born population doubled. But 57 percent of Mexican workers in 2011 earned less than $13.50 a day, and some 18 million remained in extreme poverty. Because of poverty and overpopulation, thousands of desperate Mexicans continue to cross the border to the United States each year, legally or illegally, in search of a better life. Others have taken up growing or smuggling illegal drugs.

Unlike Mexico, Cuba, led by Fidel Castro (b. 1927), built a society dominated by a powerful communist government. Castro, a onetime amateur baseball star nearly signed by a U.S. professional team who instead became a lawyer, came to power in 1959 in a revolution against a corrupt U.S.-supported dictator. Although a rich sugar planter's son, Castro allied with the Cuban Communist Party, pledging to introduce radical change; many thousands of affluent Cubans fled to the nearby United States. In 1961 Americans moved to isolate and then overthrow Castro's regime by organizing a Cuban exile military force that landed on a Cuban beach, the Bay of Pigs. But the invasion, poorly planned and enjoying little popular support in Cuba, was routed—a humiliation for the United States. Castro became a firm Soviet ally, igniting even more U.S. opposition and precipitating the Cuban Missile Crisis. In 1962 U.S. air surveillance discovered Soviet ballistic missiles with a 2,000-mile range and capable of carrying nuclear warheads. President John F. Kennedy demanded the missiles' removal, imposed a naval blockade on Cuba, and considered invading the island. With the threat of nuclear confrontation looming, the Soviets removed the missiles, defusing the crisis. In the aftermath, the United States imposed an economic boycott, supported by Cuban exiles, that still endures, cutting off Cuba from sources of trade and investment.

In the 1960s and 1970s Castro tried innovative socialist policies, known as **Castroism**, to stimulate economic development while tightly controlling the population. Castro called capitalism "repugnant, filthy, gross, alienating because it causes war, hypocrisy and competition"[15]; yet his own policies generated little surplus food and few consumer goods. Despite valiant efforts, Cubans largely failed to diversify their sugar-based economy. Nonetheless, Castroism improved life for the working classes: schools and clinics were built, literacy campaigns were mounted, and long-marginalized Afro-Cubans and

---

[15]Quoted in Sebastian Balfour, *Castro*, 2nd ed. (New York: Longman, 1995), 167.

CASTRO ADDRESSING CROWD A spellbinding orator, the Cuban leader, Fidel Castro, often recruited support for his government and policies by speaking at large rallies.

Wally McNamee/CORBIS

women gained more equality; women now constitute 60 percent of professional and technical workers and 43 percent of parliament. By the mid-1980s Cuba had the lowest infant mortality and highest literacy rates, life expectancy, and doctors per population in Latin America; its citizens lived as long as North Americans and ten years longer than Mexicans and Brazilians. Moreover, unlike in some Latin American dictatorships, no death squads murdered dissidents. However, government agencies monitored citizens and their opinions; Castro limited free expression and jailed or harassed those who defied the ban, including brave writers, homosexuals, and human rights and free speech advocates. Seeking political freedom, better-paying jobs, or higher living standards, nearly a million Cubans fled over the years, mostly to the United States; forty thousand of them left in 2013.

Castro exchanged dependence on the United States for dependence on the USSR, which poured billions of dollars into the country. Since the USSR's collapse, Cuba has struggled. With few foreign markets or sources of capital, the social welfare system cracked, and the economy crumbled despite some market reforms. Yet, frustrating his opponents, Castro remained in power for fifty years. In 2008 an ailing Castro turned over leadership to his brother Raul Castro (b. 1931), who offered some cautious reforms, sputtering toward a market economy. The regime tolerated mild criticism, leased some state-owned land to private farmers, and allowed small private enterprises like restaurants, pizza makers, and cobblers, often in homes or garages, while trimming the government work force. Legal bazaars now fill streets to serve consumers. Many urban Cubans, but not the poorest residents, have access to televisions, DVDs from Miami, Internet-linked computers, cell phones, and even (often old) cars. Critics, including most U.S. allies, have opposed the U.S. embargo, arguing that it helps Castro by reinforcing

anti-U.S. feelings and discrediting dissidents. In 2009 U.S. president Barack Obama made it easier for U.S.-based Cubans to visit the island. Many Cubans desire a freer system, but, remembering American domination from 1898 to 1959, some remain wary of the United States.

Dictatorship and Democracy: Brazil and Chile

Few Latin American nations have had as much promise and experienced as many problems as Brazil and Chile. Occupying half of South America, Brazil is Latin America's colossus, with 200 million people and its largest economy. From the mid-1940s to the mid-1960s Brazilians, despite economic crises, maintained democracy. In 1961 Joao Goulart (**jao joo-LART**) (1918–1976), a populist reformer supported by leftists, assumed the presidency, but his efforts to organize impoverished peasants and rural workers antagonized powerful landlords. The military overthrew Goulart in 1964 and imposed a harsh dictatorship for the next two decades (1964–1985), arresting some forty thousand opponents. Fearing a communist takeover, the United States encouraged the military coup because it supported authoritarian governments that emphasized economic growth and national security. Relying on brutal repression, the generals imposed censorship, outlawed political parties, and banned strikes and collective bargaining. Rightwing vigilante groups and death squads killed up to one hundred dissidents a month and tortured countless others, including labor leaders and slum dwellers.

For a decade the capitalist economy boomed, eliciting American praise of the "Brazilian miracle" as annual growth rates averaged 10 percent between 1968 and 1974 and exports shifted from natural resources, such as coffee, to manufactured goods. Industrialization relied heavily on foreign investment, technology, and markets; the United States and international lending agencies poured in $8 billion in aid. But the "miracle" depended on low wages and redistributing income upward to the rich and middle class, confirming the local saying that there is no justice for the poor. The top 10 percent enjoyed 75 percent of the income gain, while half of all households lived below the poverty line. While many people went barefoot and dressed in rags, Brazil made and exported shoes. Brazilian governments also encouraged land speculators and foreign corporations to open up the vast Amazon Basin, the world's largest tropical rain forest and river system. Logging, farming, mining, and ranching rapidly stripped virgin forest, destabilizing the environment and displacing many of the 200,000 Indians living off its resources. Brazil's South American neighbors such as Peru and Bolivia are also responsible for severe deforestation in the Amazon region.

By 1980 the "miracle" had faded; Brazil experienced an inflation rate of over 100 percent, huge balance-of-payments deficits, massive foreign debt, and sagging industrial production. Meanwhile, numerous Brazilians demanded democracy, and the Catholic Church criticized human rights violations, advocating for social justice. In 1985 democracy returned with the election of a civilian president. However, under the successive democratic governments led by moderate reformers, many problems remained unresolved; leaders feared another military coup. Inflation soared to 2,500 percent by 1994. When landless peasants seized land, well-connected landowners hired gunmen to harass them. Social inequities such as school dropout rates, malnutrition, bankrupt public health services, homelessness, and debt slavery grew. Before 2000 Brazil maintained one of the world's most unequal income distributions: the wealthiest 1 percent earned the same percentage of national income as the poorest 50 percent. Many Brazilians became disillusioned with democracy.

Wanting further reform, in 2002 Brazilians turned to the left, electing as president socialist labor leader Luis Ignacio da Silva (b. 1944), known as Lula, a former metalworker and longtime dissident. While some peasant and worker groups believed that Lula's pragmatic, moderate economic policies did too little for the poor and the environment, Lula fostered such dramatic economic growth that some observers compared Brazil to dynamic Southeast Asian nations such as Malaysia, Singapore, and Thailand. Eventually Lula's center-left policies fostered a larger middle class and improved life for many. The booming economy (the world's seventh largest), growing manufacturing, and discovery of offshore oil gave Brazil regional and international clout, restoring national self-confidence. Brazil became a major player in the G-20 group of key industrial nations and joined with Russia, India, China, and South Africa to form the BRICS bloc as an alternative to the U.S.-led Western alliance. When Lula retired in 2011, still highly popular, Brazilians elected his colleague, former leftwing dissident Dima Roussef (b. 2011) and the nation's first female leader. But while unemployment remained low, the economy stumbled (from 7.5 percent growth in 2010 to 1 percent in 2012) and inflation increased. In 2013 massive street protests erupted against corruption, inadequate public services, slowing economic growth, and lavish spending on facilities for the 2014 World Cup and 2016 summer Olympics, unsettling the political landscape. Brazilians have often shared an optimistic outlook because of the nation's size and economic potential, reflected in the saying that "God is a Brazilian." But a perennial local joke reflects cynicism: "Brazil, Country of the Future, but the future never comes."[16]

Chileans, like Brazilians, tried varied strategies, from reform to dictatorship to democracy, to foster development. Chileans enjoyed a long tradition, unusual in Latin America, of elected democratic governments sustained by a large middle class, high rates of literacy and urbanization, and multiple political parties. Nonetheless, a wealthy elite of businessmen, military officers, and landowners held political power, suppressing labor unrest. Dependent on mineral exports, especially copper, by the 1960s Chile, divided politically between the right, center, and left, had a stagnant economy in which two-thirds of Chileans

earned under $200 a year. With the 1970 elections, Chileans shifted direction and elected the Popular Unity, a coalition of six liberal, socialist, and communist parties supported by small businessmen, the urban working class, and peasants. Their winning presidential candidate, medical doctor Salvador Allende **(ah-YEN-dee)** (1908–1973), promised a "Chilean road" to socialism, with red wine and meat pies, through constitutional means in a parliamentary democracy. His regime nationalized banks and a copper industry dominated by powerful U.S. corporations; broke up underutilized ranches and farms, dividing the land among the peasant residents; supported labor unions; and provided urban shantytowns with health clinics and better schools. Both employment and economic production soared. The Popular Unity also fostered a Chilean cultural renaissance, arguing that American magazines, recordings, and films had overwhelmed Chilean-produced cultural products. A pro-Allende cultural organization protested, "Our folklore, our history, our customs, our way of living and thinking are being strangled [by] the uncontrolled invasion [of the U.S. media and popular culture]."[17]

Although democracy flourished and Allende enjoyed growing popularity, rapid reforms produced shortages of luxury goods, fostering middle-class resentment. Allende's opponents controlled the mass media and judiciary while dominating the congress. U.S. president Richard Nixon worried about Allende's friendship with Cuba's Fidel Castro and feared that Allende's socialism without revolution could spread, threatening U.S. power and economic interests. Nixon mounted an international economic embargo on Chilean exports, while the CIA spread untrue rumors, helped assassinate pro-Allende military officers, and organized strikes to paralyze the economy.

In 1973 a U.S.-supported military coup overthrew Allende, who died defending the presidential palace. The military imposed a brutal military dictatorship led by General Agusto Pinochet **(ah-GOOS-toh pin-oh-CHET)** (1915–2006) that arrested 150,000 Allende supporters, detained and tortured hundreds of political prisoners for years, and murdered thousands of dissidents, sometimes in front of other prisoners held in the national stadium. Thousands fled the country. The junta forbade labor unions and strikes, prohibited free speech and political parties, restored nationalized U.S. property, and publicly burned books and records produced by leftist Chileans. Advised by U.S. economists, Pinochet installed a free enterprise economy, similar to military-ruled Brazil's, that generated growth and moderate middle-class prosperity but also a monumental foreign debt and environmental degradation. Little of this wealth trickled down to the poor, whose living standards deteriorated. By the later 1980s, unemployment had skyrocketed to 30 percent, and 60 percent of Chileans were poor. Two observers wrote that Pinochet's Chile "remained a dual society of winners and losers. The rich, roaring through traffic in their expensive sedans, seemed to mock those left behind, trapped in fuming buses."[18]

However, a severe economic crisis undermined the regime's legitimacy, and in 1989 escalating social tensions

---

[16] The quotes are in Thomas E. Skidmore and Peter H. Smith, *Modern Latin America*, 4th ed. (New York: Oxford University Press, 1997), 147; Joseph A. Page, *The Brazilians* (Reading, MA: Addison-Wesley, 1995), 5.

[17] Quoted in David J. Morris, *We Must Make Haste—Slowly: The Process of Revolution in Chile* (New York: Vintage, 1973), 270–271.

[18] Pamela Constable and Arturo Valenzuela, *A Nation of Enemies: Chile Under Pinochet* (New York: W.W. Norton, 1991), 38.

and political protests forced an election. The resulting center-left governments, often headed by presidents from Allende's Socialist Party, retained free enterprise while boosting health, housing, education, and social spending. They reduced poverty by half and lowered unemployment; tax increases and increased welfare did not stifle high annual economic growth. Chile has become the most prosperous Latin American economy and enjoys a stable democratic system, but considerable inequality persists. In 2010 Chileans elected their first conservative president in twenty years, Sebastian Pinera, who soon faced massive student protests, led by charismatic leftist Camila Vellejo, demanding reform of an educational system favoring the wealthy. Although the parliament refused to consider their proposals, Vallejo inspired and helped activists worldwide. The 2013 elections returned former president Michelle Bachelet to power on a center-left platform, defeating the conservative candidate, also a woman. While leaders have sought closer economic ties with the United States, many Chileans remain bitter toward the Americans for having helped perpetuate a brutal military regime.

MAKE SURE YOU UNDERSTAND THESE KEY POINTS BEFORE MOVING ON

- The Mexican Revolution led to decades of single-party rule that failed to significantly help the poor, and a reformist president elected in 2000 also failed to improve their lot.

- Under Castro, communist Cuba has attempted to control its people but has also provided excellent medical care and education; however, the withdrawal of aid from the USSR in 1991 and the U.S. embargo have left its economy struggling.

- Under a brutal U.S.-supported military dictatorship, Brazil enjoyed a period of impressive growth but then experienced extreme inflation and increasing gaps between rich and poor; democracy returned in the mid-1980s, and the economy recovered in the late 1990s.

- Alarmed by the popularity of a democratically elected leftist government in Chile, the United States supported a 1973 coup there as well as the brutal military dictatorship that resulted, which rewarded the wealthy and further impoverished the poor, and which was replaced by a democratic government in 1989.

aplia

Changing Latin American and Caribbean Societies   (S)

How have Latin American and Caribbean cultures been dynamic?

Latin Americans and Caribbean peoples, while facing daunting economic problems, developed social and cultural patterns different from those of North Americans. Most still exported traditional natural resources such as oil, sugar, coffee, bananas, wool, and copper. Spanish-speaking nations, Portuguese-speaking Brazil, and English-, Dutch-, and French-speaking Caribbean societies, derived from varied mixes of peoples and traditions, often have little in common with each other but have fostered dynamic cultural forms that have gained international popularity.

Latin American Economies

Latin Americans, while struggling to achieve the affluence common in the industrialized West or eastern Asia, often enjoyed economic growth, forged rising literacy rates, and lowered infant mortality rates. More people now own televisions, even in poor neighborhoods. Nonetheless, world prices for most of their natural resource exports have declined or fluctuated over the years. Most countries have experienced at best modest growth in per capita income and productivity. To pay the bills and import luxury items, governments took out loans, eventually owing billions to international lenders. For decades populations grew around 3 percent a year, adding to the social burden and causing environmental problems. Governments tried to satisfy land hunger, mineral prospecting, and timber exploitation by treating rain forests as expendable resources. Yet, population growth has dropped considerably in recent years. Women averaged 6.0 children in 1960 and 2.3 in 2010.

Latin America has also suffered severe income inequality. By 2000 the top 10 percent earned half of all income, while 70 percent lived in poverty. Often evading taxes, the small elite class drive Rolls Royces, while the poor lack bus service. In 2000 half of Brazilians had no access to doctors; yet Rio de Janeiro became the world's plastic surgery capital catering to wealthy Brazilians and foreigners. A decade ago in Caracas, Venezuela's capital, one shopping mall serving the affluent boasted 450 stores, an amusement park, two movie theaters, and a McDonald's. But any customers coming from a slum of open sewers and tin shacks, perched a few miles away on unstable hillsides, paid half a day's wage for a Big Mac. Such inequality fueled support for leftists like Hugo Chavez. Poor peasants in some nations, their traditional crops declining in value, turned to growing coca and opium for making cocaine and heroin. But the drug trade, largely to the U.S. market, fosters political turbulence and government corruption, profiting only a few kingpins. In recent years, violence between rival drug cartels has killed many people and unsettled life, especially in Colombia and Mexico. To reduce crime, in 2013 Uruguay became the first Latin American nation to decriminalize marijuana, sparking regional debate on drug laws.

U.S. FACTORY IN MEXICO Since the 1980s growing numbers of U.S. companies have relocated industrial operations to Mexico, building many factories along the Rio Grande River that separates Mexico from Texas. In this factory, in Matamoros, Mexico, the mostly female labor force makes toys for the U.S. market.

Agriculture has remained an economic mainstay. By the 1990s, 60 percent of all agricultural land was held in large estates, mostly owned by elite families and multinational corporations, and farmed inefficiently, contributing to food shortages. Modern agriculture requires large investments for machinery, fertilizers, pesticides, and fuel; growing beans and corn to feed hungry peasants supplies inadequate revenue. Vast tracts of rain forests and farms have been transformed into cattle ranches. Latin America remains a food importer, mostly from North America, but imports fell slightly between 2002 and 2011; malnutrition causes half of all child deaths. In Peru's major city, Lima, hundreds of poor children, known as "fruit birds," desperately compete with stray dogs for spoiled fruit.

Hardship often marks rural life. A Brazilian novel captured hopelessness in the drought-tortured northeast, where, in the 1980s, life expectancy was thirty years and only two-thirds of children attended school. The herder Fabiano understands that everything prevents his escape from endless poverty: "If he could only put something aside for a few months, he would be able to get his head up. Oh, he had made plans, but that was all foolishness. Ground creepers were never meant to climb. Once the beans had been eaten and the ears of corn gnawed, there was no place to go but to the boss's cash drawer [for a loan]."[19] Unemployment and unprofitable farms generated migration to cities and made Latin America the world's most urbanized region, with 80 percent of people living in cities, often in shantytowns, by 2013. Many migrants work as shoeshine boys, cigarette vendors, car washers, or in other poorly paid work. Half the urban population lacks adequate water, housing, sanitation, and social services.

Beginning in the 1980s, many nations adopted **neoliberalism**, an economic model, encouraged by the United States, that promoted free markets, privatization, and Western investment. But although neoliberalism generated growth for a decade, more people remained stuck in poverty because neoliberals failed to curb government corruption, install honest judicial systems, foster labor-intensive industries, reduce the power of rich elites, or decrease dependence on foreign loans and investment. A few people enjoyed fabulous wealth while most remained poor. Argentina, the most ardent neoliberalism adopter, saw its economy collapse in 1998 while unemployment soared. By 2001 half of the people lived in poverty, and neoliberalism lost credibility around the region. In 2002 Argentina defaulted on its debts. But the election of pragmatic Peronist leftists in 2003 revived the economy, which grew by 9 percent a year, and in 2006 Argentina paid back money still owed to the International Monetary Fund, symbolizing recovery and a more state-oriented economy. In 2008 Argentine economic growth dwindled and the Peronists lost some support. But public spending by the Peronists, now led by Cristina Fernandez de Kirchner (b. 2007), elected president in 2007 and again in 2011, brought recovery from the 2008–2009 economic crisis. By 2014 rampant inflation and other problems brought

neoliberalism An economic model encouraged by the United States in the developing world that promoted free markets, privatization, and Western investment.

---

[19]Graciliano Ramos, *Barren Lives*, quoted in E. Bradford Burns, *Latin America: A Concise Interpretive History*, 5th ed. (Englewood Cliffs, NJ: Prentice-Hall, 1990), 231.

on another economic slide. Thanks to economic growth and job creation, Latin America's middle classes doubled to 30 percent between 2002 and 2012 while unemployment fell, but prosperity is concentrated in major cities.

Latin American Societies and Religions

Political and economic change reshaped gender relations and family life. Although men dominate governments, militaries, businesses, and the Catholic Church, women's movements have reduced gender inequality. Once considered helpless and groomed as girls to be wives and mothers, many women now do paid work, some in male-dominated trades. Millions earn money selling clothing, handicrafts, and food in small markets or from street stalls. Factories relocating from North America prefer young women, who accept lower wages and have been raised to obey. Family life has experienced strains. By the 1990s far fewer people married, especially among the poor. But divorce, banned by the Catholic Church, has remained difficult or impossible in some nations. Men still enjoy a double standard, their extramarital affairs tolerated while women's are condemned. Although abortion is illegal many places, Latin America has one of the world's highest abortion rates. Some nations, among them Brazil, Argentina, and Peru, allow abortions with some limitations. Homosexuality remains illegal and is often punished in many nations, including Castro's Cuba, but attitudes are changing; Brazil, Argentina, Uruguay, and liberal Mexico City have legalized homosexual marriage. In 2013 representatives of thirty-eight Latin American and Caribbean nations issued the Montevideo Consensus, urging support for safe abortion services, contraception, and homosexual marriage.

Gaining voting rights everywhere by 1961, women became more active in politics. In 1974 Isabel Peron (b. 1931), a former dancer who married Juan Peron after Evita's death, succeeded her late husband to become Argentina and the region's first woman president; she was ousted in a military coup in 1976. In 1990 newspaper publisher Violeta Chamorro (**vee-oh-LET-ah cha-MOR-roe**) (g. 1990–1996) was elected Nicaragua's president, and she served until 1996. In 2006 Chilean voters chose pediatrician-turned-socialist-politician Michelle Bachelet (**BAH-she-let**), a divorced mother of three and avowed agnostic whose father was murdered while she and her mother were jailed and tortured during the Pinochet years. Striking a blow for gender equity, Bachelet filled half her cabinet positions with women, including the key defense and economy ministries. Women later headed several other nations, including Brazil, Argentina, Costa Rica, Jamaica, and Trinidad. After Mexican feminists challenged inequitable laws and social practices, the legislature passed laws in 1974 guaranteeing women equal rights for jobs, salaries, and legal standing. Yet, men often resented women's empowerment; military dictatorships singled out women activists, such as Bachelet's mother, for torture and rape.

The religious landscape has become increasingly diverse. In the 1960s progressive Latin American Roman Catholics developed **liberation theology**, a movement to make the church more relevant to contemporary society and address poverty. Until the Vatican prohibited the movement in the 1980s, priests favoring liberation theology, especially in Brazil, cooperated with Marxist and liberal groups working for social justice. Meanwhile, the Catholic hierarchy generally remained conservative. While fewer attended church, many revered popular Catholic fiestas, pilgrimages, and family altars. The first Latin American to head the church, Pope Francis (pope 2013–), an Argentine known for his modest lifestyle, tango skills, soccer fandom, and concern for the poor, hoped to revitalize the faith in a region containing 40 percent of the world's Catholics. Protestantism, chiefly evangelical or pentecostal, grew rapidly with increased missionary efforts, attracting converts with its participatory, emotional services. By 2013 Protestants numbered half the population in some Central American nations, especially Guatemala and Honduras, and 22 percent in Brazil; their numbers are also growing elsewhere, including in Mexico. But their active evangelization has caused resentment among Catholic leaders. A top Brazilian cardinal worried: "We wonder with anxiety: how long will Brazil remain a Catholic country?"[20] Growing numbers of Latin Americans (15 percent in Brazil) are secular with no religious affiliation.

Brazil reflected the region's social changes and continuities. The urban population grew from about a quarter of Brazilians in 1920 to 87 percent in 2010. Migrants jammed into shantytowns, such as the notorious hillside shacks of Rio de Janeiro; despite recent rapid growth, poverty remained pervasive. By the 1980s three-fourths of Brazilians were malnourished, a third of adults had tuberculosis, a quarter suffered from parasitic diseases, and millions of abandoned or runaway children wandered city streets, living by their wits. Conditions remain bleak for many today. A substandard public health system that has neglected the rural and urban poor was a major cause of the massive protests in 2013, leading to the import of four thousand Cuban doctors. Yet, the shantytowns are also well organized, led by community activists and filled with hard-working residents seeking a better future for their children.

Although Brazilians have increasingly tolerated racial and cultural diversity, race remains a central social category. Like the United States, Brazil has never become a true racial "melting pot." Afro-Brazilians often condemn what they view as a racist society steeped in prejudice. Race often correlates with social status: whites (half the population) dominate the top brackets, blacks dominate the bottom, and mixed-descent Brazilians fall in between. However, Brazilians' flexible notion of race differs from North Americans' biological concept. Dark-skinned people can aspire to social mobility by earning a good income; as a popular local saying claims, "money lightens." Furthermore, Afro-Brazilian culture has increasingly influenced whites. Afro-Brazilian faiths linking West African gods or other African traditions with

> **liberation theology** A Latin American movement that developed in the 1960s to make Catholicism more relevant to contemporary society and to address the plight of the poor.

[20]Cardinal Claudio Hummes, quoted in Simon Romero, "A Laboratory for Revitalizing Catholicism," *New York Times*, February 14, 2013 (http://www.nytimes.com/2013/02/15/world/americas/in-brazil-growing-threats-to-catholicism.html).

Roman Catholic saints and ceremonies attract over a third of Brazilians, often devout Catholics.

The mass media and professional sports have become popular entertainments and diversion from social problems for Latin Americans. Immensely popular local television soap operas dominate prime time television viewing, with those from Brazil and Mexico gaining a large market around the world. A Brazilian anthropologist credits telenovelas, featuring affluent women with small families, for reducing fertility: "They (female characters) are all young…live well…are comfortable.…Why do they need children?"[21] Hugely popular, football (soccer) unites people of all social backgrounds. For two decades (1950s–1970s) the storied career, fluid play, and magnetic personality of Brazilian superstar Pele (b. 1940), from a poor Afro-Brazilian family, helped make football popular globally. Brazilian national teams have enjoyed the most international success of any country, winning the World Cup championships five times between 1958 and 2002 by employing a creative, teamwork-oriented strategy known as "samba football." A playwright noted how Brazilians obsessively suspend their daily lives during the World Cup, held every four years: "The nation pauses, all of it. Robbers don't rob, ghosts don't haunt, no crimes, no embezzlements, no deaths, no adulteries."[22]

Latin American and Caribbean Cultures

Creative Latin American and Caribbean cultural forms reached a global audience. Latin American literature flourished, with writers often describing social conditions and government failures. Popular Brazilian novelist Jorge Amado **(HOR-hay ah-MAH-do)** (1912–2001) blended fantasy, realism, and political commitment, providing insight into Brazil's impoverished northeast. Former journalist Gabriel García Márquez **(MAHR-kez)** (b. 1928), Nobel Prize–winning Colombian novelist, developed an international audience for imaginative books full of "magic realism" that represented possible events as if they were wonders and impossible events as commonplace. His most famous work, *One Hundred Years of Solitude* (1970), charts the history of a Colombian house, the family who lives in it, and the town where it was located through wars, changing politics, and economic crises. Some writers tested governments' tolerance. The greatest epic poem of the leftist Chilean writer and former diplomat Pablo Neruda **(neh-ROO-da)** (1904–1973), *General Song*, published in 1950, portrays the entire hemisphere's history, showing an innocent pre-Columbian America cruelly awakened by Spanish conquest. The poem romanticizes Incas, extolls the liberators who ended

New Song A Latin American musical movement based chiefly on local folk music and closely tied to progressive politics and protest; became popular in the 1960s and 1970s, especially in Chile.

Rastafarianism A religion from Jamaica that arose in 1930 and that mixed Christian, African, and local influences; Rastafarianism attracted urban slum dwellers and the rural poor by preaching a return of black people to Africa.

Spanish rule, castigates foreign capitalists (often American) as exploiters, and identifies an emerging mass struggle to establish government by and for the people rather than the rich. In 1971 Neruda won the Nobel Prize for literature, cheering his admirers and distressing those who considered his radical views a threat to society.

Other art forms also developed social consciousness. Brazil's New Cinema movement, launched in 1955, tried to replace Hollywood films with films reflecting Brazilian life. One of the movement's finest films, *Black Orpheus* (1959), which gained an international audience, employed a local popular music soundtrack to examine the annual pre-Lenten Carnival in Rio de Janeiro's shantytowns and the rich-poor divisions revealed in the different ways people celebrated Carnival. **New Song**, a musical style based chiefly on local folk music and closely tied to progressive politics and protest, gained popularity in a half-dozen countries, especially Chile, in the 1960s and 1970s. Seeking an alternative to the Anglo-American popular culture favored by the elites, musicians used indigenous Andean instruments and tunes. Chilean New Song pioneers such as Violeta Parra (1918–1967) and Victor Jara **(HAR-a)** (1932–1973) wrote or collected songs that addressed problems such as poverty and inequality (see Profile: Violeta Parra, Chilean New Song Pioneer). Jara used music to promote his political goals: "I don't sing for the love of singing, Or to show off my voice, But for the statements, Made by my honest guitar."[23]

Its leftwing connections made New Song vulnerable to changing political conditions. In 1970 Chilean New Song musicians joined the leftist Popular Unity coalition electoral campaign. New Song musicians promoted the new government's programs, such as land reform, and some toured abroad to gain foreign support. In 1973, Chile's military seized power, arresting, executing, or deporting most of the New Song musicians while criminalizing playing or listening to the music. Before thousands of other detainees held in the national stadium, soldiers publicly executed Victor Jara, symbolizing the death of free expression and the military's fear of popular culture. New Song faded as a popular music in Latin America and was replaced by local forms of rock and distinctive dance-oriented hybrid music such as *salsa* (originally from Cuba and Puerto Rico) and *meringue* from Colombia.

With diverse populations of blacks, whites, and Asians, Caribbean islands fostered creative cultural development, especially in religion and music. Jamaica proved particularly fertile soil. **Rastafarianism**, a religion mixing Christian, African, and local influences that arose in 1930, attracted the urban and rural poor by preaching a return of black people to Africa. Believers revered Emperor Ras Tafari of Ethiopia, the sole uncolonized African state in 1930. Rastafarians (Rastas) outraged Jamaica's elite by smoking ganja, an illegal drug, and sporting dreadlocked hair. Mixed with black nationalism, repatriation to Africa became more a spiritual than a physical quest. Rastafarianism became a movement of the black poor seeking to redistribute wealth.

---

[21]Immacolata Vassallo de Lopes, quoted in Juan Forero, "Birth Rate Plummets in Brazil," *New York Times*, December 29, 2012.

[22]Nelson Rodrigues, quoted in Warren Hoge, "A Whole Nation More Agitated than Spike Lee," *New York Times*, June 5, 1994, p. A1.

[23]From Jara's song "Manifiesto" ("Manifesto"). The song and the translation can be found on Jara's album *Manifiesto: Chile September 1973* (XTRA 1143, 1974).

Violeta Parra, Chilean New Song Pioneer

Born in 1918 to a poor school-teaching family, Violeta Parra was the key figure in the early development of New Song, a Chilean music based chiefly on local folk music, and a multitalented artist in many mediums, including poetry, filmmaking, tapestry, and painting. Despite her lower-middle-class background, the unconventional Parra lived and dressed like a peasant, wearing her hair long and almost uncombed. Restless and unsuited for marriage, she struggled to find the best outlet for her talents while supporting herself and her two children, Isabel and Angel (AHN-hell). After working as a commercial entertainer, she began collecting, writing, and singing folk music in the 1940s and eventually collected over three thousand songs. She had clear musical goals: "Every artist must aspire to unite his/her work in a direct contact with the public. I am content to work with the people close to me, whom I can feel, touch, talk and incorporate into my soul." Yet, unlike her protégés, such as Victor Jara, who was deeply engaged in leftwing movements, she never became directly active in politics.

VIOLETA PARRA An influential Chilean musician, folklorist, and artist, Violeta Parra is credited with founding the folk-music-oriented New Song movement, influencing many musicians in Chile and throughout Latin America.

In the early 1950s Parra began Chile's first folk music radio program and recorded her debut album, with simple guitar-accompanied arrangements. She also taught briefly at a southern Chilean university. Parra and her children introduced Andean and African American folk music to Chile after a four-year sojourn in Paris, France, where they encountered musicians from various countries. Settling with her children in Chile's capital city, Santiago, she enjoyed cooking huge pots of beans for the young Chileans who gathered around her to drink wine, discuss Chilean affairs, and exchange songs and stories. A café the Parras opened in Santiago became a meeting place for performers and other Chileans interested in New Song and leftist politics. Parra greatly influenced younger urban musicians, who began learning from her how to play traditional Andean instruments while collecting or writing their own songs; she also provided a role model for other Latin American musicians. As Cuba's top New Song musician, Silvio Rodriguez, claimed: "Violeta is fundamental. Nothing would have been as it is had it not been for Violeta."

Parra's songs displayed two essential elements of later New Song: a base in folk music and concern with Chile's social, economic, and political problems. In "Look How They Tell Us About Freedom," she critiqued the Catholic Church establishment and her nation's ills: "look how the nation's religious and political leaders brag about freedom when they are actually keeping it from us; they boast about tranquility as their power tortures us." Her music attacked such issues as police brutality, capitalism's inequalities, exploitation of Indians, and chronic conflict between Latin American governments. Yet, her songs retained an intense, highly personal, contemporary mood, both Chilean and universal.

Held in contempt by Chile's elite for her unconventional life and antiestablishment sympathies, Parra was plagued by poverty and increasing personal problems, including depression. Even her closest friends found her strong, often unpredictable personality difficult. Younger musicians began gravitating to Victor Jara and other New Song figures. Her later songs took on a more philosophical spirit. On her last album in 1966 she recorded her famous farewell, "Gracias a la Vida" (I Give Thanks to Life), a prayerlike expression of gratitude for the richness of life: "I am grateful for the life that has benefited me so much; It has given me both laughter and tears; because of this I can differentiate happiness from sadness; everybody's song is my own song." Not overtly political, the song reflected her identification with common people, becoming the underground anthem of many Latin Americans living under dictatorships. As Parra's depression deepened, she committed suicide in 1967. But her career had built a bridge between an older, peasant-based folk tradition and the developing interest of younger musicians. She may have gone, but New Song flowered in Chile and around Latin America.

THINKING ABOUT THE PROFILE

1. Why did her peers consider Parra fundamental to the evolution of New Song in Latin America?
2. How did Parra's life reflect Chilean social and political conditions?

Notes: Quotations from *Studies in Latin American Popular Culture* 2 (1983): 177–178, and 5 (1986): 117; and Nancy E. Morris, *Canto Porque es Necesario Cantar: The New Song Movement in Chile, 1973–1983* (Albuquerque: Latin American Institute, University of New Mexico, Research Paper Series No. 16, July 1984), 6.

EL MERCURIO de CHILE./Newscom

The most influential Caribbean popular music had similar mixed origins. In the 1960s Jamaicans created reggae, which blended North American rhythm and blues with Afro-Jamaican traditions and which was highlighted by a distinctive beat maintained by the bass guitar. Reggae musicians, many of them Rastas, promoted social justice, economic equality, and the freedom of Rastas to live as they liked. Reggae's international popularity owed much to Bob Marley (1945–1981), a Rasta, and his group, the Wailers, the first international superstars from a developing nation (see Chapter 26). Marley's perceptions were shaped by the status of blacks in Jamaica and the wider world and the degrading conditions of the nonwhite poor. His explosive performances and provocative lyrics offered clear messages: "Slave driver, the table is turned; Catch a fire, you gonna get burned."[24] Like Chilean New Song musicians, Marley and other reggae musicians became involved in politics. Many supported socialist Michael Manley (1924–1997), whose antibusiness policies as prime minister (1972–1978) prompted crippling U.S. sanctions that caused Jamaicans hardship. After Marley's death from cancer in 1981, many reggae musicians watered down their message. Raunchy party music soon dominated Caribbean music scenes. *Reggaeton*, a hugely popular Spanish-language music around Latin America and among Hispanics in North America, mixed reggae with rock, rap, and Latin music.

Latin America and the Caribbean in the Global System

Latin Americans and Caribbean peoples forged closer relations with one another and increased regional economic cooperation and trade, often through trade pacts. The Southern Cone Common Market, formed in 1996, included six South American nations with over 200 million people. Caribbean countries cooperated in the Caribbean Community and Common Market, formed in 1973, and Latin and North American leaders periodically met in summits to enhance cooperation on immigration, tariff reduction, suppression

reggae A popular music style that began in the 1960s and that blended North American rhythm and blues with Afro-Jamaican traditions; reggae is marked by a distinctive beat maintained by the bass guitar.

of illegal drug trafficking, and other issues. While Americans blamed Latin American drug cartels for smuggling illegal drugs, Latin Americans often resented the U.S. interventions and economic impositions they considered "Yankee imperialism." Latin American and Caribbean leaders also feared being pushed aside in a world economy dominated by North American, European, and, increasingly, Asian nations. U.S. exports to Latin America nearly matched those to Europe.

Globalization influenced Latin Americans and their economies. Asian nations, especially China, Japan, Taiwan, and South Korea, captured a growing share of Latin America's traditional overseas markets while investing in Latin America and the Caribbean. Energy-hungry China sought resources such as oil from countries like Brazil and Venezuela. In a globalized economy, a hiccup in Tokyo or New York causes a stomach ache in Ecuador or El Salvador. Latin American and Caribbean economies are particularly vulnerable to ebbs and flows in the United States. When the 2001 terrorist attacks diverted U.S. attention to the Middle East, the sudden U.S. disinterest in Latin America sparked a regional economic downturn, that reduced demand for Latin American exports. Economic gains made in the 1990s slipped away; the fifth of Latin Americans living in extreme poverty faced an even grimmer future; and leftists won elections in many countries. The 2008–2009 global economic crisis further damaged many Latin American and Caribbean economies as jobs disappeared, tourism declined, and many jobless migrants to North America returned home. Yet, some countries, most notably Brazil and Chile, have done very well over the past decade, improving their status in the global system.

Buffeted by political changes and sporadic economic crises, Latin Americans search for their identity and role in a world largely dominated by other societies. Calling on leaders to recognize the needs of all the people, regardless of class, ethnicity, and gender, and for both North and Latin Americans to find common ground with each other, the Panamanian salsa music star, lawyer, and part-time U.S. resident Ruben Blades (**blayds**) pondered the hemisphere's destiny in song: "I'm searching for America and I fear I won't find her. Those who fear truth have hidden her. While there is no justice there can be no peace. If the dream of one is the dream of all let's break the chains and begin to walk. I'm calling you, America, our future awaits us, help me to find her."[25]

[24]See Marley's album *Catch a Fire* (Island ILPS 9241, 1973).

[25]Quoted in Jan Fairley, "New Song: Music and Politics in Latin America," in *Rhythms of the World*, ed. Francis Hanly and Tim May (London: BBC Books, 1989), 90.

MAKE SURE YOU UNDERSTAND THESE KEY POINTS BEFORE MOVING ON

- Though men continue to dominate Latin American society, more women have entered the work force, and several have become national leaders.

- Brazil, Latin America's largest nation, became increasingly urban and suffered widespread poverty, with a racial divide between lighter- and darker-skinned people, but Brazilians have found escape from their problems through popular sports such as soccer.

- In the Caribbean, the Jamaican religion of Rastafarianism promoted redistribution of wealth, while a closely related musical form, reggae, frequently included calls for social justice and freedom from police interference.

- Latin American and Caribbean nations forged closer relations, signed several trade pacts, and shared an uneasy economic relationship with the United States, while Asian nations also became important competitors with and investors in their economies.

aplia

CHAPTER SUMMARY

Having emerged from World War II as the dominant superpower, the United States soon engaged in a Cold War with the Soviet Union. The campaign to contain communism fostered the growth of a powerful military and a strong government. Americans lavished aid and investment on allies and developing nations while intervening in many nations, including some in Latin America and the Caribbean, to counter revolutionary movements or overthrow left-leaning governments. While the U.S. economy flourished for decades, American society and culture rapidly changed, as ethnic minorities and women struggled for equal rights. Although shaped, like the United States, by massive immigration from Europe, especially Britain, Canadians, Australians, and New Zealanders have more liberal attitudes on social issues and, unlike Americans, have extensive social welfare systems.

Latin American and Caribbean experiences differ from those in the United States, Canada, and the Pacific Basin. Military dictatorships dominated many Latin American nations for decades. Most nations struggled to implement and sustain democracy, which became prevalent in the 1990s, and to find the right economic mix to foster economic development. While some nations enjoyed economic growth, many people remained in dire poverty. Women and nonwhites worked to improve their status, with modest success. The Latin American and Caribbean peoples also fostered dynamic cultural forms, from innovative literatures to popular musical forms, that often expressed protest and gained worldwide audiences.

KEY TERMS

domino theory (p. 726)
multilateralism (p. 726)
unilateralism (p. 726)
containment (p. 726)

Mutually Assured Destruction (p. 727)
preemptive war (p. 730)
Castroism (p. 742)
neoliberalism (p. 746)

liberation theology (p. 747)
New Song (p. 748)
Rastafarianism (p. 748)
reggae (p. 750)

MODERN VS. TRADITIONAL Wearing traditional clothing, including veils and head scarves, Egyptian women walk through downtown Cairo in 1998 in front of billboards promoting popular entertainers. The scene illustrates the encounter between Islamic customs and modern ideas in many Middle Eastern nations.

Enric Marti/AP Images

I saw the Berlin Wall fall, [Nelson] Mandela walk free. I saw a dream whose time has come change my history—so keep on dreaming. In the best of times and in the worst of times gotta keep looking at the skyline, not at the hole in the road.

—"Your Time Will Come" by South African pop group Savuka, 1993[1]

In 1987 Nigerian writer Chinua Achebe (ah-CHAY-bay) (1930–2013) dissected the underside of African politics in a controversial novel, *Anthills of the Savannah*, about a military dictatorship. *Anthills* illustrates the dangers of unaccountable, repressive power and portrays problems faced by average people throughout much of Africa, mercilessly depicting the dictatorship's immorality, vanity, and destructiveness. Achebe did not have to look far for examples: Nigerian military leaders who overthrew a civilian government in 1983 first arrested people well known as corrupt and then jailed anyone who questioned the regime's economic mismanagement and human rights abuses. Just as the racially integrated South African pop group, Savuka, could sing of dreams changing history and a new era with the end of white minority rule, Achebe urged people to struggle to attain a better life. He believed that no novel is ever politically neutral because even saying nothing about politics is a political statement affirming that everything is OK. *Anthills* argues eloquently that everything is not OK. Like various other creative writers, musicians, and artists who used their art to spur political and social change, Achebe had to live many years in exile from intolerant governments.

The problems Achebe vividly described—despotism, corruption, economic stagnation, combustible social tensions, failed promises of democracy—have applied to most sub-Saharan African and Middle Eastern nations. Between 1945 and 1975, country after country became independent or reduced the political power of Western domination. But unlike various Asian and Latin American nations, they often struggled just to survive. While innovative in cultural affairs, few successfully resolved their social and economic problems. For some, Islam became a rallying cry to assert political interests and preserve their culture. Meanwhile, to serve their own ends, global superpowers manipulated African and Middle Eastern governments and intervened to shape these regions.

IN THIS CHAPTER

The Middle East: New Nations and Old Societies
How have Arab-Israeli tensions and oil shaped contemporary Middle Eastern politics?

The Reshaping of the Middle East
Arab Nationalism and Egypt
Israel in Middle Eastern Politics
Islamic Revolution in Iran
Iraq and Regional Conflicts
Saudi Arabia, Oil, and the World

Change and Conflict in the Middle East
What roles has Islam played in the contemporary Middle East?

Ethnic and Religious Conflict
Social Change
Religion and Culture
The Middle East in the Global System

Political Change in Sub-Saharan Africa
What were the main political consequences of decolonization in sub-Saharan Africa?

Nationalism and Decolonization
Political Change and Conflict
The New South Africa

African Economies, Societies, and Cultures
What new economic, social, and cultural patterns have emerged in Africa?

Economic Change and Underdevelopment
Social Change
African Culture and Religion
Africa in the Global System

PROFILE Nelson Mandela, South African Freedom Fighter and President

WITNESS TO THE PAST Assessing Arab Development

[1]See Savuka's album *Heat, Dust and Dreams* (EMI 9777-7-98795, 1993).

The Middle East: New Nations and Old Societies

How have Arab-Israeli tensions and oil shaped contemporary Middle Eastern politics?

Few world regions have witnessed more turbulence since 1945 than the predominantly Muslim nations stretching from Morocco across North Africa and southwestern Asia to Iran and Afghanistan. Arabs have dominated most of these nations, but Turks, Iranians, Kurds, and Israeli Jews also influence the region. After World War II Middle Eastern societies ended Western colonization and asserted their own interests, often under modernizing leaders. But they also endured dictatorial governments, chronic political instability, and centuries-old hostilities between Sunni and Shi'a Muslims. Containing the

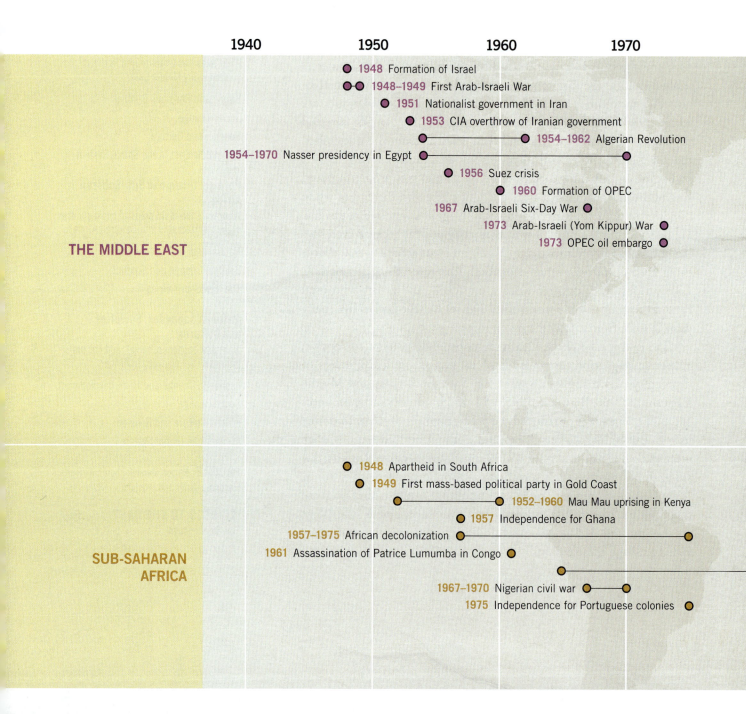

	1940	1950	1960	1970

THE MIDDLE EAST

1948 Formation of Israel
1948–1949 First Arab-Israeli War
1951 Nationalist government in Iran
1953 CIA overthrow of Iranian government
1954–1962 Algerian Revolution
1954–1970 Nasser presidency in Egypt
1956 Suez crisis
1960 Formation of OPEC
1967 Arab-Israeli Six-Day War
1973 Arab-Israeli (Yom Kippur) War
1973 OPEC oil embargo

SUB-SAHARAN AFRICA

1948 Apartheid in South Africa
1949 First mass-based political party in Gold Coast
1952–1960 Mau Mau uprising in Kenya
1957 Independence for Ghana
1957–1975 African decolonization
1961 Assassination of Patrice Lumumba in Congo
1967–1970 Nigerian civil war
1975 Independence for Portuguese colonies

world's largest oil reserves, the region also became crucial to the global system.

The Reshaping of the Middle East

In the two decades after World War II, nationalist governments replaced the remaining colonial regimes. France abandoned control of Morocco, Tunisia, Lebanon, and Syria, while Italians left Libya. During the Algerian Revolution (1954–1962), nationalist guerrillas fought 500,000 French troops to bring independence to their country, which had a large European settler population. Seeing no clear end to the

struggle, which killed 250,000 Algerians, France granted independence in 1962. Although some other nations, such as Egypt and Morocco, had a long history of national identity and unity, many states were fragile. After World War I the British formed the artificial states of Iraq, Jordan, and Palestine with arbitrary boundaries, while Afghanistan, Turkey, Lebanon, and Syria all included diverse, often feuding ethnic and religious groups.

The region's most developed and prosperous nation, Turkey, which has never been colonized, has sought an influential regional role and built formidable military forces. Turkey's prestige and power make it a major force in regional politics. However, Turkey has also abused human rights, arresting

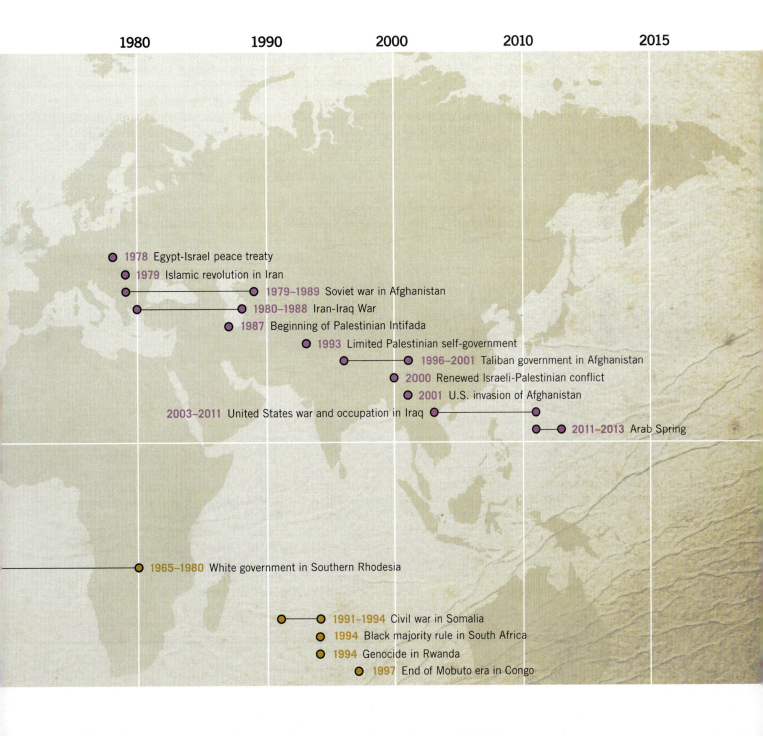

1980   1990   2000   2010   2015

1978 Egypt-Israel peace treaty
1979 Islamic revolution in Iran
1979–1989 Soviet war in Afghanistan
1980–1988 Iran-Iraq War
1987 Beginning of Palestinian Intifada
1993 Limited Palestinian self-government
1996–2001 Taliban government in Afghanistan
2000 Renewed Israeli-Palestinian conflict
2001 U.S. invasion of Afghanistan
2003–2011 United States war and occupation in Iraq
2011–2013 Arab Spring

1965–1980 White government in Southern Rhodesia

1991–1994 Civil war in Somalia
1994 Black majority rule in South Africa
1994 Genocide in Rwanda
1997 End of Mobuto era in Congo

dissidents and restricting ethnic minorities. Although it shifted from military-dominated to democratically elected governments by the 1980s, it used strict internal security laws to imprison several thousand people for political offenses. Led largely by secular politicians, Turks looked increasingly westward, joining NATO (the North Atlantic Treaty Organization), hosting U.S. military bases, and applying, so far unsuccessfully, for European Union membership. But Turkey's governments, while promoting women's rights, have also suppressed the culture and language of the largest ethnic minority, the Kurds, the 18 percent of the population who chiefly live in southeastern Turkey. Some separatist Kurds supported an insurgency that has cost 40,000 lives.

Although Turkey's 76 million people are largely Sunni Muslim, nationalist governments have long limited political activity by groups favoring an Islamic state and discouraged conservative religious customs. However, the moderate Islamic Justice and Development Party led by Recep Tayyip Erdogan (b. 1954), which came to power in 2002 and won successive elections, loosened restrictions on Muslim practices, such as by allowing devout female students to wear head scarves, while pursuing a pro-Western policy and closer ties with Europe and, more recently, Arab states that some termed an "Ottoman Revival". The gap between largely secular urbanites and more devout rural folk is wide. A prominent secular artist and activist explained in 2012: "We don't eat the same way ... We eat at tables with ladies and men sitting together and enjoying and drinking wine and making jokes and listening to either Turkish music or Beethoven or Rolling Stones or Beatles or Edith Piaf. They sit separately with men and women. They don't drink alcohol."[2] Secular Turks revere the Ataturk era, conservatives the Ottoman Empire. While the economy has rapidly grown for twenty years, in 2013 large protests erupted in Istanbul protesting Erdogan's controversial urban development projects, crackdown on journalists and dissenters, conservative social initiatives (such as limiting alcohol advertising and sales), allegations of corruption, and increasingly autocratic style.

Outside of Turkey, hopes for development and multiparty democracy have floundered as vested interests—large landowners, military leaders, most Muslim clergy—have opposed significant changes, and many people remain mired in illiteracy, poverty, and disease. However, some semidemocratic systems have emerged. Lebanese can choose between many competing warlord- or sectarian-based parties; Iranians can vote, but the regime disqualifies candidates it dislikes. In recent years both men and women in the small Persian Gulf kingdoms of Bahrain **(BAH-rain)** and Kuwait could vote for elected parliaments, and in 2009 three Kuwaiti women won seats. Due to U.S. occupation, Iraq now has an elected, although deeply factionalized, parliament with some women deputies. In Morocco, King Muhammad VI, who claims descent from the prophet Muhammad, has used a tolerant interpretation of Islam to try to modernize his nation, granting new rights to women while strengthening civil liberties and the elected parliament. However, he still controls vast power, and critics believe the reforms

were more cosmetic than substantive. Indeed, by 2013 the king, worried by political instability in other North African countries, veered back toward autocracy, arresting some critics.

Most Middle Eastern countries have rigged elections, weak parliaments, or rules marginalizing opposition candidates. Furthermore, during the Cold War the United States and the Soviet Union, attracted by the region's oil and strategic location along vital waterways like the Persian Gulf and Suez Canal, filled the power vacuum created by decolonization. Pan-Arab nationalism, based more on a shared cultural and linguistic background than political interests, has not overcome political rivalries and superpower meddling. Divided by rival Muslim sects and differing outlooks toward the West, Arabs have floundered in their quest for unity. Hence, the Middle East has become a highly combustible region subject to many strains.

All of these frustrations came to a boil with the "Arab Spring," when the self-immolation of a fed-up street vendor in Tunisia in 2010 sparked protests that replaced the dictatorial regime. Soon unrest spread to other nations, unleashing unpredictable forces that brought turmoil and instability to many nations and unsettled regional politics. In 2011 Libyans, with NATO help, fought and overthrew the long-established but quirky autocrat Muammar Gaddafi (g. 1969–2011). The Shi'ite majority in Bahrain challenged the Sunni monarchy, and protests and insurgency forced the ruler of Yemen from office. Months of protests also forced the longtime dictator from office in Egypt in 2012. Meanwhile, ethnically and religiously divided Syria erupted in civil war as Sunni protests against a government supported by various minorities fostered a brutal government response and then an insurgency and civil war. Most of these uprisings evolved into bitter struggles and polarization between factions, tribes, and sects, preventing the democracy, social justice, and human rights many protesters desired. Yet the social media that spread these "Facebook revolutions" linked people all over the region, perhaps setting a foundation for more open societies.

Arab Nationalism and Egypt

During the 1960s and 1970s, confrontation between Arab nationalism and the world's superpowers, especially the United States and Britain, was acute in Egypt, which, with 84 million people (10 percent Christians) by 2012, is the most populous Arab country. In 1954 charismatic, anti-British general Gamal Abdul Nasser **(NAS-uhr)** (1918–1970) became Egypt's leader after a military coup ended the corrupt pro-British monarchy. Nasser's frequent childhood visits to his parents' impoverished farming village sparked his sympathy for the poor and resentment of rich landlords. As a radical student and then army officer, he developed a vision of a new Egypt, free of Western domination and social inequality.

Nasser preached modernization, socialism, and unity, and his promise to improve the lives of the poor and implement land reform made him a hero in the Arab world. To generate electric power and improve flood control, Nasser used Soviet

---

[2]Bedri Baykam, quoted in Anand Giridharadas, "In Turkey, Forging a New Identity," *New York Times*, November 20, 2012.

aid to build the massive Aswan High Dam along the Nile, completed in 1970. But his nonaligned foreign policy antagonized a Cold War–obsessed United States, and his support of pan-Arab nationalism also generated wars. In 1956 Egypt took over the British-operated Suez Canal, a key artery of world commerce; while foreign ownership of the canal had symbolized Egypt's subjugation to foreign powers, Europeans considered the canal the lifeline moving oil and resources to the West from Asia. Britain, France, and Israel dispatched military forces to reclaim the canal, but the United States, which disliked Nasser but feared regional instability, and the USSR forced their withdrawal. Standing up to the West made Nasser an even greater Arab hero and leader of the developing nations seeking nonalignment, or neutrality, between the two superpowers. However, Nasser was humiliated by Israel's defeat of Egypt and its allies in a brief 1967 war. Furthermore, Nasser's social and economic reforms fostered little economic development or military strength.

Nasser's successors followed pragmatic, pro-U.S. policies. In 1978 Anwar Sadat (g. 1970–1981) signed a peace treaty with Israel brokered by U.S. president Jimmy Carter (g. 1977–1981), but he was assassinated by hardline military officers. Sadat and his successor, Hosni Mubarak, dismantled Nasser's socialist economy, and in the coming years a few well-connected capitalists became fabulously rich while the poorest became even poorer. In Cairo, the contrast grew more dramatic between glittering rich neighborhoods, featuring luxury apartments and mansions surrounded by high walls, and poor, overcrowded neighborhoods, where the most desperate families lived in huts on top of ramshackle apartment buildings. Hence, millions of Egyptians sought work in oil-rich Arab nations.

With little oil and few resources other than fertile Nile farmlands, Egypt suffered from high malnutrition and unemployment, low rates of literacy and public health, and a huge national debt. In elections candidates opposing long-entrenched president Hosni Mubarak (r. 1981–2012) were hampered by free speech limits, harassment, and arrest of dissidents. While liberals sought more democracy, Islamic militants like the Muslim Brotherhood, feeding on these frustrations, challenged the secular but corrupt, repressive government.

Egypt was not immune to the Arab Spring sweeping the region. In 2011 massive protests against Mubarak were met with violence, but eventually Mubarak fled and was arrested, the army stepped in, and, after a transition, in 2012 it introduced a more participatory system including freer elections. Although many of the protesters were secular liberals wanting a more open system, the Islamist Muslim Brotherhood won the elections and control of Parliament; one of their leaders, Mohammed Morsi, became president. But the Morsi government proved unable to revive a staggering economy and began imposing a more Islamic agenda, disillusioning or outraging many Egyptians. In 2013 massive protests erupted, generating violence between Islamists and secular liberals; the military then removed Morsi, brutally repressed the Muslim Brotherhood, and instituted military rule, dashing hopes for

democracy while arresting both Islamist and liberal critics of their harsh policies and the resulting civil strife and violence. The secular-Islamist gap made compromise difficult; many Egyptians seemed to prefer military rule to Islamist rule but dissent also grew.

Israel in Middle Eastern Politics

Israel-Arab conflict became the Middle East's most insurmountable problem, sustaining tensions for over half a century. Zionist Jews had emigrated from Europe to Palestine since the late 1800s, building cities and forming productive socialist farming settlements, but their presence triggered occasional conflicts with the Palestinian Arab majority. The Nazis' murder of 6 million Jews during World War II spurred a stronger desire for a homeland free of oppression, and in the later 1940s Jewish refugees poured into Palestine. Moderate Jewish leaders asked Britain to transfer power to them in Palestine. However, Zionist extremists practiced "gun diplomacy," using bombings and assassinations against the British, Arabs, and moderate Jews, while Arabs, opposing an Israeli state at their expense, attacked Jews. Unable to maintain order, Britain referred the Palestine question to the new Western-dominated United Nations. As the British withdrew in 1948, Jewish leaders proclaimed the establishment of Israel. Forming a multiparty democracy, Israelis gained strong Western support, and the United States has supplied generous aid ever since.

These developments sparked full-scale war in 1948–1949 between Israel and its Arab neighbors, to whom Israel was a white settler state symbolizing Western colonialism (see Map 30.1). As some 85 percent of Palestinian Arabs fled the fighting, Israelis occupied their farms and houses. Israelis won the war against the disorganized Arabs, while many Palestinian refugees (numbering some 5 million by 2012) settled in overcrowded, squalid refugee camps in Egypt, Lebanon, Jordan, and Syria, nursing their hatred of Israel. Most supported the Palestine Liberation Organization (PLO), an Arab nationalist-Muslim-Christian coalition. Neither Western nations nor Israel officially recognized or would negotiate with the PLO until the 1990s, prompting it to employ terrorism, attacking public buses and rural settlements.

Israel endured chronic confrontation with its Arab neighbors and the PLO. Palestinians still in Israel, though participating in democratic politics, were disproportionally poor. Meanwhile, thousands of Jewish immigrants arrived, many from Middle Eastern countries where they had experienced discrimination or retribution. Their arrival intensified divisions between secular and devout, European and Middle Eastern Jews. Obsessed with security, well-armed Israel devoted half its total national budget to the military. A cycle of violence followed; when the PLO attacked, Israelis bombed a Lebanon refugee camp in retaliation.

An Arab-Israeli War in 1967 further complicated regional politics, heightening conflict and reshaping Israeli society. Responding to an ill-advised attack led by Egypt and Jordan, Israel occupied the West Bank of the Jordan River; eastern

Jewish state after UN partition of Palestine, 1947

Israel after War of 1948–1949

Area controlled by Israel after Six-Day War, 1967

Israeli-occupied area after Yom Kippur War, 1973

By Egyptian-Israeli agreements of 1975 and 1979, Israel withdrew from the Sinai in 1982. In 1981 Israel annexed the Golan Heights. Through negotiations between Israel and the PLO, Jericho and the Gaza Strip were placed under Palestinian self-rule, and Israeli troops were withdrawn in 1994. In 1994 Israel and Jordan signed an agreement opening their borders and normalizing their relations.

U.S. troops, 1958, 1983–1984

Soviet occupation, 1979–1989
U.S. aid to rebels, 1980s
International and Northern Alliance forces defeat Taliban, 2001

Principal center of al-Qaeda activity, 2004–

U.S. arms sales, 1955–1978: $20.8 billion
Shah overthrown, 1979
American hostages taken, 1979–1981

U.S. and allies launch First U.S.-Iraq War, 1991

U.S. arms sales, 1980s, during Iran-Iraq War
Iraq invades Kuwait, 1990
Second U.S.-Iraq War, 2003

Oil embargo, 1973
Source of 17% of U.S. oil imports in 1975
Largest buyer of U.S. arms, 1978

Al-Qaeda headquarters, 1992–1996

Bombing of USS Cole by al-Qaeda, 2000

U.S. troops assist in relief of famine, 1992–1993.
U.S. troops withdrawn, 1994.
U.S.-backed Ethiopian invasion removes Islamist government, 2006

Members of the Organization of Petroleum Exporting Countries (OPEC)

Oil fields

ARAB-ISRAELI CONFLICT

MAP 30.1 **MIDDLE EAST OIL AND THE ARAB-ISRAELI CONFLICT** Several Middle Eastern nations, including Saudi Arabia, Iran, Iraq, Libya, and the small Persian Gulf states, are rich in oil and active members of OPEC. Israel, founded in 1948, and the neighboring Arab countries of Egypt, Jordan, and Syria have been in chronic conflict that has resulted in four wars. Israel's victory in the 1967 war allowed it to take control of Gaza, the West Bank, and the Golan Heights. © 2015 Cengage Learning

Jerusalem, filled with Jewish and Islamic holy places; the Gaza Strip, a small coastal enclave of Egypt; and the Golan Heights, a Syrian plateau overlooking northeast Israel. The new Israeli-controlled lands contained a large Arab population, a combustible situation that Israel exacerbated by treating the occupied Palestinians as a colonized people, with no political rights. In 1973 another Israeli war with Egypt and Syria proved costly to all sides.

While many Israelis wanted to trade occupied land for a permanent peace settlement, others hoped to permanently annex occupied lands as part of biblical Israel. Ultranationalist and religiously conservative Israelis, with government support, began settling on Arab land, creating another problem: thousands of Jewish settlers living amid hostile Arabs. Palestinians resent the heavily fortified settlements, guarded by Israeli soldiers, that often overlook Palestinian cities and villages from nearby hilltops. Because Israel proper has remained a democracy with a vibrant free press, Israelis heatedly debate these policies and the treatment of Arabs. In 1987 desperate Palestinians began a resistance, the **Intifada** ("Uprising"), against the Israeli occupation. Rising Islamic militancy in the occupied territories alarmed both the secular Fatah movement, the main PLO party, and Israelis. Negotiations led in 1993 to limited self-government under the PLO in some of the occupied

territories, the basis for a possible Palestinian state, and a peace agreement between Israel and Jordan.

In 2000 violence erupted again. Moderate Israelis and Palestinians lost hope as demoralizing Palestinian suicide bombings of civilian targets, such as restaurants and public buses, and Israeli reprisal attacks on Palestinian neighborhoods made life insecure for everyone. Israel built a high security fence separating it from the West Bank that incorporated some occupied territory, enraging Palestinians. In a 2006 election, Palestinians, tired of Fatah's ineffective and corrupt regime, gave the militant Islamic Hamas movement, which sponsored terrorist attacks and refused to recognize Israel's right to exist, a majority of seats in the Palestinian parliament. Soon Hamas seized Gaza, from where militants fired rockets into Israel; Fatah controlled the West Bank. An inconclusive Israeli invasion of southern Lebanon in 2006 to stop terrorist attacks, as well as a bloody, destructive military incursion in Gaza in 2008 and a blockade in 2009, hardened Israeli and Palestinian attitudes and sparked world condemnation. After a hardline Israeli government led by right-winger Benjamin Netanyahu (g. 1996–1999, 2009–) took power in 2009, prospects for negotiations to resolve issues

Intifada ("Uprising") A resistance begun in 1987 by Palestinians against the Israeli occupation.

SAIF DAHLAH/AFP/Getty Images

PALESTINIAN POLITICAL RALLY In 2011 after Arab media published hundreds of secret documents revealing Israeli-Palestinian peace talks, many Palestinians rallied to support president Mahmud Abbas. This rally was in Jenin, on the West Bank.

ebbed and flowed. With conflicting visions of how Israelis and Palestinians might coexist or form two states, no consensus for ensuring long-term peace has yet emerged.

Islamic Revolution in Iran

By the end of World War II, rival European nations had interfered with Iran, rich in oil and strategically located along the Persian Gulf, for a century, and the interference continued after the war, when Iranian politics was embroiled in a conflict between the young king, Shah Mohammed Pahlavi **(pah-LAH-vee)** (1919–1980), and nationalist reformers opposed to foreign domination. In 1951 nationalists came to power and reduced the shah to a ceremonial role; they then nationalized the British-dominated oil industry, from which Iran had received little revenue. Britain and its ally, the United States, considering the nationalists pro-USSR, cut off aid and launched a boycott to close oil markets, bringing Iran to near bankruptcy and fostering unrest. In 1953, American CIA agents secretly organized opposition among military leaders and riots against the nationalist government. Royalists overthrew the government, imprisoned its leaders, and restored the unpopular shah to power, embittering many Iranians. Shah Pahlavi, a ruthless, pleasure-loving man who lived extravagantly and dreamed of restoring Persia as a great power, allied himself with the United States, allowing American companies to control the oil industry.

The shah's three and a half decades of rule brought modernization, political repression, and a huge military force built with oil revenues. While his "white revolution" earned Western admiration because it promoted a market economy and women's rights while enlarging the middle class, it failed to improve most Iranians' living standards. While a corrupt elite siphoned off most of the development money and generous U.S. aid, 60 percent of peasants remained landless, and people flocked to the traffic- and smog-choked cities. Meanwhile, to increase national pride and attract Western tourists, the shah spent billions to renovate the splendid palaces and tombs of Persepolis, a city built for Persian kings twenty-four hundred years ago that few Iranians could afford to visit. The absolute monarch's secret police eliminated opposition, holding thousands of political prisoners. Poetess Faruq Farrukhzad **(fuh-ROOK fuh-ROOK-sad)** wrote of how intellectuals, cowed into submission, retreated into "swamps of alcohol [while] the verminous mice gnawed through the pages of gilded books, stacked in ancient closets."[3] At the same time, conservative Shi'ite leaders opposed modernization, such as unveiled women and crowded bars, as threatening Muslim culture. In 1979, as the economy slumped, strikes and protests forced the shah into exile in the United States, turning Americans and Iranians into bitter foes.

An Islamic revolution then reshaped Iran. While some Shi'ite thinkers discouraged clergy from taking political action, others promoted a clergy-governed Islamic state. Militant Shi'ite clerics, led by long-exiled Ayatollah Ruhollah Khomeini **(roo-HOLE-ah KOH-may-nee)** (1902–1989),

took power, eliminated leftists and moderate nationalists, overturned the shah's modernization, and mandated Islamic Shari'a law codes. Thousands fled abroad, many to the United States. Women were forced to wear veils and prohibited from socializing with men from outside their families. The regime also restricted other personal freedoms, prompting a popular joke: "We used to drink in public and pray in private. Now we pray in public and drink in private." Like the shah, the clerics ruled by terror, suppressed ethnic minorities, such as the mostly Sunni Kurds in the northwest, and executed opponents.

The United States became a bitter enemy after Islamic militants, who hated America for its long support of the shah, seized the U.S. Embassy in 1979 and held it and U.S. diplomats for one year. Iran's Arab neighbors, fearing Iran's territorial size, large population (77 million by 2013), military strength, and regional ambitions, were also alarmed. Now they encountered Islamic militancy aimed at their more secular governments. Animosity between mostly Sunni Arabs and mostly Shi'ite Iranians fueled tensions, sparking a catastrophic war with Iraq (1980–1988) that produced 500,000 to 1 million Iranian casualties. An Iranian program to develop nuclear power and perhaps nuclear weapons also worried the international community.

Eventually Iran mixed theocracy with democratic trappings. A more open electoral process allowed opposition parties to win parliamentary seats. With the economy floundering, by 1997 moderate reformers seeking closer ties to the outside world, democratization, and loosening of harsh laws challenged the hardline clerics who controlled the judicial and electoral systems. Young people, resenting Islamic laws, increasingly confronted restrictions on personal behavior, and young women, often unveiled or wearing fashionable head scarves, began socializing again with men. But hardliners banned reformist newspapers and disqualified reformist candidates. Shirin Ebadi **(shih-RIN ee-BOD-ee)** (b. 1947), a feminist Iranian lawyer and human rights activist, won the Nobel Peace Prize in 2003 for bravely challenging the clerical leadership and favoring reformist Islam. In 2005 Iranians elected a hardline president, Mahmoud Ahmedinijad **(mah-MOOD ah-mah-DIH-nee-zhahd)** (b. 1956), who increased nuclear capabilities, restored conservative values, banned Western music from radio and television, harassed dissidents, threatened Israel, and openly defied the United States. However, as the economy declined, reformers and hardliners continued to struggle for influence. In 2009, Ahmedinijad and the hardliners won a disputed election that many Iranians considered rigged, generating massive street protests but also intensifying repression of dissidents. The brutal civil war engulfing Iran's main regional ally, Syria, complicated relations with the West. Hoping for better relations with the outside world, in 2013 Iranians elected a more moderate cleric, Hassan Rouhani **(ha-SAN roo-HAHN-ee)**, who introduced some modest reforms and negotiated with the United States and the West over Iran's controversial nuclear program.

[3]Quoted in James Alban Bill, *The Politics of Iran: Groups, Classes and Modernization* (Columbus, OH: Charles E. Merrill, 1972), 76–77.

Iraq and Regional Conflicts

Iraq also proved a major source of regional instability. In 1958 the army overthrew an unpopular monarchy, beginning four decades of ruthless dictatorships that crushed all opposition. During this time the Sunni Arab minority of 20 percent ruled a nation with a restless Arab Shi'ite majority (60 percent) and a disaffected Sunni Kurdish minority (20 percent). The mostly Sunni Ba'ath ("Renaissance") Party, which favored socialism and Arab nationalism and strongly opposed Israel, dominated governments, fostering secular policies and some economic development and prosperity. In 1979 Saddam Hussein (1937–2006), a landless peasant's son, seized power, proving even more brutal than his predecessors.

Alarmed by the Iranian Revolution, whose leaders considered Saddam's secular regime godless, in 1980 Saddam's army invaded Iran, using poison gas against Iranian soldiers, but was unable to achieve victory. The war threatened Persian Gulf shipping lanes and hence the world oil supply. The United States, with vested interests in Iraq's oil—the world's second largest proven reserves—and hostility toward Iran, sided with Iraq, attacking Iranian shipping and arming Saddam's military. Both Iran and Iraq drafted teenagers to fight. The costs of the war were staggering: over 260,000 Iranian and 100,000 Iraqi dead, and grave damage to the Iraqi economy. The war ended in 1988 with no victor.

U.S. president George H. W. Bush (g. 1989–1993), viewing Saddam as a useful strategic ally, continued providing weapons. But in 1990 Iraq invaded prosperous, oil-rich Kuwait, ruled by an Arab royal family. Bush, worried that oil-rich Saudi Arabia might be next, launched the Persian Gulf War (1991), which drove Iraqis from Kuwait, killing perhaps 30,000 Iraqi soldiers. The war restored Americans' faith in their military, undermined by bitter defeat in Vietnam. But Saddam remained in power, persecuting dissidents and slaughtering Shi'ites and Kurds, who rebelled with U.S. encouragement; at least 30,000 Shi'ites and thousands of Kurds died. The United States and United Nations eventually gave the Kurds some military protection and autonomy in their northern region. But United Nations sanctions restricting Iraq's foreign income and ability to buy weapons undermined Iraq's economy; Iraqis struggled to acquire food and medical supplies, with thousands dying from the resulting shortages.

The Al Qaeda attack on the United States in 2001 and the resulting Afghan war germinated a larger conflict in Iraq. Charging that Saddam Hussein had weapons of mass destruction and was linked to Al Qaeda, U.S. president George W. Bush ordered an invasion and occupation of Iraq in 2003. Massive looting followed the quick U.S. victory, with museums, ancient historical sites, power plants, armories, and communications networks plundered. U.S. credibility suffered after claims about the Iraqi threat proved wrong. Inadequate planning for postwar reconstruction also forced Bush to shift troops and resources from Afghanistan. Fostering democracy, containing factional divisions, and restoring basic services such as electricity and clean water proved a challenge.

Although Saddam was captured and executed, American forces struggled to maintain order against a persistent, mostly Sunni, resistance movement and terrifying suicide bombings by foreign jihadis. Between 2003 and 2011 over 100,000, and by some estimates as many as half a million, Iraqis died, 2 million became refugees in neighboring countries, and many were forced from their neighborhoods by "ethnic cleansing." Many Iraqis, especially Shi'ites and Kurds, having hated Saddam's bloody regime, welcomed its demise, but, remembering British colonization after World War I, they also resented yet another Western occupation. While some Arab liberals hoped democracy would flower in Iraq and throughout the region, the occupation of an oil-rich Arab country, at a high cost in U.S. and Iraqi casualties, tied down the U.S. military in a quagmire. However, Iraqis then elected their own government led by Shi'ites closely tied to Iran. The new government had to handle ethnic and tribal rivalries while trying to hold the nation together and rejuvenate public services. By 2009 violence had diminished, but a large U.S. military presence remained. The Shi'ites' monopoly on power and harassment of opponents alienated many Sunnis, while the sectarian passions of the Syrian civil war next door spilled over the border. Since the last U.S. troops withdrew in 2011, Sunni-Shia conflict and jihadi violence have increased, making life dangerous once again. Groups linked to Al Qaeda have reestablished a presence, fueling sectarian tensions.

Saudi Arabia, Oil, and the World

The Persian Gulf War reinforced Saudi Arabia's close connections with the United States, which had military bases and strong economic stakes in the kingdom. Mostly bleak desert, Saudi Arabia possesses the world's largest known oil reserves. Oil revenues funded modernization and the building of highways, hospitals, and universities, so that by the 1980s the Saudis had achieved high health and literacy rates for the Middle East. Glittering shopping malls offering the latest Western fashions and electronic gadgets serve affluent urbanites, who reach them in luxury cars often driven by chauffeurs. Yet, outside cities, poor Saudis often travel by camel and sleep in tents.

Despite modernization, Saudi political and social life has remained conservative. The royal family exercises absolute power, living extravagantly, quashing dissent, and maintaining traditional customs and social patterns. Modern institutions (like television) clash with a highly puritanical, patriarchal Islamic culture. With royal support, the Wahhabis impose their rigid beliefs on religious thought, life, and education. Hostile to Western and often modern ideas, Wahhabis believe that women should stay at home under male control. Hence, although some educated women desire more freedom, they still cannot legally drive or work or study alongside men. Armed with canes, the "religious police" patrol the streets, markets, and city malls, punishing women for violating strict dress codes that require them to be covered head to foot. In the 1990s they prevented unveiled

Ba'ath ("Renaissance") A political party in the Middle East that favored socialism and Arab nationalism and strongly opposed Israel.

OIL WEALTH Saudi Arabia contains the world's largest oil operations, mostly located on or near the Persian Gulf. A Saudi worker overlooks one of the nation's many refineries, which produces the oil exports that have brought the nation wealth.

female students from fleeing a school dormitory fire, causing dozens to burn to death. Meanwhile, the Shi'ite minority, despised by the Wahhabis, has enjoyed few rights, fostering tensions. Movie theaters, concerts, and most other entertainments are banned. Saudi and Western critics believe that the narrow Islam taught in Saudi schools promotes extremism and anti-Western feeling, and by 2013 calls for liberalization and women's empowerment by some Saudi men and women had fostered some minor reforms. After a peaceful protest on Facebook, a royal edict now allows women to work as sales clerks in lingerie and cosmetic shops, a first step perhaps in expanding the female work force. But with little public transportation, men have to drive them to workplaces.

Saudi Arabia has strongly influenced the prices and availability of world oil. In 1960 the kingdom spurred formation of **OPEC** (Organization of Petroleum Exporting Countries), a cartel designed to give producers more power over oil prices and leverage over consuming nations. OPEC's members range from Middle Eastern nations such as Algeria, Iran, and the United Arab Emirates to Mexico, Nigeria, and Indonesia. In 1973 OPEC members, angry at Western support of Israel, reduced the world oil supply to raise prices, badly discomforting industrialized nations by causing long lines at gasoline stations. After the embargo ended, the world price remained high, enriching OPEC members, while the high prices forced Americans and western

OPEC (Organization of Petroleum Exporting Countries) A cartel formed in 1960 to give producers more power over the price of oil and leverage with the consuming nations.

Europeans to conserve fuel. For example, some nations promoted development of more fuel-efficient cars. But in the 1980s reduced oil consumption broke OPEC's power and prices plummeted, damaging most OPEC members' economies.

Saudi Arabia's status as the world's largest oil exporter ensured political support and profits from industrialized nations but did not guarantee Saudi prosperity; by the 1990s the Saudi economy had soured. Between 1980 and 2000 income levels fell by two-thirds, generating government benefit cuts and climbing unemployment. Meanwhile, royal family members spent money lavishly, often violating Wahhabi restrictions by cavorting in Beirut nightclubs and European casinos. Resentment of the royal family and U.S. military bases on Saudi soil has increased. Seeing little future, frustrated young people often drink alcohol, have mixed-gender parties behind closed doors, and flirt over social media. Others have embraced militant Islam, and a few have joined terrorist groups such as Al Qaeda, including most of the young men who hijacked and crashed four U.S. airliners in 2001. Al Qaeda's leader, Osama bin Laden (1957–2011), a militant Wahhabi from a wealthy Saudi family, had long raged against the U.S. military bases in Saudi Arabia. Meanwhile, the Saudis help finance embattled Sunni groups in troubled nations like Lebanon and Syria while opposing Iranian influence. Saudis also invest heavily in the U.S. and European economies, and many Saudis have studied in the West. Thanks to oil, Saudi Arabia and the industrialized nations have remained close allies despite vastly different social and political systems.

MAKE SURE YOU UNDERSTAND THESE KEY POINTS BEFORE MOVING ON

- After World War II, nationalist governments replaced many colonial regimes in the Middle East, but the region has failed to develop many working multiparty democracies.

- Traumatized by the Holocaust, many Jews moved to Palestine after World War II and established the state of Israel, which led to a war between Jews and Arabs, a mass exodus of Palestinians into refugee camps, and enduring tensions.

- After nationalists overthrew the Iranian shah, the United States helped organize a coup that returned him to power, and he ruled ruthlessly until 1979, when he was overthrown by anti-Western Islamic fundamentalists.

- From 1958 on, Iraq was ruled by ruthless military dictatorships dominated by the Sunni minority, and

in 1979 Saddam Hussein came to power, launched a costly war against Iran, and then was attacked by the United States after invading Kuwait. In 2003 the United States invaded Iraq, overthrowing Saddam but fostering sectarian tensions that increased after the U.S. withdrawal of troops in 2011.

- Saudi Arabia grew extremely wealthy from oil sales, but many citizens have remained poor, and Saudi society is dominated by extremely conservative religious leaders, some of whose followers resent the close relationship the Saudi royal family has forged with the United States.

Change and Conflict in the Middle East

What roles has Islam played in the contemporary Middle East?

In 1979 Muslims celebrated thirteen centuries of Islamic history during which they had fostered extensive trade networks, introduced and transmitted scientific knowledge, and founded powerful empires. From roughly 1850 to 1950, European powers dominated these societies, though many older traditions have remained relevant into the present. In recent decades new conflicts resulting from foreign interventions, Islamic militancy, international terrorism, and political change have unsettled the Middle East and world politics.

Ethnic and Religious Conflict

Ethnic and religious hostilities have led to long-term conflict in some societies. In Lebanon competition between a dozen rival factions and sects—Christian, Sunni, and Shi'ite—has sparked occasional political crises and civil war. A national government mostly existed only in name during the 1970s and 1980s, and Beirut, once a prosperous, free-wheeling mecca for trade, entertainment, and tourism, was devastated by factional fighting. Supporting various factions, Israel, Syria, Iran, and the United States were all sucked into the conflict. Syria stationed troops in the north and east, Israel in the south. In the 1980s the United States intervened to help a weak national government led by the largest, most pro-Western Christian faction. U.S. warships shelled areas around Beirut dominated by opposition, especially Shi'ite, factions while Marines secured the Beirut airport. The disastrous episode caused some five hundred U.S. deaths from suicide bombers and the holding of U.S. hostages.

In the 1990s the fighting ebbed and Lebanon regained some stability, but there was little national unity. However,

the U.S. and Israeli interventions energized radical Shi'ites, who formed a militant Iran-backed organization, Hezbollah (**HEZ-bo-LAH**), which shelled Israel. Israelis responded by invading Lebanon in 2006 to weaken Hezbollah, but the incursion was costly in lives on all sides and failed to destroy Hezbollah, which remained a strong force in the deeply polarized Lebanon politics. By 2013 the civil war in Syria, whose population is even more diverse, spilled over into Lebanon; as refugees poured in, various Lebanese factions supported the Syrian government or the rebels.

Syria's ethnic configuration also helped generate a violent civil war as a reaction to the "Arab Spring." Since 1970 the Assad family and the Ba'ath Party have ruled Syria with an iron fist to limit ethnic conflict and dissent while favoring the Assads' Alawite Arab community, offshoots of Shi'ism who constitute 12 percent of the Syrian population. Sunni Arabs vastly outnumber other communities, among them Christians (10 percent), Palestinians, Kurds, and various Shi'ite groups. In 2011 Sunni anger at repressive Alawite control, a terrible drought, and high unemployment (18 percent in 2012) sparked protests and, after police repression, an uprising. As the regime had with earlier uprisings, the current dictator, Bashar al-Assad (president since 2000), responded with brutal force, attacking both civilians and insurgents. Soon the insurgency fragmented into various factions, some moderates, others Islamists or jihadis linked to Al Qaeda. Fearing militant Islam, many non-Sunnis supported Assad, who used poison gas weapons. By 2013 some 100,000 Syrians were dead and 7 million were refugees inside or outside the country. The war also enflamed regional passions, with Turkey, Saudi Arabia, Iraqi Sunnis, and the Gulf kingdoms supporting Syria and Iran, Iraqi

Karim Sahib/Getty Images

ARAB ART The large monument of Revolution, in Baghdad, sculpted by a major modern Iraqi artist, Jawad Salim (1920–1961), occupies a central place in the city. Commissioned in 1958 after the overthrow of the monarchy, it celebrates the Iraqi struggle for justice and freedom and often provided a motif for Iraqi poets.

Shi'ites, Russia, and Lebanon's Hezbollah aiding Assad, raising the danger of a wider conflict.

In the Sudan, the Arab Muslim-dominated government, which imposed an Islamic state, used military force to control rebellious black African Christians and animists in the south, a conflict that resulted in 2 million deaths. In 2005 the two sides agreed to end the conflict, but rebellion erupted in the impoverished Darfur region. Aided by local Arab militias, the government launched a genocide against African Muslim farmers, earning the world's condemnation as thousands died from military assaults, disease, or starvation. In 2011 South Sudan became independent, but tensions with Sudan persist over control of oil wealth.

Another longtime ethnic conflict concerned Kurds, a large mostly Sunni ethnic group—over 30 million strong—that mostly inhabited mountain districts in Iran, Iraq, Syria, and Turkey. Although deeply divided by clan and factional rivalries, Kurds had long sought either their own nation or self-government within their countries of residence, generating constant conflict with central governments. Kurdish rebel groups were especially active in eastern Turkey, where the Turkish government, while building a national identity based on Turkish values and language, repressed Kurdish culture and language. Kurds were also restless in oil-rich northern Iraq, where the dictator, Saddam Hussein, made Kurds a special target of his repression, launching air raids and poison gas attacks against Kurdish villages. Today Iraqi Kurds enjoy some regional autonomy and prosperity but still have tense relations with the Arab-dominated national government, while Syrian Kurds are caught between two seemingly irreconcilable sides in the country's civil war.

Farther east, in Afghanistan, violence, foreign interventions, and militant Islamic movements generated instability for over three decades. From the early 1800s until 1978, kings from the largest ethnic group, the Pashtuns, loosely governed Afghanistan's diverse Sunni and Shi'a ethnic groups, which were subdivided into rival tribes. In 1978 procommunist generals seized power, forged close ties with the Soviet Union, and introduced radical social and economic reforms that challenged Islamic traditions: land reform, women's education, and replacing Islamic law with secular family law. When conservative Islamic rebels, known as **mujahidin** (moo-JAH-hi-deen) ("holy warriors"), rebelled against the pro-Soviet regime, the USSR invaded in 1979, launching decades of turbulence during which the mujahidin won small victories against the 150,000 Soviet troops. Both sides were ruthless, and indiscriminate Soviet air attacks created 5 million refugees, turning the population against the occupation. Meanwhile, the United States, Pakistan, and Arab nations sent military and financial aid to the rebels and Islamic volunteers such as wealthy Saudi Osama bin Laden. Afghanistan became an unwinnable quagmire for Soviet forces, and they withdrew in 1989, hastening the demise of Soviet communism and the Soviet empire. As the pro-Soviet government collapsed, rival mujahidin groups fought for control. The West offered little help to reconstruct the ruined country.

Pashtun militants known as the **Taliban** ("Students"), many educated in Pakistani Islamic schools, conquered much of the Pashtun south and then seized the capital, Kabul, in 1996. Eventually they extended their influence into the north, which was mostly inhabited by anti-Taliban Tajiks and Uzbeks. The puritanical Taliban introduced an especially harsh Islamic rule. Women in Kabul, who once wore jeans and T-shirts and attended universities, were now required to wear long black robes and stay at home. The Taliban banned women's education, alcohol, and music and films as sinful, executing people for even minor infractions. Although the streets were safe, life offered no joy. Reflecting their disdain for Afghanistan's pre-Islamic past, the Taliban also destroyed spectacular monumental Buddhas carved into a mountainside over a millennium ago, outraging the world.

Meanwhile, international jihadist terrorist groups, forming around radical Arab volunteers who fought with the mujahidin, made Taliban-controlled Afghanistan their base and used it to build training camps. Osama bin Laden, leader and chief financial backer of the largest group, Al Qaeda, called on Muslims to take up arms against Western regimes, whom he called "crusaders":

mujahidin ("holy warriors") Conservative Islamic rebels who rebelled against the pro-Soviet regime in Afghanistan in the 1970s and 1980s.

Taliban ("Students") A group of Pashtun religious students who organized a military force in the 1980s to fight what they considered immorality and corruption and to impose order in Afghanistan.

"Tell the Muslims everywhere that the vanguards of the warriors who are fighting the enemies of Islam belong to them."[4]

After the Al Qaeda attacks on the United States in September 2001, Americans, enjoying widespread world support, sent military forces into Afghanistan. With local anti-Taliban allies soon displacing the Taliban from the main cities, the Americans destroyed Al Qaeda bases and installed a fragile pro-Western government. But instability ensued: Taliban and Al Qaeda leaders, including bin Laden, went into hiding (U.S. special forces killed him in Pakistan in 2011), and the victors struggled to foster development and democracy, especially after the United States shifted much of its military force and development aid to Iraq. The Taliban regrouped, mounted an insurgency against the pro-Western regime and the U.S.-NATO forces supporting it, and eventually controlled large sections of the Pashtun south. As the Obama administration prepared to withdraw the remaining combat forces in 2014, the Afghan regime and the Taliban competed to win popular support and secure territory.

Social Change

Tradition still shapes gender relations and family life in the Middle East. Although four predominantly Muslim nations—Bangladesh, Pakistan, Indonesia, and Turkey—have elected women prime ministers, no Arab or Iranian women have reached this goal. Urban women operate businesses and enter the professions, especially in Turkey, Egypt, Iraq, Jordan, and Lebanon. But many women remain in the home, often secluded, their lives as daughters, wives, and mothers controlled by men. Liberals have advocated improving women's lives through education, and several nations, including Turkey, have adopted Western-influenced family laws according women divorce and child custody rights. In 2014 a new constitution in Tunisia, strongly supported by secular liberals, guaranteed gender equality. Blaming patriarchal cultural traditions for restrictions, some women activists argue that the Quran supports women's rights. But conservative Muslims have prevented liberal laws in most Middle Eastern societies. Moreover, devout women have often opposed secular feminism, believing that women are best protected by strict Islamic law. Egyptian Zainab Al-Ghazali (1917–2005) founded mosques, trained female preachers, and promoted an active women's role in public life, but her staunch support of Islamic values upset both liberal feminists and modernizing President Nasser, who had her jailed and tortured. The conflict between modernizer and traditionalist has fostered gender role confusion, as an Egyptian writer noted: "Our mothers understood their situation. We, however, are lost. We do not know whether or not we still belong to the harem, whether love is forbidden or permitted."[5]

Liberal and conservative Muslims also disagree on women's dress. To liberals the veil symbolizes female subjugation, and many urban middle- and upper-class women have adopted Western dress. But traditionalists praise the veil as essential to female modesty. In secular nations like Turkey and Egypt, women influenced by revivalist Islam have lobbied to wear the full veil or head scarf to demonstrate their piety. A young Egyptian, speaking for many religious women, claimed that "being totally covered saves me from the approaches of men and hungry looks. I feel more free, purer, and more respectable."[6] In fact, many independent-minded, well-educated women do not uncritically adopt Western ways. Liberal, well-traveled Moroccan sociologist and Quranic scholar Fatema Mernissi contended that Western women, obsessed with physical appearance, face their own clothing veil: "I thank you, Allah, for sparing me the tyranny of the 'size six harem.' I am so happy that the conservative male elite [in the Middle East] does not know about it. Imagine the [Muslim] fundamentalists switching from the veil to forcing women to fit size 6."[7]

Attitudes toward homosexuality often became more repressive. For centuries some societies tolerated, although they did not approve, homosexual activity, and writings exploring homosexual experiences circulated widely. By the late 1800s homosexuals were forced into the closet, but in the 1990s the taboo slowly diminished in some cities. Where strict gender segregation exists, people spend most of their time, and enjoy emotional bonds, with other people of the same sex, sometimes making it easier for homosexual couples to escape notice. Yet, in many countries homosexual behavior, when discovered, frequently brings jail terms or even execution.

Religion and Culture

The clash between tradition and modernity has fostered creativity in religion, music, and literature. Islam remains central to life but, despite its message of peace, social justice, and community, often proves divisive (see Map 30.2), as age-old divisions—Sunni-Shi'a, liberal-conservative, secular-devout, Sufi–anti-Sufi—remain powerful. **Islamists** have become increasingly influential in many nations. Bitter rivals of secular Muslims, they are antimodern, usually puritanical militants who seek an Islamic state. After World War I the Islamist Muslim Brotherhood spread around the region. French-educated Iranian Shi'ite Ali Shariati (**SHAR-ee-AH-tee**) (1933–1977) castigated Western democracy as subverted by the power of money but also blamed Islamic tradition for reducing women to, as he put it, the level of a washing machine. Egyptian writer Sayyid Qutb (**SIGH-eed ka-TOOB**) (1906–1966) sparked political Sunni Islam, redefining jihad ("struggle") as violent opposition to the West. Qutb lived for two years in the United States, where he found Americans friendly but was appalled by the antiblack racism and hedonism, such as heavy drinking and casual romantic relations. Returning to Egypt, Qutb promoted an Islamic state and joined the Muslim Brotherhood. Inspired by thinkers like

Islamists Antimodern, usually puritanical Islamic militants who seek an Islamic state.

---

[4]From Akram Fouad Khater, ed., *Sources in the History of the Modern Middle East* (Boston: Houghton Mifflin, 2004), 362.
[5]Latifa az-Zayyat, quoted in Wiebke Walther, *Women in Islam from Medieval to Modern Times* (Princeton: Markus Wiener, 1993), 235.
[6]Quoted in Daniel Bates and Amal Rassam, *Peoples and Cultures of the Middle East*, 2nd ed. (Upper Saddle River, NJ: Prentice-Hall, 2001), 235.
[7]Fatema Mernissi, *Scheherazade Goes West: Different Cultures, Different Harems* (New York: Washington Square Press, 2001), 219.

MAP 30.2 THE ISLAMIC WORLD The Islamic world includes not only the Middle East—western Asia and North Africa—but also countries with Muslim majorities in sub-Saharan Africa, Central Asia, and South and Southeast Asia. In addition, Muslims live in most other Eastern Hemisphere nations and in the Americas. © 2015 Cengage Learning

Qutb, the most extreme Islamists, known as jihadists, support violence against secular Muslims, Sufis, and non-Muslims they consider obstacles to imposing their rigid beliefs. One ultraconservative strand of Islamism, Salafism ("predecessors"), embraces seventh-century religious traditions but tends to favor political rather than violent action. The same social media that liberals revere also allow Salafists and other Islamists to spread their message and organize.

Resentment of repressive and corrupt governments, lack of material improvement, and Western world power have prompted a growing turn to Islam. When elections are allowed, Islamic groups with their large followings often triumph over secular parties, as happened in Palestine in 2005 and Egypt in 2012, a reason why pro-Western modernists often fear democracy. In a troubled world, the Islamic revival promises tradition, personal solace, and a just political system. Devout Muslims dominated the U.S.-installed Iraqi government. While conservative activists in Iraq closed bars, harassed unveiled women, and terrorized Christians, Sunni militants in various lands attacked followers of Sufi mysticism as heretics. Some Islamists, frustrated at home, join international terrorist groups.

While Islamic militants condemn music, dance, and other pleasures, many people—both secular and devout—enjoy popular culture, especially music. Egyptian singer Oum Kulthum

(oom KAL-thoom) (1904–1975) symbolized Arab people's feelings. Attracting a region-wide following with emotional songs of love and abandonment, Kulthum dominated Middle Eastern popular music from the 1940s through the 1960s, becoming, with Egypt's President Nasser, one of the two most popular figures among Arabs. Her recordings were always on the radio and in films. Another hugely popular figure, the Lebanese singer Fairuz **(fie-ROOZ)**, has been credited with symbolizing hope and community in that turbulent, civil war–plagued land. Israelis revered Yemen-born Shoshana Damari (1923–2006), whose optimistic songs encouraged Israeli unity, extolling the nation and its military forces.

In religiously dogmatic or ethnically divided states, popular music has sometimes stirred controversy. Iran's Islamic government, opposed to women performing in public, tried to silence all female singers, especially vocalist and film star Googoosh **(GOO-goosh)** (b. 1950), whose melancholic Westernized pop music had a huge audience during the 1960s and 1970s. The clerics destroyed all her recordings, posters, and films, turning Googoosh into a popular symbol against clerical rule. Turkey's *arabesk* pop music reflects the experiences of poor Arab and Kurdish migrants to Istanbul. One observer noted that "arabesk describes a decaying city in which poverty-stricken migrant workers are exploited and abused, and calls on its listeners to pour another glass of wine and curse fate and the world."[8] Some popular styles blend Arab and foreign forms while addressing social problems. Algeria's **rai** ("opinion") music, based on local Bedouin chants, Spanish flamenco, French café songs, Egyptian pop, and other influences, often addresses forbidden themes of sex and alcohol. Appealing to urban working-class youth in North Africa and young Arab immigrants in France, rai is despised by puritanical Islamic militants, who have forced singers into exile or even assassinated them. Rai musicians often move their base to Paris.

Middle Eastern writers have also expressed ideas forbidden in politics and religion. The novels of Egyptian Naguib Mahfuz (**nah-GEEB mah-FOOZ**) (1911–2006), a government official and journalist, addressed social problems, such as poverty, and questioned conservative religious values and blind faith, which he believed kept individuals from realizing their full potential, sparking bans on his writings in Egypt and other nations. In 1988 Mahfuz became the first Arab writer to win a Nobel Prize for literature. The political verses of Egypt's "poet of the people", Ahmed Fouad Nagm (**NEG-em**) (1929–2013), skewered national leaders and Islamists, inspiring protesters from the 1970s until today. Iranian writers often risked punishment when attacking religious hypocrisy in their satires of government and business failings. One famous Iranian novel recommended opportunism for career success: "Try to establish connections with the holders of high offices. Agree with everybody, no matter what his opinion is."[9]

The Middle East in the Global System

Middle Eastern nations have generally lagged behind much of Asia and Latin America in development. A Lebanese novelist wrote that dictatorial Arab regimes deprived people not only of dignity but also of air: the opportunity to discuss problems freely. In 2002 Arab thinkers issued an Arab Human Development Report outlining economic and social failures, including marginalization of women and limited health and education development (see Witness to the Past: Assessing Arab Development). Regional cable networks, such as Qatar-based Al Jazeera, spur debate, spread awareness of political and social developments, and promote a modern image, such as using unveiled female news anchors. Some urbanites have access to the Internet, often at cafés, and go online to access foreign news, shop, or arrange dates; Arab and Turkish chat rooms and blogs abound. Religious and political groups also use the Web to recruit support, among them Al Qaeda, which has been able to capitalize on a power vacuum and political instability to establish operations in countries like Iraq, Syria, Libya, and Yemen.

The region's economic record has been checkered. The Middle East has usually had the world's highest unemployment rate and, except for sub-Saharan Africa, slowest economic growth and lowest productivity. Only Turkey has fostered much industrialization and high economic growth. Nations with oil, such as Algeria, Iran, and Libya, have remained dangerously dependent on oil revenues for survival. Some 10 million migrant workers from other Arab countries, South Asia, and Southeast Asia work in the Gulf states; most are semiskilled or unskilled, often facing abuse and discrimination. Oil wealth often fosters political corruption, spurs autocratic leaders to oppose democracy, and sometimes funds Islamist and terrorist groups. Several small Persian Gulf states have used their oil wealth to become centers of global commerce. Dubai, one of the world's most modern, globalized cities, boasts luxury hotels, towering skyscrapers, futuristic architecture, the world's largest artificial port, local branches of Western universities, and thousands of businessmen and workers from all over the world. Yet many of the low-skilled workers, mostly from South and Southeast Asia, are treated little better than slaves, with few rights. Dubai was also hurt by the 2008–2009 world economic crisis, during which many foreigners left. Yet, the Western, Japanese, and new Chinese and Indian appetite for oil ensures that oil-rich nations will profit for years to come. Meanwhile, Middle Eastern nations without oil, such as Egypt and Lebanon, struggle to build modern economies with limited resources. Some Arab thinkers argue that democracy will only flourish in the Middle East if buttressed by social and economic change to improve living standards for the majority of people.

Past and present, tradition and modernity, have all been jumbled in the contemporary Middle East, whose people hope to preserve revered traditional patterns while harmonizing them with the modern world. An Egyptian novelist wrote that a Cairo resident has a split personality: "Half of him believes, prays, fasts and makes the pilgrimage [to Mecca]. The other half renders his values void in banks and courts and in the streets, the cinemas, perhaps even at home among his family before the television set."[10] The recent history of the Middle East, like that of India and sub-Saharan Africa, challenges the notion that contact with the modern world automatically erodes all traditional cultures, steering people inevitably toward Western models. Older patterns of life and thought persist. Observers disagree whether this persistence constitutes a barrier to progress or gives the people an anchor to deal with the destabilizing effects of change.

Islamic militancy taps unease with Western ideas. Many Muslims reject Western culture's materialistic, hedonistic values. The Iranian Revolution was the first successful attempt by an Islamic country to become totally independent of Western political, economic, social, and cultural influence. Many Iranians and Arabs agreed with Indian Muslim poet Muhammad Iqbal (**ik-BALL**) (1873–1938), who wrote in 1927: "Against Europe I protest, And the attraction of the West: Woe for Europe and her charm, Swift to capture and disarm! Earth awaits rebuilding; rise! Out of slumber deep, Arise!"[11] Militancy challenges capitalism, secularism, failed governments, and Western-style democracy. But other Muslims

rai ("opinion") A pop music of Algeria based on local Bedouin chants, Spanish flamenco, French café songs, Egyptian pop, and other influences and featuring improvised lyrics that often deal with forbidden themes of sex and alcohol.

---

[8]Martin Stokes, *The Arabesk Debate: Music and Musicians in Modern Turkey* (Oxford: Clarendon Press, 1992), 1.
[9]Sadiq Hidayat, in *Hajji Aqa*, quoted in Bill, *Politics of Iran*, 105.
[10]Naguib Mahfuz, quoted in Bates and Rassam, *Peoples and Cultures*, 199.
[11]Quoted in Frances Robinson, *The Cultural Atlas of the Islamic World Since 1500* (Alexandria, VA: Stonehenge, 1982), 158.

WITNESS TO THE PAST

Assessing Arab Development

Under the auspices of the United Nations Development Programme, a group of Arab scholars and opinion makers from the twenty-two member states of the Arab League, a regional organization, met to consider the Arab condition. In 2002 they issued the first of four planned reports, offering both a description of the Arab condition and a prescription for change. Hailed by Arab and non-Arab observers as a pathbreaking effort by Arabs to foster a debate on the inadequacies of Arab development and local barriers to progress, the first document reported great strides in many areas but also unsolved problems. This excerpt is from the Executive Summary.

The Arab Human Development Report 2002...places people squarely at the [center] of development in all its dimensions: economic, social, civil, political, and cultural. It provides a neutral forum to measure progress and deficits, propose strategies to policymakers, and draw attention to country problems that can benefit from regional solutions. It is guided by the conviction that solid analysis can contribute to the many efforts underway to mobilize the region's rich human potential. There has been considerable progress in laying the foundations for health, habitat, and education. Two notable achievements are the enormous quantitative expansion in educating the young and a conspicuous improvement in fighting death. For example, life expectancy has increased by 15 years over the last three decades, and infant mortality rates have dropped by two-thirds. Moreover, the region's growth has been "pro-poor": there is much less dire poverty (defined as an income of less than a dollar a day) than in any other developing region.

But there have been warning signs as well. Over the past twenty years, growth in per capita income was the lowest in the world except in sub-Saharan Africa...If such trends continue [into] the future, it will take the average Arab citizen 140 years to double his or her income ... The decline in productivity has been accompanied by deterioration in real wages, which has accentuated poverty. It is evident that... Arab countries have not developed as quickly or as fully as other comparable regions...The Arab region is richer than it is developed,...hobbled by a...poverty of capabilities and ... opportunities. These have their roots in three deficits:

freedom, women's empowerment, and knowledge. Growth alone will neither bridge these gaps nor set the region on the road to sustainable development.

The way forward involves tackling human capabilities and knowledge. It also involves promoting systems of good governance, those that promote, support and sustain human well-being, based on expanding human capabilities, choices, opportunities and freedoms,...especially for the poorest and most marginalized members of society. The empowerment of women must be addressed throughout ...

[The Report concludes that] People in most Arab countries live longer than the world average life expectancy of 67. However, disease and disability reduce life expectancy by between five and 11 years. Arab women have lower life expectancy than the world average ... Arab countries have made tangible progress in improving literacy:...female literacy rates tripled since 1970. Yet 65 million adults are illiterate, almost two-thirds of them women ... One out of every five Arabs lives on less than $2 per day ... Arab countries had the lowest freedom score [in the world] in the late 1990s ... [Utilization] of Arab women's capabilities through political and economic participation remains the lowest in the world ... Serious knowledge deficits include weak systems of scientific research and development.

The Arab world is at a crossroads. The fundamental choice is whether its trajectory will remain marked by inertia, as reflected in much of the present institutional context, and by ineffective policies that have produced the substantial development challenges facing the region; or whether prospects for an Arab renaissance, anchored in human development will be actively pursued.

THINKING ABOUT THE READING

1. How have Arabs done in promoting freedom, women's empowerment, and knowledge?
2. What does the report consider the major improvements and the major failures and challenges of the Arab nations?

Source: Arab Human Development Report 2002: Creating Opportunities for Future Generations (UNDP, 2002), available online at http://www.rbas.undp.org/ahdr/press_kits2002/PRExecSummary.pdf. Reprinted with permission of the United Nations Development Programme (UNDP).

---

fear militant Islamic rule, which has not delivered a better material life in countries like Iran and Sudan. In 2014 protests by secular Tunisians forced an Islamist regime to resign and reinforced multi-party democracy.

Interventions by outside powers, such as the USSR and the United States, reflect the region's oil wealth and strategic location among key waterways of world trade. Until cost-effective alternative power sources become common, all industrial economies need access to Middle Eastern oil, without which modern lifestyles would come to a screeching halt. The world community will not tolerate anything

threatening the movement of oil tankers through the Persian Gulf. While U.S. leaders have hoped that democracy will spread, instability in Iraq, Syria, and Egypt has unsettled the entire region, and perhaps strengthened Iran, while presenting foreign policy dilemmas for the United States, Europe, China, Japan, Russia, and other interested nations. Furthermore, few conflicts or persistent problems, including the Arab-Israeli conflict, sectarian rivalries, and Arab-Iranian tensions, seem resolvable anytime soon. These challenges make the Middle East a focus of world attention and, some fear, a potential tinderbox.

MAKE SURE YOU UNDERSTAND THESE KEY POINTS BEFORE MOVING ON

- The Middle East has been torn by ethnic conflict, especially in Lebanon, Syria, and the Sudan, while the Kurds in various countries have struggled to gain their own home.

- In Afghanistan, U.S.-supported Islamic rebels and Soviet-assisted communists fought for a decade until the Soviets withdrew, after which the Taliban took over much of the country and allowed terrorist groups such as Al Qaeda to base themselves there.

- After Al Qaeda's September 2001 attack on the United States, a U.S.-led invasion in Afghanistan and later in Iraq led to significant backlash and opposition to pro-Western government initiatives.

- Middle Eastern societies have been divided between Islamists and secular Muslims, and musicians and writers, popular among the people, have raised the ire of religious conservatives

- Middle Eastern societies have been torn between those who feel they have failed to adapt to the modern world and those who champion tradition and urge rejection of the modern, Western values, while the region has remained extremely important to outside powers, such as the United States, because of its oil reserves.

aplia

Political Change in Sub-Saharan Africa

What were the main political consequences of decolonization in sub-Saharan Africa?

As in the Middle East, the rise of nationalism and the consequent wave of decolonization in Africa between 1957 and 1975 reduced Western political influence, reshaping societies and politics. Countries won political independence after the British, French, Belgians, Spanish, and eventually Portuguese came to terms with rising nationalist activity. As optimistic Africans celebrated their freedom, formed governments, and hoped for a better future, some observers proclaimed the 1960s Africa's Age of Glamor. The years since have brought rapid, though often destabilizing, change. Most Africans still struggle to find the right mix of policies to resolve their problems.

Nationalism and Decolonization

Rising African nationalism sparked decolonization. European colonial powers did little to encourage national feeling, maintaining control of the diverse ethnic groups through divide and rule, while nationalists struggled to overcome the ethnic complexities within colonies with the arbitrary boundaries imposed by colonialists. The colossal slaughter in World War II undermined Western credibility, leading Africans to resent the Western powers and their pretensions of superiority, as expressed by a British official in Nigeria who argued that African "barbarism" required maintaining the "civilizing mission" into the far future. While Britain and France espoused freedom and democracy, they seldom applied these values in the colonies. After the war the British encouraged African hopes by granting independence to India and Burma and introducing local government in some African colonies. Yet most colonial governments did little to prepare Africans for true political and economic independence.

The first major changes came in the British Gold Coast. In 1948 riots began after small farmers boycotted European businesses suspected of profiteering at their expense. A rising leader with British and American university degrees, Kwame Nkrumah **(KWAH-mee nn-KROO-muh)** (1909–1972), believing only socialism could save Africa, organized a political party in 1949 but was soon arrested. However, with unrest

continuing, Britain allowed an election in 1951 for a legislative council, which was won by Nkrumah's party. After negotiations, in 1957 the Gold Coast became independent and was renamed Ghana, after the first great West African kingdom. The nation's first prime minister and Africa's hero, Nkrumah preached **pan-Africanism**, the goal of eventually forming some sort of united states of Africa.

Now it became impossible to stem the decolonizing tide. By 1963, after peaceful negotiations and workers' strikes, all British colonies in West Africa had become independent. France, having no plans to abandon its empire, fought brutal but unsuccessful wars in the 1950s to hold Vietnam and Algeria. Finally realizing that a peaceful transition might better maintain its economic influence, France gave its colonies the option of a complete break or autonomy within a French community of closely connected nations. Eventually all the French colonies became fully independent, though usually maintaining close political and economic ties to France.

In some colonies widespread violence preceded or accompanied independence. After both World War I and World War II, British settlers migrated to Kenya and took land from the Africans to establish farms. In 1952 many Gikuyu, Kenya's largest ethnic group and the group that had lost the most land, began an eight-year uprising known as the **Mau Mau Rebellion**, attacking British farmers and officials. British troops committed atrocities against pro–Mau Mau villages, ultimately killing 10,000 Gikuyu and detaining 90,000 others in harsh prison camps, where many died from disease or mistreatment. Finally realizing the futility of their cause, the British released from prison the leading nationalist leader, Jomo Kenyatta **(ken-YAH-tuh)** (ca. 1889–1978), a Gikuyu former herd boy who had studied

pan-Africanism The dream that all Africans would cooperate to eventually form some sort of united states of the continent.

Mau Mau Rebellion An eight-year uprising in the 1950s by the Gikuyu people in Kenya against British rule.

Hulton-Deutsch Collection/Corbis

MAU MAU During the 1950s Africans in Kenya, especially the Gikuyu, rebelled against British colonial rule. The British responded by detaining some 90,000 suspected rebels and sympathizers in concentration camps such as this, where many died.

Joseph Mobuto **(mo-BOO-to)** (g. 1965–1997), then became a dictator and eventually renamed the country Zaire while styling himself Mobuto Sese Seko, "Mobuto the All Powerful." Mobuto required his people to sing his praises every day at workplace or school and replaced European names and values with African ones, including exchanging Western clothes, such as ties, for traditional garb. Wearing a tie became an act of political resistance.

Meanwhile, Portugal, ruled by a fascist dictator, was reluctant to give up its empire. When revolts broke out in its three colonies—Angola, Guinea-Bissau, and Mozambique—in the 1960s, Portuguese soldiers struggled to crush them. Angola's liberation movement was divided into three rival factions based on the country's major ethnic groupings, while Marxists led the major liberation movements in Mozambique and Guinea Bissau. Visionary Guinea-Bissau revolutionary leader Amilcar Cabral **(AH-mill-CAR kah-BRAHL)** (1924–1973), a university-educated agronomist who was assassinated in 1973, emphasized educating the people to empower them, telling his followers: "Learn from life, people, books, the experiences of others, never stop learning."[12] In 1974 Portugal's war-weary army ended Portugal's dictatorship, and the new democratic, socialist-led government granted the colonies independence in 1975. In Angola, the nationalist factions fought each other for dominance for the next two decades. Mozambique's government faced a long insurgency supported by white-ruled South Africa.

The British-ruled Rhodesias and Nyasaland in southern Africa, all containing white settlers bitterly resisting equality for Africans, struggled for independence under black majority rule. Facing largely nonviolent resistance campaigns, Britain granted independence to Zambia (Northern Rhodesia) and Malawi (formerly Nyasaland) in 1963. But Southern Rhodesia's large white settler population, declaring independence in 1965, installed a white racist government that imposed stricter racial segregation and prohibited nonwhite political activity. In response, Africans took up arms in two rival Marxist-led liberation movements. By 1980 the United States and Britain had pressured the white government to allow elections, which were won by Robert Mugabe **(moo-GAH-bee)** (b. 1924), a guerrilla leader and former political prisoner. The country became independent as Zimbabwe.

anthropology in Britain. Kenya became independent in 1963, with Kenyatta the first freely elected prime minister. Britain also granted independence to its other East African colonies, Uganda and Tanzania. Many white settlers who once opposed political rights for the African majority remained in Kenya.

Violence also engulfed the Belgian Congo, a vast, natural resource–rich territory containing some two hundred ethnic groups. Belgium failed to foster an educated leadership class, encourage national consciousness, or build adequate paved roads, bridges, and telephone systems. The only Congolese leader with any national following, left-leaning former post office clerk and brewery director Patrice Lumumba **(loo-MOOM-buh)** (1925–1961), opposed economic domination by Belgian business and mining interests. In 1959 widespread rioting forced the colony's first free elections, which were won by Lumumba's party. As Lumumba took power, some Congolese troops mutinied, attacking whites, while Belgian-supported, anti-Lumumba leaders in the mineral-rich Katanga region announced Katanga's secession from the country. A United Nations peacekeeping force restored order, but in 1961 Katanga leaders, with Belgian and American complicity, abducted and murdered Lumumba, whom they viewed as pro-USSR. The Congo's new leader, Belgian- and U.S.-supported General

Political Change and Conflict

A West African scholar called the term *nation* "a magical word meant to exorcise ethnic quarrels and antagonisms—and

12Quoted in Basil Davidson, *The People's Cause: A History of Guerrillas in Africa* (Burnt Mill, UK: Longman, 1981), 165.

MAP 30.3 **CONTEMPORARY AFRICA AND THE MIDDLE EAST** Sub-Saharan and North Africa contain over forty nations. Six sub-Saharan African nations and Algeria in North Africa experienced anticolonial revolutions, and a dozen sub-Saharan nations have been racked by civil wars since independence. © 2015 Cengage Learning

as such very precious"[13]; but the magic usually failed to overcome disunity. New African nations typically experienced political and economic challenges that generated instability: coups, civil wars, and recurring famines (see Map 30.3). Until recently, military or one-party dominance has been more common than multiparty democracy. But privileged military officers have often lost touch with the population; used to giving orders, they have ruled with a heavy hand and often looted treasuries. Civilian-led one-party states can minimize ethnic divisions. While some one-party states, such as

the Congo (Zaire), have been despotisms, others have been relatively open, some offering multiple candidates for office. Some nations, such as Nigeria and Ghana, have shifted back and forth between authoritarian military dictatorships and ineffective, corrupt civilian governments. But the despotic governments have sometimes brutally mistreated their own people. During the 1970s in Uganda, poorly educated boxer-turned-general Idi Amin's **(EE-dee AH-meen)** (1925–2004) terroristic rule killed some 300,000 people, while thousands more were jailed or fled into exile.

---

[13]A. Toure, quoted in Bill Freund, *The Making of Contemporary Africa: The Development of African Society Since 1800* (Bloomington: Indiana University Press, 1984), 192.

Western-style democracy faced tremendous odds in these artificial countries with a tiny middle class and numerous poor people. Given often deteriorating economic conditions, governments had little money to spend on containing ethnic tensions or building schools, hospitals, and roads. The nationalist leaders and parties governing the new nations often lost their credibility and mass support after a few years. Hence, Ghana's Kwame Nkrumah was overthrown for economic mismanagement and an autocratic governing style, and he died in exile. Some leaders have been respected, far-sighted visionaries, such as Tanzania's Julius Nyerere **(NEE-ya-RARE-y)** (g. 1962–1985) and Mozambique's Samora Machel (g. 1975–1986), and pragmatic problem solvers, such as South Africa's first black president, Nelson Mandela, using political office largely to improve society rather than enrich themselves. However, many leaders, emulating old Africa's despotic kings, have held on to power, rigging elections or having compliant parliaments declare them presidents for life. Some, such as Zaire dictator Mobuto (g. 1965–1997) and Nigerian military dictator Sani Abacha (g. 1993–1998), were ruthless crooks, arresting or murdering opponents and plundering the public treasury. When Abacha, hopped up on Viagra, died of a heart attack while engaging in an orgy with prostitutes, few Nigerians lamented.

Competition for personal wealth fostered political instability, conflict, and social unrest. Blatant corruption, conspicuous consumption, and smuggling in government and the business sector increased income inequalities, deepening public frustrations. In some countries, government officials were known as "Mr. 10 Percent," a reference to the share of public budgets they grab. East Africans chastise the wabenzi—"people who drive a Mercedes Benz"—a privileged urban class of politicians, bureaucrats, professionals, military officers, and businessmen who manipulate their connections to amass wealth. Elites have often squandered scarce resources on importing luxuries, such as fancy cars and hard liquor, confirming the continuing appeal of Western taste and consumer goods.

However, in some societies relations between governments and the governed have improved in recent years. New grassroots nongovernmental organizations have addressed issues such as human rights and the environment. For example, by 2000 some twenty-five thousand local women's groups in Kenya pushed for improved rights and other issues, such as environmental protection. Kenyan women's rights and environmental activist Wangari Maathai **(wan-GAHR-ee MAH-thai)** won the Nobel Peace Prize in 2005 (see Chapter 26). Since few Africans can afford health insurance, poor Senegalese came together to form small mutual health organizations, negotiating with local clinics to get affordable group rates for health care. In Liberia, recovering from civil war and dictatorship, women voters helped elect economist Ellen Johnson-Sirleaf (b. 1939), a Harvard-trained banker and former United Nations official, as Africa's first woman president in 2005. Although she struggled to bring progress to a maimed nation with no piped water or electric grid and few functioning schools and hospitals, she was reelected and also won the Noble Peace Prize in 2011.

Africa's hopes and frustrations are mirrored in Nigeria, home to some 170 million people, a fifth of Africa's total population. Nigeria's ethnic and religious diversity and natural wealth have been both blessing and curse. Among the 250 Nigerian ethnic groups, about two-thirds are Hausa-Fulani, Igbo (Ibo), or Yoruba. Oil wealth has produced 80 percent of Nigeria's total revenues but has also corrupted politics and increased social inequality. Having neglected agriculture, Nigeria is now a food importer, and many Nigerians have insufficient food. Coups, countercoups, riots, political assassinations, and civil war rooted in regional and ethnic rivalries have punctuated Nigerian history. Between 1967 and 1970 a bloody civil war raged to prevent the secession of the Igbo-dominated oil-rich southeast region. The religious divide between Christians, who dominate the south, and Muslims, who control the northern states, also complicates politics. Many northern states have imposed strict Islamic law, antagonizing non-Muslims; authorities sentenced several Muslim women to death by stoning for adultery while not punishing the men involved, causing an outcry in Nigeria and around the world. Sometimes severe Christian-Muslim fighting causes the deaths of hundreds of people. Recently a militant group with possible Al Qaeda ties seeking an Islamic state, Boko Haram ("Western learning is forbidden"), has terrorized some northern districts with bombings and killings. Such religious tensions have often generated corrupt military rule that has brought stability by suppressing opposition but pushed the people hard, alternated with periods of corrupt civilian democracy that has increased political freedom but often governed ineffectively. Since 2007 civilian regimes have held power and attempted to reduce rampant corruption.

The oil industry, while creating some prosperity, has made Nigeria dependent on oil exports. A few politicians, bureaucrats, and businessmen have monopolized oil profits, fostering corruption, sometimes outright plunder of public wealth, and inequitable wealth distribution. By 2005 the top 20 percent received 56 percent of all the country's wealth, while the bottom 20 percent got only 4.4 percent. Impoverished people in southern oil-producing districts, watching sullenly as pipelines through their villages move oil to coastal ports for shipment to European and North American consumers, protest and sometimes sabotage oil pipelines, prompting military reprisals and sometimes execution of protest leaders. Local rebel groups harass the oil industry and fight the army. Disenchanted Nigerians refer to a "republic of the privileged and rich" and a "moneytocracy." After oil money created high expectations in the 1970s, world oil prices collapsed in the 1980s, forcing the nation to take on massive foreign debt. Oil prices have since rebounded.

The combination of artificial boundaries, weak national identity, and economic collapse or stagnation has produced chronic turmoil in several African nations. Liberia and Sierra Leone, once among the more stable countries, disintegrated in the 1990s. As ethnic-based rebel groups challenged governments for power, thousands fled the slaughter and the maiming

---

wabenzi ("people who drive a Mercedes Benz") A privileged urban class in Africa of politicians, bureaucrats, professionals, military officers, and businessmen who manipulate their connections to amass wealth.

of civilians; African nations like Nigeria sent in troops to bring stability. In drought-plagued Somalia, when longtime military rule collapsed in 1991, the country fragmented into regions ruled by feuding Somali clans. As the Somali economy disintegrated, thousands starved to death. Some Americans with a United Nations humanitarian mission were killed, and the United Nations withdrew in 1994, unable to forge a unified government. Somalia remained a country in name only, controlled by warlords and, more recently, engulfed in civil war involving Islamist militias linked to Al Qaeda, a weak central government, and the Ethiopian army. Desperate young men in coastal villages turned to piracy, disrupting shipping and prompting an international naval force to police the nearby seas. Somalia's violence spilled over into neighboring Kenya, where Somali and Kenyan Islamists mounted attacks on civilian targets, including a 2013 massacre in a downtown Nairobi mall. Islamists supported by Al Qaeda also seized much of northern Mali, including historic cities like Gao and Timbuktu, in 2012–2013 but were forced out by French troops. In 2013 Christian-Muslim political tensions led to massive violence in the Central African Republic, with France once again dispatching troops to a former colony to reestablish order.

Hatreds also sparked genocide in impoverished, densely populated Rwanda, divided between majority Hutus and minority Tutsis. The Belgians had ruled through Tutsi kings, and soon after independence Hutus rebelled, slaughtering thousands of Tutsis and forcing others into exile. The remaining Tutsis faced discrimination and repression. In 1994 the extremist Hutu government began a genocide against Tutsis and moderate Hutus, murdering over 500,000 people. Tutsi exiles invaded Rwanda, forcing the Hutu leaders and their followers—over 2 million—into the neighboring Congo. As a result, the new Tutsi-led government continued to face militant Congo-based Hutu resistance groups, leading to Rwandan military incursions into the Congo and support for Congolese rebel groups. In recent years various warlord militias, Congolese troops, and foreign forces have terrorized the eastern Congo, killing and raping many thousands of civilians.

The New South Africa

From World War II to the early 1990s, South Africa remained the last bastion of institutionalized white racism. The white population, in the 1990s some 15 percent of the total and divided between an Afrikaner majority (descendants of Dutch settlers) and an English minority, ruled the black majority (74 percent) and the Indians (2 percent) and mixed-descent Coloreds (9 percent). Racial inequality became more systematic after 1948, when Afrikaner nationalists, winning the white-only elections, declared full independence from Britain. A top nationalist leader claimed: "We [whites] need [Africans] because they work for us but they can never claim political rights. Not now, nor in the future."[14] Their new policy, **apartheid (uh-PAHRT-ate)** ("separate development"), established a ruthless police state to enforce racial separation; laws required all Africans to carry ID ("pass") cards specifying where they could legally reside or visit while outlawing interracial marriage and sexual relations. Apartheid created a chilling juxtaposition of white comfort and black despair.

Apartheid expanded segregation to include designated residential areas, schools, recreational facilities, and public accommodations. Urban black men were commonly housed in crowded dormitories near mines or factories where they worked or, with their families, in shantytown suburbs. While most white families lived comfortably in well-furnished apartments or houses with swimming pools, a typical house in Soweto, a dusty Johannesburg suburb, was bleak; residents used candles or gas lamps for lighting, and most had no running water. Demoralized blacks frequented the informal bars dotting African neighborhoods.

Apartheid also created what white leaders called tribal homelands, known as **bantustans**, rural reservations where black Africans had to live if not needed in the modern economy. The system allocated whites 87 percent of the nation's land, nonwhites the other 13 percent. Every year thousands of Africans were forcibly resettled to impoverished bantustans, which contained little fertile land and few jobs, hospitals, and secondary schools and where infant mortality rates were among the world's highest. Men and women were recruited on annual contracts for jobs outside the bantustans, fracturing black families. A husband and wife recruited for jobs in the same city could not legally visit each other if their ID cards restricted each to a different neighborhood.

Rich in strategic minerals such as gold, diamonds, uranium, platinum, and chrome, South Africa became Africa's most industrialized nation with the largest economy, but it had the world's most inequitable income distribution. Whites enjoyed one of the world's highest standards of living, with well-funded schools and medical centers, while Africans and the Colored and Indian minorities enjoyed few benefits. Whites controlled two-thirds of the nation's wealth and personal disposable income, while a third of Africans were unemployed. Fearing that unrest or black majority rule might threaten their billions in investments and access to lucrative resources, several industrialized countries, including the United States, Britain, and Japan, supported South Africa.

Africans resisted, often paying a price for their defiance. The police state brutalized dissidents and had the world's highest rate of execution and prisoners. Stephen Biko (1946–1977), a former medical student whose organization encouraged black pride and self-reliance, was beaten to death in police custody. Hundreds were arrested each day for "pass law" violations and held for a few days or weeks. The police violently repressed protests; imprisoned thousands of dissidents, including numerous children, often without trial; and sometimes

apartheid ("separate development") A South African policy to set up a police state to enforce racial separation.

bantustans Rural reservations in South Africa where black Africans under apartheid were required to live if they were not needed in the modern economy.

---

[14]Prime Minister John Vorster in 1968, quoted in L. S. Stavrianos, *Global Rift: The Third World Comes of Age* (New York: William Morrow, 1981), 759.

assassinated black leaders, such as lawyer Victoria Mxenge (ma-SEN-gee), who defended anti-apartheid activists. Nevertheless, various forms of defiance, including strikes, work interruptions, and sabotage, became common. Resistance was often subtle; Nobel Prize–winning white South African novelist and apartheid critic Nadine Gordimer (b. 1923) described how even domestic servants in white households protested and asserted their dignity in nonverbal ways:

> *Every household in the fine suburb had several black servants—a shifting population of pretty young housemaids whose long red nails and pertness not only asserted the indignity of being undiscovered fashion models but kept hoisted a cocky guerrilla pride against servitude to whites.*[15]

The African National Congress (ANC), the major opposition organization, remained multiracial, with some whites, Coloreds, and Indians serving in its leadership. In 1955, despairing of peaceful change, a more militant ANC leadership framed its inclusive vision in the Freedom Charter: "South Africa belongs to all who live in it, black and white."[16] But the government declared the ANC illegal, and the fierce repression forced it underground and toward violent resistance. Several main leaders, including Nelson Mandela (1918–2013), spent almost thirty years in prison for their political activities (see Profile: Nelson Mandela, South African Freedom Fighter and President). ANC women, including Mandela's wife, Winnie Mandela, often faced arrest and mistreatment.

Ultimately, international isolation, economic troubles, the need for more highly skilled black workers, and growing black unrest forced the government to relax apartheid and release Mandela from prison. Negotiations produced a new constitution requiring "one man, one vote." In 1994 white supremacy ended in the nation's first all-race elections, which installed Mandela as president and gave the ANC two-thirds of parliamentary seats. The ANC government enjoyed massive goodwill but also faced daunting challenges in healing a deeply fragmented society while restoring African pride and spirits. Mandela sought both racial reconciliation and major changes benefiting the disadvantaged black majority. He improved some services in urban black communities, such as electricity and water, and fostered a growing black upper and middle class, but critics believe he neglected addressing racial inequality while promoting racial healing. In 1999 he voluntarily retired, a still-popular figure, while the ANC retained power in free elections.

Despite these momentous changes, millions of South African blacks have felt neglected, wanting better land and services and complaining about corruption and mismanagement. Whites still earn six times more income than blacks, a quarter of South Africans lack electricity and proper housing, a fifth have no proper sanitation facilities, and half live below the poverty line. South Africa has one of the world's highest rates of HIV/AIDS, crime has rapidly increased, violent protests have erupted, and income inequality, corruption, and black unemployment have remained high. In 2009 the election of a more radical ANC leader, Jacob Zuma (b. 1942), prompted some blacks to form or join opposition parties. Zuma faced widespread discontent and strikes; in 2013, in a reminder of apartheid-era repression, the police violently crushed a strike by 80,000 miners over low wages and poor living conditions, killing 34. A union organizer charged that "the A.N.C. today is all about power … They are supposed to be here to listen to the problems of the people … But they are nowhere to be seen."[17] But while some of the goodwill of the Mandela years has faded, given the long history of repression and fear in South Africa, the rapid transition to multiparty democracy has been impressive. People all over Africa hope that the nation of 52 million (80 percent black) succeeds in healing racial wounds while spreading the wealth to all its citizens.

MAKE SURE YOU UNDERSTAND THESE KEY POINTS BEFORE MOVING ON

- Most British colonies attained independence through peaceful means, but Kenya's transition was long and violent, as was that of the Belgian Congo, Angola, Guinea-Bissau, Mozambique, and Zimbabwe.

- After independence, many African nations were ruled by military dictatorships or corrupt civilians, many nationalist leaders lost favor over time, the gap between rich and poor widened, and some nations experienced ongoing violence, disorder, and genocide.

- Nigeria, home to rival ethnic and religious groups, has experienced civil war, coups, and corrupt military rule, and while its oil reserves have brought wealth to the elite, they have hardly benefited the poor, and dependence on them led to economic problems in the 1980s.

- Under apartheid, a white minority in South Africa viciously suppressed the black majority with laws restricting their political, economic, and physical freedom, but the African National Congress, led by Nelson Mandela, resisted fiercely and ultimately won control of the government in 1994.

aplia

[15]From *Something Out There*, quoted in Jean Comaroff, *Body of Power, Spirit of Resistance: The Culture and History of a South African People* (Chicago: University of Chicago Press, 1985), vi.

[16]Quoted in Gwendolen Carter, "The Republic of South Africa: White Political Control Within the African Continent," in *Africa*, ed. Phyllis Martin and Patrick O'Meara, 2nd ed. (Bloomington: Indiana University Press, 1986), 353.

[17]Teboho Masiza, quoted in Lydia Polgreen, "Killing of Strikers Alters South Africa Politics," *New York Times*, August 16, 2013.

Nelson Mandela, South African Freedom Fighter and President

A courageous symbol of unbroken black determination, Nelson Mandela (1918–2013) changed history in the struggle against apartheid, South Africa's policy of rigid racial separation, despite severe white supremacist repression. The inspirational Mandela represented African ambitions for several generations.

Nelson Mandela was born in the Transkei reserve near South Africa's southeast coast, the son of a Xhosa **(KHO-sa)** chief. His middle name, Rolihlahla **(ROH-lee-la-la)**, meant "troublemaker." Mandela was groomed to succeed his father as chief, but, after years of hearing stories about the valor of his ancestors in war, he wanted to help with the freedom struggle. After attending a Methodist school and then earning a BA from the only college for black South Africans, he qualified as a lawyer and opened the country's first black legal practice. He also joined the African National Congress (ANC), which had, for half a century, promoted education for blacks and cautiously criticized rather than confronted the government. Mandela and his young colleagues transformed the ANC into an activist mass movement. In 1958 he married Winnie Madikizela **(MAH-dee-kee-ZEH-la)**, a Xhosa nurse, but they had only a short life together before political repression separated them.

The white government tolerated little opposition. In 1960, after police opened fire on 20,000 peaceful black protesters, killing 69 of them (including women and children), the government banned the ANC and arrested black leaders. The ANC then became an underground movement committed to violence. In 1964, found guilty of sabotage and treason, Mandela was sentenced to life in prison. In his stirring statement to the court, Mandela articulated his goals: "During my lifetime I have dedicated myself to this struggle of the African people. I have fought against [both] white and black domination. I have cherished the ideal of a democratic and free society in which all persons live together in harmony and with equal opportunities. It is an ideal for which I am prepared to die."

Mandela spent most of the next three decades in the notorious Robben Island prison off Cape Town, where he was joined by dozens of other ANC leaders and members. He turned the prison experience into an ANC school, leading political discussions and studying other freedom fighters, such as Mohandas Gandhi and Jawaharlal Nehru in India. Over the years Mandela grew into an international hero. During his imprisonment Winnie Mandela campaigned ceaselessly for black rights and her husband's release, gaining an international reputation as a freedom fighter. In 1990, after secret negotiations, a realistic new South African president, F. W. de Klerk, legalized the ANC and released Nelson Mandela from prison, and in 1993 Nelson Mandela and de Klerk shared a Nobel Peace Prize. In 1994 the first all-race elections made Nelson Mandela the first black president of South Africa. At his inauguration, he told the people: "Out of the experience of an extraordinary human disaster that lasted too long must be born a society of which all humanity will be proud. Let there be justice [and] peace for all. We must act together as a united people, for the birth of a new world. God bless Africa!"

NELSON MANDELA A symbol of black South African aspirations for nearly thirty years in prison, Mandela led the African National Congress after his release and, in 1994, was elected the nation's first black president.

David Turnley/Corbis

Forgiving and pragmatic, Mandela remained popular with most South Africans, white and black. His moderate, accommodationist style reassured whites but also disappointed some impatient blacks for conceding too much to white business and farming interests while only slowly improving black communities. Meanwhile, his marriage to Winnie became strained, in part because of her controversial activities, legal problems, and political support for a militant ANC faction that mistrusted Nelson's conciliatory policy. In 1996 Nelson and Winnie Mandela divorced. Nelson later married Grace Machel, the widow of respected Mozambique president Samora Machel, who was killed in an airplane crash.

In 1999, at the age of eighty-one, Mandela voluntarily retired from politics and moved to his native village. But family disputes over his estate and legacy clouded his reputation. In his autobiography, he wrote, "I have walked a long road to freedom. I have tried not to falter, I have made missteps along the way. After climbing a great hill, one only finds that there are many more hills to climb. With freedom come responsibilities. I dare not linger, for my long walk is not yet ended." In 2013 South Africans watched anxiously when Mandela was hospitalized with varied ills of old age. When he died in December, national leaders and admirers from around the world traveled to Johannesburg for his memorial service, celebrating with millions of South Africans his life and achievements as the creator of a new nation. The long walk taken by Nelson Mandela changed history.

THINKING ABOUT THE PROFILE

1. Why did the Mandelas become international symbols of the freedom struggle?
2. How did the Mandelas change history?

Note: Quotations from Kevin Shillington, *History of Africa*, rev. ed. (New York: St. Martin's, 1995), 405; and Nelson Mandela, *Long Walk to Freedom: The Autobiography of Nelson Mandela* (Boston: Little, Brown, 1996), 620, 625.

African Economies, Societies, and Cultures

What new economic, social, and cultural patterns have emerged in Africa?

Since the 1960s, achieving economic development has often seemed a desperate struggle rather than an exhilarating challenge. African nations have tried various strategies, including capitalism and socialism, to benefit the majority of people, often unsuccessfully. Economic problems have proliferated. Africans have also created new social and cultural forms to help deal with their problems.

Economic Change and Underdevelopment

Africa experienced severe economic problems. As during colonial times, Africans mostly supplied agricultural and mineral resources, such as cocoa and copper, to the global economy, but this trade did not foster widespread wealth. Hence, in Kenya small farmers, encouraged to replace subsistence food growing with tobacco planting, found that tobacco brought in little money, required cutting down adjacent forests, and leached nutrients from the soil. In 2004, Jane Chacha, still living in the same two-room, mud-and-thatch house she and her husband built fifteen years earlier, complained that "this is a hopeless dream. Growing tobacco has been nothing but trouble."[18]

Until recently only a few countries have enjoyed consistently robust economic growth, escaped reliance on one or two resources, or substantially raised living standards. Hence, sub-Saharan Africa contains most of the world's twenty poorest countries. With a billion people by 2012, Africans produce only 1 percent of the world's goods and services, about the same as Belgium, with 11 million people. Many sub-Saharan African countries have annual per capita incomes of under $1,000 per year, and some are under $500. Sub-Saharan Africa has also had the world's highest infant mortality and desperate poverty rates and the lowest literacy rates and average life expectancies.

The economic doldrums are linked to other problems. Until recently the region's economies generally grew slowly, but population increase is now the world's highest, over 3 percent. Half of Africans are under twenty-five. Since 10 to 15 percent of babies die before their first birthday, parents have had an incentive to have many children to provide for old-age security. And many Christian and Muslim religious leaders opposed family planning as opposed to God's will. While the population may double by 2025, new jobs, classrooms, and food supplies will not keep pace. Only a few nations have enjoyed self-sufficiency in food production; most require food imports from Europe and North America. Although women grow the bulk of the food, male farmers growing cash crops receive most government aid. Millions are chronically malnourished, and several million children die each year from hunger-related ailments. Severe drought and dried-up water sources cause dehydration, starvation, or migration. In Kenya some malnourished people eat cactus. Less than half of school-age children attend school, while millions of others work in the labor force. In addition, only a quarter of

Africans have access to electricity. Poverty means scraping by, physically and mentally exhausted by the struggle for survival.

As Africans have sought viable strategies to achieve economic development, many have maintained close economic ties to Western nations and encouraged foreign investment and free markets, what critics call neocolonial capitalism. Countries following this strategy emphasize the cash crops and minerals that dominated the colonial economy, and Westerners, especially British and French, manage or own a substantial portion of their economies. A few countries have prospered, but the political consequences have often been negative. In the 1960s and 1970s, Ivory Coast (or Côte d'Ivoire) and Kenya, hospitable to a Western presence, were rewarded with high growth and rising incomes. Ivory Coast remained a major exporter of coffee and cocoa; Kenya, with world-famous game parks, lived from tourism and exporting coffee, tea, and minerals. By the 1980s both had per capita incomes twice the African average. However, Ivory Coast rapidly logged once-verdant forests, causing less rain, and more French lived there than during colonial times, owning, along with other non-Ivoireans, most of the economy. Both countries eventually became one-party states that, while stable, grew despotic and corrupt. While the glittering major cities, Abidjan and Nairobi, had fancy restaurants, boutiques, and nightclubs, some rural people faced starvation. By the 1990s, as collapsing coffee and cocoa prices stressed their economies, protesters demanded more democracy, delicate ecologies became dangerously unbalanced, and crime rates soared. Economic development became a fading memory. Civil war engulfed Ivory Coast, intensifying Christian-Muslim and south-north divisions. Kenyans forced out a dictator and elected a reformist government that failed to fulfill most of its promises. In 2007 a disputed Kenyan election led to riots, interethnic fighting, 1,500 deaths, and 60,000 forced from their homes. Tensions between ethnic groups simmered, but, thanks partly to healthy economic growth, the 2013 election remained largely peaceful.

The Democratic Republic of the Congo (known as Zaire between 1971 and 1997) had the most disastrous experience. A huge country, with 76 million people, Congo enjoys a strategic location and rich mineral resources, but it became Africa's biggest failure. The United States and Belgium poured in billions of investment and aid to support President Mobuto, who looted the treasury and aid to amass a huge personal fortune—some 4 to 5 billion dollars—while repressing his opponents. Mobuto built palaces for himself all over the country and in Europe while hiring top French chefs to prepare his food, spending little money on schools, roads, telephones, and hospitals. Hence, the Congo suffered one of the world's highest infant mortality rates, limited health care, and widespread malnutrition. In 1997 a long-festering rebellion gained strength, forcing Mobuto into exile, where he died. Rebels took over but have done little to

---

[18]Quoted in Joe Asila," No Cash in This Crop," in *Global Studies: Africa*, ed. Wayne Edge, 2nd ed. (Guilford, CT: Dushkin, 2006), 285.

foster democracy or development. The Congo fragmented in intractable, prolonged civil war and interethnic fighting that drew in armies from neighboring countries, with rebel groups controlling large sections of the sprawling country. Over 4 million Congolese died from the fighting and collapse of medical care, causing a humanitarian crisis.

Some African nationalists pursued revolutionary or reformist strategies. Radicals argued that political institutions, businesses, and plantations inherited from colonialism, geared to transfer wealth and resources to the West, could not foster economic development; after independence more wealth still flowed out of Africa than into it. To empower Africans, they wanted to replace the colonial state with something entirely new. Various social revolutionary regimes emerged from the long wars of liberation. Looking toward China or the USSR for inspiration, Marxist revolutionary governments gained power in Angola and Mozambique. However, aided by the United States, white-ruled South Africa sponsored opposition guerrilla movements that perpetuated civil wars for several decades, leaving over 2.5 million dead in Angola and Mozambique. Blessed with coffee, diamonds, and especially oil but plagued with corruption, Angola enjoyed growth but struggled to foster development despite considerable Western investment. Since Mozambique's war ended in 1992, pragmatic Marxist leaders have introduced multiparty elections and liberalized the economy, raising per capita incomes. But regional and ethnic tensions persisted, threatening stability.

One social revolutionary state, Zimbabwe, was initially Africa's biggest success story. The Marxist-influenced government, led by liberation hero Robert Mugabe (g. 1987–), proved pragmatic for over a decade, largely respecting democracy and human rights, encouraging the white minority to stay, raising living standards and opportunities for black Zimbabweans, and exporting surplus food. But tensions between rival African ethnic groups simmered. Blacks resented continuing white ownership of the best farmland, and Mugabe became more dictatorial, using land disputes to divide the nation. As his support waned, he rigged elections, harassed or jailed opponents, and seized white-owned farms, awarding them to his cronies and supporters. Meanwhile, uncontrolled inflation made local currency worthless. Commercial agriculture collapsed, drought and cholera spread, life expectancy dropped sharply, food disappeared from shops, refugees fled to neighboring countries, and Mugabe's police drove poor blacks who favored the opposition out of the cities. The nation has remained in precarious shape, demoralizing many Zimbabweans.

Tanzania experimented with an "African" socialism compatible with African traditions, especially cooperation and mutual resource sharing. Under visionary president Julius Nyerere (1922–1999), Tanzania reorganized agriculture into cooperative villages to achieve national self-sufficiency. Nyerere encouraged some democracy in his one-party state, holding regular elections with multiple candidates running for each office or parliamentary seat. Building schools and clinics improved literacy and health to well above African norms. But Nyerere's dreams were dashed; the government became overly bureaucratic, planning proved inadequate, and many lost enthusiasm for socialism. With few imported luxury goods, life was austere compared to that in capitalist Kenya, and peasants often preferred their small family farms to collective villages. As the economy slumped, Tanzania took more foreign loans. Still admired, Nyerere retired in 1985, one of the few founding leaders to voluntarily give up power. His successors dismantled much of the socialist structure, promoted free enterprise, welcomed foreign investment and loans, and fostered a multiparty system. Yet life for most Tanzanians improved little, malnutrition became widespread, ethnic tensions intensified, and Tanzania remains a poor nation.

The most recent showcases for economic success include Ghana and Botswana. Once a symbol of failure, Ghana has made steady progress. For several decades the country experienced a roller coaster of corrupt civilian governments interspersed with military regimes. But in the 1990s the leaders gradually strengthened democracy and adopted certain policies of the Asian Little Dragons, such as Taiwan and South Korea, mixing capitalism and socialism. Helped by newly discovered oil, Ghana became increasingly prosperous: by 2009 it enjoyed one of the continent's highest annual per capita incomes, a life expectancy of fifty-nine, democratic elections, press freedom, and one of Africa's most educated populations. Botswana also made a turnaround. At independence in 1966, it was one of the world's poorest countries, with an annual per capita income of $35. Gradually, tapping ethnic traditions and rich diamond mines, Botswanans carved out a successful democracy, while the economy, health care, education, and protection of resources all steadily improved, despite deadly droughts and a serious AIDS epidemic. Today Botswanans enjoy living standards higher than in most African and many Middle Eastern, Asian, and Latin American societies. In the past decades rapid economic growth rates have raised incomes in several other poor nations as well, among them Angola, Mozambique, and Rwanda.

Social Change

Modern Africa has experienced rapid social change. More people live in cosmopolitan cities where traditional and modern attitudes meet, mix, and clash. City life attracts rural people because it offers more variety—jobs, department stores, movie theaters, nightclubs—than village life. Cities that developed as governments and commercial centers under colonialism, such as Nairobi (Kenya), Lagos (Nigeria), and Dakar (Senegal), have grown nearly 5 percent a year since 1980. Between 1965 and 2000 the percentage of Africans living in urban areas doubled to 30 percent. Cities grow so fast that services such as buses, water, power, police, schools, and health centers cannot meet peoples' needs. These problems are exemplified by Africa's largest city, Lagos, which grew from less than a million in 1965 to a megalopolis of some 12 million by 2008. A journalist described the urban chaos:

> Lagos is a vast laboratory of helter-skelter expansion … confusion and frenzy. A tiny minority of people live extremely well, in villas or plush apartments, and they go to work in gleaming skyscrapers that sit awkwardly next to traditional marketplaces. A vastly larger number of people live in appalling slums, where open sewers

may run under disintegrating floorboards. The traffic jam, or "go-slow," is a fact of life. Much of the everyday commerce occurs in this city through the windows of cars, trucks, and other vehicles.[19]

Cities also foster social changes. Interethnic mixing, even marriage, has become more common. Neighborhoods have developed their own slang, hairstyles, music, dance, art, and poetry. Institutions such as football (soccer) leagues, labor unions, and women's clubs help migrants adjust by creating a new community, replacing the villages left behind. Along sidewalks small traders hawk everything from food and drinks to cheap clothes, religious items, and music cassettes. Various nations have enjoyed international football success, while Ethiopians and Kenyans have dominated long-distance running. Africans have played in the U.S. National Basketball Association and National Football League.

Life in cities fosters different family patterns. Smaller nuclear families have often replaced the extended family of villages, and individualism increasingly challenges village traditions. Whereas before elders largely arranged marriages, now love has become a major criterion for selecting a spouse. Traditionally village men also had an incentive to gain economic status by taking more than one wife, since women did most of the routine farm work, especially the growing of food crops. Now, since urban women have no farming option, men no longer need several wives and, enjoying more educational opportunities, dominate wage labor in business and transportation.

Gender roles have changed as women have become more independent. Growing numbers have served in governments and parliaments, and sub-Saharan Africa ranks ahead of most developing nations in the percentage of women in legislative positions. Reformist former businesswoman Joyce Banda of Malawi became Africa's second female president in 2012. Some women have also achieved positions as politicians, professors, lawyers, and company heads. Kenyan Grace Ogot **(OH-got)** (b. 1930) served in parliament while writing short stories featuring heroines who confront traditional values and change. In addition to organizations for work, savings, or worship, women have formed groups to work for society's improvement. Nigerian midwife's daughter Eka Esu-Williams (b. 1950), who earned a PhD in immunology and became an academic, formed Women Against AIDS in 1988 to educate and empower women, who are more likely than men to get HIV, through workshops, schools, and support groups. Some women work in poorly paid occupations as teachers, nurses, and secretaries, but most women pursue low-wage self-employment, such as by hawking goods and keeping stalls in city markets, a female near monopoly for centuries; performing domestic work as maids, cooks, or nannies; or working in hairdressing. Living Goods, an antipoverty organization in Uganda, employs women to sell healthy goods, such as soap, deworming pills, and fortified foods to poor families. Meanwhile, many men spend long hours commuting to and from work and socializing with friends after work in bars or at club meetings. Thanks to colonial antisodomy laws, homosexuals face severe intolerance, including imprisonment and sometimes execution, in many African countries, but South African courts legalized homosexual marriage in 2005.

soukous ("to shake") A Congolese popular music that was shaped by dance rhythms from Cuba and Brazil.

African Culture and Religion

Africans have combined imported ideas with their own cultural traditions, creating works loved around the world. As Senegalese writer and president Leopold Senghor **(sah-GAWR)** (1906–2001) asked, "Who else would teach rhythm to the world that has died of machines and cannons?"[20] Urbanization, growing mass media, and the mixing of ethnic groups and outside influences have fostered exciting new popular music styles reflecting social, economic, and political realities. World-renowned South African jazz and pop singer Miriam Makeba **(muh-KAY-ba)** (1932–2008), forced to spend decades in exile, described her mission: "I live to sing about what I see and know. I don't sing politics, I sing truth."[21] Popular music styles creatively blending local and imported influences have helped Africans adjust to change while affirming their cultural values. Hence, Nigeria's *juju* music reflects Yoruba traditions while adopting Western instruments, such as electric guitars.

African popular musicians perform and sell recordings around the world. Perhaps the greatest African superstar, Senegalese Youssou N'Dour **(YOO-soo en-DOOR)** (b. 1959), often collaborates with leading Western and Arab musicians yet remains true to his roots, living in Dakar and following his tolerant Sufi Muslim faith. Some musicians are highly political. Nigerian Fela Kuti (1938–1997), whose music mixed jazz, soul, rock, and Yoruba traditions, used songs as a weapon against Nigerian governments and their Western sponsors, facing frequent arrests and beatings for his protests. Like Bob Marley, Bob Dylan, and Chile's Victor Jara, Fela gained worldwide fame for using music to attack injustice. Women have also expressed their views through music. Mali's Oumou Sangare had a massive hit with her account of a young woman torn between pleasing her parents and her loved one. In the Congo, a particularly influential (Zairean) pop music, known widely as **soukous** ("to shake"), was shaped by Cuban and Brazilian dance rhythms created by descendants of African slaves. Soukous depends heavily on the guitar as well as on traditional African songs and melodies. But Congolese musicians, unable to make a living or speak freely in their troubled homeland, have often sought their fortunes elsewhere. Soukous became a major dance music throughout Africa and among African immigrants in Europe.

Like popular musicians, writers have combined old traditions with new influences to comment on modern society, assert African identity, and influence political change. Many write in English or French to reach an international audience. Nigerian

---

[19]Sanford Unger, *Africa: The People and Politics of an Emerging Continent* (New York: Simon and Schuster, 1985), 131–132.

[20]Quoted in Richard A. Fredland, *Understanding Africa: A Political Economy Perspective* (Chicago: Burnham, 2001), 139.

[21]Quoted in John Follain, "Only the First Step for 'Mama Africa,'" *New Straits Times*, February 23, 1990.

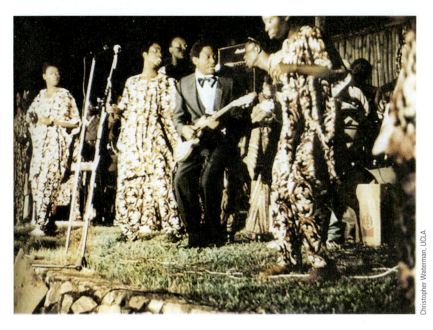

Christopher Waterman, UCLA

AFRICAN CULTURAL EXPRESSION Africans have developed diverse and vibrant popular music, often by mixing Western and local traditions. In Nigeria, juju music, played by bands such as Captain Jidi Oyo and his Yankee System in this 1982 photo, has been popular among the Yoruba people.

Wole Soyinka **(WOE-lay shaw-YING-kuh)** (b. 1934), a Yoruba poet, playwright, novelist, and sometime filmmaker who won the 1986 Nobel Prize for literature, mixed Yoruba mysticism with criticisms of Western capitalism, racism, cultural imperialism, and African failures. A former political prisoner, Soyinka denounced repressive African leaders, chastising "Nigeria's self-engorgement at the banquet of highway robberies, public executions, public floggings and other institutionalized sadisms, casual cruelties, wanton destruction."[22] Their powerful political dissent often forced both Soyinka and his Nigerian colleague Chinua Achebe to live in exile.

Writers and artists sought authentic African perspectives, among them negritude, a literary and philosophical movement first developed in the 1930s. Writer Leopold Senghor, later Senegal's first president after independence, attempted to balance Western rational thought with African approaches to knowledge, such as mysticism and animism. To Senghor, Africans needed to assert, rather than feel inferior about, their black skins and cultural traditions. Negritude influenced French artists and writers; philosopher Jean Paul Sartre praised it as a weapon against all forms of oppression.

Marxism influenced one of the best-known writers in Francophone West Africa, Senegalese Ousmane Sembene **(OOS-man sem-BEN-ee)** (1923–2007). The son of a poor fisherman who was drafted into the French army during World War II, Sembene fought in Italy and Germany. After the war he worked in France as a dockworker and became a leader of the dockworkers' union; his first novel portrayed the stevedore's hard life. Returning to Senegal, Sembene often wrote about the colonial period, expressing resistance to Western domination

and social inequality while attacking Senegal's greedy businessmen and government officials. Sembene also achieved international acclaim for films satirizing corrupt bureaucrats and the exploitation of the poor by the rich.

English-language literature flourished in South Africa and East Africa. Kenyan journalist-turned-university-professor Ngugi Wa Thiongo **(en-GOO-gee wah thee-AHN-go)** (b. 1938) explored the relationship between colonialism and social fragmentation, showing Gikuyus struggling to retain their identity, culture, and traditions while adjusting to the modern world. Once devout, Ngugi later rejected Christianity as a legacy of colonialism. His 1979 novel, *Petals of Blood*, portrays Kenya struggling to free itself from neocolonialism but also beset with corruption. His attacks on the privileged Kenyan elite allied with Western exploitation brought several jail terms and later exile.

Africans have maintained a triple religious heritage of animism/polytheism, Islam, and Christianity, all with many followers. Animists now account for perhaps 5 percent of Africans. With their links to wider worlds, Christianity and Islam are also globalizing influences, spreading Western or Middle Eastern political, social, and economic ideas. Africans often view religions in both theoretical and practical terms, adopting views that help them adjust to change.

Christianity has become Africa's largest religion, attracting over 60 percent of Africans by 2012, many of them fervent. Some countries, such as Congo, South Africa, and Uganda, are largely Christian. Christianity has proved a powerful force for social change. Mission schools have educated many leaders, influencing their world-views. However, many churches have prevented followers from practicing traditional customs. While believers often favor liberating women, many criticize progressive social views such as toleration of homosexuality. A growing number of independent churches, some blending African traditions into worship and theology, have no ties to older Western-based denominations. Promising to help members acquire wealth and happiness, some African churches have enjoyed spectacular growth, building big urban churches that attract thousands of congregants each Sunday. In a reversal of historical patterns, several evangelical churches send missionaries to revitalize Christianity in the West, establishing branches in Europe and North America. Yet many other Africans have viewed Christianity as connected to Western imperialism. According to a popular nationalist saying: "When the missionaries came the Africans had the land and the Christians had the Bible. They taught us to

> **negritude** A literary and philosophical movement to forge distinctively African views.

[22]Quoted in Tejumola Olaniyan," Narrativizing Postcoloniality: Responsibilities," *Public Culture* 5, no. 1 (Fall 1992): 47.

pray with our eyes closed. When we opened them they had the land and we had the Bible."[23]

Some 30 percent of black Africans follow Islam, a fourth of all countries having Muslim majorities. Some revivalist and Wahhabi movements have gained influence, especially in West Africa and Somalia, and some northern Nigerian states have imposed Islamic law or spawned extremist Muslim groups, sparking deadly clashes with Christian minorities and less extreme Muslims that have left several thousand dead. In 2012 jihadis linked to Al Qaeda capitalized on unrest to capture northern Mali, including ancient cities like Timbuktu, and impose harsh Islamic law while destroying ancient sites and books; French troops pushed them out in 2013.

But most Muslims and Christians remain moderate and inclusive. While politicians use religion as a wedge issue, and although Christian-Muslim clashes have occurred in several countries, tolerant relations among Christians, Muslims, and animists are more common. Hence, Yoruba Christians and Muslims mix easily and even intermarry. One sect in Lagos mixes Islam and Christianity into a blend called "Chrislam." Ethnicity often divides people more than religion.

Africa in the Global System

The Cold War rivalry between the United States and the USSR gained some African countries aid but also fostered superpower manipulation. Countries such as Congo and Angola became pawns as superpowers helped to support or remove leaders. But with the Cold War over, the Western world often ignored Africa, providing little aid and only modest investment. The wealth gap between African countries and Western industrialized nations has grown even wider than during colonial times. Today the gap between the richest Western and poorest African countries is around 400 to 1. When the world economy boomed in the 1950s and 1960s, African economies showed steady growth. Between the 1970s and 2000, however, as world prices for many African exports collapsed, African economic growth rates steadily dropped. In the past decade some countries have resumed rapid growth while others have lagged behind.

Since the 1990s Western experts have encouraged a policy of "structural adjustment" in which international lenders, such as the International Monetary Fund (IMF) and World Bank, loan nations money but require opening their economies to private investment and, to balance national budgets, reduce government spending for health, education, and farmers. The resulting hardship on average people—from eliminating money for poor children to attend village primary schools to closing local offices that aid small farmers—increases resentment both of governments and Western nations. This private investment also promotes a shift away from traditional farming to more productive modern agriculture that relies on tractors, chemical fertilizers, and new seeds, which has large environmental and social costs: marginal land is often turned into desert, and small farmers lack money to buy the modern supplies.

To obtain the cars, fashionable clothes, and electronic gadgets the urban middle and upper classes desire, African nations take out loans. As a percentage of total output, African countries had the largest foreign debts in the world in the 1990s. Yet, the world prices for most of Africa's exports, such as coffee, cotton, and tobacco from Tanzania and cocoa from Ghana, steadily dropped from the 1960s to 2000. Small farmers, such as the cotton growers in Mali, cannot compete with highly subsidized Western farmers and the tariff barriers erected in Europe, North America, and Japan against food and fiber imports from Africa. The world financial institutions implemented a debt relief program in 1996 that lowered the debt burden by three-quarters and fostered reforms and dynamism, so that today Africa as a whole has less debt than Asian and Latin American countries. Prices for exports, especially minerals and oil, rebounded by 2000, spurring faster economic growth, but the 2008–2009 global economic crisis lowered growth rates from 6.1 percent in 2007 to 2.8 percent in 2009. However, growth rebounded by 2012. Total foreign direct investment grew sixfold between 2000 and 2011.

Taking advantage of Western disinterest, in the past decade China, now Africa's largest trading partner, has made huge investments in African oil, refining, mining, timber, agriculture, and banking as well as constructing railroads, dams, bridges, and other infrastructure projects. Bilateral trade quintupled between 2000 and 2006; perhaps 750,000 Chinese now live and work in Africa, sometimes sparking resentment, kidnappings, and riots. The Chinese activity may foreshadow a change of direction for many Africans.

Africa's economic problems have diverse roots. Colonial economic policies caused severe environmental destruction, such as desertification and deforestation, while incorporating Africans into the world economy as specialized producers of minerals or cash crops for export rather than food farmers. Hence, Zambia relies on exploiting copper, Uganda coffee, Malawi tobacco, and Nigeria oil. Colonial regimes often failed to build roads, schools, and clinics. For decades bad policy decisions, poor leadership, corruption, unstable politics, and misguided advice from Western experts also contributed to the economic challenges, while the rapid spread of HIV/AIDS killed and affected millions (see Chapter 26). In some nations a third of the population has the HIV virus.

But although falling behind much of Asia and Latin America, Africans have had successes. Using foreign aid and their own resources, they have made rapid strides in literacy, social and medical services such as active birth control campaigns, and road construction. In the 1990s, some 58 percent of Africans lived on less than $1.25 per day; by 2010 the figure was 48.5 percent. But many still lived in extreme poverty. Some nations, such as South Africa and Ghana, have a feisty free press. Nations have also worked together to resolve problems. The African Union, formed in 2000 with fifty-four members, has sent peacekeeping troops into violence-torn countries. By the 1990s Africans grew skeptical about Western models of development, which were often dependent on expensive high technology, and disillusioned with socialist governments controlling economic activity. Many nations moved toward more democratic systems and private enterprise.

---

[23]Quoted in Chinweizu, *The West and the Rest of Us: White Predators, Black Slavers, and the African Elite* (New York: Vintage, 1975), 1.

However, political leadership often failed to root out corruption and poverty and foster food production. Africa also suffers a particularly acute "brain drain" as academics, students, and professionals, seeking a better life, move to Europe or North America. Thus Africans have not enjoyed complete control of

their destiny. The Ghanaian historian Jacob Ajayi **(a-JAH-yee)** laid out the challenge: "The vision of a new [African] society will need to be developed out of the African historical experience. The African is not yet master of his own fate, but neither is he completely at the mercy of fate."[24]

[24]Quoted in Jennifer Seymour Whitaker, *How Can Africa Survive?* (New York: Harper and Row, 1988), 197.

MAKE SURE YOU UNDERSTAND THESE KEY POINTS BEFORE MOVING ON

- African cities have grown rapidly and often lack necessary services, individualism has grown more common, and women have lost some of the economic value they had in agricultural villages, though some have become successful professionals.

- African musicians, writers, and artists have drawn on local traditions as well as influences from the West to create original forms, such as soukous, as well as works that criticize both Western encroachment and homegrown corruption.

- While animism has grown less influential in Africa, Christianity is the most popular religion and has

undermined traditions and been seen by some as connected to Western imperialism, while Islam is followed by 40 percent of Africans.

- The economic gap between Africa and the industrialized West continues to grow larger, and Western attempts to help Africa through the IMF and the World Bank often include requirements that harm the environment and the poor and inspire resentment, as do tariffs against African imports and the enduring colonial legacy.

aplia

CHAPTER SUMMARY

The Middle East and sub-Saharan Africa shared certain experiences, including decolonization, mass poverty, reliance on exporting natural resources, political instability, and Western intervention. Diverse developments reshaped the Middle East since 1945. Arab nationalism, especially strong in Egypt, generated conflict with the West and with Israel, which became the major Arab enemy. Arab-Israeli conflict greatly destabilized the region, while ethnic and religious divisions fostered violent struggles within nations. Islam proved most potent as a revolutionary political force in Iran, long a battleground for international rivalries over its oil supplies. The Middle East, especially the Persian Gulf region, provided much of the world's oil, fostering wealth but also global attention as world consumption increased. Oil-rich Saudi Arabia forged an alliance with the United States. Most Middle Eastern societies remained conservative but also fostered cultural creativity. Meanwhile, the

rivalry between militant and secular Muslims, and Sunnis and Shi'ites, has provided a major cleavage in many countries.

By the 1970s long-colonized African nations achieved independence under nationalist leaders. But the hopes for a better life were soon dashed. Artificially created multiethnic nations found it difficult to sustain democracy, and dictatorial governments often gained power. Most nations remained dependent on exporting one or two resources. Ambitious development plans gave way to economic stagnation and, as commodity prices fall, increasing poverty. By the early 2000s some resumed economic growth, but most nations still struggle to raise living standards for the majority of their people. South Africa was finally transformed from a racist state to a multiracial democracy. Societies urbanized, redefined family life and gender roles, and created new music and literature. Africans still search for the right mix of imported ideas and local traditions to create better lives.

KEY TERMS

Intifada (p. 759)
Ba'ath (p. 761)
OPEC (p. 762)
mujahidin (p. 764)
Taliban (p. 764)

Islamists (p. 765)
rai (p. 767)
pan-Africanism (p. 769)
Mau Mau Rebellion (p. 769)
wabenzi (p. 772)

apartheid (p. 773)
bantustans (p. 773)
soukous (p. 778)
negritude (p. 779)

31 South Asia, Southeast Asia, and Global Connections, Since 1945

Mary Cross

COMMUTING TO WORK Vietnam has largely recovered from its decades of war and has experienced increasing economic growth. These women in Hanoi are commuting to work by bicycle.

This music sings the struggle of [humanity]. This music is my life. This is the revolution we have begun. But the revolution is only a means to attain freedom, and freedom is only a means to enrich the happiness and nobility of human life.

—Hazil, the Indonesian revolutionary nationalist in Mochtar Lubis's novel *A Road with No End* (1952)[1]

In 1950 several idealistic Indonesian writers published a moving declaration promoting universal human dignity: "We [Indonesians] are the heirs to the culture of the whole world, a culture which is ours to extend and develop in our own way [by] the discarding of old and outmoded values and their replacement by new ones. Our fundamental quest is [helping] humanity."[2] These writers having witnessed the Indonesian Revolution against the Dutch (1945–1950), a nationalist struggle that achieved independence, also warned against narrow nationalism. They were inspired by irreverent Sumatran poet Chairul Anwar **(CHAI-roll ON-war)** (1922–1949), who believed the revolution had made possible a new, open society. Influenced both by Western books and Indonesian sensibilities, Anwar's pathbreaking poems stretched the Indonesian language's possibilities. But Anwar had died at twenty-seven, leaving it to others, like liberal Sumatran novelist and journalist Mochtar Lubis **(MOKE-tar LOO-bis)** (b. 1920), to carry on the campaign to blend widely admired foreign ideas with Indonesian ideas, fostering change while preserving continuity.

The declaration's noble aspirations and recognition of wider world connections reflected a new sense of possibility as colonial walls were knocked down. But the writers' idealism was soon dashed by early post–World War II realities. While South and Southeast Asians longed for human dignity, more immediate goals took precedence: securing independence, building new nations, and addressing poverty and underdevelopment. But despite false starts and conflicts, Indonesians and other South and Southeast Asian nations sought, and sometimes found, answers to their challenges while increasing their links to global networks, changing dramatically without destroying tradition.

Southern Asia is the world's most densely populated region: over 2.3 billion people live in the lands stretching from Pakistan and India to Indonesia and the Philippines. It also contains a wide array of languages, ethnic groups, religions, world-views, governments, and levels of economic development. This region of contrasts, playing an important world role for over four millennia, continues to be a cornerstone of the world economy.

---

[1]Mochtar Lubis, *A Road with No End*, translated by Anthony Johns from 1952 Indonesian edition (Chicago: Henry Regnery, 1968), 9.
[2]Quoted in Anthony Johns, "Introduction," in Lubis, *Road with No End*, 4.

The Reshaping of South Asia

What factors led to the political division of South Asia?

World War II undermined British colonialism, hastening independence for South Asians. Britain, economically drained and aware that maintaining control would come only at great cost, handed power over to local leaders. India's first prime minister, Jawaharlal Nehru **(JAH-wa-HAR-lahl NAY-roo)** (1889–1964), told his people: "A moment comes, which comes rarely in history, when we step from the old to the new, when an age ends and when the soul of a nation, long suppressed, finds utterance."[3] Yet the daunting challenges ahead tempered Nehru's idealism. India's long struggle for independence, marked by Mohandas Gandhi's (1868–1948) nonviolent philosophy, had ironically ended with Gandhi assassinated and British India divided into two separate, often hostile countries, predominantly Hindu India and largely Muslim Pakistan. Mostly Buddhist Sri Lanka and, in the 1970s, largely Muslim Bangladesh also gained independence. Each nation had achievements and failures, but the largest and most populous, India, became the regional colossus and a major player in world affairs.

[3]Quoted in John R. McLane, ed., *The Political Awakening of India* (Englewood Cliffs, NJ: Prentice-Hall, 1970), 178.

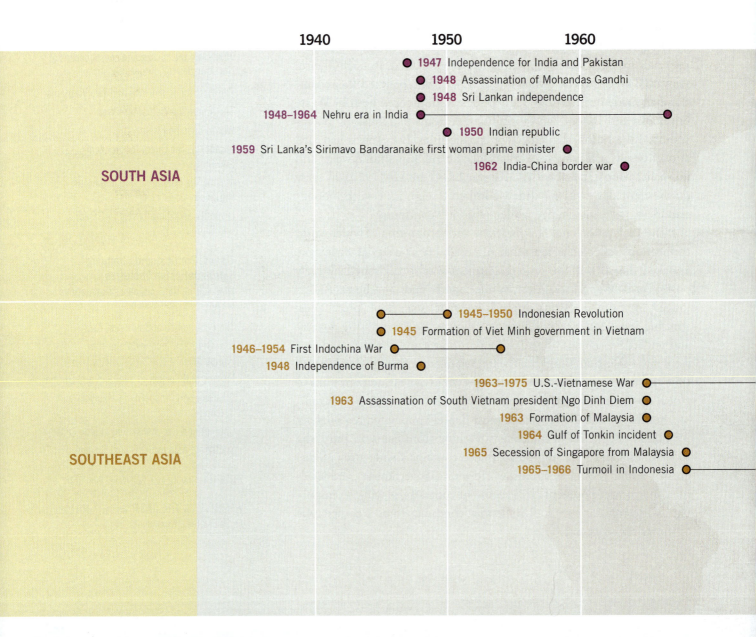

	1940	1950	1960

SOUTH ASIA

- 1947 Independence for India and Pakistan
- 1948 Assassination of Mohandas Gandhi
- 1948 Sri Lankan independence
- 1948–1964 Nehru era in India
- 1950 Indian republic
- 1959 Sri Lanka's Sirimavo Bandaranaike first woman prime minister
- 1962 India-China border war

SOUTHEAST ASIA

- 1945–1950 Indonesian Revolution
- 1945 Formation of Viet Minh government in Vietnam
- 1946–1954 First Indochina War
- 1948 Independence of Burma
- 1963–1975 U.S.-Vietnamese War
- 1963 Assassination of South Vietnam president Ngo Dinh Diem
- 1963 Formation of Malaysia
- 1964 Gulf of Tonkin incident
- 1965 Secession of Singapore from Malaysia
- 1965–1966 Turmoil in Indonesia

Decolonization and Partition

South Asia's regional unity was undermined by religious divisions. During World War II relations between the British and the mainly Hindu Indian National Congress ruptured (see Chapter 25). Fearing Hindu domination, the Muslim League pressed its case for a separate Muslim nation, to be called Pakistan. As tensions increased, rioting erupted; Muslims and Hindus began murdering each other, pulling victims from buses, shops, and homes. In Calcutta alone five thousand died. With any pretense of Hindu-Muslim unity shattered, the Muslim League leader, Mohammed Ali Jinnah (1876–1948), announced that if India were not divided it would be destroyed. As violence spread, the Congress leaders and British officials realized that some sort of partition was inevitable. In 1947 the British, Congress, and Muslim League agreed to create two independent nations, India and a Pakistan formed out of the Muslim-majority areas of eastern Bengal and the northwestern provinces along the Indus River.

Addressing his new nation, Prime Minister Nehru proclaimed: "Long years ago we made a tryst with destiny, and now the time comes when we shall redeem our pledge. At the stroke of the midnight hour, when the world sleeps, India will awake to life and freedom."[4] Pakistanis had a similar mood of renewal. But the euphoria proved short-lived as a bloodbath ensued. Muslims and Hindus had often lived side by side, but partition sparked hatreds between members of the local

---

[4]Quoted in B. N. Pandey, *The Break-up of British India* (New York: St. Martin's, 1969), 209.

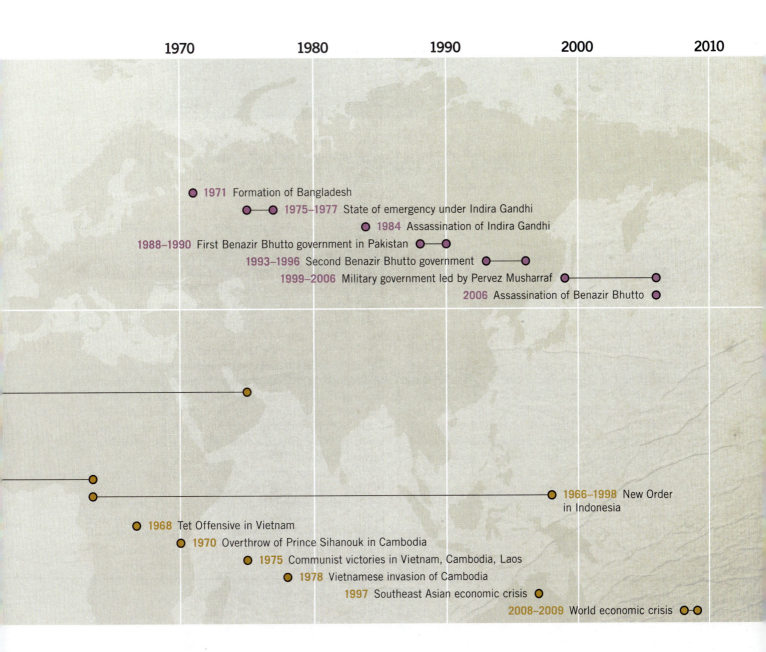

1970   1980   1990   2000   2010

1971 Formation of Bangladesh
1975–1977 State of emergency under Indira Gandhi
1984 Assassination of Indira Gandhi
1988–1990 First Benazir Bhutto government in Pakistan
1993–1996 Second Benazir Bhutto government
1999–2006 Military government led by Pervez Musharraf
2006 Assassination of Benazir Bhutto

1966–1998 New Order in Indonesia
1968 Tet Offensive in Vietnam
1970 Overthrow of Prince Sihanouk in Cambodia
1975 Communist victories in Vietnam, Cambodia, Laos
1978 Vietnamese invasion of Cambodia
1997 Southeast Asian economic crisis
2008–2009 World economic crisis

AP Images

MUSLIMS LEAVING INDIA FOR PAKISTAN DURING PARTITION As India and Pakistan split into two new nations in 1947, millions of Muslims and Hindus fled their homes to escape violence. This photo shows displaced Muslims, carrying a few meager belongings, jamming a train headed from India to Pakistan.

majority faith, who felt empowered, and religious minorities, who feared discrimination. As violence flared, Hindus and Sikhs fled Pakistan for India, while Muslims fled India for Pakistan. Altogether some 10 to 12 million refugees crossed the India-Pakistan borders. Perhaps 1 million died; 75,000 women were raped. Religious extremists attacked whole villages or trainloads of refugees.

Sixty-eight years old, Mohandas Gandhi labored to stop the killing. Moving into Delhi's Muslim quarter, he toured refugee camps without escort, read aloud from scriptures of all religions, including the Quran, and confronted Hindu mobs attacking mosques. Desperate, and hoping to send a message to everyone, Gandhi, who weighed only 113 pounds, began a fast until all the violence in Delhi stopped or he died. He quickly fell ill, but Gandhi's effort worked. After violence subsided, a substantial Muslim and Sikh minority remained in India and a Hindu and Sikh minority in Pakistan. But partition had been shattering. A Muslim poet spoke for many disillusioned people: "This is not that long looked-for break of the day. Where did that fine breeze blow from—where has it fled?"[5] Gandhi's support for Muslim victims of Hindu violence outraged Hindu extremists, who regarded Gandhi as a traitor. In January 1948, one of them gunned down Gandhi as he walked to a meeting, shocking the whole country and the world.

Despite its bloody start, India was built on a solid political foundation. Britain bequeathed to India democratic institutions, a trained civil service, a good communications system, and an educated if Westernized elite committed to modernization. India became a republic with a British-influenced constitution, led by a prime minister chosen by the majority party in an elected parliament. However, given its huge ethnic, religious, regional, and linguistic diversity (fourteen major and hundreds of minor languages), building national unity proved difficult. To accommodate the many minorities, regions, and cultures, India adopted a federal system, with elected state governments, and was officially secular with complete separation of religion and state. Kashmir, a Himalayan state on the India-Pakistan border with a Muslim majority but Hindu ruler who opted to join India, has remained a source of tension and sometimes war between India and Pakistan.

Pakistan, an artificial country with two wings separated by a thousand miles of India, confronted numerous problems. The founding leader, Jinnah, died soon after independence; his successor was assassinated. With Muslims overrepresented in the British Indian military, the army played a stronger role in Pakistan's politics than in India's. The loss of top civilian leaders, the lack of a balanced economic base, massive poverty, and geographical division made Pakistan more vulnerable than India

[5]Faiz Ahmed Faiz, quoted in Sugata Bose and Ayesha Jalal, *Modern South Asia: History, Culture, Political Economy* (New York: Routledge, 1998), 200.

to political instability and military rule. Pakistan and India also quarreled over issues from water use to trade to ownership of Kashmir.

Building a New India

India's first prime minister, Nehru, a British-educated lawyer and close associate of Gandhi, dominated Indian politics for a decade and a half (1948–1964). A gifted speaker, brilliant thinker, and democrat, Nehru was supported by the small middle class, who wanted a modern India, and the lower-class majority living in overcrowded, unhealthy urban slums or dusty villages without electricity and running water. Nehru promised to raise living standards and address the overwhelming poverty. While India lagged behind China in economic development, it preserved personal freedom. Promoting peaceful coexistence with neighbors, renouncing military aggression, and working to prevent a superpower nuclear conflict, Nehru became a major world figure. He helped found the Non-Aligned Movement of nations, such as Egypt and Indonesia, unwilling to commit to either the U.S. or Soviet camps. As India's stature grew, the Congress Party won three smashing electoral victories.

Nehru admired Western politics, literature, and dynamism but also respected India's cultural heritage and its moral strength. Raised a Hindu brahman, Nehru was nevertheless a secularist who believed that Congress should represent and serve all religions and social groups. Like Gandhi, he opposed the caste system and fought gender inequalities. Nehru convinced parliament to approve new laws on untouchability and women's rights that penalized discrimination. Untouchables, who had preferred the designation **Dalit** ("suppressed" or "ground down" people) since the 1970s, acquired special quotas in government services and universities, while Hindu women gained legal equality with men, including the right to divorce and inheritance. To discourage child marriage, Nehru set a minimum marriage age at eighteen for males and fifteen for females. But these laws, challenging centuries of tradition, were often ignored, especially in rural areas.

Mixing capitalism and socialism in what he termed a "third way," Nehru introduced a planning system to foster modern technology. While established industries remained in private hands, new public ventures built power plants and dams, which doubled power production, and irrigation canals, increasing agricultural yields by 25 percent. In the 1960s the Green Revolution of new high-yield wheat and rice dramatically increased food production. Thanks to Nehru's five-year plans, by the 1970s India produced many industrial products, including steel, and was nearly self-sufficient in food.

But some policies proved failures. Government control of the private sector through regulations gave bureaucrats great power, fostered corruption, and shackled private enterprise. Nehru failed to cultivate good relations with Pakistan or China; in 1962 Chinese troops humiliated Indian forces during a border dispute. Nehru also did not recognize that a rapidly growing population, rising from 389 million in 1941 to 434 million in 1961, undermined most of India's economic gains; he only belatedly endorsed family planning. In addition, the government built schools and universities but failed to

substantially raise literacy rates. Yet, when Nehru died in 1964, millions mourned the end of an idealistic era that had earned India world respect.

Nehru fostered a family political dynasty. With his respected successor's sudden death in 1966, the Congress selected Nehru's daughter, Indira Gandhi (1917–1984), to be the nation's first woman prime minister. She had worked closely with her father while her husband (no relation to Mohandas Gandhi) served in parliament. Mrs. Gandhi enjoyed a decade and a half in power. When her support waned in the 1967 elections, she responded with policies to win back the poor, and some of her policies improved the economy. India's smashing military victory over archenemy Pakistan also elevated her status. But mounting domestic problems precipitated increasingly harsh policies. Powerful vested interests ignored her reforms, the economy faltered, and many Indians turned against her party. In 1975 Gandhi declared a state of emergency, suspending civil rights, closing state governments, and jailing some ten thousand opposition leaders and dissidents. Meanwhile, her youngest son, Sanjay Gandhi (1946–1980), launched a controversial birth control campaign to forcibly sterilize any man with more than three children and also implemented a slum-clearance program that forced thousands out of sidewalk shanties. Both programs became deeply unpopular. In 1977 Indira lifted the emergency. After thirty years in power, the Congress Party, and with it Indira Gandhi, was voted out of office and was replaced by an uneasy coalition, including Hindu nationalists opposed to secularism. But the coalition government, solving few problems, collapsed.

When Indira Gandhi returned to power in the 1980 elections, she restored the Nehru dynasty but faced voter apathy, growing unemployment, and unrest. In 1980 Sanjay Gandhi died in a plane crash, and Indira Gandhi elevated her eldest son Rajiv (1944–1991), an apolitical airline pilot, as her heir apparent. Violence in the Punjab, India's richest state, which had a heavy Sikh population, provoked Mrs. Gandhi's final crisis. Many Sikhs, whose religion mixes Hindu and Muslim ideas, desired autonomy from India. In 1983 armed Sikh extremists occupied the Golden Temple at Amritsar (**uhm-RIT-suhr**), the holiest Sikh shrine, and turned it into a fortress, calling for an independent Sikh homeland and murdering those, including moderate Sikhs, who opposed them. The Indian army stormed the Golden Temple and reduced the temple to rubble; over a thousand militants and soldiers died in the incident.

Sikhs were shocked by the destruction of their holiest temple, and two of her Sikh guards assassinated Indira Gandhi. In response, Hindu mobs roamed Delhi, burning Sikh shops and killing thousands of Sikhs, often by pouring gasoline over them and setting them ablaze. Meanwhile, Rajiv Gandhi succeeded his mother but proved ineffective; in 1991 he was blown up by a young Sri Lankan woman who opposed India's support of the Sri Lankan government in its war against the Tamil secessionist group to which she belonged. Yet, despite this tumult, India remained a functioning democracy and thriving nation.

Dalit The designation commonly used for untouchables since the 1970s.

The Making of Pakistan and Bangladesh

Pakistan faced greater challenges than did India. Jinnah had pledged to make the nation happy and prosperous, but the leaders who followed had only limited success, thanks partly to tensions between ethnic groups who shared an Islamic faith but often little else. Hostilities flared between the nationalistic Bengalis, who dominated the east, and Punjabis and Sindhis, who dominated the west. The two regions differed in language, culture, and outlook. When the factionalized Pakistani parliament proved unworkable, military leaders took power in 1958. But dissatisfaction with military dictatorship sparked riots, prompting martial law. Moreover, Bengalis felt they did not get a fair share of the nation's resources and political power. After the **Awami League**, a Bengali nationalist party, won a majority of East Pakistan's seats in national elections, in early 1971 Pakistani troops arrested party leader Sheikh Mujiber Rahman **(shake MOO-jee-bur RAH-mun)** (1920–1975).

Hoping to crush Awami League support, troops opened fire on university dormitories and Hindu homes, causing hundreds of casualties.

Inspired by Sheikh Mujiber, the Awami League then declared independence. In response, West Pakistani troops poured into East Pakistan, terrorizing the Bengalis with massacres, arson, and rape. At least half a million Bengalis died, and the civil war caused 10 million desperate, starving refugees to flee to India. World opinion turned against Pakistan. India appealed for support of East Pakistan, armed Bengali guerrillas, and, after an ill-advised Pakistani attack on Indian airfields, sent troops into both West and East Pakistan, rapidly gaining the upper hand. Meanwhile, Pakistan received military aid from China and the United States. By the end of 1971 Pakistani troops in Bengal had surrendered to Indian forces, and the Awami League, led by Sheikh Mujibur, established a new nation, Bangladesh (Bengali Nation) (see Map 31.1).

MAKE SURE YOU UNDERSTAND THESE KEY POINTS BEFORE MOVING ON

- After World War II, when majority Muslim Pakistan broke off from majority Hindu India, widespread religious violence broke out and a dispute over the territory of Kashmir set the stage for continued tension between the two countries.

- Nehru attempted to expand the rights of women and, through a mix of capitalism and socialism, vastly increased India's industrial and agricultural output, but the population expanded at a dangerously rapid rate and not all policies were successful.

- Nehru's daughter, Indira Gandhi, was prime minister for over a decade, but she treated her opposition harshly and

was assassinated in the midst of clashes between Hindus and Sikhs, and her son and successor, Rajiv Gandhi, was also assassinated.

- East and West Pakistan were divided along ethnic lines, and a military crackdown on a Bengali nationalist party led to a bloody civil war in which India intervened on behalf of East Pakistan, which then became a separate country, Bangladesh.

aplia™

South Asian Politics and Societies

What have been the major achievements and disappointments of the South Asian nations?

Each South Asian society forged its own political role. With 1.25 billion people by 2012 and 65 percent of the subcontinent's land, the Republic of India rose to regional dominance. In the 1990s economic liberalization stimulated growth, but growing Hindu nationalism has challenged Congress Party domination, threatening its secular vision. Meanwhile, India's neighbors have struggled to achieve stability and economic development. Both Pakistan and Sri Lanka have experienced persistent ethnic violence, while India and Pakistan remain wary, building up military forces and nuclear weapons for possible use against the other. In each South Asian nation, ancient customs exist side by side with modern machines and ways of living.

Awami League A Bengali nationalist party that began the move for independence from West Pakistan.

Indian Politics and Economic Change

When India celebrated its fiftieth jubilee of independence in 1997, the president reminded his people that India's challenge was to achieve economic growth with social justice. India has been unable to mount the sort of concerted attack on mass poverty found in China. However, Indians have maintained one of the few working multiparty democracies outside industrialized nation-states, fostering lively debate and forcing candidates to appeal to voters. An Indian novelist described the campaign rhetoric leading up to elections: "The speeches were crammed with promises of every shape and size: promises of new schools, clean water, health care, land for landless peasants, powerful laws to punish any discrimination."[6] While such

[6]Rohinton Mistry, *A Fine Balance* (London: Faber, 1996), 143.

MAP 31.1 **MODERN SOUTH ASIA** India, predominantly Hindu, is the largest South Asian nation and separates the two densely populated Islamic nations of Bangladesh and Pakistan. Buddhists are the majority in Sri Lanka, just off India's southeast coast. The small kingdoms of Bhutan and Nepal are located in the Himalayan mountain range. © 2015 Cengage Learning

grandiose promises usually prove difficult to fulfill, millions of people vote, and changes in state and federal governments have regularly occurred. An Indian Muslim leader contrasted India favorably with Muslim nations: "In this country there are rights. We can demand our rights, speak out. In other countries: eat, drink, and shut up. Go to Saudi Arabia...Kuwait, Dubai, Iraq, Iran....They are all dictatorships."[7]

Scholars debate whether democracy has fostered national unity by providing a flexible system for accommodating the diverse Indian population or instead intensified differences between groups. Tensions between Hindus and Muslims and between high-caste and low-caste Hindus, manipulated by opportunistic politicians, have complicated political life. While voting has allowed the poor to put pressure on elites, elites can manipulate the system to preserve their privileges. Critics contend that democracy functions as a safety valve for popular frustration, creating the illusion of mass participation that prevents the country from attacking caste and class inequalities. Yet, lower-caste voters sometimes force officials to meet their needs, such as by paving pathways in their neighborhoods. And

[7]Mufti Shabbir Alam Sidiqi, quoted in Anand Giridharadas, "Once-Clear Thoughts Are Clouded," *New York Times*, June 19, 2009.

some state-based parties mobilize poor voters and win elections by campaigning against high-caste Hindus. Members of lower castes and Dalits serve in parliament and head state governments; one Dalit became India's president.

The Congress Party remained nationally influential but faced rivals. On the left, several communist parties often dominated politics in West Bengal and in Kerala in the southwest, repeatedly winning elections by promoting modernization and support for the poor. On the right, Hindu nationalist parties had limited success until the 1990s. In southern states various parties representing regional interests generally dominated state governments and joined federal coalitions. These regional parties, often led by local film stars, protected local languages while preserving English, understood by educated people around the country, as a national language. All parties suffered from corruption.

Since 1989 Indian politics has become more pluralistic. The major Hindu nationalist party, the **Bharatiya Janata Party** (BJP), gained influence in north India by espousing hostility to Muslims and state support for Hindu issues, such as having schools teach Indian history in accordance with Hindu traditions and religious writings. The BJP slogan, "One Nation, One People, One Culture," confronts the Gandhi-Nehru vision of a tolerant multicultural state. By the late 1990s rising political corruption, violent secessionist movements in border regions, caste conflict, and religious hostilities plagued a BJP-dominated regime. Then in 2002 major Hindu-Muslim violence left over 1,000 people dead and over 100,000 terrified Muslims, burned out of their cities, huddled in tent camps. In 2004 the Congress, led by Rajiv Gandhi's Italian-born, sari-wearing widow, Sonia Gandhi (b. 1946), a Roman Catholic who met Rajiv when both were students in England, capitalized on disenchantment among the poor and Muslims and, allied with leftist parties, defeated the ruling BJP-led coalition. A Pakistan-born Sikh economist, Manmohan Singh (b. 1932), became the first non-Hindu prime minister. The Congress government, despite its shortcomings, has offered help for the poor, such as a controversial food subsidy program.

A free press monitors politics, reporting on protests and violence. In 2005 a television station's investigation of corruption forced several members of parliament to resign, indicating a vibrant democracy. Although India was rocked by a terrorist attack on Bombay by Pakistani militants and then by the global economic crisis, in 2009 the Congress and Singh won a big electoral victory with strong support from the poor, grateful for increased spending on rural health and education. While older politicians still dominated government, a quarter of the successful parliamentary candidates were younger than forty-five. The middle class also became more assertive in politics. However, by 2013, with the Congress government suffering from factionalism, corruption, ineptitude, and various scandals, the BJP regrouped under divisive Gujarat chief minister Narendra Modi, a business-friendly free market enthusiast but strong anti-Muslim Hindu nationalist hated by minorities, but with many wealthy and middle-class supporters. Meanwhile, anti-corruption reformers founded a new party, Aam Aadmi (Common Man), that

swept state elections in Delhi in 2013 but faced uncertain prospects as a national movement challenging both the Congress and the BJP. Polls suggested that elections in 2014 swept Modi and the BJP-led coalition to power, displacing the Congress.

India has struggled to resolve economic backwardness, skyrocketing population growth, and crushing poverty for the majority. While Nehru's dream to end ignorance, poverty, and inequality of opportunity has not been fully realized, Indians can boast of many gains, especially after India changed directions economically in the 1970s. In 1956 India had to import vital foodstuffs and manufactured goods. Twenty years later it exported grain and, by 2000, made and exported its own cars, computers, and aircraft. Furthermore, India now grows enough wheat and rice to feed the entire population. The per capita income has grown from $200 in 1947 to about $1700 in 2013. To spur faster growth, Indian leaders pursued reform, deregulation, and liberalization, fostering 9 percent annual growth by 2000.

Several cities, especially Bangalore and Bombay, have become high-tech centers closely linked to global communications. Hundreds of North American and European companies, taking advantage of a growing, educated Indian middle class, especially university graduates fluent in English, have moved information and technical service jobs, such as call-in customer service and computer programming, from North America and Europe to India. Chennai (Madras), India's Detroit, ships small Fords, Nissans, and Hyundais to Africa, Europe, and Latin America. India's boom has prompted thousands of highly educated Indians living abroad to return and join its high-tech sector, often moving into spacious, newly built California-style suburbs with names like Ozone and Lake Vista. However, by 2013 growth slowed to some 4–5 percent, revealing structural limitations and demoralizing the new middle class; unlike China or South Korea, India relies on a small skilled labor pool for call centers and high-tech jobs rather than a vast cheap, unskilled labor pool for manufacturing.

Persisting social, economic, and regional inequalities have prevented equitable food distribution. Hence, when inadequate monsoon rains cause severe drought, millions of poor farmers lose income. Despite the economic revival and a growing middle class—some 200–300 million people today—many Indians have yet to enjoy its fruits. Compared to that of China, Malaysia, and South Korea, India's economy has not delivered a better life to the majority. A third to half still live below the poverty line, 40 percent have no electricity, 25 percent (including 50 percent of children under five) lack an adequate diet, and half earn less than $1.25 per day. While China nears universal literacy, only half of Indians can read and write. Despite laws against it, millions of children under twelve, mainly girls, work full-time. Although population growth is slowing, experts expect India to surpass China as the world's largest country by 2025, posing additional challenges because population growth eats away at national resources. Ironically, success in doubling life expectancy contributes to overpopulation, which causes overcrowded cities, lack of pure drinking water and adequate sanitation, and insufficient primary health care. India has half as many physicians per

Bharatiya Janata Party The major Hindu nationalist party in India.

GLOBAL COMMUNICATIONS A workroom in one of the hundreds of call centers in Indian cities such as Bangalore and Mumbai (Bombay). The workers, mostly well educated and fluent in English, field customer service calls from around the world for Western companies, many of them in the financial services, computer, and electronic businesses.

population and over twice as much infant mortality as China; Chinese live ten years longer than Indians. Lacking money, millions live in tarp and bamboo shacks in vast slums or sleep on city sidewalks. Many schools are inadequate, staffed by poorly paid teachers. While affluent Indians increasingly buy fancy imported cars to drive along newly built highways, many commuters ride on the roofs of jammed buses and trains. India's greenhouse gas emissions are expected to triple in the next two decades.

The stark contrasts between modern and traditional sectors have produced development amid underdevelopment, raising questions as to who benefits from the changes. The "haves" can afford services that strapped governments cannot provide—good schools, clean water, decent health care, efficient transport, gated communities; ambitious birth control campaigns enjoy success in cities but less in the countryside. The Green Revolution has increased output but mostly benefits big landowners, who can afford the large investments in tractors and fertilizers, while per capita calorie consumption remains well below world averages. Because Indian governments have been largely unable or unwilling to challenge powerful landlords, half the rural population has become landless. Poverty fosters growing urban crime and rural

banditry, and Maoist guerrillas challenge local police in some impoverished districts.

Economic growth and poverty also ravage the environment as cities encroach on farmland and villagers cut down trees for firewood. As in China, poor peasants protest, often violently, against governments for taking their land to build factories, often foreign-owned, and highways. The Chipko forest conservation movement, based on traditional and Gandhian principles and led mostly by women, is one of many groups working to protect the environment. A Chipko leader, the globe-trotting Sunderlal Bahugana **(SUN-dur-LOLL ba-hoo-GAH-na)**, stresses the place of people in the larger web of nature.

Indian Societies and Cultures

In his will, Jawaharlal Nehru asked that his ashes be scattered in the Ganges River because it symbolized India's millennia-old culture, ever changing and yet ever the same. Ancient traditions have persisted but also been modified, especially in modern cities, where contrasts with villages, where 70 percent of Indians live, remain stark. The growing urban middle class enjoys the recreations and technologies, from golf to video games, that are available to the affluent worldwide. As young people move around the country, often on the new national highway system, they identify less with their home region and more with India, becoming cosmopolitan. Whether living in Punjab, Calcutta, or Bangalore, educated urban young people often like the same music and buy the same consumer goods. Conservatives fumed but many urbanites cheered when Indian courts struck down laws against homosexuality in 2009; other courts reinstated them in 2013, outraging those who embrace modern social change and igniting debates about cultural traditions and Western influence.

Practices that ensure strict divisions between castes, such as avoiding physical contact or sharing food, are harder to maintain in cities than in villages. While city people often pay attention to caste, their approach to preserving it is different. Hence, many high-caste families place classified ads in national newspapers seeking marriage partners from similar backgrounds for their children, as in this example: "Suitable Brahman bride for handsome Brahman boy completing PhD (Physics). Write with biodata, photograph, horoscope."[8] Meanwhile, caste remains more firmly rooted in villages. At the bottom, untouchables (Dalits), some 20 percent of Indians, still live difficult lives, especially in villages, even though government policies to improve their status have enabled some low-caste people to succeed in high-status occupations or politics. But poor Muslims complain that they do not have access to the affirmative action programs that have helped lower-caste Hindus. The grooves of tradition run deep, particularly in rural areas; changes can bring demoralization and disorientation as well as satisfaction.

Modern life has hastened the breakup of traditional joint families, where parents lived in large compounds with their married and unmarried children and grandchildren; smaller, nuclear families have become more common. Most marriages are still arranged, but some seek family approval after selecting their own spouses. New forms of employment causing family members to move to other districts or countries have undermined family cohesion. A traditional preference for male babies continues. Today the ability of technology to determine the sex of a fetus allows many Indians preferring male children to terminate pregnancies. Experts worry that a gender-imbalanced population will experience increasing social problems.

Nehru had believed that India could progress only if women played a full part. New laws banned once-widespread customs such as polygamy, child marriage, and sati, and female literacy rose from 1 percent in 1901 to 54 percent in 2010. But some changing customs have penalized women. The requirement that new brides provide generous dowries to their in-laws, once restricted to higher castes, has become common in all castes. As a result, some families banish, injure, or kill young brides whose own families have failed to supply the promised dowries.

Domestic violence and rape are also major problems. Notions of women's rights, common in cities, are less known in villages; some villages send spies to monitor young women who migrate to cities and report on their transgressions of tradition, shaming their families. In some towns police harass unmarried couples in public parks for public displays of affection; even in Bangalore, where many educated women work in high-tech jobs, conservatives sometimes harass young women who go with friends to bars and discos. One young woman complained that "India is going through a very confused phase. There are many cultures coming at us.…But we don't all have to wear a sari every minute of the day."[9] Furthermore, few politicians address women's issues and gender violence in their campaigns. Some politicians blame women for any violence they experience.

Nevertheless, many Indian women have benefited from education, even becoming forceful leaders in such fields as journalism, business, trade unions, and the arts. Women have been elected to parliament, are guaranteed one-third of seats on village governments, and serve as chief ministers of states. In 2009 the Congress Party challenged tradition by naming a Dalit woman, former diplomat Meira Kumar, as parliament speaker. An antipatriarchy women's movement has grown for a century. The Self-Employed Women's Association, founded by Ela Bhatt in 1972, provided low-cost credit and literacy training to some of the poorest city women: the rag pickers, in-home seamstresses, and sidewalk vendors. Outside big cities, however, women have remained largely bound by tradition, expected to demonstrate submission, obedience, and absolute dedication to their husband. Women's organizations affiliated with the Hindu nationalist BJP emphasize women as mothers who produce sons and portray Muslim men as a threat to them. AIDS has rapidly become a female health problem, due largely to women being forced into prostitution to serve the sexual needs of increasingly mobile male workers such as long-haul truckers.

Religion plays a key role in Indian life. Although Hindus form a large majority, India's population also includes 180 million Muslims (15 percent), over 20 million Sikhs (2 percent), and nearly 20 million Christians. In 1998 a pilgrim at a major Hindu festival explained the passion for ancient rituals: "Our technological know-how is very well, but our ancients were understanding things much better.…Something is there…which is hidden; which I may not be able to prove technically, but which I know to be there in my soul."[10] However, religious differences have become politicized. Some upper-caste Hindus, particularly in the BJP, have used the notion of a Hindu nation to marginalize Muslims and low-caste Hindus. Violent attacks on Muslims by militant Hindus, often fundamentalists who interpret ancient Hindu religious texts literally, have caused political crises. Sometimes Muslims have initiated the violence. In 2006 Muslims protesting Danish cartoons offensive to Muslims rioted, attacking Hindu

[8]Quoted in Susan Bayly, *Caste, Society and Politics in India from the Eighteenth Century to the Modern Age* (New York: Cambridge University Press, 1999), 315.

[9]Quoted in Emily Cox, "A Rising Anger in India's Streets," *Washington Post*, May 1, 2009.

[10]A. K. Sharma, quoted in John F. Burns, "Ancient Hindu Festival Thrives in Computer-Age India," in *Global Studies: India and South Asia*, ed. James H. K. Norton, 4th ed. (Guilford, CT: Dushkin-McGraw-Hill, 1999), 178.

and Western targets. Polarizing election campaigns sometimes ignite sectarian violence as cynical politicians appeal to religious factions for support. These tensions are fueled by mass poverty among all religious groups.

Yet, Muslims occupy high positions in government, business, and the professions and play key roles in cultural expression, such as films and music. India's most famous modern artist, Tyeb Mehta (1925–2009), was a Shi'ite Muslim whose works, much of which address the Hindu-Muslim divide, sell all over the world. Yet, art can stir controversy. Many Indian galleries refuse to show the works of another acclaimed Muslim artist, Maqbool Fida Husain, because some of them depict Hindu goddesses in the nude.

Indians have eagerly embraced modern cultural forms. Indian-born novelists such as Arundhati Roy (**AH-roon-DAH-tee roy**) and Salman Rushdie achieved worldwide fame. India has also built the world's largest film industry, making about a thousand movies a year, many of them popular among both Indian emigrants and non-Indians in Southeast Asia, the Middle East, Africa, Europe, and the Caribbean. Mumbai's industry, known as Bollywood (see Profile: Raj Kapoor, Bollywood Film Star), churns out films in the major north Indian language, Hindi. But other regions make films in local languages, such as Tamil in southeast India. Many films, especially musicals, portray a fantasy world that enables viewers to forget their problem-filled real world. As one fan explained: "I love to sit in the dark and dream about what I can never possibly have. I can listen to the music, learn all the songs and forget about my troubles."[11] Religious divisions are muted in Bollywood; many leading directors, writers, singers, and stars come from Muslim backgrounds. Because of their superstar status, some film stars move into state and federal politics. Voters in southern India, and more recently north India, have favored local stars as state leaders.

Islamic Societies and Sri Lanka

South Asia's two densely populated Muslim countries, Pakistan and Bangladesh, struggled to develop and maintain stability while alternating between military dictatorships and elected civilian governments. Containing 185 million people, over 95 percent Sunni Muslims, who spoke some sixty languages, Pakistan had difficulty transforming its diverse ethnic and tribal groups into a unified nation. The longest-serving civilian leader, Zulfikar Ali Bhutto (**zool-FEE-kar AH-lee BOO-toe**) (g. 1971–1977), a Britain- and U.S.-trained lawyer from a wealthy landowning family, pursued socialist policies to help the poor. But, accusing Bhutto of corruption, the army took power and later executed him. Soviet occupation of Afghanistan in 1979 and the resulting Pakistan-supported Islamic resistance (see Chapter 30) brought more U.S. military aid to Pakistan and strengthened the military role in government. Bhutto's Oxford-educated daughter, Benazir Bhutto (**BEN-ah-ZEER BOO-toe**) (1953–2006), challenged the unpopular military regime and became prime minister in 1988, as well as later the first modern Asian leader to give birth to a child while in office. She was respected abroad but, accused of abusing power, was dismissed in 1990. Returning to power in 1993, she failed to resolve critical problems, including growing ethnic conflict and militant Sunni attacks on the small Shi'a and Christian minorities. In 1996 she was once again removed.

In 1999 the military took over and installed as president General Pervez Musharraf (**per-VEZ moo-SHAR-uff**) (g. 1999–2008), whose family had fled to Pakistan during India's partition in 1947. While introducing some economic reforms, he also largely failed to meet the persistent challenges: to halt factional violence, punish corruption, collect taxes from the wealthy, restore economic growth, solve high unemployment, improve the inadequate infrastructure (such as transportation, electricity, and education), reduce rapid population growth (2.3 percent per year), and balance the demands of both militant and secular Muslims. Although Musharraf allied with the United States after the 2001 terrorist attacks and resulting U.S. invasion of Afghanistan, many Pakistanis resented America and the West. While seeking Pakistani help against international terrorism, the United States was reluctant to remove high tariff barriers against Pakistani textiles, which accounts for nearly half of all manufacturing jobs. After popular unrest forced Musharraf out in 2006, Benazir Bhutto won free elections but was soon assassinated by a Muslim zealot. Since then the government, led by her widower, has been besieged by corruption and the rise of a Pakistani Taliban, Muslim extremists seeking a rigid theocracy; these tensions have led to terrorist attacks and Taliban-army fighting that has displaced several million refugees. The Muslim League under conservative Nawaz Sharif won the 2013 elections, promising to negotiate with rather than combat extremist groups.

Pakistani society and culture have remained conservative and deeply divided between Sufis and secular urbanites, generally moderate, and those promoting strict Islamic laws and conduct. People are prosecuted, imprisoned, or sometimes assassinated for violating strict blasphemy laws, while religious groups seen as heretics are harassed and even face violent retribution. Pakistan's cosmopolitan founding leader, Jinnah, had favored more rights for women, arguing that shutting up most Pakistani women within the house as prisoners was a crime. But leaders sharing this view were reluctant to challenge strong opposition to women's rights, especially in rural areas. In 1979 an Islamizing military government imposed discriminatory laws making rape victims guilty of adultery, a serious offense. Women enjoyed far fewer legal rights than men and were subject to honor killings, acid attacks, rape, forced marriage, and buying and selling. Soldiers attacked women's groups courageously protesting in the streets, prompting feminist poet Saeeda Gazdar (**SIGH-ee-da GAZ-dar**) to write: "The flags of mourning were flapping, the hand-maidens had rebelled.

Bollywood The Mumbai film industry.

---

[11] Quoted in Jeremy Marre and Hannah Charlton, *Beats of the Heart: Popular Music of the World* (New York: Pantheon, 1985), 150.

Raj Kapoor, Bollywood Film Star

Raj Kapoor (1924–1988) was the first real superstar of Indian film, an accomplished actor, director, producer, and all-round showman. Kapoor skillfully combined music, melodrama, and spectacle to create a cinema with huge popular, even international, appeal, especially among the poor. He was born in Peshawar, the son of one of India's most distinguished stage and film actors, Prithviraj Kapoor. The family settled in Bombay in 1929, when the Hindi-language film industry was in a formative stage (Hindi is the major language spoken in north India). At age twenty-two Kapoor entered an arranged marriage to Krishnaji. Although he had romances with actresses, the marriage endured and the couple had five children.

Handsome and vigorous, with a talent for comedy, music, and self-promotion, the young Kapoor formed his own film company in 1948 with hopes of appealing to the common person. Over the next three decades he starred in or oversaw dozens of films, many of them commercially successful. Kapoor's greatest success came during the Nehru years from the late 1940s to mid-1960s, when Indians were optimistic and looked outward. His films, often subtitled in local languages, brought him celebrity all over South Asia and in Southeast Asia, East Africa, the Middle East, the Caribbean, and the Soviet Union. Songs from his films were sung or hummed on streets of cities and small towns thousands of miles from India, and he and his female costars became popular pin-ups in the bazaars of the Arab world and folk heroes in the Soviet lands. Kapoor, like Nehru, believed that an Indian could enjoy foreign products and influences while also remaining deeply Indian. A song from his film *The Gentleman Cheat* in 1955 reflected the hero's transnational identity: "The shoes I'm wearing are made in Japan, My trousers fashioned in England. The red cap on my head is Russian. In spite of it all my heart is Indian."

Fans saw in his characters youth, optimism about life, and revolt against authority, the little man straddling the great divides of wealth and poverty, city and village, sophistication and innocence. For example, in *The Vagabond* (1951) he portrays a rebellious youth and petty thief growing up on the streets, both daring and vulnerable, charming and reckless, surviving by his wits.

RAJ KAPOOR As the most influential male lead and director in Indian films, Kapoor could attract the top actresses to star in his films. He made many films with Nargis, the two of them shown here in a 1948 musical, *Barsaat*.

The themes of Kapoor's films often touched on social problems or politics. They offered underdog heroes who were poor but also happy. These themes permeated some of his most popular films, such as *The Vagabond*, which broke box-office records in the USSR and the Middle East, where it was dubbed into Arabic, Persian, and Turkish. Like American comedians, especially Charlie Chaplin, Kapoor often portrayed a deglamorized tramp, the little man at odds with the world and hiding his pain behind a smiling face, a figure he thought "had a greater identity with the common man."

Kapoor's romanticism was evident in his sympathetic treatment of women. The heroine, often played by the actress Nargis **(NAR-ghis)** (1929–1981), a Muslim was always a central player in his films. Sometimes Kapoor presented women as strong and without flaws; as was his character's love interest, Nargis, in *The Vagabond*; at other times women were victims, exploited and tormented by religion and tradition. Kapoor argued, "We eulogize womankind as the embodiment of motherhood but we always give our women the worst treatment. They are burnt alive [in sati], treated as slaves [by men]." Yet, Kapoor's films presented sensuous actresses and opened the way to more sexually explicit scenes, shocking social conservatives.

Kapoor's career faded in the 1970s, when his style of romantic hero became old-fashioned. At the time of his death in 1988 he was making a film exploring the taboo subject of love across the India-Pakistan border, between a Hindu and a Muslim. His sons, all actors, tried to keep his banner alive and his grandson, Ranbir Kapoor, is a current heartthrob, but Bollywood moved in new directions, centering stories on men and their challenges rather than balancing strong male-female roles as Kapoor had done.

THINKING ABOUT THE PROFILE

1. Why is Kapoor often credited with spreading Indian film to other countries?
2. What social viewpoints were expressed in his films?

Notes: Quotations from Sumita S. Chakravarty, *National Identity in Indian Popular Cinema, 1947–1987* (Austin: University of Texas Press, 1993), 138, 30; and Malti Sahai, "Raj Kapoor and the Indianization of Charlie Chaplin," *East-West Film Journal* 2, no. 1 (December 1987): 64.

Those two hundred women who came out on the streets, were surrounded on all sides, besieged by armed force, [repressed by] the enemies of truth, the murderers of love."[12]

Things have improved little over the years: only 16 percent of adult women are employed outside the home, and fewer than 20 percent are literate. In some districts Islamic militants have succeeded in restricting women from voting or from attending school with males. In 2012 brave and outspoken fifteen-year-old Malala Yousafzai (MA-la-la YOU-sef-ZAI), was shot in the face for promoting girl's schools, which Muslim extremists opposed. She survived to address the United Nations, saying the assassination attempt gave her new determination and demanding that world leaders provide free education to girls. Like another Pakistani, Mukhtaran Bibi earlier (see Chapter 26), Malala Yousafzai inspired millions around the world.

Repression exists in other areas as well. Attempts by Islamic leaders to prohibit broadcasting of music by popular singers, especially women such as London-based Nazia Hassan, have fostered an ongoing debate about Westernized popular culture and women entertainers. A lively bootleg industry provides often-banned Bollywood videos to fans. Pakistan also remains a land of villages dominated by large, politically influential landowners. Although life expectancy improved from forty-three to sixty-four years between 1960 and 2012, 20 percent of Pakistanis and 30 percent of children suffer from malnutrition. With far too few public schools, many Pakistani youngsters attend Islamic madrasahs with narrow religious curriculums that teach few usable skills.

Bangladesh, overcrowded with 155 million people, has also encountered barriers to development. The mostly flat land is prone to devastating hurricanes, floods, tornados, famine, and rising sea levels due to global warming. Sheikh Mujiber Rahman hoped the nation he founded—secular, democratic, and socialist—would rapidly progress, but he was assassinated by the military. None of the governments after him, military or civilian, have succeeded in resolving many problems, and all have suffered from corruption. Several leaders have been assassinated. After 1991 democracy became the main pattern, with the two largest parties led by women. Conservative, procapitalist Khaleda Zia (ZEE-uh) (g. 1991–1996, 2001–2006), widow of an assassinated leader, heads one party, while left-leaning Sheikh Hasina Wajed (shake ha-SEE-nah WAH-jed) (g. 1996–2001, 2009–), daughter of Sheikh Mujiber Rahman, leads the Awami League. Sheikh Hasina, who promoted education, women's empowerment, and better relations with India and Pakistan, herself escaped an assassination attempt in 2004. The two women, bitter rivals, have alternated as the nation's prime minister. In 2013–2014 the feud between the two parties intensified after Sheikh Hasina's government executed several militant Muslims after controversial war crimes trials for assisting Pakistan's invasion in 1971, leading to rioting, strikes, protests, and the Khaleda Zia-led opposition's boycott of national elections. In response, Sheikh Hasina, easily re-elected thanks to the boycott, arrested some opponents, raising questions about the future of democracy in the bitterly polarized nation.

Despite political turbulence, however, Bangladesh has pioneered programs to eliminate poverty and educate children. The Grameen Bank, which gives small loans, particularly to poor women, for starting a village business, has helped millions, earning world attention (see Chapter 26). Visionary activist Fazle Hasan Abed launched a movement to improve rural life through forming cooperatives. Bangladesh also developed a huge garment industry, with the world's lowest paid labor force, serving many Western companies, accounting for three-fourths of export earnings; but some poorly constructed factories have collapsed or caught fire, killing hundreds of workers. Despite the progress, nearly half the population lives below the official poverty line.

Social and cultural issues have divided Bangladesh, which is officially a secular state with a large Hindu minority (10 percent). Historically Bengalis incorporated Hindu and Buddhist influences as well as Sufi mysticism, creating a tolerant Islam, but militant movements seeking an Islamic state gained strength in the 1990s, heightening divisions. Allied with Khaleda Zia's party, militants restricted women's rights. Public universities required women students to return to their dormitories by sunset to protect their chastity. Zia's government also prosecuted feminist writers such as medical doctor-turned-novelist Taslima Nasreen (b. 1962), who criticized religion and a conservative culture for holding Bengali women back, arguing that the basic division was between modern, rational values and irrational, blind faith. Muslim militants condemned Nasreen's writing as blasphemy against Islam, a capital offense. Nasreen fled to Europe to escape death threats. Since 1975 Bangladesh has improved gender equality, health, renewable energy, poverty rates, literacy (57 percent), and food production while doubling per capita income and reducing population growth. Yet, conflict and instability continue to plague the country. Responding to growing Islamist pressures to enforce blasphemy laws, in 2013 the government arrested "atheist" bloggers and introduced limitations on social media.

Sri Lanka shares problems of ethnic conflict and poverty with its neighbors but has generally maintained a democracy, although sometimes shaky. In 1948 the Sinhalese, some 75 percent of the population (today 21 million) and mostly Theravada Buddhists, negotiated independence from Britain, inheriting a colonial economy based on rubber and tea plantations. Sinhalese-dominated governments discriminated against the language and culture of the major ethnic minority, the mostly Hindu Tamils. In 1959 Sirimavo Bandaranaike (sree-MAH-vo BAN-dar-an-EYE-kee) (1916–2004), widow of an assassinated leader, became the world's first woman prime minister. Her enemies derided her as a "kitchen woman" who knew all about cooking but nothing about running a country; yet she dominated politics in the 1960s and 1970s.

---

[12]Quoted in Bose and Jalal, *Modern South Asia*, 232.

Successive governments promoted Sinhalese nationalism while sponsoring textile and electronics manufacturing to reduce dependence on cash crop exports. While socialist policies discouraged free enterprise, they fostered high literacy rates (92 percent), high per capita income (nearly $3,000), free education, and, by providing rice and free medical care to the poor, South Asia's longest life span (seventy-eight). Like India, Sri Lanka, with many English speakers, attracted outsourcing jobs by the 2000s. In 1983 some Tamils seeking independence for their northern and eastern region began a rebellion that kept the island in a constant state of tension, with assassinations of top political leaders and communal fighting. In 1994 Chandrika Kumaratunga **(CHAN-dree-ka koo-MAHR-a-TOON-ga)** (b. 1945), Sirimavo Bandaranaike's University of Paris–educated daughter, led her left-leaning party to victory, becoming Sri Lanka's second woman leader, but she narrowly escaped an assassination attempt in 2000.

Meanwhile, nearly sixty thousand people, many innocent civilians, died in twenty years of Tamil-Sinhalese violence. Some Buddhist clergy advocated peace and tolerance; others viewed Hindu Tamils as a threat to Buddhism. In 2009 the Sri Lankan military finally defeated the main Tamil insurgent group, bringing hope for peace. But the conflict and an increasingly authoritarian regime diminished multiethnic democracy, generated human rights violations, and alienated Tamils, making long-elusive national reconciliation even more challenging.

South Asia in the Global System

Since 1945 South Asian nations have grown in geopolitical and economic stature. Along with China and Brazil, India became a major voice in the G-20 nations. Although Nehru strode the world stage, his successors lacked his international influence. However, India became an advanced technology center, importing high-tech and service jobs from the West, and one of the most industrialized non-Western nations, exporting heavy machinery, steel, and autos while producing consumer goods for local consumption. Some Indians who provide telephone technical support to users of U.S.-made computers receive training in mastering an American accent to facilitate rapport. Even with the global recession of 2008–2009, outsourcing of jobs to India has continued, although some companies now put call centers in Sri Lanka or the Philippines, both with many educated English speakers. Every year Indian universities, some world class, turn out thousands of talented engineers and computer scientists who have built both homegrown industries and the high-tech "silicon valleys" of North America and Europe. Some of that talent has turned to innovating "green technologies" such as wind power and solar electric cars.

Experts debate whether India or China might eventually compete for world economic leadership with the United States. Some point to India's many English-speakers, solid financial system, and vibrant democracy as advantages. However, the nation's boom has added few jobs, and to become a world power, India needs to contain social tensions; greatly improve its transportation, communication, and education infrastructure; and find ways to better share the wealth and reduce rural poverty. In addition, diminishing water sources as Tibetan glaciers recede with global warming, as well as dam building and diversion that threaten glacier-fed rivers, pose a danger that requires the affected nations' working together.

South Asian technology and ingenuity have sparked scientific achievements. In 1975 the Indian government launched into orbit its first satellite, named after Aryabhata **(OUR-ya-BAH-ta)**, a major Indian scientist and mathematician over fifteen hundred years ago, and in 2013 it announced an unmanned mission to Mars. In 1998 India tested its first nuclear bomb. In response to the regional arms race, Pakistan also developed nuclear weapons, sparking international worries because Islamic militants, some with possible links to global terrorist networks, influence Pakistan's military and local and national politics. In 2004 a top Pakistani nuclear scientist admitted selling nuclear secrets to other nations.

Global and regional politics has intensified Indian-Pakistani rivalries. After 2001, when U.S. president George W. Bush justified preemptive military attacks against potential threats, ordering U.S. forces into Afghanistan and Iraq, some Indians wondered why India should not preemptively attack Pakistan: "If the United States can fly its bombs 10,000 miles to hit terrorist bases [in Afghanistan], why should India wait to knock out Pakistan's [military] bases?"[13] But while India-Pakistan relations have remained combustible, after 2000 Indian and Pakistani leaders promoted a thaw and visited each other's countries, fostering cross-border visits and sports competitions and giving hope that tensions might diminish. However, the Afghanistan conflict spilled over into Pakistan, and Islamist groups flourish among conservative Pashtuns in the tribal regions bordering Afghanistan, which was never under firm government control. Over time Islamists have extended their influence beyond the tribal areas and threaten more violence in Kashmir, alarming moderate Muslims, India, and the United States.

South Asians have made distinctive contributions to world politics. Although South Asia has maintained traditional social patterns and cultural viewpoints, at various times women have led the four major South Asian nations, all democracies some or most of the time, in a striking difference from the preference for male leaders in much of the world. Both Sri Lanka and Bangladesh have elected two different women prime ministers. Hence, while women remain disadvantaged, they enjoy more high-level political power than in other nations, a part of the great complexity of this region.

---

[13]Quoted in Stanley Wolpert, *A New History of India*, 7th ed. (New York: Oxford University Press, 2004), 462.

MAKE SURE YOU UNDERSTAND THESE KEY POINTS BEFORE MOVING ON

- India's multiparty democracy has endured despite religious and caste tensions.

- Despite great advances in agricultural and industrial production, India still suffers from extensive poverty, and its rapidly growing population is likely to perpetuate this problem.

- Pakistan has alternated between civilian and military governments and has been slow to grant women equal rights, while Bangladesh has combated poverty in spite of great challenges and has generally accepted religious minorities, though militant Muslim groups have gained influence in recent years.

- Since it became independent, Sri Lanka has been a democracy; it elected the world's first woman prime minister, and it has nurtured a well-educated, long-lived population, despite tensions between minority Tamils and majority Sinhalese.

- Though women's rights are not universal in South Asia, more South Asian women have achieved positions of great power than in other areas of the world.

Revolution, Decolonization, and New Nations in Southeast Asia

What were the causes and consequences of the struggles in Southeast Asia?

The nationalist thrust for independence produced new nations in Southeast Asia after World War II (see Map 31.2). But the euphoria proved short-lived; building states capable of improving the lives of their people had only just begun. Indochina's peoples experienced wrenching violence as France and the United States attempted to roll back revolutionary nationalism. During the First Indochina War (1946–1954), France attempted to maintain control of Vietnam against communist-led opposition but was eventually defeated. In the second and more destructive war, the United States and its Vietnamese allies waged an ultimately unsuccessful fight against communist-led Vietnamese forces, also dragging in Cambodia and Laos. Indonesia, the Philippines, Burma, and the other new nations, while often facing violent unrest, avoided such destructive warfare but also had to overcome economic underdevelopment, promote national unity in ethnically divided societies, and deal with opposition to the new ruling groups. Economic progress but also conflict and dictatorships marked the years between 1945 and 1975. The leaders also had to forge new relationships with the former colonial powers and the new Cold War superpowers—the United States and Soviet Union—as well as with nearby China.

The First Indochina War and Two Vietnams

Anticolonial revolution gripped Vietnam after World War II. In 1945 the Japanese army in southern Vietnam surrendered to British forces moving into southern Vietnam to prepare for a French return to power. Meanwhile the communist-led Viet Minh that fought the Japanese occupation captured colonial Vietnam's capital, Hanoi, and declared the end of French colonialism. Controlling much of northern Vietnam and parts of

the center and south, the Viet Minh–led government, headed by Ho Chi Minh, became the first non-French regime in over eighty years. Addressing a half-million jubilant Vietnamese gathered in Hanoi's main square, Ho quoted the U.S. Declaration of Independence, adding: "It means: All the peoples on earth are equal from birth, all the peoples have a right to live and to be happy and free."[14] Both French and American observers noted that the majority of Vietnamese supported the Viet Minh.

However, the French, desperate to retain their empire, quickly regrouped and reoccupied southern Vietnam. The Republic of China sent troops to disarm the remaining Japanese in northern Vietnam, alarming the Vietnamese, who feared a permanent presence by their traditional enemy. Using earthy language, Ho told his followers he had to patiently negotiate with the French because sniffing French manure for a while was better than eating China's all their lives. Americans, influenced by Cold War thinking and allied with France, and alarmed at Ho's association with the USSR and communism, shifted from supporting the Viet Minh during World War II to opposing all leftwing nationalists, including Ho and the Viet Minh.

Vietnam remained tense. As Ho negotiated with the French for recognition of Vietnamese independence, he also appealed to U.S. president Harry Truman for political and economic support, receiving no answer. French leaders, with allies among anticommunist Catholics and pro-Western nationalists, were determined to regain domination over all Vietnam. In 1946 Ho warned a French diplomat that a war would be costly and unwinnable: "You will kill ten of my men while we will kill one of yours, but you will be the ones who will end up exhausted."[15] During the First Indochina War (1946–1954) France attempted, with massive U.S. economic and military aid,

---

[14]Quoted in William J. Duiker, *Ho Chi Minh: A Life* (New York: Hyperion, 2000), 323.

[15]Quoted in George Donelson Moss, *Vietnam: An American Ordeal*, 4th ed. (Upper Saddle River, NJ: Prentice-Hall, 2002), 40.

MAP 31.2 MODERN SOUTHEAST ASIA Indonesia, covering thousands of islands, is the largest, most populous Southeast Asian nation. Southeast Asia also includes four other island nations (including the Philippines and Singapore), five nations on the mainland, and Malaysia, which sprawls from the Malay Peninsula to northern Borneo. © 2015 Cengage Learning

to maintain its colonial grip. Meanwhile, Americans believed in the domino theory, which predicted a communist sweep through Southeast Asia, and coveted Indochina's resources. A large military force pushed the Viet Minh out of northern cities, but their brutal tactics alienated the population, while in some rural areas the Viet Minh won peasant support by transferring land to poor villagers. The French could not overcome an outgunned but determined foe with a nationalist message. As his forces became bogged down in what observers called a "quicksand war," a French general complained that fighting the Viet Minh was "like ridding a dog of its fleas. We can pick them, drown them, and poison them, but they will be back in a few days."[16] After a major military defeat in 1954, when Viet Minh forces overwhelmed a key French base in the mountains at Dien Bien Phu and took thousands of prisoners, the French abandoned their efforts and went home.

Peace agreements negotiated at a conference in Geneva, Switzerland, in 1954 divided the country into two Vietnams. But while northern, central, and southern Vietnamese spoke different dialects and had some cultural differences, few wanted separate nations. The agreements left the Viet Minh in control of North Vietnam and provided that elections be held in 1956 to determine whether South Vietnamese wanted to join in a unified country. Ignoring the Geneva agreements, which it had not signed, the United States helped install Ngo Dinh Diem **(no dinh dee-EM)** (1901–1963), an anticommunist and longtime U.S. resident, as South Vietnam's president. Believing the widely respected Ho might win, Diem refused to hold reunification elections. Some Vietnamese opposed communist ideology, backing Diem and the United States.

North and South Vietnam differed dramatically. Ho's government built a disciplined state that addressed colonial inequalities, redistributing land from powerful landlords to poor peasants. However, the government's authoritarian style and socialist policies prompted nearly a million North Vietnamese, including many Catholics, to move to South Vietnam, where President Diem, from a wealthy Catholic family, established a government in Saigon. Americans poured in economic and military aid and, to stabilize Diem's increasingly unpopular regime, sent military advisers.

---

[16]Jacques Philippe Leclerc, quoted in James S. Olson and Randy Roberts, *Where the Domino Fell: America and Vietnam, 1945–1995*, 3rd ed. (St. James, NY: Brandywine, 1999), 28.

The rigid Diem alienated peasants by opposing most land reform. In 1960 dissidents in South Vietnam, including former Viet Minh soldiers, formed a communist-led revolutionary movement, the **National Liberation Front (NLF)**, often known as the Viet Cong, that was armed by North Vietnam. Diem responded with repression, murdering or imprisoning thousands of suspected rebels and other opponents. Buddhists resented the Diem government's pro-Catholic policies, while nationalists generally viewed Diem as an American puppet. Meanwhile, the NLF spread their influence in rural areas, assassinating government officials and brutalizing opponents.

By the early 1960s the NLF controlled large sections of South Vietnam, and thousands more American troops, still called military advisers, became more involved in combat. In 1963 U.S. leaders, judging Diem ineffective, sanctioned his overthrow by his own military officers, who killed him. As the situation deteriorated and North Vietnamese troops moved south, U.S. concerns about a possible communist sweep through Southeast Asia generated what Americans called the Vietnam War (1963–1975) and that many Vietnamese called the American War.

The American-Vietnamese War

In 1964 U.S. president Lyndon Johnson (g. 1963–1969) used an alleged North Vietnamese attack on a U.S. ship in the Gulf of Tonkin, which probably never occurred, to escalate the conflict into a full-scale military commitment (see Map 31.3). When Johnson said in 1965, "I want to leave the footprints of America there [Indochina]. We can turn the Mekong into [an economically developed] Tennessee Valley,"[17] he was reflecting a longtime American mission to change the world, spreading democracy and capitalism. However, Johnson and other U.S. leaders, civilian and military, had little understanding of the nationalism and opposition to foreign occupation that shaped the Vietnamese, who had many historical reasons for mistrusting foreign powers on "civilizing" missions. Soon the war intensified. In 1965 Johnson ordered an air war against both South and North Vietnam targets and a massive intervention of ground troops, peaking at 550,000 Americans by 1968. The conflict also drew in other outsiders. Small numbers of Australian, South Korean, and Thai troops aided the U.S. effort, while the Soviet Union and China provided North Vietnam with military supplies. However, a series of military regimes never achieved enough credibility with the South Vietnamese majority. Military supplies and North Vietnamese troops regularly moved south through the mountains of eastern Laos and Cambodia, along the Ho Chi Minh Trail.

Despite technological superiority, U.S. forces struggled to overcome the communists, often ignoring South Vietnamese leaders and the consequences of military actions; meanwhile, the South Vietnamese army, largely conscripts, proved somewhat ineffective. U.S. strategists measured success by counting the enemy dead and creating free fire zones from which civilians were ordered to evacuate, a strategy that made it hard to win Vietnamese "hearts and minds" and diminish local support for the NLF. Vietnam became the most heavily bombed nation in history; Americans dropped twice the total bomb tonnage used in World War II. In addition, the use of chemical defoliants to clear forests and wetlands, as well as the countless bomb craters, caused massive environmental damage. Thanks in part to the toxic chemicals, Vietnam today has among the world's highest rates of birth defects and cancer.

By 1967 the United States had achieved a military stalemate, but in 1968 the **Tet Offensive**, when communist forces attacked South Vietnamese cities during the Vietnamese new year, proved a turning point. Although the communists were pushed back and suffered high casualties, Tet proved a political and psychological setback for Americans. Meanwhile, for procommunist Vietnamese, the American-Vietnamese War was a continuation of the First Indochina War to expel the French and rebuild a damaged society. When the Viet Minh humbled the hated French colonizers, they gained a popularity the United States could not overcome. The communists also gained peasant support by advocating reforms. Some U.S. policies, especially the air war, which killed thousands of innocent people, backfired. One of the thousands of women NLF fighters reported: "The first days I felt ill at ease—marching in step, lobbing grenades, taking aim with my rifle, hitting the ground. But as soon as I saw the American planes come back [to bomb], my timidity left me."[18] However, many South Vietnamese supported the pro-U.S. government or rejected both sides. Pham Duy (**fam do-ee**), a folksinger who, like many South Vietnamese, disliked both the corrupt Saigon government and the often ruthless communists, wrote a song describing the war's impact on average Vietnamese: "The rain of the leaves is the tears of joy, Of the girl whose boy returns from the war. The rain on the leaves is bitter tears, When a mother hears her son is no more."[19]

The war, which generated huge budget deficits and other economic problems, bitterly divided Americans; by the late 1960s a majority had turned against the commitment to a seemingly endless quagmire that killed or injured Americans for uncertain goals. The United States began a gradual withdrawal of troops and negotiated peace agreements with North Vietnam. By 1973 U.S. ground forces had left Vietnam, and in 1975 the NLF and North Vietnam defeated the South Vietnamese forces, reunifying the country under communist leadership. Many South Vietnamese fled, nearly 2 million eventually settling in the United States. General Maxwell Taylor, former U.S. ambassador to South Vietnam, later concluded that Americans lost because, never understanding

National Liberation Front (NLF) Often known as the Viet Cong, a communist-led revolutionary movement in South Vietnam that resisted American intervention in the American-Vietnamese War.

Tet Offensive Communist attacks on major South Vietnamese cities in 1968, a turning point in the American-Vietnamese War.

---

[17]Quoted in Thomas G. Paterson et al., *American Foreign Policy: A History Since 1900*, 3rd ed. rev. (Lexington, MA: D.C. Heath, 1991), 553.

[18]Anh Vien, quoted in Arleen Eisen Bergman, *Women of Vietnam*, rev. ed. (San Francisco: Peoples Press, 1975), 123.

[19]Quoted in Neil L. Jamieson, *Understanding Vietnam* (Berkeley: University of California Press, 1993), 290.

MAP 31.3 **THE U.S.-VIETNAMESE WAR** From the early 1960s until 1975, South Vietnam, aided by thousands of U.S. troops and air power, resisted a communist-led insurgency aided by North Vietnam, which sent troops and supplies down the Ho Chi Minh Trail through Laos and Cambodia. © 2015 Cengage Learning

the Vietnamese on either side, they overestimated the effectiveness of U.S. strategies. The devastating war cost the United States 58,000 dead and 519,000 physically disabled; the Vietnamese lost around 4 million killed or wounded—10 percent of the total population. After the fighting ended, Vietnam turned to reconstruction.

War in Laos and Cambodia

Laos and Cambodia became pawns in the larger conflict between the United States and the North Vietnamese. Anticolonial sentiment grew during and after the Japanese occupation. In 1953 France, wearying of its Indochinese experience, granted Laos independence under a pro-French government dominated by the ethnic Lao majority. Cambodia gained its independence under young, charismatic, widely popular Prince Norodom Sihanouk (**SEE-uh-nook**) (1922–2012), who won the first free election in 1955. However, the Vietnam conflict eventually engulfed both countries, in part because of U.S. military interventions.

The U.S. intervention in Laos, which began in the late 1950s and continued until 1975, intensified conflict between U.S.-backed anticommunist rightwingers, neutralista, and the Pathet Lao, revolutionary nationalists allied with North Vietnam. In 1960 rightwing forces advised and equipped by the U.S. Central Intelligence Agency (CIA) seized the Laotian government as fighting intensified. Because the corrupt Laotian regime's U.S.-financed army was ineffective, Americans turned to hill peoples for recruits, among them a large faction of the Hmong. Promising permanent support and protection, the CIA recruited a secret 45,000-man army, largely Hmong, that attacked North Vietnamese forces along the Ho Chi Minh Trail and fought the Pathet Lao. Ten percent of the Hmong population, some 30,000 people, died during a conflict largely unknown to the American public. At the same time, U.S. bombing depopulated large areas, forcing many Laotians into refugee camps; the war killed some 100,000 Laotians. After 1975, when the Pathet Lao took full control of a war-weary Laos, thousands of anticommunist Laotians fled into Thailand, many later moving to the United States and other Western nations.

Cambodia also became embroiled in the Indochina conflict. President Prince Sihanouk ruled as a benevolent autocrat, maintaining peace while also writing sentimental popular songs, playing the saxophone, directing films, and publicizing his political views in foreign newspapers. But both the Vietnamese communists roaming the border area and the U.S. war planes bombing communist positions violated Cambodian neutrality. Sihanouk faced other problems. The Khmer Rouge (**kmahr roozh**) ("Red Khmers"), a communist insurgent group led by French-educated intellectuals seeking to overthrow Sihanouk, built support among impoverished peasants. Although Sihanouk remained popular among many peasants, military officers and big businessmen, resenting dictatorial rule, desired

to share in the U.S. money and arms flowing into South Vietnam, Laos, and Thailand.

In 1970 U.S.-backed generals and civilians overthrew Sihanouk, who went into exile. U.S. and South Vietnamese forces then invaded eastern Cambodia seeking Vietnamese communist bases, creating an opening for the Khmer Rouge to recruit mass support. The pro-U.S. government, dependent on U.S. aid for virtually all supplies, lacked legitimacy, while Cambodia's ineffective army suffered from corruption and low morale. To attack the Khmer Rouge, U.S. planes launched an intensive, terrifying air assault through Cambodia's agricultural heartland, killing thousands of innocent civilians. Rice production declined by almost half, raising the possibility of massive starvation. Amid the destruction, the growing Khmer Rouge recruited the displaced, shell-shocked peasants. From 1970 through 1975, between 750,000 and 1 million Cambodians, mostly civilians, perished from the conflict between the brutal Khmer Rouge and the brutal U.S.-backed government. In 1975 the Khmer Rouge seized the capital, Phnom Penh, and controlled the country until 1978.

Indonesia: The Quest for Freedom and Unity

Indonesian independence came through struggle in the late 1940s. During the Indonesian Revolution, the Dutch used massive force to suppress the nationalists, who fought back. Describing a brutal battle, a nationalist writer noted that, for the revolutionary soldiers, "everything blurred: the future and their heart-breaking struggle. They only knew that they had to murder to drive out the enemy and stop him trampling their liberated land. They killed [the Dutch soldiers] with great determination, spirit and hunger."[20] The United States, fearing regional instability, pressured Holland to grant independence in 1950.

Given the diversity of islands, peoples, and cultures, Indonesians still faced the challenge of fostering national unity and identity. Their national slogan, "unity in diversity," expressed more goal than solid reality. During the 1950s and early 1960s, the charismatic but increasingly authoritarian president Sukarno (**soo-KAHR-no**) (1902–1970) led Indonesia. A spellbinding, inspirational orator able to bring different factions together, Sukarno worked to create national solidarity in a huge nation where villagers on remote islands and cosmopolitan city dwellers on Java knew little about each other. Sukarno also sought a role on the world stage, sponsoring a major international conference at the Javan city of Bandung in 1955 to shape a Non-Aligned Movement, a middle way between the two superpowers.

However, Sukarno could not maintain stability, the

Pathet Lao Revolutionary Laotian nationalists allied with North Vietnam during the American-Vietnamese War.

Khmer Rouge ("Red Khmers") A communist insurgent group seeking to overthrow the government in Cambodia during the 1960s and 1970s.

---

[20]From Idrus, "Surabaya," in *From Surabaya to Armageddon: Indonesian Short Stories*, ed. Harry Aveling (Singapore: Heinemann, 1976), 13.

multiparty parliamentary system became divisive, and regionalism grew as outer islanders resented domination by the Javanese, who constituted over half of Indonesia's population. By the early 1960s Sukarno's nationalistic but poorly implemented economic policies had generated a severe economic crisis, deepening divisions between communist, Islamic, and military forces. A procommunist Javanese novelist described post-Revolution economic failures: "Jakarta [the capital city] reveals a grandiose display with no relationship to reality. Great plans, enormous immorality. [There are] no screws, no nuts, no bolts, no valves, and no washers for the machinery we do have."[21]

By 1965 explosive social and political pressures sparked Indonesia's greatest crisis. After a small, procommunist military faction's failed attempt to seize power, discontented generals arrested Sukarno, took over the government, and launched, with Muslim groups, a brutal campaign to eliminate all leftists, especially the large Communist Party, which was influential among poor peasants in Java. The resulting bloodbath killed perhaps half a million, including members of the unpopular Chinese minority. Thousands of leftists were held in remote prison camps for years. Sukarno died in disgrace in 1970.

Making the Philippine and Malaysian Nations

The Philippines and Malaysia both became independent but troubled nations. The Philippines achieved independence on July 4, 1946, and remained closely tied to the United States politically and economically, but it soon faced problems sustaining democracy. A small group of landowners, industrialists, and businessmen manipulated elected governments to preserve their power and protect U.S. economic interests. Free elections involved so much violence, bribery, and fraud that disillusioned Filipinos complained of "guns, goons, and gold." Nationalists believed that the continuing U.S. influence, including several military bases, hindered a truly independent Filipino identity and culture. Referring to popular U.S. films, television programs, music, comics, and books, a prominent scholar wrote that her people "sing of White Christmases and of Manhattan. Their stereos reverberate with the American Top 40."[22] Outside influences on their culture—first Spanish, then American—were often superficial, but Filipinos struggled to create a clear national identity out of diverse local languages and regions.

Economic inequality and social divisions fueled conflict. A Filipino poet portrayed the gap between rich and poor: "[For the affluent] there's pleasure and distraction, fiesta and dancing, night-long, day-long; who dares whisper that thousands have no roofs above their heads; that hunger stalks the town."[23] Only heavy U.S. assistance suppressed the communist-led Huk Rebellion (1948–1954), which capitalized on rural discontent. In the 1970s the communist New People's Army (NPA), promising radical change, controlled many rural districts, supported by rural tenant farmers

UMNO The main Malay political party in Malaysia.

and urban slum dwellers. Religious differences have also fostered conflict. While most Filipinos became Christian in Spanish times, Muslims in the southern islands often resented Christian domination, and several Muslim groups seeking autonomy or secession took up arms. In 1972 President Ferdinand Marcos (1917–1989) suspended democracy, ruling as a dictator (1972–1986) but resolving few problems.

Malayan governments proved more stable. After World War II communist-led insurgents kept the British colony on edge for a decade. In 1957, with the insurgency crushed, Malaya became independent as a federation of states led by the main Malay party, **UMNO** (United Malays National Organization). However, predominantly Chinese Singapore, a major trading center and military base, remained a British colony. In Malaya the majority Malays, nearly all Muslim, dominated politics, but Chinese, a third of the population, gained liberal citizenship rights and maintained economic power. British leaders, tired of colonial burdens, forged a merger of Singapore, two northern Borneo colonies, Sabah and Sarawak, and Malaya, creating a larger independent but geographically divided federation, Malaysia, in 1963.

Malaysians struggled to create national unity out of deep regional and ethnic divisions. Singapore withdrew in 1965, becoming independent. To reduce political tensions, sustain economic growth, and preserve stability, the leaders of the key Malayan ethnic groups—Malays, Chinese, and Indians—cooperated through allied political parties in an UMNO-dominated ruling coalition, but below the surface ethnic tensions simmered. Street fighting between Chinese and Malays following the heated 1969 election spurred a nationwide state of emergency. After 1970 Malay-dominated governments pursued policies designed to reshape Malaysia's society and economy while sporadically detaining some dissidents and banning discussion of "sensitive" ethnic relations issues.

Diversity and Dictatorship in Thailand and Burma

Thailand and Burma have also struggled to create national unity and stability. Although historical rivals, the two countries have shared some common patterns. The majority Thais (Siamese) and Burmans, both Theravada Buddhists, assert authority over diverse minorities, including hill tribes, Malay Muslims, and Chinese. Both countries have also experienced insurgencies by disaffected ethnic, religious, or communist factions.

Thailand's leaders sought to build a national culture based on Thai cultural values: reverence for Buddhism and the monarchy, respect for those in authority, and social harmony. This conservatism fostered authoritarian governments and bureaucratic inertia. Various communist and Islamic insurgent groups operated during the 1960s and 1970s in ethnic minority regions. Thanks partly to unrest, Thai politics was marked by long periods of military rule, often corrupt and oppressive, followed by short-lived democratically elected or semidemocratic

---

[21]From Pramoedya Ananta Toer, "Letter to a Friend in the Country," in Aveling, *From Surabaya*, 72.
[22]Doreen Fernandez, "Mass Culture and Cultural Policy: The Philippine Experience," *Philippine Studies* 37 (4th Quarter, 1980): 492.
[23]"The Kingdom of Mammon," in Amado V. Hernandez, *Rice Grains: Selected Poems* (New York: International Publishers, 1966), 31.

governments. In the 1970s opposition movements challenged the long-entrenched military regime. Many Thais also resented the United States, which supported the military regime and had military bases and some fifty thousand troops in the country. Free-spending American soldiers created a false prosperity, outraging staunch Buddhists with their sleazy bars, gaudy nightclubs, and brothels that often exploited poor Thai women.

In 1973 antigovernment feelings boiled over, and the military regime was overthrown following massive student-led demonstrations during which soldiers arrested protest leaders and killed or wounded over a thousand demonstrators. The collapse of military rule opened a brief era of political liberalization during which democracy and debate flourished. Progressive writers and musicians promoted what they termed "art for life," often extolling the hardworking peasants. But the fragile civilian government proved unable to resolve major problems. With society polarized between liberals and conservatives, in 1976 bloody clashes between leftist students and rightwing youth gangs sparked a military coup and martial law, during which time hundreds of students and their supporters were killed or wounded and thousands arrested. Although the

crackdown reestablished order, the massacres discredited the military.

After the destructive Japanese occupation, the British returned to Burma to reestablish their colonial control. War-weary and facing a well-armed Burmese nationalist army, they negotiated independence with charismatic nationalist leader Aung San (1915–1947) and left in 1948. But newly elected Prime Minister Aung San was assassinated by a political rival, after which U Nu (1907–1995), an idealistic Buddhist and democrat, became leader. Soon ethnic minorities, fearful of Burman domination, declared their secession and organized armies. For several decades the central government rarely controlled more than half the nation's territory as ethnic armies and communist insurgents, funded by opium revenues, battled the Burmese army. In 1962 the army seized control, suspended civil liberties, imposed censorship, claimed most of the government budget, discouraged foreign investment, and took over industries, banks, and commerce. By the 1980s, economic stagnation and political repression had fostered dissent; various secession movements continued, only to be largely suppressed in the 1990s.

MAKE SURE YOU UNDERSTAND THESE KEY POINTS BEFORE MOVING ON

- Using a questionable attack as a pretext, the United States went to war to rid Vietnam of communism, but despite vastly superior resources, the United States and its allies in South Vietnam could not triumph over the communists.

- In Laos the United States recruited Hmong hill people to fight the Pathet Lao revolutionaries, who took control of the country in 1975, while in Cambodia the United States bombed areas occupied by North Vietnamese and supported a weak, dependent government, which was overthrown in 1975 by the Khmer Rouge.

- After attaining independence, the Philippines remained strongly influenced by the United States and struggled

with economic inequality and a Muslim insurgency, while Malaysia experienced intermittent tensions between the politically dominant Malays and the economically strong Chinese.

- Thailand alternated between long periods of military rule and short periods of democratic or semidemocratic rule, while Burma endured decades of factional fighting and, since 1962, brutal military domination.

aplia

Tigers, Politics, and Changing Southeast Asian Societies

N
S

What role do the Southeast Asian nations play in the global system?

Southeast Asia changed dramatically after 1975, mixing influences from the past and from the wider world and reshaping life in both cities and villages. Indonesia, Malaysia, Singapore, and Thailand, with market economies geared to world commerce, gained reputations as dynamic "tigers." Governments stimulated economies and often became authoritarian to ensure social stability. When the fighting ended, the Indochinese had to rebuild their societies shattered by the turmoil. Vietnam eventually developed a tiger economy.

The Resurgence of Southeast Asia

Shifting their economic direction allowed several Southeast Asian nations to play greater roles in the world economy. In

1976, Indonesia, Burma, and Thailand were under military rule, Indochina's communist regimes faced monumental reconstruction, a dictator governed the Philippines, and only Malaysia and Singapore had semidemocracies. Few countries enjoyed impressive economic growth. But in the 1980s, development accelerated. Inspired by Japan's late-nineteenth-century industrialization and rapid recovery from World War II, leaders encouraged their people to "Look East," mixing capitalism and activist government to spur economic expansion. Local entrepreneurs of Chinese ancestry provided much of the initiative and capital. However, resentment by many of Chinese wealth sparked occasional anti-Chinese violence or legal restrictions. Economic growth also had drawbacks, as the industrial activity and expansion of agriculture, mining, and logging caused widespread environmental destruction. Yet, migrants crowding into cities rubbed elbows with other peoples, encouraging cultural mixing. While governments often squashed dissent and repressed personal liberties, expanding education fostered larger middle classes who sought more political influence and fostered civil society institutions concerned with human rights. A vibrant Pacific Rim included the "tiger" nations: Japan, China, Taiwan, South Korea (see Chapter 27), and eventually Vietnam. Some forecast a Pacific Century in which these nations would lead the world economically and increase their political strength.

To promote growth and stability, Southeast Asian countries cooperated as never before. Founded in 1967 by Malaysia, Indonesia, Thailand, Singapore, and the Philippines, **ASEAN** (Association of Southeast Asian Nations) promoted regional economic and political exchange among the noncommunist Southeast Asian nations. However, ASEAN's priorities shifted after the Indochina wars ended. As Vietnam, Cambodia, Laos, Burma, and tiny, oil-rich Brunei became members, ASEAN emerged as the world's fourth largest trading bloc while providing a forum for members to work out differences and deal with the wider world, especially in cultivating relations with China and Japan.

Many challenges remained. A rapidly growing population (620 million in 2012) outstripped economic growth, burdening limited resources such as food and water, especially in the Philippines, Indonesia, and Vietnam. But despite occasional violence, insurgencies, and political upheavals, the destructive earlier wars were not repeated. More open regimes eventually replaced dictatorships in most nations. In 1997 most countries faced a severe economic crisis, part of a broader collapse among Asian and world economies that resulted from poorly regulated banking systems, overconfident investments, and government favoritism toward well-placed business interests. The crisis eventually bottomed out, only to be rekindled in 2008–2009 by the larger world economic downturn, reducing demand for Southeast Asian products, causing massive job losses, slowing foreign investment, and calling into question a forthcoming Pacific Century. Southeast Asia is also one of the regions most threatened by global warming, which may foster erratic rains and will raise sea levels, flooding densely populated river deltas, lowlands, and cities like Hanoi, Bangkok, and Jakarta.

ASEAN A regional economic and political organization formed in 1967 to promote cooperation among the noncommunist Southeast Asian nations; eventually became a major trading bloc.

New Order The Indonesian government headed by President Suharto from 1966 to 1998, which mixed military and civilian leadership.

New Orders in Indonesia and the Philippines

Both Indonesia and the Philippines experienced political turbulence and social instability. Indonesia, with more than seven hundred ethnic groups and 245 million people, struggled to preserve political stability while developing economically. Between 1966 and 1998 the **New Order** government, headed by Javanese general-turned-president Suharto (1921–2008), mixed military and civilian leadership while limiting political opposition to maintain law and order. Suharto used force to repress independence movements in East Timor, a small, mostly Christian former Portuguese colony, north Sumatra, dominated by the strongly Islamic Achehnese, and West Irian (western New Guinea). However, the New Order improved Indonesia's economic position and fostered an educated urban middle class. Per capita income, life expectancy, and adult literacy increased, aided by an annual economic growth rate of nearly 5 percent by the 1990s; meanwhile, a third of Indonesians remained desperately poor, earning less than a dollar a day. Creative musicians, writers, artists, and filmmakers shaped a vibrant popular culture.

The New Order also started some negative trends. Indonesia became dependent on exporting oil, which constituted 80 percent of foreign earnings. As a result, whenever world oil prices decline, reducing the national budget, Indonesia adds to an enormous foreign debt. The rapid development of mining, forestry, and cash crop agriculture has also damaged the environment. Rain forests were clear-cut so rapidly for timber and plantations that forest fires became common, polluting the air and creating a thick, unhealthy haze that spread into neighboring nations. Meanwhile, income disparities between classes and regions widened while political and business corruption thrived. One Indonesian fiction writer satirized government officials and predatory businessmen soliciting bribes and grabbing public funds for themselves: "Indonesia, Land of Robbers. My true homeland stiff with thieves. In the future, I shall plunder while my wife shall seize."[24] The wealthy frolicked in nightclubs, casinos, and golf courses built across the street from slums or on land appropriated from powerless villages. Suharto, the son of poor peasants, became one of the world's most corrupt leaders, his family acquiring over $15 billion in assets from their business enterprises and access to public coffers.

Islam provided the chief vehicle for opposition to the New Order. Some 87 percent of Indonesians are either devout or nominal Muslims, but few have supported militant Islamist movements. Given the large Christian and Hindu minorities, Suharto discouraged Islamic radicalism as a threat to national unity. However, devout Muslims have often opposed secular policies; desiring a more Islamic approach to social, cultural, and legal matters, they denounce gambling casinos, alcoholic beverages, racy magazines and films, and scantily clad female pop singers. At the same time, a progressive, democratic strand of Islamic thought favors liberal social and political reform. Muslim liberals tap into the Javanese emphasis on harmony, consensus, and tolerance incorporated into Indonesian Islam, offering a stark contrast to the more dogmatic Islam common in Pakistan and Saudi Arabia.

By the 1990s Indonesian society suffered from increasing class and ethnic tensions, student protests, and labor unrest.

---

[24]From Taufiq Ismail's story "Stop Thief!" in *Black Clouds over the Isle of Gods and Other Modern Indonesian Short Stories*, ed. David M. E. Roskies (Armonk, NY: M.E. Sharpe, 1997), 97.

When the economy collapsed in 1997, throwing millions out of work and raising prices for essential goods, widespread rioting resulted in Suharto's resignation. Indonesia fell into turmoil, and protests and ethnic clashes proliferated. Many among the urban middle class wanted to strengthen democracy, and in 1999 free elections were held. Later, Megawati Soekarnoputri **(MEH-ga-WHA-tee soo-KAR-no-POO-tri)**, daughter of Indonesia's first president, Sukarno, became Indonesia's first woman president. Like her father, Megawati followed secular, nationalist policies but showed little faith in grassroots democracy and resolved few problems. By 2004 popular support for her regime had ebbed, and she lost to a retired Javanese general, Susilo Bambang Yudhoyono, who was reelected in 2009.

The disorderly democracy replacing the New Order brought unprecedented freedom of the press and speech. But removing restrictions allowed long-simmering ethnic hostilities to reemerge. East Timor, which had endured a long, unpopular Indonesian occupation, finally achieved independence in 1999 after Indonesian troops and militias killed thousands. Muslim-Christian conflicts caused numerous deaths, while Islamic militants capitalized on the instability to recruit support. Several terrorist bombings of popular tourist venues added to the growing tensions. Then in 2005 over 100,000 Indonesians perished from earthquakes and a deadly tidal wave, or tsunami, that destroyed cities and washed away coastal villages on Sumatra. Meanwhile, assertive Muslim conservatives increasingly harass or demand punishment for people they view as behaving immorally. These setbacks have raised questions about the long-term viability of Indonesian democracy. Yet, in 2009 voters decisively rejected anti-Western Islamist parties and reelected the centrist, secular government.

The Philippines lagged well behind the most prosperous Southeast Asian nations in economic development. Under the Ferdinand Marcos dictatorship (1972–1986), economic conditions worsened, rural poverty became more widespread, population grew rapidly, and political opposition was limited by the murder or detaining of dissidents, censorship, and rigged elections. Marcos, his family, and cronies looted the country, amassing billions. High walls built along city freeways ensured that affluent motorists would not have to view slums along the route. A tiny minority lived in palatial homes surrounded by high walls topped with broken glass and barbed wire, with gates manned by armed guards. Across the street from the glittering pavilions of Manila's Cultural Center, homeless families slept in bushes; child malnutrition increased. A Filipino novelist described impoverished, mostly landless peasants, eking out a living on unproductive land: "Nothing in the countryside had changed, not the thatched houses, not the ragged vegetation, not the stolid people. Changeless land, burning sun."[25]

As a result of all these problems, Filipinos have often migrated, temporarily or permanently, to other Asian nations, the United States, or the Middle East. Some 8 million Filipinos lived abroad by 2012, many women working as nurses, maids, or entertainers. About 2,500 Filipinos leave the country every day for overseas work. The emigrants have become part of what Filipinos ruefully call a "3D" culture, referring to the dirty (domestic work), the dangerous (factory work), and the difficult (entertainment).

The Marcos regime's failures sparked massive public protests in 1986 that restored democracy. The opposition rallied around U.S.-educated Corazon Aquino **(ah-KEE-no)** (1933–2009), whose popular politician husband had been assassinated. In a spectacular nonviolent "people's power" revolution, street demonstrations involving students, workers, businessmen, housewives, and clergy demanded justice and freedom. Marcos and his family fled into exile in the United States, which had long supported his regime. Demonstrators breaking into the presidential palace found that the dictator's wife, Imelda Marcos, a former beauty queen, owned thousands of pairs of shoes and vast stores of undergarments, symbolizing the Marcoses' waste of public resources. Mrs. Aquino became president, reestablishing democracy.

But hopes that the Philippines could resolve its problems proved illusory. The new government, while open to dissenting voices, was dominated by the wealthiest Filipinos, mostly members of the hundred or so landowning families favored during U.S. colonial rule. Mrs. Aquino, who belonged to one of these families, declined reelection in 1992. Her successors had rocky presidencies; one, a former film star with a reputation for heavy drinking, gambling, and womanizing, was impeached for corruption and vote-rigging. In 2001 another woman, Gloria Macapagal-Arroyo (b. 1947), a PhD economist and daughter of a former president, became president but also faced corruption allegations; she was reelected in 2005. Powerful women are not unusual in the Philippines, where many are prominent in politics, higher education, journalism, and small business. But in 2010 Benigno Aquino III, the son of Corazon Aquino, won the presidency on a reform platform and soon cracked down on corruption and tax evasion; Mrs. Macapagal-Arroyo faced criminal prosecution.

While many Filipinos admire the United States, others resent the continuing U.S. ties and influence. Fearing China, Aquino seeks a larger American troop presence. But a bestselling pop song reflected the opposition to what nationalists considered neocolonialism: "You just want my natural resources, And then you leave me poor and in misery. American Junk, Get it out of my bloodstream. Got to get back to who I am."[26] While democracy has returned, a free press flourishes, and the economy has improved in recent years, much of the economic growth has been eaten up by rapid population growth; the nation now has 98 million people. None of the governments have successfully addressed poverty or seemed willing to curb the activities of influential companies exploiting marine, mineral, and timber resources, often harming the environment. A local Catholic priest noted how economic exploitation and environmental destruction remained common:

---

[25]F. Sionel Jose, quoted in David G. Timberman, *A Changeless Land: Continuity and Change in Philippine Politics* (New York: M.E. Sharpe, 1991), xi.

[26]"American Junk," by the Apo Hiking Society, quoted in Craig A. Lockard, *Dance of Life: Popular Music and Politics in Southeast Asia* (Honolulu: University of Hawai'i Press, 1998), 156.

David H. Wells/Corbis

PEOPLE'S POWER DEMONSTRATION IN THE PHILIPPINES In 1986 the simmering opposition to the dictatorial government of Ferdinand Marcos reached a boiling point, resulting in massive demonstrations in Manila. Under the banner of "people's power," businesspeople, professionals, housewives, soldiers, students, and cultural figures rallied to topple the regime.

"A plunder economy, that's the post World War II Philippine history: plunder of seas, plunder of mines, plunder of forests."[27] At the same time, differences in access to health care, welfare, and related services have continued to reflect the great gaps in income between social classes and regions.

Politics and Society in Thailand and Burma

Since the 1970s the striking contrasts between prosperous Thailand and stagnant Burma have increased. In the 1950s both nations had economies of similar size and growth rates, but the gap between them has become vast. While both nations have a long history of military dictatorship, by the 1980s the Thais, finding the repressive atmosphere chilling, developed a more open semidemocratic system combining order and hierarchy, symbolized by the monarchy, with representative, accountable government. Although most successful political candidates came from wealthy families, often of Chinese ancestry, the rapidly growing urban middle class generally supported expanding democracy to gain more influence. A new constitution adopted in 1997 guaranteed civil liberties and reformed the electoral system, and a lively free press emerged.

Thailand has generally enjoyed high rates of economic growth. Despite a growing manufacturing sector, rice, rubber, tin, and timber exports remain significant. Although the Chinese minority of some 10 percent controls much wealth, Thais enjoy high per capita incomes and standards of public health by Asian standards. Thousands of people from North America and Europe come to Thailand each year for medical treatment. Yet perhaps a quarter of Thais are very poor, especially in rural areas. The economic "miracle" was built on the backs of women and children, many from rural districts, working in urban factories, the service sector, and the sex industry. Millions of Thai women have identified with the songs of popular singer Pompuang Duangjian **(POM-poo-ahn DWONG-chen)** (1961–1992), herself the product of a poor village, which often dealt with the harsh lives of poor female migrants to the city: "So lousy poor, I just have to risk my luck. Dozing on the bus, this guy starts chatting me up. Says he'll get me a good job."[28] With only two years of primary school education, Pompuang worked as a sugar-cane cutter before starting a music career. Much of her money was stolen by lovers, managers, and promoters, and she died at thirty-one unable to afford treatment for a blood disorder.

The economic collapses of 1997 and 2008–2009 threw many Thais out of work. The overcrowded capital, Bangkok, is one of Asia's most polluted cities, drenched in toxic matter from factories and automobiles despite efforts by local environmental groups to clean up the air. The nation's once-abundant rain forests disappear at a rapid rate, lamented by

[27]Quoted in Robin Broad and John Cavanaugh, *Plundering Paradise: The Struggle for the Environment in the Philippines* (Berkeley: University of California Press, 1993), xvii.

[28]Quoted in Pasuk Phongpaichit and Chris Baker, *Thailand: Economy and Politics* (Kuala Lumpur: Oxford University Press, 1995), 413–415.

WITNESS TO THE PAST

A Thai Poet's Plea for Saving the Environment

Angkhan Kalayanaphong (**AHN-kan KALL-a-YAWN-a-fong**) *(1926–2012), the most popular poet in Thailand for decades, also gained fame as an accomplished graphic artist and painter. His poems often addressed social, Buddhist, and environmental themes. In his long poem "Bangkok-Thailand," he examines Thailand and its problems in the 1970s and 1980s. The author pulls no punches in condemning Thai society for neglecting its heritage, skewing politicians, government institutions, big business, and the entertainment industry. In this section, Angkhan pleads for Thais to save the forest environment being destroyed by commercial logging.*

> Oh, I do not imagine the forest like that
> So deep, so beautiful, everything so special.
> It pertains to dreams that are beyond truth....
> Dense woods in dense forests; slowly
> The rays of half a day mix with the night.
> Strange atmosphere causing admiration.
> Loneliness up to the clouds, stillness and beauty.
> Rays of gold play upon, penetrate the tree-tops
> rays displayed in stripes, the brightness of the sun.
> I stretch out my hand drawing down clouds mixing them
>   with brandy.
> This is supreme happiness....
> The lofty trees do not think of reward for the scent of
>   their blossoms....
> Men kill the wood because they venerate money as in
>   all the world....

> The lofty trees contribute much to morals.
> They should be infinitely lauded for it.
> The trace of the ax kills. Blood runs in streams....
> You, trees, give the flattering pollen attended by scents.
> You make the sacrifice again and again.
> Do you ever respond angrily? You have accepted your
>   fate which is contemptuous of all that is beautiful.
> But troublesome are the murderers, the doers of future
>   sins.
> Greedy after money, they are blind to divine work.
> Their hearts are black to large extent, instead of being
>   honest and upright.
> They have no breeding, are lawless....
> Thailand in particular is in a very bad way.
> Because of their [commercial] value parks are "puri-
>   fied," i.e., destroyed.
> Man's blood is depraved, cursed and base.
> His ancestors are swine and dogs. It is madness to say
>   they are Thai.

THINKING ABOUT THE READING

1. What qualities does the poet attribute to the forest?
2. What motives does he attribute to the loggers and businessmen who exploit the forest environment?

Source: Klaus Wenk, *Thai Literature: An Introduction* (Bangkok: White Lotus, 1995), pp. 95–98. Copyright © 1995 Klaus Wenk. Reprinted with permission.

Thai musicians and poets (see Witness to the Past: A Thai Poet's Plea for Saving the Environment). The AIDs rate skyrockets. With fewer joining the Buddhist clergy, monks complain that consumerism is now the Thai religion. In 2001 media magnet and billionaire nationalist Thaksin Shinawrata swept into power, supported largely by big business and discontented rural voters. Although the autocratic Thaksin's populist policies helped villagers, they also created huge budget deficits, polarizing the country and sparking massive street protests, Thaksin's removal for corruption, and a temporary return of military-aligned aligned governments. These events resulted in several years of political turmoil between rival factions, deeply dividing the country and weakening democracy. In 2011 Thaksin's party, now headed by his pragmatic sister Yingluck Shinawatra, returned to power in free elections and energized economic growth, but the deep divide between the pro-Thaksin rural north and northeast and the anti-Thaksin Bangkok middle class remains dangerous. Devastating floods in 2011, an aging king, and controversies over the monarchy's role contributed to tensions that erupted again in 2013 with massive opposition street protests and demands that Yingluck's government resign, fostering more instability and threatening economic recovery in a deeply polarized nation.

Observers worried about more chaos and a political dead end, perhaps fomenting even another military coup. Yet, Thais possess a talent for political compromise, and Buddhism teaches moderation, tolerance, respect for nature, and a belief in individual worth, providing the basis for a democratic spirit, more equitable distribution of wealth, and environmental ethic.

Whatever Thailand's problems, they seem dwarfed by those of Burma, which has been ruled until recently by a harsh, corrupt military regime. In one of Asia's poorest nations, few outside the ruling group have prospered, despite the country's natural riches of timber, oil, gems, and rice. Sparked by economic decline and political repression, mass protests in 1988, led by students and Buddhist monks, demanded civil liberties; soldiers killed hundreds and jailed thousands of demonstrators. In 1990 Burma, now renamed Myanmar (**my-ahn-MAH**), under international pressure, allowed elections. Although most of its leaders were in jail, the opposition won a landslide victory. Aung San Suu Kyi (**AWNG sahn soo CHEE**) (b. 1945), the founding president's daughter and an eloquent orator, returned from England to lead democratic forces. But the military refused to hand over power, put Aung San Suu Kyi under house arrest, and jailed thousands of opposition supporters. Aung San Suu Kyi refused to compromise to end her house arrest. A courageous symbol of principled leadership, she won the Nobel Peace Prize in 1991.

The military regime remained in power, detaining opposition leaders, until 2011. Meanwhile, many Burmese long dreamed of democracy, some exchanging illicit cassettes of protest music and opposition messages from hand to hand; others, valuing stability and fearing civil war, accommodated military rule. Eventually the government began welcoming some limited foreign investment, especially in the timber and oil industries, and diminished the willingness of other countries to punish Burma for gross human rights violations. In recent years the brutal suppression of Buddhist-led protests, a refusal of foreign assistance for the victims of a devastating hurricane, and increased military assaults on ethnic minority settlements made clear that the generals would not relax their grip or modify their isolation from the world. Yet, in 2010 the junta changed direction, releasing Aung San Suu Kyi and many political prisoners and holding new elections with opposition candidates. In 2011 the junta was dissolved and a nominally civilian government installed, albeit with many military members. Hoping for more investment for modernization, the leaders improved relations with the world, and many countries lifted sanctions. Although the fragile political reforms are threatened by Buddhist attacks, some led by radical monks, on minority Muslims, as well as by restless ethnic minorities and protests against unpopular dam-building and mining projects, the 60 million Burmese finally have reason to hope that the future might be much better than the past.

Diversity and Prosperity in Malaysia and Singapore

Malaysia and Singapore, both open to the world, achieved the most political stability and economic progress. Both countries successfully diversified their economies and stimulated development while raising living standards and spreading the wealth. The two nations, once joined in the same federation, share a similar mix of ethnic groups; Malays constitute 60 percent of the 30 million Malaysians, while three-quarters of Singaporeans are Chinese. Malaysia and Singapore maintain limited democracies, holding regular elections in which the ruling parties control the voting and most of the mass media. While opposition leaders sometimes face arrest or harassment, dissidents use the Internet to spread their views. In 2008 and 2013 a multiethnic opposition coalition overcame obstacles and made electoral gains against the ruling Malay-dominated alliance in Malaysia.

Religion has often divided Malaysia's Muslim majority from the Christian, Hindu, Buddhist, and animist minority. Conflict also occurs within religious traditions. Islamic movements with dogmatic, sometimes militant views have attracted some Malays, especially rural migrants to the city alienated by a Westernized, materialistic society and seeking an anchor in an uncertain world. These movements, which encourage women to dress modestly and sometimes reject modern technology or products, often alarm secular Malays and non-Muslims. In response, Malay women's rights groups use Islamic arguments to oppose the restrictions favored by conservatives. Sisters in Islam, founded by the academic Zainab Anwar (**ZEYE-nab AN-war**), espouses freedom, justice, and equality while fighting strict interpretations of Muslim family law. Numerous women hold high government positions. At the other extreme, some aimless Malay youth mock mainstream society, wearing long hair and listening to heavy metal and hip hop music.

Supported by abundant natural resources, such as oil and tin, economic diversification, and entrepreneurial talent, Malaysia has surpassed European nations like Portugal and Hungary in national wealth. High annual growth rates have fostered relatively high per capita income and export industries employing cheap, often female, labor to make shoes, toys, and other consumer goods. The manufacturing sector has continued to grow rapidly; Malaysians even build their own automobiles. Timber and oil have become valuable export commodities. But economic growth causes toxic waste problems, severe deforestation, and air pollution.

In 1969 Chinese-Malay violence precipitated the New Economic Policy; aimed at redistributing more wealth to Malays, it fostered a substantial Malay middle class. Televisions, stereos, cell phones, and videocassette recorders became nearly universal in cities and increasingly common in rural areas. Many Malaysians have personal computers or access to Internet cafés. Official poverty rates dropped from some 50 percent in 1970 to around 20 percent by 2000. Nevertheless, the gap between rich and poor remains and may have widened. In the bustling capital city, Kuala Lumpur, jammed freeways, glittering malls, and high-rise luxury condominiums contrast with shantytown squatter settlements and shabbily dressed street hawkers hoping to sell enough of their cheap wares to buy a meal.

Restricted to a tiny island, Singapore, despite few resources, joined the world's most prosperous nations, with a standard of living second only to Japan in Asia. The numerical and political predominance of ethnic Chinese makes Singapore unique in Southeast Asia. The government, efficient and ruthless, mixes free-wheeling economic policies with an autocratic leadership that tightly controls the 5.5 million people and limits dissent. People pay a stiff fine if caught spitting, littering, or even tossing used chewing gum on the street. But the regime has also curbed inequalities, redistributing pretax income. One of the healthiest societies, enjoying the world's lowest rate of infant mortality, Singapore devotes more of its national budget to education than other nations; everyone studies English in school, and world-class universities attract international faculties. In the vanguard of the information revolution, the city has become a hub of light industry, high technology, and computer networking. Businesspeople and professionals from around the world have flocked to this globalized city, just as they flocked to Melaka centuries ago. So have lower skilled, and often poorly paid, migrant workers from around Asia, who accounted for a third of the population by 2013. In 2011, after the political opposition had better-than-expected election results, the government pledged some modest liberalization of culture and politics.

Conflict and Reconstruction in Indochina

After years of war and destruction, Vietnam, Laos, and Cambodia began to rebuild and deal with lingering tensions. In Vietnam, socialist policies failed to revitalize the economy; the reunification of North and South Vietnam proved harsh.

KUALA LUMPUR Dominated by new skyscrapers, including some of the world's tallest buildings, and a spectacular mosque, the Malaysian capital city, Kuala Lumpur, has become a prosperous center for Asian commerce and industry. Modern buildings have gradually replaced the older shop houses built decades ago. Yet, poor shantytowns have also grown apace to house the poor.

Because of mismanagement, natural disasters, a long U.S. economic embargo, and the war's devastation, between 1978 and 1985 half a million refugees, known as "boat people," risked their lives to escape Vietnam in rickety boats. After spending months or years in crowded refugee camps in Southeast Asia, most of the refugees were resettled in North America, Australia, or France.

In the 1980s the government, recognizing its failures, introduced market-oriented reforms similar to those in China favoring private enterprise and foreign investment. The reforms increased productivity, facilitated export-oriented manufacturing, fostered some urban prosperity, and ended the refugee flow. Emphasizing education more than doubled the 1945 literacy rates to 94 percent of adults. Many observers see Vietnam as becoming another "tiger" economy. But the shift from socialism widened economic inequalities, leaving most farmers living just above the poverty line. Vietnamese also debated the appropriate balance between socialist and free market policies. With the global recession of 2008–2009, Vietnamese experienced the full effects of globalization. Hundreds of former farming villages producing handicrafts for export saw their income collapse as foreign consumers cut spending.

Although Vietnam has remained an authoritarian one-party state, with little democracy, restrictions on cultural expression have loosened. Several former soldiers became rock or disco stars, and many writers addressed contemporary problems and the war's legacy in fiction. "The General Retires," a former North Vietnamese soldier's short story, caused a sensation by depicting the despair of an old soldier contemplating the new society's emptiness. The authoritarian government periodically jails dissenters and cracks down on social media.

However, the communists have expanded ties to the West and the world economy, and the United States and Vietnam have resumed diplomatic relations. Motor scooters jam urban streets; bustling Saigon, renamed Ho Chi Minh City, has enjoyed especially dynamic economic growth and prosperity. Americans now buy shrimp and underwear imported from Vietnam, and many Americans, including former soldiers and Vietnamese refugees, visit Vietnam. Hundreds of American veterans operate businesses or social service agencies in Vietnam, sometimes in partnership with former communist soldiers. Still, the ruling communists struggle to satisfy the expectations of the 90 million Vietnamese, for many of whom the war is ancient history.

In neighboring Laos, the challenge has been dealing with wartime divisions and destruction. After the Vietnam conflict, many Laotians fled into exile, among them some 300,000 Hmongs who settled in the United States. The Laotian government persecuted some remaining Hmong it believed were supporting anticommunist guerillas. While Laotian leaders have sought warmer relations with neighboring Thailand, China, and the United States, they have failed to foster a more open society or energize the economy. Rigid communists still dominate the one-party state. Several places have attracted Western tourists, but most of the 7 million Laotians remain poor. Laotians see a more successful development model when they look across the Mekong at the busy freeways, neon lights, and high-rise buildings in Thailand.

Cambodia has faced a more difficult challenge because the war was followed by fierce repression and mass murder; at the same time, badly disrupted agriculture raised the specter of widespread starvation. The communist Khmer Rouge leader

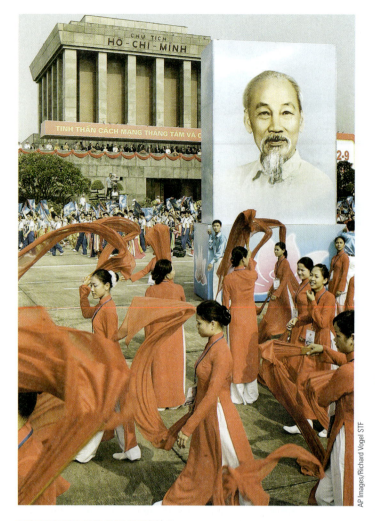

AP Images/Richard Vogel STF

HONORING HO CHI MINH These schoolgirls, dressed in traditional clothing and parading before Ho Chi Minh's mausoleum in Hanoi, are part of an annual festival to honor the leading figure of Vietnamese communism.

Pol Pot (1925–1998), hardened by brutal war, achieved power in 1975 and drove the urban population into the rural areas to farm. The Khmer Rouge's radical vision of a propertyless, classless peasant society, combined with violence against suspected dissenters and resisters, led thousands to flee into neighboring countries. The Khmer Rouge executed thousands in death camps and shot or starved many others, including common people such as peasants and taxi drivers, as well as Westernized and educated people. The regime was ultimately responsible for 1.5 to 2 million deaths, sparking comparisons with Nazi Germany.

In 1978 the Vietnamese, alarmed at Khmer Rouge territorial claims and the murder of thousands of ethnic Vietnamese in Cambodia, allied with an exile army of disaffected former Khmer Rouge, invaded Cambodia, and rapidly pushed the Khmer Rouge to the Thailand border. After liberating Cambodians from tyranny, the Vietnamese installed a less brutal communist government. But military conflict continued for years as a Khmer Rouge–dominated resistance controlled some sections of the country. Cambodia proved to be for Vietnam what Vietnam had been for the United States, an endless sinkhole of conflict that

drained scarce wealth and complicated Vietnam's relations with the West.

In the early 1990s a coalition government was formed under United Nations sponsorship, and the Khmer Rouge splintered and collapsed as a movement. While everyone welcomed the resulting peace, the government remained repressive and corrupt, tolerating some opposition but controlling the vote. Sihanouk returned from exile to become king but served largely as a symbol of Cambodia's link to its past. Life for many Cambodians remained grim as they faced everything from high fuel prices to poor education; often using social media, some people demanded more democracy and attention to social problems. While the opposition eroded the long-entrenched ruling party's majority in 2013 elections, it also protested what many observers considered a rigged system, corruption, and low wages for workers, leading to violent clashes with police. Nevertheless, the government opened the country to investment and tourism, which has brought in revenues, and has transformed Cambodia, while still haunted by past horrors, from a traumatized to a functioning society, kept afloat largely by Western tourism and aid.

Southeast Asia in the Global System

Although Southeast Asians still export the natural resources they did in colonial times, some nations have seen major economic growth through industrialization and exploitation of other resources. Oil, timber, rubber, rice, tin, sugar, and palm oil have largely replaced the gold, pepper, and spice exports of earlier centuries. The region's world role has also changed, fostering some of the fastest-growing economies. Malaysia, Thailand, Singapore, and, to some extent, Indonesia and Vietnam have become major recipients of foreign investment. Meanwhile, workers produce manufactured goods like shoes, clothing, computer chips, and sports equipment for European and North American markets. Several countries elsewhere in Asia, Africa, and Latin America now borrow economic models from the Southeast Asian "tigers." Recently Southeast Asians have begun shifting their focus from the United States to China, which they view as the rising world power with which they must cooperate. But by 2012 Chinese claims to much of the South China Sea had unsettled ASEAN, especially Vietnam and the Philippines, which also claim some of the islands, prompting closer ties with the United States as a counterweight.

Southeast Asians have influenced politics worldwide. The Indonesian Revolution forced a major colonial power to abandon its control, giving hope to colonized Africans. Vietnamese communists, in their ultimately successful fifty-year fight against French colonialism, Japanese occupation, and then U.S. intervention, stimulated a wave of revolutionary efforts, from Nicaragua to Mozambique, to overthrow Western domination. The Vietnamese struggle also inspired European and North American activists; in the 1960s, while protesting against war and inequality, a few of the more radical shouted slogans praising Ho Chi Minh. Women have long played an influential role in Southeast Asia, and political leaders like Indonesia's Megawati Soekarnoputri, Corazon Aquino in the Philippines, and Burma's Aung San Suu Kyi have become inspirations to women worldwide.

Global influences and economic development have increasingly modified lives. For example, the resident of an upscale suburb of Kuala Lumpur, Bangkok, or Manila, connected through her home computer to the information superhighway and working in a high-rise, air-conditioned office reached by driving a late-model sports car along crowded freeways, lives very differently than the peasant villager embedded in traditional society. Modern cities boast malls, supermarkets, boutiques, Hard Rock Cafes, and Planet Hollywoods.

Indonesian television features many U.S.-style reality shows, which have replaced local soap operas in the ratings. Even rural areas have become more connected to wider networks by televisions, outboard motors, motor scooters, and telephones. Yet change has often been superficial. In poor-city neighborhoods restaurants may have compact disc players and cold beer, but they may also feature traditional music and dance and serve up fiery hot curries. For every youngster who joins the fan club for a Western or local pop star, another identifies with an Islamic, Buddhist, or Christian organization, sometimes a militant one. Many people find themselves perched uneasily between the cooperative village values of the past and the competitive, materialistic modern world.

MAKE SURE YOU UNDERSTAND THESE KEY POINTS BEFORE MOVING ON

- Beginning in the late 1970s, Southeast Asia experienced rapid economic growth through a Japanese-style mix of capitalism and active government involvement, though a severe economic crisis hit the region in 1997.

- Since the 1980s, Thailand has developed a semidemocratic system and has grown economically, though it has endured widespread poverty, sexual exploitation, and sporadic political crises. Burma remained a harsh military dictatorship until 2011.

- Malaysia has taken advantage of abundant natural resources to become highly successful, surpassing some European nations in wealth, while Singapore, with fewer resources, has been even more successful through a combination of economic freedom and political restriction.

- Vietnam and Cambodia struggled after the war, but in the 1980s opened up their economies and by the 1990s had reestablished ties with the rest of the world, including the United States.

- With their rapidly growing economies, the Southeast Asian "tigers" have inspired developing nations around the world, and while most of the region has joined the modern world, tradition thrives in them as well.

aplia

CHAPTER SUMMARY

After decolonization, the societies of southern Asia struggled to shape their futures. Since Hindu and Muslim leaders could not agree on a formula for unity after independence, British India fragmented into two rival nations, predominantly Hindu India and mostly Muslim Pakistan. Under Nehru, India adopted democratic practices and modernizing policies. Indians generally sustained multiparty democracy, raised the legal status of untouchables and women, achieved a dramatic rise in food production, industrialized, and fostered high-technology enterprises. But it failed to transform rural society, distribute the fruits of economic growth equitably, and eradicate Hindu-Muslim conflict. Muslim-dominated Pakistan divided when Bangladesh broke away. Both Pakistan and Bangladesh have had difficulty maintaining democracy and generating economic development. India and Pakistan, both armed with nuclear weapons, have remained hostile neighbors.

Like South Asians, Southeast Asians also regained the independence they had lost under Western colonialism.

Vietnamese communists led by Ho Chi Minh launched a revolutionary war that eventually forced the French to leave, giving the communists control of North Vietnam. The United States, influenced by Cold War thinking, supported anticommunist South Vietnam and, in response to a growing communist insurgency, sent American troops to South Vietnam. But the United States withdrew in 1975, unable to triumph over a determined foe. The conflict caused several million casualties and major environmental damage. With the war over, Vietnam, Cambodia, and Laos, all under communist control, struggled for reconstruction. Meanwhile, Indonesia and Malaysia worked to build national unity in a complex mosaic of peoples and cultures. Burma, Thailand, and the Philippines experienced chronic unrest that often led to military or civilian dictatorships. But eventually Malaysia, Singapore, Thailand, Indonesia, and Vietnam achieved rapid economic growth, supplying natural resources and manufactured goods to the world.

KEY TERMS

Dalit (p. 787)
Awami League (p. 788)
Bharatiya Janata Party (p. 790)
Bollywood (p. 793)

National Liberation Front (NLF) (p. 799)
Tet Offensive (p. 799)
Pathet Lao (p. 801)

Khmer Rouge (p. 801)
UMNO (p. 802)
ASEAN (p. 804)
New Order (p. 804)

Globalization: For and Against

The first pictures taken from the moon in 1969, which showed the earth as a blue oasis in the middle of nowhere, made clear that humans share a single home and an interlinked future. Different kinds of networks have increasingly connected peoples across distance and borders, and globalization—the interconnections between societies, the rise in cross-border exchanges, and the creation of one world—has become a major subject of debate. Often used vaguely and inconsistently, the concept became a metaphor to explain capitalism spreading throughout the world. But to many observers, the concept has deeper meanings, describing a process that both unites and divides, creates winners and losers, and brings both new possibilities and new risks. The debates on globalization cut across political leanings and national divisions.

The Problem

Globalization inspires passionate support and bitter opposition, generating immense discussion and disagreement. The debate focuses on four questions: When did globalization begin? What are the arguments in favor of it? What are some of the major opposing views? Is the trend leading the world into a troubled era of increasing conflict or greater cooperation?

The Debate

The first question, the roots of globalization, remains disputed. Some scholars argue that its origins lie deep in the past, going back to the interconnections that slowly enveloped people from the dawn of cities and states. German historians Jurgen Osterhammel and Niels Petersson, for example, trace it back a millennium or two to the silk trade between China and the Mediterranean region, the sea trade between the Middle East and India, and the caravans crossing the deserts of Africa, all activities that moved people, ideas, artwork, natural resources, goods, and coins. By contrast, Australian Robbie Robertson argues that history changed dramatically only five hundred years ago, when the gradual linking of the world by European voyages of discovery transformed societies and economic activities. Still other scholars trace it no further back than the mid-nineteenth century, pointing to the first permanent transoceanic telegraph cable in 1866, global social movements such as feminism, and global regulatory bodies such as the Universal Postal Union. Some other writers claim that globalization did not affect most of humanity until the 1960s or later, especially after the invention of the microchip in 1972, which generated the information revolution. Whatever the roots, today a global system—defined by market capitalism, over two hundred nation-states, some four hundred international organizations, and forty thousand transnational corporations—exists with no central authority.

On the second and third questions, whether the effects are positive or negative, the debate has raged for years. Among the benefits attributed to globalization are higher living standards and the worldwide sharing of culture. British sociologist John Giddens identifies a worldwide trend toward democracy and intellectual freedom. Walter Anderson praises the opening of societies to one another, as reflected in communications satellites and the fiber-optic submarine cable system winding its way around the world. As a result, he notes, the Inuit people living in northern Alaska watch twenty-eight channels of satellite television, take courses through the Internet, and stay in touch with their families by cell phones. Free market enthusiasts, such as Indian-born, U.S.-based economist Jagdish Bhagwati, stress the fostering of economic freedom. Opposing antiglobalization movements as the misguided enemy of progress, all these thinkers complain that newspapers and television reports focus more on shuttered textile factories, as jobs move overseas, than on the African child at the computer. Bhagwati claims that when properly governed, globalization becomes a powerful force for social good, bringing prosperity to underdeveloped nations, reducing child labor, increasing literacy, and helping women by creating jobs that increase their income and status. Another enthusiast, Thomas Friedman, considers globalization a reality, not a choice, and the principal trend of the post–Cold War world, symbolized by the Lexus, a Japanese-made luxury car sold around the world. Yet, he argues, people often prefer to hold on to meaningful traditions, symbolized by the olive tree often found at the center of an Arab village, rather than embrace new ideas. To Friedman the world has gotten flat, and this level playing field has allowed over 2 billion Chinese, Indians, and Russians to contemplate eventually owning a car, house, refrigerator, and toaster, increasing competition and dramatically raising the demand for the world's resources.

The contrary views on globalization stress negative consequences. These consequences include a concentration of economic power, more poverty, and less cultural diversity. The challengers of economic globalization argue that powerful governments and multinational corporations bully the marketplace, control politics, and stack the deck in their favor. Walter LaFeber shows how U.S. basketball star Michael Jordan, whose games were broadcast all over the world, became an international phenomenon of great commercial appeal, benefiting the international corporations who used Jordan to create a demand for their expensive products, such as sneakers, often at the expense of local manufacturers making the same product. To LaFeber, the terrorist attacks on the United States, especially the World Trade Center in New York in 2001, must also be understood in the context of the growing opposition to globalization around the world as the rich become richer and the poor become poorer. Joseph Stiglitz, an ardent fan of capitalism and former World Bank official, believes that globalization can be positive but that misguided policies and the economic power of industrial nations have made free trade unfair for developing nations. Looking at other aspects of globalization, Cynthia Enloe explores the often-negative effects of tourism and U.S. military bases on women, who, enjoying fewer economic options than men, often need to sell their bodies to male tourists and soldiers to survive. James Mittelman argues that, experienced from

KUWAITI STOCK EXCHANGE Capitalism has spread widely in the world, and with it financial institutions such as investment banks and stock exchanges. The oil-rich, politically stable Persian Gulf sultanate of Kuwait has one of the most active stock exchanges.

below, globalization fosters the loss of local political control as power shifts upward and also a devaluation of a society's cultural achievements as foreign cultural products, such as music and films, become influential. All of these globalizing trends spur angry resistance, reflected in antiglobalization movements. Maori scholar Makere Stewart-Harawira emphasizes the impact, often negative, on indigenous groups in the evolving world order.

Experts also disagree about the fourth question, where globalization is taking the world. Some predict a growing divide both between and within societies. Benjamin Barber, for example, analyzes the conflict between consumerist capitalism (what he calls McWorld, after McDonald's) and tribalism or religious fundamentalism (what he terms jihad, after Islamic militants). Barber dislikes both trends: the dull homogeneity of McWorld, in which everyone, moved by capitalism and advertising, has the same tastes and ideas; and the balkanized world of jihad in which rival cultures, convinced of their own superior values and disdainful of others, struggle for dominance. Other scholars also predict tensions. John Giddens argues that the globalization of information, symbolized by the World Wide Web, that puts people in touch with others who think differently will promote a more cosmopolitan world-view respecting cultural differences but will also generate a backlash among narrow nationalists and religious fundamentalists who see only one path to truth.

Preventing conflict between the factions and lessening the growing divide between rich and poor nations require cooperation between nations. Bhagwati, for example, supports managed rather than unfettered globalization, with world leaders discussing how to foster equality as well as growth. Taking a different approach, Mittelman doubts that globalization can be managed and calls for people around the world, rather than leaders and governments, to work together to decentralize political and economic power to build a future of greater equity. Friedman agrees that no one nation, bloc, or organization is in charge of managing globalization.

Evaluating the Debate

The globalization discussion, much more than an academic debate, is a disagreement about profound transformations in the world and about what ethical and institutional principles should be applied to better organize human affairs for a brighter future. Some authors engaged in the debate have proposed catchy ideas, such as the Lexus and the olive tree, jihad and McWorld, but the reality of globalization is usually more complex. Both proponents and opponents make strong points about the consequences of globalization; other scholars believe the truth may lie somewhere in between. Globalization may indeed bring great benefits, at least to a section of the world's people. While the free flow of ideas inspires some people to demand more political rights or

(Continued)

social equality, many young women working long hours for low wages in foreign-owned factories may often prefer that life to the dead end of rural poverty. But improving the lives of those who do not benefit, as even globalization proponents Bhagwati and Friedman concede, may require action such as land reform to help poor peasants, more funding for schools, and stiffer environmental and worker protection laws to smooth the impacts on societies, cultures, and environments. Yet, the relations between business interests and their political supporters promoting globalization and the antiglobalization activists, often from worker or peasant backgrounds, remain tense. Local, national, regional, and global forces are intermingling in new and complex ways that may necessitate new ways of thinking.

THINKING ABOUT THE CONTROVERSY

1. When did globalization begin?
2. What are the positive arguments for globalization?
3. What main points do opponents make?

Exploring the Controversy

Among the key historical studies are Robbie Robertson, *The Three Waves of Globalization: A History of a Developing Global Consciousness* (New York: Zed Books, 2003), and Jurgen Osterhammel and Niels P. Petersson, *Globalization: A Short History* (Princeton: Princeton University Press, 2009). Some of the major proponents are John Giddens, *Runaway World: How Globalization Is Reshaping Our Lives* (London: Routledge, 2000); Walter Truett Anderson, *All Connected Now: Life in the First Global Civilization* (Boulder, CO: Westview Press, 2001); Jagdish Bhagwati, *In Defense of Globalization* (New York: Oxford University Press, 2004); and Thomas L. Friedman, *The Lexus and the Olive Tree: Understanding Globalization* (New York: Anchor, 2000) and *The World Is Flat 3.0: A Brief History of the Twenty-First Century* (New York: Farrar, Straus, and Giroux, 2007). Skeptics questioning the benefits include Walter LaFeber, *Michael Jordan and the New Global Capitalism*, new and expanded ed. (New York: W.W. Norton, 2005); Joseph E. Stiglitz, *Globalization and Its Discontents* (New York: W.W. Norton, 1993) and *Making Globalization Work* (New York: W.W. Norton, 2007); Cynthia Enloe, *Bananas, Beaches and Bases: Making Feminist Sense of International Politics*, updated ed. (Berkeley: University of California Press, 2001) and *Globalization and Militarism: Feminists Make the Link* (Lanham, MD: Rowman and Littlefield, 2007); James H. Mittelman, *The Globalization Syndrome: Transformation and Resistance* (Princeton: Princeton University Press, 2000); and Makere Stewart-Harawiri, *The New Imperial Order: Indigenous Responses to Globalization* (London: Zed, 2005). For one view of future trends, see Benjamin R. Barber, *Jihad vs. McWorld* (New York: Times Books, 1995). On globalization generally and the debates about it, see Thomas Hyland Eriksen, *Globalization: The Key Concepts* (New York: Berg, 2007); David Held, ed., *A Globalizing World? Culture, Economics, Politics* (New York: Routledge, 2000); Held and Anthony McGraw, *Globalization/Anti-Globalization: Beyond the Great Divide*, 2nd ed. (London: Polity, 2007); McGraw and Held, *Globalization Theory: Approaches and Controversies* (London: Polity, 2007); Mark Kesselman, ed., *The Politics of Globalization: A Reader* (Boston: Houghton Mifflin, 2007); George Ritzer, *Globalization: A Basic Text* (Hoboken, NJ: John Wiley, 2009); Robert K. Schaeffer, *Understanding Globalization: The Social Consequences of Political, Economic, and Environmental Change*, 4th ed. (Lanham, MD: Rowman and Littlefield, 2009); Lui Hebron and John F. Stack, Jr., *Globalization*, 2nd ed. (New York: Pearson, 2010); and Manfred B. Steger, *Globalization: A Very Short Introduction* (New York: Oxford University Press, 2003).

Index